TERRA MADRE

1,600 Food Communities

Slow Food Editore

Editors
John Irving, Serena Milano,
Bianca Minerdo, Grazia Novellini,
Raffaella Ponzio

Area editors
Francesca Baldereschi,
Michela Blengetti, Paolo Bolzacchini,
Silvia Monasterolo, Séverine Petit,
Lia Poggio, Federica Tomatis,
Sara Tramontini, Lilia Smelkova,
Cinzia Scaffidi, Veronica Veneziano

Editorial desk
Elena Aniere, Stefania Barroero,
Cristina Battaglino, Daniela Battaglio,
Simone Beccaria, Alessandro Cecchini,
Elisabetta Dutto Mel, Makalé Faber,
Andrea Ferrandi, Federica Frigerio,
Carlo Gaia, Tiziano Gaia, Elisa Gallo,
Giancarlo Gariglio, Kathy Gilsinan,
Kelly Hrajnoha, Cerise Mayo,
Marta Mancini, Mariagiulia Mariani,
Ermina Martini, Monica Mascarino,
Clarissa Monnati, Karina Morales Torres,
Bess Mucke, Miki Nakano, Linda Nano,
Mauro Pizzato, Angelo Surrusca,
Petra Tanos, Amy Thompson,
Piero Sardo, Victoria Smelkova,
Winnie Yang

Photographs
Agenzia Grazia Neri, Fabio Aceto,
Valter Arbali, Fabio Artusi,
Carlo Avataneo, Giovanni Bellingeri,
Giacomo Bergamo, Paolo Bolzacchini,
Marco Bruzzo, Giuseppe Cannoni,
Antonello Carboni, Valerio Chiarini,
Giuseppe Cucco, Rémi Denecheau,
Paolo Di Croce, Paola Di Fabio,
Czarnego Dunajaca, Carlo Fanti,
Giuseppe Fassino, Salvatore Fazio,
Anya Fernald, Andrea Ferrandi,
Ezio Ferreri, Nicola Ferrero, Carlo Gaia,
Giulio Gelardi, Tino Gerbaldo,
Francisco Klimscha, Przemek Krzakiewicz,
Jean-Claude Le Berre, Giuseppe Leone,
Fabio Liverani, Alberto Lotti,
Marcello Marengo, Maria Stella Marotta,
Silvia Monasterolo, Silvio Marocchino,
Serena Milano, Miki Nakano,
Claudio Pastrone, Cristiana Peano,
Cristian Pennacchio, Séverine Petit,
Alberto Peroli, Livio Piatta,
Manfredo Pinzauti, Lia Poggio,
Raffaella Ponzio, Fabio Rinaldi,
Armando Rotoletti, Toty Ruggieri,
Andrea Samaritani, Loreta Sardo,
Marco Sasia, Lilia Smelkova,
Franco Tanel, Sara Tramontini,
Antonio Trivigno, Walter Turcato,
Paola Vanzo

Editorial Coordination
Maria Vittoria Negro, Gigi Piumatti

Art Director
Dante Albieri

Layout
Scriba Studio – Bra (Cuneo)

Graphics
Maurizio Burdese, Francesco Perona

Photolithography
Imago – Marene (Cuneo)

Cover
photo Harry Gruyaert, © Contrasto

Printing
Rotolito Lombarda – Pioltello (Milan)

Printed in October 2006

Copyright © 2006
Slow Food® Editore
All rights reserved

Slow Food Editore srl
Via della Mendicità Istruita 14-45
12042 Bra (Cuneo) – Italy
Tel. +39 0172 419611
Fax +39 0172 411218
www.slowfood.com
www.terramadre2006.org
blog.terramadre2006.org

ISBN 88-8499-118-8

General coodination
Paolo Di Croce

Area coordination

Slow Food Italy, Slow Food USA, Slow Food France,
Slow Food Germany, Slow Food Japan, Slow Food Switzerland,
Slow Food UK, Ana and Hugo Cetrángolo (Argentina),
Agnesa Sargsyan (Armenia),Vanda Evison, Jamie Kronborg,
Pauline Tresise (Australia),
Luigi Eusebi, Roberta Marins de Sá, Margarida Nogueira (Brazil),
Francisco Klimscha (Chile), Anna Rita Hadjigavriel (Cyprus),
Silvana Grispino (Dominican Republic), Sonia Lehmann (Ecuador),
Gilbert Dallarosa, Jean Lhéritier (France),
Ramaz NiKoladze, Maka Stamateli, (Georgia)
Hans-Werner Bunz, Dinah Epperlein, Otto Geisel,
Walter Kress (Germany),
Zoi and Yiorgos Hatziyannakis, Marios Kalfoglou (Greece),
Zoltan Erdos (Hungary),
Maya Goburdhum, Poonam Pande, Minoo Sahoo (India),
Giana Ferguson (Ireland), Francesco Amonti, Stefano Asaro,
Sonia Chellini, Silvia De Paolis, Luca Fabbri, Danilo Gasparini,
Giovanna Licheri, Cristiana Peano, Pippo Privitera, Vito Trotta (Italy),
Vladimir Levin (Kazakhstan), Samuel Karanja Muhunyu (Kenya),
Kim Lhin Wha (Korea), Kamal Mouzawak (Lebanon),
José Iturriaga de La Fuente (Mexico), Marjolein Kooistra,
Andrea Van Gemst (Netherlands), Graham Harris (New Zealand)
Terje Inderhaug, Ove Fosså (Norway), Mario Edgar Tapia Nuñez,
Moises Quispe Quispe (Peru), Jacek Szklarek (Poland),
Virgínia Kristensen (Portugal), Nadezhda Zhdanova (Russia),
Nebojsa Davcik (Serbia), Germán Arrien, Ismael Ferrer,
Nacho Lánderer, Valentí Mongay Castro (Spain), Ola Buckard,
Christina Gaitan (Sweden), Meret Bisseger (Switzerland),
Pam Rodway (United Kingdom), Michael Dimock (United States),
Titina Nuñez (Uruguay), Yuriy and Marina Tsoy (Uzbekistan)

Collaborators

Serena Alaimo, Andrea Alfieri, Chiara Appendino,
Concetta Baiamonte, Silvio Barbero, Maura Biancotto, Laura Bonino,
Dino Borri, Fabiana Brandino, Roberto Burdese, Valter Cambieri,
Chiara Cauda, Silvia Ceriani, Alberto Chiappa, Carla Coccolo,
Stefano Colmo, Valeria Cometti, Daniela Corso, Raimondo Cusmano,
Richard Egnar, Patrice Ekoka, Francesca Farkas, Alberto Farinasso,
Nicola Ferrero, Dario Ferro, Manuela Fissore, Tiziana Gazzera,
Jane Karanja, Eugenio Mailler, Ishida Masayoshi, Elena Marino,
Silvio Marocchino, Daria Mascotto, Valeria Melucci,
Cristiano Meneghin, Fabio Merafino, Simona Milvo,
Alessandro Monchiero, Valter Musso, Paola Nano, Fabio Palladino,
Cristiana Peano, Stefano Pescarmona, Luciano Piana, Ivan Piasentin,
Simona Piasentin, José Carlos Redon, Olivia Reviglio, Serena Rinaldi,
Paola Rinaudo, Fiona Richmond, Claudia Saglietti,
Riccardo Sauvaigne, Fabio Torta, Eric Vassallo, Francesca Vespa,
Carmen Wallace, Dana Ziemel

Terra Madre Foundation
Italian Ministry of Agriculture and Forestry
Italian Development Cooperation – Ministry of Foreign Affairs
Piedmont Regional Authority
City of Turin
Slow Food

The Terra Madre Network

Thanks to the generosity of many institutions, companies and individuals, the Terra Madre network is taking shape.
And it is thanks to that network that it is possible for food community delegates, cooks and universities of developing countries to take part in Terra Madre 2006.

In Piedmont...
Alessandria Provincial Authority
Asti Provincial Authority
Biella Provincial Authority
Cuneo Provincial Authority
Novara Provincial Authority
Turin Provincial Authority
Verbano Cusio Ossola Provincial Authority
Vercelli Provincial Authority
Langa delle Valli Mountain Community (Cuneo)
Val Pellice Mountain Community (Turin)
Valli Po Bronda and Infernotto
    Mountain Community (Cuneo)
Consorzio Comunità Collinare del Roero (Cuneo)

Unione dei Comuni
    Comunità Collinare Valtriversa (Asti)
Unione dei Comuni del Fossanese (Cuneo)
Unione dei Comuni di Langa e Barolo (Cuneo)
Acqui Terme (Alessandria)
Alba (Cuneo)
Albiano d'Ivrea (Turin)
Alessandria
Alice Bel Colle (Alessandria)
Alpignano (Turin)
Andrate (Turin)
Angrogna (Turin)
Antignano (Asti)
Asti

Baldichieri d'Asti (Asti)
Baldissero d'Alba (Cuneo)
Banchette (Turin)
Barge (Cuneo)
Barolo (Cuneo)
Bene Vagienna (Cuneo)
Bergolo (Cuneo)
Berzano San Pietro (Asti)
Bibiana (Turin)
Biella
Bobbio Pellice (Turin)
Bollengo (Turin)
Borgofranco d'Ivrea (Turin)
Bricherasio (Turin)

Burolo (Turin)
Buttigliera Alta (Turin)
Calamandrana (Asti)
Calosso (Asti)
Caluso (Turin)
Camerano Casasco (Asti)
Canale (Cuneo)
Cantarana (Asti)
Carignano (Turin)
Carmagnola (Turin)
Carrù (Cuneo)
Casalborgone (Turin)
Caselle Torinese (Turin)
Castagnito (Cuneo)
Castellero (Asti)
Castelletto Stura (Cuneo)
Castelletto Uzzone (Cuneo)
Castellinaldo (Cuneo)
Castello di Annone (Asti)
Castelnuovo Bormida (Alessandria)
Castiglione Falletto (Cuneo)
Castino (Cuneo)
Cavallermaggiore (Cuneo)
Cavour (Turin)
Cercenasco (Turin)
Ceresole d'Alba (Cuneo)
Cerro Tanaro (Asti)
Cervere (Cuneo)
Cherasco (Cuneo)
Chiusano d'Asti (Asti)
Chivasso (Turin)
Cinaglio (Asti)
Ciriè (Turin)
Clavesana (Cuneo)
Collegno (Turin)
Corneliano d'Alba (Cuneo)
Corsione (Asti)
Cortandone (Asti)
Cortanze (Asti)
Cortazzone (Asti)
Cortemilia (Cuneo)
Cossano Belbo (Cuneo)
Cossombrato (Asti)
Cuneo

Dogliani (Cuneo)
Druento (Turin)
Ferrere (Asti)
Fossano (Cuneo)
Frinco (Asti)
Gorzegno (Cuneo)
Gottasecca (Cuneo)
Govone (Cuneo)
Grinzane Cavour (Cuneo)
Grugliasco (Turin)
Guarene (Cuneo)
Incisa Scapaccino (Asti)
Ivrea (Turin)
Lagnasco (Cuneo)
La Morra (Cuneo)
Levice (Cuneo)
Luserna San Giovanni (Turin)
Lusernetta (Turin)
Magliano Alfieri (Cuneo)
Magliano Alpi (Cuneo)
Maglione (Turin)
Maretto (Asti)
Margarita (Cuneo)
Masio (Alessandria)
Monale (Asti)
Moncalvo (Asti)
Monchiero (Cuneo)
Mondovì (Cuneo)
Monesiglio (Cuneo)
Monforte d'Alba (Cuneo)
Montà (Cuneo)
Montaldo Roero (Cuneo)
Montalto Dora (Turin)
Montechiaro d'Asti (Asti)
Montelupo Albese (Cuneo)
Monteu Roero (Cuneo)
Monticello d'Alba (Cuneo)
Morozzo (Cuneo)
Narzole (Cuneo)
Niella Tanaro (Cuneo)
Nomaglio (Turin)
Novara
Novello (Cuneo)
Palazzo Canavese (Turin)

Pancalieri (Turin)
Pavone Canavese (Turin)
Perletto (Cuneo)
Pezzolo Valle Uzzone (Cuneo)
Pianezza (Turin)
Piasco (Cuneo)
Piea (Asti)
Pinerolo (Turin)
Piobesi d'Alba (Cuneo)
Piossasco (Turin)
Piozzo (Cuneo)
Piscina (Turin)
Pocapaglia (Cuneo)
Poirino (Turin)
Priocca (Cuneo)
Prunetto (Cuneo)
Racconigi (Cuneo)
Refrancore (Asti)
Rivalta di Torino (Turin)
Rivoli (Turin)
Roatto (Asti)
Rocca de' Baldi (Cuneo)
Rocchetta Belbo (Cuneo)
Rocchetta Tanaro (Asti)
Roddi (Cuneo)
Roddino (Cuneo)
Rodello (Cuneo)
Rorà (Turin)
Rosta (Turin)
Saliceto (Cuneo)
Saluzzo (Cuneo)
Samone Torinese (Turin)
San Gillio (Turin)
Sanfrè (Cuneo)
Sant'Albano Stura (Cuneo)
Santa Vittoria d'Alba (Cuneo)
Santena (Turin)
Santo Stefano Belbo (Cuneo)
Santo Stefano Roero (Cuneo)
Savigliano (Cuneo)
Scarnafigi (Cuneo)
Serralunga d'Alba (Cuneo)
Settime (Asti)
Settimo Torinese (Turin)

Settimo Rottaro (Turin)
Sinio (Cuneo)
Soglio (Asti)
Sommariva del Bosco (Cuneo)
Sommariva Perno (Cuneo)
Strambino (Turin)
Torre Bormida (Cuneo)
Traversella (Turin)
Trinità (Cuneo)
Val della Torre (Turin)
Venaria Reale (Turin)
Verbania
Vercelli
Verduno (Cuneo)
Verzuolo (Cuneo)
Vezza d'Alba (Cuneo)
Vico Canavese (Turin)
Villafranca d'Asti (Asti)
Villanova d'Asti (Asti)
Villa San Secondo (Asti)
Villarbasse (Turin)
Villar Pellice (Turin)

Slow Cities
Abbiategrasso (Milan)
Acqualagna (Pesaro-Urbino)
Acquapendente (Viterbo)
Amalfi (Salerno)
Amelia (Terni)
Anghiari (Arezzo)
Barga (Lucca)
Borgo Val di Taro (Parma)
Bra (Cuneo)
Brisighella (Ravenna)
Bucine (Arezza)
Caiazzo (Caserta)
Casalbeltrame (Novara)
Castel Morrone (Caserta)
Castel San Pietro Terme (Bologna)
Castelnovo ne' Monti (Reggio Emilia)
Castelnuovo Berardenga (Siena)
Castiglione del Lago (Perugia)
Chiavenna (Sondrio)
Chiaverano (Turin)

Città della Pieve (Perugia)
Civitella in Val di Chiana (Arezzo)
Cutigliano (Pistoia)
Fiumicino (Rome)
Fontanellato (Parma)
Francavilla al Mare (Chieti)
Galeata (Forlì-Cesena)
Giffoni Valle Piana (Salerno)
Giuliano Teatino (Chieti)
Greve in Chianti (Florence)
Guardiagrele (Chieti)
Levanto (La Spezia)
Massa Marittima (Grosseto)
Monte Castello di Vibio (Perugia)
Montefalco (Perugia)
Orvieto (Terni)
Pellegrino Parmense (Parma)
Penne (Pescara)
Pianella (Pescara)
Pollica (Salerno)
Positano (Salerno)
Pratovecchio (Arezzo)
San Daniele del Friuli (Udine)
San Miniato (Pisa)
San Vincenzo (Livorno)
Sangemini (Terni)
Santa Sofia (Forlì-Cesena)
Suvereto (Livorno)
Teglio (Sondrio)
Todi (Perugia)
Torgiano (Perugia)
Trani (Bari)
Trevi (Perugia)
Zibello (Parm)

Italian metropolises
Bologna
Florence
Turin

Italian towns and cities
Altare (Savona)
Bagno di Romagna (Forlì-Cesena)
Bardineto (Savona)

Bolzano
Bormida (Savona)
Cairo Montenotte (Savona)
Calizzano (Savona)
Carcare (Savona)
Cengio (Savona)
Cinisello Balsamo (Milan)
Alta Valle Bormida
    Mountain Community (Savona)
Cosseria (Savona)
Dego (Savona)
Forlimpopoli (Forlì-Cesena)
La Spezia
Lastra a Signa (Florence)
Livorno
Mallare (Savona)
Massimino (Savona)
Millesimo (Savona)
Montevarchi (Arezzo)
Murialdo (Savona)
Osiglia (Savona)
Pallare (Savona)
Pelago (Fi)
Piana Crixia (Savona)
Plodio (Savona)
Pontassieve (Florence)
Roccavignale (Savona)
Rufina (Florence)
San Giuliano Milanese (Milan)
San Giuliano Terme (Pisa)
Scandicci (Florence)
Terricciola (Pisa)
Vernio (Prato)

Friends of Terra Madre
A.S.P. Asti Servizi Pubblici
AAPI - Associazione Apicoltori
    Professionisti Italiani
Alan & Michela Abrams
Adina World Beat Beverages
AITR, Associazione Italiana
    Turismo Responsabile
Alcisa Salumi
Amici in Tavola

ANCI, Associazione Nazionale Comuni Italiani
Apilombardia
Aspromiele - Associazione Produttori
    Miele Piemonte
Associazione Arcobaleno onlus
Associazione Ecoredia
Gruppo d'Acquisto Solidale
Asti Turismo - ATL
ATL Canavese e Valli di Lanzo
Azienda Agricola Apicoltura
    di Paternoster Andrea
Azienda Agricola Fratelli Muratori
Azienda Agricola Malvirà
Azienda Agricola Masciarelli
Annabella Bassani
Blulab
Brescia con Gusto
Bruno Bronzini
California Vegetable Specialties
Camera di Commercio, Industria,
    Artigianato e Agricoltura di Torino
CGIL Piemonte
The Christensen Fund
CISL Piemonte
Cittadellarte - Fondazione Pistoletto
CUNEOA Nazionale Alimentare
CUNEOA Torino
Comieco
Consorzio CTM Altromercato
Consorzio del Prosciutto di San Daniele
Consorzio Parco Lombardo
    della Valle del Ticino
Consorzio Tutela Provolone Val Padana
Coop Italia
Cooperativa della Rava e della Fava
Cooperativa Sociale Vedogiovane
Cooperativa Viaggi Solidali S.C.S. onlus
Silvia D'Ambra
F.lli De Cecco
Peter & Pat De Garmo
Michael Dimock
F.A.I. Fondo per l'Ambiente Italiano
    Sezione di Masino

Fabrica
Famiglia Damilano
Paul & Kelly Flemming
Fondazione Biella The Art of Excellence
Fondazione Cassa di Risparmio di Asti
Fondazione Cassa di Risparmio di Biella
Foundation for Global Community
Lynne Frame & Rick Hoskins
Gal Montiferru Barigadu Sinis
G. Cravero
The Investors' Circle Foundation
Istituto Italo Latino Americano
Istituto Italiano per l'Africa e l'Oriente
Deborah Koons Garcia
Patrizia Giordano
Paola Giubergia
Peter Glidewell
Eugenio Guarducci
Icario Società Agricola
Lavazza
Legacoop Piemonte
Lindt & Sprungli
Lily Films
Lurisia
m.r. Service
Marchesi srl Cous Cous
Paolo Masarati
Piero Masarati
Maddalena Mazzeschi
William & Marie McGlashan
Metropolis
Michele Chiarlo
Mila
Hans & Kate Morris
Giulio Muttoni
Giuseppe Muttoni
Ogawa Kingi
Organic Valley
ORS
Osservatorio Ligure Pesca e Mare
Panta Rhea Foundation
    Pro Organics/Sunopta
Produttori Moscato d'Asti Associati S.C.A.

Provincial Authority of Ascoli Piceno -
    Agriculture Department
Provincial Authority of Bologna
Putumayo
Edoardo Ramolfo
R.E.A. Torino
Reale Mutua Assicurazioni
Bruce Reizenman & Rose Gallagher
Rekordata
Rivera Azienda Vinicola
Peter & Melita Rogers
Prosciutto Rosa
Alice & William Russell-Shapiro
Nancy Schaub
Bruce Sherman
Sicily Regional Authority - Regional Agriculture
    and Forestry Department
Slow Food Predia:
Bitto of the Bitto Valleys (Sondrio)
Bottarga of Orbetello (Grosseto)
Goose in Onto (Treviso)
Graukäse of the Aurina Valley(Bolzano)
Monti Sibillini Pink Apples(Ascoli Piceno)
Monte Veronese (Verona)
Ur-Paarl (Bolzano)
SMAT
David & Louise Smith
Società Azienda Agricola Tenuta Villanova
Richard & CJ Theis
Mima Toscano
Lucia Turati
Tuscany Regional Authority - ARSIA
UIL Piemonte
UNAAPI - Unione Nazionale Associazioni
    Apicoltori Italiani
Unione Industriale Torino
Venchi
WIFI-Company
Felicia Woytak & Steven Rasmussen
Zenit Informatica

Osterias and Restaurants

A Casa tu Martinu - Taviano (Lecce)
A Maidda - Lentini (Siracusa)
Abraxas - Pozzuoli (Naples)
Al Bersagliere - Verona
Al Caminetto - Follina (Treviso)
Al Gambero Rosso - Bagno di Romagna (Forlì-Cesena)
Alla Torre - Romagnano Sesia (Novara)
Allo Scoglio - Bogliaco (Brescia)
Antica Osteria Casa di Lucia - Acquate (Lecco)
Antica Osteria dell'Orsa - Savigliano (Cuneo)
Antica Osteria Italia - Cocquio Trevisago (Varese)
Antica Trattoria al Bosco - Saonara (Padua)
Antica Trattoria dei Mosto - Ne (Genoa)
Antica Trattoria di' Tramway - Signa (Florence)
Antica Trattoria La Pergolina - Capriano del Colle (Brescia)
Antiche Sere - Turin
Antipastoteca di Mare - Trieste
Armonia - Bajardo (Imperia)
Bancogiro - Venice
Bandini - Portacomaro (Asti)
Belsito - Serrone (Frosinone)
Belvedere - Monte San Savino (Arezzo)
Boccondivino - Bra (Cuneo)
Ca' del Re - Verduno (Cuneo)
Ca' Derton - Asolo (Treviso)
Caffè La Crepa - Isola Dovarese (Cremona)
Campanini - Busseto (Parma)
Castello - Serle (Brescia)
Conti - Roncadelle (Brescia)
Cracco Peck - Milano (Milan)
Da Amerigo - Savigno (Bologna)
Da Bortolino - Viadana (Mantua)
Dâ Casetta - Borgio Verezzi (Savona)
Da Checco - Cori (Latina)
Da Conte - Mira (Venice)
Da Fefè - Bacoli (Naples)
Da Gagliano - Sarteano (Siena)
Da Maria - Fano (Pesaro-Urbino)
Da Paeto - Pianiga (Venice)
Da Pippo - Fontanegli (Genoa)
Da Roberto - Barbianello (Pavia)
Dai Saletta - Turin
Del Belbo Bardon - San Marzano Oliveto (Asti)

Devetak - Savogna d'Isonzo (Gorizia)
DiVino Amore - Frosinone
Dorfnerhof - Montagna (Bolzano)
El Purtù - Orzinuovi (Brescia)
Enoteca dal Mizio - Pistoia
Fenesta Verde - Giugliano in Campania (Naples)
Gardenia - Caluso (Turin)
Giardini - Piode (Vercelli)
Hosteria Il Carroccio - Siena
Hosteria La Vecchia Ròta - Marciano della Chiana (Arezzo)
Hotel Bellevue - Cogne (Aosta)
Il Bacco Felice - Foligno (Perugia)
Il Casolare - Bacoli (Naples)
Il Cibreo - Florencerenze
Il Focolare di Loretta and Riccardo D'Ambra -
    Barano d'Ischia (Naples)
Il Giardino da Felicin - Monforte d'Alba (Cuneo)
Il Giardino degli Ulivi - Castelraimondo (Macerata)
Il Moro - Capriata d'Orba (Alessandria)
Il Rifugio - Nuoro
Il Tempo Ritrovato - Bordighera (Imperia)
'L Bunet - Bergolo (Cuneo)
La Betulla - Trana (Turin)
La Bomboniera - Civitavecchia (Rome)
La Brinca - Ne (Genoa)
La Cantina del Rondò - Neive (Cuneo)
La Coccinella - Serravalle Langhe (Cuneo)
La Pergola - Capaccio (Salerno)
La Piazzetta del Sole - Farnese (Viterbo)
La Ragnatela - Mirano (Venice)
La Rosa Rossa - Verolavecchia (Brescia)
La Solita Zuppa - Chiusi (Siena)
La Subida - Cormons (Gorizia)
La Tavernetta - Spezzano della Sila (Cosenza)
La Torre - Viterbo
L'Acquario - Castiglione del Lago (Perugia)
Le Due Colonne - Truccazzano (Milan)
Le Quattro Fontane - Casagiove (Caserta)
Le Rive - Pederobba (Treviso)
Lo Spiedo - Bagnoli Irpino (Avellino)
Lo Stuzzichino - Massa Lubrense (Naples)
Locanda agli Angeli - Gardone Riviera (Brescia)
Locanda delle Tre Chiavi - Isera (Trento)
Locanda del Vegnòt - Borgo San Giacomo (Brescia)

Locanda dell'Olmo - Bosco Marengo (Alessandria)
Locanda La Clusaz - Gignod (Aosta)
Locanda Mariella - Calestano (Parma)
Luigina - Genoa
Mammarosa - San Casciano in Val di Pesa (Florence)
Mangiando Mangiando - Greve in Chianti (Florence)
Marsupino - Briaglia (Cuneo)
Masseria di Parco di Castro - Fasano (Brescia)
Moro - Venezia Mestre
Nerina - Romeno (Trento)
Ostaria da Mariano - Venezia Mestre
Osteria de l'Umbreleèr - Cicognolo (Cremona)
Osteria del Caffè Casolani - Casole d'Elsa (Siena)
Osteria del Crotto - Morbegno (Sondrio)
Osteria del Divin Porcello - Masera (Viterbo)
Osteria del Quartino - Brescia
Osteria del Tempo Perso - Casalvieri (Frosinone)
Osteria del Treno - Milan
Osteria del Velodromo Vecchio - Rome
Osteria della Villetta - Palazzolo sull'Oglio (Brescia)
Osteria dell'Acquasanta - Mele (Genoa)
Osteria dell'Arco - Alba (Cuneo)
Osteria di Mezzo - Salò (Brescia)
Osteria di Salvatore Cucco - Gravina in Puglia (Bari)
Osteria La Piazzetta - Valle dell'Angelo (Salerno)
Pace - Sambuco (Cuneo)
Pantagruele - Brindisi
Pinocchio - Borgomanero (Novara)
Prosciutteria Dok Dall'Ava - San Daniele del Friuli (Udine)
Ristorante del Mercato da Maurizio - Cravanzana (Cuneo)
Ristorante Schiffini - La Spezia
Saltini - Pomponesco (Mantua)
Silvio La Storia a Tavola - Cutigliano (Pistoia)
Taverna Colonna - Paliano (Frosinone)
Taverna di Fra' Fiusch - Moncalieri (Turin)
Torre Ferano - Vico Equense (Naples)
Trattoria alle Rose - Salò (Brescia)
Trattoria Belvedere - Borgosesia (Vercelli)
Trattoria degli Amici - Saint-Vincent (Aosta)
Trattoria Dino - Scandicci (Florence)
Trattoria Di Pietro - Melito Irpino (Avellino)
Trattoria Società - Verzuolo (Cuneo)
Trattoria Visconti - Ambivere (Bergamo)
Vecchio Mulino - Castelnuovo di Garfagnana (Lucca)

Vicolo Duomo - Caltanissetta
Vineria della Signora in Rosso - Nizza Monferrato (Asti)
Vino e Camino - Bracciano (Rome)
Vite & Vitello - Siracusa

Slow Food
Slow Food Italy National Association
Slow Food USA National Association

Convivia
Brisbane (Australia)
Gold Coast (Australia)
Lungau (Austria)
Sud Est et Principauté de Monaco (France)
Munich (Germany)
Ulm (Germany)
Miyagi (Japan)
Nara (Japan)
East Cork (Ireland)
Fingal-Howth (Ireland)
Tipperary (Ireland)
West Cork (Ireland)
Del Garraf (Spain)
Norra Bohuslän (Sweden)
Zürcher Oberland (Switzerland)
West Gothenburg (Sweden)
Amsterdam (Paesi Bassi)
Devon (United Kingdom)
Dorset (United Kingdom)
Oxon (United Kingdom)
Saltire-Ayrshire (United Kingdom)
Somerset (United Kingdom)
Chicago (USA)
Hawaii (USA)
Marin Petaluma (USA)
Napa Valley (USA)
Portland (USA)
Russian River (USA)
San Diego (USA)
San Francisco (USA)
Valley of the Moon (USA)
Yolo (USA)

National Coordinating Committees

Emilia Romagna
Friuli Venezia Giulia
Lombardy
Piedmont and Val d'Aosta
Veneto

Italian Convivia

Alassio, Albenga e Finale (Savona)
Alberobello (Bari)
Alta Irpinia (Avellino)
Appennino Reggiano (Reggio Emilia)
Artusiana (Forlì-Cesena)
Assago (Milan)
Baronia di Vico (Avellino)
Bassa Bresciana (Brescia)
Basso Mantovano (Mantua)
Belluno
Bergamasco (Bergamo)
Bologna
Bra e Alba (Cuneo)
Brescia
Cagliari
Campi Flegrei (Naples)
Canavese (Turin)
Capodimonte (Viterbo)
Caserta
Casperia Sabina (Rimini)
Castelfranco (Treviso)
Centese (Ferrara)
Cesena
Ciampino (Rome)

Cinisello Balsamo (Milan)
Ciriè Valli Lanzo (Turin)
Civitavecchia (Rome)
Colline Alfieri (Asti)
Conegliano (Treviso)
Costa degli Etruschi (Livorno)
Costa del Vesuvio (Naples)
Cremonese (Cremona)
Dogliani (Cuneo)
Forlì
Frascati (Rome)
Garfagnana (Lucca)
Godo (Ravenna)
Lago d'Iseo (Brescia)
Legnano (Milan)
Mantova
Marino (Rome)
Merano (Bolzano)
Milan
Modena
Montereglo (Grosseto)
Monza e Brianza (Milan)
Morene del Garda (Brescia)
Oglio e Franciacorta (Brescia)
Padova
Parmense (Parma)
Pavia
Pinerolese (Turin)
Pistoia
Provinces of Treviso and Belluno
Pugliese (Bari)
Ravenna

Reggio Emilia
Riviera del Brenta (Venice)
Sanremo (Imperia)
Scandicci (Florence)
Siena
Siracusa
Terra d'Otranto (Lecce)
Terracina (Latina)
Torinese Nord Est
Torino Città
Treviso
Trieste
Val Leogra (Vicenza)
Val Nervia e Otto Luoghi (Imperia)
Valdemone (Messina)
Valle Caudina - Libero Masi (Benevento)
Valsesia (Vercelli)
Valtellina (Sondrio)
Vercelli
Verona e Villafranca (Verona)
Vicentino (Vicenza)
Vigevano e Lomellina (Pavia)
Viterbo e della Tuscia (Viterbo)
Vittorio Veneto (Treviso)

Horizons of Compatibility

The role of agriculture and food has taken on new meanings in society. New spaces for interaction between agrifood production and the community have been opened round food and its productive, cultural, social and local dimensions. These new spaces express new opportunities to promote products and their local identities, prompting possible horizons of compatibility among models designed to develop agricultural and rural fabrics.

The new trajectories that are transforming exchange and consumption processes create not only dangers but also outstanding opportunities for sustainable growth.

The progressive assertion of new sensitivities within consumer models, boosted by the unprecedented growth in the number of opportunities for cultural integration and access to knowledge, has produced new interpretations that enhance the relationship between food production and sustainable development.

In this respect, Terra Madre is an event of enormous importance, a way of exploring the issues in question and building a new perspective for the role of agriculture and food, thereby improving discussion and integration between the components of society that are carrying forward this process today.

Paolo De Castro
Minister of Agriculture, Food and Forestry

A New Cooperation

One of the aims of the present millennium has to be the reinforcement and radical innovation of international cooperation.

What is needed is cooperation founded on bilateral relations between countries such as to promote relations among local communities, cultures and experiences, thus enabling us to address the world's serious problems together. Environmental and food problems top the agenda: we need to create an alternative economy based on the protection of common goods such as the earth, food, water and energy.

It is necessary to follow the path they staked out years ago with the Via Campesina in Mexico to develop an active critique of a model of agricultural globalization that makes thousands of peasants and farmers slaves to the multinationals, denying their identity and dignity.

Hence Terra Madre, an event at which the world's food identities meet to attract attention to common goods and emphatically reassert the values of community and food sovereignty. The big job of protecting crops, hence the earth, food and related cultures demands the direct commitment of all those who are not prepared to passively accept global, all-standardizing food that denies the differences in the women and the men of this earth of ours.

The link between savvy and savoir and the rights of food sovereignty are fundamental for local communities whose only form of defense is the full affirmation of their diverse origins.

Patrizia Sentinelli
Deputy Minister of Foreign Affairs

A Chance to Meet

For the second time, welcome to Turin and Piedmont to the representatives of the food communities, ambassadors of Terra Madre, producers of quality, tradition and biodiversity!

Farmers, fisherfolk, and breeders from the weakest parts of the planet, threatened by homologation, offended by environmental pollution and exploitation. The public-private Salone del Gusto-Terra Madre partnership offers a place for them to speak, a chance to meet, an occasion for exchange and alliance: in short, an opportunity for drawing up a strategy of quality to defend typical products and protect consumers. It's a commercial gamble and a cultural challenge insofar as the civilization of taste has cast cones of light on food forgotten or devalued by the metropolitan lifestyle — too often restless, fast, chaotic and 'over-the-top'.

The return of Terra Madre coincides with the sixth Salone del Gusto. For these two events the commitment of the Piedmont Regional Authority and the other main regional bodies has been and is huge. For the values expressed by the Salone and the Terra Madre meeting are consistent, if not in symbiosis, with the policies to guarantee, protect and promote quality developed by the regional government over the years, in conjunction with business associations and local bodies.

Our warm, very warm welcome to food communities is an act of hospitable receptiveness to virtuous globalization, a phenomenon we have grown to know and admire through new international forms of what the Salone del Gusto 2006 slogan dubs as 'good, clean and fair' commerce.

Mercedes Bresso
President of the Piedmont Regional Authority

In the Heart of Turin

Turin is happy to host this second edition of Terra Madre, World Meeting of Food Communities: an event of the very highest level, undoubtedly unique in the world agrifood calendar.

In the five days of Terra Madre, thousands of people from all five continents will have the chance to talk and discuss fundamental issues such as the protection of cultural identities bound to food and gastronomic traditions, the respect for biodiversity, the defense of the equilibrium of the planet and its resources and the need to guarantee the working conditions of fair and decorous working conditions.

A novelty this year is that we have asked the people of Turin to welcome to and host in their homes some of the delegates to create what we believe is a unique opportunity to get a closer understanding of the event and enter into contact with people who represent cultures, traditions and stories, so distant hence so interesting. I am happy to say that lots of people have adhered enthusiastically to the initiative, confirming not only growing interest in the issues in question, but also the spirit of kindness and hospitality previously expressed during the Winter Olympics earlier this year.

We believe in Terra Madre and precisely for this reason we have decided, in conjunction with Slow Food, the Ministry of Agriculture and Forestry, the Ministry of Foreign Affairs and the Piedmont Regional Authority, to set up a special foundation – the Terra Madre Foundation – to organize this and future editions and thus raise the profile of such an invaluable experience.

Sergio Chiamparino
Mayor of Turin

The Great Network

We are living in an era in which we can download knowledge, information and data from the Worldwide Web at the flick of a finger. Yet the printed page still plays a fundamental role, expressing ideas and concepts, telling stories and describing feelings. Every book has an importance all of its own, but the book you are holding in your hands represents something different, something grander: it contains details of the extraordinary and painstaking labor of millions of people – farmers, shepherds, fishermen – from many parts of the globe and reveals the profound significance of Terra Madre. It describes the daily, constant commitment of 1,600 food communities that, through economics of small scale, defend biodiversity. the dignity of the rural world – a heritage of traditional knowledge and knowhow of inestimable value.

It is an important document not only for the stories it tells but also as the distinctive sign of the uniqueness of Terra Madre. It is the translation into written words of a network that self-generates, grows, develops, giving life to a close-knit web of solidarity, exchange, information and, in some cases, protest. The nodes of the network are neither political institutions nor trade unions, but food communities gathered together into a single community with planning skills and great practical sense.

Let no one underestimate the small tangible things these outstanding human beings are capable of achieving. At a moment in time in which distorted development is proving itself unsustainable, the food communities are a dam capable of checking the menace of an environmental disaster already foretold. The book of Terra Madre, which recounts the small gestures of thousands of producers in harmony with nature and the environment, is the instrument to make this extraordinary reality known.

This list of communities and products may give birth to a new alliance between food producers and food buyers, a relationship founded on complicity and brotherhood that turns the consumers of yesterday into the co-producers of today, ready to support with their choices anyone determined to practice agriculture that is good, clean and socially sustainable.

Carlo Petrini
President Slow Food International

Reader's Guide

This book, published in Italian and English to accompany the second Terra Madre world meeting (Turin, October 26-30), contains fact sheets (divided by continent and country and arranged in alphabetical order) for all the 1,600 food communities taking part. At the end of each description are supplied details of the production area in question and, where possible, a community contact person (complete with telephone number and/or e-mail address). It is our belief that circulating this information is a powerful means of strengthening the Terra Madre network.

300 food communities are also presidia, projects launched by the Slow Food Foundation for Biodiversity to support small producers (farmers, breeders, fishermen, cheesemakers, agrifood artisans and so on) and support products in danger of extinction. We have dedicated a whole page to each of these community-presidia, with which we have been following a common route for some years now. In that time, producers' associations have come into being, production protocols have been drawn up, production techniques have been improved with the help of consultants and expert and producers have taken part in a number of international events, often finding new market outlets. In short, these are positive, reproducible examples for all food communities to follow.

In some countries, the community fact sheets are followed by those of delegations which, albeit not representing the world of production, take an active part in the Turin meeting. They include various associations that play an important role in disseminating the principles on which the Terra Madre network is founded. In the sector dedicated to the United States, two insets outline the significance of farmers' market and CSA (Community Supported Agriculture). In Italy, likewise, a fact sheet describes the school garden educational project. On pages 23-24, you will find an overview of the countries of origin of the communities taking part in Terra Madre 2006 while, at the end of the book, two indices – one by nation, the other general – list all the communities in alphabetical order, highlighting those corresponding to presidia in blue.

In the first pages of the book, following prefaces by representatives of the five bodies that combine to form the Terra Madre Foundation (Italian Ministry for Agriculture, Food and Forestry, Italian Cooperation for Development-Ministry of Foreign Affairs, Piedmont Regional Authority, City of Turin, Slow Food), you will find a list of all the local bodies, companies, osterias, restaurants, Slow Food presidia and so on that have given their support – large or small – to Terra Madre.

The book ends with a list of all those who have contributed in some way to the organization of Terra Madre: producers' associations and syndicates, non-government organizations, foundations and so on. For each we have included an e-mail contact so that they, in turn, can become active members of the network.

www.terramadre2006.org
blog.terramadre2006.org

Getting To Know The World

Getting to know food communities means getting to know the world. Food communities don't confine themselves to providing us with what we eat, but ensure our survival and that of the planet we live on. By getting to know them, we rediscover the importance of very simple but vital elements such as the earth and water. It is they, the communities, the repositories of farming and fishing techniques in harmony with the environment, of breeding systems respectful of animal well-being and slow, complex processing methods, that permit the production of bread, cured meats, cheeses, cakes and biscuits that are excellent, unique and unrepeatable. An expression of ancient cultures, the communities preserve language, dialect, music and tradition; they have deep roots in their areas of origin and have thus always sought to preserve them too.

We have tracked down 1,600 communities in every corner of the planet: from the reindeer breeders of Magadan to the hatahata fishermen of the port of Kitaura, from the raisin producers of Herat to the Camaldolite monks of Nola, from North American farmers' markets to dabbawala communities, who every day get on their bikes and deliver about 100,000 packed meals to the office workers of Mumbai. In this book, we introduce you to them one by one.

Together, the communities are at the forefront of a new agriculture and a new food production philosophy based on taste quality, sustainability and social justice. Together, they wage important battles: for the free circulation of information, for fair trade, for the right to water, for GMO-less farming, for the conservation of native breeds, the protection of origin and the defense of mountain pastures and so on.

Bu they have to be able to liaise and talk and work together. Left alone they are more fragile, marginal to society, crushed by the rules of the global market, by the industrial logics of agriculture, fishing, breeding and mass production. Terra Madre offers precisely this: a possibility for world food communities to exchange information, ideas and solutions. It is democratic network of players who speak freely and strengthen each other reciprocally.

Of course Terra Madre is also a major event: a world meeting of food communities held every two years in Turin. The first edition, staged in 2004, attracted 5,000 people from all over the world. The second – to be held at the Oval in Turin from October 26-30 2006 – is organized and financed by the Italian Ministry of Agriculture, Food and Forestry, Italian Cooperation fro Development-Ministry of Foreign Affairs, the Piedmont Regional Authority, the City of Turin and Slow Food.

1,600 food communities from 150 countries are involved at Terra Madre 2006, as well as 1,000 cooks and chefs and over 200 universities. Broadening Terra Madre to kitchen experts and official science is a 'political' choice. The first we ask to become aware of the situation of agriculture round the world, of the continuous erosion of biodiversity, of the risks of homologation that a globalized market involves, and of the disarming ignorance of the new generations about such issues. Official science we ask to listen, to put its knowledge on the table, to find possible solutions to the big problems of the world's small producers and to be receptive to traditional wisdom and to grant it equal dignity.

Contents

Africa **25**
Algeria 26
Benin 26
Burkina Faso 29
Burundi 34
Cameroon 35
Cape Verde 38
Central African Republic 39
Chad 39
Comoros 41
Côte d'Ivoire 41
Congo, Democratic Republic 42
Djibouti 53
Egypt 43, **90**
Eritrea 44
Ethiopia 44
Gabon 47
Gambia 49
Ghana 50
Guinea 53
Kenya 56
Lesotho 63
Lybia 64
Madagascar 64, **91**
Malawi 65
Mali 66
Mauritania 69, **94**
Morocco 68, **93**
Namibia 70
Niger 70
Nigeria 72
Rwanda 72
Senegal 73
Seychelles 78
Somalia 79
South Africa 79
Sudan 80
Swaziland 81

Tanzania 81
Togo 85
Tunisia 85
Uganda 86
Zambia 88
Zimbabwe 88

Americas **95**
Argentina 96, **216**
Belize 108
Bolivia 108, **219**
Brazil 110, **221**
Canada 125, **227**
Chile 135, **228**
Colombia 138
Costa Rica 141
Cuba 142
Dominican Republic 144, **233**
Ecuador 144, **234**
El Salvador 147
Guatemala 148, **235**
Haiti 149
Honduras 150
Jamaica 148
Mexico 150, **237**
Nicaragua 160
Panama 161
Paraguay 162
Peru 162, **239**
United States 166, **243**
Uruguay 213
Venezuela 215, **248**

Asia **249**
Afghanistan 250
Armenia 251, **303**
Azerbaijan 253
Bangladesh 254

Bhutan 254
Cambodia 255
China... 255, 304
Philippines 257
Georgia 258
Japan... 261
Jordan 269
India 269, 305
Indonesia 276
Iran 277
Israel 278
Kazakhstan 279
Kirghizia 280
Korea 256
Laos... 283
Lebanon..................................... 284, 307
Malaysia 289, 309
Mongolia 289
Nepal 290
Pakistan 291
Palestine 291
Sri Lanka 293
Syria 293
Tagikistan 294
Taiwan 296
Thailand..................................... 297
Turkmenistan 299
Uzbekistan 299
Viet Nam 302

Europe **311**
Albania 312
Austria....................................... 314
Belgium 315
Belorus....................................... 316, 454
Bosnia and Herzegovina 318, 455
Bulgaria 320
Czech Republic........................... 323

Cyprus 457
Croatia....................................... 325, 458
Denmark 328
Estonia....................................... 330
Finland 330
France 333, 459
Germany 342
Greece 346, 467
Hungary 451, 697
Iceland....................................... 354
Ireland 350, 469
Italy 355, 470
Latvia 391
Lithuania 392
Macedonia 393
Malta 393
Moldavia 394
Montenegro 395
Netherlands 398, 673
Norway 395, 669
Poland 400, 677
Portugal 403, 679
Romania 412, 687
Russia 414
Serbia 428
Slovakia 429
Slovenia 430
Spain.. 432, 689
Sweden 442, 694
Switzerland 446, 695
Turkey 448
Ukraine 449
United Kingdom.......................... 404, 681

Oceania **699**
Australia..................................... 700
New Zealand 704
Palau 704

Africa

Béni-Isguen Oasis Date Producers

An evolution of the Béni-Isguen Tazdait Club (*tazdait* is the name for the date palm in Mozabit), the community brings together around 60growers, palm grove owners, processors and date merchants from the oasis. It has promoted and carries out, under the auspices of the international working group Growing Diversity, a project around the date palm which is the symbolic tree of the Saharan oases. It is believed that there are almost one thousand varieties of which, up to now, 48 have been selected and amongst which are those called tamjouhert, tazoggart, ouarous, babati, ajoujil, deglet nour, medjhoul, dalt, tazerzait and taneslit. Reproduction is achieved by separating and interring the buds at the base of the plant but it may also be spontaneous through the date stones. Plantations are fertilized with organic materials: palm remnants, cuttings, sheep, goat and, to a lesser degree, cattle droppings.

PRODUCTION AREA
Mzab, in the Ghardaïa district

COMMUNITY COORDINATOR
Baelhadj Tirichine
tirichinebelhadj@yahoo.fr

Atacora Mountain Flower Honey Producers

On the Atacora massif in the north of Benin, the honey plants (neré, shea, cashew, mango…) are subjected to great care and attention. The greater part of the honey comes from the colonies of *Apis mellifera adansonii* (the African bee) living inside tree cavities, termitaries, under baobab branches or in the roofs of houses. The remainder is collected in bee hives made from natural materials such as pumpkin stalks, palm leaves or clay although, in some cases, modern langstroth hives are used. The community numbers about 600 bee keepers, each of whom is responsible for a number of between five and seven hives. The extraction of the honey from the combs, pouring into barrels and then into bottles and sales are all tasks of the women. The Wamma ethnic group makes great use of honey during its circumcision ceremonies.

PRODUCTION AREA
Natitingou, Atacora Department

COMMUNITY COORDINATOR
H.M. Prosper Monde
tel. +229 97579129
mondeprospere@yahoo.fr

Atacora Mountain Rice Producers

The community brings together the women who produce and commercialise the large grained Atacora rice in the 39 villages of the area of Tanguiéta in the northwest of the country. A number of varieties of *Oryza glaberrima* (African rice) survive in this area either because they reproduce spontaneously or are planted alongside other cultivated rice. The rice grains are steamed and dried first in the sun and then in the shade. Mountain rice is greatly valued and forms the basis of traditional recipes. Rice boiled with black-eyed peas and served with sauces of either *wagassi* cheese or chili peppers fried in groundnut oil is called *watche en dendi*. *Mon habrou* is a dish made with boiled whole grains of rice served with groundnut sauces, local cheese, goat, guinea fowl or game.

PRODUCTION AREA
Tanguiéta, Atacora Department

COMMUNITY COORDINATOR
Adijoua Moutouama
tel. +229 90950726
mondeprospere@yahoo.fr

Cotonou Healthy Food Producers and Distributors

Since 1992, the community has been structured around a family run retail outlet in Cotonou, in the commercial area of Littoral, and uses a network of suppliers providing ecological and traditional foods from more than 10,000 farmers, breeders, processors, cooks and teaching farms. Amongst the products, bought by at least 500 customers, are honey, groundnut and palm oil, shea butter, cashew and pineapple syrups, cane plantation mouse meat, néré sauce, soya biscuits, dried baobab and okra, yam, cassava, white maize, sorghum and soya flours... Many products are sold with labels showing their place of origin such as, for example, *Mono zomi* is an aromatized palm oil, a specialty of the Adja women of this area, used for flavoring black-eyed peas, yam tubers and boiled cassava.

PRODUCTION AREA
Cotonou, Littoral Department

COMMUNITY COORDINATOR
Virginie Amoussou
tel. +229 97072826
mondeprospere@yahoo.fr

Fruit and Vegetable Producers

The organizational structure behind this community is that of the *maisons nourricières*. Their aim is to guarantee a varied, healthy and nutritious alimentation for the local population through the cultivation of local varieties of fruit and vegetables. It is formed by around twenty villages and although there is no specialized growing of any particular product, what unites it is the sharing of principles of quality and awareness of the nutritious and medicinal properties of the plants. It also aims to maintain those traditions surrounding the magical, protective and auspicious characteristics of the products. The spreading of cultivations and the growth of new *maisons nourricières* by both imitation and the desire to own similar plants as those grown by the community participants, is encouraged by a continuous free exchange of seeds and seedlings.

PRODUCTION AREA
Godomey, Natitingou, Cotonou, Matéri and other cities in the country.

COMMUNITY COORDINATOR
Monde Kocou Eustache
tel. +229 90950726
mondeprospere@yahoo.fr

Honvié Angolan Pea Growers

Angolan or Tropical peas (*Cajanus cajan*) are a legume of Asian origin that have been grown in Africa and the Antilles. Their long pods contain between five and eight slightly flattened seeds which range from pale green to dark red. The roots of the plants capture nitrogen and, therefore, contribute to rendering the soil more fertile. The higher stalks create a biomass that also enriches the earth. Cultivation of the plant in Benin began on the Adja plateaux in the southeast of the country where the impoverishment of the soil had become of serious concern. From here it was imported to Honvié by the village's founder, Kintogandou. In the Goun language, the Angolan pea is called *adjayi* – meaning Adja pea. 35 members of the Ayidoté cooperative grow the peas in Honvié (of which, 24 are women who also sell the product) and are supported by the Graap-Benin NGO.

PRODUCTION AREA
Adjarra in the Ouémé Department

COMMUNITY COORDINATOR
Lydie Codjo
tel. +229 90021460
graapbenin@hotmail.com

Kalalé Peul Wagassi Cheesemakers

Within a community of around 68,000 of the Peul and Gando tribes who breed cattle (97,000 heads) and grow crops, the Peul women produce a cheese – *wagassi* (*gassiré* or *gassarou* in the local languages) using a rennet obtained from a plant, the Sodom apple (*Calotropis procera*). Although the plant is widespread in Benin only the Peul know how to extract its lactic acid. To make the cheese, milk is heated for five minutes (freshly milked from zebu cows of the indigenous *borgou* breed) and then the rennet (diluted in a little milk) is added. After half an hour, the fire is stirred up and the mixture is boiled for a further five minutes. The result is then left to drain in a sieve until the following day. The forms can be colored red by immerging them in water where either maize or sorghum leaves have been boiled.

PRODUCTION AREA
Kalalé, Borgou Department

COMMUNITY COORDINATOR
H.M. Prosper Monde
tel. + 229 97579129
mondeprospere@yahoo.fr

Matéri Mountain Rice Producers

Matéri is an area of the hill chain of Atacora in the northwest of Benin. The community brings together 58 villages where mountain rice – the most consumed food in the area - is grown. The manual working of the soil seeks to make the seed bed as homogeneous as possible and to ensure that the plants retain water. In the past, seed planting was carried out during June and July but now, due to climatic changes, it takes place in August. Two traditional recipes are produced with this rice – *watche en dendi* and *mon habrou*. In the former, the rice is boiled with black-eyed peas and is served with a sauce of *wagassi* cheese or chili peppers fried in groundnut oil. In the latter, the rice is boiled whole in a large amount of water and is eaten with a variety of sauces, local cheese, goat, guinea fowl or game.

PRODUCTION AREA
Matéri, Atacora Department

COMMUNITY COORDINATOR
Gilbert Sahgui
tel. +229 97579129
mondeprospere@yahoo.fr

Sakété Yovogari Producers

Cassava is a shrub of the Euphorbiaceae family, originally from Brazil. It arrived in Africa during the slave trade period and is grown in all the tropical regions for its large underground trunks which are rich with starch. The peeled rhizome is minced, cooked and dried in the sun to produce a flour – *gari* – widely used in African dishes. By adding pineapple before it is cooked, the Mignonmidé cooperative produces *yovogari* which looks like and is used in the same way as normal *gari* but tastes much better. The cooperative which is supported by the Graap-Benin NGO is composed of 47 producers of whom 38 are women. Each producer participates in the commercialization of the product in which are contained two prime materials (the pineapples come mainly from Ahita) of which are abundant in the area. The widespread use of *yovogari* could contribute to countering the malnutrition that plagues Sakété.

PRODUCTION AREA
Sakété, Plateau Department

COMMUNITY COORDINATOR
Yves-Constant Atchade
tel. +229 90918708
graapbenin@hotmail.com - actpr2002@yahoo.fr

Bambara Pea Producers of Bobo-Dioulasso

The Bambara is a dish that the Senoufo, a population settled in the west of the country, offer to foreigners whilst waiting for the main meal to be ready. It appears as a whitish mass with the consistency of bread or pastry. The essential ingredient is a flour made by squashing or pounding Bambara seeds, a legume (*Voandzeia subterranea*) with African origins produced mainly in Nigeria and Burkina Faso. The dried pulp is turned into a very liquid paste to which is added salt and soumbala (locust seeds) and then poured into a saucepan made by the local village blacksmiths. It is put over the fire and, after a while, it is stirred so that the upper part of the contents is cooked directly by the flames. When it is ready, a few balls or shea butter or drops of oil are added. It is cut with a knife and served in slices.

PRODUCTION AREA
Bobo-Dioulasso, Houet Province

COMMUNITY COORDINATOR
Moussa Traore
tel. +226 76614844
gogwadjo@yahoo.fr

Banfora Region fruit and cereal producers and processors

Wouol, in Turkish, means reciprocal help or solidarity and Wouol is the name of the association whose members, 1,200 people of various ethnic groups, live on subsistence farming integrated by a small amount of animal breeding, artisan work and fishing. The main products, both dried by the women, are fonio and mangoes. Fonio (*Digitaria exilis*) is an ancient cereal whose limited need for water and nutrients makes it ideal for a system of organic agricultural crop rotation. Until recently it has been the ritual food of weddings and other ceremonies but has now been threatened by rice and other less traditional products. The community grows it between the mango trees, whose fruits have been dried since 1992 – in response to a crisis of over production – and exported to Europe since 1996.

PRODUCTION AREA
Banfora Region

COMMUNITY COORDINATOR
Mamadou Traore
tel. +226 20918014 – 287 8807620
rvlats@yahoo.fr

Baobab Leaf and Shea Tree Larvae Gatherers

The leaves of the Baobab which, in the Doula language are called *cira foulabourou*, are gathered mainly by women and can be eaten either fresh or dried. In this second form, they are made into a powder which is used in making sauces for maize or millet paste or rice. Both fresh and dried and ground, Baobab leaves are the ingredients of numerous dishes and baby foods. Another baby food is the powder made by finely grinding Shea tree larvae once they have been dried in the sun. The consumption of these insect larvae is a traditional Bobo diet and is in a period of rapid expansion. The larvae are collected every morning under the Shea trees, boiled in water and potash and left out in the sun. They are eaten as a substitute for meat, often between slices of bread like a sandwich.

PRODUCTION AREA
Bobo-Dioulasso, Houet Province

COMMUNITY COORDINATOR
Moussa Traore
tel. +226 76614844
gogwadjo@yahoo.fr

Black-eyed Pea (Niebé) Growers

The black-eyed pea (*Vigna unguiculata*) is a pulse widely grown throughout all the tropical and subtropical areas of the world but its greatest production area is Africa where 90% of world production is concentrated. Niebé is a French name whilst in Moorish it is called benga. It is grown in fairly infertile soil for its ability to capture atmospheric nitrogen and alongside sorghum which protects it from its most damaging parasite, the caterpillar. The black-eyed pea is an important source of vegetable proteins and is gastronomically considerably versatile. The community of 12 individuals produces around three tons a year and collaborates with research institutes in the study and selection of the varieties.

PRODUCTION AREA
Oubritenga Province

COMMUNITY COORDINATOR
Moussa Ouedraogo
tel. +226 50364319
moussasegnam@hotmail.com

Dried Mango Producers of Ouagadougou

Gie (Groupement d'Intérêt économique) Naffa, since the year 2000, has brought into an association around thirty companies, mainly run by women, each of which employees an average of around a dozen people and uses between three and four gas fired dries for treating mangoes bought fresh from producers. The mango (*Mangifera indica*) is an extremely common tree in Burkina Faso, particularly in the southwest regions (Bobo-Dioulasso, Orodara). There are numerous varieties of which four are suitable for drying: Amélie or Governor (the earliest with a green peel flecked with orange and a dark orange, soft and fibreless flesh), Kent, Lippens and Broogt. The production is certified as organic and the annual 200 tons of dried mangoes are destined almost exclusively for export to Switzerland, France and the UK.

PRODUCTION AREA
Ouagadougou

COMMUNITY COORDINATORS
Barry Mariam Rosemonde Rita Eveline
tel. +226 70249410
fiab@zcp.bf
rose_eclat@yahoo.fr

Entomophagus Women of the Bobo-Dioulasso Region

In Burkina Faso, during the rainy season whilst awaiting the September-November harvests, people eat both wild fruits and insects. All the indigenous people, except for the Bobo, eat winged termites mainly of the *Bellicositermes bellicosus* species whilst others are fed to chicks and young guinea fowl. The Bobo, a tribe to which the thirty women of the community belong, eat rather the larvae of a Lepidoptera (*Cirina butyrospermi*) that lives exclusively on shea tree leaves. The larvae are much awaited and the first arrivals are a treat for the whole village. They are gathered before their metamorphosis into cocoons, immerged in boiling water, drained, dried and then fried in oil. They serve as an accompaniment to a number of dishes and are also used as a filling in sandwiches.

PRODUCTION AREA
Bobo-Dioulasso, Houet Province

Fonio and Palm Wine Producers of Orodara

A number of groups of producers and processors of edible plants belong to the Association pour le Développement du Département de Kourinion. Fonio is a short cycle graminaceous (between 45 and 90 days) that is scatter seeded during the rainy season and its grains are used to make couscous, focaccia and tô, the country's symbolic dish. The seeds of the Bambara, a legume (*Voandzeia subterranea*) are boiled, fresh or dried, or made into flour for crepes, purees and soups. From the dried petals of the *Hibiscus sabdariffa* flowers is made bissap, a refreshing drink served during important ceremonies. The lymph of the Borasso palm (*Borassus akeassii*) is collected twice a day by making an incision in the trunk. It is then sweetened with sugar and left to ferment and is the basis of bandji, an alcoholic drink.

PRODUCTION AREA
Orodara, Kenedougou Province

COMMUNITY COORDINATOR
Chantal Kabore-Zoungrana
tel. + 226 70723271
cykabore@yahoo.fr

Forest Food Promoters

The Amicale des Forestières du Burkina Faso (Amifob) was created in 1995 and is a professional organization of environmental researchers whose aim is to promote forest products and, in particular, those for human consumption. It works in collaboration with about a dozen base organizations, one of which – a group of Nabonswendé women – manages a botanical garden together with Amifob. The community has developed initiatives, with regard to chefs and restaurateurs, for the appreciation of spontaneous legumes, wild fruits and vegetable fats. The products are collected and processed for domestic family consumption but are also sold in local markets and in the cities. Some, such as baobab leaves, vouka (*Bombax costatum*) and kaga (*Detarium microcarpum*), are also exported to neighboring countries.

PRODUCTION AREA
Ouagadougou

COMMUNITY COORDINATOR
Kardiatou Kabore
tel. +226 50356036 – 70233282
amifob_bf@yahoo.fr - kaborekardiatou@yahoo.fr

Jujube Bread Producers

A group of Tuareg women in the village of Tin Akoff, in the northern province of Oudalan, decided to contribute to the defense of local biodiversity by preparing a curious sweet made with jujubes. The Tin Akoff women are members of an association – Tin Hinan – which has set itself the task of defending and making the most of local tree species. Amongst these, the *Ziziphus mauritiana* or jujube tree, produces a fruit that is not of any particular value. The women use only the external part, the pod, which is cooked in the stomach of a kid. Once well cleaned, the stomach is filled with the pods and interred. A wood fire is lit above it and burns slowly throughout the night. The morning after, it is extracted, the outer casing is removed, and what remains is a sweet – jujube bread.

PRODUCTION AREA
Tin Akoff, Oudalan Province

COMMUNITY COORDINATOR
Fatima Mint Sidi
tel. + 226 70128526
tinhinanb@yahoo.fr

Okra Growers of Tanlili

The Union Namanegbzanga des Groupements Villageois de Tanlili (Ungvt), founded in 1992, currently coordinates 44 groups of 26 villages in the central plateaux with a total of 3,625 individuals. It promotes and populariZes agro-pastoral and forestry methods, defends and enhances the activities of its members and provides them with support and assistance. The most significant elements produced by the community's peasants are a legume, okra (*Hibiscus esculentus*) and a cereal, pearl millet (*Pennisetum typhoides*). The best okra grows between June and October or between November and February. It is planted directly as seeds and is harvested two months later with an excellent yield and a good market. Okra is eaten with other legumes or with aubergine leaves and is made into a condiment for millet paste (*tô*) and rice. The leaves are also edible and nutritious.

PRODUCTION AREA
Zitenga, Oubritenga Province

COMMUNITY COORDINATOR
Tinouigou Yacouba Zoungrana
tel. +226 50342829 – 70263779
yacoubaz@yahoo.fr

Organic Sesame Producers of Gulmu

Composed, in the eastern part of the country, of 10 groups of 15 people each devoted to production and 10 concerned with commercialization, both men and women, the community produces sesame by using organic methods, quality certified by the Ministry for Agriculture of Burkina Faso. The sesame (*Sesamum indicum*) is an oleaginous plant that produces capsules containing small, oval, white- or cream-colored seeds in the amount of between 600 and 1,300 kilos per hectare, providing a percentage of oil of between 50 and 53%. The sesame can be used in the production of various foods such as cakes, oil and chicken feed.

PRODUCTION AREA
Gulmu Region

COMMUNITY COORDINATOR
Ouoba Larba
tel. +226 70241631
Gfa_etse_ouoba@yahoo.fr

Organic Sesame Producers of Kongoussi

There are 815 peasants and 24 village communities belonging to the Association Wendin-Songdé (Aws) which, in the central northern region of Kongoussi, grow organic sesame together with potatoes, beans, onions and tomatoes. The sesame is planted on as yet uncultivated terrain or on yellow ochre sands of stony or clayey areas. It is fertilized with organic waste and there must not be any fields treated with chemicals within a distance of 300 metres. Pounded or the ash of Neem leaves are used as anti-parasites. Each grower and each peasant organization of the association has a field and, therefore, the production is both collective and individual at the same time. The harvest takes place in October-November and the sesame is put out to dry in warehouses. Its processing into oil, sauces, couscous and sugared balls is carried out by the women in the association.

PRODUCTION AREA
Kongoussi Region

COMMUNITY COORDINATOR
Nana Oumarou
tel. +226 70147316 – 40459247
inadesbf@fasonet.bf

Ouagadougou Cheesemakers

The dairy, with its headquarters in the capital, is a family business created in 1974 by Regina Edith Ouedraogo after a brief period of training in a Breton dairy. 21 individuals, of whom 16 are women, work together in processing cow and Zebu milk with traditional methods. The milk is supplied daily by cooperatives of Peul herders who have often given up their nomadic life to settle in the peripheries of the capital in order to facilitate the sales of their products. Thanks to the commitment of the community and the knowledge gained about specific dairy products, the weekly amount of milk processed has risen from 20 to 300 litres and the traditional fresh cheeses are now accompanied by the production, still fresh, of cheeses mixed with cream and yogurt.

PRODUCTION AREA
Ouagadougou

COMMUNITY COORDINATOR
Regina Edith Ouedraogo
tel. +226 50342860
nomagina@yahoo.fr – nomagina@hotmail.com

Ouagadougou Peul Breeders

The Fulbe or Peul descend from a nomadic tribe of either Berber or Ethiopian origins and, today, constitute around 10% of the population of Burkina Faso. They are, above all, herders and cattle traders and the herd is at the centre of their social structure. To the presence of the Peul is linked the breed of cattle with huge hollow horns depicted in the ancient cave drawings of the Sahara. A principal element of the Fulbe diet is milk which is consumed fresh, curdled or made into butter, whilst the excess is exchanged with land working peasants who grow cereals. The community is made up of 25 people settled on the outskirts of the capital Ouagadougou and produces fresh milk (*biissoum*) from pure local breeds (Zebu Peul, Goodal) or, occasionally, breeds crossed with Tarantaise, Montbéliarde, Alpine Browns or Holsteins.

PRODUCTION AREA
Ouagadougou

COMMUNITY COORDINATOR
Regina Edith Ouedraogo
tel. +226 50342860
nomagina@yahoo.fr - nomagina@hotmail.com

Pearl Millet Growers of Tanlili

Agriculture, breeding, protection of the environment (reforesting, nurseries, hydro-geological recovery, conservation of water and soils), credit and consultancy on investments for peasants, technical preparation: these are the main intervention areas of the Ungvt, an association active in the 26 villages of the Tanlili area. Many of the 3,625 members of the community grow a cereal, pearl millet (*Pennisetum typhoides*) that is eaten as paste, couscous, focaccia and even as a fermented drink. It originally came from the tropical regions of western Africa and *Pennisetum typhoides* is the most widely grown millet in the world, mainly due to its great ability to resist drought. The kernel contains a relatively large germ which is rich in protein and, above all, fats providing it with a high nutritional value.

PRODUCTION AREA
Zitenga, Oubritenga Province

COMMUNITY COORDINATOR
Tinouigou Yacouba Zoungrana
tel. +226 50342829 – 70263779
yacoubaz@yahoo.fr

Peul Zebu Cattle Breeders

The group of Peul speakers, traditionally nomadic and devoted to herding throughout a large part of western Africa, have not renounced their pastoral roots despite a growing process of increasingly sedentary lifestyle. The traditions and the socio-economic structure of the Peul are strongly influenced by a complex and strong relationship with the animals in their herds which are considered the most important of their resources and wealth and, for this reason, are rarely killed. Raising mainly local Zebu breeds, the five breeders who constitute the community, produce around 16,000 litres of *biissoum* (the name for fresh milk in the Moorish language of Burkina), which is then sold to local processors for the production of cheese and yoghurt.

PRODUCTION AREA
Ouagadougou

COMMUNITY COORDINATOR
Ouedraogo Nour al Ayatt
tel. +226 50342860
nomagina@yahoo.fr - nomagina@hotmail.com

COMMUNITY COORDINATOR
Suzanne Sanou Pale
tel. +226 20972014
palesuzanne@yahoo.fr

Shea Butter Producers

The community, member of the Fédération Nationale des Industries Agroalimentaires et de Transformation du Burkina (Fiab) associates more than 1,000 women who collect shea nuts and treat them to extract the so-called butter. Traditionally used as a local food, this vegetable fat is also a valuable export product used by both cosmetics and sweet making factories alike. The activities of harvesting and extraction employ 3-4,000 women in rural areas and have an impact on the nation's commercial balance sheet (the main buyers being Europe and Canada) to the tune of seven million dollars a year. The community produces conventional butter, organic butter, untreated nuts and soaps made by an emulsification of the excess with potash extracted from the ashes of various vegetables.

PRODUCTION AREA
Mossi Plateaux and other areas of the country

COMMUNITY COORDINATOR
Stéphane Badioubié Bayala
tel. +226 70324858 - 50368209
bayalastephane@gmail.com - fiab@zcp.bf

Soumbala Producers

The locust bean tree (*Parkia biglobosa*) grows in sand soil to 20 meters and produces long, flat pods which are slightly curved, rich in glucose, mineral salts and vitamins. The seeds, equally nutritious, are used as a condiment and were once used as a coffee surrogate. In Burkina Faso, they are harvested, selected and dried in the sun and the seeds are then boiled and placed into jars where, after three or four days, they become ball shaped. These are called Soumbala and are sold in restaurants and markets and are used in the making of practically all the sauces made throughout the country. Soumbala rice is extremely popular in the cities. The balls can be made into a powder and used with other ingredients (salt, dried fish, chili peppers...) to flavor ready meals.

PRODUCTION AREA
Bobo-Dioulasso and surroundings, Houet Province

COMMUNITY COORDINATOR
Moussa Traore
tel. +226 76614844
gogwadjo@yahoo.fr

Zaban and Palm Juice Producers

The forest has consistently provided the African populations with numerous spontaneous edible products. Particularly appreciated are the more or less fermented and alcoholic fruits juices that can be produced by collecting the liquid that oozes out of various plants. The community has specialized in the production and limited distribution of a juice, locally known as Zaban, made from liana (*Saba senegalensis*). Zaban is rapidly spreading to the cities and is particularly popular amongst students and those who do not drink alcohol. Bandji is made in the same way from the lymph of the Ronier palm (*Borassus aethiopum*) and it can be consumed either fresh or after a fermentation of varying lengths of time.

PRODUCTION AREA
Bobo-Dioulasso and surroundings, Houet Province

COMMUNITY COORDINATOR
Moussa Traore
tel. +226 76614844
gogwadjo@yahoo.fr

Zamené Producers

The Zamené is a plant that grows spontaneously in several areas of Burkina Faso, from the north to the south, Ouahigouya to Bobo-Dioulasso. Its small seeds are collected and dried or used fresh. By boiling them, one obtains a much sort-after and liked sauce, rarely found in restaurants due to the brevity of the period during which it is produced. It is traditionally used in the ceremonies that punctuate the social life cycle (weddings, baptisms and circumcisions) and on festivities. Zamené sauce is increasingly considered a luxury item due to its use in official refreshments and cocktail events. It can also be eaten as meal in itself, other than as a sauce, and is mainly used in the regions of Sourou, Nayala and Bobo-Dioulasso and is often eaten together with gomeré, a type of bean pancake.

PRODUCTION AREA
Houet Province

COMMUNITY COORDINATOR
Moussa Traore
tel. +226 76614844
gogwadjo@yahoo.fr

Banana Beer Producers of Cibitoke

In the banana producing province of Cibitoke, most of the bananas are used to produce a fermented drink, widely consumed throughout the whole of Burundi. At least 80,000 of the 400,000 inhabitants of the province are involved in the work of the community which produces both natural and fermented banana juice. The best variety for the extraction of juice is Igitsiri. The bananas are harvested when very ripe and are left to rest for four days. They are then roasted, without burning them, in a special oven (*urugarama*) or on a shelf exposed to the kitchen fire. The fruits are then peeled and the flesh is squashed with graminaceous leaves in a hollowed out tree trunk. The juice is filtered and pasteurized or left to ferment by mixing it with sorghum flour with funghi (saccaromiceti). The alcohol content ranges from 2-6 degrees in *urwarwa* to 12 degrees in *insongo*.

PRODUCTION AREA
Cibitoke Province

COMMUNITY COORDINATOR
Emmanuel Nahaio
tel. +257 593246

Coffee Producers of the province of Ngozi

This community, called Dufatane Munda (meaning solidarity in the Kirundi language), is composed of 72 small coffee growers, 40 men and 32 women, who have met to work together to improve their financial situations. The main product is Arabica coffee, introduced to Burundi in 1930. The plantations can be found on the central plateau in the province of Ngozi at an altitude of between 1,500 and 2,000 meters above sea level with a somewhat mild temperature. They are generally in open spaces but, in some instances, are shaded by Calliandra and Grevillea plants. A very recent crop, introduced to the area in the 1980s, is rice of which numerous white varieties are produced. Both products are commercialized nationwide.

PRODUCTION AREA
Ngozi Province

COMMUNITY COORDINATOR
Chantal Nduwimana
tel. +257 096585
Nducha2003@yahoo.fr

Farmers and breeders of Shombo, Mutumba and Nyabikere

The community is a federation of 13 cooperatives, associating 4,700 families of peasants in three localities of the province of Karuzi. The most important activities are animal breeding and the multiplication of seeds. The three centers for the production and selection of beef, cross breeds Ankolé cows (Sangas is a typical breed of the area) with Sahiwal bulls (a Zebu breed of Indian origins that has been present in Africa for a considerable length of time). Of the three centres for goat selection, two cross breed local goats with Boer or Galan rams, whilst the third breeds pure Galans. The sheep breeding centre prefers the local breed of fat tails (Intama). The centers for the multiplication of seeds produce potato, rice, bean and cassava seeds. Of particular importance is the variety of cassava which is resistant to the *mosaico severo* virus.

PRODUCTION AREA
Shombo, Mutumba and Nyabikere, Karuzi Province

COMMUNITY COORDINATOR
Petronille Kibwa
tel. +257 948790
petroki@yahoo.fr

Bambara Pea Producers of Djogona

The eight members of this community, part of the Massa people, are a group in the north of Cameroon who grow and partially transform a number of legume varieties. Despite the fact that the largest crop is millet (around 4,000 kilos a year), the Bambara pea (*Voandzeia subterranea*) and Niebé are also grown. Planted during July, the seeds of the Bambara pea germinate within 4-6 days and flower within a month. The harvest is usually carried out in October. For a rapid consumption, the fresh pods are boiled or they can be sold on the market either fresh or after drying. The dry fruits are normally made into flours of varying consistencies to be used in a number of recipes. In each small, local market there is now a retail point for the sale of ground pea paste which is often eaten for breakfast.

PRODUCTION AREA
Djogona, Extrême-Nord Province

COMMUNITY COORDINATOR
Yanmanga Soussia
tel. +237 2296475
ahmadmat@yahoo.fr

Cassava Producers of Nyanon

In the coastal area inhabited mainly by the Basso and Bakoko tribes, the growing of cassava is very common. The plant, which can grow to a height of 5 metres, produces tubers of up to 50 centimeters with a diameter of between 5-10 centimeters, thanks to which they can resist long periods of drought. The distinction between the sweet and bitter varieties lies in the greater present of a cyanide derivate in the lymph and tuber of the bitter species. However, this does not prevent it being grown more than the other due to its greater productivity. The procedure for eliminating the toxin requires the immersion of the tuber in running water or the drying of the root after it has been grated. The tuber is extirpated throughout the seasons by digging a hole about one meter wide around the plant. The most common way of serving cassava is in boiled sticks enveloped in vegetable leaves – a sort of poor-man's bread.

PRODUCTION AREA
Ndom, Littoral Province

COMMUNITY COORDINATOR
Sabine Ntollo Meka
fspe@yahoo.fr

Desert Date Leaf Gatherers

The desert date (*Balanites aegyptiaca*) is a thorny tree of the Zigofillacee family, widespread throughout many areas of Africa. As well as the small fruits similar to olives, which are edible and used to produce a much sought after oil, the leaves also play an important role in the alimentation of Cameroon. During the dry season, the tree loses its leaves leaving space for buds that are gathered by cutting the branches on which they grow and are then eaten in two ways. The leaves can be eaten fresh as vegetables for sauces and accompaniments for meat or beans or they can be cooked after being dried in the sun for at least three days. The dry leaves can be kept for up to a year and normally accompany dry meat. The five women of the community produce around 500 kilos of leaves per year.

PRODUCTION AREA
Bangana (Yagoua) Extrême-Nord Province

COMMUNITY COORDINATOR
Balamba Mahounde
tel. +237 2296475
ahmadmat@yahoo.fr

Growers and Processors of Black-Eyed Beans

The community comprises numerous local tribes but also those from other areas of Cameroon: the indigenous Mabng and Dibom tribes have been expanded by the arrival, over the years, of the Bamileké, Bassa, Boulou, Bétis and Haoussa tribes. Amongst the crops, the black-eyed or Egyptian bean stands out due to its consumption by numerous tribes. It is grown at the end of the crop rotation cycle after the soil has been freed of the remains of the preceding crops. After harvest, the bean is dried during the daytime and brought it at night to keep it from any excess damp. After three days, the pods break and the beans can be separated and preserved with addition of ash to keep them free of insects and parasites. The portion of the crop that is not sold is eaten in the form of kokii, a round shaped paste that each tribe cooks in a different manner and adding different condiments.

PRODUCTION AREA
Nkondjock, Nkam Department, Littoral Province

COMMUNITY COORDINATOR
Wamba Guy Jacques
tel. +237 9915763
guywamba@hotmail.com

Guiziga Bald-Neck Chicken Breeders

The Guiziga are a tribe from the Diamaré plains and grow cereals (in the dry season) and legumes (in the rainy season). They also raise small ruminants and chickens on a free-range basis. A characteristic breed is that of bald-neck chickens who are still used as sacrifices in ritual ceremonies. During the day, they range in the courtyards or the surrounding fields pecking at insects, larvae, cereal grains and quenching their thirst in troughs made from earth, hollowed wood or old plates. In the evenings they are brought into sleep in either the kitchen or small chicken coops where the hens lay eggs, sitting on between 8 and 12 for about 20-21 days. The animals are not killed before they are at least six months old. Their meat is traditionally eaten with millet couscous after being cooked with pounded okra or sesame paste.

PRODUCTION AREA
Moutourwa, Mayo-Kani Department, Extrême-Nord Province

COMMUNITY COORDINATOR
Jean Abdou
tel. +237 2291871
acracam@braouz.net

Guiziga Millet Growers

As a result of contact with the Fulbe, millet is now the principal food of the Guiziga. The cereal, of the *Pennisetum typhoides* variety, is planted in seed beds towards the end of August and is then planted out in karal – a silica-rich soil fertilized with ash from grass cut and burnt in the fields. In October, the men make holes in the ground with jujube sticks or steel bars, the children fill the holes with water and the women then plant out the seedlings. The millet grows in the dry season only with the reserves of that initial water and, although there are not too many weeds, the fields are weeded once in December. Between March and April, the crop is cut, dried, threshed and sifted in the fields. The millet is transported home on mule-back and stored in granaries or bags. It is used, crushed, to make couscous to be combined with vegetables.

PRODUCTION AREA
Moussoutourk, Mayo-Kani Department, Extrême-Nord Province

COMMUNITY COORDINATOR
Pierre Guidang Walkoua
tel. +237 7919893
acracam@braouz.net

Honey Producers of Danay

In the corridor formed by the northern most territories of Cameroon that divide Nigeria and Chad, immediately south of Lake Chad, this group of seven men produces around 80 liters of honey a year. It is locally known as yumna and is produced by placing the hives on the branches of the trees on the river banks and by spreading wax over the inside of the hives to attract the bees. When the honey is in production, the hives are moved to stable supports and, after four months, the producers can harvest it. The blossoms on the trees in the area – mangoes, cashews, African mahogany and others – give this honey a particular clear brown colour that is greatly valued in the region.

PRODUCTION AREA
Danay (Yagoua), Extrême-Nord Province

COMMUNITY COORDINATOR
Etienne Kawaye
tel. +237 2296475
acracam@braouz.net

Niebé (Black-Eyed Peas) Producers of Moutourwa

The Guiziga group of Moutourwa, one of the largest and most homogeneous of the tribe, is one of the many populations living in the plains of Daimaré in northern Cameroon. The main crop is the white bean, commonly known as Niebé and widespread throughout many countries of western Africa. Grown on its own or with sorghum or cotton, Niebé is not treated with chemical insecticides since the robustness of the plant allows the use of natural products such as Neem oil (*Azadirachta indica*) mixed with chili pepper, or boiled tobacco mixed with a small part of soap. Niebé can be eaten with sauces, as pancakes (*kossé*) or as a substitute for meat thanks to its high protein content.

PRODUCTION AREA
Moutourwa, Northern Province

COMMUNITY COORDINATOR
Ruth Esther Elise Bille Sike
tel. +237 9813760
billesike@yahoo.fr

Ovangoul Okok Producers

The women of the community devote their attentions to growing *Gnetum africanum* and *bucholzianum*, an evergreen climber with considerable nutritional and pharmacological properties. A spontaneous plant of the African forests, the okok is also propagated by taking cuttings and is grown either on its own or together with other species. As it is a climber, the fields are prepared with supports which are either living or of dead wood. Living supports are preferred as they can enrich the soil and are put in place up to six months before the cuttings are planted. Gnetum leaves are exported to Europe, despite their very short shelf life, and can been eaten either raw or finely chopped and added to soups or other dishes. They are also used in herbal teas and compresses to combat numerous ailments and can be fermented to make a highly alcoholic drink.

PRODUCTION AREA
Akono, North West Province

COMMUNITY COORDINATOR
Françoise Yolande Ngono Onana
ofrany@yahoo.fr

Paradise Grain Producers

Organized in the Bamenda Community Food-Medicinal Plants Association, the community's producers have been brought together to build a strong and sustainable local food system that can guarantee economic, nutritious and appropriate foods throughout the years. As well as neem, cashews and gnetum (an evergreen climber), the community produces 'Paradise grains' or alligator pepper (*Afromomum melegueta*) which is an indigenous spice. The bush, which can grow to a metre, produces reddish-brown, irregularly shaped berries which are strongly aromatic and pungent. Paradise grains, together with other spices, are used in the cure of diseases such as diabetes (when mixed with kola nuts) and beri beri (when mixed with ginger). Whilst part of the production is consumed by the producers themselves, the rest is sold locally, nationally and through a system of farmers' markets.

PRODUCTION AREA
Bamenda, North-West Province

COMMUNITY COORDINATOR
Sylvester Beng Kum
Kumsb2000@yahoo.com

Rice and Sorghum Producers of Bizili

Composed of around 300 individuals living in the extreme north of Cameroon, the cereal producers union began in 1992 with the aim of facilitating the cultivation of rice and sorghum. These products are planted in areas not subject to flooding, a little before the rainy season, and are harvested in autumn. They have the advantage of being kept at length in personal and communal granaries, whilst a part of the produce is kept back for the following planting. After husking, the waste is used for feeding the animals and the stalks for the building of roofs and small doorways. The community members have a network of solidarity available to them for the exchange of seeds and small jobs of work, together with the possibility of technical training and of joining the collective sale of the harvest.

PRODUCTION AREA
Bizili (Maroua), Extrême-Nord Province

COMMUNITY COORDINATOR
Bambe Gilbert
Cropsec2002@yahoo.fr

Goat Cheese Producers of Santo Antão

The 66 families of the community work in one of the highest and most arid areas of the island of Santo Antão. With such climatic and environmental conditions, only goats can survive and the methods for working with the milk are reduced to a minimum. It is necessary to economize with every small about of water, there is no wood for a fire, the milk is curdled raw as soon as it is milked at room temperature, there are no rooms for ageing the cheeses and, therefore, goats cheeses are produced to be sold fresh, using rennet produced by on the farm and salvaged forms. Nonetheless, all phases of production are carried out scrupulously and with a suitable knowledge of the surrounding environment. The outcome is a richly aromatic cheese with traces of grasses, a clear taste and a good structure – a cheese that recalls the origins of shepherding and which is perfect in its unembellished nature.

PRODUCTION AREA
Planato Norte, Ilha de Santo Antão

COMMUNITY COORDINATOR
João Ramos Coelho
tel. +238 9931228
Bolona.project.cv@gmail.com

Wine Producers of Chã das Caldeiras

Wine growing, on the island of Fogo, was introduced by the Portuguese colonizers in the 16th century and in the 17th century its wine was exported as far as Brazil. This community, comprising 30 small producers united in the association Chã das Caldeiras, produces around 30,000 liters of wine, 400 litres of distilled and 300 liters of grape juice every year. The traditional vines are Moscatel Preta and Preta Tradicional (with red grapes), Moscatel Branca and Branca Tradicional (with white grapes). Thanks to the volcanic soil, dry climate and a wine making method that has clearly improved in the last few years as a consequence of the intervention by Italian Cooperatives and the Cospe NGO, the association produces good bodied wines (red, white and rosé) with a considerable alcohol content.

PRODUCTION AREA
Chã das Caldeiras, Santa Catarina, Ilha do Fogo

COMMUNITY COORDINATOR
Neves Pires Monteiro Rosandro Damasceno
c/o Adega
tel. +238 2821533
assoagricha@yahoo.com.br

Cassava Growers

The Force Tranquille association brings together 640 women and youngsters from 38 groups of producers in six prefectures. Cassava, the staple food of the republic, is grown by 291 farmers, organized into 16 trading groups, and 21 independent growers. The whole plant is harvested and the fresh leaves are eaten fresh or dried in sauces or flatbreads. The cassava is then processed into flour, hence baked into bread. The community grows many other edible plants using rigorously traditional methods: corn, rice, yam, tomato, pepper, chili pepper, sweet pepper, pumpkin, banana, gombo and so on. Five cooks are currently promoting the community's produce.

PRODUCTION AREA
Bangui

COMMUNITY COORDINATOR
Clotaire Rodonne Siribi
tel. +236 043854
crosiribi@yahoo.fr

Kanembou Gatherers of Lake Chad Blue Algae

An agro-pastoral ethnic group with Sahelian origins, the Kanembou have a well structured political and administrative organization and carry out commercial activities. The artisan food is the work of the women who grind cereals to make flour and butter from milk. The female components of the community also undertake the collection of Spirulina or blue algae, which has been known and consumed for centuries in Chad where it is called dihé. The algae develop and multiply rapidly in the stagnant waters of the lake area, rich with carbonate sodium. Its high protein content makes it an important food source and, after it has been collected, it is dried and sold in wafer form. It is also used as a sauce to be eaten with maize or millet bread.

PRODUCTION AREA
Lac and Kanem Regions

COMMUNITY COORDINATOR
Laba Millalem
c/o Mahamat Seid Kidigodi
tel. +235 6279332
Kiseid2000@yahoo.fr

Kanembou Kouri Cattle Breeders

The Kanembou represent around 60% of the populations settled on the banks of Lake Chad and are 140,000 people occupied with the growing of cereals and legumes and with animal breeding. The women take care of the transformation (into flour and butter) of the products and gathering blue algae. Over and above commerce, the activity for which the Kanembou are well known even in the surrounding countries, the breeding and raising of the indigenous breed of Kouri cattle, characterized by their considerable size, light color and great lyre-shaped horns, is particularly important. Every Kouri cow produced between 4 and 6 liters of milk per day which is consumed either fresh or made into butter or curdled milk. Their flesh, to prolong its shelf life, is dried. Free range raising, typical of the Sahel, is particularly suitable for the hydro-geological conditions of the lake area.

PRODUCTION AREA
Lac and Kanem Regions

COMMUNITY COORDINATOR
Mahamat Seid Kidigodi
tel. +235 6279332
Kiseid2000@yahoo.fr

Lake Chad Maize Producers

The community is made up of farmers of the Kanembou tribe, a largely Muslim population linked to the historic reign of Kanem-Bornou. At the foundation of a complex socio-political structure, the Kanembou are organized in Groupement d'Intérêt Économique (Gie) in groups of villages and in wider inter-village structures. Maize, a fundamental food of the Kanembou, is grown by the men and processed by the women who use the inedible parts of the plant as fuel and fodder for the animals. The cobs are grilled or processed into flour for making biri paste, bouloum semolina or a sort of couscous. Maize dishes are frequently flavored with sauces made from blue algae, okra or niebé. During the unproductive season, the Kanembou are occupied with commerce both locally and in the bordering countries.

PRODUCTION AREA
Bol, Lac Region

COMMUNITY COORDINATOR
Zakaria Moussa Djoukouma Ali
c/o Mahamat Seid Kidigodi
tel. +235 6279332
Kiseid2000@yahoo.fr

PRODUCTION AREA
Lac Region

COMMUNITY COORDINATOR
Fadjack Malloum
c/o Mahamat Seid Kidigodi
tel. +235 6279332
Kiseid2000@yahoo.fr

Lake Chad Millet Producers

The agro-pastoral population of the Kanembou live around Lake Chad. The ancient roots of this people can be seen in the complex socio-political structure of its society which sees the division into tribes, smaller clans and then into families. The union of different clans gives life to a district, run by a head of district. The villages are led by a chief, though there is an intermediary figure, the head of the land, who manages the wealth of the village, the distribution of land and the settlement of conflicts. From all this, can be sensed the importance that the role of agriculture has for this community in which 31,000 tons of millet is produced every year subsequently made into flour, an essential element of local gastronomy.

Moroni Producers

Situated in northeast Madagascar, the Comoros are uncontaminated volcanic islands with an and a wonderfully rich seabed. Around the capital, Moroni, the community composed of around a thousand producers, works mainly in the fields of fishing, agriculture, pastry making and the production of fruit juices. Fish is sold fresh, dried or smoked whilst the greatest grown agricultural product is the banana, of the precious Kontrikè variety. Pastry making is mainly rice based whilst fruit juices are obtained exclusively from the tropical fruits on the island, particularly the wild orange. The concentrated juice is extracted from the citrus fruits to which sugar and natural aromas are then added. All the products are sold exclusively on the local market and for family consumption.

PRODUCTION AREA
Moroni, Ngazidja

COMMUNITY COORDINATOR
Mohamed Nafion Abdoulhalim
tel. +269 720449 - 720783
nafionhad@yahoo.fr

Dried Fish Producers of Kingabwa

The 476 producers of this community catch fish and transform it according to traditional methods of drying and salting. Almost 50 years ago, in this area closely connected to the waters of the River Congo, saw the introduction of the *Heterotis niloticus* (called *konga ya sika* in the local language), a fish that can grow to almost a meter in length and lives in calm, vegetation covered, fresh water and which is caught with creels or large webbed nets. Cut into small pieces, the fish is wrapped in leaves, often cassava leaves, and aromatized with salt and chili pepper to make *liboke*, a typical local dish that is much loved. The fish is also consumed in the form of *makayabu* – the equivalent of salt cod. By collaborating with the women who sell the fish, the community has ensured a consistent commercialization of its catch.

PRODUCTION AREA
Kingabwa, Kinshasa

COMMUNITY COORDINATOR
Jean-Baptiste Maganga
tel. +243 818801695

Tanganyika Fishermen

Supported by Human Dignity in the World, the community comprises more than 600 small producers whose activities are closely linked to the overwhelming influence of Lake Tanganyika. Fishing is the main activity of the greater part of the riverside population, given the exceptionally large amount of fish in the lake, both in the shallow waters near the banks and in the deeper reaches. The fishing community uses traditional methods, alternating the use of fishing rods and nets and catch fish of the *Lates* species, similar to the Nile perch, local varieties of *Solothrissa* and *Lamenotrissa* as well as Tanganyika shrimps. The sales of fish have gone beyond local needs and the various areas of the immense Congo are distinguished by their different methods of preparing fish based dishes: fresh, dried, in salt or in soups, in the *mwamba* (baked) manner in the Low Congo and grilled in the Kasai.

PRODUCTION AREA
Kalemie, Katanga

COMMUNITY COORDINATOR
Jean Pierre Kapalay
tel. +243 997169167
jpkapalay@yahoo.fr
inadesformation@if-congo.net - jbmaganga@yahoo.fr

Cassava and Yam producers of Anyama

This community brings together 4,000 people of different nationalities – Ivory Coast, Burkina Faso, Mali and Togo – who all work in the production, transformation and commercialisation of a number of products. The main two are cassava and yams, essential tubers of local alimentation, and both linked to the Akan tribe who arrived in the Ivory Coast from Ghana at the end of the war with the Ahoussa. Each year the Akan people celebrate the yam festival since its cultivation effectively marks the beginning of the new year. Cassava is eaten every day, cooked in various ways and, in particular, its flour is used to make Attiéké, a type of couscous. This community also grows papayas and passion fruit.

PRODUCTION AREA
Anyama, Abidjan Department

COMMUNITY COORDINATOR
Yapo Lazare
tel. +225 23557484
equipegds@africaonline.co.ci - equipegds@yahoo.fr

Cocoa producers in Tiassalé

The community comprises 200 small producers. The cocoa seedlings are transplanted to the shade of the banana trees and start producing after around three years. Four months passes between flowering and the harvest. The beans are harvested manually and then split in two to extract their white flesh with the help of a machete. At this stage, fermentation begins – and is crucial to the ultimate quality of the product – and can take place inside wooden boxes or on a bed of banana leaves and lasts six days. On the seventh day, the cocoa beans are placed on a grid in the sun for the drying phase (about one week). The community's production is around 250 tons a year.

PRODUCTION AREA
Tiassalé Department

COMMUNITY COORDINATOR
Sekongo Fonibe
tel. +225 5632833
sekongofonybi@yahoo.fr

Coffee and Cocoa growers in Daloa

The Kavokiva cooperative, with its headquarters in Gonaté, unites 6,000 small producers of coffee and cocoa in the region. Both species (*Theobroma cacao* and *Coffea Arabica*) are planted on soil rich with the humus of the forest areas, initially in nurseries where the damp seeds, wrapped in sacks, remain for eight months. From their transplant to the first harvest, three years will pass. The fruits are harvested manually and, if the case of coffee, dried before being sent to the warehouse for husking. The cocoa beans are, on the other hand, wrapped in banana leaves and left to ferment for six days after which they are transported in vans to the drying rooms. Dried and crisp, they are put in sacks and taken to the central warehouse for subsequent preparations or exportation although the smaller beans and the cocoa powder is eliminated from each sack before this occurs.

PRODUCTION AREA
Daloa Department

COMMUNITY COORDINATOR
Fulgence N'guessan
tel. +225 22412081
fulgence@aviso.ci

Fruit Juice producers of Abidjan

The community brings together 180 women who produce drinks made from three tropical plants: tamarind, ginger and karkade. The *Tamarindus indica* (called tomidji in the local language) is a tall tree with rare leaves and clusters of red flowers. The fruit is a legume which contains, as well as hard seeds, a gelatinous reddish-brown flesh which, when ripe, is mixed with water to obtain an aromatic cold drink. *Zingiber officinale* (gnamakoudji) is a herbaceous plant with creeping rhizomes that the women use fresh – it is crushed and left to macerate in water to which sugar is subsequently added. Ginger juice is drunk iced. The infusion made with the dried hibiscus flowers of the Karkade (*Hibiscus sabdariffa*, locally known as bissap) is another refreshing drink.

PRODUCTION AREA
Abidjan Department

COMMUNITY COORDINATOR
Hien Victorine Ouattara
tel. +225 5018017
Hien_victorine@yahoo.fr

Animal breeders and milk and dairy producers of Djibouti

The community of eight people raises 115 head of cattle of which 40 are mixed breed calves and 65 African, Dutch and mixed breed cows. They are fed on crushed grain, dates, grass growing around the farm, millet grains and other cereals bought in the city. Once a month, a calf is sold as meat whilst the sale of milk, yogurt, curdled milk and butter is constant (sold on the farm to two clients who take it so market). The cows are milked manually twice a day. The milk is bottled in mineral water glass bottles. The by-products of the butter making process are used to fatten the horses and as traditional medicines. The community possesses a similar farm in Ethiopia at Dire Dawa.

PRODUCTION AREA
Djibouti

COMMUNITY COORDINATOR
Mohamed Hassan Djama
tel. +253 831441
omar_hassan dj@yahoo.fr

Bakers and Confectioners of Alexandria

Village of Hope is an eco-village working in activities linked to sustainable agriculture and involves a group of disabled young men and women. These youngsters work mainly in the local bakery where they produce a number of traditional cakes and pastries. The association, composes of 12 individuals, prepares the classic *omali*, a pastry made with puff or short pastry, milk and a variety of nuts. Legend has it that this pastry has its origins in the times of the Queen Om Ali who is supposed to have had it made to celebrate the assassination of her husband King Aybak's second wife. Amongst the other products are the *fetteeer meshaltet*, which are eaten with cheese or filled with honey and jam, and also *hawawsy*, sandwiches filled with minced meat and baked in the oven.

PRODUCTION AREA
El Iskandarîa

COMMUNITY COORDINATOR
Thabet Nada Alfy
tel. +20 33930807 - 12449182
nadathabet@hotmail.com

Growers of Wadi El Rayan

By means of the Land Reclamation policies of the Egyptian government in the 1950s, some stretches of the Saharan territories were provided with infrastructures to render them capable of cultivation and were given over to peasant families to grow maize, corn, olives, vegetables and medicinal plants (in particular, camomile). The draining of Wadi El Rayan, lying at about 140 kilometers southeast of Cairo, provided a virgin soil that was otherwise inhabitable, thanks to two artificial lakes and an integrated irrigation system supplying water both to the fields and for human consumption. In two villages, little more than one kilometer apart, lived around 50 peasants, of whom 18 live in a special protected area. Around fifty farms sell their certified organic products abroad.

PRODUCTION AREA
Wadi El Rayan, Youssef El Sediq District, Fayoum Governorship

COMMUNITY COORDINATOR
Mohamed El Medany
tel. +20 846368507
medanyfao@yahoo.co.uk

Olive Producers of Sinai

The family community of Tamr Henna is part of a project for sustainable development in desert areas, centered around the conservation of natural resources through the cultivation of olive groves introduced by the Romans more than 2,000 years ago. The pilot project, created with the aim of reducing the levels of poverty and improving the social conditions of the Bedouin groups subsequent to the reforms concerning them, began with the assignment of almost 1,000 acres of olive groves, cultivated partially with bio-dynamic and partially with organic methods. A large number of women are involved in this activity, particularly with regard to the operations of processing the olives. The fruit, green and fleshy, are harvested and pitted manually and can be sold both naturally or dressed with lemon juice, garlic, thyme and other spices.

PRODUCTION AREA
Tamr Henna, Et-Toor Governorship

COMMUNITY COORDINATOR
Daniel Khair Samia
tel. +20 102260919
sdselwanes@yahoo.com

Organic Vegetable and Aromatic Herb Producers of Fayoum

Located in the governorate of Fayoum, in central northern Egypt, the community is present throughout the country. Camomile flowers are picked singularly, placed in thin layers of palm sticks and are dried in the shade. Onions are interred in the winter and harvested in May, a month after the leaves have dried and bent over. After the harvest, the onions are laid out at the ends of the rows until the leaves have dried completely so that they can then be cut and prepared. Mint, the aromatic herb that is most common and used in local cuisine, is collected five times a year and dried with the same methods. The community has the Egyptian certification of is organic agriculture status from the Egyptian Centre for Organic Agriculture (Ecoa).

PRODUCTION AREA
Fayoum Governorate

COMMUNITY COORDINATOR
Ashour El Sayed
tel. +20 846338169
Eoa002@hotmail.com

Vegetable Producers of Midrisien

In Midrisien there are 400 inhabitants in an arid and stony area and seven women who are united in a cooperative cultivating and equal number of kitchen gardens. They began this activity thanks to a micro credit project run by the National Union of Eritrean women (Nuew) and, having repaid the loan by selling their products (lettuces, carrots, potatoes, onions, chard, cabbages...) in the Asmara markets, they contribute to the support of both their families and the village as a whole. The fields are worked traditionally and manually, without agricultural machinery (at the very most they will have a plough pulled by a very thin cow) and without chemical products. The kitchen gardens are kept extremely well and between the rows of plants there are small, dug out irrigation channels. Until a few years ago, the women had to carry buckets of water to the fields in order to irrigate but they now have a pump which greatly simplifies their labor.

PRODUCTION AREA
Midrisien, Asmara (Asmera)

COMMUNITY COORDINATOR
Belainesh Seyoum
tel. +291 1125444
bseyoum@nuew.org

Coffee and Forest Honey Producers of Dollo Mena

On the Mena-Angetu Bale Mountains in the southern part of Ethiopia, around 300 peasants have come together in a cooperative and harvest the coffee that grows spontaneously in the forest. The peasants use neither pesticides nor weed killers and collect the fruit manually when they are ripe although the work is hindered by the presence of baboons who love it. They produce around 2,500 tons of coffee per year in the form of beans dried in the sun and of which a very small part is put aside for family consumption. In the same area, other than coffee, a group of beekeepers collect honey by hanging the hives on the high trunks of the trees in the forest. The honey undergoes an exposure to the sun to permit a slight filtration.

PRODUCTION AREA
Mena-Angetu, Oromia Region

COMMUNITY COORDINATOR
Eshetu Demissie
tel. +251 223311155
eshetudemissie@yahoo.com

Coffee Producers of the Golocha Forest

Ethiopia is the country where coffee originated and, therefore, the only place in the world where wild plants can be found. In the mountain forest of the Arsi-Golocha (Oromia, the central southern region of the country) *Coffea arabica* grows spontaneously at an altitude of 1700-1800 meters above sea level. No fertilizers or chemical products are used and the coffee is harvested manually. The around 536 members of the community are organized in a cooperative and live on the sales of coffee (certified organic) which is sold raw to intermediaries in the capital, Addis Ababa, or cities closer by. A small part of the harvest is consumed by the families living in the forest where the coffee beans are crushed with a wooden mortar and pestle and toasted in the homes.

PRODUCTION AREA
Arsi-Golocha, Oromia Region, Arsi District

COMMUNITY COORDINATOR
Abebe Taffa
tel. +251 223311155

Euphorbia Honey Producers of Tigrai

The Tigrai region is located in the extreme north of Ethiopia on the border with Eritrea and is mainly inhabited by the Tigrino people. Here there is a community of 10 people who produce around 5,000 kilos of Euphorbia honey per year. Honey production (*kicha me ar* in the local dialect) has deep roots in Ethiopian history, so much so that an ancient Egyptian legend cites Abyssinia (today, Ethiopia) are the land giving origins to honey and wax. The bees have selected natural places for their hives and, thanks to the abundance of Euphorbia plants on which they live, they have populated the area. The honey produced by the community, following traditional methods of collection, is very white with a creamy and caramelized consistency and a flavor of citrus fruits – particularly citron. The community also produces bees' wax.

PRODUCTION AREA
Wukro, Tigrai Region

COMMUNITY COORDINATOR
Haleka Alem Abreha
tel. +251 0344430505
rutateven@yahoo.com

Hard Wheat Producers in Ejerre

The community involves around 300 peasants and 30 retailers working on the cultivation and commercialization of various varieties of hard wheat. The community is structured in a cooperative and its aim is the recovery and selection of ancient local varieties which have been substituted by softer wheat. The wheat is grown in rotation with legumes and teff (a local cereal) in accordance with sustainable agricultural methods. One of the most interesting varieties is black wheat which has dark grains ranging from brown to a bluish colour and which is highly resistant to both salty soils and drought. With the black corn, the community members produce a wholemeal bread traditionally called *deffo dabo*. The community takes great care over the conservation of the seeds obtained either through the seed bank or directly from other peasants.

PRODUCTION AREA
Ejerre, Oromia Region, Arsi District

COMMUNITY COORDINATOR
Aseffa Zerihun
tel. +251 115502288

Honey Producers of the Wonchi Volcano

A couple of hours southeast of Addis Ababa, the road climbs up between pastures and fields of the 'false banana tree' (a tree similar to the banana tree of which the leaves and roots are used) when suddenly the magnificent crater of Wonchi appears: a ring of verdant steep slopes with a deep blue lake at their base. For a few years, a co-operative of 21 men have been organizing visits to the Park and they also work on the maintenance of the roads and paths. The volcano's second resource is honey, harvested in December and sold in honeycombs. The producers also build the hives with large cylinders of bamboo and banana tree leaves. The honey is reddish with an intense, slightly bitter taste. A Slow Food Presidium is being planned to improve the quality of the product, organize its packaging and sales and to promote eco-tourism around the volcano.

PRODUCTION AREA
Wonchi, Woreda District, Oromia Region

COMMUNITY COORDINATOR
Miressa Himeskel Igo
tel. +251 911868460

Incense and Myrrh Gatherers in the Filtu Area

The semi-nomadic shepherds living in the most eastern area of Ethiopia move around following the erratic rains in search of pastures. They breed and sell cattle, goats and camels from the latter of which they produce milk, meat and skins. During the dry season, the community works on the collection of the natural resins that can be found in trees without damaging them. There are different types of resin amongst which are white, yellow and black incense, myrrh and Arabian gum. The area is historically known for the number of plants with aromatic resins and for its commerce in incense. It is well known that the Egyptians bought these products from Ethiopia to use in their mummification processes. Today, many incense gatherers are discouraged by the extremely low prices that products reach, particularly in consideration of the complex process surrounding their collection.

PRODUCTION AREA
Filtu, Somali Region

COMMUNITY COORDINATOR
Abdidaad Ibrahim Bulale
tel. +251 911173491
pcae@ethionet.et

Kollo Producers of Dinsho

Bale is the most important Ethiopian region for the growing of barley (it is no coincidence that the only production of Ethiopian beer is in this area) and the village of Dinsho is unanimously considered the best area for the production of kollo, or toasted barley. The seeds are soaked in boiling water for two to three minutes (30 kilos to every 10 liters of water) and are then toasted on a huge, circular iron plate placed directly over the flames on a stone or clay support. The women responsible for the preparation continually stir the seeds over the five for about 10-15 minutes with a wooden stick with a curved point. Once the seeds have been toasted, they are crushed in a mortar for a few minutes. There are about fifty producers and they sell the kollo in the streets (9 birr per kilo).

PRODUCTION AREA
Dinsho, Bale Park, Oromia Region

COMMUNITY COORDINATOR
Eshetu Demissie
tel. +251 223311155
eshetudemissie@yahoo.com

Teff Producers of Debre Zeit

The Alfa Gowa cooperative brings together 58 peasants (41 men and 17 women) and sells teff, wheat, barley and vegetables in an open market at Debre Zeit thanks to Oxfam financial support. The main product is teff, white or red, and which represents 75% of sales, followed by wheat, barley, chickpeas and a number of local vegetables. Teff is an ancient cereal with miniscule grains that are little bigger than a grain of sand. Its cultivation requires repeated plowing with oxen in May, fertilization, planning in June and the harvest (manual with a sickle) in November. After the harvest, the stalks are placed on a platform of hardened cattle dung and are crushed by oxen. To divide the chaff from the grains, wooden paddles and a sieve are used. With teff flour, the national Ethiopian bread, 'njera, is made.

PRODUCTION AREA
Debre Zeit, Oromia Region

COMMUNITY COORDINATOR
Abebe Tedla Biruk
tel. +251 114336481
alfat@ethionet.et

Banana Growers of Mbenga

In the village of Mbenga, in northern Gabon, an association of banana producers has been created which brings together around forty peasants, mainly women. The association manages the whole production line, from the growing to commercialization. The bananas are planted on a flat and well irrigated terrain, using a gem from the adult tree. Every day, the women go through the fields to manually pull up the weeds and to cut off any excess leaves. After 12 months the first crop is ready for harvest. Three of the varieties grown belong to the species *Musa sapientium* which is the most common, whilst other are *Musa paradisiaca* which produces plantain bananas which are only eaten once cooked. There are also sweet bananas, those universally recognised, a pink figue which is purplish and highly perfumed and the atora, a local variety of the sweet banana.

PRODUCTION AREA
Mbenga, Woleu-Ntem Province

COMMUNITY COORDINATOR
Meye Mbote Philomene - tel. +241 06954994

Cane Sugar Growers and Processors of Doumandzou

The community brings together eight producers, 12 processors and eight wholesalers of case sugar (*Saccharum officinarum*), a plant whose introduction to Gabon goes back to the slave trade period. The cuttings are placed in the ground which has previously been roughly tilled and ploughed. The harvest is carried out between nine and twelve months later and the canes are transported to the village in baskets made from lianas. Part of the crop is consumed as it is and the rest is made into syrup which can be added to pineapple juice or left the four days in a barrel with bitter woody essences and maize to make a fermented drink. The waste left over from the sugar canes are placed around fruit trees during the rainy season and are used to retain the water that will be needed in the dry season. The same waste is used to make a material which is used as toilet paper.

PRODUCTION AREA
Doumandzou, Woleu-Ntem Province

COMMUNITY COORDINATOR
Angone Eva Noel Maucklère
tel. +241 07948105 - gedergabon@yahoo.fr

Cassava Growers and Processors of Makokou

Composed of farmers, the community mainly works on the small scale crop growing, the transformation and sale of cassava – called *mbong* in the Fang language. Cassava is a shrub belonging to the Eupohorbiacee family and is grown for both is tubers and its leaves. The roots are rich with starch which is used in the both the textiles and food industries. The plant is grown above all in the area near to the Equator. When the tubers are mature, they are extracted from the ground and immersed in water for several days in order to remove any impurities. Once dried, they are cooked and wrapped in leaves before being eaten. Cassava leaves are used both as a tropical medicine and as food, with the addition of spices.

PRODUCTION AREA
Makokou, Ogooué-Ivindo Province

COMMUNITY COORDINATOR
Fidele Nzeng Biteghe
tel. +241 07298903
gedergabon@yahoo.fr

Coconut Processors of Bissok

Drinks, sweets, oil and body milk: this is the range of products made by the community which brings together around 20 processors and retailers of the derivates of the coconut (*Cocos nugifera*), a tropical palm tree that can grow to a height of 25 meters. The milk to be drunk is produced by mixing it with water, boiling lightly and filtering the coconut flesh that has been manually peeled. The grated seeds are used in the preparation of two sweets: one a mixture of coconut and sugar, caramelized and cut into pieces; the other is a mixture of coconut, sugar and egg whites beaten until stiff and then baked in the oven. From the ripe nuts, once they have been liberated from the fibrous outer layer and broken apart, cosmetics are produced.

PRODUCTION AREA
Oyem, Woleu-Ntem Province

COMMUNITY COORDINATOR
Mélanie Zang Minko
tel. +241 06657532
gedergabon@yahoo.fr

Karkade Growers

Karkade (*Hibiscus sardariffa*) is a tropical African malvaceous whose flowers, when dried, are used to prepare a thirst quenching infusion. The bush grows to the height of around a meter and a half and has a green or yellowish trunk which can be smooth or thorny according to the variety. The leaves are oval and the fruit is a capsule surrounded by a fleshy calyx when ripe. It reproduces through seeds but has no need of a nursery. Traditional in Gabon is the syrup of a mother o pearl redness that is obtained by leaving the dried karkade fruits in water for 6-12 hours. The solution is then sugared and perfumed with mint leaves and it is drunk as a remedy against anemia. The community, composed of about ten growers and merchants, also grows okra and amaranth, plants which are popular with the Fang people who uses the leaves as anticoagulants for snake bites.

PRODUCTION AREA
Libreville, Estuaire Province

COMMUNITY COORDINATOR
Judith Nkare Emane
tel. +241 07846215 - 06111061
gedergabon@yahoo.fr

Oil Palm Producers and Processors of Lambaréné

The oil palm (*Elais guineensis*) reproduces through seeding either spontaneously or in plantations (the first of which in Gabon go back to 1931).The fruit is a drupe whose mesocarp contains a red oily substance whilst the seed, wrapped in a woody shell provides the better known palm oil. The red or raw oil is extracted by crushing the flesh and it can be divided into two elements: a liquid used also as a food substance and a solid, which is used to make soaps. The oil obtained by breaking up the nuts is black when worked by local artisans (carried out by the small community with the aid of an agronomist) and pale yellow in the industrial version – locally it is only used for medicinal purposes. From the trunks of unproductive trees is extracted a whitish lymph which if fermented with pieces of wood and bark and produces a palm wine that is drunk at markets and festivities. The nuts are used to make *gnembwe*, a traditional soup.

PRODUCTION AREA
Lambaréné, Moyen-Ogooué Province

COMMUNITY COORDINATOR
Jean Okoue
tel. +241 07906555
jeanokoue@yahoo.fr - gedergabon@yahoo.fr

Taro Producers of Obout-Essangui

The Les Communautaires association has, amongst its members, this community of growers and retailers of taro, a herbaceous plant with Asian origins introduced into daily African life as a result of the slave trade. Taro is a tuber that grows mainly in the subtropical region and is grown for its roots which provide a flour with a taste similar to that of the sweet potato which is much used in Gabon's cuisine. Taro leaves also play an important role in rural eating and are grown and sold in the local markets. They are about 70 centimeters long and grown on the upper part of the plant. They are collected slightly earlier than the tuber and cooked like spinach

PRODUCTION AREA
Obout-Essangui, Woleu-Ntem Province

COMMUNITY COORDINATOR
Hursule Medza Ollomo Juna
tel. +241 07575667
medza.ursule@caramail.com - gedergabon@yahoo.fr

Traditional Spice producers in N'kart and Ngomessi

This small community is composed of 12 women who work processing and selling a number of traditional herbs and spices. In particular, they transform the fruit, roots and bark of the essoun (*Scorodophuleus zenkeri*), a spontaneous forest tree distinguishable by its yellow leaves. The powder produced from the fruit, roots and pieces of bark are mixed and traditionally used to flavour numerous local dishes. They also grow messep (*Ocimum gratissimum*, a type of basil whose dried leaves are excellent for aromatizing strongly flavored meat such as mutton), numerous varieties of chili pepper and ossang (*Dinophora spenneroides*), of which the roots and leaves are used.

PRODUCTION AREA
N'kart and Ngomessi, Mitzic, Woleu-Ntem Province

COMMUNITY COORDINATOR
Rosalie Awa Nang Angone
tel. +241 07870034
gedergabon@yahoo.fr

Wild Mango Gatherers of the Doum District

In the province of Woleu-Ntem, the most northern of Gabon, the wild mango (*Irvigia gabonenis*) is a formidable resource for the local populations of Bantu and Pygmies. The elders look for the trees in the forest, the youngsters collect the fruit and the women prepare them. Of the fruit – called *ndock* in the local dialect –the fresh cotyledon is used for sauces and the nut is used to produce, after a long process of drying and grinding, a paste called *ekima ndock*. This paste, also called *dika* bread or chocolate, solidifies at the end of the process In the shape of a container and can be kept for many months. During the very last phases of drying, an oil appears on the surface of the paste which is gradually collected with a spoon and used for cooking.

PRODUCTION AREA
Doum District, Woleu-Ntem Province

COMMUNITY COORDINATOR
Eva Mbeng Lucien
tel. +241 07418039
lucieneva1@yahoo.fr

Producers and Processors of Banjul

The National Association of Food Processors is a base organization which brings together beekeepers, animal breeders, vegetable growers, shellfish gatherers and processors of cereals and fruit from the municipality of Kanifing. Thanks to a series of training activities, these producers apply and promote sustainable agricultural methods. The area in which they work most is that of beekeeping which has traditionally been in the area due to the curative properties of honey and the use of wax and the breeding of local cattle and sheep breeds for the production of meat and ghee, a type of clarified butter – both of which are essential elements of the Gambian diet.

PRODUCTION AREA
Kanifing Municipal Council, Banjul

COMMUNITY COORDINATOR
Cham Alhagi
tel. +220 9936835
chamkaddy2004@yahoo.co.uk

Producers and Processors of Brikama

The sustainable agricultural development and the promotion of the territory are the focus of the interest of this community. The producers and processors of Alla Tentu Kaffo work on the one hand to organize training courses, initiatives to facilitate access to market for the peasants and activities of tourist promotion. On the other, they grow a variety of traditional products such as, in particular, cereals (amongst which are early and late millet, maize and sorghum) but also cashews, sesame and cassava. Fishing in both fresh water and the sea are equally important and they catch, over and above barracudas and the South African tilapia, also the bonga fish (*Clupea fimbriata bowdwich*), particularly during the period when the Gambia River overflows.

PRODUCTION AREA
Brikama, Western division

COMMUNITY COORDINATOR
Cham Alhagi
tel. +220 9936835
chamkaddy2004@yahoo.co.uk

Producers from the Methodist Mission of Kerewan

In Kerewan, at 60 km from the capita Banjul, the community brings together small producers and processors in a cottage industry system. Its main activity is the growing of mangoes, cashews, citrus fruits and vegetables. The Gambian Republic is one of the main producers of mangoes whose cultivation has, however, been reduced during the last few years due to the introduction of other crops. Harvested between April and August, according to the type of transformation, mangoes will become a tasty chutney (spiced sauce) or a jam. With regard to vegetables, the community produces and sells in the local markets several types of lettuce and tomatoes, amongst which is the famous bitter tomato only found in this area.

PRODUCTION AREA
Kerewan, North Bank Division

COMMUNITY COORDINATOR
Cham Alhagi
tel. + 220 9936835
chamkaddy2004@yahoo.co.uk

Animal Breeders of Amuyaokope

The population inhabiting the area of Amuyaokope (90 kilometers from Accra) live by raising cattle, sheep, goats, pigs and poultry in a free range regime. In order to integrate their income, the 40 members of the community also grow vegetables. The manure produced buy the animals is used to fertilize the fields. There is neither running water nor electricity in this area and, after butchering the animals, the women wash the meat and keep it overnight covered with salt and spices. It is then hung from the ceiling of the kitchens so that it is slowly smoked. This process permits it to be kept for six to eight months and it is used mainly for the preparation of a baked soup. Another specialty of the area is *chinchinga*, a type of kebab. The largest city in Amuyaokope is Sege. The community is part of the Development Action Association.

PRODUCTION AREA
Sege, Amuyaokope, Greater Accra and Volta Regions

COMMUNITY COORDINATOR
Agbovi Eva Ametepey
c/o Lydia Sasu
tel. +233 21315894
daa@africaonline.com.gh

Fish Smokers of Kokrobite

The fish, bought on the beaches, are placed on wooden trays and layers of metal netting piled up one on top of the other above a mud oven. For each oven there is a maximum of 15 trays for a total of 100-160 kilos of fresh fish. The smoking takes about 10-18 hours at a low temperature. The order of the trays is changed about two to four times in order that all the fish is evenly smoked. The result is a product that can be kept for six months. The community is part of the Development Action Association, a federation of associations with a percentage of 98% women who work in Greater Accra to ensure a just remuneration for the workers and to help them deal with problems linked to safety of the food products, diversification of incomes, environmental deterioration and HIV contagion.

PRODUCTION AREA
Kokrobite, Greater Accra Region

COMMUNITY COORDINATOR
Cecilia Agbeshie
c/o Lydia Sasu
tel. +233 21315894
daa@africaonline.com.gh

Cassava Processors of Obom

The area of Obom, composed mainly of small rural villages, is located in the Greater Accra region and is famous for the production of cassava, a tuber defined as the food of the poor. Obom supplies the famous market of Kasoa in Central Ghana with the main part of its huge quantity of cassava paste. The fresh cassava sticks are cut in pieces of around 15 centimeters and are planted with the buds facing upwards and covered with earth. No fertilizers are used. The harvest is carried out after six to nine months. The cassava is peeled, washed, grated and place is sacks to expel the water. A this point it is ready to be used. There are many local recipes in which it is used: gari, agbelikakro, tapioka, yakayaka, fufu. The community is a member of the Development Action Association.

PRODUCTION AREA
Obom, Greater Accra Region

COMMUNITY COORDINATOR
Mary Kale
c/o Lydia Sasu
tel. +233 21315894
daa@africaonline.com.gh

Fishermen and Animal Breeders of Nyuiyui

Originally living on the banks of the artificial Lake Volta, at almost 350 kilometers from the capital Accra, the community of fishermen has moved to Nyuiyui in the area of Ada, close to the Atlantic estuary of the River Volta. Traditionally devoted to fishing and the preparation of the fish, the members of the community have been able to diversify their production by raising cattle, thanks to the considerable availability of both water and pastures. The herds are tended by a Peul shepherd and, equally, the method of producing wagassi cheese also comes from the Peul. Fish is smoked on wood fires and subsequently salted and dried in the sun for up to two or three weeks.

PRODUCTION AREA
Nyuiyui, Eastern Region

COMMUNITY COORDINATOR
Adjokatse David Kwao
tel. +233 244771375
akunzule@yahoo.co.uk

Maize Producers from Donkokrom

Donkokrom, at a little more than 200 kilometers from the capital Accra, is considered the granary of Ghana for its vast production of cereals, groundnuts, beans and cassava. In this area a community, formed into an association of around 500 producers of maize and three processors, live and work. Maize is a continuous crop with two harvests a year: the first planting takes place from April to June and the second, less fertile, from August to November. Abro, as maize is locally known, matures in 120 days and the preparation of the soil, the planting and the harvest are all done manually. Maize flour is produced by the community's processors and is the ingredient of many local dishes. A type of cassava locally called *bankye* is also grown.

PRODUCTION AREA
Donkokrom, Eastern Region

COMMUNITY COORDINATOR
Biribia Kwaku
c/o Anthony Akunzule
tel. +233 244771375
akunzule@yahoo.co.uk

Pineapple Growers from Obodan

At around 50 kilometers from the capital, in a highly productive agricultural area, the community accompanies the growing of cassava and maize for its own consumption with growing crops to be sold. In particular, the peasants have specialized in the production of pineapples and, to a lesser degree, pepper and palm oil. Mainly propagated by suckers and hand picked, the pineapple plants are placed in regular rows on a soil that has previously been tilled using hoes and short swords and, only rarely with the use of tractors. After the harvest, which is also manual, the fruit are packaged and ready for transformation into fruit juices and fruit salads or for immediate consumption.

PRODUCTION AREA
Obodan, Eastern Region

COMMUNITY COORDINATOR
Anthony Akunzule
tel. +233 244771375
akunzule@yahoo.co.uk

Pineapple Growers from the Central Region

In 2005 the Ghana Association of Modena (Italy) founded Ghanacoop, one of the first Italian experiences of cooperation in development by immigrants. This cooperative promotes Fair Trade products and organizes initiatives of solidarity between Italy and Ghana. The end of 2006, in the village of Gomoa Simbrofo (Central Region) will see the creation of an agricultural firm for the growing of pineapples of the smooth cayenne variety that was domesticated by Venezuelan natives and is preferred due to the sweetness of its flesh. It has been grown for centuries in Ghana and is eaten either fresh or as the ingredient of a number of sweets. One of the most common recipes uses pineapples, bananas, chocolate and rum. Both the rind and the flesh are used in some villages as a treatment for malaria fevers. Thanks to Ghanacoop, 30 growers from the country sell around 15,000 tons of pineapples a year to Italy with the Transfair certification.

PRODUCTION AREA
Central Region

COMMUNITY COORDINATOR
Thomas McCarthy
tel. +39 059279076 - tmccarthy@oltrelab.it

Plantain Banana Growers of Amanease

Lake Volta, one of the largest artificial lakes in the world, is the main source of irrigation for the eastern regions of Ghana and is essential for animal raising, agriculture and fishing. South of the lake the villages of Amanease, Osino and Nyanyano are well known for the production of plantains, taro and a local maize. It is here that a community of 50 farmers, men and women, produce plantain bananas. The dishes made with this fruit are common throughout the country: fried plantain with beans is locally called red red and, in the urban centers is is usual to cook it in the streets and sell it together with peanuts. On a number of days of the week the community's women go to the capital Accra to sell their plantains on stalls in the markets of Mokola and Adabraka.

PRODUCTION AREA
Eastern Region

COMMUNITY COORDINATOR
Victoria Appiah
c/o Lydia Sasu
tel. +233 21315894 - daa@africaonline.com.gh

Salt Producers and Processors of Nyanyano

Nyanyano is famous for its production of salt that takes place on the beach without the use of chemicals. In the past, people arrived from the north of the country to work in the salt mines. Today, the young people of the area have revived this activity, making it economically viable again. Traditional production methods have remained unchanged: the sea water is pumped into natural basins dug out of the clayey soil located in the less rainy area. Here the sea water is left to evaporate for about five days. As soon as the salt crystals have formed, they are collected and stored. The women use the salt for preserving fish (perch and kobi). The community is part of the Development Action Association.

PRODUCTION AREA
Nyanyano, Central Region

COMMUNITY COORDINATOR
Kottah Ebenezer
c/o Lydia Sasu
tel. +233 21315894
daa@africaonline.com.gh

Vegetable Growers of Okushiebiade

The Okushiebiade Association brings together farms growing vegetables to be sold in local markets and involves – between peasants and collaborators, around 200 individuals. Okushiebiade and the surrounding villages are well known for the production and sale of fresh vegetables and women come from Accra, about 20 kilometers away, to buy the vegetables which will then be resold in the city's markets. Over and above local varieties of eggplant and peppers, they also grow okra, a plant belonging to the Malvaceae family whose fruit, a capsule is similar to a brilliant green pepper with longitudinal raised ridges. It has a wealth of small white seeds and must be harvested a few days after flowering since, otherwise, it becomes woody and inedible.

PRODUCTION AREA
Okushiebiade, Amasaman, Greater Accra Region

COMMUNITY COORDINATOR
Adotei Brown
c/o Lydia Sasu
tel. +233 21315894
daa@africaonline.com.gh

Beekeepers of Sampirin

The community is composed of 30 peasants and two merchants of the village of Sampiring, in the Poreko quarter, 10 kilometers northeast of Labé, on the central Fouta Djalon plateau. The traditional activity of this area is the collection of honey and other by-products of bees that feed off wild plants and inhabit natural hives made in tree trunks. When the honey is collected the hive is brought down to the ground and opened. The combs are cut and placed in a recipient. The honey (n'djuri in Peul) is collected with a slight filtering. It is for family use and to sweeten the white bread used in religious ceremonies and as a medicine for the treatment of malaria, gastric infections and light burns. By boiling the combs once the honey has been extracted, the community produces wax (kaagné), used by local artisans.

PRODUCTION AREA
Labé Region

COMMUNITY COORDINATOR
Abdoul Gadiri Diallo
tel. +224 60572236
saliouporeko@yahoo.fr

Chilli Pepper Growers of Niégueré

More than 300 peasants, mainly women, are organized in an economic interest group supported by the NGO Communauté nourriciére du Foutah Djallon. Their main product is the chili pepper (Capsicum anuum), which is grown mainly on light soils with a rich humus. It is planted in nurseries and planted out after 45-65 days in double rows between 40-50 centimeters apart. The vegetative cycle lasts about five to six months and the harvest is gradual from March to October-November. When they are ripe, the fruit are hand harvested and left to dry in the sun (or in ovens during the winter). Chilli peppers are grown together with maize and cassava. Only organic fertilizers are used and the fertility of the soil is revived by alternating leaving the field fallow. The community also produces sweet potatoes and other vegetables.

PRODUCTION AREA
Lélouma, Labé Region

COMMUNITY COORDINATOR
Mamadou Saliou Diallo
tel. +224 60572236
saliouporeko@yahoo.fr

Citrus Fruit Growers of the Pita Prefecture

The Fouta Djallon plateau has a relatively mild climate and good water resources and, thanks to these characteristics, the growing of citrus fruits has grown over time. However, a serious fungal infection, cercosporiosis, has devastated the crops. In order to react to this situation, about ten years ago an economic interest group (Gie) was created in the village of Mamou, of the Peulh tribe east of Conakry, with the aim of recuperating citrus fruit growing with sustainable methods capable of defeating the disease. In a field of two and a half hectares, orange varieties that can now be termed as local (valince, malimbo, valenna sokotoro), tangerines and lemons (kathiou) have been planted. Production has restarted with reasonably good results and the sale of the fruit provides a good integration to the income provided by vegetables, mangoes and avocados in the area.

PRODUCTION AREA
Pita Prefecture, Mamou Region

COMMUNITY COORDINATOR
Bah Amadou Sadio
tel. +224 60572236

Defenders of the Néré and Souombara producers of Fouta Djalon

A typical tree of the Savana, the néré (*Parkia biglobosa* or *Vitellaria paradoxa*) is threatened by deforestation and its indiscriminate use as fuel. The men of 16 villages of the Fouta Djalon plateau are working in its defense, whilst 150 women brought together in 18 associations work in gathering the seeds and making soumbara, a traditional condiment. The network is completed by a community of 25 chefs who use traditional cooking in the cities of the five prefectures and in the capital Conakry. The soumbara is sold by two women's associations with headquarters in Wéndou and Ley Miro. The community hopes to recuperate the festivities that were once held in the villages in honor of the néré, which is also used for its medicinal properties.

PRODUCTION AREA
Labé and Conakry Regions

COMMUNITY COORDINATOR
Mamadou Mouctar Sow
tel. +224 60294281
smamadoumouctar@yahoo.fr

Fishermen of Boulbinet

Boulbinet is a port of the capital, Conakry, and is the oldest on the Guinean coast. It was once the place where all the fish destined for the interior arrived but, today, is used to embark all the products for export. A rock barrier defends it from the sea, creating a natural lagoon. In the lagoon's dock lies a fleet of around 3,400 Boulbinet fishermen, more than 350 boats of between 5 and 22 meters with 8 to 40 cc outboard motors. The catch, certified as organic, is about 25,000 tons a year and includes, as well as the bonga (*Ethmalose fimbriata*), a clupeid much eaten in Guinea, the red-banded seabream, red snappers and a torpedo shaped fish, *Arius heudelotii*. The former two are preserved and lightly smoked as well as eaten fresh.

PRODUCTION AREA
Conakry

COMMUNITY COORDINATOR
Mamayawa Sandouno
tel. +224 60342192 - 30451606
smamayawa@yahoo.fr

Fonio Growers and Processors of Fouta Djalon

Fonio (*Digitaria exilis*) is a poacea with a very thin stalk and tiny kernel traditionally grown by the Peul populations of Fouta Djalon, the mountainous area whose inhabitants are farmers and nomadic animal breeders. The miniscule grains of fonio are closely wrapped in glumes that need to be eliminated. Peeling the grains is a task of the women and, up until recently, it was a long, tiring and wasteful job: the grains were crushed in a mortar mixed with sand and then washed many times using vast amounts of water. Nowadays a machine is used to grate the membranes away. In local cuisine, fonio is frequently associated with okra and groundnuts and occupies an important role in both ceremonies and in food for the sick.

PRODUCTION AREA
Labé Region

COMMUNITY COORDINATOR
Mamadou Saliou Diallo
tel. +224 60572236
saliouporeko@yahoo.fr

Ginger Growers and Processors

Ginger is a herbaceous perennial whose rhizomes are irregular and lumpy with a strongly aromatic taste which has made of common use in the cuisine of many countries throughout the world. Ginger is also claimed to have both medicinal and aphrodisiac properties. In Guinea, the historic area of cultivation coincides with the eastern part of the country. In the community, supported by the NGO Association des Femmes pour le Développement Rural Intégré (Afdri), 15 work on the harvesting and commercialization of the raw product whilst 84 women work on its transformation and a further 16 on the sale of dried or powdered ginger and a type of sorbet called djindjan. This is made by diluting the flesh of the rhizomes in water, adding lemon juice and sugar and refrigerating the liquid. The production of infusions is currently being planned.

PRODUCTION AREA
Forécariah Region

COMMUNITY COORDINATOR
Gnama Conde
tel. +224 64227364
hadjagnama@yahoo.fr

N'dama Cow Milk and Cheesemakers

This community – with 127 members of which 97 are women – revolves around a dairy created in 2002 with the support of FAO. The primary material is cow milk from the local N'dama breed: a small, rustic animal that produces around half a liter of milk a day. The animals are put out to pasture in the winter and in the dry season are fed on the waste left from the fonio harvest, rice, potatoes and groundnuts. The main products of the dairy are yoghurt, curdled milk and a series of fresh and matured cheeses. The traditions of pastoral activities and the production of fresh and curdled milk in this area are very ancient and are linked to the nomadic tribe of the Peul. The other dairy products are recent introductions.

PRODUCTION AREA
Pita, Fouta Djallon Region

COMMUNITY COORDINATOR
Bah Mamadou Alpha
tel. +224 60528078

Sintin-Sitirin Producers

The aronga (Harungana madagascariensis, locally called soungala) is a common plant of the Fouta Djalon forests. By diluting with water the flesh of the fruit, red drupes the size of a pepper corn, a drink is produced called sintin-sitirin which is energizing and refreshing. The harvest and preparation is the work of the women. Since 2002 the recuperation of this ancient tradition has involved the members of the Tata 2 cooperative. Today, its activities have widened to include around 400 people; the women harvest, process and sell the fruit, while the men protect the plants and market the drupes. The community also produces a type of flatbread made with cotton seeds, maize flour, ginger and groundnut paste.

PRODUCTION AREA
Labé and Conakry Regions

COMMUNITY COORDINATOR
Boubacar Camara
tel. +224 30452047
bappacaro@yahoo.fr

Soumbara Producers of Lélouma

Soumbara (oddji in Peul) is a condiment made from seeds of the néré, a spontaneous tree of the Savana. Called scientifically Parkia biglobosa or Vitellaria paradoxa, it is so profoundly linked to the areas of Parawol that some villages carry its local name. The seeds, contained in bunches of pods, are boiled, peeled, washed and left to ferment in banana or ceiba (eriodendrum) leaves. They are subsequently roasted, crushed and sieved to produce a powder or small balls. Nutritious and energizing, soumbara flavors all kinds of dishes but, above all, the sauces of Guinean cuisine. The community comprises 66 women and 11 men and produces 75 hundredweights of soumbara per year which is sold to merchants in the region.

PRODUCTION AREA
Lélouma, Labé Region

COMMUNITY COORDINATOR
Mamadou Saliou Diallo
tel. +224 60572236
saliouporeko@yahoo.fr

Taro Growers of Fello Diounguel

Taro is the vulgar name of *Colocasia esculenta*, a plant of the Aracee family which produces rhizomes with a high content of starch, calcium and iron. In Fouta Djalon it is one of the species most grown by the women, together with maize, cassava, okra and potatoes, in small lots of land surrounded by hedges near their homes. The seedlings are planted at the beginning of the rainy season in deep holes of between 5 and 10 centimeters. Only organic fertilizers made from straw and compost. As well as taro (*diabéré foutah* in the local language), the 30 women of the community also grow a plant of the same family and with similar characteristics, the makabo (diabéré kooku, whose scientific name is *Xanthosoma sagittifolium*). The rhizomes are eaten boiled, fried or pureed. The young leaves are also edible and are make into a sauce.

PRODUCTION AREA
Pita Prefecture, Fouta Djallon Region

COMMUNITY COORDINATOR
Mamadou Saidou Sow
tel. +224 60597659
sow_ms@yahoo.fr

Baobab Jam Producers of Kibwezi

The community came together to produce a local and lower cost alternative to margarine and other spreadable products. Baobab jam is produced by mixing the fruit powder with an equal amount of sugar diluted with water or milk and flavored with lemon juice. After a slow boiling, the product is served on bread or as an accompaniment to tubers such as taro, cassava and sweet potatoes. The baobab, a tree of exceptional size, grows spontaneously from the coast up to altitudes of 1,200 meters above sea level and is one of the most long living plants in the world, thanks to its resistance to drought. From various parts of the plant it is possible to make numerous objects of everyday use such as fiber ropes, baskets, musical instruments, containers, dyes and waterproof hats.

PRODUCTION AREA
Kibwezi, Eastern Province

COMMUNITY COORDINATOR
Nzamalu Priscilla Nthenya
tel. +254 721404058
nzamalupn@yahoo.com

Camel Breeders of the Salato Tribe

This community of Salato women with around 104 members, lives in northern Kenya in an arid area which receives fewer than 500 millimeters of rain per year. They work as herders and sell milk, meat and pelts. The animals most suitable for surviving in these extreme conditions and of being bred are camels. A fairly costly dish, *nyirinyiri,* typical of Kenyan nomadic cuisine, is prepared on festivities or special occasions: the meat is cooked in oil until is has expelled all its water content and is then spiced making it possible to preserve it at length. With the cheese made from camel milk, a type of sweet that is ideal for mothers and babies is also prepared.

PRODUCTION AREA
Ngurunit, Samburu District

COMMUNITY COORDINATOR
Laura Lemunyete
tel. +254 725461738
lemunyete@wananchi.com

Cereals Growers of Kathonzweni

This network of seven small communities in the District of Machakos was created in 1999 to promote the sales of local products, reducing the distribution chain and encouraging direct access to the markets. Strangled by the power of the wholesalers, around 200 small producers brought together around the village of Kathonzweni decided to unite in a structured consortium that would provide them with the means of facing the difficulties of the marketplace. Once established, the group began to work on food safety and the preservation of local seeds for the production of higher quality cereals that were more suitable for resistance to the dangers of the extremely dry local climate. In collaboration with the NGO, Inades Formation, the group strengthened its agricultural knowledge and is working on the distribution of its gastronomic products to the villages.

PRODUCTION AREA
Machakos District, Central Province

COMMUNITY COORDINATOR
Omondi Vincent Elias
tel. +254 4421595 - 722623121
voluxafwa@yahoo.co.uk

Cow and Camel Breeders

Principally belonging to the pastoral tribes of the Borana and Redille, the almost 3,000 members of this community participate in the raising, working and sales of the milk and flesh of dromedaries and cows, in accordance with a strict division of tasks. The young men tend the animals, the elders look after the milk and its preserving, sales are managed by an organized group of youngsters whilst the adult men look are responsible for the pastures and the fattening of the animals. The methods used in working an preserving the products are still those dictated by the necessities of a nomadic, pastoral life. The flesh is cut into narrow strips and fried in accordance with a process that renders them still edible after more than eight months. Even the milk is smoked in a gourd container together with a particular kind of wood that aids its preservation. Alternatively, the milk undergoes a acidifying process that prolongs is shelf life and increases its value.

PRODUCTION AREA
Nairobi

COMMUNITY COORDINATOR
Wario Qalicha Gugu
tel. +254 020317182
klmc@livestockcouncil.org - qalicha@livestockcouncil.org

Farmers of the Arid Areas of Kitui

The community is composed of the inhabitants of several villages around the city of Kutui, an area populated by the Kamba tribe, one of the three main ethnic groups of Kenya. Structured as a self-supporting group, the small community grows local products with the purpose of preserving the surplus for periods of drought and generic scarcity of resources. In some instances, the almost 50 members of the community manage to produce a surplus that has been sold to merchants in the vicinities, generating a small source of income that is divided out proportionally between them. The crops include mangoes, cassava and bananas: of which the first two, in particular, are highly resistant to dry and arid climates and are easily preserved by being dried in the sun. In effect, cassava is boiled and made into flour or is lightly salted and eaten directly.

PRODUCTION AREA
Kitui Dirstrict, Central Province

COMMUNITY COORDINATOR
Wambua Elizabeth Nduku
tel. +254 723938046
Liziduku2005@yahoo.com

Fish Farmers of Kisumu

A community formed by the union of four self-supporting groups which, in 1999, dug out the first tank for fish breeding on the plateau of Kisumu at between 1,800 and 2,100 metres above sea level. The young tilapia and cat fish, provided by the Moi University, are turned into the tanks whose shapes follow the formation of the terrain and are then fed with vegetable fibers and cereals, as well as the plankton that spontaneously develops in the water enriched with natural fertilizers. The fish, fried in simsim oil or boiled with the addition of cream, contribute to the increase in the vitamin element of the local diet and represent a traditional form of nutrition of those living around the lakes. The fish are sold locally, either fresh or after being smoked, permitting the distribution of the profits to the members of the community and for the salaries of those working on the fish tanks.

PRODUCTION AREA
Kisumu, Nyanza Province

COMMUNITY COORDINATOR
Machuka Evans Ochoki
tel. +254 5343083
necofakenya@yahoo.com

Herb and Fruit Gatherers of the Rift Valley forest

The community is composed of the inhabitants of the forests and their surroundings who gather fruit, herbs and medicinal plants as well as hunting small animals. The current process of diversification in order to protect the forest consists in the attempt to bring productions within the confines of farms. The main products sold or bartered with bordering communities are black nightshade (a herbaceous plant of which both the fruit and the leaves are eaten), the Cape Gooseberry, a wild fruit rich in vitamins with which the community hopes to make in jam in the future and the African plum. Of the latter, the bark as well as the fruits is used by drying and breaking it down in a mortar to use in medicines for both humans and animals.

PRODUCTION AREA
Rift Valley Province

COMMUNITY COORDINATOR
Clement Kariuki Kimone
tel. +254 51721537
cofeg2002@yahoo.com

Indigenous Chicken Breeders of Kilifi

The families making up this small community were brought together to recover and maintain alive one of the area's traditions: the free range breeding of local varieties of chickens. The community is particularly involved in a process of selecting examples, achieved by marking the eggs of the strongest, healthiest species with the best reproductive capacities, hatching them and enriching their feed with maize and insects. Once the chickens are adults, the selected chickens are sold locally whilst the greater part are distributed amongst the community to encourage an improved production. As well as being used in well known ways, chicken is traditionally used to make soups said to be beneficial for pregnant women.

PRODUCTION AREA
Kilifi, Coast Province

COMMUNITY COORDINATOR
Mwamachi Samson
tel. +254 733542571
samwamachi@yahoo.com

Indigenous Chicken Breeders of Machakos

The women of three villages in the Mwala area have come together to give life to the community which has earned the recognition of the Ministry for Cultural Affairs as the women's Group Ngenda. Its aim is to improve its status and economic conditions through chicken breeding. This type of work effectively represents a considerable percentage of local livestock breeding and is also an activity which, in this area, is traditionally the responsibility of women. The community members take turns in the construction and maintenance of the chicken coops where the birds are housed overnight. The chickens belong to indigenous breeds and are sold either to individuals or to local restaurants. The community has recently attempted to start up honey production has led a leading role in the formation of the southwest Kenya Slow Food Convivium.

PRODUCTION AREA
Machakos District, Central Province

COMMUNITY COORDINATOR
Mutuku Julius Manthi
tel. +254 735785703
inadeskenya@copperbelt.net

Macadamia Nut Producers and Processors

The introduction of the Macadamia nut into central Kenya took place in the 1980s and permitted the families previously growing coffee to convert from an increasingly less profitable production dominated by the large multi-nationals. In this way, the 120 families of the communities have been able to increase their income and improve their health and living situations by earning a small margin of profit. The Macadamia plant begins to produce around three kilos of nuts after five years and can eventually produce around 50 kilos when it reaches 15 years of life. The pleasant tasting nut can be eaten fresh or toasted or can be worked to produce an oil which, once filtered through a cloth, is used in local cuisine.

PRODUCTION AREA
Embu, Central Province

COMMUNITY COORDINATOR
Waweru Stanley Peter Gakori
tel. +254 722663684
gakori@yahoo.com

Nettle Growers of the Rift Valley

Eight groups of women are part of this community, together with two groups of young people and four self-supporting groups, for a total of 420 members to which must be added a further 1,200 part-time workers. The harvest previously took place in the nearby government owned Mau forest. But, over the last ten years, the government has taxed the harvest at over 40% and, therefore, with the support of the international association Networking for Ecofarming in Africa (Necofa), the community has domesticated the cultivation of nettles in its own farms, adopting organic methods. The nettle leaves constitute a foodstuff rich in iron and calcium, ideal for pregnant, breast-feeding women and children. As well as being used to make local dishes, the nettles are also used in infusions and medicinal preparations to cure hypertension and diabetes.

PRODUCTION AREA
Molo, Rift Valley Province

COMMUNITY COORDINATOR
Beatrice Wangari Kamau
tel. +254 721958247
necofakenya@yahoo.com

North Turkana Shepherds

The shepherds of North Turkana, on the borders of Uganda, Sudan and Ethiopia, occupy one of the most arid areas of Kenya where animal raising represents the only activity which can generate some income. Further difficulties arise from its peripheral location, the serious lack of any infrastructures and organised markets for the commercialization of their products and by the frequent theft of animals in the border areas. Thanks to an Italian project lead by Amref, Terra Nuova and Cooperazione allo Sviluppo, a community comprising more than 1,000 shepherds has created for its own slaughterhouse for the processing of meat with sustainable methods. The purpose of the cooperative is to reduce the poverty of the pastoral groups, promoting the development of a market for local animals and thereby contributing to the reduction of conflict situations for the area's populations.

PRODUCTION AREA
Lomidat and Lokichoggio, Rift Valley Province

COMMUNITY COORDINATOR
David Lopua Ekulan
tel. +254 735952912
lomidatcoop@yahoo.co.uk

Orange Sweet Potato Producers

The 70 members of this small community located around the city of Thika in central Kenya, grow a particular sweet potato with exceptional nutritional value. The orange flashed variety of sweet potato was introduced specifically in the area to reduce the vitamin deficit of the local diet. The orange color of the peel is effectively an indication of the high vitamin content of the tuber. Grown in well drained soil fertilized with natural compost, the orange flashed grow up to altitudes of 2,000 meters above sea level, taking between three to six months to ripen. However, after just two months, the vitamin and protein rich leaves are cut and used as fodder for sheep and milk cows. The potatoes are eaten raw, dried in the sun or processed into sweets and bread.

PRODUCTION AREA
Thika, Central Province

COMMUNITY COORDINATOR
Kinyua Wamuyu Kinyua
tel. +254 733718546
rkkinyu@yahoo.com

Organic Farmers of Marsabit

Working both in agricultural and in livestock, the members of this community autonomously produce a good part of the fertiliser used in their small fields and, at the same time, the fodder required for fattening their cattle, goats and camels. Due to the severe drought of the fast few years, the inhabitants of the area of Marsabit grow varieties that can resist with hardly any rain, such as teff (a local cereal that does not contain gluten), wheat, barley, peas, cartamo (a subspecies of saffron), cassava and sweet potatoes. The work is divided up between different groups who, on a rotation basis, are responsible for the various phases of the cultivation process. Their most characteristic product, prepared by every family and, therefore, rarely sold, is *dabo*, a bread made with teff flour or wheat which is fermented before use.

PRODUCTION AREA
Marsabit District, Rift Valley Province

COMMUNITY COORDINATOR
Omar Boru Kutara
tel. +254 735422716
Omarkutara@yahoo.com

Organic Infusion Producers of the Meru Region

Meru Herbs is a cooperative of peasants created in 1991 with the purpose of covering the costs of the irrigation project in the Meru area, at the feet of Mount Kenya. As well as growing crops to be sold in the local markets, the peasants have specialized in karkade – an untraditional crop for the area – and in the growing of camomile and lemon grass infusions sold through Fair Trade channels. The production, which has obtained organic certification from the English Soil Association, also comprises dried chili peppers, tropical fruit jams and tomato sauce. In this way, the association manages to repay the costs of the irrigation project and to make it a more capillary system. The community comprises 190 members, 43 of whom work full time and 100 are seasonal workers for Meru Herbs.

PRODUCTION AREA
Meru, Central Province

COMMUNITY COORDINATOR
Diana Kagendo Mucee
tel. +254 4442081
meruherbs@maf.or.ke

Organic Medicinal Food and Herb Producers

The community associates producers from three different provinces of the country. All its 160 members organically produce foods and herbs with therapeutic qualities. Amongst the principal products are various kinds of infusions. From the nettles (*Urtica dioica*) growing naturally in the shady areas rich with water, the community members gather, dry and mince the leaves and then package them. Lemon grass (*Cymbopogon citratus*) undergoes a similar treatment. A considerable amount of finely chopped garlic as also produced and sold every year. A simple procedure is followed comprising an initial drying of the garlic cloves after which they are turned into powder. In order to provide their products with added value, the community members work in collaboration with doctors and pharmacists of the respective localities.

PRODUCTION AREA
Coast, Eastern and Western Provinces

COMMUNITY COORDINATOR
Lucy Muchoki
tel. +254 0208632700
lmuchoki@icipe.org

Organic Producers of the Suburban Areas of Gachie

The area of Gachie, run by the Karuri Town Council, borders on the most peripheral suburbs of Nairobi and is characterized by a very high population density which reveal many of the elements and social problems typical of such situations throughout Africa. The community of organic producers, composed of 46 members, was formed with the purpose of exploring and developing the opportunities for a small-scale production for family consumption and marketing in the surrounding areas. The typical products of this area are grown without fertilisers or chemical pesticides whilst they are preserved mainly by drying in the sun. The community produces dried groundnuts with the addition of salt and pepper, fresh or dehydrated bananas, honey and milk derivates such as yoghurt, butter and cheese.

PRODUCTION AREA
Gachie, Nairobi

COMMUNITY COORDINATOR
Kinyanjui Stanley Nghete
tel. +254 207121685
coskenya@yahoo.com

Potato and Pea Growers of Nakuru

The 80 farmers of this group belong to three communities in the area of Nakura, on the eastern highlands of the Rift Valley. The purpose of the community is to increase its production in accordance with natural principles, to train for and establish an organic and biodiverse agriculture and, above all, to autonomously manage the sales process and limiting external mediation. In effect, during the colonial period, the area was an important one for agriculture but was in the hands of a few European absent landowners. The community, in an attempt to facilitate the development of small scale agriculture, has specialized in growing potatoes and peas produced with the use of natural fertilizers and the effective micro organisms most suited to the climate, altitude and volcanic terrain of the area.

PRODUCTION AREA
Nakuru, Rift Valley Province

COMMUNITY COORDINATOR
Wambuguh Dameris Wangeci
tel. +254 722474295
mauforesta@yahoo.com

Pumpkin Growers of the Arid Areas of Homa Bay and Kilify

The community works on the banks of Lake Victoria and on the ocean coast of the Kilify region and specializes in the growing of pumpkins that are particularly suitable for areas of very little rain. The local varieties produced by the community are greatly valued because they grow rapidly, are easily transportable (thanks to their hard skin) and can be kept for more than a year. Furthermore, at a local level, the pumpkins represent a complete food: as well as the fruit, the leaves are also eaten since they are traditionally considered as improving fertility whilst the seeds have a number of traditional medicinal uses. The community has an important role in the conservation of crop seeds suitable for arid areas and is distinguished by its widespread commitment to didactic activities in the schools through the organization of school kitchen gardens and educating about healthy food.

PRODUCTION AREA
Homa Bay, Nyanza Province and Kilify, Coast Province

COMMUNITY COORDINATOR
Nderitu Stanley Mwaura
tel. +254 721283661
smwauranderitu@yahoo.com

Seed Promoters and Savers in Molo and Makueni

In the semi-arid arid of the Rift Valley, occupied in the colonial period by extensive crops of the European producers, the communities of Molo and Makueni have come together to recuperate traditional methods of preserving and reproducing local seeds. The activities, supported by the organizations Necofa and Inades, are carried out by around 300 people divided into groups of women and self-supporting groups. As well as reproducing examples of cassava and mango, that of the hyacinth bean *Dolichos lablab*) is particularly interesting as, in Europe it is considered an ornamental plant, whilst in Africa it is used for both cooking and as animal fodder. In order to avoid the damage caused by insects and bacteria, wood ash, wild chrysanthemum or African pyrethrum are used.

PRODUCTION AREA
Rift Valley Province

COMMUNITY COORDINATOR
Muhunyu Samuel Karanja
tel. +254 722647112
muhunyusk@yahoo.com

Sesame Producers of Mount Elgon

The community is composed of 120 small farmers and their families. The sesame is planted in March and harvested around July. The stalks are set out to dry on a canvas (*sikhali*) and are then cut and gathered into stacks (*kamalisi*). Once dried, the threshing takes place. By burning the stubble, a salt is produced that is traditionally used to favour vegetable dishes. The sesame seeds are fried and stone ground and the resultant paste, called *kamasikhisikhi*, is eaten spread on bread or with ugali, a type of maize flour cake. A combination of *kamasikhisikhi* and water is mixed with pulses such as black-eyed peas. Elgon sesame is sold, as well as in bordering countries, in the most important markets of Kisumu, Nakuru and Nairobi.

PRODUCTION AREA
Kitale, Western Province

COMMUNITY COORDINATOR
Ignatius Maina Katasi
tel. +254 721355424
mainakatasi@yahoo.com

Sustainable Food Producers of Kangemi

The community of sustainable farmers created in 1922 has made its strongest point the high number of families that make up many of its components (around 2,200). Associated to Pelum-Kenya, an association for the ecology of land uses, this community acts in turn as a focus point for the numerous groups of self-supporting farmers who work within it. The choice of adopting the Leisa method (sustainable agriculture with a low external input) is justified by the desire of its members to protect their own habitat and health, but derives also from clear economic requirements. The crops grown are large in number: bananas, taro, sugar cane, coffee, yam, maize and beans.

PRODUCTION AREA
Central Province

COMMUNITY COORDINATOR
Kamau Mary
tel. +254 6730541
sacdep@iconnect.co.ke

Taro Producers

The 70 members of the community resident in the urban area of Nairobi, grow taro alongside small rivulets, ponds and damp areas where few other crops can survive. At the moment of harvesting, new plants are sown and will be ready after six months. The edible parts of taro are the tuber which is rich in starch and the leaves which are used either as a vegetable accompaniment or as natural plates on which food is served. Taro is disappearing due to the reduction in damp areas and by its substitution with products of foreign origin, which are less delicate and quicker to grow and cook. Furthermore, taro must always be boiled to eliminate the toxins present in the raw root. The community of producers, as well as preserving an increasingly rare local product, contribute to the protection of the areas traditionally used for its production.

PRODUCTION AREA
Nairobi

COMMUNITY COORDINATOR
Wanjama Daniel Njoroge
tel. +254 721618569
danielwanjama@yahoo.ca

Traditional Animal By-product Producers of the Rift Valley

Lying on the borders between the Rift Valley and Central Kenya, the Nyandarua plateau has an almost temperate climate which has always been an ideal area for raising cattle and sheep. For this reason, the local populations of Kikuyu and Kalenjin are well versed in the methods of preserving animal products. The main products of the 650 families of the community are strips of sheep meat, zebu and, to a lesser degree, chicken and the derivates of milk such as ghee (liquefied butter) and yoghurt. The meat requires boiling in sheep's fat and an immersion in honey or it is covered with a thin film of the same fat. Yoghurt is produced by fermenting milk for three-five days in containers whose interiors have been smoked with charcoal. The community also breeds fish in two water basins.

PRODUCTION AREA
Nyandarua Plateau, Rift Valley Province

COMMUNITY COORDINATOR
Mwangi John Paul Munene
tel. +254 722391302
munenejpm1@yahoo.com

Traditional Beekeepers of Pokot

The Pokot, with around 200 beekeepers, are a minor tribe of a wider community living in the Rift Valley. Honey is an important element in the traditional local alimentation and is used for the production of medicines and local beer. The wax, on the other hand, is used to repair tools. The beekeepers place considerable value on the natural resources of the area, opposing the cutting of the abundant and diverse indigenous flora on which the bees feed, concentrated in the area of the Cherangany Hills. Thanks to the assistance of the local NGO, the Sustainable Mobilization of Agricultural Resource Technologies (SMART), the community is modernizing its equipment and production methods, attempting to reach local markets autonomously and eliminating the mediation of distributors.

PRODUCTION AREA
Kapenguria, Rift Valley Province

COMMUNITY COORDINATOR
Namianya Jack Wafula
tel. +254 720471715
jackson_wafula@yahoo.com

Vegetable Growers of Embu

The idea inspiring the 260 members of this community to unite their individual strengths was that of protecting traditional Kenyan agriculture through the growing of local and traditional vegetables and the multiplication and distribution of seeds. Amongst the varieties grown by this community at the feet of Mount Kenya are black nightshade, spider weed and witch weed. These three plants, as well as being used in traditional cooking, have considerable medicinal properties: black nightshade leaves, for example, are used for stomach aches and tonsillitis, the berries are rubbed on children's gums when they are teething and the roots are boiled and added to milk as a natural tonic. Spider weed is very nutritious and rich in minerals and proteins and is particularly good for breastfeeding women.

PRODUCTION AREA
Central Province

COMMUNITY COORDINATORS
Ojienda Leah Wanjiru
Samuel Karanja Muhunyu
tel. +254 722752009
ciruojienda@yahoo.com

Waterlily Gatherers of the Baringo District

The small agro-pastoral tribe of the Ilchamus inhabits the banks and islands of Lake Baringo, one of the seven in the Rift Valley in central western Kenya. The Ilchamus tribe's economy is closely linked to the water of the lake and its surrounding rivers as it permits them to carry out, other than fishing, subsistence farming and also provides pastures for family-based animal raising activity. The community, in the periods of great drought, also resorts to the gathering of spontaneous products, amongst which water lilies are an important element as they populate the shallow waters along the river banks. The hand ground seeds are made into highly nutritious flour.

PRODUCTION AREA
Baringo District, Rift Valley Province

COMMUNITY COORDINATOR
Tenges Tomson
tel. +254 722676965
lemarkoko@yahoo.com

Wild Mushroom Gatherers of Western Kenya

The peasants of western Kenya usually integrate their farming activities by gathering the mushrooms growing in vast numbers during the rainy season. These mainly belong to the *Termitomyces* family and grow on the walls or in the vicinity of termitaries or on fallen tree trunks. The collected mushrooms can be cooked fresh, dried or smoked. After an initial drying, they are covered with salt and left out again in the sun or smoked. Dried mushrooms are usually flavored with the ash of banana leaves, dried banana skins or maize cobs. They are traditionally packaged in banana leaves and mushrooms preserved in this way can be used in the periods of famine or sold at local markets.

PRODUCTION AREA
Western Province

COMMUNITY COORDINATOR
Sikuku Dominic Ngosia
tel. +254 735835678
sdngosia@yahoo.com

Vegetable Producers of Maseru

The community was created by and is composed of ten women brought together for the purpose of producing typical crops and selling the excess produce in order to generate profit. Amongst the vegetables grown, the main production is of nettles, traditionally grown by the Basotho and widely used as a vegetable accompaniment or to flavor foods. Nettles were chosen, not only due to their widespread local usage but also for the ease with which they can be grown and the little care that they require. Assisted by the nutrition sector and health safety department of the Ministry for Agriculture, the community's women are also responsible for raising pigs and sheep and carry out a small activity of dressmaking. The profits are divided up proportionally amongst the associated members.

PRODUCTION AREA
Maseru, Maero District

COMMUNITY COORDINATOR
Agnes Bereng Libuseng Malianakoena
tel. +266 22314610 - 22320673
libusengb@yahoo.com

Local Date Variety Producers

Libya is the country that conserves the highest number of local date varieties: from fleshy, to be eaten fresh (grown along the coast), to semi-soft (hinterland) to fruits for drying (oases). The varieties cultivated – 400 according to the national Palm Center, 25 of which are marketed – are those described by Italians from 1926 to 1930, but their number has begun to drop due to lack of water and because old plants have not been replaced. This community is made up of small coastal producers. The most interesting varieties are the saidi (fleshy with a smooth yellow-brown skin and a sweet though interesting flavor with pleasant grassy notes) and the khadrai (a smaller green fruit, less sweet than the saidi, with hints of citrus, minerals and spices).

PRODUCTION AREA
Libyan coast

COMMUNITY COORDINATOR
Ahmed Ezarug Endogali
tel. +218 2036 2157
e.endogali@dpodico.com

Tuareg Breeders and Growers of Ghat

The oasis of Ghat is in the south of Libya, 30 kilometers from the border with Algeria. The result of thousands of years of wisdom and knowledge, it consists of plots of 5-10 date palms (the varieties cultivated are mostly for drying, such as amjog, allulu and emeli, which can be conserved for up to ten years), surrounded by rectangular fields irrigated by canals, where fava beans, onions, garlic, tomatoes, eggplant, melons and millet are grown. The Tuareg mainly devote themselves to rearing goats, sheep and camels. Their women prepare an extraordinary variety of breads, such as fitat (wafer-thin and crisp) tammasì and tannur (baked on the inside walls of an underground terracotta oven) and use mortar-pressed dates (*karun*) to produce a highly nutritional flour and *alacò* cheese (with the addition of goat's milk).

PRODUCTION
Ghat Region

COMMUNITY COORDINATOR
Mahmud Mohamed Ali Al Sadeq
tel. +218 092 604 0732

Pink Rice Producers

Pink rice is a variety grown around Lake Alaotra. Its very limited production is fairly recent and the result of a series of experiments carried out by Jean-Baptiste Rakotomandimby, a peasant of the Sahamamy municipality. Jean-Baptiste found a grain of this mysterious rice in 1993 in a sack bought from a traveling merchant and subsequently tried to grow it. After several attempts, he finally grew the first ten kilos of rice in 1995. The grains, characterized by a light pink color, become decidedly more interesting from an organoleptic point of view after cooking. For this reason, the Koloharena cooperative – which has already started up a Red Rice Slow Food Presidium – has decided to ascertain its commercial potential by presenting it at a number of food fairs in Italy and Switzerland.

PRODUCTION AREA
Amparafaravola and Sahamamy, Alaotra Mangoro Region, Toamasina Province

COMMUNITY COORDINATOR
Randrianarivelo Jules
tel. +261 331246557

Red Rice Producers of Antanafisaka

The Antanafisaka community, which has benefited from around three years of support from the Italian Granello di Senape association, brings together about 100 families divided into eight groups. Red rice, grown on terraces at almost 1,200 meters above sea level, is used in the school canteens of their children (200 boys and girls) and is also sold. With the profits, the families pay for the rent of the land and buy basic necessities. The cultivation methods are very simple and do not require the use of mechanical tools but, rather, rely on animal and human labor with the use of organic composts are as fertilizers. Once harvested, the rice is hand cleaned: the plants are first beaten against a tree trunk or rock and then the grains are crushed in a mortar to eliminate the chaff.

PRODUCTION AREA
Antanafisaka, Antambolo, Antananarivo Province

COMMUNITY COORDINATOR
Associazione Granello di Senape
tel. +39 017244599
gdsmad@blueline.mg

Strawberry Producers of Antsimondrano

Strawberries have been grown on a family scale for quite some time in the area around Antananarivo, the Madagascan capital. In the 1950s the French colonists grew these crops without, however, carrying out works of improvement or structuring. Successive local attempts to increase and improve the production failed due to sickness in the plants and cyclical market crises. Eventually, in 1999, Fonavotana, a consortium of 20 associations of producers was created to renew strawberry production (in 2004, 714 tons were harvested) in an area covering ten square kilometers. The variety grown is the traditional gasy strawberry (called *voalobo-jaza* in the local tongue) which has small, vivid red and finely punctuated with an intense, lasting perfume.

PRODUCTION AREA
Antananarivo Province

COMMUNITY COORDINATOR
Edline Ravelonirina
tel. +261 331183355 - 202220901
tefvsaina.mr@simicro.mg - saha.filiere@iris.mg

Fruit Juice, Jam and Purée Producers

140 farmers are members of the Ngolowindo cooperative which grows tomatoes and local fruits on 17 hectares of land together with 35 who work on their processing. There are five products: jujube jam and juice, baobab jam and juice and tomato purée. The jujube and baoban are typical trees of the area. Hand harvested, the fruit are then squeezed in a press, which separates the stones from the flesh. This is then sieved to make jam whilst the juice is sterilized with the addition of salt, sugar and conserving agents (citric acid and sodium benzoate) before bottling. The tomato purée is made from very ripe fruit with few seeds, grown with organic and non-organic fertilizers. The denser flesh is separated from the juice with a press and, as before, salt, citric acid and sodium benzoate are added.

PRODUCTION AREA
Salima, Centre

COMMUNITY COORDINATOR
Mercy Butao
tel. +265 1263303
cospengolowindo@mw.celtelplus.com

Honey and Fruit Juice Producers of Mwanza

The considerable demand for wood as fuel for the nearby commercial city of Blantyre has caused serious problems of deforestation in the Mawanza district. In order to save the remaining trees and replant those already cut down, the Wildlife and Environmental Society of Malawi began, in 1997, together with the local communities, a project of organization of the natural resources of east Mwanza. The project has resulted in some guinea fowl farms, enterprises for the production of baobab (*malambe*) and tamarind (*bwemba*) juice and two types of honey: forest honey which is light brown and made from *miombo*, which grows in the dry forest (with the addition of *Jubernadia globiflora* and *Bauhinia thonningi*) and mountain honey which is dark brown and made from the flowers of *Brachystegia* plants growing in the damp plateau forests.

PRODUCTION AREA
Mwanza East, South

COMMUNITY COORDINATOR
Herbert Mwalukomo
tel. +265 1643502
wesm-hq@africa-online.net

Cereal and Legume growers and processors

Around 100 people are employed in working and supplying the primary materials as well as merchants have as their focus point small transformation units whose purpose is the enhancement of their products. Beginning with cereals grown without recourse to fertilisers or chemical anti-parasites, the community produces dried fonio, precooked fonio and rice, flour and fragments of maize and millet. One particular product is *djouka*, a mixture of fonio and steamed and then dried groundnuts. The rice is used to produce a couscous powder enriched with aromatic herbs. The community belongs to Fenatram (Fédération Nationale des Transformateurs du Mali), and also benefits from the collaboration of the NGOs Afrique Verte and Sassakawa Global 2000.

PRODUCTION AREA
Bamako District

COMMUNITY COORDINATOR
Aïssata Thiam Dem
tel. +223 2219760
afriqueverte@afribone.net.ml - dem@afribone.net.ml

Cereal producers and merchants of Bamako and Ségou

The work of the community – 50 producers, wholesalers and retailers brought together in a cooperative – directly interacts with more than 5,000 consumers. Apart from rice, a water crop that requires both fertilisers and chemical treatments, all the products can be considered organic. Millet of the *Pennisetum americanum* variety (pearl millet called in the local dialect *séguifa, sofila sigui* or *gadiaba*) and colored grain sorghum (with the same dialect names) are amongst the main food cultures of Mali and are eaten in a number of ways: tô, couscous, pastes, *dégué* (a cream), *dolo* (beer). Fonio (*Digitaria exilis*) is another traditional crop although it only represents 2% of the national cereal production.

PRODUCTION AREA
Bamako District and the Ségou Region

COMMUNITY COORDINATOR
Mama Kone
tel. +223 2219760
afriqueverte@afribone.net.ml - dem@afribone.net.ml

Dogon Onion Growers

One hundred kilometres east of Moptì, near the border with Burkina Faso, lives the Dogon people in an extremely hostile environment. More than a third of the region is bare rock whilst another third is composed of soil never any deeper than 10 centimetres. In this arid area the Dogon have managed to create real oases of green with crop-growing terraces and little stone dykes for collecting water. Vegetable growing is a mainly female activity and one of the main food crops is millet (made into *tô* – a sort of polenta). However, even during the dry season, thanks to ingenious hydraulic solutions (the *zai* method), the community manages to grow Dogon onions which are a type of shallot.

PRODUCTION AREA
Bandiagara, Mopti Region

COMMUNITY COORDINATOR
Mamadou Guindo
tel. +223 6052659
pdcomamadou@yahoo.fr

Goat Cheese and Dried Meat Producers of Gargando

60 women make up the community, assisted by the Tin Hinan NGO, and are dedicated, as well as to artisan items, to the production of dried beef and Tuareg goat's milk cheese. For the latter, a kid stomach is used as rennet, cooked in some milk. The mixture is then transferred to a skin bag from which is taken the required amount for the coagulation of the milk. The mass is than pressed in as sieve made from stalks and woven leather strips and left to dry out in the shade. In the same way, the women dry the meat of young cattle for a week, cut into slender strips. Subsequently, the meeat is kept for a month in a sack. It is eaten during the long camel journeys and, in a soup with butter and cereals, is a typical Tuareg dish.

PRODUCTION AREA
Gargando, Tomboctou Region

COMMUNITY COORDINATOR
Teghaichite Walet Ehiya
tinhinanbf@yahoo.fr

Leaf Growers and Processors of Baguinéda

The community is composed of around one thousand women working in twenty villages through local associations with the purpose of achieving alimentary self sufficiency and a balanced diet by consuming only fruit and vegetables produced during three months of the year. As well as fruit (mangoes, papaya and bananas), legumes and cereals (making flour used for baby food from millet) the village associations grow and dry in the sun onion, aubergine and the particularly nutritious baobab and Moringa leaves. To set up the structure, the women used 'microcredits' from the Tanima 2000 association in the form of seeds which were returned in the form of dried products. With hibiscus flowers and ginger they make traditional drinks (*dableni*, *ngamacou*) which are consumed on festive occasions.

PRODUCTION AREA
Surrounds of Kati, Koulikoro Region

COMMUNITY COORDINATOR
Fanny Bréchard
tel. +33 681011150
fanny.brechard@wanadoo.fr

Mango and Vegetable Producers

This association involves around 70 individuals – producers and merchants – and works with the NGO Afrique Vert Mali, which offers its support to guarantee the quality of the products, improve packaging and to find new market outlets. The main products are mangoes, tomatoes and shallots. All three are sold fresh, dried or in brine. Mangoes are also made into jam (with the fresh flesh, sugar and lemon juice) and the tomatoes are made into juice and concentrate. None of the recipes requires the addition of either aromas or preservatives. The tomatoes and shallots in brine may be flavored with a few bay leaves, pepper grains and garlic.

PRODUCTION AREA
Bamako District

COMMUNITY COORDINATOR
Mariam Kalifa Traore
tel. +223 2219760
afriquevert@afribone.net.ml

Missira Market

The capital of the Republic of Mali, Bamako, is situated on the north bank of the Niger. The city has a population of about a million inhabitants and, besides two large-scale markets, Marché Rose and Marché de Médine, boasts a small old-fashioned market in its Missira quarter. Here it's possible to find all the typical products of Mali, from karité butter to fish, from artisan jewelry to incense, to medicinal herbs to fruit and dried local vegetables. In 2000 producers and traders, led by the former Minister of Culture Aminata Traoré, formed an association to rehabilitate and manage the market. The name of the association is Yeleen, which in the Bambara language means 'light'. Thanks to local artists, the market has been restructured with the red stones typical of the area. The recovery project is supported by the Slow Food Foundation for Biodiversity.

PRODUCTION AREA
Mali

COMMUNITY COORDINATOR
Yeleen Association
famapemissira@yahoo.fr

Camel Breeders and Milk Producers of Nouakchott

The breeding of camels around the capital of Mauritania is a modern conversion of an ancient activity following the massive urbanization that affected the nomadic population whose main food was milk. Numerous breeders possess and manager, in an area surrounding the capital, herds of dromedaries in groups of 20-30 heads which are left to graze freely, without fencing or stable structures. Camel milk is sold directly to passers-by or to intermediaries who sell it - raw milk has a higher price than pasteurized milk. The community is also trying to appreciate, limit and counter the negative effects that this activity has had on biodiversity.

PRODUCTION AREA
Nouakchott

COMMUNITY COORDINATOR
Mohamed Ould Tati
tel. +222 6512041
tiviski@opt.mr

Cheese and Honey Producers of the Mid-Atlas Mountains

13 peasant women, with the support of Réseau Marocain d'Economie Sociale et Solidaire (Remesse), have come together to produce cow cheese, honey and jams. Honey is a traditional product of this mountain area and is rich with floral essences. The community has brought back to life another two traditional activities: weaving and wool dying – both highly symbolic skills for the region's inhabitants who were nomadic shepherds up to about fifty years ago. Conversely, the cheese making method – which requires pasteurizing the milk, the addition of rennet, preserving in brine and ageing – was introduced by a French cheesemaker.

PRODUCTION AREA
El Ksiba, Béni Mellal Province

COMMUNITY COORDINATOR
Mustapha Yacobi
tel. +212 68196589
mustapha_y@hotmail.com

Dried Fruit Producers of Taounate

This community from northern Morocco is made up of 120 women. Thanks to a project financed by the United Nations and the Moroccan Commerce and Industry Ministry, it has been equipped with a food dryer partially powered by solar energy and partly by diesel. With this equipment, the women dry figs and plums having first carefully picked the fruit according to its size and consistency. The consumption of both fruits is particularly linked to two periods of the year: figs are an important food in the month of Ramadan and during the Achoura festivities (the start of the lunar year), whilst prunes are often served with dishes during weddings or baptisms.

PRODUCTION AREA
Taounate Province

COMMUNITY COORDINATOR
Saida Tayebi
tel. +212 65431921
saida_tayebi@yahoo.fr

Goat Breeders of Souss-Massa-Draa

The women's cooperative Tamghart Worgh works in the territory of the *douar* (village) of Jouabre, on the banks of the *oued* (water course) Massa, on the edges of the Souss-Massa National Park. Created in January 2006, the community has manager to buy in Fez its first goat herd thanks to the support of the Mohammed VI foundation. A smll part of the milk produced is kept by the women and drunk fresh or processed to produce cheese for their families although almost all is sold to a dairy. Commercial relations have been established thanks to the Jouaber association for development following the collaboration with a vet and a sales agent.

PRODUCTION AREA
Souss-Massa-Draa Province

COMMUNITY COORDINATOR
Amara Malika
tel. +212 64203600
talibi1@hotmail.com

Mussel Fishermen from the Tiznit Province

Mirletf is a fishing village on the Atlantic coast, south of Agadir and still untouched by mass tourism. There are wide beaches and long stretches of sheer cliffs rising out of the sea where mollusks and, in particular, mussels abound. The mussels are ripped from the rocks by hand with the help of a few basic tools and then separated from the shells and steamed in sterilized steel containers. Once cold they are packaged and sent to the local markets. A sun dried mussel is also produced as a more traditional product and part of the harvest (around 10 tons a year) is sold fresh. The Tifaouine association works with the fishermen – 46 women and nine men – to rationalize production, improve quality and guarantee a just social development.

PRODUCTION AREA
Mirleft, Tiznit Province

COMMUNITY COORDINATOR
Moulay Mohamed Elouassifi
tel. +212 66021965
aboumaria2006@yahoo.com

Farmers and Animal Breeders in the Khomas Region

In the mountain chain of Khomas, west of Windhoek, a community composed of 50 individuals farms and raises animals in accordance with organic and sustainable agricultural methods, assisted by the Necofa organization. This helps peasants by organizing training sessions on technologies and sustainable crop methods and promotes the exchange of experiences between African farmers. The community raises cattle without intensive methods using only primary materials as fodder. They grown millet, one of the most common cereals in the country and a number of fruits such as watermelons and *eembe*, a fruit similar to grapes which the men and women of the community make into jams and juices. The Marula tree, with its edible nuts, is also present in the region.

PRODUCTION AREA
Windhoek, Khomas Region

COMMUNITY COORDINATOR
Frans Persendt
tel. +264 612063894
fpersendt@unam.na

Cheese and Curdled Milk Producers of Toukounous

The community brings into an association 29 zebu azawak breeders in the village of Toukounous, close to Filingué. A part of the milk is made into cheese and the rest into curdled milk. The products are sold in situ or sent to urban agglomerates (Niamey and Filingué).The cheese is called *tchoukou* and is a dry product made with milk and veal rennet. It is formed into thin parallelepiped about three to five millimeters thick according to the amount of milk used (half or a full liter). The curdled milk is made by mixing fresh milk with a small amount of the previous day's curdled milk. The association is supported by the Toukounous animal raising station and participates in a series of Nigerian and international projects.

PRODUCTION AREA
Tillabéri District

COMMUNITY COORDINATOR
Ousseina Saidou
tel. +227 929062
ousseysk@refer.ne - ousseyks@yahoo.fr

Kouri Cattle Breeders of Sayam

Large, with a light-colored coat and large lyre-shaped horns, the Kouri is a bull-like breed typical of the areas around Lake Chad, currently at risk of extinction due partially to the frequent cross breeding with local zebu breeds. The last thousand heads of Kouri still existing in Niger are raised in the Centre Secondaire de Multiplication du Bétail of Sayam, in the Diffa District in the very far east of the county. The centre which employs 50 civil servants works in research aimed at the selection and more widespread use of the breed which has undergone a very large amount of crossbreeding, particularly with the m'bororo zebu. The animals produce milk and a hard cheese made with veal rennet.

PRODUCTION AREA
Diffa District

COMMUNITY COORDINATOR
Mahaman Salissou Haboubacar
princekouri@yahoo.fr

Milk Producers of Kirkissoye

Located on the right of the Niger, down valley from the capital Niamey, the animal raising station of Kirkissoye was created in 1966 in order to carry out applied research on the production of fodder and its genetic potential for the azawak zebu breed with the aim of providing the city with milk and of improving domestic fattening. The station is the focus point for the milk cooperative Kirkissoye whose 28 members raise 243 heads of cows, cattle, veal, bullocks and bulls – all of the azawak breed. This is a typical Niger breed, indigenous of the Azawak Valley whose propensity for milk production has caused their multiplication throughout the country. The almost 79,000 liters of milk produced annually are sold locally and, for the purposes of transformation, to the Société de Lait de Niger (Solani).

PRODUCTION AREA
Tillabéri District

COMMUNITY COORDINATOR
Traore Assane
tel. +227 977088
agtraore@intnet.ne

Takommar Cheese Producers of Timia

Timia is a village on the Air Massif in the Nigerian Sahara, where around 600 women of ages ranging from 15 to 60 divided into 30 groups, work as shepherds. They are all Tuareg Kel Ewey and work particularly on the semi-nomadic raising of goats and the transformation of their milk. The main products are milk, cheese (an important nutritional element which is eaten either fresh or matured), meat (when the animals are killed either on festivities or when one of the goats is ill) and butter. The skins are used to make small necklaces with gris-gris as amulets. The community also produces artisan objects with local primary materials such as palm leaf mats.

PRODUCTION AREA
Air Massif, Agadez District

COMMUNITY COORDINATOR
Amoumene Salek
tel. +227 276684

Tuareg Producers of Milk, Meat and Cereals

The almost 3,000 members of the community are organized in several groups forming part of an association named after the legendary mother of the Tuareg, Tin Hinan. Their main source of sustenance is the nomadic raising of animals. With the milk of goats, sheep and cows, curdled for two to three hours, the breeders produce a cheese which can be seasoned for up to two years. The meat is cut into slices and dried for four to five days. From wheat and millet flour is made a form of bread (*togulla*) which can be kept for a long time. It is made by mixing the flour with salted water to obtain a solid paste, which is then divided into pieces of weights varying from one to three kilos. The resulting flatbread is then buried in the hot sand where it bakes for at least an hour.

PRODUCTION AREA
Agadez, Tahoua and Tillabéri Districts

COMMUNITY COORDINATOR
Habsatou Aboubacar
tel. +227 884204
tinhinanniger@yahoo.fr

Beekeepers of Ijebu-Ode

In southern Nigeria, covered mostly by woods and forests, the seasonal rains start in June and last until September, thanks to the Atlantic winds. This area sees the concentration of the main cities of the country, amongst which is Ijebu-Ode. The community's 15 beekeepers come from different tribes and have formed a company in which 10 processors also participate. The hives, for more than one hundred colonies are spread all over the region. The producers harvest the honey from the trays, hand filter it and package it with the company's brand name. Each beekeeper then sells his own wild flower honey in the local markets and to individual customers. According to local cultural traditions, honey has beneficial effects on health and, for this reason, it is used as a medicine and during traditional ceremonies.

PRODUCTION AREA
Ijebu-Ode, Ogun Department

COMMUNITY COORDINATOR
Adebisi Data Adekunle
tel. +44 7710900597
Saraounia1@tiscali.co.uk

Sorghum Drink Producers of Nyakinama

In Nyakinama there are about 200 small juice, beer and other sorghum by-product producers. The three representatives of the community buy the cereal from local growers and make drinks destined mainly for domestic consumption. The rest is sold to local retailers. The normally red grains are dried and then left to soak for 24 hours in water and ash to make them turn black. They are then drained, washed thoroughly, dried again in the sole for about ten days and then ground. In order to make 20 litres of juice, 10 kilos of flour and 30 litres of water are required. The water is brought to the boil and then divided into two separate parts: one is left to cool and the other is mixed with the flour in a large wooden basin until it becomes a sort of paste which is then diluted with the cold water. The drink is ready after 12 hours resting. Sorghum beer is made by adding yeast to the juice.

PRODUCTION AREA
Ruhengeri Prefecture, North Province

COMMUNITY COORDINATOR
Clément Ernest Habiyaremye
tel. +250 08481513
elacza@yahoo.fr - csanyakinama@yahoo.fr

Artisan Fishermen of Saint-Louis

Around 3,000 fishermen, processors and retailers form the community working in the north of the country under the auspices of the Fédération Nationale des Groupements d'Intérêt Économique de Pêche du Sénégal, in the enhancement of the fishing resources and its sustainable management. The *Sardinella aurita*, one of the Clupeidae species which undertakes large-scale migrations and *Cymbium glans*, a single valve mollusk of the tropical seas are locally widely consumed and form – dried or fermented – an essential ingredient of Senegalese rice dishes. The white spotted octopus (*Octopus macropus*) and the white grouper (*Serranus aeneus*) are caught mainly for exportation. The mollusc is sold in Europe and Asia and can be dried or salted. For the grouper, increasingly rare, protection measures are currently under development.

PRODUCTION AREA
Saint-Louis Region

COMMUNITY COORDINATOR
El Hadji Amadou Wade
tel. +221 8321100
fenagiepeche@sentoo.sn - alawade61@yahoo.fr

Artisan Fishermen of Ziguinchor

The community, associated to the Fédération Nationale des Groupements d'Intérêt Économique de Pêche du Sénégal, comprises 560 fishermen, processors and small retailers. Amongst the species caught and preserved with traditional methods and procedures, is the round sardinella (*Sardinella aurita*), the fundamental element of the daily, national dish (rice with fermented fish). It is fished throughout most of the year with trawling or surrounding nets and, after grilling, it can be smoked or dried. A gastropod, *Cymbium glans*, is caught with sleeping or immersion nets and is a traditional ingredient of Senegalese cuisine although it is also exported to Europe and Asia. The other species are the white-spotted octopus (*Octopus macropus*) and the white grouper (*Serranus aeneus*): the latter, of great commercial value, should be protected as it is at risk of extinction.

PRODUCTION AREA
Ziguinchor Region

COMMUNITY COORDINATOR
El Hadji Amadou Wade
tel. +221 8321100
fenagiepeche@sentoo.sn - alawade61@yahoo.fr

Cereal, Legume and Vegetable Growers of Keur Massar

The eight members of the Massaci association (three are seasonal workers) grow millet, groundnuts and vegetables. The cereal is sown on the association's three fields at the beginning of the rainy season, harvested and stored in granaries for the organized sale to merchants. It is the ingredient of dishes such as *laakh*, which is accompanied by curdled milk. The groundnuts are harvested twice a year and are partially stored for sale and partially reused as seeds. The kitchen gardens in Sébikotane, are the responsibility of the community's three women. They have a nursery and exclusively use the scales and heads of smoked sardinella bought from the fish processors of Bargny as fertilizer. Tomatoes, beans, cabbages, onions and potatoes are harvested and placed in crates or sacks.

PRODUCTION AREA
Rufisque District, Dakar Region

COMMUNITY COORDINATOR
Aïssatou Thior
tel. +221 4492163

Fish processors and sellers

More than 25,000 women of the riverside areas form the community which belongs to the Union Nationale des Operatrices de la Fenagie Pêche. The fish products most frequently treated are round sardinella, salmon bass, a type of shark of the *Carcharhinus* species and a series of shell fish (Noah's ark, mangrove oysters, murexes...) The management of the latter is the work of the women from their harvest in the water tanks or amongst the coastal vegetation during the low tide either manually or with the help of small machetes. The shells are then taken to the village, boiled and opened to extract the mollusks to be dried. The fish undergo a traditional treatment: dry salted or in brine, grilled and dried (*ketiakh*) or smoked (*methorah*), fermented in small pieces (*guedj*) or whole (*tambadiang*).

PRODUCTION AREA
Departments of Dakar and Fatick

COMMUNITY COORDINATOR
Awa Djigal
tel. +221 8321100
djigalawa@yahoo.fr

Fonio Producers of Kedougou

The community is composed of 945 peasants who grow fonio, a graminaceous, on 1,131 hectares and are organized in 36 groups of producers, each of which belongs to a village and participates in a network for harvesting and sales. They grow three species of Poaceae, *Digitaria exilis*, *Digitaria iburua* and *Brachiaria deflexa*. The crops are basically manual by broadcast on a lightly tilled soil. Growth is rapid and needs only one or two weedings. The ears, cut by the men with sickles, are gathered into stacks and put out to dry on wooden platforms. The crop is threshed with sticks or by crushing underfoot on areas of beaten earth of clay covered with cow dung. The grains are sieved by the women to clean them and stored in the granaries. An association for the promotion of fonio was founded in Senegal in 2005.

PRODUCTION AREA
Tambacounda Region

COMMUNITY COORDINATOR
Madieng Seck
tel. +221 8256908
syfia@sentoo.sn

Fruit Growers of the Diouloulou District

The southern regions of Senegal are characterized by a climate suitable for fruit trees which are often to be found growing amongst the forest trees. The Association des Planteurs de l'Arrondissement de Diouloulou (Apad) associates 171 producers from three rural communities (Diouloulou, Kafountine e Djignaky) in order to encourage, whilst respecting the environment, the development of fruit growing and beekeeping. The most interesting products are the kent, keitt and haden devis mango varieties and other early varieties (sold in Italy with a Fair Trade label) and citrus fruits. With regard to beekeeping, the community encourages the use of hives that can be accessed without recourse to the traditional method of smoking, which creates considerable risks for the forests.

PRODUCTION AREA
Bignona District, Ziguinchor Region

COMMUNITY COORDINATOR
Mamadou Diatta
tel. +221 9913467
gie_apad@hotmail.com - cospesen@sentoo.sn

Groundnut Paste and Oil Producers of the Diourbel Region

Although an area with a large production of groundnuts, Diourbel is a very poor area. Both rainfall and soil fertility are very low and centuries of monoculture of groundnuts for exportation are impoverished the other crops. Only a few peasants can collect sufficient to feed their families for more than six month. The Unione Régionale des Associations Paysannes de Diourbel is composed of 36 groups with 2,200 members. The transformation of the groundnuts into paste and oil tend tends to link production more closely to local consumption. The paste, made by pressing the toasted groundnuts, is the base element of a condiment (mafé) for white rice which is the daily dish of Senegal. The production of oil, as an alternative to that of the nationalized industry currently being privatized, follows ancient family traditions.

PRODUCTION AREA
Diourbel Region

COMMUNITY COORDINATOR
Marie Thérèse Niane
tel. +221 9736304
urapd@sentoo.sn

Karkade Growers and Processors of the Dakar Region

Karkade (*Hibiscus sabdariffa* is its scientific name, *bissap* its Wolof name) is a herbaceous plant possibly originally from Central America, now widespread throughout many tropical regions. In Senegal it is grown mainly where there are large groundnut plantations and also serves to mark out the fields. A drink is made from the red calyx variety whilst the green calyx variety is made into a condiment for rice and fonio dishes. The localities of Dangalma and Lambaye, at around one hundred kilometers from Dakar, are famous for karkade where both the cultivation and transformation are a female prerogative. From the red calyx of the bissap, various types of tonic drinks are made. Syrup is prepared by placing the calyx to soak in water for six to seven hours, stirring it now and again. The liquid is then filtered, transferred to buckets, diluted and sugared. It is lightly boiled for 30 seconds at 100°C and then bottled.

PRODUCTION AREA
Dakar Region

COMMUNITY COORDINATOR
Madieng Seck
tel. +221 8256908
syfia@sentoo.sn

Milk and Butter Producers of Koumpentoum

The Entente de Koumpentoum works through 49 groups and 12 committees with a total of 1,280 individuals in an area straddling the groundnuts plantations and the wooded pastures. The massive production of groundnuts, beguan in the colonial period and continued after independence, has caused the abandonment of traditional cereals. However, neither has there been any policies for the integration of agriculture and stock raising. As a result, Senegal is now a greater importer of both rice and powdered milk. In order to correct this tendency, the community produces organic milk, natural curdled milk and cow milk butter without additives. The curdled milk (*soow*) and butter (*diiw gnoor*), of a rather liquid consistency, is a good accompaniment to traditional dishes such as rice with fermented fish and millet paste.

PRODUCTION AREA
Tambacounda Region

COMMUNITY COORDINATOR
Ousseynou Gory
tel. +221 9815047
fongstamba@yahoo.fr

Millet and Maize Growers and Processors of the Thiès Region

Created in 1985, the Union des Groupements Paysans de Mekhé has 42 village associations with a total of 5,000 individuals. Amongst its activities is the transformation of agricultural products with traditional methods, the main crops being millet, maize and groundnuts. Millet undergoes various kinds of milling which produce flour (*soungouf*), semolina (*sanxal*), a rather larger grained semolina (*thiacry*) and couscous (*thiéré*). Couscous called *thiéré mbooxë* is also made with maize flour whose crushed grains are the origins of the so called maize rice (*thiébou mbooxë*). The work is carried out on family run farms and the community makes use of a self-managed credit and savings system.

PRODUCTION AREA
Thiès Region

COMMUNITY COORDINATOR
Fatou Binta Niane
tel. +221 9555113
ugpm@sentoo.sn

Niebé Producers in the Louga Region

There are around 600 members of the Association des Paysans de la Région de Louga, a sub-Saharan area exploited for more than a century for the production of groundnuts. The peasants grow several varieties (mougne and ndiambour are amongst the most traditional) of black-eyed pea, a legume (*Vigna unguiculata*) locally called niebé and grown in fields of cereals such as millet and sorghum. Niebé is much used in Senegalese cuisine: it can be eaten fresh, with or without its pod; the dried grains are cooked alone or with other legumes, cereals or meat. In collaboration with the NGO Apecs, the community is experimenting with mushroom derived fertilisers which should provide the plant with a better nutritional content.

PRODUCTION AREA
Louga Region

COMMUNITY COORDINATOR
Assane Sylla
tel. +221 6419325
assane.asylla@yahoo.fr - assane.asylla@hotmail.com

Peul Animal Breeders and Milk Producers in the Louga Region

The Peul tribe women, seven breeders and eight processors, are united in an association which aims to enhance zootechnic resources and their derivates for the benefit of the family farms. At the base of the transformation activities is fresh milk, collected in the owned farms or, occasionally, from other producers in the Darha area. The milk is sold directly after a brief heating or is left to curdle or is made into yoghurt. The curdled milk (*kosaam kaadam*) is produced by keeping the milk in hermetically closed stockpots for one or two days until it becomes sold, greasy and slightly acidic. It is then poured into buckets or sacks for sale. With the addition of lactic bacteria, sugar and aromas, yoghurt is obtained although this is a new product which the association is developing with the help of specialised methods.

PRODUCTION AREA
Keur Momar Sarr, Louga District and Region

COMMUNITY COORDINATOR
Awa Diallo
tel. +221 5695314
awapoulo@yahoo.fr

Preserved Fish Producers and Sellers of Fatick

The traditional methods for preserving fish in Senegal are numerous. The community's women – around 50 – use them all but with a preference for the methods called ketiakh (grilling followed by drying) and guedj (fermentation in brine and drying). The first method is used particularly with round sardinella (*Sardinella aurita*)and the second with salmon bass (*Argyrosomus regius*). The sardinella is grilled, the head and scales are removed, it is covered in salt and then dried in the sun. It can also be slowly cooked in two phases and then smoked. The salmon bass is gutted and cut into pieces and then left for 48 hours in a closed tank, exposed to the sun with a saline solution of 15-20% of its weight. The subsequent drying lasts between three to five days. Guedj, with rice, is the ingredient of tiébou diene, the national dish.

PRODUCTION AREA
Fatick Region

COMMUNITY COORDINATOR
Awa Djigal
tel. +221 8321100 - 5615288
djigalawa@yahoo.fr

Producers and Processors of Diakhao

The Jeunes Producteurs et Transformateurs de Diakhao association works to improve the quality of food and promote its availability to the local population. The 12 members of the community, of whom 10 are women, produce juices and syrups, fruit and vegetable composts and cereal derivates. The fruits are made into juices or syrups by immerging them in hot water and filtering the liquid and are grown locally, except for the mangoes, which come from Thiès. Jams and conserves are made by pureeing or leaving whole mangoes, watermelons, baobab fruits, carrots, celery and aubergines after they have been cooked. Millet, maize and sorghum are bought from local producers. The women pound the grains in mortars to eliminate the husks, after which they are sieved in large baskets and washed in running water. After a more or less lengthy drying in the sun, they are ground and milled to make flour powder for soups, couscous or laakh.

PRODUCTION AREA
Fatick Region

COMMUNITY COORDINATOR
Juliette Paule Zingan
tel. +221 6847080
zinganjulie@yahoo.fr

Rice Processors of Podor

Created in 1987, the Union des Jeunes Agriculteurs de Koyli-Wirndé has 4,287 members of which 2,605 women, grouped into 22 village associations. With their activities of transformation, rice is obtained from the raw crop – eaten locally like millet – and a flour used again like the semolina made from millet, to make various forms of couscous. The whole cereal grains, before husking, are first processed into white rice and then ground. Traditional condiments for couscous (thiéré) in Senegal are groundnut sauce, tomato sauce (typical of the Wolof, the largest tribe in the country and the Serer) and curdled milk.

PRODUCTION AREA
Podor, Saint-Louis Region

COMMUNITY COORDINATOR
Nadjirou Sall
tel. +221 9643003

Shea growers of Kedougou

The Karite (*Vitellaria paradoxa*) is a tall tree growing exclusively in Africa but whose fruits provide products used throughout the world: butter, soaps, creams, body milk and conditioners and shampoo... The plant can grow to a height of 20 metres and live up to 150 years but its nuts are only productive after 50 years. In the Kedougou District, 700 kilometres south of Dakar, the presence of this tree is linked to the Bassari tribe. Growing, harvest, transformation and commercialization are traditionally the responsibility of the women. For the sale of their products, the community, which can count on 150 inhabitants of three villages, is supported by the company Maison du Karité, with headquarters in Dakar.

PRODUCTION AREA
Kedougou District, Tambacounda Region

COMMUNITY COORDINATOR
Taïb Cherif Diop
tel. +221 8231829
maisonkarite@yahoo.fr

Vegetable anf Fruit Producers and Processors of Thiès

The Takku Liggeey Awafrul association works to improve the value of the Thiès Region's products. It is composed of five women and benefits from the collaboration of six fruit and vegetable growers to produce drinks, conserves and jams. Amongst the juices and fruit syrups the most popular are those extracted from dried karkade flowers (bissap), a small plant traditionally grown by women. Other drinks made from tamarind, mangoes, guava and ginger which is bought from Guinean merchants. Jams are made from karkade, oranges, watermelons, mangoes, guava and papaya, whilst the conserves are made with chili peppers, beans, tomatoes, carrots, onions and aubergines. One particular compote is made by cooking the sweet baobab potato and lemon juice.

PRODUCTION AREA
Thiès Region

COMMUNITY COORDINATOR
Juliette Paule Zingan
tel. +221 6847080
zinganjulie@yahoo.fr

Producers from the Island of Mahé

Comprising 150 individuals, the community produces a large variety of vegetables, tropical fruit and legumes including sweet potatoes, cassava and spices. It also includes chicken and pig breeders. The community members are united in the Seychelles Farmers Association (SFA), registered in 2002 with the purpose of providing representatives for growers and stock raisers particularly with regard to the problems of marketing, production costs and the availability of agricultural products. The SFA, in a subsequent series of consultations with the government, contributed to the implementation of the Farmers' Incentive Act of 2005, which guarantees a favorable commercial taxation regime, social security funds and agricultural work regulations.

PRODUCTION AREA
Island of Mahé

COMMUNITY COORDINATOR
Serge Benstrong
tel. +248 515020
sergebenstrong@seychelles.sc

Banana Producers of Lower Shabelle and Lower Jubba

Before the civil war, the growing of bananas was concentrated in two areas, Lower Shabelle and Lower Jubba, on an overall surface area of around 7,000 hectares. The bananas were destined for exportation to Europe and Saudi Arabia but, over the past 15 years, the Somalia growers' association has been dependent exclusively on the very poor local market. The two varieties grown are called bouyo and grand micheal. A second important product, above all in Lower Shabelle, is the watermelon, which is harvested from December to April. Each farm is also dedicated to stock raising and beekeeping.

PRODUCTION AREA
Shabeellaha Hoose and Jubbada Hoose Regions

COMMUNITY COORDINATOR
Omar Mohamed Oday
tel. +252 1236142
adahir@yahoo.com

Beekeepers of the Pacaltsdorp District

The founding members of the community are passionate beekeepers from their infancy. They are small farmers who, penalized by the racial laws since 1944, have at last managed to set up both production and commercialisation. The main area of beekeeping is the Pacaltsdorp District near the city of George. The bees (above all the *Apis mellifera capensis* species) extract pollen and nectar from the flowers of bluegum, canola, rape, citrus and fynbos – which in Afrikaans means thin bushes and refers to the needle shaped, narrow leaves of many plants in the regions which indicate a biome of more than 8,000 species. As well as honey, the community produces wax, propolis and various derivates for gastronomic and pharmaceutical uses.

PRODUCTION AREA
Pacaltsdorp, Western Cape

COMMUNITY COORDINATOR
Japie Hollander
tel. +27 448781061 - 827034515
mjbfarming@webmail.co.za

Organic Producers of Klein Karoo

The Karoo, divided into the Large and Smallo Karoo, is an arid region in inland South Africa. The Klein Karoo Organic Initiative (Kkoi), which brings together around 60 farmers (although their number is steadily increasing) is encouraging a conversion to the growing of crops since the goats and ostriches are one of the main reasons for the desertification of the area. Its objective is to transform the entire region into a vast zone of mainly sustainable, organic agriculture. The Karoo is considered an exemplar of biodiversity with a vast variety of indigenous species. The community grows and produces, above all, olives and their derivates (oil and paste), three varieties of chili pepper (jalapeno, inchanga cayenne and habanero), organic fruit and vegetable. Furthermore, they also raise Dorper sheep with organic methods.

PRODUCTION AREA
Klein Karoo, Western Cape

COMMUNITY COORDINATOR
Elizabeth Susanna Eglington
tel. +27 217151953 - 836533635
lizeglington@netconnect.co.za

Rooibos Producers of Suid Bokkeveld

Created in 2001, thanks to 14 members of the community, the cooperative Heiveld aims to produce Rooibos tea with traditional methods selling it in Europe and thereby improving the living conditions of its associates. The community is composed of around 500 small landowners and land workers who live and work in somewhat isolated conditions in Suid Bokkeveld, an arid and drought ridden area about 75 kilometers from the nearest village. Many members of the community pass most of their time working in the large agricultural farms to earn more. The tea is made from about 95% cultivated and 5% wild Rooibos and all the production is certified by Naturland and the Fairtrade Labelling Organization (Flo). As well as producing tea, the community grows wheat and raises sheep and goats.

PRODUCTION AREA
Surroundings of Nieuwoudtville, Northern Cape

COMMUNITY COORDINATOR
Noel Oettle
tel. +27 272181117
dryland@global.co.za

Rooibos Producers of Wupperthal

Created by missionaries in 1830, the community is made up of around a thousand small farmers who live in the isolated villages of the mountain around Wupperthal and make Rooibos tea with traditional and organic methods from the leaves and buds of the *Aspalathus linearis*, an indigenous plant typical of the sandstone mountains of western South Africa. All the lands contained within the boundaries of the old mission belong to the Moravian Church of South Africa. The greater part of Rooibos is grown in the lands that the Church lets to the peasants at a symbolic price whilst the rest of the harvest comes from wild Rooibos. The tea is certified organic and fair trade by the Fairtrade Labelling Organization (FLO) and is sold both in South Africa and Europe since 1998.

PRODUCTION AREA
Surroundings of Wupperthal, Western Cape

COMMUNITY COORDINATOR
Noel Oettle
tel. +27 272181117 - 836938676
dryland@global.co.za

Cereal and Fruit Producers of Wad Medani

Composed of 200 members (producers, technicians and consumers) this community refers to the international Necofa association and is to be found in Wad Medani, in the Gezira agricultural region. Their principal products are sorghum, wheat and the fruit of the baobab (also called *tabaldi*, whose scientific name is *Adansonia digitata*). Sorghum – the second most important crop in Africa – is a cereal with various uses: it is mostly eaten fermented as a sort of porridge, but can be the ingredient of breads, sweets, and couscous. The wheat is made into flour and is used for the production of bread. The baobab fruit is dried, soaked in water, sugared and processed into a fresh, summer drink.

PRODUCTION AREA
Wad Medani, Gezira

COMMUNITY COORDINATOR
Abdalla Ibrahim El Hagwa
tel. +249 912536014
elhagwa@yahoo.com

Traditional Food producers, processors and cooks of Shewula

The community uses sustainable methods for growing traditional varieties of sorghum, amathapa (a tuber similar to the potato), imbuya (a wild vegetable gathered during the rainy season) and the jugo bean (tindlubu), rich with protein and, for this reason, used as a substitute for meat. The community also produces honey and fruit jams from the wild forest trees, amongst which is the Marula. The promotion of products is entrusted to the Shewula Mountain Camp, a tourist structure, which belongs to the community. The recovery of traditional crops is a part of a wider attempt to bring the food up to a secure state of health in a context of crisis due to the spread of the Aids virus.

PRODUCTION AREA
Shewula, Lubombo District

COMMUNITY COORDINATOR
Nomsa Mabila
tel. +268 6031931
shewula@realnet.co.sz

Vegetable and Legume Producers of Kambhoke

Kambhoke (around 5,000 inhabitants) is in central Swaziland, amongst the Hlatikhulu mountains and the great plain of the River Usutu, where the ancient reign of the Mamba lived. The community is made from an association of which 20 peasants are members and who, with sustainable and traditional methods, grow various indigenous legumes and cereals. The 40 hectares of land are equally divided amongst maize, sorghum, the protein rich jugo bean (tindlubu in the local dialect) and the black-eyed bean (a small legume of the Vigna species, here called tinhlumaya). Around 30 tons of maize, 5 of sorghum, 4 of jugo beans and 2 black eyed peasare produced. The aim of the community is to promote sustainable agricultural methods and the recovery traditional cultures throughout the country.

PRODUCTION AREA
Kambhoke, Shiselweni District

COMMUNITY COORDINATOR
Nomsa Mabila
tel. +268 6031931
shewula@realnet.co.sz

Bamboo Wine Producers of Njombe

As well as growing various self-supporting crops, this community is specialised in the production of bamboo wine (bambù), harvested and worked on a family basis and sold in the surroundings to ensure a financial income. Growing spontaneously, without chemical composts or weed killers, the bamboo is cut 10 centimeters below its summit to extract the lymph and is left to ferment for five days until it is processed into a clear liquid, collected every morning and late afternoon. Although the drink is ready to be consumed, it can be preserved further to increase its alcoholic content. Traditionally linked to the Bena tribe, the bamboo wine is drunk both by men and women. The community is part of the Tanzania Organic Certification Association (Tancert).

PRODUCTION AREA
Njombe, Iringa Region

COMMUNITY COORDINATOR
Mtama Leonard Yuda
tel. +255 784490275
lm@tancert.org

Barabaig shepherds

The Barabaig are a small agro-pastoral population in the area around Mount Hanang, in central northern Tanzania. Despite the increasing process of abandonment of their nomadic life, a good number still lead a nomadic or transhumant existence, finding nutriment from their herds of cattle and sheep. As well as milk, meat and blood, fundamental foods for their nutriment, the Barabaig use the animal skins from which they produce objects, clothing and repairs. Animal raising is frequently accompanied by a subsistence agriculture concentrated mainly on growing maize in small lots of land which, in contrast to the night recoveries for the animals, are not protected by thorny hedges. For this reason, the Barabaig often build their huts on the edges of the fields to protect the crops from predators.

PRODUCTION AREA
Hanang District, Manyara Region

COMMUNITY COORDINATOR
Linda Darema
tel. +255 744294069 - 754294069
daremalinda@yahoo.com

Cassava and Coffee Producers of the Ileje District

Urafiki (friendship) is an association of 25 producers formed in 2001 thanks to the support of the local Irdo organisation. The association mainly sells cassava (manioc) and coffee. After the harvest, the cassava roots are washed, peeled, soaked and dried in the sun. The resultant product, with a high energy content, is sold in the dry season in 25 kilo sacks in the markets of Mbalizi and Mbeya (through the association) or in local markets (by individual producers). 20% of the overall production is destined for domestic consumption. Urafiki harvests and sells around 1,500 kilos of coffee (*Coffea arabica*) each season. 95% is old in the Moshi market, fresh or naturally dried whilst the rest is toasted and sold in the local market. The association is working to obtain organic certification.

PRODUCTION AREA
Magoga, Spande, Chibila and Luswisi, Ileje District, Mbeya Region

COMMUNITY COORDINATOR
Kibona Amanulas
tel. +255 744251390
amanucleus@yahoo.it

Cereal and Legume Growers of the Kiteto District

The community is a cooperative called Nabulu (growth) and is composed of 15 Masai women brought together in 2005 thanks to an assistance program run by Women Development for Science and Technology (Wodsta). The community puts together a detailed work program for each season and meets every month to discuss growing methods, marketing and running costs. The methods used are traditional, such as bio-dynamic intercropping: only natural compost is used rather than chemical fertilisers. Once dried and packaged, a small proportion of the maize, soya and white beans are sold to the families of the Kujungu and Lengatei villages and the nearby shops and markets. The larger proportion is sold to wholesalers who resell it in cities such as Tanga, Dar es Salaam and Arusha.

PRODUCTION AREA
Loolera, Kiteto District, Manyara Region

COMMUNITY COORDINATOR
Kibona Amanulas
tel. +255 744251390
amanucleus@yahoo.com

Cheese and Milk Producers of Njombe

The Njombe Livestock Farmer Association (Njolifa) is a cooperative of milk cattle breeders which are both indigenous (zebu) and not (Friesian, Jersey) which is co-proprietor of a dairy. The milk undergoes a series of quality tests every morning and, if it does not come up to the standard, it is withdrawn. Both the full fat pasteurized milk (maziwa) and the yoghurt (*maziwa ya ngando*) made by adding milk fermentations to milk heated to 95°C, are distributed in vases, bottles or plastic bags to children in schools, orphanages and the hospitals of Njombe. The production of cheese (*jibini*) involves two types: one mature and one fresh. The former are a type of soft and a type of hard cheese, hand made in special forms using natural rennet, fermentations and salt. The fresh cheese is similar to mozzarella and is also handmade with the same ingredients.

PRODUCTION AREA
Njombe, Iringa Region

COMMUNITY COORDINATOR
Gerion Efrehimu Nisilu
tel. +255 745482750
njombemilkfactory@gmail.com

Fruit and Vegetable Producers of Morogoro

The Uluguru mountains, with a high-density population and essential water resources for the inhabitants of Morogoro and Dar es Salaam, have an intensive production of fruit and vegetables. The community brings together numerous small scale productions, supporting them in the application of sustainable methods in agriculture such as the collection of rain water in order to avoid a conflict of water use between the rural and urban populations, the use of natural compost such as hemp and organic pesticides such as neem. The main crops of the community are pineapples (fresh or sun dried), cooking bananas, plums (from which juices and alcoholic drinks are made) and beans. The community is also responsible for training and collaboration with universities and agrifood research institutes.

PRODUCTION AREA
Uluguru Mountains, Morogoro Region

COMMUNITY COORDINATOR
Mdanku Idd Saleh
tel. +255 744879306
iddmdanku@yahoo.com

Growers and Stock Breeders of Ngurudoto and Kikatiti

The Unoin of women's groups for development in Ngurudoto and Kikatiti is a community created in 1995 and formed of two cooperatives, Umangu and Dakika, of which 36 women are members. Umangu is concerned with the organic growing of fruit and vegetables(mangoes, papaya, avocados, bananas, oranges, cabbages, carrots, peppers and tomatoes), the raising of 45 pigs, the fishing of klapia (the most common fish in Lake Victoria) and the harvesting of honey from 47 hives. Dakika is responsible for the transformation, packaging and sales of products to local and regional shops. The solar dryer built by Dakika enables both fruit and fish to be dried – the latter being subsequently smoked. The profits from sales are divided up equally amongst the members.

PRODUCTION AREA
Ngurudoto and Kikatiti, Arumeru District, Arusha Region

COMMUNITY COORDINATOR
Kibona Amanulas
tel. +255 744251390
amanucleus@yahoo.com

Hibiscus Growers and Processors of the Pwani Regio

The community works not far from Dar es Salam, in one of the less developed areas of Tanzania. It is composed of 26 people, 20 small farmers and six processorswho work together for the promotion of their organic products all made with Hibiscus, a spontaneous plant growing in various areas of the country. The range of products includes tea made with dried flowers which can be drunk either hot or cold, with or without sugar; juice, made with an infusion of fresh and dried petals; wine made by fermenting the juice with yeasts and sugar. Both juice and wine should be drunk cold. The populations of central Tanzania and the coastal region use Hibiscus for medicinal purposes to cure anaemia and kidney diseases. The flowers are not easy to keep but can be harvested twice a year due to the double rainy season.

PRODUCTION AREA
Kibaha, Pwani Region

COMMUNITY COORDINATOR
Hawa Kimolo
tel. +255 232402716
resnafom@yahoo.co.uk

Masai Farmers of the Arusha Region

Thanks to the cultural exchanges of the Arusha Region Environment Conservation Network (Arecon) and other associations, the Masai who live a semi-nomadic life raising animals in the semiarid land between Tanzania and Kenya, have begun the organic cultivation of vegetables and legumes. Amongst these are the black-eyed pea (*kunde*) and the lablab (*mbaazi*), which grow in plain lands with little rain. The weeding is carried out only once before the seeds germinate and the harvest takes place four months after planting. These crops, rich in vitamins and with a good protein content are eaten fresh or are kept for periods of drought. Of the lablab are eaten the leaves, fresh or dried and the seeds, used to make biscuits.

PRODUCTION AREA
Arusha Region

COMMUNITY COORDINATOR
Zuhura Chitanda
tel. +255 2741650201
areconn@yahoo.com

Milk and Nilk By-Product Producers of the Hai District

With its 250 members, this community is the largest milk product co-operative in northern Tanzania. It produces, packages and sells milk, yoghurt and butter on the southwest slopes of Kilimanjaro. Created in 1998 from the union of 75 people, it is mainly composed of women (the few men have administrative responsibilities) responsible for the production line from the milking to the creation of labels. The cows are raised wild with organic methods. Their milk – every member owns from two to ten heads – is mainly destined for family consumption whilst the remainder is partially sold as fresh milk to the local villages and partially given to the cooperative to make into butter, yogurt and fermented milk.

PRODUCTION AREA
Nronga and other villages in the Hai and Moshi Districts, Kilimanjaro Region

COMMUNITY COORDINATOR
Kibona Amanulas
tel. +255 744251390
amanucleus@yahoo.com

Cassava Growers and Processors of Attitogon

The community, a cooperative, organizes 589 producers and 309 processors and merchants of villages with a population of 24,000 people, dedicated to agriculture and the breeding of mutton and goats. Cassava (*Manihot esculenta*), grown for its large starchy tubers, is planted at the beginning of the rainy season whilst at its end, the remainders of the harvest and the weeds are buried. The land is fertilized with organic material and weeded two weeks after planting. The cassava roots can be harvested at any time but the harvest often coincides with the dry season. They are kept, buried, for up to three months. They are made into a paste (*foufou*), tapioca and flour with which different breads are made. The community also produces maize, tomatoes and *sodabi* a distilled palm wine.

PRODUCTION AREA
Maritime Region, Lacs Prefecture

COMMUNITY COORDINATOR
Kokouvi Abotsy Ahlanko
tel. +228 2275074
inadesformation@if-togo.net

Yam Growers of Kpéssi

Dioscorea cayennensis rotundata is a species of yam of which various varieties are grown in Togo: kratsi, gnalabou, alassorao and kokou.. It is a herbaceous plants with rhizomes which can grow to 20 kilos in weight and are eaten boiled, crushed, fried or baked. As well as providing a valuable source of starch, yams are the central point of a festivity still celebrated to recall the myth of the Kpéssi, one of the community's tribes (together with the Kabyé, Losso and the Ifé). The species is propagated by cuttings, which are planted in holes as deep as 10 meters, two or three months before the start of the rainy season. The land is weeded and the trunks are supported with sticks. The rhizomes are harvested when the leaves turn yellow. The community of 505 producers, brought together in a cooperative, also grows maize, rice and okra.

PRODUCTION AREA
Plateaux Region, East Mono Prefecture

COMMUNITY COORDINATOR
Adufu Kossi Sena
tel. +228 2259216
sena.adufu@if-togo.net

Producers of Djerba Island

The community, created in 1976, has as its objective, the harmonious development of the island, the safeguarding of its traditions and the promotion of the region culturally, socially and economically. The vegetation of Djerba is less poor than that of the interior of the country and its landscape is dominated by olives and date palm, the occasional orchard and, kitchen gardens where there is sufficient water. A number of local varieties survive on the island: lemsi palms, matata, aguiwa and rotbi, biféres figs, tounsi vines and stakasli (which can be reproduced by cuttings thanks to the absence of phylloxera), apples of the sweet Djerba and Chami varieties. Fishing is also important for the economy and the cooking traditions of the island. There are numerous local recipes, from the versatile *zommita*, a toasted barley mixed with lentils, to dried meat called *kadid*.

PRODUCTION AREA
Houmt-Suk, Djerba Island, Madanin Governorate

COMMUNITY COORDINATOR
Ben Tenfous Aziza
tel. +216 75620940
assidje@planet.tn

Banana Growers of the Kampala District

Bananas are an indispensable food source for the Ugandan population and almost a third of the cultivated land in the country grows them. In the hilly land north of Lake Victoria, a community of around 200 farmers produces gonja bananas – a variety which is highly sensitive to its environmental conditions which requires considerable efforts for its growth. The lots of land are only a few hectares which the producers cultivate as a form of subsistence farming. The international network International Network for the Improvement of Banana and Plantain (INIBAP), programs for the improvement of the bananas and the plantain variety and actively works with the community to perfect preservation methods and to strength the methods of sustainable growing.

PRODUCTION AREA
Kampala District

COMMUNITY COORDINATOR
Anne Kalanzi
tel. +256 772305860
annekalanzi@yahoo.com

Coffee Producers of Kibinge

The Kibinge Coffee Farmers Association, member of the National Union of Coffee Agribusiness and Farm Enterprises, unites 47 groups of coffee producers, each of which involves about thirty growers for a total of around 1,500 individuals. The association allows the growers to contract the price and to be more competitive. The variety grown is the Robusta, rich in caffeine with a strong and full bodied flavor, which grows spontaneously in the central area of the country and was spread by Europeans to all the Ugandan regions. The dimensions of this production are very small and the peasants are helped in their work by members of their families. Since 2006 the Kibinge producers have Utz Kapeh certification guaranteeing a sustainable crop for both the environment and the consumer.

PRODUCTION AREA
Kibinge, District of Masaka

COMMUNITY COORDINATOR
Hermant Mrema
tel. +256 41236199 - 712301494
mrema@ugandacoffee.org

Fishermen and Stock Breeders of Kasokwe

The 150 members of this community work mainly fishing in fresh water, transforming the fish (byt drying, salting and smoking) and raising African zebu and Ankole cows. These are distinguished by their long curved horns and are very rustic animals with more than one use: they provide meat (eaten fresh or dried over a wood fire) and milk (an average of four liters a day) which is processed into ghee. The community, to a lesser degree, also farms producing mangoes, avocados and sweet potatoes (which, wrapped in banana leaves, are one of the most traditional local foods – *lumonde*). All their activities are sustainable: the crops do not require chemical treatments and it is forbidden to cut or burn trees.

PRODUCTION AREA
Kasokwe, Kayunga District

COMMUNITY COORDINATOR
Lillian Sarah Nalubega
tel. +256 782058490
kasokwefishingcommunity@yahoo.com

Honey Producers of Soroti

This community lies in the Soroti District, near Lake Kyoga, and was created in 2004 with the purpose of sustaining the small honey collectors. It brings together 150 peasants although the number of people involved in the training courses is very high. Honey is a very ancient product of this area, but, through the traditional methods of collection – which requires the use of hollow trunks as hives, their sealing and the subsequent destruction of the colony with fire – results in a highly contaminated product. The community now collects and works a number of types of honey –wild flowers, mango, acacia, eucalyptus – that are destined for the local market.

PRODUCTION AREA
Soroti District

COMMUNITY COORDINATOR
Auta Deo Gratias
tel. +256 782202590
deoauta@yahoo.com

Local Chicken Breeders of Mukono

In Uganda chickens play an important role in the economy and family traditions. When a guest arrives, for example, a chicken is cooked and, when a woman marries, the witness gives a cockerel to the bride's brother. This community works to promote the raising of local breeds and collaborates with technicians, academics and local banks. Six breeds of chicken are raised amongst which the kakofu (white and black, lujumba (red and black), lusingosingo (with a featherless neck, enzirugavu (black). The community also raises ducks, guinea fowl and turkeys. The animals are free to range in the open and, thanks to this form of farming, both their meat and their eggs are of excellent quality.

PRODUCTION AREA
Mukono, Mukono District

COMMUNITY COORDINATOR
Silver Nganda
tel. +256 772620309
ngandasilver@yahoo.com - isekitto@hotmail.com

Organe Flesh Sweet Potato Growers of Luwero

The community is composed of 35 women joined in an association which grows sweet potatoes, or batata, a herbaceous creeper of the Convolvulacee family which produces highly nutritious tubers. In the Luwero area, the variety of tuber with an orange-colored flesh is grown and can be sold fresh, harvested after four to five months after planting to be eaten boiled or roasted or processed into oven products with the addition of wheat flour or into juice. This is obtained by steaming the roots, whipping and adding to the compote aromatized water with fresh fruit. Another of the community women's activities consists in the preparation and sale to peasants of the area, material for propagating a disease free sweet potato since the numerous attacks of parasites obliges new planting every year.

PRODUCTION AREA
Luwero, Luwero District

COMMUNITY COORDINATOR
Joweria Namubiru Ssekiyanja
tel. +256 712878095
womenngo2004@yahoo.com

Vegetable and Fruit growers and processors in the Masaka District

This community is located in the fertile region of Masaka, on the western coast of Lake Victoria in southern Uganda. Its 52 members (amongst which are 34 women) work on the organic growing of pineapples, red African aubergines (locally called *nakatti*, scientific name *Solanum aethiopicum*) and local varieties of tomato, in particular, two types similar to cherry tomatoes, one red and one yellow. The community uses cow dung and the waste of coffee production as fertilizers. The products are sold fresh or processed thanks to the recently introduced solar dryers.

PRODUCTION AREA
Masaka District

COMMUNITY COORDINATOR
Peter Lusembo
tel. +256 772423448
mknardc@africaonline.co.ug

Wild Fruit Jam Producers

In the Ugandan territory, near the capital Kampala that stretches along a long hilly area, the tropical climate is not only suitable for the growing of bananas but also encourages the spontaneous growth of berries and other wild fruits. The women of the community steam and roast the gonja bananas, a very sweet local variety. Furthermore, they also prepare jams and jellies for everyday use with the wild fruits. According to the rules of an ancient local tradition, some wild fruits are used in the preparation of bland medicines used purely by the community's families. The sale of jams and jellies is exclusively local in the small markets organized by the producers..

PRODUCTION AREA
Kampala

COMMUNITY COORDINATOR
Joseph Kajubi
tel. +256 782430333
kajubij@yahoo.com

Honey Producers of Kabompo

In the Lunda tongue (still spoken in some areas of Zambia, Angola, parts of the Congo and Zimbabwe) there are 60 different words for honey, demonstrating the ancient traditions of beekeeping in the area. Traditionally, the hives are made with bark and hung on trees in the forest. The community beekeepers, located in Kabompo along the river of the same name, are able to climb up the trees to collect the honey without either frightening or damaging the bees. The main products are honey and wax and is sold on both local and international markets (in the UK) with a Fair Trade certification.

PRODUCTION AREA
Kabompo

COMMUNITY COORDINATOR
Bob Jeremiah Malichi
tel. +260 8375085
mail@tropicalforest.com - nwbp@coppernet.zm

Gatherers of Mopane Worms

Due to the characteristic shape of its leaves, the mopane (*Colophospermum mopane*) is also known as the butterfly tree. The larvae of a lepidopteron of the *Gonimbrasia* species feed on its leaves and are considered edible and very good by the farming communities of Zimbabwe, Botswana e Namibia. In the Gwanda District, an association managed by a committee of seven people works on gathering, working and packaging the mopane worms which it then sells in local, national and international markets. Before being sold, the worms are pressed to remove their innards, boiled in salted water and dried. From the marula seeds, typical of the area, the community also produces an oil suitable both for gastronomic and cosmetic uses.

PRODUCTION AREA
Gwanda District, Matabeleland South Province

COMMUNITY COORDINATOR
Liberty Shelton
tel. +263 11790025
libertyshelton04@yahoo.com

Ilala and Marula Wine Producers

Uchema is made from an indigenous palm called ilala. The producers lightly dig around the trunk, cut the palm down to a small trunk and collect the lymph that flows out in bottles. The best uchema is that made in the spring. To permit its regrowth, different plants are cut each year. Makumbi is a wine made with marula (*Sclerocarya birrea*). Harvested whilst still unripe, the fruit of this plant are kept in containers until they turn yellow, after which they are peeled and squeezed. Once the seeds have been removed, the juice is put to ferment in sealed vases. Part of the harvest is destined for exportation and supplies the South African wine company Amarula. The uchema and makumbi wine producers part of the network of communities Campfire (Community Areas Management Programme for Indigenous Resources).

PRODUCTION AREA
Chiredzi District, Masving Province and Beitbridge District, Matabeleland South Province

COMMUNITY COORDINATOR
Metheuseli Maphala
tel. +263 313411
413677@ecoweb.co.zw

Makoni Tea Producers

Makoni tea is an infusion classified as black tea in accordance with international standards. It is produced organically: the leaves are collected in baskets of a perennial, the *Fadogia ancylantha*, widespread around the feet of the mountains in the Makoni District far from cultivated fields with chemical pesticides. Traditionally the harvest is the responsibility of the women. Used both as a drink and a medicine, it has no caffeine and a high energy and mineral salt (particularly zinc) content. The producers of Makoni tea are part of the network of communities Campfire (Community Areas Management Programme for Indigenous Resources).

PRODUCTION AREA
Makoni District, Manicaland Province

COMMUNITY COORDINATOR
Metheuseli Maphala
tel. +263 313411
413677@ecoweb.co.zw

Natural Oil Producers in the Chivi District

The community is composed of the Hazvidihope and Tomboedza groups with 373 growers and six processors. Their main activities consist in the growing and transformation of marula plants (here called *mapfura*), parinari (*chakata*) and baobab (*mumbuyu*). All the crops are certified as organic. From the marula seeds, which can also be eaten raw, both an oil (used in the cosmetics industry) and a paste are made. The latter is used in place of groundnut butter in rural areas during periods of drought. Marula fruits are used to make jams and, by fermentation, to make a traditional wine called mukumbi. Parinari seeds are also used to extract oil, which is an excellent nutriment for pigs.

PRODUCTION AREA
Chiv District, Masvingo Province

COMMUNITY COORDINATOR
Florate Ndakadhleyi Whindizi
tel. +263 0513250
zwp@telco.co.zw - zvishwp@mweb.co.zw

Siwa Dates

The great Siwa oasis (300,000 date palms and 70,000 olive trees) is in the desert area of northwestern Egypt, just a few kilometers from the Libyan border. This important archeological site and ancient caravan stop has been known since ancient times for the abundance of its brackish waters and its lively social and religious life. There are 13 villages in the oasis, whose 5,000 hectares of gardens are divided into plots (*hattia*) and connected to irrigation wells, which used to be natural and are now artificially excavated. The main cultivars of dates, the most important crop, are the *siwi*, the *frehi* and the *azzawi*, all indigenous. Three other important varieties, cultivated to a lesser degree and therefore at risk of vanishing from the oasis, are the *ghazaal* (a semi-hard pulp), the *amnzou* (an early variety that starts bearing fruit in September) and the *takdat* (late variety, whose very soft pup is ripe in December-January). According to the type, the dates are eaten fresh (in this case only consumed locally) or oven-dried at about 70°C. The inhabitants of the oasis gather them by hand, climbing up the trunks of the palm trees with the aid of belts made of palm fiber. A staple in the local tradition, the dates are the basis for preparations such as *elhuji* (eggs, olive oil and dates), *tarfant* (bread, olive oil and dates), and *tagilla* (flour, olive oil, water and dates). During Ramadan, they are eaten in the evening to break the fast. The production and sale of the dates is organized by the Scdec association and promoted by Italian Development Cooperation. In addition to allocating micro credit, this association supervises a project of computer literacy and is the privileged partner for Italian and non-Italian cooperation projects. The Presidium intends to promote the finest dates from the oasis on national and international markets. Regulations will be drawn up to control cultivation, an association of small producers will be formed and – in the medium term–a common date drying facility will be established to allow producers to control the entire production chain through to exportation. Siwa dates are already on the international market thanks to circuits of Sustainable Exchanges in Italy and Alternative Trade in certain other European countries.

PRODUCTION AREA
Oases of Siwa

PRESIDIUM COORDINATORS
Anwar Youssef Sarhan
tel. +20 04604600010 - 0460460007
anwarscd@yahoo.com
Salvo Monachino
tel. +39 3488741515
s.monachino@scambisostenibili.itt

PRESIDIUM SUPPORTED BY
Gran Sasso-Laga National Park (Abruzzo, Italy)

Andasibe Red Rice

Pale red in color and known as *vary mena* in dialect, this rice is considered indigenous to the island and is probably a hybrid of local varieties of wild red rice and the white *japonicas* of the *Oryza sativa* species, introduced by the Indonesians in around the year 1000. Vitamin-rich with a pleasant hazelnut flavor, it is the most sought after variety on the local market. Rice accounts for almost 70% of the daily calorie requirement of Malagasy farmers, who eat it three times a day. It is eaten in a soup made with wild herbs for breakfast, flavored with salt and hot pepper at lunch, and for dinner served with boiled chicken, fried eggs, lentils and cassava leaves crushed and cooked in palm oil. The farmers also habitually drink its cooking water, *ranon 'apango*. The rice also possesses important ritual and religious meanings. Today the cultivation of *vary mena* is increasingly rare because of its scanty yields and low market prices. The little that arrives in the city, where they mainly eat white rice imported from Pakistan, is belittled for its rustic quality and imperfect processing. Nevertheless, there is a potential for greater yields of *vary mena* and, given its excellent organoleptic qualities, it could become an important resource for the island. The Presidium combines an innovative approach to cultivation, the so-called *Système de riziculture intensive* (SRI), with the promotion of five varieties of indigenous red rice. The project arose from collaboration with the Koloharena Tongalaza association, which represents about 300 farmers in the towns of Ambatavola, Beforona and Andasibe, near the Analamazotra-Andasibe nature reserve. The Presidium has acquired equipment for threshing, husking and packaging the rice to allow Malagasy farmers to improve the quality of the final product, hence a rice capable of competing with imported product.

PRODUCTION AREA
Ambatavola, Beforona and Andasibe, province of Tamatave

PRESIDIUM COORDINATOR
Hasiniaina Ramparandrandrana
tel. +261 202203228
hasmireille@mel.wanadoo.mg - hasmireille@yahoo.fr

PRESIDIUM SUPPORTED BY
Three Italian towns – Bagnacavallo (Ravenna), Brisighella (Ravenna), Fontanellato (Parma) – and the Po Delta Regional Park of Emilia-Romagna

TECHNICAL PARTNER
Risi & Co-Gli Aironi (Lignana, Vercelli, Piemonte, Italia)

Mananara Vanilla

Intense hints of plum, dried fruit and cloves make this one of the finest vanillas in the world. Brought to the island by French colonies around 1840, it has found fertile ground in the damp rain forests of northern Madagascar. It now guarantees more than two thirds of the world's production on ever larger plantations, which have supplanted the cultivations in the heart of the forest and the shade of the forest trees. In the Mananara North Biosphere Reserve, created by UNESCO at the northeastern tip of the island, many farmers still practice the traditional method of cultivation, working small plots of land with 20-40 plants each in remote villages that are connected to the port only by footpaths. The vanilla buds, pollinated by hand with a stick or tweezers, turn into capsules of seeds similar to bean pods. The fruit is immersed in hot water when still green, then covered and left in a warm place for two or three weeks. This way the pods become soft and black and take on an intense aroma. They are then wrapped in wool cloths and left in a warm dry place to ooze moisture and release vanillin, the principle aromatic component of the spice. During this phase, the women rub the pods one by one with their fingers, cleaning them and making them smooth and supple. The position of Mananara and the existence of the reserve have helped keep alive this traditional practice which, unlike the farming associated with the ruinous 'cut and burn' method, it has little environmental impact. But it also makes it difficult to sell the product except to local distributors. The Presidium is working with a group of 360 farmers to improve the farming methods and help producers organize the sale and promotion of this spice. By creating a cooperative and making it easier for producers to sell the product directly, the Presidium seeks to ensure that these farmers have a better profit margin to reinvest in the local community.

PRODUCTION AREA
15 villages in the Mananara-Nord Biosphere Reserve

PRESIDIUM COORDINATORS
Herman Mulder
tel. +261 202260889 - 202261205
intercop.suisse@iris.mg
Jürg Brand
brand@wanadoo.mg

PRESIDIUM SUPPORTED BY
Three Italian towns – Bagnacavallo (Ravenna), Brisighella (Ravenna), Fontanellato (Parma) – and the Po Delta Regional Park of Emilia-Romagna

Imraguen Women's Bottarga

The Imraguens (Imrâgan) are nomadic fisherfolk who follow the great schools of golden grey mullets and umbrines as they swim past Banc d'Arguin along the northern coast of Mauritania, where the dunes of the Sahara fade away into the Atlantic. The Mauris, the country's predominant Berber population, are mainly shepherds, and only the Imraguen have made fishing their livelihood. In Banc d'Arguin – made a National Park in the 1970s – traditional fishing techniques still survive. Only the Imraguen are permitted to fish there, on foot or with their motorless boats (*lanches*). From October to December, when the schools of mullets swim past the coast, a dozen men go into the water dragging a net, which once closed as a sack imprisons the fish in a death chamber. A school of mullets was once sighted from the shore and dolphins helped the fishermen push it towards the coast. The traditional method of fishing without boats and the non-polluting use of *lanches* is threatened, however, by the industrial trawlers that illegally enter the waters of Banc d'Arguin. The fishing is done exclusively by men, but women take care of processing the fish. The Imraguen women use the ovarian sacks of the mullets to produce a botargo, which is mostly bought by middlemen and exported to North Africa or to western countries. The Presidium has started working with a co-operative of Imraguen women from Nouadhibou, the second largest city in Mauritania. Supervised by the local NGO Mauritanie 2000, the women buy the mullets from the fishermen on the beach or at the port and then take care of the pickling and drying. But their work is underpaid today. Slow Food, with the collaboration of the Presidium producers of Orbetello botargo (Grosseto, Tuscany, Italy), are trying to help improve production by providing adequate equipment. The aim is to find alternative markets and autonomously manage the sale of the processed products.

PRODUCTION AREA
Villages of Banc d'Arguin and Nouadhibou

PRESIDIUM COORDINATOR
Nedwa Moctar Nech
ongmauritanie2000@mauritel.mr

Argan Oil

Argan oil has a golden color and an intense flavor of toasted hazelnuts. Similar to the olive tree, the argan is only found on the southern coast of Morocco, between Safi to the north and Goulimime to the south. The nuts ripen between July and August and their oil is a staple ingredient in Berber cooking. A few drops of the oil are added to couscous at the end of cooking, to the *tajine* of fish and meat, and to cruditées. With honey and almonds, it goes into the preparation of *amlou beldi*, a cream that is still offered to visitors with bread and mint tea as a sign of welcome. In the countryside it is commonly used as a first food for newborns. It is also used as a hair dye and a skin moisturizer. The market price is much higher than that of olive oil because 50 kilos of nuts are needed to produce a half liter of the oil, and the processing is long and laborious. The latter job is mainly carried out by women, who break the shells with the aid of a stone, remove the skins and then crush the nuts. A small amount of lukewarm water is then added to the paste and the mixture is pressed in a small homemade mill consisting of two rotating stones. A few of the cooperatives with more sophisticated tools, albeit still rudimentary, have improved the quality of the product considerably in the last couple of years. In particular, some Berber women have formed a cooperative in Tamanar, where the oil that each of them makes for their family is now produced with modern equipment. The results are better in terms of quality and conservation, and provide the women with an important source of additional income. The Presidium supports this kind of work by looking for new market outlets for the argan oil. In addition to the social and economic aim of the project, it also has an environmental importance. The Arganeraie, in fact, is a forest of about 20 million trees, which UNESCO has declared a Biosphere Reserve; an important bulwark against the unrelenting advance of the Sahara desert.

PRODUCTION AREA
Provinces of Agadir, Essaouira, Taroudant and Tidzi Ait Baha

PRESIDIUM COORDINATOR
Zoubida Charrouf
tel. +212 37682848
zcharrouf@menara.ma

PRESIDIUM SUPPORTED BY
Piedmont Regional Authority (Italy)

TECHNICAL PARTNER
Olio Roi (Badalucco, Imperia, Liguria, Italy) - Organic Oils (Mugnano, Perugia, Umbria, Italy)

Americas

Andean Potato growers

The Puna, the arid semi-desert steppe in the Andes in northwest Argentina is the site of the cooperative formed by 50 native families in the area of Jujuy. Its members are sharing their traditions and knowledge with the aim of saving and cultivating Andean varieties which are threatened with extinction. Varieties like the *kiwicha* (or *quiwicha*), the *quinoa*, the *maca* and the various varieties of Andean potato with a very high yield. The income generated by the demand for these products (10 tons a month) has improved the quality of life of the local people, demonstrating that saving farming traditions is also useful from an economic point of view.

PRODUCTION AREA
Province of Jujuy

COMMUNITY COORDINATOR
Hugo Cetrangolo
tel. +5411 4771-2944
hcetrangolo@yahoo.com

Caiman farmers

The work of the 9 members of this community is known as Proyecto Yacaré. The process begins by collecting wild caiman eggs which are then incubated artificially. The small animals which emerge are reared in captivity and, after about a year, some of them (more than the number that would have survived if they had been left in the wild, and not until they are large enough to cope with predators) are released back into the wild in their original habitat. The others are sold for their meat and their skin and part of the money from this goes toward the project and various studies that are being carried out on this species. The project started in 1990, with the aim of increasing the numbers of *Caiman latirostris*, locally called *yacaré overo*, and to preserve the ecosystem in which they live.

PRODUCTION AREA
Santa Fé, province of Santa Fé

COMMUNITY COORDINATOR
Pablo Ariel Siroski Silva
tel. +54 342 498 2520
latirostris@arnet.com.ar

Cake-makers of Trelew

Trelew is one of the most important towns in the Province of Chubut. Situated in Argentine Patagonia, the town was founded in 1886 by immigrants from Wales and now has a population of about 90,000. The community of cake-makers based here run a small workshop that makes cakes and other confectionery using local, organically produced raw materials. Its main product is the Welsh cake, made according to an original recipe brought here with the immigrants from Wales in the early 19th century. They produce about 6 tons of cakes a year, part of which is sold on the international market.

PRODUCTION AREA
Trelew, province of Chubut

COMMUNITY COORDINATOR
Hernan Filguiero
tel. +54 296 543 3489
lagalesahfr@yahoo.com.ar

Carob Flour producers

Colonia Ismael Sánchez is a rural village in the municipality of Ibarreta, in Argentine Chaco, where a group of 12 young people have a farm. They produce honey, aromatic herbs and, especially, carob flour. To make it they use the carob (*Prosopis alba*), a tree which has always been associated with local food and culture. In fact, the indigenous people here used to use the fresh fruit of the carob to make drinks, food and sweet products, were fond of the honey flavored by the nectar from its flowers, and used to make furniture with wood from the carob. The carob has a special place in local myths and legends associated with supernatural events. While the fruit was harvested, between November and December, which was the beginning of the period of abundance, the carob was celebrated with special ceremonies and festivals.

PRODUCTION AREA
Ibarreta, province of Formosa

COMMUNITY COORDINATOR
Sebastián Carenzo
tel. +54 114 833 5935
sebastian.carenzo@gmail.com

Charqui producers

This community is formed by 28 families, who are all involved in rearing cattle. They process their own meat, both for their own consumption and for sale. The animals are reared according to the ancient practice of transhumance and the meat is dried in the traditional way to make *charqui*. First the meat is cut into very thin slices or strips and the fat and blood is removed. Then it is hung up in the sun in a well-ventilated place and protected by mosquito nets, until the meat becomes dark. Then it is preserved between layers of salt, with the occasional addition of pepper, chili pepper and pepper, or, more rarely, between layers of honey and propolis. The community also makes a smoked version of *charqui*. It can be eaten as it is, or soaked in water and cooked.

PRODUCTION AREA
Las Animas, Valles de Altura

COMMUNITY COORDINATOR
Bernardo Cachagua
tel. +54 388 154 207 786
Bncachagua@Yahoo.Com.Ar

Cheese-makers of Estación Yeruá

In the north of Argentina, there is a region which, because it is situated between several rivers, is called Mesopotamia. As we can imagine, the fact that there is plenty of water makes the land very fertile. In fact, this is one of the largest cereal-producing areas in the world. 60% of Argentine rice is produced in the Province of Entre Ríos alone. In an area with an abundance of rich pasture, livestock rearing is also common. The cattle farms here produce 4.5 million head of cattle a year. But in this land of huge numbers, there are still a few small-scale activities, like the small farm run by Señor Debortoli, where the milk produced on the farm is used to make a cheese he has named after himself: Don Benito. Like all the cheese made in Argentina, this one is based on a classic cheese of the Old Continent: in this case, the all-Italian *mozzarella*.

PRODUCTION AREA
Estación Yeruá, province of Entre Ríos

COMMUNITY COORDINATOR
Alcide Benito Debortoli
tel. +54 345 156 251 818

Cheese-makers of Maciá

The association is based in a town in the Province of Entre Ríos, called Maciá, and involves 200 families who work together and rely on the continuous consultancy of a technical expert to improve the quality of their products. The business began by producing a hard cheese with cow's milk, to which other cheeses (with special flavors, semi-hard or soft) were added when this no longer guaranteed sufficient income. Most of the cheese is sold directly to the consumer and, since the producers don't have enough space to increase the numbers of dairy cattle, they guarantee profitability by concentrating on quality. In this way, they can make their products different to other similar products on the market, and can sell them at a higher-than-average price.

PRODUCTION AREA
Maciá, province of Entre Ríos

COMMUNITY COORDINATOR
José Isidro Vittori
tel. +54 344 546 1394
sproduccion@virtual-net.com.ar

Edible wild plant gatherers

According to figures published by the WHO, we currently consume and sell less than 1% of existing vegetable varieties, despite the fact that many more varieties than that are edible. On the basis of this information, in 1989, four researchers of the Conicet (Consejo Nacional de Investigaciones Científicas y Técnicas) began to catalogue edible plant varieties in Patagonia. They succeeded in identifying 600 species which are usually regarded as weeds and which, on the contrary, are excellent from the point of view of human nourishment, since they are full of vitamins and other nutritious principles. These herbs and plants could constitute an excellent food supplement, especially for the economically underprivileged. The aim of the work of this community is to draw attention to this "new" nutritional resource, encourage people to collect and transform these varieties and educate young people and chefs about their potential.

PRODUCTION AREA
San Carlos de Bariloche, province of Río Negro

COMMUNITY COORDINATOR
Eduardo Rapoport
tel. +54 2944 41 437 - rapaporteduardo@speedy.com.ar

Farmers, growers and preserve producers of San Javier

All the products of the community of San Javier, in the far north of Argentina, are organically produced. The main product is sugar cane. It is cultivated for between four and seven years, depending on the variety, and the ground is then allowed to rest until it becomes fertile again. The vegetables grown are destined mainly for consumption by the growers, whereas the maize, wheat, soya and sunflowers are used as fodder for animals (cattle, pigs and poultry) and is also partly used for bartering with other producers. In addition to agriculture and livestock rearing, the farms also transform their products. They make tomato sauce, eggplant and cucumber preserves, jam, sweets and liqueurs, and pasta, with flour bought from outside and their own eggs.

PRODUCTION AREA
San Javier, province of Misiones

COMMUNITY COORDINATOR
Sonia María Jara
tel. +54 375 415 659 875-375 515 412 040
soniamariajara@hotmail.com

Fruit and vegetable producers of El Hoyo

El Hoyo is situated in the area known as the Precordillera, in the northwest of the Province of Chubut, and owes its name to the configuration of the land, which, being surrounded by high mountains, is rather like a hole (*hoyo* in Castilian Spanish). Its privileged position, sheltered from the wind and only 200 m above sea-level, means that the area has a very mild climate which, combined with the fertility of the land, makes it ideal for agricultural activities. The members of this community cultivate organic fruit and vegetables using only manual techniques, and without any chemicals. They use their products to make preserves and jam, bottling the products and labeling them by hand. They also gather fruit from wild plants to make comfectionery, jellies, tisanes and fruit juice. They sell their products in neighboring villages, and deliver them to their customers' homes.

PRODUCTION AREA
El Hoyo, province of Chubut

COMMUNITY COORDINATOR
Mauro Diego Ferencich
tel. +54 294 447 1148
huertafresca@yahoo.com.ar

Fruit producers and farm tourism operators

30 small-scale fruit producers in the Province of Misiones, who are almost all owners of plots of land no larger than 2 hectares, have set up activities in tourism, which they run alongside their normal fruit-farming business. As well as growing papaya, pineapple and grapes, they have begun to supply a restaurant service based on local cuisine, and to produce confectionery, cheese and other craft products, which they sell directly on the farm or in tourist resorts in the region. These activities, conducted by members of the family, have enabled the women of the community to attain higher status, and to emerge from the lifestyle to which they have been restricted for centuries. They also provide employment for young people and an alternative to migrating to the towns in search of work

PRODUCTION AREA
Alba Posse, Bonpland and Santa Ana, province of Misiones

COMMUNITY COORDINATOR
María Inés Montenegro
tel. +54 375 540 4910
mimontenegro@correo.inta.gov.ar

Goat farmers of the Valle di Uco

This community is an extended family of about 20 people who live in the Valle de Uco, an area in the Province of Mendoza, situated between the Cordillera Frontal and the region of Huayquerías. They rear and sell goat's meat. The animals are fed on natural food and, when they have been butchered, the meat is sold either fresh, smoked or flavored with aromatic herbs. The smoking of the meat is the only process that is handled externally. The producers themselves deal with the business of selling the meat, both directly, on a local level, and through markets of farm produce. Meat is a traditional local food, especially goat's meat and meat from the wild *guanco*, a local type of llama.

PRODUCTION AREA
Valle de Uco, province of Mendoza

COMMUNITY COORDINATOR
Raul Javier Rodríguez
socios@slowfoodmendoza.com.ar

Guaraní ka'aguy poty producers of Kuñá Pirú

According to the estimates of the Encuentro Nacional de Pastoral Aborígen (Endepa), there are more than 700 indigenous communities in Argentina. The Guaraní are one of the most numerous ethnic groups. About 3,000 people, who live in small communities, usually in settlements, earn a living through farming, fishing and collecting honey and fruit. The indigenous Guaraní Ka'aguy poty community of Kuñá Pirú comprises 40 families, a total of about 190 people, who produce and sell craft objects and cultivate maize, manioc, potatoes and vegetables for the community. The growth in population, together with the irrational exploitation of the rainforest, has reduced the area and amount of resources available to the community. As a result, it has had to become more dependent on the industrial society.

PRODUCTION AREA
Aristobulo del Valle, province of Misiones

COMMUNITY COORDINATOR
Cirilo Duarte
tel. +54 3755 470 195
muniadelvalle@yahoo.com

Home-brewed Beer producers

Potrerillos is situated in the Province of Mendoza, in an area where the economy is based on agriculture, livestock rearing and craft industries. There is almost no large-scale industry. A small family community in this area makes home-made beer in the traditional way. They use water from the glaciers, which is absolutely pure and contains none of the traces of chlorine found in water in the towns. The community makes three types of beer: pale beer, which is a deep golden color, has a slightly malty flavor, and tastes slightly bitter, with an after-taste with a hint of vanilla; red beer, which is a lovely amber color, with a strong taste, with hints of caramel, with a spicy, fruity after-taste; and black pearly-colored beer with a creamy froth, that tastes of dried and withered fruit, coffee and chocolate.

PRODUCTION AREA
Potrerillos, province of Mendoza

COMMUNITY COORDINATOR
Eduardo Maccari
tel. +54 261 432 0449 - info@cervezajerome.com

Honey producers

The bee-hives of this community are in the south of the Province of Buenos Aires, in areas which are uncontaminated by chemicals, where the fields are not cultivated and only a few of which are located close to pasture used as grazing land. As a result, the honey they produce is completely natural. To collect the honey, the hives are taken to a center authorized by the Senasa, the national body which certifies quality and healthy environments in the agricultural and livestock farming sphere. Here, the honey is separated from the wax, filtered, put into special containers and analyzed. Under the Amerinda trade-mark, the association sells four different types of honey: Pampa (from the southeast of the province), Silva (from the forest in the delta of the River Paraná), La federal (made of honey from several different locations) and Susurros del monte (from a mountain beyond the River Colorado).

PRODUCTION AREA
Bahía Blanca, province of Buenos Aires

COMMUNITY COORDINATOR
María Dela Larsen
tel. +54 223 475 8979
mdlarsen@hotmail.com

Jam producers of Juella

Over the centuries, the people who live in the Quebrada de Humahuaca have selected the fruit varieties best suited to the environment and which give the best results from an organoleptic point of view. Six families in Juella have decided to use some particularly tasty fruit varieties to make two different kinds of sweet products. Using apples and pears, or sometimes just apples, they make *panes de dulce*, a sort of very solid quince jam, and they use peaches to make jam. They do all the processing manually, with copper pans and wooden utensils. Finally, the products are sold in the production area and in the surrounding region.

PRODUCTION AREA
Juella, Quebrada de Humahuaca, province of Jujuy

COMMUNITY COORDINATOR
Eugenio Banos
tel. +54 114 554 4727
terramadre06@yahoo.com.ar

Kiwicha and quinoa growers of the Quebrada de Humahuaca

The Quebrada de Humahuaca, a valley in the Andes which stretches for 155 km into the Province of Jujuy, is an oasis of natural and cultural biodiversity, where rare and ancient varieties of plants still survive. They include the kiwicha (or quiwicha) and the quinoa, which, even today, still form the staple diet of the indigenous people of this area. The two species are very similar, and have a very high protein content and an extraordinary capacity to adapt to the Andean habitat. For 12 years, this community has been working very hard to preserve and promote them. Since the market for kiwicha and quinoa flour is very variable, and does not guarantee sufficient income, they are trying to use the flour to make other products, like biscuits and bread, in small workshops.

PRODUCTION AREA
Quebrada de Humahuaca, province of Jujuy

COMMUNITY COORDINATOR
Armando Alvarez Mamani
tel. +54 388 495 5072
pircatlcara@arnet.com.ar

Manioc growers and processors of Misiones

The community is a cooperative, the Cooperativa San Alberto, and its members are 200 manioc producers in the Province of Misiones. The plant which they cultivate (Manihot esculenta) has a fairly steady yield and the harvesting season lasts a long time. Its high starch content means that it is a very nutritious food, both for humans and animals. Manioc grows in places with a warm climate. The white flesh of the roots is edible. 65% of manioc is water while the other 35% is a dry substance. It can be prepared in many different ways (boiled, baked, fried) or processed into flour and tapioca (a very digestible energy-giving food). This community uses it to make flour, and uses the flour to make sweet and savory foods. All the rest of the plant can be used as fodder for animals.

PRODUCTION AREA
Puerto Rico, province of Misiones

COMMUNITY COORDINATOR
José Reis
tel. +54 374 342 0204
coopsalberto@prico.com.ar

Muña liqueur producers

In 1984, the indigenous Krolla community of Tumbaya decide to take steps to defend their land from national compulsory-purchase laws. After 14 years of struggle and legal battles, it has been acknowledged that the land belongs to the indigenous farmers. Today, the community of Tumbaya is formed by 120 families who, in addition to cultivating and preserving traditional varieties of maize (including capia), produce a digestive liqueur from a kind of mint, known locally as muña. It is a bush belonging to the Lamiacaeae family, which grows between 2,500 and 3,500 meters above sea-level throughout the Andes. This liqueur is drunk at festivals and celebrations, especially during the Festival of the Dead, which is a fundamental moment in the religious calendar of the Krolla people.

PRODUCTION AREA
Tumbaya, province of Jujuy

COMMUNITY COORDINATOR
Celestina Nieves Abalos
tel. +54 388 8499 6026
celestinajuy@hotmail.com

Mushroom growers

In the Province of Jujuy, a small association of 13 farmers grows mushrooms (especially the girgolas variety) and sells them, either fresh or dried, or in the form of preserves. The mushrooms are grown in humidified environments where the temperature is controlled, on a substratum consisting of jute sacks stuffed with straw. Organic methods are employed and, currently, production amounts to about 20 tons a year. For the time being, every farmer sells his/her own products, but work is in progress to form a cooperative which can sell on behalf of the whole community, achieving economies of scale and broadening the area of distribution, which, at the moment coincides with the area of production.

PRODUCTION AREA
San Salvador de Jujuy, province of Jujuy

COMMUNITY COORDINATOR
Guilliermo Fumagalli
tel. +54 388 492 2067
fuma@imagine.com.ar

Oca growers of Coctaca

The community of Coctaca, located in the Department of Humahuaca, in the far north of Argentina, has always been an important center for agricultural production. The farmers who belong to it follow the rules laid down by their forefathers, based on an intelligent use of natural resources. One of their main products is the *oca*, a tuber native to the Andes, also called the "red potato". It is grown on beautifully preserved terraces built by the pre-Hispanic peoples. The community wants to increase production of *oca* and its derivatives – mainly flour and sweet products – and to revive old farming traditions. Women are also involved in this project and are trying to preserve traditional recipes and flavors.

PRODUCTION AREA
Coctaca, province of Jujuy

COMMUNITY COORDINATOR
Donato Gutiérrez
tel. +54 388 155 814 288
donatopgutierrez@yahoo.com.ar

Oca growers of Iruya

The two communities of the town of Iruya, called Colnazuli and Nazareno, are associations of small-scale producers who grow *oca*, a typical tuber of the Andes similar to a potato. The members of the community cultivate small plots of land using organic methods, using animal dung as fertilizer and ecological, sustainable methods for fighting the diseases which attack the plants. *Oca* can be eaten raw or in a semi-finished form that can be used to make jam and cakes. Most of the crop is consumed by the growers' families, but some is sold on the local market.

PRODUCTION AREA
Iruya, province of Salta

COMMUNITY COORDINATOR
Elsa Estrada
tel. +54 388 5482 001
maguijuy@arnet.com.ar

Organic honey producers

In the impenetrable Parque Chaqueño, in the north of the Province of Chaco, 75 families of bee-keepers have formed a community called Miel de la Tierra. The organization involves about 400 people in villages scattered around the area, all of whom are of the indigenous Qom people. The rich biodiversity of the area and its abundance of plant varieties enables them to produce polyflora honey with a unique flavor, which is sold in containers or cans, although in this last case, it has to be outsourced to be canned. Honey is a traditional activity here. The community uses hives built by the bee-keepers themselves, which make it easier to collect the honey and generate a higher yield. This honey has been awarded organic certification by the Organización Internacional Agropecuaria.

PRODUCTION AREA
Province of Chaco

COMMUNITY COORDINATOR
Mario Segundo
tel. +54 385 1560 96686
fdp-sol@yahoo.com.ar

Organic wine producers of Maipú

In recent years, in the Province of Mendoza, many small, family wineries have developed which, to give a new slant to their business, have invested in organic vine-growing and wine-production. Generally speaking they have limited, very high-quality production, which they achieve through a combination of artisan techniques and new technologies. Every single one of the 10 wineries which belongs to the community relies on technical experts. In total, annual production amounts to about 600,000 l, which is sold in Argentina and abroad.

PRODUCTION AREA
Maipú, province of Mendoza

COMMUNITY COORDINATOR
Aníbal Alejandro Catania
tel. +54 261 424 3472
acatania@mendoza.inta.gov.ar

Organic wine producers of Mendoza

The wines made by the Cecchin family are the result of experience which has been handed down for three generations. This family is still producing wine using traditional, natural, artisan methods. No chemicals are used whatsoever, either to grow the grapes (fertilizer, weedkiller or sprays) or in the wine-cellar. All the substances used are natural. The family's wineries and vineyards, where the raw materials are grown, are in the areas of Maipú, Junín and Lujan de Cuyo. All the wines produced here have been certified by the Organización Internacional Agropecuaria (OIA), the National Organic Program (NOP), which enables the wines to be sold on the American market, and the International Federation of Organic Agriculture Movements (IFOAM), which enables them to be sold in Europe.

PRODUCTION AREA
Province of Mendoza

COMMUNITY COORDINATOR
Oscar Alberto Cecchin
tel. +54 261 497 6707
gerencia@bodegacecchin.com.ar

Pheasant farmers

In the southeast of the Province of Buenos Aires, in the town of Santa Clara del Mar, there is a small community which specializes in poultry farming, and produces mainly pheasants and home-made paté. The farms rear the poultry, giving them as much freedom to roam as possible. When they are born, the chicks are taken outside to large open areas where they are fed on maize and soya. They are given neither antibiotics nor anabolic steroids. When they are four months old, they are killed in special facilities certified by the State. The final products are frozen pheasant and paté, either plain or flavored with herbs, which the community sells on a national and international scale.

PRODUCTION AREA
Santa Clara del Mar, province of Buenos Aires

COMMUNITY COORDINATOR
Ricardo Alberto Diez
tel. +54 223 451 1647
ricardo@mardelplata.com

Producers of cane-sugar honey and cane-sugar

The producers of the community, who have formed a cooperative, own a total of 400 hectares of land, half of which is used to grow sugar cane. For a long time they sold the harvest to people who had the equipment to produce sugar, but now they are launching a project which will enable them to produce honey and cane-sugar themselves (here they call it *panela*). The "honey" is produced by putting the stalks of the sugar cane in a press to extract the juice. This is then cooked in copper or steel pots over a fire of bagassa, an energy source that is economic and clean. In this way, no part of the plant is wasted. When the product has reached the consistency similar to that of bee's honey, it is put into containers, ready for sale. Sugar, on the other hand, is obtained by allowing the juice extracted from the cane to crystallize.

PRODUCTION AREA
Famaillá, province of Tucumán

COMMUNITY COORDINATOR
Juan Silverio Ascacena
tel. +54 386 346 1175
juansilverioescacena@hotmail.com

Producers of chocolate and other cocoa derivatives

The Chocolate Fenix community of Buenos Aires is a family-run company which has been producing cocoa derivatives, made according to traditional recipes, for more than a century. The cocoa, which arrives in selected grains of extremely high quality straight from the countries of origin (Venezuela, Ecuador and Brazil), is toasted by hand and is subsequently ground so as to obtain a pure, natural paste. This is mixed with sugar and left to solidify. To promote this product, the community takes advantage of the help of expert chefs who work in Argentina's top cookery schools. Total production is about 1,000 tons a year and the products are sold mainly on the domestic market, both directly and through middle-men.

PRODUCTION AREA
Buenos Aires

COMMUNITY COORDINATOR
Josè Rodrigo Salgado
tel. +54 114 305 3329
jrsalgado@chocolatesfenix.com

Producers of dulce de leche

The community that produces dulce de leche, in the town of Dina Huapi, is a small association which produces and transforms food. Situated in Argentine Patagonia, which has a dry climate, the community comprises about 130 people. As well as dulce de leche, a traditional cream dessert made by cooking milk and sugar together very slowly, other important products of the community include smoked trout, liqueurs and preserves made with locally-grown fruit. All the products are made using traditional artisan techniques with a low impact on the environment. They are sold mainly on the local market.

PRODUCTION AREA
Dina Huapi, province of Entre Ríos

COMMUNITY COORDINATOR
Analia Garcia
tel. +54 114 554 4727
terramadre06@yahoo.com.ar

Producers of extra-virgin olive oil

In Argentina, they have only been growing olives for about two hundred years but, in the Province of Mendoza, like vine-growing, it is already an important tradition. The 20 members of the La Tebaida association continue to use the production technique begun by the Spanish immigrants who first introduced olive growing to this country. For example, there must be no longer than 12 hours between harvesting the olives, which is done by hand, and pressing them, which is done with old stone olive-presses. Also, according to the rules of the producers of the community, at least 8 kg of olives are needed to produce one liter of extra-virgin olive oil.

PRODUCTION AREA
San Martín, province of Mendoza

COMMUNITY COORDINATOR
Martin Miguel Argerich
tel. +54 262 342 2952
miguel.argerich@molinolatebaida.com

Producers of fruit-flavored honey

The Valdés Peninsula, situated in Argentine Patagonia, is a natural paradise which is famous for its colonies of penguins and sea-lions. This is where the five members of the community live and work. They are bee-keepers and farmers who work using traditional methods and add neither preservatives nor chemicals to their products. Together they have formed an association which, every year, produces about 1 ton of fruit-flavored honey a year. They sell it directly on the local market, or indirectly, through middle-men, on the national market.

PRODUCTION AREA
Valdés Peninsula, province of Chubut

COMMUNITY COORDINATOR
Carlos Luis Maldonado
tel. +54 296 51540 2136
apifrutpatagonia@yahoo.com

Producers of goat's milk and cheese

Six dairy farmers and a cheese factory form this community in the Province of Santiago del Estero. Rearing goats is a traditional activity in this area. They produce 200 l of milk a day and 500 kg of fresh, semi-hard and hard cheese a month. They sell their products on the local and national markets, but also rely on middle-men to participate in local and national fairs. They try to associate their products with other craft products made in the province, such as baskets and wooden chopping-boards. The community makes a product which has been part of the local tradition as long as anyone can remember, but their facilities and the procedures they use ensure the highest level of hygiene. The cheeses are vacuum-packed in special bags so that they last longer.

PRODUCTION AREA
San Carlos, province of Santiago del Estero

COMMUNITY COORDINATOR
Pablo María Usandivaras
tel. +54 385 156 096686
pablousandivaras@hotmail.com

Producers of honey and related products

This cooperative of small-scale bee-keepers in the Province of Tucumán, in the northwest of Argentina, is formed by three indigenous Wichí communities. About a hundred families, a total of 400 people, produce honey and other substances from the industry of bees. The hives are placed in lemon groves where the bees suck the nectar from the lemon-blossom to make honey. The cooperative also collects the pollen of *Schinopsis lorentzii* (a typical tree species of the area, called *quebracho colorado*), royal jelly and propolis from the hives. Argentina's last grave economic crisis drove many bee-keepers, who previously produced only for family consumption, to undertake production on a commercial scale and join the cooperative.

PRODUCTION AREA
Famaillá, province of Tucumán

COMMUNITY COORDINATOR
Alejandro Raúl Alvarez
tel. +54 381 432 3554
aalvarez@correo.inta.gov.ar

Producers of honey, royal jelly and propolis

Situated 200 km from Salta, the provincial capital, El Galpón has a co-operative of 31 small-scale bee-keepers who produce a dark honey with a strong flavor in a natural environment which is completely free of contamination. The cooperative also collects royal jelly and propolis from the hives. Royal jelly, produced by the bees to feed the queen bee, has energy-giving properties for humans thanks to the high content of vitamins, sugar and trace elements. Propolis, a substance which the bees collect from trees, is made of aromatic resin, wax and essential oil. Traditionally, it is attributed with having anti-oxydant, anti-inflammatory, anaesthetic and antibiotic properties. The products of the cooperative are certified by the Fair Trade Label Organization (FLO).

PRODUCTION AREA
El Galpón, province of Salta

COMMUNITY COORDINATOR
Carlos Gustavo Cabrera
tel. +54 386 346 1396
paolapena2003@yahoo.com.ar

Producers of jam and spicy sweet and sour preserves

This community lives in an area with luxuriant vegetation, consisting mainly of endemic species, in the Andean Cordillera of Patagonia, near Lago Puelo, which has the same name as the town where the members of the community live. The local economy is based essentially on tourism and on fruit production. This last sector is the one in which the community operates. The fruit is grown on farms in the area and, when it has been harvested, is taken to small workshops and cooked with sugar to make home-made jam. They use a similar process, but add vinegar and a few spices, to make spicy sweet and sour sauces. These products are sold both directly, on the local and national market, and indirectly, through middle-men.

PRODUCTION AREA
Lago Puelo, province of Chubut

COMMUNITY COORDINATOR
Dolores Graciela Sarabia
tel. +54 294 415 511 320
elcipres_dulces@yahoo.com.ar

Producers of jam made from forest fruits

The Province of Misiones lies in the region of the Litoral, between Paraguay and Brazil, and stretches as far as the Rio Iguaçu. Most of it is a plateau surrounded by the Paraná, Uruguay and Iguaçu rivers and is almost completely covered by thick forest. The population is concentrated mainly along the River Paraná, which is the best communication route in the region. The community of jam producers of this province is an association of 120 families who cultivate the land and rear livestock near the town of Andresito. Using wild or organically cultivated forest fruits and using traditional recipes, the association makes jam, which is its main product and is sold on the local and national market.

PRODUCTION AREA
Andresito, province of Misiones

COMMUNITY COORDINATOR
Ramón Godoy Sixto
tel. +54 374 115 631 904

Producers of olives and extra-virgin olive oil

The Cuenca del Pichanas is a quiet valley situated at 800 m above sea-level, in the Province of Cordoba. Its paedoclimatic conditions are ideal for growing olives. It is no coincidence that the main job of the more than 150 people who form this community is growing olives. 30% of total production (about 1,000 tons a year) is sold as eating olives, the remaining 70% is sold to local companies who use them to make olive oil. The association has received important certification awards, including certification for organic production from the United States Ministry of Agriculture.

PRODUCTION AREA
Department of Cruz de Eje, North of Cordoba

COMMUNITY COORDINATOR
Rodolfo Pedro Nieves
tel. +54 354 949 5091
pasoviejo@arnet.com.ar

Producers of sheep's cheese and lamb

This group of producers started their business in the 1990s because of the need to diversify local production, traditionally based on wool, and provide a solution to the falling price of wool on the world market. With this in mind, research was carried out with the aim of creating an area for milk production. By crossing two breeds of dairy cattle (the Texel and the Fresian), a new breed was created, which is being reared by this community. Its milk, which is obtained by carrying out strict controls at every stage of production, is used to produce about 3,500 kg of cheese a year. In parallel to this activity, the community rears and sells lambs, also for dairy production and grows alfalfa in irrigated fields which are artificially flooded, to feed their own animals and sell to other cattle farmers.

PRODUCTION AREA
Trelew, province of Chubut

COMMUNITY COORDINATOR
Lidia Mercedes Astutti
tel. +54 2965 1555 0346-1551 5436
lidiaastutti@yahoo.com.ar

Producers of sweet products and liqueurs

The identity of the area where this community is based is inhabited by people of two very different traditions: the indigenous people, who have always been farmers, and the Italian and Spanish immigrants, who constitute the majority of the population. The main activities locally are agriculture and livestock rearing. The influence of the Europeans is particularly evident in the techniques used to transform the raw materials produced locally. This community produces confectionery, jams, jellies and syrups. It also makes alcoholic drinks, such as grappa, obtained by distilling local fruit, without adding any colorants or artificial aromas. 250 people are involved in these activities, which are supported by two NGOs: Centro Interdisciplinario para el Desarrollo Humano y Productivo (Cidehp) and Ferias y Seminarios de Producciones Alternativas (Fespal).

PRODUCTION AREA
Rosario, province of Santa Fé

COMMUNITY COORDINATOR
Hugo Alberto Alejandro Don Gazzaniga
tel. +54 341 4561859-155629928
hdon@ciudad.com.ar

Producers of traditional local wines

The community is an association of producers of grapes and wines associated with Argentina. It includes wineries in various areas, scattered throughout the nation, including Cuyo (in the Province of Mendoza), and some areas of Patagonia and the Province of Salta. In total, about 500 people are involved. They all make wines which superbly reflect the territorial wine characteristics of each region. The aim is to improve the already very good quality of Argentine wines by using production technologies which are as close as possible to artisan techniques. The wines produced are sold on the national and international market.

PRODUCTION AREA
Province of Salta, Mendoza and some areas of Patagonia

COMMUNITY COORDINATOR
Maria Cristina Barón
tel. +54 4553 1161
gabriela@ficadelmarques.com.ar

Producers of vegetables and regional specialties

The main aim of the Feria Agroartesanal Trabum Ruka association, which has 250 members, is producing, transforming and marketing regional products. The vegetables, which are completely free of contamination from chemicals, since they are cultivated without fertilizer in fields which are irrigated by water of excellent quality, are sold fresh. The production surplus is carefully selected and used to produce vegetable preserves in cans, and pickles. The other products of the cooperative are local gastronomic specialties: *empanadas* (a type of filled pasta with different fillings), local raw meat, finely chopped with a heaviy knife, and home-made bread. Most of the sweet products are made with indigenous fruits, the most popular being rose-hip oil.

PRODUCTION AREA
Zapala, province of Neuquén

COMMUNITY COORDINATOR
Sergio Daniel Silva
tel. +54 294 242 4067
sergiodsilvazapala@yahoo.com.ar

Producers of wines, fruit and vegetables

In Argentina, they have been making wines for centuries, but wine-making didn't become a serious economic proposition until the wave of migration from Europe, when the Italians, French, Spanish and Germans arrived. In this context, the Province of Mendoza is the most productive in the country. Some of the most respected producers in this province live in the area of Luján de Cuyo, south of the provincial capital. The family business which forms this community is situated precisely in this area, at Ugarteche. It grows Malbec grapes (using both organic and traditional methods, but always with the highest regard for quality and health regulations) and Chardonnay, and makes organic wine, but also grows vegetables, using the crop rotation technique, and fruit (especially walnuts and plums).

PRODUCTION AREA
Ugarteche, municipality of Luján de Cuyo, province of Mendoza

COMMUNITY COORDINATOR
José Antonio Blanco Moreno
tel. +54 261 4991 009
andalhue@hotmail.com

Shellfish farmers

At the end of Bahía Camarones, on Argentina's east coast, half-way between the towns of Trelew and Comodoro, is Camarones, a small town traditionally associated with fishing. Shellfish, in particular, has always been part of the local culinary tradition, but it has only recently become necessary to farm shellfish because of the excessive exploitation of fish resources. This community is an association which involves more than 100 people in the production of the typical shellfish of Patagonia, including Patagonian mussels (*cholgas*) and a flat kind of oyster which is threatened with extinction. The fish-farms respect ecological procedures which ensure that the fish and their natural environment are protected. The products are sold fresh on the local market.

PRODUCTION AREA
Camarones, province of Chubut

COMMUNITY COORDINATOR
Daniel Figliuolo
tel. +54 297 496 3025
joapatagonia@hotmail.com

Smoked food producers of Rosario

Rosario, where this family business is based, is the largest town in the Province of Santa Fé. Here, the community produces smoked foods, along with meat, fish, cheese and vegetables. All the products processed here come from the local region, including caiman meat, which they buy from a farm in the same province. Its meat is smoked with warm smoke from a mixture of sawdust and branches of citrus trees. The *boga*, which is fished in the River Paraná, is treated in a similar way. It is smoked for about six hours, depending on its size, and flavored with bay twigs. This product is also used to make a kind of paté. The community also smokes a semi-hard cheese with cold smoke, along with some vegetables, such as sun-dried tomatoes.

PRODUCTION AREA
Rosario, province of Santa Fé

COMMUNITY COORDINATOR
Oscar Jorge Caviglia
tel. +54 341 454 5405
ojcaviglia@yahoo.com.ar

Traditional food producers of Oberá

The characteristics of the people who live in the Province of Misiones are the result of the flows of people who migrated from Europe. Although, on the one hand, the various identities came into contact with each other, influencing each other and creating a common cultural heritage, on the other, each community maintained close links with its original traditions and recreated them in their new home, using the raw materials that were available. This strange phenomenon led to the creation of the Federación de Colectividades, an organization formed by the representatives of 15 communities of immigrants who live in the province. Each one of these makes the typical dishes of the country of origin, selling them directly to consumers during the Immigrant festival held every year in Oberá and at other local fairs.

PRODUCTION AREA
Oberá, province of Misiones

COMMUNITY COORDINATOR
Elsa Beatriz Delgado de Komatsu
tel. +54 375 542 1848
federacion@fiestadelinmigrante.com.ar

Vegetable growers of Corrientes

This community of Corrientes is a group of small-scale farmers who are creating an association to improve the production and marketing of their vegetables. At the moment, their vegetables are sold through the wholesale market in town and the costs aren't high because the market is close to the area where the vegetables are produced. The products produced by the community include tomatoes, chili peppers, lettuces and beet, which are cultivated in glass-houses where the temperature and the amount of light, the levels of humidity and carbon dioxide are kept under constant control. Depending on the season, beet is also grown in the fields, in the shade, using natural fertilizers. Periodically, the water used for irrigation is analyzed .

PRODUCTION AREA
Corrientes, province of Corrientes

COMMUNITY COORDINATOR
Hector Araujo
tel. +54 378 343 4953
tito_araujo@laclinica.com.ar

Vegetable growers of the Pereyra Iraola Provincial Park

The Pereyra Iraola Provincial Park, in the Province of Buenos Aires, is home to the approximately 200 families who form this community. About 800 hectares of the park is devoted to agriculture and livestock rearing. Each family cultivates small plots of land of between 8 and 14 hectares, but, after the harvest, the crops are sold collectively. The community has also created initiatives to encourage rural tourism so as to create alternative employment for the young people of the area and combat migration towards large towns in search of employment.

PRODUCTION AREA
Berazategui, province of Buenos Aires

COMMUNITY COORDINATOR
Cecilia Corina Gelabert
tel. +54 114 541 1567
gelaber@agro.uba.ar

Yerba mate growers

In the town of Santo Pipó, some Yerba mate producers have formed a cooperative which, through all its members, "owns" about 4,000 hectares of land. The area, which is entirely devoted to growing mate, stretches between the town where the community is based and the towns of Gobernador Roca, Polana and Jardín América. Currently, directly and indirectly, the community involves more than 2,000 people and has drying facilities and mills where all the mate collected by the members is processed. Production is quite high: about 7,000 tons a year, which the cooperative sells in Argentina and abroad.

PRODUCTION AREA
Santo Pipó, province of Misiones

COMMUNITY COORDINATOR
Nestor José Munaretto
tel. +54 375 542 4395
nestor_munaretto@yahoo.com.ar

Cocoa producers

This community, situated in the District of Toledo, is a cooperative formed by a group of Maya people. There are about 950 member cocoa producers who collaborate with various local and international NGOs (including Trust and Sustainable Harvest International), and important local organizations. The members of the cooperative grow cocoa on small plots of land of 2 or 3 hectares, using organic methods certified by the British company Soil Association Certification Limited, which are environmentally friendly and help to preserve the biodiversity of the region. Overall, they produce about 35 tons of cocoa a year. It is sold – both locally and on an international level – by a single distributor: Green and Blacks.

PRODUCTION AREA
Punta Gorda, district of Toledo

COMMUNITY COORDINATOR
Ansel Dubon
tel. +501 722 2992
tcga@btl.net

Coffee producers of Yungas

Yungas is a sub-tropical area situated on the eastern slopes of the Andes, where the climate is ideal for growing coffee at altitude (between 1,000 and 1,800 m above sea-level). 95% of the coffee grown in Bolivia comes from this area. Coffee has been grown here since 1780, when it arrived with some Africans who were fleeing from slavery in Brazil. In 1991, Fecafeb (Federación de Caficultores Exportadores de Bolivia) was created with the aim of helping small-scale coffee producers to access the national and international market with a quality product at a sustainable price. The association represents 30 organizations, involving a total of 43,500 people who produce arabica coffee, mainly of the criolla varietal.

PRODUCTION AREA
Yungas Region, department of La Paz

COMMUNITY COORDINATOR
Elías Mamani Flores
tel. +591 2284 6310
fecafeb@gmail.com

Goat farmers of Tarija

Although goats have been common in Bolivia since the arrival of the first Spanish colonists, in the Province of Tarija, for most of the 20th century, goat-farming was not a widespread economic activity. Any goats that were reared were destined merely for family consumption. In 1997, an association was formed in Tarija which adopted highly productive farming techniques based on selecting the best animals, increasing the number of pastures protected by fences and shelters, producing fodder, and more frequent, more thorough veterinary controls. In this part of Bolivia, the diet of the population has improved thanks to goat's meat and cheese made from goat's milk. Although some of these products are consumed by the farmers' families, the rest is sold throughout the region.

PRODUCTION AREA
Tarija, department of Tarija

COMMUNITY COORDINATOR
Antonio Marcos Bass Werner Montecinos
tel. +591 4663 1446-4664 5837
mbwerner58@hotmail.com

Potato growers of Araca

The community is formed by 350 indigenous families of the Aymara culture who live in an area of the Province of Loayza called Araca. The farmers cultivate various vegetables, the most important of which are potatoes, which have played a fundamental role in the economy and the diet of people living in the Andes since ancient times. The area in which the association operates is situated at different altitudes, between 400 m and 4,500 m above sea-level. This makes it possible to grow crops at different times of the year, using different farming methods. Some of the potatoes produced are destined for family consumption, part as seed potatoes for the next crop and part for the production of *chuño* or *della tunta*. These products are obtained by desiccating the potato, enabling it to keep for a long time, and is part of the traditional indigenous diet.

PRODUCTION AREA
Araca, municipality of Cairoma, department of La Paz

COMMUNITY COORDINATOR
Alfonso Espinal Coaquira
tel. +591 2242 1277
alfoespinal@gmail.com

Wheat producers and processors of Totora

For the inhabitants of Cochabamba, wheat has always been a fundamental part of the daily diet. In 2003, problems cause by a floundering market forced the Asociación de Productores de Trigo de Totora, which involves 125 families of small-scale wheat producers, to concentrate on wheat derivatives, such as wholemeal flour, bread and pasta. This enabled the association to gain access to more remunerative markets and to sell their products to the school canteens in the town.

PRODUCTION AREA
Totora, department of Cochabamba

COMMUNITY COORDINATOR
José Germán Pardo Bustamante
tel. +591 476 2914
apt@cochabamba-bolivia.net

Women bakers of San Javier

The association has 18 women members, but, in all, including the people on temporary contracts and producers who supply the raw materials, 200 people are involved in its activities. The women make and sell oven-baked products from the tradition of eastern Bolivia, including cuñapé and bizcocho de maíz. There are two types of cuñapé, made with yucca starch, is a sort of bread, mixed with eggs and cheese: the softer type, which is eaten after it has been baked once, and another type, which is crunchy and will keep for longer, which is baked two more times. Bizcocho de maíz looks like bread, but is made with maize flour, eggs and butter. All the raw materials used are produced by local small-scale farmers and growers who are mostly indigenous people.

PRODUCTION AREA
San Javier, department of Santa Cruz

COMMUNITY COORDINATOR
Claudia Ranaboldo
tel. +591 2289 0158
ranaboldo@megalink.com

Abaetetuba Açaí and Cupuaçu by-product producers

Abaetetuba is a town with a population of about 125,000, founded in the 18th century on the edge of the Bay of Marapatá, where the water of the Tocantins and Abaeté Rivers meet. The town is an important center of trade for the products of the Amazon rainforest. The producers of açaí and cupuaçu by-products have formed a cooperative which comprises 850 families of producers of tropical fruits and andiroba oil. The andiroba tree (Carapa guianensis) grows naturally in the Amazon rainforest. It produces a fruit rather like a large walnut which is rich in oil. The essence of the andiroba is extracted and traditionally used by the indigenous people for medicinal purposes. These products are organically produced and are certified by the Guaranteed Organic Certification Agency.

PRODUCTION AREA
Abaetetuba, state of Pará

COMMUNITY COORDINATOR
João José Corrêa
tel. +55 9140053763
jcorrea@fase-pa.org.br

Babaçu by-products producers

The community is formed of people who hand-make the by-products of the babaçu (Orbignya martiana), a tropical palm of enormous economic value insofar as every part of the plant can be exploited. It can be used to make oil for cooking, cosmetics, flour (for making cakes, bread and puddings), vegetable carbon, soap, paper, and craft products. Three cooperatives, two associations and another informal group in the region of Médio Mearim in the State of Maranhão belong to Assema, the organization which coordinates production and runs training initiatives. The 1,549 families of the community manage to earn a reasonable living from activities associated with the babaçu palm. A babaçu promotion center has been set up in the capital of the State of Maranhão, São Luís, where by-products from the palm are displayed and sold.

PRODUCTION AREA
Medio Mearim, state of Maranhão

COMMUNITY COORDINATOR
Fracinaldo Ferreira de Matos
tel. +55 9936423612
gentedefibra@assema.org.br

Beiju and Bolachinas de Goma producers

The community comprises about 50 families, all members of the Association of Boa Hora and Adjacências, who make manioc by-products. The territory in question comprises about 20 municipalities located around the town of São Gonçalo dos Campos, in the State of Bahia. The producers are participating in the Projecto Mandioca, the aim of which is to promote and spread the artisan techniques used to prepare this staple food. The most important specialties include beiju (or biju), which is produced using the starch from manioc roots, tapioca flour, bolachinhas de goma, which are rather like manioc fritters, and manioc flour, of which the community produces about 1,000 tons a year.

PRODUCTION AREA
São Gonçalo dos Campos, state of Bahia

COMMUNITY COORDINATOR
Joselito Motta Da Silva
tel. +55 7536218043
joselito@cnpmf.embrapa.br

Brazil Nut and Copaìba Oil producers

This cooperative, created in 2001, is based in Rio Branco, in the north of Brazil. It comprises 1,890 families who earn a living by gathering Brazil nuts (castanhas do Brasil) and other products such as copaíba oil and rubber. The castanha do Brasil is the fruit of the castanheira, a tree which can grow to a height of 40 m. It is a traditional, highly nutritious product and is used in cooking to make rissoles and in other meat dishes. Copaíba oil, which is used particularly in the cosmetics market, is used to make soap and balsams, and is used by the native people of the rainforest for therapeutic purposes. The community works in cooperation with the CTA (Centro de Tecnologia Avançada), WWF and the Instituto Brasileiro de Meio Ambiente.

PRODUCTION AREA
Rio Branco, state of Acre

COMMUNITY COORDINATOR
Mouzinho Gerliano
tel. +55 6832217164
gerlianunes@bol.com.br

Brazil Nut producers

Capeb, founded in 1996, is a cooperative which works with associations of small-scale producers – about 360 – of castanhas do Brasil, better known as Brazil nuts. The piñata, a tree native to the Amazonian rainforest, grows to a height of 45 m and has a trunk which can reach 2 m in diameter. The fruit contains between 15 and 24 seeds with woody shells, which are in fact a kind of almond with a very pleasant flavor. The fruits, which are an important source of food for the local people who live in the forest and gather them when they fall to the ground. Each fruit weighs about 1.5 kg. Another product of the cooperative is copaíba oil, which is used as a medicinal balsam. All the products of the cooperative are certified by the FSC (Forest Stewardship Council) and Imaflora (Instituto de Manejo e Certificação Florestal e Agrícola) and bear their labels.

PRODUCTION AREA
Rio Branco, state of Acre

COMMUNITY COORDINATOR
Odete Da Silva Santos
tel. +55 683546-81128081
capeb@yahoo.com.br

Cacimbas Pequi producers

The pequi fruit (Caryocar brasiliense coriaceum), which is collected when it falls to the ground, contains an oil that is used in cooking and to produce cosmetics. The pequi is a typical feature of the culture and gastronomy of the Sertanejos, who live in the sertão, the Brazilian savanna. The tree is common throughout the Cerrado, while the fruit – which has a strong perfume and a characteristic flavor – contains between one and four seeds enclosed in a pulp which is cooked and used to make savory dishes. The community of Cacimbas comprises about 1,000 producers, who apply ecological criteria to the collection, processing and sale of pequi by-products, an ancient tradition here. The pequi is also used in caseira medicine and features in religious and cultural events and at local trade fairs.

PRODUCTION AREA
Cacimbas, state of Ceará

COMMUNITY COORDINATOR
Maria Araujo Ferrer
tel. +55 8896129451
ferrermaria@bol.com.br

Cametá fruit by-products producers

The community comprises several families who have formed a cooperative. They collect and process fruit, including the açaí and the cupuaçu. The açaí is the fruit of a palm that grows in the Amazon rainforest (Euterpe oleracea) It resembles a blueberry and is rich in vitamins, mineral salts and antioxidants, and has always been eaten by the Indians. When processed into juice and mixed with waraná, it is an extremely rich source of energy and, in summer, can replace a meal. The cupuaçu is the fruit of another tree (Theobroma grandiflorum), which is related to the cocoa tree (Theobroma cacao). It has always been part of the diet of the people of the Amazon rainforest. In Brazil and Peru, the pulp is used to make ice-cream, fruit juice, pralines, creams, jellies and cakes, while the seeds are used to make a sort of chocolate, called cupulate. The community also produces cocoa and andiroba (Carapa guianensis) oil.

PRODUCTION AREA
Cametá, state of Pará

COMMUNITY COORDINATOR
José Hermínio Dias Feio
tel. +55 9137811069
jherminio_br@yahoo.com.br

Cananéia Oyster gatherers

The community is formed by about 40 gatherers descended from slaves who settled near the town of Cananéia in the 18th century. Oyster selling is the local people's most important source of income, and in 1998 the highly organized community decided to set up the Cooperativa dos Produtores de Ostras de Cananéia (Cooperostra). Once the oysters have been collected, they are reared in special 'nurseries'. When they reach the optimum size, they are cleaned and washed by members of the cooperative and then sold to restaurants on the coast of the State of São Paolo. The women in the community use them to prepare delicious oyster specialties for tourists, including torta de ostra, or pão de ostra, and farofa de ostra.

PRODUCTION AREA
Cananéia, state of São Paulo

COMMUNITY COORDINATOR
Fernandez Thaís Almeida Cardoso
tel. +55 1338513708
thaisalmeidacardoso@yahoo.com.br

Cantagalo Fava do Vale producers

The village of Cantagalo is a community of 25 farming families who work on the land and rear livestock. This is a quilombola community, descended from people who were slaves during the colonial period. The agricultural work is organized by a consortium – with a rotation of different crops – on an itinerant basis: each year the crops are sown in different areas to allow the soil to rest. The fava do vale (*Vicia faba*) is one of the traditional crops farmed here. It is sown in long rows in small fields and is harvested manually after about 75 days. It is a tropical leguminous plant similar to a broad bean, with a high nutritional value which, for the poorer social classes, represents an alternative to the carioca bean as a source of protein and vitamins. It is normally included in soups, sauces and salads or served as a purée.

PRODUCTION AREA
Cantagalo, state of Maranhão

COMMUNITY COORDINATOR
Henrique Paulo Da Silva Coelho
tel. +55 9891399919
phscoelho@ig.com.br

Centro Popular de Saúde Yanten aromatic herbs producers

The community comprises 40 small-scale producers, most of whom are women, who live in the countryside around the town of Medianeira, in the west of the State of Paraná, in the south of Brazil. Aided by a group of specialists (including pharmacists and agronomists), the producers are members of the Centro Popular de Saúde Yanten of Medianeira, created in the eighties with the aim of increasing the cultivation and use of medicinal plants. The community produces various types of herbs for teas and tisanes, spices to flavor food and plants used in phytotherapeutic products such as *waraná* and artichoke pills. To begin with, producers marketed their own products individually on the local market, but later created an association to distribute them through participation in trade fairs and markets.

PRODUCTION AREA
Medianeira, state of Paraná

COMMUNITY COORDINATOR
Teolide Parizotto Turcatel
tel. +55 4532644125-32642806
teolidept@yahoo.com.br

Cerrado fruit gatherers

In the Brazilian Cerrado inthe States of Maranhão and Tocantins, this community of about 6,000 Timbra Indians from seven tribes (Apinajé, Krikati, Canela Apānjekrá, Canela Rancôkamekrá, Gavião Pykobjê, Gavião Parakatejê and Krahô) and 300 farming families grows and picks fruit. Every year the community produces 130 tons of pulp from the typical tropical fruits of the Cerrado, including abacaxi (pineapple), maracuja, cashew nut, tamarind, buriti (fruit of the aguaje palm), goiaba (guava or Indian pear) and the fruit of the cajá tree. The FrutaSã company processes and freezes the pulp supplied by the community and sells it to consumers or fruit juice producers.

PRODUCTION AREA
Brazilian Cerrado, states of Maranhão and Tocantins

COMMUNITY COORDINATOR
Jaime García Siqueira Junior
tel. +55 6133497769
jaime.siqueira@trabalhoindigenista.org.br

Chapecó small-scale farmers

The Apaco, an association of small-scale farmers in the west of the State of Santa Catarina, is a non-profit NGO, the aim of which is to encourage the small-scale farmers of the region to adopt ecological farming principles. The association was formed in 1989 and involves about 4,500 farmers who live in small communities. It is trying to combat the predominant agricultural model, based on an enormous concentration of wealth and land and the large-scale exploitation of environmental resources. The association was formed thanks to the support of the labor unions, local social movements and the Church. It is organized into 85 groups of agricultural cooperation. The members of the community earn a livelihood by making cheese and by-products from pigs raised on natural feed, and growing many varieties of fruit, especially local fruits threatened with extinction.

PRODUCTION AREA
Chapecó, state of Santa Catarina

COMMUNITY COORDINATOR
Paulo Ernesto Hubner
tel. +55 493322-0154
apaco@apaco.org.br

Cupuaçu producers and processors

The APA (Association of Alternative Producers) represents a total of 250 people from the communities of six municipalities in the central region of the State of Rondônia. This is the part of the Amazonian rainforest that has been most affected by the deforestation of the last few decades. Other factors contributing to the destruction of the environment include the use of chemical fertilizers, the appalling practice of starting fires of massive proportions and a culture that preaches monoculture and intensive farming. The APA supports alternative ecological farming principles in its cultivation of fruit such as *cupuaçu, araça-boi, graviola, acerola, açai* and banana. The *cupuaçu* (*Teobroma grandiflorum*), a plant native to the Amazon rainforest that grows to a height of about 8 m, begins to bear fruit after three years. The fruits weigh between 300 g and 43 kg. The pulp of the fruit is used to make fruit juice, ice-cream, cakes, liqueurs and jam.

PRODUCTION AREA
Porto Velho, state of Rondônia

COMMUNITY COORDINATOR
Antônio Abílio Siqueira
tel. +55 6934611844
apa@ouronet.com.br

Cupuaçu producers and processors

The community comprises about 1,000 people who produce and process cupuaçú (*Theobroma grandiflorum*), the fruits of a tree similar to the cocoa tree, which have always been part of the diet of the indigenous Amazonian people. The pulp of the fruit, which is creamy and has an exotic taste, can be eaten raw, turned into juices or used for other food such as ice-cream, creams and cakes. The seeds are used to make a kind of butter with a high oleic acid content. The pulp and seeds are also used to make a kind of chocolate. Another product made by the community is palmito de pupunha, namely the inside of the stem of the fruit (pupunha) of a species of tropical palm, the *Guilialma speciosa*, which is typical of the north of Brazil. It looks like a kind of palm heart and is removed by hand because the product is extremely delicate.

PRODUCTION AREA
Porto Velho, state of Rondônia

COMMUNITY COORDINATOR
Hamilton Condack
tel. +55 6932531007-6932531046
hcondack@yahoo.com.br

Farinha d'Água producers

Located in the municipality of Bragança, which comprises six districts, the community makes manioc by-products. Manioc cultivation is the main activity in this area, where a subsistence economy prevails. A typical ingredient in traditional indigenous cooking in the Amazonian region, farinha d'água is obtained by leaving manioc roots in water for between three and eight days, after which it is processed and kneaded manually in traditional containers called *tipiti*. It is then cooked in a special oven. This food constitutes the energy base of the diet of the people in the Amazonian region, and is used in sweet and savory recipes. It is marketed directly by the producers, members of the Projecto Mandioca, the aim of which is to promote the traditional production of manioc flour nationwide.

PRODUCTION AREA
Bragança, state of Pará

COMMUNITY COORDINATOR
Benedito Batista Da Silva
tel. +55 9188559507
nafaz@eletronet.com.br

Feira de Santana fruit producers and processors

The Rede de Productoras de Bahia, consisting of 170 producers organized into groups run by women, is based in Feira de Santana. It operates in seven municipalities in the State of Bahia and collaborates with women's associations to promote the role of women in business. It is active in two sectors, traditional craft skills and food, and the aim is to increase local farm production. The community makes cakes with tropical fruits (mango, *umbú*, orange, banana), manioc by-products, creams, jams and preserves. All the products are made by hand and are the result of traditional local knowledge that has been handed down for generations. The raw materials are produced with the utmost respect for the environment, without any synthetic or chemical substances.

PRODUCTION AREA
Feira de Santana, state of Bahia

COMMUNITY COORDINATOR
Alves Santos Silva Neide
tel. +55 7534218640 - rprodbahia@yahoo.com.br

Florianópolis Manioc Flour producers

The community, which comprises about 50 families, is based around Santo Antonio de Lisboa, on the island of Santa Catarina. The Engenho do Casarão is the center for the activities of the farmers who produce manioc flour, which is a staple of the diet of the local people. Following the rapid process of industrialization on the island from the middle of the last century, most of the artisan manioc flour workshops were closed down. During the last few decades, products historically associated with the area have been promoted, including this flour, which is mentioned in the accounts written by early missionaries and travelers. An *engenho de farinha*, driven by draught animals, has been designed to produce a fine white flour, similar to wheat flour.

PRODUCTION AREA
Florianópolis, state of Santa Catarina

COMMUNITY COORDINATOR
Claudio Agenor De Andrade
tel. +55 4832352572
engenhoandrade@gmail.com

Honey and Ouricuri producers

The community, which comprises 400 families (about 2,000 people), in the area known as Diamantina del Sertão, a semi-arid region in the State of Bahia, mainly produces honey and grows ouricuri, a palm native to the region, which yields a nut the size of a hazelnut, as well as various types of fruit, milk, meat, fish products and cheese. The inside of the ouricuri is used in cooking: it can be eaten raw, boiled or toasted. The palm also produces an oil which is used in many typical Brazilian dishes. The honey is produced organically, by bees which have interbred with African bees and by mandaçaia bees (which are native to Brazil). When it has been collected, it is centrifuged, put into jars and marketed locally either by the beekeepers themselves or through cooperatives.

PRODUCTION AREA
Capim Grosso, state of Bahia

COMMUNITY COORDINATOR
Souza Alves Josenaide
tel. +55 7436510225
josa.alves@ig.com.br

Itápolis Orange Juice producers

The Coagrosol association of Itápolis is a cooperative with about 80 members who work in the State of São Paulo. Formed in the year 2000, it acts as an umbrella organization for dynamic, enterprising young people who produce fruit and fruit by-products which are interesting and competitive in social and qualitative terms. The Itápolis area, where the temperature is high and which is constantly exposed to the sun, is ideal for growing citrus fruits, such as mandarins, oranges, pineapples and limes. Coagrosol products are certified as being organically grown, and produced on a Fair Trade basis by internationally recognized bodies. All the fruit can be picked manually several times year, thanks to the favorable climate. The cooperative also organizes social projects to confant child malnutrition and holds evening courses to teach children and adults to read, write and use computers.

PRODUCTION AREA
Itápolis, state of São Paulo

COMMUNITY COORDINATOR
Reginaldo Vicentim
tel. +55 1632624700
reginaldo@coagrosol.com.br

Iúna coffee producers

This is a community of coffee producers who belong to the federation of community associations of Iuna and Irupi – called Faci. It is a sort of consortium of 27 associations involving about 1,000 farming families in the southeast of the State of Espirito Santo. They produce certified organic Fair Trade arabica coffee. The coffee is grown at an altitude of approximately 600 m. It is picked and sieved by hand, either with rollers or sleves (called *peneiras*). Growing coffee is a traditional activity in the area of Iuna and Irupi. This is confirmed by the large number of trade fairs in the sector, seminars about coffee and prizes for quality coffee which are organized every year. During the coffee harvesting season, the members of Faci employ temporary laborers who are paid by piece-work, earn a regular wage with social security contributions, and are guaranteed the support of the labor unions.

PRODUCTION AREA
Southeast of the state of Espirito Santo

COMMUNITY COORDINATOR
José Augusto Santana
tel. +55 2835452343
faci.iuna@bol.com.br

Jatobá Flour producers

Agrotec is a community comprising 21 farmers and plant gatherers in a pilot area of 125 hectares in the Cerrado biome in the area of Diorama, in the west of the State of Goiás. 76% of this area contains protected flora and fauna. The range of products includes medicinal and other plants that are used for phytotherapy in local doctors' surgeries, and *jatobá* flour, dessicated *pequi*, toasted *castanha de baru*, crystallized cashew nuts, and by-products from local species of fauna bred in areas of the Cerrado. The *jatobá* (*Hymenaea stignocarpa*) is a typical leguminous plant of the Cerrado, which is eaten by humans in the form of flour and is also popular with local monkeys, who eat it by breaking open the rind of the fruit, gouging out the pulp and scattering the seeds on the ground below.

PRODUCTION AREA
Diorama, state of Goiás

COMMUNITY COORDINATOR
Venderlei Pereira De Castro
tel. +55 6436891165
agrotec@persogo.com.br

Krahô Sweet Potato Flour producers

This indigenous Krahô community comprises 2,000 people from 19 villages in the northeast of the State of Tocantins. Farming is the main source of subsistence of the Krahô people, who also hunt, fish and gather fruit and berries. Sweet potato flour is made between April and June. Once the potatoes have been harvested, they are washed, wrapped in banana leaves and cooked over burning embers. Afterwards they are peeled and crushed by hand. Then the flour is left to dry for three days on mats made from the leaves of the *catù*, a local palm. The mats are placed on special racks and sometimes covered with nets to prevent dust and insects coming into contact with the flour. The flour is kept in containers called *pocotú*, straw bags made from the same palm leaves as the drying mats, woven by hand by the women of the villages.

PRODUCTION AREA
Northeast of the state of Tocantins

COMMUNITY COORDINATOR
Terezinha Dias Aparecida Borges
tel. +55 6134484789
dias@cenargen.embrapa.br

Lages Pine Nut producers

The Brazilian pine (*Araucaria angustifolia*) produces nuts, called *pinhão*, which are collected from April to July. This food is eaten by birds and rodents which scatter the kernels on the ground. The *pinhão* is used in many typical regional dishes, including *sapecada*, which also contains the dried leaves of the Brazilian pine. This dish is very popular and is a traditional feature of the national *pinhão* festival, which has been held for the last 18 years in the State of Santa Catarina, attracting as many as 300,000 people to the town of Lages. The community comprises 573 farming families, who own small plots of land and who sell their products through local cooperatives, either whole or in a processed form.

PRODUCTION AREA
Lages, state of Santa Catarina

COMMUNITY COORDINATOR
Eliane Niehues
tel. +55 4932785007
elianeniehues@yahoo.com.br

Lagoa Seca Caju Passa producers

In the north of the State of Bahia, in the village of Lagoa Seca, 33 farmers grow tropical fruits, manioc, beans, maize and cashew nuts. The community collaborates closely with local artisan confectionery and *caju* (cashew nut) jam producers. After the cashew nuts have been harvested and passed the first processing phases, the liquid is extracted from the nuts and boiled with sugar over a low heat for three days. Then it is left to dry in the sun for another three days before being packed by hand. *Caju passa* is a traditional product of the northeast of Brazil and the recipe has been handed down for generations. The community is collaborating with other organizations, such as Cealnor, and local administrations to promote made products.

PRODUCTION AREA
Lagoa Seca, state of Bahia

COMMUNITY COORDINATOR
Ramos Valdice
tel. +55 7534261719
cealnor.comercio@terra.br

Lima Duarte Honey producers

This association consists of 25 people, who work on the Mata reserve in the State of Minas Gerais, in the southeast of Brazil. They produce honey, propolis and pollen in areas with flowering trees or areas used for grazing. Once the honey and propolis have been collected, they are subjected to a gentle centrifuge process, decanted, then put into jars. For centuries, honey, which is historically associated with the area, has been used by the local people both as food and in traditional medicine. Pollen is collected on cloths placed at the entrance to the hives, and is then frozen at a temperature of -5°C. Finally, the moisture is removed. All the products are marketed directly on a local scale. The community is associated with Abio, the Associação dos Produtores Biológicos, in the State of Rio de Janeiro.

PRODUCTION AREA
Lima Duarte, state of Minas Gerais

COMMUNITY COORDINATOR
Emidio Barreto de Carvalho
tel. +55 3136897440
luzflora@uai.com.br

Macaúba Oil producers

The macaúba is a native species of Brazilian palm that can grow to a height of 15 m. Used as an ornamental plant, it yields edible fruits, which contain a kind of oil, similar to olive oil, which is used in the food and pharmaceutical sectors. The community of the State of Minas Gerais, in the southeast, processes the by-products of this unusual palm. The oil is extracted and filtered mechanically without any chemicals being added, so that its falvor and aroma remain unchanged. The community belongs to the Centro de Agricultura Alternativa do Norte de Minas, an important NGOs which supports farming family organizations in the State, offers agronomic consultancy and supplies tools to improve the marketing of their products.

PRODUCTION AREA
Monte Claros, state of Minas Gerais

COMMUNITY COORDINATOR
Aparecido De Souza Alves
tel. +55 3832232285
gradeserto@caa.org.br

Mata Atlântica resource promoters

Vale do Ribeira is situated in the *mata atlântica*, the native forest of the Brazilian coast. It is inhabited by an extremely varied population, including Guaraní, Tupinambá and Tupiniquin Indians, ethnic groups such as the *Caiçaras*, *Quilombolas* and *Caipiras* and many immigrant communities. Despite its countless resources, the economy of the region is the least developed in the State of São Paulo. For this reason, a network of alternative activities is being created, especially in the sphere of ecotourism. Food tourism is being encouraged by promoting traditional products and directly involving small-scale producers. Through projects like Banana, Barro e Mandioca: quatro roteiros para conhecer or Vale do Ribeira, traditional crops like quilombola rice, manioc and bananas are being promoted.

PRODUCTION AREA
Vale do Ribeira, state of São Paulo

COMMUNITY COORDINATOR
Paulo Marcos Noronha Serpa
tel. +55 1137271982
serpapaulo@hotmail.com

Melipona bee's honey producers

18 villages in the State of Maranhão, in the northeast of Brazil, belong to the community. They produce quality honey, which was once used by the Indians for treating respiratory ailments. This honey (*natmel*), sold under the name of 'Meliponina', the pure production of which is guaranteed, can be distinguished from ordinary honey because it is more acidic, less sweet and less solid. Thanks to the support of the environmentalist NGO, Amavida, efforts are being made to combine the production of honey with other local products, such as fruit and vegetables, by creating small workshops produce cakes and jams as part of a strategy defined as an 'ecosystemic production structure'. About 200 people work in the community and are attempting to combat the threat posed by mass-produced products from soya and eucalyptus monocultures.

PRODUCTION AREA
State of Maranhão

COMMUNITY COORDINATOR
Fátima De Maria Carvalho
tel. +55 9834691615
amavida@amavida.org.br

Monte Claros fruit producers and processors

The 900 producers involved in the Grande Sertão cooperative grow fruit for preserves. The cooperative was formed with the aim of promoting the sustainable social and economic development of the area, and to improve the quality of life of the small-scale producers and their families who belong to the cooperative. Training and technical and scientific consultancy are important factors in bringing this about. The community works by growing fruit using organic methods and respecting the principles of ecological farming. The job of selling the fruit preserves is entrusted to a distributor (Conab), which makes sure they reach the national market.

PRODUCTION AREA
Monte Claros, state of Minas Gerais

COMMUNITY COORDINATOR
Carlos Avila
tel. +55 3832236880
joaoavila@caa.org.br

Montenegro Mandarin Juice producers

The Montenegro mandarin is the result of a natural mutation, discovered in 1940 at Campo do Meio in the municipality of Montenegro (Vale do Caí, Rio Grande do Sul) by João Edwino Derlam, a farmer of German origin. Today, this species of mandarin, which matures late in the year, in September and October, is extremely tasty and has a very hard rind, is threatened with extinction. The area of production of the mandarin, which is the second-most common variety grown here, encompasses 20 municipalities in the Vale do Caí. The Ecocitrus cooperative markets citrus fruits, mostly Montenegro mandarins, throughout the region. Each year 1,000 tons of citrus fruit are produced for consumption, while another 400 tons are destined for sale as fruit juice.

PRODUCTION AREA
Vale do Caí, state of Rio Grande do Sul

COMMUNITY COORDINATOR
Adriano Martins Da Silva
tel. +55 5136324824
comercial_ecocitrus@terra.com.br

Pareci Novo fruit farmers and processors

In the little town of Pareci Novo, in the State of Rio Grande do Sul, the community comprises 12 families of farmers, who cultivate fruit trees (such as bergamot, orange and maracuja) using organic methods, and 18 families who process the fruit. The products derived include fruit juice, which is made by extracting the liquid part of the fruit just after it has been harvested, pasteurizing it quickly and bottling it in glass jars without any preservatives. The community also uses the organically grown fruit to make ice-cream and creamy desserts, sometimes with the addition of Muscovado sugar (unrefined sugar similar to molasses). The products, which have all been awarded Ecovida and Ecocert certification, are sold at large trade fairs like the one at Porto Alegre, or through cooperatives.

PRODUCTION AREA
Pareci Novo, state of Rio Grande do Sul

COMMUNITY COORDINATOR
Maria Helena Da Rocha
tel. +55 5199330333
novocitrus@yahoo.com.br

Pintadas Honey producers

The community of Pintadas, in the State of Bahia, comprises about 50 families who keep bees and produce honey. Bee-keeping constitutes an extra source of income for the farmers, who know they can rely on honey even if other crops fail in this arid region. There are about 300 beehives and the bees belong to the species *Apis mellifera*, though, over the years, these have been inter-bred with African species. The producers all belong to the Pintadas Beekeepers' Association and deliver their product – about 4 tons a year – to the local Honey Workshop, where the honey is put into a centrifuge to remove the water and then put into jars. The product is distributed by the Agroindustriale Pintadas cooperative under the Mel do Sertão label all over Brazil, but is also sold directly at local markets and fairs.

PRODUCTION AREA
Pintadas, state of Bahia

COMMUNITY COORDINATOR
Nereide Segala Coelho
tel. +55 7536932215
sadepintadas@yahoo.com.br

Pirarucu fishermen

Since 1993, more than 100 fishermen have joined the Associação de Silves pela Preservação Ambiental e Cultural, an association which has set itself the task of safeguarding the freshwater ecosystem and the fishing of *pirarucu* in the Silves area. The *pirarucu* (*Arapaima gigas*), which is indigenous to the Amazon basin, is one of the largest freshwater fish in the world. It can measure more than 2 m in length and weigh anything up to 125 kg. The meat, which is a traditional part of the diet of the *Riberinhos*, an Amazonian tribe, is eaten raw, or dried and salted, rather like salted cod. Other parts of the fish, such as the scales, are used in local crafts. The ossified tongue is used to grate *guaranà* sticks. Since the *pirarucu* is a protected species, the sale of its meat is prohibited between September and May.

PRODUCTION AREA
Silves, state of Amazonas

COMMUNITY COORDINATOR
Maria Gabriella Pettazzoni
tel. +55 9232346562-9296031840
amazonas@tin.it

Pirenópolis fruit preserve producers

The community comprises about ten women who produce fruit preserves. Their work is part of an ecological farming project called Promessa do Futuro, proposed and implemented by a group of small-scale producers in the region of Caxambu in the municipality of Pirenópolis. The aim of the project is to promote the traditional products of the area, including *cagaita*, a typical fruit of the Cerrado. The community is especially interesting from a social point of view, since the women involved in producing the preserves and processing *baru* nuts are properly paid. The products are sold informally in small quantities, so that the women can also devote themselves to other activities.

PRODUCTION AREA
Pirenópolis, state of Goiás

COMMUNITY COORDINATOR
Katia Karam
tel. +55 0623311388
katia_karam@hotmail.com

Poço Fundo coffee producers

In 1991, an association was founded by 74 families of producers in the regions of Machado and Poço Fundo, in the south of the State of Minas Gerais. The aim of the association, which is a member of organizations such as the Organic Cooperative of Machado and Acob (Associação de Cafeicultura Orgânica do Brasil) is to promote the coffee they produce, which amounts to 1,500-2,000 sacks of coffee a year. In Machado, Poço Fundo, Santo Antonio do Amparo and Viçosa, small farms grow and pick high-quality organic Montanhas de Minas Gerais coffee, one of the most aromatic varieties in the world. Their products carry the BCS and Transfair certification labels and are destined for Fair Trade.

PRODUCTION AREA
Poço Fundo, state of Minas Gerais

COMMUNITY COORDINATOR
Luiz Severiano Célio
tel. +55 3532832113
assprodutores@axtelecom.com.br

Praia Grande Valley banana producers

In the south of the State of Santa Catarina, 150 people, belonging to 35 families of farmers who use ecological farming methods, form the community of Mampituba Valley. As elsewhere in the south of Brazil, production here is based on ecological farming criteria combined, in this particular case, with policies geared to promoting farm tourism and local craft industries. Thanks to the region's sub-tropical climate, its main product is the banana, which is sold as fruit or processed into cakes or the traditional bananada ('banana-passa' or dried bananas). Sometimes it is combined with palm hearts. The bananas are organically grown, using natural organic fertilizers. Other foods produced by the community according to the same ecological farming principles include legumes, cane sugar and honey.

PRODUCTION AREA
Praia Grande Valley, state of Santa Catarina

COMMUNITY COORDINATOR
Silvana Ferrigo De Fátima
tel. +55 4835320333
silvanaferrigo@ecovida.org.br

Rapadura de Melado producers

In the State of Paraná, sugar cane was the first product to be cultivated by the local people. The association of producers of rapadura de melado, of which numerous families in the area are members, has existed for more than 20 years. Rapadura is a brown sugar produced in the plantations of the State of Paranà in southern Brazil. After it has been collected, it is solidified into a brick shape to which other ingredients — such as papaya or orange juice, manioc or peanuts — can be added. Rapadura is highly nutritious. Annual production amounts to about 18,000 kg, which is consumed by the farmers' families or sold locally.

PRODUCTION AREA
Rio Branco do Sul, state of Paraná

COMMUNITY COORDINATOR
Antonio Stresser
tel. +55 04133482509
Fepar@netpat.com.br

Red Chilli Pepper producers

The CIR is the council of the indigenous peoples of Roraima, the region of the Amazon rainforest where they are most strongly concentrated. It includes eight ethnic groups, including the Yanomami, the Makuxi, the Wapixana and the Wai-Wai. The council, formed 20 years ago, now represents more than 20,000 Indians. The most symbolic region is Raposa-Serra do Sol, where there has been a great deal of violence against Indians in recent years. Here they produce the malagueta chili pepper (called capsicum or pimi 'ro in the local dialect), which has been used in Makuxi recipes since ancient times. The peppers are dessicated, ground, collected and packaged for the consumer market. An educational initiative involving local schools attended by indigenous children is in progress to enable the chili pepper to regain its original cultural value, thanks to the pimenteiras, women who live in Makuxi villages who still know how peppers were traditionally used.

PRODUCTION AREA
Raposa-Serra do Sol, state of Roraima

COMMUNITY COORDINATOR
Ribeiro do Nascimento Filho Herundino
tel. +55 9536265489
heribeiro@technet.com.br

Rio Real tropical fruit and juice producers

Cealnor is a consortium which acts as an umbrella organization for 22 associations in the north of the State of Bahia, comprising about 800 farming families who grow fruit – orange, maracuja, pineapple, mango and mandarin – and make fruit-products. They farm according to ecological farming criteria, combining organic methods with ecological sustainability. Cealnor is structured like a grassroots cooperative and, for many years, has belonged to the Fair Trade circuit. Cealnor entrusts the job of processing the fruit, especially in the case of juices for export, to two companies located close by. Until a few years ago, a great orange festival used to be held in the region, with parades and events linked to local products. Cealnor hopes to revive this tradition in 2006.

PRODUCTION AREA
Rio Real, state of Bahia

COMMUNITY COORDINATOR
Simões Da Silva Walmir
tel. +55 7534261719
cealnor.comercio@terra.com.br

Santa Lizia do Itanhi fishermen

In the State of Sergipe, in the Nordeste, the northeast of Brazil, about 350 km north of Salvador, the coastal strip consists of broad beaches and dunes and has a typically tropical climate and vegetation. The community, which comprises about 1,000 people, lives almost exclusively from artisan fishing and collecting *aratu* (a small crab), *sururu* and *siri* (shellfish and crustaceans) and *caranguejo* (another species of crab). Recently, they have begun to breed the *sururu*, a delicious edible Brazilian lake shellfish, as an economic alternative to catching crabs and shellfish. In any case, efforts are being made to promote production of the *catado de aratu*, which is traditionally produced and processed by women, due to a decline in the production of *caranguejo* crabs.

PRODUCTION AREA
Santa Lizia do Itanhi, state of Sergipe

COMMUNITY COORDINATOR
Daniel Freire do Amor Cardoso
tel. +55 7999881725
danielfreiredoamor@yahoo.com.br

Santa Luzia Jam producers

The community is based at Cidade Ocidental, in the State of Goiás, and has ten members who collaborate with associations like the Secretaria de Agricoltura de Cidade Ocidental and Agenciarural. The jam made in Santa Luzia is a traditional kind of sweet quince preserve. The recipe, typical of the region of Luziania, in the State of Goiás, has been handed down for generations. A traditional variety of quince is used which grows particularly well in the climate of the Luziania plateau. Quinces ripen between January and February. The fruit is picked, pre-cooked and put into tin containers. In the course of the year, it is then processed into jam in the traditional way in the houses of the producers, according to demand. The product is marketed mainly on a local scale.

PRODUCTION AREA
Cidade Ocidental, state of Goiás

COMMUNITY COORDINATOR
João Antonino Araujo
tel. +55 36251632
antonino@bol.com.br

Santana Velha Bacurí gatherers

In Santana do Maranhão, in the northeast of Brazil, this community of about 50 familiesis mainly involved in farming. As well as growing vegetables, the members of the community gather the fruits of the *bacuri* (*Platonia insignis*), a tree valued for its yellow wood. The fruit of the *bacuri*, which is similar to the papaya, is oval, with a thick, yellow skin, and white flesh containing brown, rather oily seeds. It has an unusually acidic, sweetish taste. The fruit's organoleptic properties are remarkable and it is rich in phosphorous, iron and Vitamin C. The pulp can be eaten raw or used to make sweets, juice, liqueurs and sorbets.

PRODUCTION AREA
Santana do Maranhão, state of Maranhão

COMMUNITY COORDINATOR
Vera Antônia Cláudia Ferreira
tel. +55 34881019
mary.figueiredo@mmda.gov.br

Santa Rosa de Lima organic producers

The community of Santa Rosa de Lima, in the State of Santa Catarina, consists of about 100 farmers who are mostly descended from German and Italian families. They produce fruit, cakes, ice-cream, legumes and cereals, and process poultry reared on small farms. The raw materials are grown, selected, processed and wrapped by small companies belonging to members of the community. The Nutrition Department of the Southern University of Santa Caterina is trying to promote the products and market them on a national scale through Brazilian supermarket chains under the Ecocert label, which guarantees organically produced foods.

PRODUCTION AREA
Santa Rosa de Lima, state of Santa Catarina

COMMUNITY COORDINATOR
Maia Lunardi Adilson
tel. +55 4836540107
adolson@agreco.com.br

Serra do Salitre cheesemakers

The community is made up of about 20 families of small-scale producers, who, for several generations, have made cheese from raw milk. They participate in almost all the phases of the milk and cheese production chain. The families have been producing dairy products in the mountainous regions of Serra da Canastra, Serra do Salitre e Serro, in the State of Minas Gerais, for about 150 years. The cheese is made by hand from raw milk straight from the milking, to which powdered rennet is added. The cheese can be kept for weeks or months at a time. The cheeses, which weigh about a kilo, are dry-salted and left to dry for about one day. The length of the maturation process varies depending on the type of cheese desired.

PRODUCTION AREA
Serra do Salitre, state of Minas Gerais

COMMUNITY COORDINATOR
Eustáquio Galvão da Silva
tel. +55 3134841013
Galvao.e@gmail.com

Serra Gaucha Grape producers

The community of producers and consumers of this unusual grape variety (*Vitis labrusca*, known as Isabel) in the municipality of Antônio Prado lives in Serra Gaucha, an area with a large population of German and Italian immigrants. It comprises 35 farmers and consumers who are particularly keen on using ecological farming techniques and are concerned about the environment and biodiversity. The community also organizes training initiatives, during which suitable traditional farming techniques are discussed and cookery courses. During meetings and festivals, it also prepares typical dishes with maize, tomatoes, beans, strawberries and Isabel grapes, which are used to make fruit juice, wine, cakes and vinegar. 40% of the world's Isabel grapes are currently grown in Serra Gaucha.

PRODUCTION AREA
Serra Gaucha, state of Rio Grande do Sul

COMMUNITY COORDINATOR
Cesar Augusto Volpato
tel. +55 5481340664
c.ecologico@terra.com.br

Small-scale Cashew Nut producers

In the State of Piauí, north of Bahia, in the northeast of Brazil, the vegetation consists mainly of *caatinga* — a word in the Tupy language meaning 'gray forest' — trees which have dried up and have no leaves, except during the rainy season. This is the habitat of the *cajueíro* tree and its fruit, the *castanha de caju* (cashew nut). Near the town of Picos, 200 people from 40 families, who belong to a cooperative of small-scale producers, collect 30 tons of cashew nuts a year. After they have been harvested, the nuts are taken to a depot, dried in an oven at 90°C, sorted according to size and color, and wrapped in vacuum packs. Cashew nuts have a high nutritional value and are used in confectionery, biscuits and sorbets. They are also delicious toasted and salted.

PRODUCTION AREA
Picos, state of Piauí

COMMUNITY COORDINATOR
Estevão Araújo Rocha
tel. +55 8934224370
estevão_coasa@hotmail.com

Spices producers

Located in the central corridor of the *mata atlàntica* on the coastal strip of the central-southern of Bahia, in the municipality of Taperoá, the Progetto Onça (which stands for Organizzazione Nuclei Comunità Agricole, but also means 'jaguar' in Portuguese) began by supporting small-scale producers. For 16 years it has been working on behalf of communities of farmers who want to abandon conventional farming, which leads to the impoverishment of the soil and a lack of resources for the producers, and embark on a new type of farming in harmony with the climatic, topographical, end environmental conditions of the area. These farmers now practice organic farming in agro-forestry systems, which respect eco-systems, and are organized as an association. The main crops are spices, *waraná*, chili peppers, tubers and palm oil.

PRODUCTION AREA
Taperoá, state of Bahia

COMMUNITY COORDINATOR
Santos Edvaldo
tel. +55 7536641694
projetoonca@ig.com.br

Sugar Cane growers

The Cooperagrepa cooperative comprises 300 farming families who live in the municipalities of Portal Amazônia, in the State of Mato Grosso. The 1,000 people involved produce organic food according to ecological farming practices and try to combine the possibility of earning a fair living with sustainable activities which help to preserve the biome of the Amazonian rainforest. The main products of the community are cane sugar, honey, *guaranà*, coffee and Brazil nuts. Sugar cane is cultivated according to the principles of ecological farming. The cane is harvested manually using scythes and machetes and is processed by a small artisan company, which ensures that the sugar's nutritional value, color and flavor are preserved.

PRODUCTION AREA
Portal Amazônia, state of Mato Grosso

COMMUNITY COORDINATOR
Teixeira Vagner Meira
tel. +55 6635341884
vagnermpa@yahoo.com.br

Teófilo Otoni young farmers

The Itamunhec community, which operates in the *fazendas* (coffee farms) around the town of Teófilo Otoni, a semi-arid area in the southeast, belongs to the association called Aprender Produzir Juntos (APJ – 'learning to produce together'), created in 1984 by a Roman Catholic mission. The aim was to help deprived young people and children by employing them in activities to help them in the future. To begin with, on-the-job training involved cutting and processing the precious stones mined in the local area. Later, the running of the project was taken over by lay Brazilian nationals and, since 2004, the activities of the association have been extended to rural areas. Two cooperatives have been set up to produce fruit and vegetables and breed small domestic animals. All the products of the community are sold on the national market.

PRODUCTION AREA
Teófilo Otoni, state of Minas Gerais

COMMUNITY COORDINATOR
Joana Alves Louback
tel. +55 3335228015
apjuntos@apjuntos.org.br

Turvo Pine Nut gatherers

In Turvo, a little town in the State of Paraná, more than 4,000 people are involved in a project to develop the economy of the area by gathering natural products such as Brazilian pine nuts, medicinal herbs for tisanes and yerba mate, a product of great economic, environmental and cultural importance for the southern states of Brazil. Unlike their European counterparts, Brazilian pine nuts are the fruits of a tree of the species *Araucaria angustifolia*, which is native to Brazil. Because its flesh is rich in starch, it is a staple of the local diet. Historical and archeological research has shown that the nuts have been used by the indigenous people here for thousands of years. The flesh of the nut can be turned into flour, which is used in confectionery and in various types of bread. In areas where the araucaria is very common, the pine nuts are cooked and then preserved in brine and vinegar.

PRODUCTION AREA
Turvo, state of Paraná

COMMUNITY COORDINATOR
Eurich Roseli Cordeiro
tel. +55 4236421318
roselieurich@yahoo.com.br

Vale do Piancó Red Rice producers

Vale do Piancó is an area in the south of the State of Paraíba famous for its production of *arroz vermelho* (red rice), a member of the *Oryza sativa* species. This variety, which was introduced by the Portuguese in the 17th century, is grown and consumed in the semi-arid areas of the northeast of Brazil. It can be distinguished from white rice because of its color and its unusual flavor. In the last few decades, as a result of the spread of urbanization and the increasing popularity of white rice, the cultivation of red rice has fallen dramatically — by one third in the State of Paraíba alone. The community involves about 5,000 small-scale producers who cultivate small plots of land. Part of the rice grown is consumed by the farmers' families and the rest is sold locally.

PRODUCTION AREA
Vale do Piancó, state of Paraiba

COMMUNITY COORDINATOR
José Almeida Pereira
tel. +55 8632251141
almeida@cpamn.embrapa.br

Valente Manioc Flour producers

The Apaeb association of Valente comprises about 750 families of small-scale farmers. Well known in Brazil and worldwide, it has existed for 26 years and has won many prizes for its work in promoting the sustainable development of the *sertão* of the northeast of Brazil. The main activity in this area is the processing of agave leaves to make rugs, carpets and other craft products. Another product line is associated with manioc, a tropical plant with edible roots, which are used as they are or made into flour. Facilities exist for producing manioc flour and promoting its use in typical local recipes: in fish dishes (*pirão*), with beans (*feijão tropeiro*), or it can also be baked or fried. Manioc starch is used to make a popular Brazilian specialty called *pão de queijo*, or cheese bread.

PRODUCTION AREA
Valente, state of Bahia

COMMUNITY COORDINATOR
Luca Giovanni Allegro
tel. +55 7132479668
allegro@apaeb.com.br

Vitoria De Santo Antão producers

The cooperative, which is based in Vitoria de Santo Antão, in the State of Pernambuco, in the northeast of Brazil, has 118 members. They mainly produce fruit, vegetables, and legumes according to organic farming methods. These crops constitute the only source of income for these small-scale producers. The tropical fruits produced here, which include banana, mango, coconut and peanut, are sold fresh and also processed for use in sweets and cakes. Manioc is sold as flour and is the staple of the diet of people in the cities and countryside in the northeast of Brazil. The community also produces pumpkins, which are used with other fruits to make typical local cakes and sweets.

PRODUCTION AREA
Vitoria De Santo Antão, state of Pernambuco

COMMUNITY COORDINATOR
Giovanni Baroni
tel. +55 58134445165
giovanni.baroni@gmail.com

Xingu Park fruit producers

The Xingu Park is the third-largest indigenous park in Brazil. It is inhabited by 5000 indigenous people representing 16 different ethnic types and 204 tribes. The Kaiabi grow tropical fruit and roots and are hunters and fishermen. The community of fruit producers has 1,100 members. One of the main crops is the peanut (*Arachis hypogaea*), which is regarded as a gift from the god of cultivated fields. After they have been harvested, the peanuts are eaten raw, toasted or ground to make a sort of polenta, which is eaten with millet, sweet potatoes or rice. Alternatively, they can be mixed with manioc and roasted on a hot plate or wrapped in banana leaves to make *pane canapé*. The association is endeavoring to ensure that the 36 varieties of peanuts currently known are recognized and protected.

PRODUCTION AREA
Gaúcha do Norte, state of Mato Grosso

COMMUNITY COORDINATOR
Kaiabi Tuiaraiup
tel. +55 63478 1948
atix@brturbo.com.br

Yerba Mate growers and processors

The community of Santa Maria de Oeste, in the central region of the State of Paranà, involves 500 families and belongs to the Movement of Landless Farm Workers, a network of small Brazilian communities which process and sell their own products. Since 1984, the community has been participating in a project with the aim of deriving economic benefit from the traditional cultivation of yerba mate. The product is collected, dried and sold as the basic ingredient for making *chimarrão*. Also known as *mate* or *amargo*, this traditional drink of the Guaraní Indians consists of yerba mate infused in boiling water. It is drunk hot in a small cup called a *mate* or *porongo*, using a metal or cane straw (*bombilla*).

PRODUCTION AREA
Santa Maria de Oeste, state of Paraná

COMMUNITY COORDINATOR
Luiz Zenaide Gomes
tel. +55 4236441177
produtosdaterra@anca.org.br

Nós Existimos

This movement was founded in recent years on the State of Roraima (Norte) in the Amazon, to try to forge a strategic alliance in a land where conflict and the abuse of power are daily events, amid indigenous populations, urban social movements (trades unions, grass roots associations, NGOs, social religious groups), rural organizations (movements of peasant women and family groups of simple farmers). Nós Existimos is a movement-forum which, for the first time in Roraima history, is attempting to assert the civil, human, economic and political rights of social classes (indios, farmers, urban organizations) that have always been persecuted by the local oligarchies (big landowners, gold-diggers, armed forces), and that have never been able to pool their forces, presenting themselves as a single interlocutor for the rights of the people represented.

AREA OF ACTIVITY
State of Roraima

ASSOCIATION COORDINATOR
Andrea Vasconcelos
tel. +55 9532240060
andref_vasconcelos@yahoo.com.br

Acton Biodynamic Food producers

The community, comprising around 150 members, practices and promotes biodynamic agriculture following the principles laid down by Rudolph Steiner. Biodynamic agriculture is based on the conviction that a farm is a living organism, a closed, self-nourishing system, lying within the greater cosmic living organism to whose influences it is subject. A biodynamic farmer has to be aware of these influences and adopt methods to encourage them. This will result in more fertile, more vigorous soils and healthier crops. The community's foodstuffs include vegetables, cereals and milk products such as yogurt, cheeses and ice creams. Part of this milk comes from the indigenous Canadian cow breed, which has less than 1,000 head remaining. Most of the sales take place through a Community Supported Agriculture scheme.

PRODUCTION AREA
Acton, Ontario

COMMUNITY COORDINATOR
Leslie Moskovits
tel. +1 5198561384
moskovitsleslie@hotmail.com

Alberta bakers

The industrialization of food production in Canada has turned leavened bread into a mass market product. Yet although white bread looks good it is not particularly nourishing and has to be enriched with vitamins and minerals. It was its lack of taste and nutritional value that brought the small bakers of this community to diversify their range and increase the quality of the ingredients they use in their breads. Hence they produce traditional bread from wheatflour which is grown and milled locally. The sourdough is prepared with a "mother" yeast which receives a daily addition of stone-milled organic flour. The dough is left for 24 hours to rise slowly and is baked each morning. Some of the bread goes for own consumption, the rest is sold locally.

PRODUCTION AREA
Alberta

COMMUNITY COORDINATOR
Melissa Cheah
tel. +1 4036802409
lisacheah@hotmail.com

Alberta beekeepers and mead producers

Alberta's beekeeping community produces honey and various derivatives, making everything as naturally as possible and keeping processing to a minimum. Everything, from the beekeeping through to the packaging of the finished goods, takes place on their small farms. The honey, the core of their activity, is sold both in its pure state and in other forms, such as mead, which is a specialty hereabouts. Mead, also known as hydromel, is an ancient, natural alcoholic drink based on water, honey and yeast. There are also versions, called melomel, which contain fruit, and others, called methoglin, with natural spices and herbs. The community's other products include pollen, propolis and beeswax. The pollen is particularly rich in proteins and vitamins. It is collected from the hives at the time when it is most plentiful, so that the natural equilibrium of the system is not disturbed. Propolis is a natural antibiotic, antifungal and antiviral, and is scraped out from the hives after the honey has been collected.

PRODUCTION AREA
Alberta

COMMUNITY COORDINATOR
Cherie Andrews
tel. +1 4039950830
chinookhoneyco@nucleus.com

Alberta Bison breeders

The bison, also known as the American buffalo, is a native of the great North American prairies. Local populations venerated its power and beauty, and hunted only what was necessary for their survival. The skins were used to make shields, saddles and shoes, and the hair for ropes and pillows. But in the 18th century, when the European explorers began to conquer North America's more westerly regions, the number of bison began to diminish drastically. The animals were considered a threat to their farms and their cultivated crops, and were killed in large quantities. Now, though, there is a conservation program underway and bison have been reintroduced into protected areas, parks and private farms, where the community's breeders let them graze freely.

PRODUCTION AREA
Alberta

COMMUNITY COORDINATOR
Edward Buchan
tel. +1 7803512115

Alberta breeders

Livestock rearing on the vast prairies of Canada and the United States has always been of great importance, to both the native populations and the European immigrants. Even now raising animals forms the main source of income for most farmers. The community's breeders rear diverse breeds inlcuding North American Plains bison, Red Poll and Canadian Lynch Lineback cattle, and British Large Black and Tamworth pigs. The animals range free and graze on the prairies, which gives their meat excellent flavor. They often move to new pastures to reduce the problem of parasites and to keep the soil healthy. The meat is sold in Calgary and at the local markets held in more rural areas.

PRODUCTION AREA
Alberta

COMMUNITY COORDINATOR
Jerry Kitt
tel. +1 7803562239
jkitt@telusplanet.net

Alberta Cattle breeders

The Canadian prairies have been populated by bison for thousands of years but it was only with the arrival of the European populations that they started being raised in captivity, especially in the valleys and on the lowest mountain slopes. There are still many communities of breeders remaining in these areas who let their animals graze freely but their herds now comprise various breeds of cattle. The Alberta community uses their meat to prepare jerky, a preserved food which was part of the traditional diet of the native populations. The meat is dried, being reduced practically to a powder and mixed with hot fat. Originally, the drying took place in the open air, using the heat of the sun, but very soon changed to smoking over various types of wood.

PRODUCTION AREA
Canadian Rockies, Alberta

COMMUNITY COORDINATOR
Zona Armstrong
tel. +1 4038437769
craigarm1967@telus.net

Alberta Lamb breeders

The lambs reared by the community are of the Barbados breed. This name might imply that they are of Caribbean origin, but in fact they are thought to derive from Africa. The Barbados was probably introduced into North America at the start of the 20th century, however it has now become one of the breeds at risk of extinction there. The community, numbering just two members, has been rearing and selling the breed for 13 years, taking an attentive, sensitive, ecological approach to their activity. They use Maremmana breed dogs, which are naturally predisposed towards protecting livestock, to keep predators away; the animals graze freely on fresh grass in the summer months; they are fed on locally produced hay and barley in winter; the fields are subject to crop rotation to ensure the natural restoration of soil nutrients.

PRODUCTION AREA
Alberta

COMMUNITY COORDINATOR
Linda and Denis Jabs
tel. +1 4037282398
cakadu@telusplanet.net

Alberta organic breeders

The community is composed primarily of three families in central Alberta who raise poultry, cattle, lambs, pigs and bison but also includes the many Alberta families who buy their meat at farmers' markets. The animals are reared as in times past, ranging free or driven daily to open air grazing. All the meat has organic certification. The community breeders aim to build up lasting relationships with their clients and work to promote taste education. Their goods can be found at the Calgary farmers' market.

PRODUCTION AREA
Alberta

COMMUNITY COORDINATOR
Sheila Hamilton
tel. +1 7806729799
sunworks@telusplanet.net

British Columbia farmers' markets producers

British Columbia's temperature climate lends itself well to agriculture, as is evidenced by the more than 300 products being sold at farmers' markets and in Community Supported Agriculture schemes in the province. The Fraser Valley is primarily noted for its dairy produce and berry fruits, principally raspberries, blackberries and strawberries; while the Okanagan valley grows mainly stone fruits and vines. Farming in the Cariboo region is more directed towards livestock rearing and grain cultivation; while organic farming is more prominent on Vancouver Island, which has numerous dairies producing a range of milk products and several flower markets. Farmers' markets are a way of creating a direct link between producers and consumers. and increasing the sense of identity and solidarity within the community.

PRODUCTION AREA
British Columbia

COMMUNITY COORDINATOR
Erin Nichols
tel. +1 6047420645
erin@eatlocal.org

British Columbia food producers

The British Columbia community numbers over 300 members, 100 producers and 100 volunteers, who all work in direct liaison with the non-profit FarmFolk/CityFolk Society. Its projects include protecting farmland, promoting access to the land, and establishing direct relationships between producers and consumers. The community also has a particular interest in the collection and conservation of seeds. Its members' products include various varieties of salad greens, seasonal vegetables, aromatic herbs, edible flowers, and plants, both cultivated and wild, for forage. These are mainly sold direct to local restaurants, and at farmers' markets. All the products have organic certification.

PRODUCTION AREA
Vancouver, British Columbia

COMMUNITY COORDINATOR
Heather Pritchard
tel. +1 6045879057
sustain@ffcf.bc.ca

Cape Breton farmers' market producers

Until a short time ago Cape Breton Island was dominated by its coal and steel industries. But its inhabitants came to realize the importance of locally-produced food and a farmers' market, with 25 stands, was set up in Sydney. The bread is made artisanally with organic ingredients, the flours being milled on the nearby mainland; the chickens come from the Margaree rural area and are moved on tent-like structures with a rotating base that provides them continuously with fresh ground. The other meats sold are beef from Scottish Highland cattle (a breed which arrived in the 18th century from the town of Louisbour) and Berkshire pork. Then there are the celebrated cranberries, which hailed initially from a farm on Madame Island.

PRODUCTION AREA
Sydney, Cape Breton, Nova Scotia

COMMUNITY COORDINATOR
Sharon MacDonald
tel. +1 9025642080
sharrick@ns.sympatico.ca

Dufferin Grove farmers' market producers

The Dufferin Grove farmers' market, in Dufferin Grove park in Toronto, is renowned for its oven where anyone can bake their bread. But it also offers most of the organic produce grown in the area. The 20 farmers who set up stall there every Thursday afternoon are members of an organization for the defense of seeds, which documents and uses plants that are of particular importance to Canada. They grow vegetables, including 25 varieties of tomato, fruits, grain, about 50 aromatic and medicinal herbs, and other indigenous Ontario plants, such as *Anemone canadensis*. The members additionally organize periodical events tied to local food products, in liaison with the Toronto Slow Food Convivium.

PRODUCTION AREA
Toronto, Ontario

COMMUNITY COORDINATOR
Colette Murphy
tel. +1 4165041653
grow@uharvest.ca

Eastern Seaboard farmers' markets producers

This community extends along the four provinces of Canada's eastern seaboard: Newfoundland and Labrador, New Brunswick, Prince Edward Island and Nova Scotia. The first typically produces molasses cookies, hard tack and Screech (a traditional, rum-based alcoholic drink); New Brunswick's markets abound with seaweeds, fern extracts and local fish; Malpèque oysters, lobsters, potatoes and mussels are the leading products from Prince Edward Island; while the stalls of Nova Scotia are bright with Tancook Island cabbages, wild blueberries, smoked salmon and shellfish. There are also numerous livestock farmers in the community who sell a wide range of meats, coming from Highland breed cows and bulls right down to free-range chickens.

PRODUCTION AREA
Newfoundland and Labrador, Nova Scotia, New Brunswick and Prince Edward Island

COMMUNITY COORDINATOR
Paul Colville
tel. +1 9028254401
coldspring@ns.sympatico.ca

Grand Manan Island Lobster fishers

Grand Manan is an island in the Gulf of Maine, in the deep waters of Fundy Bay. The area has the highest tides in the world, which give rise to a fascinating, ever-changing marine landscape. This unique environment, where cool Atlantic currents bring their influence to bear on the lands and climate, has been home to lobster fishing for centuries. The season officially opens on the second Tuesday in November but in reality divides into two distinct periods, one from mid November to mid January, the other from the last week of April to the end of June. The 120 or so small boats fishing the area are dedicated solely to lobster fishing, and use sustainable methods. Their catch supplies many of the small restaurants around the bay.

PRODUCTION AREA
Grand Manan Island, New Brunswick

COMMUNITY COORDINATOR
James Pickering
tel. +1 5066625555
jim@grandmananlobster.com

Gulf Islands farmers' markets producers

The Gulf Islands form part of the archipelago lying between Vancouver Island and British Columbia's Lower Mainland. They are home to a group of livestock and crop farmers who manage and ensure the sustainability of the foods produced in the Island Trust Area, an ecological preserve. The 470-odd islands forming the archipelago have limited water resources and there is not a great deal of cultivable land, so the range of local fruits and vegetables produced is not huge. They are, though, all organic. The vegetables are led by tomatoes, garlic and salad greens; then there is lamb, cheese, and eggs from indigenous chicken breeds. These can all be found at farmers' markets. In addition, farmers sometimes sell them directly at the roadside.

PRODUCTION AREA
Gulf Islands, British Columbia

COMMUNITY COORDINATOR
Michelle Masselink
tel. +1 2506296934
hopebayfarm@cablelan.net

Gull Valley Vegetable growers

Alberta province is known for its fertile soils and its livestock rearing but the sudden growth in its economy following the discovery of oil has drawn people away from agriculture. The farmers in the cooperative forming this community grow vegetables without the use of any pesticides, herbicides, fungicides or genetically modified seeds. Organic methods are used to keep plants healthy and pollination is carried out by bumble bees. Some of the crops are grown in greenhouses, which are heated by large coal boilers. The produce includes lettuce, over 15 varieties of tomatoes and a number of cucumber varieties, sales taking place at farmers' markets.

PRODUCTION AREA
Gull Valley, Alberta

COMMUNITY COORDINATOR
Scott Epple
tel. +1 4036851418
sjnsons@telus.net

Hagersville Wild Plant gatherers

The Six Nations community has always been dedicated to activities linked with the soil, most notably the cultivation and gathering of aromatic and medicinal plants. Its food education programs, aimed at the younger generation, aim to promote the traditional diet of the native populations, with its long-standing reliance on the nutritional value of wild fruits. With this objective, and preservation of the culture of the original North American populations, in mind, Sweet Grass Gardens, a small farm run by a native family, decided to specialize in the production and sale of foods that date back to pre-European times. Everything is gathered from a territory within a 90-kilometer radius and includes pollens and barks, roots and leaves from various plants, herbs (including angelica) and berries, hyacinth, ginger, wild garlic, Indian hemp, field onions and cardoons, all growing wild.

PRODUCTION AREA
Hagersville, Ontario

COMMUNITY COORDINATOR
Kenneth Parker
tel. +1 5194454828
info@sweetgrassgardens.com

Ice Cider producers

The community began its activities around 30 years ago, producing and selling ice cider, a product typical of Québec, where the freezing winter temperatures allow the apples (mostly of the Macintosh or Spartan varieties) to gain sufficient sugar concentrations. Ice cider can be made in two ways, by crio-concentration or crio-extraction, depending on whether it is the apples or their juice which is left in the open air to freeze. Either way, a thick syrup is formed which ferments slowly for months until it reaches around 12% alcohol. In 2001 the Association des Cidriculteurs Artisans du Québec (Québec Artisan Cidermakers) determined the official definition of what constitutes an ice cider (or *cidre de glace*) clearly distinguishing it both from traditional ciders and from Eiswein/Icewines.

PRODUCTION AREA
Montérégie, Laurentides and Cantons-de-l'Est, Québec

COMMUNITY COORDINATOR
François Pouliot
tel. +1 4502472899
fpouliot@cidreglace.com

Lake Superior fishermen

The Thunder Bay Fish Shop, overlooking Lake Superior, is a small enterprise which has been selling freshwater fish for generations. The entire Great Lakes area comprises the largest freshwater fish reserve in the world and contains a vast range of fish breeds, all of the highest quality; but the preference of local restaurateurs for the practicality of frozen salmon fillets prevents the wealth of this resource being turned to best advantage. It was immigrant fishermen from Finland who introduced traditional, eco-compatible fishing methods to Thunder Bay: no use of colorants or other chemicals, no use of electricity, brining solely with seawater, and smoking for 8-15 hours over alder wood. The most choice fish of the bay, apart from trout, is the delicious lake whitefish.

PRODUCTION AREA
Thunder Bay, Lake Superior, Ontario

COMMUNITY COORDINATOR
Lisa Karkkainen
tel. +1 8079832214
thefishshop@tbaytel.net

Newfoundland organic producers

Newfoundland is a large island lying off the northeastern seaboard of North America. Its food community is based on the Avalon peninsula, whose rather severe climate leads to a short growing season. The members nevertheless grow a wide range of vegetables and aromatic herbs, making use of the opportunities given by both open-air and greenhouse cultivation. They have been using organic methods for over 20 years and have gradually increased their client base, drawing in students at Memorial University, small food shops and local restaurants. They have also set up a Community Supported Agriculture scheme which already involves 55 families. The community belongs to the Canadian Organic Growers Association and works with a number of seed conservation organizations.

PRODUCTION AREA
Newfoundland, Newfoundland and Labrador

COMMUNITY COORDINATOR
Melba Rabinowitz
tel. +1 7098952884
organicfarm@nl.rogers.com

Niagara Wine producers

A group of independent grape-growers from the lands of Lake Ontario and Niagara province, an area recognized by UNESCO as a World Biosphere Reserve, and a zone which has recently gained note for its Rieslings and Eiswein/Icewines, have come together with the object of ensuring that vine cultivation remains traditional and their small crops are hand-picked. Winemaking in Niagara started at the beginning of the 19th century, the Speck family being among the pioneers. Today the group's members grow and vinify Cabernet, Merlot, Chardonnay (this latter barrique fermented with careful re-immersion of the yeasts) and, especially, Riesling Eiswein, made from grapes left on the vines to over-ripen until they freeze in winter, thereby further concentrating their sugars.

PRODUCTION AREA
Saint Catharines, Ontario

COMMUNITY COORDINATOR
Paul Decampo
tel. +1 4166571596
decampo@idirect.com

Nova Scotia and Ontario Maple Syrup producers

Of the 13 indigenous North American maple species, syrup can be made from just four: the sugar maple, the black cedar maple, and the red and silver maples. Their bark is tapped to release its sap, which is then boiled down until a rich syrup results. Maple syrup is a natural sweetener, like molasses (although it has fewer calories), and formed an important part of the native populations' diet. Its main constituents are saccharose, and organic acids, vitamins and minerals. There are about 30 producers, joined in the North American Maple Syrup Council. The community members own small, family-run farms of no more than a few hundred acres. Once boiled, the syrup is simply bottled into containers of between 40 milliliters and four liters, and sold, both locally and throughout the country.

PRODUCTION AREA
Nova Scotia and Ontario

COMMUNITY COORDINATOR
Susanne Robinson
tel. +1 5195297857
robinmap@hurontel.on.ca

Nova Scotia Wild Blueberry gatherers

The Canadian Atlantic coast of Nova Scotia has a wealth of berry fruits, especially the dwarf blueberry, of which various varieties are found. The fruit, which is renowned for its antioxidant properties, grows spontaneously. The community's activities are directed entirely towards its picking and sale. Blueberries were an important part of the diet of the ancient native populations and also gave them a means of exchange in trading with adjacent areas. The widespread use of synthetic treatments to increase and force blueberry production has created serious dangers for both the fruit and the soil, which has become eroded and impoverished. The community's organic gatherers naturally use no chemicals. They pick the fruit twice a year and sell the berries fresh, and in sweetmeats such as tarts, muffins and pancakes.

PRODUCTION AREA
Nova Scotia

COMMUNITY COORDINATOR
Barbara Jack
tel. +1 9025462475
hinjack@ns.sympatico.ca

Ontario farmers' market producers

The community is made up of 14 farms, employing 75 people, who supply around 150 families in a Community Supported Agriculture (CSA) scheme and also sell their goods at a farmers' market. The first one in the area was in the small town of Kingston – in 1780. At this time it became normal in Ontario to buy foods directly from the producer, which gave a wide range of choice and cheaper prices. These days the farmers' markets have vegetables, meats, flowers, fruit, butter, jams and syrups, all with organic certification; the CSA schemes run complementary to them.

PRODUCTION AREA
Lucknow, Ontario

COMMUNITY COORDINATOR
Michael Hubbard
tel. +1 5199418298
maranatha.farms@sympatico.ca

Ontario producers and consumers

Fourteen small farmers from central-southern Ontario belong to a co-operative, called CRAFT, which acts as a Community Supported Agriculture (CSA) scheme whereby consumers pay a fixed sum to receive fresh local farm produce. The farms are each of between 25 and 100 acres and produce a wide range of goods, including vegetables, meats of all kinds, grain and hay. In this part of Ontario the growing season starts at the end of April and sometimes finishes in November. All the community members farm organically and some have organic or bio-dynamic certification. As well as their CSA sales, they also sell at farmers' markets and to shops.

PRODUCTION AREA
Ontario

COMMUNITY COORDINATOR
Chris Krucker
tel. +1 9053048048
manorun@hwcn.org

Ontario small-scale brewers

This community of microbrewers is distinguished by its concentration on organic methods and its concern for the environment, both in terms of waste-water management and its research into low-impact energy sources. One special product, made from local ingredients, is a light-colored beer with cranberries and maple syrup. The breweries are constantly researching new ways of recycling by-products into livestock feed, fertilizers and irrigation water. The better-known establishments have become popular destinations for Canadian beer-lovers wanting a countryside break. Distribution is at local level.

PRODUCTION AREA
Ontario

COMMUNITY COORDINATOR
John Graham
tel. +1 7056539950
info@churchkeybrewing.com

Ontario small-scale farmers

There are very few small-scale, family-run farms remaining in Ontario which practice sustainable agriculture. The community, represented by McCully's Hill Farm, is working actively to keep the area's family-run farms alive through the promotion of rural education programs and the creation of a direct sales system. Maple syrup is one of the community's main products. The sap is collected from the trees by channeling it through slim tubes and it is then boiled down in the traditional way. The resulting syrup, about 3,000 liters a year, is bottled *in situ*. The producers also raise various indigenous livestock breeds, including Black Angus calves and Tamworth pigs, and rabbits, chickens and lambs. They additional make preserves, chutneys, pickles and fruit jams, all using traditional preservation methods

PRODUCTION AREA
Saint Marys, Ontario

COMMUNITY COORDINATOR
David Pullen
tel. +1 5192843179
mcfarm@cyg.net

Ontario Wild Plant gatherers

In North American wild plants are picked both for own consumption and for sale. The gathering progresses with the seasons: chickweed, wild onion, wild garlic, violets, mustard and dandelion are harvested at the beginning of spring, followed by sorrel, hops, pigweed, mallow, clover, plane and nettles. Fruits and nuts appear with the arrival of winter, as do dandelion roots. The gatherers – women, children and adult farmers – come from the native populations and live in rural localities. The community practices sustainable harvesting methods – sustainable for each particular plant species (only plants whose survival is not in danger are picked) and also for the pickers, whose livelihood depends on a thriving source of wild foods. The community members additionally educate the public about taste, healthy eating and the benefits to be derived from wild plant gathering.

PRODUCTION AREA
Ontario

COMMUNITY COORDINATOR
Jonathan Forbes
tel. +1 4169279106
forbes@wildfoods.ca

Perth County dairy farmers

Perth County lies in southeast Ontario, between lakes Huron and Erie. Farmers have been raising livestock in its temperate climate for 160 years, but the tendency is towards large farming enterprises. Fortunately there remains a number, albeit small, of artisan dairies whose cheeses are made from sheep's and goats' milk. The community is composed primarily of 12 sheep farmers who milk their sheep by hand and send it immediately to the dairies. Their animals do not eat silage. Average production is 300 kilos a week. The cheeses are ripened underground and then sold in Stratford and the rest of Ontario, at markets and in wine bars, restaurants and shops. The community also includes those consumers who buy the cheeses at the dairy door, and those who work with the Toronto Slow Food Convivium in sending them to local chefs.

PRODUCTION AREA
Perth County, Ontario

COMMUNITY COORDINATOR
Ruth Klahsen
tel. +1 5195957920
monfortedairy@cyg.net

Saint-Camille farmers' markets producers

Clé des Champs is a solidarity cooperative supplying products and services to the small farmers and inhabitants of the town and province of Saint-Camille. It works to develop agricultural activity by fostering the sale of farm produce, both locally and regionally. A collection of funds enabled the community to open a sales center in the town which has become a focus for the farmers' goods, all of which are organically produced and come from numerous traditional varieties. Most notably there are pulses, cereals, green vegetables, potatoes and foods, such as mushrooms, which grow wild. These are all also sold in the province's farmers' markets and through a Community Supported Agriculture scheme.

PRODUCTION AREA
Saint-Camille, Québec

COMMUNITY COORDINATOR
Henri-Paul Bellerose
tel. +1 8198282677
cledeschamps@globetrotter.net

Seed conservers

The community groups organic growers from the provinces of Nova Scotia, New Brunswick and Prince Edward Island, who collect and conserve seeds from the leading local tuber and green vegetable varieties. It aims to combat the spread of monocultures, which create genetic impoverishment. To this end it organizes meetings for the exchange and sale of seeds, and participates actively in local farmers' markets. The emblem of the community is most probably its large number of bean varieties (which include Jacob's Cattle), pulses having always been a staple of the North American diet. The seed bank also includes local potato varieties, for example Island Sunshine and Bluenose, Jerusalem artichokes and about a hundred tomato varieties.

PRODUCTION AREA
Nova Scotia, New Brunswick and Prince Edward Island

COMMUNITY COORDINATOR
Janet Wallace
tel. +1 5067343361
janet@cog.ca

South Alberta food producers and restaurateurs

The Calgary River Café is an institution of more than local renown. The restaurant is supplied by 65 producers of local organic foodstuffs, and has become a multi-faceted organism in which butchers, fishermen, growers, bakers, cheese-makers, distillers and cooks come together in a sustainable productive network. The cooking at the River Café concentrates on specialties linked with its territory, with particular interest in the culinary traditions of the native populations. There are meat and game (venison, musk ox, bison, pheasant, partridge, duck), cereals (Red Fife wheat, Hamilton barley, canola, oats), organic butter, green vegetables and tubers, wild herbs, edible flowers and berries. The 60 or so River Café staff do more than prepare delicious meals: they also take care of the restaurant's vegetable garden and arrange food education activities.

PRODUCTION AREA
Calgary, Alberta

COMMUNITY COORDINATOR
Sal Howel
tel. +1 4032617670
sal@river-café.com

Southwest Vancouver fishermen and gatherers

Vancouver Island lies off the Canadian Pacific seaboard and has a long tradition of fishing, which was an occupation of the native populations even before the arrival of the European settlers. But the community does not just fish, it gathers seaweed too, most notably *porphyra*, also known as laver, nori or black seaweed. This formed an important source of nutrition for the natives and is still an ingredient in a number of local dishes. The community members additionally gather traditional wild forest foods, including berries, mushrooms and aromatic herbs. Then they produce mead (hydromel), an alcoholic drink based on honey, to which fruit is sometimes added. The community is pledged to promote traditional food products so that sustainable development can be fostered and dependence on imported goods reduced.

PRODUCTION AREA
Sooke, British Columbia

COMMUNITY COORDINATOR
Philip Sinclair
tel. +1 2506423421
sinclair@sookeharbourhouse.com

Toronto organic producers

Foodshare, the leading Canadian food safety organization, is working to improve access to healthy, sustainable foods, by creating a direct link from field to table. The Good Food Box is a shopping basket in which one can buy organic produce in line with one's needs and preferences, but predominantly ultra-fresh fruit and vegetables, . There are small, medium, family-sized and wellness Boxes available, this latter aimed at women undergoing cancer treatments. About 800 Boxes a week are distributed, with a group of 120 volunteers delivering them to wholesalers and another 40 or so filling them. Foodshare also has a catering service and has opened two Salad Bars. This is part of a program to supply elementary school children with lunches prepared from organic produce. It additionally aims to get them involved in visiting farms.

PRODUCTION AREA
Toronto, Ontario

COMMUNITY COORDINATOR
Debbie Field
tel. +1 4163921628
debbie@foodshare.net

Vancouver Wild Plant gatherers

The community groups around 1,500 gatherers, processors, cooks, university lecturers, NGOs and associations, who work to promote and conserve the wild food products of the Canadian Pacific seaboard, especially those from the Cowichan and Comox valleys. Following artisanal methods which are not greatly different from those used by the native populations, numerous spontaneously growing fruits, mostly blueberries, blackberries and huckleberries (including the dwarf varieties), are processed into jams, compotes and jellies, or dried in the sun and used to make sauces and condiments. There are also mushrooms: chanterelles, with their pretty partridge-eye color, their convex cap and their inwardly turned rim, are real delicacies.

PRODUCTION AREA
Cowichan and Comox Valleys, British Columbia

COMMUNITY COORDINATOR
Ken Jensen
tel. +1 2502181017
naturestreat@shaw.ca

Yukon bakers

The artisan bakers of Yukon are an integral part of a regional Community Supported Agriculture (CSA) scheme, for which they produce around 16 types of bread, principally rye, all from local flours, all traditional and all wood-baked. Apart from their sweet bakery products, which are made with white wheatflour, the range is based on sourdough. Back in 1898, during the times of the gold rush which swept through the area, the native tribes used to eat a flatbread called Bannock (still much admired) which was made with sourdough and enriched with lard plus berries or sultanas. Sourdough was used because it was the only raising agent that could survive their long treks through the mountains and the cold winter temperatures.

PRODUCTION AREA
Whitehorse, Yukon

COMMUNITY COORDINATOR
Suat Tuzlak
tel. +1 8676686871
alpine@yknet.ca

Yukon farmers' market producers

The word Yukon comes from the language of the native populations and means "large river", referring to what is now called the Yukon river, in whose watershed much of the territory lies. The growing season is short but productive; and even though the lands are mainly mountainous, and in part covered with glaciers, there is cultivation of a huge variety of high quality local products, including all sorts of vegetables, most particularly numerous types of brightly colored tubers. To these must be added two products essential to the local diet: cranberry syrup and birch syrup. All these products can be found at farmers' markets but some producers sell their goods directly at the farm gate, bringing consumers a wide choice that ranges from elk and bison meat to goat's cheese.

PRODUCTION AREA
Yukon

COMMUNITY COORDINATOR
Michael King
tel. +1 8676674145
michael@beannorth.com

Yukon food tradition promulgators

The main aims of the community are to maintain and promote traditional dietary habits, and to promulgate the cultural heritage of the native populations, taking the message into homes, especially to the younger generation, and into collective social structures such as hospitals. It regularly organizes cultural programs which discuss the community's history and its traditional activities, these being led by the gathering of wild fruits and medicinal herbs, but also involving hunting, fishing and food processing.

PRODUCTION AREA
Whitehorse, Yukon

COMMUNITY COORDINATOR
Barb Buyck
tel. +1 867633003

Biological wine producers

Wine production in a privileged area of the VI region of Chile, Valley Colchagua, is a family run business. The geographic position between two high mountain chains that form a corridor leading to the ocean, creates the ideal climate for cultivating the vines: mild temperatures, no frost, rain concentrated in the cold season, lots of water for irrigation, and no pollution all form the picture of an idyllic place to produce biological wine as they do here. Without pesticides, they are hand picked and all production phases are totally manual. The company produces wine from Cabernet Franc, Carmenére and Syrah grapes, for home consumption and sales to the local market.

PRODUCTION AREA
Placilla e San Ferdinando, VI region (O'Higgins)

COMMUNITY COORDINATOR
Alejandro Caerlos
tel. +56 97888619
castillodelaguaclara@gmail.com

Garlic growers in Chilote

The 12 members of this small association are mainly women, producing a special variety of garlic *Allium ampeloprasum*. The majority of them are housewives who divide their time between their housework and farming. Totally manual production methods are used, from preparing the soil, with the help of the oxen, to sowing in March and April, and the harvest in December or January. They use only natural fertilizer, such as manure or the seaweed they collect at low tide. The garlic they cultivate is also called elephant due to its large size: each head has at most six cloves, weighing around 120 grams each. A fete dedicated to the product is held every year on the island.

PRODUCTION AREA
Queilén, island of Chiloé, X region (Los Lagos)

COMMUNITY COORDINATOR
Patricio Andrés Contreras Silvas
tel. +56 65671243
pcontreras@indap.cl

Mapuche Black Quinoa growers in Southern Chile

Black quinoa (*Chenopodium quinoa wild*) is an endemic herbaceous plant in the Andes area, and the seeds are normally eaten, which are rich in protein and cooked using the recipes for rice, or are processed into flour or fermented to produce an alcoholic drink. The community of Mapuche farmers – who call the variety they have selected and traditionally grown dawe or zawe – do not have a formal organization, but work with a renewed cooperation each year, with meetings where they exchange seeds and discus how to deal with quinoa and how to market it. Besides internal consumption, the peasants sell it to the local markets and, in particular, to the hotels which appreciate its quality and nutritional properties.

PRODUCTION AREA
Gorbea, Lautaro, Lumaco, Nueva Imperial, Temuco and Villarrica, IX region (La Aruacanía)

COMMUNITY COORDINATOR
Max Felipe Thomet Isla
tel. +56 45248796
mthomet@cetsur.org

Mushroom pickers

Among the various products belonging to Mapuche traditions, mushrooms stand out, which the 200 members of this community still pick and sell today. The *Ramaria flava*, which they call changle, grows in the nearby damp woods and, as their survival is continuously threatened, it is in risk of extinction. The *Cyttaria espinosae*, which they call digueñe, grows on the tree trunks and is picked in the spring. Besides the mushrooms, another main product for the community are peas. All these products are eaten and sold fresh or dried, and help protect the local traditions and biodiversity, and they are valorized by special gastronomic events.

PRODUCTION AREA
Villarrica, IX region (La Araucanía); Panguipulli, X region (Los Lagos)

COMMUNITY COORDINATOR
Pablo Alex Flores Silva
tel. +56 45411830
pfloresl@puc.cl

País grape producers

País grapes are the most common variety in Chile, especially in the Biobio region, where they arrived around 500 years ago. The grapes have a tough skin, medium acidity, with a perfume of ripe berries and dark chocolate, the flavor is strong and distinct. It is a very hardy variety and perfect for the climate and soil features. In Guarilihue and Caravanchel, in the Coelemu countryside where peasants have been growing them for centuries, there is a farming community that grows them with natural manual methods. There are around 300 people who are convinced that vine and wine production is fundamental for local traditions and should be safeguarded and valorized. Besides wine, the país grapes are used to make fruit juice, liqueur, cooked must and a highly appreciated vinegar.

PRODUCTION AREA
Coelemu, VIII region (Biobío)

COMMUNITY COORDINATOR
Margarita Yañez
tel. +56 42430320
myanezmonje@yahoo.es

Pichilemu Seaweed pickers

Pichilemu is a town overlooking the ocean, and seaweed has always been a basic part of their diet, and still today the local women dedicate their time to picking them. Among the varieties they pick, with methods handed down over the generations, the main one is *Durvillaea antarctica*, which they call cochayuyo. It is very firm, pulpy and elastic seaweed, used in various recipes in the kitchen, from mixed salads to rich first courses, like vegetarian paella. Cochayuyo has nutritional properties that make it an important element in their daily diet: it has good contents of iodine, calcium, iron and magnesium and is rich in proteins and fibers.

PRODUCTION AREA
Pichilemu, VI region (O'Higgins)

COMMUNITY COORDINATOR
Loreto Isabel Puebla Muñoz
tel. +56 72842586
loretopuebla@hotmail.com

Pine nut producers

There are about 70 members of the Mapuche community who pick pine nuts and use them in various food preparations. The seeds are those found in very old trees, of the *Araucaria araucana* species, known locally as Chilean Pine, and very important in their traditions. Just think, the Pehuenche population, born from the Mapuche, took its name from this custom: in local dialect it means people of the pehuén, or pine nut. Now a permit is needed to harvest them, and once it has been obtained the expedition sets off into the woods and stays away for several days. The pine nuts are extracted from the cones and then stored in the harvesters' houses, where they are processed into flour or put in jars with syrup.

PRODUCTION AREA
Villarrica, IX region (La Araucanía); Panguipulli, X region (Los Lagos)

COMMUNITY COORDINATOR
Mario Caliñanco Huenumán
tel. +56 45411830
sumario14@gmail.com

Potato growers in Chiloé

Five Ancud families on the island of Chiloé (the largest in its archipelago), have joined together in a farming cooperative, where the women look after the farming and the men the cattle breeding. Among the vegetables they grow, the most important is the potato (*Solanum tuberosum*), an endemic product with numerous different varieties in shape, size, perfume, color and consistency. Some of the island farmers still remember that besides the numerous different types of potatoes that were grown there were also the wild ones that were picked along the roadsides and in the woods. The cooperative aims at keeping alive and promoting knowledge of this food and cultural heritage, aided by cooperation from a few local restaurants.

PRODUCTION AREA
Ancud, Island of Chiloé, X region (Los Lagos)

COMMUNITY COORDINATOR
Patricio Andrés Contreras Silva
tel. +56 65671243
pcontreras@indap.cl

Producers of Chilean Hazelnuts

The community is formed of about 40 farming families who live in the areas of Hualapulli and Calfutúe, in the rural area of Villarrica, and the majority of them belong to the Mapuche ethnic group. Besides farming they also breed cattle, make handicraft products and collect the wild berries. Their most important activity, deep rooted in Mapuche history, is picking the Chilean hazelnuts (*Gevuina avellana*) and transforming them into products used personally and sold to local markets. They use the hazelnuts to make a creamy spread, flour and a sort of coffee, but they also toast them to make them crisp. A lot of these families have now started cultivating them themselves.

PRODUCTION AREA
Villarrica, IX region (La Araucanía)

COMMUNITY COORDINATOR
Héctor Marín Manquecoy
tel. +56 45411830
biodiversidad@chile.com

Producers of palustrine blueberries

In the gastronomic traditions of the Mapuche people, a certain fruit has always been picked and processed by them: palustrine blueberries (*Ugni molinae*), which grow throughout Chile and are very perfumed, small, round with a deep red color. This community if formed of small Mapuche farmers – mainly women – who look after numerous different jobs, cattle breeding, weaving, organizing traditional ceremonies and feasts, but their most typical and important job is the harvest and processing of this wild blueberry, which some of them now cultivate as well. They use them to make syrup, a liqueur (called enmurtado or murato), jams and jellies, which are mainly for home consumption, but a small part is also sold to the local market.

PRODUCTION AREA
Villarrica, IX region (La Araucanía)

COMMUNITY COORDINATOR
Pablo Alex Flores Silva
tel. +56 45411830
pflores@puc.cl

Seed preservers

In three regions in Southern Chile: Biobío, La Aruacnía and Los Lagos, a few women live who dedicate their time to preserving a good part of their local heritage. The *curadoras*, which belong to the local Mapuche population, conserving a large amount of seeds of different varieties, and twice a year, at the beginning of spring and autumn, they get together to exchange their products and knowledge. They know when the seeds should be sown, the soil they should be planted in and the amount of water and sun they need. Their aim is to preserve the seeds that have been selected over the centuries, to protect their biodiversity and prevent the use of transgenic seeds. They also keep local gastronomy alive, cooperating with a group of Chilean chefs.

PRODUCTION AREA
Cañete, Coelemu and Tomé, VIII region (Biobío); Cholchol, Gorbea, Lautaro, Lumaco and Temuco, IX region (La Aruacanía); Liquiñe, X region (Los Lagos)

COMMUNITY COORDINATOR
Isolde Perez Ovalle
tel. +56 45248796
iperez@cetsur.org

Arhuaca farmers

The Arhuaca are an indigenous people of the Sierra Nevada, in the north of Colombia, with their own form of government and a traditional language and culture. They call themselves Ijka, which means "men of corn", as this cereal crop has always formed the basis of their diet and world view. The four colours the cereal may have – yellow, coffee brown, black and white – underpin the Ijka cosmogony and the organization of their life. They consider corn to be a sacred food and use it in magical and religious rites, as well as for medicinal purposes. The Ijka cultivate corn at various altitudes, exploiting all the territory's site climates, and use the crop in a wide range of foods, including arepa, a sort of fritter, and chicha, a fermented beverage.

PRODUCTION AREA
Departments of La Guajira, Magdalena and Cesar

COMMUNITY COORDINATOR
Moises Villafañe (Kaku Zarbatum)
tel. +57 12186593
slowfoodcolombia@yahoo.com

Blueberry pickers

Blueberries of the *Vaccinium meridionale* variety, which are very common in Colombia where they are known as agraz or mortiño, are picked by hand from spontaneous plants growing in the woods. The five producers in this community sell a small portion of their fruit fresh at local and national markets but send most of the crop to the El Robledal company, which processes it into jam by stewing it with sugar without chemical additives. The mortiño is found in an increasingly limited area and is at risk of extinction. This is why the association collaborates with academics and researchers from the faculty of agriculture at the Universidad Nacional de Colombia, who are studying the variety's genetic profile.

PRODUCTION AREA
Raquira and Tinjacá, department of Boyacá

COMMUNITY COORDINATOR
Gustavo Adolfo Ligarreto Moreno
tel. +57 13165000
galigarretom@unal.edu.co

Coarse Cane Sugar producers of La Vega

The production of coarse cane sugar, known locally as panela, is an activity whose roots lie deep in Columbia's past. In the La Vega area, cane sugar is grown using natural methods on small plots. After the harvest, it is pressed to extract the juice. The juice is then sieved and boiled until it reaches the required degree of concentration. Finally, it is powdered. The end product is sold mainly on the local and regional markets but an export plan is being drafted with the collaboration of Andines, a French fair trade organisation. The community also grows another traditional product, chayote (*Sechium edule*), and is recovering the ancient recipes for cooking it.

PRODUCTION AREA
La Vega, department of Cauca

COMMUNITY COORDINATOR
Dennis Marcela Bejarano Sánchez
tel. +57 3124680423
evasiembra@yahoo.es

Cocoa producers and pig and sheep breeders

El Tesoro, the community of Fr Gianfranco Testa, is situated near Melgar, a town in the department of Tolima, about 100 kilometres from Bogotá. It is a non-profit foundation that produces organic cocoa and farms various breeds of pigs and sheep typical of the zone, with the professional support of the university. The community's most important product is cocoa (1.2 tons per year), which is part-processed – it is fermented and dried – before it is sold to local companies. The pigs are farmed for meat and the sheep for milk, which is used to make cheese.

PRODUCTION AREA
Melgar, department of Tolima

COMMUNITY COORDINATOR
José Ricardo Yafi Rojas
tel. +57 14296511
gianfrancotesta2001@yahoo.com

Fruit and vegetable producers and processors

The varieties of fruit and vegetables grown by the Tinjacá community have always been available and consumed locally, but the members of this family business use them to make jams and pickles, adding value. The Peruvian groundcherry (*Physalis peruviana*) is planted and harvested by hand and then hulled, washed and split in two. It is left to stand with a little sugar. It is then stewed to make a jam, which is packed in jars without chemical additives. Blueberries of the *Vaccinium floribundum* variety are processed in a similar fashion whereas the tamarillo or tree tomato (*Cyphomandra betacea*) is conserved in jars with a syrup of water and sugar. Sweet peppers are cooked in vinegar and preserved in oil.

PRODUCTION AREA
Tinjacá, department of Boyacá

COMMUNITY COORDINATOR
Andrés Uribe Salazar
tel. + 57 3123505534
andruribe48@yahoo.com

Fruit producers and processors

The 100 members of the Sumapaz association grow and process local fruit using traditional agricultural and gastronomic knowledge. The fruit is picked by hand and stored before being processed at a communal facility. Association members themselves distribute the products at fairs or the market in the Bogotá botanical gardens. Most of the products sold are jams and yoghurts prepared by processing local varieties of blackberry, blueberry (mortiño) and uva camarona (*Macleania rupestris*). Once much prized and eaten fresh, uva camarona experienced a period of neglect before it was rediscovered, partly thanks to the efforts of the association.

PRODUCTION AREA
Province of Sumapaz, department of Cundinamarca

COMMUNITY COORDINATOR
Jesús Iván Ortiz Poveda
tel. +57 16741089
jesusivanortizpoveda@yahoo.com.ar

Producers of aromatic herbs

The members of this community are united, organized and supported by the Sociedad Orgánicos de Santander (SAT), which aims to ensure they enjoy appropriate working, wage and living conditions. To that end, SAT organizes training workshops on the production and conservation of quality farm products. The community produces many kinds of aromatic herbs, including basil, oregano, thyme and dill traditionally used for the natural treatment of illnesses, and distributes them fresh, dried or in sauces. The principles underpinning the methods of cultivation are respect for the environment, especially soil and water, the use of unpolluted water and organic fertilizers, and the associated cultivation of different varieties.

PRODUCTION AREA
Bucaramanga, department of Santander

COMMUNITY COORDINATOR
Carlos Andrés Arias Bustos
tel. +57 7647811
andresarias111@yahoo.com

Vegetable farmers of Cundinamarca

The members of this community in the department of Cundimarca live in various villages, breeding animals and farming, their main source of income. They grow some flowers but the main crops are vegetables that over the years have adapted to the area's severe climate. The fields lie at altitudes between 2,500 and 2,800 metres and the average temperature is 12-15°C. The community, which is assisted by qualified professionals, was formed in the 1990s to distribute its products effectively in the face of competition from large-scale producers. Community members collaborate with academics and students on projects to safeguard their farming tradition, and with the municipality of Bogotá to improve city-dwellers' diets.

PRODUCTION AREA
Cota, Cogua, Zipaquirá, Guasca, Chía, Sesquile, Tausa, Tenjo and Nemocón, department of Cundinamarca

COMMUNITY COORDINATOR
Marila Segura Abril
tel. +57 16929860
seguraabril@gmail.com

Vegetable farmers of Sabana de Bogotá

Sabana de Bogotá is a plateau at an average altitude of 2,600 metres. The river Bogotá, which crosses it from north to south, feeds a large number of lagoons and ponds, creating a temperate climate and making the land fertile. A community of small-scale farmers on this plateau has contributed to solving the serious malnutrition problems of the local population. The farmers' main products are high-altitude vegetables, most of them organic, including white cabbage, salad leaves, carrots, sugar beet, red onions, spinach, broccoli and radish. The community has also set up 26 education centres, mainly for young people, where the rules of a healthy, varied, natural diet are taught.

PRODUCTION AREA
Sabana de Bogotá, department of Cundinamarca

COMMUNITY COORDINATOR
María Consuelo Vergar Holguin
tel. +57 16813851
maconnet74@yahoo.com

ZERI FOUNDATION, COFFEE-PRODUCING CENTER

The Zeri Foundation (Zero Emissions Research and Initiatives) is a network of scholars and professional people who, faced with the ever more numerous problems of our planet, are trying to find sustainable solutions for society and the environment, inspired by the designs of nature, that limit waste wherever possible. In Colombia, the organization intervened in a moment of crisis on the coffee market, starting up production that exploits harvesting waste, and crops that can be grown alongside coffee, such as bananas, mushrooms and a type of fast-growing bamboo (*Gaudua angustifolia*), which represents a renewable resource and an excellent building material. The most significant building constructed with this type of bamboo is the Pabellón Zeri, designed by Simón Vélez for Expo Hanover 2000.

AREA OF ACTIVITY
Manizales, department of Caldas

ASSOCIATION COORDINATOR
Carlos Bernal
tel. +57 12588919
bernalzeri@cable.net.co

Organic producers of Talamanca

The Asociación de Pequeños Productores de Talamanca is an umbrella organisation for more than 1,000 small-scale organic farmers in the Talamanca area, in the south of Costa Rica. Most belong to one of two indigenous local peoples, the Bribri and the Cabécar. Farming is based on the joint cultivation of several crops, of which the most important is cocoa, the mainstay of the local economy and culture. The cacao tree is sacred and features in all ceremonies. It is cultivated with araza and pejibaye (*Bactris gasipaes*) trees, in the shade of timber and banana trees, particularly the Gros Mitchel variety. Harvesting involves all members of the household.

PRODUCTION AREA
Bribri, province of Talamanca

COMMUNITY COORDINATOR
Walter Rodríguez Vargas
tel. +506 7510435
walter@appta.org

Raw milk cheesemakers of Turrialba

The Turrialba community has about 200 members. They make a soft, cream-coloured cheese from raw milk using artisanal methods, unchanged for a century, which bring out the flavour, aroma and uniqueness of the raw material. Some 90% of members are directly involved in cheesemaking and contribute to the production of 150 tons of cheese each year, which is sold on the domestic market and abroad.

PRODUCTION AREA
Santa Cruz, province of Cartago

COMMUNITY COORDINATOR
Marvin Blanco Murillo
tel. +506 2852612
mblanco@infoagro.net

Sugar cane growers of Jaris de Mora

Founded in 1990, the Asprodulce association unites 80 producers and processors from the Jaris de Mora area in the province of San José. The main source of income, along with fruit production and pig breeding, growing sugar cane, a traditional activity now less widely practised than in the past. Selected canes ground at 18 small local mills yield a high quality, intense brown sugar that is highly prized and reasonably remunerative.

PRODUCTION AREA
Jaris de Mora, province of San José

COMMUNITY COORDINATOR
Johnny José Alpizar Salazar
tel. +506 4162020
asprodulce@cedeco.or.cr

Sugar cane producers of San Ramón

The 670 members of this community belong to a cooperative that owns the country's smallest sugar cane factory (there are 16 factories in Costa Rica and a total of 7,000 producers). Production is mostly for the internal market and self-consumption, but each year a small proportion (8%) is exported to Europe. The plants are spaced one metre apart. After one year, the canes are harvested manually using an ordinary knife. They are then ground, and their juice extracted and crystallized by evaporation. The cooperative is supported by the Liga Agrícola e Industrial de la Caña de Azúcar, which was formed in 1965 to coordinate the production and distribution of sugar cane in Costa Rica.

PRODUCTION AREA
San Ramón, province of Alajuela

COMMUNITY COORDINATOR
Jesús María Villalobos Gamboa
tel. +506 4455617
ingenio@racsa.co.cr

Asociación de Cooperativas sin Fronteras

The Asociación de Cooperativas sin Fronteras has its headquarters in Costa Rica, but groups together 18 organizations of small producers operating in a number of Latin American countries: Brazil, Argentina, Nicaragua, Costa Rica, Guatemala, Panama and Peru. Its objective is to promote an exchange of experience and collaboration between members, helping them to acquire knowledge and to market their products, and to obtain the Designation of Origin for their organic products. The most important of these are coffee, which is cultivated in a natural state up to an altitude of 2000 meters; cocoa, which grows in the shade of the tropical forests, two types of cane sugar (the natural raw variety and the white industrial variety), and several types of fruit which is sold fresh or used to make jams and juices.

AREA OF ACTIVITY
San José, province of San José

ASSOCIATION COORDINATOR
Hugo Vicente Valdés Cifuentes
tel. +506 236 5198
h.valdes@cedeco.or.cr

Agricultural machinery producers

The community produces animal-drawn farm machinery and utensils whose action on the soil is innovative with respect to traditional tools. The vertical action of an ordinary plough turns over the top layer of soil and mixes it, but the new version cuts the soil vertically and horizontally without turning it over, leaving the remains of the crop on the surface. This safeguards the soil's natural characteristics, encourages the accumulation of organic material, ensures the survival of microorganisms in the soil and reduces emissions of greenhouse gases, laying the foundations for sustainable farming. The machines are the result of 30 years of research, and the joint efforts of agronomists, biologists and mechanics.

PRODUCTION AREA
Ciudad de La Habana

COMMUNITY COORDINATOR
José Arnaldo Zuaznabar García
tel. +53 451111-451731-973104
prodmec@sih.cu

Farmers and stock breeders of Santa Barbara-Campo Florido

Economic difficulties during the 1990s meant that in many parts of the island, including Santa Barbara, the area of land used for farming increased. The eastern part of the province of Ciudad de La Habana is little industrialized and has an ancient tradition of farming and animal breeding. Although the soil is not very fertile and unsuitable for intensive farming, it is possible to grow food for self-consumption, thanks in part to the abundant availability of water. The community farms pigs, rabbits, goats (mainly for milk), sheep, hens (mainly for eggs), all from breeds selected for their resistance to the tropical climate. It also grows vegetables, wheat and cereals for self-consumption and to feed the animals. Lack of access to chemical fertilizers and pesticides has prompted the adoption of organic methods.

PRODUCTION AREA
Habana del Este, province of Ciudad de La Habana

COMMUNITY COORDINATOR
Aurelia María Castellanos Quintero
tel. +53 5378733214
filial@acpahav.co.cu

Producers of conserved foods

The community project for the conservation of foodstuffs, condiments and medicinal plants came into being in 1995 in the Pogolotti district of Mairanao. The island's economic and food situation was critical. The project's founders attempted a solution by circulating knowledge and experience to other members of the community through workshops, fairs, exhibitions, meetings and the media. Today, the project's scope extends beyond the district and involves the whole of the country. Producers do not use chemical additives and prepare their conserves to personal recipes, utilizing classic conservation processes such as sun-drying, fermentation, pasteurization, immersion in vinegar, sugaring and salting.

PRODUCTION AREA
Marianao, province of Ciudad de La Habana

COMMUNITY COORDINATOR
José Antonio Lama Martínez
tel. +53 2609068
conserva@ceniai.inf.cu

Tropical fruit farmers

The community comprises two associations, the Circulo de Interés Amigos de la Naturaleza and the Comité de Investigación Agrícola Local, which set up the Fruticultura Comunitaria Participativa project. The initiative aims to educate people about their relationship with the environment, safeguard vegetable varieties at risk of extinction and develop small-scale rural industry to add value to production. The community's most representative product is the marañon or cashew (*Anacardium occidentale*), which has a range of uses as a food. Its juice is drunk and it is eaten as a fresh fruit (the edible part is actually a hypertrophy of the flower stem) or in the form of toasted seeds from the nut that constitutes the terminal part. All products are for self-consumption and for sale in local markets.

PRODUCTION AREA
Peralejo, province of Granma

COMMUNITY COORDINATOR
Narciso Aguilera Marín
tel. +53 2367605
leonelalejo.grm@infomed.sld.cu

Urban farmers

The community of San José de las Lajas owes its name to the highly urbanized nature of the area. Farming has always been very important and has experienced remarkable growth over the past decade. The community's main objective is the economic and social development of the region through the production and distribution of local fruit and vegetables while protecting the environment and ensuring food safety. The members of the organization grow organic products, including various vegetables, garlic, parsley and guava, a tropical plant whose elongated fruit has a yellow-green skin and red pulp. The soil is fertilized with earthworm humus produced on members' own farms. Pest control is carried out using natural methods.

PRODUCTION AREA
San José de las Lajas, province of La Habana

COMMUNITY COORDINATOR
Rafael Ojeda Suárez
tel. +53 78732109
rafael.ojeda@infomed.sld.cu

PROYECTO COMUNITARIO DE CONSERVACIÓN DE ALIMENTOS

It was 1995 when the community project for the conservation of food, spices and herbs was started in Barrio Pogolotti, Marianao, in the province of Ciudad de La Habana. The economic and food situation on the island was very critical and the founders of the project tried to find a solution by spreading knowledge and sharing experience with the other members of the community, through laboratories, fairs, exhibitions, meetings and recourse to the media. Today the project's scope of action has spread outside the original district and involves the entire country. The information campaigns now focus on traditional recipes and classic conservation techniques: drying in the sun, fermentation, pasteurizing, pickling, and the addition of sugar and salt, but not chemicals.

AREA OF ACTIVITY
The entire country

ASSOCIATION COORDINATOR
José Antonio Lama Martínez
tel. +53 2609068
conserva@ceniai.inf.cu

Coffee producers from the upper basin of the Yuna river

The Asociación de Caficultores la Independencia (Asocain) was set up on 31 October 1998, after hurricane George had caused a considerable drop in coffee production. The communities involved in the association are based around Bonao, in the Yuna river basin, where coffee has always been one of the most important crops. The 800 producers in the association battle to gain fair prices for their coffee, to be able to sell without intermediaries and to improve quality. The coffee is an Arabica, composed of 60% Typica and 40% Caturra, both fairly large-sized beans. The coffee has an intense aroma and a fruity flavor, medium acidity, and remains long on the palate. The most important of the other products grown by community members is rice, one of the country's staples.

PRODUCTION AREA
Bonao, province of Monseñor Nouel

COMMUNITY COORDINATOR
Luis Henríque Núñez
tel. +1809 5258625
asocain@hotmail.com

Jamao Coffee producers

The rural territory of Jamao lies in the zone of La Loma, in the province of Salcedo, and divides into the outer (Jamao Afuera) and upper (Jamao Arriba) areas. The principal product of the community living here is a fully-flavored Arabica coffee with an intense, long-lasting aroma and a nutty aftertaste. The beans are grown at between 700 and 1,400 meters. They also grow shaded by other plants. This brings crop diversification, thereby protecting biodiversity and reducing the risk of diseases. One of the most important of the plants used to shade the coffee is avocado, *Persea americana*, which requires little attention and is harvested at a different period from the coffee crop. Hence growers gain a second source of income.

PRODUCTION AREA
Jamao, province of Salcedo

COMMUNITY COORDINATOR
Gregorio Camilo González
tel. +1809 5773414
coscafe@jamao.com

Andean vegetable and cereal farmers

In the north of Ecuador on a plateau about 2,400 metres above sea level, local people have created a project that in many respects is reminiscent of Slow Food's school gardens. At the initiative of UNORCAC, an organization of indigenous peoples founded in 1977, household or school-run vegetable gardens have been set up in 12 native communities. The products, which include all the typical high-altitude vegetables and a number of Andean cereal crops, are used above all to improve children's diet, but some are sold locally to ensure new economic resources for the population. Farming complies with the rules of integrated pest management and special attention is devoted to water management.

PRODUCTION AREA
Canton of Cotacachi, province of Imbabura

COMMUNITY COORDINATOR
María Teresa Farinango Guandinango
tel. +593 62916664
antonella.ronco@ucodep.org

Cereal farmers of Chimborazo

In each of the 102 communities in the indigenous rural part of the province of Chimborazo, women's associations have been set up for cereal farming and the production of a children's food called Cereal Nutrivital. Using production systems inspired by the ancient techniques of the Kitchwa natives, about 5,000 women grow various types of herbaceous plants and cereals that have been the basis of the local diet since ancient times. Important crops are protein-rich quinoa, and tarwi or chocho, the Andean lupin (*Lupinus mutabilis*). The women also have a facility for making flour and Cereal Nutrivital, obtained by mixing three types of flour: quinoa, fava beans and barley. The preparation, diluted in warm water, is given to children under eight years old.

PRODUCTION AREA
Riobamba, Guamote, Colta, Tixan and Alausí, province of Chimborazo

COMMUNITY COORDINATOR
María Eugenia Lima Garzón
tel. +593 22468421
fundamyf@andinanet.net

Cocoa producers of Nord Esmeraldas

Aprocane is an association founded in 2000 that today has 429 small-scale member producers of Nacional cocoa, most of them African-Ecuadorians, in various parts of the north of the province of Esmeraldas. The association's initial aim was to protect woodland threatened by indiscriminate deforestation. Subsequently, it expanded into the production of cocoa, a traditional crop in the area. Ecuador's particularly aromatic and spicy Nacional cocoa bean is one of the best in the world. Association producers grow and process the bean from fermentation and drying to packaging in jute sacks, which are then sold on the international market, principally in Switzerland and Italy.

PRODUCTION AREA
Cantons of Eloy Alfaro, San Lorenzo and Rioverde, province of Esmeraldas

COMMUNITY COORDINATOR
Néstor Lemos
tel. + 593 62786027-62786811
jmeston@yahoo.com

Coffee producers of the South

Four associations of small-scale southern Ecuadorian coffee producers (APECAM, APECAP, PROCAFEQ and PROCAP) joined forces to form the Federación regional de asociaciones de pequeños cafetaleros del Sur (FAPECAFES). Arabica coffee is farmed and processed to obtain an organic product. FAPECAFES markets five types, one originally from Vilcabamba. This part of Ecuador is outstandingly suitable for growing very high quality coffee. Plantations are located between 800 and 2,100 metres above sea level, the climate is subtropical, the temperature ranges from 18 to 24 °C and the rainfall of about 1,200 cubic millimetres a year encourages abundant vegetation.

PRODUCTION AREA
Provinces of Loja, El Oro and Zamora Chinchipe

COMMUNITY COORDINATOR
Roberto Jiménez
tel. +593 72583478-62786027
rvjimenz@fapecafes.org.ec

Indigenous farmers of Cotacachi

The farmers of 44 rural communities have set up the Unión de organizaciones campesinas indígenas de Cotachi (UNORCAC) and produce largely for self-consumption, selling only products that are excess to requirements. Their main crops are corn and vetch, which form the basis of the local diet and for which traditional techniques are used. The community also cultivates blackberries from the Andes, which are used to make jam for sale. Some of the women are setting up an association to process farm products, for example to produce sambo seeds (a variety of pumpkin common in Ecuador) and creams based on medicinal plants. The group also farms about 6,000 guinea pigs a year for self-consumption, raising them in groups of 11 in small cages.

PRODUCTION AREA
Canton of Cotacachi, province of Imbabura

COMMUNITY COORDINATOR
Hugo Fabián Carrera Rueda
tel. +593 62916012
unorcacrrnn@hotmail.com

Producers of aromatic herbs

Made up mainly of women, this community is called Jambi Kiwa and brings together about 600 families, almost all native Puruhaes. Activity focuses on the production of medicinal and aromatic plants, teas, infusions and essential oils, as well as smaller quantities of shampoos and creams. The herbs used for the purpose are grown using natural methods or picked to criteria of sustainability in an area whose many ecosystems and climates endow it with an incredible wealth of biodiversity. The herbs are processed at a facility owned by the organization and marketed both domestically and internationally. The selection of raw materials and the various recipes used are based on traditional knowledge that has belonged to this native population since time immemorial.

PRODUCTION AREA
Riobamba, province of Chimborazo

COMMUNITY COORDINATOR
Rosa Gauman
tel. +593 32951026
jambikiwa@ch.pro.ec

Producers of honey and derived products

The Cotacachi beekeepers' association comprises about 200 native families who have been producing honey for several years. The organization's hives are located on the slopes of the Cotacachi volcano (4,944 metres) at the Cotacachi-Cayapas reserve, one of the world's ten most important bioregions. Beekeeping was little practised in the area until a few years ago but today has become an important source of income that has enabled the community's members to improve their living conditions and conserve the environment. Production is sold directly on the local market, and in recent years has extended to the rest of Ecuador. The range of products includes honey (3,000 kilograms a year), pollen (200 kilograms) and delicious artisanal honey nougat bars (100 kilograms a year).

PRODUCTION AREA
Canton of Cotacachi, province of Imbabura

COMMUNITY COORDINATOR
Luis Guillermo Grijalva Cevallos
tel. + 593 062915602
grijalva63@yahoo.es

Producers of Salinas

Until the 1970s, the main economic activity at Salinas was the extraction and sale of salt. The population lived in poverty: infant mortality was running at 45% and 85% of the population was illiterate. In late 1971, change came with the creation of the first of the 28 cooperatives that make up the present community. Through this organization, local residents have become owners of the land and equipment they use to produce milk, cheese, dried mushrooms, chocolate, tea, infusions, salt, jams, cold meats and livestock. Currently, there are 7,400 people (75% of the local population) involved in the community's economic activities. The distribution network extends over the whole of Ecuador.

PRODUCTION AREA
Salinas, province of Bolívar

COMMUNITY COORDINATOR
Luis Alfonso González Oña
tel. +593 32390020

Quinoa farmers of Chimborazo

Quinoa is a herbaceous plant from the Andes which the Incas held sacred. Today, it is grown mainly in Ecuador, Bolivia and Peru. The seeds are highly nutritious, gluten-free and rich in proteins, carbohydrates, unsaturated fats, vitamins, fibre and minerals. The small-scale producers of the Taita Chimborazo community (the name means "Father Chimborazo", from the volcano after which the province is named) are mainly indigenous Puruhaes who live and grow quinoa with other products at about 4,000 metres above sea level. The techniques employed are traditional and manual. No chemical fertilizers or pesticides are used, ensuring health-giving, high-quality products. The quinoa is sold mainly in France and the United States.

PRODUCTION AREA
Riobamba, province of Chimborazo

COMMUNITY COORDINATOR
Jenny Arias
tel. +593 32961608-32960221-32960247
ferpe@erpe.org.ec

Quinoa farmers of San Nicolas de Ichubamba

The community has 40 members who practise agricultural and livestock farming, especially quinoa farming and alpaca breeding. Supported by FEPP, an Ecuadorian fund that assists native and African-Ecuadorian farmers' organizations, the community believes it is necessary to differentiate production to encourage rural life. For this reason, it has focused on quinoa, which is rich in nutritional elements, an excellent crop for safeguarding the quality and stability of the soil, and has a wide range of uses. Quinoa may be used to make oils or flour and in a vast range of food preparations. Alpaca has an equally wide range of uses. The meat may be eaten fresh in sausages, the skin is used to make leather and the dung produces manure.

PRODUCTION AREA
San Nicolas de Ichubamba, province of Chimborazo

COMMUNITY COORDINATOR
Iván Marcelo García Viscarra
tel. +593 23227911
igarcia@fepp.org.ec
exportaciones@salinerito.com

Producers of dehydrated fruit .

Ten women work together in the department of Chalatenango in a small business called Prodesol, which produces dehydrated fruit. Thanks to the CORDES foundation, set up in the late 1980s to promote sustainable development, sex equality and respect for the environment, there has been a remarkable increase in the number of fruit trees, such as papaya, pineapple, mango, banana and coconut, in the local area. The initiative has brought great benefits to the community, making greater quantities of locally produced raw materials available. The process for making the finished product is straightforward. The fruit is sliced and put into solar ovens, which are therefore perfectly compatible with the environment, where it remains for two to four days. It is then packaged and sold locally.

PRODUCTION AREA
Guargila, department of Chalatenango

COMMUNITY COORDINATOR
Yanett Rodríguez de Flores
tel. + 503 22358262
cordes.ri@telesal.net

Producers of cashew nuts

Anacardium occidentale is a tropical plant that produces what appear to be two fruits joined together, one fresh and the other dry. In fact, although the fresh part is edible and has a pleasant flavour, it is not a true fruit but a swollen flower stem. The actual fruit is the second part, an oily seed protected by a kidney-shaped shell. The production of these seeds, known as cashews, is the main activity of the Tecoluca community, supported by the CORDES foundation. Sixty farmers are involved in growing and processing. The first stage is discarding the hard shell of the seeds. These are then roasted and the film that covers them is removed. The seeds are classified into whole, half and split categories, and finally packed for sale on the international market.

PRODUCTION AREA
Tecoluca, department of San Vicente

COMMUNITY COORDINATOR
Fredy Orlando López
tel. +503 22358262
cordes.ri@telesal.net

Producers of coarse cane sugar

The CORDES foundation supports a group of 12 producers of coarse cane sugar at Tejutepeque. This kind of sugar, known as panela, has long been a feature of the local gastronomic tradition. It is used to sweeten typical beverages like coffee and atoles, a drink made from corn flour cooked in water or milk, or snack foods such as pumpkin or banana cakes. Traditionally, panela was shaped into a small cone wrapped in the leaves that cover the corncob. Today, panela is sold as small granules in packets. Recently, the producers have accomplished a leap forward in quality and acquired capacity to carry out the entire production process independently, from growing sugar cane to refining the sugar.

PRODUCTION AREA
Tejutepeque, department of Cabañas

COMMUNITY COORDINATOR
David Sibrián
tel. +503 22358262·
cordes.ri@telesal.net

Producers of honey

Forty-six beekeepers in the department of La Libertad and 12 in Cuscatlán produce honey with the support of the CORDES foundation, which over the past ten years has planted fruit trees in several parts of the country. Native trees such as the ipê and maquilishuat (*Tabebuia rosea*) have been supplemented by persimmons, medlars, bananas and various citrus fruit trees. This makes it possible for beekeepers to produce high-quality honey if they have the necessary equipment and workers to extract, filter and package the product.

PRODUCTION AREA
Tamanique and Comasuaga, department of La Libertad; Sichitoto and Cinquera, department of Cuscatlán

COMMUNITY COORDINATOR
Adrián Martínez Valencia
tel. +503 22358262
cordes.ri@telesal.net

Growers and processors of medicinal plants

Created in 2003, the Casa Barillense de las Mujeres cooperative is formed of 35 women who grow medicinal plants and 10 who process them to make different products: creams, ointment, shampoo, liquid soap, tinctures and cough syrups. They cultivate the herbs without any chemical products and only manual methods are used to transform them, respecting the ancient traditions of the Maya people. That old civilization not only used certain herbs for holy ceremonies, but also appreciated their therapeutic qualities. Among the large number of varieties the most important are, pot marigold, basil, fennel, camomile, lemon-balm, mint, thyme, rue and another plant similar to tarragon (*Tajetes lucida*), traditionally used against stomach pains and colic.

PRODUCTION AREA
Barillas, department of Huehuetenango

COMMUNITY COORDINATOR
Rafaela Pérez Escalante
tel. +502 77802796
casabmujeres@hotmail.com

Pacaya and pepper growers

Amidst the highlands of San Cristóbal Verapaz, the 200 members of the Asociación de Caficultores de Tamahu e San Cristóbal keep alive cultivations that have been handed down over the centuries, such as pepper and pacaya, an eatable palm that grows at 1200 meters altitude and higher. In the various dialects it is called chem chem, ixqui quib, qui'b, pacaya is an important source of vitamins. It is used in several Guatemala traditional recipes; it can be eaten salcochada, i.e. seasoned with lemon and salt. The pepper is used as a spice and for preserving food products and is also used to treat mal de ojo, an eye illness that hits children in that area.

PRODUCTION AREA
Cobán, department of Alta Verapaz

COMMUNITY COORDINATOR
Williams Picón Soberanis
tel. +502 79504301
icpguate@yahoo.com

Southwest Honey producers

The 135 small beekeepers in the Cooperative Producción Integral Apicultores del Sur Occidente (Copiasuro) are spread around the three departments of Huehuetenango, San Marcos and Quetzaltenango. To make the honey, the bees process the nectar gathered in their honey bag with their digestive juices, it is then regurgitated and deposited in the honeycomb. The resulting mixture is very syrupy, contains fructose, glucose, saccharine and other sugars, besides a large amount of water and other minor components, such as vitamins, minerals and aromatic principles. The structure of the hives where the bees are kept by the cooperative means the best moisture level is maintained of 17-18.5%. Their honey is sold to international markets.

PRODUCTION AREA
Departments of Huehuetenango, San Marcos and Quetzaltenango

COMMUNITY COORDINATOR
Álvaro Milto Almengor Escobar
tel. +502 77227326
copiasurorl@hotmail.com

Northern cocoa producers

Haiti is the poorest country in the Caribbean, with an extremely high rate of unemployment and a farming sector that faces considerable challenges. The soil is relatively poor, there are no advanced irrigation systems and machinery is scarce. Fertile soil is mainly used to grow products for export. Cocoa produced by the FECCANO community in the north of Haiti is sold on the international market, although some is distributed domestically or used for self-consumption. FECCANO is a federation of six cooperatives representing 3,800 small producers, more than one third of whom are women. They produce a total of 250 tons of Fair Trade-certified cocoa each year.

PRODUCTION AREA
Cap-Haïtien, Nord department

COMMUNITY COORDINATOR
Guito Gilot
tel. +509 4111074
guitog@yahoo.fr

Farmers, fishers and artisans of La Ceiba

The Garífuna community comprises 450,000 people in 64 villages along the northern coast of Honduras. Originating in the Antilles, where Caribbean islanders interbred with a group of slaves who arrived from Africa in the second half of the eighteenth century, the community conserves its original social structure, language and traditions. Community members work mainly in farming, fishing and craft manufacture. These activities are performed in compliance with a social division of labour. The men prepare the ground, fish and process raw materials while women sow, tend and harvest the field crops, and cook and sell the community's products. One of the group's traditional foods is a yucca cake called casabe ("ereba" in the Garífuna language).

PRODUCTION AREA
La Ceiba, department of Atlántida

COMMUNITY COORDINATOR
José Ángel Manaiza-Casildo
tel. I 504 4145434
josemanaiza@yahoo.es

Growers of organic products

The Treasure Beach farmers' association was formed in January 2006 to grow organic products, especially legumes (mainly peas) and vegetables, including tomatoes, broccoli and peppers. Association farmers use traditional, natural methods such as mulching and collecting rainwater to combat the area's droughts. The association rejects the chemical fertilizers and pesticides generally used elsewhere on the island, considering them to be pollutants of the soil and prejudicial to human health. The aim of the association is to expand the market for organic products by establishing commercial relations with tourism-related businesses in the area and raising awareness of organic products.

PRODUCTION AREA
Saint Elizabeth, district of Treasure Beach

COMMUNITY COORDINATOR
Elizabeth Solms
tel. +1876 3521375
lizathon@aol.com

Rastafarian producers of Ital Food

In the language of the Rastafarians, a political and religious movement that grew up in Jamaica in the 1930s, Ital derives from "vital". The word indicates the natural, pure, clean qualities that Rastafarian food must have because dietary rules strictly forbid chemical additives, salt, meat – especially pork – and blood. The community has 12 members who produce alcoholic beverages by fermenting herbs, roots and fruits such as plums, mangos, bananas and cashews that they grow themselves, various hot powders from spices such as turmeric, ginger or pepper to use both in cooking and for medication, and a characteristic sauce known as jerk.

PRODUCTION AREA
Bunkers Hill, district of Trelawny

COMMUNITY COORDINATOR
Markus Braun
tel. +1876 5393802
markusbraun@cwjamaica.com

Agave and Mescal producers of Chilapa de Álvarez

The150 members of this community are spread between four municipalities near to Chilapa de Álvarez: 110 of these grow agaves and the others use them to make mescal. The plants are seeded in nurseries and then planted in open spaces without creating plantations or monocultures. In order to make mescal, mature agave is crushed with a pestle and then allowed to ferment in 250 liter wooden barrels. After a period of between 3 to 15 days, it is then distilled twice in copper alembics. Each producer decides what alcohol content he wants (usually between 48 and 52 %). The liquor's taste depends on the kind of agave that was used to produce it, the conditions in which the plant grew and the preparation method used to make the liquor.

PRODUCTION AREA
Chilapa de Álvarez, state of Guerrero

COMMUNITY COORDINATOR
Refugio Calzada
tel. +52 567 475 1227
macarena@laneta.apc.org

Agave Honey and Jam producers

This community is located in an area with an arid climate where it rarely rains, and if it does, then only during the months of July and August. The only possible crop here is agave. These food producers, all of which are women and nearly all of which belong to the Otomí ethnic group, sow, harvest and process this endemic plant that is highly resistant to drought and use it to make honey and jam. The honey is a concentrate of the juice extracted from the agave: very high in vitamins and minerals, it can be used as a substitute for sugar. It is also believed locally to have curative properties for several illnesses such as osteoporosis, diabetes and respiratory disorders. The jam is made by cooking the pulp of agave fruits, which are oval in shape with a sweet taste and a meaty texture.

PRODUCTION AREA
Valle del Mezquital, state of Hidalgo

COMMUNITY COORDINATOR
María Consepción Pérez Matínez
tel. +52 555 661 2061
scontreras@bioplaneta.com

Avocado growers

The avocado is a fruit that originates from Latin America. According to the variety it can be oval, spherical or pear-shaped. The members of the Cupanda cooperative produce two different varieties: Criollo and, above all, Hass. The Hass avocado is oval with a strong, shiny skin that turns black or dark purple when the fruit is mature; the flesh is light yellow. It has a high fat content (30%), and is also high in water, vitamins and mineral salts. The farmers of this community practice organic farming and receive technical assistance from the cooperative, particularly with regards to phytosanitary treatments. The organization sells its products across the nation and has been exporting them abroad to places such as France, Costa Rica and Canada, for over 15 years.

PRODUCTION AREA
Tacambaro, state of Michoacán

COMMUNITY COORDINATOR
Leovigildo Ortega Trejo
tel. +52 459 596 0047
cupanda@prodigy.net.mx

Chaya growers

The area around the coastal town of Tututepec is inhabited by the Mixteca indigenous population and is characterized by its great cultural wealth and extraordinary natural resources, which have been disappearing over the last few decades. The 32 families that form the Sociedad de Solidaridad Social (SSS) have started promoting initiatives encouraging the rational use of resources and preserving agricultural, gastronomic and craft knowledge. The community's main product is Chaya, a plant rich in protein, vitamin A and iron whose leaves are used in local cuisine. Other products include two legumes: Moringa, whose leaves, pods and seeds are eaten, and the *Mucuna pruriens*, which is used both in cuisine and medicine.

PRODUCTION AREA
Tututepec, state of Oaxaca

COMMUNITY COORDINATOR
Hilario Felipe Cruz Alavez
tel. +52 954 541 0065
ecosta@laneta.apc.org

Chili Pepper cultivators

The chili pepper is one of the main ingredients of the oldest Mexican gastronomic tradition. This community is formed of four work groups with a total of 40 people (20 of which are women) that form two distinct companies. All of these people are engaged in the cultivation of a kind of chili pepper known as Chile manzano (*Capsicum pubescens*). It has a characteristic apple shape, orange skin and black seeds. This is a perennial plant that is cultivated alongside fruit trees such as avocado and peach trees. It is grown in vegetable gardens no larger than five hectares at an altitude of at least 2000 meters above sea level. Once seeding has been carried out, it needs a further 70 days before the seedlings can be planted. Three months after that the first chilies are ready to harvest and from then on the chilies are produced all year round.

PRODUCTION AREA
Zitácuaro, state of Michoacán

COMMUNITY COORDINATOR
Jacobo Sánchez Martínez
tel. +52 715 157 3922
jacobo_sanchezmartinez@yahoo.com.mx

Coffee and chocolate producers of San Rafael Toltepec

San Rafael Toltepec, an area belonging to the municipality of San Pedro Pochutla, is situated in Southern Oaxaca, at 400 meters above sea level. Numbering around 800 inhabitants, it is a small collection of wooden houses with roofs made from palm leaves, surrounded by luxuriant vegetation. Here there is a cooperative formed of 100 producers engaged in the production of coffee and the preparation of chocolate products made with cocoa, cinnamon, raw cane sugar and sometimes almonds. The coffee is grown at between 900 to 2000 meters above sea level. By blending the Caracolillo and Robusta varieties, the producers obtain a high quality product. The community has plans to organize a route through the plantations so that visitors can learn all about coffee and its production.

PRODUCTION AREA
San Pedro Pochutla, state of Oaxaca

COMMUNITY COORDINATOR
José Iturriaga de la Fuente
tel. +52 777 382 0316-777 382 6082
jniturriagaf@yahoo.com.mx

Coffee producers of Huatusco

Bourbon, Typica, Caturra and Garnica are the most common varieties of coffee grown in the region of Huatusco, which has been involved in the cultivation of this crop for several generations. These plants require allot of care, both during the cultivation (pruning, cleaning, fertilization and reseeding), and during the harvest, which keeps the cultivators, busy from October to March. The first harvest takes place about three or four years after sowing, but the plants only produce coffee that is fit for sale after seven years. The Pequeños Productores de Café, Agropecuaria, Forestal y de Agroindustria association, which is made up of nearly 2000 local coffee growers aims to manage a centre where the association's members can roast and grind their coffee. It also hopes to create two brands that will distinguish their coffee and give it added value.

PRODUCTION AREA
Huatusco, state of Veracruz

COMMUNITY COORDINATOR
Angelino Espinoza Mata
tel. +52 273 734 2355
uregional@prodigy.net.mx

Desiccated locust producers

The traditional preparation of insect-based foods, which the members of this community are involved in, belongs to an entomophagous culture. They gather the locusts (*Sphenarium purpurascens*) in the cornfields, wash them, select them and then cook them with salt and lemon; they are finally desiccated and then packed into jars. The small insects can also be minced and combined with other ingredients such as iodized salt, to make a powder used for seasoning food. Agave worms are roasted and ground and then can be salted and combined with chili to make a powder or mixed with chili, cooked green tomatoes, salt and lemon to make a sauce. The locusts are rich in protein and are a good substitute for meat, which is very expensive in these areas.

PRODUCTION AREA
Oaxaca de Juárez, state of Oaxaca

COMMUNITY COORDINATOR
Hugo Sandoval Bolaños
tel. +52 951 515 9507
chapuguin@hotmail.com

Ecological food producers of Xonacatlán

Using organic techniques and tools, this group of 18 food producers in the Xonacatlán area is dedicated to cultivation, animal breeding and the processing of agricultural produce. It therefore sells fresh produce as well as prepared foods and preserves. The prickly pears, which are cultivated in a natural way, are harvested, de-spined, washed and cut into pieces. They then add vinegar, vegetables and chili and pack the mixture into glass jars. They also prepare jam using a variety of cherries known locally as Capulín, and use chopped chilies (*Capsicum anum*) together with oil, garlic and onion to make a spicy sauce. In four different farms they also breed rabbits, which are sold butchered or cooked, according to the customers needs.

PRODUCTION AREA
Xonacatlán, state of México

COMMUNITY COORDINATOR
Laura Margarita Perea Avila
tel. +52 722 267 3030
lauavat@yahoo.com.mx

Farmers and fishermen of Escuinapa

This community is formed of three organizations that unite several different cooperatives for a total of 94 members. The members of this community carry out various different activities in Sinaloa State. In land basins of about five hectares in size they breed white shrimps in salty water, feeding them a balanced diet that is rich in protein. They also fish in the lagoons, cultivate chili peppers (harvested three to four times a year for a total yield of 20-30 metric tons per year), and different kinds of mangoes. The mango trees don't require many treatments and don't even need to be irrigated because of the rainwater they receive. All the foods this community produces are typical of the Escuinapa area, whose gastronomy is well known - especially for its prawn rolls.

PRODUCTION AREA
Escuinapa, state of Sinaloa

COMMUNITY COORDINATOR
Horacio Arturo García Padilla
tel. +52 695 953 9326
scontreras@bioplaneta.com

Flor de Jamaica producers

The poetic Mexican name Flor de Jamaica indicates the *Hibiscus sabdariffa* (commonly known as Roselle). The ruby red flower cups of this plant are dried and used to make a herbal infusion, which creates a beverage with extraordinary medicinal properties. The Flor de Jamaica, is extremely rich in ascorbic acid, citric acid and tartaric acid. It is a kind of natural aspirin with notable emollient, sedative and anti-inflammatory properties. The Ejido de Algodon de Oropeo community, formed of 300 farmers with high rates of illiteracy and poverty, has started the organic cultivation and sale of sesame and above all Flor de Jamaica, whose cultivation, harvest, processing and drying is carried out exclusively by hand.

PRODUCTION AREA
Tierra Caliente, state of Michoacán

COMMUNITY COORDINATOR
Edoardo Lombardi
tel. +52 443 334 5815
cooperativaoropeo@yahoo.com

Herbs, spices and passion fruit growers

This community is situated in an area of Northern Oaxaca traditionally inhabited by the Mazateca indigenous population. It is a humid area particularly well suited to coffee cultivation. During the economic crisis brought about by the drop in the price of coffee in the 1990's, the community went back to autochthonous cultivations such as fruit trees and roots. Today they cultivate medicinal plants and agricultural products with high protein content in order to balance the community's diet. The main products, which thrive in humid tropical climates, are passion fruit, ginger, turmeric and cardamom. These are processed and turned into syrups, jams, liquors and natural colorants. The products are then sold in the traditional fairs of Oaxaca and also in other Mexican states, thanks to the support of Red Bioplaneta.

PRODUCTION AREA
Santa María Chilchotla, state of Oaxaca

COMMUNITY COORDINATOR
María Antonia Oviedo Mendiola
tel. +52 555 661 2061
maoviedom@hotmail.com

Honey producers

The Kabitah cooperative unites different communities of producers made up exclusively of indigenous Mayan people. They are mainly based in the town of Hopelchen, in the State of Campeche (Yucatan peninsula). Their activities mainly involve the production of honey, and the 45 producers involved in this cooperative can rely on the support of several NGOs and associations such as the Bioplaneta network. As well as honey, the community produces tomatoes, watermelons, and corn. Thanks to several intermediaries they sell their products internationally as well as locally.

PRODUCTION AREA
Hopelchen, state of Campeche

COMMUNITY COORDINATOR
Félix Patrón Uicab
tel. +52 996 822 0229
kabitah_2@hotmail.com

Maíz azul producers

This association includes 28 families living in the rural area known as La Ventanilla. They are involved in the conservation and production of local varieties of criollo corn that have been selected during the course of the centuries. There are five different kinds of corn according to a myth of the Huichol people (descendants of the Aztecs): white, yellow, red, spotted and *azul* (blue). The flour made from this last variety is considered to be particularly well suited to the production of a basic element of Mexican cuisine: the tortilla. Bluish in color and full of flavor, the grains of corn are boiled in water with a little lime until they shed their skins. The mixture is then processed after it has been left to rest for around twelve hours. The community also runs a restaurant, El maiz azul, where they prepare traditional dishes.

PRODUCTION AREA
Santa María Tonameca, state of Oaxaca

COMMUNITY COORDINATOR
Trinidad Cortés Hernández
tel. +52 555 661 2061
proyecto_ventanilla@hotmail.com

Mescal producers of Teúl de González Ortega

The municipality of Teúl de González Ortega is situated in the southern part of Zacatecas, at almost 2000 meters above sea level. It is home to the 100 members of an association that produces mescal and sells it both locally and nationally. A dozen different varieties of agave, the endemic plant that has been used to make beverages since the pre-Columbian era, can be used to make it. With the arrival of the Spanish, the practice of distillation and the consequent creation of mescal also arrived here. This community uses the *Agave tequilana*, which is cooked, fermented and distilled, and then finally left to rest in barrels. Mescal is considered as an indispensable beverage for religious occasions such as baptisms and weddings even today.

PRODUCTION AREA
Teúl de González Ortega, state of Zacatecas

COMMUNITY COORDINATOR
Saúl Héctor Romo Vallejo
tel. +52 551 041 4812
saulromo@terra.com.mx

Mescal producers of Tlacolula

The agave, which is used to produce mescal, was widely cultivated and formed an important part of the autochthonous population's diet even before the arrival of the colonists. The whole of the plant was used, and the fruits were used to make fruit juice and a dessert known as Mezcalli. Mescal derives from the distillation of this fruit juice and takes its name from the dessert. In Tlacolula today there is a true example of a mescal-producing district: several organizations and numerous producers collaborate to produce one of the oldest and most famous liquors in the world. There are around 7000 agave growers and mescal producers, they are joined by more than 39,000 others (35% of the population of Tlacolula), who are involved in various stages of production; they produce around a million liters of mescal each year.

PRODUCTION AREA
Tlacolula, state of Oaxaca

COMMUNITY COORDINATOR
Eric Adalid Hernández Cortés
tel. +52 951 562 0146
mezcalmistique@yahoo.com.mx

Milk producers of Chiapas

The municipality of Tecpatán is situated in Zoque, a green region with a humid climate in Northern Chiapas, the State responsible for 19% of the nation's milk production. 1100 producers live and work here and form part of an association that sells milk under the brand name of Prado Verde. These are small-scale producers that allow their cows to pasture in fields that have not been treated with chemicals. They are also fighting for these areas to be re-forested. The breeders raise their animals out in the open without using genetically modified products or administering hormones. They also leave the calves with their mothers in order to stimulate the production of milk. Once it has been milked, the milk is then pasteurized, chilled and then packed and sold all across the Country.

PRODUCTION AREA
Tecpatán, state of Chiapas

COMMUNITY COORDINATOR
Rubiel Estrada Méndez
tel. +52 968 661 0234
rubielestrada@yahoo.com

Mushroom growers of Zitácuaro

Thanks to its wide range of different climates, Mexico is rich with mushrooms. This traditional food has been part of the heritage of the indigenous populations ever since the pre-Hispanic era. Half the entire mushroom production of Latin America comes from here. In two small centers in the municipality of Zitácuaro, Coatepec de Morelos and La Encarnación, six producers have created a work group (not yet formalized) formed of five men and one woman. The group cultivates the *Pleurotus ostreatus* variety of mushrooms, which mainly grow on the trunks of rotting trees or other plant substratum such as hay. They are shaped like large ears, can be either coffee or blue-green in color and have a reproductive cycle of three months. The community mostly sells them on the local market.

PRODUCTION AREA
Zitácuaro, state of Michoacán

COMMUNITY COORDINATOR
José Luis Arroyo Carlon
tel. +52 715 116 0237
setasarroyo@hotmail.com

Natural animal-based coloring producers

The cochineal is a small parasitic insect that feeds on plants - succulent plants in particular. In this area it generally feeds on the sap of the nopal or prickly pear. This small insect is used to produce cochineal red coloring, which has been used as a colorant for a long time both in the textile and food industries. It was approved in Europe with the seal E-120 and as natural red n. 4 by the United States FDA. The natural, animal-based colorant producers of Oaxaca community is an association of 30 producers dedicated to breeding this insect. The production phase (which has been certified organic) involves gathering the insects by delicately removing them from the plants, drying them, cleaning them and then grinding them. The 400 kilograms that this community produces annually is also sold internationally.

PRODUCTION AREA
San Bartolo Coyotepec, state of Oaxaca

COMMUNITY COORDINATOR
Ignacio del Rio y Dueñas
tel. +52 951 551 0030
info@aztecacolor.com

Organic cocoa and chocolate producers

This network of cocoa producers, processors and merchants was set up in collaboration with academic and institutional bodies. It is based in Villahermosa and includes over 500 members. What sets this organization apart is its use of natural methods to create a completely organic product. This allows it to achieve a higher price on the international market and thereby benefit the entire production chain. The greatest of care is given to the protection of natural resources within the community, the soil and traditional production techniques in particular. The processing of cocoa into chocolate, an activity carried out predominately by women, gives added value to this high quality product. The cocoa is mixed with cane sugar and pepper and then worked until the ingredients have blended into a uniform mixture.

PRODUCTION AREA
Villahermosa, state of Tabasco

COMMUNITY COORDINATOR
Alma Rosa Garcés Medina
tel. +52 993 314 9625
atcovillahermosa@yahoo.com.mx

Organic coffee producers

Situated in the region of Oaxaca, the town of Putla has around 1800 inhabitants and is surrounded by rural landscapes. Its 1500 hectares of land is mostly used for the cultivation of coffee, but also for corn and sugar cane. The cooperative is made up of 28 producers that use organic and sustainable farming methods. Thanks to the technical support of NGOs and various associations, they have also been granted organic certification. The 270 tons of coffee produced each year are distributed directly by the cooperative on a local and regional scale, and through the intermediation of the Bioplaneta network, throughout all of Mexico.

PRODUCTION AREA
Putla de Guerrero, state of Oaxaca

COMMUNITY COORDINATOR
Maldonado Eudin
tel. +52 555 661 6170
scontreras@Bioplaneta.com

Organic food producers of Tlayacapan

This community was created with aim of producing organic food in a sustainable manner, without the use of chemical substances either during cultivation or in processing the food. Its ten members, most of whom are women, are also involved in safeguarding local plant varieties and selecting the best seeds year after year. The area's good climate, the abundance of water and sunshine as well as the great wealth of natural resources allow for the sowing of many different plant varieties. As well as fruit, the community's main products include blue and yellow corn (whose flour is used to make *tortillas*), vegetables and spices (which are used to make sauces and preserves) and honey.

PRODUCTION AREA
Tlayacapan, state of Morelos

COMMUNITY COORDINATOR
Sandra Contreras Martínez
tel. +52 555 671 6873
scontreras@bioplaneta.com

Organic fruit promoters

The Colectivo Pinpinaxi is an association that promotes the cultivation and consumption of organic produce. The association has recently focused its promotional and research activities on criollo avocado cultivations. This cultivar is at risk of extinction because almost all the avocado plantations are converting to the *Persea americana*, the biggest and most fructiferous avocado variety. The *Persea mexicana*, despite being the original variety in Mexico (it was domesticated in Michoacán State), and the fact that is rich in mono-unsaturated fats, is less profitable to produce. The aim of this organization is to catalogue the last criollo avocado cultivators, organize them into an association and promote the sale of the original avocado with consumers.

PRODUCTION AREA
Uruapan, state of Michoacán

COMMUNITY COORDINATOR
Bautista Villegas
tel. +52 452 523 6108
lamacadamia@yahoo.com.mx

Peanut growers and processors

This community is a social enterprise that was founded in 1997. It involves ten food producers that live near the town of Santa María Colotepec, in Oaxaca State. Having been dedicated to the production of peanuts for some time, this community chose to give an added value to their production by transforming the nuts into natural and flavored creams. The community members also decided to improve their cultivation methods by ceasing to use chemical products and focusing on an organic and sustainable production. The products are sold both locally and nationally.

PRODUCTION AREA
Santa María Colotepec, state of Oaxaca

COMMUNITY COORDINATOR
Librada Cortés Ríos
tel. +52 555 661 6170
scontreras@bioplaneta.com

Pez Blanco fishermen

The Pez blanco fish lives in lake Pátzcuaro and nowhere else in the world. This community aims to safeguard the species, which is in danger of extinction. This fish is literally worshipped by the local fishermen given the formidable prices it fetches in comparison to other fish from the same lake. Arturo Chacón Torres and Catalina Rosas Monge, biologists from the University of Michoacán research institute for natural resources, are trying to defend the species by combating overfishing, the abuse of fishing season rules, pollution and the deterioration of the lake (in the last twenty years the water level has gone down by two and a half meters). They are also involved in a project to set up a protected nature reserve with the help of nine ex-fishermen and two other biologists.

PRODUCTION AREA
Pátzcuaro, state of Michoacán

COMMUNITY COORDINATOR
Catalina Rosas Monge
tel. +52 443 324 1570
catalina_compesca@michoacan.gob.mx

Prickly Pear cultivators and processors

The area of Chapantongo borders between two very different ecosystems: one of oak and conifer forests, and the other semi desert (which is now predominant). The *Opuntia joconostle* variety of prickly pear was a fundamental food source for the indigenous people that used to live in the desert areas. The community chose to honor this tradition and start cultivating this fruit. The plants are highly resistant to drought and have many positive effects on the body (the fruit is rich with vitamin C), and also on the land where they are grown, preventing erosion and stabilizing the soil. In order to increase sales, the community also processes these fruits to make sweet and savory preserves, honey, jam and liquors.

PRODUCTION AREA
Chapantongo, state of Hidalgo

COMMUNITY COORDINATOR
Yunuén Carrillo Quiroz
tel. +52 559 115 3667
yoconostle@yahoo.com.mx

Prickly Pear growers of Tlaxco

The prickly pears produced by this community, formed of an association with 38 members, are cultivated in a natural way and processed without the use of any chemical substances or preservatives. The prickly pear, which originates from Latin America, is an egg-shaped, spiny fruit with a hard flesh that varies in color according to the variety. The community uses this fruit to add flavor to the corn tortillas they produce, which are around 14 centimeters in diameter. The tortillas are soft and pale green in color, with a slight taste of herbs that comes from the addition of the prickly pears; they are sold in vacuum packs. By combining these two basic elements of Mexican gastronomy they have created a healthy product that can be used to compliment many different dishes. The production process is industrial but is controlled by technicians that use traditional methods.

PRODUCTION AREA
Tlaxco, state of Tlaxcala

COMMUNITY COORDINATOR
Gustavo Rosete Olvera
tel. +52 555 631 5266
qusarturrosete@yahoo.com.mx

Red Lobster fishermen

The Federación Regional de Cooperativas de la Industria Pesquera Baja California (Fedecoop) is a group of nine cooperatives with 1500 members including fishermen, technicians, employees and managers. Fishing for red lobster, a traditional ingredient of the local cuisine (especially in Puerto Nuevo), takes place between September and February using special traps laid out on the sea floor. The captured animals are then measured to check they exceed the minimum size stipulated by the law. The lobsters are sold live, frozen or cooked whole; the greatest of care is taken when transporting these animals so as not to damage them and thus compromise their quality. The food producers of this community, who have been working together for 50 years, have received Marine Stewardship Council (Msc) certification.

PRODUCTION AREA
Ensenada, state of Baja California

COMMUNITY COORDINATOR
Mario Roberto Ramade Villanueva
tel. +52 646 176 2076
fedecoopbc@prodigy.net.mx

Rice and zucchini cultivators

San Pedro Aytec is one of the ten areas that make up the district of Huamuxtitlán, which together with Alpoyeca and Tlapa forms the region of Cañada. With a population of just 1800 inhabitants, San Pedro is a village whose economy is based on agriculture: in fact 90% of the population is involved in farming or animal breeding. The Rural Farmers of San Pedro Aytec Company is made up of 29 members who are involved in the production of rice, zucchini, corn and beans. The formation of this company has allowed these food producers to work in an organized manner during the various phases of production, thereby increasing productivity – they now produce around 150 metric tons of rice each year – and widening their sales network.

PRODUCTION AREA
San Pedro Aytec, state of Guerrero

COMMUNITY COORDINATOR
Francisco Merino Cruz
tel. +52 757 49 4019
arroz_gro@hotmail.com

Salt producers

Colima is one of the smallest States in Mexico, with a surface area only slightly larger than Molise. It has been inhabited since long before the Spanish colonization and the production of salt practiced along the Pacific coast here dates back to the pre-Colombian era. Today there are 500 workers involved in the Salina de la Santa Cruz salt production community, which extracts around 50,000 tons of organically certified salt each year using completely traditional techniques. However, the production that the community is most proud of (and justifiably so), is the flor de sal, of which they produce "just" 100 tons each year. This product is obtained by delicately gathering by hand the thin layer of salt that solidifies on the surface of the salt-water basins.

PRODUCTION AREA
Colima, state of Colima

COMMUNITY COORDINATOR
Mariano De La Garza Orozco
tel. +52 333 611 0908
mariano@bluepoinsalt.com

Sheep's cheese makers

This group of producers, which forms part of a rural development company, received funding in 2003 to agronomically redevelop a 64-hectare tract of land. Their first concern was how to optimize the water resources. It was then decided to use the excellent forage provided by the land to feed a herd of semi-domesticated sheep. They use the pasteurized sheep's milk to make cheeses that are matured for four months. Some parts of the land are not used for pasture and in these areas they cultivate criollo corn and medicinal asparagus. The rewards this community receives come not so much from the cheese making but rather from the satisfaction of being able to manage a difficult area in an absolutely sustainable manner, with integrated agriculture and good economic returns.

PRODUCTION AREA
El Marqués, state of Querétaro

COMMUNITY COORDINATOR
Javier Pérez Rocha Malcher
tel. +52 442 21 75611
ranchosantamarina@yahoo.com.mx

Traditional mescal producers of Durango

Mescal is made from agave plants, just like tequila. The difference between the two spirits lies in the different manufacturing methods employed but above all in the different type of agave used. The Mexican agave is made up of a whole universe of different varieties and species much like the vine in other parts of the world. Each mescal-producing region leaves its own unique mark on the product. This is also true of the mescal produced in Durango using a variety of agave with the same name. The 13,000 liters of mescal they produce here each year is a tiny amount when compared to the national production of millions of liters. it is however very characteristic and completely traditional. The heart is taken from mature agaves (from six to eight years of age), and cooked in pits along with red-hot volcanic rocks; it is then ground and distilled twice. This is a long and laborious process that allows the fruit to absorb the flavors of the earth and smoke. The product is sold locally.

PRODUCTION AREA
Nombre de Dios, state of Durango

COMMUNITY COORDINATOR
Alejandro Solis Lozano
tel. +52 618 146 4308
metzcalelmalpais@yahoo.com.mx

AIRES DE CAMPO

Aires de Campo is a company whose main offices are in San Pedro de los Pinos, in the State of México, which distributes more than 300 certified products, many of which are organic. It works for about twenty organizations which group together micro-firms, family farms, communities and cooperatives, and markets their products on both the international and the domestic market, where it relies on a network of exclusive stores known as Biocentros. The products (dairy products, jams, honey, meat, eggs, cereal, baked goods, dehydrated foods, pulses, herbs, coffee, fruit drinks) are certified by institutes such as Bioagricert, Naturland, Organic Crop Improvement Association (Ocia), Lacon, Certimex, Imo and Quality Assurance Institute (Qai).

AREA OF ACTIVITY
State of México

ASSOCIATION COORDINATOR
Marcela Valdés Villarreal Schwarz
tel. +52 5526140122
marcela@airesdecampo.com

BIONEXOS

This association supports Mexican craftsmen by introducing manufacturing organization and marketing development projects for small manufacturers who work in the fields of handicrafts, traditional agriculture and organic farming. Its main activity is to offer technical-scientific and managerial consultancy and training to the various regional handicrafts organizations, with particular emphasis on the problems related to the certification of products. The association has its main offices in the federal capital, but operates all over the country; over 5000 families of producers are involved in the network, and numerous NGOs and other associations collaborate on the various projects.

AREA OF ACTIVITY
The entire country

ASSOCIATION COORDINATOR
Muñoz Pablo
tel. +52 5526140122
pablo@bionexos.org

BIOPLANETA

Bioplaneta is a network of community cooperatives involved in various sectors, including agro-food. Through this network, the cooperatives specialize in the use of agronomic techniques that respect the environment, concentrating on recovering and improving traditional farming and food processing methods. Bioplaneta is also a marketing concern that draws together 68 indigenous and family communities and cooperatives, making a total of about 200 rural communities in 14 Mexican States. The inter-community network employs various distribution channels: the organic market, the Fair Trade market and the conventional market.

AREA OF ACTIVITY
Much of the country

ASSOCIATION COORDINATOR
Hector Marsilli Esquivel
tel. +52 56616170
hmarselli@bioplaneta.com

FUNDACIÓN PARA LA PRODUCTIVIDAD EN EL CAMPO

The Foundation for Productivity in rural areas assists the populations who live in very marginal and poor areas. These populations have very few resources, which are insufficient to meet their basic needs, a fundamental condition to guarantee the development of the community. The activities of the Foundation focus in particular on spreading understanding of farming methods and of agricultural micro-banking, primarily through technical assistance but also through organizational, technical and financial training. The main goal is to ensure that although they come from an environment of pure subsistence, these products can acquire added value and be introduced into the country's main economic channels.

AREA OF ACTIVITY
States of Hidalgo, Chiapas, Michoacán, Puebla, Oaxaca

ASSOCIATION COORDINATOR
Roberto Ramirez Rojas Velasco
tel. +52 55233898
rramirezrojas@apoyoalcampo.org.mx

FUNDACIÓN RENACIMIENTO

This Foundation provides food and lodging for street children, with the goal of eventually reintegrating needy young people into society through education and training. Its activities concentrate on encouraging the integration of the young guests, offering them suitable professional training, which is essential if they are enter the working world. To this end, Renacimiento has set up a small firm to produce organic bread, which has been certified by the Italian Bioagricert institute. The bread is sold locally and this generates resources that can be reinvested in the institutional activities.

AREA OF ACTIVITY
Mexico City

ASSOCIATION COORDINATOR
Antoine Pierre-Marie Dornier Mathieu
tel. +52 26140122
montmaudit@hotmail.com

Banana growers of Altagracia

About 5,500 Nicaraguan families live on the island of Ometepe, which is formed by two volcanoes in Central America's largest lake. The local diet is based mainly on consumption of *Amphilophus citrinellus*, a fish from the Cyclides family, and bananas. In the municipality of Altagracia alone, there are 3,000 banana farmers. For the island's inhabitants, the main source of income is working in the plantations, which first went into production in the 1960s and reached a peak of activity in the 1980s. At Altagracia, an association of 15 farmers grows bananas of the *Musa paradisiaca* variety, also known as giant horn, both for self-consumption and for sale through intermediaries. There are 15 sales staff.

PRODUCTION AREA
Altagracia, department of Rivas

COMMUNITY COORDINATOR
Martín Antonio Juárez Ponce
tel. +505 5694118
volcanes@ibw.com.ni

Coffee growers of Estelí

Forty cooperatives belong to the Promotora de Desarollo Cooperativo (PRODECOOP) at Las Segovias, which unites 2,300 Arabica coffee growers in 10 municipalities in the department of Estelí. Coffee is harvested once a year, when ripening is at its peak, to ensure high quality. The seed is extracted from the fruit by wet processing. The cherries are fermented in water, dried and then cleaned. PRODECOOP takes care of marketing, also assisting members through a programme for the promotion of production techniques based on respect for the environment. It strives to increase the contribution of women and provides help to improve workers' living conditions.

PRODUCTION AREA
Department of Estelí

COMMUNITY COORDINATOR
Ramos Merlig Presa
tel. +505 7133268
info@prodecoop.com

Producers of cocoa and chocolate

A network of producers of cocoa and chocolate has been set up in the department of Matagalpa. The project is called Valle de Chocolate and was formed at the initiative of El Castillo del Cacao, a company that makes chocolates and is now planning to extend collaboration to other producers in the region and the rest of Nicaragua. The cocoa is organic and comes from the La Campesina cooperative. Processing is by hand and the raw materials are mainly organic, although it is not yet possible to source all of them in Nicaragua. No preservatives are used. Distribution is supported by several NGOs, the Liga Cooperativa de Estados Unidos de América (CLUSA), the Asociación para la Diversificación y Desarrollo Agrícolo Comunal (ADDAC) and the Asociación de Pueblos en Acción Comunitaria (PAC).

PRODUCTION AREA
Department of Matagalpa

COMMUNITY COORDINATOR
Harm Jan Van Oudenhoven
tel. +505 7723529
harm@elcastillodelcacao.com

Producers of honey

One of the positive aspects of honey production is its low cost. The investment required is modest and the only item that inflates costs is transport for distributing the end product. This is one of the reasons why honey production has in recent years become crucial for the Nicaraguan economy, particularly in the export sector. Boaco is the collection centre where the 98 members of the Apibo community sell their organic honey. In order to benefit from this positive trend, the association has shifted from artisanal production to intensive farming, still carried out using natural methods. The association is striving to increase its membership and expand its markets in Nicaragua and abroad by selling its products at a fairer price.

PRODUCTION AREA
Department of Boaco

COMMUNITY COORDINATOR
Vidal Salina Ruiz
tel. +505 6530083
apibo@tmx.com.ni

Cocoa producers of Bocas del Toro

The 2,000 producers of the Bocas del Toro community grow cocoa on plantations diversified with medicinal plants, fruit and timber trees to increase economic returns, ensure subsistence and safeguard the harvest. Economically, the most important of the plants that shade the cacao trees are bananas, which are still harvested using traditional methods. Cocoa producers harvest the ripe berries on their own land, extract the seeds and leave them to ferment for five or six days. The seeds then go into a solar dryer to reduce their humidity before selection and transfer to the collection centres. The producers' cooperative distributes to north America and to some European markets.

PRODUCTION AREA
Almirante. province of Bocas del Toro

COMMUNITY COORDINATOR
Abelardo Vigil Aguilar
tel. +507 7583719-65609304
abelardovigil@gmail.com

Producers of cane sugar

The community of the district of Arroyos y Esteros in the Cordillera department has been producing cane sugar for some time. Traditionally, the product is used to make a beverage called caña paraguayana. In the past decade, production has focused on organic cane sugar and sesame, and important international certifications have been obtained. Currently, about 4,500 people are employed in production and processing. Annual output is significant, with about 1,500 tons of sugar produced each year. Products are distributed and consumed on the local, domestic and international markets.

PRODUCTION AREA
Arroyos y Esteros, department of Cordillera

COMMUNITY COORDINATOR
Andrés Gonzales Aguilera
tel. +595 510272115
agonzalez_py@yahoo.com

Producers of herbs and infusions

The use of herbs for medicinal and other purposes is part of the heritage of the indigenous populations of Latin America. Even today, herbs are used in the prevention of disease and as tonics. The small Minbipá community of associated producers of medicinal herbs was created by farmers in the department of Caaguazú to improve the yields and quality of their products. Members have obtained organic certification and annual output is around 30 tons. Some members of the community have set up an association to process and distribute their products.

PRODUCTION AREA
Repatriación, department of Caaguazú

COMMUNITY COORDINATOR
Nestor Gustavo Fretes Benites
tel. +595 971265721
gustavofretesb@yahooo.com

Bean farmers of Chiclayo

The community has 26 members who grow various kinds of legume. The main product is frejoles (beans), which are eaten on almost every day in the area. The most traditional cultivar is pallar (*Phaseolus lunatus*), a flat, white kidney bean. In the pre-Incan Mochica culture, different coloured pallar seeds were used for an archaic form of writing. The same people, which lived on the coast of Peru, even dedicated a god to this legume, Yan-Pallek, who is portrayed as a white navigator dressed in elegant green robes. Naturally enough, the Peruvian kitchen has many bean-based recipes. One of the most popular is tacu tacu, a base of beans and rice garnished with various ingredients.

PRODUCTION AREA
Chiclayo, department of Lambayeque

COMMUNITY COORDINATOR
Salvador José Sánchez Serna
tel. +51 44221868
salvadorarpelltrujilloperu@hotmail.com

Camu-camu growers of Ucayali

About 30 of the 118 households that make up the community grow camu-camu (*Myrciaria dubia*) exclusively. The others pursue various other activities such as fishing, aquaculture, honey production, fruit juice making and rice growing. The camu-camu bush is two to three metres tall. It grows in the marshy zones of the Amazon forest, yielding a small round fruit with a yellow-red skin. It is a spontaneous plant that has only been cultivated for a few years, since its medicinal properties and very high vitamin C content were discovered. The fruit may be eaten fresh or used to make sweets, ice cream, beverages or even feed for fish. Every year, a camu-camu fair is held at Yarinacocha.

PRODUCTION AREA
Pucallpa, department of Ucayali

COMMUNITY COORDINATOR
Silverio Flavio Trejo Prado
tel. +51 61578328
trejoprado@hotmail.com

Chuin Flour and Starch producers of Yanallpa

Chuin is the local name for *Pachyrhizus tuberosus*, a legume that grows in tropical climates and represents a major food resource in the Amazonian areas of Peru. The Yanallpa community, located in the Ucayali river basin in the district of Jenaro Herrera, in the province of Requena, grows chuin either as a single crop or with other farm crops. Cultivation methods are natural, and the product is organic. Processing techniques come from the local oral tradition. Chuin roots are used in cooking as a side dish for a number of recipes. The flour and the starch extracted from it have excellent nutritional properties as they are protein-rich, gluten-free and easy to digest.

PRODUCTION AREA
Yanallpa, department of Loreto

COMMUNITY COORDINATOR
Isabel Consuelo Oré Balbín
tel. +51 65267733
iore@iiap.org.pe

Corn growers

The most important of the many agricultural products grown by the 50 families that belong to the association is corn, which is one of the staple foods of the Peruvian Andes. The valleys of the Andes, especially the Urubamba river valley, have a unique variety of corn, paraky or white corn, with very large, flavoursome kernels. In Peru, many different cultivars of corn are grown, each having established itself by adapting to the specific microclimate of a given area. The corn is sown in August and September and the harvest takes place in February and March. The community of corn growers markets its own products, and organizes training and refresher courses in collaboration with the Asociación Nacional de Productores Ecológicos (ANPE).

PRODUCTION AREA
Departments of Apurímac, Cusco, Junín and Huancavelica

COMMUNITY COORDINATOR
María Eliana Grajeda Puelles
tel. +51 84247211
egrajeda@conam.gob.pe

Growers of medicinal plants

The Vicos community is on the west-facing slope of the Cordillera Blanca about 450 kilometres from Lima in north-central Peru. About 5,600 people living at altitudes of 2,800 to 5,000 metres belong to the community. The wide range of altitudes makes it possible to cultivate many varieties of cereals, tubers, roots, legumes and vegetables, and to breed various animals. Medicinal herbs are very important crops, and are an integral part of the traditional medicine still practised in the area. Much ancient lore is attached to these herbs. For example, the leaves of *Alnus acuminata* are used to prepare poultices for tumours and abscesses while infusions of *Gentianella alborosea* (known as *hercampuri*) purify the blood and reduce liver inflammation.

PRODUCTION AREA
Vicos, department of Ancash

COMMUNITY COORDINATOR
María Beatríz Rojas Berrocal
tel. +51 43443059
bearojasberrocal@hotmail.com

Mashua producers of Tuti

The community comprises about 100 households involved in a range of projects to revive mashua production. Mashua is the dialect name for isaño (*Tropaeolum tuberosum*), a plant with edible tubers. It grows in the Andes only above an altitude of 3,000 metres and its growing cycle is very similar to that of the potato. Known and prized for its curative properties since the time of the Incas, mashua is eaten mainly in the form of soups after it has dried in the sun for a period of time to concentrate its sugar content. Today, mashua is available in juice, flour, bread and dehydrated form. The community is seeking certification.

PRODUCTION AREA
Tuti, department of Arequipa

COMMUNITY COORDINATOR
Antonio Quispe Capira
tel. +51 54531103
kantuas@yahoo.com

Organic vegetable farmers

The 50 producers and 20 processors in this community grow vegetables using organic methods. Products are for self-consumption and sale in local markets. The soil is prepared with compost, manure or harvest waste. Special shelters are then built to protect the products – onions, beet, spinach, carrots, cabbage and basil – from bad weather, disease and parasites, and to conserve the dampness of the soil. The Asociación Nacional de Productores Ecológicos (ANPE) of Perù collaborates with the community, supplying support and consultancy from technicians specializing in organic production, distribution and gastronomy. Visits to the vegetable gardens are organized to enable customers to see the production methods for themselves.

PRODUCTION AREA
Departments of Lima, Arequipa, Lambayeque and Cusco

COMMUNITY COORDINATOR
María Eugenia Calla Alvis
tel. +51 54445785
mari_uc@yahoo.com

Producers of citrus fruits

The community comprises just over 30 individuals who grow, pick and market oranges, tangerines and in smaller quantities, avocados. Citrus fruits arrived in the New World from the Far East in 1493, reaching Peru in 1609. Production extends throughout the tropical and subtropical regions of nearly the entire planet. The community grows citrus fruits, medicinal herbs and other fruit trees. Over the past 30 years, the land area in Peru dedicated to citrus fruits has expanded enormously. Between 2003 and 2005, citrus exports doubled. This is having a beneficial impact on the country's economy. The community aims to make its own fruit identifiable locally, safeguarding the environment and striving to take advantage of this positive phase.

PRODUCTION AREA
Department of Piura

COMMUNITY COORDINATOR
Pedro Faustino Francia Zevallos
tel. +51 15308843
riccifrancia@hotmail.com

Producers of organic cocoa

The association comprises 25 producers and 10 processors of organic cocoa who operate in an area of Peru with particularly favourable environmental conditions, the region of Cajamarca. *Theobroma cacao* is a plant of the Sterculiaceae family that is native to Latin America. The trees begin to bear fruit, known as cherries, four or five years after planting. After the harvest, the cherries are allowed to stand for a few days. They are then opened to extract the seeds, which should ferment with the pulp that surrounds them. Five or six days later, the seeds are dried until the film that covers them opens. They are then roasted and finally ground into cocoa. The product obtained is sold or used in the production of chocolate bars or cocoa liquor.

PRODUCTION AREA
Department of Cajamarca

COMMUNITY COORDINATOR
Mario Tapia Guevara
tel. +51 769593748
marte24@yahoo.es

Producers of special organic coffee

The community brings together 280 producers and 40 processors of Arabica coffee with a pure genetic profile identical to the variety imported into Latin America from Ethiopia. In Peru, this special coffee is grown at an altitude of between 1,200 and 1,800 metres. Its large beans, assertive, attractively acidic aroma and flavour are obtained by picking the fruit between May and August. Organic farming methods are used. The plantations are protected by shade trees, weeds are removed with special tools or by cover cropping, and natural fertilizers are used. Natural pest and disease controls are also adopted. The environment and ecosystems are safeguarded by diversifying surrounding crops as much as possible, and the plantations are sited near woodlands.

PRODUCTION AREA
Satipo, department of Junín; Villa Rica, department of Pasco; Canchaque, department of Piura

COMMUNITY COORDINATOR
Edgardo Eutimio Cáceres Parraguez
tel. +51 12419786
caceresparraguez@yahoo.com

Yaku tayta fishers and fish processors

In Quechua, the native South American language still used by more than nine and a half million people, yaku tayta means "fathers of the water". They are the people who monitor fishing in the Pacaya Samiria national park. The Manco Capac community, in the north-eastern region of Loreto, comprises 18 people in charge of monitoring enforcement of the regulations imposed to protect the area's aquatic species. The paiche (*Arapaima gigas*), known as pirarucu in Brazil, and the tambaqui (*Colossoma macropomum*) are registered and fished using nets designed to catch the each species when it has grown to an appropriate size. Tambuqui are eaten only after drying and salting. Members of the community also monitor the eggs that the taricaya turtles (*Podocnemis unifilis*) lay on the banks of the rivers.

PRODUCTION AREA
Iquitos, department of Loreto

COMMUNITY COORDINATOR
Elena Braiato
tel. +39 3389459910
elena.braiato@gmx.net

Alaskan Wild Salmon Fishermen

This community consists of the Cape Cleare Fishery, a four-person independent business that cooperates with other Pacific Northwest wild fishermen and environmental groups. A member of Cape Cleare has been catching salmon with hook and line and processing it onboard for the past 29 years. All the fish Cape Cleare sells are caught one at a time and promptly flash frozen at sea. This community is active in working with groups to enlighten citizens about sustainable seafood and healthy ocean issues.

PRODUCTION AREA
Sitka, Alaska; Port Townsend, Washington State

COMMUNITY COORDINATOR
Joyce Gustafson
joycegustafson@hotmail.com

Arizona Seedsavers and Growers

In Northern Arizona, the Bioregional Lifeways Network is made up of hundreds of families in communities across Arizona. These families run projects to promote food security and preserve traditional seeds and food heritage. Their various endeavors provide healthy foods to local communities who have little access, create young leaders, and promote sustainability. Members of the Lifeways Network believe that the communities within the bioregion of Flagstaff, Navajo Nation, Hopi Nation, and surrounding areas have the opportunity and necessity to integrate projects and share resources. They can create a healthy, interconnected community if they come together to move on a collective vision. Growers in this community produce an array of agricultural products; some raise Churro Sheep, other gather wild foods, and some grow traditional medicinal plants and the three sisters crops – corn, beans and squash.

PRODUCTION AREA
Arizona

COMMUNITY COORDINATOR
Daniel Rosen
daniel_rosen@mac.com

Aroostook County Wheat Growers

This community of three growers, two bakeries, one distributor and one community college in Aroostook County, Maine represents a re-establishment of wheat in what was once a large grain-growing region referred to as the Food Basket of New England. Most grain production eventually moved west, but this community believes that wheat is still a viable crop for the regional food system. Community members practice crop rotation and under sow clover to facilitate soil build-up. The community harvests its wheat with a combine and stone-mills on the farm. In addition it grows oats and rye that the community processes into rolled oats and rye flour. All of its value-added products have organic certification through Maine Organic Farmers and Gardeners Association (MOFGA).

PRODUCTION AREA
Aroostook County, Maine

COMMUNITY COORDINATOR
Angela Wotton
amwotton@earthlink.net

Artisan Cheesemakers from the Uplands of Southwestern Wisconsin

Wisconsin has a 160 years history of dedication to the craft of dairying. Currently the popularity of artisan and farmstead dairy products in Wisconsin is rising. Rolling hills, lush pasturelands and the clean water in Wisconsin help farmers produce top-quality milk for cheese making. A small but growing number of producers and cheesemakers craft products from the milk of animals allowed to graze and feed only on fresh pasture grasses. The Wisconsin Dairy Artisan Network provides current and future Wisconsin dairy food artisans with education, promotes their craft, and advocates for regulations that benefit their operations. Fantome Farms began almost 20 years ago with a single goat. Now they raise their goats on pasture and use the fresh milk to make cheese. The farmers of Uplands Cheese Company in Dodgeville, Wisconsin began making cheese in 2000. Their cows graze on pastures from early spring through the fall. The company makes Pleasant Ridge Reserve, an alpine Gruyère-style cheese made during pasture growing months with the milk of their grass-fed cows. At Bleu Mont Dairy they make cheeses with the organic milk of their cows.

PRODUCTION AREA
Dane and Iowa Counties, Wisconsin

COMMUNITY COORDINATOR
Susan Boldt
susanboldt@slowfoodwisconsin.org

Asheville Producers

Asheville, North Carolina has an active community of food producers who are exploring ways to preserve Asheville's food heritage. This community believes in keeping foods local. These brewers, bakers, wild food gatherers, and activists are helping make Asheville into place with its own very distinctive food culture. The Asheville Brewing Company opened over 10 years ago as part of a resurgence of micro-breweries in the southeast of the United States. The ales are 'real ales', unfiltered and alive. The brewery operates on a small-scale, selling their ales to the local community, thus eliminating the environmental stressors of extensive packaging and transportation. The Appalachian Sustainable Agriculture Project (ASAP) involves over 300 members, including farmers, bakers, wine producers, grocers and educators across the Appalachian Mountains. ASAP promotes local agriculture through marketing campaigns, school garden projects, various events, and publications. The Ramp Project of the Smoky Mountain Native Plant Association brings together a group of over 40 members who grow, collect, process, and market Appalachian native plants. The association provides education about native species and produces value-added products using locally grown, sustainably harvested plants. Natural Bridge Bakery was the first bakery in the region with a wood-fired open. Flat Rock Village Bakery bakes breads in a wood-fired brick oven. All their breads are worked by hand for at least a portion of the kneading process. They use wild yeasts and organic flours from North Carolina growers and millers whenever possible.

PRODUCTION AREA
Asheville, North Carolina

COMMUNITY COORDINATOR
Kelly Davis
keldavis@verizon.net

Austin Farmers

The community of Boggy Creek Farm consists of two principle farmers and eight employees. They raise 80 hens in the hen house and grow certified organic vegetables and fruits. There are two separate farms, one 75 miles east of Austin, Texas and the other on five-acres in the center of urban Austin. The food that is grown at Boggy Creek Farm feeds approximately 600 people each week. The farm grows over a thousand Roma tomato plants from seed; they are harvested, cut in half and smoke-dried. Tomatoes are marinated in olive oil and packed. The farmers at Boggy Creek believe in the importance of urban farms, which allow city dwellers access to agriculture as it is happening.

PRODUCTION AREA
Austin, Texas

COMMUNITY COORDINATOR
Carol Ann Sayle
carolann@boggycreekfarm.com

Berkshire and Taconic Region Biodynamic Farmers

Three small-scale organic farms situated in the Berkshire Hills of Massachusetts and foothills of the Taconic Mountains of New York have come together to create a community that practices sustainable agriculture and shares its resources. Moon In The Pond Organic Farm and Berle Farm, both 15-year-old operations, and North Plain Farm each has only one to four workers. As a community their farming practices unite traditional, sustainable methods with modern technology to create a system that benefits their animals and land, and produces healthy foods. At North Plain Farm, they rotate heritage-breed grass fed animals from pasture to pasture, leaving some fields to grow back in order to provide habitat for wildlife. Together the three farms produce cheese, dairy milk, meats, poultry, vegetables, legumes, cereal grains, honey, and maple syrup. They sell and distribute their products within a 70-mile radius.

PRODUCTION AREA
Berkshire, Massachusetts; Taconic, New York State

COMMUNITY COORDINATOR
Sean Stanton
seanstanton@hotmail.com

Big Sandy Grain and Field Crop Producers

This community of American grain producers supports sustainable farming methods and growing for taste and quality rather than yield. Across the country these farmers are using cover crops extensively in order to improve the richness of the soil. No-till farming and compost have also been introduced to protect the land. Hard red winter wheat, oats, millet, barley, corn, soy, beans and peas are grown in varying quantities based on geography and climate considerations. Many community farmers are exploring organic farming as the important alternative to industrialized, standardized grain production.

PRODUCTION AREA
Big Sandy, Montana

COMMUNITY COORDINATOR
Bob Quinn
bob.quinn@kamut.com

Bolinas Farmers

The Regenerative Design Institute (RDI) operates a 17 acre farm in Bolinas, on the California Coast. RDI is a non-profit educational organization that focuses on teaching people how to build community models that address human needs while regenerating and improving the surrounding environment. Their farm has a mature orchard with over 200 heirloom fruit and nut trees, two pastures, a community kitchen and greenhouse. The community entails five farm managers, 15 student volunteers and 10community volunteers who grow certified organic foods including garlic, chard, apples and strawberries, which they sell at the local food community and to Commonweal, a healing retreat center for people with chronic and possible terminal illnesses such as cancer and HIV/AIDS.

PRODUCTION AREA
Bolinas, California

COMMUNITY COORDINATOR
Penny Livingston
penny@regenerativedesign.org

Boulder Farmers

Cure Organic Farm is a small family farm located on the fertile, high plains of Boulder, Colorado. Using organic and biodynamic methods, they grow over 90 varieties of vegetables, berries and herbs on 10 acres. The farm raises 150 pastured laying hens, and tend several honey beehives. Farmers at Cure Organic Farm focus on growing the most highest quality produce possible, while working to maintain and encourage natural diversity. The farm provides food to over 100 families through its Community Supported Agriculture program. It also supplies produce to elders in need in the community, local restaurants, grocery stores and the Boulder Farmers Market. The farm offers educational classes, tours and volunteer opportunities in order to connect local people with their food source. The Kitchen Café, a restaurant in Boulder that creates simple dishes, is a regular customer of the farm. The cafe brings ingredients grown in the community to the table.

PRODUCTION AREA
Boulder, Colorado

COMMUNITY COORDINATOR
Anne Pendleton
cureorganicfarm@yahoo.com

Brentwood Organic Fruit Growers

Frog Hollow Farm is a 120-acre organic farm located in Brentwood, California on the Sacramento River Delta, an area known for producing delicious stone fruits. The farm produces 25 varieties of organic peaches, nectarines, cherries, apricots, plums, pears, and table grapes. There are over 30 year-round employees at Frog Hollow. The farm has diversified its operations by building a processing kitchen and starting a Community Supported Agriculture (CSA) program. In 1999, Frog Hollow created a line of jams, chutneys and marmalades. With the fruit that cannot be sold at market, they make fruit pastries in their farm kitchen. Frog Hollow Farm products are sold to the local San Francisco Bay Area community at stores, restaurants and farmers' markets which are part of the community.

PRODUCTION AREA
Brentwood, California

COMMUNITY COORDINATOR
Rebecca Courchesne
becky@froghollow.com

Bristol Bay Wild Salmon Fishermen

Bristol Bay is home to the world's largest sustainable wild salmon fishery. Under the guidance of a strict conservation model legislated by the Alaska Department of Fish and Game, the community members fish for wild sockeye salmon in 20-foot vessels with hand-operated gillnets. Sockeye salmon have been an increasingly important economic component of Bristol Bay for several centuries and a primary subsistence for the native Alaskan families. The community – made of fishermen and processors – is committed to the sustainable harvest of wild salmon and to consumer education. Sockeye salmon is sold according to an affordable pricing structure that is based on volume sales to make its wild sockeye an affordable choice for family meals. Its marketing targets neighborhood and community groups.

PRODUCTION AREA
Bristol Bay, Alaska

COMMUNITY COORDINATORS
Christopher Nicolson
christopher@redsalmon.com
Nadine LaPira-Wolos
wildnredsalmon@aol.com
Anne Mosness
eatwildfish@aol.com

Brooklyn Seedsavers and Gardeners

Since 1914 children have continuously tended a garden within the walls of the Brooklyn Botanic Garden. It is the oldest children's garden in the United States and possibly the world. Currently, the organic garden is in partnership with Slow Food to teach children about the importance of America's food heritage and of locally produced fresh food. The garden features many of the fruits and vegetables on The Slow Food Ark of Taste including the Moon and Starts watermelon, the Burbank tomato, the Cherokee purple tomato, the German Pink tomato, the Boston Marrow squash, and Wenk's hot pepper. The Children's Garden holds a true Johnny Appleseed apple tree, grafted from a tree farmer Johnny Chapman planted in Upstate New York. This living cultural treasure serves as a continual reminder to children of their national food heritage and the power of planting a single seed.

PRODUCTION AREA
New York City, New York State

COMMUNITY COORDINATOR
Adrian Almquist
adrianalmquist@aol.com

Brooklyn Urban Farmers

Added Value is a non-profit organization that works with the youth of South Brooklyn to help them engage with their community and provide locally grown foods to neighborhood citizens. Since its opening, Added Value has provided long-term training to more than 85 neighborhood teenagers. The non-profit together with neighborhood young people have helped revitalize local parks, processed vacant lands into vibrant Urban Farms, improved Red Hook citizens' access to healthy, safe and affordable food, and begun to grow an economy that supports the needs of the community. Currently Added Value operates two Farmers' Markets that features produce grown on Red Hook Community Farm by its youth leadership team as well as products from other regional farmers including fresh milk, yogurt and ice cream, a full selection of fruit and pasture raised meats. The Red Hook Farmers Market was established in June 2001. It serves as the sole provider of fresh produce for neighborhood residents.

PRODUCTION AREA
Brooklyn, New York

COMMUNITY COORDINATOR
Ian Marvy
imarvy@added-value.org

Burlington Farmers

The Intervale Center stands at the center of a community of 22 farmers across twelve farms. The Center's workers run a variety of projects and ventures to restore agricultural land and provide jobs, healthy food, and clean energy to the Burlington community. The Intervale itself is a parcel of more than 700 acres within the city of Burlington, Vermont that was first cultivated as agricultural land more than 1,000 years ago by the Abenaki Indians. Since 1988 the modern Intervale Center community has reclaimed over 325 acres of agricultural land. Intervale farmers seed, grow, harvest and deliver themselves. They are in partnership with Vermont Fresh Network, an association that connects farmers directly to local chefs and restaurants. One farm specializes in pick-you-own berries, another grows dry beans, rye, and oats and sells straw to local farms as a cover crop, and another raises chickens, which it moves between its farm fields to assist in weed and pest control. Half of the Intervale Farms have organic certification, although all are required to farm organically.

PRODUCTION AREA
Burlington, Vermont

COMMUNITY COORDINATOR
Mara Welton
weltons@halfpintfarm.com

California Ethnic Minority Farmers

This community is made up of farmers from the two greatest agricultural regions of California: Central Coast and San Joaquin Valley. These agricultural regions include some of the highest-grossing land in all of California, yet the underserved, minority farmers who farm this land face great barriers to success in the state. The Central Coast is home to some of the largest and most successful representatives of the agricultural industry. The San Joaquin valley is one of the most productive agricultural regions in the world, with over 120,000 people who work in the agricultural sector on over 18,000 farms. There is another side to the agriculture of the San Joaquin Valley, one made up of smaller farms, many of them with ethnic-minority operators: 30% of Fresno county farmers are members of an ethnic minority, of which 5% are Afrio-American, 12% are Southeast Asian and 17% are Hispanic. The minority farmers in the valley are disproportionately small landholders: Asian, Hispanic, Afro-American, and American Indian farmers operate nearly 50% of small farms. Latino farmers in the Central Coast are a fast-growing segment, However, they remain limited by their relatively small size and lack of capitalization. The Hmong growers in the California tend to be new immigrants and to work farms that are a fraction of the size of most in San Joaquin. The average size of a Hmong farm is 3.25 acres, compared to a county average of 175-acre farms. The Afro-American farmers are a more consolidated presence in the Valley, and many of the farming families in Fresno and Tulare County have been growers in the region for three generations. This delegation, coordinated by the California-based non-profit Community Alliance with Family Farmers, has brought together 10 ethnic minority farmers for a learning experience focused on direct marketing and networking.

PRODUCTION AREA
Central Coast and San Joaquin Valley, California

COMMUNITY COORDINATOR
Anya Fernald
anya@caff.org

Californian Artisan Bread Bakers

The community of bread bakers at the Acme Bread Company in Berkeley, Californi,a has produced artisan breads for the past 23 years. Seven years ago the community began supporting organic and sustainable agriculture by purchasing over 3 million pounds of organic flour a year milled from identity-preserved wheat selected by lot according to flavor and functional criteria. The bakers pay farmers virtually twice as much for their flour as they would otherwise receive. All of Acme Bread Company's breads are hand-molded, most baked in stone-hearth deck ovens, and about half are naturally leavened from wild yeast starters. The community comprises over 150 persons (growers and bakers) at four locations. The bakery has avoided centralizing its production so that the breads stay as near to their locations of sale as possible.

PRODUCTION AREA
Berkeley, California

COMMUNITY COORDINATOR
Steve Sullivan
stevacme@aol.com

Camarillo Organic Farmers

The McGraths are fifth generation farmers who grow a diverse selection of organic produce and flowers, including 15 varieties of lettuce, 4 varieties of carrots, 2 of strawberries, numerous varieties of winter squash, and beets. The 300-acre ranch in Camarillo, California was established in 1871. The McGrath family and its employees manually harvest all of the produce; they collaborate with other farmers of the area and organize and sell at eight farmers markets and over 40 restaurants in Southern California.

PRODUCTION AREA
Ventura County, California

COMMUNITY COORDINATOR
Philip McGrath
mcgrath.familyfarms@verizon.net

Capay Valley Farmers and Ranchers

23 farms and ranches in Capay Valley, California, joined together to launch the Capay Valley Grown label in 2004. Their aim is to promote high-quality farm products that maximize freshness. This community of growers seeks to offer costumers the choice to buy local products grown by farmers who work for long-term environmental sustainability. Full Belly Farm is a member of the Capay Valley Community. At Full Belly, farmers have been growing certified organic vegetables, fruits, flowers, herbs, sheep and nuts on 200 acres since 1985. They employ 25-50 people, 20 of whom have been with the farm for 15 years or more. Working with other local producers to launch the Capay Valley Grown brand is one several projects that the farmers participate in to improve the quality of their community. The farm also runs a Community Supported Agriculture program and once a month they make deliveries of produce to three food bank organizations that provide food assistance to low-income seniors in Oakland, California.

PRODUCTION AREA
Capay Valley, California

COMMUNITY COORDINATOR
Judith Redmond
judith@fullbellyfarm.com

Cape Cod Hook Fishermen

This Cape Cod, Massachusetts' community is made up of 2,000 commercial fishermen who use hook and line. These fishermen employ methods that are more time consuming than the use of nets, which destroy fish habitat, because they are dedicated to environmental sustainability. The community members catch wild cod and haddock and deliver their catch fresh to a filet house for immediate processing and sale. They catch lobsters wild, which they store and then sell while still alive. The commercial distribution of codfish and haddock caught on hook and line has a long and distinguished history in New England: both fish have been central to the trade and sustenance of the region's populace for centuries. This community of fishermen, bound together as a non-profit and cooperative, are working to build a future in which sustainably harvested wild fish will re-establish itself as a staple of the regional diet. They seek to educate the public about the importance of healthy ecosystems, connect consumers to the processes that bring them the fish that they are eating, and promote changes in regulation that disallow traditional hook fishing.

PRODUCTION AREA
Chatham, Massachusetts

COMMUNITY COORDINATOR
Peter Baker
baker@ccchfa.org

Cascades Farmers' Market Producers

Approximately 500 growers come together to form the Cascades Farmers' Market community. One of its members is Ninety Farms which began in 1993 in Western Washington State with some of the first Katahdin Hair sheep on the West Coast. Ninety Farms raises nearly 900 purebred Katahdin lambs on pasture. It sells its grass fed beef, heritage breed Katahdin lambs, and naturally raised veal at local markets. In 1995 Ninety Farms started growing a few artichokes in a garden plot. Now they grow a diverse array of herbicide and pesticide free vegetables for a Community Supported Agriculture program and for sale to restaurants in the Seattle area. As development springs up on every side of the farm, the growers work hard to educate their community on the benefits of local agriculture and the importance of sustainable land stewardship.

PRODUCTION AREA
Arlington, Washington State

COMMUNITY COORDINATOR
Linda Neuzing
ninetyfarms@aol.com

Catskills Region Agriculture Promoters

The community puts together the members of Pure Catskills, a campaign sponsored by the Watershed Agricultural Council to mobilize support for fresh food products grown, raised and manufactured in the Catskill Mountain Region. A group of one hundred and fifty farmers, chefs, educators, and others are involved in promoting "Pure Catskills" as a regional label. The following are two of the farms that receive the Pure Catskills designation: Stoneledge Farm grows organic vegetables and fruits for restaurants and CSA customers. Once a year they invite all the New York City CSA members to the farm for a tour. Ti Na nOg Farm is a family farm near Walton, New York that raises heritage breed pigs, sheep, cows, turkeys and chickens.

PRODUCTION AREA
Walton, Catskill Mountains, New York State

COMMUNITY COORDINATOR
Allison Bennett
allisonbennett@nycwatershed.org

Central Appalachian Farmers' Market Organic Farmers

The community of Anthon Central Appalachian Farmers is at work to transition from an economy dependent on coal mining and tobacco farming to one rooted in organic agriculture, grass-based poultry and meat production, and other more sustainable enterprises. Appalachia was once a self-reliant region where local people grew and raised the vegetables, fruits, meats, and dairy they needed. The community includes a network of forty certified organic produce farmers, 50 farmers in transition to organic, 20 pasture-based meat and poultry farmers, and a number of direct marketers. All are at work to regain Central Appalachia's self-reliance while creating new opportunities for family farmers and other local entrepreneurs. The farmer community is active in the development of its community farmers markets. In addition, it provides nearly 60,000 pounds of organic produce each year to the regional Food Bank.

PRODUCTION AREA
Central Appalachian region, Virginia and Tennessee

COMMUNITY COORDINATOR
Anthony Flaccavento - asd@eva.org

Central Coast Heritage Poultry Producers

The 'Buy Fresh, Buy Local' campaign is a project of CAFF (Community Alliance with Family Farmers). It works to create a regional food identity and promote the sales of local, fresh, nutritious foods. In the process, CAFF seeks to strengthen the local economy, support endangered family farms, and protect the environment. 52 farmers, 15 farmers markets, 8 grocers and 13 restaurants have come together to participate in the campaign. Jim Dunlop and Rebecca Thistlewaite of TLC Ranch in Watsonville, California, are partners with CAFF and members of the campaign. They raise broiler chickens on organic pasture, moving the chickens daily in bottomless pens so that they always have access to fresh, organic grass. They raise Low Cornish, Black and Red Broilers, and some heritage varieties. TLC Ranchers also raise pigs, 650 laying hens for organic eggs, and between 50-75 heritage turkeys annually.

PRODUCTION AREA
Watsonville, California

COMMUNITY COORDINATOR
Jim Dunlop - tasteslikechickenranch@yahoo.com

Central Indiana Organic Farmers

A core group of sustainable and organic activists farmers in central Indiana has come together to sell products directly to consumers. In 2003 they established the Winters Farmers Market at Traders Point Creamery on the north side of Indianapolis. It was the first venue in the region for local farmers to sell their products during the winter and the first dedicated solely to small-scale sustainable organic and natural producers. The Traders Point Green Market now operates year-round. The success of the market has encouraged several small conventional farmers in the area to transition to organic. It is also responsible for the increase in the number of local chefs who use local organically produced products in their restaurants. Among its members, the Apple Family Farm is a third generation farm near McCordsville, Indiana. They raise pastured chickens, sheep, beef and dairy cows. Traders Point Farm Organics and Creamery is a family owned dairy which produces pure, fresh non-homogenized whole milk, yogurts, ice creams, and cheeses.

PRODUCTION AREA
Central Indiana, Indiana

COMMUNITY COORDINATOR
David Robb - davidRobb@netdirect.net

Central New Jersey Ice Cream Makers and Vegetable Growers

The Community of Sustainable Farmers and Ice Cream Makers of Central New Jersey is an informal association of approximately 50 chefs, farmers, local brewers, coffee roasters and livestock farmers from the Central New Jersey region who are committed to reemphasizing the processes that bring food from the field to the table. One of the farms, Cherry Grove Organic, is a certified organic farm that produces a variety of vegetables for a local CSA, a farmers market, and other local businesses. The farm grows over 25 varieties of mostly heirloom tomatoes, helping to preserve New Jersey's tradition of high-quality tomato growing. The Bent Spoon specialized in making small batches of artisan ice cream and sorbet using eggs from local farms, hormone-free dairy products from a nearby co-op, and herbs grown just down the road.

PRODUCTION AREA
Princeton, New Jersey

COMMUNITY COORDINATOR
Gabrielle Carbone - thebentspoon@verizon.net

Central Valley Peach and Raisin Growers

The San Joaquin Valley of California is the largest peach and nectarine growing area in the United Sates. Millions of boxes of tree fruit are grown there annually, and almost all the world's raisins are grown specifically in the Fresno region. At the Masumoto Family Farm, Mas and Marcy Masumoto grow 25 acres of certified organic peaches and nectarines and 45 acres of certified organic grapes that are sun-dried or cured on the vine. Because these family farmers strive to preserve old flavors and tastes, they grow exclusively heirloom variety fruits known for their outstanding flavor and balance of acidity and sugars. Their Sun Crest peach was one of the first species included in the United States Slow Food Ark of Taste.

PRODUCTION AREA
Central Valley, California

COMMUNITY COORDINATOR
Mas Masumoto
masumoto@aol.com

Chattanooga Breeders

Historically, the Southeast of the United States has been known for its forested pork and cured hams. This community of ten people, mostly family members, raises pigs in the forests of Chattanooga, Tennessee. They are at work to develop high quality cured ham and sausage products. They also raise grass-fed beef and lamb without using any antibiotics. The community raises rare heritage breed animals including Milking Devons cows and Gloustershire Old Spot pigs. Biodynamic principles to guide the farm operation, which also produces vegetables for a Community Supported Agriculture program using only farm-generated compost.

PRODUCTION AREA
Chattanooga, Tennessee

COMMUNITY COORDINATOR
Bill Keener
keener@chatt.com

Chattanooga Cooperative Farmers

Started in 1998, Crabtree Farms is a non-profit organization that runs a demonstration farm and community garden on 22 acres in the Clifton Hills neighborhood near downtown Chattanooga, Tennessee. The non-profit offers workshops and hosts farmers markets and various events put on by Slow Food and other sustainable agriculture groups. The community grows nearly 200 varieties of vegetables, flowers, fruits, and herbs on the farm and garden. Many varieties found at Crabtree Farms have histories tied with the Southern United States and are not otherwise commercially available.

PRODUCTION AREA
Chattanooga, Tennessee

COMMUNITY COORDINATOR
Vanessa Mercer
vmercer@crabtreefarms.org

Chattanooga Organic Bread Bakers

The community is made up by a group of cereal growers, millers, herbs and vegetable growers, and by a local bakery. The four employees at Niedlov's Breadworks, an artisan bakery in Chattanooga, Tennessee, produce 50,000 lbs of naturally leavened, handcrafted, and hearth baked organic bread each year following a traditional recipe. Their breads are made from stone-ground organic whole grain flours milled by a small regional mill, the Lindley Mills of Graham, North Carolina. Niedlov's artisan breads contain only three ingredients: flour, water, and salt. They are leavened with a sourdough culture that was started six years ago in Chattanooga and has been maintained with only organic whole flour and water since. The Niedlov's Breadworks community sources organic garlic, honey, tomatoes and herbs from local farmers. Many of Chattanooga's fine-dining establishments serve Niedlov's breads.

PRODUCTION AREA
Chattanooga, Tennessee

COMMUNITY COORDINATOR
John Sweet
jsweet@niedlovs.com

Chicago Green City Farmers' Market Producers

The community is a venue for local producers who operate around Chicago to sell their organic or all-natural products directly to the public. Fifty-five producers come together twice a week at the south end of Chicago's Lincoln Park for the market. Chicago Green City Market makes a diverse range of high quality, locally farmed products available to Chicago's citizens, chefs, restaurateurs, and food organizations. Among its members, John and Pat Sondgeroth of Heartland Meats are fourth generation farmers who continue the family tradition of raising cattle on their fully integrated livestock farm. They raise their cattle without hormones and feed them all-natural, non-GMO corn that they grow on the farm. They process the meat at the farm's own USDA-inspected plant.

PRODUCTION AREA
Chicago, Illinois

COMMUNITY COORDINATOR
Carolyn Zezima - admin@chicagogreencitymarket.org

Chicago Producers

The organic farmers, cheesemakers and meat producers who are part of the community share a dedication to preserving food traditions brought to the state by the first group of European settlers in the 1800s. They employ sustainable farming methods that help preserve the environment. Some of the farmers work within North Central Illinois Small Organic Farmers, an affiliation of four of organic growers of wheat, oats, barley, corn, hay, buckwheat, flax, and soybeans. The growers sell their products directly to consumers and to select restaurants in Chicago. The Woodford County Organic Farmers Community is a network of family farmers that are actively recovering sustainable farming traditions. Prairie Fruits Farm covers seven acres of rich prairie soil in the heart of Central Illinois. They sell their products through local markets, including the Urbana Farmers Market, as well as at some restaurants and retail locations in the Chicago area. Triple S Farms is a 200-acre diversified organic operation in Stewardson, Indiana, that produces dozens of varieties of organic fruits and vegetables, grains, pork, beef, chickens, turkeys and ducks.

PRODUCTION AREA
Illinois

COMMUNITY COORDINATOR
Joel Smith - jasmith@jasmith.net

Cornwall Hollow Breeders

This 100-acre plot in the northwest Hills of Connecticut has been farmed since the mid-1700s. For years the small family dairy farm shipped its milk to a distributor and lost contact with it from that point on. Two years ago the family decided to eliminate the 'middle man'. It scaled back the size of its herd and began to distribute its own non-homogenized milk and cream and produce its own cheeses. Hautboy Hill raises its cows without the use of antibiotics or hormones. The farm also has several hundred free-range chickens that produce brown eggs for local consumption. At its farm stand, Hautboy Hill sells pesticide and herbicide free produce in season and its own pastured pork and beef. The community sells its products through a scheme of Community Supported Agriculture.

PRODUCTION AREA
Cornwall Hollow, Connecticut

COMMUNITY COORDINATOR
Allyn Hurlburt
hautboyhill@optonline.net

Corona Ranchers

The community of New Mexico Ranchers is represented by Ranney Ranch, a family-operated cattle ranch dedicated to raising healthy, entirely grass-fed and grass-finished beef. The range is managed according to holistic and sustainable land management practices, using rotational grazing principles. At Ranney Ranch they build on a long tradition of family cattle ranching in the high New Mexico mesa country. Calves of traditional breeds are born and raised on the open range. The beef is humanely handled, processed and dry-aged; it is packaged and shipped according to customer specifications. Members of the community belong to the American Grassfed Association, a nation-wide organization grouping cattle, bison, goats and sheep raised by farmers who feed the animals nothing but milk and grass or grass-type hay from birth to harvest.

PRODUCTION AREA
Corona, New Mexico

COMMUNITY COORDINATOR
Nancy Levi Ranney - ranneyranch@gmail.com

Creswell Farmers

The growers at Sweetwater Farm and Nursery seek to capture the finest tastes and highest nutrition levels they can by growing organic foods and maintaining soil health. On 26,000 square feet of greenhouses and cultivated acreage, Sweetwater practices open pollinating farming. Six year round and five seasonal employees grow organic vegetables, fruits and herbs, raise chickens for eggs, harvest wild foods, and produce vegetable preserves. They replenish the soil through composting, the use of rock powders, and seed saving. The Farm and Nursury supplies its harvests to 150 subscribers to its Community Supported Agriculture (CSA) program, or about 300-350 people. In the 1880s, the grandfather of Sweetwater's owner immigrated to the United States, bringing with him seeds from his home in the Tatry Mountains of Czechoslovakia. Sweetwater continues to grow and nurture those prize 'Grandfather Beans'.

PRODUCTION AREA
Creswell, Oregon

COMMUNITY COORDINATOR
John Karlik - swth2o@earthlink.net

Cromwell Vegetable Growers

The community is represented by a seven-acre certified organic farm, which has operated in Cromwell, Connecticut since 1986 and is today the last remaining farm in the town. At Upper Forty Farm, a small handful of producers grow hundreds of varieties of heirloom, open-pollinated and ethnic vegetables. Almost all of the heirloom vegetables have cultural and regional backgrounds that make them historically important. The Upper Forty farmers are passionate about educating the customer on the benefits of eating organically, locally, and in season and the joy of trying new varieties of vegetables. Each year they host a 'Tomato Taste' sponsored by Slow Food Connecticut.

PRODUCTION AREA
Cromwell, Connecticut

COMMUNITY COORDINATOR
Kathryn Caruso - upperfortyfarm@sbcglobal.net

Cuyahoga County Farmers

The Community of Farmers, Producers & Markets of the Ohio & Erie National Heritage Canalway represent a broad spectrum of local-based producers, each sourcing its products to a local audience and working to build a solid, sustainable food community. A group of various farms work within the community. Curly Tail Organic Farm is a 114-acre farm in Knox County that raises certified organic heritage breed pastured pork. Cross Point Ecology Center sits on a 130-acre historic farmstead in Bath, Ohio and runs a 10-acre CSA organic farm and is committed to environmental education and sustainable agriculture. Larksong Dairy Farm, located near the Amish community of Fredericksburg, is an organic operation where the dairy farmers practice intensive and rotational grazing. Basket of Life is a Community Supported Agriculture (CSA) Farm in the Cuyahoga Valley. Its twenty-five CSA members come from three surrounding counties in Northeastern Ohio.

PRODUCTION AREA
Cuyahoga County, Ohio

COMMUNITY COORDINATOR
Kari Moore
kmoore@cvcountryside.org

Dalton Small Grain and Row Crop Growers

This community consists of forty certified organic farmers in western Nebraska who raise crops including hard red and white winter wheat, amaranth, millet, oats, blue corn, pinto beans, kidney beans, barley, rye and golden flax. Small grains, most of which are grown on dry land, have been raised in western Nebraska for over 150 years; these crops are the basic foundation of the area's economy. This community grows soil building plants such as clover, alfalfa, and peas in rotation to build the soil's organic matter and increase its fertility. Their grains are processed into flours, breakfast cereals, and other products which are marketed locally.

PRODUCTION AREA
Dalton, Western Nebraska

COMMUNITY COORDINATOR
Marva Holt
organics@daltontel.net

Davenport Organic Berry Growers

The community is represented by Swanton Berry Farm, a certified organic strawberry and vegetable farm serving the San Francisco Bay Area of California. Founded in 1983, Swanton Berry Farm now encompasses 20 acres of strawberries, 8 acres of olallieberries and blackberries, 15 acres of broccoli and cauliflower, 15 acres of artichokes, 3 acres of peas, and 3 acres of kiwis. In 1998, Swanton Berry Farm was the first organic farm to sign a contract with the United Farm Workers, AFL-CIO. Today, all of the farm's 50 unionized employees have access to an ownership program via the profit-sharing plan. The (AFL-CIO) is a voluntary federation of 53 national and international labor unions. Today's unions represent nearly 9 millinions represent nearly 9 million working women and men of every race and ethnicity and from every walk of life.

PRODUCTION AREA
Davenport, California

COMMUNITY COORDINATOR
Jim Cochran
jimcochran50@hotmail.com

Dungeness and Calallam County Organic Farmers

Nash's Organic Produce was established in the 1970s. It is a 400-acre diversified organic farm that serves as the heart of the Sequim-Dungeness Valley organic agricultural community. This farm's small crew grows a variety of vegetables and produces eggs, chickens, pigs, seed crops, forage, and cover crops. Nash's Organic Produce uses bi-products from local crabbing and small-scale dairy operations. They sell their produce at a farm stand, local farmers' markets, Puget Consumers Cooperative in Seattle, and through a CSA program. Nash Huber – the leader of the community – is actively keeping farming alive in Calallam County on the North Olympic Penninsula of Washington State through his extensive work in farmland protection campaigns and involvement in the local land trust. He has secured long-term leases and conservation easements on his 400 acres so that future generations can continue to farm the land.

PRODUCTION AREA
Sequim, Washington State

COMMUNITY COORDINATOR
Nash Huber
orca@olympus.net

Eastern Colorado Plains Lamb Breeders

Prairie Natural Lamb is a small family-run sheep operation in the eastern plains of Colorado. The family raises 60-70 lambs per year, allowing ewes and lambs to graze on pasture. They supplement their diets with hay and finish them on a combination of high-protein alfalfa hay and additive-free, soy-free grain. They do not use antibiotics, artificial hormones, or animal by-products in feed. Sheep have played a historically important role in the lives of Colorado farm and ranch families, their wool and meat providing the local community with sustenance. The family sells directly to consumers after the meat has been custom cut and wrapped in a family-owned USDA approved facility. Together with other breeders and farmers of the area, they sell their products through the local farmers' markets.

PRODUCTION AREA
Strasburg, Colorado

COMMUNITY COORDINATOR
Marilyn Wentz
marilyn.wentz@hughes.com

East Meredith Pig and Turkey Farmers

Skate Creek Farm is located on 120 acres in Delaware County, New York in the northern Catskill region. It sits on the historic site of a 1920s era dairy, and the farmers are currently at work to preserve the architecturally significant buildings. At Skate Creek Farm, the farmers raise beef, lamb, Berkshire pork, and heritage turkeys including Red Bourbon Reds, Blue Slate, Standard Bronze and Black Spanish. All of the livestock is raised without the use of antibiotics, growth hormones, or other drugs, and with free access to pasture. The turkeys, the Farm's primary focus, are raised for the Thanksgiving holiday; they roam freely on fresh grass. In addition, Skate Creek raises bull calves from a local dairy for sale as pastured veal. Skate Creek Farm sells its meat at farmers' markets, through a mail order system, at various New York State stores and restaurants, and directly at the farm.

PRODUCTION AREA
East Meredith, Delaware County, New York State

COMMUNITY COORDINATOR
Amy Kenyon - skatecreekfarm@earthlink.net

Esparto Vine Growers and Wine Makers

The community is represented by Orfila Vineyard and Winery, which was started by a member of the original committee of the California Wine Institute, a public policy advocacy association of California wineries. The Wine Institute brings together the resources of 915 wineries and affiliated businesses to support legislative and regulatory advocacy, market development, media relations, scientific research, and education programs that benefit the entire California wine sector. The owners of the Orfila Vineyard and Winery are currently studying the possibility of transitioning to biodynamic agriculture. The Winery produces a wide variety including the Viognier Cuvee 'Lotus', one of America's first true Rhone-style wines using the classic three whites (Viognier, Marsanne and Roussanne), on 70 acres in the San Pasqual Valley of Southern California.

PRODUCTION AREA
San Diego County, California

COMMUNITY COORDINATOR
Leone Santoro - ewinemaker@aol.com

Florida Panhandle Farmers

Zebra Truck Farm is a Community Supported Agriculture (CSA) endeavor of eight farmers on several farms in the Jefferson and Leon County areas of Florida's Panhandle. Forty-five Community Supported Agriculture shareholders receive Zebra Truck Farm's organically grown seasonal fruits and vegetables, canned and jellied products, free-range poultry, organic eggs, fruit, honey, hand-made goats' milk cheeses, and grass-fed non-antibiotic beef. This community of farmers trains other local farmers in natural and organic farming methods. The farms are part of Local Harvest, a country-wide project aimed at sourcing fresh, healthy and flavorful food to the consumers all over the United States. Their website lists farmers' markets, family farms and other sources of sustainably grown food, taking into account the issue of food miles, according to which consumers can buy food produced in their area.

PRODUCTION AREA
Jefferson and Leon County, Florida

COMMUNITY COORDINATOR
Penny Orr
porr@fsu.edu

Fourth Corner Farmers' Market Producers

Fourth Corner is located north of Seattle, Washington. The Fourth Corner Farmers' Market began with a small group of Italian immigrants who farmed small lots of land at the turn of the century. Today, approximately 75-100 farmers in the Fourth Corner region produce hazelnuts and raspberries, high quality dairy products, and over 150 varieties of traditional and heirloom vegetables and flowers. In particolar, Uprising Seeds, a vendor at the Fourth Corner Farmers' Market, recently began providing local Northwest gardeners and farmers with regionally adapted, organically grown seeds. Alongside commercial standard varieties, Uprising Seeds believes lesser known heirloom vegetables have a vital place in the cultural identity of the Pacific Northwest.

PRODUCTION AREA
Bellingham, Fourth Corner, Washington State

COMMUNITY COORDINATOR
Brian Campbell
meowtos@riseup.net

Georgia Family Farmers

The Slow Food Atlanta Georgia Convivium promotes sustainability and biodiversity by endorsing and supporting local growers who use responsible, eco-friendly production methods. The community also works to safeguard the culinary traditions of the area through various events and educational workshops. The region's agricultural heritage reflects the blending of Native American, African American, Asian, and European immigrant populations. The majority of the community's growers have small family farms where they strive to preserve a farming heritage that is being lost because of the dominance of corporate agriculture and urban sprawl. Among the members of the community is Farmers Fresh, a network of farmers and food producers who work to create sales opportunities for small farmers of high quality foods. Member farms and producers offer their products through a CSA program and at several farmers markets. Another member of the community is White Oak Pastures, a natural grass-fed beef operation that uses rotational grazing. Sweet Grass Dairy is a family-run farm that handmakes award winning cheeses with milk from its two herds of goats and select milking cows. The animals are free-range. Five Seasons Brewery produces handcrafted beers that it sells locally. With over 30 different types of beers and a restaurant, this brewery has gained local and regional praise. Tamworth Farm raises pigs in open lots and fields and feeds them pure, non-GMO grains with no animal by-products.

PRODUCTION AREA
Georgia

COMMUNITY COORDINATOR
Julie Shaffer - indiasjules@gmail.com

Gulf of Mexico Seafood Harvesters

The Gulf of Mexico Seafood Harvesters are shrimpers, oystermen, fishers and crabbers from the second largest seafood production area in the United States. The community's main products are white and brown shrimp caught with trawls and then sold fresh locally or to dockside buyers who freeze them. An individual owns each fishing boat in the Gulf and operates it with his or her own small crew. Fishermen of the community harvest and process oysters and reef fish such as amberjacks, snappers, and porgies. Seafood is a vital component of regional food culture. Because of the devastating effects of Hurricanes Katrina and Rita this community has the difficult and important task of coming together to rebuild a struggling industry.

PRODUCTION AREA
Galliano and Violet, Louisiana; Fort Myers, Florida

COMMUNITY COORDINATOR
Margaret Curole - mbcurole@myviscom.com

Gulf South Blueberry Growers

This community is made up of members of the Gulf South Blueberry Growers Association, a group of 210 producers who grow indigenous rabbit eye blueberries both organically and conventionally. Members of the community planted the first managed acres of blueberry bushes in 1982. The farmer members now grow over 2,400 acres of the local blueberries in the southeastern United States. The highest concentration of these orchards is in the southern half of Mississippi State where the rabbit eye blueberry grows well in the acidic, sandy soils. Bees pollinate the blooms so farmers use earth-friendly methods of field management to preserve healthy native and domesticated bee populations. Most of the fruit is grown on small acreages on small farms. Farmers harvest and market independently or through cooperatives.

PRODUCTION AREA
Mississippi

COMMUNITY COORDINATOR
Amy Phelps - mercury3rd@aol.com

Hancock Educators

This year the founder of Norway Hill Garden in Hancock, New Hampshire, is piloting a project to build a greenhouse and school garden at Wells School in Peterborough, New Hampshire and a garden and garden shed at Crotched Mountain Rehabilitation Center in Greenfield, New Hampshire. At the two sites, students will learn science, history, and geography hand-in-hand with stewardship of the land and the value of locally grown food. The project seeks to become a model for all schools in the Monadnock Region.

PRODUCTION AREA
Monadnock, New Hampshire

COMMUNITY COORDINATOR
Kin Schilling - kinschilling@verizon.net

Healdsburg Farmers' Market Producers

This community entails 60 plus farmers and purveyors who produce a wide variety of products including honey, garlic, onions, peaches, pork, lamb, mushrooms, flowers and other fruits and vegetables. The Healdsburg Farmers Market provides these small-scale local farmers with the rare opportunity to reach local consumers directly. The farmers who participate in the market share a desire to produce the best tasting, freshest, most interesting, and diverse products possible in a manner that benefits the community and the earth. At the farmers' market they are able to share that mission with the community that eats their foods. Wine grape agriculture has come to dominate the local landscape. By displaying a wide range of well-crafted products at the market, these farmers remind local community members of the diverse possibilities of the land. While some producers sell their products nationally, all agree that the farmers' market is their most important venue.

PRODUCTION AREA
Sonoma County, California

COMMUNITY COORDINATOR
Bill Hawn
astibill@directway.com

Herscher Poultry Farmers

The community is represented by a family farm raising poultry and by the butchers who process the meat. Dennis and JoAnn Dickman have been farming for over 41 years on a farm 75 miles southwest of Chicago. The two have been supplying fresh, multi-colored sweet corn to local markets for over 15 years. In 1999 they began raising fresh pastured chickens and turkeys. Their poultry feed on organic grasses and are not given antibiotics, growth stimulants, or steroids. Because grass is a natural detoxifier, the Dickmans' chickens are higher in omega-3 fatty acids, have less fat and more substance to their meat than grain-fed birds. The Dickmans' goal as farmers is to provide customers with most nutritious product possible. They use a federally licensed processing facility that a small Amish family owns and operates.

PRODUCTION AREA
Herscher, Illinois

COMMUNITY COORDINATOR
JoAnn Dickman - djdickman@netzero.net

Homestead Tropical Fruit Growers

This community is made up of a two-person management team, a plant collector, a garden manager, and fifteen volunteers who work together to grow heirloom cultivars and land races of tropical fruit crops. Fairchild Tropical Botanic Garden is a living collection of tropical fruits assembled after decades of plant collecting and collaboration with growers around the tropical world. The community promotes the long-term conservation and use of tropical fruits. It uses sustainable field practices and processes its harvests into an array of value-added products. Mangos are Fairchild's largest produced fruit; there are over 350 cultivars, ten wild crop relatives, and many landraces on their acreage. Mango trees are grown in the field under sustainable field practices. Their avocado collection includes over 150 local cultivars. Fairchild Tropical Botanic Garden puts on an international festival that celebrates the history, traditions, culinary uses, arts and culture of each of its primary fruit varieties: mango, avocado, jack fruit, and mamey sapote.

PRODUCTION AREA
Homestead, Florida

COMMUNITY COORDINATOR
Richard Campbell - rcampbell@fairchildgarden.org

Honey Producers

Bee Raw Honey is a small, New York-based organization that supports eight artisan beekeepers from around the United States who provide raw, unfiltered honeys made from single flower varieties. Bee Raw has been working with individual beekeepers since 1999 to bring a diverse assortment of varietal honeys into the marketplace, from buckwheat honey from Washington State's Yakima Valley to Saw Palmetto honey from the Florida wetlands. Other bee keepers produce basswood, blueberry, buckwheat, desert wildflower and cranberry honey. Bee Raw Honey seeks to preserve and extend the rich beekeeping heritage represented in each region of the United States. The bee keepers working within Bee Raw Honey sell their products directly at their farm shops or through Bee Raw Honey website.

PRODUCTION AREA
Various locations

COMMUNITY COORDINATOR
Zeke Freeman
zbee@beeraw.com

Hudson Valley Agricultural Educators

Hearty Roots Community Farm is a place where local community members connect with the land and one another through the Community Supported Agriculture (CSA) program. Members of Hearty Roots CSA visit the farm every week during the growing season to pick up a CSA share of naturally grown produce, freshly harvested by the farmers. Hearty Roots strives to keep locally grown produce affordable for everyone and offers alternative payment options for those living on a low income. In addition to their local CSA program, the farmers sell their greens at the Montgomery Place farm stand and several local restaurants. Once a week, from June through November, they deliver produce to Brooklyn, where city CSA members pick up shares at the Red Shed Community Garden in the Williamsburg/Greenpoint neighborhood.

PRODUCTION AREA
Tivoli, Hudson Valley, New York State

COMMUNITY COORDINATOR
Benjamin Shute
benjamin@heartyroots.com

Illinois Artisan Cheesemakers

The Community of Illinois Artisan Cheesemakers consists of the members of the Prairie Pure Cheese Company, a partnership between three families. The company was formed in 2004 to produce artisan cheeses for people in the Chicago metropolitan area. Two small, family-owned dairies provide the milk: the Aves Family milks approximately 90 cows, and the Fitzgerald family milks an 80-cow herd. Both feed their cows primarily home grown forages and grains and do not inject artificial growth hormone. They are located in northern Illinois, just outside the town of Belvidere. They dairy farm families and their veterinarian work with a small cheese plant, Edelweiss Town Hall Dairy, in Monticello, Wisconsin. Their first batch of artisan cheese was available in 2004, and since then they have marketed and sold their products in seasonal outlets across Illinois. Prairie Pure Cheese Company makes a creamy brick-style German cheese, and Cheddar.

PRODUCTION AREA
Belvidere, Illinois

COMMUNITY COORDINATOR
Brian Gerloff - seneca@interaccess.com

Indiana Uplands Farmers

The Indiana Uplands is a hilly, undulating area in south central Indiana that is not suitable for large-scale mono-crop industrial farming because of the rocky soil and landscape. As a result, a diverse community of small independent family farmers has emerged. These producers are united by their participation in the Bloomington Farmers Market. Bloomington is a large university town that hosts a year-round producer-only market with more than 100 vendors. The market has been a vital part of the community since 1975. Heartland Family Farm grows organic heirloom tomatoes, eggplants, peppers, and salad greens that it sells at the market and through the farm's CSA program. Local chefs work with the farm to custom create salad mixes. The farmers also raise chickens for eggs and meat. Harvest Moon Flower Farm grows culinary herbs and edible flowers including squash blossoms, gem marigolds, Johnny-jump-ups (viola family) and nasturtiums. They also grow a wide selection of vegetables for sale at the farmers market.

PRODUCTION AREA
Indiana Uplands, Indiana

COMMUNITY COORDINATOR
Christine Barbour - barbour@indiana.edu

International Food Producers in National Parks

This community represents a first effort to recognize that there are food producers around the world operating within national parks. Many of these producers have been living and farming the same land for generations, long before the establishment of the national park. Across the world there are many cases of park managers collaborating with NGOs and other national and regional organizations to protect these traditional producers and their modes of life. In some cases producers have been able to brand their products with reference to the park. Mexican Blue Corn, raw milk cheddar cheese, olive oil and lentils are among the products these traditional producers grow and create.

PRODUCTION AREA
Various countries

COMMUNITY COORDINATOR
Jeffrey Roberts
cowcreek@attglobal.net

Iowa City Farmers

Laura Dowd heads Local Food Connection, a charity organization that collects Community Supported Agriculture (CSA) shares and donates them to underprivileged families in Iowa City. Local Foods Connection (LFC) was founded in 1999 in Iowa City, but touches the lives of people in Johnson, Washington, Linn and Jefferson Counties. LFC purchases produce, meat products and other goods from small family farmers and donates these goods to needy families. Their purpose is twofold: to champion small family farmers who use environmentally-friendly farming methods, and to put high-quality, fresh food into the hands of people who cannot afford it. LFC enrolls clients in CSAs, through which they receive weekly boxes of vegetables, bread or eggs for 4 to 5 months. Clients receive chickens and turkeys but are also offered educational opportunities, which include readings and movies on nutrition and agriculture, farm visits, cook books, volunteer experience, cooking classes and more.

PRODUCTION AREA
Iowa City, Iowa

COMMUNITY COORDINATOR
Laura Dowd
localfoodsconnection@yahoo.com

Jacksonville Farmers

Noah Valley Farm is a small, diversified farm in Calhoun County, Alabama. This community of one farmer and his workers strives to develop a sustainable food system that respects the natural balance of plants, animals, soil, water and air. Both a Monsanto Company chemical plant and the US Army's chemical weapons depot/incinerator are near the farm, causing Noah's Valley huge challenges and threatening the health of the local environment. Noah Valley Farm stands firm as a sustainable enterprise despite the difficulties posed by its corporate and military neighbors. The farm's main products are heirloom tomatoes, summer peas, carrots and chanterelle mushrooms. The farm is Certified Naturally Grown and all of its products are grown organically. Noah Valley sells to Community Supported Agriculture (CSA) members and local chefs and at a local farmers' market.

PRODUCTION AREA
Jacksonville, Alabama

COMMUNITY COORDINATOR
Simon Bevis - nohavalleyfarm@gmail.com

Kalona Organic Sprout Growers

The community of organic sprout growers operates in Kalona, Iowa, and is made up of a farmer who grows the vegetable on his organic farm, and a group of local restaurateurs who buy the primary products from the farm. James Nisly grows 20 different varieties of organic sprouts, from sweet pea to arugula to popcorn sprouts, and wheat grass in hot houses near Kalona. Through a program offered by Alliant Energy (a company encouraging energy conservation), 25% of the power Nisly uses in his green houses is generated by the wind. Nisly sells his sprouts to groceries and 20 restaurants.

PRODUCTION AREA
Kalona, Iowa

COMMUNITY COORDINATOR
James Nisly - organicgreens@earthlink.net

Lebanon Heirloom Apple Growers and Cider Producers

The family farmers at Poverty Lane Orchards in rural New Hampshire grow 85-100 varieties of apples. They are first-generation apple growers and leaders in the planting of rare and heirloom varieties. They sell their apples as is and pressed and fermented as cider. Thanks to Poverty Lane Orchards, apples including Spitzenbergs, Golden Russets, Wicksons, and Pomme Grise now have a strong market in gourmet shops and restaurants. The farm uses an integrated pest management system. They make their hard ciders in the regional American tradition by fermenting their apples with neutral champagne yeast at cool temperatures for better flavor. A visit to Bullmer Ciders, the best-known cider producer in England, taught the farmers how to choose apples for cider.

PRODUCTION AREA
Lebanon, New Hampshire

COMMUNITY COORDINATOR
Louisa Spencer - lspencer@farnumhillciders.com

Little Rock Agricultural Educators

The Dunbar Educational Urban Farm is a community garden at a multiracial urban school in an economically depressed neighborhood of South Little Rock, Arkansas. At Dunbar, educators teach kindergarten through 8th grade students the fundamentals of sustainable agriculture and the importance of good nutrition. Students also work a summer first job as part of the school's Life Skills program. The intensive training program in organic gardening, leadership, and entrepreneurship enables youth to learn about the nurturing environment of community while developing the technical skills to produce fresh food.

PRODUCTION AREA
Little Rock, Arkansas

COMMUNITY COORDINATOR
Sylvia Blain - sblain@auger-ar.org

Los Angeles Educators

The Watts Garden Club is an agricultural education facility in Watts, California in South Central Los Angeles. The facility is in a community where drug warfare and gangs run rampant, welfare recipients make up 90% of the population, and the HIV/AID infection rate has risen to 70%. The neighborhood is completely denatured, and filled with housing projects. The only foods available to the Watts community are fast foods and processed foods. Since 1992, the Watts Garden Club has built over 2,067 gardens, and this year they are opening a farmers' market. They seek to teach the community how to grow its own organic foods and to eat real, natural foods. On their gardens, community members grow vegetables for their community's consumption. They also create value-added products including pesto, salsa, and coleslaw. The Club hires exclusively people who have been convicted of a felony and helps them turn around their lives.

PRODUCTION AREA
Los Angeles, California

COMMUNITY COORDINATOR
Anna Marie Carter - wattsgardenclub@hotmail.com

Louisiana Farmers, Shrimpers, and Restaurateurs

Hurricane Katrina was one of the largest natural disasters the United States has endured in its history. Through its Terra Madre Relief Fund, Slow Food USA has awarded 12 grants to local fishermen, farmers and restaurateurs to help them reconstruct their businesses and rebuild of their food system. The recipients include Isabel and Miguel Mendez, the only growers of the Louisiana strawberry, a Slow Food Ark of Taste product, Pete and Clara Gerica, local shrimpers, God's Vineyard Community Garden, and Mrs. Leah Chase of Dooky Chase restaurant. Each has been an active part of New Orleans' long and rich food history. The recipients face tremendous difficulties in their daily lives, but each continues forward with determination. Together they represent the possibility of a revitalized New Orleans food system.

PRODUCTION AREA
Louisiana

COMMUNITY COORDINATOR
Poppy Tooker - poppy@poppytooker.com

Madera Growers, Bakers, and Wine Grape Growers

Historically, Madera has been a high industrial production area. The 10 producers in this food community are exceptional examples of farmers and producers who emphasize quality over quantity. John Texiera of Lone Willow Ranch produces 350 varieties of heirloom tomatoes on a small organic farm on the west side of the San Joaquin Valley. For 10 years he has supplied tomatoes for the West Coast's largest tomato event. Patrick and Margaret Bourrell of La Boulangerie have owned the Fresno community's highest quality artisan bakery for the past 25 years. They grind their own grain, use some organic flours, and source local fresh fruits for their pastries. Gina Nonini of Marian Farm in Fresno, California, grows two local grape varieties using biodynamic methods. Sharlyn and Lou Pasquale of Il Giardino Organics grow organic vegetables for restaurants and markets.

PRODUCTION AREA
Madera County, California

COMMUNITY COORDINATOR
Thomas Willey - mrwilley@tdwilleyfarms.com

Madison Educators

Initiated in October 2002 at the Slow Food Salone del Gusto, this is the first sister city partnership organized by Slow Food. Since Madison, Wisconsin and Mantua, Italy became Slow Food sister cities, members from both communities have shared food traditions, put on taste education events, and established a visitor exchange program. Both cities promote artisan products of their respective regions in the sister city. In October 2005, visitor chefs from Mantova put on cooking demonstrations and a food-sampling event in Madison. At the Madison Food and Wine show, chefs from both cities paired Mantovan products with local artisan ingredients and vegetables in the dishes they served attendees. Community members from the two cities share a common agenda to sustain biodiversity and support Slow Food's goals of good, clean, and just food. Among their projects to meet those ends, Slow Food Madison established a demonstration garden at Middleton High School in Wisconsin. In Italy, Slow Food members established a school garden in Pegognaga.

PRODUCTION AREA
Madison, Wisconsin

COMMUNITY COORDINATOR
Susan Boldt - susanboldt@slowfoodwisconsin.org

Maine Chocolatiers

In Aroostook County, Maine, a woman began her own artisan chocolate sauce business after discovering the difference between fine flavor cocoas and conventional ones. All of product line is made with organic ingredients and half with fair trade cocoa. She sources cocoa from small-scale organic farmers in Central America and the Caribbean regions who grow cacao using traditional agricultural methods. The cacao is shade grown under rainforest canopy using intercropping and integrated pest management practices. The farmers harvest the cacao by hand and ferment it using banana leaves. The cacao is then dried and pressed to produce cacao liquor before it undergoes additional processing.

PRODUCTION AREA
Aroostook County, Maine

COMMUNITY COORDINATOR
Angela Wotton - amwotton@earthlink.net

Maine Organic Potato Farmers

With a 200-year tradition of potato growing, Maine was the number one potato producing state in the nation until 50 years ago. There are still more potatoes grown in Aroostook County, Maine than in any other county in the United States. Within the county there is a community of certified-organic, small-scale potato farmers who are committed to agricultural sustainability and crop diversity. The approximately 125 members who make up these organic family farms grow and harvest potatoes using simple, sustainable practices. They use wheat and oats as rotation crops in a tradition that Maine farmers have applied for 200 years.

PRODUCTION AREA
Aroostook County, Maine

COMMUNITY COORDINATOR
Jim Gerritsen - jim@woodprairie.com

Maine Organic Producers

With over 5000 members, the Maine Organic Farmers and Gardeners Association (MOFGA) is the largest state level organic association in the United States. The heart of the community consists of about 500 small, diverse, organic farms that are smaller in scale than the national average. The community also includes several thousand households who focus their energies on home food production. The MOFGA counts among its membership leaders in local farmers markets, seed saving and biodiversity preservation, and the Community Supported Agriculture (CSA) movement. At every level, members are at work to build bridges between farmers and eaters. The associations put on an annual harvest festival, the Common Ground Country Fair, that draws 50,000 people to Unity, Maine, each September. The organic farming movement in Maine is now 35-years-old. Today, nearly five percent of Maine's farmers are certified organic, with 15% of the state's dairy farmers in that category. Most of the products the farmers and gardeners produce have been grown in the state for 300 to 400 years, a few of them truly indigenous to the region.

PRODUCTION AREA
Maine

COMMUNITY COORDINATOR
Russell Libby - rlibby@mofga.org

Marin and Sonoma County Olive Oil Producers

The community of Californian olive oil producers is represented by McEvoy Ranch, a farm which marries traditional methods with innovative engineering to produce a singular, certified-organic Extra Virgin olive oil. This richly complex oil has a medium body with a mild, savory bitterness and a distinct, yet delicate pungency. The appearance is grass green at harvest, mellowing to a greenish gold after a resting period of a few months. The Ranch encompasses 17 orchards across 550 acres in Northern California, west of Petaluma. At McEvoy Ranch, workers blend together six varietals in their onsite blade and stone olive oil mills. The Ranch does not allow chemical processing of its olives and has voluntarily adopted the International Olive Oil Council's stringent rules for extra virgin olive oil processing. The products of the farms are sold at the farm shop and at the Ferry Plaza Farmers' Market in San Francisco.

PRODUCTION AREA
Petaluma, California

COMMUNITY COORDINATOR
Christina Cavallaro - christina@mcevoyranch.com

Marin County Grassfed Livestock Ranchers

This community comprises two husband-and-wife operations that supply the local community with their high-quality, natural beef, poultry and pork. Dave and Julie Evans of the 'H' Ranch and Dan Bagley and Liz Cunninghame of Clark Summit Farm employ the rotational grazing system to raise cows on certified organic pastures. The meat is then butchered locally. In addition, both ranches raise diverse breeds of certified, free-range organic hens, relocating the flocks to fresh pasture every day. They raise pigs in a stress-free environment and have the meat processed at one of the community family's cut and wrap facilities. The beef, chicken, eggs and pork are all sold locally. In addition, Julie Evans runs Point Reyes Preserves, selling sauces, condiments, vegetables and fruits preserves made with local, seasonal ingredients.

PRODUCTION AREA
Marin County, California

COMMUNITY COORDINATOR
David Evans - david@marinsunfarms.com

Marin County Producers

The Community of Marin Organics is an association of Marin County organic food producers whose livelihood is based on respect for nature and a sense of place. For over a century the fertile valleys and lush grassy hills of Marin County have been home to thriving family farms and dairies, although in the past 50 years many small farming operations have gone out of business because of economic competition from industrial agriculture. Marin Organics was formed in 1999 by a group of over 30 certified organic farmers and ranchers who produce a variety of products including meat, poultry, fish, shellfish, olive oil, wine, honey, bread, dairy, cheese, vegetables, fruits and wild foods. Marin Organic provides practical support to these producers with its recognizable label for products. It also offers educational programs for community members and information on transitioning from non-organic to organic practices and marketing help for farmers. Marin Organics is dedicated to creating the first all-organic county in the nation. They would like to see organic foods in Marin schools, hospitals and prisons, and for every Marin County resident to know three producers by face and name.

PRODUCTION AREA
Marin County, California

COMMUNITY COORDINATOR
Helge Hellberg - helge@marinorganic.org

Marin County Vegetable Growers

This community entails 30 plus producers, farm laborers, distributors and state employees working in Marin County, north of the San Francisco Bay Area. As a community they grow and distribute a highly diverse selection of certified organic cool and warm weather crops such as tomatoes, bell peppers and melons. They are seed-savers and proponents of heirloom varieties, having grown the same varieties of fruits and vegetables since one of these operations began over 150 years ago. It is the oldest certified organic operation in California.

PRODUCTION AREA
Marin County, California

COMMUNITY COORDINATOR
Jesse Kuhn - jesse@marinroots.com

Marin County Wine Grape Growers

This community consists of grape growers and vintners at three vineyards in Marin County, California. All three grow and process on a small-scale using sustainable methods. The three vineyards grow grapes including Pinot Noir and Chardonnay. The community sells grapes, wine, grass-fed lamb, and grass-fed rabbit. They have won numerous awards for their wines and other products. Among the membership is Stubbs Vineyard, the first certified organic vineyard in Marin County. A few miles inland from Tomales bay, the vines are planted in a valley surrounded by steeply rising hills. This topography and location provides a unique microclimate for the fruit which results in a long, cool growing season, and in a long hang time for the fruit. The fruit is quite intense, and is pleasingly high in acidity. The soil profile is moderately fertile and is mostly decomposed marine sedimentary material.

PRODUCTION AREA
Marin County, California

COMMUNITY COORDINATOR
Mary & Tom Stubbs - mary@stubbsvineyard.com

Marshall Organic Dairy Farmers

The eighty members of the Straus Dairy Cooperative produce fully sustainable, pasture-based organic dairy products. They make their products as naturally as possible using simple techniques and keeping ingredients to a minimum. The cooperative grazes its cows on organic pastures. They process their artisan butter without any additives in a 1950s small batch churn. Their butter contains 85-86% butterfat content and less moisture than any butter on the US market. The cooperative makes its yogurts without thickeners, just milk and live cultures. Its super premium organic ice creams are made in small batches using only organic ingredients and no emulsifiers, thickeners or colorings. Point Reyes County has been famous since the turn of the 19th century for its unique and flavorful butter. Unfortunately, over the years the number of dairies has declined precipitously. Today, only 28 dairies are left in the county. The Straus Dairy, one of the remaining few, was the first organic dairy in the western United States. Ellen Straus, co-founder of the farm, started the first agricultural land trust in the US, the Marin Agricultural Land Trust.

PRODUCTION AREA
Marshall, Marin County, California

COMMUNITY COORDINATOR
Albert Straus - albert@strausmilk.com

Martha's Vineyard Aquaculturists

The Wampanoag people have harvested shellfish on Martha's Vineyard for millennia. A community of small-scale aquaculturalists continues that tradition using sustainable, natural production methods in coastal bays and ponds. The community includes approximately 300 shellfish aquaculture producers and 25 members of the Slow Food Martha's Vineyard Convivium. Together they work to provide high quality, fresh, local products to the region's eaters, and their success has kept industrial-scale shellfish operations out of Massachusetts. Their products include eastern oysters, bay scallops, hard clams and cultured bivalve shellfish. Their various endeavors help to support the local economy, bolster the area's shellfish population, and preserve New England's culinary heritage.

PRODUCTION AREA
Massachusetts

COMMUNITY COORDINATOR
Richard Karney - mvsg@adelphia.net

Maui Pineapple Growers

This community represented by Maui Land and Pineapple Company (MLP) community, headed by David Cole, is the strongest force in creating a self-sufficient, diversified local food economy for Hawaii. Pineapple agriculture dominates thousands of acres on all the main Hawaiian Islands. It is in the hands of small number of large companies. The leader of the community is a Hawaiian native who returned to the islands in 2003 after revitalizing a farm in Virginia. He took the helm of MLP and began a full-throttle campaign to awaken Hawaiians to the importance of self-sufficiency and agricultural variety and to inspire all local citizens and growers to become active in building a sustainable future. Nearly 90% of Hawaii's food and nearly all of its fuel for transportation and energy production are imported from elsewhere. MLP now embraces the notion of diversified local production as a means to strengthen the economy and provide food security.

PRODUCTION AREA
Maui, Hawaii

COMMUNITY COORDINATOR
David Cole - dcole@mlpmaui.com

Mayan Corn Growers

Ocean Song Farm and Wilderness Center is a non-profit learning center located in the coastal hills of Western Sonoma County in Northern California. At Ocean Song Organics Farm they grow over 75 heirloom vegetables, grains and flower varieties in small-scale hand tilled plots. Ocean Song Farm is a worker-based CSA; all workers are compensated with vegetables and other produce from the farm. Seeds from their harvests are deposited into a seed bank for community distribution. The Motherseed Project on the farm provides sanctuary to the biological and cultural heritage of the Mayan peoples of Chiapas: Ocean Song has a living seed bank of five varieties of Zapatista GMO-free corn. Ocean Song works in partnership with the Zapatista Community of Chiapas to help preserve their indigenous Mayan corn seed. The project began in the 1990s when it was discovered that GE corn had begun to contaminate indigenous Mayan corn varieties. The corn is processed for grinding as food for the local community and for seed.

PRODUCTION AREA
Occidental, Sonoma County, California

COMMUNITY COORDINATOR
Benjamin Fahrer - benja77@earthlink.net

Miami Student Farmers

The Growing Connection is a grassroots project developed by the Food and Agriculture Organization of the United Nations and the American Horticultural Society. Students in the United States, Mexico, Ghana, Senegal, and the Dominican Republic communicate with each other over the internet; they are a global growing community, each group using low-cost, water efficient and sustainable food growing techniques in its respective school or community garden. The students share their experiences with each other using IT connectivity. At Miami Country Day School in Miami, Florida, 400 students grow Moringa trees and Cape Gooseberry tomatoes, a rare variety, in their school garden. They are a part of The Growing Connection network. The students prepare food grown in the organic gardens in one-of-a-kind solar ovens.

PRODUCTION AREA
Miami, Florida

COMMUNITY COORDINATOR
Rowena Gerber - gerberr@miamicountyday.org

Michigan Cider Makers

The Michigan Cider Makers' Guild is a grass-roots organization of twenty-three cider producers in Michigan State. The guild restricts membership to those who meet its stringent quality standards; members must attend a cider school at Michigan State University, where they learn the latest concepts in sanitation and other quality-assurance techniques. Apple cider was a centerpiece of the food culture of the United States at its founding. The first cider mills in Michigan date back to the 1800s. The Michigan Cider Makers Guild seeks to ensure that traditional cider making continues into the future. The Dexter Cider Mill in Dexter, Michigan is a 115-year-old mill and a member of the guild. At Dexter, millers press cider in a wooden oak press with the apples of local growers. They sell their cider, over 20 varieties of fresh apples, organic vegetables, and baked goods such as apple pie at the mill.

PRODUCTION AREA
Michigan

COMMUNITY COORDINATOR
Nancy Koziski-Steinhauer - steinhaueer489@cs.com

Michigan Specialty Grain Growers and Processors

This community unites two producers, five small distributors, and one processor of specialty grains in central Michigan. The Bloomer family grows red and white popcorn and soybeans on their farm near Ann Arbor. Specialty grains are important to the biodiversity of agriculture in central Michigan. The Bloomers have chosen to grow both red and white popcorns for their hull characteristics and not for yield or kernel size. Both are traditionally bred corn varieties. They also grow non-GMO soybeans that they harvest and clean on the farm and then dry roast in a convection system for processing into a line of value-added products, from dry-roasted soy nuts with organic sea salt to honey ginger soy nuts. They are at work with a loc al Michigan chocolate manufacturer, Gilbert Chocolates of Ja

PRODUCTION AREA
Morrilton, Ozark Mountains, Arkansas

COMMUNITY COORDINATOR
Ragan Sutterfield
ragan@adamafarm.com

Mississippi Cooperative Farmers

This community has more than 100 mainly African American members who range in age from 25 to 91. They are brought together through their participation in the Indian Springs Farmers' Association, a marketing and buying cooperative of farmers operating in southern Mississippi who are committed to sustainable, regional food production. The farms range in size from 10 to 1,600 acres. Their principal crops include watermelons, kale, jalapeno peppers, corn, collards, okra, and other vegetables suited to the area. Member farmers bring their produce to the Association's facilities for packaging and shipping. The community belongs to The Federation of Southern Cooperatives/Land Assistance Fund, a larger organization licensed in sixteen states throughout the southeast of the United States whose mission is the development of self-supporting communities; the organization provides assistance especially for African Americans to help them retain their land.

PRODUCTION AREA
Petal, Mississippi

COMMUNITY COORDINATOR
Ben Burkett
benburkett@earthlink.net

Morrilton Livestock Breeders

Located in the Ozark Mountains of Arkansas, the Adema Farm community raises a variety of animals including chickens for eggs and meat, pigs, sheep and cattle. They breed Katahdin Hair Sheep, an heritage breed animal that is known for its wonderful flavor. Native to the United States, these sheep are well adapted to the region because they have a high heat tolerance. The producers of the community also raise chickens on pasture: they and given plenty of access to green grass. This results in full flavored eggs. The cattle raised on the farms are 100% grass fed.

PRODUCTION AREA
Morrilton, Ozark Mountains, Arkansas

COMMUNITY COORDINATOR
Ragan Sutterfield
ragan@adamafarm.com

Napa Valley Farmers and Producers

The members of this community are growers and producers in the Napa Valley with a dedication to the quality of their products and to local, sustainable production. For several generations Gary and Giny Heitz of Shypoke Vineyard have been growing Charbono grape in the area. Charbono grapes are at risk of extinction and thanks to the work of the Heitzes, they have been boarded onto the Slow Food USA Ark of Taste. Silverado Brewing uses organic ingredients to craft an array of artisan beers. The owners run a restaurant that follows Slow Food principles. Marshall Honey Farm makes over 20 varieties of honey. Beekepers harvest small quantities of high quality natural honey, which is sold pure and raw. Long Meadow Ranch is one of the few remaining integrated farms in the Napa Valley. This certified organic farm raises cattle and chickens, grows tomatoes, melons, grapes and olives, and produces wine, olive oils and vinegars. Grandpa Jacks Farm sells fresh, free-range eggs and organic vegetables at the local farmers market and to its CSA members. Goat's Leap Dairy was started in 1972. They raise LaMancha breed goats. In 1992 the farmers began making seven of varieties farmstead goat's milk cheeses.

PRODUCTION AREA
Napa Valley

COMMUNITY COORDINATOR
Gary Heitz
ggheitz@comcast.net

Native Plants and Medicinal Herbs Gatherers

Honopua Farm is located in the Waimea Puukapu Farm Lots, a district in North Kohala that is leased to native Hawaiians by the State of Hawaii Department of Hawaiian Homelands. Waimea is the primary vegetable growing area on the island of Hawaii. Marie McDonald and her husband Bill grow a wide range of vegetables for the local market on 9.75 acres of land. They specialize in native plants used for *kapa* making (*kapa* is the traditional bark cloth made by native Hawaiians for their clothing), natural dyes, and traditional medicine. Honopua Farm sells directly to consumers in their community through farmers markets and restaurants.

PRODUCTION AREA
Waimea (Kamuela), Hawaii

COMMUNITY COORDINATOR
Roen Hufford - honopua@msn.com

New Britain Organic Farmers

Urban Oaks Organic Farm is located in one of the poorest and oldest neighborhoods in New Britain, Connecticut. Once a booming industrial city, New Britain has been ravaged by the money-saving tactics of modern multi-national corporations. The community that remains in place is multi-cultural, reflecting waves of immigration from the turn of the 19th century through today, initially from Europe and more recently from Latin America. The community's diverse cultural make-up is part of what drives the farmers' achievements in growing heirloom and imported varieties of produce. Urban Oaks sees itself as part of three larger communities: certified organic specialty growers, urban farmers, and local food systems activists. Its members believe in the holistic benefits of urban agriculture; by providing fresh foods to its local community, Urban Oaks saves fossil fuels that would be used for transport and connects local citizens to their food sources. The Farm works directly with local chefs, offering a year-round supply of various products, delivers wholesale, runs a CSA, and sells from its on-site farm stand.

PRODUCTION AREA
New Britain, Connecticut

COMMUNITY COORDINATOR
Anthony Morris - urbanoaks@earthlink.net

New Florence Lamb Breeders

The community is represented by Prairie Grass Farm, a small family owned farm that produces grass fed lamb, and free-range eggs. They also offer blackberries, raspberries, strawberries and tomatoes during the summer season. They sell an array of lamb products, including summer sausage, lamb kabobs, racks, and stew meat. The Hillebrands raise nearly 700 lambs a year on their 520-acre farm near New Florence, Missouri. David Hillebrand – the leader of the community – grew up on this farm, which has been in the family for three generations. As a kid, his parents focused mostly on row crops, though they kept some livestock, and often while the others left home each morning to tend the field crops, David stayed behind to take care of the chickens. His interest in raising sheep came from his grandfather, who was the first in his family to raise lamb. Prairie Grass Farm's grass fed lambs and free-range eggs are served up in some of the area's finest restaurants, which collaborate with other local farmers.

PRODUCTION AREA
New Florence, Missouri

COMMUNITY COORDINATOR
David Hillebrand - lambguy@newflorence.com

FARMERS' MARKETS

A farmers' market is a venue where a group of local farmers and food producers gather to sell their products once or twice a week. Most are operated during the growing season specific to the region. They are often held at designated public places such as parks and parking lots, and sometimes include live musical performances, cooking demonstrations, and other presentations. Farmers' markets enable producers to market their products directly to their local community, making them an important sales outlet for small-scale agricultural producers across the United States. At the markets, producers are able to sell specialty products including fruits, vegetables, baked goods, meats, farmstead cheeses, and local traditional foods. Community members get the chance to meet local farmers, purchase fresh, seasonal products, and support their local economies. In recent years, the number of farmers markets in the United States has grown dramatically. The 2004 National Farmers' Market Directory lists over 3,700 farmers markets in operation in the United States.

New Hampshire Farmers

Two farms, Willow Pond Community Farm and Sunnyfield Farm, have come together to form the Community of New Hampshire farmers. Both farms are run with a focus on social responsibility, community support, and sustainable land stewardship. Willow Pond Community Farm is the only vegetable farm operating in Brentwood, New Hampshire. The farm has a CSA program on 3 acres, providing the 45 participating local families with 190 varieties of different crops. Sunnyfield Farm sits on a former dairy farm from the 1940s. The farm had gone unused for 5 years when the Crotched Mountain Foundation founded Sunnyfield. The Foundation leases protected land in exchange for sustainable land stewardship. Sunnyfield farmers grow and hand harvest salad greens, onions, potatoes and tomatoes according to organic methods. In addition they raise a few bull calves, hens, and pigs, and tend ten dairy cows. The farm works with organizations that provide support for disabled individuals, in turn providing job training and employment for the handicapped on the farm. Sales occur at the farm and at a local farmers market.

PRODUCTION AREA
Brentwood and Peterborough, New Hampshire

COMMUNITY COORDINATORS
Kathleen Sullivan
willowpondfarmer@yahoo.com
Karen Holmes
rdsunnyfield@yahoo.com

New Mexican Benedictine Brewers

Monks from Christ in the Desert Monastery in Abiquiu, New Mexico and Pecos Benedictine Monastery in Pecos have formed the Abbey Beverage Company with brew master Brad Kraus. The Abbey Beverage Company brews traditional Belgian-style ale that has been brewed in monasteries in Belgium and France for hundreds of years. The ale is made in small batches at the Pecos Benedictine Monastery; it is brewed from water, malted barley and hops, and then fermented with yeast originally from the Trappist Monastery brewery of Orval in Belgium. Currently the community self-distributes its ale. It is only available on draft in Santa Fe restaurants, but soon Abbey Beverage plans to package it into bottles and distribute regionally. The sales of Abbey ales provide income for the monasteries and make them more self-sufficient. 75% of the company's profits go to the Benedictine Foundation of New Mexico.

PRODUCTION AREA
Abiquiu Pecos, New Mexico

COMMUNITY COORDINATOR
M. Brad Kraus
krausbrew@earthlink.net

New Mexican Greenthread Growers and Gatherers

Greenthread is an herb native to the arid Southwest of the United States. The Ancestral Puebloans (Anasazi) who dwelled in the Southwest over 1,000 years ago used greenthread to brew a delightful, relaxing infusion for daily drinking. This drink is also known as Navajo Tea, Hopi tea or Indian Tea, as it is traditionally brewed by the Navajo, Hopi and Pueblo peoples. The Greenthread plant is appropriately named for its leaves, which are thread-thin and dusty green in color. There are many different species of the Greenthread plant that are used throughout much of New Mexico, Arizona, and Colorado; the genus, Thelesperma, is native to North America. Traditionally, the plant is harvested as the flower buds open. It is then washed and dried in the sun. Once fully dried, the plant is folded into small tied bundles that are steeped in about six cups of water for five to ten minutes. Unsweetened, the tea tastes slightly sweet and mild, aromatic like a standard green tea. Medicinally, Greenthread tea is a mild diuretic and is consequently recognized as beneficial for the kidneys. It is similarly known to purify the blood. In September 2005 the High Desert Farmers' Greenthread was added to the Slow Food USA Ark of Taste.

PRODUCTION AREA
Gallup, New Mexico

COMMUNITY COORDINATOR
Steve Heil
heil@highdesertfarmers.com

New Orleans Urban Gardeners

God's Vineyard Community Garden was started in 1997 in a lower income, predominately African American neighborhood of New Orleans, Louisiana to involve young men in the community in labor-intensive work and in nourishing the land. The garden project grew rap-idly, soon involving 35 boys ages 11 to 19 years old. Hurricane Katrina severely damaged God's Vineyard Garden. As a Terra Madre Relief Fund recipient they received a grant to help put the production back in business. In 2000 the community started a food bank, offering local residence okra, corn and eggplant from the garden. In 2002 with a grant from USDA they began producing St. Thomas Seven Pepper Hot Sauce. The sauce is made with peppers that grow in the garden. Every aspect of production is done within the community, from growing the peppers, preparing the hot sauce, labeling and bottling the product, and selling it at the local farmers market. All proceeds from the sale of the hot sauce support God's Vineyard and provide college scholarships for the young men who work in the garden.

PRODUCTION AREA
New Orleans, Louisiana

COMMUNITY COORDINATOR
Earl Antwine - godsvineyard1997@yahoo.com

New Prague Organic Cattle and Dairy Farmers

The community is made up of a family farm raising cattle for the production of milk, and of another farm who process and retails the meat. Cedar Summit Farm is a fourth generation family-run business that has been in operation since 1926. In 1974 the family stopped using pesticides and converted the farm to an organic grass-based operation. The Cedar Summit Farm and Creamery employs 17 persons for the production, processing and distribution of its dairy products including fluid milk, cream, seven flavors of yogurt and ice cream. The milk is non-homogenized and sold in returnable glass bottles. The dairy also provides the community with a variety of beef and pork products. Lorentz Meats of Cannonfalls, Minnesota and Odenthal Meats of Montgomery, Minnesota process their steers and hogs for retail sales.

PRODUCTION AREA
New Prague, Minnesota

COMMUNITY COORDINATOR
David Minar - daveandflo@cedarsummit.com

New York City Greenmarket Farmers

Greenmarket is a program of the Council on the Environment of New York City that has organized and managed open-air farmers markets in New York City since 1976. The program promotes regional agriculture and ensures a continuing supply of fresh, local produce for New Yorkers. Greenmarket provides the region's small family farmers with venues to sell their fruits, vegetables and other farm products directly to urban citizens. The Community of Greenmarket Farmers includes around 170 farmer participants. The farms that will be representing this vast membership at Terra Madre 2006 are Eckerton Hill Farm in northeast Pennsylvania, which produces over 50 varieties of heirloom tomatoes, Keith's Farm in Orange County, New York, and Honey Hollow Farm, which specializes in heirloom produce varieties and foraged plants including fiddlehead ferns, ramps and mushrooms.

PRODUCTION AREA
New York State, New Jersey, Pennsylvania, Connecticut

COMMUNITY COORDINATOR
Gabrielle Langholtz - glangholtz@greenmarket.cc

New York City Organic Producers

Just Food is a New York City non-profit organization that addresses regional farm and food issues in order to build a more just food system. The non-profit facilitates Community Supported Agriculture (CSA) programs whereby family farmers sell their produce directly to consumers in New York City neighborhoods. Just Food has helped to start over 30 CSA programs in the city, and this number continues to increase as it starts additional sites with new groups and new farmers every year. Its membership includes forty farmers who supply over 8000 people through 42 CSA programs. Two farms will represent this broad and diverse group at Terra Madre 2006. The community is represented by Garden of Eve Farm, growing certified organic produce on the east end of Long Island, and by Windflower Farm, a small organic farm on 38 acres in the Taconic Hill country of New York State between Saratoga Springs and the Vermont border.

PRODUCTION AREA
New York City, New York State

COMMUNITY COORDINATOR
Paula Lukats - paula@justfood.org

North Carolina Piedmont Triad Food Producers

North Carolina Piedmont Triad area was once a thriving agrarian community composed of many small farms, dairies, orchards, orphanage farms, markets and small supporting business. A group of over 75 food growers, farmers markets, school gardens, Presidia, Ark and Raft members, and at least 30 cooperating restaurants are at work to revive the community. All the producers are committed to sustainable practices. Their primary products are cheese, meat and poultry, vegetables, and wool. The food producers of this community make a variety of remarkable products. Goat Lady Dairy is a small-scale family farm that makes award-winning cheeses. The dairy is committed to sustainable practice in pasturage, feed, energy creation and conservation and water and resource recycling. Rising Meadow is a family farm with a herd of 200 Navajo Churro Sheep, a breed designated in the Slow Food Ark. The Rising Meadow farmers also raise whey-fed Ossabaws, a hog breed developed at local university in Greensboro to create an alternative to the large-scale hog operations of North Carolina. The North Carolina Piedmont Triad community of growers work together on many levels: Rising Meadows ossabaws hog are fed the whey from the cheese making process at Goat Lady Dairy.

PRODUCTION AREA
Piedmont Triad, North Carolina

COMMUNITY COORDINATOR
Charlie Headington - ceheadin@uncg.edu

Northern California Aromatic, Culinary and Healing Herbs Growers

This community of four farmers produces plants for healing salves, body products, essential oils, hydrosols and delicious condiments. They work in collaboration with the Aromatic Plant Project, a project based in San Francisco. This is a non-profit educational organization working to support American agriculture and its natural products.

Among their top-quality, imaginative products are lavender salt, a food flavoring made of French grey salt ground with dried organic lavender, and azuline, which when distilled into an essential oil serves as an anticancer agent. Many of the beneficial uses of the plants the community grows have been known by natural healers for centuries and passed on through generations. However, some such as the cancer treatment properties of azuline are recent discoveries.

PRODUCTION AREA
Dixon, Davis, California

COMMUNITY COORDINATOR
Walker Nigel - organic@eatwell.com

North San Juan Fruit Growers

At Heaven and Earth Farm, Amigo Bob Cantisano and his family grow organic vegetables, herbs, olives and flowers, tend bees and raise chickens on 3.5-acres at 2,500 feet in the Northern Sierra Mountains. Heaven and Earth Farm has a 40-member organic CSA program. The family operates a processing facility where they make preserves, fermented foods, raw foods, sprouts and olive oils, which they provide with their fresh produce to CSA members and sell to approximately 12 local restaurants, two produce distributors and six natural food stores. They also offer community outreach and education programs. Amigo Bob is one of the founders of the Ecological Farming Conference (Eco-Farm), the largest conference for sustainable farmers on the West Coast.

PRODUCTION AREA
North San Juan, California

COMMUNITY COORDINATOR
Amigo Bob Cantisano - orgamigo@jps.net

Norwich Dairy Farmers

Evans Farmhouse Creamery is a certified organic, family-run dairy farm located in upstate New York. Chenengo County's primary agricultural focus has long been dairying, but recent years have seen the closure of over half of the area's small family farms. The Evans family has been instrumental in preserving small family farms by educating members of its community about value added dairy products. The community is dedicated to sustainable agricultural practices, as well as to producing top quality, healthy dairy products. Their yogurt is non-homogenized which allows the cream to rise to the top. Their unsalted butter is made from gently pasteurized cream in small, 30-gallon batches. At the creamery they also bottle non-homogenized, gently pasteurized milk and make Chenango County's historic Monterey Jack cheese. The Evans Farmhouse Creamery has been a model for and advisor to other families interested in producing organic and value added dairy products such as fluid milk, yogurt, butter, and crème fraiche.

PRODUCTION AREA
Norwich, Chenengo County, New York State

COMMUNITY COORDINATOR
Dave Evans - tel. +1 607 3345339

O'ahu Food Producers

The Hawaian island of O'ahu is becoming increasingl urban. Several farmers and producers have made significant contributions to preserving and developing local agriculture. At Ma'o Organic Farm, Gary and Kukui Maunakea-Forth produce a variety of organic fruits and vegetables which they supply to their local farmers markets and restaurants. They also work with Waianae youth to teach them about local food traditions and get them involved in organic farming. Together Gary and Kukui have established a local cafe, Aloha Aina, one of the few non-fast food joints in Waianae.

PRODUCTION AREA
Waianae, O'ahu, Hawaii

COMMUNITY COORDINATOR
Kukui Maunakea-Forth - waianaeorganic@hawaii.rr.com

Ojai Valley Pixie Growers

This community of 22 family farms, which have formed a loose-knit organization called the Ojai Pixie Growers Association, is working to create and strengthen the market for the Pixie Mandarin tangerine, grown in the Ojai Valley in Southern California, and to foster a regional identity for the flavorful fruit. They came together as an association in the mid-1990s, and from that point forward the Pixie Mandarin began to develop commercial success. Pixie is one of the latest maturing citrus varieties, ripening in March, April and May when they are harvested by hand. Small, firm, seedless fruits grow on vigorous trees. The rind is thick and pale orange to yellowish orange and it is very easy to peel. Because the color is light and the season is late, many consumers pass up the ripe Pixies, thinking they are faded leftovers from winter's high tangerine season. Some of these Ojai Pixie Tangerine growers are organic and some are not but all use integrated pest management. The community has worked extensively with non-governmental organizations that are devoted to introducing locally grown fresh produce into Ventura County public school lunch programs.

PRODUCTION AREA
Ojai Valley, California

COMMUNITY COORDINATOR
Jim Churchill - jrchurchill@earthlink.net

Oregon and California Biodynamic Growers

The North Coast Biodynamic Farmers are approximately 64 farms linked together by their Demeter Biodynamic certification. Demeter's mission is to foster and encourage holistic, biodynamic methods of food production. They offer certification to farms, gardens, processors, and traders. Demeter encourages farmers to work with an understanding of the whole farm as a living organism and as part of the living earth. The delegates who will represent the larger Demeter community include Ceago Vineyard in Clear Lake, California, Frey Vineyard in Mendocino, California, Elk Creamery in Elk, California, and Hoskins Berry Farm in Philomath, Oregon. These four producers grow biodynamic grapes, raise a goatherd and make artisan cheeses, and grow blackberries, some of which become fruit spreads and vinegars. Some of the community members were instrumental in establishing the GMO free zone in Mendocino County, California.

PRODUCTION AREA
Oregon; California

COMMUNITY COORDINATOR
Jim Fullmer - jfullmer@peak.org

Pescadero Goat Dairy Farmers

Dee Harley started farming 14 years ago with six goats, and today she and her husband own 220 American Alpine goats that roam on nine acres of pasture at Harley Farms in Pescadero, California. The two rebuilt a 1910 cow dairy farm, and their property now houses a cheesemaking room and milking parlor. Although there are not other producers in the community, the work carried out by the dairy is crucial: Harley Farms is in fact the last remaining dairy farm in San Mateo County. The goats each produce a gallon of milk per day, which makes one pound of cheese. Milk from the goatherd is turned into cheese using traditional methods with cheesecloth bags to separate the curds from the whey. The cheese is handmade in rounds and often includes edible flowers, fruits, herbs, and flavorings from the garden. They make fresh *chevre* in various forms.

PRODUCTION AREA
Pescadero, San Mateo, California

COMMUNITY COORDINATOR
Deborah Harley - dee@harleyfarms.com

Petaluma Geese and Pekin Duck Breeders

This community consists of the sustainable poultry producers at Reichardt Duck Farm. Jim Reichardt and five farmers currently operate the farm on more than 300 acres home on Middle Two Rock Road in Petaluma, California. They raise Pekin duck, Guinea hens, and heritage geese without growth hormones or stimulants in open buildings. The birds are bred, hatched, raised and processed on the farm in a humane environment. Pekin duck has been raised in the Petaluma region since the 1870s. In 1901, Reichardt's great grandfather started one of the first operations in San Francisco, and the family has remained in the business since, establishing a poultry tradition for the area. Reichardt Duck Farm sells its poultry directly to chefs in the San Francisco Bay Area, who are also part of the community.

PRODUCTION AREA
Petaluma, California

COMMUNITY COORDINATOR
Jim Reichardt - scpducks@aol.com

Philadelphia Growers

These individuals represent just a few of the many food artisans and sustainable farmers who make up the community. They are at the top of their fields, employing innovative sustainable farming, brewing, and harvesting techniques while paying heed to Philadelphia's rich culinary heritage. Branch Creek Farm is a member of the Pennsylvania Association for Sustainable Agriculture (PASA). These family farmers grow heirloom crops—both organic micro vegetables and herbs — on 21 acres in Perkasie, Pennsylvania. Another member, Charlestown Cooperative Farm (also a member of the PASA) is a family-run farm that uses sustainable practices to grow vegetables and fruits. Other members are brewers: Heavyweight Brewery employs traditional brewing methods to create unfiltered beers that the brewers let mature in the bottles. Yards Brewery creates a wide-selection of English and Belgian beers that are naturally cask and bottle conditioned. One of their outstanding projects has been to reproduce accurately three historic ales from recipes created by American Founding Fathers, including one from Benjamin Franklin's original recipe for Spruce Beer.

PRODUCTION AREA
Philadelphia, Pennsylvania

COMMUNITY COORDINATOR
Bill Anderson - broadwaterfarm@mac.com

Pittsboro Educators

The community is represented by The Sustainable Farming Program at Central Carolina Community College in Pittsboro, North Carolina, which teaches beginning farmers sustainable, organic farming methods. It began in 1995 thanks to the collaborative efforts of farmers, consumers, community organizations, and the community college. The school is surrounded by a diverse group of farms that practice sustainable agriculture. There are about 20 full-time students and 75 part-time students who work with fellow classmates to plant, cultivate, and harvest a variety of produce in the school's garden. In its classes the school promotes biodiversity of plants, animals, and soil life. The program teaches the technical skills needed to develop and manage a profitable, environmentally sound and community-based small farm or agricultural business.

PRODUCTION AREA
Pittsboro, North Carolina

COMMUNITY COORDINATOR
Robin Kahanowich - rkohanowich@cccc.edu

Pittsburgh Educators

The community is represented by Grow Pittsburg, a small collaborative of urban growers that provides classes and apprenticeships for teens and young adults in Pittsburgh, Pennsylvania. Grow Pittsburgh teaches classes at two demonstration sites, Mildred's Daughters Urban Farm and Garden Dreams. Mildred's Daughters is a five-acre farm deeded since 1875 in the Lawrenceville/Stanton Heights area of Pittsburgh. There, students and farmers grow and market herbs, vegetables, fruits and free-range eggs. Garden Dreams, which was created on two reclaimed lots in Wilkinsburg, is a quarter acre market garden with a licensed greenhouse. Here participants grow and market naturally grown vegetables and specialty and heirloom seedlings. They also provide products and services for backyard gardens. Grow Pittsburgh's hand-on classes serve as a tool for community revitalization. On the farm and garden, students learn about sustainable urban agriculture, local food security, and the health benefits, both environmental and personal, of a local-based sustainable food system.

PRODUCTION AREA
Pittsburgh, Pennsylvania

COMMUNITY COORDINATOR
Randa Shannon - mildredsdaughters@earthlink.net

Point Reyes Seashore Oyster Harvesters

This community comprises the family members and fishermen who operate both Drakes Bay Oyster Company and Lunny Farm in Point Reyes, California. The community grows oysters afloat, off the shore bottom, in order to protect sub-aquatic vegetation. It performs its entire oyster processing on-farm. In addition, it raises a closed herd of organic, grass-fed cattle on the family ranch. The meat is processed locally. On Lunny Farm they also grow organic Green Globe artichokes, an heirloom variety. Artichokes were grown in Point Reyes in the past and after a fifty-year absence the community reintroduced the vegetable.

PRODUCTION AREA
Point Reyes, California

COMMUNITY COORDINATOR
Kevin Lunny - Kevin@drakesbayoyster.com

Potter Valley Ranchers

For the past 25 years, Mac Magruder has been raising grass-finished beef on both irrigated pastures and open hill ground, which allows for year-round grazing for the cattle in a holistic rotational system. He is a fourth-generation rancher on his family's Mendocino County property. All the animals are born and raised on the ranch or purchased from a similar program. They receive neither hormonal implants nor antibiotic feed additives and are at least 18 months old before they are harvested. The cattle are fattened on the ranch and processed locally. Much of the beef is sold to independent grocery stores and restaurants, with about a third of the total production sold directly to local individuals, packaged and frozen.

PRODUCTION AREA
Potter Valley, Mendocino County, California

COMMUNITY COORDINATOR
Mac Magruder - magruderranch@pacific.net

Purcellville Livestock Breeders and Farmers

The pastures of Mountain View Farm are nestled below Virginia's Blue Ridge and surrounded by hundreds of acres of woodlands and wetlands. At Mountain View Farm, a small, family-run farm, animals are raised on high-quality grasses and legumes in an integrated, rotational system. This process of grazing and re-growth encourages the development of rich soils, maintains the vigor of the grasses, and increases the diversity of grass species. The farmers are self-employed and lease their land from a nature preserve, the Blue Ridge Center for Environmental Stewardship, in exchange for hosting educational programs. At Mountain View family farmers raise lamb, turkeys, cattle, broiler chickens and laying hens and grow heirloom varieties of fruits and vegetables including melon, corn and bean varieties that are essential to historical Appalachian cuisine. The Farm's produce is sold to local restaurants and distributed through a Community Supported Agriculture (CSA) program.

PRODUCTION AREA
Purcellville, Virginia

COMMUNITY COORDINATOR
Shawna DeWitt - shawna_dewitt@yahoo.com

Redland Tropical Fruit Growers

Because of its southern location, the Redland area of South Florida has been the only area of the United States dedicated to the production of tropical fruits and vegetables. Gaby's Farm, a family run operation, grows mango, passion fruit, and white and black sapote, all fruits that originate in tropical and subtropical regions of the planet. Gaby's Farm sells fresh fruit locally and uses these fruits to manufacture ice creams and sorbets. Because tropical fruits are highly perishable, by creating a line of ice creams Gaby's Farm extends their shelf life and economic value. The growers use their own fruit and those of nearby farms in the Redland area. Gaby's Farm has received a grant from the US Department of Agriculture to assist in the promotion of tropical fruits, most of which are unknown in the other parts of the country.

PRODUCTION AREA
Redland, Florida

COMMUNITY COORDINATOR
Gabrielle Berryer - info@gabysfarm.com

Rhode Island Dairy Farmers

Farm Fresh Rhode Island is an organization that runs five farmers markets in Providence and others in Woonsocket and Central Falls, Rhode Island. In an additional project to link local farmers with potential buyers, Farm Fresh has created a searchable database of locally grown foods which gives Rhode Island's small and specialty farmers greater exposure and market access. The Rhody Fresh Dairy Cooperative is one of the groups that work with Farm Fresh. The cooperative was created to preserve, protect, and promote dairy farming in Rhode Island. Thirty years ago there were over 100 dairy farms in Rhode Island, but currently only 18 remain. Four farmers came together to create Rhody Fresh. One of the members also runs a milk transportation business. The cooperative convinced a large grocery retailer, Stop and Shop, to carry its local milk, and the result has been proof of the profound success that can occur when locally grown foods are made more accessible.

PRODUCTION AREA
Providence, Rhode Island

COMMUNITY COORDINATOR
Noah Fuller - noah@farmfreshri.org

Russian River Wine Grape Growers

The community is represented by the Davis Bynum Winery, which is serving as the representative of the Russian River Valley Wine Grape Growers Association, a group of 74 wineries and 161 vineyard owners dedicated to protecting and enriching the region's sustainable agricultural community. Davis Bynum was one of the first wineries to practice organic and biodynamic farming in the area. In 1973 it was the first vineyard to recognize its connection to the region with the now important Russian River label. Davis Bynum Winery promotes the belief that food and wine are part of a larger circle of enjoyment that includes family, friends, and community.

PRODUCTION AREA
Mendocino County, California

COMMUNITY COORDINATOR
Hampton Bynum - hampton@davisbynum.com

Sabinal Farmers and Ranchers

In South Texas, Ranch de la Chuparrosa is a family owned and operated farm with 30-members who participate in their Community Supported Agriculture (CSA) program. The farmers use sustainable practices to raise heritage turkeys, chickens for eggs and meat and to grow over 50 varieties of vegetables and many of heirloom tomatoes. They raise poultry breeds including Aracauna, Rhode Island Red, Production Reds, Gold Sex Link, Barred Rocks, Silver Spangled Hamburgs, Anconas, and Buff Orpingtons. There are 750 hens that lay nearly 180 eggs every daily. These hens have a mobile "Inn of the Hens" that keep them happy with plenty of fresh air and new grass every week. They have a crew that processes their poultry on the farm. They deliver the birds fresh to customers. The Ranch began raising heritage breed turkeys in cooperation with the Slow Food International's Save the Turkey project. Many of the turkey varieties are making a comeback because customers have rediscovered their deliciousness.

PRODUCTION AREA
Sabinal, Texas

COMMUNITY COORDINATOR
Robin Bowman - robin@goodfoodfarm.com

Saint Louis Brewers

Stephen and Sara Hale of the Saint Lewis Brewery and Tap Room brew mostly traditional style ales and lagers, which they package on a small scale. The 10-person-operated brewery ships all of its beers within a four-hour radius; the brewers aim to provide their local region with the freshest, best tasting beer available, and thus do not pasteurize their product. In their brewpub they use mostly foods from local purveyors who are part of the same community, and their on-premise garden. They have received a grant for an upcoming spent-grain composting project. The brewpub hosts a weekly farmers market during the summer and a monthly one during the winter.

PRODUCTION AREA
Saint Louis, Missouri

COMMUNITY COORDINATOR
Stephen Hale - slowstephen@sbcglobal.net

Saint Paul Farmer's Market Lamb and Sheep Breeders

On the border of Wisconsin and Minnesota in the Coulee Region (an area of about 20,000 square miles in western Wisconsin, northeastern Iowa, southeastern Minnesota, and extreme northwestern Illinois, which was by-passed by the last continental glaciers) of West Central Wisconsin, family farmers raise a flock of more than 800 sheep and lamb at Promised Land Farm, a cooperative farm. Farmers of the community manage the flock without the use of antibiotic feed, hormone implants, or steroids. These animals graze on lush rolling organic pastures on the ridge tops of Mississippi River bluffs. Promised Land Farm has its lamb processed at a local family-run USDA-inspected meat facility. The community sells much of its lamb at the Saint Paul Farmers' Market, one of the oldest farmers markets in the United States.

PRODUCTION AREA
Cochrane, Wisconsin

COMMUNITY COORDINATOR
Steve Schotthofer - plfarm@mwt.net

San Diego Organic Farmers

Stephenie Caughlin began Seabreeze Organic Farm on two-acres south of Del Mar, California in 1988. She grows hundreds of varieties of diverse vegetables for year-round distribution to the approximately 70 subscribers to her Community Supported Agriculture (CSA) program. Along with vegetables, she also grows strawberries, mulberries, blackberries, avocados, cherimoyas, guavas, hundreds of varieties of annual and perennial flowers, various herbs and small poultry for eggs. The work carried out by Stephenie Caughlin is crucial: currently, Seabreeze Organic Farm is the only farm left producing coastal food in San Diego.

PRODUCTION AREA
Del Mar, San Diego, California

COMMUNITY COORDINATOR
Stephenie Caughlin - info@seabreezed.com

San Diego Organic Tangelo Growers

The Community of Organic Tangelo Growers comprises four growers and two packing houses in Poway, California. The farmers grow organic tangelos – a hybrid between a mandarin orange and either a pomelo or a grapefruit – in a citrus and avocado grove that was planted over 30 years ago. The tangelo may have originated in Southeast Asia over 3,500 years ago. The fruits look like good-sized, oblong oranges and have a tangerine taste, but are very juicy, to the point of not providing much flesh but producing excellent and plentiful juice. Once the grove filled an entire valley in Poway, but now only the land of the four growers of this community remains.

PRODUCTION AREA
Poway, San Diego, California

COMMUNITY COORDINATOR
Rhonda Farrar - rhonda@farrarfinancials.com

San Francisco Brewers

Magnolia Brewery was opened in 1997 in the Haight-Ashbury neighborhood of San Francisco, California. The brewery specializes in hand-crafted American interpretations of classic British ales, from the Blue Bell Bitter to the hoppy Prescription Pale Ale. They use the Maris Otter variety of English pale malt, and heirloom barley that is floor-malted in the traditional manner by Thomas Fawcett & Sons of Yorkshire, England. The Magnolia Brewery is part of a larger community of American craft breweries that preserve traditional brewing methods while forging their own American styles and offer more flavorful alternatives to mass-produced beer.

PRODUCTION AREA
San Francisco, California

COMMUNITY COORDINATOR
David McLean - dave@magnoliapub.com

San Francisco Educators

The Center for Urban Education about Sustainable Agriculture (CUESA) is a non-profit in San Francisco that sponsors the Ferry Plaza Farmers Market and conducts education and outreach on sustainable food systems. This community consists of over 80 farmers, 35 food artisans, 15 volunteers, and over 20,000 consumers who shop at the market each week. The Ferry Plaza Farmers Market is critical to the survival of many of the area's small farmers who rely on the opportunity to sell their products directly. These farmers' products represent the best of local agriculture and regional food traditions. The 120 market vendors are selected based on their commitment to and demonstration of sustainable practices. Everything Under the Sun is a farm on 30-40 leased acres in Winters, California, where they grow stone fruits, vegetables, roots, brassicas, nuts, persimmons, greens, alliums, nightshades, figs, corn and hard squash to name a few.

PRODUCTION AREA
San Francisco, California

COMMUNITY COORDINATOR
William Crepps - everunderthesun@aol.com

San Francisco National Parks Producers

As the largest urban national park in North America, the Golden Gate National Parks are committed to being a bridge between the fecund rural landscape to the north and south and the vibrant and hungry population of San Francisco. Covering more than 75,500 acres, they attract over 17 million visitors per year. In May 2006, the Food from the Parks Initiative was formed to create an integrated park-wide food program that enhances the extraordinary park experience by educating visitors, not only on the environment, but also on food production. The Initiative is working closely with the Point Reyes National Seashore to enable the 17 food service facilities in the park to purchase and serve the bounty produced by unique food artisans. In addition to providing food from its neighbors to the millions of park visitors, the initiative has established criteria to ensure a food program that is both sustainable and just.

PRODUCTION AREA
San Francisco, California

COMMUNITY COORDINATOR
Larry Bain - larry@nextcourse.org

San Francisco Organic Fruit Growers

In 1979, Rick and Kristie Knoll converted a weedy 10-acre alfalfa field about 60 miles east of San Francisco into a productive, diverse, biodynamic farm. Knoll Farms is in an area where the weather allows a 12-month growing season so the farm remains in production year-round. Most of what the Knolls grow is sold to wholesalers and can be found in the San Francisco Bay Area's natural food stores. Their diverse product line includes artichokes, green garlic and bulb garlic, rosemary, four kinds of mint, sage, tarragon, figs – Adriatic, black mission, brown turkey, and kadota – five varieties of apricots, snow queen and white rose nectarines, flowers, salad greens, and firewood. The main focus of the farm is on the health and tilth of the soil. In addition, they work with the Brentwood Agricultural Land Trust to revitalize farming in there are and to put brakes on development of the area's farmland.

PRODUCTION AREA
Brentwood, California

COMMUNITY COORDINATOR
Kristie Knoll - kristie@knollorganics.com

Santa Cruz River Producers

The Santa Cruz River Food Community consists of members who are involved in food production for local consumption using direct markets. Four members of Forever Yong Farm, fifty of San Xavier Cooperative Farm, four of Desert Harvesters, fourteen of the Community Food Bank and the Community Food Security Center and Garden, twelve from the Santa Cruz River Farmers' Market, and 30 home and market gardeners share a commitment to sustainable practices and an interest in native and culturally valued foods. Community members grow crops including purslane, mesquite pods, Ajo Rojo garlic, and Pima Club Wheat. Many of these crops are grown organically. Mesquite pods grow on Native Velvet Mesquite trees. The pods are milled in their entirety in a hammer mill or by hand on stone. The flour has a sweet and nutty flavor; it is used in baking and in a hot beverage called Atole and made into cereal. The majority of crops community members grow are historically linked to the Santa Cruz River Valley near Tucson, Arizona. Agricultural settlements have been found in the valley that date from 1000 BC Over centuries these crops have adapted to the Sonora Desert environment. They are highly valued by the local Native Americans, people of Mexican decent, and recent Mexican immigrants.

PRODUCTION AREA
Tucson, Arizona

COMMUNITY COORDINATOR
Vanga Garland - vgarland@communityfoodbank.com

Santa Fe Educators

In Santa Fe, New Mexico, as in many communities across the United States, there is a rise in the prevalence of overweight and nutrition-related diseases in children. Intent on fighting these negative trends, this community of about 50 community activists, educators, and food producers brings farmers to classrooms, establishes and run school gardens, plans field trips to farms, and works to facilitate the purchase of local farm foods to be served in school cafeterias. Their efforts assist the farming community and increase the health of school children who learn the skills and arts of cooking, the difference between fresh foods and processed foods, and where their local foods come from.

PRODUCTION AREA
Santa Fe, New Mexico

COMMUNITY COORDINATOR
Le Adams - ladams@cybermesa.com

Santa Fe Farmers' Market Producers

The Santa Fe Farmers' Market began with a handful of farmers in the late 1960s and is now New Mexico's largest farmers market. The Community comprises over 100 active vendors who feature hundreds of different agricultural products at their stands. In 2002 the Market began operating year-round, further meeting Santa Fe's demand for fresh, local produce. The Market assures its customers that they are buying directly from the local producers. The following are some of the members of the Farmers' Market Community: One Straw Farm has been selling organic produce and flowers at the Santa Fe Farmers' Market for 10 years; they also sell to local restaurants and through a CSA program. Sweetwood Dairy produces raw goats milk cheeses. Harmony Farm grows chilies, greens, tomatoes, summer squash and a variety of other vegetables, which they sell at the Santa Fe Farmers' Market and to local restaurants. Chilies are New Mexico's state vegetable; many strains are regionally specific, such as the Chimayo Chile, and have been perpetuated by careful seed saving and generational inheritance. Many of New Mexico's chili fields are irrigated with water that flows through a system of canals (*acequias*) that has existed for hundreds of years.

PRODUCTION AREA
Santa Fe, New Mexico

COMMUNITY COORDINATOR
Deborah Madison - deorahmadison@earthlink.net

Santa Rosa Livestock Breeders and Vegetable Growers

Sol Food Farms in Sebastopol, California is a classic and diverse market garden, producing organic vegetables, cut flowers and herbs. Laura Neale, Andy Szymanowicz, and Leo Goldsmith, three young friends in partnership, supply certified organic, high quality produce to their immediate community through two farmers markets and a small CSA program. They grow Early Girl tomatoes, a dry-farm tomato that thrives in Sonoma County, an area with little summer rainfall. Sol Food farmers have educated many local producers about dry farming. Their other products include carrots, lettuce, cabbage, broccoli, kale, chard, collards, leeks, beets, fresh beans, eggplants, peppers, cucumbers, squash, basil, cilantro, dill, parsley, turnips, radishes and mustard. Triple 'T' Ranch and Farm is a small family farm in Santa Rosa, California run by Larry Tristano. On the farm, the Tristano family grows certified organic Early Girl hybrid tomatoes, lettuce, sweet bell peppers, round of Hungary peppers, Goliath Jalapenos, and winter greens such as kale, collards, chard, broccoli, and broccoli rabe. All of the products are sold at the local level to restaurants and farmers' markets.

PRODUCTION AREA
Santa Rosa and Sebastopol, California

COMMUNITY COORDINATOR
Larry Tristano Sr. - ltristano@aol.com

Sausalito Cooks and Fishermen

Fish is a restaurant in Sausalito, California devoted to serving only responsibly harvested, sustainable seafood. The restaurant owners are licensed commercial fishermen who fish for their own Wild Pacific King Salmon and other species of fish with hook and line on the restaurant's boat. In addition, Fish purchases organic produce, breads, cheeses, meats, and additional sustainable seafood from local vendors as much as possible. The members of the community are concerned about the environment: the restaurant converts vegetable oil from the fryers into biodiesel fuel for local fishing boats and its own vehicles.

PRODUCTION AREA
Sausalito, Marin County, California

COMMUNITY COORDINATOR
Kenny Belou - kenny@331fish.com

Shepherdstown Fruit Growers

This biodynamic farm in West Virginia grows heirloom variety vegetables for CSA members. The small farm hosts interns each year who receive an intensive education in biodynamic farming and gardening as well as room, board and a monthly stipend. Fresh and Local is located 8 miles from the confluence of the Potomac and Shenandoah rivers, and offers its customers the opportunity to visit the farms and meeting the producers. Members of the CSA pay in advance of the season for a weekly share of the farms' harvest, from early June through mid-October. Shares contain a variety of seasonal foods, picked that morning. A share provides most of the salad and vegetable needs for a couple or a small family for a week.?Each box comes with a newsletter (to be e-mailed this season!) detailing what's inside and how to cook, bake, serve and store the produce.

PRODUCTION AREA
Shepherdstown, West Virginia

COMMUNITY COORDINATOR
Allan Balliett - allan@freshandlocalcsa.com

Shushan Pig Breeders

Flying Pig Farm is a family-owned and operated farm in Shushan, New York that uses sustainable methods to raise heritage breed pigs. Of the fifteen pig breeds grown in the United States in the 1930s, six have gone extinct, making some of the heritage breeds very rare and precious. Flying Pig Farm raises the pigs outdoors, allowing them to feed on pasture. Pork from these breeds has more moisture than the pork from conventional hybrids. In 2003, Flying Pig Farm co-founded Farm to Chef Express, a New York State Department of Agriculture and Markets grant-funded organization, which became Farm to Chef, Inc., a private company owned by farmers and chefs. For a fee, Farm to Chef market farmers' goods to city restaurants and provides once a week delivery to participating New York City chefs.

PRODUCTION AREA
Shushan, New York

COMMUNITY COORDINATOR
Jennifer Small - jen@flyingpigsfarm.com

Socorro Organic Poultry Producers

At the Pollo Real Ranch in Socorro, New Mexico, the farm family raise heritage turkeys, chickens, and organic vegetables and native and traditional red and green chilies. Their turkeys are bred, incubated and hatched at the ranch. They raise the chickens on organic grains and organic pastures. The chicken flocks eat bugs, larvae, weeds, and seeds, helping produce healthy sustainable soils for the ranch's vegetable production. Pollo Real Ranch vegetables are distributed through a CSA program and at farmers markets. The breeders of the community are part of a breeding program which developed in France and is called Label Rouge. This program provides premium products to consumers, increases farmer income, and strengthens rural development. It consists of many regional producer-oriented alliances, which produce and market their own branded products under a common label. In the US, a grassroots 'pastured poultry' movement has been growing since the early 1990s. Poultry raised on pasture are processed on-farm and direct marketed, creating supplemental income on small diversified family farms. The *Label Rouge* program emphasizes quality attributes such as taste and food safety, and free-range production practices. The main reason for the superior taste are use of slow-growing birds instead of the fast-growing birds used in the conventional industry. The meat is flavorful and firm, but not tough.

PRODUCTION AREA
Socorro, New Mexico

COMMUNITY COORDINATOR
Tracey Hamilton - polloreal@zianet.com

Sonoma County Brewers

Vinnie and Natalie Cilurzo of Russian River Brewing Company in Santa Rosa, California make twenty seasonal ales without chemicals or artificial flavorings. Several of their beers contain local fruits such as cherries and pluots, a fruit developed in Sonoma County. The Cilurzos have built a close-knit community: approximately 30 local people work with them – the growers, the producers at the brewery and brewpub. In addition, they are in collaboration to develop a Harvest Ale with a 96-year-old local hop grower who grows nearly extinct native hop varieties. Hops were the main agricultural product in Sonoma County, California in the 1940s. Due to the invention of the harvester machine, the hop fields were moved to areas with more flat land. Sonoma's agricultural focus shifted from hops to prunes to apples, and now grapes overrun the agricultural landscape. To fight the trend of a grape monoculture and defend the biodiversity of the area, Russian River Brewing Company and another microbrewer have brought hop growing back to Sonoma County.

PRODUCTION AREA
Sonoma County, California

COMMUNITY COORDINATOR
Vinnie & Natalie Cilurzo - ncilurzo@russianriverbrewing.com

Sonoma County Poultry Breeders

The community of Sonoma poultry breeders is represented by Paine Farm in the Sonoma Valley of Northern California, a small, owner-operated farm that has been supplying quality, naturally grown poultry directly to Francisco Bay area restaurants since 1979. Paine Farm specializes in raising squab. The farm's breeding flock has been genetically closed for over 20 years. The birds are harvested once a week, processed locally and delivered the same day on ice to San Francisco Bay Area restaurants that are dedicated to supporting local farms.

PRODUCTION AREA
Sonoma Valley, California

COMMUNITY COORDINATOR
Phillip Paine
dmccomponents@aol.com

South Atlantic Farmers' Market Producers

This community consists of ten farm producers and two off farm processors that run Riverview Farms, a certified organic farm. Most community members are part of a family that has raised animals and grown grains and vegetables on the same plot for the past thirty years. The family sells to local restaurants, at local farmers markets, and to families that participate in its Community Supported Agriculture (CSA) program. Its pigs are all heritage breed animals, raised on pasture and fed corn, beans and vegetables from the farm. The family sends its pigs to a local family-owned slaughterhouse for processing and cures the meat themselves. Additionally, the farmers teach workshops on sustainable farming in partnership with Georgia Organics, Biodynamics, and Slow Food.

PRODUCTION AREA
Ranger, Georgia

COMMUNITY COORDINATOR
Charlotte Swancy - singingfrog@earthlink.net

Southern High Plains Grassfed Livestock Breeders

This is a community of grass-fed, natural meat producers working to improve soil, wildlife habitat, and to maintain the complexity of plants in the grasslands. The prairie grasslands have a history of grazing buffalo, elk, antelope and deer. After the land was opened for settlement during the land run of the 1890s, prairie lands were fenced and plowed, and have been farmed and grazed continually since then. These producers are working to restore prairie ecosystems by using grazing methods that mimic the movement and behavior of those wild herds of grazing animals. Benessere Farms and Walnut Creek Farms sell their meat directly to consumers and nationally through distributors.

PRODUCTION AREA
Waynoka, Oklahoma

COMMUNITY COORDINATOR
Kim Barker - barker_k@hotmail.com

South Florida Organic Farmers

The community is represented by Three Sisters Farm, where farmers grow heirloom tomatoes, vegetables and tropical fruits on a small scale. The farm sells directly to local chefs and at farmers markets and participates in a Community Supported Agriculture (CSA) program. The community members are actively involved in seed saving and education. They promote and plant sustainable organic gardens at schools and provide heirloom plants and instruction to students in traditional and sustainable growing methods. One of Three Sisters' main products is lychee, which can be difficult to grow because the tree's root system is very close to the surface and vulnerable to the intense weather common in Florida. Three Sisters Farm employs heavy mulching and seasonal pruning to protect the trees; lychees are harvested by hand as the fruit ripens. In addition, Three Sisters Farm has one of the only certified organic greenhouses in South Florida.

PRODUCTION AREA
Redland, Florida

COMMUNITY COORDINATOR
Rachael Middleton - raemiddleton@yahoo.com

South Londonderry Organic Vegetable and Herb Growers

Anjali Biodynamic Farm sits in the Green Mountains of Vermont on a 10-acre slope above the West River in the village of South Londonderry. This small farm has grown organic heirloom vegetables, culinary and medicinal herbs, berries and melons for the past nine years. The two-member community also raises chickens for eggs, harvests shiitake and oyster mushrooms, creates value-added products including Rhubarb Ginger Chutney and Garlic Honey, and runs a medicinal herbal company on the farm. They provide their products to local chefs and restaurants, offer CSA members the opportunity to volunteer, teach hands-on farm education classes, and recently hosted a Vermont Fresh Network dinner on the farm.

PRODUCTION AREA
South Londonderry, Vermont

COMMUNITY COORDINATOR
Emmett Dunbar - edunbar71@verizon.net

Standing Rock Reservation Bison Ranchers

The community is made up of three ranchers working within the Standing Rock Reservation in North Dakota. Three individuals work together at Standing Rock Bison Ranch in North Dakota to raise and process buffalo in a sustainable and traditional way. Buffalo is a vital food for the cultural, spiritual, and physical well being of the Lakota community. Bison ranchers at Standing Rock distribute bison meat to Lakota tribal members and customers who value their practices: they follow Lakota traditions, holding ceremonies to the bison, conducting prayers, and working to create reciprocal relationships between themselves and the animals.

PRODUCTION AREA
Fort Yates, North Dakota

COMMUNITY COORDINATOR
Linda Jones - lindaj@sbci.edu

Tallahassee Region Farmers and Heirloom Seed Savers

Native Natural Farm is a 100-acre diversified farm in the Tallahassee Region. One family has practiced sustainable agriculture on the same land since 1826 across eight generations. At Native Naturals they organically grow primarily heirloom varieties of vegetables and fruits and raise chickens and cattle using a sustainable rotation system. Native Naturals participates in Tallahassee area local growers markets and cooperates with the Florida A&M University Small Farm Program, hosting on-farm workshops on a regular basis. They have also worked with a regional group to preserve agricultural lands from urban sprawl and incompatible development.

PRODUCTION AREA
Lamont, Florida

COMMUNITY COORDINATOR
Susan Anderson - nativenaturals@joimail.com

Tea Purveyors

This community is made up of tea buyers and distributors who are concerned with the loss of traditional tea making skills in China and Southeast Asia. Many North American distributors travel to remote tea growing regions and work directly with tea farmers. Recently, in some tea-producing areas, farmers have left their tea to wilt simply because they can't afford processing costs. By distributing tea from small scale, sustainable farms, individual farmers are able to make a living, while practicing an age-old tradition.

PRODUCTION AREA
Cornwall Bridge, Connecticut

COMMUNITY COORDINATOR
Beckwith Sebastian -- sdorje@aol.com

Tomato Seed Savers and Growers

This food community is dedicated to the preservation of heirloom tomato varieties. Over the past years, many tomato seed varieties had become unavailable commercially, but thanks to the efforts of this network of seed companies, nurseries, and small regional growers, working closely with Seed Savers Exchange, many heirloom varieties are reentering the marketplace. The farmers that grow tomatoes from these seeds use organic and biodynamic methods, paying meticulous attention to labeling in order to maintain the correct identification of varieties. They allow the tomato fruit to fully mature, and once ripe, process it by hand in order to safely remove seeds. Many of the names of heirloom tomato varieties contain a history of the plant. Some names indicate the place of origin such as Kentucky Potato Leaf. Others indicate the family or person who created the variety, such as Cooper's Special, a pink tomato created in 1913 by a Florida Farmer. Many of these stories of origin are passed on through the listings in the Seed Savers Exchange yearbook.

PRODUCTION AREA
Napa Valley, California

COMMUNITY COORDINATOR
Jeff Dawson - jeff@roundpond.com

Triangle Farmers' Market Producers

The community consists of seven vendor-run farmers markets with over 250 participating farmers, gardeners, ranchers, and food artisans. The markets offer a direct retail outlet for local farmers, many who have been selling at the markets for 25 years. Many farmers of the community grow heirloom fruits and vegetables and raise heirloom hogs, chickens and cows. They produce cheeses, pickles, relishes, fruit butters, preserves and jellies. The Triangle Farmers' Market community has been working with its Slow Food local chapter and several agriculturally oriented non-profits to help its greater community foster an awareness of the local foods in their midst. The community collaborates with the sustainable meat producers of Central North Carolina, a rapidly growing community in a region that has been a major meat producing area since the 1700s. This community brings together more than one hundred meat producers, four red meat processors, and one poultry processor. They sell to restaurants, locally owned groceries and farmers markets.

PRODUCTION AREA
Triangle Area, North Carolina

COMMUNITY COORDINATOR
Andrea Reusing - andrea@lanternrestaurant.com

Upper Columbia Poultry Breeders

This is a community of approximately 100 growers, educators, and market managers in Stevens County in Northwest Washington who are commmitted to sustainable production. During the first 30 years of the 20th century millions of pounds of fruit were being shipped from this area, but the construction of the Grand Coulee Damn caused the flooding and destruction of endless tracts of orchard land. The remaining orchardists were struggling and are now getting back on their feet by beginning to market directly. Some members of this community grow organic apples, cherries, peaches, and pears, others raise poultry; some make goat cheese in the traditional European manner and others raise grass-fed beef.

PRODUCTION AREA
Stevens County, Upper Columbia, Washington State

COMMUNITY COORDINATOR
Albert Kowitz - akowitz@centurytel.net

Upper Connecticut River Valley Meat Producers

Members of this community in the Upper Connecticut River Valley are committed to raising animals that thrive in a pasture-based system that compliments the local climate. The community involves 45 farms and three processors. Many community members raise animals that have been bred for generations for adaptation to the area. Though many of the small farmers in the area have disappeared in the last 20 years, those remaining are playing a fundamental role in the burgeoning local food economy. Beef, sheep and pigs are rotated through pastures so that they have access to fresh grass regularly. Animals are also given access to annual forage crops to extend the time they spend on pasture and to supplement their grass diet. Pigs are fed grain as well. The animals are processed in one of two slaughterhouses that serve the region. Community members create a number of value-added products such as ham and bacon, which are traditionally cured in a brine containing maple syrup—an economically and culturally important regional product—and smoked with maple wood.

PRODUCTION AREA
Connecticut River Valley, Connecticut

COMMUNITY COORDINATOR
Chip Conquest - chip@farmersdiner.com

Vacaville Breeders

This community comprises a small-scale producer of grass-fed Highland cows, Tamworth pigs, lambs and goats, and heritage turkeys. Ted Fuller, the sole farmer at Highland Hills, is dedicated to the humane and ecologically responsible production of his animals. All the livestock and poultry are raised on open pasture on 205 acres near Vacaville, in Solano County, California. Fuller is dedicated to preserving these heritage and rare breeds and to educating consumers about the benefits of supporting species diversity.

PRODUCTION AREA
Vacaville, California

COMMUNITY COORDINATOR
Ted Fuller - mailbox@highlandhillfarm.com

Vermont Bread Bakers

The small state of Vermont is home to a number of small-scale bread bakers; many have been established over the past 25 years. The community of Vermont Bread Bakers currently includes four bakers committed to using sustainably grown non-GMO grains and to baking breads without using additives, flavor enhancers or preservatives. The community expects its membership to grow. By devoting themselves to thoughtful production methods to create outstanding artisan products, these bakers have helped Vermont develop a reputation as an important place for baking.

PRODUCTION AREA
Vermont

COMMUNITY COORDINATOR
Jeremy Gulley - threegoodbeans@yahoo.com

Vermont Farmers and Consumers

The Vermont Fresh Network is the nation's first state wide farm-to-restaurant program. Founded in 1996 by the Vermont Department of Agriculture, Food and Markets at the New England Culinary Institute and incorporated in 1999, the Network is currently under the direction of a board of dedicated farmers, chefs and consumers. The farmers in the network grow and produce a variety of products in a number of ways; some items are heritage breeds, some certified organic, but all are grown in Vermont. The community membership totals around 96 farmers and food producers and 180 Vermont chefs, colleges and food co-ops. All have a dedication to creating a vibrant community that preserves the state's agricultural heritage and working landscape. The Networks diverse projects create direct links between farmers and restaurants and promote fair prices for quality local products. Its aim is to create a thriving local food system by populating the state's landscape with a farms and restaurants that work together to provide fresh, flavorful, high quality food to Vermont's citizens and visitors. Member chefs highlight the local products on their menus so that eaters can make informed decisions when dining out.

PRODUCTION AREA
Vermont

COMMUNITY COORDINATOR
Meghan Sheradin - meghan@vermontfresh.net

Vermont Maple Syrup Producers

Maggie Brook Sugarworks specializes in producing organic maple sugar. The tradition of boiling maple tree sap into sugar traces all the way back to the Abenaki People, the native inhabitants of the land. Maple syrup continues to be a centerpiece of Vermont culture and history. Maggie Brooks Sugarworks is a family-run operation of people personally invested in the quality of their products and the health of their forests. Four to eight family members and friends tap maple trees in a sustainably managed forest and market Maggie Brook syrup. In turn their syrup production contributes to the biodiversity of the woodlot and makes the forest a greater financial resource. The wood from their plots is harvested according to the standards of Vermont Family Forests, the local green lumber certifying agency, and milled and distributed locally.

PRODUCTION AREA
Vermont

COMMUNITY COORDINATOR
Calen Elder - calelder@gmail.com

Vermont Organic Producers

The Northeast Organic Farming Association of Vermont (NOFA-VT) is a non-profit organization that unites a community of 384 organic producers, gardeners and consumers in Vermont. As a whole, the community is dedicated to producing high quality foods, supporting local food systems and maintaining a viable agricultural economy in Vermont. One of the community farms, owned by the Stevens family (members of NOFA-VT) operates Golden Russet Farm, a certified organic greenhouse and market garden. They grow a wide variety of vegetables on 8-10 acres and sell 95% of their produce and plants within 15 miles of their rural farm.

PRODUCTION AREA
Vermont

COMMUNITY COORDINATOR
Enid Wonnacott - elila@sover.net

Vermont Wild Food Gatherers

This community comprises several hundred people in Vermont and the greater region of New England who harvest wild foods. They are not part of a formal association, but rather are united by common experiences and practices. The wild food gatherers supply their families, village markets, and chef-owned restaurants with the natural bounty of their landscape, from fiddlehead ferns and ramps, wild greens and tubers to various wild mushrooms and berries. Their work reintroduces indigenous foods to eaters and makes possible the continued appreciation of wild foods. The community members know it is to their advantage to protect the natural habitat and many actively work to protect it. Nova Kim and Les Hook, founders of VT Native, have started a Wild Foods CSA program year-round, and offer regular classes to culinary schools throughout the area.

PRODUCTION AREA
Vermont

COMMUNITY COORDINATOR
Kim Nova - wildorganic@yahoo.com

Vernon Artisan Bakers and Cheesemakers

The community is represented by Bobolink Dairy and Bakeyard, a family-run operation where farmers raise old breed cows on 200 acres of native New Jersey pasture grass, make raw milk artisan cheeses from the milk, and bake rustic breads in a wood-fire oven. The cheeses are produced daily from April through November and aged 3-15 months in a cellar. The community bakes 12 types of rustic breads using organically grown grains, natural ferments and yeast, locally grown produce, and Bobolink cheese. Bobolink also runs an internship program for future farmers, cheese makers, and bakers.

PRODUCTION AREA
Vernon, New Jersey

COMMUNITY COORDINATOR
Nina White - nina@cowsoutside.com

Virgin Islands Farmers

The Virgin Islands Sustainable Farm Institute on Saint Croix Island is a study-abroad school with hands-on courses in agro-ecology and related sciences. It encompasses a 100-acre Caribbean organic farm. This community of farmers, students, educators and residents believes that an education in the production of local agriculture is the first step toward building a vital community and achieving long term sustainability for the island. The producers harvest mango, papaya, passion fruit, and hot peppers and produce mango wine, papaya and passion fruit juices, hot sauce, vinegars, oils and more. Due to the isolated nature of the islands, people on Saint Croix have been growing fruits and vegetables and harvesting from the wild for their own consumption for centuries. In recent times St. Croix has become dependent on an expensive importation scheme for its residents, importing much of its fruits and vegetables. This community is attempting to create a base of local and sustainable produce to make the island more self-sufficient, to improve local food security, and to preserve the agricultural knowledge and seed heritage of St. Croix.

PRODUCTION AREA
St. Croix, Virgin Islands

COMMUNITY COORDINATOR
Ben Jones - farmnotfight@yahoo.com

Waipi'o Valley Piko Poi Producers

The Mock Chew family has been raising wetland taro for four generations in the Waipi'o Valley on the big island of Hawai`i. Approximately twenty farmers remain in the valley producing 15% of the state's taro. There were once more than 300 varieties of taro, but now only a few are grown. The amout of taro being produced in Hawaii is declining due to adverse weather conditions, various diseases and pests, and a decline in the interest level of younger generations to become taro farmers. Kanani and Kalai Mock Chew are part of the future for taro; they are young farmers dedicated to continuing their family business. The labor-intensive process requires cultivation and maintenance primarily by hand. The farmers then brings its taro to a small facility where they produce poi, a taro root paste. They send Mokuwai Piko Poi, as the product is labeled, out to neighboring towns and farmers markets for distribution. Poi taro is a staple of the Hawaiian diet, nutritious and easily digestible. Hawaiians offer it as the first food to their babies and the last to their elderly. It has been said that without poi there would be no Hawaiian culture.

PRODUCTION AREA
Waipio Valley, Hawaii

COMMUNITY COORDINATOR
Kanani Mock Chew - nanikyla@msn.com

Waiahole Taro Growers

The Waianu Farm, a partnership of two brothers, is one of the last two taro farms on O'ahu Island, Hawaii. The farm sits in the Waiahole Valley, once famous as a taro growing area. Taro is a flooded crop that requires about 15 months to mature and is traditionally eaten as poi, a paste made by pounding and grinding. The families of the Waianu Farm were pioneers in rebuilding *taro loi* (patches) in Hawaii and in fighting for the return of water that had been diverted for sugar plantations. They received grant money to create the Waiahole Poi factory, which processes taro into poi once a week and provides local citizens with part time jobs. Along with organic taro the farmers grow papaya, banana, breadfruit, honey, coffee, cacao, and much more. They sell much of their harvest at Peoples Open Markets, a city run network of around 30 markets that rotate to mostly high-density, low-income neighborhoods.

PRODUCTION AREA
Waiahole Valley, O'ahu, Hawaii

COMMUNITY COORDINATOR
Paul Reppun - lollydr@hotmail.com

Waltham Organic Farmers

This community consists of 200 organic Community Supported Agriculture farms on the fringe of Boston's urban area. The urban residents of Boston have historically enjoyed fresh produce from local farms. These CSA continue that tradition, the young farmers working side by side with CSA member volunteers to grow and harvest organic vegetables on the farms' 1,000 productive acres. The importance of the community is defined by its location in an urban environment. The promotion of the concept of community farms is central to their mission: the farmers of the community believe that farming is a valuable and honorable occupation; they subscribe to farming methods that respects natural systems and enhance the health of the environment. They also seek to reconnect people with the knowledge of how food is produced: children and adults learn about plants, food production and farming.

PRODUCTION AREA
Waltham, Massachusetts

COMMUNITY COORDINATOR
Amanda Cather - farmmanager@communityfarms.org

Washington Chinook Fishermen

The Washington Trollers Association represents 80 fishermen who harvest salmon off the Washington State coast using traditional low-impact selective gear. This Trollers community supplies the Washington State market with high quality, regionally distinct fish. Nearby fish smokers and restaurants prize the unique 'marbled salmon', a breed of Chinook that has a one-of-a-kind flesh coloration. Marbled salmon describes a Chinook or 'King' salmon (*Onchorhynchus tshawytscha*) that exhibits flesh pigmentation that is neither the characteristic red/orange nor the less common white flesh. Rather, it is comprised of varying amounts of both colorations; 'marbled' through the body. Generally the flesh along the backbone contains more red areas and the white dominates along the back and belly. The Trollers Association is in partnership with the Makah Native American nation who process much of their catch. The Washington Trollers Association and the Makah Natives have joined their efforts in promoting the salmon that they catch from Washington waters.

PRODUCTION AREA
Washington State

COMMUNITY COORDINATOR
Jeremy Brown - fvoneandall@hotmail.com

Waxhaw Organic Farmers

A ten-person family works together on this small, diversified farm, producing organic vegetables, small fruits, pastured poultry and pork. They offer their products through a CSA program, a farmers market, and by selling directly to local restaurants. All their products are certified organic. New Town Farms Organic is in Waxhaw, a town in a once rural county in North Carolina that is now the second fastest growing county in the United States. Only a few farms remain in the rapidly developing area. New Town Farms Organic has been highly involved in promoting organic farming as an alternative mode of production to agribusiness. The farm's family leaders helped found the Matthews Community Farmers Market in 1992.

PRODUCTION AREA
Waxhaw, North Carolina

COMMUNITY COORDINATOR
Samuel Koenigsberg - newtownfarms@alltel.net

Westchester County Farmers, Chefs, and Educators

Since its public opening in 2004, Stone Barns Center for Food and Agriculture has been successfully teaching, demonstrating and promoting sustainable, community-based food production to a mixed audience of small-scale farmers, school children, aspiring chefs and everyday eaters. The Stone Barns Center is on 80 acres of pasture, woodland and cultivated fields in New York's Westchester County. Nestled in the center of the property are its namesake stone barns; converted from 1920s farm buildings, the stone barns now serve as home to the Center's educational and culinary spaces. The community members put an emphasis in all their activities on a direct farm-to-table relationship. The Center operates on three integrated levels of production and consumption: the farm and grass-fed livestock program, the not-for-profit education center, and the adjoining restaurant, Blue Hill at Stone Barns.

PRODUCTION AREA
Pocantico Hills, New York State

COMMUNITY COORDINATOR
Nena Johnson - info@stonebarnscenter.org

West Chester Herb Gatherers and Honey Producers

The community is represented by Cross Creek Farm is a small, family-run farm in West Chester, Pennsylvania that provides seasonal, fresh culinary herbs and honey to local restaurants. Christine and Mark Miller and their son Edward garden without the use of chemicals. In July they harvest their first honey crop and in October their second, a crop of autumn herbal honey. They sell honey in its raw form, strained but not heated. Cross Creek Farm delivers its fresh and hand-picked herbs including garlic chives, lemongrass, pineapple sage, lemon balm, and many varieties of basil, from May until November. They have close relationships with many members of the local restaurant community who often recognize the farm on their menus.

PRODUCTION AREA
West Chester, Pennsylvania

COMMUNITY COORDINATOR
Christine Miller - crossckfrm@aol.com

West Concord Breeders

Big Woods Bison Farm, Cedar Summit Farm, Callister Farm, Talking Oak Farm, Hill and Vale Farm, Pastures A' Plenty Farm, and Pasture-land Co-op are a few of the 14 family farms and five processors that make up this community in West Concord, Minnesota. The community raises chickens, turkeys, laying hens, and beef cattle that they market directly to consumers. Callister Farm was established in 1856 by the same family that runs the operation today. The family farm has its own USDA inspected processing plant where community farmers bring their animals to be slaughtered. Callister Farm specializes in chickens and fresh turkeys that are ordered in advance for the Thanksgiving holiday.

PRODUCTION AREA
West Concord, Minnesota

COMMUNITY COORDINATOR
Lori Callister - henhouse@clear.lakes.com

Wheatland Farmers

This community entails the family farmers of Fresh Farm in Wheatland, California and the 25 members who subscribe to the farm's Community Supported Agriculture (CSA) program. Fresh Farm is a fifth-generation family-run farm that has been productive since 1854. During the summer months the Muck family grows and harvests by hand peaches, berries, tomatoes, peppers, eggplants, squash, pears, apples, cucumbers and melons on a two-acre plot. Many of the varieties of melons are rare, heirloom types considered to have historical value for the region. The Muck Family also grows and hand-cleans potatoes, corn, greens, lettuce, and garlic, beans, peanuts and a variety of herbs. Many of the crops grow between the farm's olive trees that date to the mid-1800s. From the fruit of these old trees, Fresh Farm presses its own olive oil for members. Besides their regular pick ups, the 25 CSA members interact with the farmers during special on-farm events and farm tours.

PRODUCTION AREA
Wheatland, California

COMMUNITY COORDINATOR
James Muck - muckster34@hotmail.com

COMMUNITY SUPPORTED AGRICULTURE

Community Supported Agriculture (CSA) is a system whereby local citizens invest money in a nearby farm at the start of the growing season to help cover its production costs. In turn, during the growing season they receive a weekly selection known as a "share" of fresh, locally grown, seasonal produce directly from the farm. By becoming members (also known as "shareholders" or "subscribers") of a CSA program, citizens enable local farmers to receive a fair wage and maintain or transition to ecologically responsible practices. CSA programs ensure that community members have a direct link with their food, farming community, and the natural landscape and seasons. Most CSA farms are small-scale operations that grow organic produce. Alongside fresh vegetables, CSA farms sometimes offer or sell flowers, fruits, herbs, honey, meats, eggs, milk, cheese, and baked goods. Some CSA programs require that members work a small number of hours on the farm or help distribute the shares during the growing season. Robyn Van En, a farmer from Massachusetts, introduced the CSA system to the United States in 1985, and today there are over 1,700 CSA programs across the country.

Willamette Valley Lamb Breeders

The Community of Willamette Valley Lamb Breeders consists of two family farms in the southern Willamette Valley. The lush grass pastures made possible by Oregon's mild climate and abundant rainfall enable the farmers to graze lambs exclusively on pesticide free pastures nearly year round. The breeders never apply hormones or sub-therapeutic antibiotics nor feed their lamb with GMO grown grains. The meat is processed in small batches at a USDA inspected facility where it is not irradiated or gassed. In order to maximize flavor and tenderness, carcasses are dry aged whole for six days. The lamb is then cut and wrapped, and either delivered fresh the next day or quick-frozen. Cattail Creek has provided lamb to Chez Panisse restaurant since 1985. The primary breed at Cattail Creek is the Romney breed, an old English down sheep known for its sweet and mild flavor. The community also raises a limited amount of Navajo-Churro, a heritage breed that is on the Slow Food Ark of Taste. Navajo-Churro sheep were North America's earliest domesticated farm animal. Descended from the Churra, an ancient Iberian breed, they were introduced to North America by the Spanish in the 1500s. This breed is extremely hardy and lives lightly on the land, requiring less water and grass than other sheep breeds.

PRODUCTION AREA
Willamette Valley. Oregon

COMMUNITY COORDINATOR
John Neumeister - jneumeister@earthlink.net

Willamette Valley Wine Grape Growers

The community is made of the Willamette Valley's exemplary sustainable food producers. These are vineyardists, dairymen, and farmers: all of which create high-quality products using sustainable practices. The Deep Roots Coalition is an association of Oregon Winegrowers who are committed to the production of table wines from grapes grown without irrigation in order to preserve local water resources. The Dairy Farmers of the Willamette Valley make farmstead cheese from their own milk supply. Their cows graze on organic pastures, and the milk goes directly from the dairy into the cheese room at the Willamette Valley Cheese Company where it is vat heated. The cheeses are aged on wooden shelves and develop a natural rind. The 47th Avenue Farm manages several pieces of land within the Portland, Oregon metro area. The CSA farm started a plot ten years ago in the Woodstock neighborhood of Southeast Portland. Sauvie Island Organics is a group of growers committed to producing food in an environmentally, socially, and economically sustainable manner. They cultivate nine acres of public land on an island 15 miles from downtown Portland. Sauvie Island Organic sells food directly to the Portland community through a CSA and and has relationships with several local restaurants. They offer the opportunity for consumers to build a relationship with the farm through weekly newsletters, farm tours and potlucks.

PRODUCTION AREA
Portland, Salem and Sauvie Island, Willamette Valley, Oregon

COMMUNITY COORDINATOR
Katherine Duemling - katherine@slowfoodportland.com

Wind River Indian Reservation Farmers and Ranchers

The Lander Valley is nestled against the foothills of the Wind River Mountains. The town of Lander, formerly called Pushroot, is on the banks of the Pop Agie River. Agriculture is the bedrock of the Lander Valley community, but production is dominated by the export of beef calves for feedlot and alfala hay. The Slow Food Wyoming Pushroot Convivium is focused on reviving the rich agricultural traditions of the area as well as shedding light on the sustainable hunting and gathering practices that once sustained the valley's population. Wild River Indian Reservation is a more than 1.7 million-acre stretch that sits northwest of Lander. Wyoming's only Indian Reservation, Wild River is home to the Eastern Shoshone and Northern Arapaho tribes. Twin Creek Ranch and Lodge is a member of the community of producers of high-quality local goods that has sprung in response to the diversification of Lander's population. Twin Creek Ranch and Lodge provides ranch-raised food to its guests and community members. The ranchers raise beef, pork, and poultry, make goat cheese, and grow vegetables.

PRODUCTION AREA
Lander, Wyoming

COMMUNITY COORDINATOR
Andrea Malmberg - andrea@homelander.org

Windsor Fruit Growers

This community is a small bio-diverse farm in Windsor, California, growing 100 varieties of organic fruits. Four people live and work on-site. The farmers strive to help build a strong local community by offering internships, community volunteer days, classes, events, social gatherings, and tours, all of which connect local people to the farm. They use rabbit manure from the farm to fertilize their Golden Muscat, Black Emerald Seedless, Interlaken, Bronx Seedless, and many other varieties of grapes not found in local stores, as well as blueberries, pears, and many varieties of plums. They participate in the Sonoma County farmers' market and Sonoma County Herb Exchange.

PRODUCTION AREA
Windsor, Sonoma County, California

COMMUNITY COORDINATOR
Ana Stayton - ana@goldennectar.com

Winters Organic Walnut and Vegetable Growers

This community consists of Craig McNamara of Sierra Orchards, a diversified farm near Winters, California. On 450-acres at Sierra Orchards, McNamara grows and processes primarily fresh organic walnuts and grape rootstock using cover crops and compost fertilization. McNamara helped to structure a biologically integrated orchard system that became the model for UC/SAREP (Sustainable Agriculture Research and Education Program). In 1993 he also developed a program called FARMS in partnership with University of California Davis, Yolo County Resource Conservation District, and the California Foundation for Agriculture in the Classroom. FARMS introduces high school students and teachers to the principles of sustainable agriculture and Integrated Pest Management practices through student-directed research projects conducted largely at Sierra Orchards.

PRODUCTION AREA
Winters, California

COMMUNITY COORDINATOR
Craig McNamara - farming@sbcglobal.net

Wrightstown Organic Farmers

Anchor Run Community Supported Agriculture (CSA) farms a total of 12 acres on the Anchor Run Farm Preserve. The farm was acquired in 1996 and 1998 with the support of two local families, the township's residents and Board of Supervisors, and Bucks County Open Space Funds. Wrightstown Township is committed to protecting local farmland and encouraging environmentally responsible practices. 150 households participate in the Anchor Run CSA program. Anchor Run CSA brings together farmers and community members in a mutually beneficial relationship that ensures fair compensation for the farmers while providing the community with 60 varieties of vegetables for six months of the year. The Community of Anchor Run All the produce is grown without fertilizers, pesticides, herbicides or genetically modified organisms. They make use of compost, cover crops, and crop rotation to promote healthy soil and plants. Their goal is to sustain the environment while building community.

PRODUCTION AREA
Wrightstown, Pennsylvania

COMMUNITY COORDINATOR
Tali Adini - talyon@juno.com

Yukon River Salmon Fishermen

This community is made up of 900 commercial permit holders who fish for salmon in the Yukon River, seven processors, and a Fishermen's Association that represents 42 rural communities with 100-900 residents each. The fishermen are Yupik Eskimos of the Lower Yukon. The Yukon River originates in British Columbia in the Yukon Territory of Canada, traverses the interior of Alaska and empties into the Bering Sea in Western Alaska. Salmon from the Yukon River are prized for their rich flavor and bright orange-red color. Members of the community produce a range of smoked salmon products.

PRODUCTION AREA
Yukon River, Alaska

COMMUNITY COORDINATOR
Jill Klein - jill@yukonsalmon.org

FOOD JUSTICE

Food Justice is a network of organizations working across the United States to address the challenges communities face. Many involve young people and local citizens in local sustainable agricultural projects, from community gardens and urban farms to food distribution ventures and farmers markets. Each group works with the fundamental belief that everyone in every community deserves access to healthy and affordable foods. Community Food Security Coalition is based in Venice, California: it is a non-profit dedicated to building strong, sustainable, local and regional food systems that ensure access to affordable foods for all people. The Boston Food Project works each year with thousands of volunteers to farm on several lots in urban Boston and on 31 acres in rural Lincoln, Massachusetts. Oregon Food Bank recovers food from farmers, manufacturers, wholesalers, retailers, individuals and government sources, which it distributes to 20 regional food banks across Oregon, helping low-income individuals. CSA Learning Center offers hands-on programs as part of its Agroecology Education for Youth, Adults & Families. In addition, CSA runs the Food Security Harvest Shares Program, which creates affordable access for low-income families to fresh and nutritious vegetables. The People's Grocery is an organization in West Oakland, California that develops creative solutions to the daily health, environmental and economic challenges of the community. Among their projects, the People's Grocery runs the Mobile Market, an organic grocery store on wheels that travels around West Oakland three times a week with staple goods, healthy snacks, and fresh produce. World Hunger Year is a leading advocate for innovative solutions to hunger and poverty. WHY has the only centralized, nationwide database of innovative organizations working on food, nutrition and agriculture issues. WHY has helped to raise more than $6 million, initiated countless media connections.

AREA OF ACTIVITY
California, Oregon, Wisconsin, Illinois, Massachussets, New York State

ASSOCIATIONS COORDINATORS
Food Security Coalition Andy Fisher
andy@foodsecurity.org
The People's Grocery Jason Uribe
jason@peoplesgrocery.org
Oregon Food Bank Sharon Thornberry
sthorn1953@earthlink.net
CSA Learning Center at Angelic Organics Rasha Abdulhadi
rasha@csalearningcenter.org
Growing Power Will Allen
will@growingpower.org
The Boston Food Project Patricia Gray
patgray@thefoodproject.org
World Hunger Year Peter Mann
peter@worldhungeryear.org

NATIVE NORTH AMERICAN INDIGENOUS DELEGATION

Since the beginning of time, Indigenous peoples have been instructed to nurture the relationship with their relatives. The continuity of this relationship has been disrupted by colonialism, in the practices of the scorched earth military campaigns which destroyed their orchards and fields, or Manoomin (wild rice) and the destruction of the great buffalo herd and taking of land. The creation of industrialized and invalid food systems in North America and the Pacific has been at the cost of their sustainable traditional agricultural and harvesting systems. Indigenous Hopi, Zuni, Keresan, Dine, Tewa and Haudenosaunee farmers grow ancient varieties of corn, beans and squash which will now be the foundation of a post-colonial agriculture. Indigenous harvesters of wild rice and taro farmers continue their work to protect sacred foods from both genetic engineering and patenting. All food producers carrying original seeds are facing the same battle: seed sovereignty. They are working with their relatives, the Buffalo Nation and the Salmon Nation and Agriculturalists to restore their lands and waters. The delegation of indigenous farmers and harvesters are intent upon feeding future generations.

AREA OF ACTIVITY
Various states

ASSOCIATION COORDINATOR
Jill Martus-Ninham
jmartus@oneidanation.org

RENEWING AMERICAN FOOD TRADITIONS

RAFT is a partnership of seven of the most accomplished US food, agriculture and conservation organizations, which have joined together to identify, restore and promote America's endangered heritage foods for their cultural and genetic value. RAFT projects work with farmers, fishermen, chefs, and consumers around the United States to develop and promote conservation strategies, sustainable food production, public policy initiatives, and market based incentives.

AREA OF ACTIVITY
New York; Massachusetts; Virginia; North Carolina; Arizona; Washington State; California

ASSOCIATION COORDINATOR
Makalé Faber
makale@slowfoodusa.org

Fishermen and processors of the Laguna de Rocha

The Asociación de Pescadores Artesanales de las lagunas Costeras (Apalco) is the name of an organization formed by 20 families, where both men and women are involved in the activities of fishing and fish-farming in this coastal lagoon. They are continuing activities which have been practiced in the area for decades and which have been improved by technical support from universities (the University of the República Oriental of Uruguay and the Brazilian University of Río Grande do Sul). The community fishes for gray mullet and smokes them in the traditional way (a process which began as a means of preserving food), farm a local variety of shrimp (called *camarones rosados*), catch crabs and process the meat, and fish for atherines, which are particularly delicious fried. These products are mainly sold on the local market to restaurants, since traditional regional cuisine is based on fish.

PRODUCTION AREA
Rocha, department of Rocha

COMMUNITY COORDINATOR
Ángel Javier Vitancurt de los Santos
tel +598 472 3133
javiervitancurt@yahoo.com

Ñandú farmers

The ñandú is a bird rather like an ostrich, which is native to South America. It is common in the plains of Brazil, Uruguay and Argentina, and on the high plateaus of the Andes, but indiscriminate hunting in recent decades has reduced its numbers alarmingly. Only in recent years, thanks to repopulating programs and the renewed interest of public opinion, have ñandú numbers begun to increase again. The community of San Carlos, a small family business which produces foods made with meat, including the meat of this bird, bases all its activities on ecological farming principles, and also sells its products on the international market.

PRODUCTION AREA
San Carlos, department of Maldonado

COMMUNITY COORDINATOR
Mendiburu Nair
tel. +598 410 2681
criaderodevovo1@adinet.com.uy

Producers of Colonia Valdense

In 1850, a colony of Waldensians from Piemonte founded the town of Colonia Valdense in Uruguay. In 1915, an agricultural cooperative was formed which now has 700 producer members. Their work is based on using natural techniques which are environmentally friendly and ensure the high quality of their products. This applies not only to crop cultivation but also to the transformation of the raw materials. Their main products include bee's honey, fresh fruit and vegetables grown in the open, cereals, seeds and cheese made with raw milk from cows which spend all year outside grazing on open pastureland. The cooperative, called Sofoval, sells the products of the members of the community and offers them technical assistance.

PRODUCTION AREA
Colonia Valdense, department of Colonia

COMMUNITY COORDINATOR
Luis Horacio Jourdan Ricca
tel. +598 558 8884
sofoval@sofoval.com

Producers of goat's cheese

Cerro Negro is a cheese cooperative which obtains a large number of different products by transforming goat's milk from its members. It pays particular attention to ensure that the pasture where the goats graze is healthy, and, indeed, the whole production process. In this way, they ensure that the cheese conserves its excellent quality and organoleptic properties, which have enabled it to acquire an excellent reputation on the national market. More than 40 people are involved in the community, including producers, technical experts and factory staff. The main products are a *chêvre*-type cheese, of which they produce 15 tons a year, and a cheese made from cream, of which they produce about 18 tons. The cheese is sold nationwide.

PRODUCTION AREA
Villa Rodríguez, department of San José

COMMUNITY COORDINATOR
Ciro Alejandro Rodríguez Hernández
tel. +598 2707 8482
cerron@adinet.com.uy

Vegetable and legume growers

The Department of Canelones is situated in the south of the country, on the border with the Province of Montevideo. The economy of the area is based mainly on agriculture, especially vines, fruit, vegetables, cereals and tobacco. The producers of Los Cerrillos, a small town 40 km from Montevideo, is a free association of 10 farmers who grow vegetables (mainly tomatoes, peppers, lettuces and cauliflower) and legumes, using sustainable, organic farming methods, and save and preserve seeds of indigenous varieties. They sell their products mostly on a national scale, both through small-scale middle-men and large-scale distribution channels.

PRODUCTION AREA
Los Cerrillos, department of Canelones

COMMUNITY COORDINATOR
Hans Hugentobler
tel. +598 336 2516
swisfarm@hotmail.com

Wine producers of San Juan

Washed by the Río de la Plata, Colonia is one of the most prestigious wine-producing areas in Uruguay. There are more than 370 wineries, covering an area of about 10,000 hectares. The Los Cerros de San Juan winery is one of the oldest and best renowned. It started more than 150 years ago and concentrates especially on the production of Tannat, a complex, robust, very fruity wine. Since the early 20th century, wine production has been based on an ingenious steam-driven system for keeping the must cool, which highlights the fruitiness of the wine. This was probably one of the first systems to control the temperature through refrigeration. Currently, the winery produces about 500,000 bottles a year, which it sells on the national and international market.

PRODUCTION AREA
San Juan, department of Colonia

COMMUNITY COORDINATOR
Estela De Frutos Cis
tel. +598 7109 609
info@loscerrosdesanjuan.com.uy - esteladefrutos@hotmail.com

Artisanal producers of Cocuy

The members of this community are located in various villages in Lara, mainly in the municipality of Urduneta. More than 500 artisanal producers are organized in a number of associations and cooperatives, the largest of which, with 50 members, is the Asociación Civil de Productores del Municipio Urdaneta (ACIPRACOMUR). Products are obtained by processing *Agave cocui*, an endemic plant used since pre-Columbian times as a food and medicine. Distilled juice from cooking some parts of the plant yield a liquor called cocuy. The fruits, washed several times to remove some of the bitterness and cooked in water, vinegar, salt, sugar and spices, are conserved in jars. The community collaborates with the Asociación de Productores de Licores de Caripe.

PRODUCTION AREA
State of Lara

COMMUNITY COORDINATOR
Héctor Lucindo Pineda García
tel. +58 4145127547
recordandoelayer47@yahoo.es

Casabe Galleta producers

The native peoples who lived in the eastern part of Venezuela before Columbus' arrival prepared and ate casabe every day. In various forms, the food is still part of the Venezuelan diet. Casabe galleta is a crunchy round dry bread made of yucca flour. It is three to five centimetres thick with a diameter ranging from 25 centimetres to almost a metre. The colour varies from white to toasty brown. There are three main producers in Barlovento in three different towns: Managua, Calabaza and Palo Quemao. Casabe galleta is produced mainly for self-consumption and the local market, but contact is being established with other markets in Venezuela to open new distribution channels. All three collaborate with the Acción Campesina NGO.

PRODUCTION AREA
Managua, Calabaza and Palo Quemado, state of Miranda

COMMUNITY COORDINATOR
Manuel Gómez Naranjo
tel. +58 2126712509
beduino53@yahoo.com

Chocolate producers of San José de Barlovento

Mis Poemas is a small, family-run artisanal producer located in the Barlovento region, a particularly attractive part of Venezuela. It has a lively cultural atmosphere because the traditions that arrived with slaves from Africa still survive. Dance, song and ancient rituals thrive especially in the San José area. The entire region also has a historic vocation for growing and processing cocoa, which Mis Poemas interprets in an extremely original way. Using pure Barlovento cocoa, cocoa butter, cane sugar with no chemical additives, the 15 individuals involved in the business make exquisitely packaged chocolate products, designing the necessary machinery themselves.

PRODUCTION AREA
San José de Barlovento, state of Miranda

COMMUNITY COORDINATOR
Luisa Amanda González de García
tel. +58 4129356472
luisamandadegarcia@hotmail.com

Preserve producers of Monte Carmelo

All 1,200 members of this community in the state of Lara in northern Venezuela are women. For generations, residents in their village in a mountainous area about 1,000 metres above sea level have been active farmers supplying the local and regional markets. Inspired by this heritage, the women have set up an association that produces fruit and vegetable preserves, ranging from figs in syrup, which are stewed in sugared water and vacuum-packed in glass jars, to wild blackberry jam, tomato sauce and pickled vegetables. The community collaborates with Red de Educación Popular entre Mujeres de América Latina y el Caribe (REPEM) and Red de Aliados de los Parques (RAP), since the location, Monte Carmelo, is near to the Yacambú national park.

PRODUCTION AREA
Monte Carmelo, state of Lara

COMMUNITY COORDINATOR
Gaudy María García
tel. +58 2535145950
gaudyg101@yahoo.com

Andean Corn

Corn, along with potatoes, has always formed the staple diet of the Andes, where the culinary tradition has played a decisive role in safeguarding a high degree of biodiversity. There are many different varieties of corn– *capia, blanco criollo, amarillo socorro, morocho, amarillo de ocho, chullpi* – each of which has its own particular role, both in cooking, ensuring a varied diet albeit based on a single ingredient, and during local festivals. *Capia* is used to make *tortillas, tijtinchas* (for the festival of San Santiago on July 25) and *capias*; *amarillo* is used to make *tamales* and *chicha* (traditionally drunk during carnival); *blanco criollo* is the main ingredient of *mazamorra* (a sweet dating back to colonial times) and *locro*, which is popular throughout Argentina.

Andean cornis grown in small fields and the farmers use sustainable farming methods. They still use traditional tools such as *arados de palos* drawn by mules or horses. Corn is sown by hand at the beginning of October and harvested in April. The cobs are left to dry, the ears are separated from the cob and the husk is removed. Thanks to the creation of the Presidium in 2002 and the initiative of Julián Cámara Hernández, professor of botany at the University of Buenos Aires, a group of corn growers from San José (in the Province of Catamarca) has been able to purchase some small husking machines which make the final, tedious task less arduous. Only in the case of *capia* corn, whose ears are extremely delicate, is the operation still performed by hand. First they are cooked, after which the skin is removed and they are left to dry in the sun. Coordinated by Slow Food convivium leader Hugo Cetrángolo and agronomist Juan Caseres, in just a few years the Presidium has achieved extraordinary results. There is now an Asociación de Productores de Maíces Andinos Argentinos with its own protocol and logo. The production system has improved thanks to the introduction of the husking machines and a new method of conserving corn. With the assistance of agronomist and chef Mayu Bacigalupo, many traditional recipes using corn have been recovered and, thanks to the Buenos Aires Nord convivium, the products of the Presidium are now being promoted in local restaurants.

PRODUCTION AREA
Santa Maria San José, province of Catamarca

PRESIDIUM COORDINATOR
Hugo Cetrángolo
tel. +54 1147712944
hcetrangolo@yahoo.com

PRESIDIUM SUPPORTED BY
Guido Berlucchi (Corte Franca, Brescia, Lombardy, Italy)

Quebrada de Humahuaca Andean Potatoes

Today the crops grown in the Andes near Quebrada de Humahuaca – in the center of the Province of Jujuy, close to Argentina's northernmost border – constitute a resource of incalculable value in terms of genetic heritage and economic potential. Besides many varieties of potatoes and maize, they also include *kiwicha*, *quinoa*, *oca* and *papa lisa*, which date back to the time of the *conquistadores*. The cultivation of many of these species was prohibited because they were associated with forms of superstition. The first evidence of the selection and cultivation of potatoes in the area of the Quebrada has been dated to 4,000 years ago, when, traditionally, every generation would grow a particular type of potato and collect the seeds, thus ensuring the survival of the species. Many types have been lost, and the ones that have survived belong to the *Solanum tuberosum andigena* species (though it is not known whether this is a species in its own right or a sub-species) and have a higher-than-average protein content. In 1996, the Cauqueva Cooperative was set up with the aim of improving the standard of living of people living in the Quebrada area by marketing not only the potatoes grown by local farmers, but also local maize, *oca* and *papa lisa*. In 2002, Cauqueva was selected as one of the finalists for the Slow Food Award for the Defense of Biodiversity. Early in 2004, a Presidium was created which identified five kinds of potato being grown at an altitude of between 2,100 m and 3,800 m: *papa azul* (the sweetest-tasting of them all), *papa señorita*, *cuarentilla*, *tuni morada* and *chacarera*. During its first year of business, each one of the 12 producers belonging to the Presidium was given enough seed to enable them to devote a quarter of a hectare to each of the five species of potato, as well as receiving advice about how to prepare the soil, sow the seed and harvest the crop. The technical experts of the cooperative, especially those from the Faculty of Agricultural Sciences of the University of Jujuy, laid on training courses to teach farmers how to grow particular crops, why quality is important, and how to select and market their crops. The Presidium has been promoting Andean potatoes in restaurants and on the national market, as well as their processed counterparts (potatoes which have been scalded in boiling water), which can be exported and sold on the international market.

PRODUCTION AREA
Tumbaya, Tilcara and Humahuaca, province of Jujuy, Northwest Argentina

PRESIDIUM COORDINATOR
Javier Rodríguez
tel. +54 3884955097
jrcau@imagine.com.ar

Yacón

This ancient Andean root with a vaguely melony flavor is called *aricoma* or *aricuma* in the local dialect and, in Spanish, as *yacón* (pronounced 'chaconne'), *arboloco*, *chicama* or *jiquimilla*. It can be grown in any season – usually it is rotated with other crops such as maize or potatoes – although, in the Central Andes, it grows best between August and September. The ground is prepared with a *taclla*, a simple plough once used by the Incas, and the bulbs are planted in the furrows. The plant is a shrub with a slender trunk and green leaves and grows to a height of one and a half meters. The edible part of the plant is the root: when the brown skin has been removed, the yellow flesh inside is sweet and juicy, with a pear-like consistency. If it is harvested carefully and stored in a cool, dark place, it will keep for months. As it ripens, it gradually becomes sweeter, thanks to the transformation of the starch it contains, a process which can be speeded up by exposing it to sunlight. After several days in the sun (the skin must become wrinkly), it can be eaten raw or processed into juice, jam, jelly or *escabece* (a savoury dish). The leaves are dried and used to make a delicious, aromatic tea. *Yacón* is tasty, versatile and has important dietetic properties. It contains insulin, for example, and is used to prepare special foods for diabetics. In order to grow, it needs very damp soil and plenty of fertilizer, which is why it grows well in the southern part of Quebrada de Humahuaca. The most important production areas are around Barcena and, more particularly, Volcán. Slow Food, in partnership with the Fundandes association (*Fundación para el Ambiente Natural y el Desarollo*, Foundation for the Natural Environment and Development), intends to re-launch *yacón* production and raise public awareness of its benefits in the hope of increasing consumption. Just over 30 farmers in the Quebrada area are involved in the Presidium. Using land long since abandoned (or used for growing other crops), they now grow and process *yacón*. Thanks to the Presidium, a producers' association has been set up and a protocol drawn up for growing and processing this versatile root.

PRODUCTION AREA
San Salvador de Jujuy, Volcán and Barcena, province of Jujuy, Northwest Argentina

PRESIDIUM COORDINATOR
Magda Alejandra Choque Vilca
(Fundandes)
tel. +54 3884257538
magui@imagine.com.ar

Pando Nut

These ivory-colored, kidney-shaped nuts have a reddish-brown skin and a woody shell and are enclosed within a coccus, the fruit of the *Bertholletia* plant, a species endemic to the Amazon jungle. Since it grows to a height of 40 meters, its thick canopy shelters the undergrowth from the sun's rays and the rain. When it ripens (between November and February), the coccus falls off the tree and can be harvested. A special stick is used to remove it from the ground and avoid snake bites. The men who collect the nuts slice it open with machetes and pour the nuts (each coccus contains between 15 and 20) into large, hand-woven baskets, which they then carry home on their shoulders. The nuts are sorted according to size and left to dry in a simple hand-made frame for about two weeks. When they have been shelled with mechanical nut-crackers, the farmers divide the nuts and wrap them. They can be eaten in their natural state or are used to make traditional nut-bars and *brigadeiros* (nuts covered with cocoa and sugar, which also come in a less common version covered with *cupuaçu*, the extremely sweet flesh of another fruit found in the rainforest). The presidium has launched a project to promote the Brazil nut and protect the rainforest from being cleared by land-owners keen to create grazing land for rearing livestock. Work in the Pando area – an area of Bolivia on the border with Brazil – began thanks to the NGO called ACRA (Association for Rural Cooperation in Africa and Latin America) and involves about 150 families of nut gatherers in 15 communities, all members of the Coinacapa cooperative. The Presidium has set up an artisan workshop to produce and market typical sweets based on the Brazil nut on the local market. The first stage of the project involved training a group of producers on the spot while the second stage involved a trip to Italy for two women, both members of the Presidium, to gain professional experience. Furthermore, a machine has been sent to Pando which will enable producers to process the wild cocoa and dried fruits available locally into a paste.

PRODUCTION AREA
Cobija and Porvenir, Pando district

PRESIDIUM COORDINATORS
Casildo Quispe Nina
tel. +591 38422698
coinacapa@cotas.net
Maria Cristina Negro
tel. +39 0227000291
mariacristinanegro@acra.it

TECHNICAL PARTNER
Laboratorio di Resistenza Dolciaria (Alba, Cuneo, Piedmont, Italy)

Potosí Llama

People have been eating llama meat for 6,000 years. After the Spanish conquest, when sheep, cattle and horses were introduced to the American continent, this practice was gradually abandoned, but has been preserved by the people of the high Andes. Llamas are grazing animals and their meat (rich in protein and low in fat and cholesterol) can either be cooked as it is, or processed into *charque*, which is tasty, spicy and keeps well. It used to be bartered in exchange for products of the valley (maize, manioc and corn). Every family knows how to make *charque* using either a dry-salting process or by soaking the meat in brine and then drying it in the sun or in freezing temperatures. Since 1997, an NGO called ACRA (Association for Rural Cooperation in Africa and Latin America) has been operating in the Potosí district of Bolivia to help breeders of camelids, especially llamas, and ensure a commercial outlet for their products. To begin with, they concentrated on wool production (from the *k'ara* breed) and, later, on meat production (from the *thampull* breed). Potosí is a district fraught with problems: the gradual erosion of the pasture-land, the blocking of its exports, competition from imported meat and from alpaca wool for clothing, and the harsh climate have brought the local economy to a virtual standstill. Slow Food is supporting ACRA's efforts by promoting *charque*, safeguarding the age-long culture surrounding llama-breeding and defending the Andean eco-system. In fact, the quality of llama wool and llama meat is closely linked to grazing. About 1,000 llama breeders now belong to ARCCA (Regional Association of Camelid Breeders). If a commercial outlet is to be found for their products, rational breeding methods, veterinary controls and clinics and new techniques for spinning and weaving the wool and drying and processing the meat must be introduced. In the course of 2005 and 2006, the Presidium participated in a number of local trade fairs and has been promoting *charque* in restaurants in La Paz and environs.

PRODUCTION AREA
Provinces of Daniel Campos, Antonio Quijarro, Nor Lipez, Enrique Baldivieso, Sud Lipez, Potosí district

PRESIDIUM COORDINATORS
Maria Cristina Negro
tel. +39 0227000291
mariacristinanegro@acra.it
Japhet Zapana
tel. +591 22421277
japhet63@hotmail.com

Barù Nut

The Cerrado, the typical maquis vegetation that covers most of central Brazil, has much in common with the African savanna and the Australian outback, although the level of biodiversity is much greater and the vegetation more luxuriant. Its many plant species include the Barù (*Dipterys alata*), a large leguminous tree whose fruits mature between September and October and which contain a nut with a delicate flavor: the *castanha de Barù*. The *castanha* can be toasted, so that it acquires a flavor similar to that of peanuts or cashew nuts, or used raw to prepare typical sweets made with cane sugar and milk, like the *Pé-de-Moleque* and the *Paçoquinha*. Unfortunately, the Cerrado *baruzeiro* is disappearing as it is being felled for commercial purposes and on account of the spread of intensive farming of single cereal crops. Along with other fruits native to the Cerrado, the *baruzeiro* is now the subject of study, research and testing by the Cerrado branch of EMBRAPA (the Brazilian Ministry of Agriculture's network of agricultural research centers). The presidium was launched in the State of Goiás, in particular in the area round Pirenópolis, in collaboration with two associations: the ADCC (Associação de Desenvolvimento Comunitário do Caxambu) and the CENESC (Centro de Estudos e Exploração Sustentável do Cerrado). The first project, in the Caxambu region, involves five families in gathering, processing and selling the *castanha*. The second brings together farmers, researchers and environmentalists interested in introducing sustainabòe techniques to manage the resources of the Cerrado. In 1988, a book of recipes was published in Pirenópolis which explains how to make typical dishes using the *castanha de Barù* and other fruits of the Cerrado. The most important project in this area involved 150 families in seven towns, in a program which involves the sustainable collection of Barù nuts. In 2006, the town also held the first Barù Nut Festival. Thanks to the presidium, which aims to strengthen the infrastructures needed to process and promote it locally and on an international scale, the Barù nut is commercialized by a number of small farmers.

PRODUCTION AREA
Pirenópolis, State of Goiás, Central-West Brazil

PRESIDIUM COORDINATORS
Roberta Marins de Sá
tel. +55 6121919881 - 81572556
roberta.sa@mda.gov.br
Katia Karam Toralles
katia_karam@hotmail.com promessadefuturo@hotmail.com
Luis Carrazza
tel. +55 6133278085
luis@ispn.org.br

PRESIDIUM SUPPORTED BY
Veneto Regional Authority (Italy), Tenute Niccolai (San Gimignano, Siena, Tuscany, Italy)

UNDER THE AEGIS OF
Brazilian Ministry of Agricultural Development

Canapù Bean

This is a kind of bean (*Vigna unguiculata*), a West African species introduced to Brazil by African slaves in the 16th century, which spread throughout the northeast of the country. EMBRAPA – the Brazilian Ministry of Agriculture's network of agricultural research centers – has identified 300 local populations. They include the canapù cowpea, cultivated in a semi-arid area in the south of the State of Piauí, which has an excellent flavor and an unusual texture. The size of an ear of maize and roughly oval in shape, the cowpea can be pale green, pink or even light bronze in color. When cooked, it becomes dark brown with tinges of purple and is soft and flavorsome, with hints of freshly cut grass, hay and walnut. The whole process, from the planting to the harvest, is executed entirely by hand, without chemical treatments of any kind. Maize, manioc, rice and cashew nuts are grown in the same region (during the first four years of growing, cashew plants and canapù cowpeas are planted side by side, after which the cashews provide too much shade). Canapù cowpeas can be eaten fresh or dried, and are used in several traditional recipes, such as *mugunzá*, usually served at festivals, in which they are cooked with maize and pork rind. Although cowpeas tend to be grown in people's vegetable plots and consumed in private homes, they tend to be marketed almost exclusively at local fairs and markets. The Presidium has made its first moves in the towns of Picos and Campogrande (in the State of Piauí) thanks to EMBRAPA and in collaboration with Picos branch of Emater (the Rural Development Association of the State of Piauí). The canapù cowpea is interesting because of its flavor and aroma, the fact that it can be farmed in a sustainable way (it is cultivated in a completely natural way) and its strong link with local identity and culture. The aim of the Presidium is to organize a nucleus of producers, draw up a production protocol, providing advice about how the cowpeas can be grown, and to promote the product on the local, national and international market.

PRODUCTION AREA
Towns in the State of Piauí, Northeast Brazil

PRESIDIUM COORDINATORS
Roberta Marins de Sá
tel. +55 6121919881 - 6181572556
roberta.sa@mda.gov.br
José Antonio de Sousa Batista (Emater)
tel. +55 894224453
emater-picos@emater.pi.gov.br

PRESIDIUM SUPPORTED BY
Veneto Regional Authority (Italy) - the Comunità Montana del Trasimeno-Medio Tevere (Italy) - the town of Corciano (province of Perugia, Italy) - and the Slow Food Trasimeno Convivium (Italy)

UNDER THE AEGIS OF
Brazilian Ministry of Agricultural Development

Juçara Palm Heart

The most traditional type of palm and the one that has the best quality heart, the *juçara* (*Euterpe edulis*) grows naturally in the few surviving areas of Atlantic forest in the south of Brazil. It is also the species at highest risk: only in a few areas are palm hearts harvested by native Indios using sustainable methods. In the Ribeira Valley, the *palmiteros* are not Indios and the harvesting is both intensive and clandestine. For some years now, the Guaraní village of Silveira has been planting small nurseries in the forest in an attempt to reconstruct the population of traditional palm trees – besides the *juçara*, the *jerivá* and the *pindo ovy* (or blue palm) – as well as growing sweet potatoes, maize and manioc. The *juçara* suffers direct sunlight and requires no special treatments. It has a straight, slender, greyish-white trunk and grows to a height of approximately 15 meters. Before the heart can be harvested (this involves cutting off the tallest part of the trunk and removing the bark with a machete, effectively killing it), the gatherers must wait eight or ten years. Every six months, the seeds are gathered (usually local kids climb skillfully to the top of the tree and remove the bunches of purplish fruit). No part of the *juçara* is wasted: the leaves are used for making beds and chairs, the wood is used for building houses, and the sour berries are processed into fruit juice. The *juçara* palm is cut just before it is sold, and the heart is sold fresh, usually on the spot, or to the owner of a local restaurant, for a maximum of 5-10 reais (1.5-3 euros). It can be eaten raw (with honey), boiled, grilled over the embers of a fire or fried. The Presidium hopes to repeat the successful experiments conducted in the Boa Vista and Silveira reserves (an area of 948 hectares with a population of about 300 people) where, with the support of the indigenous organization Instituto Teko Arandù, villages chiefs are helping to increase the presence of the *juçara* palm, by creating nurseries in the forest and growing at least two new palms for every one cut down. The inhabitants of the reserves have almost finished writing a handbook containing advice about growing and harvesting this palm, which is also going to be translated into the Guaraní language. They have also launched a program to train families living in the surrounding villages.

PRODUCTION AREA

The Guaraní reserves of Rio Silveira (municipality of São Sebastião) and Boa Vista (Ubatuba), State of São Paulo, Southeast Region

PRESIDIUM COORDINATORS
Roberta Marins de Sá
tel. +55 6121919881 - 6181572556
roberta.sa@mda.gov.br
Maurício Fonseca
tel. + 55 1138153848
mafon@uol.com.br

PRESIDIUM SUPPORTED BY
Veneto Regional Authority (Italy)

UNDER THE AEGIS OF
Brazilian Ministry of Agricultural Development

Sateré Mawé
Canudo Bee's Honey

According to an old Indian legend, when Anumaré Hit went up into Heaven to be transformed into the sun, he invited his sister Uniawamoni to follow him. She decided to remain on the Earth in the form of a bee so that she could help the Sateré Mawé Indians to look after the sacred waraná forests. These small, wild, stingless bees are responsible for pollinating at least 80% of the flora in Amazonia. The canudo bee plays a particularly important role. It is part of the local population of *Scaptotrigona*, a sub-family of the *Meliponinae*, which includes 300 species of tropical American species, all of which are very small and stingless. Canudo bees are kept in the villages of the Sateré Mawé Indians to safeguard the honey of the Maya, which is very liquid, aromatic and tasty. Mayan beekeepers used to collect wild honey in the tropical rainforest, in Yucatán in Central America, long before Europeans introduced the *Apis mellifera*. According to documents written before the arrival of the Spanish, there were hundreds of *jobones* (hives in holes in trees), from which honey and bee's wax used to be extracted. Today, the original bee species has been almost completely replaced by honey bees, although the substance produced by canudo bees is so different from honey that, in this case, honey is really a misnomer. Each species of *Meliponinae* produces a different nectar. The nectar produced by canudo bees has a high water and sugar content, a high level of acidity and medicinal properties. A few years ago, together with the Sateré Mawé Indians, the Slow Food Foundation for Biodiversity formed a presidium to protect waraná sticks. The two projects are closely linked, since the nectar is obtained from the flowers of the waranà plant. So far, canudo bees have been domesticated in about 15 villages and the aim is to extend canudo bee domestication to the 80 villages in the area. The presidium intends to preserve these bees and the Amazonian rainforest to ensure that the Indians have an economic resource. To solve the problem of humidity, which makes the nectar difficult to preserve, the Foundation has involved the bee expert Dr Rémy Vandame and begun tests to remove humidity from the product so that it can be sold commercially.

PRODUCTION AREA
The native land of Andirá Marau, in the basin of the two rivers of the same name, State of Amazonas-Pará, North Brazil

PRESIDIUM COORDINATORS
Maurizio Fraboni
tel. +55 926154763 - 9288042688
acopiama@horizon.com.br
Roberta Marins de Sá
tel. +55 6121919881 - 6181572556
roberta.sa@mda.gov.br

PRESIDIUM SUPPORTED BY
Veneto Regional Authority (Italy)

UNDER THE AEGIS OF
Brazilian Ministry of Agricultural Development

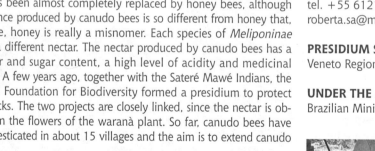

Sateré Mawé Native Waraná

Called *waraná* (meaning the fount of all wisdom) in the indigenous language, *Paullinia cupana sorbilis* has been grown (though it would be more exact to talk about semi-domestication) for hundreds of years in the ancient lands of the Sateré Mawé Indians, a tribe of some 8,000 people who live in about 80 villages in the north of Brazil. The plant is a creeper which grows naturally in the forest to a height of approximately 12 meters. The Indians collect the small plants which grow from seeds landing at the bottom of the tree and take them to clearings in the forest where they transplant them. The white flowers give way to bunches of red fruits which are gathered just before they are ripe, after which the flesh is removed and the seeds are washed. The black seeds are dried in terracotta ovens, the outer skin is removed and they are then crushed in a mortar and made into loaves or long sticks of various sizes (ranging from 100 g to 1 kg). At this stage they are laid on aromatic wooden shelves and, when the time comes to use them, grated using rough basalt stones. Waraná is rich in caffeine, phosphorous, potassium, vitamins and tannin and acts on the nervous system, helping to combat fatigue and stimulate cerebral activity. The powder obtained from the ground seeds can be dissolved in water or diluted in fresh or dried fruit juices. The seed extract is used to make syrups and long drinks. The honey made from the waraná flowers is most unusual. It is produced by small, wild stingless bees called Canudo, without whose totally spontaneous efforts, 80% of the Amazonian flora would disappear. The Presidium was created thanks to the NGO ACRA (Association for Rural Cooperation in Africa and Latin America) and the producers are members of the Conselho geral da tribo Sateré Mawé. The aim is to safeguard the authentic waraná produced in the land where it grows naturally by the people who discovered its virtues so long ago, and who also invented the most suitable techniques for growing and processing it. If the Presidium succeeds in its aim, this is equivalent to saying that it will guarantee not only the survival of the species, which risks being radically impoverished from a genetic point of view, but also the culture of a people threatened by the onslaught of huge, multinational companies. The Presidium is promoting and trying to encourage more widespread use of the traditional waraná stick by presenting it to barmen worldwide.

PRODUCTION AREA
The native land of Andirá Marau, in the basin of the two rivers of the same name, State of Amazonas-Pará, North Brazil

PRESIDIUM COORDINATORS
Maurizio Fraboni
tel. +55 926154763 - 9288042688
acopiama@horizon.com.br
Maria Cristina Negro
tel. +39 0227000291
mariacristinanegro@acra.it

PRESIDIUM SUPPORTED BY
Veneto Regional Authority (Italy)

UNDER THE AEGIS OF
Brazilian Ministry of Agricultural Development

Umbù

Also known as *imbù*, this fruit is native to northeast Brazil and is typical of the *caatinga*, the maquis of this semi-arid region Sertão. The name comes from a word of the dialect spoken by the Tupi Guaraní Indians, *y-mb-u*, which means 'tree that gives drink'. This tree, with its umbrella-shaped foliage, has a special root system which forms large tubers capable of storing up to 3,000 liters of water during the rainy season, so that it can withstand long periods of drought. An important resource in one of the poorest, driest areas of Brazil, where agriculture, based on maize, beans and manioc, suffers from cyclical periods of drought. The fruits of the tree are round and vary in size, from that of a cherry to that of a lemon, with a smooth, green or yellow skin and juicy, aromatic, sweet-sour flesh. They are picked by hand and can either be eaten raw or made into preserves. Traditionally, they are cooked until the skin separates from the flesh. Then the liquid is drained off, cane sugar is added and cooking continues until it forms a gelatin (*geléia*). If the flesh is separated from the pips and sugar is added, it can be cooked for a long time until becomes a slightly bitter, dense cream (*doce*). Umbù can also be used to make fruit juice, *vinagre* (obtained by cooking the fruits when they are past their best), *marmelada* (obtained by piling up strips of the flesh that have been dried in the sun) and, with the addition of sugar, a compôte (*umbu em calda*). The flesh of fresh fruit or *vinagre*, milk and sugar are used to make the traditional *umbuzada*, which is sometimes eaten instead of the evening meal. The Cooper-Cuc cooperative has 59 member-cum-producers who collect the umbù from the local communities, and transform it into high-quality products. Thanks to the Slow Food Foundation and the NGO Horizon 3000, in the first months of 2006, small workshops were established to complete the first stages of processing, after which the semi-processed fruit is delivered to the cooperative. Since the Presidium participated at the Salone del Gusto in Turin in 2004 Hall of Taste and Aux Origines du Goût, organized in Montpellier by Slow Food France in 2005, jars of umbù have begun to travel around the world.

PRODUCTION AREA
Towns in the Sertão Bahiano area, State of Bahia, Northeast Brazil

PRESIDIUM COORDINATORS
Roberta Marins de Sá
tel. +55 6121919881 - 6181572556
roberta.sa@mda.gov.br
Erwin and Catharina Gross
tel. +55 746731296
procuc@lkn.com.br

PRESIDIUM SUPPORTED BY
Veneto Regional Authority (Italy)

UNDER THE AEGIS OF
Brazilian Ministry
of Agricultural Development

Red Fife Wheat

The first person to sow this type of wheat in Canada was a farmer called David Fife, who had brought a few seeds with him from Scotland. The species is first documented in 1840 in the context of the region of Otonabee, now in Central Ontario. Given its resemblance to the Ukrainian variety, *halychanka*, this variety of wheat may be descended from the Ukrainian species. Another school of thought maintains that it is an accidental hybrid. The red fife (the name may refer to the Kingdom of Fife) is robust and resistant to disease. It is bright red when mature and has a higher yield than any other variety of wheat ever grown in Canada. What's more, it tastes good and, milled into flour, in the form of flour,

cooks very well. As a result, it is very popular with farmers, millers and bakers alike. The flat, fertile plains of the Canadian prairies have guaranteed a quality harvest over the years, despite the extremely cold climate. Government agronomists are convinced that the properties of red fife and its capacity to adapt to the extreme weather conditions mean that it is the only forerunner of cultivated varieties of wheat. And it has survived thanks to a few organic farmers scattered around the country. The Red Fife Presidium is the first one in Canada, and was created to re-launch red fife by introducing it to artisan bakeries. It has supported the efforts of farmers who grow the wheat and has succeeded in increasing the amount of seed to such an extent that it can now be marketed. The bread promoted by the presidium is kneaded and shaped by hand and baked in a stone oven. It has a yellow outer crust and smells of wheat and herbs. It has a strong, slightly acidic taste, with hints of spices, aniseed and fennel. To promote the high quality and excellent taste of artisan bread made from red fife flour, the presidium organized an Artisan Bread Tour which visited six Canadian towns. The presidium has applied to the Canadian Wheat Board for legal recognition of this wheat variety and has launched a campaign with the aim of spreading the idea of growing and processing red wheat on the Canadian prairies.

PRODUCTION AREA
Central Ontario and the southern range of the provinces of Alberta, Saskatchewan and Manitoba

PRESIDIUM COORDINATOR
Mara Jernigan
tel. +01 2507434267
engeler@telus.net

Blue Egg Hen

The area of Temuco, capital of Region IX (La Araucanía), where large numbers of indigenous Mapuche people live, you often see eggs with pale-blue or pale-green shells for sale at local markets. This unusual color is transmitted by the O (olive) gene and it is thought that the original hen of this kind was *Gallus araucanus*, but it is not clear whether the Araucana hen – which is small, has no tail and has 2 tufts beside its ears, a feature that led it to be re-christened *inauris* (meaning 'with an earring') – is an indigenous breed or the result of years of selection, having been crossed with hens supplied, apparently, by the last chief of the Mapuche, Michiqueo-Toro-Mellin. And how did the domestic hen reach South America? Was it thanks to the Spanish *conquistadors* or Dutch pirates in the 16th and 17th centuries? Or, by sea, from Japan, in about 3200 BC? Or did it come from the Mongolian steppes via the isthmus of what is now the Bering Strait 40,000 years ago? It is a mystery for breeders and researchers alike. The pale-blue eggs are interesting for another reason. Hens that lay colored eggs will not tolerate an intensive farming environment. This being so, the pale-blue (or pale-green) color is a sign of quality and ensures yolks that are yellow, very large and absolutely delicious. The presidium was set up in collaboration with the local Temuco branch of the NGO Cet Sur to promote the eggs and encourage research into the selection of the *araucana* breed through the *curadoras de semillas*, who collect and safeguard samples of the region's plant and animal biodiversity. In 2004, an important cooperation project was set up with the Valdarno Hen Presidium to organize visits and exchanges. The *curadoras* (who are already working on the task of conserving the various indigenous plant varieties) have undertaken to rear small groups of hens that lay blue eggs with the idea of selling the eggs on the national market, and will collaborate on research and selection initiatives.

PRODUCTION AREA
Region VIII (Bio Bio) and region IX (La Araucanía)

PRESIDIUM COORDINATORS
Max Thomet
tel. +56 45248835
mthomet@cetsur.org
Francisco Klimscha
tel. +56 99198471
slowfoodchile@hotmail.com

Calbuco Black-Bordered Oyster

If you drive for 1,200 km south from Santiago towards the end of the world, you come to the port of Calbuco, in Region X (Los Lagos), where you will discover an archipelago of islands inhabited by fishermen. If you set sail from the port in a small boat, in an hour you will reach the beautiful little island of Chiduapi: emerald green fields, wooden houses looking out to sea, a church, a school, a cemetery. Nothing else. No hotels, restaurants or shops, no electricity or telephones. Just occasional days of sunshine which alternate with days when it rains and an icy wind blows. Here, the tradition of collecting wild oysters has been handed down for at least four generations. During low tide (twice a day), the water in the bays of the island retreats as much as 300 meters, leaving the oyster beds bare. When this happens, the fishermen begin the task of selecting the largest oysters and bringing them nearer to the shore, where enclosures marked with stones have been made for keeping them until they are sold. A net running around the edge of each enclosure, topped with white buoys, shows the divers where the oysters are even during high tide. These oysters are smaller than the ones we know in the rest of the world, they have a stronger taste and have a more highly-developed muscle. Calbuco oysters can easily be recognized because, when they are opened, they have a distinctive black fringe. The technique used for collecting these molluscs respects the natural cycles of the reefs. They may only be collected in the autumn and winter months (when oysters do not reproduce), and only the largest oysters at least three years old may be collected. However this traditional practice of gathering wild oysters is in danger of being abandoned. The presidium was set up with the idea of organizing the few remaining oyster fishermen, giving them an official trade-mark which distinguishes the black-edged oyster, ensuring that there are commercial outlets which are willing to pay more for an excellent product – on the market today, wild and cultivated oysters are sold at the same price – and preserve an ancient, sustainable system of fishing. Furthermore, the presidium hopes to encourage the various institutions to bring pressure to bear so that the islands of the Calbuco archipelago can benefit from primary services such as electricity, gas and a telephone line.

PRODUCTION AREA
Calbuco Archipelago, region X (Los Lagos)

PRESIDIUM COORDINATORS
Francisco Klimscha
tel. +56 99198471
slowfoodchile@hotmail.com
Alejandro Soto Velasquez
tel. +56 29465038

Merquén

This universal condiment of Mapuche cuisine is an aromatic mixture in powder form, which never contains less than 70% of *aji*, a long, curved, pointed chili pepper, called *caciocavra* locally. These hot peppers are grown throughout the region and are harvested in February, when they are bright red. As they dry in the sun, they become purple, after which they are smoked for half-an-hour over a hot fire in wicker baskets in a special smoking shed. They are then dried a bit more in the sun and finely ground, although they used to be pounded for a long time with a stone mortar and pestle. At this stage they are mixed with fresh coriander, which is also slightly smoked and then ground, and sea salt, which must never constitute more than 20% of the mixture. In the past *merquén* was a common sight on tables in Chile and was used to spice up soups, fried dishes, meat and salads. But, gradually, it has disappeared, possibly because it is associated with the poverty of the past, which most people would prefer to forget. However, if you go to the market in Temuco, the town with the highest percentage of Mapuche Indians, you will find not only pale-blue eggs, home-woven fabrics, ancient musical instruments with a strange military sound and Arcuana hens but also plenty of *merquén*, with its sweet, spicy smell. The presidium was constituted thanks to the NGO Cet Sur, with the idea of bringing back the authentic recipe of this spicy powder, which replaces cumin as a substitute for coriander and the use of too much salt. First, it hopes to promote production of *merquén* in the area where it has traditionally been made by encouraging the Mapuche communities to start growing *caciocavra* and coriander again, and inviting the few artisans who still make *merquén* to use only locally grown ingredients. Secondly, it hopes to attract the attention of the best restaurants in Chile and elsewhere in South America, persuade them to serve *merquén* to their customers, either as a table condiment or as an ingredient in tempting new recipes.

PRODUCTION AREA
Temuco, province of Cautin, region IX (La Araucanía)

PRESIDIUM COORDINATORS
Max Thomet
tel. +56 45248835
mthomet@cetsur.org
Francisco Klimscha
tel. +56 99198471
slowfoodchile@hotmail.com

Purén White Strawberry

In central southern Chile, in Region IX (La Araucanía), near the town of Purén, people have grown white strawberries, forerunners of all the cultivated varieties around the globe, for hundreds of years. In fact, large, modern-day strawberries were invented only fairly recently (in the 18th and 19th centuries), whereas the fruit grown prior to the discovery of the New World were tiny wild strawberries (*Fragaria vesca*). The American *Fragraria virginiana* was crossed with the white Chilean *chiloensis* in Brest, France, in 1766, to produce the *ananassa*. These were subsequently cross-bred several times, until they became the large, red variety we know today. The white, Chilean strawberry is round with a small point. The pale skin is sometimes pink, but, more often than not, ivory-colored with red or pink spots. It has a pleasant, delicate, grassy smell and a subtle flavor. It is grown on 14 hectares of land near Purén, in an area called the Manzanal, sheltered by the Cordillera Nahuelbuta, the mountain range overlooking the ocean. The ground is steep and the fields are located between plots of forested woodland, where the soil is poor and clayey. White strawberries do not require any spraying, fertilizer or irrigation and are harvested between November 20 and mid-January. Locally, they are associated with Christmas and New Year, like mandarin oranges in other parts of the globe. They are sold directly by the producers in the fields, or at local markets or trade fairs. The aim of the Presidium is to raise awareness of this fruit, encourage more people to grow and eat it and promote it further afield. Once it would have been impossible to order white strawberries in a local trattoria or a restaurant in the city, but by organizing a series of initiatives, Slow Food Chile hopes to promote them in eateries throughout the country, especially in Santiago. Slow Food experts, technical specialists and members of the Comité de Pequeños Agricultores de Frutilla Blanca are working together to compile a producers' handbook. They guarantee that the strawberries are healthy food, given that the farmers who grow them use no chemicals of any kind.

PRODUCTION AREA
Purén, province of Malleco, region IX (La Araucanía)

PRESIDIUM COORDINATORS
Roberto Giacomozzi
tel. +56 99699187-45793344
rgiacomo1@hotmail.com
Francisco Klimscha
tel. +56 99198471
slowfoodchile@hotmail.com

Robinson Crusoe Island Seafood

People on the island have been fishing for at least three centuries. The place is most famous for its lobster (*Jasus frontalis*), which has been caught here since at east the 18th century, and is only to be found here and off the islands of Desventuradas (San Felix and Sant'Ambrosio), three days' sail to the north. *Jasus* lobsters are caught at a depth of 50-100 meters, using long, narrow, wooden boats built on the island by the Chamorro family. The fishermen let down into the sea rectangular lobster pots, made with the branches of a local tree called the *maqui*. Subsequently the pots are hauled up using a motor, a job that used to be done manually. On Robinson Crusoe Island, lobster fishing is only permitted between October 1 and May 14 and the lobsters that are caught must be at least 12-14 years old. The sea around this island also contains other species of indigenous fish, mollusks and crustaceans which are equally interesting in terms of their taste and flavor. In particular, the golden crab (*Geryon quinquedens*), which is caught at a depth of 500-600 meters, using the same wooden traps, the black sea urchin (*Aspidodiadena microtuberculatum*) and, lastly, the delicious, but little-known breca (*Cheilodactylus gayi*) and the vidriola (yellow tail amberjack), both of which are caught using the *espinel*, a very long hook. Getting to the only town on the island (about 400 km from terra firma) involves a two-and-a-half-hour flight from Santiago, half-an-hour on foot and an hour by boat. The island constitutes a unique ecosystem with many native species of algae, birds, mammals, fish and crustaceans, which the presidium is seeking to protect. It hopes to do this by promoting the island's fish resources without emphasizing lobster-fishing unduly since – despite restrictions – stocks risk being seriously depleted. For this purpose, the presidium intends to establish a communal fish-processing workshop.

Furthermore, in 2004, a joint project began with the Bottarga Presidium of Orbetello, as a result of which there have been many exchange visits as part of a wider program of international exchanges between small-time producers of international presidia and Italian producers of a similar kind. Today, the entire Juan Fernández archipelago is protected as a national park and UNESCO World Biosphere Reserve, a fact that bodes well for the preservation of biodiversity on the island,

PRODUCTION AREA
Robinson Crusoe Island, Juan Fernández Archipelago, region V (Valparaíso)

PRESIDIUM COORDINATORS
Juan Torres de Rodt
jtorresderodt@yahoo.es
Francisco Klimscha
tel. +56 99198471
slowfoodchile@hotmail.com

PRESIDIUM SUPPORTED BY
Bottarga Presidium Orbetello (Grosseto, Tuscany, Italy)

Sierra Cafetalera Coffee

The Dominican Republic is situated in the eastern part of Hispaniola, the island in the center of the Greater Antilles Archipelago. Sull'isola caraibica ilNella zona,One of the traditional areas for growing coffee is the Sierra di Neyba, situated in part of the provinces of Elías Piña, San Juan, Indipendencia and Bahoruco. The presidium was created in the area around Los Bolos – the Sierra Cafetelera – which lies across the border of the provinces of Indipendencia and Bahoruco. Here, at an altitude of between 1,000 m and 1,400 m, small-scale producers, organized into associations and cooperatives, grow excellent *arabica typica* and *caturra* coffee on sandy and clayey soil in the shade of tall trees. After the 'cherries' have been picked, the pulp and skin is removed, the beans are fermented for a short time, washed and dried. No chemical treatments are involved. In the early 'nineties, there were more than 400 families in this area growing coffee. Then, as a result of mass emigration towards the cities, the plantations were replaced with pasture and short-cycle crops like the *yautia*, a local species of tuber, leading to deforestation, impoverished soil, and a diminished water supply. In order to produce better quality coffee, the plantations were moved higher up, incentives were offered to farmers to produce the *typica* and *caturra* varieties, and tall trees were introduced. The project to promote the coffee grown in the Sierra Cafetalera was started thanks to the NGO Ucodep of Arezzo, an association formed to promote international solidarity and cooperation, which has been active in the area for years. The interlocutors in the Dominican Republic are 12 associations (Nucleo Neyba), representing more than 500 families of producers and operating in nine communities in the provinces of Independencia and Bahoruco. As well as the Huehuetenango coffee project, the presidium is involved in the Regional Network Project which supports associations of small-scale coffee producers, promoted by the IAO (Istituto Agronomico per l'Oltremare or Overseas Agricultural Institute) with Slow Food, Ucodep and the Tuscany Regional Authority, and financed by the Italian Ministry of Foreign Affairs. The aim of the presidium, whose first task was to draw up a production protocol, is to improve the quality of life of small-scale coffee producers.

PRODUCTION AREA
Los Bolos, Sierra de Neyba, provinces of Independencia and Bahoruco

PRESIDIUM COORDINATORS
Carlo Simonetti
tel. +39 0553220895 - 0553245133 - 3494219887
carlo.simonetti@ucodep.org
Silvana Grispino
tel. +1 8095258118 – 8092962168 - 8092506180
silvana.grispino@ucodep.org

Cacao Nacional

Cacao nacional descends from the first plants cultivated by the Mayans in South America. It is a particularly delicate cacao found only in Ecuador, which explains the patriotic name *nacional*. Genetically it is a *forastero,* a variety characterized by robust and vigorous plants, but the flavor and aroma of the chocolate that derives from it has a quality rivaled only by the legendary *criollo.* The province of Napo, today the production center of *cacao nacional,* is in the heart of Ecuadorian Amazonia. Much of its population is indigenous, consisting mainly of the Quichua, followed by the Quijos and Chibcha ethnic groups. Its geographic position has contributed to the province's cultural isolation. Even today, the only way to reach the provincial capital of Tena is by taking a bus from Quito along a bumpy dirt road. Nevertheless, the isolation has preserved the last remaining plants of *nacional,* which survive in the forests, while in other regions of the country they have gradually been replaced by more productive and disease-resistant hybrids. The presidium was formed in collaboration with the Quichuas of the Kallari cooperative to safeguard the by now rare trees yielding *nacional* and to help the indigenous communities improve the methods for fermenting and drying the cacao beans, thus helping to boost prices. The province of Napo is running a serious environmental risk because of the recent discovery of oil reserves, so the Kallari growers are also striving to show that cacao production can be an important economic alternative, as well as helping conserve the area's valuable ecosystem. Today, with the support of the Slow Food Foundation for Biodiversity, *nacional* producers can now count on a centralized facility for drying the beans.

PRODUCTION AREA
Quechua villages near Tena, province of Napo

PRESIDIUM COORDINATOR
Diego Grefa
tel. +593 93098740
diegogrefa@hotmail.com

PRESIDIUM SUPPORTED BY
L'Insieme Association (La Morra, Cuneo, Piedmont, Italy)

TECHNICAL PARTNER
Max Felchlin AG, Guido Gobino (Turin, Piedmont, Italy)

Huehuetenango Highland Coffee

The Jesuits introduced coffee to Guatemala in 1773 and today the country produces some of the finest coffee in the world. One of the best regions for coffee production is Huehuetenango, at the foot of the Cuchumatanes, the highest non-volcanic mountain range in Central America. The coffee grows at altitudes up to 1900 meters, in the shade of forest trees, so the beans ripen without receiving too much sun. The worldwide slump in coffee prices in recent years has endangered the survival of the indigenous population, descendants of the Mayans, whose livelihood depends on coffee production. In order to protect and valorize the highland coffee, a presidium of eight cooperatives of producers was established in 2002. The members drew up a regulatory framework listing the areas best suited for production and the crus yielding the best beans in the region, obtained from *Coffea Arabica* (*typica*, *bourbon* and *caturra* varieties). The berries are hand-picked one by one and then placed in wicker baskets tied around the harvester's waist. Then the beans are extracted from the berries by a gentle fermentation process, starting no more than four hours after harvesting and lasting 24 to 36 hours. After removal of the coffee berry's flesh, the beans are dried in the sun for at least three days, continuously turned over with a rake. Then they are placed in sacks for exportation. In Italy the coffee is roasted by a few artisans and also at the Vallette Prison in Turin (thanks to the Pausa Café cooperative), away to safeguard biodiversity through social commitment. A wood oven was set up in the prison and the in-mates process the raw beans under the guidance of the Tuscan coffee roaster Andrea Trinci, the first of many to support the project. Generally middlemen earn more than the growers, but in this case half of the proceeds from the cooperative return to the Guatemalan producers themselves. Huehuetenango highland coffee is served in bars, coffee shops and restaurants all over Italy, and since May 2005 can also be found on the shelves of some of the Coop supermarkets. The TransFair label guarantees that the coffee processing did not engender exploitation or poverty in the southern areas of the world and that it was acquired according to fair trade criteria.

PRODUCTION AREA
Western plateau of Huehuetenango, municipalities of San Pedro Necta, La Libertad, Cuilco, La Democracia, Todos Santos Cuchumatanes

PRESIDIUM COORDINATORS
Marco Ferrero
tel. +39 01119711488
marzia_sica@hotmail.com
Manrique Lopez Castillo
tel. +502 7643103
mlopez@guatemais.org

PRESIDIUM SUPPORTED BY
Italian Ministry of Foreign Affairs,
General Directorate
for Development and
Cooperation, Coop, Iao

TECHNICAL PARTNERS
Rancilio Macchine per caffè
(Italia, Andrea Trinci (Agliana,
Pistoia, Tuscany, Italy)

Ixcán Cardamom

Oscar Kloeffer, a young German, brought cardamom to Guatemala at the beginning of the 20th century to be used as a flavoring for medicine, and it very quickly spread to the north and coastal region of the country. The zone of Ixcán, in the department of El Quiché, inhabited by indigenous farmers of different ethnic groups, produces an excellent product that was in great demand in the last decade by the United States, Europe and Arab countries. In the past five years the market fell off, causing a drastic reduction in the selling price with social and economic consequences. Today cardamom cultivations cover 32% of the farmland and involve just under 50% of the population, who are forced to sell the product at cost price. The cardamom grows in damp tropical zones on spontaneous bushes of the Zinziberaceae family. The little dark seeds are contained in triangular pods, which preserve their sweet-sour aroma reminiscent of lemon. It is grown at altitudes of between 600 and 1,500 meters. Harvested manually three times a year, in October, November and December, it is dried for 24 hours and then prepared for sale (as seeds or powder). In cooking it is used to flavor rice pilaf, meat dishes, pickled fish, *vin brûlé*, bread and pastries. When ground, the seeds serve as a base for curry. An Arab tradition, maintained by the Bedouins, is to put a few of the seeds in the spout of the coffee maker to flavor the coffee as it is poured into the cup. The presidium involves five of the Ixcán communities, where a total of 130 families grow the green cardamom, the finest variety. The producers are guided by the *Asociacion Integral de Productores Organicos de Ixcán* (ASIPOI), a local organization set up in 2000, and can also count on the support of CEFA, an Italian NGO. Presidium coordinator and director of ASIPOI, Miguel de Miguel, selected the communities and families to be involved in production and with them established a regulatory framework for production.

PRODUCTION AREA
Ixcán, department of El Quiché

PRESIDIUM COORDINATOR
Miguel de Miguel
tel. +502 8000394
migueldemi@hotmail.com

Chinantla Vanilla

The vanilla plant is an orchid that needs heat, humidity and shade: filtered rather than direct sunlight. Vanilla was once widely grown throughout the country and women used it to perfume the oil of the *mamey*, to make their hair silky. The cultivation of vanilla was given up in the 19th century, but resumed in the 1990s. Chinantla, the only region in the world where you can find wild vanilla, is the zone of greatest genetic diversity. Called *kuo li gm* in the Chinanteco dialect (the scientific name is *Vanilla planifolia*), it grows on tree props in the thick of the forest. It is a hermaphroditic plant, but a very thin membrane (*rostelo*) separates the female and male sexual organs. In the early morning hours between the end of March and the beginning of May you need to lift the membrane with a toothpick and prod it gently with the forefinger to pollinate three or four flowers in each cluster. The ripe fruit, which is meaty, yellow in color and 15 to 25 centimeters long, contains an enormous quantity of tiny seeds. Immediately following the harvest, the pods are baked for six or eight hours at 63-65°C and then placed in the sun for two months, making them soft, flexible, aromatic and coffee-colored. The presidium began from Rancho Grande, a community of 200 people guided by agronomist Raúl Manuel Antonio, who received the Slow Food Award for Biodiversity in 2000. It is now working with the Communities of Cerro Verde and Flor Batavia (also involving Arroyo Tambor and San Felipe Usila producers in coming years) and focuses on the vanilla production chain. In 2004, it began drafting a production protocol, and an initial group of producers– the Guardiani della Selva – has also drawn up an internal protocol. The presidium producers take training courses with experts in the field and can count on the University of California and the Center for Tropical Studies (Citro) of Veracruz for the identification of the different varieties of vanilla and the Tuxtepec Istituto Tecnológico Agropecuario n. 3 for technical assistance.

PRODUCTION AREA
San Felipe Usila, San Juan Bautista, Valle Nacional, San Andrés Teutila, San Andrés Teotilapan, San Pedro Ixcatlán, State of Oaxaca

PRESIDIUM COORDINATOR
Elías García Martínez
tel. +52 2878753681
elias_garciam@hotmail.com

TECHNICAL PARTNER
Baiocco A. & Figlio (Sesto San Giovanni, Milan, Lombardy, Italy)

Tehuacán Amaranth

As early as pre-Columbian times, Tehuacán valley was known for its fertile and water-rich terrain, which was why the nomads of Central America chose it as the place to cultivate amaranth, corn and beans. With the arrival of the *conquistadores*, the cultivation of amaranth was prohibited and corn and beans began to be grown extensively, gradually impoverishing the zone. Protein-rich amaranth requires less water than maize and several parts of the plant can be used as well. The *Amaranthus hypocondriacus* variety, native to Tehuacán, grows to a height of two or three meters, has large green leaves and magnificent flowers. The seedlings can be eaten as a vegetable, and the leaves, which contain more iron than spinach, are an important food for children. They are eaten in salads, in soups or dried and used as spices. The toasted seeds are used in the preparation of traditional sweets like *alegria*, or flour can be obtained to make tortillas (mixed with Maize flour), cakes and biscuits. Being gluten-free, amaranth is also used as an ingredient in bread, pasta and biscuits for people with celiac disease. The slow work of recovering certain varieties of amaranth began in 1980 thanks to Alternatives (*Alternativas y procesos de participación social*), which has organized cooperatives in 60 villages, involving 1100 indigenous families in the Mixteca region. Each family plants a maximum of one quarter hectare of amaranth and on the rest of the allotted land a mixture of corn, beans, peppers and squash. The cooperatives then join forces to produce amaranth-based foods under the common label of Quali, which in the *náhuatl* language means good. In addition to helping design the machines to process the amaranth, the presidium works to raise the profile of the *alegria* sweet and also tests products for people with celiac disease – a project realized with the University of Milan thanks to the support of the Cariplo Foundation. Moreover, the presidium is creating a center for the display, cultivation and sale of amaranth inside a Museo del Agua, which will also be home to other Mexican Presidia.

PRODUCTION AREA
Tehuacán Valley, State of Puebla

PRESIDIUM COORDINATOR
Raúl Hernandez Garciadiego
tel. +52 2383712550
raulhdezg@laneta.apc.org

Andean Kañihua

The *kañihua* is a chenopod that grows at over 3,800 meters in the southern strip of the Peruvian Andes and the highlands of Bolivia. No more than a half a meter in height, the leaves and stems are streaked with bright spots of red and yellow. The plant is well suited to the soil and climatic conditions in the zone, capable of withstanding drought, saline terrain and low temperatures. And it is unique because the microscopic grains (one millimeter in diameter) yield a very fine brown flour. Known as *kañihuaco* in Quechuan dialect, the flour is used in the preparation of dry-baked goods (*kispiño*), cakes, soups, and even hot drinks. The pre-Columbian populations began cultivating *kañihua* at the beginning of 1000 BC. Since then it has been a primary source of food for the inhabitants of the Andes because its very high protein content makes it a good partial substitute for animal proteins like milk, which are difficult to find. Unfortunately, current agro-industrial processes cannot guarantee the quality of the final product, which loses much of its original nutritional value when it is processed. Today the *kañihua* occupies about 2,000 hectares in Peru (distributed between the departments of Puno, Cusco, Apurimac and Huancavelica). This is just half of what was produced ten years ago because the cultivations have given way to forage species for animal husbandry. The grains are so small that many are lost during the often manual harvesting, so the Slow Food Foundation for Biodiversity has helped presidium producers purchase a small threshing machine to harvest and clean the *kañihua*. The presidium has also planned various informative and promotional activities, aimed primarily at the Peruvian people, to recognize the nutritional value of the *kañihua* and the importance of including it in the daily diet. This will be done by distributing promotional material, proposing *kañihua*-based recipes, experimenting with alternative by-products (the grains can be puffed up and used as the basis for a light snack), and making it easier for producers to take part in local and international trade fairs.

PRODUCTION AREA
Ayaviri, Cupi and Santa Rosa, province of Melgar, department of Puno, Sur

PRESIDIUM COORDINATOR
Elisbán Felix Lino Alarico
tel. +51 563082
elisbanlino845@hotmail.com

Andean Sweet Potatoes

According to a popular legend, when the first Inca, Manco Cápac, emerged from Lake Titicaca with his spouse Mama Ocllo to found the empire, the first thing the god Wircocha taught him was how to grow maize in the lowlands and potatoes up high. Native to the central Andes (Peru, Bolivia), the potatoes are cultivated on all the mountains in the country and symbolize the agricultural and gastronomic culture of the Andean people. The farmers selected more than 900 varieties belonging to eight different species, all singular in terms of color, shape, flavor, and use (in the west, on the other hand, only the *Solanum tuberosum* is known and cultivated). Given this enormous wealth, it was decided to choose only a handful of representative varieties, particularly interesting from an agronomic and organoleptic perspective, and develop a limited promotional project that would serve as the driving force for the other varieties. Worthy of mention is the *mactillo* (elongated shape, purple skin and floury cream-colored pulp streaked with violet), the *pitiquiña* (skin wrinkled by deep furrows and eyes, yellow pulp), the *choclluscha* (bright red skin and pulp streaked with the same color) and the *chapiña* (black outside, blue-black inside). The latter two are particularly suited for frying. The presidium, set up in collaboration with ANPE (Asociación Nacional de Productores Ecológicos), initially involved farmers in efforts to improve seed quality and draw up a regulatory framework to guarantee the origin, genuineness (no chemical fertilizers or special treatments are used) and quality of the final product (e.g. the potatoes must be grown above 3,200 meters of altitude). The next objective will be the processing of quality by-products (the Foundation will provide economic assistance to create a small processing plant) and a graphic study of suitable packaging to increase the market share of products whose diversity is difficult to recognize and understand.

PRODUCTION AREA
Ecological areas of Quechua, Suni and Puna, in Lares valley, province of Calca, department of Cusco

PRESIDIUM COORDINATOR
Moisés Quispe
tel. +511 4235756
arpec_cusco@hotmail.com

San Marcos Andean Fruit

The Cajamarca region, at the foot of the Andes, conserves a great variety of edible plants, many unfamiliar or entirely unknown, including numerous fruits of various colors and shapes. The variety is tied to the richness of the ecosystems, but also to the way pre-Columbian peoples viewed the world. The respect that the Inca culture has for the relationship between man and environment has helped preserve the extraordinary biodiversity of the Andes. Among the indigenous species, the presidium has selected three fruit trees, interesting both when eaten fresh and because of the way they are processed: the *tomatillo*, the *poro poro* and the *pushgay*. The tomatillo (*Physalis peruviana*) a round berry surrounded by a papyrus-like calyx, looks like a small Chinese lantern. Slightly acidic and refreshing, it is particularly suited to preparing sweet-sour relishes to accompany fish or meat, as well as for jams, ice cream, liqueurs and fermented drinks. The poro poro (*Passiflora pinnastipula*) is a perennial vine with showy flowers and whose light yellow oblong fruit can be added to salads. The pulp, which is filled with tiny seeds, has an intense and persistent aroma, and can be used to make thirst-quenching drinks, jams and sorbets. Finally, the pushgay (*Vaccinium floribundum*) is a small, wild shrub that grows in the highest and rockiest zone of Cajamarca. It produces fruit similar to European blueberries and, like them, can be used to make jams, liqueurs and sorbets but is also worthy of accompanying meat dishes. The presidium already has a regulatory framework in place for the cultivation of these species, which will be followed by the drafting of a production protocol for the by-products (juices, gelatins, jams). Soon a graphic project will be worked out together with the producers, making it possible to put the presidium fruit and their derivatives under a single label and packaging. In the medium term, the presidium will help the producers create an association and will send technicians to regulate the quality of the by-products and their packaging.

PRODUCTION AREA
San Marcos, department of Cajamarca

PRESIDIUM COORDINATORS
Rubén Figueroa Llanos
tel. +51 356224
figruben@mixmail.com
Florentino Napoléon Machiuca Vilchez
tel. + 51 76588169
mavinasm@hotmail.com

Traditional Chuño Blanco

The method of preparing *chuño* has very ancient origins and has been mentioned ever since the first Spanish chroniclers visited the Andes in the 16th century. The complex processing technique makes it possible to freeze-dry the potatoes by taking advantage of very sudden changes in temperature. The tubers are exposed to frost at night (at altitudes and in seasons when temperatures drop below 15° C), then to the light and heat of day and then put in icy river waters. This process dehydrates the potato over time, making it white and very lightweight like a pumice stone. The tuber can be conserved in this condition for as many as 10 years and only needs to be soaked in water before cooking. Preserving the potato for a long time is not the only advantage of this age-old method. It is also the only way to be able to eat the so-called bitter potatoes. These tubers have a very high glycol-alkaloid content that must be eliminated to make them edible, something only this treatment can do. Today the *chuño* (*moraya* in Quechuan dialect, *tunta* in Aymaran dialect) is mainly sold on the Bolivian market, where consumption is greatest, and is also made with sweet potatoes from outside the zone of origin, which yield a product of poorer quality. Despite their abundance, very few producers can carry out the long, repetitive and delicate operation needed to gauarntee a perfect product (the potatoes can easily rot and give off unpleasant flavors and odors). This is why the Presidium involves two different productive entities: a valley community that procures the bitter potatoes and a mountain community that processes them into *chuño*, facilitating the freezing by taking advantage of the cold river waters flowing near the village. By working together, the two groups are able to produce an excellent product that the farmers can sell in the large cities and promote locally among the tourists.

PRODUCTION AREA
Department of Puno, Sur

PRESIDIUM COORDINATOR
Alipio Canahua
tel. +51 51368946
alipiocanahua@yahoo.es

American Raw Milk Cheeses

The common denominator is the use of raw milk, either home-produced or from neighboring dairy farms. The first American cheeses were made according to Dutch or English recipes, and later by going back to Italian and German methods. In the last 200 years, cheesemakers in the United States have 'domesticated' famous European artisan cheeses (Parmigiano, Taleggio, Limburger) by inventing American equivalents (Dry Jack, Teleme, Brick...). In the 1970s a new school of cheesemakers started making unique cheeses that tell the history of the region. The cheeses can be compact or soft, with a crust that is washed or pressed, of enormous size (as much as 80 pounds) or very small (barely a quarter of a pound), wrapped in leaves, covered with ashes or rubbed with salt. Hand-crafted and of excellent quality, they generally come from small, family-run dairies. The cheese is produced daily and then sold to local markets and large restaurants. In many cases, the market forces the producers to offer as many as 10-12 types of cheese, sometimes by processing the milk from just 25 cows. Since it is illegal to sell cheeses made from unpasteurized milk unless they have been aged for at least two months, the cheesemakers run the risk of no longer being able to use raw milk. The lack of a regional identity and the fact that producers are scattered around various parts of the country and have problems communicating with one another encouraged Slow Food to launch a project with new objectives. Isolated geographically, and with very different experiences behind them, the 30 cheese makers in the presidium are united by the need to deal with a confusing health directive and the considerable problems of how to increase sales. In order to improve the quality of raw milk cheeses the presidium is working with a group of tasters, made up of cheesemakers and Slow Food experts, who select the best products each year. They are the ambassadors of the project, setting an example of quality for the producers and representing the presidium during various events.

PRODUCTION AREA

California, Connecticut, Indiana, New Jersey, North Carolina, Oregon, Vermont, Virginia, Wisconsin

PRESIDIUM COORDINATORS

Robert La Valva
tel. +1 7182608000
rlavalva@earthlink.net
Jeffrey Roberts
tel. +1 8022230248
cowcreek@attglobal.net

Anishinaabeg Manoomin

Water rice (*Zizania palustris*) is actually an aquatic herb and not rice in the literal sense (genus *Oryza*). Like rice, it grows in shallow water and in flooded fields, but is higher in protein and contains fewer carbohydrates. It is the main means of sustenance for the Native American Anishinaabeg (also known as Ojibwe), who consider it sacred and harvest it at the end of summer along the shores of the many lakes in their region, the White Earth Reservation. It is said that the natives who used to live in eastern Minnesota moved out of the area after a prophecy ordered them to settle 'where the good berry grows in the water'. And *manoomin* means precisely good berry. Couples – often husband and wife – harvest the rice by canoe. The 'mower' at the stem pushes the canoe through the expanse of rice, and the 'beater' at the stern strikes the plants so the grains fall into the bottom of the canoe. At the end of the day, two expert harvesters can manage to gather 250 kilos of rice. The fresh grains, green in color, are then hulled and left to dry over a wood fire. The *manoomin*, with its complex flavor having hints of smoke and brushwood, is carefully cooked so the grains do not break apart. Owing to the domestication of the cereal, more than 95% of production in the United States is from cultivated fields. But the Anishinaabeg still harvest authentic wild rice in the traditional way the presidium promotes at some of the lakes in northern Minnesota. This traditional product is threatened both by competition from cultivated varieties and the destruction of the natural ecosystems caused by the proliferation of recreational areas around the lake, the construction of levees and agricultural dis-

charges. The presidium works very closely with Native Harvest's White Earth Land Recovery Project to promote the consumption of traditionally harvested and processed wild rice.

PRODUCTION AREA
Lands of the Anishinaabeg tribe, Minnesota

PRESIDIUM COORDINATOR
Andrea Hanks
tel. +1 2183752600

PRESIDIUM SPONSORED BY
Consorzio Tutela Vini Oltrepò Pavese
(Broni, Pavia, Lombardy, Italy)

Cape May Oyster

Cape May is the tip of a narrow peninsula sheltering Delaware Bay to the east, where the fresh water from the Delaware River meets the sea and goes on to flow through the states of Pennsylvania, New Jersey and Delaware. The presidium was set up to protect a historic bay activity, oyster farming. The Cape May oysters, called *salt* because they are exposed to the salt waters of the Atlantic, are firmer and tastier than most of the New Jersey oysters farmed near the mouth of the Delaware, where the water is less saline. In colonial times the bay mollusks were gathered in casks and loaded on wagons for Philadelphia, where they supplied a flourishing trade. It was a big business in the city, and the roads were often layered with shells. The oysters were eaten raw, stewed, pickled or deep-fried in oil and served with chicken salad. The activity declined sharply during the Great Depression because of over-fishing, pollution, warmer waters and the onslaught of parasites. The oysters became smaller and their numbers diminished. According to some studies, the oyster farms in the upper bay area were ruined during the Second World War when motor boats replaced sail boats. But today the waters of Cape May are quite clean again thanks to environmental programs in the three states. As a result, oysters can be farmed in shallow waters by placing them in nets hung from racks and by feeding them naturally without artificial ingredients or antibiotics. The success of the new sustainable oyster farms is a sign of the renewed health of the bay, which Slow Food intends to give new vigor by supporting the activity of the few remaining fisherman and by boosting the local and international oyster market.

PRODUCTION AREA
Cape May, Delaware Bay, New Jersey

PRESIDIUM COORDINATORS
Hansjakob Werlen
tel. +1 6103288612
hwerlen1@swarthmore.edu
Jim Weaver
tel. +1 6094521515
jim@trepiani.com

Navajo-Churro Sheep

The Navajo-Churro sheep was introduced by Spanish explorers to the Rio Grande Valley, in New Mexico in the 16th century. It constitutes an important part of the history of the Hispanic communities of Pueblo and Diné (called Navajo in the native American language) in the southwest of the United States. For 400 years, this sheep, referred to as the *ganado menor churro*, a descendant of the ancient Iberian breed, the *churra*, has been reared by Hispanic shepherds in New Mexico and Arizona according to the traditional methods of transhumance and grazing. This is a hardy sheep, living lightly on the land and requires less water and food than other breeds. It has very long legs, thin bones and a fleece of varying natural colors. Its meat is lean, with a distinctive, sweet lamb flavor. Traditionally, it is eaten when it is 20-24 months old and this reduces its commercial value because consumers tend to think that it is less tender than lamb. Furthermore, the *Navajo-Churro* produces large quantities of milk and high-quality wool. Once there were 2 million of them, but, during the last 30 years, the breed has seriously declined for two main reasons: first, the breed declined because of a federally imposed interbreeding initiative, and, second, a program which had the aim of weakening the Navajo culture. As a result, by the 1970s, there were only 450 Navajo-Churro sheep left in the United States. Now, about 65 flocks in the Navajo Nation, the Navajo reserve which lies between Arizona and New Mexico, include animals of the breed registered with the Diné *be'iiná*, an association which works closely with the presidium, with the aim of selling 200 Navajo-Churro sheep a year to restaurants in the region.

The project also involves the registration of pure animals of the Navajo Nation. A website is currently being prepared which will include a list of breeders of Navajo-Churro lambs who want to sell part of their stock directly to consumers, restaurants, farmers' markets and the programs of Community Supported Agriculture.

PRODUCTION AREA
Navajo Nation Reserve, Arizona and New Mexico

PRESIDIUM COORDINATORS
Gary Nabhan
gary.nabhan@nau.edu
Gay Chanler
mchanler@cybertrails.com

Sonoma County Gravenstein Apple

The climate of Sonoma County, in California, is ideal for growing the Gravenstein apple which is 'venerated' by the inhabitants of Sebastopol, who name streets, festivals and schools after it and hold a parade every year to celebrate the flowering of the apple trees. The apple has a sweet and tart flavor and a greenish-yellow skin with red striations. It ripens at the end of July and can be processed into apple juice and desserts. Once, more than 7,000 acres of land in Sonoma County were planted with Gravenstein apple orchards, but now just under 1,000 are left. The cause of this serious decline in this Danish apple variety – introduced to the county in 1811 by Russian trappers – is that they are extremely delicate and perishable, with the result that consumers tend to favor Red Delicious. What's more, many orchards have been replaced by vineyards, which are more profitable. In the United States this County is a stronghold of the movement for sustainable agriculture, but it is hard for the local community to maintain agricultural biodiversity because of the high production costs and the fact that there are many middle-men. Despite the importance of the Gravenstein, only eight producers still grow them commercially. One of the farms of the Presidium, which has been operating since 1979, is run by the Kolling family, which grows and picks manually organically grown Gravensteins and 25 other indigenous varieties of apple. Like other apple farmers, they transform them into apple juice, cider and vinegar and sell them to a local bakery and restaurants in the vicinity. The presidium aims to find new markets for the people who grow this kind of apple. The project involves growers and consumers of apples who intend to promote sustainable agriculture. Together, they hope to raise the awareness of consumers about agricultural biodiversity and are working together to create a market on a national scale. Bodies collaborating with the Presidium, as well as Slow Food USA, include the University of California Cooperative Extension, the AG Innovations Network, the Community Alliance with Family Farmers and Santa Rosa Junior College.

PRODUCTION AREA
Sebastopol, Sonoma County, California

PRESIDIUM COORDINATOR
Paula Shatkin
pdshat@sonic.net

Barlovento Cacao

According to early explorers, the cacao bean was used as a form of currency in Venezuela, which shows just how important cacao was to the local economy. And the Spanish understood the commercial value of cacao, which quickly became the chief export product. Later on, however, the low yield per hectare and competition from new countries like Indonesia and Malaya pushed Venezuela to the bottom of the list of producers. Along with Ecuador, Panama and Colombia, it provides less than 5% of world production by now. But it continues to offer one of the best cacaos in the world, particularly the varieties cultivated in the northwestern part of the country (the *caracas* and *carenero superior*), which account for 30% of Venezuelan productionhe Presidium was started in collaboration with Cesvi, an NGO in the Barlovento region, which is the strip of coast east of Caracas and a very interesting area in terms of culture. Whole communities of people have transformed the region into a center of African folklore steeped in Catholicism, voodoo and devil worship. The presidium will purchase fermentation cases and driers and draw up a protocol for the cultivation and processing of the cacao. Contacts have already been established with European artisan companies, which will buy their supply of cacao directly from the producer and thus ensure better prices. The presidium will help research activities aimed at mapping out the different varieties of plants in the area that best typify the *carenero superior*, helping producers to replace the plants that are no longer productive.

PRODUCTION AREA
Barlovento and Acevedo, State of Miranda

PRESIDIUM COORDINATOR
Manuel Gomez
tel. +58 2126712509
cesvivenezuela@cesvi.org

Asia

Jalalabad Olive Oil producers

Jalalabad is located in the central-eastern province of Nangarhar, near the Pakistani border. There has been an oil mill in the area ever since 1931, when it was opened by the Ministry of Agriculture, and it was also used during the Soviet occupation. Because of the historical events in the country the oil mill later fell into disuse until 2002, when it became part of an Italian Development Cooperation project. The aim of the project is to restore and modernize the oil mill so that all of the 2200 hectares can be cultivated. The hope is to produce not only extra virgin olive oil but also products preserved in oil.

PRODUCTION AREA
District of Jalalabad, province di Nangarhar

COMMUNITY COORDINATORS
Gul Ghulam
tel. +93 799382598
ab_ghulamgul@yahoo.com
Abdul Ahad Abdul Ahmad
tel. +93 799344698
ahmad_loqmani@yahoo.com

Pistachio producers of Badghis

The community was founded and is supported by the Heart Conservation Corps association, which aims to preserve the 90,000 hectares of natural pistachio forests in the province of Badghis. This area is situated in north-western Afghanistan, at the border with Turkmenistan and the provinces of Faryab, Ghowr and Herat. It is here that the pistachio originated and where one can find evidence of its harvesting in texts from over five hundred years ago. The planting method has not changed and nor have the operations associated with the harvesting and drying the pistachios, which is only done by hand and at specific times of the year. There are more than 700 members of the community. They are mainly involved in harvesting the pistachios, maintaining the forests and selling the products, all activities that hold considerable weight in the regional economy.

PRODUCTION AREA
Province of Badghis

COMMUNITY COORDINATOR
Mohammed Naser
tel. +93 040225874
naserjami2003@yahoo.com

Raisin producers of Herat

The name of Herat, a city in northwestern Afghanistan, has always been associated with particular varieties of grape typical of a region in which wine growing has been favored by the temperate climate and by a series of techniques used to protect the plants from strong winds and excessive sun. Historically the grapes were produced for withering, which was done by putting the grape bunches on cane racks in shady, well-ventilated places. The withering techniques were codified five hundred years ago in an agrarian manual, the *Er-shadozaraa*, and since then very little has changed. The community numbers about 7,500 small-scale producers who grow a hundred or so varieties of *Vitis vinifera*. All of the varieties are seedless and have a very high sugar content, characteristics that make this production all but unique.

PRODUCTION AREA
Province of Herat

COMMUNITY COORDINATOR
Mohammed Naser Jami
tel. +93 040225874
naserjami2003@yahoo.com

Ararat Valley fruit growers

The climate in the zone favors the cultivation of a great variety of fruit, including cherries, apricots, peaches, figs, apples, pears and walnuts. Numerous ancient species, all excellent and highly-prized, have been domesticated in fertile Ararat Valley. The four women who started the community and their families take care of growing local varieties both for their own personal use and to sell on the local and national market. Given the availability of so much fruit has given rise to many methods for conserving the summer and autumn harvested fruit for the winter months: *muraba* (a fruit preserve) and *alani* (a holiday sweet), to mention the most traditional. Jams, dried and candied fruit, and syrups are also produced without the use of preservatives.

PRODUCTION AREA
Ararat

COMMUNITY COORDINATOR
Sargsyan Anzhela
tel. +374 10733322
grant_tapan@armencell.am

Ararat Valley seed and vegetable producers

The community works in Ararat Valley, the main farming region in the country. It aims to protect seeds and local species, to cultivate vegetables by traditional methods that call for the use of organic fertilizers, and to preserve the foods. For historical, geographic, climatic and ritual reason, preserving the fruit of the land in Armenia is a very common practice and a genuine tradition. The farmers involved in the project plan to expand the areas that can be cultivated and oppose the use of GMOs. The products, *in primis* tomatoes and different varieties of fresh or canned beans, are used locally and sold on the national market.

PRODUCTION AREA
Ararat

COMMUNITY COORDINATOR
Shahazizyan Rubik
tel. +374 10227460
grant_tapan@armencell.am

Breeders and fruit growers of Aragatsotn

The members of this community – a little more than ten families – are in the region of Armenia that takes its name from Aragat, the highest mountain in the country (4090 m). The area has been famous for fruit growing for thousands of years. Many domesticated fruit species are tied to the region, especially the apricot, but also cherries and most likely grapes. The community grows various vegetables (eggplants, potatoes, tomatoes...) and breeds cows, goats and pigs in addition to cultivating a number of local fruit varieties (peaches, apricots, apples, pears, cherries). The fruit is eaten fresh, but also dried, candied or in syrup.

PRODUCTION AREA
Aragatsotn

COMMUNITY COORDINATOR
Avetisyan Zhanna
tel. +374 91471231
grant_tapan@armencell.am

Honey producers of central Armenia

Beekeeping in Armenia is a very old activity, whose traditional methods have been handed down from one generation to the next. The community is made up of about twenty people – a few producers and their families – who raise the most common bee species, the yellow and the fulva. The sweet, floral scented honey, which is made without additives, is a dark yellow color with reddish traces. Widely used in the local traditional cuisine to make a particular white bread, a number of sweet specialties, and for cooking meats, it is sold both locally and nationally. Using only local ingredients, the community also produces beeswax, which is used as a medicinal remedy because of its recognized therapeutic properties.

PRODUCTION AREA
Aragatsotn, Kotayk', Ararat

COMMUNITY COORDINATOR
Galstyan Ashot
tel. +374 23296501
grant_tapan@armencell.am

Lake Sevan fishermen

The region of Lake Sevan, in eastern Armenia, is traditionally toed to fishing. In the most prolific years, the zone accounts for 90% of national fish production. Nevertheless, climate changes and the creation of a reservoir for hydroelectric energy are putting the most typical and preferred varieties of fish at risk. Fishing on the lake is prohibited by now because of the dramatic drop in the water level, and a reserve aims to protect the ecosystem and the more traditional and rarer species. To safeguard the secular and very profitable fishing business, a consortium of fishermen is trying to revive the local varieties of trout, white fish and *scardola* by raising and fishing them in small natural lakes fed by underground springs located just outside the reserve.

PRODUCTION AREA
Lake Sevan, Geghark'unik'

COMMUNITY COORDINATOR
Mikayelyan Mikayel
tel. +374 91218485
grant_tapan@armencell.am

Local wheat producers

In the semi-mountainous region of Ararat a community of growers is trying to revive the production of spring and winter wheat. They are varieties already known in ancient times, whose cultivation made it possible to produce flour even in the more difficult months. Today the community has started making the flours again. The work is doubly important because the rediscovery of these ancient cereal varieties, which Armenia has many of, also offers the possibility of studying the evolution that led to the present-day cultivars. Armenia is in the vanguard in cereal research. By way of illustration, it is worth mentioning the Erubini reserve, where a team of researchers has identified traces of seeds dating to 40-60,000 years ago.

PRODUCTION AREA
Ararat

COMMUNITY COORDINATOR
Martirosyan Gayane
tel. +374 93432026
grant_tapan@armencell.am

Southern Armenia winegrowers

Pages from the Old Testament and more recent discoveries of cellars and the remains of casks in archeological sites are evidence of the very ancient history of wine making in Armenian farming. Wine making is still very popular and widespread in the country today, to the point that at least forty different species of vine are cultivated. This community in southern Armenia, which involves about one hundred producers and a winery, is trying to preserve some of the traditional varieties, particularly the *areni* (red berry), the *mshaleni* and the *hargi* (white berry). The winery produces various types of more or less long-lived, dry and fortified wines.

PRODUCTION AREA
Vaiots' Dzor

COMMUNITY COORDINATOR
Sargsyan Lyova
tel. +374 93804420
grant_tapan@armencell.am

Indigenous sheep breeders

The indigenous sheep of the Karabakh are crucial for the people in the villages of southern Azerbaijan, near the Iranian border. The shepherds spend most of the year in the high mountain pastures. They make cheeses with the sheep's milk, while the fat concentrated around the tail is one of the main ingredients of *plov*, a local rice dish. And the meat of this sheep is tender, mellow and low in cholesterol. The cheese is preserved in sheepskins that are turned inside out, which means the natural rennet passes from the hide to the milk. The cheese is made for home consumption or sold in the neighboring villages. The breeders from the village of Sis are united in a cooperative of 20 people who breed and raise the sheep.

PRODUCTION AREA
Sis, district of Shemakha

COMMUNITY COORDINATOR
Karimov Shahmar Rakhman
tel. +99 417655008
azer.garayev@rec-caucasus.org

Ismailli beekeepers

There would appear to be a long tradition of beekeeping in the Caucasus regions. Even today it plays a fundamental role in supporting small communities of villages that are not sufficiently well-organized and have to rely on street traders to sell their product in city markets. In the province of Ismailli the beekeepers are united in a cooperative (27 members) that produces the honey. The product, which according to the local people also has curative properties, is made from field flowers, lime shrub and fruit trees. In addition to honey, the producers are also involved in other activities typical of the zone: making mulberry and plum vodka, preparing jams and gathering wild plants.

PRODUCTION AREA
District of Ismailli

COMMUNITY COORDINATOR
Azer Garayev
tel. +99 4124493741
azer.garayev@rec-caucasus.org

Mazoni (fermented milk) producers

Mazoni is the most common fermented drink in Azerbaijan, and the Caucasus regions in general. The flavor of the *mazoni* varies from region to region because of the bacterial flora that determines its acidity. In the central-eastern district of Ismailli it is made with the milk from the small local cows, famous for the high fat content in the milk. *Mazoni* is also the base for other products such as butter, a typical sweet ricotta and a salted ricotta flavored with mountain herbs (shor). One of the community's products is *pendir*, a white cheese similar to pecorino. The producers in the village of Eniel are united in a cooperative, aimed mostly at selling their preparations on the local market.

PRODUCTION AREA
Eniel, district of Ismailli

COMMUNITY COORDINATOR
Soltanov Ahmadagha
tel. +99 4503831263
azer.garayev@rec-caucasus.org

Sis village fruit growers

The village of Sis, in the district of Shemakha, is known for its fruit orchards. The fruit is used to prepare jams, fruit juices and distillates (fruit vodka), which are made for personal use, or sold locally and sometimes nationally. The village is part of a pilot project of the Regional Environmental Center for the Caucasus. The producers are united in a cooperative of 15 people, which prepares wild mulberry vodka, fruit juices and dried fruit. The zone is also famous for the production of silk and for the wild mulberries. The wild varieties of cornel, quince, strawberry and cherry are used to make traditional jams (*murabba*).

PRODUCTION AREA
Sis, district of Shemakha

COMMUNITY COORDINATOR
Garayev Alkhan
tel. +99 4506306744
azer.garayev@rec-caucasus.org

Barisal producers

The Barisal area is traversed by rivers and streams frequently subject to flooding that often causes the loss of agricultural land, the only source of sustenance for entire families. Added to this is are serious health problems and a lack of drinking water, meaning that most of the population lives below the poverty line. The Bikalpa Unnayan Karmashuchi, whose importance is a sustainable development approach, brings together numerous families of small-scale producers. The B.U.K. offers its members training and assistance, making them sensitive to the themes of sustainable rural development, alimentary sovereignty and farming that respects the environment. It also tries to facilitate market access for the local products, which are chiefly foods like rice, wheat and legumes.

PRODUCTION AREA
Barisal Division

COMMUNITY COORDINATOR
Alam Qazi Shamsul Alam
tel. +880 28126964
bikalpa@bdcom.com

Magura producers

This community, which refers to the Greenfoods association, is a group of more than 3,000 small-scale food producers, processors and consumers who live in remote rural zones in the southwest of the country, without electricity, paved roads and communication means. They have plots of land available that are smaller than 2 hectares and practice subsistence farming based on crops tied to the local diet like rice, legumes and vegetables. The challenge is to promote sustainable production that respects the environment, which can unite producers and consumers, and which can get local cooks and shopkeepers involved in selling the families' excess products.

PRODUCTION AREA
Distretto di Magura

COMMUNITY COORDINATOR
Biswas Subash Chandra
tel. +880 48863075
asd_bangladesh@yahoo.com

Paro Red Rice producers

Throughout Bhutan rice is cultivated wherever possible, but Paro red rice is considered to be of better quality because the very high altitudes (2200 meters) permit it to grow and accumulate for a longer period of time than usual. For centuries production was mainly for home consumption and the surplus rice was sold in neighboring Tibet. The rice is cultivated during the monsoon season, when the rains ensure the best habitat. All of the farming is done manually and after the harvest the rice can dry for as long as two months before being threshed and refined. Red rice is short grained and has no gluten, making it similar to brown rice even though the cooking time is shorter.

PRODUCTION AREA
District of Paro

COMMUNITY COORDINATOR
Tashi Wangchuk
tel. +975 8271464
tashiw@gmail.com - ctp@druknet.bt

Takeo organic rice producers

The Taso Organic Rice Producer Group has fifteen members, including four women; a community that grows local varieties of rice (*Oryza sativa*), without chemical fertilizers or pesticides, in southern Cambodia. The quality of the products is also guaranteed by the support of the non-governmental Community Economic Development Assistance Corporation (Cedac), involved in safeguarding local resources and developing organic farming. It also tries to combat domestic violence and encourage growers to cooperate with each other to improve the yields and profits. Chicken are raised ,and at the beginning and end of the rainy season various vegetables are also cultivated in the region, including Chinese cabbage, tomatoes and cucumbers.

PRODUCTION AREA
Province of Takeo

COMMUNITY COORDINATOR
Or Thy
tel. +855 23880916
cedacnetwork@online.com.kh

Organic beekeepers of the northeast

Ruikang is a cooperative made up of 200 beekeers who make organic honeys in Shandong, Jilin and Heilongjiang provinces. More than 30,000 colonies of domestic bees gather nectar and pollinate in nature reserves in eastern and northeastern China, far from pollution. Part of the nectar comes from the Changbai Mountains at the border with North Korea and Siberia, an uncontaminated area where there are more than 300 medicinal plant species suited for honey production. The organic certified production consists of acacia and lime shrub honey, royal jelly, propolis, beeswax and pollen that the cooperative exports to Europe and the United States. The pollen in particular is gathered from a large variety of herbs and flowers in China's largest forest, the Xing'anling, at the Siberian border.

PRODUCTION AREA
Heilongjiang, Jilin and Shandong provinces

COMMUNITY COORDINATOR
Chen Jing
tel. +86 2584580141
xiao@ofdc.org.cn

Abkhazia Tea producers

Abkhazia is formally an autonomous Republic of Georgia, but in reality it is independent and maintains control over much of its own territory. The Republic of Abkhazia is on the Black Sea, in Transcaucasia, a vast region of central-western Asia and one of the northernmost areas with tea cultivations. The community consists of artisans from the village of Duripsh, who harvest the tea, and four workers who process it. This product has the characteristics of both Chinese and Indian teas: the aroma of the first and the tartness of the second. The community produces three types: classic black, unfermented green, and *oolong* (a semi-fermented green tea). All of the work is done by hand and without the use of chemical additives. The tea is sold locally and in the nation's capital.

PRODUCTION AREA
Duripsh, Republic of Abkhazia

COMMUNITY COORDINATOR
Gamgija Astamur
tel. +7 9184043443
nmon@teanadin.ru

Aromatic Herb growers

The Gardabani district, where the community operates, has Tbilisi, the capital of the country, as its district capital as well. It is located in southern Georgia, at the Armenian and Azerbaijan border. The members of the community produce aromatic herbs, including mint, coriander and thyme. The plants are carefully harvested, dried in the shade (hot sun could damage them) and are then blended in various proportions to obtain seasonings that add fragrance to Georgian cooking. *Adgika* is a typical blend of dried sweet pepper, black pepper, garlic, anise and coriander. The community's products are for personal consumption and sold locally.

PRODUCTION AREA
Kvemo Kartli, district of Gardabani

COMMUNITY COORDINATOR
Liana Darashvili
tel. +995 22663433
mszgc@access.sanet.ge

Cheese producers of the Tush ethnic group

The Kakheti region, which occupies the easternmost part of Georgia, at the Russian border, is known for its wine making and livestock breeding. The Georgian cow's milk or sheep's milk cheeses are: *imeretian*, *suluguni* (layered, or thin, flat and round, or even smoked) and *chechili* (braided cheese). Other dairy products worth mentioning are butter and melted butter. The ethnic group in this small area of Georgia is the Tush. The breeders are united in an association whose aim is to safeguard traditional method of making *guda* cheese and promote it on the market, to valorize the meat and wool of sheep, and to form long-lasting ties between producers and consumers.

PRODUCTION AREA
District of Akhmeta, region of Kakheti

COMMUNITY COORDINATOR
David Tchitava
tel. +995 32253319
dtchitava@yahoo.co.uk

Imereti beekeepers

The vast region of Imereti, in central Georgia, is a mixture of flat lands and forest covered mountains. The beekeeper association, founded in 1999, now has 250 members and sells honey made by Caucasus bees both locally and in the capital, Tbilisi. The association also provides consultancy, organizes courses and seminars (with foreign experts as well) and publishes a newsletter. The community includes a dozen people from the village of Didi Dzhikhaishi. The members, who own 30 hives on average, produce honey, pollens and wax. Acacia and chestnut honeys are the most common types, but honey made with officinal herbs or lime tree are not unusual.

PRODUCTION AREA
Region of Imereti

COMMUNITY COORDINATOR
David Sanadze
tel. +995 23179566
mszgc@access.sanet.ge

Imereti wine growers

The development of wine growing in the Georgian territory started in the copper age, between 4 B.C. and 5 B.C., and there are more than 500 varieties of vine. The ones traditionally cultivated in the Imereti region, in central Georgia, are tsolikauri and tsitska. The community includes many families from the district of Tersola. The wine is made according to an ancient Georgian technique. The grapes are crushed by foot in a large receptacle (*saznekheli*) and then the must is put into large, cone-shaped terracotta amphorae (*kvevri*), and buried in the cellar so that only the opening of the amphoraremains above the floor. The earth keeps the temperature a constant 14°C during the fermentation and conservation. Produced this way, the wine is oxidized and can age for a long time, improving its characteristics.

PRODUCTION AREA
Imereti region

COMMUNITY COORDINATOR
Nikoladze Ramaz
tel. +995 93944841

Kakheti wine growers

Wine growing in Georgia dates to the Neolithic Age and the region where it is practiced the most is the Kakheti, in the eastern part of the country. At Kardanakhi, a famous wine growing village, the 30 growers of the community produce about 120 hectoliters of wine each year, especially dry and semi-dry wines. The wide range of indigenous vines includes more than 500 varieties. One of the best is the *rkatsiteli* grape. Mixed with *mtsvane* and other varieties, it yields the *Tsinandali*, *Vazisubani*, and *Gurjaani* wines. It is also the main ingredient for distilling brandy. *Saperavi* is one of the oldest varieties of grape grown in Georgia. The best Georgian dry, semi-dry and semi-sweet red wines are obtained from this grape, as are dessert wines like *Muzukani* and *Kindzmarauli*

PRODUCTION AREA
Kardanakhi, region of Kakheti

COMMUNITY COORDINATOR
Kacharava Elguja
tel. +995 25322759
ipruidze@ird.ge

Kartli fruit growers

In central-eastern Georgia, the best farming region is the Kartli, filled with plateus and hills, where the climate and the lay of the land are well-suited to growing fruit trees and grape vines. The community is composed of families from the Khashuri and Kaspi districts. Some of the producers have been trying to organize a kind of structured cooperative, but without success so far. Apples are the most important fruit crop, most of which the *kadil sinap* variety, probably of Turkish origin. They are red apples having a rather long oval shape, with which the members of the community also produce apple juice. Quinces (*koshmi*) are also grown and used for making excellent preserves. Selling is organized at the local level, but the products are marketed abroad.

PRODUCTION AREA
Districts of Khashuri and Kaspi, region of Kartli

COMMUNITY COORDINATOR
Loladze Vazha
tel. +995 93412359
mszgc@access.sanet.ge

Khoni Honey producers

The community counts five families who each own about thirty hives and produce five-seven tons of honey overall each year. The bees are of the *Mellifera caucasica* species, native to the deep valleys of Mingrelia and the mountains in northwest Georgia. The beekeepers not only produce honey, which they sell directly in the capital, Tbilisi, but have tried to diversify the activity by raising queen bees. The honeys vary according to the altitude, with acacia and chestnut being the most common. Imereti is the main farming region in the country and includes both mountainous zones and flat lands, where the weather is hot and humid in the summer and mild in the winter. The patrimony of forests – beech, oak, chestnut – is among the richest in Georgia.

PRODUCTION AREA
Khoni, region of Imereti

COMMUNITY COORDINATOR
Gogoberidze Teimuraz
tel. +995 32292136
gogober@geo.net.ge

Racha Ham producers

Pig breeding is one of the main activities around Racha, a mountainous region at the Russian border covered with thick oak woods, where the pigs providing the famous hams graze. The village of Chiora has 178 families, almost all involved in the laborious production. Salted and smokes for 40 days with pine and oak bark, the meat has an intense flavor and aroma and keeps a long time. The village is also known for its cultivation of a bean, the *zulispira*, which belongs to the *Vigna* genus and thus precedes the arrival of beans from America. Resistant to the extreme temperatures, unlike other legumes it can be cultivated at high altitudes. The seeds in the pods are dried and made into flour for bread.

PRODUCTION AREA
Chiora, district of Ambrolauri

COMMUNITY COORDINATOR
Rekhviashvili Bakur
tel. +995 99799360
georgianslowfood@yahoo.com

Samtskhe-Javakheti Wheat producers

The wheat growing culture in Georgia is very old and very important. The country still preserves three of the four wild wheat varieties existing in the world. The community of producers is made up of a dozen farmers in the Samtskhe-Javakheti, who formed an association in 2004. The Samtskhe-Javakheti region is in the southern part of the country, near the Armenian and Turkish border; a plateau where the climate is sever and separated from the rest of Georgia by the southern Caucasus Mountains. The wheat varieties that are grown are *ziteli doli*, a winter wheat, and *dika*. A tasty, top-quality bread is made from these grains and sold through a network of shops and farmers' markets.

PRODUCTION AREA
Village of Tsnisi, region of Samtskhe-Javakheti

COMMUNITY COORDINATOR
Peradze Bidzina
tel. +995 32954589
crop@elkana.org.ge

Tbilisi organic producers

Founded in Tbilisi in 1993, Elkana is an association of farmers that practice and promote organic farming. Since 1998, the association has also had a small mobile unit (Dika) to protect agroalimentary biodiversity. They have recovered hundreds of varieties of indigenous species that risked extinction: wheat, barley, *panico*, beans, chickpeas and lentils. Cereals and legumes are grown on small plots of land, and a member of Elkana usually has no more than five hectares of owned or rented fields.

The association is betting on the commercial opportunities of biocompatible production and organizes two fairs at Tbilisi each year, where farmers present and sell the fruits of their labor.

PRODUCTION AREA
Tbilisi

COMMUNITY COORDINATOR
Dundua Tamaz
tel. +995 32527157
manager@elkana.org.ge

Wild Fruit and Herb gatherers

The community comes from the Imereti region and numbers 29 families involved in gathering wild herbs and woodland berries, as well as producing infusions. They pick the new leaves of wild berries on Unagira Mountain and at the foot of Mount Brolisqedi and leave them to exsiccate in the driest and darkest corner of the house. After five or six hours they hand-press the leaves and allow them to dry for another four or five weeks. The very tannic black raspberry infusion is made in this way. Almost 80% of production is sold to the city markets and the rest is for family consumption.

PRODUCTION AREA
Region of Imereti

COMMUNITY COORDINATOR
Kravishvili Nestan
georgianslowfood@yahoo.com

Amaranth growers of Agastyamuni

This community of 1150 people is devoted to growing and processing amaranth seeds (the women in particular involved in the latter). When toasted and ground, the light colored, tiny lens-shaped seeds of this hardy annual are used for preparing a variety of breads, including the traditional unleavened chapati, as well as sweets and focaccias. Briefly heated in a pan, the seeds burst open like popcorn, becoming one of the ingredients of muesli, together with peanuts, raisins, lotus seeds and honey. Like buckwheat, *Amaranthus sp.* belongs to the group of gluten-free, but high protein pseudocereals. The plant, which reaches two meters in height, is grown throughout the hilly regions in the State of Uttaranchal.

PRODUCTION AREA
Agastyamuni, State of Uttaranchal

COMMUNITY COORDINATOR
Chandra Shekhar Bhatt
tel. +91 9412934477
navslow@yahoo.co.in

Banda Wheat growers

About a hundred members of an association make up this small community of farmers, which use traditional methods to grow and processes the local variety of wheat known as *katiya* (*Triticum spp.*). It is the only type of wheat that can grow in this region because of the lack of water for irrigation. The small, dark, easy to digest lightweight grains are much higher in protein, minerals and carbohydrates than hybrid varieties. They are processed into flour, bran and used for making biscuits. The cereal is also eaten as *daliya*: after being washed and toasted, the grains are coarsely chopped by hand with millstones, which are commonplace in the homes in the region.

PRODUCTION AREA
Banda, region of Bundelkhand, State of Uttar Pradesh

COMMUNITY COORDINATOR
Krishan Bir Chaudhary
tel. +91 1124359509
navslow@yahoo.co.in

Bamboo producers of Sikkim

The 600 members of the community are involved in growing and processing bamboo in the mountainous region of northeastern Sikkim. The bamboo shoots are harvested in the summer, when they are edible, and after being boiled with curcuma to eliminate the bitter taste are cut into pieces to make *tama*, a typical food sold in the local markets from June to September. *Mesu*, on the other hand, has a characteristic sour taste and is made from shoots that have undergone anaerobic fermentation for one or two weeks. It can be seasoned with mustard oil and spices and served with rice. Depending on the variety, the bamboo plant is also used by the local communities to firm up the terrain and escarpments, as fencing, and for making baskets and mats.

PRODUCTION AREA
Gangtok, State of Sikkim

COMMUNITY COORDINATOR
Jagannath Dhakal
tel. +91 3592231519
jdhakjal69@yahoo.co.in

Barley growers of Ladakh

In the land of high mountain passes, amidst the peaks of the western Himalayas and the vast Tibetan plain, there are more than 100,000 people involved in this community. The cultivation of barley, a staple of the Ladakhi diet, is particularly suited to the high elevations (up to 4000 m) and semi-desert terrain. *Tsampa*, the flour made by toasting and grinding the barley in water mills, is used for preparing soups, pasta and bread. Beer, *chang*, is made with the fermented grains. The members of the community also produce butter, cheese and goat's meat. These same products for personal consumption and local sale have been in the region for over a thousand years.

PRODUCTION AREA
Leh, State of Ladakh

COMMUNITY COORDINATOR
Tsering Dolma
tel. +91 1982252749
kagabanurbo@yahoo.com

Bundelkhand producers of seeds for oil

More than 500 farmers are involved in cultivating flax and sesame plants for producing oil. The small, flat sesame (*Sesamum indicum*) seeds are used in many dishes, on top of bread and in fritters, and the oil rich in sesamine, an antioxidant, is extracted from them. Delicate sweets made with sesame oil, the symbol of love and tenderness, are exchanged on 14 January during *Makar Sankranti*, the national holiday celebrating the moment when the sun starts its journey in the northern hemisphere. An oil containing linolenic acid, which is very healthy for the body's circulatory and immune systems, is extracted from the seeds of the flax plant (*Linum usitatissimum*).

PRODUCTION AREA
Banda, region of Bundelkhand, State of Uttar Pradesh

COMMUNITY COORDINATOR
Mahendra Tewari
tel. +91 9415949183
navslow@yahoo.co.in

Chitrakoot breeders

The more than 400 people in the association are involved in raising indigenous breeds of cows, important for work in the fields and milk production. The *Gir* cow, native to Gujarat (a State on the western coast), has long hanging ears, horns that curve back and then twist at the tip, and a white and red dappled coat. The cow produces an average of 1590 kilos of milk per lactation period. The *sahiwal*, considered the best milk cow in India and Pakistan and producing 2270 kilos of milk, is known for its resistance to hot weather and parasites. And the milk from these animals has fewer fatty acids than milk from crossbreeds.

PRODUCTION AREA
Chitrakoot, State of Uttar Pradesh

COMMUNITY COORDINATOR
Chhote Singh
tel. +91 7670265623
navslow@yahoo.co.in

Coconut and Spice producers

The members of the community – about 250 – grow coconut palms and spices such as black pepper and nutmeg. Many of the culinary specialties of Kerala would not be complete without these products. Ever since ancient times the State has excelled in the production of coconuts, sold as is or processed into a variety of products: oil, cream, milk, jams, and fermented and unfermented drinks. Thanks to the sun and the climate in the zone, the pepper plant, a climber, produces black meaty grains, which are harvested when ripe and then dried. Highly aromatic, they are used in cooking and in aromatherapy. The evergreen *Myristica fragrans* plant produces the meaty, yellowish nutmeg berries, used in cooking as a spice and as the main ingredient in ayurvedic medicine.

PRODUCTION AREA
Alleppey and Kanjirappally, State of Kerala

COMMUNITY COORDINATOR
Sudha Soni
tel. +91 47722677735
sonisudha@yahoo.com

Cumin and Fennel seed growers of Rajasthan Beawar

More than 500 growers in this community are involved in organically growing these two spices. Cumin (*Cuminum cyminum*), one of the most typical spices in India, is a small grassy plant whose fruit is used for seasoning meats, onions, legumes and especially lentils. The small, dry, dark, oval-shaped grains have an intense flavor and a warm penetrating aroma. The little cylindrical, yellow-greed fennel seeds smell like anise, but a little less sweet and are used to make breads, pastry, liqueurs and for seasoning soups and pan roasted or grilled meat, especially pork. They also stimulate digestion and tone up the intestines.

PRODUCTION AREA
Beawar, State of Rajasthan

COMMUNITY COORDINATOR
Rashmi Sharma
tel. +91 1462256792
navslow@yahoo.co.in

Himachal Pradesh growers of local Walnut varieties

In this remote northern region, a few varieties of walnut trees have adapted to the very high altitudes (5000-6000 m). The community consists of about 150 people, mainly women, involved in growing and selling the walnuts. After harvesting, the fruit of the walnut tree (*Juglans regia*) is covered with leaves from the plant and then sprayed with water for a week. The hull is then separated from the kernels by hand. They are eaten whole or made into flour and used to add fragrance to sweets and spicy dishes. The fruit of the almond tree (*Prunus amygdalus*), both the sweet and bitter varieties, is used for preparing bread and sweets. Since they cannot grow cereals at such high altitudes, the walnuts are the basis of this rural community's economy.

PRODUCTION AREA
Pangi, district of Kinnaur, State of Himachal Pradesh

COMMUNITY COORDINATOR
Vidya Devi
tel. +91 1786228922
navslow@yahoo.co.in

Karnataka Coffee growers

The community is represented by a cooperative of 200 coffee growers, and many of the plantations have belonged to the same family for generations. Two varieties of coffee are grown: *Coffea arabica* and *Coffea canephora*, more commonly known as *robusta*. The plant of *arabica* grows slowly at high elevations and its beans are highly prized. Coffee from the more robust, disease-resistant *canephora* variety has a bitterer taste and more caffeine. The plant takes five to six years to flower and produce cherries, which are harvested by hand. The economy of the zone depends on coffee and practically all the inhabitants work as farm laborers paid by the day. They say that the seven coffee beans a Muslim Indian brought home when returning from Mecca gave rise to coffee cultivation in Southern India.

PRODUCTION AREA
Virajpeth and Ammathi, region of Coorg, State of Karnataka

COMMUNITY COORDINATOR
Diya Sharma
tel. +91 9820308366
diyasharma@yahoo.com

Karnataka Spice producers

The more than 700 members of the community grow spices like black pepper, cardamom and vanilla. *Piper nigrum*, native to the Keral region in southern India, has prevailed in the cuisine for centuries. The local variety of perennial cardamom (*Elettaria cardamomum*) produces green pods that contain small dark seeds. Thanks to the warm climate, the soil and the regular rainfall, Indian cardamom is very aromatic. As seeds or a powder, it is used in many desserts and meat dishes, and cardamom oil is also used in ayurvedic medicine. Along with black pepper it is one of the spices in curry powder. *Vanilla planifolia*, a plant of the Orchidacee family, produces a black pod about twenty centimeters long that is used to add aroma to sweets.

PRODUCTION AREA
Sunticoppa, region of Coorg, State of Karnataka

COMMUNITY COORDINATOR
Reetha Balsavar
tel. +91 9820058042
rbalsavar@gmail.com

Kashmir Saffron producers

A spice, a natural colorant and a plant with medicinal properties, saffron has been grown in this region for centuries. The oldest book of Indian history mentions it as long ago as the times of Alexander the Great's invasion in 326 B.C. The most important religious ceremonies call for the use of saffron. The Muslims of Kashmir serve tea with saffron during weddings and holidays, and the Hindu kings of the past used to decorate their foreheads with it when they were crowned. More than 500 members of the community are involved in the difficult cultivation of this plant, which need a particular terrain and climate and constant care. The precious red stamens are found inside the violet flower of *Crocus sativus*, which is picked by hand in the autumn. 50,000 stamens are needed to produce 100 grams of saffron, which is why the product is so costly.

PRODUCTION AREA
Srinagar, State of Jammu and Kashmir

COMMUNITY COORDINATOR
Gulam Hassan Dar
tel. +91 1352749931
navslow@yahoo.co.in

Kotagiri Honey producers

In the northwestern part of the State of Tamil Nadu, amidst the dense vegetation of the Nilgiris hills (a Biosphere Reserve), the indigenous community of Irulas and Kurumbas gather the honey produced by a wild variety of bee (*Apis dorsata*). In the past these groups lived in the forest, feeding on its products, and honey was an important commodity to trade with the other communities in the area. Today, having settled at the edges of the forest, the Irulas and Kurumbas continue to practice this traditional activity. To reach the honeycombs built by the bees on trees and high rocks, they make cords and ladders out of plants. Gathered from April to July before the monsoon season, the honey is sold directly and indirectly at the local level. During this phase the community is given assistance so that the product is purchased at a fair price.

PRODUCTION AREA
Kotagiri, State of Tamil Nadu

COMMUNITY COORDINATOR
Sadhasivan Sarasasmeeta
tel. +91 4266275297
mathew@keystone-foundation.org

Legume growers of Uttar Pradesh

Two local varieties of legumes are organically grown in this area of the country by over two hundred people: the tropical pea (*Cajanus cajan*), called *arhar* or *tur*, and the lentil (*Lens esculenta*) called *masoor*. The first, the seeds and pods of which are both edible, has been known for over 3000 years. Smaller than hybrids from the United States, it is eaten both fresh and dried and used to make flour and as forage and fertilizer. The lentils, an excellent source of vegetable fiber, are the basic ingredient for one of the most widespread dishes in the country, the *dhal*, a spiced soup eaten as a side dish or with *chapati* and rice. Both of these native varieties of legume need less water than the hybrids, and can also grow in semi-desert zones.

PRODUCTION AREA
Eastern sector of the State of Uttar Pradesh

COMMUNITY COORDINATOR
Udai Pratap Singh
tel. +91 9415661807
navslow@yahoo.co.in

Mango growers of the pre-Himalayan areas

The mango (*Mangifera indica*), which has always been closely tied to Indian culture, is an evergreen tree that produces rounded, oval or kidney-shaped fruit, according to the variety. The most popular ones in India are the *alphonso*, *jeengira*, *dussehri*, *totapuri*, and *neelam*. The color varies from green to red to yellow according to how much it has ripened, and the soft and compact yellow-orange pulp is tangy sweet and intensely aromatic. The mango is very perishable and must be kept at cool temperatures to be able to reach the more distant markets. It is eaten fresh or can be made into juices and preserves and become an ingredient in sweets, sorbets and ice cream. In India the mango is the symbol of love and giving someone a basket of this fruit is considered a gesture of friendship.

PRODUCTION AREA
Dehra Dun, State of Uttaranchal

COMMUNITY COORDINATOR
Kumar Anand
tel. +91 9897196778
navslow@yahoo.co.in

Medicinal herb and vegetable growers

The more than 2000 members of the community come from various rural villages and live off of the sale of their organically grown products. The root of the *Saussurea lappa*, commonly known as costus, is a perennial herb that grows between 2600 and 3000 meters that is used to produce an oil having diuretic and antiseptic properties. The root of *Rauvolfia serpentine* is used as a snake bite antidote and to combat rheumatism, epilepsy and hypertension. The gel from the meaty, succulent *Aloe vera*, an evergreen perennial, has been used for centuries to cure burns, herpes and psoriasis. In addition to growing medicinal herbs, the community also raises indigenous vegetables and legumes, whose seeds are protected and saved.

PRODUCTION AREA
Yamuna Ghati, State of Uttaranchal

COMMUNITY COORDINATOR
R.S. Rawat
tel. +91 01360258123
navslow@yahoo.co.in

Millet and Buckwheat growers of Kotdwara

The community is a group of 5000 people who live in various Himalayan regions of Garhwal. Millet (*Echinochloa frumentacea*) cultivations became popular in this area due to the steep slopes of the hills, which are subject to landslides making it impossible to grow rice. The barnyard variety of millet grows so quickly that it can be harvested four months after seeding and adapts to different kinds of soil. In recipes, it can be used as a rice substitute. Buckwheat (*Fagopyrum esculentum*) is a vitamin and mineral rich food, and the black cuticle of the grain contains lysine, an essential amino acid. Buckwheat flour is used for preparing *chilare* (a kind of bread), vegetable fritters and sweets.

PRODUCTION AREA
Kotdwara, State of Uttaranchal

COMMUNITY COORDINATOR
Darban Singh Negi
tel. +91 09411368312
navslow@yahoo.co.in

Mumbai ready-to-eat food distributors

Every day about 2,000 men, the *dabbawalla*, distribute over 100,000 ready-to-eat meals in Mumbai (formerly Bombay). Picked up from the customer's home in the morning, they are delivered directly to the office before lunchtime. Transport is made possible by the use of the *dabba*, a vertical tin lunchbox that holds four or five aluminum receptacles that keep the various lunch courses hot. A series of simple symbols on each container mark its destination. The organization of delivering the food, though very complicated, is in fact managed by illiterate people who used to be farmers from the village of Pune. In order to cross the city quickly, in a relay system in which each *dabba* changes hands at least four times, the *dabbawalla* load the trays of 40 containers on bicycles, carriages and hand carts.

PRODUCTION AREA
Mumbai (Bombay), State of Maharashtra

COMMUNITY COORDINATOR
Raghunath Medge
tel. +91 9869152163
rdmedgedabbawalla@yahoo.co.in

Orissa rice and vegetable producers

Despite the rapid mechanization of the farming sector, this State on the eastern coast has an economy based on small-scale farming. The members of the community come from over 300 villages in the zone and are organized in an association that grows organic cereals and vegetables. The local varieties of rice (*Oryza sativa indica*) are processed in different ways by successive processes of soaking, steaming, sun drying and husking. In the region, rice is eaten at every meal and is the main ingredient in many specialties prepared for the numerous annual festivals tied to the work in the fields. The community also grows legumes like chickpeas and peas, and oilseeds from peanut and mustard plants.

PRODUCTION AREA
Balasore, State of Orissa

COMMUNITY COORDINATOR
Kusum Misra
tel. +91 6782264867
kusummisrapanigrahi@yahoo.co.in

Rajma growers of Uttaranchal

In the Himalayan region of Garhwal, on the plateaus around the village of Chakrata (2100 m), the community of 2000 small-scale farmers, many of whom women, grow about 50 varieties of *rajma*, or bean (*Phaseolus vulgaris*), which differ in color, shape and size. For centuries the region has been known for the cultivation of this annual plant, whose protein-rich legumes ripen quickly and can be harvested after 4-6 weeks from seeding. The highly prized *chakrata* variety in particular grows only in this area. The beans are used to prepare *rajma masala*, a traditional, highly spiced dish with a creamy consistency that is served hot with bread, *roti*, *chapati* or steamed rice.

PRODUCTION AREA
Chakrata, region of Garhwal, State of Uttaranchal

COMMUNITY COORDINATOR
Virendra Pawar
tel. +91 9412154906
navslow@yahoo.co.in

Sugar cane growers and processors

Sugar cane is found everywhere in this part of Uttar Pradesh. The *Saccharum officinarum* is an indigenous plant of Southeast Asia similar to bamboo cane. The members of the community cultivate it and extract its juice, which is a cloudy dark brown color, rich in sucrose, vitamins and mineral salts. It is boiled slowly to evaporate the water and eliminate any impurities, without the use of chemical agents. When the juice boils, it is scooped up with a large ladle and poured on a circular area of stone having a diameter of two meters and then worked with a wooden spatula. To obtain *shakkar*, a light brown powder, baking soda is added to bleach the juice and prevent it from thickening too much. Or it is left to coagulate further to make *gur*, shaped little breads that look like toffee.

PRODUCTION AREA
Merrut, Barote, Baghpat, State of Uttar Pradesh

COMMUNITY COORDINATOR
Rakesh Singh
tel. +91 1234251894
singh_rakesh@rediffmail.com

Turmeric producers of Erode

The approximately 700 members of the community are involved in growing organic turmeric and processing the tuber. A perennial herb, *Curcuma longa* has a long underground rhizome, 20 centimeters in diameter, consisting of the characteristically yellow tuber and numerous roots. Once harvested, the tuber is boiled for over an hour, dried in the sun for 6-8 days and then pulverized. The spice, which has been produced in southeastern India for centuries, is very commonly used in cooking since it is one of the main ingredients of curry powder. It has a spicy, bitter taste. It is also used in ayurvedic medicine because of its preventive and therapeutic properties, especially as a cicatrizing and anti-inflammatory agent. The community also produces three local varieties of organically grown rice.

PRODUCTION AREA
Erode, State of Tamil Nadu

COMMUNITY COORDINATOR
Ramasamy Selvam
tel. +91 46363502
thulir@rediffmail.com
organic_network@riseup.net

Varanasi producers of dairy products and sweets

For centuries, half of the milk produced in the country has been used for preparing a variety of foods, especially sweets and certain regional specialties. Thanks to techniques for curding (hot and cold), drying and fermenting, which have been handed down for generations, milk is made into by-products that keep can be kept after several days. *Khoa*, obtained from the rapid evaporation of the liquid, is the most common one and is used as an ingredient in *mithais*, various traditional solid sweets. In the Varanasi region, about 20,000 members of the community are involved in the artisan production of dairy products and traditional sweets based on cow's milk, buffalo's milk and goat's milk, to which sugar, dried fruit, herbs and spices are added.

PRODUCTION AREA
Varanasi, State of Uttar Pradesh

COMMUNITY COORDINATOR
Rajendra Kumar Pandey
tel. +91 5422570923
birambsdc@yahoo.com

Wild Fruit gatherers of Chitrakoot

In the dense forest surrounding Chitrakoot, at the border between Madhya Pradesh and Uttar Pradesh, there are a variety of wild plants like *amla* or *aonla* (*Emblica officinalis*), *mahua* (*Madhuka indica*) and other medicinal herbs. *Amla* has been used in ayurvedic medicine for thousands of years as an anti-inflammatory and anti-pyretic agent. Its round fruit, rich in vitamin C, is made into jams, gelatins and candies and is also an ingredient in cake; the tart juice is added as a seasoning to foods during cooking. *Mahua* flowers are used to treat diabetes. The community of 400 people includes those who gather the wild herbs and fruit and those who organically grow the plants on their own land in the villages and then process the products.

PRODUCTION AREA
Satna, State of Madhya Pradesh

COMMUNITY COORDINATOR
Nandita Pathak
tel. +91 7670265477
udyamita@chitrakoot.org – drichitrakoot@chitrakoot.org

Aceh Coffee producers

At the northern tip of Sumatra Island, in the hills of the autonomous Aceh territory, coffee production is being revived after more than three decades of guerilla warfare between separatists and the military that caused many of the farmers to abandon the fields. Today coffee plants are cultivated on nearly 50,000 hectares of terrain in the area by 60,000 families, who grow and sell the harvest to a network of middlemen that takes the product to the national market to be sold. Aceh coffee, husked in water and quick dried, has low acidity, and the rich volcanic soil gives it a strong character, with hints of fruit. The community, which is a cooperative, involves about 3,000 producers and aims to reach 10,000 members. It is striving to obtain the Fair Trade certification so it can ensure the producers fair remuneration.

PRODUCTION AREA
Nanggroe Aceh Darussalam, Sumatra

COMMUNITY COORDINATOR
Bachtiar Usman
bachtiarusman98@yahoo.com

Martabak producers of Java

Martabak is a typical Indian dish of Muslim origin that is very common in Malaysia and Singapore. This sort of Indonesian pizza is still made in the traditional way in the Banten region of Java Island: a thin dough filled with meat (usually mutton), seasoned with garlic and onion and fried or baked until brown and served with cucumbers, raw onions and a curry sauce. *Martabaks* can also be sweet, or stuffed with cheese, chocolate or peanuts. The community involves 20 people in the Pandeglang area, who produce about 30 *martabak* a day for their own personal use or to be sold locally.

PRODUCTION AREA
Kelurahan, Pandeglang, Banten, Jawa

COMMUNITY COORDINATOR
Riza V. Tjahjadi
tel. +62 218296545
biotani@rad.net.id - biotani2004a@yahoo.com

Rice and Sweet Potato growers of Bali

Having developed by following the Tri Hita Karana Balinese philosophy, *subak* is a traditional way of managing irrigated areas so that the local cultivation methods are kept alive. The Wangaya Betan community includes 103 family farms where local white and red varieties of rice and sweet potatoes are grown using traditional methods. The land is worked with the help of oxen and is seeded and harvested by hand. The only fertilizers the farmers use is the dung of the farm-raised animals. The livestock employed for the field work and the fertilizing is the *sapi bali*, or banteng oxen (*Bos sondaicus*) from the Malay archipelago. They have a characteristic black coat, white legs, and very small horns that bend backwards.

PRODUCTION AREA
Tabanan, Bali

COMMUNITY COORDINATOR
Kharisma Karyadijaya
tel. +62 361753269
adi_kh@hotmail.com

Shrimp raisers of Java Island

For the inhabitants of Sidoarjo, a town in the east of Java Island, shrimp raising is one of the main resources, along with mackerel, sardine, tuna and carp fishing. The more than two hundred water farmers of the community use non-intensive production methods: the larva of *udang windu* (the local name of shrimp) are deposited in the ponds and only fed plankton, without the help of chemical foods. When mature, the little crustaceans are collected with the traditional bamboo traps and sent to the processor who weighs, selects and cleans the product before freezing it. Thanks to their excellent flavor, the Sidoarjo shrimp are known, appreciated and thus sold even outside of the local market.

PRODUCTION AREA
Sidoarjo, Jawa Timur, Java

COMMUNITY COORDINATOR
Ida Bagus Gde Mahendra Sutha
tel. +62 315942711
altertradeindonesia@yahoo.com

Tempeh producers of Yogyakarta

In the central part of Java Island, near the city of Yogyakarta, *tempeh* is still being made in the traditional way. This dish based on fermented soy is also eaten in Sumatra, Singapore and New Caledonia, as well as in Holland where it was introduced by Indonesian immigrants in 1940. In the traditional recipe the soy seeds are softened, mashed finely and then cooked. Then an acidifying liquid and a mold (mushroom) are added and the mixture is spread out and left to ferment for about 24 hours at 30° C. *Tempeh* is served with flat bread and can be roasted, fried or used to prepare vegetable soups. The community, which has about twenty people who produce for home consumption and direct sale, is trying to promote an ancient and unique Indonesian culinary tradition.

PRODUCTION AREA
Yogyakarta, Java

COMMUNITY COORDINATOR
Mohammad Rois
tel. +62 218296545
biotani@rad.net.id - biotani2004a@yahoo.com

Garmsar Cereal growers

The Garmsar plain is an important zone for cereal and cotton production. The farmers' reckless use of pesticides has had serious repercussions in the area in recent years, also affecting the lives of the other inhabitants. So a group of growers and technicians, supported by the local NGO Cenesta (Iranian Centre for Sustainable Development), is trying to promote a form of sustainable agriculture through producer and consumer awareness. The principal organic crops are cereals, especially wheat and barley, which are traditionally grown in the zone and so basic to the local diet that they are often depicted on rugs and copper plates. Wheat and flour have always had an almost sacred role in the area.

PRODUCTION AREA
Garmsar, province of Semnan

COMMUNITY COORDINATOR
Ahmad Taheri
tel. +98 2324225639
ahmad@cenesta.org

Khorasan Spice producers

Khorasan, which in Persian means "the place where the sun rises", is the largest province and one of the most densely populated regions in Iran. It is bordered to the north by Turkmenistan and to the east by Afghanistan. The population density is partly due to the attraction of Mashhad, the capital, a holy city for the Shiites, but also because the weather and territorial conditions are favorable for agriculture. In particular they grow saffron (95% of world production), green cumin, *berberè* hot peppers and zibibbo grapes. The spices are home grown and the products are then given to a cooperative that takes care of the marketing. The community is supported by the Agrarian University of Mashhad. The Second International Symposium on Saffron is being held in Mashhad in October 2006.

PRODUCTION AREA
Province of Khorasan

COMMUNITY COORDINATOR
Parviz Rezvani Moghaddam
tel. +98 5118814967
prm93@yahoo.com

Nomadic shepherds of Fars

In Iran, nomadism is still very common and many communities live on livestock breeding (cows, camels, buffaloes, donkeys), using them for their hides, meat, milk and dairy products. The mobility of the shepherds and the herds is essential for protecting the pastureland. The animals trample the terrain, transporting the seeds of wild plants and fertilizing the soil. The fact that many tribes now lead a sedentary life has contributed to desertification. For this reason nomadic communities are protected by the international organization World Alliance of Mobil People (WAIMP), which works with Cenesta in Iran. The Shesh Bayli tribe belongs to the Qashai Tribe Confederation, Turkmen tribes that move between Fars, in Southern Iran, and the winter pastures near the Persian Gulf.

PRODUCTION AREA
Province of Fars

COMMUNITY COORDINATOR
Catherine Razavi Khadija
tel. +98 2122964114 – 2122964115 - 2122964116
khadija@cenesta.org

Goat's Milk Cheese producers of Mount Eitan

This small community is made up of three people, who run a farm where 170 goats are raised in the wild. The goats were introduced twenty years ago and are a crossbreed of the male *anglo-nubiana* and the female *Cyprus*, very well-suited to the pastures in the area. The farm is located on the slopes of Mount Eitan, west of Jerusalem near the springs of the Sataf River, an area that has been cultivated for thousands of years. Shai Seltzer (Slow Food Award for the Defense of Biodiversity) and its collaborators produce wine and extra virgin olive oil, cultivate an organic vegetable garden on the slopes terraced with dry stone and produce cheeses that age for a few months in natural caves. The goat's cheese aged wrapped in grape leaves, in the residue of wine fermentation, or in ashes.

PRODUCTION ARE
Mount Eitan, Judea

COMMUNITY COORDINATOR
Zeltzer Shai
tel. +972 544403762

Olive Oil producers of Galilee

The community unites 60 Arab farmers who grow the centuries old *surri* olive tree. In addition to organic olive oil, they also produce honey, cakes of oil soap and *za'atar*, a mixture of marjoram, sesame, sumac, olive oil and salt. Used as a seasoning for soups, meats and salads, *za'atar* is also an ingredient in one of the most common dishes in Galilee: *manakish*, a topping for Arab bread. The producers are part of the Sindyanna association, founded in 1996 by a group of Jewish and Palestinian women in Majd al Krum, a West Bank village. Sindyanna is involved in selling products through fair trade markets. The objective of Sindyanna (meaning oak in Arabic) is to see that the Arab population receives a fair income, help them improve the quality of their products and preserve their own territory.

PRODUCTION AREA
Western Galilee

COMMUNITY COORDINATOR
Hadas Lahav
tel. +972 46516784
sindyan@netvision.net.il

Traditional producers of Ela Valley

The small landowners of the community live in Ela Valley, famous for being the place where David fought Goliath according to the Biblical tradition. This community, which still practices sustainable farming, works in central Israel, about 14 miles west of Jerusalem. It produces olive oil, wine (vineyards have been grown for thousands of years in Israel) and vegetables. It also raises goats and rams for both meat and milk, which is made into organic dairy products. The cheeses are made mainly for home consumption, while the other ingredients are sold locally.

PRODUCTION AREA
Ela Valley, Jerusalem

COMMUNITY COORDINATOR
Ra'anan Mallek
tel. +972 544642695
siegcran@yahoo.com

Aguni Island Sea Salt producers

To defend the chemical salt industry, government monopoly banned all traditional salt production in 1971. Artisan production of natural salt was also abolished in the Riukyu archipelago after the territory was returned to the Japanese government in 1972. Labor groups, working with university professors, have long battled to obtain a repeal. In 1997, after the State Company was privatized, natural salt began to be produced in Japan legally again. On Aguni Island (20 minutes by plane from Okinawa), 30 people extract it from the sea water. The water is pumped onto a structure made of bamboo branches to facilitate evaporation and is then reheated so the unrefined salt can be removed. The liquid residue is sold as dietary supplements and cosmetics.

PRODUCTION AREA
Aguni, Okinawa prefecture

COMMUNITY COORDINATOR
Koshin Odo
tel. +81 989882160
kaien@thesmis.ocn.ne.jp

Amarume Leek producers

About twenty producers are members of the Nokyo cooperative, which wants to protect this local variety of leek that has been replaced by other higher yield varieties over the years. Both sweet and spicy, tender, fragrant and flavorful, this leek has always been grown in the Amarume area. Seeded at the beginning of September, it is transplanted to the fields in April. The high water level in the subsoil does not make vertical cultivation possible. As such, between August and September, when it has grown sufficiently, the leek is interred at a 30 degree incline according to a technique devised by a local agronomist. As it grows it looks for light, becoming curved. Each producer then collects the seeds from his own production, dries them, and then selects and saves the best.

PRODUCTION AREA
Iwakiri, suburb of Sendai, and surrounding areas (Aoba, Miyagino, Wakabayashi, Tashiro), Miyagi prefecture

COMMUNITY COORDINATOR
Seiichi Sekiuchi
tel. +81 222558930

Aigamo method Rice producers

This community is a cooperative of about seventy rice producers who work in the zone of Fukukoa, on Kyushu Island, about two hours by boat from Korea. Managed by the researcher Takao Furono, it practices and promotes the Aigamo method of rice cultivation. The method calls for raising ducks and fish (like the Crucian carp and Japanese loach) in the rice paddies to contain the number of insects and other parasites and avoid using chemical agents. This method increases the productivity of the paddy and two other productions, fish and ducks, give the grower additional income. Recently Furuno has started traveling in order to publicize his cultivation methods in other countries as well.

PRODUCTION AREA
Katsura-gawa, Fukuoka prefecture (Kyushu)

COMMUNITY COORDINATOR
Takao Furuno
tel. +81 948652018
furuno@d4.dion.ne.jp

Ancient Rice variety growers

In past centuries, when the rice plants were in flower, the Kyushu Island fields must have been full of color. Archeologists have found a*ka mai* (red rice) seeds in storehouses dating to 2000 years ago, while black rice (*kuro mai*) and green rice (*midori mai*, which has purple flowers and grains rich in chlorophyll) were mentioned in 17th century catalogues. The community has recovered these ancient varieties, tied not only to everyday use but also to Shinto ritual practices. The 11 farmers have also revived the custom of using reeds (yoshi, kaya, ashi) as fertilizers. The reeds grow so profusely along the Rokkaku River that they are a potential threat in the case of floods. The nearly 20 tons of rice produced annually is certified organic.

PRODUCTION AREA
Saga prefecture

COMMUNITY COORDINATOR
Akiko Eguchi
tel. +81 952864560
takedomi@vip.saganet.ne.jp

Chikuma Apricot growers

In the zone of Mori, a suburb of Chikuma, apricots were being cultivated as early as the 18th century. According to tradition, Sanada Yukimichi of the Datè family, who lived during the Genna period (1615-1624), is responsible for having introduced this crop in the zone. Back then apricots were used for the seed, the basis for certain medicines and the practice of eating the pulp came later. The community is composed of families that organically grow both the native variety and the *heiwa*, which was introduced in the 19th century. The soil is not aerated and is organically fertilized, and only natural antiparasitic agents are used. The area has always been famous for the apricots and is a popular tourist destination when the trees are blossoming. For the past 40 years the apricot festival (Anzu Matsuri) has been organized here.

PRODUCTION AREA
Chikuma, Nagano prefecture

COMMUNITY COORDINATOR
Akiko Nishimura
tel. +81 262723381
abricot@gaea.ocn.ne.jp

Daikon growers of Akka

The community is made up of farmers who continue to grow the local variety of daikon in the traditional way and a group of people working to preserve the local food traditions. Only 30 growers manage to sell the *akkajidaikon*, while the other farmers keep very small cultivations only for their own personal consumption. This variety of *Raphanus sativus* is unusual because of the deep red color of the root. It is harvested from October to November and after being boiled is traditionally immersed in the local river waters to eliminate the sour taste. Then it is left to dry in the winter wind. The leaves, also dried in the wind, are finely chopped to make *onighiri* (rice ball) and *hoshiba* soup (dried leaf).

PRODUCTION AREA
Iwaizumi, suburb of Akka, Iwate prefecture

COMMUNITY COORDINATOR
Akemi Kamura
tel. +81 194242045
motegi-kz@ryusendo-water.co.jp

Daikon growers of Miura

The community of daikon growers of Miura, a small peninsula in the Gulf of Tokyo, is made up of eight members of a cooperative. The daikon, or giant radish (*Raphanus sativus*), is an autumn-winter vegetable that has always been a staple of the Japanese diet. This local variety, officially recognized in 1902 but historically documented since the Edo Age (1600-1868), is long and white and weighs about three kilos. The crop was abandoned because the long, thin root was very difficult to harvest. A few dozen farmers on the peninsula continue to grow it, but only the members of the community are working to safeguard it and valorize it as a food.

PRODUCTION AREA
Miura, province of Kanagawa

COMMUNITY COORDINATOR
Tomoko Yoshida
tel. +81 468880229

Dried Persimmon producers

They are called *hachiyagaki* because they are as sweet as honey (*hachi* means bee). And as long ago as the 9th century, the fame of their sweetness gave the name to the village they come from. Production, already reduced in the 19th century, risked ceasing altogether during the Second World War. The last trees were saved by a family of farmers, who founded an association in 1977 whose members today include 87 producers and processors of the Megumino farming cooperative. After the harvest in November-December, the persimmons are left to ripen for another five days. Peeled with a special knife, they are smoked for twenty minutes with sulphur. They are dried in the shade for 15 days and in the sun for another 20, brushed with a small broom periodically to make them soft and to remove the excess sugar.

PRODUCTION AREA
Hachiya and part of Minokamo, Gifu prefecture

COMMUNITY COORDINATOR
Kuraichi Horibe
tel. +81 574255020

Hatahata fishermen and sauce producers

At one time *hatahata* (a member of the Trichodontidae species) was a staple of the local diet and very much in demand. But starting in the mid-1970s, the *hatahata* catch declined so much that it was nearly non-existent. To prevent its extinction, between 1992 and 1995 the fishermen of Kitaura harbor banned *hatahata* fishing along the coast of Akita prefecture in front of the Sea of Japan. Hatahata isinglass (*shottsuru*) is a local specialty. It is made by using *hatahata* fished in December, when they return to the area to lay their eggs. Filled with protein then, they are ideally suited to making this substance. After being caught they are cleaned, salted and arranged in a container that is covered and pressed. The isinglass is ready after about two years.

PRODUCTION AREA
Akita prefecture

COMMUNITY COORDINATOR
Hideki Sugiyama
tel. +81 185273003
sugi@pref.akita.lg.jp

Hokkaido Maize growers

Longfellow and *sapporo hachiretsu*, two local ecotypes of eight-row maize, were fairly common on Hokkaido Island before the Second World War, but very rare today. They belong to the *frint nord* variety, with hard, shiny, glasslike kernels, which was imported from the United States in 1891 by Arthur A. Brigham, an agronomy professor in Sapporo. The crop dates to the epoch when the Island was first cultivated and the growers selected the seeds that yielded the largest kernels. Not as sweet as other types, it is eaten roasted with soy sauce, dried in soups, mixed with rice, or made into flour used for making dumplings (*dango*). The market is limited because the kernels harden after two days and are difficult to sell. The community unites five growers still producing these unusual types of maize.

PRODUCTION AREA
Memuro-cyo, Hokkaido prefecture

COMMUNITY COORDINATOR
Eiji Sanbu
tel. +81 116230988
eijismb@ybb.ne.jp

Japanese organic tea producers

As part of the Ichien-Iccha projects, the Radix association has united organic tea producers from the best farming regions in Japan. The objective is to restore the value of *terroir* for tea cultivations as well, an idea that has been abandoned by modern production methods. The added value of these productions is guaranteed by the organic growing method. Tea is in fact one of the crops most seriously affected by the use of chemical agents. They cannot be eliminated by washing the leaves as this would cause a loss of flavor and aroma. This project also aims to deal with other problems arising from the modernization of tea cultivation, such as the standardization of taste and the loss of biodiversity.

PRODUCTION AREA
Japan

COMMUNITY COORDINATOR
Amane Takeuchi
tel. +81 353994631
takeuchi@radix-jp.org

Kobutakana producers of Unzen

Brassica juncea is commonly known as Indian mustard. The plant originated in China, but over one thousand years ago spread to Japan (where it is called *takana*), acclimating well to the western zone, especially Kyushu Island. *Unzen kobutakana* is an ecotype that originated in Unzen (the ancient name of Azuma). It has thick wavy, bright yellow-green leaves and central ribs where irregularly sized nodes (*kobu*) develop. Because of this "abnormality", but mainly because it was less profitable than other varieties, Indian mustard was on the verge of extinction. Fortunately the seeds were recovered, and the Unzen Kobutakana Saisei project team saw to it that this vegetable would be cultivated again. It is eaten in salads, sautéed in oil, lightly pickled or salted (*tsukemono*).

PRODUCTION AREA
Azuma (Unzen), Nagasaki prefecture

COMMUNITY COORDINATOR
Hidetomo Shibata
tel. +81 957383111
h-shibata@city.unzen.nagasaki.jp

Organic growers and breeders of Ayacho

The town of Ayacho is situated in a heavily wooded mountainous zone in central-southern Kyushu Island. The organic farming movement began in the city a good forty years ago with the aim of encouraging the inhabitants to eat food that was as natural as possible. Now all of the school cafeterias in Ayacho serve the children organic rice. The farmers from the surrounding areas are also involved in growing vegetables and breeding pigs, always using natural methods. This community of farmers, breeders, cooks, agronomists and architects aims to make the city the emblem of the defence of biodiversity in Japan.

PRODUCTION AREA
Aya, Miyazaki prefecture

COMMUNITY COORDINATOR
Kouno Toshiro
tel. +81 985318086
teruha@miyazaki-aya-slowfood.jp

Organic growers of Saitama

At Saitama, in the mountainous Kanto area northwest of Tokyo, about twenty farmers belonging to the Nihon Noen association grow organic vegetables. The vegetables are raised without the use of any chemical agents or animal by-products and are sold directly on the local market. The community has expanded its activities and opened a restaurant and a small factory for processing the products. They produce a variety of foods (mainly for their own personal consumption), such as rice, soy, lettuce, tomatoes, carrots, turnips, melons, eggplants and eggs from organically raised hens. Their processed foods include tofu, miso, soy sauce, pickled vegetables and mayonnaise.

PRODUCTION AREA
Province of Saitama

COMMUNITY COORDINATOR
Nancy Hachisu
tel. +81 495771539
nancy@gol.com

Organic growers of Uzumasa

This small community of growers works on a farm where they practice and promote organic, sustainable agriculture. They grow about twenty seasonal vegetables, including tomatoes, onions, *shiso* (purple basil), okra, and *kamonasu* (Kyoto eggplant).The Uzumasa area has a flourishing tradition of vegetable growing, as is evident from some of the local ceremonies: during the Zuiki Matsuri festival (4 October) a temple made of vegetables is carried in the procession. The community members follow the principle of crop rotation, periodically controlling the condition of the soil and limiting the use of fertilizers (always natural) to protect the environment. Their certified organic products are used in the finest restaurants in the area.

PRODUCTION AREA
Uzumasa, Kyoto prefecture

COMMUNITY COORDINATOR
Gen'ichi Nagasawa
tel. +81 758810479
chiiho@kyotoslowfood.com

Sakè Rice producers

The community of 60 rice growers and sakè producers is trying to recover an ancient variety of rice called *kameno-*o, which was used in the past to prepare the typical Japanese liquor. *Kameno-o*, which some of the modern cultivars derive from, is a *uruchimai* type of rice. It is grown in the Mizuhara rice paddies near the city of Fukushima (Honshu Island); a district where various agricultural projects have been developed related to healthy food and ecocompatible tourism. The sakè factory is 290 years old. The harvested rice is steamed and fermented with yeasts the company has always used. After the distillation and filtering, it is left to age for more than six months. The sakè is an essential part of the local farm festivals.

PRODUCTION AREA
Fukushima prefecture

COMMUNITY COORDINATOR
Yujin Yusa
tel. +81 422410391
yujin@okunomatsu.co.jp

Salted Anchovy producers of the Gulf of Tachibana

Sweet potatoes and salted anchovies (*etari*) used to be the daily food for the local farmers. And in the Azuma zone, on Kyushu Island, the most important product is still *iriko, etari*, dried Japanese anchovy (*Engraulis japonicus*) used for making broths and soups. The fish not used for *iriko* become *etari no shiokara*, salted and fermented anchovies destined for personal consumption. A few families of fishermen have taken up this method again, using anchovies caught in the Gulf of Tachibana. After rinsing the anchovies in sea water, they arrange them in large barrels with salt and a covering of straw, which facilitates the fermentation. Then they close the containers and put stones on top. After about one month, when a white powder has formed on the covers, the anchovies are ready. Refrigerated, they can keep for even three years.

PRODUCTION AREA
Azuma (Unzen), Nagasaki prefecture

COMMUNITY COORDINATOR
Hidetomo Shibata
tel. +81 957383111
h-shibata@city.unzen.nagasaki.jp

Smoked Goby producers of the Gulf of Nagatsura

Of the 291 types of goby in Japan, the *mahaze* (*Acanthogobius flavimanus*) in particular has found a favorable habitat along the eastern coast of Honshu Island, especially in the Gulf of Nagatsura. Here, in front of the sea teeming with algae and plankton, is a 1300 hectare wood of broad-leafed trees. A traditional technique in the zone, *yakihaze*, is still practiced by the three families in the community. The method calls for roasting the fish, threaded on wooden sticks with the belly turned towards the fire, and then smoking them. Goby preserved like this make an excellent broth and a *zoni* soup, typically served on New Year's Day in Sendai, the capital of the prefecture. The ingredient and the recipes are threatened by the sea pollution and the economic crisis that has struck the fishing industry.

PRODUCTION AREA
Gulf of Nagatsura, Ishinomaki, Miyagi prefecture

COMMUNITY COORDINATOR
Teruko Sakaki
tel. +81 225652543

Tankaku cattle breeders

Tankaku beef is lean but very flavorful. This robust breed resists the cold, is ideally suited to being raised in the wild and is very attentive to its young. It would be extinct by now had it not been for the intervention of the community members. They take care of raising the animals on certain farms, where they are free to graze from spring to autumn, and fatten them on others, in special stalls, where the animals are fed forage from the local pastures. The community's headquarters is in Iwaizumi, a village in the Iwate prefecture, but the livestock breeding extends to the territories of Aomori and Hokkaido. In addition to about seventy breeders, the community includes processors, researchers and distributors who try to promote other local products as well.

PRODUCTION AREA
Prefectures of Iwate, Aomori, Hokkaido

COMMUNITY COORDINATOR
Kazuto Motegi
tel. +81 194224432
motegi-kz@ryusendo-water.co.jp

Unzen seed savers

Nine people work at the Tane-no-Shizen noen (Natural seed farm). Some are involved with production and others with home delivery of the products, and the protection and exchange of seeds. More than 80 different vegetables are cultivated on the two hectares of land. The varieties of greatest interest are some regional ecotypes of radish, turnip and Chinese cabbage risking extinction because of competition from more productive hybrids. The daikon or giant radish arrived in Japan from China 1250 years ago, and adapting to the microclimate divided into numerous local subtypes. The one that the community is trying to save from standardization is the red daikon of Itsuki. Similar attention is being given to the *kabu* turnip and *tojin-na* (Nagasaki cabbage).

PRODUCTION AREA
Azuma (Unzen), Nagasaki prefecture

COMMUNITY COORDINATOR
Masatoshi Iwasaki
tel. +81 957383937

Yuko growers

All that is known about the *yuko*, which has never been classi-fied botanically, is that it is a wild citrus fruit, probably used by the Jesuits. The tree (3-4 meters high) bears fruit that is similar to a small orange. The porous skin is a light yellow col-or as is the very fragrant pulp full of seeds. The slightly sour juice is drunk unsweetened by sucking it through a straw stuck into the fruit halves, and it is also used as a lemon juice sub-stitute for seasoning fish.. Until 60 years ago the Sotome area was filled with these trees, which blossom in early June and bear fruit from October to March, but they were cut down to prevent hybridization with the tangerine trees. The Ferme de Sotomi growers have taken a census of the last remaining plants and created nurseries to recover this ancient tree.

PRODUCTION AREA
Sotome, Nagasaki prefecture

COMMUNITY COORDINATOR
Sugino Hiu
tel. +81 959250575

Spice producers of Deir Alla

In the Jordan Valley this community is made up of families that are neighbors or related to each other and who gather herbs and wild plants (thyme, rosemary, wild fennel, roses) in the mountains or on the plain near the village. After they are picked, the herbs are dried in the shade, ground and put up in bottles and then sold at the local markets. A very popular snack is bread sprinkled with *zatar*, a blend of thyme, sesame seeds and *sumac*, a lemon-flavored spice made by grinding the dried berries of the sumac shrub (*Rhus coriaria*), a shrub of the Anacardiaceae family.

PRODUCTION AREA

Deir Alla, governorship of Al Balqa

COMMUNITY COORDINATOR

Safran Jaser Mahmoud Alsalem
khaldoun2004@yahoo.com

Kazakh nomadic breeders

Ever since ancient times the Kazakhs have been considered the experts of nomadic breeding. Of all the animals that grazed in the steppe, the fat-tailed sheep and lambs were especially prized. At Jangeldy, in the Karasay region near Lake Aral, where summer temperatures can be as high as 47°C, the transhumant shepherding of livestock makes it possible to reclaim the areas near the village, recovering terrain impoverished by excessive exploitation, and produce excellent lamb, beef and horse meat. The Kazakhs are among the few populations in the world to raise horses for food, and many of the dishes in their cuisine are based on horse meat: *bieshbarmak, kazy, shuzuk, karta, kuyardak*. The 148 breeders in the community produce meat for themselves and to be sold locally.

PRODUCTION AREA

Jangeldy, Kyzil-Qrda

COMMUNITY COORDINATOR

Yesmyrzayev Sadyk
tel. +7 3272997472
levin@nursat.kz

Northern Kazakhstan producers

The region of northern Kazakhstan borders Russia. In this flat and arid territory a few families have formed a farm (Arkaluk), which now numbers about sixty people. The head of the community is also president of the region's farming association. The primary activities are wheat growing and livestock breeding. The community raises the fat-tailed *edilbajevskaya* sheep and produces mutton tail fat for their personal use and to sell at local markets. The community's horses provide the milk for making *kumys*, slightly alcoholic fermented milk.

PRODUCTION AREA

Petropavlovsk, Northern Kazakhstan

COMMUNITY COORDINATOR

Zhussiyev Bessembe
tel. +7 3152344706
ard_olga@mail.ru

Uralsk producers

In eastern Kazakhstan, in the area of Uralsk, 816 producers are members of the Giajuk Shaurasu association, whose purposes include protecting members' rights, helping gain access to markets and legal assistance. The community is involved in growing wheat and barley and livestock breeding. Traditionally nomads, since the middle of the 19th century the Kazakhs have been involved in farming. Kazakh cooking is based on horse meat and horse milk. The horse meat products (smoked and salted meat, sausages) keep well and can be eaten every day. The horse milk is used for making *kumys*, fermented mare's milk, which is put into bags made of horse hide (*torsukan*) or goatskin (*saba*). These bags filled with milk are attached to the saddles and left to bounce around.

PRODUCTION AREA
Uralsk, Oral

COMMUNITY COORDINATOR
Umarov Berik
tel. +7 3112519411
uralskfsf@nursat.kz

Chon-Alaj yak breeders

Chon-Alaj is near the Pamir mountain range, one of the highest in the world. Even though the zone is subtropical, it is close to desert areas and very far from major sources of water, which creates an arid, continental climate. Yaks are the only animals that can survive at these altitudes. Very resistant to the cold, they have little grazing land but the grass is very nutritious. The Chon-Alaj community of breeders consists of various families from the village who also raise camels along with the yaks. Yak milk is used to make a fermented drink, *airan*, and a dry cheese, *kurut*. Yak meat is often the only kind of meat the shepherds eat. The yak products are mainly produced for home consumption or sold locally.

PRODUCTION AREA
District of Chon-Alaj, province of Osh

COMMUNITY COORDINATOR
Osmonov Jalil
tel. +996 323421488
microfinanceosh@rambler.ru

Gulcho beekeepers

The Osh region is in the northeastern part of the Pamir-Alai mountain range and includes the hills of Fergana Valley. The city and the region of Osh are part of the routes that the caravans followed along the Silk Road. Beekeeping is an important source of income in a country where most of the population lives on farming. All of the producers are members of an association of beekeepers. The Gulcho community receives concrete help from the Aga Khan Foundation in the form of microcredits and thematic courses. The honey is made for home consumption and also sold locally.

PRODUCTION AREA
Province of Osh

COMMUNITY COORDINATOR
Jurabaev Farkhad
tel. +996 502211221
microfinanceosh@rambler.ru

Issyk-Kul fishermen

The province of Issyk-Kul occupies a vast territory in the central-northern and central-eastern part of the Republic, at the border of Kazakhstan and China. It is situated in the Tien Shan mountains (the Heavenly Mountains), at 1500 meters above sea level. Extraordinary Lake Issyk-Kul never freezes in winter thanks to the presence of some hot springs. The lake is both a nature park and a place for fishing, and in the 1990s the local inhabitants started raising *sevana* and *peled* trout there. And the local cuisine is based precisely on fish. The community has official permission to fish and sell both at a national level and on the Issyk-Kul shores, which is a very popular tourist spot.

PRODUCTION AREA
Province of Issyk-Kul

COMMUNITY COORDINATOR
Aida Jamankulova
tel. +996 32346255

Kirghis indigenous sheep breeders

The mountainous region of Alaj and Chon-Alaj is famous for the semi-nomadic shepherds that retreat to the mountains during the summer with their families and their herds, staying in the traditional *yurte* (round tents). On average, a family raises 50-100 sheep for meat consumption. The sheep are sold live at the local market or purchased from the itinerant tradesmen who go up to the mountains to bring sugar, salt and to buy meat. The Aga Khan Foundation manages some small shepherd assistance projects, like courses and microcredits. The small, black *kirghis* sheep is known for the thick layer of fat that accumulates near the tail. The fat is used in many traditional dishes, the most famous of which is the rice dish *plov*.

PRODUCTION AREA
Districts of Alaj and Chon-Alaj, province of Osh

COMMUNITY COORDINATOR
Murzaliev Joldosh
tel. +996 323426053
microfinanceosh@rambler.ru

Producers of Fermented Kumys

In the mountainous zone of Alaj, mare's milk is used to make a traditional drink called fermented *kumys*, and is also the basis for a local dry ricotta, *kurut*. The *kumys* is made for home consumption and sold to itinerant tradesmen, who take it to the Osh market. With the help of the Aga Khan Foundation the product is now also sold at some kiosks along the road to Tajikistan. The *kumys* is made in a sheepskin, usually whole and closed at the bottom, which can be used for years. This skin imparts ferments to the milk, which develops an intense flavor and slight alcohol content in just a few hours. The little balls of sun-dried *Kurut* cheese keep for months, and if dissolved in a little water can be used to make a refreshing soft drink.

PRODUCTION AREA
District of Alaj, province of Osh

COMMUNITY COORDINATOR
Maksutov Saipidin
tel. +996 323426289
microfinanceosh@rambler.ru

Talas Bean producers

The province of Talas is distinguished by the Tien Shan mountain range, and the altitude is always above 500 meters. Livestock breeding (sheep, cows, horses) developed here because of the mountainous terrain, while in the valleys it is possible to cultivate the irrigated lands. In the 1990s many farmers got together, organizing private companies and apportioning lands suitable for agriculture, which occupy only 12% of the territory. The Talas community of producers grows various types of legumes: beans and peas above all. The most common crops are beans, which are used in everyday cooking and for special occasions. The beans are sold throughout the country.

PRODUCTION AREA
Province of Talas

COMMUNITY COORDINATOR
Kasymbaev Talantbek
tel. +996 502575859
microfinanceosh@rambler.ru

Usgen Rice producers

Usgen rice is produced in the Kirghis region of the same name by a group of farmers that belong to a local association. The rice is cultivated entirely by hand, from the sowing to the threshing. No herbicides are used and the work is done by women hired for the season. An important collaboration exists with the Aga Khan Foundation, which has been operating in the area for a few years now. The rice, which is used to make *plov*, the national dish of Kirghizstan, has a sweet taste and is the color of terracotta because of the clay soil it grows in. The rice is sold (not in an organized way for now) at the Osh market, one of the largest in central Asia. It is also bought by itinerant tradesmen, who export it to Turkey and Russia.

PRODUCTION AREA
District of Usgen, province of Osh

COMMUNITY COORDINATOR
Madaminov Osmonali
tel. +996 502242001
microfinanceosh@rambler.ru

Wild fruit and herb gatherers

In Jalal-Abad is the world's largest natural walnut forest, a wealth of biodiversity: alongside the walnut trees are more than 1800 different plant species. To preserve this genetic wealth, small companies were formed in 1999 to cultivate and process such riches of the forest as nuts, fruit, berries, honey, wild herbs and medicinal plants. In the community of 120 members, 80% of whom are women, everyone is involved in producing fruit and berry jams, freshly squeezed fruit juices without preservatives, walnut oil, mountain honey from wild plants, teas and infusions from medicinal and wild plants. All the products carry the Dary Liesa quality seal and are in great demand at a national level.

PRODUCTION AREA
Province of Jalal-Abad

COMMUNITY COORDINATOR
Ismailova Gulmira
tel. +996 372251864
lesproducts@elcat2.bishkek.su

Producers and processors of food for school cafeterias

The community involves about eighty growers, processors, cooks and distributors, who work in different ways to provide healthy, tasty dishes to the local school cafeterias. The food served in the lunchrooms of the Korean elementary and middle schools has been rather problematic for years by now because of a lack of hygiene, healthiness and nutritional value. The situation changed when Mr. Park decided to grow fruit and vegetables organically and use the ingredients in traditional dishes. As a result, 330,000 meals are supplied to the school cafeterias today. One of the most popular dishes is *bibim bap*, a Korean recipe based on steamed rice, various vegetables, beef and eggs.

PRODUCTION AREA
Daegu-si, province of Northern Kyongsang

COMMUNITY COORDINATOR
Kim Chin Wha
tel. +82 231446658-182896942
chinwkim@hotmail.com

Producers and processors of local cabbages and radishes

For over fifty years, the eleven families in the community have been growing a number of different vegetables and rice. In recent years, to cope with frequent market fluctuations caused by competition with its big neighbor China, they decided to organically grow only local cabbages and radishes. At the beginning it was not easy, but the excellent quality of the produce convinced a good number of consumers to pay higher prices to have them. In addition to selling the fresh vegetables, today the community is also involved in making and selling dishes based on cabbages and radishes. These vegetables can be cooked in many different ways, but are used mainly for the traditional Korean *kimchi*, made with vegetables (cabbage, radishes, onion, leeks, garlic), hot peppers and water cress.

PRODUCTION AREA
Jisan-ri, province of Kyonggi

COMMUNITY COORDINATOR
Kim Ji Yong
tel. +82 231446658-182896942
chinwkim@hotmail.com

Sea Salt producers

Thanks to the high tides and the long muddy beaches, ever since the 17th century the western coast of the Korean peninsula was known as an important area for producing natural sea salt. The people used to build wells of mud there, where the sea water would turn into salt because of the strong sun. But although the final product was excellent, it was not a profit-making activity and was therefore abandoned during the 19th century. The new demand for natural products has encouraged a limited number of families for now to revive this traditional activity again. The sea water from the wells (50m wide and one and a half meters deep) evaporates in just a few days. The salt that forms is collected in rice bags, which permit it to dry completely, and then it is preserved in wooden containers.

PRODUCTION AREA
Sorae, Icheon-si, province of Kyonggi

COMMUNITY COORDINATOR
Koo Jong Woo
tel. +82 231446658-182896942
chinwkim@hotmail.com

Bolaven Coffee producers

The Jhai Coffee Farmers Cooperative, a community of coffee producers in the southern part of the Bolaven highlands, originated at the initiative of the Jhai Foundation. The aim is to grow, process and sell the product autonomously, eliminating the middlemen from the production chain. Many of the farmers belong to the Lao Vahn or Laven ethnic group, one of the most numerous of the highland indigenous groups. This is the origin of the name Bolaven, or rather the place of the Laven. The plantations of the Arabic variety of coffee were introduced by the French when they ruled the area in the 20th century. Cultivated at 800-1000 meters above sea level, the plants produce abundant fruit after the fifth year. The JCFC, with about 530 members from 12 villages, pays 30 workers and teaches them to process coffee.

PRODUCTION AREA
District of Paksong, province of Champasak

COMMUNITY COORDINATOR
Dengkayaphichith Vorasone
tel. +856 209820106
vorasone@hotmail.com

Paksong Tea producers

The Southern Lao Farmers Group is a cooperative of green and black tea producers in the district of Paksong, on the Bolaven plateau. More than one hundred families residing in several villages and composed of two to four members, are involved in growing and processing the product, which is sold locally and exported. The tea leaves can be harvested after the plant is two years old, at an interval of 1-15 days depending on the amount of rainfall. The terrain best suited for the plantations are at an altitude of 800-1000 meters. The processing method is simple: the leaves are left to dry in the sun and then desiccated at high temperatures. Tea cultivation was introduced in the country during the French colonization.

PRODUCTION AREA
District of Paksong, province of Champasak

COMMUNITY COORDINATOR
Bouasone Maniseng
tel. +856 205360808
vorasone@hotmail.com

Vientiane organic growers

Since 1996, the Lao Farmers' Products cooperative has been the only organization in the country interested in purchasing farmers' surplus products, processing them and selling them both locally and in Europe through the network of fair trade markets. The am is to help farmers rise above the subsistence economy they have always lived in and provide incentives for protecting organically grown local varieties. The Lao Farmers' product range includes various kinds of rice as well as a few fruit, especially bananas and pineapples, dried or processed into jams, juices and liqueurs. The Lao Farmers' Products has a delegation of farmers on its board of directors and counts about 1550 members.

PRODUCTION AREA
Province of Vientiane

COMMUNITY COORDINATOR
Inpeng Silasane
tel. +856 202407546
vorasone@hotmail.com

Beekeepers of Jdeideh

The community unites eight beekeepers of the Habib family, who for over three generations have perpetuated the tradition of using earthenware jars as hives. The containers are shaped like an amphora. The bees, which are the *Apis mellifera syriaca* variety and smaller than European ones, go into the mouth of the jars and work inside. The jars are covered with jute cloths to protect them from the sun. The inside of the jar is divided into sections by filters, so the honey is removed in disks. The bottom is closed with a wooden plug that the beekeeper removes when it is time to take out the wax disks covered with honey. The community's hives are found in various zones of Lebanon and produce honey of various floral essences.

PRODUCTION AREA
Jdeideh, governorship of Beirut, and various other places in the country

COMMUNITY COORDINATOR
Maurice Habib
tel. +961 3718907
info@soukeltayeb.com

Chanklich Cheese producers

The seven members of the Moussa family are still making *chanklich* cheese the traditional way near the Syrian border. This goat's milk cheese seasoned with thyme is typical in northern Lebanon. The family raises about eighty *baladi* goats in the local pastures and use raw goat's milk to prepare this cheese, which keeps for over a year. *Chanklich* is not made from the milk but rather yoghurt or whey, which are left to dry until covered with mold. Similar to an aged feta, the cheese is then sprinkled with dried wild thyme. It is eaten with salads of tomatoes, onion and olive oil. The cheese is sold directly at the farm or in a small boutique in Chadra.

PRODUCTION AREA
Chadra, district of Aakkar, governorship of the North

COMMUNITY COORDINATOR
Samira Moussa
tel. +961 3436076

Chlifa growers

The Mattar farm is one of the first organic farms in Lebanon. It is located in the village of Chlifa, in Bekaa Valley, next to the ancient city of Baalbeck and not far from the legendary cedars of Lebanon forest (unfortunately very much reduced in size by now). The Mattar farm is a fine example not only because of the organic production, but also its organization, which involves all the members of the family and the neighbors, a total of 18 fruit and vegetable growers. Twenty years ago, during the civil war, this region was famous for the numerous illegal cultivations, later replaced by olive groves and vegetable plots.

PRODUCTION AREA
Chlifa, governorship of Bekaa

COMMUNITY COORDINATOR
Samira Aakoury
info@soukeltayeb.com

Farmers' market of Beirut

There are many markets in the old city of Beirut, but they are markets where only shopkeepers sell. But at Souk el tayeb (*tayeb* in Arabic means good), the protagonists are small-scale producers. From these farmers, bakers, and cheese makers 40 people in all, one can buy traditional and natural products that are organically grown, fresh and seasonal. Soul el tayeb is a place where these small-scale quality producers can get together and an important informative moment for consumers, who specific projects are dedicated to. The outdoor market is held every Saturday morning in the village of Saifi (Georges Haddad Street, below Burj el Ghazal) and in the Hamra quarter on Tuesday mornings. Other markets are found in the cities of Byblos, Batroun, Tripoli and Saida.

PRODUCTION AREA
Governorship of Beirut

COMMUNITY COORDINATOR
Kamal Mouzawak
tel. +961 3340198
kamalm@cyberia.net.lb

Female producers of Mouneh

The community is represented by the Ateliers association of Western Bekaa, formed by four women who practice the *mouneh* tradition. The term indicates an art of processing and a group of culinary practices (that usually only the women know) applied to the stocks of food each family had to procure to cope with the continuous succession of times of plenty and times of want. The traditional method for producing mouneh for home consumption, once an essential part of the diet in rural zones, is now in rapid decline. Until the 1950s, each family made *mouneh*, which was used as goods to exchange with other products or sold at the farmers' markets of the villages.
The products of the cooperative are sold at the Souk el Tayeb market of itinerant organic products.

PRODUCTION AREA
Zone west of Bekaa Valley, governorship of Bekaa

COMMUNITY COORDINATOR
Saber Nada
tel. +961 1486455

Female producers of Serdeleh

Serdeleh is a traditional dairy product from the Chouf Mountains, where many herds of goats have always grazed. The community is made up of seven female Druze producers from the village of Niha, some of whom also raise *baladi* goats, a local breed. The *serdeleh* is made from March to November from fresh *baladi* goat's milk, and prepared in large earthenware jars without the addition of any ferments. It is a very long process: the raw milk is filtered, salted and stirred again. Once a week, or at most every ten days, the whey is removed by letting it drain out of the bottom of the jar. Then fresh milk is added and the process is repeated. After six months the contents of the earthenware jar are transferred to glass jars full of olive oil.

PRODUCTION AREA
Niha, governorship of the South

COMMUNITY COORDINATORS
Abla Izzat Majed
Kamal Mouzawak
tel. +961 3340198
kamalm@cyberia.net.lb

Fruit growers of Kab Elias

The Arc en Ciel di Kab Elias cooperative unites 42 growers involved in the cultivation of plums, apples, peaches and potatoes. Their small farms are supervised by agronomists form the cooperative, who provide the members farm equipment and training. In the future the cooperative intends to manage the sale of the fruit. The Bekaa and in particular the village of Kab Elias have always been known for the production of small, very sweet plums, which the Arab writer Amin Rihani mentions in his novels. This variety of plum also risks extinction, as do the *njass* pear and the *kharma* persimmon, only sold locally or purchased directly from the growers.

PRODUCTION AREA
Kab Elias, governorship of Bekaa

COMMUNITY COORDINATOR
Manar Dagher
manar_dag@hotmail.com

Herb gatherers of Adonis Valley

Adonis Valley, today called the Nahr Ibrahim River valley, is an area of wild, uncontaminated nature at the source of the river about 50 kilometers north of Beirut, between the cities of Byblos and Afqa. According to the Greek myths, Adonis was killed right on the banks of this river. Today it is one of the most interesting tourist destinations in Lebanon, characterized by imposing Roman ruins. Six producers from Adonis Valley gather wild edible herbs, mainly thyme, which are the basis for some of the country's traditional dishes. The members of the community also produce a sour pomegranate molasses and preserve traditional Lebanese recipes.

PRODUCTION AREA
Adonis Valley, governorship of Mount Lebanon

COMMUNITY COORDINATOR
Fadi Daw
fadydaw@hotmail.com

Mouneh producers

The community consists of six people, all from the same family, who grow legumes in a completely natural way at Jebcheit, in the southern part of the country. The legumes are then processed into *mouneh* products, a word that comes from the verb *mana*, meaning supply, which designates all of the provisions obtained by using traditional conservation methods. These provisions, especially vegetables in oil or salt and tomato concentrate, are made in summer to be eaten in winter. *Mouneh* is an art of preparation, of processing, that follows various culinary techniques which only the women know the secret of. The jars of food are sold locally. Other community products are *labneh* goat's milk cheese, stuffed eggplants, jams, compotes and syrups. The community produces no more than 700 kilos of preserved foods a year, which are sold locally and nationally at farmers' markets.

PRODUCTION AREA
Jebcheit, governorship of the South

COMMUNITY COORDINATOR
Ali Fahs
tel. +961 3885980
info@soukeltayeb.com

Mount Kesrouan producers

Mama Therra is a small family business in Jounieh with six people who produce traditional jams made with fruit they grow themselves or purchase from nearby growers. The Sarkis are also beekeepers (producing honey with terracotta hives) and bake *maamoul*, traditional ritual biscuits for both the Christian and Muslim Lebanese population. The Christians eat them at Easter, the Muslims for the feast of Eid el Kebir or Eid al Adha (the mutton feast). The bran biscuits are filled with walnuts, pistachios or dates.

PRODUCTION AREA
Jounieh, governorship of Mount Lebanon

COMMUNITY COORDINATOR
Thérèse Sarkis
tel. +961 3692628
mamatherra@hotmail.com

Organic food producers

World Vision is a Christian association present in various countries, with projects that primarily focus on the well-being of children. It has been active in Lebanon, especially in the north, ever since 1975. In Lebanon its activity concentrates on the well-being of war refugees, who it gave food, medicines and clothes to during the Lebanese War. After peace came in 1991, World Vision became actively involved in the process of returning lands, and at the end of the 1990s it created a network of collaboration among the various communities, with projects for education, organic farming and training. The community of Lebanese organic food producers is one of the World Vision projects. It unites 200 small-scale Lebanese farmers and producers, who mainly make apple juice and other fruit juices.

PRODUCTION AREA
The entire country

COMMUNITY COORDINATOR
Khater Wajdi
tel. +961 4401980
wajdi_khater@wvi.org

Organic food producers and distributors

In collaboration with the Faculty of Agriculture and Food Sciences of the American University of Beirut, the Supported Agriculture Community has launched the Healthy Basket project to support organic producers and to sell their products. The aim is to help organic growers earn a steady income, protect the environment and provide consumers healthy food products. The community relies on a network of local farmers in which each "shareholder" buys a quota of the crop at the beginning of the season. After payment, the shareholders are given a weekly basket containing at least eight varieties of fruit, vegetables and eggs, all produced naturally and quality certified. It is not possible to choose what goes into the basket, which depends on the seasonality of the products.

PRODUCTION AREA
The entire country

COMMUNITY COORDINATOR
Touma Rania
rania.touma@gmail.com

Organic food producers of Beirut

The 25 producers in the community are part of the Association for Lebanese Organic Agriculture (ALOA), whose members include growers, processors and development agencies. Its aims are to provide assistance and to promote and carry out research in the organic agricultural sector in Lebanon. ALOA also works with the Swiss government to offer market outlets for organic products at both the local and national level. Founded in 2005, the association unites Beirut producers mainly involved in growing cereals and legumes and producing olive oil and organic preserves. Currently the products are sold locally.

PRODUCTION AREA
Beirut

COMMUNITY COORDINATOR
Omeira Nada
tel. +961 3351821
aloalebanon@yahoo.com

Pine Nut producers of Rachaya el Wadi

Rachaya el Wadi is a village of about 6,000 at the foot of Mount Hermon, inhabited mainly by Druze and made up of typical stone houses with red roofs. The five members of the community are involved in farming and gathering pine nuts in the conifer woods at high altitudes. The pine nuts, called *snoubar* in the local language, are a very important ingredient in traditional Lebanese cooking and pastry making, but their use is on the decline. The indigenous pine nuts are very rare and are therefore expensive. The cones are harvested by hand from November to spring, when the pine cones are closed. After the cones are broken the seeds are removed, husked and cleaned.

PRODUCTION AREA
Rachaya el Wadi, governorship of Nabatiye

COMMUNITY COORDINATOR
Hussein Abou Mansour
tel. +961 3972146
info@soukeltayeb.com

Pine Nut producers of Rmeileh

Rmeileh is famous for its beaches, but also for the cedar, oak and pine forests in the Chouf Mountains, where the largest nature reserve in Lebanon can be found. The community is composed of 200 gatherers of pine nuts (*snoubar*), which are highly prized in this zone. The pine trees belong to a species called Metn pines that are found nowhere else, and the pine nuts are particularly flavorful. The wild pine nuts, the *snoubar barri*, are dark and have a pleasantly resinous taste. The community also preserves the ancient tradition of baking bread in ovens stoked with pine wood and branches give the bread an unusual resinous aroma and taste.

PRODUCTION AREA
Rmeileh, governorship of the South

COMMUNITY COORDINATOR
Massoud Massoud
tel. +961 3516392
info@soukeltayeb.com

Small-scale fishermen of Batroun

Batroun is an ancient Phoenician port about fifty kilometers north of Byblos (Juba¥l), very well-known in the past for the fishing of sponges, exported throughout Europe. Today this kind of fishing no longer exists because the sea is polluted. Fifty years ago fishermen dressed in very heavy diving suits (over 65 kilos) still dived down to more than 200 meters to collect the sponges on the sea bed. When they resurfaced, they washed the sponges in fresh water, tread upon them for hours to flatten them and then dried them in the sun. Today the sponges are still present on the bottom, but are small and die before reaching the right size. Using small boats, the 93 members of the Batroun community confine themselves to catching tuna, mollusks, squid, cuttlefish and octopus, with October and November being the best months for fishing.

PRODUCTION AREA
Batroun, governorship of the North

COMMUNITY COORDINATOR
Assal Assal
tel. +961 3690776

Traditional Bread producers

Walid Atayah is an architect who has always been attentive to food quality. After many experiences around the world, he decided to reintroduce traditional bread making in his native country of Lebanon. He opened a bakery in Lebanon, Bread Republic, which the whole community revolves around. His specialties also include a few foreign breads, but the traditional Lebanese bread deserves particular mention. It is prepared as it has been for thousands of years, by mixing flour and water with the mother yeast. Once the dough has risen it is shaped into large round loaves similar to the ones that were eaten in these places over two thousand years ago. The flours come from a local variety of wheat, *salamouni*, cultivated by organic growers who are members of Healthy Basket.

PRODUCTION AREA
Beirut

COMMUNITY COORDINATOR
Walid Atayah
tel. +961 1201520
info@breadrepublic.com

Kampung fruit producers

Although it is quite close to very modern Kuala Lumpur, the Ishak property, in Perak, is immersed in lush vegetation. Associated with the NGO Cetdem (Centre for Environment Technology and Development Malaysia), the community has been organically growing tropical fruit for a few years now. One and a half hectares of land are planted with *pitaya* (dragon fruit, *Hylocereus undatus*), a species native to Central America but widespread in Southeast Asia by now, which has curious, deep pink fruit that are eaten raw. The rest of the land, another one and a half hectares is used to raise organic local fruit trees like the mango, the durian (*Durio zibethinus*) and the *rambutan* (*Nephelium lappaceum*).

PRODUCTION AREA
Kampung, State of Perak

COMMUNITY COORDINATOR
Bin Din Ishak
tel. +60 377292850
ishakdin@hotmail.com

Selangor vegetable growers

The community is part of the still meager number of organic producers existing in the country, all gathered around the NGO Cetdem (Centre for Environment Technology and Development Malaysia). The 3 hectares of land are used to cultivate organic fruit and vegetables, including okra, eggplant, beans, *nagka* (jackfruit) and papaya. The products are consumed locally by private individuals who buy them directly from the community and, in part, sold to wholesalers in the zone.

PRODUCTION AREA
Batu Arang, State of Selangor

COMMUNITY COORDINATOR
Tan Hwee Noi
tel. + 60 378757767
of@cetdem.org.my

Nomadic shepherds

In southern Mongolia, at the Gobi Desert borders, there are still families who practice nomadic sheep farming. This community is a group of about thirty people who seasonally dedicate themselves to nomadism and raising herds of goats, sheep, horses and camels; the very animals that enable the nomads to survive. In addition to using their meat and hides, the community also produces dairy product like: *tarag*, acid milk similar to yoghurt; *kumiss*, a fermented drink traditionally made with mare's milk, butter from camel's milk and dried milk curds cut in pieces.

PRODUCTION AREA
Province of Bayankhongor

COMMUNITY COORDINATOR
Chimeddorj Altanchimeg
tel. +976 11329477
altan0220@yahoo.com

Chitwan producers

The region of Terai, in southern Nepal, is home to the indigenous Tharu people. Over the centuries these traditional fishermen have developed a profound awareness of the relationship between food and health and have always helped to maintain the local biodiversity. The 200 members of the community are still involved in river fishing and fish farming using traditional methods (like traps) and with total respect for the environment. The catch is consumed by the family, often shared with neighbors and at times sold locally. The fish can be eaten fresh or can be dried and preserved in mustard oil, in wooden or earthenware containers.

PRODUCTION AREA
District of Chitwan, zone of Narayani

COMMUNITY COORDINATOR
Ghimire Ishwor Bhakta
tel. +977 14384783
ghimireib2003@yahoo.com

Gorkha district producers

The indigenous Magar communities are scattered all over the country and their presence in the Gorkha district, the region of the Manaka-mana Bhgawati temple, dates to the period of the Nepalese Petty Kingdoms. The communities chose to settle in the hilly zones and start farming and breeding livestock, using sustainable production methods aimed at selecting local varieties of plants best suited in terms of food safety. One of these crops is the Indian *panico* (finger millet), a small graminaceous plant that is harvested in autumn and grows well here thanks to the abundant rainfall. The flour is used to make bread (*dhosa*) and porridge (*dhindo*), at times mixed with tender nettle leaves to create a nutritious food that is high in iron and easy to digest.

PRODUCTION AREA
District of Gorkha, zone of Gandaki

COMMUNITY COORDINATOR
Aryal Badri Prasad
tel. +977 56531977
vkaryal2006@yahoo.com

Lalitpur Dafne Paper producers

The approximately 250 members of the community, many of whom are women, produce *lokta kagaz*, or dafne paper, a parchment paper made from the bark of *Daphne bholua* or *dafne papiracea*, a Himalayan mountain shrub. Only gathered every three to four years, the bark is covered with water and boiled with caustic soda and alum; the paste is then dried in the sun. For twenty years or so the process has been carried out in a sustainable way: in various districts the cutting and production are planned by special Forest Users Groups. The community is grouped around the Mahaguthi association. In Italy, dafne paper is sold by the non-profit cultural association Ram, with which Slow Food has started making sustainable packaging by using the very paper of this community.

PRODUCTION AREA
District of Lalitpur, zone of Bagmati

COMMUNITY COORDINATOR
Chitrakar Sunil
tel. +977 15533197 - 5532981
sguthi@mos.com.np - mguthi@mos.com.np

Madhuvan producers

Madhuvan Ecovillage Network is a network of ecovillages in the southern part of the country at the Indian border. It was set up to create a tie between the 15 localities where producers work with an eye to the environment and sustainability. Production is aimed mainly at cultivating cereals and legumes, the main staples in the Nepalese diet. These products include *mansuli* rice, maize conserved in the traditional bamboo containers called *thankro* or *suli*, wheat and soy. Today the Madhuvan Network has 45 producers who meet monthly to discuss problems associated with production and to exchange technical advice. The aim is to include another 60 producers in the group soon.

PRODUCTION AREA
Narayani zone

COMMUNITY COORDINATOR
Khand Bandana Kumari
tel. + 977 156532737
khandbandana@yahoo.com

Kinnow producers

One of the most familiar products of northern Punjab is *kinnow*, a local variety of tangerine (*Citrus reticulata* Blanco), also known on international markets. This fruit differs from other citrus varieties because of the skin, which is so thin the fruit can be eaten unpeeled, the juiciness of the pulp and the high Vitamin C content. The pulp is perfect for making preserves, sauces and desserts, while the peel can be used for cosmetics and ointments. The extraordinary flavor of this citrus fruit is made even more exceptional by the totally natural method of cultivation the community applies.

PRODUCTION AREA
Mandi Bahauddin, Punjab

COMMUNITY COORDINATOR
Ahmad Ijaz
tel. + 92 3334345368
drijaz2002@yahoo.com

Punjab Rice growers

Around Gujranwala, a small city in northeastern Punjab almost at the Indian Kashmir border, a particular kind of local rice has been cultivated for many generations: *basmati chawal*. Sown in June, it is harvested in the months of October and November and then dried and processed. Although rice accounts for most of its production, the community also grows wheat (seeded in November-December and harvested between April and mid-May) and various types of legumes. Fifteen families (mainly owners of small plots of land) are involved in the activity, but there are also paid workers who receive fair pay as well as health insurance.

PRODUCTION AREA
Gujranwala, Punjab

COMMUNITY COORDINATOR
Zahoor Imran
tel. + 92 544435103
drijaz2002@yahoo.com

Bayta Olive Oil producers

Palestine is particularly well-suited to olive growing, and one still finds large stone presses and millenary olive groves in the area, evidence that olive oil was already being produced in Roman times. Olive oil production is most common among the very poor Arab populations, particularly in the villages in northern Palestine. The olive tress can produce even without irrigation, which is essential in an area where there is very little water. The harvest season goes from October to December. The 40 small farms of the community produce extra virgin olive oil, and a few artisans from Nablus also make oil soap. The products are sold through fair trade channels with the help of the NGO Parc (Palestinian Agricultural Relief Committees).

PRODUCTION AREA
Bayta, district of Nablus

COMMUNITY COORDINATOR
Abu-Ghazaleh Saleem Yousef Ibrahim
saleem@pal-arc.org

Jenin Almond growers

In northern Palestine, in the province of Jenin, a variety of almond has always been cultivated that is known as *om al-fahim* (like the village of the same name in the Palestinian zone separating Israel from the West Bank). Also called *hassan al-asaad*, the variety is particularly well-suited to growing in arid zones as it needs no irrigation. The almonds ripen in July. After the harvest, the fruit is set out to dry, and then the women of the community take care of the shelling, selecting, smoking and packaging. The community includes 35 fruit growers joined in a cooperative. The products are sold through fair trade channels with the help of the NGO Parc (Palestinian Agricultural Relief Committees).

PRODUCTION AREA
Province of Jenin

COMMUNITY COORDINATOR
Al Ahmad Samer
tel. +970 22963840
saleem@pal-arc.org

Jericho Date producers

Growing date palms and processing the fruit is one of the most profitable activities for the Arab populations in Jordan Valley. The date palm prefers territories with a very hot climate and this is the lowest zone on the planet. The community is formed by 25 small farms that grow different varieties. The one that is most highly prized is the *medjoul*, with its large, sweet, tender and particularly succulent fruit. When ripe, the color varies from light to dark brown. Harvested from October to November, the main difficulty is procuring the seeds to increase the crops. The dates are sold through fair trade channels with the help of the NGO Parc (Palestinian Agricultural Relief Committees).

PRODUCTION AREA
Jericho and the Jordan River Valley

COMMUNITY COORDINATOR
Samir Barakat
tel. +970 22963840
saleem@pal-arc.org

Jericho traditional food producers

The YWCA, founded in Great Britain in 1855, is one of the world's largest international women's associations. A Christian organization, but open to all religious faiths, its objective is to assist and improve the living conditions of women everywhere. With more than 25 million members today, it has been in Palestine since 1918. Following the *Intifada* in 2001, it started a food project to help women and to create work and commercial opportunities at a time when there were tight restrictions on the movements of the Arab population. The community of Palestinian women in the YWCA produces traditional foods like couscous, *ajweh* (date dough) and honey, and gathers and dries thyme, mint and *ruta canina*. The community has 15 women, 18 farmers and three tradesmen.

PRODUCTION AREA
Jericho, West Bank

COMMUNITY COORDINATOR
Mekel Abeer
tel. + 972 22322784
nazar_halteh@hotmail.com

Tubas shepherds and Cheese producers

The community involves over 160 small-scale sheep and goat breeders supervised by veterinarians and agronomist of the Palestinian Livestock Development Centre, a NGO whose objective is to train breeders and improve the quality of the local dairy products. The shepherds mainly produce yoghurt (*leban*), which is made into *lebaneh-glool* cheese. The method calls for the yoghurt to be drained of water by being placed in a cloth sack for a few days in a cool place. After the salting, small, two centimeter balls of cheese are formed, which are preserved in olive oil. Butter (*zebdeh*) is also made by churning the *leban* with a goatskin tool called a *kerbeh*.

PRODUCTION AREA
Districts of Nablus, Tubas and Jenin

COMMUNITY COORDINATOR
Abu-Al Zulof George
tel. +972 2407530
george@dci-pal.org

LAND RESEARCH CENTER

The Land Research Center was created in Jerusalem in 1986 as an Annex to the Arab Studies Society. It is an independent no-profit NGO that works in the West Bank (including East Jerusalem) and the Gaza Strip. Its main goal is to promote and develop Palestinian agriculture. Its many projects focusing on agriculture in desert areas have included the organization of conferences that help to train experts in agriculture and soil protection.

AREA OF ACTIVITY
West Bank and Gaza Strip

ASSOCIATION COORDINATOR
Murad Al-Housani
lrc@palnet.com

Balangon Banana and Sugar producers of Negros Island

Sixty per cent of all Philippine sugar is produced on Negros Island. This monoculture was the cause of the serious economic crisis that hit the Island in the mid-1980s when sugar prices slumped. It was only thanks to Japanese consumer cooperatives like Alter Trade that the situation was gradually restored. Alter Trade intervened by promoting organic farming and the diversification of crops and by favoring the formation of trade agreements, including international ones. Characterized by high quality standards and certified by international bodies, production now concentrates on a particular type of banana called *balangon* (1800 tons) as well as sugar (c. 2000 tons a year). An important feature is the protection of the 5,000 workers employed in the sector.

PRODUCTION AREA
Province of Bacolod, Negros Island, Western Visayas

COMMUNITY COORDINATOR
Marthine Lopez Edwin
tel. +63 344410051
atfinc@gmail.com - atcor@info.com.ph

Oton Banana Chips and Sugar producers

Ever since 1991 the Panay Fair Trade Corporation (PFTC) has been working to coordinate the productive and marketing activities of the Panay Island farming communities. Set up as an association of women, today it provides technical and economic support to improve the living conditions of the local producers. The activities of the PFTC benefit 7000 farmers and workers involved in processing local products like *mascobado* (very sweet and low-calorie unrefined sugar) and banana chips, a local variety of the *saba* banana. The PFTC promote organic farming and opposes the use of GMOs, pesticides and synthetic fertilizers. The association also defends traditional culinary practices and opposes mechanized processes, in defence of local labor.

PRODUCTION AREA
Oton, province of Iloilo, Panay Island, Western Visayas

COMMUNITY COORDINATOR
Angel Panganiban
tel. +63 333363911
pnyfair@skyinet.net

Pangasinan producers

Pangasinan, a province in the central plains of Luzon, is a zone of primary importance for rice production. The members of the community are small-scale farmers associated with Agtalon, a NGO that works to promote sustainable farming. Thanks to this collaboration, there has been a rediscovery of indigenous rice varieties and eco-compatible farming methods, the antithesis of the large-scale farming that developed after the green revolution. 150 producers, processors and distributors are involved in the community's activities. Rice accounts for most of the production, followed by pork, fruit, vegetables and natural fertilizers made from the decomposition of farm refuse by earthworms.

PRODUCTION AREA
Pangasinan, Luzon Island, Central Luzon

COMMUNITY COORDINATOR
Victoria Padilla
tel. +63 755194987
agtalon_inc@yahoo.com

Rice and Cashew producers of Palawan

The members of the community descend from groups of colonies from various zones in the Philippines that settled these territories, bringing with them their knowledge that gradually became a single culture, the fruit of common experiences. Rice and cashes are the two crops that characterize the community. The organically grown rice, the main resource, is chiefly for personal consumption. To preserve its flavor, consistency and nutrients, the rice is kept intact, with little processing. The cashews are the cash crop for the community. Each farm has from 100 to 400 trees, most of which are centuries old. The flesh of the fruit is used as feed for the small animals raised on the farm, while the cashew seed is separated from the flesh and sold directly to the processors.

PRODUCTION AREA
Northern Palawan Island, Southern Tagalog

COMMUNITY COORDINATOR
Laurence Padilla
tel. +63 484348362
oyen.padilla@gmail.com

Small-scale fishermen

Pamalakaya is an important association of small businessmen involved in fishing, fish-farming and selling fish products. Communities scattered about several provinces in the country are members of the association in the country, with more than 80,000 fishermen involved in the activities. One of the most important species is the wild or farm-raised large grey mullet (milk fish), 5,000 tons of which are caught each year. The association has no commercial partners and is totally self-sufficient in terms of production and distribution. It recognizes the importance of water as a source of life and fights for the protection of marine resources by promoting traditional and sustainable fishing methods.

PRODUCTION AREA
Provinces di Samar, Leyte, Albay, Sorsogon, Rizal and Laguna

COMMUNITY COORDINATOR
Luna Jr. Servillano
tel. +63 24368915
pampil@skyinet.net

Coconut producers of the South

The community brings together more than 700 people from various zones in the Southern part of the country who grow palms and process the coconuts. The fruit is harvested 13 months after the plant flowers, shelled, dried and then cut into small pieces before being packaged. Mainly women are involved in this activity, which is also a form of social enfranchisement. The community works with the Siyath Foundation, set up in 1985 to offer technical training to small-scale artisans and to farmers, especially women. Since the terrible tsunami of 2004, the Foundation has been helping the families of fishermen and farmers who lost everything in the disaster.

PRODUCTION AREA
Colombo, Kurunagala, Kandy and Galle

COMMUNITY COORDINATOR
Indika De Costa
tel. +94 112667176
siyath@zeynet.com

Negombo Spice producers

Sri Lanka has always been known for the cultivation of tea and spices, which since the 18th century have been the primary food export. Podie, which in the Cingalese language means small, is the name of the non-profit organization that harvests spices on the western coast and exports them to Europe, Australia, New Zealand and the United States through the fair trade circuit. Founded in 1974, it helps farmers during the cultivation phases, but especially during commercial negotiations by trying to have the products sold without any middlemen. This activity involves about 1,125 people, who mainly produce hot peppers, cinnamon, white and black pepper and curcuma.

PRODUCTION AREA
Negombo

COMMUNITY COORDINATOR
Fernando Piyonkara Wedage Tyrell Delukshan
tel. +94 312233773
tyrell@sltnet.lk

Pelmadulla Tea producers

In the south of the country, around Pelmadulla, there are 75 families cultivating about 50 hectares of land, producing organic tea and trying to restore soil quality, which has been eroded after years of chemical fertilizer use. Sri Lanka produces excellent tea and the plantations though widespread in the south are present throughout the island. *Mihirasa* is the organic tea produced by this community, which includes about 800 farmers and processors. It is sold directly at the local level.

PRODUCTION AREA
Pelmadulla, Ratnapura

COMMUNITY COORDINATOR
Suranjan Kodithuwakku
tel. +94 112817156
suranjan@greensl.net

Tadef dairy producers

Sheep and goat breeding is an integral part of the farming system in Syria and one of the major sources of income for the communities. Dairy product producers in the area of El Bab are small-scale breeders who also own fields (from 5-20 hectares) cultivated with wheat, cumin, and chickpeas. Their main resource is the dairy products they produce from sheep breeding: milk, yoghurt, butter and cheese (mainly acid, made from yoghurt mixed with salt), which are also the bases for all Middle Eastern cooking. In Syria they raise the *assawi* breed of sheep, valued both for its high fertility rate and its excellent meat and milk.

PRODUCTION AREA
Tadef, El Bab, district of Halab

COMMUNITY COORDINATOR
Abdel El Hawish
tel. +963 212213433
s.rihawi@cgiar.org

Yuen Foong Yu Biotech organic producers

Producing organic vegetables with reduced pesticide content from "a healthy land, a healthy body and a healthy lifestyle" standpoint is the objective of the Yfy Biotech Company of Taipei. Thanks to the wealth of natural resources they obtain top quality products, which are also sold abroad. Eggs from free-range chickens, organic bread and rice, handmade *tagliatella* pasta, fruit, vinegar without additives, sauces, and snacks made with officinal herbs are just a few of their products. Families receive the foods directly at their homes. The community is also involved in training the producers, (above all native Taiwanese of the Taiya ethnic group) and consumers through good food education, in part by way of a monthly magazine that has stories about food and farmers.

PRODUCTION AREA
T'aipei

COMMUNITY COORDINATOR
Stephanie Ho
tel. +886 223961166 - 223963588
yichiaho@yfy.com

Badakhshan fruit growers

The province of Badakhshan boasts a great variety of fruit: apricots, apples, pears, indigenous varieties of cherries. The fruit is used dried and for preparing jams and marmalades. Tajikistan apricots are very famous and also found at the markets in Moscow. Projects for the organized and rational production of jams and marmalades have been started with the help of the Aga Khan Foundation. Near Khorog they are putting up jams made from the village fruit by using only a wood burning fire in the courtyard and no gas or electricity. For now there is no certificate of origin or quality, but they intend to request it and expect to get it soon.

PRODUCTION AREA
Province of Badakhshan, region of Gorno-Badakhshan

COMMUNITY COORDINATOR
Kodirova Usnoro
tel. +992 352222699
msdpgbao@akdn.org

Ishkashim Black Pea producers

The black peas are the basis for the traditional Pamir dish known as *osh*, a sort of tagliatelle handmade at home by the women and once one of the m main local foods. The irregularly shaped grey-black peas are sold at the Khorog market and in a few other large cities. The flour is ground by hand and the *osh* can be cooked with a little salt and chives and served immediately, or it can be dried. Every morning, an *osh* soup prepared the same day is served in the cafés at the Khorog market. This dish is being eaten less and less now both because young people prefer "modern foods" and because it takes a very long time to prepare.

Langar Wheat growers

In the Pamir valleys, at 3000 meters, only one indigenous variety of wheat can grow in the poor terrain with no need of fertilizers. Resistant to disease and drought, it is cultivated in every village to make flat bread that is baked in a round oven. The yield of the wheat is not high, but is certain nevertheless, and it is not necessary to buy new seeds each year because the seeds from the harvested wheat can be used. The flour from Langar wheat is a bit darker than usual and the flavor of the bread, which keeps very well, is very unusual. Occasionally the bread is sold at the local markets.

PRODUCTION AREA
Region of Gorno-Badakhshan

COMMUNITY COORDINATOR
Shambieva Zumrat
msdspkhorog@akdn.org

PRODUCTION AREA
Region of Gorno-Badakhshan

COMMUNITY COORDINATOR
Abdulloev Sheroz
tel. +992 93 5002529
sheroz.abdulloev@akdn.org

Khorog Mulberry growers

Every household grows wild mulberry (white and black), but Porshniovo is the most famous place for *pekht*, also called *tut piz*, a sweet made with ground white mulberry flour and walnuts. Before the arrival of sugar, at the time of the civil war, it was used as a sweetener in tea and in jams. *Tutovniza* vodka, another product made from wild mulberry, is very tasty because of the high sugar content of the berries.

PRODUCTION AREA
Region of Gorno-Badakhshan

COMMUNITY COORDINATOR
Rahimjonova Mohira
tel. +992 352224161
msdspkhorog@akdn.org

Murgab breeders and dairy producers

6,000 yak and sheep breeders live in the district of Murgab at the remarkable altitude of 3600 meters above sea level. Many *kishlak* (villages) in the district are scattered in the canyons of the surrounding valleys and to reach them it takes several hours or days of walking. The most common products are *airan* (fermented milk, acid curd), *ravgan* and *ravgan maska* (butter and melted butter), *chaka* (ricotta) and *kurut* (dry ricotta). One of the main breeding problems is the lack of suitable pastures. The same spiny shrubs the animals eat are used for heating the houses. The products are for home consumption or sold to itinerant tradesmen or at the Murgab market.

PRODUCTION AREA
District of Murgab, region of Gorno-Badakhshan

COMMUNITY COORDINATOR
Tagaev Turdubay
tel. +992 355421036
msdspkhorog@akdn.org

Rasht Valley fruit growers

Rasht Valley has always been famous for its fruit orchards. The local varieties of *kandak* apricots are left to dry directly on the trees and are ready to eat as soon as they are harvested. And the Garm pears are of excellent quality. Every family has an orchard with about thirty pear trees and twenty apple trees or so. During the civil war, 70% of the orchards were cut down for firewood. Today the Rasht Valley fruit growers are working to replant the fruit trees, but it is a difficult process. Important assistance is being given by the Aga Khan Foundation, which works with the farmers on seeds, grafts and microcredit. The dried apricots and the other fruit are sold locally and in the capital, Dushanbe.

PRODUCTION AREA
District of Garm

COMMUNITY COORDINATOR
Javarieva Ruqiyamo
tel. +992 35222699
ruqiy.javarieva@akdn.org

Hin Lad Nai farmers

The community is composed of about twenty families of the Karen ethnic group (one of the two main indigenous groups in northern Thailand, along with the Pakakeryor). The village is involved in hunting, livestock breeding, bamboo harvesting, and growing rice, vegetables and tea in total harmony with the natural surroundings and without the use of chemical agents. The rice cultivations are arranged as privately owned fields, and the head of each family also plants the tea in the forest. The bamboo, on the other hand, is collectively owned. The community primarily produces for its own personal use, and only sells surplus products. The tea is sold as green leaves or dried, the bamboo shoots fresh or boiled. The entire community takes part in the tea drying and the boiling of the bamboo shoots.

PRODUCTION AREA
Wiang Papao, province of Chiang Rai

COMMUNITY COORDINATOR
Od-ompanich Walaiporn
tel. +66 25911195
walai_04@yahoo.com
annet@ksc.co.th

Muk Island fishermen

The community consists of about 300 inhabitants of Muk Island, which is inside the Had Chao Mai National Marine Park, struck by the tsunami of 2004. The village is involved in small-scale fishing and fish processing. The communal work of processing the fish is mainly performed by the women. Various foods are prepared from the fish caught along the coast (prawns, shrimp, crabs, anchovies, langoustines, imperial blackfish), including a fresh fish paste (*am prik pa yang*) based on shrimp and *pla keng* (imperial blackfish), sun-dried shrimp (an ingredient in many Thai dishes) and a kind of shrimp crackers. All the products are sold locally and outside the village.

PRODUCTION AREA
Muk Island, province of Trang

COMMUNITY COORDINATOR
Pannarai Supaporn
tel. +66 99767578
annet@ksc.co.th

Nan fruit growers

The community is made up of about 200 families from Nam province, in northern Thailand, mainly involved in organic fruit growing. Lichees, oranges, mangoes and bananas are the main crops, but the families also gather herbs, grow rice and raise livestock. The province is known in particular for the production of the Nan orange, a golden-orange variety that has been cultivated here since the end of the 15th century. The mangoes cultivated here are also indigenous, but are common throughout the country. The community was organized in 1994 and is a member of the organic growers' association of Chiengmai province. It uses no pesticides but instead grows plants that keep harmful insects away from the crops. Animal manure is used as a fertilizer.

PRODUCTION AREA
Province of Nan

COMMUNITY COORDINATOR
Songsikhwa Sawian
tel. +66 14721426
annet@ksc.co.th

Ranong-Chumporn tropical fruit growers

Tropical fruit growing is very common in Thailand. In the area of Ranong-Chumporn, 300 families (members of the Local Agroforestry, Southern Alternative Agriculture Network) cultivate durian, rambutan and mangoes in their gardens and fields, as well as coffee and local vegetables. One of the most commonly grown indigenous vegetables is *pak mieng*, whose leaves (similar to those of the mango tree) can be eaten raw or cooked. Sweet and tasty, it is high in Vitamin A, protein and calcium. The bush is grown near the mango, durian or rambutan trees. Another important crop is *petai* (*Parkia speciosa*), a legume native to this zone. Like *pak mieng*, it is sold in order to buy rice from other parts of the country.

PRODUCTION AREA
Province of Ranong-Chumporn

COMMUNITY COORDINATOR
Suthonthanyakorn Auaiporn
tel. +66 18207006
annet@ksc.co.th

Srisaket organic rice producers

The community, which is part of a network of organic producers called Asoke, consists of 600 families who live in Srisaket province and grow five indigenous types of rice and other non-native varieties. The local *dang sam phan* rice has been cultivated for thousands of years by the Suai ethnic group. The red grains of this gluten-free rice are small and slightly rounded. The rice crop, which is rotated with crops of legumes, is harvested between November and December. The producers of the community also grow herbs for making detergents, medicines and tea, which they sell or use themselves. The field work and processing the rice and herbs is a community effort. The members of the community are not paid, but the community provides them with food and housing.

PRODUCTION AREA
Province of Srisaket

COMMUNITY COORDINATOR
Singkam Un-Uea
Tel. +66 45635767
annet@ksc.co.th

Suphanburi White and Red Jasmine Rice

The 200 families from the village of Ban Nong Jang in the province of Suphanburi are involved in producing rice from organic cultivations. The community also selects and produces seeds that it then sells to its members, and develops techniques for improving productivity. A dozen local varieties of rice have been cultivated in this zone for 150-200 years or more, including white jasmine and red jasmine, *luang lao kwan*, *kao arkard*, and *luang thoang*. A few recently introduced, non-native varieties are also grown. No pesticides or chemical fertilizers are used, but only manure and compost. The community has also organized a field school to teach people the techniques of rice growing.

PRODUCTION AREA
Ban Nong Jang, province of Suphanburi

COMMUNITY COORDINATOR
Siripatra Day-cha
tel. +66 35597193
daycha@loxinfo.co.th

Yasothon organic rice producers

Rice is the main crop in northeastern Thailand and is produced for both personal use and to be sold. Over ten years ago, the Northeast Organic Rice Growing Farmer Group (composed of 500 families) started growing rice organically and produces two kinds of rice, with and without gluten. Rice with gluten is the staple of the Thai diet and 70 local varieties are grown. The most common is the very productive and resistant lao *tak*, with small rounded grains, which has been used for more than 100 years primarily to make ceremonial desserts. The gluten-free varieties, grown mainly to be sold, are the delicately fragrant jasmine and a variety with rosy-red grains, appropriately called red jasmine.

PRODUCTION AREA
Province of Yasothon

COMMUNITY COORDINATOR
Kittisiri Areerat
tel. +66 95845344
areerat_siri@hotmail.com

Wheat producers

The community is in the region of Ashkhabad, the capital. Wheat is the historical crop in the country and archeological finds attest to the existence of wheat seeds as early as 3 B.C. The members of the community are involved in all the phases of making wheat or rye bread. They cultivate, harvest and process the wheat, make the bread, and sell it in the local shops. The national bread, called *chiama churek*, is a round or oval focaccia about thirty centimeters in diameter. Churek bread is made with *hamur maja* ferment, which means the bread stays fresh for several days even with a hot climate. The members of the community are united in an association that has 3,000 members at the national level.

PRODUCTION AREA
Ahal Welayati

COMMUNITY COORDINATOR
Orayev Orazgeldy
tel. +993 865553206
wsultan@online.tm

Chimgan nomadic breeders

The region of Tashkent is in northeastern Uzbekistan between the Tian Shan Mountain range and the Syrdarya River. The inhabitants of Chimgan (2000 m) have preserved some of the features of nomadic life. The community is composed of five families who raise horses. By processing the milk and the meat they obtain the most typical products of the Uzbek nomadic culture: *kumys*, a slightly alcoholic fermented milk and *kasu*, a horse meat sausage that can be kept at room temperature. Made by the communities, the sausages are sold at the local market to be eaten especially during the winter.

PRODUCTION AREA
Chimgan, province of Tashkent

COMMUNITY COORDINATOR
Rejepov Bahtiyor
tel. +998 27423164
chimgan2020@mail.ru

Khalva producers of Yangikishlok

The community was formed around a small family business that operates thanks to the work of about fifteen members and a few collaborators. The community's most characteristic product is *khalva*, a sweet made with sugar, water, butter, flour and a variety of roots. White in color, it has paper thin layers that are put together in a rectangular shape. Since all of the ingredients (from the flour to the butter) are produced by the community itself, the sweet has an extraordinary taste. And the addition of dried roots makes it unusual in that it is very nutritious and high in vitamins. Traditionally *khalva* is served at weddings and other holidays and can be purchased locally.

PRODUCTION AREA
Yangikishlok, province of Jizzakh

COMMUNITY COORDINATOR
Narsiev Asror
nature@albatros.uz

Khashtak producers of Brichmulla

In the southwestern part of the Tian Shan Mountains they grow walnuts, almonds and a few rare, indigenous grape vines, which have adapted to the particular weather and soil conditions in the area. About 4000 people live in Brichmulla, one of the largest and most remote villages in the region. It is known mainly for the production of *khashtak*, a sweet only found at the Alaj market and sold by a reliable person of the village. *Khashtak* is very popular with the tourists who visit the village. It is made with particular varieties of hazelnuts or mountain almonds, apricots and raisins. When honey is added, the mixture is put inside a dried apricot, cut in half and then closed by squeezing it tightly. The complete recipe is kept a secret and is handed down from one generation to the next.

PRODUCTION AREA
Brichmulla, province of Tashkent

COMMUNITY COORDINATOR
Odinaev Djura
tel. +998 27439413
brichmulla2020@mail.ru

Khumsan Cheese producers

The Tashkent region (city and province of the same name) in northeastern Uzbekistan is famous for the production of milk. On the banks of the Ugam River, about 80 kilometers from the capital, is the village of Khumsan (pop. 3000). It is surrounded by pastures where the cows, goats and sheep raised in a wild state go to graze. The milk is used to make cheeses used for personal consumption and also sold nationally. *Kurt* (dry ricotta), *susma* (a kind of ricotta) and butter with the addition of honey are just a few of the products. The shepherds work with the local NGO Rabat Malik and with the Tashkent Slow Food convivium.

PRODUCTION AREA
Khumsan, province of Tahskent

COMMUNITY COORDINATOR
Ashurov Salokhiddin
tel. +998 27437266
humsan2020@mail.ru

Producers of Karluk Melon Sweets

The Kashkadarya region is located on the slopes of the Pamir Mountains, and the village of Karluk is found in the steppe, where the soil favors the cultivation of melons. The community is composed of the members of three families, about thirty in all. Its main activity is producing melon sweets. The basic ingredient is the pulp of the ripe fruit, to which flour or seeds are added. The mixture is then cooked for a long time to obtain a dense, deep red purée, which is mixed so that it loses the excess liquid. Another typical sweet prepared with melon is *kovun kok*, made with the raw pulp. All of the products have curative properties. They are good for the kidneys and liver and increase the hemoglobin level.

PRODUCTION AREA
Karluk, province of Kashkadarya

COMMUNITY COORDINATOR
Hamitov Gaibulla
tel. +998 752276227
gaybulla_hamitov@rambler.ru

Sesame oil producers

The heart of sesame oil production, the main vegetable oil produced in Uzbekistan, is the mountainous region surrounding the city of Samarkand, very close to the Tajikistan border. The community of sesame oil producers includes 500 families of the Paiaryk district, who are organized in a cooperative. In a country where the principal activity is livestock breeding, lately there has been a growing interest in producing oils such as sunflower oil, castor oil and others still. Sesame oil is made from the plants of the same name, which contain up to 60% vegetable oil and 15-20% carbohydrates. It is made by pressing the seeds and used to prepare, season and preserve and food. The oil is homemade and sold all over the country.

PRODUCTION AREA
District of Paiaryk, province of Samarkand

COMMUNITY COORDINATOR
Atakhojayev Alisher
tel. +998 662331152
akme@rol.uz

Sheep breeders and dairy producers

Near saline Lake Aral, in Karakalpakstan (an autonomous republic of Uzbekistan), there is a community of shepherds who have remained faithful to their traditions by raising local breeds of sheep and growing a variety of native vegetables. The work is complicated by the difficult environmental situation resulting from the drying up of the lake in recent years. A family community of 12 individuals distinguish themselves by processing milk, from which they produce *katyk* (a fermented milk beverage) and *kurt* a ricotta made of fermented sheep's milk, goat's milk or cow's milk. The milk is brought to a boil over low heat and when it has coagulated it is put into a cloth to drip. The ricotta can be salted or eaten as a sweet.

PRODUCTION AREA
Republic of Karakalpakstan

COMMUNITY COORDINATOR
Sarsenbaev Izbasar
tel. +998 436512188
izbazar@rol.uz

Western Tian Shan wine growers

At the foot of the western Tian Shan Mountains, there are forty families who belong to a community dedicated to mountain viticulture. The dry terrain cultivated by the community is in constant need of water and this affects the flavor of the harvested grapes, making them very sweet. The high-yield grapes are sold to companies specialized in wine making, and the varieties not used for making wine are processed by the local inhabitants. One of the best known products is *kishmish*, a variety of raisin that can be white or black. And they prepare a traditional Uzbek dish, the *dolma*, with the young grape leaves. The products are sold both locally and regionally.

PRODUCTION AREA
Western Tian Shan, province of Tashkent

COMMUNITY COORDINATOR
Shamsutdinov Sirojiddin
tel. +998 27563063
nature@albatros.uz

Chicken breeders of Hoa Binh

More than 570 families raise chickens at Nam Son and in Bac Son village. They belong to the Muong minority ethnic group, which breed pigs, cows and chicken in addition to farming (mainly rice grown on plots of terraced land). For one hundred years there have been four varieties of *ca* (chicken in the Muong language), all small sized (from 500 grams to 1 kilo): *ca khem, ca kien, ca nao* and ca *cai*. They grow in the wild for three months, feeding on organic grasses and plants. The meat is tasty and usually grilled, steamed or mixed with bamboo juice (*bang chua*). On each chicken farm a specific rule is in force to prevent diseases and preserve the original characteristics of the chickens: the animals that are taken out of the area to be sold can no longer return to the village of origin.

PRODUCTION AREA
Hoa Binh province

COMMUNITY COORDINATOR
Ino Mayu
tel. +84 47260283
jvchanoi@fpt.vn - phucsen@yahoo.co.jp

Green Tea producers of Di Nau and Son Thuy

The farmers in Phu Tho province have been producing tea since 1890, when the first plantation was started at Thin Cuong. In the years that followed this crop spread rapidly until it played an important role in the country's economy. Today the excessive use of pesticides has caused Vietnamese tea prices to decline by 25-30% compared with tea from other countries. And the situation is still very serious for small-scale farmers, who have greater difficulty accessing the market. The producers in the region have united in the Ipm Tea Club association to try to produce "healthy" green tea (keeping pesticide use to a minimum) that can be sold at a fairer price. The association also trains farmers and favors ties between producers, companies, districts and provincial authorities.

PRODUCTION AREA
Phu Tho province

COMMUNITY COORDINATOR
Tran Manh Hung
tel. +84 47199627
hungucodep@fpt.vn

Organic Rice producers of Hai Phong

The duck is one of the Vietnamese farmers' best friends because it eats snails and weeds that are harmful to the rice. This is why over 1500 producers in the city of Hai Phong use a farming method that integrates duck breeding and rice growing. Instead of using pesticides and fertilizers, the farmers set the ducks free in the rice paddies to protect their crop. This very ancient technique known as *aigamo* is very common in China, but was practically unknown in Viet Nam until 1993. That was when Takao Furono first started the method on 20 farms, which then became ever more numerous. Rice is the staple of the Vietnamese diet, and is consumed in its natural state, but also as spaghetti (*pho* or *bun*) and wine (*ruou nep*).

PRODUCTION AREA
Hai Phong

COMMUNITY COORDINATOR
Ino Mayu
tel. +84 47260283
jvchanoi@fpt.vn – phucsen@yahoo.co.jp

Motal

Sheep and goat breeding is a primary source of sustenance for the populations of the hilly and mountainous zones of Armenia. The Aragatsotn and Ararat regions are filled with fruit orchards and, at higher altitudes, pasturelands, where goats with long curved horns (a spiral shape in the males) and a thick coat (white, black or brown) graze freely from spring and well into autumn. Milked by hand, their excellent milk is used for making Motal. A bit of cow's rennet is added to the milk while it is still warm, and after a half an hour the curd is broken up into large chunks and the whey strained off. Then the curd is put on a cloth and pressed under a weight for at least 15 minutes. After that, it is cut into little pieces and left in salt for at least 40 days. The cheese is then crumbled with the hands and seasoned with crushed dried mint, thyme and tarragon. In some cases, wild garlic is added to the curd before the salting. Finally, the cheese is packed into terracotta amphorae, which are sealed with *lavash*, a very thin traditional bread, or with the leaves of walnut trees or with beeswax. The containers are then turned upside down and put on a layer of ashes in cool, dry cellars, where the motal can age for six months or more. Before being used, the containers are boiled, warmed in the oven and greased inside with sour cream (mutton fat used to be used) Each producer raises from 40 to 150 goats, and the cheese goes to private individuals or intermediaries. Often it is simply removed from the brine because of a lack of time and resources for conserving it in terracotta. The presidium was set up in collaboration with Eco-Club Tapan, a NGO involving five shepherds. The presidium intends to bring the producers out of their atavistic isolation, improve the conditions for processing the cheese and obtain the necessary health authorizations for the national and international market. It plans to restore a cellar, which will become a place for aging the cheese, and draw up a regulatory framework for the traditional way of making the cheese with pure goat's milk and a salting period that lasts at least 40 days.

PRODUCTION AREA
Provinces of Aragatsotn and Ararat

PRESIDIUM COORDINATORS
Agnessa and Hrant Sargsyan
tel. +374 10733322 - 91206862
agnessa_sh@yahoo.com - tapan@list.ru

PRESIDIUM SUPPORTED BY
Beppino Occelli (Farigliano, Cuneo, Piedmont, Italy)

TECHNICAL PARTNER
Avec–pvs (Veterinary association for cooperation with developing countries)

Tibetan Plateau Yak Cheese

The grasslands where the yak graze is extraordinarily green to be at an altitude of 4,500 meters. And it is so level that from miles away you can make out the tents of the nomad shepherds, who owe their survival to these animals with their thick coats of black and white. The shepherds use the animals for their wool and meat and the milk (of the *dri*, the female) for making yogurt, butter (excellent when fresh and after a year of aging), a very hard, almost granite-like cheese that is a useful provision to have at hand during long journeys. The dried excrement is also used as fuel. For breakfast the shepherds eat *tsampa*, a dense cream made by heating grains of barley that puff up on the hot sand, whole milk and a little butter. Not far from the highland pastures, at a small dairy in Qinghai province, one hour from the famous monastery of Ragya, some Tibetan cheese makers process the fresh milk from the shepherds. Rich in vitamins and mineral salts, it is exceptionally pure because the calf sucks the mother's udder for a couple of minutes before and after the milking. The cheese is fragrant and has a rustic taste. When aged, it takes on a pronounced grassy flavor and a delicate scent of fat. The presidium was set up to improve the production of the small cheesemakers and to sell the yak cheese locally and in western countries. Since the products cannot easily commercialized on account of the distance between the dairy and potential markets, one of the presidium's objectives is to perfect a cheese that can withstand a good period of aging. It is a challenge that cheese technicians and veterinarians have been attempting to win for three years by now. Thanks to their efforts, a type of semi-hard cheese has been produced for a couple of years now. At present they are trying to improve quality by carrying out research on the milk and water used in production and by training personnel.

PRODUCTION AREA
County of Maqin, Golok prefecture, Qinghai province

PRESIDIUM COORDINATOR
Paola Vanzo
pVanzo@trace.org

PRESIDIUM SUPPORTED BY
Trace Foundation

TECHNICAL PARTNER
Avec–pvs (Veterinary association for cooperation with developing countries)

Dehra Dun Basmati Rice

Rice is believed to have been cultivated in India since 8000 BC and has always been a staple of the diet. Basmati rice, selected by Indian farmers, comes in about 100 varieties that differ in terms of color (from light yellow to dark brown) and aroma (from jasmine to sandalwood). The grains are finer and longer than other kinds of rice and they remain light and separated after cooking. It is cultivated in the States of Uttaranchal (on the steepest slopes of the Himalayas), Uttar Pradesh, Haryana and Punjab in terraced fields supported by walls of clay, mud and grass (with a few openings to allow for the flow of water). The crops are grown in rotation with peas and wheat or with mustard and wheat, and cultivated using simple tools like some sickles, a wooden plow pulled by an ox, and a cart. Local dishes that exalt its aroma include the *khichdi*, with *moong* beans, cardamom, *garam masala* and cashew nuts, which is prepared for the harvest festival of Sankranti, and the *kheer*, a sweet rice and milk pudding often flavored with cardamom, ground almonds and raisins. Urbanization, over using pesticides and fertilizers, and the production of hybrids like *kasmati* and *texmati* have all seriously endangered the basmati. The presidium was established in collaboration with Navdanya (which means nine seeds), the foundation created by Vandana Shiva, which brings together more than 60,000 farmers, promoting seed banks throughout northern India and forms of sustainable and biological agriculture. The presidium producers – 173 so far –have selected three indigenous varieties of basmati: the *punjab*, a light yellow fragrant rice, the *desi*, with traces of white flowers and sandalwood, and the *kasturi*, with a hint of mint and lemon. They intend to promote these varieties on the national and internal market through events, dinners and publications, and have drawn up a regulatory framework of common production. In 2005 the Slow Food Foundation for Biodiversity financed the purchase of a machine to vacuum-pack the rice.

PRODUCTION AREA
Dehradun and Haridwar, State of Uttaranchal; Saharanpur, State of Uttar Pradesh

PRESIDIUM COORDINATOR
Maya Goburdhun
tel. +91 1126853772
navslow @yahoo.co.in

TECHNICAL PARTNER
Risi & Co-Gli Aironi (Lignana, Vercelli, Piedmont, Italy)

Orissa Mustard Oil Pickles

In Indian culture, mustard symbolizes rebirth. For the spring festival in April, when the beautiful yellow flowers bloom, everyone wears this color. A versatile and resistant plant, it is grown throughout the country, but especially in the northern States of Rajasthan and Uttar Pradesh (even though sugar cane has partially substituted the cultivations in this latter region). Dried in the sun for a couple of days and then cold pressed in small oil presses, the seeds are made into an oil that is used for frying *pakoras* (vegetables in batter) and the *hilsa* fish, for seasoning, and for preserving fruit, vegetables, herbs and berries. Among the oldest preparations are the pickles (*achar* in Hindi) of mangoes, bananas, lemons, onions, bamboo or other ingredients, spiced with turmeric, coriander, fennel, cumin, and ground salt and then mixed with mustard oil. Made with one ingredient or with a mix of fruit and vegetables, they can be more or less hot and spicy and are sometimes sweet-sour. After the fruit and vegetables have been washed, everything is cut into chunks, seasoned with the various spices according to the zone and the recipe, and left to marinate in the mustard oil. The presidium was established to support a group of women who produce the traditional *achar* of the Balasore region, in Orissa, a State in central-eastern India facing the Bay of Bengal. They use the mustard oil to preserve tropical fruit typical of Southeast Asia, including the large jackfruit (*Artocarpus heterophyllus*) with the yellow peel, the ber (*Ziziphus mauritiana*), a sweet, yellow stone fruit, and the mango. The pickles are served with traditional dishes like the *chapatti* and the *paranthas* (Indian breads) meat, fish, and to flavor soups. An industrial version, often with the addition of preservatives, can be found on the Indian and international market. Set up in collaboration with Navdanya, the foundation created by Vandana Shiva, the aim of the presidium is to preserve the traditional method of preparation. It involves a group of mustard oil producers and about forty women who prepare the pickles using artisan methods.

PRODUCTION AREA

Mustard cultivation: villages of Deshma, Peenali, Kirawal and Pipalya, in Rajasthan; villages of Chandanheri, Rohta, Siwal Khas and Baraut, in Uttar Pradesh; pickles production: Orissa

PRESIDIUM COORDINATORS

Poonam Pande
tel. +91 1126535422
poonam.pande@gmail.com poonam_pandey3@rediffmail.com
Kusum Misra
tel. +91 6782264867
kusummisrapanigrahi@yahoo.co.in

Darfiyeh

In the hinterland, where the oldest cedars of Lebanon grow, is the mountain chain of Mount Lebanon, traditionally a Maronite stronghold. Here, raw milk from Baladi goats is still used to produce darfiyeh, a cheese which is matured inside a clean, salted goatskin (*dariff*). The milk is filtered and left to rest for a minimum of 24 ore. Rennet is added and it is left to coagulate at 30°C-35°C. The curd is processed by hand: it is broken up for the first time, squeezed and shaped in the hands until it forms a ball, and is left to dry. It is salted, then broken up a second time, this time with a knife, and left to rest for about 12 hours. The left-over whey is heated to make *arichi*, a sort of ricotta, which can be eaten as it is or sweetened with sugar. Meanwhile the goatskin is washed and sprinkled with salt. The legs of the goatskin are tied together so that only the neck of the skin is left open. The cheeses and the *arichi* are placed inside the goatskin in alternate layers. The cheeses are matured in damp caves for a minimum of a month to a maximum of six months. Darfiyeh production involves input from the whole family. The father usually butchers the goats, the children look after the flock and the mother sees to the cheese-making. The fresh cheeses are usually sold in the butcher's shops in town, where you can also buy goat's meat. The presidium was formed to protect this traditional way of producing an ancient cheese which is threatened with extinction. The project, which, in time, will involve all darfiyeh producers, will work on several fronts. One of the aims is to help solve the problem of finding grazing for the goats, which must be regulated rather than prohibited. An important reference point for the presidium is the Souk El Tayeb, Lebanon's first farmers' market, which was closed during the war but is expected to re-open shortly.

PRODUCTION AREA
Mountains of Northern Lebanon: Bcharré, Ehden, Inata

PRESIDIUM COORDINATOR
Kamal Mouzawak
tel. +961 3340198
kamalm@cyberia.net.lb

PRESIDIUM SUPPORTED BY
Tuscan Regional Authority, Italy

Kechek el fouqara Cheese

On the south coast of Lebanon, a few kilometers from the ancient city of Tyre, is Majedl el Zoun, a small Muslim farming community. Kechek el fouqara or 'poor man's cheese', also known as *jebnet el burghol* (burghul cheese), which actually contains no milk whatsoever, has been made here for as long as anyone can remember. Corn is fermented in water for at least eight hours and cooked in a cauldron over a wood fire. After four or five hours, it is put out in the sun to dry on large white sheets, after which it is taken to the mill and processed into burghul (crushed, fermented corn). Water and salt are added and it is left to ferment again for between 2 and 4 weeks, depending on the season. It is ground, left to ferment for another week, and then kneaded by hand until it becomes a uniform, elastic mass. This can be flavored with thyme, cumin, orange flowers, sesame seeds, or red or black pepper. The mixture is kneaded into a large ball, which is then divided into smaller balls. These are kept under the extra-virgin olive oil produced by local farmers. Poor man's cheese is one of the products of the *mune*, from the verb *mana*, which means to accumulate provisions, and refers to the food reserves which every family used to accumulate to survive periods of famine. The term *mune* refers to a series of cooking techniques which used to be handed down from mother to daughter. The Presidium was formed because only four or five people still knew about

this ancient culinary technique for survival. Today, its aims have changed: the producers involved in the project live in the Province of Tyre and have had to abandon their houses and their land as a result of bombardments during the recent war. The aim, now, is to help the members of the small cooperative to get back to work on their land. As soon as it proves possible to start up *kechek* production again, the Presidium will devise ways to promote and market the product. The Christian and Muslim producers of the Earth&Co cooperative bought their corn and oil from local Muslim farmers, who do not spray their crops with insecticides. Their *kechek el fouqara* was the best on the market. An important reference point for the Presidium is the Souk El Tayeb, Lebanon's first farmers' market, which was closed during the war but is expected to re-open shortly.

PRODUCTION AREA
Majedl el Zoun, district of Tyre

PRESIDIUM COORDINATOR
Nelly Chemali
tel. +961 3814341 - 4404257
nellychemaly@yahoo.com

Bario Rice

Bario rice grows at 1,100 meters of altitude on the remote highlands of Bareo, in the heart of Borneo, where it is cultivated by the families of the small Kelabit tribe (fewer than 5,000 people). Output is low: from two to three tons per hectare, as compared with the ten tons obtained from commercial hybrids used in the rest of the world. The terraces have been carved into the mountainsides and the water reaches the fields through a complex system of bamboo conduits. As tradition would have it, different cultivars are often grown together on the same plot of land. The rice is sown in July, after the fields have been ploughed by buffalo, and then harvested in January. For the Malayan farmers, the sowing and transplanting hold a sacred significance and they celebrate the occasion with various ceremonies. In addition, during the growing season, rituals are performed to protect the crop from evil spirits. The grains of bario rice are very small, white and opaque. Popular in the Sarawak, it is the perfect ingredient for puddings and sweet cakes and is prepared by the finest Malayan cooks. They know how to bring out the best of its unusual consistency in traditional recipes like *lemang*, a dense mass of rice wrapped in banana leaves and cooked in bamboo canes. An indigenous product, cultivated by hand without the use of chemicals or herbicides, the bario is an important example of biodiversity. The presidium was set up to protect it and provide concrete assistance to the growers by publicizing the product on the Malayan market through information campaigns, dinners and primarily local events. Most of the Malayans, in fact, cannot tell the difference between original bario rice (of optimum quality and elevated price) from the other lesser varieties often sold as bario. The scarce production of rice in relation to consumption has encouraged the Malayan government to block the exportation of indigenous varieties. This situation and the meager production means the activities of the Presidium are carried out first and foremost at the local level.

PRODUCTION AREA
Highlands of Kelabit, Sarawak

PRESIDIUM COORDINATOR
Gien Kheng Teo
tel. +60 82611171
tfanfare@tm.net.my

PRESIDIUM SUPPORTED BY
Guido Berlucchi (Corte Franca, Brescia, Lombardiy, Italy)

TECHNICAL PARTNER
Risi & Co-Gli Aironi (Lignana, Vercelli, Piedmont, Italy)

Rimbàs Black Pepper

Black pepper is possibly the most well known and commonly used spice in the world. A patrimony in the kitchens of diverse and distant peoples, it represents a fourth of the commerce in the sector, making it the most important spice of all in economic terms. Not everyone knows where it comes from however. Native to southeast Asia, *Piper nigrum* spread to Malaya over 2,000 years ago in the fertile zone of the Sarawak (one of the two Malayan states on the island of Borneo), where it is still cultivated on about 13,000 hectares. Rimbàs is an inland agricultural region, far from the large urban areas. This is where the Ibans, the most numerous native population in Sarawak, live and still cultivate *kuching*, a local variety of black pepper. The village of Babu Sedebau is composed of 12 families all living under the same roof in the characteristic lake dwelling structure called a longhouse; a fine example of the Ibans' strong sense of community. It is the village chief who decrees the ownership of the land to the first person who cultivates it, sees to it that the passage from father to son takes place properly and that all the fields around the longhouse are cultivated. The fields of pepper are small (about one hectare with 200-300 plants) and the rows are arranged on a gentle slope, which is essential to avoid the excess water in the soil caused by the abundant tropical rains. The plant, in the form of a bush, grows around an pole of ironwood, the hardest and most resistant wood in nature and the only one that can withstand the equatorial climate. The grains of pepper are gathered when the green color begins to turn a straw yellow. Then they are washed and left to dry in the sun. Pepper requires a great deal of work, and as a crop is less profitable than rubber trees or palm oil. Unlike rice, it is not a primary commodity so the families only devote their spare time to it. The aim of the presidium is to improve the quality of pepper by increasing the number of annual harvests and improving the processing, from washing to drying, so producers can fetch better prices.

PRODUCTION AREA
Babu Sedebau, Rimbàs, Sarawak

PRESIDIUM COORDINATOR
Mulokanak Saban
tel. +60 82575395
tfanfare@tm.net.my

PRESIDIUM SUPPORTED BY
Rome Chamber of Commerce for Industry, Handicraft
and Agriculture (Latium, Italy)

Europe

Dukati Black Goat breeders

The community is formed of 30 shepherds and two dairymen from the village of Dukati in southern Albania. The Dukati Black Goat is a biotype which over the centuries has become well adapted to the particular natural conditions of the extensive pastureland of the Karaburuni peninsula. The community rears the animals following traditional methods which date back to the times of the Illyrians. From them they obtain milk, the much admired *mish keci* (kid meat) and a particularly tasty feta (*dhjate dhie*), one of the most renowned in Albania. Production is currently 300 tonnes a year of meat and 600 of feta but there is potential for four times these amounts. The community is directed towards gaining organic certification for these products and to attracting tourists to the area.

PRODUCTION AREA
Dukati, Vlorë district

COMMUNITY COORDINATOR
Aranit Kulluri
tel. +355 692075570
auledavlore@yahoo.com

Elbasan Olive Oil producers

The Elbasan Agricultural Federation (FBE) was formed from three associations, totaling 380 olive growers, in the areas of Shirgjan, Gostime, Belesh and Mollas. Its aim is to improve and raise the profile of the district's local products, most notably its olive oil. There are three communal oil mills, equipped with small-medium size continuous cycle oil extractors. The oil is analyzed for its acidity level and then left to settle naturally in stainless steel bins. The olives grown by the members are mostly the local varieties, Koker Madhe, Elbasanit and Mixan. Oil production has long traditions in the Elbasan district, as can be seen from the remains of ancient wooden oil mills and terracotta storage jars which are to be found in the cellars of old houses. There is also a traditional olive oil-based dessert called *fuli*.

PRODUCTION AREA
Shirgjan, Gostime, Belesh and Mollas, Elbasan district

COMMUNITY COORDINATOR
Dhimiter Piligriu
tel. +355 682299269
shbe_elbasane@hotmail.com

Iljare and Sukes grape-growers

The community is formed of 70 grape-growers organized into two associations based in the villages of Iljare and Sukes. The Italian NGO Cesvi is working in the area to restore grape-growing and winemaking traditions, which had been almost completely lost in recent years, and two new cellars and a number of new vineyards have been created. However the Përmet district is not just renowned for its wine but even more so for its raki. The wine comes from the first pressing of the grapes; the remainder goes into the raki. This is held in 250-liter tanks, where it referments during the cold weather, and is then distilled. The most important grape variety in Iljare is Debine, which comes in both black and white versions; in Sukes the most famed indigenous variety was Sianbel but this has now almost disappeared.

PRODUCTION AREA
Iljare and Sukes, Përmet district

COMMUNITY COORDINATOR
Marku Shkelzen
tel. +355 682040761
zenmarku@yahoo.com

Lepushe Food producers

At 1,250 meters, Lepushe is the highest village in the Albanian Alps – and in the whole country. Just 70 inhabitants now remain (the younger generation having moved away) and they produce cheeses, raki (a plum spirit), sauerkraut, potatoes and wild herb infusions called *caj*. One product of particular note is *mishavin*, a fermented cows' milk cheese which, together with sauerkraut, pork and raki, supplies the nourishment needed to survive the freezing winters. There is also *jardun*, sheep's milk which is salted and condensed over a low heat, and which is mostly consumed by children. Raki is the supreme ritual drink and is made with red plums that are picked in October, left to ferment for a month and then distilled. The herbs used for the infusions are oregano and St. John's wort (*Hypericum maculatum*), dried out of the sun.

PRODUCTION AREA
Lepushe, Shkoder district

COMMUNITY COORDINATOR
Gjystina Grishaj
tel. +381 169586403

Novosele Olive Oil producers

Vlorë is the leading district in Albania for olive oil production. In Novosele 7,000 of the 12,000 inhabitants cultivate olives and an area of 135 square kilometers has been declared a protected zone. The Quality Olive Oil Kanina association groups 84 small growers from three villages – Trevllazer, Cerkovina and Skrofotina – who have inherited a long tradition of olive and grape cultivation. The members of the community own 4,500 olive trees and, with support from FAO and organic farming organizations, use natural cultivation techniques. A fifth of the harvest is used to make organically certified extra-virgin olive oil, some of which is sold abroad.

PRODUCTION AREA
Novosele, Vlorë district

COMMUNITY COORDINATOR
Musa Vesaf
tel. +355 692294213
info@musaioliveoil.org

Përmet Food producers

The community is based in the Përmet district, 230 kilometers from Tirana, an area close to the Greek border and, during the last world war, the Italo-Greek front. The zone is noted for the production of wine, raki (the local spirit) and cheeses, especially *kaqkavall* (a pressed sheep's cheese made with natural rennet), *dhjath* and *bardhe* (a feta-like cheese in brine). Another two products of interest are *gliko* (a range of fruit- and vegetable-based preserves made from plums, watermelon, grapes, walnuts, cherries, eggplant...) and rosewater (Përmet is also known as the city of roses). The conflicts of recent years hit the area hard, leading to serious economic recession and considerable depopulation.

PRODUCTION AREA
Përmet

COMMUNITY COORDINATOR
Marku Shkelzen
tel. +355 682040761
zenmarku@yahoo.com

Zadrima beekeepers

Zadrima, in northern Albania, has excellent conditions for beekeeping and the practice is widespread among families, who gained their expertise during the time of state planning. The Lezhe district beekeepers' association, working in conjunction with the Ucodep NGO based in Arezzo (Tuscany, Italy), is working to ensure that the honey produced is qualitatively and commercially sound. That of highest renown is the sage honey, which comes from two hill zones and is produced between mid May and mid June. Some of the 511 beekeepers in the community also produce the Kalmet bean. This is additionally the name of a grape variety which is now grown only very sporadically since much of the vineyard land was destroyed during the disturbances of the 1990s.

PRODUCTION AREA
Lezhe and Shkoder

COMMUNITY COORDINATOR
Hila Hile
tel. +355 682247022
sorinel.ghetau@ucodep.org

Bread bakers of Sarleinsbach

The Mauracher traditional bakery in Sarleinsbach started researching grains and traditional methods for the preparation of oven-baked products back in 1980, but making bread in the Hof (the courtyard, traditionally of a farm or farmhouse) dates back to the 17th century. The community is made up of around fifty people connected with five families of bakers, millers and organic farmers. As well as ordinary bread, they offer a wide range of more specialized products: brown bread, red wheat bread, garlic flavored crispy sticks and sweet pastries filled with custard cream and covered in dark chocolate. The most important ingredient of all is rye. This hardy mountain cereal is used to prepare the sour dough that forms part of a peculiar, old dietary custom, which has made a comeback into the daily diet of local people from the mountains and beyond.

PRODUCTION AREA
Sarleinsbach, Oberösterreich

COMMUNITY COORDINATOR
Josef Eder
tel. +43 7283 8466
josef.eder@mauracherhof.com

Cheese makers of the Salzburg region

The consortium for the protection and promotion of Austrian un-pasteurized cheeses is made up of around twenty-five people. Across different sectors and despite strict hygiene laws, the association supports several small-scale, local cheese makers and sellers that produce milk according to organic standards. There is a wide range of products, all connected with milk, whose wide consumption in Austria is strongly linked to the daily dietary habits of the entire country. Most sales take place directly at the cheese makers' farms or in local farmers' markets. The milk is always un-pasteurized and is used to produce very different kinds of cheese – hard or soft, spreadable, fresh or mature, sweet, sour – all of which are linked to the traditional flavors of the Salzburg area. Radstädter, Pinzgauer and Topfnkäs are the most popular cheeses.

PRODUCTION AREA
Salzburg

COMMUNITY COORDINATOR
Niki Rettenbacher
tel. +43 62446475
fam.rettenbacher@utanet.at

Farmers of Lungau

In Lungau, the southernmost district of the Salzburg area, 25 small cultivators have united to promote their products. As well as being organic, the products retain strong links with the ancient values of the local food tradition. Theirs is an internally organized network for the exchange of products, the organization of the farmers' markets and above all the natural and traditional manufacture of basic ingredients. Their organic products span every sector of food production. The cheeses are mostly made from alpine pasture milk; the cereals feature a regional variety of rye known as Tauernroggen, which once ground and processed into a sour dough, is used to make wholemeal bread and oven-baked desserts such as the traditional Sunday biscuits of Lungau. They also produce sausages and salami, vegetables, aromatic herbs and honey.

PRODUCTION AREA
Lungau, Salzburg

COMMUNITY COORDINATOR
Günther Naynar
tel. +43 6483219
hiasnhof@tele2.at

Seed preservation and distribution specialists

The Arche Noah (Noah's Arc) association collects, propagates, and promotes the exchange of old fruit and vegetable varieties in order re-establish their cultivation in gardens and vegetable gardens. The aim of this association is therefore the promotion of regional varieties as an alternative to industrial monoculture. It was created 12 years ago to support not only agricultural biodiversity, but aesthetic and culinary diversity as well. Arche Noah has a collection of around 6500 seeds of plant varieties from central Europe and the East: hundreds of these varieties are also cultivated in the Langenlois organic garden. The association organizes specialist conferences, seminars, exhibitions and markets. It also publishes the "Arche Noah Nachrichten" magazine and several manuals on its collection of around 980 rare fruits and vegetables and 500 ornamental plants and grasses. These varieties are no longer available commercially but can be sourced through contacts provided by the association.

PRODUCTION AREA
Schieltern, Niederösterreich

COMMUNITY COORDINATOR
Peter Zipser
tel. +43 2734 8626-2734 8613
peter.zipser@arche-noah.at

Vineyard garlic cultivators

Weingarten-Knofl and Weingarten-Knoblauch are the Austrian terms for vineyard garlic, a variety of *Allium sativum* that has been cultivated here for over one hundred years. As the name suggests this variety is grown in the terraced vineyards of Wachau and Weinviertel. The soil here is rich with gravel from the old riverbed of the Danube and this is what gives the garlic its intense, hot, spiced flavor and long conservation properties. The bulbs are planted at the end of autumn, usually near the posts supporting the vines, and are either weeded by hand or with tools that won't damage the bulbs (this variety is more delicate that common garlic). It is harvested between June and July. Vineyard garlic has always been a essential part of the local wine producers' diet: it used to be served in *Heurigen* or with bread, meat and lard as a hearty meal to be eaten in the vineyards and wine cellars of the territory.

PRODUCTION AREA
Wachau and Weinviertel, Niederösterreich

COMMUNITY COORDINATOR
Karin Kuna
tel. +43 18125730-38
karin.kuna@global2000.at

Producers of traditional Liegi Syrup

On the Herve plateau in the hilly area that separates Belgium from Holland, they have been cultivating fruit trees since Roman times. Mainly apples and pears, these fruits are used to make a product that is considered as a regional specialty both in Vallonia as well as Limburg: Liegi syrup. Despite the prevalence of standardization (less fresh fruit and the addition of sugar and artificial flavorings), in this industry, some producers and cultivators of autochthonous fruit still make this product using the traditional recipe and ancient preparation method. Five families see their apples and pears all the way from the tree to the marketing of the finished product. Between mid September and the beginning of November, the fruit is gathered and then boiled in copper cauldrons to concentrate the fruit pulp. As well as the syrup, which is often used to compliment the local cheeses, the community also produces jams and fresh fruit juices.

PRODUCTION AREA
Limburg

COMMUNITY COORDINATOR
Boris Balancier
borisbalancier@hotmail.com

Promoters of typical products

This community is represented by the Origin association, which is formed of over 100 producers from 24 different countries that decided to create an international body to safeguard and promote PGI (protected geographical indication) products. Origin is a network for the exchange of information between producers the world over. Its aim is to promote PGI as a tool for the development and protection of local products and knowledge. The organization provides technical assistance to producers and maintains contact with a series of international organizations. Origin represents a wide range of different products: from alcoholic beverages to coffee, from cocoa to cheese and from rice to salami. The organization collaborates with Italian producers of Parmigiano Reggiano, Columbian coffee growers and Basmati rice growers in India.

PRODUCTION AREA
Worldwide

COMMUNITY COORDINATOR
Ester Olivas Cáceres
tel. +32 22854694
secretariat@origin-gi.com

Small-scale brewers of Flanders

This community is made up of five master brewers that all work in the ancient, traditional, family-run brewery of Verhaeghe-Vichte in southwest Flanders. The beer is produced according to the traditional Flemish method, using high quality basic ingredients – water, malt and hops – that are all sourced locally. Their aim is to improve existing beers and create more superior quality beers, by using exclusively local techniques and ingredients. The double fermentation process is fundamental to their production; it gives the beer a mellow, fruity flavor without obscuring its individual flavor, aroma and visual qualities. As well as the traditional Flemish beers matured in oak barrels, they also produce a number of special beers such as the Duchesse de Bourgogne, a ruby red ale, the Petrus and the Rodenbach, to make up a total annual production of 65,000 hectoliters.

PRODUCTION AREA
Vichte, West Flanders

COMMUNITY COORDINATOR
Karl Verhaeghe
tel. +32 56777032
info@brouwerijverhaeghe.be

Central Belorus beekeepers

Belorus' beekeepers are joined in the association The Belorusian Bees, based in the capital Minsk. This has an important role in organizing fairs and circulating information on the qualities and properties of the country's honey. The community too is based in the centre of the country, where the vast plains give both lime-blossom and poly-floral honeys. For some, beekeeping forms the principal source of income, for others it sidelines livestock and crop farming. The association has published the book *His Highness Honey*. Sales of honey take place via private contacts or at markets and the income supplements the finances of the local farming families.

PRODUCTION AREA
Minsk

COMMUNITY COORDINATOR
Vladimir Kamenkov
tel. +375 296531105
danilov@gastronom.by

Kobrin Food producers

The Kobrin producers' community operates in the Polessie zone. This is in the province of Brest, in southwestern Belorus, near the Polish border. Polessie is famous for its woodland and its marshlands but it is also historically known for various types of bread and for marinated vegetables. The community has around ten members who rear pigs, chickens, ducks and geese. There is additionally a rye bread produced, called *bokhan*. One of the favorite vegetables is marinated cucumbers. These are prepared following ancient recipes using oak leaves, sour black cherries, raspberries, horseradish, wild fennel and garlic. Sales are local and direct.

PRODUCTION AREA
Kobrin, Brest province

COMMUNITY COORDINATOR
Nina Hlavatskaya
tel. +375 164274201
alesiahakim@yahoo.com

Minsk Food producers

The community is based in the village of Sloboda in the district of Smolevichi, not far from the capital, Minsk. It is set up as a cooperative, involving 300 crop farmers and cattle and pig breeders. Beside tiny, privately farmed plots are communally cultivated lands and pasture used for grazing. The foodstuffs are sold both locally and nationally, although most is for own consumption. The specialties include pork *saltison*, a kidney, liver, heart and ears sausage; *prasnyk*, an unleavened bread; and a fresh cheese based on cottage cheese.

PRODUCTION AREA
Smolevichi, Minsk province

COMMUNITY COORDINATOR
Sergey Luchenok
tel. +375 172866405
luchenok4@tut.by

Producers of local varieties of fruit and vegetables

The Ostrovez district community is composed of about 30 people, centered on the village of Kovali (the word means "smith"). The producers' activities include the selection, distribution and conservation of seeds and other means of propagating indigenous varieties of potato, onion, cabbage and beetroot, and of apples, pears, plums, cherries, sour cherries and small fruit such as gooseberries, blackberries, redcurrants and raspberries. Everything is family-grown, with helpers only taken on for seasonal work, and organic certification is of great importance. The goods are distributed through a chain of shops, at trade fairs and at farmers' markets, all of this organized by the association.

PRODUCTION AREA
Ostrovez, Grodno province

COMMUNITY COORDINATOR
Chaslau Labachevski
tel. +375 159120259
danilov@gastronom.by

Producers of traditional foodstuffs

This all-female community works to maintain traditional systems of production, preservation and sale of a large range of local produce. It is set up as an association which, in 2002, included around 300 people. It organizes seminars, guided farm visits, a food festival and other educational activities, all in support of organic agriculture, which is of growing importance in Belorus. There is production of milk, cheese, fruit, vegetables and spirits, for which there is a long tradition going back to the 15th century. Sales are organized locally. The group is linked with the Dudutki museum, near Minsk, which is involved with historic research on traditional Belarusian foods and recipes.

PRODUCTION AREA
Grodno and Minsk

COMMUNITY COORDINATOR
Valerya Klizunova
tel. +375 172510076
info@ruralbelarus.by

Bihac beekeepers

Beekeeping has been practiced for centuries in Bosnia but modern beekeeping arrived in 1884 when the first beehives with movable frames were made in Bihac, and by the start of the 20th century the country had the largest number of hives per capita in Europe. Today, all Bihac's beekeepers produce their honey by hand and have anything from a few hundred hives down to fewer than ten. Just two are equipped for nomadism and none concentrates on single-flower honeys. The community groups a hundred or so of them and is an association pledged to spread relevant technical knowledge and improve the conditions surrounding extraction of the honey and its bottling. It also supports the need to protect the sector from substances which are passed off as honey.

PRODUCTION AREA
Bihac, Una-Sana canton

COMMUNITY COORDINATOR
Semsudin Delic
tel. +387 37223816
sorirel.ghetau@ucodep.org

Growers of the Poljak Bean from Trebinje

The Petrovo Polje cooperative groups around 50 growers who produce wine, cheese and vegetables, beans in particular, in the area south of Trebinje, along the Croatian border. The Poljak bean is a variously colored dwarf variety with a wrinkly skin. It is found throughout the Balkans, with some morphological and color variations, but cultivation is centered in the hot, dry lands of Dalmatia and Herzegovina where it was widespread until 20 years ago. It's a hardly plant and doesn't need fertilization or irrigation, indeed their use, especially at certain times of the vegetative cycle, can actually reduce yields. The cooperative's cheese is called *?kripavac* and is made with unpasteurized sheep's milk, which comes either from the Pramenka breed or from mixed herds; the name derives from the noise the cheese makes when eaten.

PRODUCTION AREA
Trebinje, Republic of Srpska

COMMUNITY COORDINATOR
Jovo Runjevac
tel. +387 59257103

Laksevine Fruit growers

The Tresnja Produkt cooperative is in Laksevine, not far from Mostar, and was founded in 2002 to boost local agriculture. It now has 130 members, who cultivate 265 hectares, growing indigenous varieties of grapes, cherries, figs and pomegranates. The restoration of these indigenous varieties is helped by the cooperative's nursery which propagates plants for the local market as well as its members. The cooperative gives its members technical assistance on renovating vineyards and orchards that suffered war damage and on new plantings. The wine comes from the Zilavka grape and is sold locally. The cooperative is a partner of the Cefa NGO, which works for the development of organic and integrated pest management farming systems; this alliance has led to several producers already benefiting from organic certification.

PRODUCTION AREA
Laksevine, Erzegovina-Neretva canton

COMMUNITY COORDINATOR
Dragan Supljeglav
tel. +387 36480575
dragan.s@bih.net.ba

Livno Cheese producers

The community is formed of around 30 dairy farmers from Livansko Polje (the Livno plain) and a smaller number from the zone of Giamoc. The cheese is produced on the Cicar mountains and the Livno, Tomis-lavgrad and Glamoc plateaux, following a tradition that goes back to the 19th century, and which involves using a mix of milk from the Pramenka sheep with 20% of cows' milk. The sheep are only milked for part of the year, between middle-to-end May and early-to-middle October. Unpasteurized milk is generally used, although some dairies do now pasteurize. The cheese has the typical aroma and taste of goat cheeses and is used in soups as well as for eating on its own. It is often served thinly sliced with smoked charcuterie. The Ucodep NGO is supervising plans for the formation of a producers' consortium.

PRODUCTION AREA
Livno, Erzegovina-Neretva canton

COMMUNITY COORDINATOR
Stanko Ivankovic
tel. +387 36325015
stankoivankovic@yahoo.com

Raspberry growers and processors

Bratunac is on the west bank of the Drina, which marks the border separating Serbia from Bosnia and Herzegovina, and is the center of a zone specializing in small fruit cultivation. Until 1991 over 1,500 tonnes of raspberries were produced each year, and almost similar quantities of blackberries, blueberries and strawberries, but then came the carnage of the war and the activity was thrown into crisis. Now, a project supported by Bosnian and Italian NGOs is redeveloping this fruit cultivation, with the additional aim of encouraging the return of refugees. The Insieme Bratunac cooperative groups around 350 Serb and Muslim families who grow the Willamette and Heritage raspberry varieties and sell them frozen, or as jams – without using any preservatives or thickeners. The fruit bushes are mostly double-arch trained, farming techniques are traditional and the berries are hand picked.

PRODUCTION AREA
Bratunac, Republic of Srpska

COMMUNITY COORDINATOR
Skender Hot
tel. +387 61880056
cooperativainsieme@yahoo.com

Travnik Cheese producers

Travnik cheese is produced exclusively in the Mount Vlasic area and has long traditions. It is made with milk from the Pramenka sheep and the Busa cow, both local breeds. The rennet comes from a secret recipe; it is known only that it is composed of 17 different animal and vegetable ingredients. The fresh curd forms a mass of about 20 kilos which is then divided into one- or two-kilo cubes and placed in brine, in characteristic wooden containers. The cheese is sold in these containers only in the Travnik area; for sale further afield it is cut into half-kilo pieces and packaged, with its brine, in plastic bags. Cheesemaking and sales are handled by Eco-Vlasic, a breeders' organization. Some of the cheese will shortly be able to benefit from organic certification.

PRODUCTION AREA
Travnik, Central Bosnia canton

COMMUNITY COORDINATOR
Akif Konjalic
tel. +387 61890981

Elena Ham producers

The town of Elena rises on the northern Balkan slopes, between the Danube and Maritsa valleys, not far from Lake Jovkovci. One farm in the village of Harvalovtsi has returned to traditional pig rearing, which was compromised by the years of political turbulence. There are seven members, joined in a cooperative, whose few animals are destined almost entirely for own consumption. The pigs feed on acorns, hazelnuts and barley, and are butchered shortly before Christmas. The shoulders and haunches are salted and left in semi-underground caves; the shoulders are eaten in spring, but the haunches remain until summer when they are brought out to dry in the sun. They are then lightly covered with a flour-based paste and return to the coldest part of the caves until the depths of winter where they become ready for eating.

PRODUCTION AREA
Elena, Veliko Turnovo region

COMMUNITY COORDINATOR
George Georgiev
tel. +359 888550055
jopybg@yahoo.com

Haskovo cheese-makers

Feta cheese in Bulgaria is used in most salads and in many local dishes but the traditional version, from goats' milk, is produced only in certain areas. One of these is Haskovo, in Thrace, in the southeast of the country, whose lands give excellent pasture. The six small farms in the community produce goats' milk cheese in 900-gram square pats, sold mostly locally but also in some shops in Sofia. Even rarer is sheep's milk feta, kept in pottery containers. Yeasts are added to the curd and this is then poured into terracotta jugs of up to two liters to ripen, the jugs being sealed with wax. Once ready, the cheese is sold in its original container.

PRODUCTION AREA
Haskovo

COMMUNITY COORDINATOR
Dimcio Stoyanov Gogov
tel. +359 888916143
kami_24@abv.bg

Karakachan nomadic breeders

The community is from a small nomadic ethnic group traditionally dedicated to sheep farming in the Balkans. The members live on Mount Pirin, the second highest peak in Bulgaria, and rear indigenous breeds, most notably the Karakachan, the oldest sheep breed in southeastern Europe, and one which is not unlike the Mouflon. In most cases the flocks are taken up to altitudes of 2,000 meters and are driven dozens of kilometers between summer and winter. The Karakachan is a hardy sheep with a black coat. Its milk is used to make yogurt and other local produce: a young white cheese kept in brine; the yellow Balkan cheese *kashkaval*; and *tulum* – or *tomarotiri* – which is preserved in sheepskins. The community, which is overseen by the Bbps Semperviva NGO, also raises Kalofer goats.

PRODUCTION AREA
Monte Pirin, Blagoevgrad region

COMMUNITY COORDINATOR
Sider Sedefchev
tel. +359 888788121
semperviva@bluelink.net

Rhodope Mountains Bean producers

The community is formed of a cooperative of bean growers living and working in the Upper Arda valley. Traditional activities in the area are milk production and the cultivation of potatoes and beans (*Phaseolus coccineus*). The same techniques have been used in growing the beans for over 250 years: fertilization with manure, irrigation with water from the river, and winding the plant stalks around pine canes. The quality of the soil and the ideal temperatures give rise to an excellent bean, which is used in a number of local recipes. Various initiatives have been undertaken to maintain and raise awareness of the traditions surrounding the bean, including a popular festival, organized each year in the village of Smolyan.

PRODUCTION AREA
Smylian, Smolyan region

COMMUNITY COORDINATOR
Bisser Bekyarov
tel. +359 889218799
bekyarovb@abv.bg

Rhodope Mountains Tahan (sesame cream) producers

Sesame (*Sesamum indicum*) is a herbaceous plant of tropical origins which today is grown in many of the world's warmer areas. Its small, oval, flat, yellow seeds, covered by a capsule, are one of the oldest seasonings used by man. They yield an oil of high nutritional value and, in Middle Eastern and Balkan countries, are also used to make a kind of purée, known as *tahan* or *tahina* (tahini). In Bulgaria sesame is grown only on the southern slopes of the Rhodope mountains, on the border with Greece and Turkey. Growers from the three small farms that make up the community use organic methods and produce their *tahan* without any additives, cooking and hot-pressing the seeds. The result is a coffee-colored cream which may be eaten on its own or mixed with honey, and is also used in marinades and sauces.

PRODUCTION AREA
Ivajlovgrad and adjacent townships, Haskovo region

COMMUNITY COORDINATOR
Nikola Yankov Ivanov
tel. +359 888318671
kami_24@abv.bg

Rose Jam producers

The cultivation of roses, primarily for rose oil production, is of ancient tradition in Bulgaria. In the times of the Ottoman Empire rose cultivation was of fundamental importance to the economy of the Bratzigovo area, which lies at the foot of the Rhodope Mountains. But during the last century roses were progressively abandoned for fruit trees. Then, around ten years ago, a number of growers from Bjaga, a center of 2,000 inhabitants, northwest of the Rhodope, decided to restore cultivation. Now 60 growers, joined in a cooperative, produce jams, syrups and oils from the petals of the Damask roses which they hand pick during the mild weather of late spring.

PRODUCTION AREA
Bratzigovo, Pazardzhik region

COMMUNITY COORDINATOR
Valeri Varadinov
tel. +359 888903700
varadinov-v@abv.bg

Smilyan dairy farmers

This is a cooperative of 450 breeders and producers of hand-made cheeses, all of whom live and work in the Upper Arda valley. The milk comes mainly from the Rhodope cattle breed, a hybrid obtained in the 1950s from a cross of the local Rhodope Shorthorn and the American Jersey. The milk, partially skimmed, is coagulated and, after an hour and a half, the temperature is gradually raised so that it cooks. Once the curd breaks up it is removed and cut into roughly 200-gram pieces. These are left for three or four days for the whey to drain out and the cheeses to turn yellow. They then ripen in juniper wood barrels for four or five months. A small amount of sheep's milk cheese is produced between the months of May and September, following the same method.

PRODUCTION AREA
Smilyan, Smolyan region

COMMUNITY COORDINATOR
Veneta Peteva
tel. +359 30183870

Troyan beekeepers

The association groups 230 beekeepers and honey producers. Troyan is in the center of Bulgaria, straddling the regions of Sofia and Gabrovo. It's a mountainous zone, with a temperate-continental climate, and has long beekeeping traditions. The honey produced is poly-floral and sometimes has hazelnuts or toasted sesame seeds added. The community also produces honeydew. Communal hives are now utilized; in the past characteristic hives known as *travni* were used.

PRODUCTION AREA
Troyan, in the Sofia and Gabrovo regions

COMMUNITY COORDINATOR
Vassil Radoichevski
tel. +359 878770210
beeingbg@yandex.ru

Troyan Rakya producers

The community is formed of about ten families from the village of Balabansko (on Mount Stara Planina, eight kilometers from the town of Troyan) who produce rakya, a plum spirit, using traditional methods. Plum trees have been grown at the foot of the mountain for over a century and in the past every family produced its own rakya. Now production is mainly industrial but a few small farmers still make their own, for family consumption and for sale locally. The plums are small and very sweet, coming from the *Prunus domestica* and *Prunus insititia* varieties. They are picked in October and November, fermented in wooden barrels and then distilled. The plums, stoned, are also used to produce prunes, which are dried on wooden shelves.

PRODUCTION AREA
Balabansko, Lovech region

COMMUNITY COORDINATOR
Nada Nachevska
tel. +359 8893121118
nada_nachevska@abv.bg

Yogurt producers

The community is situated around the city of Troyan in central Bulgaria, 100 kilometers east of Sofia. It numbers 160 breeders and processors. The mountainous terrain and its abundant pasture give ideal conditions for rearing cattle, goats and sheep. The milk from the cows and goats in particular gives an excellent traditional-style yogurt whether natural (called Bulgarian) or a fruit yogurt, this latter produced by adding jams made from wild berry fruits (blueberries, raspberries…) grown in the same area.

PRODUCTION AREA
Troyan, in the Sofia and Gabrovo regions

COMMUNITY COORDINATOR
Mihovski Tzvetoslav
tel. +359 67028915
mihovsky@mail.bg

Crowns of Diocletian producers

The town of Solin, a short way north of Spalato, still retains important links with its ancient history when, called Salona, it formed the heart of the Roman colony of Illyria. The city of Roman times is recalled not just by its amphitheatre but also by the crops grown in its fields and the dishes prepared in its kitchens. The gentle slopes surrounding the town are carpeted with olive trees and their oil is an important ingredient in local specialties. The community has set up a mechanized oil mill which is now used communally. Some of the oil goes into sweetmeats whose recipe dates back to Roman times. The basic ingredients are bitter almonds, dried figs, carobs, honey, bay and sage liqueur. These delicacies are known as Crowns of Diocletian, named after the emperor who, around 300 b.C., nominated the region of Spalato as his summer residence.

PRODUCTION AREA
Solin, Splitsko-dalmatinska Zupanija

COMMUNITY COORDINATOR
Ingrid Badurina
tel. +385 98228386
ingrid.badurina@1001delicija.com

Isle of Unije food producers

Unije is one of the westernmost islands of the Croatian archipelago in the upper Adriatic. The landscape is mountainous and soils are limestone-based. In its southwest lies the small peninsula of Polje, where the soils are fertile and which has a source of drinking water. The rest of the island is covered with Mediterranean scrub. The flora and fauna on Unije and in the sea surrounding it are completely uncontaminated, helped by the fact that no motorized transport is allowed on the island. But unemployment has reduced the thousand inhabitants that there were at the beginning of the 20th century to a mere 80. About 20 of these are members of the community. It includes producers, breeders, fishermen and processors, all of whom work to safeguard and promote their island's natural resources. Recently the members have returned to harvesting olives from the indigenous Greek varieties Orcola (Orkula) and Lussino (Starovjerka).

PRODUCTION AREA
Isle of Unije

COMMUNITY COORDINATOR
Robert Nikolic
tel. +385 51235717
robert.nikolic@ri.htnet.hr

Ljubitovica Garlic producers

The village of Ljubitovica sits in a sea of green and gold, furnished by its surrounding vegetation and the broom that in summer carpets the hills around Trogir, a delightful medieval town now under UNESCO protection. Over the last few years most of its inhabitants have moved to the cities, and few are now left to cultivate its harsh lands. Yet the name of Ljubitovica has always been associated with garlic and the variety grown here is renowned throughout Dalmatia. The community brings together those few garlic growers still remaining in Ljubitovica. Members are currently working on a program to promote the variety throughout the country and abroad, their objective being to increase sales to the point where they can gain sufficient income to ensure that cultivation continues.

PRODUCTION AREA
Ljubitovica, Splitsko-dalmatinska Zupanija

COMMUNITY COORDINATOR
Viljac Ante
tel. +385 21895720
gianinicola@yahoo.it

Momjan Muscat producers

Istria's dessert wines are led by two indigenous varieties, Porec Muscat and Momjan Muscat, which are also known by their Italian names, Moscato di Parenzo and Moscato di Momiamo. Momjan lies in Croatian Istria, a few kilometers from the Slovene border, and here around 20 grape-growers are working to relaunch the variety, and its wine, which, it would appear, was known to the Court of Vienna in centuries past. The community members are small-scale growers with, maximum, 1,500 vines, which they cultivate by traditional techniques. The grapes are hand picked, pressed and left to macerate for anything between 24 and 62 hours. The resultant sweet or semi-sweet wine is sold directly by each producer.

PRODUCTION AREA
Buje, Istarska Zupanija

COMMUNITY COORDINATOR
Simon Brajko
tel. +385 981877928
stefano.brajko@odlikasi.hr

Producers of Extra-Virgin Olive Oil from the Bianchera Istriana olive

Olive cultivation is of ancient origin in Istria, dating back to the time when it was colonized by the Romans. Although many groves were abandoned during the last century, things are now changing and there are new plantings and the arrival of new small-scale growers. The 60 farmers who form the community come from the lands stretching between Buie and Dignano, where there are two annual food-based festivals. The members make oil by traditional methods, using the Bianchera Istriana grape, a variety that has been ever-present here. The olives are hand picked and brought rapidly to the mill to avoid the oil becoming rancid or having any other defect. The oil is mostly sold on the local market.

PRODUCTION AREA
Buje and Vodnjan (Dignàn), Istarska Zupanija

COMMUNITY COORDINATOR
Kristian Brajko
tel. +385 52779077
stefano.brajko@oldlikasi.hr

Slavonia Kulin producers

Kulin, or Kulen, traditionally comes from the region of Slavonia and is possibly the most prized sausage in Croatia. The producers in the community are grouped into a cooperative and produce their Kulen from the best cuts of pig, together with salt, garlic and sweet and hot paprika. The animals, which often roam wild in the Slavonian oak forests, are from the Mangulica and Slavonia Black indigenous breeds. The sausage is completely natural and the skins come from the intestine, preferentially from the appendix. It is smoked for about a month and then left to mature for a further six. Kulin has gained a Ministry of Agriculture Geographical Indication of Typicity.

PRODUCTION AREA
Slavonski Brod, Brodsko-posavska Zupanija

COMMUNITY COORDINATOR
Tomislav Galovic
tel. +385 98229257
katarina.galovic@lura.hr

Small-scale fishermen from Istria

After the fall of the State fishing industry, which had been set up in the 1950s, a large number of fishermen equipped themselves with nets and small boats and carried on fishing on their own. Currently around 200 of them, who fish the upper Adriatic, mainly around Trieste, most of them from the Italian-speaking minority, are joined together in a cooperative . They use a wide range of fishing techniques and the catch is of excellent quality, thanks to the ideal climate and natural conditions. The range of fish is led by soles, scallops, squid, cuttlefish, sea bass, gilt-head bream, turbot, red mullet, gray mullet, oysters and variegated scallops.

PRODUCTION AREA
Istarska Zupanija

COMMUNITY COORDINATOR
Roberto Susel
tel. +385 914431213

Wild Berry fruit processors

The uncontaminated vegetation of the Croat mountains gives abundant quantities of juicy berry fruits. The quantities demanded by the international market have induced many Croats to abandon their traditional wild fruit picking, and turn instead to the less laborious cultivation of imported varieties. In some parts of the country, though, wild berries are still patiently picked in the woods and processed into delicious preserves and drinks. Indeed, the community has an innovative approach which has taken it beyond the arena of family consumption and led it to turn to processed foodstuffs which can be sold throughout the country. Its members include a woman producing jam from the zone of Lika, a producer of a juniper spirit from a village on the Slovene border, and a man producing a wild blueberry syrup from Skrad.

PRODUCTION AREA
Primorsko-goranska Zupanija and Licko-senjska Zupanija

COMMUNITY COORDINATOR
Kurbekovic Nedzib
tel. +385 51810351
gorje@ri.t-com.hr

Boretice grape-growers and winemakers

Boretice is a village in south Moravia, in the heart of Central Europe's oldest and best viticultural area, where grapes were grown as far back as the 9th century. Here the Trojak family grows a number of typical Central European grapes (Gruner Veltliner, Neuburger, Silvaner, Welsch Riesling and Blaufrankisch) and produces a range of wines using traditional vinification techniques, with even the yeasts being produced on the estate. The property divides into two: one part has sandy soils which are particularly suitable for whites; the other has soils rich in magnesium, which are idea for reds.

PRODUCTION AREA
Boretice, Jihomoravsky kraj

COMMUNITY COORDINATOR
Richard Stavek
tel. +420 602582589
richard.stavek@vinarskyobzor.cz

Chrámce fruit producers

This farm, founded in the 17th-century, is still run by the family who took it over in 1829, becoming organic in the 1990s. It originally concentrated on growing a number of local fruit varieties. Then, more recently, it also started to raise sheep for wool, meat and manure. Mostly there are just four people who tend the farm but the whole village of Chramáce gets involved when it comes to the picking and processing. The fruits grown – apples, pears (most notably the Koporecka, Ananaska and Salander varieties), morello cherries, apricots and plums – produce jams, fruit juices, dried fruits and alcoholic drinks.

PRODUCTION AREA
Chrámce, Karlovarsky kraj

COMMUNITY COORDINATOR
Jirí Syrovátka
tel. +420 723875817
info@zameckesadychramce.com

Breeders and crop farmers

This community, joined in a cooperative, farms using sustainable methods and with respect for the land. It rears indigenous sheep and goat breeds which graze on pasture; it grows and harvests vegetables, such as millet, buckwheat, mallow and hops, which are not often found but are of medicinal as well as nutritional benefit; and it manages game reserves through selective control and hunting. On the pasturelands it also rears geese of the indigenous Bohemia breed, which is noted for the quality of its meat. Goose keeping has ancient traditions in the area, although these were lost during the years of socialism.

PRODUCTION AREA
Jihoãesky kraj and Jihomoravsky kraj

COMMUNITY COORDINATOR
Boris Hucko
tel. +420 732748495
hucko@af.czu.cz

Jablonec nad Nisou bread makers

The Hradecky family, from the town of Jablonec nad Nisou, make bread using exclusively local flours. Their only assistance comes from two associates who handle sales. In 1999 they added a macrobiotic bread to their range. This comes entirely from sprouted grain, from which all impurities are removed. Their policy is to use oil instead of the more common pig's lard; to avoid all preservatives, colorings, emulsifiers and yeasts; and to ensure that flavor is enhanced purely by salt and cumin rather than chemical additives. The community initially sold the bread simply to local shops but is now trying to increase its distribution area and is offering regular supplies of fresh bread to a wider spread of restaurants, shops and private individuals.

PRODUCTION AREA
Jablonec nad Nisou, Liberecky kraj

COMMUNITY COORDINATOR
Tomas Hradecky
tel. +420 483319660
tomas.hradecky@volny.cz

Kutná Hora wine producers

Kutná Hora is a glorious Bohemian town lying a few dozen kilometers from Prague. It is ideally suited to viticulture, especially because of its mild climate. The community is formed of five people who produce wine by traditional methods and who are trying to relaunch and redevelop local viticulture. Cuvée Barborka is a deep red dessert wine; Traminer Cerveny is sweet and soft; Svatovavrinecké (its name in the Czech Republic and Slovakia) or Saint Laurent, is a characterful wine with an intense, silky taste; Müller Thurgau has good acidity and aromatic, floral notes.

PRODUCTION AREA
Kutná Hora, Stredocesky kraj

COMMUNITY COORDINATOR
Stanislava Rudolfská
tel. +420 736536489
vinokutnahora@seznam.cz

Prague organic producers

The Rezonance association groups 12 companies which acquire organic produce from small farms in the mountains and distribute it, either fresh or processed, to restaurants and specialized shops in and around Prague. Their dairy products include yogurt, ricotta and spiced young cheeses, all made by local methods from unpasteurized goats' milk; and *brynza*, a quark-like cheese made daily from sheep's milk, also unpasteurized. They also handle vegetables, bread, spices and buckwheat, these too coming from small mountain communities who thereby gain an important source of income from their sale. None of the foods has any chemical additives and all have Kez organic certification.

PRODUCTION AREA
Praga, Stredocesky kraj

COMMUNITY COORDINATOR
Sarka Dittrichova
tel. +420 608106141
sarka.dittrichova@volny.cz

Cider makers of Fejø

This community is made up of a group of apple growers and cider makers on the island of Fejø, north of Lolland. The apples, which are mostly Danish varieties, are grown over roughly three hectares of land and the fermented beverage takes about six months to produce. During the last century the island has acquired a certain popularity for its apples, which are mainly used to produce cider but are also used to make jams and fruit preserves. Cider was originally produced using French apples: choosing Danish ones was intended to give cider a decidedly more national character. Two years ago they started producing a completely additive-free organic cider. The fermented apple juice is placed in Champagne bottles and allowed to ferment for at least two months before going on sale.

PRODUCTION AREA
Island of Fejø, Storstrøm Amt

COMMUNITY COORDINATOR
Winter Kai
tel. +45 54722121
kai@kernegaarden.dk

Food producers of Bornholm

This community is based in Åakirkeby, a town on the island of Bornholm, in the Baltic Sea. Its members are also responsible for the distribution of the island's high quality produce – mostly vegetables and fish. Fishing takes place from the cliffs or from fishing boats where sea trout, salmon, cod, needlefish, sole and eels are caught. One of Bornholm's traditional products is smoked herring, which has been produced here since the Middle Ages. It has always been sought after and was exported in large quantities when the basic ingredient, the silver herring, was abundant. There were once around 50 smoke houses on the island, 25 of which were concentrated in the village of Gudhjem. Today there are far fewer, but most of these remaining smoke houses now have a wider range of activity. Smoked herring is excellent when heated in the oven, skinned by hand, seasoned with salt and accompanied by radishes and a raw egg yolk.

PRODUCTION AREA
Island of Bornholm

COMMUNITY COORDINATOR
Hans Jørgen Jensen
tel. +45 20423370
hjj@leader.dk

Food producers of Greenland

This community revolves around a small group of people involved in finding and developing several typical local products. Meat, a fundamental part of the diet at these latitudes, is salted by hand and matured naturally. Particular specialties include musk ox heart and tongue and haunch of reindeer. Aromatic herbs also play an important role in local cuisine. Many parts of the arctic angelica (known as the ginseng of the north), including the seeds, roots, stem and leaves are used to make various different products such as: jam, wine, flavorings for butter and curative infusions. Thyme, another very important herb in local tradition, is gathered between July and August, dried and used for making honey, aromatic baths, balsamic oils, soups, meat sauces, alcoholic drinks and as an antiseptic.

PRODUCTION AREA
Nuuk

COMMUNITY COORDINATOR
Anne Sofie Hardenberg
tel. +299 322808
ansohardenberg@greennet.gl

Food producers of the island of Fyn

This community is made up of two cooperatives that are mainly involved in the production of Rygeost, a traditional cheese produced exclusively on the island of Fyn, and the cultivation of Filippa apples, the fruit of a tree that was cultivated for the first time in a Danish garden in 1880. Rygeost is made using sour milk smoked over oat straw: it is eaten with rye bread, chives and radishes, or as a dessert with jam or rose jelly. Filippa apples have pale yellow skin with crunchy, juicy, white pulp and a sweet and sour flavor. The production is very limited and this variety is not available in shops. The island of Fyn has a long tradition of producing food (meat, fish, vegetables, fruit and cheese) and is known as the garden of Denmark because of its numerous apple, pear and cherry orchards.

PRODUCTION AREA
Island of Fyn, Fyns Amt

COMMUNITY COORDINATOR
Torben Folkmann
tel. +45 62222918
tf@phs.dk

Fruit growers of Lilleø

The Frugt fra Lilleø cooperative brings together five fruit farms on the island of Lilleø, north of the island of Lolland. Despite the excellent quality of the fruit that ripens here in the mild climate of the Danish southern coast, this cultivation was abandoned for economic reasons. The community aims to stimulate a new interest in the use of fruit in cuisine. They are currently reviving ancient local varieties of apples, pears and plums, which were replaced by other varieties better suited to industrial farming techniques. Products are sold with the cooperative's labels and the name of fruit grower is indicated on the packaging. The products come from trees that are over twenty years old. Fruit trees are normally cut down at between seven and ten years of age because their productivity decreases as they get older.

PRODUCTION AREA
Island of Lilleø, Fyns Amt

COMMUNITY COORDINATOR
Andreas Harder
tel. +45 22353714
andreas@meyerfood.dk

Organic produce distributors of Barrit

The Aarstiderne (seasons) association has been delivering 25.000 boxes of top quality organic produce (fruit, vegetables, fish, meat, wine, cheese etc.), each week to peoples' homes in the town of Barrit, on the east coast of the Jutland peninsula, since 1999. Customers can choose between 600 products that are delivered along with information on the farms that produced them, the production techniques employed, the recipes used to make them and biographic statements about the cultivators. The association employs 110 people, providing organic farmers with a commercial outlet and enticing consumers to buy quality food. The products they sell include the Diverse Raavarer range, a brand with a series of products that have been certified organic by the farms of Barritskov, Billeslund and Krogerup including: wheat flour, rye flour, oats and nettle tea.

PRODUCTION AREA
Vejle Amt

COMMUNITY COORDINATOR
Thomas Harttung
tel. +45 702660066
th@aarstiderne.com

Dried and Smoked Flounder Producers

Fish is one of the most widespread foods in Estonia and one of its most important resources, particularly when dried or smoked. Flounder (*lest* in Estonian), caught between mid June and September, is one of the species most often used for smoking or dying. On the island of Saaremaa, the country's largest, there are still some families who smoke flounder at home. The community is formed of seven people from Nasva, a village on the Nasva river, who carry out this process traditionally. The flounder is cleaned, baked for an hour in an oven and then smoked gently over alder on a stone hearth. It is best enjoyed spread with butter and served with baked potatoes in their skins. Dried flounder is prepared by first salting it, using either dry salt or brine, and then hanging it in the open air for a week. It is eaten cut into small strips, partnered by beer.

PRODUCTION AREA
Nasva, Saaremaa island

COMMUNITY COORDINATOR
Tiina Mai
tel. +372 5265511
valgeee@hot.ee

Bakers and food cultivators of Ekenås and Nagu

This small group is made up of several bakers-patissiers and food cultivators on the Åland Islands. Bread, a fundamental part of the Nordic diet, is made using traditional methods with a strong preference for rye, the main ingredient of Scandinavian bakery. Soft, ring-shaped rolls and thin, crispy sheets are some their most popular oven-baked specialties, which are also sold on the Åland archipelago. These traditional breads have connections with different cultures (Swedish, Russian etc.) but still retain close links with their Finnish origins. Worth noting among the agricultural products are the Arielle potatoes. This autochthonous variety was proclaimed as the best potato variety in the archipelago in 2005 and is sought after far beyond the regional borders. The Bakers and cultivators that form this community are members of the Skärgårdssmak association, which promotes its products by means of training workshops and aims to support and raise awareness about traditional varieties.

PRODUCTION AREA
Ekenås and Nagu, Ahvenanmaa, province of Åland

COMMUNITY COORDINATOR
Marika Sundqvivst
tel. +358 1814986
marika.sundqvist@skargarddssmak.com

Bakers of Parainen

Varsinais-Suomi, literally translated as "Finland proper", is a bilingual area whose population has managed to maintain their Finnish roots despite having been dominated for a long time by the Swedes and the Russians. Here bread making is based around brown or wholemeal bread, which is typical of the northern European dietary tradition. The employment of natural methods and a respect for tradition are the founding principles of the small Axo bakery. The secret of their bread lies with the dough, which is softened with milk that is allowed to rest for at least two days before it is used. This trick gives the products prepared in the oven each day a longer life and a better fragrance. One of their specialties is rye bread, which is shaped into soft, round, flat loaves with a hole in the centre. In the past these loaves were stored by piling them up on poles in farm attics. The Finn Crisp, a thin bread also made from rye, is produced by using fermenting milk.

PRODUCTION AREA
Parainen, Länsi-Suomi

COMMUNITY COORDINATOR
Maria Axo
tel. +358 201552540
maria.axo@axo.fi

Beekeepers of Pirkanmaa

Three members of a family from Mouhijärvi, in the region of Pirkanmaa, have been professional beekeepers for many years now and have widened their activities to include the gathering of wild herbs and fruits. Their main product is honey, but this small company also offers pollen, propolis, wax candles and aromatic essential oils for use in baths and saunas. Produced by bees that gather the nectar of local flowers, the honey is collected in a completely natural way with refining processes reduced to a minimum and always carried out at very low temperatures. Different kinds of berries and other wild fruits that have been growing in this region for centuries, such as the cranberry for example, are used to make naturally flavored honey. The honey they make is both for the family itself as well as for sale: specialized channels and a network of farmers' markets also take it across the regional borders.

PRODUCTION AREA
Mouhijärvi, Pirkanmaa, Länsi-Suomi

COMMUNITY COORDINATOR
Marika Sundqvivst
tel. +358 1814986
marika.sundqvist@skargarddssmak.com

Fishermen of the Åland archipelago

The islands at the entrance of the Gulf of Bothnia, whose ownership was contested by Sweden and Russia up until the last century, are now harmoniously divided between Sweden and Finland. Despite the fact that over 50% of the population speaks Swedish, a good portion of inhabitants still maintain Finnish customs and traditions. Fishing is the main activity that eastern and western slopes of the archipelago have in common. In the past it was the primary source of subsistence and is a rich economic and cultural resource still today. The oldest and most traditional form of fishing is linked to the herring, which together with rye bread was the principle food source of the Scandinavian population. Considered as a poor man's food for many years, the herring is now eaten both as a light snack (even in the morning), as well as a starter or main course, and is often accompanied by sour cream and aromatic herbs.

PRODUCTION AREA
Ahvenanmaa, province of Åland

COMMUNITY COORDINATOR
Marika Sundqvivst
tel. +358 1814986
marika.sundqvist@skargarddssmak.com

Food producers and distributors of Åland

Skärgårdssmak, or "flavors of the archipelago", is an association of restaurateurs, shop owners, and agricultural and livestock farmers based in the islands spread out between Sweden and southwest Finland. Its aim is to promote the region through its quality products and to generate a tourist industry connected with the local gastronomic traditions. Food producers, restaurateurs and merchants can display the white wave (the mark of quality awarded by the organization) only after they have undergone a strict selection process. One of the main products they deal with are potatoes, which have been cultivated by farmers of the Finnish Åland for around forty years. They are usually eaten with fresh herrings and butter and accompanied with a glass of vodka on special occasions. Other products range from bakery products to fish, from cheese to meat and from aromatic herbs to alcoholic beverages.

PRODUCTION AREA
Ahvenanmaa, province of Åland; also the Swedish counties of Stockholm, Södermanland and Uppsala

COMMUNITY COORDINATOR
Marika Sundqvivst
tel. +358 1814986
marika.sundqvist@skargarddssmak.com

Sausage and Salami producers of Turku

Within a radius of 50 kilometers of town of Turku in southwest Finland around two hundred animal breeders raise cows, turkeys, chickens, wild boar, bison, sheep, ostriches and goats. They also supply local hunters and some butchers with game (deer, elk and roe deer). They produce cured meats, which they sell in small quantities to the restaurants of Turku and Tampere or directly to the public. Their traditional salami, a kind of black pudding, is called verimakkara, and they make three different kinds of sausage, laukkamakkara, ruusinamakkara and keskiaikamakkara. This last one dates back to the Middle Ages and is made each year in July, during the week dedicated to that period in history. The main ingredient of this sausage is pork, which is roughly ground and then flavored with fresh herbs, salt and pepper. It is usually grilled and served with raw cabbage leaves.

PRODUCTION AREA
Turku, Lånsi-Suomi

COMMUNITY COORDINATOR
Geick Gero
tel. +358 407314461
gero.geick@labskaus.inet.fi

Snail farmers of Lumijoki

This small community is formed of two snail farmers from Lumijoki, a village south of Oulu, the capital of the province of the same name. In this town on the northern coast of Finland, facing the Gulf of Bothnia, there is a old farm where they have been using traditional methods to breed snails for many years. There is also a restaurant that opened some time ago, which uses snails to create delicious recipes. The snails are carefully prepared: after being immersed in boiling water and shelled, they are marinated in herbs, spices and white wine and then incorporated into a paste made from garlic butter and locally produced blue cheese, and then finally placed in the oven. Snails bred in the Lumijoki farm are not for sale and can only be tasted in the restaurant attached to the farm.

PRODUCTION AREA
Lumijoki, province of Oulu

COMMUNITY COORDINATOR
Marika Sundqvivst
tel. +358 1814986
marika.sundqvist@skargarddssmak.com

Basque Pig breeders and processors

The Basque pig breed (Porc Basque, Euskal Xerria) has been present for centuries in the western Pyrenees between France and Spain, but 20 years ago it had almost disappeared. Then a group of 70 breeders, 12 small-scale processors and one delicatessen owner formed an association to revive it, adopting rules for its breeding and applying for AC status. The pigs roam free for almost a year, eating grass, acorns and chestnuts. They are mostly bred for their ham, which is obtained by salting the haunches, these weighing at least ten kilos. The hams are matured for at least 16 months in the open air, benefiting from the hot, dry *föhn* wind that blows through the mountains. The Association de Développement de la Filière Porc Basque works in association with Euskal Herriko Laborantxa Ganbara, which operates in a similar way on the Navarra (Spanish) side of the mountains.

PRODUCTION AREA
Pays Basque (Euskal Herria): Pyrénées-Atlantiques (France), Navarra (Spain)

COMMUNITY COORDINATOR
Christian Aguerre
tel. +33 559939243
aguerre.christian@wanadoo.fr

Béarn Cattle breeders

The community comprises around 30 breeders grouped into the Association Intercommunale pour la Sauveguarde de la Race Bovine Béarnaise. There are currently just 128 head of the breed remaining, scattered in mixed herds; this compares with 300,000 at the start of the 20th century. The Béarn cow is hardy and fairly small, with attractive big horns, a straw-colored coat and white rings around the eyes. It is descended from the ancient Pyrenean Blonde and is the cattle breed best adapted to high altitudes. There are no longer any herds formed solely of Béarns, there aren't even any cheeses made solely from their milk. Therefore the community is working towards bringing back such a cheese which, as those who once ate it remember, was very rich with intense floral and herby aromas.

PRODUCTION AREA
Haut-Béarn (in particolar the Aspe and Lourdios valleys, up to 2,500 meters), Pyrénées-Atlantiques, Aquitaine

COMMUNITY COORDINATOR
Bernard Cimorra
tel. +33 559399958
slowfood.biarn@wanadoo.fr

Bleu de Queyras producers

Queyras is a valley in the Hautes-Alpes département, separated from Italy's Val Varaita by the Col de l'Agnel. A nature park since 1977, it currently comprises 11 townships. Although the area has always been devoted to tourism, there is a strong desire among its inhabitants to preserve its traditional farming activities, especially those tied to cheese-making. The community groups those producing Bleu di Queyras, a blue cows' cheese. The cattle are from the Tarine and Abondance breeds, and graze on mountain pasture, and a large number of the breeders still practice transhumance. The cheese, which is creamy and has abundant blue veining, has come to symbolize the quality of local dairy farming. As well as being part of the French Ark of Taste, Bleu di Queyras has also been certified by the Parc Naturel Régional du Queyras.

PRODUCTION AREA
Queyras, Hautes-Alpes, Provence-Alpes-Côte d'Azur

COMMUNITY COORDINATOR
Philippe Rostain
tel. +33 492579232
philippe@slowfood.fr

Breeders of Hardy Cattle from the Catalan Pyrénées

There are 50 breeders, 30 cowherds and two dealers in the Rosée des Pyrénées Catalanes association. At the heart of their activity, which is carried out on the eastern side of the mountain chain that separates France from Spain, are calves, cows and bulls, all from the hardy breeds Aubrac, Gasconne and Brune. The first of these originated in the Aubrac mountains in the southern Central Massif (Aveyron), the Gasconne came from the Pyrenean part of Gascony, while the Brune, descended from Alpine breeds, has been found on French mountain slopes since 1830. Apart from mother's milk, the calves feed only on local herbs and cereals, and pass much of their life grazing with the cows. They are butchered at five to eight months old, giving tender, flavorsome, pink-colored veal whose quality has been certified and which is under application for AC status.

PRODUCTION AREA
Prades, Pyrénées-Orientales, Languedoc-Roussillon

COMMUNITY COORDINATOR
Gilbert Lanau
tel. +33 468397440
info@gites-ruraux-catalogne.com

Breton Pie Noir Cattle breeders

The community comprises 350 farmers in the historic Vannetais zone of Brittany who raise the local Pie Noir cattle breed. About 20 of them are dairy farmers, another group is primarily involved in direct sales of the meat. There also exist other Pie Noirs reared in mixed milk-cow herds; others again are raised by simple amateurs, although in very small numbers The community is formed into the Société des Éleveurs de la Race Bovine Bretonne Pie Noir. One of its typical products is a buttermilk-like product sold under the name *Gwell*, but the more traditional cheeses are led by a *tomme*, pressed, not cooked, and one made with milk curd that recalls a Saint-Marcellin. The community's products are mainly for own consumption and direct sale in the region, most notably at the Douarnenez market, 20 kilometers north of Quimper.

PRODUCTION AREA
Morbihan and Finistère, Bretagne

COMMUNITY COORDINATOR
Jacques Cochy
tel. +33 240457344
cochy.jacques@wanadoo.fr

Brittany seaweed gatherers and processors

There are hundreds of people along the Breton coastlands involved in gathering and distributing edible seaweeds, and raising awareness of their benefits, and several more in seaweed aquaculture and processing. The geological conformation of the coastlands and the seabed, together with the tides and currents in the area, gives rise to seaweeds of great quality, variety and value. A quarter of the production is *kombou*, a brown seaweed from the species *Laminaria digitata*, which is used in sauces, soups, drinks and *bara-mor*, a traditional bread. The rest comes from around 20 other species of which the most important are *wakamé* (a cultivated species originating in Japan), sea lettuce, *Lithophyllum lichenoides*, dulse, *Himanthalia elongata* and porphyra.

PRODUCTION AREA
Bretagne and Manche, Basse-Normandie

COMMUNITY COORDINATOR
Matéo Magariños
tel. +33 467871139
contact@algues-tao.org

Châteauneuf-du-Pape producers

The community is formed of around 300 grape-growers whose grapes are used to made Châteauneuf-du-Pape, together with enologists and representatives of associations involved in the wine's production and sale throughout the world, an activity that involves 1,000 paid workers and five commercial undertakings. Production takes place on 3,200 hectares of vineyard in an area of the Rhône valley in Provence bordered by the towns of Orange and Avignon. The vines grow on gentle hills, and the soils are covered with round stones. Most Châteauneuf-du-Pape is red, with just 4% white, and is made from any of 13 grape varieties, mostly grown on small family-owned plots. It gained AC back in 1936. The wine has great ageing potential and is renowned worldwide for its excellence. Indeed, more than half the production is exported.

PRODUCTION AREA
Vaucluse, Provence-Alpes-Côte d'Azur

COMMUNITY COORDINATOR
Michel Blanc
tel. +33 490837221
michel@chateauneuf.com

Espelette Chili Pepper producers

Ten townships in the western Pyrenees are involved in the cultivation, processing and packaging of the Espelette chili pepper (*ezpeletako biperra* in Basque), which has appellation contrôlée status. The Espelette is the only hot pepper used as a spice to be grown in France and comes, as do all the varieties of *Capsicum annuum*, from America, probably from Mexico, arriving in the region in the 16th century. It belongs to the Gorria variety and grows in open fields on hand-weeded soils which are neither irrigated nor are subjected to any chemical treatments. The harvest lasts from October to December and the pepper undergoes a series of controls before sale, which include taste tests. It may be sold fresh or powdered; for the latter it needs to dry for at least 15 days in the open air. The community is formed of 90 growers, two processors and one sales cooperative.

PRODUCTION AREA
10 townships in Pays Basque, Pyrénées-Atlantiques, Aquitaine

COMMUNITY COORDINATOR
Gilles Billaud
tel. +33 559933013
billaud.gilles@fre.fr

Forain Pink Garlic producers from the Tarn

Lautrec, in the Tarn département of the Midi-Pyrénées region, is celebrated for the production of a glorious garlic, pink-speckled and with even-sized cloves. Its flavor, refined and slightly sweet, and its delicate aroma, make it just as appealing to the palate as it is to the eye. Unlike most garlic, which is plaited into strings for keeping, the Tarn's pink garlic is formed into *manouilles*, bunches, which will hang for several months in local kitchens. Most growers in the zone use mainstream, selected and certified varieties, for their pink garlic; only a couple of producers, who form the community, still use seeds of the traditional variety, Forain, having to reproduce them each year themselves. Their garlic is excluded from using the Protected Geographical Indication "Ail Rose di Lautrec" and from the "Label Rouge" quality certification system. The community therefore acts to defend the use of these local seeds.

PRODUCTION AREA
Lautrec, Tarn, Midi-Pyrénées

COMMUNITY COORDINATOR
Jean-Pierre Py
tel. +33 563759444
gianinicola@yahoo.it

Growers of grapes using animal traction

The 40 members of the community, who are scattered throughout France, are grouped in an association called L'Attraction Animale, whose title is a word-play between "la traction" and "l'attraction". All members grow their grapes using organic or biodynamic methods, employ indigenous yeasts for winemaking, and use no chemicals, either in their vineyards or in the cellar, apart from small quantities of sulfur dioxide when necessary. The unusual aspect is that they choose to work the fields using horse-drawn machinery. The group runs courses on animal traction to grape-growers throughout France (but especially in the Loire Valley) and forms a sounding-board for the exchange of ideas on all aspects of viticulture.

PRODUCTION AREA
Throughout the country

COMMUNITY COORDINATOR
Olivier Cousin
tel. +33 241594909
ocousinvin@wanadoo.fr

Haut-Languedoc food producers, breeders and restaurateurs

Art et Saveur groups 20 or so food producers, breeders and restaurateurs from the Haut-Languedoc, a region where nature provides a fascinating contrast, with the nearby Mediterranean in one direction and the southern rim of the Massif Centrale, which dominates the landscape, in the other. The producers and local restaurateurs work closely together, all the foods are processed *in situ* and local produce is given a high profile. The foodstuffs, which are grown using organic or ecologically responsible methods, include traditional old vegetable varieties, chestnuts, the Pardhailan black turnip (a Slow Food Presidium), free range chickens and trout raised in mountain streams. The community operates in close contact with Assiette de Pays, an association set up in the interest of consumers, based on the concept of partnership, reciprocal trust and professionalism among food producers and restaurateurs.

PRODUCTION AREA
Haut-Languedoc, west Hérault, Languedoc-Roussillon

COMMUNITY COORDINATOR
Hervé Leroy
tel. +33 467239207
ladonisrouge@wanadoo.fr

Jurançon White Wine producers

The Route des Vins du Jurançon community is formed of 60 independent producers, an enologist and four sales specialists, who have been working together for more than 15 years. Its prime objective is to improve the quality of the white wines throughout the area, which extends over 40 kilometers of the historical Béarn district, from Pau to the Pyrenees. The wines may be dry or sweet and are made from the Manseng variety, grown on sloping terraces and vinified using traditional methods. A further aim of the community is to devise marketing strategies that will assist its small producers, such as Wine Day, which attracts 9,000 visitors. The next step will then be to draw into the community other small-scale products, such as the Roussane de Monein peach, which comes within the French Ark of Taste.

PRODUCTION AREA
Pyrénées-Atlantiques, Aquitaine

COMMUNITY COORDINATOR
Gilbert Dalla Rosa
tel. +33 559026439
gilbert.dallarosa@wanadoo.fr

Loire basin fishermen

The community is formed of an association of 20 professional fishermen who use selective, eco-compatible, artisanal methods. Their trademark, Poissons Sauvages du Bassin de la Loire, guarantees that the fish is extremely fresh, of very high quality and comes from uncontaminated waters. During the stormy nights of fall and winter when the river is in spate, the fishermen make for the shoals of eels on their way to their reproduction sites in the Sargasso sea, fishing them with bag nets, but manage to catch only 13% . Between January and March, when the river rises again, they fish lampreys, using wicker or plastic creels. In spring comes shad fishing, using traditional barrier nets, or similar. Instead trawl nets or sweep nets are used to catch small fish for frying (gudgeon, bleak...)

PRODUCTION AREA
Pays de la Loire-Centre

COMMUNITY COORDINATOR
Philippe Boisneau
tel. +33 247238609
philippe.boisneau@wanadoo.fr

Maine Anjou Cattle breeders

The community, involving a dozen people from the Pays de la Loire region, is not only involved in rearing the Maine Anjou breed but in protecting it and increasing its numbers, given that the number of head started to fall in the 1970s and has now diminished considerably. Now that there is a resurgence of interest in the Maine Anjou and it has gained appellation contrôlée recognition it is more the traditional rearing method used by the community's farmers that is at risk: the livestock are exclusively grass fed and not butchered before 30 months old. The meat has excellent flavor, thanks to a considerable quantity of intramuscular fat. Most of the farms raising the Maine Anjou breed are concentrated in seven Pays de la Loir départements: Ile-et-Vilaine, Mayenne, Sarthe, Loire-Atlantique, Maine-et-Loire, Deux-Sèvres and Vendée.

PRODUCTION AREA
Pays de la Loire

COMMUNITY COORDINATOR
Albéric Valais
tel. +33 243072294
upra-maine-anjou@unimedia.fr

Mercantour Massif Cheese producers

The Mercantour Massif, along the far west of the Alpine rim, is home to a wide range of dairy farming activities. Around 15 small producers in the area are dedicated to the production and sale (direct or at local markets) of high quality cheeses. The most important of these are the cows' milk *tommes*. These are non-cooked, pressed cheeses which are mostly produced during the summer months from cattle grazing on mountain pasture. Each producer and each valley gives a cheese of individual characteristics: the aroma of *genepì*, a grey or a yellow rind, Tomme de Brigue or Tomme de Vésubie... One unusual product is *cachaille*, produced mainly in the area around Ubaye, which is made from small pieces of different cheeses, seeped in *genepì* liqueur and left to ferment. There are also numerous goats' and sheep's milk cheeses.

PRODUCTION AREA
Mercantour, Alpes-Maritimes and Alpes de Haute-Provence, Provence-Alpes-Côte d'Azur

COMMUNITY COORDINATOR
Huges Fenouillaires
tel. +33 493021814
fromagerie.roria@wanadoo.fr

Mercantour Olive growers

Olive growing has been documented for over 2000 years in what is now the Alpes-Maritimes département, and has always been an important part of the economy of Nice and the Côte d'Azur. The ten members of the community work on the Mercantour Massif, the northerly limit for olive cultivation. The trees are almost all of the Cailletier variety, the only one permitted under the Olive di Nice AC, apart from a few examples of ancient local varieties that survived the severe frosts of 1956. The Cailletier, or Small Nice Olive, grows on the southern part of the massif and is well adapted to its marginal climate; additionally, traditional mountain olive cultivation methods are used, bringing maximum sun exposure. As well as olive oil, the community produces table olives preserved in brine and olive paste.

PRODUCTION AREA
Mercantour, Alpes-Maritimes, Provence-Alpes-Côte d'Azur

COMMUNITY COORDINATOR
Frédéric Soffiotti
tel. +33 493040881
frederic.soffiotti@wanadoo.fr

Pays Basque food producers

The Idoki association, based at Saint-Palais-su-Mer, groups about 100 small food producers who already have a general Charte de Qualité (Quality Charter) and specific production regulations, and who are seeking to create a collective means for increasing the added value of their products. The members produce a wide range of fresh and processed foods derived from milk, meats and grapes. Of particular interest is Ossau-Iraty, an AC cheese made with milk from local sheep breeds (Manech Tête Noire, Manech Tête Rouge, Basco-Béarnaise) whose feed is strictly controlled. The community also produces cows' and goats' cheeses, and raises pigeons, chickens, ducks, pigs, calves, rams and lambs. Those with vines can make the AC wine Irouléguy. Some members additionally produce herbs.

PRODUCTION AREA
Pays Basque, Pyrénées-Atlantiques, Aquitaine

COMMUNITY COORDINATOR
Maider Duguine
tel. +33 559658547
arrapitz@free.fr

Pays de Thau Oyster breeders

The community is primarily dedicated to breeding oysters in the lagoon in the center of the Gulf of Lyon. There are 900 hectares dedicated to the culture, using a system of semi-immersed tables or *palafittes*, the typical southern French system for mussel breeding. The oysters are sold under the name Bouzigue, the locality where the activity initiated. As well as its 750 oyster breeders the community also includes producers of the white wine, Picpoul di Pinet, made from the indigenous Picpoul grape, the perfect accompaniment to the oyster. The basin is surrounded by a 500-hectare, brackish, nature reserve. Some of the Thau basin oyster breeders have joined together to improve working conditions for the women producers and to adopt rules that respect the environment as well as the quality of their product.

PRODUCTION AREA
Thau Lagoon, Sète, Hérault, Languedoc-Roussilon

COMMUNITY COORDINATOR
Manuel Di Vecchi Staraz
tel. +33 665157838
manuel.divecchi@ensam.inra.fr

Producers of the Sweet Basque Chili Pepper

The community groups around 20 producers of the sweet chili pepper, *biper etzia*, from the Pays Basque agricultural region and neighboring Seignanx. The variety has been progressively selected and adapted to local conditions by generations of small farmers, often amateurs. These days, whether picked while still green or when more mature and red, it forms an essential part of local cooking, being used in dishes such as omelets, *piperade* (a sort of pepper-based ratatouille) and *axoa*, a Basque beef stew. The community members, who have formed themselves into a union, have created a Charte de Qualité (Quality Charter) for the pepper, a set of production rules that ensures a good, clean product, which is produced by hand and involves the use of only natural fertilizers.

PRODUCTION AREA
Landes and Pyrénées-Atlantiques, Aquitaine

COMMUNITY COORDINATOR
Jean Michel Urruty
tel. + 33 559376569
aguerra.christian@wanadoo.fr

Provençal Goat breeders and producers of Banon Cheese

The community comprises 40 producers of Banon and *tomme* from Haute-Provence, who come under the Syndicat Interprofessionnel de Défense et de Promotion du Banon. They are divided into 18 cheese-makers using milk from their own goats, 19 milk producers, two processors and one maturer. Banon, whose name comes from a village in the Alpes de Haute-Provence département, is a goats' cheese which is ripened in chestnut leaves. The Provencal goats are very hardy animals which are well adapted to the region's dry, windy climate; and the wide variety of wild plants (lavender, thyme...) growing in its soils give their milk, and the cheeses made from it, great flavor. The producers have succeeded in obtaining AC recognition for Banon and this, plus the interest it stimulated, has led to a revival of the *tomme* too.

PRODUCTION AREA
Alpes de Haute-Provence, Provence-Alpes-Côte d'Azur

COMMUNITY COORDINATOR
Joël Corbon
tel. +33 492730154
joel.corbon@wanadoo.fr

Provence vegetable producers and consumers

The Les Olivades AMAP (Association pour le Maintien de l'Agriculture Paysanne) is a "proximity network" and involves three organic/biodynamic vegetable growers, each of which has a pool of around 60 consumers who underpin its activities. The vegetables are grown on market gardens on the outskirts of towns, a practice which is at risk of disappearing; yet, where they can be maintained, traditional landscapes and culture will be preserved too. At the beginning of the season every consumer in the group commits to purchasing a part of what is produced, which is received as a weekly basket of goods. It is a fair trade system which combines production ethics and social ethics. Les Olivades, created five years ago, is the largest AMAP in France in terms of the number of baskets distributed, and has become the model for the 300 or so AMAPs currently in existence.

PRODUCTION AREA
Var, Provence-Alpes-Côte d'Azur

COMMUNITY COORDINATOR
Denise Vuillon
tel. +33 494300313
denise@olivades.com

Pyrenean Goat breeders

The hardy Pyrenean goat, historically found throughout the entire Pyrenees mountain chain, has always formed an important part of the local diet and been widely used in its cooking. The principal products of the community's 150 members, who work in the mountain highlands, are goats' cheeses, kid meat and, in smaller measure, charcuterie and pâtés. The animals feed mainly on mountain pasture. The cheeses are made between April and fall; the *crottins* are made with a milk curd, the *tomes*, which are pressed but not cooked, with a rennet curd. The kids follow their mothers to the summer pasture before being sold at between three and seven months old. The community breeders, and others sympathetic to their cause, are coordinated by the La Chèvre de Race Pyrénéenne association.

PRODUCTION AREA
Ariège and Hautes-Pyrénées, Midi-Pyrénées, and Pyrénées-Atlantiques, Aquitaine

COMMUNITY COORDINATOR
Monique Lahitette
tel. +33 559396413
slowfood.biarn@wanadoo.fr

Seed producers

The community, based in Alès, in Languedoc, comprises around 30 organic producers of seeds from ancient fruit and vegetable varieties, together with a network of voluntary associates who sell them at fairs throughout France, all grouped in the Kokopelli association. This was founded in 1999 and is pledged to the production and free circulation of seeds, and the protection of biodiversity in vegetable matter. It lists 2,500 varieties, all with organic certification; numerous others are sold directly by members who reproduce and grow one or more particular types. An important part of Kokopelli's work is the gifting of seed varieties to Third World countries, especially India and parts of Africa, where the association runs training activities and seed collection centers.

PRODUCTION AREA
Throughout the country

COMMUNITY COORDINATOR
Jacques Debeaud
tel. +33 466300055
Kokopelli.semences@wanadoo.fr

Tanche Olive Oil producers

Olive production around Nyons, a township once under the rule of the Dauphin and now part of the Drôme département, has long been of note and its olive groves now cover 600 hectares. Both the olives and their oil received a certificate of provenance in 1968 and then, in 1994, gained AC status. The Nyons cooperative groups more than a thousand producers and associate workers; there are others who produce oil within the delimited area but prefer not to apply for AC recognition. The variety grown for both oil and table olives is Tanche, a small, dark-colored variety with a wrinkly skin. The fruit is handpicked and cold-pressed, and the oil extracted in vertical presses. The virgin oil is then allowed to settle naturally, the aqueous juices and solids separating out without the use of centrifuges.

PRODUCTION AREA
Drôme, Rhône-Alpes

COMMUNITY COORDINATOR
Philippe du Roy de Bliquy
tel. +33 688235313
philippe.duroy@free.fr

Transhumance shepherds from Les Trois Vallées Béarnaises

The Association des Bergers et Éléveurs Transhumants des Trois Vallées, which was formed in the 1990s to defend the interests of the shepherds and dairy farmers of the high mountain lands, groups 60 of the 200 shepherds in the region who practice transhumance. The animals – sheep, goats and cattle, all of indigenous breeds – are reared for the production of cheeses. Traditional methods are used for mountain cheeses, but their superb quality has no official certification and is not reflected in their price. The transhumance lasts from June to September, and additional journeys are undertaken whenever fresh pasture is required. The mountain cheeses are made in huts which have no electricity and which are traditionally disinfected with stinging nettles. Each morning that morning's milking, together with the milk from the previous evening, is placed in a cauldron where the cheese-making takes place. After being salted the new cheeses are left in cool locations to ripen.

PRODUCTION AREA
Ossau, Aspe and Bareteous valleys, between 1,500 and 2,500 meters, Haut-Béarn, Pyrénées-Atlantiques, Aquitaine

COMMUNITY COORDINATOR
Joseph Paroix
tel. +33 559826424
slowfood.biarn@wanadoo.fr

Trébons Sweet Onion producers

The community is a cooperative grouping around 15 farmers from the Adour valley who produce the Trébons sweet onion. The village of Trébons is close to Bagnères-de-Bigorre where growers traditionally acquired seeds of the variety. It is elongated, has a sweet taste and is eaten between May and September, initially fresh and later dried. The sprouts are used for food too, and are picked in the spring. All picking and packing is carried out by hand. In the past, the onion formed subsistence farming: the only income came from the small quantities left after family consumption, which were sold on local markets. Today the Trébons sweet onion is at risk of extinction and the cooperative's objectives are to safeguard its survival; to ensure that their work, which is a source of pride, continues; and to set up collective working methods.

PRODUCTION AREA
Trébons, Hautes-Pyrénées, Midi-Pyrénées

COMMUNITY COORDINATOR
Christian Duboé
tel. +33 562910880
chduboe@wanadoo.fr

CHEMIN FAISANT

The artistic duo Chemin Faisant (Along the way) is made up of Frédéric Gana and Tifenn Hervouët, and its activities reflect a huge commitment to sustainable agriculture. Frédéric is a photographer while Tiffen is an actress and narrator; they have traveled all over France together, with their art, exploring different types of agricultural production that respect the environment. During their first tour in 2005, they visited 82 farms, and in the Summer of 2006, they traveled the country with a theatrical performance that was born out of their first meetings.

AREA OF ACTIVITY
The entire Country

COORDINATOR
Frédéric Gana
tel. +33 609424973
cheminfaisant@loalabouche.org

Ahle Wurscht producers of Northern Assia

Long considered as a fundamental part of local culinary culture, the Ahle Wurscht is a salami made from pork meat and fat taken from adult pigs weighing at least 150 kilos. The meat and fat is ground and seasoned with saltpeter, salt, pepper, sugar, garlic soaked in cognac or rum, and sometimes also with mustard or cumin seed. It is then stuffed into guts of various different sizes and left to mature for between two to nine months in clay-walled cells; it is also sometimes smoked over birch wood. The sanitary-hygiene restrictions brought in the 1960's and the advent of more profitable industrial butchery techniques led to the reduced consumption of this traditional salami. The community, an association of animal breeders, merchants and quality inspectors, aims to preserve the traditional food culture of Assia, where they still breed the local variety of pig and still prepare the Ahle Wurscht using traditional methods.

PRODUCTION AREA
North Hessen

COMMUNITY COORDINATOR
Gerhard Müller-Lang
tel. +49 56518980
info@muller-land.de

Animal breeders and dairy farmers of Langenburg

The community of Langenburg, on the Hohenlohe plateau in Baden-Württembug, is made up of around fifteen people including animal breeders, dairy farmers and butchers involved with East Friesian sheep (Ostfriesisch). The animals are raised to produce unpasteurized cheeses, sausages, salami and choice cuts of meat. The cheese production includes blue cheese (made from sheep's milk and animal rennet, enriched with mould cultures and matured for at least three months), hard rock (an extra mature and particularly hard cheese) and agrino (made with sea salt and formed into special shapes). The sheep and lambs graze freely on the Jagsttal enjoying a cool dry climate. The mutton salami, made by five different organic butchers, is produced using natural gut. A small network of delicatessens, butcher shops and regional markets handles the community's produce.

PRODUCTION AREA
Langenburg, Baden-Württemberg

COMMUNITY COORDINATOR
Norbert Fischer
tel. +49 7905475
roque-blue@gmx.de

Bakers of Nordrhein-Westfalen

The Cibaria bakery in Münster sources the ingredients for its bakery produce – cereals and eggs – directly from four local farmers. The bakery employs around forty women who take care of the various phases of production including: the daily grinding of the cereals in the bakery's two mills, the preparation of around 30 different kinds of wholemeal, rye, corn and spelt breads and the direct sale of the finished products. The bakery also collaborates closely with local schools, in providing dietary education, whilst a network of canteens, regional markets and organic produce retailers provides the ideal outlet for the sale of their products. Wholemeal brown bread comes in numerous different variations in most Northern European countries. Here however, it maintains a particularly strong link with the past dietary customs of this region, especially around the town of Münster, which is well known for its substantial and hearty cuisine.

PRODUCTION AREA
Nordrhein-Westfalen

COMMUNITY COORDINATOR
Rike Kappler
tel. +49 25167547
rike.kappler@cibaria.de

Beekeepers of Baden-Württemberg

Several selected, traditional beekeepers based in South Germany have united to form an association to safeguard the traditional production of honey and challenge the use of GM products. Honey is produced raw, and only when it is produced with great care can it avoid being manipulated and drastically changed. The honey made by Deutscher Berufs- und Erwerbsimkerbund comes in around forty different varieties, which are selected in close association with the local vegetation. In fact, the beekeepers of Baden-Württemberg also gather and select wild aromatic and medicinal herbs as well as making honey. Distribution takes place via a network of small local markets and, despite the fact that the size of the association has grown over the past few years to include over 200 producers, the selection criteria are as strict as ever and are based entirely on organic methods of production.

PRODUCTION AREA
Baden-Württemberg

COMMUNITY COORDINATOR
Jürgen Binder
tel. + 49 1701857424
juergen.georg.binder@web.de

Beekeepers of Nordrhein-Westfalen

Only one quarter of the demand for honey in Germany is satisfied by the national production. At the same time the bee breeding in Northern Renania, which has been involved in this business for over a century, has reduced by over 80% in the past decade. The beekeepers of this community work near the small town of Much. They employ traditional methods without using chemical substances or antibiotics and only use organic acids for mite disinfestation. Moving honeycombs and thermal treatments on the finished product are not allowed either. Made by bees that gather the nectar of regional plant species with excellent balsamic properties (bitter almond, clover, eucalyptus and lime tree), the honey is sold through a network of organic shops and supermarkets. It is available in different seasonal varieties: early (available from the beginning of June), summer (end of July), forest (collected every seven years during the hottest months of the year); they also produce pollen and honeydew.

PRODUCTION AREA
Much, Nordrhein-Westfalen

COMMUNITY COORDINATOR
Marianne Kehres
tel. +49 220682855
b.kehres@bgkev.de

Breeders of the Colored Pigs of Bentheim

In Northern Renania they raise an autochthonous, medium-sized kind of pig with broad dangling ears and white spots and circular grey markings on its body. The animals are long-lived, have a thick layer of fat and produce meat with a high fat content. This is the colored pig of Bentheim. The rapid decline in numbers of this breed witnessed in the last few years and the impossibility of cross-breeding with other varieties have driven several producers to form an association to protect this valuable resource. The community is made up of five breeders, a butcher and a merchant. The association is involved in raising these pigs as well as a local breed of cattle; they also handle the butchering and direct sale of the finished products. They make around one thousand products each year from smoked frankfurters to ham on the bone. The products are air-dried and matured for a period of between three months to one year and are seasoned only with sea salt and organic spices.

PRODUCTION AREA
Nordrhein Westfalen

COMMUNITY COORDINATOR
Maria Büning
tel. +49 2554 8620
mariabuening@web.de

Cattle farmers of Limpurg

This association is formed of around sixty breeders who are also involved in the direct marketing of the meat they produce. The cattle, which take their name from the county of Limpurg, south of Schwäbisch Hall, an area that was annexed by the Württemberg kingdom in 1806, derive from a cross between the local red breed and the Allgäuer breed. Medium-sized and very strong, they are also known as Lein valley cattle. The Lein is a river that flows through the green hills and steep slopes of Hohenlohe, where the oldest cattle breed of Baden-Württemberg continues to thrive. The pasturing and feed, which is exclusively hay-based and without any soya or silage added even in winter, produce extremely tender and juicy meat. Two traditional companies butcher and sell the Limpurger Beouf de Hohenlohe protected brand meat.

PRODUCTION AREA
Hohenlohe, Schwäbisch Hall, Baden-Württemberg

COMMUNITY COORDINATOR
Dieter Kraft
tel. +49 790470007519
Limpurger@Rind-BW.de

Franconia Goat breeders

In the small town of Seybothenreuth ten people belonging to five different families raise a local breed of goat known as the Franconia goat (Frankenziege), as well as processing the milk and meat they produce. The Würnsreuth company employs organic farming methods: the animals are allowed to graze freely for the entire summer; they are fed with natural foods and butchered on the farm. The cheese-making business produces different kinds of fresh goat's cheeses, which can either be eaten on their own or as part of traditional meat dishes. The cheese is made by processing the goat's milk and is sold by the families directly both within and outside the region or origin. The meat is used to prepare a particularly tasty dish, Bocksbraten, which is a recognized specialty throughout Germany but originates from the southwestern area of Bavaria.

PRODUCTION AREA
Seybothenreuth, Bayern

COMMUNITY COORDINATOR
Robert Knöbel
tel. +49 9209 823
info@ziegenhof-wuernsreuth.de

Goat breeders and cheese makers of Irmelshausen

The preparation of various different kinds of un-pasteurized goat's cheeses and the raising of ancient autochthonous breeds (Toggenburger and Turingia) are the activities that link fifteen or so dairymen and animal breeders of Lower Franconia in Southern Germany. Goat products have a very long history in this region, which is reflected in the main local dishes. The fresh cheese known as Gäßkäse in the local dialect is made with the simple addition of natural spices, mainly garlic, horseradish, pepper and chili pepper. Another version of this cheese is made by maturing the cheese in dry, ventilated rooms for at least three weeks. The goat's meat is processed according to organic regulations in a small butcher shop near Irmelshausen. The cheeses and meat are sold by members of the community at local markets and through a few intermediaries.

PRODUCTION AREA
Irmelshausen, Bayern

COMMUNITY COORDINATOR
Anne Schöneberg
tel. +49 9764 1095
haschoeneberg@aol.com

Milbenkäse producers

Milbenkäse, or cheese with mites, is a true delicacy that has been produced in the Altenburger region of Turingia, on the border with Sassonia-Anhalt, for over three hundred years. It starts of as a low-fat, fresh, desiccated cheese made from goat's sheep's or cow's milk. The cheese is then matured in wooden boxes where it is brought into contact with special mites that aid the maturation process, give the cheese its distinctive aroma and give the cheese its long conservation properties. This difficult process takes from between three to six months to complete and requires an enormous amount of care. This cheese can only be made from the spring to the autumn, as the mites are not active during the winter. The average yearly production is between one and three thousand cheeses, which the Milbenkäse Conservation Consortium (made up of six families of dairy farmers), supports by directly organizing the sale of these products on the local market.

PRODUCTION AREA
Würchwitz, Sachsen-Anhalt

COMMUNITY COORDINATOR
Christian Schmelzer
tel. +49 170 5858793
christianschmelzer@gmx.de

Peat bog Sheep breeders of Diepholz

In the district of Diepholz, a nature reserve in Lower Saxony, the owners of three farms have joined forces to protect the Diepholzer Moorschnucke, a breed of sheep at risk of extinction. The landscape of this region is made up of heathland and wetland and is mostly covered by grass and birch trees. In the past, the land that these sheep used to graze was rich with peat – this is why the breed was named Moorschnucke (peat bog sheep). The animals are only allowed to graze on areas that have not been treated with chemicals. Accelerated growth and intensive farming techniques are not used. The roasted meat of Diepholz sheep is very tender; it has a slightly gamey taste and solid consistency. The varieties of grass that the sheep eat – heather, cotton grass, fiorin and aromatic calamus – provides them with good reserves of unsaturated fatty acids.

PRODUCTION AREA
Diepholz, Niedersachsen

COMMUNITY COORDINATOR
Dau Kai
tel. +495492 890
kd@hotel-toewerland.de

Potato growers of Svevia

This community is made up of around twenty farmers involved in the organic cultivation of rare, regional and local potato and vegetable varieties in the Kocher valley, on the border with Austria and Switzerland. They concentrate mainly on different kinds of potato, which were once widely diffused in the area but that are now under threat. The tubers are marketed directly, through a network that brings farmers into contact with traditional restaurants and delicatessens, Slow Food members and regional organic produce markets. These varieties are well suited to organic cultivation; they are not overly delicate and have a good resistance to disease. They are classified according to the consistency of the flesh (floury potatoes, firm and semi-firm potatoes), the harvest period (new or late harvest) and the color of the skin (red, light brown etc.). Each of these categories is then divided into four of five sub-categories.

PRODUCTION AREA
Baden-Württemberg

COMMUNITY COORDINATOR
Walter Kress
tel. +49 7139452464
kress@haaghof.com

Promoters of the regional produce of Oberes Werntal

The municipalities that overlook the Oberes Werntal have organized to form the Pro Bio Oberes consortium for the promotion of the traditional and organic products of their valley, situated in Lower Franconia. Although horticulture is quite well developed in this area, the raising of pigs and cattle plays a fundamental role here. The meat, in particular that of the Franconia yellow cattle, is used to make tasty sausages and salamis: Leberwurst (made from liver), Greifenwurst and Bauernweißer. All of these products are prepared by hand using exclusively local aromatic herbs and natural gut. These sausages, which can also be lightly smoked, are usually eaten roasted. Four organic animal breeders, a butcher and several collaborators (forming a total of 14 people), are involved in producing these products both for the respective families and for direct sale on the local market.

PRODUCTION AREA
Oberes Werntal, Unterfranken, Bayern

COMMUNITY COORDINATOR
Thomas Hemmerich
tel. +49 9721 941587
thomas.hemmerich@gmx.de

Snail farmers of the Swabian Alb

The Albschneck, in other words the snail of Swabia, is at the centre of a project that involves a butcher, three delicatessens, the Lautertal Tourist Board, a themed museum and a scientific committee, as well as three snail farmers. The culinary tradition of Swabian Alb (Schwäbische Alb) has many different dishes based on these snails – soups, hot and cold appetizers, pasta sauces – which during the Middle Ages were known all over Europe as the Swabian oyster. Regulations governing the collection of these snails as well as a registered mark protect the snails from initial checks that are carried out on the eggs right up to their sale through protected channels. Today there are five areas involved in the low-density breeding of these snails. In these areas the snails can grow by feeding on wild herbs for a period of at least two years before they are sold fresh, frozen or shelled.

PRODUCTION AREA
Schwäbische Alb, Baden-Württemberg

COMMUNITY COORDINATOR
Roman Lenz
tel. +49 7022212680
R.Lenz@uisgruppe.de

Spelt farmers of Franconia

Several farmers from Boxberg in Southern Germany have united to form an association dedicated to the cultivation and traditional processing of a cereal that many people have never heard of. Grünkern, also known as large spelt, is dried green spelt or rather spelt that has been harvested early and put through a drying process. More than five hundred years ago farmers used a single kind of local spelt called Bauländer Spelz. The members of this community cultivate this same variety on calcareous land and harvest this so-called farmer's spelt before it is fully mature and then dry it at 120-180°C in ovens fuelled by beech wood. The spelt is then crushed and dried once again, until it becomes a transparent green color. Spelt can be used in soups, pies, risottos and dressings for vegetable flans and salads.

PRODUCTION AREA
Boxberg, Baden-Württemberg

COMMUNITY COORDINATOR
Dietmar Hofmann
tel. +49 7930517
r-b-hofmann@web.de

Aspra Spitia food producers and processors

Aspra Spitia (which means "white houses") is a residential settlement created following the development of the Pechiné industrial estate in a remote corner of the Sterea Ellada, one of the most mountainous parts of Greece. The community is composed of eight women who produce over 40 foodstuffs following ancient recipes and using only organic local ingredients. Their products include *glikoxina kolokithakia*, made with sweet-sour zucchini; *oinomelo*, a condiment from wine and honey; and *tirokafteri* a sauce based on cheese, chili and olive oil. Their activities have a dual role: to give Aspra Spitia an identity, and to instill a new conscience into local consumers with regard to organic produce.

PRODUCTION AREA
Aspra Spitia, Fokida prefecture

COMMUNITY COORDINATOR
Maria Marinou
tel. +30 6979003882

Ios Caper producers

The island of Ios is an hour's ferry ride from Santorini. The caper plants (*Capparis spinosa*) grow wild on the rocky soils, their well-developed, highly-resistant root system allowing them to burgeon between stones and in cracks in walls. The plants carry out an important role in maintaining the water content of the soil, their wide leaves forming a dense carpet that limits transpiration. The people of Ios habitually collect caper flowers, leaves and fruit to flavor their dishes, but there is only one woman, assisted by her family, who produces capers commercially. The flower buds appear from May to August and are picked by hand, one by one, then preserved in salt and vinegar. The same procedure is used for the *kaparofila*, the leaves, although these are first blanched.

PRODUCTION AREA
Isle of Ios, Cyclades

COMMUNITY COORDINATOR
Claudine Pousseos
tel. +30 2286091469
caparios@yahoo.gr

Kavala Asparagus growers

Kavala is a city in northern Greece and the main port of eastern Macedonia. Here asparagus has been known and cultivated since ancient times: it is referred to in *History of Plants*, a work by Theophrastus of Eressos dating from 300 b.C., and it was often a votive offering in Egypt, Greece and the Roman Empire for good fortune and fertility (asparagus is considered to be a potent aphrodisiac). Today the community, joined in an association, has 25 members who grow two-thirds of the country's entire production of organically certified asparagus. As well as growing and selling it, they are involved in various promotional activities with cooks and restaurants, both locally and nationally, to encourage asparagus consumption.

PRODUCTION AREA
Kavala

COMMUNITY COORDINATOR
Fotis Litsos
tel. +30 6975873666
nestosp@otenet.gr

Kos grape growers

Kos is the third largest island in the Dodecanese and enjoys a marvelous climate, along with that of Rhodes and Crete one of the best in the Mediterranean. Its inhabitants farmed the land until the mid-1950s when the invasion of mass tourism led to the almost complete abandonment of agriculture, viticulture in particular. As a result the island is at risk of losing a vast food heritage. Now, this community, numbering about 15 people, has decided to combat the decline and improve the state of Kos's wines. They have replanted a hundred or so hectares of vineyard, some with indigenous varieties, some not, and are making several styles of wine, mostly white.

PRODUCTION AREA
Isle of Kos, Dodekanissa

COMMUNITY COORDINATOR
Maria Triantafyllopoulos
tel. +30 6948821669

Kythera beekeepers

The community is formed of around 20 producers, joined in an association, who use modern rational beekeeping methods. "Modern" here means the use of wooden hives which allow the honeycomb to be extracted safely, although the technique was developed by the ancient Greeks. The rocky slopes of the island of Kythera provide the bees with a vast number of aromatic Mediterranean plants from which to gain pollen. The one that most truly typifies Kythera honey is thyme. This flowers in June and July, carpeting the hills in a glorious mauve color and leading to the production of a unique, exceptionally fine, single-flower honey. When bottled it has a deep amber hue, an intense, flowery, spicy aroma from the thymol it contains and an unforgettable flavor.

PRODUCTION AREA
Isle of Kythera

COMMUNITY COORDINATOR
Yannis Protopsaltis
tel. +30 6977692745

Ladotyri Cheese producers

Mytato (a term which in Homeric times meant a sheepfold and/or a shepherd's dwelling) is the most ancient village on the island of Kythera, a place full of caves and an ideal spot for sheep farming. But now there is only one dairy farmer left producing *ladotyri*, a part-cooked, pressed cheese which is one of the rarest and most admired in Greece. The curd is broken up into corn-kernel size pieces and heated to 50°C. The cheeses, shaped like a small head (*kefalaki*) are first brined, then dry salted, and periodically turned and washed with salted water. When they have ripened sufficiently, they are put into a mix of olive oil and grape must where they stay for almost two months; this gives them a particularly spicy taste.

PRODUCTION AREA
Mytato, isle of Kythera

COMMUNITY COORDINATOR
Heleni Petrocheilos
tel. +30 2736033010

Lakonia Siglino producers

Siglino, a cured meat product that is almost certainly a legacy of the ancestral period, is still prepared traditionally in almost all households in Sparta, at least in those which still rear and fatten a pig. The animals are fed on milk, figs and kitchen leftovers, and so give flavorsome meat, much of which is eaten fresh at Christmas time, or prior to Lent. What remains is cut into strips and placed under salt for a few days before cooking with wine, water, oil, rosemary, pepper, cloves and orange peel. It is then put in small barrels, covered with oil (or lard) and a pinch of cumin. The resulting Siglino is used in omelets along with onions and tomatoes, and is the ever-present symbol of welcome to guests on dining room tables.

PRODUCTION AREA
Sparta, Laconia prefecture

COMMUNITY COORDINATOR
Maria Karambela
tel. +30 6948040478
karabmar@yahoo.gr

Local variety & breed conservers

Peliti (the word means "oak" in the Pontos dialect and the name was inspired by a large tree in the village of Dasotò) was founded in 1995 and is now one of the most important Greek NGOs. Its objectives are the collection, conservation and distribution of indigenous vegetable varieties and animal breeds. The organization arranges explorative missions to the most isolated parts of Greece. Some of the seeds from local varieties found during these missions go to the germplasm bank, the rest are assigned to Peliti's 150 associated farmers. The community members work throughout the country, circulating information, organizing meetings (including popular festivals) for seed exchange and publishing a catalogue of associated farms which gives details of producers, regions and varieties.

PRODUCTION AREA
Paranesti, Drama prefecture

COMMUNITY COORDINATOR
Panagiotis Sainatoudis
tel. +30 2524022059
peliti@peliti.gr

Messolongi Gray Mullet Roe producers

The community is based along the northwestern coast of the Greek peninsula, and comprises 15 fishermen and processors who use ancient methods to prepare gray mullet roe. The precious egg sacs of the female fish (called *bafes* in the local dialect) are put on ice as soon as they are extracted. They are washed and delicately shaped, then left to dry until their humidity has dropped by 40%, when they are dropped into liquefied bees wax at 150°C. This enables the roe to keep for a long time without losing any aroma or color. The earliest writings relating to Messolonghi gray mullet roe go back to the 12th century, coming from travelers who had the fortune to try this rare delight. It remains the pinnacle of the local diet to this day.

PRODUCTION AREA
Messolongi-Aitoliko Lagoon, Aetolia-Acarnania prefecture

COMMUNITY COORDINATOR
Zafiris Trikalinos
tel. +30 2109518574
info@trikalinos.gr

Monopigado food producers and processors

The Perek association is made up of about 30 women, under the charismatic guidance of Maria Mouratidou, whose background, like many other Macedonians, is interwoven with that of the Pontians, who fled from the region when the Soviets arrived after the second world war. The community produces milk and eggs from animals kept unpenned and prepares many foodstuffs, all from local organic ingredients, using traditional Pontos recipes. They include bread made with a 67-year-old starter culture, which is stone-baked in old wooden ovens; yogurt, inoculated with a *Lactobacillus* from the 1930s; and various traditional types of pasta, most notably *evriste*, a sort of dry, non-egg tagliatelle, rolled out with a special rolling pin.

PRODUCTION AREA
Monopigado, Halkidiki prefecture

COMMUNITY COORDINATOR
Maria Mouratidou
tel. +30 2396025305

Samos Olive and Grape growers

This community of six people cultivates vines and olive trees organically. The main grape variety used is the White Muscat, which most notably makes the sweet wine Samos. This comes from grapes which are left to dry on the vine for 4-5 days after they become fully ripe, stimulating a short natural fermentation inside the berries. The wine is aged in old oak barrels for at least two years. The same variety, again semi-dried, is used to make Pettimessi, a dense, sweet product of ancient origins that has almost disappeared. The community's oil, produced with the local Dopia olive variety, has an intense aroma of freshly mown hay, almonds and citrus. The community has also set up the Samos Culinary Club to increase awareness of the island's food products made from traditional local recipes.

PRODUCTION AREA
Ampelos, isle of Samos

COMMUNITY COORDINATOR
Pantelis Termat
tel. +30 2273094381
dopia@samos.nl

Tinos Pasta producers

Tinos is noted for its wealth of artistic splendors but also for its food traditions. Its hand-made pasta is particularly renowned, as are its many dishes based on the artichokes which abound on the island. Until 70 years ago, when industrialized pasta-making processes first arrived, pasta was made on a small workshop on the island. Over time this raised the importance of its pasta to the point where it became the island's distinguishing product. The aim of this all-female community is to preserve this gastronomic heritage and pass it on to the following generations. All the ingredients used in producing the pasta are organic. The community makes vermicelli, spaghetti and *chylopites* (short tagliatelle), all hand-rolled and dried by the island's sun and sea breezes. It also produces fruit and vegetable preserves including artichokes in oil, capers and dried tomatoes.

PRODUCTION AREA
Isle of Tinos, Cyclades

COMMUNITY COORDINATOR
Josefina Delatola
tel. +30 69777371581

Zakynthos dairymen

This community of almost 200 people, comprising breeders, shepherds, small-scale cheese-makers and distributors, works together to promote Ladotyri and Pretza, the two renowned, historic cheeses of Zakynthos. The first evidence of their production comes from the 17th century: originally nearly all those living in the hilly part of the island, with its wealth of inviting pasture, owned small mixed flocks of goats and sheep. And every family used the milk from their flocks to make cheese for their own needs, selling any excess in the larger inhabited centers. Ladotyri (made from a mix of goats' and sheep's milk and kept under oil) is still used in several local recipes while Pretza (a young goats' cheese) is ideal in hot weather.

PRODUCTION AREA
Lithakia, Kiliomeno and other townships, isle of Zakynthos

COMMUNITY COORDINATOR
Sotiris Kitrilakis
tel. +30 6944563677
kitrilak@earthlink.net

MEDITERRANEAN ASSOCIATION FOR SOIL HEALTH

Mash is the acronym of this no-profit association to protect the quality of the soil, which has its headquarters in Crete. Starting from the assumption (formulated by the American Rodale Institute) that healthy soil=healthy food=healthy people, the association talks with everyone who is involved in the health of the soil, those responsible and those who benefit from it, through regional groups of experts and researchers in this field. These groups provide farmers with information and support on how to apply organic cultivation methods, or those with a low environmental impact, in their farms. The tourism industry, which clearly relies on the health of the natural resources (earth, water, air) is involved in projects designed to promote sustainable farming and responsible tourism. And finally, Mash dedicates a great deal of its resources to educating in schools, professional people and families, to ensure that the general public will come to understand and accept that the health of the soil means the health of the community.

AREA OF ACTIVITY
Rethymno, Crete

ASSOCIATION COORDINATOR
Kostas G. Bouyouris
tel. +30 6947275821
info@edaphon.com

OIKO BIO

Born spontaneously in September 2002, this is a self-run network that now involves about forty people in different parts of Greece: farmers, artisans and cooperative producers who work side by side in order to keep alive the small-scale output of excellent products in their native country. A couple of official meetings are held every year to plan activities, which include participation in local fairs and markets, visits to the areas of production, but above all the creation of alternative market niches, where quality products can be promoted better. The farmers who belong to Oiko Bio adopt organic farming disciplines, and share the problems and limits of eco-compatible products with the cooperative producers, and today they can also count on a small shop where most of their output is now sold.

AREA OF ACTIVITY
The entire Country

ASSOCIATION COORDINATOR
Anna Chacholoy
tel. +30 6947443082
a_kritamo@hotmail.com

Baranya cheeses and traditional food producers

This community is located in Baranya country in southern Hungary, and is made up of eight producers whose task is to collect the mushrooms, black truffles, medicinal herbs and small fruits such as elderberries, cornelian cherries and other wild berries that grow in the 57 hectares of forest available to them, near the village of Kárász. The producers are building a small workshop for the production of jams, fruit juices and preserves to be made with the forest produce. An organic business in the village of Zselic also forms part of the community, raising ibex in the wild for the production of meat and semi-matured cheeses flavored with black pepper or paprika, with dried plums and apples or cep mushrooms wrapped in cabbage or broad-leafed garlic leaves.

PRODUCTION AREA
Baranya County

COMMUNITY COORDINATOR
Erdei Sandor
tel. +36 205499728

Breeders of indigenous Poultry breeds

Poultry has been reared in Hungary probably since the 11th century, and started with imports from the Asiatic area. Over time, crossbreeding with several varieties from the Mediterranean has led to the present-day poultry-types. At the beginning of the twentieth century, in order to fight off competition from other European breeds, the more resistant varieties – and also the more efficient ones from the point of view of egg production - were selected. The damage caused by World War II and the introduction of foreign varieties then put the work of selection in jeopardy, and only the institutions assigned to the control of agricultural quality managed to avoid the danger. Today, this association of 60 producers continues the work of safeguarding breeds, and also protects other types of poultry-breeding that has been going on in this country for centuries, such as turkeys, geese and ducks.

PRODUCTION AREA
Gödöllő, Pest County

COMMUNITY COORDINATOR
Istvan Szabolcs
tel. +36 302581542
szabolcistvan@t-email.hu

Breeders of the indigenous Gray Cattle breed

The Hungarian Gray is one of the most important breeds of indigenous cattle in Hungary. For a long time, it was exported into Western Europe, where it was appreciated for the high quality of its meat, but because of the introduction of new crossbreeds, it has been in danger of extinction. Only the reclamation work carried out by Professor Imre Bodó and later, by the Hungarian Association of Gray Cattle Breeders has prevented this. Currently, there are around 6000 animals reared by the 300 members of the Association who make up this community. Its meat, dried or combined with pork fat from the Mangalica breed of pigs, is used to produce sausages, - generally hot and spicy - while the fresh meat is grilled or stewed and flavored with paprika.

PRODUCTION AREA
Budapest, Pest County

COMMUNITY COORDINATOR
Imre Bodó
tel. +36 304450276
bodoi@hu.inter.net

Organic cereal producers

In Békés province in South-west Hungary, there is a cooperative near the town of Gyula, producing organic cereals and breeding poultry. The community's products are used in the preparation of certain types of pasta – based on flour, salt, water and eggs – that are typical of the Hungarian cooking tradition and are still eaten nowadays, on a daily basis, by the country people and shepherds. The pastas they produce are cut and processed in various ways: *tarhonya* are small gnocchi, irregular in shape, and with a more or less intense yellow color depending on the number of eggs used, and they are served in soups or meat dishes; *lebbencs* are wide and flat in shape and are also eaten in soups or with potatoes.

PRODUCTION AREA
Gyula, Békés County

COMMUNITY COORDINATOR
Simon János
tel. +36 309553831
simon@mail.globonet.hu

Organic producers in the Jászság region

This community, located in the Jászság area around 80 kilometers east of Budapest, comprises the Kossuth cooperative, made up of breeders and growers who use traditional, organic methods. The community's products give an idea of the region's food heritage, with cereals and pulses (such as wheat, maize, peas, and sunflower and pumpkin seeds), local breeds of animals (the Gray breed of cow, Mangalica pigs, goats, geese and chickens) and hams, salami and other sausages obtained from their meats. The community comprises around 30 people, who are also involved in lesser, but fundamental activities such as the preparation of jams, compotes and preserves based on herbs and wild berries – one of which is the famous elder-syrup.

PRODUCTION AREA
Jászárokszallas, Jász-Nagykun-Szolnok County

COMMUNITY COORDINATOR
Gábor Farkas
tel. +36 204430323
bfarkasgabor@yahoo.de

Organic vegetable producers

The Open Garden Foundation originated in Gödöllő, a small town in northern Hungary located a few kilometers east of Budapest. It is concerned with organic vegetable cultivation (potatoes, carrots, onions, beetroot and celeriac) in an area of around 7 hectares surround by woodland. The Foundation has created an important link between the farmers and the families of consumers, who are directly involved in the organization and purchase crates of fresh vegetables. A newsletter, a Website, a series of events for the community, an organic cafeteria and a children's summer camp round off the Foundation's activities.

PRODUCTION AREA
Gödöllő, Pest County

COMMUNITY COORDINATOR
Rita Harangi
tel. +36 203998131
harangirita@gmail.com

Penyige Plum Compote producers

Penyige plum compote (szilvalekvár) is made with the Besztercei and Penyige or Nemtudom varieties, which also grow in the wild. At the end of August, after the harvest, some of the fruit is pressed and cooked slowly in a copper pan. As soon as the fruit starts to break up, other whole plums are added, and the cooking is continued until the skins and stones are separated from the pulp. The compote is then sieved and the juice obtained from this (cibere) is thickened, with constant stirring. Several families take turns to stir the compote, which is ready when it "veils" the spoon. It is poured into small clay pots (szilke) and will keep for years. It is dark blue, almost black in color, with a dense consistency and an aromatic flavor; it is used as a filling for cakes or eaten at breakfast with bread and sour cream.

PRODUCTION AREA
Penyige, Tarpa, Kölcse, Milota, Kisar and Cégénydanyád, Szabolcs-Szatmár-Bereg

COMMUNITY COORDINATOR
Petra Tanos
p.tanos@studenti.unisg.it
Katalin Körösi
tel. +36 303269562
penyige@mailbox.hu

Szeged Paprika producers

This community is made up of four producers' cooperatives that grow Szeged paprika, and two producers who transform it into powder form. The variety gets its name from the Hungarian town where it was planted over 250 years ago by Franciscan monks. It was already widespread both here and elsewhere at the end of the nineteenth century, and was initially used as a medicine, but soon became popular in cooking as well. Its distinctive characteristics are its bright red color and its intense flavor, both of which are due to the soil in the Szeged area – enriched with minerals from the Tisza river – and to the sunny climate of the area. The processing of the fruit is a very laborious procedure: it is sown in March and harvested in September, and then the fruits are dried and finely crushed with grindstones; finally, the powder is sieved and packed.

PRODUCTION AREA
Szeged, Csongrád County

COMMUNITY COORDINATOR
Tibor Huszka
tel. +36 302575884
thuszka@invitel.hu

Tokaj-Hegyalja winegrowers

The members of this community are eight producers situated in the region of Tokaj-Hegyalja, which gives its name to the wine and has pedoclimatic features that are particularly suitable for wine-production, with its clayey soil, volcanic subsoil and a favorable microclimate. Factors contributing to this are the southern exposure of the slopes and their proximity to the Tisza and Bodrog rivers. Tokaj is a sweet, white wine, produced with grapes that have dried naturally on the plant, thanks to the action of *Botrytis cinerea* mould, and then added to the pure grape-must. In order for it to be good, it has to be refined for at least three years in oak barrels. The businesses in the community are all small or medium-sized, but unlike most small producers, who sell their grapes to large companies, these make and bottle the wine within their own organizations.

PRODUCTION AREA
Mád, Borsod-Abaúj-Zemplén County

COMMUNITY COORDINATOR
Norbert Monyok
tel. +36 47548033
monyokpinceszet@t-online.hu

Traditional food producers

Paloc Flavors is an association with over 100 members – country people, housewives, cooks and retailers – who produce, process and market handmade gastronomic specialties from their region (the Cserhát) in North Hungary. They make blackcurrant, redcurrant and apricot jams, they distill Palina (a liqueur similar to grappa), they raise breeds of cattle (such as the Hungarian Gray), pigs (like the Mangalica) and sheep (such as the racka or the merino); from the latter, they make fresh or smoked pecorino cheeses. The work of the association is aimed at making gastronomic traditions a factor for increasing the value of the area, not only by promoting the products in restaurants and sales outlets, but also making them a tourist attraction.

PRODUCTION AREA
Kozárd, Nógrád County

COMMUNITY COORDINATOR
Pal Hajas
tel. +36 302104308
euragro@globonet.hu

Breeders of Icelandic Goats and Sheeps

Icelandic sheep belong to one of the oldest breeds and have remained unchanged during the one thousand years of Iceland's isolation. They were once widely bred for their milk. Icelandic goats also date back to the time of the island's first human settlements. They faced extinction at the end of the 19th century and after a slow recovery they still number less than 400 heads today. The members of this community are working towards reviving the Icelandic dairy tradition and produce a series of traditional cheeses such as the Geitamjolk and Geitaostur goat's cheeses and the Saudemjolk sheep's cheese. The animals are fed naturally with aromatic calamus, willow, moss and berries. During the summer months they are allowed to graze freely in the mountains, whilst during the winter they are kept in farms and fed with food that was set aside during the summer.

PRODUCTION AREA
The Western Regions

COMMUNITY COORDINATOR
Ólafur Dyrmundsson
tel. +354 5630317
ord@bondi.is

Animal breeders and dairy farmers of North Kerry

In the northern part of Kerry, a predominately rural county of Munster, this community sets a good example for other food producers by providing information about alternative agricultural methods. The group's members raise cows, make un-pasteurized cheese and cultivate vegetables and lettuces, supplying local restaurants and markets with their produce. One particular cheese they produce is called Beal, a traditional hard, crumbly cheese made from un-pasteurized milk from organically raised cows. The rind is washed with water and salt; the cheese is matured for at least one month and can be preserved for up to a year, after which time it can develop blue veins. This cheese is produced exclusively by the Beal Lodge farm. It is mainly sold at the farm itself, in local shops and in farmers' markets. The name Beal refers to the town on the mouth of the River Shannon in which the cheese is produced.

PRODUCTION AREA
Kerry, province of Munster

COMMUNITY COORDINATOR
Kate Carmody
tel. +353 6841137
cait@eircom.net

Bellingham Blue cheese makers

This community is formed of around fifteen dairy farmers based in County Louth, in the northeast of the country, who have united to protect the area's ancient traditions. There are texts dating back to the 18th century describing the cheeses that were once produced in Ireland. In the 1970's several dairy farmers formed an association and began producing cheese again on a small scale in the rural parts of the island, thereby increasing the number of active dairy farms. The cheeses were often given invented names but were made using traditional techniques. This is how the Bellingham Blue was created. This cheese, made from un-pasteurized cows milk and flavored with herbs, is now very popular with consumers. It is sold in local farmers' markets and in a shop in Dublin.

PRODUCTION AREA
Louth, province of Leinster

COMMUNITY COORDINATOR
Peter Thomas
tel. +353 429372343
glydefarm@eircom.net

Cheese makers of West Cork

Based in the western part of County Cork, the members of this community are involved in animal breeding, organic fruit and vegetable cultivation and the production of meat and cold meats. One farmer in particular produces the Bolg Doire, a pork sausage smoked over birch or oak wood. Others produce Gubbeen, a cheese whose name derives from the Gaelic gobin, which refers to the name of the bay west of Schull where the cheese is made. After milking in the morning, the milk is brought to the dairy and poured into containers where the bacterial cultures and rennet are added. The manufacturing process requires a great amount of care: the rind must be washed every day so that the cheese can develop its characteristic flavor. The food producers collaborate with the Irish farmers' markets association for the sale of their produce.

PRODUCTION AREA
Cork, Province of Munster

COMMUNITY COORDINATOR
Giana Ferguson
tel. +353 2828231
gubbeencheese@eircom.net

Dairy farmers of Wicklow and Kilkenny

This community is formed of 20 food producers based in the southeastern counties of Wicklow and Kilkenny. They have not formed any kind of association regarding pasteurized or un-pasteurized cheeses, but their work nonetheless forms part of the battle to save a kind of production that is representative of the territory and rooted in traditions dating back to at least 18th century. In the 1970's an association of dairy farmers re-introduced small-scale cheese making to rural parts of Ireland, in a short space of time the number of active dairy farms has grown to about thirty today. This community is mainly involved in the production of two cows' milk cheeses known as Lavistown and Croghan. Even though these cheeses have a history that is only about twenty years old, they represent an important step in the preservation of the island's dairy farming tradition.

PRODUCTION AREA
Wicklow and Kilkenny, Province of Leinster

COMMUNITY COORDINATOR
Olivia Goodwillie
tel. +353 567765145
lavistownhouse@eircom.net

Food producers and educators of County Clare

This community is made up of around fifty food producers and educators that work in close collaboration with each other to promote the production and sale of traditional and quality foods amongst the consumers of County Clare in the province of Munster. The group works not only to spread awareness about manufacturers of quality foods but also to educate the food producers themselves, encouraging them to pay more attention to local food and introduce their products to the county's farmers' markets. The members of this community dedicate themselves to the production of a wide range of Irish products such as bread, cheese, smoked foods, butter and many others. Most of these products are sold at farmers' markets, with the aim of making the whole country's food production and distribution network sustainable in the years to come.

PRODUCTION AREA
Clare, Province of Munster

COMMUNITY COORDINATOR
Michael Gleeson
tel. +353 659056611
michael.gleeson@eiri.org

Food producers of County Tipperary

In County Tipperary, around thirty food producers work alongside cooks and teachers as part of a community that aims to promote taste education in schools. There is evidence dating back as far as the 17th century of a kind of butter produced by the local farmers that was so famous at the time that it was exported to Sweden, Denmark and France. Several members of this community produce Im Baile, or traditional butter, as well as soda bread, a typically Irish bread made using bicarbonate of soda instead of yeast. It is made by mixing together flour, bicarbonate of soda, salt and buttermilk: the lactic acid reacts with the bicarbonate of soda causing the bread to rise. It is usually served hot with butter. These and other products made by the community are sold in small local shops or at farmers' markets, and are also served in local restaurants.

PRODUCTION AREA
Tipperary, Province of Munster

COMMUNITY COORDINATOR
Peter Ward
tel. +353 6732596
peter@countrychoice.com

Organic farmers and growers of the West of Ireland

The West of Ireland Organic Farmers and Growers Association is formed of around 200 organic food producers dedicated to raising animals and growing vegetables. The community collaborates with the Carnaun National School, the only school in Ireland to have been granted organic certification. Environmental education programs have been part of the school's study plan for years and many students have gone on exchange programs with other European schools as part of an initiative known as "I eat therefore I am", whose central theme is food. The region in which the community operates has a rich tradition of zootechnics and dairy farming; fruits and vegetables also used to be cultivated here. In the last fifteen years the association's food producers have breathed new life into these traditional products as well as the local farmers' markets.

PRODUCTION AREA
The West Counties

COMMUNITY COORDINATOR
Kathleen Curran
tel. +353 935 5707
ccurran@ireland.com

Organic farmers of Rossinver

The Rossinver community of organic food producers is based in County Leitrim, Northern Ireland. Atlantic Organics is an association of over 150 local organic food producers, animal breeders, farmers and butchers. All the members of this association work towards the sustainable production of food that respects the local dietary culture. The food producers of this community place particular importance on raising local breeds of domestic animals. Some, for example, raise Irish Maol cattle; this breed has been raised in Ireland since the Viking era and is now at risk of extinction. Others raise Roscommon cattle, which have also been bred on the island for centuries. The products are sold directly from the association's headquarters and also in local farmers' markets.

PRODUCTION AREA
Rossinver, County Leitrim, Province of Connacht

COMMUNITY COORDINATOR
Lucie Kennedy
tel. +353 719855113
lucie@atlanticorganics.com

Organic food producers of County Leitrim

The Organic Centre association was founded in 1995 to promote organic farming in County Leitrim, in Northwest Ireland. Its members cultivate organic vegetables and herbs over 19 acres of land. They sell their produce through a system of community supported agriculture, which allows customers to order seasonal produce and have it delivered to their homes on a weekly basis. The produce is also sold to local shops and restaurants. Given the fundamental role of potatoes in Ireland, each year the farmers organize a festival on St Patrick's day (17th of March), to celebrate them. They also organize the Green Festival, which usually takes place in September and celebrates the area's history, culture and gastronomy. As well as promoting natural foods, the Organic Centre organizes organic farming courses and demonstrations.

PRODUCTION AREA
Leitrim, province of Connacht

COMMUNITY COORDINATOR
Helen Pinoff
tel. +353 719854338
organiccentre@eircom.net

Organic food producers of the Northwest

The Community Food Project represents nine urban vegetable gardens in which around 150 people are engaged in the production of organic fruits and vegetables; they also teach consumers how to make the best use of these products. The aim of the Cfp is to increase awareness of organic cultivation, the importance of the seasonal nature of the local produce and the nutritional benefits of eating more fruits and vegetables. The members of this community meet at least once a week in the urban vegetable gardens of the northwestern counties. The educational work carried out by the Cfp consists of publishing leaflets and magazines about the cultivation, use and preservation of vegetables. The producers are also involved in the development of school vegetable garden projects in 6 local primary schools.

PRODUCTION AREA
Leitrim and Sligo, Provinces of Connacht, Donegal, province of Ulster; Fermanagh, Northern Ireland

COMMUNITY COORDINATOR
Hans Wieland
tel. +353 719854338
hansorganiccentre@eircom.net

Seed savers

This community is represented by Issa (the Irish Seed Savers Association), which was set up in 1991 in County Clare, in the western part of the island. In 1997 the Foundation for the Conservation of Irish Genetic Resources and the Issa initiated a project to bring 48 Irish cereal varieties back into use. Also thanks to the association's support, in 1996 a collection of autochthonous apples, including the Appletown wonder and Ballyvaughan seedling varieties, was started at the University College of Dublin. With regards to cereals, four farmers are currently cultivating the Sonas and Tyrone tawny oat varieties and the Schmidt rye variety. Other cultivars of autochthonous Irish cereal varieties collected by the Issa include the Stormont arrow, Victor, Scotch potato, Eire, Avena strigosa, Cafferies and Wexford tawny oat varieties; the Old Irish and Glasnevin barley varieties; and the Carroll, Fane, Finion and April bearded wheat varieties.

PRODUCTION AREA
Clare, province of Munster

COMMUNITY COORDINATOR
Lydia Monemurri
tel. +353 61921866
info@irishseedsavers.ie

Sustainable food producers and consumers of Dublin

Sustainable Ireland is a cooperative based in Dublin and formed of 100 food producers and 2500 consumers. It was formed with aim of promoting sustainable living and agricultural methods in Ireland, starting off with the capital. The cooperative runs the Cultivate Sustainable Living and Learning Centre, in which the producers provide information and organize courses on sustainable farming. One of their main projects is the Green Map of Dublin, which will be available on the Internet and will provide information on traditional food producers, farmers' markets and companies that distribute quality foods. The cooperative also publishes books and magazines about food, holds courses on renewable energy and sustainable living and organizes events such as the Festival for Sustainable Living.

PRODUCTION AREA
Dublin, province of Leinster

COMMUNITY COORDINATOR
Sarah Fleming
tel. +353 16746415 - sfleming1706@gmail.com

Sustainable food promoters of County Clare

In County Clare, in the province of Munster, there is a small community made up of food producers, consumers and members of the Slow Food Erne-Garavogue convivium. This community is actively involved in the promotion of sustainable food that is produced in a manner that respects the environment, local traditions and animal welfare. Chefs, specialist resellers and other organizations such as the Organic Centre, the Green Living Festival and Green Box all collaborate with this community. Green Box is a project aimed at creating a network of local craftsmen and food producers, as well as guesthouses, bed & breakfasts and family-run hotels all across the country. The community promotes cultural exchange between people from different parts of Ireland that have different backgrounds, contributing to peace in the Country. It also organizes film and documentary screenings, conferences and seminars.

PRODUCTION AREA
Clare, province of Munster

COMMUNITY COORDINATOR
Oliver Moore
tel. +353 6568 42492
moore.oliver@care2.com

Sustainable food promoters of Cloughjordan

This community is formed of 10 inhabitants of Cloughjordan (County Tipperary) that have joined a project known as The Village. These people – some of whom are food producers and others not – have moved to the historic village of Cloughjordan with the aim of turning it into a model of sustainable living and food production. There are currently 132 dwellings in Cloughjordan, and three further public buildings are soon to be finished. The food producers are creating an organic farm with a fruit orchard (it will bear its first fruits in the next few years) and a farmers' market where members of the community and people from nearby villages can buy their produce. The aim is to create a sustainable village that will set an example for others not only with regards to the environment and food production but also for research and education purposes.

PRODUCTION AREA
Cloughjordan, County Tipperary, province of Munster

COMMUNITY COORDINATOR
Davie Phillip
tel. +353 876340697
davie@thevillage.ie

Andarinos producers of Usini

In the area of Logudoro, a few miles from Sassari, Usini is famous for its wines (Vermentino, Cannonau, Cagnulari), oil, artichokes and traditional local bread, pasta and sweets. Here most families and an artisan workshop still make andarinos, a sort of hand-made fusillo (spiral-shape of pasta) with durum wheat semolina, water and salt. The ingredients are mixed together for a long time until the dough becomes smooth and elastic. Then little pieces of dough are made into a long, thin shape, and are then rolled rapidly over a grooved surface which gives them a spiral shape. They are then left to dry in the open air, in special flat baskets called canistreddos. This classic pasta is made for festivals, and is usually served with ghisadu, a sauce made by frying together meat and tomatoes, with grated pecorino cheese.

PRODUCTION AREA
Usini, province of Sassari

COMMUNITY COORDINATOR
Salvatore Piras
tel. +39 079 382023
Pastificiopais@tiscali.it

Ansonica wine producers of the Isola del Giglio

On the island, which is a popular tourist destination, farmers are still cultivating varieties which are extremely old. One of these is the ansonica vine, a grape variety which is much more common in Sicily, where it is called inzolia. This wine has certainly been produced on the island for a very long time. In a book published in the 16th century by Andrea Bacci, *Storia Naturale dei Vini* (A Natural History of Wine), the writer mentions a white wine which Pope Paul III was very fond of. The vineyards are situated on small plots of land which a few producers have preserved or reconstructed according to traditional principles. All the processing is done by hand and the wine is produced without stabilizers or being filtered. Ansonica is a lovely deep amber color, with a high alcohol content and plenty of body. It has a wonderfully aromatic bouquet and a dry, slightly bitter taste.

PRODUCTION AREA
Isola del Giglio, province of Grosseto

COMMUNITY COORDINATOR
Francesco Garfagna
tel. +39 0564 806041

Aole and carp fishers of Lake Garda

Professional fishing, an important if not unique source of income in the past for people living on the shores of Lake Garda, is now experiencing a decline. This is partly because many of the traditions handed down by the fishermen have been lost and partly because of the different dietary habits of residents and tourists. The Cooperativa fra Pescatori del Garda, which has about 30 members, is trying to combat the decline in fishing. It sells shad, eels, fresh and processed whitefish; also Lake Garda carp, a member of the Salmonidae family which is endemic to the lake, and àole, a small, slender fish of the Cyprinidae (minnow) family which, for centuries, along with twaite shad, ensured the survival of the local people. The fishing methods used are traditional and do not harm the ecosystem. They use nets called remattino and volantino, and another special net, the bertovelli, for eels. Species threatened with extinction are not fished during the reproduction season and the catch is limited to market demand.

PRODUCTION AREA
Lake Garda, province of Verona

COMMUNITY COORDINATOR
Sergio Vernesoni
tel. +39 045 7420068
sergiovernesoni@libero.it

Artichoke growers of Chiusure

The community has about 50 members who grow the morello artichoke, which seems to thrive here, in the land of the Crete Senesi. Famous since the Middle Ages, artichoke cultivation is mentioned in documents kept at the Abbey of Monte Oliveto Maggiore, where it was cultivated intensively until after WWII. The artichokes were grown on the land below Monte Oliveto Maggiore and San Giovanni d'Asso, which generated 200,000 artichoke plants a year. After that, production diminished, reaching a record low of 250 plants a year. In 2003, the municipal administration of Asciano, in collaboration with a group volunteer group of local gardening enthusiasts from the village, who have now formed the Associazione Castello di Chiusure, began to make efforts to relaunch the cultivation of this type of artichoke.

PRODUCTION AREA
Chiusure, in the municipality of Asciano, province of Siena

COMMUNITY COORDINATOR
Ivano Scalabrelli
tel. +39 0577 707071
i.scalabrelli@virgilio.it

Artichoke growers of Perinaldo

The consortium was formed by nine producers who grow a variety of artichoke which can be distinguished by its purple leaves without prickles. They are collected from locally grown plants within the territory of the municipality between May and June. This type of artichoke originated in Provence, and was brought here by Napoleon's troops as they marched through Italy. It will withstand very low temperatures as well as drought, and requires no chemical treatments. These artichokes, which are a feature of every vegetable garden in Perinaldo, are included in many local recipes: in salad with flakes of Parmesan cheese, fried, stewed or baked in the oven. They go particularly well with meat and game and with the local Rossese and Vermentino wines. The cultivation of artichokes is controlled by a set of regulations which guarantees its traceability.

PRODUCTION AREA
Perinaldo, province of Imperia

COMMUNITY COORDINATOR
Francesco Guglielmi
tel. +39 0184 672234-338 3981160
info@francescoguglielmi.com

Artisan brewers

In Italy, companies producing artisan beer are highly diversified but share one common technical feature which differentiates their products from industrially produced beer: the fact that the finished product is not pasteurized. In the varied artisan brewing scenario, some artisans have developed specialist knowledge about beer and show sensitivity to the issues of sustainable production. For example, care about the origin of the ingredients (often chosen from what is available locally or procure them from ethical foreign markets), care about safety throughout the various stages of production, respect – creativeness often comes into play here – for the roots and traditions of the art of home-brewing, and interest in comparing their own products with those of other brewers and artisans of other gastronomic sectors.

PRODUCTION AREA
The whole of Italy

COMMUNITY COORDINATORS
Luca Giaccone
giaccone@gem.it
Enrico Lovera
enrico.lovera@libero.it

Artisan Cupeta producers of Montepaone

The members of the community are about 20 producers of the raw materials required to make this traditional kind of nougat, which dates from at least the 18th century, and the only remaining mastro cupetaro (master artisan) of the area. The cupeta is produced with honey, sesame seeds, flour and cooked must (almonds and citrus peel are a modern addition). The ingredients are used to make a sweet that was typically eaten at Christmas, once called the torrone dei poveri (poor man's nougat), but it can now be bought all the year round. The community intends to re-launch the ancient art of making cupeta, which is now declining because of a shortage of new artisans, to prevent the figure of the mastro cupetaro, a skill handed down from father to son, and which contributed in the past to the development of the productive fabric of the area, from disappearing.

PRODUCTION AREA
Montepaone, province of Catanzaro

COMMUNITY COORDINATOR
Francesco Migliarese
tel. +39 0967 520595
info@oliomigliarese.it

Asparagus growers of Cilavegna

In Lomellina, the alluvia deposits of the Ticino River provide the ideal substratum for an early asparagus ecotype from Argenteuil, a type of asparagus that has been grown in the Po Valley since the Napoleonic era (although, apparently, Cilavegna was famous for its asparagus centuries ago). Technically speaking, asparagus comes in three colors: green, white and purple. The asparagus from Cilavegna is white with a purple tip, and is often identified as asparago rosa (pink asparagus). The 11 members of the community are producers who belong to the Conpac consortium and grow asparagus in the traditional way, without using any chemicals or machinery. They collect the turions, that is, the buds which develop on the rhizome of the plant, with a special tool which makes it possible to detach them without damaging the plant while they are still under the surface. For almost 40 years, in May, an asparagus festival has been held at Cilavegna: the Sagra dell'Asparago.

PRODUCTION AREA
Cilavegna, province of Pavia

COMMUNITY COORDINATOR
Giampiero Campana
tel. +39 038 196 665

Bakers of Lentini

In the area of Lentini and Carlentini, about 15 local bakers use old stone ovens and traditional artisan methods to make bread based on durum wheat semolina, made with the flour left over from making pasta. The bread made in Lentini contains durum wheat semolina, salt, water and lievito madre (known as crescente). When the ingredients have been mixed well together, the dough is left to rise for a couple of hours and is then baked for 45 minutes in ovens fired with olive-wood and almond shells. The soft part of the bread is compact but full of holes, while the crust is soft and thin. As well as the bakers, about 60 other people are involved in the community, who help to make this bread, which is now very limited because of the laboriousness of the method and the scarcity of stone ovens which are still functioning. In fact, hygiene regulations are very strict with the artisans who continue this ancient art.

PRODUCTION AREA
Lentini and Carlentini, province of Siracusa

COMMUNITY COORDINATOR
Salvatore Giuffrida
tel. +39 095 783 3609
slowlentini@tiscali.it

Bean and vegetable growers of Pignone

In the history of Pignone, a town in the Val di Vara, beans – especially borlotti and cannellini beans, whose seeds have been handed down for centuries – played an important part in the local economy. Until the 1950s, between the end of July and the end of September, as many as 200,000 kg of them were sold, not only at the markets of La Spezia but at the markets in Milan, Reggio Emilia and Modena. The 18 members of the community have decided to relaunch this bean variety and are in the process of organizing a sales structure. In addition to beans, they also grow potatoes and an ecotype of maize for flour, called granturco dell'asciutto. A project is being coordinated by the municipal administration, with the participation of the Province of La Spezia, the Comunità Montana and, for the technical side, the Pallodola company. By making an analysis of the land, the seeds and traditional cultivation methods, they hope to unveil the secrets of the particularly high quality of these products.

PRODUCTION AREA
Pignone, province of La Spezia

COMMUNITY COORDINATOR
Agnese Barilari
tel. +39 0187 887623
pignonescuola@tin.it

Bean growers of Lucchesia

The community was formed as part of the Associazione degli Agricoltori Custodi, the aim of which is to save, promote and spread knowledge about local varieties of beans. In three years, thanks to the germoplasm bank of the Regione Toscana and a great deal of patient research, 17 varieties of bean have been saved: mange-tout, beans that have to be shelled, eaten fresh or dried, and beans that can be eaten either way. They are picked when they are mature, and are dried on the farm. Or they may be picked gradually, as the different varieties ripen. Beans that are consumed dry are cleaned by hand and are preserved with a treatment that brings them to below 0°C to prevent insect larvae from developing. They are used in many local recipes, including zuppa alla frantoiana, minestra di farro, farinata, and i topi affogati.

PRODUCTION AREA
Province of Lucca

COMMUNITY COORDINATOR
Marco Del Pistoia
tel. +39 0583 496753-329 7399748
custodilucca@katamail.com

Bean growers of Paganica

The association U monte deju rre, created in 2005, was named after a game which children used to play on the threshing-ground of farms when the beans were being harvested: rre deju monte was the name given to anyone who managed to stand on the top of the pile of discarded bean plants. It has 44 members, about 10 of whom are farmers. There are two ecotypes of the *Phaseolus vulgaris* in question: fagioli a olio and fagiolo a pane (or a pisello). The first type – which produces dark brown or hazel-colored kidney-shaped beans, with a tough pod and a strong flavor – are used to make typical dishes (fagioli con le cotiche, tagliarelli e fagioli). The second type of bean is very tender, ivory white in color and is excellent in salad. The association wants to relaunch the cultivation of these beans which, in the 'fifties, represented an important source of income for the local people.

PRODUCTION AREA
Paganica, province of L'Aquila

COMMUNITY COORDINATOR
Maria Grazia Palmerini
tel. +39 347 1633143
mariagraziapalmerini@virgilio.it

Beekeepers of eastern Sicily

The honey from wild Iblean Mountain thyme has been famous since Ancient times and was eulogized in the verses of Virgil, Ovid and Theocritus. The plant, Thymus capitatus, grows in dry, stony habitats and grows in profusion among the quarries of the Monti Iblei. In July and August, the bees transform its nectar into dense, sweet-smelling honey (called satra or satru in dialect). The beekeepers of the community move the bee-hives up to locations in the mountains. This traditional nomadic cycle is also followed for other types of honey according to the flowering season: chestnut (in this case the hives are moved north to the Monti Nebrodi) and orange-blossom (nectar is collected from the orange-blossom in orange plantations in the plain between Floridia and Syracuse).

PRODUCTION AREA
Provinces of Siracusa, Catania and Messina

COMMUNITY COORDINATOR
Rosa Sutera
tel. +39 0931 949804-339 2691711

Beekeepers of Gran Sasso and Monti della Laga

The excellent quality of the honey from the mountains of the Abruzzo is associated with the unspoiled environment and the altitude. The community consists of three farms run by families who practice bee-keeping in three different areas of the park: the farms of Caterina Vittorini at Arischia, Carlo Alberto Pietrangeli at Poggio Cancelli di Campotosto, and Beniamino D'Eramo at Camarda. Each farm has a small, well-equipped workshop where the honey is processed. Polyflora and dandelion honey are produced by taking the bee-hives to locations in the mountains. The honey is poured into glass jars of various sizes. In the case of honey made from gentians, snowdrops and dog-roses, which is produced in the appropriate season and sold through local chemist's, the hives are placed on the slopes of Monte Jenca, at an altitude of 1,500 m.

PRODUCTION AREA
Arischia, Poggio Cancelli di Campotosto, Camarda, province of L'Aquila

COMMUNITY COORDINATOR
Domenico Picco
tel. +39 0862 607410

Biscuit producers of Venafro

The historical memory of the community of Venafro has identified a special biscuit made here which is very popular during popular festivals and weddings. It is a sort of twisted tarallo made with flour, water, salt, lievito madre, wild fennel and extra-virgin olive oil produced with local olives of the aurina cultivar. The dough is made into little sticks which are twisted round to form small rings. Once they have risen sufficiently, the biscuits are tossed briefly into boiling water. They cook for a short time in the water and then float to the surface. Then they are fished out, and left to dry on a cloth for a couple of hours, after which they are baked in a wood-fired oven until they turn a golden brown. The biscuits are produced by all the local families, but three wood ovens have kept alive the tradition for a mainly local market.

PRODUCTION AREA
Venafro, province of Isernia

COMMUNITY COORDINATOR
Giuseppe Riccitiello
tel. +39 0865 900377-335 7802582

Biodynamic wine producers of eastern Sicily

Sicily, with its incredible variety of landscape and climate, is the ideal place to introduce and develop vines which have become acclimatized here, expressing their characteristics to the full. Two wineries in eastern Sicily produce wine according to biodynamic principles, and place importance on the land, the age of the vineyard and the paedoclimatic conditions of the area, as well as the type of vine: all fundamental factors which determine and restrict the amount of work needed to produce the crop. The farmers avoid preparing the land in a way that disturbs it unnecessarily, they avoid hoeing where possible, and never use fertilizers containing elements that would upset the natural balance. No selected yeast strains or additives are used in any of the stages of wine-making, including the bottling.

PRODUCTION AREA
Provinces of Catania and Ragusa

COMMUNITY COORDINATOR
Giusto Occhipinti
tel. +39 0932 876145
info@cosvittoria.it

Botìro producers of Primiero

Written and oral sources of the 18th and 19th centuries confirm the widescale production of botìro (burro) – destined for local consumption and export to Venice – in the malghe (mountain dairies) of Primiero, in the east of the Trentino. After WWII, production for sale diminished drastically, and finally ground to a complete halt in the 1980s. The community involves about 100 people: livestock breeders who take their flocks up to high Alpine pastures in the summer, cheese-makers, restaurant owners and the Caseificio di Primiero which represents local milk producers. They belong to Qb, a committee for promoting the culture of food in Primiero, which supports the production of botìro for commercial ends as co-producers. Botìro is made in summer, when the cows are grazing the Alpine pastures, with unpasteurized cream. The cream is separated by letting it rise to the surface and is made into butter using a zangola or wooden butter churn.

PRODUCTION AREA
The Alps around Primiero, province of Trento

COMMUNITY COORDINATOR
Gianfranco Bettega
tel. +39 0439 762425
gianco@primiero.net

Bread bakers of Genzano

The bread made in all the ovens of Genzano, a town in the area of the Castelli Romani, on the south-facing slopes of the Colli Albani, is the only bread in Italy that has been certified with a DOP (Protected Designation of Origin) label. It is made using natural yeast and a biga, the mixture of water and flour made beforehand and left to ferment, which is then added to the rest of the wheat flour, salt and water. The dough is kneaded for 20-30 minutes and then left to rise for an hour. The dough is then shaped into large round or long thin loaves, dusted with coarse or fine bran and left to rise again in wooden boxes. Finally, it is cooked at 320°C. 14 bakers belong to the Consorzio di Tutela del Pane Casereccio di Genzano, but only five of them produce the IGP-certified bread. In mid-September there is a festival which celebrates this important part of the local gastronomic culture.

PRODUCTION AREA
Genzano di Roma, province of Rome

COMMUNITY COORDINATOR
Marco Bocchini
tel. +39 0693 953204
ferruzzi@ferruzzifranca.191.it

Breeders and cheese-makers of the Valnerina

Until a few decades ago, livestock rearing here was associated with transhumance towards the plains of the Maremma and Lazio. Today, the animals of the Valnerina are only taken up to higher pastures in the summer. While cow's milk is collected daily by the local dairies, goat and ewe's milk is processed by the farmers, about ten of whom are members of the community. Their products include pecorino di Norcia made with raw milk, curdled at 40°C and matured for between four and six months (the cheese made in summer, called formaggio del pastore, matures in caves for as long as a year), the pure saffron-flavored cheese of Cascia, and the ricotta salata of Norcia. When the whey has been drained off, the ricotta is hung up in cotton cloths for 12 days, then pressed and left to dry for another 12 days. Finally it is dry-salted and left to mature in a cellar for another 20-30 days.

PRODUCTION AREA
Norcia, Cascia and other towns in the Valnerina, province of Perugia

COMMUNITY COORDINATOR
Francesco Rossi
tel. +39 0743 76681

Breeders and producers of Montefeltro

The community comprises two farms in the area of Montefeltro and another on the edge of it, in the Val Marecchia. They rear animals of breeds threatened with extinction, such as the cinta senese pig, the bovino marchigiano and the Ancona. Hen. A large area of land is used for grazing and crops of fodder and the animals are reared out in the open and fed with natural products. No chemicals or GM foods are used. Every stage of the production process is carefully monitored, resulting in tender meat with the right amount of marbling and high nutritional value, and salamis and other cured meats including salsiccia di fegato: this is made by hand in the traditional way with 30% of liver, tongue, heart, and red meat, which is matured naturally, without preservatives or additives of any kind. They also make caciotta cheese – made with either pure cow's milk or mixed with goat's milk – and pecorino, curdled with cardoon flowers, a time-tested local tradition.

PRODUCTION AREA
Montefeltro, province of Urbino

COMMUNITY COORDINATOR
Luigia Minnetti
tel. +39 0722 4441
calbianchino@libero.it

Breeders of black Calabrian pigs

The members of the community are salami and pork butchers and breeders of black Calabrian pigs, an indigenous race which has been saved thanks to the efforts of technical experts of the region and interest on the part of local breeders. The animals, which are rustic and suited to being bred half-wild, are fed exclusively with feed made up of cereals and legumes. They provide high-quality meat to a group of local salami and pork butchers who make traditional salamis and cured meats such as sausage (lucanica), soppressata dolce and soppressata piccante, capocollo, gelatina, ciccioli (vaguely similar to crackling) and other cured meats. The tradition of rearing black pigs here is particularly strong around Acri. The market of Cosenza, where the herds of pigs used to be taken every Friday (known as the mercanzie) accompanied by pig farmers playing their horns, used to be an important event, given the great salami-making tradition of the Cosenza area.

PRODUCTION AREA
Province of Cosenza

COMMUNITY COORDINATOR
Francesco Monaco
tel. +39 0984 950870
arssacsdacri@libero.it

Breeders of calvana cattle

The work of the breeders' community is supported by public organizations, the Comunità Montana Val Bisenzio and the Province of Prato. The calvana breed, after years of decline and having been threatened with extinction, is now experiencing a revival. Now, the number of farms interested in breeding these animals is increasing constantly. Calvana cattle adapt well to living in a rural environment and are slaughtered at between 24 and 36 months. The bovina calvana label can only be applied to cattle reared and slaughtered in the Provinces of Florence, Prato and Pistoia, which have been fed on fresh or preserved natural local raw ingredients. The regulations do not allow them to be fed on silage, additives to boost growth or any animal derivatives apart from cow's milk, which is used only until the calves are weaned.

PRODUCTION AREA
Provinces of Prato, Florence and Pistoia

COMMUNITY COORDINATOR
Ferdinando Ciani
tel. +39 0573 34864
lorenzociani@interfree.it

Breeders of cornella bianca sheep

The cornella bianca is an old breed of sheep of the Emilian Appenines which is used for meat and milk. It is now threatened with extinction. According to a recent survey conducted by vets working for the national health service in the Val d'Enza, there are still a few hundred cornella bianca sheep, especially in the provinces of Reggio Emilia and Modena, but also in the provinces of Ferrara, Rovigo and Bologna. The community has about 30 members: breeders who keep small numbers of cornelle in their herds and vets who are interested in saving the breed. A project has been launched in the province of Reggio Emilia, which involves enthusiasts of the livestock sector, breeders, vets and the Istituto Agrario Zanelli di Reggio Emilia, with the aim of saving and promoting the breed, by promoting the production and sale of pecorino cheese and cured meat from the breed.

PRODUCTION AREA
Provinces of Reggio Emilia and Modena

COMMUNITY COORDINATOR
Andrea Iotti
tel. +39 335 6744525
iottian@ausl.re.it

Breeders of grigio alpina cattle

Today, numbers of the grigio alpina breed of cattle are reduced to a few thousand heads and, in 2004, the European Union officially recognized that it was threatened with extinction. The population of grigio alpina cattle is concentrated in the province of Bolzano, is also present in the province of Trento and is dotted around in small numbers throughout the Alpine Chain. It is a rustic, frugal animal, suited to the most difficult grazing conditions and has a high yield of milk which is excellent for making cheese, or drunk fresh, and meat. Its coat is a pale silvery color with darker rings around the eyes around the neck and on the shoulders and flanks. There are more than 1,200 breeders in Italy – 900 in the province of Bolzano – all of whom belong to the Associazione Nazionale Allevatori Bovini di Razza Grigio Alpina, which also keeps a genealogical record of the breed.

PRODUCTION AREA
Province of Bolzano

COMMUNITY COORDINATOR
Gottfried Hainz
tel. +39 0471 980490
grigio_alpina@dnet.it

Breeders of pezzata rossa of Oropa

In the north of Piedmont, a number of farmers still breed the pezzata rossa, a breed of dairy cattle native to the Biella mountains. The breed is included in the FAO list of rare breeds and has existed in the area for centuries, being suited, on account of its rustic and frugal nature, to the difficult grazing environment of this area. It can be distinguished by the red patches in its coat – which can vary from orange to dark red – with jagged edges, whereas the head, legs, belly and the end of its tail are white. It has a small head with a straight profile and horns which curve up and forwards. There are about 240 registered breeders in the provinces of Biella and Vercelli and the Registro Anagrafico delle Popolazioni Bovine Autoctone has counted more than 4,000 brood females out of a total of approximately 7,000 heads of cattle. With the milk produced by the pezzata rossa, the breeders produce excellent cheeses (toma and maccagno) and butter.

PRODUCTION AREA
Valli dell'Elvo and Valle del Cervo, province of Biella

COMMUNITY COORDINATOR
Ermanno Raffo
tel. +39 0161 54605
ermanno.raffo@email.it

Breeders of varzese cow

The members of the community are breeders, vets and a cheese producer who are trying to save an indigenous cattle breed, the numbers of which have fallen from 40,000 (recorded in the sixties) to the current 150 heads. The varzese cow, called the muntagnina in dialect, is also known as the tortonese, ottonese or cabellotta. Its area of origin is an area of the Appenines which lies in four different regions: Lombardy, Emilia Romagna, Liguria and Piedmont. Today, the herds are concentrated in the Valle Staffora. The dramatic fall in the numbers of the varzese, which is a small, rustic animal with a wheat-colored coat, is due to farm mechanization, the depopulation of rural areas, and the decision that the animals should be reared to produce meat, milk, toma cheese made with raw milk, with the addition, in some cases, of goat or ewe's milk.

PRODUCTION AREA
Valle Staffora, province of Pavia

COMMUNITY COORDINATOR
Lino Verardo
tel. +39 0383 59548

Cheese and olive producers of the land between the two lakes

The community involves about 30 producers in the area between Lake Garda and Lake d'Idro, long known for its cheese production but which, on the side facing Lake Garda, is also famous for its olives. The members of the community, who have formed a consortium, the Produttori della Terra tra i Due Laghi, transform cow's milk into tombea, a large round cheese made with raw milk weighing between 7 kg and 14 kg, with a crust that varies in color between straw yellow and dark brown. The unusual thing about this cheese is that saffron is added to the curd during the process and the cheeses are also oiled occasionally while they are aging. Other cheeses produced by the community include fresh cheeses, mature cheeses and cheeses made with goat's milk, which are always made with milk from the Valle Sabbia and the Valle Vestino.

PRODUCTION AREA
The area between Lake Garda and Lake d'Idro, province of Brescia

COMMUNITY COORDINATOR
Luciano Salvadori
tel. +39 339 6988300
luciano.salvadori@coldiretti.it

Cheese and salami makers of the Mugello

Agricampus is a project involving the farming community with a strong social commitment. The members of the cooperative – breeders, producers and cheese-makers – have launched this activity to help socially disadvantaged young people to acquire the experience in the sector of organic farming so that they can find employment more easily. The community is involved in the following activities: sheep-rearing to produce ewe's milk ricotta, rearing cinta senese pigs to produce meat with which to make salami and other cured meats; farm holiday activities and providing hospitality for disadvantaged young people; involving local people in the area by organizing cultural meetings about the problems of immigration and the environment; restoring grazing land and producing seed to cultivate vegetables for animal fodder.

PRODUCTION AREA
Barberino del Mugello, province of Florence

COMMUNITY COORDINATOR
Giovanni Capponi
tel. +39 329 4132798
giovanni.capponi@libero.it

Cheese producers of the Alto Salento

Eight people have created the Consorzio Alto Salento, which offers consumers top-quality cheese production, including pampanella, a very fresh curd cheese, which is collected in fuscelli: containers just before it is broken up. In the past it was used instead of money when giving change and the term comes from the Latin *pampinus* (meaning vine tendril) because, in Ancient times, pampanella was sold wrapped in vine leaves or fig leaves. They also produce fresh ricotta from the whey left over from the day's cheese processing, which is heated to 90°C, and strong ricotta, obtained by aging the fresh variety and adding salt. It is processed manually every three or four days for a minimum of three months and the strong taste varies depending on the length of aging. This cheese is excellent for flavoring orecchiette (local ear-shaped pasta) or on bruschette (toasted bread drizzled with olive oil).

PRODUCTION AREA
San Vito dei Normanni, province of Brindisi

COMMUNITY COORDINATOR
Francesco Cito
tel. +39 328 6160548
cito.francesco@libero.it

Cheese producers of the Carso Triestino

The last 20 years has seen a revival of cheese production on the Karst. Prior to that, cheese production had virtually disappeared as all the milk was sold to Trieste. The community comprises nine farmers who transform sheep, goat and cow's milk themselves into various types of cheese. The animals are fed on fodder from permanent meadows on the plateau which, with their more than 1,600 essences guarantee that the milk products have a very special taste. The milk is processed raw and turned into about 15 types of cheese, both fresh and matured, the names of which bely the historical influence of the nearby Slovenian community (jamar, tabor, zepek, mlet). The farmers are helping to safeguard and maintain an area which would otherwise decline, because, on the Karst, it is difficult to grow anything apart from vines.

PRODUCTION AREA
Karst plateau above Trieste, province of Trieste

COMMUNITY COORDINATOR
Dario Zidaric
tel. +39 040 201178
zidaric@tiscali.it

Cheese producers of the Mugello and the Val di Sieve

The areas of the Mugello and the Val di Sieve are the names given to the upper and lower reaches of the Sieve River. This valley with its hilly and, further up, mountainous landscape has always been used for rearing livestock, especially sheep and goats. Goats are traditionally reared higher up the valley in the Mugello, and let graze from spring until the autumn. The farmers also produce cheese made from raw ewe's, goat's and mixed ewe and goat's milk which are matured on the premises. Only a few people still practice this tradition, all of whom are members of this community. They intend to carry on this tradition, producing small quantities of cheese of extremely high quality.

PRODUCTION AREA
Area of the Mugello and the Val di Sieve, province of Florence

COMMUNITY COORDINATOR
Francesco Lecca
tel. +39 055 8046505

Cheese producers of the Valle Elvo and the Serra

The Valley of the River Elvo and the long moraine – the Serra – which separates the Biella region from the Canavese is a uniform area of great environmental interest. Since 2003, the Ecomuseo Valle Elvo e Serra has been conducting research into local cheese-production, involving eight breeders-cum-cheese-makers. In 2005 they formed a consortium (Lattevivo) and drew up a manifesto summarizing the criteria behind their work. Butter, toma magra and ricotta are made with raw milk from the pezzata rossa d'Oropa, an indigenous breed of cow, which is threatened with extinction and is now protected. The three products, which are all associated with one another, are at the center of the initiatives being launched to promote the community. Some breeders also make cheese with raw goat's milk, transforming it into cheeses which are coagulated by inoculating the milk with rennet.

PRODUCTION AREA
15 municipalities in the province of Biella

COMMUNITY COORDINATOR
Giuseppe Pidello
tel. +39 015 2568107
giuseppe.pidello@libero.it

Chefs of Volterra detention center

The community comprises about 15 of the inmates and some of the guards who, after the positive theatrical experience of the Compagnia della Fortezza, have decided to learn about cuisine with the aim of promoting the local dishes of the regions they come from. They have learned about wine-tasting, oil-tasting and cheese-tasting, how to lay a table, serve at table and ensure that everything in the dining-room is in perfect order. The families of the detainees also participate actively by procuring the local products required to prepare regional dishes. For the time being, they organize special evenings in the prison, when the detainees not only prepare the evening meal, but describe the recipes behind the various dishes to their fellow diners. They also sell many products locally. The participants hope to organize a tour of Italy, provided this is approved by current laws.

PRODUCTION AREA
Volterra, province of Pisa

COMMUNITY COORDINATOR
Leonardo Dell'Aiuto
tel. +39 0588 86384
leonardodellaiuto@virgilio.it

Chestnut flour producers of Pratomagno

The community comprises eight chestnut gatherers, millers, bakers and other transformers and retailers. The perella, marrone di Loro ciuffenna, mondiglione, raggiolana and pistolese cultivated varieties of chestnut are used to make flour. The first three cultivars are indigenous to the area of Pratomagno while the others can also be found in other parts of Tuscany. They are all threatened with extinction because of their high sensitivity to pathogenic agents. The community wants to preserve these varieties and pass on the traditional way of producing chestnut flour. First the chestnuts are put in special drying sheds with a fire that burns only chestnut wood. Then they skins are removed. They are then roasted in a wood oven, and ground in local water-powered mills with stone mill-stones.

PRODUCTION AREA
The area of Pratomagno, province of Arezzo

COMMUNITY COORDINATOR
Viviano Venturi
tel. +39 0559 172277-335 373280
radici.radici@tin.it

KEEPERS OF PEASANT WISDOM

These communities which grew up around school gardens involve producers, cooks, teachers, parents and grandparents. All of whom pledge to teach each other to share traditional peasant knowledge ansd transmit it to the younger generations. The project got underway in San Mauro Torinese, where children grow native strawberries, raise rabbits and sell their produce to the local woodland fruit fair. Strawberries — the Ribera strawberry to be precise — also dominate the 400 sq m garden in Caltanissetta in Sicily, together with chickpeas and oranges. Other communities are situated in the Turin hills, in Pegognaga and Mira near Fossano, in Piedmont, and in Dolceacqua, in Liguria. Also in Liguria, a community was recently set up involving teachers, farmers and parents from nine communes on the plain of Albenga to grant children the pleasure of getting to know and taste the fruits of the soil they themselves cultivated. The Community Coordinator is Davide Ghirardi (d.ghirardi@slowfood.it)

Chestnut flour producers of the Garfagnana

Carpinese, pontecosi, mazzangala, pelosora, verdola, rossola, nerona, capannaccia: these are all varieties of chestnut which can be processed into flour, grown in the 21 municipalities of the mountains behind Lucca in the designated production area. The award of the DOP (Protected Designation of Origin) label confirms the close link between the area and the particular properties of farina di neccio (chestnut flour). For centuries, the albero del pane (bread tree) provided the staple of the diet of the people of the Garfagnana. The whole area is littered with buildings – drying huts (metati) and mills – once used for drying and grinding chestnuts. The flour produced by the 45 members of the community is extremely fine to the touch and the palate. The color varies from white to dark ivory, and it has a typical chestnutty smell. It is used to make polenta, bread, a flat chestnut cake called castagnaccio and is cooked in milk to make manfrigoli.

PRODUCTION AREA
Castelnuovo di Garfagnana, province of Lucca

COMMUNITY COORDINATOR
Giovambattista Terni
tel. +39 329 3075752
info@poderesanbiagio.com

Chestnut producers of Combai

The community members are producers, consumers, the Pro loco and two cooperatives: in all, 150 people are involved in producing and selling these chestnuts – fruit of a much prized type of chestnut obtained by selection – which is cultivated all over the Alpine foothills near Treviso, particularly around Combai. The community was started in the village of Miane in 1995 and has devised its own rules for chestnut farming in a way that safeguards the environment, prefers prevention to chemical treatments, and hopes to obtain official organic status as soon as possible. Chestnuts destined to be sold fresh are sorted according to size and consumed roasted or boiled, or are processed into sweets and jam. And they are the main ingredient of mondoi (chestnuts in broth), the traditional soup of Combai.

PRODUCTION AREA
Combai, municipality of Miane, province of Treviso

COMMUNITY COORDINATOR
Gianni Pagos
tel. +39 0438 960056
info@marronedicombai.it

Chestnut producers of the Valcamonica

Chestnuts have always been an important resource in the upper Valle dell'Oglio. Chestnuts are cultivated throughout the region, as far as Edolo and Corteno Golgi in the north (local ecotypes include the catòt bianco and catòt rosso, the platella and the barrera). They were once used as food and as a trading commodity in the plain around Brescia, where chestnut flour was exchanged for maize flour. After a period of abandon, chestnut cultivation is now showing signs of returning thanks to the efforts of the consortium formed by the owners of chestnut forests in the valley. The consortium hopes to bring ancient chestnut trees back into production. The members of the community are also involved in processing chestnuts to produce flour, biscuits and a kind of chestnut grappa.

PRODUCTION AREA
Valcamonica, province of Brescia

COMMUNITY COORDINATOR
Pio Valeriano Cattane
tel. +39 0364 486010
consorziocastagna@tin.it

Cinta senese pig breeders

The cinta senese, the only Tuscan pig breed to avoid extinction, originated in the woods of the mountains round Siena, between Monteriggioni, the city itself, Sovicille and Casole d'Elsa. Bred in a natural or semi-natural state, it has probably interbred down the centuries with wild boars and pigs in the neighboring Maremma area. Today, cinta senese pigs grow and live in a free state as they used to do, feeding on wild herbs and acorns. Thanks to breeding in the natural or semi-natural state, the meat is evenly veined with fat, with an outstanding flavor and aroma. Cinta pork, evenly veined with fat, is tasty and aromatic. A whole range of cured meats are made with the various parts of the animal: lardo, rigatino, guanciale, prosciutto, salame, capocollo, and so on.

PRODUCTION AREA
Tuscany

COMMUNITY COORDINATOR
Marco Bechi
tel. +39 3394977937
slowfoodsiena@email.it

Custodian Farmers of ancient farming practices of Vallo di Diano

The Custodian Farmers of the community, who have not yet formed a cooperative but who are supported by the Museo delle Antiche Coltivazioni of Sassano, have formed a consortium for their small-scale production so that they can sell their products to the agriturismi: holiday farms in the Parco del Cilento e Vallo di Diano. They grow about 70 different varieties of bean, the legacy of the many different cultures and civilizations that have passed through southern Italy. The beans, which may be of one, two or more colors, are mixed and sown by hand. They are planted next to maize so that they have a support to grow up, and are harvested when the plants are dry. They also cultivate wheat – durum wheat, common wheat and an intermediate variety – and pears. The pears are gathered when they are still hard and are kept in large terracotta jars. They are used to make various salads, including one that is traditional at Christmas, with pickled peppers, anchovies and green olives.

PRODUCTION AREA
Parco del Cilento e Vallo di Diano, province of Salerno

COMMUNITY COORDINATOR
Nicola Di Novella
tel. +39 0975 72288-340 9379077
dinerbe@virgilio.it

Custodian Farmers of old varieties and local breeds of Forlì-Cesena

The community comprises about 70 farmers who belong to the project of Agricoltori Custodi di Vecchie Varietà e Razze Locali begun by the Centrale-Osservatorio Agroambientale and sustained by the Province of Forlì-Cesena, and the municipalities of Forlì and Cesena. The aim is to save local varieties from extinction by encouraging, where possible, their re-introduction to the market. Thanks to the project, the brightly colored Romagnolo hen, traditionally free range, is on the increase, as is the cultivation of varieties which are indigenous to the area, like scipiona, spadoncina and volpina pears, the Faenza blackberry, and the beautiful Cesena peach, which has white flesh and a bright red skin.

PRODUCTION AREA
Province of Forlì-Cesena

COMMUNITY COORDINATOR
Tiziana Nasolini
tel. +39 0547 380637
info@osservatorioagroambientale.org

Farmers and breeders of San Miniato

The community consists of farmers and breeders who intend to save old crop varieties and livestock breeds threatened with extinction, and craftsmen who transform and sell their products directly in the area on a local, provincial and regional level. The members of the community – about 15 farmers who have agreed to ban all types of poisons and pesticides – breed chianina cattle, cinta senese pigs, gray pigs and Livorno hens. Some of the main products they hope to introduce to restaurants, markets and shops are artichokes, cereals, legumes, fruit, extra-virgin olive oil, cheese, salamis and preserved meats, and vegetable preserves. In particular, the kind of artichoke grown here was probably first cultivated between 1870 and 1890 and has always been an important feature of the agriculture of this region.

PRODUCTION AREA
San Miniato, province of Pisa

COMMUNITY COORDINATOR
Serse Dainelli
tel. +39 0571 485000
info@carpareto.it

Farmers of Gran Sasso and Monti della Laga

Two cooperatives belong to the community, the Cooperativa Rinascita '78 and Le Carni del Parco. The former breeds free-range pigs and cattle and semi-wild sheep on more than 600 hectares of land at an altitude of approximately 2,000 m. It employs five people who organically produce and sell beef, veal and lamb, and cured pork-meat, including mortadella di Accumoli (as from this year, some of the pigs are used by a producer to make mortadella di Campotosto, a Slow Food Presidium). They also process ewe's milk to make ricotta and fresh cheeses and mature cheeses which are matured for between 6 months and a year. The second cooperative breeds free-range cattle and sheep, allowing them to graze in the spring and summer on the pastures of the uncontaminated area of the municipality of Arischia, and sells the meat produced in its own butchery.

PRODUCTION AREA
Illica, in the municipality of Accumoli, province of Rieti; Arischia, province of L'Aquila

COMMUNITY COORDINATORS
Antonio Valentini
tel. +39 0746 80625
Donatella Zaccagno
tel. +39 0862 607455

Farro and mulberry growers of the Brescia plain

The L'Antica Terra cooperative is trying to revive the cultivation of old varieties of cereals, like farro (*Triticum monococcum*). It also collects and transforms wild herbs. It has recently launched a project with the Istituto per la Gelsicoltura di Milano (Milan Institute of Mulberry Cultivation) to try to revive a crop which was traditionally grown in the Brescia plain, and was once associated with the flourishing activity of breeding silkworms and producing silk. By collecting 3,500 cuttings, they hope to create a historic mulberry plantation. They hope to harvest the mulberries, and turn them into jam and syrup, and the leaves, which can be used to feed the mora romagnola pigs reared by the cooperative.

PRODUCTION AREA
Cigole, province of Brescia

COMMUNITY COORDINATOR
Riccardo Geminati
tel. +39 030 9038463
info@lanticaterra.it

Farro growers of the Garfagnana

The community comprises growers and transformers of farro (emmer, *Triticum dicoccum*), one of the three varietals generically referred to as farro and the progenitors of the durum and common wheat varieties we know today. Together with barley, farro is the oldest cereal known to Man and, in the Garfagnana, its characteristics have remained unaltered over the centuries. It is sown in autumn – the crops need no treatments of any kind – and it is harvested the following summer. It is sown like wheat, either by being scattered or is planted in rows. The final process is the pearling, which separates the glume from the caryopsis to obtain the typical spotted grain. Farro is one of the main features of the traditional cuisine of the Garfagnana. It is eaten in various kinds of soups or with mushrooms.

PRODUCTION AREA
Garfagnana, province of Lucca

COMMUNITY COORDINATOR
Carlo Tonelli
tel. +39 0583 65189
tonelli15@interfree.it

Fatulì producers of the Val Saviore

Fatulì is a semi-cooked cheese coagulated with rennet, made with full-fat milk of the capra bionda dell'Adamello, a breed of goat which is indigenous to the Valcamonica and the surrounding area. Traditionally it is smoked on special racks over fires of green juniper branches. It is aged for between one and six months. The community is formed by five farms in the Val Saviore, within the territory of the Parco Regionale dell'Adamello, who still breed the capra bionda dell'Adamello and use their milk to make fatulì. These Adamello goats produce about 760,00 l of milk a year, of which fatulì only uses a small proportion.

PRODUCTION AREA
Val Saviore, province of Brescia

COMMUNITY COORDINATOR
Guido Calvi
tel. +39 0364 324013
guido.calvi@parcoadamello.it

Fishermen of Capo Teulada

The Pescatori San Giuseppe cooperative (22 members) practices small-scale fishing along the south coast of Sardinia in the lagoons of Porto Pino, not far from the Island of Sant'Antioco. Much of the area used for fishing coincides with the area off the NATO shooting range at Capo Teulada, the main cause of disturbance to fishing (aircraft carriers sailing to and fro and no payment of damages). The 10 boats belonging to the members of the cooperative are equipped with setnets, fish-traps and boulters. In the lagoon, repopulation takes place naturally, without the use of any special feed. Fish species include eels, bass, gilthead, five species of mullet (gray mullet, su lione, su rabellu, sa birumbula and sa conchedda), striped bream, white bream, goby, crabs and red mullet. The fish are caught using fish-traps or using setnets, trammel nets, bartevello nets, and fish-traps. The fish is sold directly to private customers and local restaurants. Only the large eels called capitoni are sold in Naples.

PRODUCTION AREA
Coast off the municipalities of Teulada, province of Cagliari; Sant'Anna Arresi, province of Carbonia-Iglesias

COMMUNITY COORDINATOR
Pietro Paolo Di Giovanni
tel. +39 070 9270553

Fishermen of Lake Trasimeno

Lake Trasimeno, Italy's fourth-largest lake, has been suffering for years from a constant decline in the level of the lake. It will only be possible to save it if less water is drawn off for irrigating agricultural land. The fishermen of the lake are taking action to prevent the relentless impoverishment of the lake from an ecological and environmental point of view by talking about the environmental problems to the public and identifying possible solutions. The Alba cooperative has about 40 members who work as fishermen and in the transformation of the catch, an activity pursued by the people who live around the lake since ancient times. Tench, Boyer's sand-smelt, perch, eels and carp are caught using traditional methods which do not harm the lake's fragile ecosystem – a vertical net called an altana, fish traps and a hook and line – and are sold fresh, whole or filleted, or are smoked and processed into paté.

PRODUCTION AREA
Lake Trasimeno, province of Perugia

COMMUNITY COORDINATOR
Aurelio Cocchini
tel. +39 075 8476005
aureliodellago@libero.it

Fishermen of the Straits of Messina

The fishermen who work in the Straits of Messina still use traditional methods and hand-made boats and materials to catch swordfish. The swordfish rise to the surface in the waters of the Mediterranean to reproduce, and then head south along the coasts of Calabria and Sicily. They are fished from May to August using strong little boats with four oars, called feluche or passerelle, which have a look-out mast 25 m high and a horizontal gangway almost 30 m long projecting from the prow of the boat, from which they throw the harpoon. As well as fishermen, the community represents the few remaining craftsmen who still know how to make the wicker fish-traps and the boats used to catch fish and cephalopods. The community comprises 35 fishermen and the last 7 craftsmen.

PRODUCTION AREA
Straits of Messina, Calabria and Sicily

COMMUNITY COORDINATOR
Stellario Capillo
tel. +39 090 7761696
stellocapillo@virgilio.it

Fishermen of Tortolì

Since 1944, in the area around Nuorese, in Tortolì and Arbatax, there has been an active fishermen's cooperative (Società Cooperativa di Produzione e di Lavoro dei Pescatori), whose members fish an area of sea of 240 hectares. The fish caught in this area – gray mullet (used for bottarga), eels, gilthead and sea bass – has always been regarded as being of very high quality and, in 50 years, the cooperative has grown considerably. It is now called the Cooperativa Pescatori di Tortolì and has never lost sight of the purpose behind its foundation: namely that of ensuring work and a dignified way of life for its members. The bottarga (fish roe of the grey mullet) di Tortolì is produced exclusively in the lagoon of the same name and is taken from gray mullet caught in fish-traps. The eggs are salted and dried for 2 weeks. The bottarga is sold locally, but the cooperative is increasing production with a view to offering its products to an ever broader market.

PRODUCTION AREA
Laguna di Tortolì, province of Nuoro

COMMUNITY COORDINATOR
Francesco Selenu
tel. +39 0782 667827
coop.pescatortoli@tiscali.it

Florentine tripe producers

Trippa and lampredotto, two types of typical Florentine street food, are made with various parts of a cow's stomach. In Tuscany, tripe is made with part of the rumen, the croce, and the reticulum (cuffia). Lampredotto is made from the abomasum (the actual glandular stomach), especially from gala and spannocchia. After the animal has been slaughtered, the parts in question are cleaned and boiled for the first time in special workshops. Traditionally, selling tripe and lampredotto, the first in a sauce and the second in the classic bread roll, is done by the few remaining master tripe-makers, about ten of whom still sell these local specialties from mobile shops. They are traditional familiar figures who, despite the problems of conforming to strict hygiene laws and changes in eating habits, continue to sell their products to passers-by.

PRODUCTION AREA
Florence and the surrounding area, province of Florence

COMMUNITY COORDINATOR
Leonardo Torrini
tel. +39 338 3361036
leonardo.torrini1@tin.it

Fruit producers of Mount Etna

This community of fruit producers who cultivate fruit on land inside the Parco dell'Etna have formed an association with about 50 members, who include fruit producers, transformers and distributors. The best-known crops are apples (called puma da muntagna in dialect) of indigenous varieties such as the gelato cola, the cola, the gelato, the cirino, the ruggia, the turco and the rotularu, all of which are picked by hand. They are small but very aromatic. Old varieties of cherries are also grown on the slopes of Mount Etna: the maiolina, the napoleona and the raffiuna. Fruit has been grown on Mount Etna since at least the 18th century. The orchards are cultivated without any irrigation except rainwater, many according to organic principles, at altitudes of between 800 m and 1,400 m on the slopes of the volcano.

PRODUCTION AREA
The slopes of Mount Etna, province of Catania

COMMUNITY COORDINATOR
Salvino Barbagallo
tel. +39 095 938773

Grano solina growers of the Abruzzo mountains

The community members are about a hundred growers scattered throughout the Appenine mountains of the Abruzzo, from the border with Lazio, in the north, to the borders with Molise, in the south. They belong to the Consorzio Produttori Solina d'Abruzzo. The consortium is concerned with the cultivation of varieties which are indigenous to the Abruzzo, in particular solina, a variety of common wheat, which is resistant to the cold, rustic, and produces a limited but constant yield even on infertile ground. It is particularly suited to organic farming methods. It is added to boiled potatoes and lievito madre to make the typical bread of the mountainous regions of the Abruzzo. The consortium also cultivates a mountain variety of durum wheat, wholemeal barley, farro, rye, lentils, chickpeas and beans.

PRODUCTION AREA
Appenine mountains of the Abruzzo

COMMUNITY COORDINATOR
Donato Domenico Silveri
tel. +39 864 33332
silverid@arssa-mail.it

Greek breeders and pork butchers of Calabria

The community of Greek breeders and pork butchers of Calabria – who live and work in the towns of Motta San Giovanni and Brancaleone, the part of Calabria facing the Ionian Sea – are continuing an ancient tradition that dates back to the times of Magna Grecia. A characteristic shared by all the salamis and other cured meats made in this area is the use of wild fennel from the mountains of Aspromonte (called to màtharo in dialect), dried red chili pepper (to pipeddhi) and black pepper. These herbs and spices are used to make capocollo, guanciale, soppressata, salsiccia, pancetta and 'nduja. In these towns inhabited by people of Greek origin, most of the families still make their own salamis and cured meats at home, but a few also produce pork products for the local market, using pigs from local farms where the pigs are reared organically.

PRODUCTION AREA
Area between Motta San Giovanni and Brancaleone, province of Reggio Calabria

COMMUNITY COORDINATOR
Francesco Riggio
tel. +39 0965 712304
agririggio@libero.it

Growers of cappello del prete pumpkins

Commonly grown in the domestic gardens of the lower Po Valley until after the last war, cappello del prete pumpkins have a greenish-gray skin and a variable shape on account of the low level of genetic selection. The characteristics of the flesh – which is orangey-yellow, with a floury consistency and low in fiber – make it ideal for making the traditional tortelli di zucca of this area. The cultivation of these pumpkins had almost died out when the Istituto Tecnico Agrario di Reggio Emilia conducted a study which involved selecting the variety, reconstructing historical testimonials, reproducing the seeds and cultivating the pumpkins. Two farming cooperatives in the area are now involved in trying to revive it. Farmers in the provinces of Mantua and Parma have also been contacted, and supplied with free seed. The cappello del prete pumpkin, has not yet been sold through traditional large-scale distribution channels and the seeds are not yet commercially available.

PRODUCTION AREA
Province of Reggio Emilia and the surrounding area

COMMUNITY COORDINATOR
Mirco Marconi
tel. +39 0522 944203-340 5530549
info@slowfoodreggio.it

Growers of Controne beans

The Controne bean is small, round and very white, without any marks or eyes, and can be distinguished by its extreme digestibility and its very fine skin. It was introduced to the Valle del Calore in the first half of the 16th century, was cultivated by the Benedictine monks of the Abbey of San Nicola di Controne, and can still be found in this town near Salerno. The community is formed by about 50 producers, who continue to cultivate the beans in the traditional way in the original area. They are sown in the first ten days of July and harvested in November. At the bean festival organized every year in the last week of November, you can buy and taste typical local dishes made with the local beans: fagioli al tozzetto, fagioli e scarola, pasta e fagioli and lagane e fagioli.

PRODUCTION AREA
Part of the municipality of Controne, province of Salerno

COMMUNITY COORDINATOR
Michele Ferrante
tel. +39 0828 772122

Growers of durum wheat and bakers of Oristano

The members of the community are growers of traditional durum wheat varieties such as senatore cappelli, bronte, flaminio and sorriso, which were brought to Sardinia in the early 20th century, local mills with stone mill-wheels and bakers who make bread in traditional shapes using lievito madre (a piece of risen dough set aside from the last baking). Traditional bread is usually based on su coccoi, a type of bread with a stiff dough, which is made into various shapes, often a loaf or a ring. Although every town makes different shapes of bread, they all have lots of points, and can be almost lace-like in their complexity, and is achieved by using scissors. If they are made for children they are made into animal shapes, while flower and crown shapes are for weddings, christenings and other special occasions. The bread may rise for as much as seven hours. Because of this, the bread will last for up to five days or more.

PRODUCTION AREA
Province of Oristano

COMMUNITY COORDINATOR
FRANCESCO MELONI
tel. +39 333 4849909
sucoccoi@tiscali.it

Growers of Lamon beans and agordino barley

The members of the community are members of the Consorzio di Tutela del Fagiolo di Lamon e Coltivatori di Orzo Agordino, who collaborate with the Ipsaa of Feltre. The bean belongs to the family of borlotti beans and includes four ecotypes: spagnolet, spagnol, calonega and canalino. Introduced to the Val Belluna in the early 16th century, they are still grown in the area below the Dolomites of Belluno. Agordino barley, which is common in the area of Ágordo, after which it was named long ago, can be distinguished because its individual plants can be traced to a single ecotype; a distichous pale white barley sown in spring, with a glassy consistency, which has to be skinned (and not peeled) using special equipment and a traditional technique. Both products are grown on marginal strips of land which are difficult for machines to reach, using mainly manual traditional methods which are compatible with ecological principles.

PRODUCTION AREA
The Dolomites, province of Belluno

COMMUNITY COORDINATOR
Stefano Sanson
tel. +39 0439 300946
stefanoss@libero.it

Growers of marano maize

The Consorzio di Tutela del Mais Marano has 22 members – 18 producers and 4 supporters – and concerns the production of the plain below the mountains of the province of Vicenza, between Schio and Bassano. It was set up to protect this variety of maize (selected by Antonio Fioretti in Marano Vicentino in 1890) which, despite the fact that it is grown in other parts of the Po Valley, has a very high percentage of genetic interference. The Consorzio carries out controls on the crops of its members and the mill which grinds and packages the flour to ensure that the crop and the processing respect the regulations. Production amounts to 60,000 kg of flour a year, of which 10,000 kg are produced organically and the others using the "integrated fight" method. Some of the flour is sold by the producer members, on the farm or at local markets, and some by the Cantina Sociale Val Leogra, of which the consortium is a member.

PRODUCTION AREA
The plain near Marano Vicentino, province of Vicenza

COMMUNITY COORDINATOR
Giandomenico Cortiana
tel. +39 0444 976465
giandoc1@virgilio.it

Growers of pericina pears

The pericina pear is one of the oldest fruit varieties in the area of the Picentino but it is now being promoted and revived by the community of Giffoni Sei Casali. These medium-size pears with their fine, sweet flesh are harvested at the end of August and in September. They are laid on racks in the sun and are then cooked in the oven to make them keep better. They are eaten all the year round and are one of the ingredients of calzoncelli, the traditional Christmas dessert, made of puff pastry with a filling of pears and boiled chestnuts, sugar, pine nuts, cocoa, liqueur and cinnamon. The community has organized a census of the few remaining trees and is trying to protect them. The local council has asked its citizens to look after these trees and on no account to chop any of them down. A field has been planted with pericina pear trees with a view to collecting the seed.

PRODUCTION AREA
Giffoni Sei Casali, province of Salerno

COMMUNITY COORDINATOR
Rosario D'Acunto
tel. +39 089 883568
sindaco@comune.giffoniseicasali.it

Growers of old maize varieties of Piedmont

This non-profit-making association has about 20 members, who are producers and transformers, who cultivate old varieties of maize organically and biodynamically. They include ottofile bianco, giallo and rosso, pignoletto giallo and rosso, ostenga and nostrano dell'Isola. These types of maize mature late, produce a high yield when ground and have a particularly intense flavor. An enormous amount of work is required to keep the different varieties pure. Each year, the farmers select the best cobs, some of which will be distributed to other growers to use as seed in the following year. Stone mills are used to transform the maize, a process which enhances the organoleptic and nutritional properties of the flour. A natural product without any additives or preservatives, it is used to make polenta, paste di meliga (cakes) and bread.

PRODUCTION AREA
Municipalities in the provinces of Turin and Cuneo

COMMUNITY COORDINATOR
Renzo Sobrino
tel. +39 0173 50118
info@ilmulinosobrino.it

Growers of piccolo farro

Its scientific name is *Triticum monococcum monococcum* and it belongs to the Graminacee family. This was possibly one of the very first cereals to be cultivated by Man. With the passing of time, it has gradually been replaced by more productive varieties of durum and common wheat. As a result, this variety has almost disappeared. The idea of re-introducing it was sparked off by research conducted by an international group of scholars, including Italian scientists, who drew attention to its organoleptic and nutritional properties. When cultivated in an organic, biodynamic way, it is certified as Demeter. The flour yield of piccolo farro, once the husks have been removed, is similar to that of common wheat. Making bread with only this kind of flour requires a natural rising method, using acidic lievito madre (a piece of risen dough left over from a previous batch of baking). Bread and other products made with piccolo farro flour, which are well tolerated by people who are allergic to gluten, are sold locally and on a national scale.

PRODUCTION AREA
Piedmont

COMMUNITY COORDINATOR
Renzo Sobrino
tel. +39 0173 50118
info@ilmulinosobrino.it

Growers of red Cetica potatoes

Some 20 growers who cultivate the red Cetica potato have formed a consortium. This old cultivated potato variety (*Solanum tuberosum*) can be distinguished by its globular shape, its dark red skin and its milk-white flesh marked with pink concentric rings. It is mentioned in guide-books and cookery books of the 19th century. The red Cetica potato is cultivated in the Tuscan Appenines above 500 m, preferably on land close to chestnut woods. Since WWII, this variety has gradually been replaced by varieties from Northern Europe and the U.S.A. In 2001, a project was launched to revive the cultivation of this vegetable with its slightly salty flavor, and promote it in the gastronomic sphere. It does not disintegrate when boiled and is ideal for making gnocchi and the typical tortelli di patate casentinesi.

PRODUCTION AREA
Cetica, in the municipality of Castel San Niccolò, and some of the towns in the Casentino, province of Arezzo

COMMUNITY COORDINATOR
Riccardo Borghini
tel. +39 335 6153974
info@patatarossadicetica.it

Lady chefs of popular festivals

The community of chefs is formed by about 20 female chefs who have inherited an ancient tradition: that of the women whose job it was to cook for important occasions in the countryside and who, today, cook traditional dishes at religious festivals and other popular events and in agriturismi (holiday farms). In the 19th century, they cooked lunches in the houses of Umbrian towns for the most important family occasions (christenings, weddings), combining experience with local raw materials and producing veritable masterpieces of rural cuisine. During the first decades of the 20th century, their gastronomic know-how was contaminated by bourgeois influences as a result of the cookery books written by Artusi, which increased the elegance of traditional country dishes. Today, their work still constitutes a blend of the popular culinary tradition and a profound sense of conviviality.

PRODUCTION AREA
Umbria

COMMUNITY COORDINATOR
Maria Rita Battistacci
tel. +39 335 6458985

Maize flour producers of Storo

The Agri 90 cooperative was formed in Storo and has about 100 members from towns in the Valle del Chiese. They work in the field of producing, transforming and selling farina gialla di Storo, made from an old maize variety and cultivated by many families in the area for private consumption and selling locally. The cooperative has introduced many regions to this specialty grown in Storo. Typically, it is bright red in color – unlike any other type of maize grow in the plain – and so is the polenta made from this flour. It became famous without any form of advertising because it is used to make carbonera at local festivals. The flour is also used to make biscuits and bread. Now the number of members has increased, and also the number of products: strawberries, raspberries, redcurrants, blueberries, some vegetables and marroni di Darzo (a large form of chestnut), which are unknown outside the province of Trento.

PRODUCTION AREA
Storo, province of Trento

COMMUNITY COORDINATOR
Vigilio Giovanelli
tel. +39 329 0509005
info@agri90.it

Maize growers of Vanoi-Primiero

In the 1960s onwards, as a result of the depopulation of the valleys, there was a fall in the cultivation of granturco (maize). In 2005, about 30 people supported an initiative to try to re-introduce the cultivation of granturco to the valleys of Vanoi and Primiero on an experimental basis, thanks to the restoration of an old water-mill in the area. During the first year, various types of granturco seeds were sown without using any fertilizers or chemical pesticides, in an attempt to identify the indigenous varieties and estimate their yield. Today, the number of growers has increased to 50. The growers are also trying to use the by-products of granturco, such as the leaves, in traditional crafts. This effort is being supported by the Ecomuseo del Vanoi and the Comitato per la Cultura del Cibo in Primiero.

PRODUCTION AREA
Valleys of Vanoi and Primiero, province of Trento

COMMUNITY COORDINATOR
Adriana Stefani
tel. +39 328 3624017
adriana.stefani@libero.it

Malga dairymen and shepherds of the Lagorai mountains

This is a free association with about 20 members which organizes cultural and research activities. In 2004, it drew up a set of production regulations with a collective trade-mark which identifies a cheese produced in nine malghe (mountain dairies) between the central and western Lagorai mountains. Its symbol – a stylized cow's face with three slices of cheese – is branded on the cheese along with a circle containing the words Originale Malghe del Lagorai, the name of the malga where it was made and the altitude of the dairy. The cheese is made by hand during the three summer months using cow's milk from cows that graze in the Alpine pastures of the Lagorai mountains in the middle of the Valsugana. Initially, the flavor of this semi-fat cheese is mild, but becomes increasingly strong and aromatized with aging. The butiro (butter) made of pure cream and the ricotta made in these mountain dairies are also excellent.

PRODUCTION AREA
Telve, province of Trento

COMMUNITY COORDINATOR
Laura Zanetti
tel. +39 349 5363542
lm.zanetti@libero.it

Medicinal herb growers of the parks of Sicily

The parks of the Monti Nebrodi, the Monti Madonie, Mount Etna and the Monti dell'Alcantara are all ideal habitats for wild medicinal herbs but the collection of these herbs in the past has led to a dangerous decline in their numbers. This was the reason for forming the consortium Flora Sicula, which cultivates some of the local species organically: origano, sage, thyme, mint, rosemary, saffron, basil mint, psyllium husk and wild fennel. The herbs are gathered manually and left to dry naturally in a dry environment. Later they are packed and sold. All the products carry the seal of the consortium.

PRODUCTION AREA
The regional parks of Sicily

COMMUNITY COORDINATOR
Sergio Argento
tel. +39 347 3007987
argentos@hotmail.com

Moscato of Siracusa producers

The community members are about 20 producers of Moscato wine belonging to farms in the municipality of Siracusa. This wine, which is one of Sicily's, and indeed Italy's, oldest wines, is produced from grapes grown using the bush or espalier vine-training system, which are left to shrivel up on the plant for a while before being picked. Because the grapes are very sweet, they are often attacked by wasps or other insects. The grapes have to be removed from the stalks to prevent their unpleasant flavor entering the wine, and are then delicately pressed. Moscato is a sweet, slightly oily yellow wine with hints of amber, with a high alcohol grade – a minimum of 15 degrees, as dictated by the regulations – which releases an intense perfume of fruit jam, dried figs and candied fruit. In 1973, it acquired the DOC (Controlled Designation of Origin) label. It goes particularly well with patisserie and cakes made with almond paste.

PRODUCTION AREA
Siracusa

COMMUNITY COORDINATOR
Fausto Consiglio
tel. +39 0931 744508-335 458000
faustomansio@tiscali.it

Mostarda of Mantua producers

Campanina apples or quinces, or passacrassana pears, sugar, lemon, mustard oil, cloves and cinnamon: these are the ingredients of the mostarda they make in Mantua, the only mostarda worthy of tortelli di zucca. It is based on a medieval recipe and, in this region, known as the "Bassa", is a traditional way of keeping fruit for the winter or for family celebrations. The 30 producers of the community make it according to the classic recipe of the Oltrepò Mantovano, the area south of the River Po, around Mantova. The apples or pears are peeled, cut into slices and boiled with sugar (600 g per kilo of fruit), slices of lemon and spices. The syrup is thickened three times, pouring it over the fruit each time, and is boiled for another quarter of an hour at the end. When it has cooled, the mustard oil is added and the mostarda is poured into glass jars, which should be kept in a cool, dark place.

PRODUCTION AREA
Mantova, province of Mantua

COMMUNITY COORDINATOR
Massimo Truzzi
tel. +39 329 3176082
massimo.truzzi@slowfoodbassomantovano.it

Mussel-farmers of La Spezia

Formed in 1983, the Mitilicoltori Spezzini cooperative has more than a century of experience in mussel-farming, an activity which has been practiced in the Bay of La Spezia since 1887. The members of the cooperative are all professional fishermen. The aim is to improve the sale of shellfish, by participating in the process of selling to wholesale and retail companies and guaranteeing the quality and safety, in terms of human health, of the products sold. The most common species of mussels in the Mediterranean are *Mytilus edulis* and *Mytilus galloprovincialis*, which have always been farmed in the bay in the traditional way. Here, where the water is calm, not too salty and rich in nutrients (phytoplancton and zooplancton), the conditions are ideal for farming shellfish. In particular, there is a form of micro-algae in this area which forms part of the diet of the mussels farmed here, giving them an unusual delicate marine flavor.

PRODUCTION AREA
Bay of La Spezia

COMMUNITY COORDINATOR
Enrico Faggioni
tel. +39 0187 971577
mitilicoltori@libero.it

Neapolitan vegetable growers

The community is formed by about 30 vegetable growers who grow indigenous varieties of vegetables: huge, tender, succulent Neapolitan pumpkins, fagioli a formella, a special kind of bean which grows like a creeper, originally from Guatemala and similar to a pea, spogna bianca maize, with grains like mother-of-pearl... together with other varieties of peppers, tomatoes and eggplants which were once commonly grown in the region. Today, these varieties are all disappearing from markets and tables. The seeds, having been carefully saved and selected, thanks to a project sponsored by the Regione Campania, have been supplied to some cooperatives (Pomar, Dani Coop and Agrigenus) in the provinces of Naples and Salerno, who have started to grow and sell their products in the markets of Naples.

PRODUCTION AREA
Acerra, Marigliano and Sarno, provinces of Naples and Salerno

COMMUNITY COORDINATOR
Vito Trotta
tel. +39 081 8044295-340 6001837
workinprogress@alice.it

Nomadic shepherds of Piedmont

The members of the community are about 40 shepherds who still practice nomadic sheep-rearing, moving along on foot throughout the year, from the Alpine pastures to the plain, in search of new pastures for their flocks. The sheep live out in the open and are fed on fresh grass. Traditionally, the shepherds and their flocks, which often contain four or five hundred sheep, spend the winters on the hills around Asti and along the course of the River Po, arriving as far as the Lomellina. Once upon a time, as well as meat, they also produced ricotta and cheese. Now nomadic shepherds no longer make cheese because it is impossible to comply with current hygiene regulations without a permanent base. The sheep are still sold for meat but no distinction is made between this type of meat and the meat of animals reared in sheds and fed on silage and cattle feed.

PRODUCTION AREA
Mountains and foothills of Piedmont

COMMUNITY COORDINATOR
Marzia Verona
tel. +39 347 1506370-333 9926978
mail@marziamontagna.it

Olive farmers of the province of Pescara

The Le Terre delle Grandi Abbazie cooperative, which was recently equipped with a new pressing and packaging system, has about 60 members, who are all olive farmers. They have got together with the aim of producing an excellent product at a reasonable price. The trees of indigenous olive varieties, such as carpinetana, posola and posolella, which are suited to the prevailing paedoclimatic conditions of the area and whose olives have optimal characteristics for being processed into extra-virgin olive oil, grow at an altitude of between 500 m and 750 m. The area in question, where olives have always been grown, includes eight municipalities situated on the southeast slopes of Gran Sasso, within the territory of the Park of the same name. The Park logo appears on the labels of the three types of extra-virgin olive oil produced here, which are excellent both from an organoleptic and chemical standpoint.

PRODUCTION AREA
Eight municipalities in the province of Pescara

COMMUNITY COORDINATOR
Tito Nunzio Perinetti
tel. +39 085 849121 - leterredellegrandiabbazie@virgilio.it

Olive farmers of Umbria

Umbria and olives are inextricably linked by the legacy of the Franciscan and Benedictine monasteries, but also by pagan influences. Olive cultivation has shaped the landscape of the region and is associated with many traditional rites, legends and recipes. The indigenous varieties, still represented by trees centuries old, were also used for products other than oil, such as the ice-dried olive which was seasoned for family consumption, and has now been replaced by olives which are heat-dried on an industrial scale. The olive farmers of the community, who number about 100, own olive-groves of the dolce agogia, nostrale di Riali, rajo, gentile di Anghiari and sanfelice olive varieties. The olive harvest, which is performed by hand or using devices which simplify the task, takes place between October and December and the olives are pressed within 24 hours of being picked, in modern olive-presses with a two-way decanter, or traditional oil-presses.

PRODUCTION AREA
Upper Tiber Valley, the Eugubino-Gualdese area, Lake Trasimeno, the area around Narnia, the Monti Martani, provinces of Perugia and Terni

COMMUNITY COORDINATOR
Saverio Pandolfi
tel. +39 328 2752616 - saveriopandolfi@inwind.it

Organic fruit of Lessinia producers

The 15 producers who form this community are trying to revive old local varieties and promote organic mountain farming. Traditional cultivated varieties – the rosa gentile and decio apple, and the miso and trentosso pear – which have always featured in private gardens, are in danger of disappearing. The gentile variety starts producing fruit when the tree is still quite young and its fruits mature in the second half of September. The decio apple, which probably originated in Lazio, produces perfumed, very tasty fruit. The miso pear, which is grown above 500 m, produces small pears which are harvested at the end of September. The trentosso pear grows well in any kind of soil, and is resistant to the cold and to the insect *Psylla pyri*. Its fruits mature in late autumn and can be conserved (this also applies to miso pears) under straw, in the dark, so that they can be eaten during the winter.

PRODUCTION AREA
Lessinia, province of Verona

COMMUNITY COORDINATOR
Roberto Marchesini
tel +39 045 7755350 - girotto.roberto@libero.it

Organic growers of the Abbazia di Monteveglio

A group of farmers in the Val Samoggia, a hilly area west of Bologna, is setting up a consortium to convert its entire production to organic farming and open it up to farm tourism. The community of organic farmers has restored old orchards of indigenous apples, pears and cherries, together with vineyards and olive-groves, within the area of the Parco Regionale dell'Abbazia di Monteveglio. The extraordinary number of crops produced by the community include, in particular, abbondanza and rosa romana apples, butirra, coscia and spadina pears, and paradisa, saslà and angela grapes. The community also produces jam, wine and olive oil, all of which are organically produced and the farmers teach people about farming on the premises.

PRODUCTION AREA
Monteveglio and Val Samoggia, province of Bologna

COMMUNITY COORDINATOR
Claudio Meli
tel. +39 051 6701012 -lafaggiola@tin.it

Organic producers and fishermen of the Riserva di Torre Guaceto

Under the supervision of the Consorzio di Gestione della Riserva, eight farmers and a cooperative which operates an olive oil press have launched a project to revive the ancient olive-groves of the area. The farmers involved use organic methods of farming with no irrigation apart from that of rainwater to cultivate about 16 hectares of olive-groves. It lies in a plain of olive-groves hundreds of years old situated between the provinces of Bari and Brindisi, an area of great beauty and environmental importance. The oil obtained from these trees is not filtered, apart from natural filtering resulting from being decanted, and is sold with the Riserva di Torre Guaceto trade-mark. The farmers are also reviving other traditional vegetables and cereals of the area, which are also being cultivated organically. A group of small-scale fishermen who are authorized to fish in the waters of the marine reserve also belong to the community.

PRODUCTION AREA
Riserva Naturale di Torre Guaceto, province of Brindisi

COMMUNITY COORDINATOR
Mariano Di Latte
tel. +39 348 0391539 - mariodilatte@alice.it

Organic producers and transformers of Foresto

About a dozen people are involved in this community. They are organic vegetable growers who are keen to save old vegetable varieties and preserve rural traditions (such as the vegetable patch in the gardens of private homes, planting useful plants beside hedges and collecting the fruits), and artisans who organically transform the various products from these activities into preserves. Wild plants in the project include the cherry plum (*Prunus cerasifera myrabolana*) of the Rosaceae family, which produces round red and yellow fruit with acidic, juicy flesh, and is gathered in July and August, which is used to make jams, juices, ice-cream and cakes. For many years they have cultivated the zucca barucca marina di Chioggia, a kind of pumpkin which is excellent in risottos, tortelli and saor de suca baruca, made with white onions, raisins, pine nuts, vinegar and white wine.

PRODUCTION AREA
Cona and part of Cavarzere, province of Venice

COMMUNITY COORDINATOR
Guido Fidora
tel. +39 0426 509136 - fidora@libero.it

Organic producers of the Agro Romano

Agricoltura Nuova is the name of the cooperative with about 40 members who work in the field of producing, transforming and selling their products directly to consumers. It was set up with the aim of producing genuine, healthy food with full respect for the environment. They produce a wide range of products, all of which carry the AIAB certification: vegetables, fruit, cereals, milk, yogurt, cheese, honey, bread, pasta, cakes and sweets, lamb, veal, pork and eggs. One of the cooperative's most characteristic products is the caciofiore della campagna romana, a cheese made with raw ewe's milk and curdled using rennet derived from plants, a Slow Food Presidium. The cooperative also organizes educational activities for schools. School groups can visit all the various production activities and attend workshops to learn about making bread and cheese.

PRODUCTION AREA
Rome

COMMUNITY COORDINATOR
Carlo Patacconi
tel. +39 06 5070453 - agricolturanuova@tin.it

Ottofile maize growers of Antignano

With the arrival in Italy of American maize hybrids, the cultivation of the indigenous ottofile maize – so called because the corn-cobis covered with eight rows of grains – was gradually abandoned. At Antignano, about 40 people – including producers, the Pro loco and the Cooperativa Antignano Prodotto Tipico – have launched a project to promote and protect this variety of maize and its derivatives, by supporting the production and sale of flour and other products (tagliatelle, bread, biscuits). The maize is cultivated naturally, without using weed-killer or pesticides, and the only fertilizer used is dung. There are two stages to the drying process: first the cobs are spread out on nets about 40-50 cm above the ground; later the grains of corn are removed and are left on the ground to dry. The fact that the maize is stone-ground exalts the organoleptic characteristics of the cereal and ensures that all the parts of the grain remain in the flour.

PRODUCTION AREA
Antignano, province of Asti

COMMUNITY COORDINATOR
Roberto Orecchia
tel. +39 011 546984 roberto@prolocoantignano.it

Pasta producers of Gragnano

Gragnano, in the province of Naples, is a town with a long tradition of pasta production, and one of the most important in Italy. This ancient tradition dates from the 9th century, when the first mills were built on the streams that flow down from the Monti Lattari. This favored the local development of artisan pasta production. The women of Gragnano became expert pasta makers, while the men specialized in perfecting natural drying techniques. Today, many companies produce highly prized pasta on a vast scale, but have abandoned manual production. However, there are still a few pasta makers who know how to make these famous fusilli, with a simple metal device and three rapid movements of the forearm. Just seven of them continue to make fusilli in the old-fashioned way for two companies which have supplied the artisans with workshops.

PRODUCTION AREA
Gragnano, province of Naples

COMMUNITY COORDINATOR
Carmela Rita Abagnale
tel. +39 081 8710157-347 1135440
carmelarita.abagnale@email.it

Pecorino producers of the Casentino

The community comprises 15 small farms which rear sheep on the pastures of the Casentino, much of which lies within the territory of the Parco Nazionale delle Foreste Casentinesi. In the past this area was often used by shepherds and their flocks during the summer. Today's breeders are also producers of pecorino and raviggiolo made with raw milk. Pecorino, a semi-hard cheese, is produced in forms weighing about one or two kilos, which, on average, are consumed having been matured for between 20 days and anything up to six months. The raviggiolo, on the other hand, is a soft, fresh cheese, always made with ewe's milk, which is traditionally kept on a bed of ferns and eaten the day it is made. The sheep reared in this area are of the appenninica breed, with a few massese and sarda sheep.

PRODUCTION AREA
Casentino, province of Arezzo

COMMUNITY COORDINATOR
Lorenzo Cipriani
tel. +39 328 0332284 - lorenzo.linda@virgilio.it

Producers and breeders of Migliarino San Rossore Massaciuccoli

The community is formed by a group of small-scale producers, breeders and beekeepers who live in the protected area of the Parco di Migliarino San Rossore Massaciuccoli. The area is particularly suited to the organic cultivation of pine nuts. They are harvested in a traditional, natural way which enables them to retain their organoleptic properties. The beekeepers produce miele di spiaggia (beach honey), an organically produced honey with a pale amber color and a strong taste reminiscent of the perfume of the essential oils of the plants of the Mediterranean maquis, from which the bees take their nectar. An indigenous breed of cow, the mucco pisano, is also bred on the estate. It produces exceptionally tender, flavorsome meat. The sheep on the estate also provide milk which is used to produce an excellent pecorino made with raw ewe's milk.

PRODUCTION AREA
Parco Regionale di Migliarino San Rossore Massaciuccoli, province of Pisa

COMMUNITY COORDINATOR
Paolo Cassola
tel. +39 050 819354-050 819287 - p.cassola@cpr.it

Producers of barena honey from the Venetian lagoon

On the islands of the Venetian lagoon, wild and domesticated bees have been around for a very long time. Moving bee-hives from one site to another on special boats is a historic feature of the area. The barene are areas of clayey, sandy land which are often submerged at high tide, but are covered with halophilous vegetation formed by such plants as sea aster, sea-lavender and a Venetian variety of samphire. These peculiar associations of plants are reflected in the unique taste of the honey produced from their flowers in the summer. At the end of the summer, some organic beekeepers place bee-hives on poles in the middle of the barene of the lagoon, to prevent the nectar from halophilous plants being mixed with other types of nectar, such as ivy, which flowers at the same time. A small proportion of the production is processed into ice-cream by two artisan ice-cream makers who collaborate with the community.

RODUCTION AREA
The central southern area of the Venetian lagoon, province of Venice

COMMUNITY COORDINATOR
Aldo Bustaffa
tel. +39 335 7360196 - boldog@libero.it

Producers of Bose Monastery

In the province of Biella, for many years there has been a monastic community of men and women from different Christian faiths who search for God through celibacy, fraternal communion and obeying the Gospel. At Bose everyone works, and those who are not employed outside the community work inside creating craft products or working on the land. The vegetable garden and the orchard provide food for the members of the community and its guests. Enzo Bianchi, the Prior of Bose, has traveled widely and studied a great deal, and encountered new products, tastes and perfumes on his travels. Today, the community is trying to offer new, different tastes and smells with preserves which are made with excellent raw materials. One example is Rose of Damascus jam, which has become very popular.

PRODUCTION AREA
Bose, province of Biella

COMMUNITY COORDINATOR
Enzo Bianchi
tel. +39 015 679185 - info@monasterodibose.it

Producers of Grecìa Salentina

In the area known as Grecìa Salentina, a group of nine municipalities in the province of Lecce with a minority of Greek-speaking people (who speak griko, a dialect of Greek origin), there is a community of producers of cereals, vegetables, legumes and olives, and bread-makers who still make a traditional type of bread by hand, called scèblasti. All these products are produced in an area with a very thin, very fertile layer of topsoil (about 70-150 cm deep) and a marl subsoil which is also used to build the stone ovens in which the scèblasti is baked. The community has about 15 member producers who, assisted by their colleagues, continue to cultivate wheat varieties such as senatore cappelli and capinera, and olive varieties like cellina di Nardò and ogliarola leccese.

PRODUCTION AREA
The nine municipalities of Grecìa Salentina, province of Lecce

COMMUNITY COORDINATOR
Gino Di Mitri
tel. +39 0836 667059 - ginodimitri@tiscalinet.it

Producers of piantone di Falerone olives

The community which represents the Associazione Falerio Picenus is formed by farmers who grow the indigenous variety of olive called piantone di Falerone. The name dates back to an area of land in Roman times called Falerio Picenus. Traditional production techniques in the olive-press go hand-in-hand with organic or integrated methods of cultivation. Annual production, much of which comes from olive trees hundreds of years old, is very small indeed, about 200 kg. The olives are picked manually and the olives are pressed in the following 24 hours. The pressing takes place in an old continuous type of oil-press. The oil obtained is slightly fruity, mild at first, slightly spicy with a pleasant bitter after-taste. The community promotes many activities geared to promoting the area in which this historic variety is grown.

PRODUCTION AREA
Area between the municipalities of Falerone and Montegiorgio, province of Ascoli Piceno

COMMUNITY COORDINATOR
Meri Ruggeri
tel. +39 071 2073196 - meriruggeri@libero.it

Producers of the Agro Nolano below Vesuvius

The community is composed of about 20 farmers – cooks, transformers and co-producers – who operate in the towns below Vesuvius and in the broad, flat plain which stretches from the volcano as far as the foot of the Partenio mountains. Many traditional crops are grown in the vegetable patches and orchards around Nola which are being safeguarded by the community: pellecchiella apricots of Monte Somma (called cresommele), Acerra artichokes (called mammarelle, which are small, have no prickles and have very tender leaves), catalanesca grapes, Sorrento walnuts, mortarella and san giovanni hazelnuts (used to make creams for use in pastry-making and ice-cream), pomodorini da serbo and many other vegetables – scarole piane (a kind of flat endive), fennel, cauliflower and friarielli (a kind of pepper) – which grow on the lava terraces which have formed over the centuries and are particularly delicious.

PRODUCTION AREA
Municipalities below Vesuvius, province of Naples

COMMUNITY COORDINATOR
Giuseppe Nota
tel. +39 081 8994166 - giuseppe.nota@libero.it

Producers of the Crete Senesi

The community was formed as a result of the initiative of ten or more producers and transformers and the association founded by them (I Colori delle Crete). It focuses on the production of oil, wine, chianina beef, cinta senese and maiale grigio pork, salamis and cured meats, ewe and goat's milk cheeses, vegetables, legumes, cereals, truffles and saffron in the municipalities of Asciano, Rapolano Terme, San Giovanni d'Asso, Monteroni d'Arbia, Buonconvento, Murlo and Montalcino. The cattle are reared half-wild, the pigs are reared wild, the cheese, made with raw milk, smells of wild herbs, while the oil is from cold-pressed olives – of the frantoio, correggiolo, moraiolo and leccino varieties – and are picked by hand. The vegetables, legumes, and cereals are all farmed organically and biodynamically. The local Custodian Farmers have achieved important results in terms of saving of old cultivated varieties.

PRODUCTION AREA
Seven municipalities in the province of Siena

COMMUNITY COORDINATOR
Alessandro Draghi
tel. +39 0577 704791 - alessandro@molinello.com

Producers of the Val di Non

The community is made up of seven producers and one restaurant owner who collaborate in the organization of dinners and other events. The products are all of excellent quality, starting from the mortandela of the Val di Non (a Slow Food Presidium), a salami weighing about 200 g with a strong smoky taste and the shape of a rissole. Then there is the groppello di Revò, an indigenous variety of vine that is resistant to the cold, which is cultivated along the edge of the Lake of Santa Giustina, the grapes of which are added to cren and kaiser pears to make a spicy sauce called ravanada. The mild, tasty cheese called monteson is made with full-fat milk from cows fed only on hay from high pastures, and rennet from a goat's stomach. The apples grown here are used to make apple vinegar. The also grow radicchio rosso di montagna and, moving onto sweet things, rhododendron honey and brezdel, a ring-shaped cake dusted with sugar which is de rigueur at local weddings and first communion celebrations.

PRODUCTION AREA
Val di Non, province of Trento

COMMUNITY COORDINATOR
Sandro Di Nuzzo
tel. +39 0463 510111-339 4595395 - info@albergonerina.it

Producers of the Val Martello

This side valley of the Val Venosta, within the territory of the Parco Nazionale dello Stelvio, has a population of just 900, most of whom still live in traditional masi (mountain farmhouses) in the countryside. Famous at the beginning of last century for its rye, the farming economy of the valley has suffered countless changes because of floods and diseases which have destroyed the crops. Today, the main activity is dairy farming and fruit and vegetable production. The 66 members of the vegetable cooperative manage the production, made by every maso, of small fruits apricots, cauliflower and radicchio (a kind of chicory). The crops are monitored by the Centro Sperimentale Laimburg and are based on farming methods which respect the environment. Building development here is also subjected to strict environmental restrictions.

PRODUCTION AREA
Val Martello, province of Bolzano

COMMUNITY COORDINATOR
Peter Gamper
tel. +39 0473 744523
leander.martell@gvcc.net

Producers of Torchiato di Fregona wine

The community consists of 14 small-scale producers who belong to a consortium which still guarantees that all the wines are made using traditional methods. The companies that produce the wine are almost all family run, and produce this passito wine with a DOC (Controlled Designation of Origin) label by pressing prosecco, verdiso, boschera and other grape varietals from local types of vines such as perera and uva dall'ocio. The bunches of grapes, which are harvested in October, are strung up one by one or laid on mats in dry, well-ventilated places. Any grapes that are moldy or damaged are removed and the bunches are left to dry until the following March or April. The grapes are then gently pressed in hand presses with a yield that does not exceed 25%. The must is put in small wooden casks until the beginning of the following year, when the wine is bottled.

PRODUCTION AREA
Fregona, Cappella Maggiore and Sarmede, province of Treviso

COMMUNITY COORDINATOR
Stefania Pollini
tel. +39 0438 581738 - stefaniapollini@libero.it

Producers on land confiscated from the Mafia

300 hectares of land confiscated by the Italian state from organized crime have been entrusted to cooperatives involved in the Libera Terra, network of associations, names and numbers against the Mafia, promoted by don Luigi Ciotti, which brings together more than 1,000 projects of social and political commitment. The land has been reclaimed both socially and agronomically and converted to eco-friendly organic practices. They yield wheat for pasta, vegetables and fruit, wine and oil, preserves and lots of other produce. Over the years law-abiding members of the community have been involved in a method of working which has turned the confiscated property into a precious resource for the economic development of the area the creation of a new awareness of the need for law and order.

PRODUCTION AREA
Sicily

COMMUNITY COORDINATOR
Libera Terra
tel. +39 0918577655 - libera@libera.it

Red garlic growers of Sulmona

This ecotype is one of the finest types of garlic grown in Italy. In the past, it was a fundamental component of the flourishing vegetable-growing sector of the Valle Peligna. The bulbs of aglio rosso di Sulmona are enclosed in a wine-red skin. It is keeps particularly well (even for a year if kept in a cool dry place) but is especially known for its very intensive smell, which is due to the high concentration of allicin. It is hung up in plaits, which originally had 52 bulbs of garlic, one for every week of the year, which is proof of its tendency to last. At Sulmona, about 30 growers set aside the seed and continue to plant this increasingly rare type of garlic. Many of them are elderly farmers, but there are also some young growers who, having inherited farms from their parents, feel it is their duty to continue to cultivate this typical traditional crop.

PRODUCTION AREA
Sulmona, province of L'Aquila

COMMUNITY COORDINATOR
Antonella Di Censo
tel. +39 0864 212077 - info@agliorossodisulmona.it

Red sausage producers of Castelpoto

In Castelpoto, in Sannio, about 50 of the inhabitants still produce a pork product from an exclusive recipe which has been handed down for centuries by the families who live there. The pigs, reared by individual families or on small farms, are fed on cereals, fruit and vegetables. The slaughtering and processing of the meat take place from November to January. The cuts used to make this sausage (shoulder, haunch, loin, filet and back of the neck) are chopped finely and mixed with salt, wild fennel, garlic, pepper and polvere di peperone. This last ingredient is made by picking sweet peppers before they mature, leaving them to turn red in the sun, and, in November, roasting them in a wood oven fed with oak, olive and vine-wood, after which they are ground. The sausage, made using natural gut and flattened with a rolling pin, is hung up to dry and mature in the wine-cellars of the town.

PRODUCTION AREA
Castelpoto, province of Benevento

COMMUNITY COORDINATOR
Antonio Muccio
tel. +39 333 6639810 - antonio.muccio@gmail.com

Rice-farmers, vegetable growers and transformers of the Lomellina

About 15 people belong to the community coordinated by Luca Sormani, who has designed and is supervising the construction of two farms, with the aim of saving crops and farming methods which date from the 17th century. They cultivate the rice – gigante di Vercelli and lencino, progenitor of the carnaroli variety – used in typical local dishes, tender fragrant white purple-tipped Cilavegna asparagus, which don't require mulching, weed-killer or chemical fertilizer, and sweet red Breme onions, which require an enormous amount of work, are hand sown, have to be transplanted during particular phases of the moon, and are harvested from June to August. Some members of the community are concerned with transforming the products for family consumption and sell their products locally and on a national level.

PRODUCTION AREA
Lomellina, province of Pavia

COMMUNITY COORDINATOR
Luca Sormani
tel. +39 0381 112695 - lsormani@interzona.com

Roero madernassa pear producers

20 madernassa pear producers have formed the Cooperativa Roero Ortofrutta, which protects, produces and sells fresh and processed fruit. The name of this ancient indigenous variety of the Roero, madernassa, comes from the hilly area facing east between the towns of Guarene and Castagnito, where it first appeared, according to fairly reliable sources, in 1784. It is a small pear with a yellowish skin with reddish tinges red on the part of the fruit exposed to the sun, dotted with rust-colored spots, with compact, whitish-yellow, slightly tannic-tasting flesh. It is harvested in October and reacts well to being cooked – in wine, with cinnamon and cloves – and being processed into jam, and the traditional cognà of Piedmont (a sort of chutney). The latter is excellent spread on bread for tea or eaten with bollito misto (traditional boiled meats).

PRODUCTION AREA
Canale, province of Cuneo

COMMUNITY COORDINATOR
Marinella Anselmo
tel. +39 0173 611295

Roventino producers of Scandicci

The roventino is a specialty made by frying pig's blood (it can be sweet or savory). Its name (which means "red hot") comes from the fact that the pan used for frying it must be very hot. Once made when pigs were slaughtered, it used to be one of the most common street foods in the east of Tuscany and especially in Florence, together with bread rolls filled with another Florentine specialty. lampredotto. Changes in eating habits and EU hygiene regulations, which limit the use of fresh blood after slaughtering, had effectively signed its death warrant. Thanks to this community, it has been possible to set up a local production chain for the cinta senese pig in the area of Scandicci. The pigs are reared, slaughtered and the blood is collected. Then, the maestro roventinaio (master roventino maker) makes the sanguinaccio (blood sausage). The recent closure of the slaughterhouse of Montespertoli has broken the chain of production, so it's back to square one.

PRODUCTION AREA
Scandicci, province of Florence

COMMUNITY COORDINATOR
Andrea Terreni
tel. +39 055 8729005 - a.terreni@cia.it

Saffron growers of Cascia

The Associazione dello Zafferano di Cascia, established in 2003, represents 26 farms situated in the area around the town and in the mountains of the Umbrian Appenines where the *Crocus sativus* is cultivated. The farms take care of the whole production chain, from the cultivation of the flowers to the sale of the saffron stems, under a registered trade-mark. The cultivation of *Crocus* in this area, which is documented as early as the Middle Ages, was at the base of a dense trading network in the 16th century. Today the production and processing is still done by hand. The bulbs are removed from the ground at the end of July and planted again in August, having been carefully selected. The flowers are collected between the end of October and November, but only in the early hours of the morning. That same day, the stems are separated from the flower and dried over warm embers at a temperature which must not exceed 45°C.

PRODUCTION AREA
Cascia and other towns in the Umbrian Appenines, province of Perugia

COMMUNITY COORDINATOR
Gianluca Polidori
tel. +39 0743 274134 - g.polidori@castellodiporeta.it

San Patrignano producers

Since 1978, San Patrignano has received over 20,000 youngsters with drug problems, without discrimination and free of charge. Rehabilitation is supplemented by general and vocational training. Learning a trade is never an end unto itself here, but rather a tool to grow up and reintegrate into society. The number of courses has increased in the course of time: no longer just agricultural and craft training, but now over 50 opportunities for professional growth. Agrifood training has achieved levels of excellence in specific sectors and the center's wines, cheeses (goat's, sheep's and cow's), cured mora romagnola pork and extra virgin olive oil have been acclaimed all over Italy and abroad.

PRODUCTION AREA
Coriano, province of Rimini

COMMUNITY COORDINATOR
Piero Prenna
tel. +39 0541 362362 - pprenna@sanpatrignano.org

Sea snail fishermen of Francavilla al Mare

The members of the Cooperativa di Piccola Pesca Sirena use traditional techniques to catch fish used for fish soup and sea snails. They use setnets, fish-traps for cuttlefish, boulters for hake, gronchi, scorpion fish, ray and turbot, and cerchietti – fish-traps in the shape of a truncated cone – for sea snails. The cooperative has about 20 members, whose wives and children are also involved, selling the fish on the quay and collecting and packing the sea snails: a total of about 40 people. A protocol agreement drawn up between the fishermen and the local restaurants guarantees a supply of fresh fish during the summer months. Other people who have signed the protocol include local farmers, olive oil producers, wine producers and consumer associations which are sensitive to the importance of purchasing the products of the local area.

PRODUCTION AREA
Francavilla al Mare, province of Chieti

COMMUNITY COORDINATOR
Donato Nunziato
tel. +39 085 4913613

Sheep and goat breeders of the Valle d'Aosta

The sheep and goat section of Arev (Association Régionale Eleveurs Valdô-tains) has 300 breeder members, some of whom rear indigenous breeds. It keeps a careful eye on the register of the various breeds – the rosset sheep and valdostana and alpina comune goats – and the genealogical record of saanen and camosciata delle Alpi goats. It controls the products made by the farmers, supplying technical assistance and promoting their products (goat's cheese and motzetta, and rosset wool). In the future, it plans to draw up a set of regulations for using the trade-mark of the sheep and goat sector, which will establish the number of animals that is sustainable per hectare of farmland from the point of view of the environment and the health and hygiene of the animals, remedy the absence of penalties for problems of food safety and issue authorizations to the farms belonging to the association for production based on the regulations.

PRODUCTION AREA
Valle d'Aosta

COMMUNITY COORDINATOR
Diego Bovard
tel. +39 0165 34510 - d.bovard@arev.it

Shepherds and cheese-makers of the Alto Volterrano

For years, this agricultural sheep-rearing community in the Alto Volterra-no, has been trying to save the pomarancina sheep, an indigenous breed now threatened with extinction, by devoting special attention to maintaining the environmental characteristics of the area. The pomarancina sheep is a white, medium-size sheep with a narrow head, no horns and a straight profile, although rams tend look more ram-like. Their ears are small and narrow, held horizontally or hang down slightly. It has a fairly long body and long, solid limbs. This rustic breed is bred mainly for meat. The shepherds use the milk from these sheep and from others reared in the area of the Balze Volterrane to make an excellent pecorino with raw milk which can be consumed at various stages of maturation.

PRODUCTION AREA
Balze Volterrane, province of Pisa

COMMUNITY COORDINATOR
Carlo Gazzarrini
tel. +39 0571 34497-338 3650355 - red@leonet.it

Shepherds of the Abruzzo Appenines

For thousands of years, the hinterland of the Abruzzo has been associated with the grazing of flocks and traditional transhumance. The community members are small-scale breeders of sheep and goats who transform their products into high-quality raw milk cheeses, salamis and cured meats and fresh meat. Production is based on certified organic farms where the animals are allowed to graze freely. About 40 people are involved in rearing the livestock, processing and selling the pecorino cheese, smoked ricotta, sheep's meat sausage and fresh lamb in the Valle del Sagittario. In a region which has many protected areas but is also threatened with depopulation and decline, the revival of traditional sheep-rearing is helping to preserve a way of life that is thousands of years old, along with the environmental heritage, and provides the local people with an alternative means of earning a living.

PRODUCTION AREA
Anversa degli Abruzzi, Cocullo, Scanno, Villalago, province of L'Aquila

COMMUNITY COORDINATOR
Nunzio Marcelli
tel. +39 329 3805825 - nunziomarcelli@yahoo.it

Siddi pasta makers

This community brings together 40 or so pasta makers from the village of Siddi and durum wheat growers from the cereal growing area of La Marmilla. The semolina, water and a pinch of salt are hand-kneaded by the women of Siddi to create a soft, even dough from which they make marraconis fibaus and long thin spaghetti. The production and consumption of artisan pasta made with durum wheat are linked to the most important feast days of La Marmilla; the marraconis fibaus in particular are eaten in commemoration of the dead. Thanks to a project by Ersat of Oristano, varieties of historically cultivated durum wheat, among which the most common is senatore cappelli, are being recovered, and the local cereal production chain is being revived.

PRODUCTION AREA
Siddi and Marmilla, province of Oristano

COMMUNITY COORDINATOR
Marco Pisanu
tel. +39 348 7735613 - coopvillasilli@tiscali.it

Strawberry growers of Maletto

Maletto is famous for its strawberries. For more than a century, local fruit and vegetable growers have cultivated a variety of strawberry that originated from the French madame moutot variety. It is a medium-size, light red fruit with a greenish tip, and of very high quality, but is extremely perishable. Once it has been picked, it must be consumed within a day. For this reason, it is only known on the markets of the Catania area. It has an intense, harmonious flavor and smell. These strawberries are grown using the "integrated fight" method at an altitude of approximately 1,000 m, on the slopes of Mount Etna, mainly on dry land in small plots close to woods. A nursery has been built at an altitude of 1,500 m with the aim of selecting the strawberry which is closest to the old madame moutot variety so that a certified, more healthy variety can be offered to producers for planting.

PRODUCTION AREA
Maletto, province of Catania

COMMUNITY COORDINATOR
Giovanni Tripoli
tel. +39 333 601935

Terra/Terra market

For more than a year, the terra/Terra structure has organized a market in the area of Forte Prenestino, at Centocelle, which is held every third Sunday of the month from September to June. The people who come to sell their wares are producers of farm products and food, artisans from Central and Southern Italy, and fair trading operators. The aim is to give continuity and stability to an alternative kind of market based on a short time-to-market, and total transparency and traceability in terms of the product, the price and the social context. The producers all display their own home-made certificate which is an information sheet, different for every category, with information about the company, and its products. Products on sale include fruit and vegetables, wine, oil, cheese, salamis and cured meats, honey, cosmetics made with natural ingredients books and small craft products.

PRODUCTION AREA
Centre and South of Country

COMMUNITY COORDINATOR
Antonio Lepore
tel. +39 347 2927168 - lepore.tonino@libero.it

Traditional Florentine Schiacciata producers

A project has been launched in the Tuscan capital to revive and safeguard the schiacciate da forno which are traditionally made in Florence and the surrounding countryside. The project concerns two types of schiacciata, one savory and one sweet, effectively two different ways of using the same dough. The schiacciata all'olio is available all the year round, while the schiacciata all'uva, made with grapes, is only made during the period of the grape harvest. The project involves all the bakers who still make the bread dough base, preferably using natural yeast (lievito madre), roll it out by hand and cook it in wood ovens.

PRODUCTION AREA
Florence and the surrounding area, province of Florence

COMMUNITY COORDINATOR
Cristiano Maestrini
tel. +39 328 7078084 - maestrini@aidanet.com

Traditional vegetable growers of Chioggia

The community involves about a dozen producers and colleagues who cultivate traditional vegetables using organic farming methods near Chioggia. This area used to be an important area for vegetable production, as we know from the Regolamenti della scuola degli ortolani di Chioggia (Regulations of the Vegetable-growers' school of Chioggia), written between 1567 and 1689. Here they cultivate the zucca barucca marina di Chioggia (a kind of pumpkin, cited in the 18th century by Goldoni in some of his plays), which was selected in the sandy soil of the area and is included in many old local recipes, three ecotypes of the white onion – maggenga, agostana and musona –, aromatic celery, which is dark green and shorter than normal celery, the pomodoro del Gorzone, a large, rounded tomato suitable for baking in the oven, and erbette rave, delicate sweet red beetroot with a whitish-pink pulp and concentric red rings.

PRODUCTION AREA
Chioggia and the surrounding area, provinces of Venice and Padua

COMMUNITY COORDINATOR
Marino Boscolo Bacchetto
tel. +39 041 4965493
marcoboscolo@tiscalinet.it

Traditional vegetable growers of Mount Etna

The community has 20 members who grow traditional vegetables on the slopes of Mount Etna. This unusual habitat, with its lava-based soil with a high iron content, gives a special quality to crops grown here: unusually bright colors and remarkable organoleptic properties. The cavolfiore violetto catanese (purple Catania cauliflower) is grown mainly for the local market. The black broccoli or Broccolo di Jaci is used to make the traditional schiacciata served for lunch on Christmas Day in the Catania area. The cavolo vecchio (old cabbage) is a perennial plant, which is grown on dry ground at the edges of vineyards on the slopes of Mount Etna, or in domestic gardens, while the cavolo rapa is perhaps the most common vegetable of the area and is grown on at least ten hectares of land. The growers reproduce the seeds themselves, and, in so doing, are preserving a unique heritage in terms of biodiversity.

PRODUCTION AREA
Farmland on the slopes of Mount Etna, province of Catania

COMMUNITY COORDINATOR
Ferdinando Branca
tel. +39 339 5012092 - fbranca@unict.it

Turchesa potato growers of Gran Sasso and Monti della Laga

The *Solanum tuberosum* – of the turchesa biotype –, which was once commonly grown in the mountains of the Parco Nazionale del Gran Sasso, has now virtually disappeared, having been replaced by potato varieties with a higher yield. This tuber has a high resistance to parasites, a dark purple skin and white flesh. Since 2001, the Park Authority has been involved in a project to revive the variety, having found the last examples of the turchesa potato at San Pietro di Isola del Gran Sasso and, after more painstaking research, at San Giorgio di Crognaleto, in the Monti della Laga. Since 2005, the ACF cooperative of Assergi, which has about 15 members, has begun to cultivate the potato in two fields within the territory of the Park, with the collaboration of the so-called Custodian Farmers, who know the territory backwards. Its high starch content and low water content mean that the turchesa is ideal for making gnocchi or baking in hot ashes.

PRODUCTION AREA
Assergi, province of L'Aquila

COMMUNITY COORDINATOR
Angelo Fiordigigli
tel. +39 0862 606211 - info@coopacf.it

Typical foods of Troina producers

A mountain town of the Sicilian hinterland, on the south-facing slopes of the Monti Nebrodi, Troina has preserved a range of gastronomy rooted in its longstanding agricultural and pastoral tradition. Here they still grow the cicerchia (rumanedda), an old variety of leguminous plant, the flour from which, mixed with chickpea flour, is used with vegetables, pigskin or sausage to make piciocia, a very thick local soup. Milk products made here include ricotta, coagulated with latex from the fig tree. The vastedda cu sammucu or nfigghiulata, which is celebrated by the Pro loco in a special festival, is a large, round form of focaccia stuffed with fresh toma cheese, salami and elderberry flowers, which are also scattered on the surface. Prickly pears are boiled for a long time and filtered repeatedly to make a kind of cooked wine which is the main ingredient of nfasciatieddi, traditional sweets which are consumed in honor of St Sylvester, the patron saint of Troina.

PRODUCTION AREA
Troina, province of Enna

COMMUNITY COORDINATOR
Antonino Rizzo
tel. +39 0935 653944-329 9741185

Vegetable growers of the Eremo dei Camaldolesi of Nola

The community, which has about 25 members, includes the Camaldolesi monks of the Eremo (Hermitage) and lay volunteers who help them to cultivate aromatic herbs and vegetables. The monastery owns several hectares of land which have been cultivated by monks for at least 400 years, where there varieties are still grown which are indigenous to the area: two types of bean, the fagiolo a formella and the fagiolo "dei sette anni" (which resprouts at the base for seven years after the original planting), two types of maize, spogna rossa and spogna nera, the pomodoro piennolo giallo and varieties of pumpkin – centenarie and del prete – both of which are creepers and planted under bamboo trellises. Origano is grown on terraces, and is harvested when it is in flower, dried in the shade, broken up into tiny pieces, sieved and packed, mainly by hand.

PRODUCTION AREA
Nola, province of Naples

COMMUNITY COORDINATOR
Padre Giuseppe Pizza
tel. +39 081 8299216 - camaldolivisciano@libero.it

Vegetable growers of the Giudecca detention center

The Rio Terà dei Pensieri cooperative has been operating since 1994 inside this Venetian prison and involves about 70 people: volunteers, external members and fe inmates. In the orto delle meraviglie (garden of wonders), as this piece of land has been christened, formerly used as a garden by the old Convento delle Convertite, they grow vegetables, fruit, flowers and medicinal herbs which are also used in the cosmetics workshop to produce essential oils and plant extracts. All the products are grown using organic farming methods and cropping techniques – combinations of crops and crop rotation – geared to keeping the land fertile. They make compost to use as fertilizer. The cooperative has managed to ensure that every stage of production, from the sowing to the harvest and sale of its products, is done by the inmates, who, thanks to Article 21, also run the stall outside the detention center.

PRODUCTION AREA
Venice

COMMUNITY COORDINATOR
Vania Carlot
tel. +39 0415 211333 - riotera@libero.it

Vinegrowers and producers of the Langa

In the higher hills of the Langhe area, in the Belbo, Bormida and Uzzone valleys, there are old terraces which are still planted with vines. The community is formed by a consortium and involves seven wineries and small-scale vine-growers who cultivate vines on terraces, all of whom are participating in a project to save and preserve these old terraced vineyards. The vineyards are mainly planted with dolcetto vines and the wine made from grapes grown here can be distinguished because of the words "vitigni dei terrazzamenti" (terraced vineyards) on the label. Some of the vineyards, which are all situated above 250 m, have been certified as organic. The others are cultivated using the "integrated management and fight" method.

PRODUCTION AREA
The Belbo, Bormida and Uzzone valleys in the Langhe, province of Cuneo

COMMUNITY COORDINATOR
Felicino Bianco
tel. +39 0141 88356 - felicinobianco@terrenostrescrrl.it

Vinegrowers of the Pollino

The community of vinegrowers of the Pollino comprises about 80 producers who are trying to revive an old local vine variety, the magliocco canino, which in the dialect of Albanian origin the locals call vera puglinit. The vines, planted using the bush vine-training system, are grown in a hilly area at an altitude of between 400 m and 800 m within the territory of the Parco Nazionale del Pollino. The vineyards are planted very close together, are manually cultivated. The grapes are picked by hand, and are carefully processed in the wine-cellar. The wines of the winery, which processes all the grapes grown in the area, are almost all made from this vine variety, although a few are made using aglianico grapes. The University of Cosenza is conducting research to try to identify a clone. Apparently this grape variety may actually be a type called lacrima di Castrovillari.

PRODUCTION AREA
Frascineto, province of Cosenza

COMMUNITY COORDINATOR
Natale Braile
tel. +39 0981 38035 - info@vinopollino.com

Walnut growers of Bleggio

The Cooperativa Produttori Giudicariesi, which has been operating since 1977, collects and finds commercial outlets for the products of the area known as the Giudicarie Esteriori, between Lake Garda and the mountain ranges of Adamello and Brenta. Its members – who number about 100, virtually all the farmers in the valley – produce walnuts and potatoes. Walnut cultivation in this area is documented in documents dating back to the Middle Ages. In the 16th century, a battle which took place in the area was even called the "guerra delle noci" (or battle of the walnuts). The walnut grown around Bleggio is smaller than normal walnuts and has a kernel of optimum size. Walnut trees tend to be planted along the edges of fields. The walnuts are collected by hand in September and October by beating the branches with sticks, so as not to damage the trees or the walnuts. Once collected, the nuts are dried and spread out on mats in the ere (attics) under the roofs of the farmhouses.

PRODUCTION AREA
Giudicarie Esteriori, province of Trento

COMMUNITY COORDINATOR
Rodolfo Brochetti
tel. +39 0465 701793 - info@copagtrentino.it

Wild fruit gatherers of the Alto Tevere

At Monte Santa Maria Tiberina and other towns in the upper reaches of the Tiber, close to the border with Tuscany, the collecting of wild fruits – wild chestnuts, mushrooms, truffles and wild herbs – has been an important factor in the local economy and the local culture for centuries. The community, which consists of about 50 people, is continuing and promoting this tradition partly as a way of bringing people together. The wild products collected, which are celebrated in autumn with a woodland festival, include the Lippiano chestnut (in the village of Monte Santa Maria Tiberina), the marzola truffle, a wide variety of mushrooms (porcino, ovolo, galletto, prugnolo...) and the buds of the creeper old-man's beard, which is used to flavor omelets.

PRODUCTION AREA
Woodland areas in the upper reaches of the River Tiber, province of Perugia

COMMUNITY COORDINATOR
Rinaldo Mancini
tel. +39 338 8522130 - mancinirinaldo@virgilio.it

Wine producers
of the Valle d'Aosta mountains

The association of Viticulteurs Encaveurs was formed by a group of wine producers to protect and promote the wines of the Valle d'Aosta. It involves 33 small-scale wineries in the valley which place particular importance on the quality and typical characteristics of the wines produced in the area. These wine-makers have a very close relationship with the land and deal with all the various stages of production, from the vineyard to the wine-cellar and also selling the products to consumers. The association participates in the regional planning of grape-production, champions improvement in the quality of the grapes produced by its members with a particular focus on indigenous grape varieties, promotes new developments in the field of wine-production and endeavors to preserve and promote the traditional techniques used to cultivate vines in the mountains.

PRODUCTION AREA
Vineyards in the mountains of the Valle d'Aosta

COMMUNITY COORDINATOR
Costantino Charrère
tel. +39 0165 902274 - info@lescretesvins.it

Women's traditional food market

The Associazione Donne in Campo was formed by small farms run almost exclusively by women – most of them certified as organic farms – who share a commitment to farming according to sustainable methods and protecting old traditions. They do this by reviving old recipes and saving old cultivated varieties threatened with extinction. The association organizes a small market in Turin in Via Cesare Battisti and Piazza Carlo Alberto, once a month, in March, June, September and December, which provides the opportunity to present a little-known side of farming and enables the public to taste traditional products. The products for sale are all grown or processed in the Region of Piedmont: fruit and vegetables in season, preserves, honey and related products, wine, cow and goat's cheese, bread and different kinds of flour, cakes, rice, oil, and salamis and cured meats.

PRODUCTION AREA
Piedmont

COMMUNITY COORDINATOR
Raffaella Firpo
tel. +39 0141 997447 - cascinapiola@inwind.it

Young farmers of the Alto Savio

This is a voluntary group of farmers who run about 50 farms run on organic and biodynamic principles, on which they still rear breeds threatened with extinction – the Romagnolo calf, donkey and hen, and the Apennine sheep – and grow old fruit varieties – the giovanazza and ghiacciola pear, the musona apple – and vegetables like the verdolino bean, the pomodoro dell'inverno and the pomodoro gigante. The community deals in a number of products which are closely linked to this particular area: cheese, meat, salamis and cured meats, bread and cakes, and chestnuts with an IGP (Protected Geographic Indication) label. Alfero chestnuts, which come from a very old chestnut wood, the largest in the province, are particularly prized. They are sold fresh or are dried in special drying huts called metati and processed into flour. They also produce donkey's milk, which is used as an alternative to cow's milk, and is suitable for children with allergies to cow's milk.

PRODUCTION AREA
Alto Savio, province of Forlì-Cesena

COMMUNITY COORDINATOR
Sergio Guidi
tel. +39 348 7334726 - sguidi@fo.arpa.emr.it

Janu sier producers

In Latvian, janu sier means John's cheese: this strange name derives from the fact that it was once traditional to eat this cheese and drink beer at the Midsummer night's festival named after this particular saint. Once always made by women, it is now a traditional, popular, very exclusive Latvian product. It is still made in the region of Kurzeme, by heating cow's milk (without letting it boil) and adding rennet, salt, cumin, whole eggs and butter or sour cream. It is usually round, with a diameter of between 20 cm and 40 cm. The rind is a vivid canary-yellow, which becomes yellower as it ages. It can be eaten very fresh, when it is still warm, with a little honey, or after a few weeks of aging. The community – 48 cheese-makers who are supplied with milk by 623 dairy farmers – produces about 20,000 kg of cheese a year.

PRODUCTION AREA
District of Saldus

COMMUNITY COORDINATOR
Ausma Meiere
tel. +371 29291371
ausma@siaozols.lv

Rye bread producers

The community is formed by a small country baker's which has been making rye bread, in particular, for 20 years, and a farm where some of the vital ingredients for the bread are grown: the two businesses involve a total of about 60 people. Rye bread, which is very common throughout Latvia, is unleavened and is made according to a recipe which is very like the traditional one. Out of the 2-2.5 tons of bread produced every day, only about 15% is made from organic ingredients. In addition to bread, the community also makes a special product that is from this area: *skrandrausi*, little cakes made with rye flour, grated carrots and potatoes. They are very popular and are made especially for festivals.

PRODUCTION AREA
Varme, district of Kuldiga

COMMUNITY COORDINATOR
Dainis Abolinis
tel. +371 29463388
zklingeris@kuldiga.lv

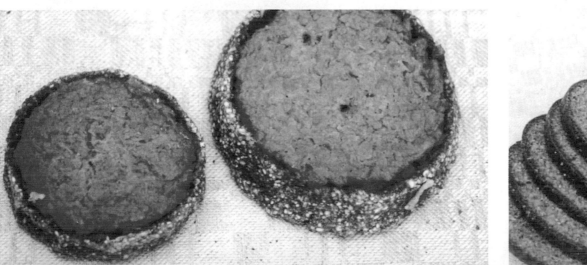

Black bread producers

At Daujenai, a village in the north of Lithuania, a small company is still using traditional techniques to produce *namine dona*, the traditional type of black bread which was once made at home. Shaped by hand into large rectangular loaves weighing 4 kg or 5 kg, it is very dark in color, has a coffee-colored crust and a dark brown inside. It is made using locally produced wholemeal flour, sourdough, water, salt, a little sugar and cumin seeds. The dough is leavened in wooden tubs (*kubilas*) for at least 24 hours (in winter, for as long as 36 hours) and is baked in a wood-fired oven. You can clearly taste and smell the cumin, the natural aromas and a hint of caramel. Dry bread is fermented and used to make a traditional drink called *ghirà* which – along with beer – is drunk at mealtime.

PRODUCTION AREA
Pasvalys, county of Panevòlys

COMMUNITY COORDINATOR
Stankeviciene Vita
tel. +370 68745198
info@saimeta.lt

Sheep farmers of Radviliskis

The community is a cooperative which operates in the northwest of Lithuania, collecting lambs from its breeder members, slaughtering them and selling the fresh meat to restaurants in the area. The cooperative also collects and processes the meat of sheep reared for dairy purposes, transforming the meat into smoked salami, ham and other traditional specialties to sell on the local market. The breeders and the cooperative are all members of the Lithuanian Association of Sheep Farmers, which has about 130 members and is involved in saving and augmenting the numbers of traditional indigenous breeds – like the black-headed Lithuanian sheep, a breed reared for its wool – numbers of which were decimated by the fact that many breeders abandoned sheep-farming during the Communist period.

PRODUCTION AREA
Radviliskis, county of Siauliu

COMMUNITY COORDINATOR
Kristina Milisiuniene
tel. +370 68626460
milisiunas@takas.it

Vinegrowers of Tikvesh

Tikvesh has the driest climate in the Balkans. The high temperatures (in summer they can reach 40°C) and the rich soil make it an area particularly suitable for growing vines. The most common vine variety is vranec, an indigenous vine which produces black grapes which is also grown in Montenegro and in some of the other countries of former Yugoslavia. Grapes from these vines produce deep red wines with lots of body, which mature particularly well in oak casks. The community of indigenous vine-growers of Negotino, represented by Cantina Bovin, uses this grape varietal to make Dissan, which has a deep ruby red color and a bouquet of red fruits and berries. Vranec, mixed with Merlot and Cabernet Sauvignon, is also used to produce another wine called Alexander.

PRODUCTION AREA
Tikvesh, Kavadarci region

COMMUNITY COORDINATOR
Kiril Bogevski
tel. +389 70324 116
kermes@bovin.com.mk

Traditional food promoters of the island of Gozo

This community is represented by AGER, a foundation based on this island that works in collaboration with other organizations and local people to breathe life into an ecological and agricultural project known as The Gozo Experience. The aim is to promote the island's economy and gastronomy by encouraging responsible tourism in the rural areas of Gozo. Over the course of the centuries the Arabs, Italians and Spanish have influenced the island's cuisine. This project will allow tourists to discover what these rural villages have to offer in the way of gastronomy, and sample specialties including: Mellusa, a kind of fermented milk used in the preparation of a dessert called Gbejna fuq ftira, and Tin imqadded or dried figs. Visitors will be able to actively participate in the preparation of food on the farms.

PRODUCTION AREA
Island of Gozo

COMMUNITY COORDINATOR
Victor Galea
tel. +356 79017017 - ager.foundation@gmail.com

Wine makers of La Valletta

The Meridiana wine company only uses grapes from its own vineyards situated in Ta'Qali, a village located at the centre of the main island, and on the island of Gozo. The cultivation and winemaking processes are carefully monitored to guarantee the authenticity and sustainability of the wines that they produce. Their wines include the Isis Chardonnay, the Mistral Chardonnay, the Melqart Cabernet Sauvignon and Merlot, the Bel Syrah, the Nexus Merlot, and the Celsius Cabernet Sauvignon. The red wines are aged in barrique with moderation. In 1994, this company was the first of its kind in Malta to dedicate itself to the sustainable production of wine. Up until that time, so-called Maltese wines were produced by blending local and imported grapes with sugar, water and flavorings. The owner of a restaurant in the capital that prepares traditional dishes, sources his wine, oil and honey from local producers and also forms part of this community.

PRODUCTION AREA
La Valletta

COMMUNITY COORDINATOR
Mark Miceli Farrugia
tel. +356 2141 3550 - markmf@onvol.net

Fruit and vegetable producers

In the district of Cantemir, about 50 farmers cultivate indigenous varieties of vines, fruit and vegetables. They have formed an association called Kurpeshteanka, which is the name of their village. The main crops are tomatoes, grapes and pears. They make preserves with the tomatoes and the pears. Tomatoes are preserved with aromatic herbs or pickled, while the pears are processed into fruit juice and jam. They grow table grapes which are eaten fresh. These producers collaborate with other farms in the region. To make it easier to sell their products, the producers have formed a cooperative called Prut Grup, through which they distribute their fruit and vegetables to local shops and, through middle-men, sell them on an international scale.

PRODUCTION AREA
Kurpesht', district of Cantemir

COMMUNITY COORDINATOR
Andone Vasile
tel. +373 79049582
bahnarudan@mail.ru

Indigenous vinegrowers

In Moldavia, vines cover 30% of the land. The district of Cantemir has about 50 vinegrowers who cultivate indigenous varieties. They have formed a cooperative which has its headquarters in the village of Kapaklija, in the south of the country. The aim of the cooperative is to unite the wine producers and help them to market their products. For a long time the grapes were collected by large companies which turned them into low-quality wines. Now, the grapes are harvested as table grapes, as well as for wine-production. The main cultivar is *moldavia* (with dark blue grapes), which matures late in the autumn. The community also produces vegetable oil. Part of the production is consumed by the families who produce it, while the rest is sold on the national market and to the Commonwealth of Independent States (CIS).

PRODUCTION AREA
District of Cantemir

COMMUNITY COORDINATOR
Bahnaru Dan
tel. + 373 27322343
bahnarudan@mail.ru

Producers of Teleneflti

The community is formed by 21 people, who are all related, from the village of Gilicheni, in the district of Teleneflti. On their own land and land leased from the government, they grow sunflowers, maize, water-melons and various types of vegetables. Wheat is a traditional Moldavian crop. These farmers grow it to produce wheat, hay, straw, bran, cattle feed and, of course, flour, which is used for making both pasta and bread. Part of the production is consumed by the producers' families and the rest is sold on the local market and through middle-men.

PRODUCTION AREA
Gilicheni, district of Teleneflti

COMMUNITY COORDINATOR
Golub Aleksandru
tel. +373 25866275
stelagolub@yahoo.com

Ham producers of Tivat

In the little town of Tivat, situated in the middle of the Gulf of Kotor, a small community of about ten people are still making the traditional *prsut* of Tivat, a smoked ham which is made by hand and is an important ingredient in many local dishes. Once the legs of pork have been cut open to remove the bone and sewn up again, they are rubbed with sea salt. Then they are put into a press so that they lose some of their moisture. After a total of about four weeks, during which they are pressed several times, the hams are put into a smoking room where they remain for three or four months to be smoked over olive and juniper wood. Finally, the hams are hung up in a dry place to mature.

PRODUCTION AREA
Tivat, Boka Kotorska

COMMUNITY COORDINATOR
Magdalena Sindik
tel. +381 82672731
micin@cg.yu

Boeren-Leidse cheese makers

Boeren-Leidse is a cheese made from skimmed milk, flavored with cumin seeds and ripened for between three months and two years. The milk comes from several milkings. The cream is skimmed off for butter and the milk is then heated to 30°C, with rennet and enzymes being added. After a few hours the curd is broken up, and salt is added and mixed in by hand. The mass is then placed in large moulds in layers, alternated with cumin and other spices. Once pressed, the cheeses are removed and rounded with a special tool called a *zakper*. At this point they are branded on their upper crust and the rinds are treated so they become a dark red color. Thus finished, each cheese weighs about ten kilos. The cheesemakers' community is centered on the city of Leyden in southern Holland.

PRODUCTION AREA
Leyden, Zuid-Holland

COMMUNITY COORDINATOR
Vandelugt Huib
tel. +31 206234870
hulbson@xs4all.nl

Dutch brewers

Holland is famed worldwide for its light, dry, pale beers from large breweries, but for some time now it has also been brewing more characterful beers, which are far from international norms. The community is formed of a small group of microbreweries, who brew their beers according to traditional methods. The master brewers of these small companies belong to PINT, a leading Dutch beer consumers' association which promotes traditionally brewed beers. PINT also organizes the bock fair each October or November in Amsterdam (bock is a bottom-fermented malt beer). PINT was founded in 1980 and now has 3,000 members in Holland but is also active in other countries and is part of the European Beer Consumers Union.

PRODUCTION AREA
Amsterdam, Noord-Holland

COMMUNITY COORDINATOR
Thornton Guy
tel. +31 651088220
guy.thornton@inter.nl.net

Edam and Remeker cheesemakers

The community brings together a small group of cheesemakers and maturers who principally make unpasteurized Edam, a cows' milk cheese typical of Holland. They use only full-fat milk and add hot whey instead of water, followed by rennet. After breaking up the whey, it is heated to 37°C, set into characteristic two-kilo molds, pressed for four or five hours and then left in brine for five days, before being ripened for at least nine months. The community members also produce Remeker, another cows' milk cheese, which is ripened for between two months and two years. The Dutch unpasteurized cheese producers' association, which also has an interest in traditional Gouda, a Slow Food Presidium, is supporting these last few dairymen who still produce hand-made cheeses.

PRODUCTION AREA
Noord-Holland

COMMUNITY COORDINATOR
Marjolein Kooistra
tel. +31 614553832
info@boerengoudseoplegkaas.nl

Friesian Islands fishermen

Although the Friesian Islands are divided between Germany, Holland and Denmark, they form a single archipelago and frame Europe's largest estuary, surrounding the mouths of the Ems, the Weber and the Elbe. The Dutch part comprises a large natural protected reserve, although its ecosystem was once at risk from its oil and gas reserves. Weddeland, the western part, forms a natural barrier to the northern coast of the Dutch mainland. There is a small fishing community on these islands that for some years now has been building up a trading network, selling certified fish breeds at local markets; only a small proportion goes through distributors and beyond the region. The fishing is small-scale and takes place in the coastal waters. Sea bass and gray mullet are sold fresh or traditionally smoked.

PRODUCTION AREA
Wadden Islands, Friesland

COMMUNITY COORDINATOR
Jan Geertsema-Rodenburg
tel. +31 651485729
internos@shipmail.nl

Groningen Goat breeders and cheesemakers

Despite the authorities' controls and the pressures on them to pasteurize their milk, some of the goat breeders in Groningen (the name of both the province and its capital city), in northeast Holland, continue to produce unpasteurized cheeses, relying on the protection given by an ancient production technique which gives cheese of excellent quality. This is sold at farmers' markets. The goats are used for meat too, which is also sold at farmers' markets as well as to a number of specialized butchers who use organic methods. The principal product obtained is tasty goat sausages. For some years now this small distribution network has been supplying chefs from the best restaurants in the area with cheeses, sausages and fresh meat.

PRODUCTION AREA
Groningen

COMMUNITY COORDINATOR
Dragt Sander
tel. +31 651797305
info@machedoux.nl

Growers of traditional greenhouse grape varieties

Westlandse Druif groups 16 cultivators (ten semi-professional and six amateur) of table grapes grown in greenhouses. In southern Holland, where fruit production has been of note since the 17th century, greenhouses – the first one in glass being built in 1888 – characterized the landscape until the first decades of the 20th century when the arrival of open-air ripened grapes from southern Europe put a halt on the cultivation. Today greenhouse cultivation of the principal varieties – the white muscat of Alexandrie and the black alicante, frankenthaler and golden champion – covers a mere 10 hectares. Everything is carried out by hand; the greenhouses are warmed before the grapes are picked to improve their quality and durability, and the berries are covered with an unusual "dew".

PRODUCTION AREA
Monster, Zuid-Holland

COMMUNITY COORDINATOR
Jan Wolf
tel. +31 624691232
jw.sfdh@bureauwolf.nl

Sheep breeders from the Drenthe moorlands

The northwesterly Dutch province of Drenthe is primarily moorland, conditions which led to the establishment of one of the oldest sheep breeds in western Europe, also called the Drenthe. The animal is comparatively small and has a brown, reddish or black coat; it is the only breed in Holland whose rams have horns. These days the Drenthe is mostly reared for its meat although the wool is used too. The sheep are raised in close contact with the environment and suckle their lambs. The meat is sold at local farmers' markets. The presence of the sheep on the moorlands and their daily grazing on its flora ensures preservation of the landscape. The breeders come under SZH, the Dutch association for the protection of rare breeds.

PRODUCTION AREA
Drenthe

COMMUNITY COORDINATOR
Andrea Van Gemst
tel. +31 513464723
andrea@slowfood.nl

Unpasteurized cheesemakers

In the northern Dutch province of Groningen, in the area stretching between Groningen itself and Ambd Delden, there is a centuries' old tradition for unpasteurized cheeses, mainly from an indigenous goat breed, but the craft is now at danger from current legislation with its restrictive food hygiene laws. As a result, production has plummeted and the minimal quantities remaining are only partially overseen and recognized nationally. A group of breeders and dairymen has therefore taken up tutelage of this important traditional product. The most typical product is a soft goats' cheese with local herbs, made entirely by hand. Distribution takes place within the region, using direct channels.

PRODUCTION AREA
Groningen

COMMUNITY COORDINATOR
Herman Van Koeveringe
tel. +31 743764566
info@wolverlei.nl

Unpasteurized cheese producers and maturers

Petit Doruvael is an unpasteurized, soft cows' milk cheese with an unusual coating of red bacteria. It undergoes a light pressing and ripens for almost three months, giving three-kilo rounds. Making cheese from unpasteurized milk has deep roots in Holland, especially in the northwest where Jersey cows (which are similar to Friesians but smaller) are reared organically. Their milk goes into the traditional cheeses of Edam, Gouda and Remeker. The producers' group and the dairies involved in the project work to protect naturally-made traditional products; they support the Slow Food Aged Gouda Presidium; and they organize meetings for those involved in production and run educational sessions open to the public.

PRODUCTION AREA
Noord-Holland

COMMUNITY COORDINATOR
Marjolein Kooistra
tel. +31 614553832
info@boerengoudseoplegkaas.nl

Vechtdal food producers

A group of small farms in Overijssel have created an integrated network offering foods that are produced with respect for the environment. Organic growers, farmers' markets and local eateries using local produce bring focus onto the landscape, the culture and the nature of food supplies. The typical diet of Zolle, Dalfsen, Ommen, Hardenberg and Staphorst, in the Vecht river basin, gains its characteristics from cardoons, Terschelling cranberries, mushrooms, milk, sausages, water and cereals. Cattle are mainly raised for milk, while a real specialty is the Pietrain pig, organically reared. Its meat is usually cured giving smoked Vechtdal ham, made with salt and honey; sausages, which contain local herbs, especially rosemary and wild fennel; and pâtés, including a sweet type made with added berries.

PRODUCTION AREA
Overijssel

COMMUNITY COORDINATOR
Harry Donkers
tel. +31 628638919
info@vechtdalproducten.nl

Bakers of spelt bread

Belonging to the same genus as wheat (*Triticum*), spelt is often seen as a precursor to this cereal with a higher resistance to frost and parasites; it comes in three varieties, *T. monococcum*, *dicoccum* and *spelta*. This community is formed of a group of farmers dedicated to the cultivation of spelt in the Ullandhaug Kulturpark, a nature reserve near Stavanger, the capital of the county of Rogaland in southwest Norway. One member of the community specializes in the cultivation of ancient cereal varieties; he also makes his own flour. He is joined by the Jakobs Bakery, which produces speltbrød (spelt bread) and traditional desserts made from spelt. At the moment their production is very limited and is sold directly through the bakery or at local farmers' markets.

PRODUCTION AREA
Stavanger, county of Rogaland

COMMUNITY COORDINATOR
Jostein Hertwig
tel. +47 5187 3898
jostein@ullandhaug-gard.no

Cider makers of Hardanger

The Hardanger fiord is the second longest in Norway. English monks probably introduced the cultivation of cider apples along its coastline in the 12th century. Legislation brought in 1920 restricted the production of this beverage. In the last ten years cider has regained popularity and the Hardanger siderprodusentlag (the association of cider makers of Hardanger) was set up. Its 25 members are involved in all the phases of production: they cultivate the apples, press them and make cider using traditional methods. The apples belong to an autochthonous variety cultivated in southern Europe and are more acidic and tannic than modern apples. They reach maturation around September-October, are pressed and put into small tanks with the addition of 4-6% sugar to produce cider with an alcohol content of 6-8% and a pronounced apple flavor.

PRODUCTION AREA
Ulvik, county of Hordaland

COMMUNITY COORDINATOR
Asbjørn Børsheim
tel. +47 91102215
Asbjorn.Borsheim@hordaland-f.kommune.no

Dried salt-cured cod producers of Kristiansund

Kristiansund, is the best place in Norway for the production of dried salt-cured cod, they also have a museum here dedicated to the specialty, known locally as Klippfisk. The fishing of Atlantic cod (*Gadus morhua*) takes place during the months of February and March. The cod used to produce dried salt-cured cod are disemboweled, drained of blood and eviscerated before being left to dry on the cliffs and then salted. It is a long and laborious process and the final product is classified into three different categories according to its quality: superior extra, superior and imperial. In the past the economy of Kristiansund was based around the production of Klippfisk, but this industry has declined notably in recent years, so much so in fact that two small companies went out of business in 2005. If this ancient technique is not protected, both the product as well as the traditional knowledge behind it will be lost forever.

PRODUCTION AREA
Kristiansund, county of Møre og Romsdal

COMMUNITY COORDINATOR
Knut Garshol
tel. +47 93202630 - garshol@eunet.no

Farmers and animal breeders of Lom

Lom is a village of 700 inhabitants in the county of Oppland, in the mountainous area of central Norway. The food producers of this community are dedicated to the cultivation of cereal crops and some also breed pigs and goats to produce ham and cheese. Lom has an ancient tradition of cereal cultivation thanks to the supply of water that is channeled into the fields from the mountains. The excellent quality flours ground in the local mill provide the village bakery with the necessary ingredients to make several traditional local breads. The pork, which is fed with the same cereals, is used to produce smoked hams. During the summer months, the cows bred in the mountains surrounding the village provide the milk needed to produce traditional cheeses such as Kvit taegerost.

PRODUCTION AREA
Lom, county of Oppland

COMMUNITY COORDINATOR
Hans Brimi
tel. +47 91137558 - ha-brimi@online.no

Mussel fishermen
of the Hardanger Fiord

Hardanger skjeldyrkarlag was set up in 2001 and now has 30 members. Up until 2001 the Hardanger fiord –179 kilometers long and characterized by a particularly mild climate and extensive fruit tree plantations – was closed to fishing because the waters were not considered to be pure. They were recently declared suitable for fishing and the members of this association were authorized to fish there. The mussels of the Hardanger fiord are of a superior quality than those of other areas. They are between four and eight centimeters in length, have oval shells that are usually free from sand and mud and range from blue to black in color. The thickness depends on the age of the mollusk. The flesh can be creamy yellow or orange in color and every part of it can be eaten; the accumulation of energy reserves makes it particularly tasty.

PRODUCTION AREA
Ulvik, county of Hordaland

COMMUNITY COORDINATOR
Sven-Helge Pedersen
tel. +47 5652 5375
ven.helge@granvin.org

Producers of organic jams and fruit juices

This community is formed of a group of organic food producers that work in the area of the Ullandhaug Kulturpark, a nature reserve near Stavanger, the capital of the county of Rogaland in southwest Norway. This community is made up of three organic food associations: Skansen urtehage, Ullandhaug gård and Økologiske dagligvarer. The members of the community are dedicated to the cultivation of herbs and berries that are used to produce jams, Hylleblomsaft (black elderberry juice) and Solbærsyltetøy (blackcurrant juice). The community's products are sold directly to consumers in the park or through the farmers' markets of western Norway. There is also a botanical garden in the Ullandhaug Kulturpark where research is carried out on plant varieties that were historically cultivated in the area.

PRODUCTION AREA
Stavanger, county of Rogaland

COMMUNITY COORDINATOR
Helge Ole Bergesen
tel. +47 5156 2924
helge.ole.bergesen@gmail.com

Pultost producers
of Hedmark and Oppland

This community is made up of a network of twenty traditional cheese makers engaged in the production of Pultost, a traditional Norwegian cheese made in the southeastern regions of Hedmark and Oppland. Pultost is a sour clotted cheese: the soured milk is heated to 60°C, the curd is then drained in a cloth for one day, crumbled and then allowed to ferment. The mass must be stirred every day to guarantee uniform fermentation. Cumin seed is added after a couple of days, this stops the fermentation as well as adding flavor. This kind of cheese has been produced in all over Norway for centuries: the cheese made in Hedmark in particular is cited in a 18th century text as being the best in the Country.

PRODUCTION AREA
The counties of Hedmark and Oppland

COMMUNITY COORDINATOR
Maria Sundal
tel. +47 6255 1206 - maria.sundal@fmhe.no

Ringerik Potato growers

Ringerike, situated 50 kilometers to the northwest of Oslo, is famous for the cultivation of small potatoes with red skin, yellow flesh and lots of sprouts. Their origins are unknown but it is thought they derive from a variety brought to Ringerike from the Oslo botanical gardens in1867. They are low-yield potatoes and are more expensive than other varieties on sale in the region. The Ringerik is considered as a delicacy and is usually served with traditional dishes such as fish and game. Six cultivators have formed an association to select, pack and sell the potatoes. In 2004 they asked for this autochthonous potato variety to be granted PDO (protected denomination of origin) status. They have also outlined production regulations, which state that only potatoes grown and packed in the municipalities of Ringerike and Hole can be sold as Ringerik potatoes.

PRODUCTION AREA
Ringerike and Hole, county of Buskerud

COMMUNITY COORDINATOR
Ottar Riis Strøm
tel. +47 32135186 - orstroem@online.no

Traditional Norwegian fishermen

The Norsk Tradisjonsfisk association has its headquarters at Bergen, in Hordaland (a county in the southwest), but operates along the entire coast of Norway. Formed of fishermen and craftsmen that work according to tradition, Norsk Tradisjonsfisk works with 50 companies involved in the processing of fish. It offers an "excellent product" guarantee, assuring the end consumer that they have purchased a high quality and environmentally friendly product. The group places great emphasis on the importance of research in this sector as well as the history and culture surrounding fish products. The fishermen mainly catch crabs and scallops that they either process directly according to traditional techniques or deliver to craftsmen where they are marinated in salt, dried or smoked.

PRODUCTION AREA
The coastal areas of the Country

COMMUNITY COORDINATOR
Terje Inderhaug
tel. +47 5523 9997
terje.inderhaug@hordaland-f.kommune.no

Apple growers of the Wisla Park

More than 60% of European apple production comes from Poland, where more than 50 varieties of apple are still grown. This is due, on the one hand, to the fact that it has a climate particularly well suited to this fruit, and, on the other, to the traditional importance of apples in Polish gastronomy. The community is formed by 25 apple growers who farm in the Wisla (Vistula) Park (in the north of Poland), where the apple orchards pre-date WWII. The apple-trees are very tall and the fruit is harvested every two years. The work of the community has helped to save a unique part of our heritage, not only for Poland, but Europe as a whole.

PRODUCTION AREA
Wisla Park, Kujawsko-Pomorze

COMMUNITY COORDINATOR
Jaroslaw Pajakowsk
zarzad@tpdw.pl

Apple-juice producers of Kalisz

Poland is Europe's largest producer of apples and almost has a monopoly (more than 90%) on the production of apple concentrate. The "apple-juice" commonly sold in shops all over Europe is, in fact, a concentrate, while artisans of this community make pure apple juice. In the Kalisz area (about100 km from Poznaƒ, in Wielkopolskie, literally Great Poland) there are still two producers who make apple-juice from fresh apples without using any additives. The apples belong to a local variety with a very high acidic content. The pulp is pressed but not filtered. No sugar is added while the apples are being processed. The finished product is a unique kind of fruit juice, which compares excellently with even the most famous fruit juices made in Germany or the Alto Adige (South Tyrol).

PRODUCTION AREA
Kalisz, Wielkopolskie

COMMUNITY COORDINATOR
Andrzej Plonka
teso@teso.com.pl

Carp breeders of Zator

At Zator, a little town on the Wisla (Vistula) River about 50 km from Kraków, is one of the oldest carp breeding-grounds in Europe. They are first mentioned in documents dating from the 12th century. Connected by a system of artificial lakes to the river, this kind of fish-farming was renowned when Kraków was still capital of Poland. Apparently Zator carp were one of the favorite fish dishes at court. But, even today, their fame is not restricted to the production area. Before WWII, carp from Zator won several international competitions. Since the fall of the Communist regime, fish farmers have been trying to promote this type of fish, which has always been part of the Polish gastronomic tradition, especially at Christmas.

PRODUCTION AREA
Zator, Malopolska

COMMUNITY COORDINATOR
Makuch Maruisz
tel. +48 507 058 469
promocja@zator.iap.pl

Growers and transformers of buck wheat

In Poland it is traditional to serve boiled buck wheat with meat. Before potatoes were introduced, this cereal was a staple of the local diet. Not many people know that a special kind of honey is made with the nectar from its flowers, which is only made in this area. It is very dark honey, rather like honey made from chestnut flowers, with an unmistakably strong taste. Buck wheat honey is usually eaten for breakfast and often accompanies fresh cheese, but it is also used to make typical cakes for Easter. The community (about 40 beekeepers and 30 buck wheat growers) operate in two different parts of Poland: in the great Masurian Lake District in the northeast of the country, and in the Roztocze Mountains in the southeast.

PRODUCTION AREA
Mazury, Warminsko-Mazurskie, and Roztocze, Podkarpackie

COMMUNITY COORDINATOR
Remigiusz Dutkowiak
pasieka@dutkowiak.pl

Organic producers of Mazovia

In Mazovia, in the heart of Poland, at Grzybów, Ewa Smuk Stratenwerth runs a farm where six people produce organic products by hand: bread, cheese, salami and cured meats and vegetables (especially pumpkins). All the bread is made with various kinds of wholemeal flour, leavened naturally and baked in traditional wood-fired stoves. The flour is organically produced and stone-ground on the premises. What's more, the farm produces other types of bread made with oats, greens and garlic. The farm is the headquarters of the ecological cultural association Ziarno, which promotes initiatives to teach people about the countryside and organizes educational activities for kids in collaboration with organic producers in the region. Founded in 1995, the association has received many international tributes.

PRODUCTION AREA
Grzybów, Mazowieckie

COMMUNITY COORDINATOR
Ewa Smuk Stratenwerth
tel. +48 242 778 196
ewapeter@poczta.onet.pl

Pradnicki bakers

Poland is famous even beyond its borders for its delicious bread made with sourdough. In Kraków, there are still four bakers who make a traditional type of bread called pradnicki. Oval or round in shape, it weighs about 6 kg and has a strong flavor. It is usually made with rye flour and will keep for more than 10 days, thanks to its very thick crust. Once they used to cook it on straw, whereas, nowadays, they use rye bran. The story goes that the first loaf of pradnicki was usually made on the day that the first rye harvest of the season was delivered to the king in his residence at Wawel Castle, now part of Kraków. Recently, pradnicki bakers have been very successful on the local market and all the best bread shops in the city now sell this traditional kind of bread.

PRODUCTION AREA
Kraków, Malopolskie

COMMUNITY COORDINATOR
Antoni Madej
poczta@piekarnia-madej.com.pl

Producers of kielbasa lisiecka

Kielbasa lisiecka is a typical kind of Polish salami, which was already documented in the 17th century. It is made by marinating pork for three weeks and then cutting it into small pieces. It is then stuffed into calf's gut, smoked and seasoned with herbs and spices. The finished product is a salami with a low fat content. It may be served cold, with horseradish or mustard, or hot (boiled or baked in the oven, grilled or used to make soups and stews). The community is formed by 15 producers from two towns, Liszki and Czernichow, both less than 30 km from Kraków. In 2005, the producers of the community formed a consortium, with the aim of saving this traditional product and technique and having greater control over the various stages of production.

PRODUCTION AREA
Liszki and Czernichow, Malopolskie

COMMUNITY COORDINATOR
Stanislaw Madry
tel. +48 507 058 469

Producers of wegierka plum jam

The community operates in the area of Kruszewo, a flat area in southeast Poland with many forests and lakes where there are many legends associated with the old Slav peoples. The plums used to make this jam are from an indigenous variety called wegierka, which are more acidic than the plums normally sold, of Greek, Spanish or Italian origin. The special flavor of the jam is due to a special recipe. When the plums have been picked, they are put into a huge copper cauldron with a diameter of about 1.5 m and are left to cook over a flame for more than 24 hours, without any sugar being added. Today, there are only five producers left who still produce jam in this traditional way.

PRODUCTION AREA
Kruszewo, Lubelskie

COMMUNITY COORDINATOR
Eugieniusz Mientkiewicz
ugin@o2.pl

Producers of wizajny cheese

Also known as "yellow cheese", wizajny is produced with raw cow's milk, and is sometimes flavored with local herbs and spices (cumin, thyme, marjoram). Wizajny cheese is named after one of the two areas in which the community operates (the other is Rutka Tartan), in the autonomous area of Suwalki, 30 km from the border with Lithuania. Here, the cheese-making tradition dates back to at least the 19th century, but, nowadays, cheese-makers do not have an easy life, because of the very strict EU laws. 30 farmers and breeders have formed an association to help each other, promote their products and try to overcome bureaucratic problems. The farms have between10 and 20 hectares of land and each producer has between two and 20 cows. Many breeds are represented, but the association is trying to save the old red Polish cow. The cattle are fed on grass and cereals (wheat, rye, barley and oats) and the cows are milked by hand.

PRODUCTION AREA
Suwalki Voivodeship

COMMUNITY COORDINATOR
Maria Micielica
miciel1@wp.pl

Swinia zlotnicka pigs breeders

The swinia zlotnicka is a very old breed of pig which has remained virtually unchanged over the years. It was introduced to Poland from the area of Vilnius, in Lithuania, by breeders who, after WWI, moved to Pomorze (Pomerania, a region in the north of Poland stretching as far as the Baltic Sea). Pigs of the swinia zlotnicka breed produce extremely good, tender and flavorsome pork. The fat is well distributed and the meat is particularly good when fried. Another advantage of this breed is that it adapts perfectly to adverse climatic and environmental conditions. Currently there are no more than 300 of them, shared among five breeders. They are periodically controlled by livestock experts.

PRODUCTION AREA
Pomorze

COMMUNITY COORDINATOR
Marek Gasiorowski
tel. +48 608 673 455

Batata doce producers of Aljezur

Aljezur, the coastal strip at the southwest tip of Portugal, is the largest sweet-potato producing area in the country. Thanks to the extraordinary paedoclimatic conditions there, the roots of the plant *Ipomoea batatas* are particularly tasty, to the extent that the batata doce of Aljezur has been awarded the DOP (Protected Designation of Origin) label. The community, whose area of production lies within the territory of the Parque Natural do Sudoeste Alentejano e Costa Vicentina, must take the credit for promoting this local variety. This potato, which has a red skin and yellow flesh, was traditionally consumed by the people who grew them and was therefore relegated to a rural family-run economy. The objective has been achieved thanks to the collaboration of local restaurants, the interest of the media and the Festival da Batata-doce de Aljezur, now in its ninth year.

PRODUCTION AREA
Aljezur, district of Faro

COMMUNITY COORDINATOR
Rogério António Marques Rosa
tel. +351 2829 91288 - rogério.rosa@cm-aljezur.pt

Broa de milho producers of Arcos de Valdevez

In the high, inaccessible north of Portugal, maize, which is grown in private gardens and never in whole fields, has traditionally been regarded as an alternative to wheat. At Arcos de Valdevez, close to the Spanish border, the old tradition of making maize bread is still alive and well. To make *broa de milho*, you need four measures of maize to one of rye, the grain must be stone-ground and worked into a dough with sourdough. The loaves are baked in old stone ovens fired with oak, heather and broom. The loaves have a streaky gold and brown crust, and a yeasty smell with hints of toasted maize and caramel. Inside, the bread is firm, crumbly and a grayish-yellow color. Excellent with traditional local gastronomic specialties, such as ham, sardines, fried salt cod, this far-from-modern type of bread has every right to a place on board the Ark of Taste.

PRODUCTION AREA
Arcos de Valdevez, district of Viana do Castelo

COMMUNITY COORDINATOR
Jorge Miranda
tel. +351 2585 20503 - geral@ardal.pt

Oyster gatherers of Setúbal

Collecting oysters in the estuary of the River Sado is a very old tradition. This activity reached its peak in the 1960s when more than 4,000 were involved in rearing and gathering oysters, which are especially popular in France. At that time, they exported as much as 50,000 tons of oysters a year. Then suddenly, everything ground to a halt. The industrial boom, together with bad management of environmental resources, leading to high levels of water pollution, brought the oysters of Setúbal to the brink of extinction. Now, a community of 10 people, supported by the Lisbon University and the Arrábida Slow Food convivium, has decided to revive this activity. There is hardly any local competition, the status of the water has improved and the oysters, which are given no food supplements, are healthy again.

PRODUCTION AREA
Setúbal, district of Setúbal

COMMUNITY COORDINATOR
Mário Brito Pinheiro
tel. +351 9329 59100
pinerose@netvisao.pt

Rock-salt producers of the Rio Maior

The story of these saltpans began more than 200 million years ago, when the sea withdrew from the Serra dos Candeeiros, leaving behind a layer of rock-salt 60 m below the ground. When the river that flows through it surfaces, it is seven times more salty than sea water. The salt of the Rio Maior was first used long before the time of Christ, but it was the Romans who built the facilities needed to extract the salt. This method was improved by the Arabs (711 AD) who made innovations that are still used today. The community continues to work in those ancient little buildings made of pine-wood, which are protected for their historic and cultural value. This salt is important not only because of its mineral value, but also because it is produced using artisan methods which are centuries old.

PRODUCTION AREA
Serra dos Candeeiros, district of Santarém

COMMUNITY COORDINATOR
Casimiro Fróis Ferreira
tel. +35 1243 991692 - coop.sal.riomaior@sapo.pt

Sea salt producers of Castro Marim

The community, formed by about 30 people who formed an association in 1999, extracts sea salt from the Atlantic Ocean. Most of the stretch of coastline where the salt is produced lies within the territory of two Natural Parks. The work is all done by hand, so that the landscape and the organoleptic properties of the salt are preserved. Because they don't use bulldozers or tractors, the sea salt and the *fleur de sel* (small salt crystals collected soon after they have formed) produced here have a high calcium and magnesium content, unlike salt produced on an industrial scale. Industrial salt has to be treated with cleansing and whitening agents and is almost pure sodium chloride. The community is trying to obtain international certification for its product and save the saltpans of Castro Marim so that they can be included in the Atlantic Salt Route, which incorporates eleven coastal towns from Brittany to the Canary Islands.

PRODUCTION AREA
Castro Marim, district of Faro

COMMUNITY COORDINATOR
Jacinto Palma Dias
tel. +351 2815 31022 - acintodias@hotmail.com

Breeders and cheese producers of Brusturoasa

At Brusturoasa, a town with 3,700 inhabitants in the east of Romania, the main activities are agriculture and rearing livestock. In the five neighboring villages which form the community there are about 1,200 small farms, all of which rear sheep and cattle which, in summer, are taken up to graze in the mountains. The cattle belong to the *baltata romaneasca* and the Romanian brown breeds, while the sheep are mainly *tsigai*, Romanian *zackel* or *tsurcana zackel*, with an extremely soft fleece. The farms with a larger number of animals and higher milk production make a mixed cow and ewe's milk cheese called *branza*, which is preserved in pine-bark or sheep's bladders.

PRODUCTION AREA
Brusturoasa, province of Bacàu

COMMUNITY COORDINATOR
Camelia Zamfir
tel. +40 236 462 564-745 075 753 - earthfriends@rdslink.ro

Cabbage growers and transformers of Bucovina

One of the most important activities in the Romanian district of Bucovina is growing and transforming vegetables. The towns of Husi and Hartop specialize in organic nurseries, whereas Iaslovat and Spataresti are more renowned for their vegetable preserves. Cabbages (in the local red, white and winter varieties), cucumbers and beet, par-boiled and thinly sliced, are the most common vegetables used for making preserves. The producers of the community put the cabbages with a few maize-cobs into vats or concrete wood-lined tanks lined tanks full of salt water, and leave them there for between one and ten months. The brine they make for preserving cucumbers may be flavored with horseradish, wild fennel, thyme, celery, garlic or chili pepper.

Producers of Vâlcea

The people forming this community are about 40 small-scale producers in the Province of Vâlcea, a region partly occupied by the Transylvanian Alps with the River Olt flowing through it. They all practice traditional farming activities: bee-keeping (they produce acacia, lime, peppermint, pine and sunflower honey, honey derivatives and honeydew), apple-growing (including several local varieties, such as *parmen*, *cretesc* and *domnesc*), bread-making and brewing, producing beer which is fermented twice using local malt and hops.

PRODUCTION AREA
Province of Vâlcea

COMMUNITY COORDINATOR
Alexandrina Sirbu
tel. +40 744 993 123
asirbu@yahoo.com

PRODUCTION AREA
Province of Suceava

COMMUNITY COORDINATOR
Bruma Ion
tel. +40 230 544 155 - andabruma@yahoo.com

Organic milk, cheese and bread producers

Started three years ago, the Culture and Ecology Foundation is a non-profit-making organization offering support and training to farmers to enable them develop forms of sustainable farming. One of its main projects is to create a training farm for the young people of Boiu, a village in the Province of Moie inhabited by Romanians and Hungarians. 30 hectares of land here are cultivated organically to grow cereals, various types of salad, turnips, onions, peas and roses (to make rose-petal jam). Another aim of the organization is to save and promote local products, such as naturally leavened bread made with local wheat, organic milk and fresh cheeses (*urda* and *telemea*).

PRODUCTION AREA
Province of Mures

COMMUNITY COORDINATOR
Wolfgang Raddotz
tel. +40 742 132 440
culteco@birotec.ro

Airan Producers

In the autonomous Republic of Karachaevo-Cherkessia, in the northern Caucasus, the members of this community raise cows and produce airan, a traditional, lightly alcoholic drink, made from milk which has fermented following the addition of a small amount of the previous day's airan. Historically it is consumed as a refreshing drink (*susap*), in meat sauces (*tuzluk*) or mixed with pieces of bread (*cianciulgian gurdzun*). It is also used medicinally, for example to treat respiratory illnesses. The community brings together a group of family-run businesses which produce a total of 2,000 liters of airan a year, some of which they drink themselves and some of which is sold.

PRODUCTION AREA
Republic of Karachaevo-Cherkessia

COMMUNITY COORDINATOR
Fatima Borlakova
tel. +7 9151002505
colipso777@yahoo.com

Bashkirian Honey Producers

The community of around 25 people is concerned with harvesting wild honey and raising bees inside hollows carved out of the trunks of trees. Wild honey, rich in fructose and glucose, gains special value from its maturity, as the honey is gathered just once during the season. At the start of the fall the hives are checked; usually each family of bees produces no more than five kilos of honey. It's sold in local shops and markets, as well as forming part of the diet of the astronauts on the international space station.

PRODUCTION AREA
Bashkir Autonomous Republic

COMMUNITY COORDINATOR
Bragina Nadezhda
tel. +7 3472336017
nadezhda_bragina@mail.ru

Beekeepers and collectors in Zabajkalie

The community of producers in Zabajkalie has settled near the large and deep Bajkal Lake. The community produces honey and collects wild herbs. There are 25 beekeepers who produce wildflower honey and other products (pollen, wax, bee's milk). They also make an alcoholic drink using medovukha honey, from a recipe which is handed down from generation to generation. The herbs are used to make tea. The products of the community have obtained the international certificate for environmental conservation.

PRODUCTION AREA
Zabajkalie, Irkutsk province, Sibir

COMMUNITY COORDINATOR
Tatyana Novoderezkina
tel. +7 4953016581
interzakaz367@mail.ru

Beekeepers in Krasnoznamensk

The beekeeper community in Krasnoznamensk comes from the remote village of Dobrovolsk, in the northwestern Kaliningrad region, on the border with Poland and Lithuania. The Krasnoznamensk area is covered in forests; the environment, vegetation and climate are ideal for beekeeping. In the village many families produce honey, wax and bee-glue. Each family also has a vegetable garden, grows wheat and potatoes and possesses some cows and pigs for family consumption. The community, with 72 beekeepers, produces different types of honey: linden flower, clover or wildflower honey. The best product is sold in specialized shops and in pharmacies.

PRODUCTION AREA
Krasnoznamensk, Kaliningrad province

COMMUNITY COORDINATOR
Vasili Dederya
tel. +7 9052443129
kenig_raisa@pochta.ru

Beekeepers in the Urals

Beekeepers in the Urals come from the village of Brod, in the Kamensk district. It sits amongst the oldest mountains in the world, on the border between Europe and Asia. The vegetation is unique, and it influences the quality of meat and milk and certain types of plants used in honey. The area has been inhabited since the Nineteenth Century, when the European-Russian population moved to these remote parts. The Sverdlovsk region was one of the most important in the whole country for the production of honey after the 1917 revolution. The beekeeper community in the southern Urals, born a few years ago, groups together thirty families with 20-30 hives each on average. It produces wildflower honey for family consumption or to be sold locally.

PRODUCTION AREA
Brod, Sverdlovsk province

COMMUNITY COORDINATOR
Vladimir Artamonov
tel. +7 9126360581
galgena@bk.ru

Biodynamic Producers

The farm Givaja Zemlia (Living Earth) is the center of the community, located 130 kilometers south of Moscow in Tula. Founded in 1991 to show the possibility of developing biodynamic agriculture in Russia, today a community of six people cultivates 100 hectares of land, formerly part of a *kolkhoz*. They produce fresh milk, which they take to the local market, and also sell various dairy products (like sour cream, yogurt and cottage cheese), meat (lard and offal), vegetables, tubers, barley and wheat, some of which are distributed nationally. In collaboration with other communities they organize educational seminars and seek to involve young people in the private agricultural sector.

PRODUCTION AREA
Tula province

COMMUNITY COORDINATOR
Markus Shumaker
tel. +7 9056245901
bolotovo@mail.ru

Bread Producers

The central regions of Russia are known for their wheat fields, and the community follows the whole production chain from the planting to the grinding of the flour, all the way up to the baking of the bread. All the bread-making phases are managed by a group of people who work in the fields growing the grain and in the mills and the bakeries, producing the final product. They produce a small quantity of bread (about 2,500 kilos a year), which means they can maintain a high quality standard and the unique flavor of every loaf. Two particular kinds of bread are produced in Saratov Oblast, *kalatch saratovski* and round *prazdnicnuj* loaves for holidays. The members of the community distribute the bread though a network of shops.

PRODUCTION AREA
Saratov province

COMMUNITY COORDINATOR
Aleksey Ponomarenko
tel. +7 453724813
alexei.pon@list.ru

Breeders of Kabardino-Balkaria

The confederal republic of Kabardino-Balkaria occupies the mountainous area of Caucasian Russia almost on the border with Georgia. The breeding of cattle, sheep and goats is the principal source of livelihood of the population. The animals, bred for milk and meat, have acclimatized themselves to the harsh temperatures of the mountains, which can drop to as low as 30° below zero. The most popular local breeds include the white cow and the red-brown cow. The production of fermented milk (gifi-airan), yogurt (zhuurt) and cheese is also an important activity. The community originates from the village of Bulungu, in the district of Chegem. The connections between the family clans are very strong and the co-operation, which is based on friendship and family relationships, is rather widespread. The products are destined for local consumption and the local market.

PRODUCTION AREA
District of Chegem, Kabardino-Balkaria

COMMUNITY COORDINATOR
Alim Zalikhanov
tel. +7 9165541901
bulungu@yandex.ru

Butter Producers of Vologda

The oblast of Vologda, noted for Vologodskoje butter, is found in the heart of European Russia. The community of producers is made up of different farms in the village of Borisovo-Sudskoe. The variegated black local cows graze on the large surrounding pastures, and willowherb, St. John's wort and hundreds of other herbs give an unmistakable hazelnut flavor to the Vologda butter. It's history goes back centuries; in the 19th century a Russian nobleman brought back the secrets of butter-making from Normandy, and initially it was produced following that recipe, but it has changed over time. The butter, made from cream, is noted in the whole country for its unique flavor. It is produced in small quantities and distributed at a national level.

PRODUCTION AREA
Vologda province

COMMUNITY COORDINATOR
Sergey Yushkevich
tel. +7 8174341363
accor@vologda.ru

Cheese Producers of Kaliningrad

Kaliningrad Oblast borders Poland and Lithuania and is historically known for livestock raising. The community includes 20 people who manage family farms, raising cows and goats and feeding them only with natural fodder. From their milk they make a range of dairy products, including yogurt, fresh ricotta, cheeses, fresh milk, butter and cream. The fresh and aged cheeses are produced only from raw milk, heated to 36°C, and with animal rennet. The best cheese for aging is rubanochnuj, which is eaten after four to six months. The community consumes some of its production and sells the rest at Kaliningrad market. They also raise pigs and make honey for themselves.

PRODUCTION AREA
Kaliningrad province

COMMUNITY COORDINATOR
Timofey Fartishev
tel. +7 9216120818
timofej.FTL@mail.ru

Cheese Producers of Ossetia

The people of the Caucasus mountains, around the borders of the Republic of North Ossetia-Alania, have traditionally raised livestock and made cheese. The majority of the cheesemakers currently working in the southern heights of the Stavropol plateau have joined in an association which helps them with marketing. The community of Ossetia cheese producers is made up of families who own a total of 180 cows and 30 sheep. The community produces meat, cheese, butter and wool, which are then sold in the capital of Ossetia. For next year the community plans to increase the number of sheep and they are building winter stables. They would like to increase the cheese production, setting up a small dairy to process the milk from nearby villages.

PRODUCTION AREA
Stavropol Krai

COMMUNITY COORDINATOR
Hetag Dzutcev
tel. +7 9284804647

Cucumber Producers of Suzdal

Thanks to its fertile soil, Vladimir Oblast has always been noted for horticulture. The city of Suzdal, northeast of Moscow, is one of the oldest in the country. Apart from attracting many tourists with a rich historical and cultural heritage, it is also famous for its cucumbers. It could be found on the tables of the tzars, and even today the cucumber, raw or tinned, is one of the basic ingredients of the Russian diet and a symbol of traditional cuisine. The community is made up of a small group of farmers, supported by the mayor of the city. They are working to set up a cooperative of cucumber producers which will be responsible for the whole production chain, from cultivation to canning, all respecting traditional methods.

PRODUCTION AREA
Suzdal, Vladimir province

COMMUNITY COORDINATOR
Roman Kuzmin
tel. +7 9038334870
roman_k@pisem.net

Fishermen in the Gizhiga river

In Magadan, the Russian far eastern region bordering on the Ohotsk sea, the regional natives' Association – whose first foundation came about in Ola in 1989, but was then formally established in 1993 and now encompasses 6300 associates – sustains and develops the indigenous community's fishing activity. The associates belong to the Eveni ethnic group, which has inhabited these areas for ages, and only a century ago has started mingling with the Russian culture. The effort put in by the Vzmoriye group in the Magadan (20 blood-related associates), founded by its current leader Alexander Avdonin - the first to set up a cooperation for the production and sales of the prestigious red caviar and fish, mainly salmon - is noteworthy.

PRODUCTION AREA
Magadan province

COMMUNITY COORDINATOR
Andrey Khalkachan
tel. + 7 4132663324
akhalkachan@gmail.com

Fishermen of Smolensk

A community of fishermen in the region of Smolensk was created to fish in the rivers and lakes of the area in order to offer the Moscow market fresh fish instead of the more common frozen or farmed. The community which works in the village of Gagarin is made up of 15 people who catch the fish and salt, dry or smoke them according to the traditional methods of the village. In order to respect the seasonality of the fish a smokehouse has been set up for the community. The freshwater fish is cleaned, salted and dried outside on wooden sticks before being smoked with aromatic roots and herbs.

PRODUCTION AREA
Smolensk province

COMMUNITY COORDINATOR
Andreev Vadim
tel. +7 9039112852
interzakaz367@mail.ru

Geese breeders

The Suzdal breeders have set up an association setting themselves a number of goals: to protect the purity of the indigenous geese by collaborating with the research institutes and a number of genetic geese farms, reintroduce goose meat on the local market and help the breeders coming from the 13 regions of the Country to organize the production and distribution of the end products. The geese, which have decreased in number by 37% in the last fifteen years, are bred free range in pastures and lakes and the quality of their meat is high thanks to their low-cholesterol diet. 22 species of geese are preserved in the farms of the community members. The main products are the meat, fresh or smoked, goose fat and liver. The community is attempting to overcome the difficulties encountered during slaughtering and distribution.

PRODUCTION AREA
Suzdal, Vladimir province

COMMUNITY COORDINATOR
Pavel Devyatov
tel. +7 49231209
root@devyatov.souzdal.elcom.ru

Goat breeders

Before 1917, European Russia was one of the areas with the highest concentration of goat farms, despite the opinion that these animals destroy the pastures and damage the soil. During the period of collectivization the number of goats was drastically reduced and only the rural population continued to breed them in small numbers. Interest in these animals returned in the early Nineties. The community includes a number of farming companies located in the vast plains crossed by the River Volga, with the pulsing heart of the city of Tolyatti at its center. Currently, the milk is the only commercialized product (it is sold in shops and distributed in the schools), but the possibility of working it to produce cheese is being considered.

PRODUCTION AREA
District of Tolyatti

COMMUNITY COORDINATOR
Nataliya Markelova
tel. +7 8482719193
pallada@infopac.ru

Gray cow breeders of Altaj

The Republic of Altaj is located in Central Asia, on the border with the Siberian coniferous forests, the kazake steppes and the Mongolian desert. In the past this region was widely populated by the gray cow, belonging to the family of the ancient *Bos Taurus primigenius*, considered the oldest race on earth. At one time the animals grazed all year in the unconfined spaces, resistant to the high and low temperatures. Today, however, only a few hundred of this breed remains. Scientists of the Academy of Russian Sciences, collaborators of an experimental breed and a few local producers form part of the community. The farming community breeds the surviving cattle trying to protect the breed and recover its genetic purity.

PRODUCTION AREA
Republic of Altaj

COMMUNITY COORDINATOR
Yuriy Stolpovsky
tel. +7 9104715438
stolpovsky@hotbox.ru

Herb Gatherers of Kamchatka

In the extreme east of Russia is the remote, volcanic region of Kamchatka, home to the largest populations of wild salmon and brown bears in the world and known for its aromatic wild herbs. Gathering these herbs is the traditional activity of the indigenous Evens people. The Fito-tè community in the Bystrinksy district produces traditional infusions without any additives; the same activity is carried out by three connected families in the village of Anavgaj. The members of the community are actively working to obtain certification for the wild herbs and also to profitably employ local people while at the same time helping revive a traditional way of life.

PRODUCTION AREA
District of Bystrinksy, Kamchatka Peninsula

COMMUNITY COORDINATOR
Nina Banakanova
tel. +7 4154223262
bnpark@mail.kamchatka.ru

Horse breeders

The community is composed of eight people joined in the Botash association, which manages the breeding of Karachaevo horses, in the Northern Caucasus. Horse meat has always been eaten in large quantities by the shepherds of the hill country. They use it to prepare different by-products, including various kinds of sausage. The meat normally used comes from horses that have never been saddled, because its taste is softer and more delicate. The k'azy sausage is prepared cutting the ribs with the meat and leaving the blood to drain for 5-7 hours. The intestine is washed and put into salted water for a few hours. Salt, pepper and garlic is added and the meat is placed in the intestine. These sausages can be smoked or dried, but are eaten cooked only. The community produces 800 kilos a year, distributing them in the shops and to private clients.

PRODUCTION AREA
Republic of Karachaevo-Cherkessia

COMMUNITY COORDINATOR
Tekeev Azretali
tel. +7 8787724148
etnos@list.ru

Kaliningrad Fishermen

Kaliningrad is a flat region on the Baltic Sea, which, thanks to its special legal status has enjoyed economic development based mainly on fishing and agriculture. The community consists of private agricultural farms which breed and kill fish and also carry out fishing in the Baltic Sea. They fish zander, Baltic Sea herring, sprat, cod, brama, which can be salted or smoked. In order to prepare the Baltic Sea herring, the fish fillets are pickled for 3-5 days, then cut into small pieces and put in jars in oil and spices. Both fresh and treated fish is sold in the region.

PRODUCTION AREA
Kaliningrad province

COMMUNITY COORDINATOR
Anna Dobrinets
tel. +7 4012911494
kenig_raisa@pochta.ru

Karachaeva sheep farming in the Cherkessia region

One of the main agricultural areas in Russia is the Caucasian Republic of Karaãajevo-âerkessia: two thirds of the inhabitants (about 400 000) live on sheep farming in the mountainous areas of Karachaevo and on crops in the Cherkessia valleys. Farmers have grouped together in order to protect the black Karachaevo breed, used for milk, meat and wool production. Animals are medium-sized: the males weigh 60 to 70 Kilos, females between 45 and 50. In the community there are 350 people who look after the sheep; there is also a group which treats and sells meat. The work is carried out in family farms, free from the use of chemical additives, but the meat keeps for long. Its sale is local all over the Republic.

PRODUCTION AREA
Republic of Karachaevo-Cherkessia

COMMUNITY COORDINATOR
Tekeeva Khadzhat
tel. +7 9265315572
etnos@list.ru

Khalva Producers of Karachaevo-Cherkessia

The community, in the Republic of Karachaevo-Cherkessia, is distinguished by the strong ties and cooperation between the different family clans of which it is comprised. The 25 members produce and market this traditional sweet, which is prepared for family consumption and for selling in the city and small local restaurants. This sweet is considered an excellent gift, and there are many different recipes. The main ingredients are flour, sugar and butter, to which honey, hazelnuts, dried apricots and raisins are added. Everything is mixed by hand: quality khalva takes time and hard work.

PRODUCTION AREA
Republic of Karachaevo-Cherkessia

COMMUNITY COORDINATOR
Albert Bayramkulov
tel. +7 9289115465
etnos@list.ru

Organic Producers

The association of organic producers in Russia, which now has 40 members, was created in 2003 with the aim of helping farmers obtain certifications and improving organization at a national level. The association is primarily concerned with production, processing, sales, certification and education. To resolve the biggest problem, the marketing of products like potatoes, cabbage, buckwheat, tomatoes and cucumbers, an internet site was created which the farmers can use to access the market, share information and exchange opinions. The initiative was a success and has contributed to the growth of the association. The everyday foods, vegetables, fruit, dairy products, meat and cereals are sold at a national level.

PRODUCTION AREA
Moscow

COMMUNITY COORDINATOR
Andrey Khodus
tel. +7 4959940397
info@biodynamic.ru

Organic Producers of Kaliningrad

Kaliningrad, on the Baltic coast, is home to this community of farmers and private companies, about 15 people in total. They are involved in livestock farming, milk and dairy production, cultivating fruit trees and collecting wild berries. Native Chiorno-Piostrye breed cows are raised organically and their milk used for cheese, butter and ricotta. The farmed and wild fruit is used to make non-alcoholic beverages, spirits and ciders, including a wine made from fruit and berries, with added sugar, which can reach an alcohol content of between 16 and 18°C. Among the community's projects is the creation of an ecological village, which will produce sustainable, good-quality food.

PRODUCTION AREA
Kaliningrad province

COMMUNITY COORDINATOR
Raisa Guseva
tel. +7 9114518750
kenig_raisa@pochta.ru

Preserves Producers of Kamchatka

The Kamchatka Peninsula, in the north of Russia, has a harsh climate. The indigenous Itelmen people are seeking to protect their interests and have united in an organization called Vale Yjkoal. The current 10 members are concerned with harvesting, processing and selling various foods. Traditionally they are fishers, hunters and foragers, and collect up to 100 different kinds of plants and berries, all used in the traditional Itelmen cuisine. They make jam from the fruits of the Kamchatka trillium (*Trillium camschatcense*), a plant with just one flower and a green, pyramidal fruit. The lightly acidic preserve is used in cakes and stirred into tea. The fruits can also be dried.

PRODUCTION AREA
Kamchatka Peninsula

COMMUNITY COORDINATOR
Liudmila Shishkina
tel. +7 9619614281
ekonomika7@mail.ru

Preserves Producers of Shoria

Gornaya Shoria is a mountainous territory in the south of Kemerovo Oblast, in southern Siberia. Around 40 people have grouped together to make the most of the products of the forest, gathering and preserve wild berries like blueberries, raspberries, red and black currants and honeysuckle, which are commonly used in the local cuisine. They prepare excellent preserves, varying according to the season and the quantity of the harvest, working in groups and sharing out the tasks of gathering and processing in order to make the best use the experience of the producers. The currants grow by the river bank, the blueberries on the hillsides and the raspberries found on the slopes of the mountains have a distinctive fragrance and have an excellent flavor. The jams are found for sale in some of the region's shops.

PRODUCTION AREA
Gornaya Shoria, Kemorovo province

COMMUNITY COORDINATOR
Elena Malyavko
tel. +7 3847545369
ecolist@mail.ru

Producers of Goat's Milk Ricotta

The community works in the southern Urals, which are considered to be among the oldest mountains in the world. The community comes from the village of Brod and is made up of about 10 people who dedicate themselves to raising goats for milk. They use a traditional recipe for preparing goat ricotta with lactic coagulation. They also produce sour milk, called *prostokvasha*: the fresh milk is left to ferment for some hours in a ceramic container together with some added *prostokvasha* from the previous day. In the summer it's left at room temperature while in the winter it's placed inside a Russian stove, an ancient kind of wood-fired oven. The community is registered as a producers' union and provides technical consultancy to the members. The production is destined for family consumption and sold at a local level, in the district of Kamensk.

PRODUCTION AREA
District of Kamensk, Sverdlovsk province

COMMUNITY COORDINATOR
Olga Podosenova
tel. +7 3432175125
olga_mox@mail.ru

Producers of Pine Nut Oil

Gornaya Shoria is located in the south of Kemerovo Oblast, in Siberia, and is home to an indigenous population called Shors. Around 15,000 people are gathered in an association to defend their interests. Historically their main activities were hunting, fishing and gathering. Foraging, particularly for pine nuts, is still very important to them today. The families move for weeks to the taiga to collect the nuts needed for pressing oil. The 10-year-old community is made up of 20 families and now brings together the gatherers, the processors and the sellers of the final product. The harvest is from August 20 to the end of September. Together with the cold-pressed pine-nut oil, the community also makes pine-nut milk. The association offers consultancy and helps organize the harvest.

PRODUCTION AREA
Gornaya Shoria, Kemerovo province

COMMUNITY COORDINATOR
Mihail Tunekov
tel. +7 3847543873

Producers of Pskov

The community is located in the suburbs of the city of Pskov, on the banks of the Velikaya River. Close to the Baltic countries, this is considered one of the most unspoiled parts of northeastern Russia. The climate varies according to the season and influences the choice of what to cultivate and the yield. The community is organized as a farm and until 1992 was a kind of *kolkhoz*. With more than 75 years of experience in the production, transformation and conservation of agricultural products, the farm is used for both growing vegetables and raising animals. Pskov milk is noted for its low fat and high protein. The products are sold on the local market.

PRODUCTION AREA
Pskov province

COMMUNITY COORDINATOR
Alexander Zadontsev
tel. +7 8112223898
afz_psc@yahoo.com

Producers of Reindeer Cheese

In the west of the Republic of Tuva, a few kilometers from Mongolia, Adir-Kazhig has had little contact with the rest of the world for centuries. In this rural village the typical houses are simple wooden yurts covered with reindeer hides. The farmers who live here get almost everything they need to survive from the reindeer: clothes, milk and cheese. The community works in a remote zone on the edge of the taiga and the tundra. Making reindeer cheese requires much time and energy. For example one animal gives 200 milliliters of milk per milking and two days are needed to collect enough for the cheesemaking process. The cheese is then hung in the highest part of the yurt to be conserved.

PRODUCTION AREA
Republic of Tuva

COMMUNITY COORDINATOR
Dorzu Choduraa
tel. +7 9133416795
choduraa2003@mail.ru

Producers of Siberian Pine Nuts

Altai is a Siberian republic near to China and Mongolia, with a landscape dominated by the taiga, forests of firs, larches, pines and Siberian cedars. The population of the region collects the Siberian cedar's nuts, which are a true delicacy. The community's activities begin in Siberia and finish in Moscow, where the nuts are packaged and most of them sold. In 2004 an association was created to promote the careful use of the resources of the Altai taiga. The community is trying to conserve traditional recipes and to maintain the use of the foods which help them adapt to Siberia's severe climate. The people collect berries, mushrooms and ferns, all for their own consumption. Their first foray onto the national market has been with the pine nuts.

PRODUCTION AREA
Republic of Altaj

COMMUNITY COORDINATOR
Andrey Pronkin
tel. +7 9262039703
kapron777@yandex.ru

Reindeer farmers in the Kola Peninsula

In the Kola peninsula in northwestern Russia, almost on the border with Finland, stretches the Lapp district of Lovozersky, which boasts the best reindeer pastures of the entire Murmansk region, where the indigenous population of Laplanders still live. The community was founded in the Twenties. Nowadays it is made up of 350 people divided into two cooperatives: Tundra, which only groups farmers of the villages of Lovozero, and Olenevod, which includes members in villages all around. Reindeer meat can be used following national recipes. The final products obtained from reindeer meat are sausages, heart, liver, smoked fillet, tongue and stroganina (frozen meat strips).

PRODUCTION AREA
Kola Peninsula

COMMUNITY COORDINATOR
Startsev Vitaly
tel. +7 8153830279
tundra@com.mels.ru

Reindeer farmers in the Magadan region

In northeast Russia the Magadan region, the main gold-bearing area in Russia, is hilly, covered in larch woods and tundra and inhabited by the Eveni, traditionally reindeer breeders and fishermen. The number of reindeer from which they get meat and clothing is decreasing drastically: of 90 000 at the start of the Nineties, there are barely 15 000 remaining. Local authorities have intervened by creating a reindeer farm of the irbychan breed with 12 000 reindeer, of which 3000 have private owners. Reindeer meat, the staple diet, may be eaten fresh or dried, or else it may be frozen. The community is trying to encourage farmers (roughly 250 today) to organize the use and production of dried or frozen meat.

PRODUCTION AREA
Magadan province

COMMUNITY COORDINATOR
Lilia Shcherbakova
tel. +7 41324822736
lsherbakova2004@mail.ru

Rye Producers of Vologda

The Vologda climate favors the cultivation of rye and barley. In 1998 a program was launched to provide support to the farmers of the Verkhovazh'ye district, a few hundred kilometers north of Moscow. To encourage the cultivation of rye and the production of bread and to ensure food production for the entire region, in 2000 the cooperative Millestones was created, which owns a mill in which rye from four local farms is ground. Today the community includes 20 farms which grow rye and produce flour and bread. The cooperative also makes machines available which facilitate breadmaking, albeit in limited quantities. The farmers have also created green farms which don't use chemicals.

PRODUCTION AREA
District of Verkhovazh'ye, Vologda province

COMMUNITY COORDINATOR
Sergey Belyakov
tel. +7 8172724405
accor@vologda.ru

Salmon Fishermen of Kamchatka

An unspoiled land of fire and ice in the far east of Russia, Kamchatka has 29 active volcanoes. It is home to the Tarja community, which has long fished and sold the region's wild salmon. Out of the 40 tons of fish caught every year, half are consumed by the community themselves, and the other half sold. The wild salmon found here are different from other varieties of salmon on the market, with an incredibly high level of quality and a rich store of vitamins and mineral salts, and need to be protected. The Tarja community also fishes nerka, kizhuch, keta, gorbusha, treska (cod), kambala and a white fish known as terpug.

PRODUCTION AREA
Kamchatka Peninsula

COMMUNITY COORDINATOR
Elena Posvolskaya
tel. +7 4153527176
tarya@vilgus.kamchatka.ru

Salted Fern Producers

In Kemerovo Oblast there is a community of producers of salted ferns, with about 30 people involved in the gathering and processing of bracken ferns. The plants are cut before they have fully opened, when they only about one centimeter off the ground. They are immediately immersed in brine at the harvesting site, usually in a wooden container with a weighted lid. On average about a kilo of salt is used for 300 grams of fresh ferns. The finished brined bracken ferns are packaged in glass jars. The ferns are eaten fried and used in salads. The salted ferns are distributed nationally.

PRODUCTION AREA
Kemerovo province

COMMUNITY COORDINATOR
Iakov Malyavko
tel. +7 3847530685
ecolist@mail.ru

Talkan Producers of Tashtagol

Gornaya Shoria is in the south of Siberia, and its indigenous population, the Shors, produce talkan. Talkan is flour made from toasted barley, and is much used in traditional dishes. The barley is toasted in a flat tin (*korgush*), crushed in a mortar, stripped and ground by hand. Talkan is pale brown, and is eaten with tea, water, milk and butter as well as sour cream. Talkan is also used in preparing drinks, and though once very common is becoming harder to find. The community is trying to preserve the traditional processing methods, and the producers are united in a tribal community, called Shin Col, which protects its rights.

PRODUCTION AREA
Gornaya Shoria, Kemerevo province

COMMUNITY COORDINATOR
Valentina Kurdakova
tel. +7 9069279144
mep@nvkz.net

Tuva sheep farmers

Not far from Kyzyl, capital of the Russian Federal Republic of Tuva, almost on the border with Mongolia, lives a nomadic population devoted to sheep, cow and goat farming from which cured meats and dairy products are made, partly for the people's own use, partly for the market and distribution in schools. In particular, there is a cheese called byshtak, made from both ewe and cow's milks, which doesn't keep longer than a week. The milk used in making this kind of cheese is from indigenous animals which are not susceptible to diseases. The community is made up of a number of family members. Among other problems in the community there is also that of preserving perishable cheeses. Thanks to the local research institute work is being carried out to set up the first gene-bank of Tuva's regional breeds.

PRODUCTION AREA
Republic of Tuva

COMMUNITY COORDINATOR
Dorzu Choduraa
tel. +7 9133416795
choduraa2003@mail.ru

Watermelon Producers

In Kamyshin in the south of European Russia, this community is made up of a few family-run businesses on the banks of the River Volga and was created in 1996 when the members bought the land around their country houses. In the busiest period they employ around 50 seasonal workers. Different kinds of watermelon are cultivated, the most common kind being Astrakanski. A local specialty is brined watermelon: In the fall the fruits are placed in small barrels, covered with chopped cabbage and salt, weighed down and left for two months to produce an excellent appetizer. Jam is also made from the watermelon rinds. All the production is sold locally.

PRODUCTION AREA
Kamyshin, Volgograd province

COMMUNITY COORDINATOR
Valery Alekseenko
tel. +7 4953403987
valtuz@mail.ru

Yak Cheese Producers of Tuva

In the south of Siberia on the border with Mongolia, the Republic of Tuva is farther from the sea than anywhere else in the world, and has a continental climate. In the Mongun-Taiga region 250 families of nomad farmers live in yurts (typical round tents) and raise yaks, wild, long-haired bison which range freely in the mountains and are very resistant to the harshest cold. With their milk the farmers produce cheese – byshtak, kurut and aarji – to be consumed at home, bartered and sold annually at the fair in the capital Kyzyl. The cheeses are a fundamental source of protein for the nomad's diet, and in Tuva they say that with a leather bag (in which the cheeses can last for many years) full of kurut you can live for six months.

PRODUCTION AREA
Mongun-Taiga, Republic of Tuva

COMMUNITY COORDINATOR
Dorzu Choduraa
tel. +7 9133416795
choduraa2003@mail.ru

GERMOPLASM BANK OF SAINT PETERSBURG

The Vavilov Institute of Research (Vir) of Saint Petersburg has an immense germoplasm collection and is in third place in the world with its archive of 341,000 genotypes. Activities began way back in 1894 and were not interrupted even during the German occupation; scientists in countries all over the world have collected both the oldest, most resistant varieties, those born from cross-fertilization by farmers and hybrids created by the Institute itself. Vir relies on the work of 15 experimental stations all over Russia, which work to preserve the genetic heritage. One of the main goals of the Institute is to preserve varieties on the spot (on farm). There are 43 hybridization centers in Russia alone. When a country loses a native variety for any reason, the institute replaces it, free of charge.

AREA OF ACTIVITY
The entire Country

COORDINATOR
Maria Girenko
tel. +7 8124765343

Backa bread producers

In the Baāka area, in northwestern Vojvodina, a baker's association is involved in protecting two types of bread, whose recipes have been handed down orally. *Burek* bread is made up of layers of dough (*kora*) filled with meat or cheese. There is also a fruit version, usually made with cherries, which is excellent a half hour after it has been taken out of the oven. *Pogaca* is reserved for family and religious holidays like Easter and Christmas, and is made with wheat and corn flour, eggs and yeast.

PRODUCTION AREA
Subotica, Northern Baāka district; Novi Sad, Southern Baāka district

COMMUNITY COORDINATOR
Branko Zujovic
tel. +38 16411 47484
zujovic@eunet.yu

Indigenous livestock breeders of Srem

In the Srem region, near the city of Sremska Mitrovica, is the Zasavica nature reserve, where the NGO Nature Conservation Movement raise two indigenous breeds of livestock. The first is the swallow-bellied *mangalica* pig, a crossbreed of the white *mangalica* (common in Hungary and the Balkans) and the black pig of the Srem zone. The second is the *podolica* cow, a very rustic breed of cattle native to Eastern Europe. The community is composed of nine breeders who also produce the typical pork sausages of Srem. Sold in pairs, they are known as "half-meter sausages" because they are 25 centimeters long.

PRODUCTION AREA
Srem district

COMMUNITY COORDINATOR
Slobodan Simic
tel. +381 6351 4847
zasavica@zasavica.org.yu

Kajmak cheese producers

This community is located in the city of Topola, 80 km from Belgrade in the Sumadija region, where the main source of income has always been livestock breeding. Its members are 250 breeders and cheese producers, who own no more than 5 animals each and use a system based on free-grazing in the summer months and stabling in winter. The cheese producers of the community make *kajmak* with the milk from their own cows (at times with sheep's milk added). This traditional creamy cheese is made by boiling the milk, collecting the curd and having it ripen in special containers. There are two versions: fresh *kajmak* and one that has been aged for 15-20 days. Many cheese makers make *kajmak* only for their personal use, but a few also sell it at local markets or to restaurants in Belgrade.

PRODUCTION AREA
Topola, Western Baāka district

COMMUNITY COORDINATOR
Senad Hopic
tel. +381 1133 41875
senad@grolink.se

Pozegaca Plum growers of Topola

The *pozegaca* plum, an ecotype of the *Prunus insititia* species, is very common throughout the Balkans and other Eastern European countries. Introduced in Serbia at the beginning of the 19th century, the *pozegaca* is smaller than other varieties on the market, but its pit is so minute that the percentage of pulp per fruit is actually higher. It is made around the city of Topola, south of Belgrade, by about 100 growers from the Bio Top association. No chemical agents are used in their orchards, which cover 80 hectares of land, because the plant itself is very resistant to pathogens. In addition to being eaten fresh, thanks to the high sugar content the plums are also dried and used for making a traditional jam called *pekmez*.

PRODUCTION AREA
Topola, Western Baāka district

COMMUNITY COORDINATOR
Senad Hopic
tel. +381 1133 41875
senad@grolink.se

Vojvodina organic producers

These producers grow, process and sell local varieties of fruit, vegetables and cereals in an effort to promote sustainable farming and preserve the culinary traditions of the country. One of their products worth mentioning is sunflower seed oil, made by cold pressing the seeds and produced in small quantities using only artisan methods. Another is *slatko*, a traditional Serbian jam made with plums, apricots, cherries and quinces. All of the community's products have been a part of the Vojvodina regional cuisine for centuries and today are sold both locally and nationally.

PRODUCTION AREA
Vojvodina region

COMMUNITY COORDINATOR
Nebosja Davcik
tel. +381 6415 07481
davcik@suonline.net - ndavcik@yahoo.com

Bryndza producers

This ewe's milk cheese, which was being made back in the 18th century, is produced on both the Polish and Slovak sides of the Tatra Mountains. It was once made by reusing less than perfect cheese forms, but today is made with whole, raw sheep's milk to which come cow's milk has been added. It does not have a particular shape, but rather is a granular cheese that can be used as a spread. Sold a couple of weeks after being made, it is eaten on bread or with potatoes. The nine producers of the community make it with milk from their own sheep, raised on high mountain grass in the summer and cereals in the winter.

PRODUCTION AREA
Ruzomberok, region of Îilina

COMMUNITY COORDINATOR
Peter Lajda
tel. +421 444 324 614
peter.lajda@pobox.sk

Organic cereal producers

The producers of the community founded their own family farm 10 years ago in the city of Nitra (a hundred miles or so from the capital Bratislava), with the aim of producing organic cereals and flours without the use of pesticides. They get the wheat, maize and spelt from organic growers and grind them in a community mill. The final product is used mainly for making bread. Their production of flours, which are also sold in other European countries, has increased from an initial 500 kilos per annum to 20,000 kilos at present.

PRODUCTION AREA
Nitra, region of Nitra

COMMUNITY COORDINATOR
Ruzena Klìmová
tel. +421 376 559 591
biola@biola.sk

Oscadnica sheep breeders

The Oscadnica farm cooperative is in northern Slovakia, near the city of âadca, a mountainous area filled with forests, rivers and streams. Its members organically raise sheep and lambs to produce milk and meat (also exported at Easter). The sheep farm covers 500 hectares of fields and pastures, where the animals graze on fresh forage integrated with cereals from organic cultivations. The cooperative is also getting ready to start an agritourism, where they will offer typical Slovak foods made from organic products.

PRODUCTION AREA
Oscadnica, region of Îilina

COMMUNITY COORDINATOR
Kulla L'ubomìr
tel. +421 905 948 991
rdoscadnica@gmail.com

Droze bread producers

Flour made from kamut, an ancient cereal having a sweet taste reminiscent of hazelnut and butter, is the main ingredient of *droze*, a traditional unleavened bread made with semi-wild apples (zlate rosce). The nearly round loaves weigh three kilos and were once baked in a wood burning oven in the black kitchen, so called because of the color it acquired from being a place for cooking meals as well as smoking cheese. At Kamnik, a beautiful black kitchen is the heart of the Budnarjeva Hisa (Budnarjeva shepherd's house), now a house museum and showcase of traditional Slovenian cooking. The idea for the project came from a group of 35 farmers who continue producing droze and potica, a traditional sweet filled with ground walnuts, sour cream, honey and tarragon.

PRODUCTION AREA
Kamnik, Gorenjska region

COMMUNITY COORDINATOR
Iva Subelj-Kramar
tel. +386 1831 2062
dednina@volja.net

Goriska Brda wine producers

Goriska Brda, on the Slovenian side of Collio, is an ideal region for growing grapevines. Its low hills face Friuli and the warm Adriatic wind, and the Giulie Alps and the plateaus of Zavni (Tarnova) protect it from inclement weather and the cold. The limestone-marl terrain offers ideal conditions for producing fine wines. The wine growers of the community cultivate the vines in the most natural way possible, accepting low yields in exchange for excellent grapes. The symbol of the wine growing tradition in this zone is the ribolla gialla, an indigenous variety of grape (*ribuele* in Friuli dialect, rébula in Slovenian) used for making a fruity, sweet and refreshing white wine.

PRODUCTION AREA
Goriska Brda, Goriska region

COMMUNITY COORDINATOR
Marjan Simcic
tel. +386 5395 9200
info@simcic.si

Organic producers of Stiria

This association, founded in 1996, has numerous organic farmers and breeders of the Maribor zone. Their main products are: buckwheat flour (*darja* cultivar); millet, whose grains are eaten fresh or made into flour; traditional varieties of apples used for making juices, vinegar and cider; local breeds of hens, raised for their small eggs and firm, tender meat; squash seed oil. The community has been involved in a number of projects in recent years, the most important of which is the weekly market of organic products, which over 20 farmers take part in. It is also preparing a series of training courses for school-aged children.

PRODUCTION AREA
Maribor, Stiria region

COMMUNITY COORDINATOR
Matjaz Turinek
tel. +386 4196 0972
matjazturinek@yahoo.com

Velika Planina cheese producers

On the Velika Planina plateau there is only a small church and a thousand mountain huts (typical low, round buildings with cone-shaped roofs) Today most of these houses are vacation homes for the people of Ljubljana; only about fifty or so are still used for raising cows and making cheese. The 65 shepherds of this community, who are members of the Dednina association, produce two types. *Trnic*, made from sour cow's milk, without added whey, and shaped like an onion with a tool called *pisava*, is a broken curd cheese that is smoked in a fireplace. *Laski-sir*, made with cow's milk and whey, is a fresh cheese shaped in large rounds that smells somewhat of pine. Both are made for personal consumption and for sale.

PRODUCTION AREA
Kamnik, Gorenjska region

COMMUNITY COORDINATOR
Reza Mali
tel. +386 1832 5015

Wild fruit and berry gatherers and processors

The Slovenian mountains of Primorska, at the Croatian border, are home to a community of about 50 wild fruit and berry gatherers and processors. Juniper berries, olives, strawberries, raspberries, blackberries, dog rose, blueberries and elderberries all grow wild here, and the methods for gathering and processing them are handed down from father to son. The community distills juniper berries to make essential oils and gins, macerates blueberries in grain alcohol to obtain a sweet liqueur and hand-pick olives and cold press them the same day to produce olive oil.

The jams are made in the traditional way with five different types of fruit and little sugar. The products are usually sold at local fairs.

PRODUCTION AREA
Koper, Obalno-Kraska region

COMMUNITY COORDINATOR
Primoz Koren
tel. +386 4138 7678
primoz.koren@koper.si

Álava pony meat farmers

The Basque mountain pony (called the *euskal herriko mendiko zaldia* in the Basque language) is an indigenous breed which is left to graze wild for most of the year and is now threatened with extinction. In the Province of Álava, horses are still used as draught animals, for riding and for meat production: the more rustic the breed, the better the meat. Mountain pony foals reared for meat are born and grow up out in the open, where they are fed on mare's milk, straw and cereals. They are slaughtered between 6 and 18 months, when they weigh an average of 165 kg, and provide lean, tender, digestible, healthy and flavorsome meat. Since1992, some chefs in the area have been involved in relaunching this traditional product and the *Red de consumidores de carne de potro de Okina* (Network of Okina pony meat consumers) is about to become operational.

PRODUCTION AREA
Province of Álava (Araba), the Basque Country (Euskadi)

COMMUNITY COORDINATOR
Amaia Arrizabalaga Fernandez de Mendiola
tel. +34 615717712

Álava Txakolí producers

The name of Txakolí first appears in a document in 864. It's a white wine which is best drunk young, with a strong fruity flavor and a perfume with slight hints of herbs and flowers, and a noticeable but balanced amount of acidity. At the beginning of the 20th century, the formerly flourishing wine-production of the area suddenly declined. The vine diseases of oidium, phyloxera and peronospora reduced the 550 hectares recorded in the census of 1877 to 95. In 1988, when the producers' association was founded, there were fewer than 2 hectares. But the action taken was so decisive and effective that, today, the producers of this Basque wine (only about 50 of them) can count on the protection of the AOC (Controlled Origin Label), with which they certify 280,000 l of wine, almost all of which is consumed on the local market.

PRODUCTION AREA
Aiara, Artziniega, Amurrio, Laudio and Okondo, province of Álava (Araba), the Basque Country (Euskadi)

COMMUNITY COORDINATOR
José Antonio Merino Belaustegui
tel. +34 656789372
merino@txakolidealava.com

Alta Anoia cigronet growers

The Alta Anoia area lies between Tarragona and Barcelona, not far from the coast. It contains twelve rural municipalities. The community was formed four years ago, when 25 people formed an association to protect an old variety of chickpea, the *cigronet* (the Catalan equivalent of a small chickpea). In the past, it was cultivated alternately with winter cereals and, more often than not, was consumed by the growers rather than being sold. This small, round legume has a uniform texture and a strong flavor. It triples its volume when cooked, but it doesn't lose its skin or go mushy. Today, the initiatives organized by the community are supported by local institutions and involve many restaurant owners, who are helping to promote the Alta Anoia *cigronet* further afield.

PRODUCTION AREA
Alta Anoia, Cataluña

COMMUNITY COORDINATOR
Rosa Centelles Vilaseca
tel. +34 938680366
martac@altaanoia.info

Ancient olive-tree farmers

The province of Castellón is famous for its ancient olive trees, some of them centuries old, which are, sadly and increasingly, being uprooted to decorate gardens and terraces elsewhere. A group of 25 olive growers has got together to try to defend these living monuments. They produce an oil that is made purely with olives from ancient, catalogued trees, situated in the Maestrat region. The harvest has to be planned in advance, in order to establish the precise date and the time when the olives must arrive at the olive-press. By doing this, they can be sure that the olives will be processed rapidly and delicately, without any delays, when they may become bruised or moldy, or go bad. The community is being supported in its task of protecting this small crop, by the Amics de l'Olivera association, with which it organizes tastings with experts and visits to the oldest olive groves, which are part of the cultural heritage of the region.

PRODUCTION AREA
Castellón, region of Valencia

COMMUNITY COORDINATOR
Ramón Mampel Dellà
tel. +34 609282916
clotdensimo@intercoop.es

Aragonese wheat growers and bakers

Aragonese wheat (*Trigo aragón*) was once the most common wheat variety in the Los Monegros area. Not only that, but even French bakers used to come here to buy the flour. Despite its excellent organoleptic and nutritional characteristics (it contains up to 17% of protein), during the 1980s, cultivation of this wheat took a sudden downturn following the introduction of varieties with a higher yield. One family preserved the original seeds and, thanks to the collaboration of farmers, and the genius of the late Juan José Marcén, Aragonese wheat was saved from extinction. The five members of the community continue to cultivate Aragonese wheat according to the principles of organic farming and sell it in the form of stone-ground flour and bread made with sourdough.

PRODUCTION AREA
Leciñena, province of Saragoza, Aragón

COMMUNITY COORDINATOR
Ana Marcén Murillo
tel. +34 653618913
ecomonegros@hotmail.com

Artzai gazta cheese producers

The community is formed by 110 breeders and cheese-makers who, for more than ten years, have been trying to defend a production system which is native to the area. Their *artzai gazta*, or *queso de pastor* (shepherd's cheese), is a DOP *Idiazábal* cheese made with raw milk only from the *lacha* sheep, a rustic breed of prehistoric origin which has a low yield (100 l per season, from February to June) of excellent milk. Its meat is also popular. The shepherds sell the lambs and use the meat of the adults to make *gorria* and *ondua*, two traditional salamis. The *artzai gazta* is a firm type of ewe's milk cheese weighing 1-2 kg, with a slightly acidic, never bitter taste, which is sometimes smoked, after at least three months of aging. By letting it ferment, they make a spicy sort of cheese sold under the name of *gaztazaharra* (which means "old cheese" in the Basque language).

PRODUCTION AREA
The Basque Country (Euskadi) and the Comunidad Foral de Navarra (Nafarroako Foru Komunitaten)

COMMUNITY COORDINATOR
Eduardo Urarte Egurcegui
tel. +34 945251790
eurarte@euskalnet.net

Asturias spelt producers

An association of 22 farmers is keeping alive one of the oldest products of Asturias, spelt (*Triticum spelta*), which is one of the species closest to common wheat, also from the point of view of its chromosomes. This makes its flour particularly suitable for making bread, cakes and other sweets. Spelt first appeared in the region during the Iron Age and, until less than a century ago, it played a fundamental role in the rural economy of the area. Then cheese production gained the upper hand, so that farmers had to devote larger areas to maize as feed for dairy cattle. As a result, *Triticum spelta*, a winter cereal which grows well on poor, land with little fertilizer, but which is sown and harvested entirely by hand (with *mesorias*, two poles tied together with string), fell into a slow decline.

PRODUCTION AREA
Grado and nearby towns, principality of Asturias

COMMUNITY COORDINATOR
Rafael Estrada Álvarez
tel. +34 647821759
estracar3@hotmail.com

Caper growers of Ballobar

Traditionally, in the Ballobar area, capers were used for domestic consumption. But now, some of the growers have formed a cooperative and have decided to try and sell them, in order to preserve a traditional activity and save a local variety which is now in danger of dying out. What makes growing capers so difficult is the fact that they are creepers, and have prickles, which makes them very difficult to harvest mechanically. But the plant constitutes a very important resource for this area, which is one of the most arid in the whole of Aragòn. The fact that capers tolerate drought so well and their prized organoleptic properties (the buds of the flowers, which are harvested before they open out prima) mean that they are an excellent crop both from the point of view of sustainability and the local economy.

PRODUCTION AREA
Ballobar, Aragón

COMMUNITY COORDINATOR
Miguel Angel Salas Gracia
tel. +34 650401917
plrsbera@terra.es

Casín cheese producers

Queso casín, named after the municipality of Caso, is probably one of Spain's oldest cheeses. The first written testimonials date from 1320. Despite this, today it has survived as a home-made cheese, and, thanks to a dairy run only by women (a mother and her four daughters), is about to obtain DOP (Protected Designation of Origin) status. To make it they use milk from casina cattle, a local breed, and rennet from a pig's stomach. The process involves the curd being mixed every seven days, for a minimum of two and a maximum of ten weeks. When it is mixed for the last time, the cheese is given the desired shape without any need for a mold. The result is a cheese with a strong, spicy, enduring taste.

PRODUCTION AREA
Campo de Caso, principality of Asturias

COMMUNITY COORDINATOR
María de los Angeles Alvarez Martínez
tel. +34 985608068
marigel@complejoreciegos.com

Cheese producers of the Sierra de Espadán

The community has been operating for about 15 years in the Sierra de Espadán Natural Park. It consists of a dairy operated by five individuals and three families who produce excellent cheeses with raw milk. Queso tronchón, which is even quoted in Don Quijote, is made with the same recipe used by shepherds practicing transhumance: a coagulant derived from the cardoon, and milk from murciana goats fed on grass and fodder produced on the farm. Queso espadán, a cheese made from goat's milk, is aged in bark, which makes it very creamy and gives it an unusual flavor. Peña blanca, made of ewe's milk, takes a long time to coagulate, which gives it a complex, strong after-taste. With these and other recipes, the community hopes to guarantee the continuation of this unique kind cheese production, with the aim of promoting the characteristics of local raw materials.

PRODUCTION AREA
Almedíjar, province of Castellón, region of Valencia

COMMUNITY COORDINATOR
Angel Valeriano Rojo
tel. +34 964137050
queseria@queserialoscorrales.com

Cocoa transformers

The community, formed 26 years ago, has two Spanish members and about 100 members who belong to native families of the Amazon rainforest in Brazil. Together, they form the Asociaçao dos Moradores da Vila de Mapia, which collects and ferments cocoa beans from the banks of three tributaries of the River Purús. The cocoa is processed in two different ways, using a combination of Maya traditions and European recipes. The Maya chocolate is particularly interesting, produced with cocoa berries, maize, peanuts, and sugar ground with the metate (an old type of hand- mill) and traditionally consumed as a drink. The community sells it in bars with the addition of a little European-style chocolate. The group organizes professional training courses and adaptation and support courses for people who want to get back to a rural way of life.

PRODUCTION AREA
Torá, province of Lleida, Cataluña

COMMUNITY COORDINATOR
María Antonia Zacarelli Sichel
tel. +34 680958357
lavalldor@hotmail.com

Euskal Oiloa chicken farmers

This community was formed by about ten founder members, Basque farmers who have decided to devote their efforts to a chicken breed which originated in their area in the Neolithic period and is now threatened with extinction. The *euskal oiloa* is a breed reared for its meat and eggs, which produces between 209 and 220 eggs a year and reaches a weight of 2 kg after 14-16 weeks. It has red wattles and yellow feet, but the plumage changes according to the distribution range. In fact, five types of Basque chicken have been identified: *beltza*, *gorria*, *lepasoila*, *marraduna* and *zimarra*. The main cause of its decline is competition from commercial products which are not indigenous, but which have obtained quality certificates and exploit the image of the *euskal oiloa*. The fact that some famous Basque chefs are interested in this breed is very encouraging.

PRODUCTION AREA
Lezama, the Basque Country (Euskadi)

COMMUNITY COORDINATOR
Asier Saez Dañobeitia
tel. +34 944556126
liburutegia@lezama.org

Extensive system farmers, Sierra di Guara Cheese

The Sierra di Guara, in the Aragonese province of Huesca, dotted with precipices and gorges, is an area traditionally used for grazing. The increasing tendency for people to abandon this traditional activity is having serious environmental consequences, including the loss of biodiversity, the impoverishment of the landscape, and an increased risk of forest fires. As a result, the few farmers left are combining livestock rearing, conducted entirely with the extensive farming system, with projects to save degraded areas of forest by using it as grazing land. Their products, which are part of the farming culture of the area, all come from animals left to graze freely. The *ternasco lactante de Guara*, a lamb killed when it no more than 4 months old, the *masito*, an 8-month old castrated lamb (certified as organic), the *latón del Perineo*, a pig fattened for more than 120 days, and the *añojo sierra guara*, a sturdy calf of the *Pirenaica* breed requiring only minimal care.

PRODUCTION AREA
Sierra de Guara, Aragón

COMMUNITY COORDINATOR
José Luis Gracia Chapullé
tel. +34 646971998
chapulle@terra.es

Farmers of Asturian breeds

This community acts as an umbrella organization for several associations of farmers of indigenous Asturian breeds, from the *oveya xalda* to the *gochu asturcelta*. Over the centuries, such breeds constituted the basis of the family economy in Asturia. As often happens, these indigenous breeds were gradually ousted by more productive foreign breeds suited to intensive farming techniques. Attempts to save them were often regarded as a form of exaggerated local pride or a mad form of nationalism. Only now is it recognized that this community, led by farmer Antón Álvarez Sevilla, has prevented an important part of our genetic and cultural heritage from disappearing completely. Here are a few of them: the ancient Celtic pony (*asturcón* or Asturian pony), traditionally used as a draught animal, the Asturian pig (*gochu asturcelta*), which is perfectly adapted to being reared wild in the woods on the Atlantic coast, and the breed of dairy sheep (*oveya xalda*), which has made some of the cheeses from this area famous.

PRODUCTION AREA
Oviedo, principality of Asturias

COMMUNITY COORDINATOR
Antón Álvarez Sevilla
tel. +34 637805552
anton.as@telecable.es

Farmers of Huesca poultry breeds

32 farmers have formed the *Asociación de Criadores de Aves de Razas Locales Amenazadas de Huesca*. Until the beginning of last century, the *Sobrarbe* hen and the *oscense* turkey were in great demand for their meat and eggs. Now the community is trying to save them from extinction. Today there are less than 600 pure examples of the hen breed and just under half that number of the turkey breed, despite the fact that these breeds were selected over a long time for their ability to survive with only minimal care. So that they are not forgotten, the farmers enter the best examples of the breeds for competitions, agricultural shows and auctions and distribute their products in food shops and restaurants, whereas, to save the breeds from extinction, they are setting up all kinds of different projects. In the case of the hen, it also risks dying out because of the high level of casual interbreeding that has taken place over the years.

PRODUCTION AREA
Province of Huesca, Aragón

COMMUNITY COORDINATOR
Ricardo Azón Pardo
tel. +34 600697090
azon@monegros.net

Fishermen of Mar de Lira

Lira is a village at the mouth of the River Corcubión, on the Costa da Morte. Since 2001, the confraternity of fishermen who live and work here has been involved in the creation of a marine reserve which allows some fishing, but preserves the area's fish resources. Their main activity is catching octopus, prawns and devil crabs in fish-traps, and selling them through the company Lonxanet, in which they are shareholders, and which distributes the products within 24 hours of it being caught. But their plans do not stop there. The founder members of the International Network of Fishing Communities for Sustainable Development (Recopades) conducts activities associated with fish tourism, runs courses for schoolkids and is setting up a network of Galician restaurants to promote sea conservation.

PRODUCTION AREA
Lira, Carnota, province of Pontevedra, Galicia

COMMUNITY COORDINATOR
Emilio Louro Lamela
tel. +34 635600076
emiliolouro@mardelira.net

Galicia seafood gatherers

Formed in 2005 by a group of four young people, the community intends to protect and promote a special fishing technique: gathering seafood in apnea (while the fisherman holds his breath). This type of fishing is carried out manually at close range, ensuring that all the products are carefully selected and that the impact on the environment is zero. As he collects them, the diver selects each mollusk one by one, according to size, the period of reproduction and the maximum quantities allowed. The top product is the *navaja* (of the *Ensis arcuatus* species, related to the razor clam), but clams and seaweed are gathered and sold using the same technique. The members of the community are approaching the owners of local restaurants, to whom they can provide a high-quality product which is completely traceable and obtained using techniques that are ecologically sustainable.

PRODUCTION AREA
Province of Pontevedra, Galicia

COMMUNITY COORDINATOR
Xosé Xulian Ferradás Vilas
tel. +34 629104463   629104420
artesanosdomar@gmail.com

Gallecs farmers

The 744 hectares of farmland of Gallecs, outside Barcelona, acts as an organic corridor with important environmental, scenic, cultural and educational implications for the city's inhabitants. Having been public property since the 1960s, the area is now involved in plans to support and defend the agricultural and forest ecosystems. As a result, about 30 producers in this region have to comply with very strict laws governing sustainable soil management. They are also participating in plans to save traditional vegetable varieties and an indigenous breed of hen. Some of their most interesting products are the Bufet potato, Gallecs bread made with wheat and barley, *coca de Sant Galdric*, a traditional cake made with local hazelnuts, and Mistela del Gallecs, a sweet red wine made with grapes from a local vine variety.

PRODUCTION AREA
Gallecs, Barcelona, Cataluña

COMMUNITY COORDINATOR
Marina Duñach Torras
tel. +34 615679508
marinadt@terra.es

Garraf vegetable producers

During the first half of the last century, the countryside on the edge of Barcelona still supplied the city markets with large amounts of fresh produce. Today few people still cultivate the land, which is increasingly being eaten up for development as holiday homes or dormitory areas for people working in the great metropolis. Only about ten small-scale farmers still grow the local varieties of vegetables which are included in many traditional recipes. Nowadays they are frequently replaced by more commercial cultivated varieties. Crunchy white endives, tasty cabbages similar to beet leaves, lettuces and tiny chickpeas, *col de brotó, col verde, espigall, escarola perruqueta* (or *cabello de ángel*) are just some of the vegetables grown by the group. The farmers are full of bright ideas about new initiatives to encourage people to talk about their special products. They hold recipe competitions, organize tasting sessions with experts and improvise courses in the middle of the weekly market.

PRODUCTION AREA
Vilanova i la Geltrú, Cataluña

COMMUNITY COORDINATOR
Montserrat Marcé Sabadell
tel. +34 938140301

Lágrima de Costa de Gipúzkoa pea farmers

Farmers in the Basque Country have tended their vegetable patches since time immemorial, selling their produce at fairs and local markets. Five of them are now trying to save a variety of pea called *lágrima de Costa de Gipúzkoa*: a product with unique organoleptic properties, which is the result of the area's proximity to the ocean and the *shirimiri*, the persistent rain which falls in the Cantabrian region (facing the Bay of Biscay). This legume, which has always been acknowledged as a vital part of the local vegetation, was once a favorite food with the aristocracy who used to come here on holiday, during the Belle Époque. Apparently the peas used to be harvested with scissors so as not to spoil their delicate flavor. Obviously they are no longer harvested like that. But the dynamism of these young organic farmers suggests that the fate of the *lágrima de Costa*, which has aroused the interest of many Basque restaurant owners, may be on the upturn.

PRODUCTION AREA
Getaria, the Basque Country (Euskadi)

COMMUNITY COORDINATOR
Jaime Burgaña Pinto
tel. +34 943140289
aroasc@euskalnet.net

Millo corvo growers and transformers

The Asociación Sociocultural Deportiva e Xuvenil de Meiro is formed by 150 people who, in nine years, have succeeded in saving the *millo corvo*, a local variety of maize that is resistant to hard soil and extreme climates, and has black cobs. For centuries, this small seed constituted the staple diet not only of domestic animals but, in particular, the local people, and is still celebrated at traditional festivals, and in legends and songs. For this reason, the community treats all its activities as a game, involving everyone, old and young alike. To prepare the land for sowing, they use the last pair of oxen in Morrazo. Weeding, harvesting and the job of removing the ears from the cob is all done manually. The corn is ground in the old water-driven mill at Meiro. They make bread with the flour, using sourdough to leaven it, and bake the bread in wood-fired ovens. So the younger generations can still taste the traditional *empanada de millo corvo*.

PRODUCTION AREA
Meiro, Bueu, province of Pontevedra, Galicia

COMMUNITY COORDINATOR
Victoria Martínez Barreiro
tel. +34 637558957
meirocorvo@gmail.com

Nomadic shepherds

This community is symbolic of a type of production that is under serious threat here, as in many other countries where intensive farming has gained the upper hand. In Spain, too, transhumance has guaranteed the survival of breeds that are used to living out in the open and moving large distances, and are not, therefore, suited to being shut up in a shed or field. For example, *churra* sheep, and *morucha*, *sayaguesa* or *zamorana* cattle. Now their movements are restricted by EU laws, by new laws governing livestock rearing, by the spread of urbanization and by the fact that many of the old drove roads are disappearing. A catalyzing element in this sphere, where there is so much going on (projects, associations, meetings and efforts to create a unique network involving all the nomadic shepherds around the globe) is the charismatic figure of Jesús Garzón.

PRODUCTION AREA
Cabezón de la Sal, Cantabria

COMMUNITY COORDINATOR
Jesús Garzón Heydt
tel. +34 659209095
pastores.sinfronteras@pastos.org

Organic vegetable producers of Ademuz

The Ceaga cooperative operates in the Rincón de Ademuz, a rural area on the border with Aragona and Castile which has a special micro-climate. It produces vegetables, aromatic herbs, apples and almonds, and rears a few head of cattle for meat and dairy products. Its products include the indigenous cultivated variety (registered in 1903) of apple called *esperiega*, the pink *morado de Castielfabib* tomato, which is sweet and juicy, the *guirra* sheep, which has almost dyed out, reared for its meat and its milk, and the *blanca serrana celtibérica goat*, renowned for its meat. The farmers and technical experts who form the community want to promote rural development and organic farming through initiatives geared to preserving biodiversity, food education and sustainable tourism, through a fascinating project entitled El Rincón de la Biodiversidad (Biodiversity Corner).

PRODUCTION AREA
Castielfabib, region of Valencia

COMMUNITY COORDINATOR
Cesáreo Casino Esteban
tel. +34 978783504
info@elrincondelabiodiversidad.org

Pink Álava bean producers

Beans are a symbol of the renowned gastronomic tradition of the Basque Country. They have been grown here for centuries, and were often allowed to climb up maize stalks, which they used for support. The *alavesa* variety is one of the most outstanding in its category. It is grown between Álava and Burgos, in small family-owned vegetable patches, by about 600 farmers who supplement their crops of cereals and potatoes by selling these beans. They are sown in May and ready for harvesting in late September. The beans are picked and removed from their pods entirely by hand. The red earth, which is typical of this area and the ecological production techniques used result in a product of extremely high quality. Pink Álava beans are small and oval with a fine flesh and a thin skin, but their consistency means that they can be cooked for a long time without disintegrating. For more than ten years there has been a festival at Pobes which celebrates the *alubia pinta alavesa* or spotted Álava bean.

PRODUCTION AREA
Vitoria (Gasteiz), the Basque Country (Euskadi)

COMMUNITY COORDINATOR
Lorenzo Martínez de Salinas Ocio
tel. +34 945293080
lsalinas@garlan.es

Producers of carranzana sheep's cheese

The community, formed by four shepherds from Biscaglia, centers around an elderly lady who is the last person who knows how to produce this cheese. It is a small ewe's milk cheese (about 9 cm in diameter), which is matured for two to three months in a ventilated environment. It smells vaguely of vanilla, milk and aromatic herbs, while, on the palate, it has a strong, buttery flavor. But not only the cheese is in danger of dying out: also the sheep that supply the milk. There are only 250 black-faced *carranzana* sheep left, kept in five separate flocks. They are exceptionally good dairy sheep, with an average yield of about 160-170 l per cycle. The breed first appears in an etching reproduced by the *Ilustración Española*, published for the Concurso de Ganados de Santander in 1872.

PRODUCTION AREA
Güeñes and Sodupe, the Basque Country (Euskadi)

COMMUNITY COORDINATOR
Mariano Gómez Fernandez
tel. + 34 630034500
mariano.gomez@bizkaia.net

Sea salt producers of Añana

The saltpans of Añana are a lovely sight: 120 hectares on the hillside, covered with wooden terraces. The salt water is conveyed along wooden channels and left in the saltpans to evaporate. The first information we have about the saltpans dates from the Roman period, whereas the medieval custom of using salt as currency resulted in the Salinas de Añana being given the status of a town in 1140. Since 1999, the activities of the saltpans have been guaranteed by 86 landowners who are working to save the historic and cultural heritage of the area, as well as the salt production. The association they have formed, Salineros Gatzagak de Añana, publishes information and organizes the Añana Salt Festival, which involves tasting workshops for kids, guided tours and tastings..

PRODUCTION AREA
Añana, province of Álava (Araba), the Basque Country (Euskadi)

COMMUNITY COORDINATOR
Valentín Angulo Pérez de Nanclares
tel. + 34 945351321
gatzagak@gatzagak.com

Traditional preserve producers of Muro de Alcoy

Muro de Alcoy is a little town in the Sierra Mariola, situated between the Serpis and Agres rivers. The 10 members of the community have formed a cooperative and produce traditional vegetable preserves. *Pericana*, in addition to being a traditional dish of the area, is also the name of the cooperative: based on dried peppers, salt cod, garlic and olive oil, it was the dish the peasants used to take with them to the fields when the time came to cut the wheat. Other specialties include *espençat* (another preserve based on roasted peppers), *dolç de tomaca* (tomatoes preserved in a syrup with lemon and cinnamon) and sun-dried tomatoes flavored with herbs gathered on the Sierra Mariola. As well as defending the gastronomic heritage of the area through its work, because so many of its recipes are based on peppers, the community is revitalizing local production of this vegetable, which had declined significantly in the previous 20 years.

PRODUCTION AREA
Muro de Alcoy, province of Alicante, region of Valencia

COMMUNITY COORDINATOR
Miguel Ángel Rebagliato Giménez
tel. +34 649875039
trotex@trotex.e.telefonica.net

Vine and olive farmers of Urgell

The community, which now has 45 members, who are producers and supporters, began more than 30 years ago with the aim of defending the traditional semi-arid crops of the Urgell area, the vine and the olive. The working group, half of whom are disabled, manages 35 hectares of land, a wine-cellar and an oil-press. Here they produce white wine with grapes from Catalan vine varieties (*macabeo, parellada*) some of which come from very old vineyards, as well as oil and olives of the local *arbequina* variety. According to the members of the community, producing excellent wine and oil improves the image of the area, protects its environmental heritage (by repairing drystone walls and preserving terraces by continuing to work them, for example), but, more particularly, it demonstrates the agricultural value of an area largely forgotten by the farming community at large, because it is arid and mountainous.

PRODUCTION AREA
Vallbona de les Monges, province of Lleida, Cataluña

COMMUNITY COORDINATOR
Carles Ahumada Batlle
tel. +34 973330276
carles@olivera.org

Zalla purple onion growers

The community is formed by six producers who have set up an association to protect a vegetable of extremely high quality that has virtually disappeared. The onion from Zalla, a town in the Basque province of Biscaglia, has a purple bulb of medium size which is conical with a pointed base. They are harvested in July and August but are available throughout the year. Although the crop is mainly consumed by the growers, they are sometimes to be found at local markets. Traditionally they are plaited into strings of 12 bulbs, especially in the pig-slaughtering (*txarribodas*) season, when they are used for making the traditional *morcillas de Las Encartaciones*, a typical local kind of blood sausage. Juicy and flavorsome, but not sharp in taste, the Zalla onion goes particularly well in salad, and, when added to soups, produces a delicate oniony flavor.

PRODUCTION AREA
Zalla, the Basque Country (Euskadi)

COMMUNITY COORDINATOR
Mariano Gómez Fernandez
tel. + 34 630034500
mariano.gomez@bizkaia.net

ARTZAIN MUNDUA

Artzain Mundua, The World Shepherd Forum, an autonomous section of the World Rural Forum, is an association created to sustain the value and right to survival of one of the oldest professions in the world: sheep-farming. Artzain Mundua intends to create a pastoral culture, setting up a documentation center which can provide those who are interested with all the possible information about the history and traditions of this archaic and complex world, generating a network of links with institutional research, management and information centers which can support the projects of the Shepherd Forum.

AREA OF ACTIVITY
Arantzazu, País Vasco

ASSOCIATION COORDINATOR
Mirén Elgarresta Larrabide
tel. +34 943038801
artzainmundua@pyme.net

DORONDÓN MONEGROS

The Dorondón Monegros association was created recently, drawing together producers of environment-friendly food operating in the province of Los Monegros in Aragon. The producers are assisted by a group of researchers and technicians with whom they establish promotional programs, organize seminars and training courses, and create networks of contacts and collaboration with other organizations, to encourage the entrepreneurial development of a virtuous form of agriculture that respects the environment, a concept which includes the territory and biodiversity, that maintains traditions and safeguards local varieties and species.

AREA OF ACTIVITY
Comarca di Los Monegros, Aragon

ASSOCIATION COORDINATOR
María Estrella Bernal Cuenca
tel. +34 658081626
bercue@unizar.es

Biological producers

Founded in 1985 by biological farmers, Ekologiska Lantbrukarna i Sverige focuses on practices and methods for producing and growing biological products, developing the social fabric of the local agricultural community and broadening the sales network for its products. The overall aim is to promote biological agriculture and protect the interests of farmers involved in it. Safeguarding and strengthening these types of practice is a fundamental element in consolidating an awareness shared by producers and co-producers who believe in the many values associated with sustainable agriculture. In Ekologiska Lantbrukarna there are 2,500 producers of meat, cheese, cereals and vegetables. The association is also involved in developing rural policies, research, education, information and the organized growth of the sector it safeguards.

PRODUCTION AREA
Uppsala

COMMUNITY COORDINATOR
Lennart Westerdahl
tel. +46 224741356
lennart.westerdahl@u.lrf.se

Craft producers of upplandskubb

The community is made up of four cereal farmers, a bakery that produces upplandskubb and a restaurant serving local dishes. Upplandskubb is the traditional bread from Uppland, the well-known province lying on the east coast of Sweden. It's prepared using wheat and rye flour and is unique compared with other types of oven-baked bread as this bread is steamed in a cylindrical container for several hours. After it is cooked it's cut into four pieces, which accounts for its characteristic shape. The finished product is brown in color; it's a very moist type of bread that keeps for a long time. It used to be made on the majority of farms in this area and was eaten especially during the Christmas period.

PRODUCTION AREA
Uppland, Uppsala

COMMUNITY COORDINATOR
Kaja Carlsson
kaja.carlson@ica-kvantum.granby.se

Food producers and distributors on the Stockholm archipelago

Restaurants, shopkeepers, farmers and breeders working on the islands between Sweden and Finlandhave formed the Skärgårdssmak association (Tastes of the archipelago) to promote that area quality gastronomy by also involving the tourism sector. Among the products there are fruit liqueurs, especially made with apples, pears, red currant and local types of berry (*vogelberen*). The range also includes a unique liqueur made with biologically grown pears aged in Swedish oak barrels, and a blackcurrant liqueur. The distillery is housed in an old barn with a small restaurant next door. Another resource is obviously fishing, thank to which a small family firm sells the famous Nämdö archipelago trout and salmon that are smoked near the fish farm.

PRODUCTION AREA
Stockholm, Södermanland, Uppsala; also Finnish Åland

COMMUNITY COORDINATOR
Tjulander Gun
tel. +46 85715 2061
gun_tjulander@hotmail.com

Growers of early varieties of cereal crops

This community of 120 people includes growers, producers and transformers who are working to safeguard the cultivation and end-use of certain early varieties of Swedish cereals particularly suited for bread-making. Crops are grown in accordance with the canons of biological agriculture and, sometimes, biodynamics. Community members also harvest crops, mill the grain (to produce wholemeal flour), bake bread (using natural yeast) and sell their products. The cereal varieties are the result of centuries of selection by farmers working on the two large Baltic islands of Öland and Gotland. The huge task of protecting these varieties has the support of Alnarp University of Agrarian Sciences.

PRODUCTION AREA
Öland, Kalmar; Gotland

COMMUNITY COORDINATOR
Hans Larsson
tel. +46 40415255
Hans.Larsson@allkorn.se

Halland county producers

The Falkenberg food community is in the county of Halland, in the southwestern part of the country facing the Kattegat, the section of sea between Sweden and the Danish peninsular of Jutland. The main, most representative products of gastronomic traditions of this group are cereals, especially spelt, grown according to longstanding biological methods and used to make various types of local bread distributed through an internal network. The many herds of cows has led to production of a type of ice cream prepared entirely from local milk and cream. Lastly, a further important product for this community is rape-oil grown by strictly controlled biological methods.

PRODUCTION AREA
Falkenberg, Halland

COMMUNITY COORDINATOR
Jan-Olof Andersson
tel. +46 346 886409
jan-olof.andersson@falkenberg.se

Jämtland goat's milk cheese makers

Seasoned goat's milk cheese id a traditional product of mountain villages in the county of Jämtland. Once Sweden could boast over 130,00 heads of goat that in less than one century have now fallen to 5,000, of which 1,000 are in Jämtland. Community cheese makers mainly raise the Svensk Lantras breed, also known as the Swedish goat and considered a breed in risk of extinction. During summer months animals feed in the fields, on moors and in forests: this makes their milk very rich indeed. Untreated milk is used to make the cheese: the curd is pressed, dried and turned from time to time. The forms mature in natural underground cells for a period ranging from three to seven months during which they develop a mold. From whey left from producing the cheese they make cream spreads and cottage cheese.

PRODUCTION AREA
Jämtland

COMMUNITY COORDINATOR
Gert Andersson
tel. +46 644 91058
gert@rocketmail.com

Koster Island producers

The Koster Islands lie off the coast of the famous province of Bohuslän in the county of Västra Götaland, where farmers and breeders have formed a small cooperative to promote and support the very varied local biological production. In particular they produce various types of vegetable, such as lettuce and tomatoes, that are sold both fresh and processed. Processing occupies many of the cooperative's members, above all in producing jams. Lastly, chicken rearing is based on a biological approach even during periods when chickens cannot be reared free-range outside. Egg production in part finds an outlet in a small network of local consumers and partly in the islands' bakeries.

PRODUCTION AREA
Koster Islands, Västra Götaland

COMMUNITY COORDINATOR
Helena von Bothmer
tel. +46 52620599
helena@kosterstradgardar.se

Lake Vänern fishermen

Lake Vänern is Sweden and northern Europe's largest lake, with its jagged shoreline and hundreds of islands, the largest of which is Kållandsö in the southern section. The two fishermen forming this community – sons, grandchildren and great grandchildren of fishermen – capture salmon and other freshwater species that then also transform into smoked products and botargo. In addition to salmon the lake also a source of perch and burbot. The catch is either sold fresh or part of it is smoked: a by no means small quantity is used to make fish roe products for which there is quite a demand from local restaurants. The fishermen sell their catch directly, mainly to retail customers, some restaurants and in local markets.

PRODUCTION AREA
Kållandsö, Västra Götaland

COMMUNITY COORDINATOR
Kjell Åke Jonsson
tel. +46 51010203-705515490
noa@brevet.nu

Linderöd pig breeders

The community comprises a group of breeders, experts in rare breeds and Slow Food members whose aim is to save the Linderöd pig. This is one of Sweden's four autochthonous breeds of pig that has been raised in Scania, the country's southernmost region, for thousands of years. The Linderöd is small, with strong legs and showy black spots marking its gray-white or light brown skin. Once it used to be the staple breed for farms and was raised mainly for meat production. Currently there are about 70 breeders, the majority of whom have no more than a couple of sows and a male, which means the total population is about 200 animals. The Linderöd's meat is used to produce rökt linderödssidfläsk (a kind of bacon) and spickenskinka (a smoked sausage).

PRODUCTION AREA
Scania

COMMUNITY COORDINATOR
Annette Nilsson
tel. +46 42136466-706920936
slowfood@telia.com

Öland Island bean growers

Bean growers on the island of Imports of commercial varieties of bean represent the major threat for the survival of the brown bean that has been grown on the island of Öland since at least 1890 (however, it's mentioned in historical records dating from the XVIIth century). The mild climate of this island lying off the southeastern coast of Sweden is the ideal habitat for this legume grown over a total area of about 600 hectares. It's sown in late May and harvested in September, then the beans are left to dry directly in the field and later stored ready for sale. The community only includes two farmers although interest in this product is gradually increasing thanks to the support of university research that is trying to encourage new growers.

PRODUCTION AREA
Öland, Kalmar

COMMUNITY COORDINATOR
Fredrik Fogelberg
tel. +46 18247315
Fredrik.Fogelberg@hihm.no

Promoters of Gävleborg products

The project involves the community in the county of Gävleborg in central Sweden that aims to promote the area's unique and craft products by helping to set up a network of small producers. Blackcurrants, red currants and blackberries grow in this area's marshlands that are used to prepare the typical wine people drink warm and spiced with cardamom, orange peel and cinnamon during winter festivities. Another distinctive food is Baltic Sea herring, smoked by craftsmen over alder and red-pine fires, and served according to tradition with mustard, dill and sour cream. And, of course, not forgetting Hälsing cake, a mixture of milk, whey and flour cooked slowly in the oven and served with a fruit sauce or cloudberry jam.

PRODUCTION AREA
Gävleborg

COMMUNITY COORDINATOR
Anita Hörnstein
tel. +46 26122217
anita.hornstein@hush.se

Promoters of sustainable agriculture and stock farming

The Swedish Federation of Farmers and Stock Farmers has about 50,000 members throughout the country and works to promote the strategic growth of agriculture. In particular it works on coordinating the various agricultural cooperatives and smallholders as regards sustainable food production. Another part of the Federation's mission is to conduct research into trends and changes in the eating habits of Swedish consumers, focusing on primary resources such as cereals, meat, cheese and vegetables.

PRODUCTION AREA
Stockholm

COMMUNITY COORDINATOR
Jan-Olof Bengtsson
tel. +46 707574835
jan-olof.bengtsson@glocalnet.net

Promoters of Swedish food products

This community represents a network for the promotion of Swedish food products and is coordinated by various national bodies: the University of Agrarian Sciences, the Federation for Rural Development, several agricultural associations and the Federation of Swedish Farmers. The aim is to promote sustainable and rural development, production of quality foods and distribution of Sweden's regional products on a countrywide basis. A number of activities are organized to further these aims: markets, food fairs, food appreciation courses in schools, seminars on the environmental impact of food production, updates on development of small-scale production, setting up farmers' associations.

PRODUCTION AREA
Throughout Sweden

COMMUNITY COORDINATOR
Charlotte Lagerberg Fogelberg
tel. +46 18671648
charlotte.lagerberg@cul.slu.se

Small producers from the Kolmården region

Kolmården is an extensive forested area south-west of Stockholm, lying between the counties of Södermanland and Östergötland, two of the country's main agricultural areas. The community representing this area is made up of an association of small producers, mainly farmers, while only one person works part-time on office work. The main aim is to promote and extend small-scale production of quality products obtained by traditional, ecological methods for distribution in surrounding areas. Another activity of this association is raising local domesticated breeds of animal for both milk and meat production and to protect very old breeds from the danger of extinction.

PRODUCTION AREA
Norrköping, Östergötland

COMMUNITY COORDINATOR
Åke Karlsson
tel. +46 11391674
krokerksgard@telia.com

Södermanland cereal growers and bakers

The small county of Södermanland (chief town of Nyköping) lying on Sweden's east coast, south-west of Stockholm, is where a 25-strong food community works to produce and mill cereals and bake bread. The flout mill, known as *Saltå Kvarn*, and bakery adopt biodynamic methods and form part of the anthroposophic community of Järna. So bread and other bakery products are produced from biological flours. In total the group offers 75 different products and 15 types of bread, including the very thin and crisp traditional Swedish rye bread. Products are sold directly at both local and national level.

PRODUCTION AREA
Södermanland

COMMUNITY COORDINATOR
Johan Ununger
tel. +46 708 306 121
johan.ununger@saltakvar.se

Sörmland producers

Sörmlands Matkluster is a group of farmers, cooks and other people involved in food production. Some produce wheat and spelt: grain is milled in an 18th century stone-grinding flour mill and bread and other traditional Sörmland specialties are produced from the flour (Sörmland is the popular name for Södermanland, a county in the south-east of Sweden). Other grow rape, the seeds of which are dried, cleaned and stored before the start of pressing by a process that not only grinds the seeds but also removes the husks. What remains is then pressed in a similar manner to the process used for olive oil. The oil is left to settle for at least 24 days, then filtered and bottled. At this point it's ready for sale. Other community members also produce vinegar and cider from a Swedish variety of apple.

PRODUCTION AREA
Södermanland

COMMUNITY COORDINATOR
Carina Dalunde
tel. +46 15823030
aakerman.dalunde@ekolantbruk.se

Västmanland producers

A group of 34 small local producers support a project to promote small-scale agriculture in the Lake Mälaren area. In addition to organizing training activities, seminars and meetings, the project intends to set up sales outlets in support of local products through farmer's markets. The first market organized has been a great success and now attracts over 2,000 visitors every Saturday. Among the community's products there are various types of cereal (wheat, rye, spelt), all milled by craft workers to be processed into bakery products; beverages made from fruit (apples and pears) cultivated using biological methods and jams (bilberry, strawberry); vegetables, among which the famous Västerås cucumber; sausages made from local breeds of sheep, cattle and pigs; fresh fish or smoked according to traditional techniques.

PRODUCTION AREA
Västerås, Västmanland

COMMUNITY COORDINATOR
Agneta Pettersson
tel. +46 22712206
agnetapettersson@telia.com

Västra Götaland cheese makers

A group of cattle breeders and cheese makers in the county of Västra Götaland have set up their own independent organization to create a network to develop the local economy and farming community. The product linking cattle breeders to cheese makers is an ancient recipe known as *kalvdans*. Kalvdans puddings and cakes are sweets made from cow's colostrum, the unprocessed residue from the udder after the cow gives birth, flavored with local herbs and a small quantity of sugar, then cooked slowly in the oven. Served warm, *kalvdans* cake is considered a very nutritious, invigorating food. As the Västra Götaland region has the highest number of cattle in Sweden milk has always been a fundamental part of the diet in which colostrum is part of a very ancient tradition that was already alive back in Viking times.

PRODUCTION AREA
Vänersborg, Västra Götaland

COMMUNITY COORDINATOR
Christina Börjeson
tel. +43 51323375
christinaborjeson@telia.se

Beer producers and consumers

This community is represented by the Berne section of the European Beer Consumers Union, an association that came into being in 1990 with the merger of the British Camra (Campaign for Real Ale), the Belgian OPB (Objectieve Beer Proevers) and the Dutch Pint (Promotie Informatie Traditioneel Bier). The EBCU is linked to other similar organizations in Sweden, Finland, Denmark and Italy, which are all united in a common project: to work for the defense and promotion of traditional types of beer produced at local level. Through these organizations, the EBCU represents 70,000 beer consumers. A further main objective of its program is to widen consumer knowledge not only about the quality of beer and other alcoholic drinks (in particular, cider), but also about drinking awareness.

PRODUCTION AREA
Bern

COMMUNITY COORDINATOR
Mousson Laurent
tel. +41 3516882 - 313072221
laurent.mousson@bluewin.ch

Conservers of traditional apple and pear varieties

This community in the Aubonne district of French Switzerland started to become interested in collecting indigenous varieties of fruit, and in particular, apples and pears, right back in the 1980s. Although today there are several similar businesses, at that time this was one of the very first projects for collecting and preserving the national fruit-growing heritage. Through the initiative of two gardeners who coordinate the community's activities, two orchards, planted with ancient varieties, were introduced into the national botanic garden in Aubonne. This initiative soon became an active, permanent undertaking to safeguard and protect a growing number of traditional Swiss varieties that were slowly disappearing. Over the following years, numerous species of walnut – also ancient - have been successfully included in this type of reserve.

PRODUCTION AREA
Prangins, Vaud

COMMUNITY COORDINATOR
Roger Corbaz
tel. +41 223614524

Maize farmers in the Rhine valley

In the Rhine valley part of Switzerland, overlooking Lake Constance, they cultivate Riebelmais (called *türgge* in the local dialect), a variety of maize that was in the past considered one of the mainstays of the staple diet. This variety apparently came to Switzerland by way of Spain shortly after the conquest of the Americas, and became one of the main cereal crops in Switzerland thanks to the valley's mild microclimate, with its good degree of humidity. The community comprises around twenty members – farmers, millers and those who work in the Riebelmais harvesting centers. The whole of the production is conveyed to a center that controls its quality and deals with the processes of drying and washing. Three mills have the task of grinding it, obtaining a beige-white bran that differs from polenta flour, which is very yellow and not as tasty.

PRODUCTION AREA
Salez, Sankt Gallen

COMMUNITY COORDINATOR
Urs Bolliger
tel. +41 712293550
produktion@culinarium.com

Organic producers in the Canton of Ticino

The Bio Ticino association is made up of a relatively widespread community of producers, processors and salesmen who, in close contact with consumers, are involved in the various activities of cereal growing, cheese-making, bread-making and selling. They are united by a commitment to work with organic methods and respect for the region's food traditions. The most outstanding of their products is without doubt the Ticino red maize, obtained from an ancient local variety of maize that is organically grown, harvested and subjected to a natural drying process while it is still whole, in the form of cobs. Subsequently, it may be processed into toasted flakes (*arrosto di mais* or corn flakes) or into flour to be used for biscuits, breads or traditional polenta.

PRODUCTION AREA
Canton of Ticino

COMMUNITY COORDINATOR
Mario Tognetti
tel. +41 91582170
colombera@dplanet.ch

Producers in Val Lumnezia

In Val Lumnezia, the "valley of the light" in the Romansch area of the Grisons canton, the Talina Lumnezia company brings together nine producers who have formed a network to link their various activities. Alpkäse (called, in dialect, *caschiel d'alp*) and Geisskäse (*caschiel caura*) are hard cheeses produced in summer with milk from cows reared on mountain pastures. The meat for Trockenwürste – sausages made with white wine and matured in cool cellars – is from sheep, cows and pigs that are native to the valley and that spend the summer in the mountain pastures and the winter in large sheds where they can move around freely. All of the animals are bred and slaughtered according to organic methods. Honey, mountain herbs and the traditional hazelnut cake complete the rich food scenario of the region. The Pro Val Lumnezia organization also deals with employment and working conditions in the area.

PRODUCTION AREA
Lumnezia, Graubünden

COMMUNITY COORDINATOR
Marcus Caduff
tel. +41 793047091
info@lumnezia.ch

Promoters of typical Sankt Gallen products

The aim of the Culinarium association, comprising around 200 small producers and 4 restaurateurs, is to support the typical, traditional products of the region, to guarantee and control their quality and promote their sustainability. Traditionally, the Sankt Gallen area has always been highly developed from the farming point of view, but in the last fifty years it has undergone a rationalization process that has favored indigenous production. Culinarium supports and promotes various activities, including the production and sale of one of the rare varieties of tuber, the Blaue Sankt Gallen potato – typical of this area and characteristic because of its light blue color that gives a blue "tint" to soups and timbales. Other products are Blodderchäs cheese, Baumanns Reinette and Jakobiapfel apples, and Weltspärgler Birne pears, which all come from a long local cultural and food tradition.

PRODUCTION AREA
Sankt Gallen, Bodensee and Rheintal

COMMUNITY COORDINATOR
Andreas Allenspach
tel. +41 712293550
geschaeftsleitung@culinarium.com

Raw milk Raclette cheese producers

The Bruson Fromagerie is very well known in the Valais canton. The family who manage the shop belonging to the milk suppliers are directly concerned in the preparation of the cheeses, which include two traditionally ancient types. The first of these is Bagnes, used for "raclette" – the famous dish made with melted cheese. Currently, various industrially-produced Raclette cheeses can be found on sale, but these are quite different from those at the Bruson shop This is a semi-hard cheese, made according to the traditional method – meaning with raw milk and natural enzymes, and matured in cool, dry cellars for at least four months. The second cheese in the Brusonintze Tomme, which is also made with raw milk, but is a soft cheese curdled at the same temperature as when it was milked. After immersion in salt water, the Tomme is matured for at least 60 days.

PRODUCTION AREA
Bruson, Valais

COMMUNITY COORDINATOR
Eddy Baillifard
tel. +41 277761470

Traditional distilled liquor promoters

The Schnaps Forum works to promote consumption, improve the quality and restore the traditional production methods of the most popular alcoholic drinks in Switzerland. The most outstanding of these are cherry-based distilled liquors, of which there are several types in existence. Kirsch is obtained by harvesting a local variety of wild black cherry from the end of June to mid-August. The unpeeled fruit is allowed to steep for a period of between two and four weeks, and the fermented mixture is then distilled in a classic copper still. A much-liked variant on this is Kirsch Cuvée Humbel K111, obtained from 111 different varieties of cherry. We can get an idea from this product of the complex heritage of varieties of this fruit in Switzerland.

PRODUCTION AREA
Zürich

COMMUNITY COORDINATOR
Stefan Keller
c/o Ursula Frei
tel. +41 44780 6366
info@stefan.keller.name

Ararat Apricot producers

The very fertile Igdir plain in eastern Anatolia extends from the Kars plateau to Mount Ararat At one time apricots, almost all of small size, were the most important crop (128 cultivars have been counted). But invasions and wars destroyed the cultivations and today the apricots are international varieties. And a serious problem in this area is the high salt and mineral content of the soil. To make it productive and reintroduce the ancient apricots, the Alagoz family covered the terrain with sodium carbonate and in the following years grew wheat. Afterwards they planted traditional varieties of apricots, but the disorder in the 1990s forced them to suspend the activity. Today Haydar Alagoz owns 50 apricot trees and more than 500 small plants. In addition to apricots, the community grows lover, which makes the soil more productive and feeds about one hundred cows.

PRODUCTION AREA
Igdir, Dogu Anadolu

COMMUNITY COORDINATOR
Haydar Alagoz
tel. +90 5359754616
hikmetalagoz@gmail.com

Kars Cheese producers

The Kars region, at the Armenian border, has been used for sheep farming, cattle breeding and cheese making for centuries. It was ruled more than once by the Russians, who governed the area until 1918 and influenced the culture and local traditions. The community is made up of eight breeder-dairy producers. The Koculu family raises cows in the wild in summer and since 1920 has produced kars gravyeri, one of the historic cheeses in the region. This cheese with the dark crust is made from whole raw cow's milk. Well-suited to long aging (at least 10 months), it has large holes like French gruyère and tastes like emmental. A fresher cheese, kasar, is eaten 30 days after it is made.

PRODUCTION AREA
Kars, Dogu Anadolu

COMMUNITY COORDINATOR
Ilhan Koculu
tel. +90 5325016213
ikarayazi@gmail.com

Buffalo breeders

Buffalos are thought to have arrived in the Ukraine 750 years ago, with the migrating Tartar and Mongol nomads. Today few remain in the Carpathian mountains, which were once full of farms raising native buffalo. But in Transcarpathia (Zakarpatie), in the extreme West of the country, in a area that spreads over three districts – Khust, Tiachev and Rakhov – 12 people recently set up an association to safeguard this traditional activity. The goals are: to increase the number of animals in the area, to safeguard the pastures for the herds and to organize the production of milk and cheese. The members of the association now produce fresh and fermented milk (buffalo cows give about six liters a day), sour cream and fresh cheese.

PRODUCTION AREA
Khustsk, Tiachev and Rakhov, province of Zakarpatie

COMMUNITY COORDINATOR
Valeriy Bovt
tel. +380 974411657

Tulum Cheese producers of Tire

Deri tulum, the most well-known Turkish cheese, has been made for centuries all over the country with goat's milk or sheep's milk, or a mixture (Aegean deri tulum has a more delicate flavor because it is made with a blend of cow's and sheep's milk). The cheese is unusual because after the curd is pressed it is cut into small cubes and then layered in a sewn goatskin, with each layer carefully salted. It is eaten after being aged for about 6 months in a cool place. The community is composed of 35 producers who live near the city of Tire, about thirty kilometers from Izmir (ancient Smyrna). The community also produces ricotta (tatli lor) and yoghurt (süzme yogurt).

PRODUCTION AREA
Tire, province of Izmir, Marmara ve Ege Kiyilari

COMMUNITY COORDINATOR
Handan Turkeli
tel. +90 5353037650
handanturkeli@ttnet.net.tr

Carpathian beekeepers

The Ukrainian province of Transcarpathia (Zakarpatie) in the Carpathian mountains, the largest mountain chain in Europe after the Alps, is renowned for its many national parks and ancient woods, which are ideal for beekeeping. All the active honey producers in this area belong to a national association of beekeepers which organizes numerous local and national fairs to promote their products. The community of Carpathian beekeepers is made up of 63 members, who produce polyflora and acacia honey, pollen, beeswax, propolis, royal jelly and bee poison.

PRODUCTION AREA
Rakhov, province of Zakarpatie

COMMUNITY COORDINATOR
Dmytro Ihnatyuk
tel. +380 673123141

Crimean Wine producers

In the Crimean Autonomous Republic (Avtonomna Respublika Krym), on the northern coast of the Black Sea, there is a community that draws together makers, producers and merchants of the local wine. This area, at the foot of the mountains and the Alushta valley, is particularly suitable for vine growing, and a number of red (Cabernet, Saperavi and Morastel), white (Pinot Gris), dessert rosé (white and red Muskat) and sweet wines (those made with raisin grapes and Heres, which is left to age for a year under a layer of yeast, and has a golden color with a slight greenish tint and an alcoholic strength of 19.5%).

PRODUCTION AREA
Avtonomna Respublika Krym

COMMUNITY COORDINATOR
Nataliya Gordets'ka
tel. +380 671308495
sim_skifia@mail.ru

Rakhov Bryndza producers

The rearing of native sheep and the production of bryndza and ricotta from raw milk are traditional activities in the Carpathian mountains, that are now in difficulty because the sheep produce excellent quality milk but in small quantities: it takes about 250 sheep to produce 40 liters. In order to guarantee the survival of this activity, 275 farmers and dairymen have formed an association and they pasture their animals up in the mountains at an altitude of 1500 to 1700 meters. They make bryndza by adding rennet, or ryndza, to the milk which is then placed near to the fire and, after salting, the forms are left to ripen for a short time. The cheese is destined to local consumption, to be sold directly to tourists, and for local festivities, in particular the celebrations in its honor that are organized in Rakhov in September.

PRODUCTION AREA
Rakhov, province of Zakarpatie

COMMUNITY COORDINATOR
Vasyl Khoma
tel. +380 969647603
card@rakhiv.ukrtel.net

Aberdeenshire breeders and crop farmers

The community is formed of about 20 producers who raise Oxford Sandy and Black pigs and Aberdeen Angus cattle, using natural feeding methods; who bake handmade bread; and who grow fruit and vegetables. All the produce is sold at local farmers' markets. The Oxford Sandy and Blacks are of particular importance. The breed was once widespread in Aberdeenshire but became extinct there around 1960. Fifteen years or so later a group of nostalgic breeders started to crossbreed with the hope of eventually being able to regain pedigree examples. A society for restoration of the breed was founded and this gained recognition by the British Pig Association, which unites those raising pig breeds at risk of extinction. Nevertheless, there is as yet no official recognition for the animals as so far there are no pure pedigree examples.

PRODUCTION AREA
Aberdeenshire, Scotland

COMMUNITY COORDINATOR
Dugie Foreman
tel. +44 1975581149
dugie@warkfarm.co.uk

Anglesey Sea Salt producers

Anglesey is an island in the Irish sea, close to the Welsh coast. The Anglesey Sea Salt Company has combined new techniques with traditional methods to develop improved processes for harvesting its salt, and produces the only organically certified sea salt in the UK. Its Halen Môn sea salt is formed of pure, white crystals and is completely additive-free. The water that laps the island's coasts is pumped ashore to large reservoirs and resting tanks, where it is filtered and boiled. The resulting concentrated saline solution is heated to steam and then transferred to a container so that the crystals can form completely. It is then harvested, dried, checked, packaged and distributed for sale. Anglesey Sea Salt also produces smoked and spiced salts.

PRODUCTION AREA
Isle of Anglesey, Wales

COMMUNITY COORDINATOR
David Lea-Wilson
tel. +44 1248430871
David@seasalt.co.uk

Artisan cornmillers

The Traditional Cornmillers Guild groups about 30 millers in the United Kingdom who use windmills and stone grinders to produce high quality flours. Most of its members use locally-grown organic and biodynamic cereals. One indispensable condition for belonging to the association is that the mills are operational and not used simply for demonstration purposes. Stone-milled flour is processed slowly so that, unlike in high-tech modern mills, the natural oils in the cereals are preserved. The flours (rye, barley, spelt and bran) are sold directly to the public at the mill's shop and at farmers' markets.

PRODUCTION AREA
Throughout the country

COMMUNITY COORDINATOR
Marie-Christine Austin
tel. +44 1652640177
trueloafbakery@aol.com

Ayrshire food producers

The community is formed of the producers in the Ayrshire Food Network, which was founded in 2002 to promote the use of local foodstuffs in the restaurants, hotels and shops along the 70 miles of the Firth of Clyde (the Clyde estuary), in southwest Scotland. The producers mainly sell their goods at the weekly markets in the county where stalls abound with beef, lamb, pork, game, bacon, fish, shellfish, vegetables, eggs and smoked specialties. The most typical foodstuff is probably Dunlop, a hard, cows' milk cheese that, until 1930, was made in over 300 farms in the area. Its production is not dissimilar to that of Cheddar but it is pressed for a shorter time and ripens for four to 12 months.

PRODUCTION AREA
North Ayrshire, Scotland

COMMUNITY COORDINATOR
Howard Wilkinson
tel. +44 1560485858
Howard.Wilkinson2@btinternet.com

Beer brewers and drinkers

In 1990 the Campaign for Real Ale, from Britain, the Objectieve Beer Proevers, from Belgium, and the Association Promotie Informatie Traditioneel Bier, from Holland, joined forces in the European Beer Consumers Union (EBCU). Other organizations, from Sweden, Finland, Switzerland, Denmark, the United Kingdom and Italy now also belong to the EBCU, bringing its overall membership to 70,000 beer drinkers. The organization is based in the UK but is active in several European countries; its aim is to maintain the culture of beer and it pays particular attention to small-scale producers, be they local, regional or national. It also actively promotes traditional beers and supports those brewing high quality beers of recognized local or national styles.

PRODUCTION AREA
Throughout the country

COMMUNITY COORDINATOR
Terry Lock
tel. +44 7976607575
terrya.lock@ntlworld.com

Berkshire cereal farmers

Doves Farm at Hungerford, about 100 kilometers west of London, grows wheat, spelt and several ancient varieties of barley and rye; and produces flour from all of them. The farm has 122 hectares, all organically certified, and is part of a program to protect the national flora and fauna. It also belongs to the Berkshire Food Group, a network of producers in the county who promote the production and consumption of local produce. The Group also works with children, in particular creating a database of farms in Berkshire where children and their teachers can have lessons in how food is produced. The organization is additionally involved with chefs and farmers' markets in the area, promoting the concepts of sustainability and shortening the supply chain.

PRODUCTION AREA
Berkshire, England

COMMUNITY COORDINATOR
Clare Marriage
tel. +44 1488684880
mail@dovesfarm.co.uk

Berkshire farmers

The community comes from Sheepdrove Organic Farm at Lambourn in Berkshire, about a hundred kilometers west of London. Sheepdrove is an organic farm with sheep, free-range chickens and pigs, reared in fields where crop rotation is practiced. The community concentrates on rare British breeds (Gloucester Old Spot and Oxford Sandy and Black pigs, Aberdeen Angus cattle, Shetland sheep) and uses renewable energy sources (solar power for heating and cooking, eco-compatible building materials, electrically powered vehicles). There are mail order sales and great importance is placed on traceability.

PRODUCTION AREA
Berkshire, England

COMMUNITY COORDINATOR
Juliet Kindersley
tel. +44 1488674726
juliet.Kindersley@sheepdrove.com

Cambridgeshire beekeepers

The Cambridgeshire Beekeepers' Association was founded in 1881 when hives were still being made of wicker or straw and in order to extract the honey each year the bees were killed. The aim of the Association was therefore to bring in more intelligent, more humane systems. It now runs training courses for its members, arranges annual meetings, demonstrations and conferences, and publishes a newsletter. Member beekeepers spread their message to the public through country fairs and by giving lessons at local schools. Their farms are generally small and the honey produced, around 800 kilos a year, is sold through the county consumer association.

PRODUCTION AREA
Cambridgeshire, England

COMMUNITY COORDINATOR
Mary Dicks
tel. +44 1223262884
mooselink@gmail.com

Cider Apple growers

The community is formed of six fruit farmers from Cambridgeshire, Herefordshire and East Sussex, all in southern England, who are battling to maintain apple growing and cider production, which are at the heart of the country's gastronomic heritage and culture. They grow ancient varieties of pears and plums as well as apples, all organically, and supply over 50 cider makers from Norfolk, Suffolk, Kent, Gloucestershire and Sussex, counties which also have historic ties with fruit production. English farmers have been making cider for centuries but commercial production only began in the 1930s. This became industrialized in the 1970s. Non-industrial cider comes from single apple varieties and the taste varies considerably depending on the variety chosen.

PRODUCTION AREA
Cambridgeshire, Herefordshire and East Sussex, England

COMMUNITY COORDINATOR
Andrea Falter
tel. +44 1487740319
andrea@falter.cc

Cornwall fishermen

A group of fishermen on the Cornwall coast is dedicated to catching burbots, crabs, black merlins, turbots and gray mullets, using small boats with large-mesh trammel nets. The fish are frozen immediately on being caught and delivered to clients (shops and restaurants in southern England) that evening or the following morning; other fish, including pollock, are smoked. The fish is not only of excellent quality but minimal environmental impact is involved in catching it. The community has recently started selling to a number of high quality restaurants, raising hopes that the period of crisis surrounding local fishing is starting to pass.

PRODUCTION AREA
Cornwall, England

COMMUNITY COORDINATOR
Dylan Bean
tel. +44 1326231067
dbean@f2s.com

Cornwall food producers

The community is formed of bakers using local ingredients; farmers rearing milk cows for butter, cheese and clotted cream; and a wine producer; all of whom work collaboratively with other producers in the zone. The wine producer, Camel Valley vineyard, is of particular importance for the region's gastronomic revival, and leading its range is a traditional method sparkling wine, Brut Cornwall. Recently the community has become a catalyst for quality improvements in the county. An emblematic case is that of a producer from Penzance who was stopped from selling non-pasteurized milk to five shops in the area. The producer, the five shopkeepers and the restaurants associated with the community took up the cudgels internationally against the ruling.

PRODUCTION AREA
Bodmin, Cornwall, England

COMMUNITY COORDINATOR
Bob Lindo
tel. +44 120877959
bob@camelvalley.com

Cumberland Sausage producers

The Cumberland Sausage Association brings together 15 pig breeders and butchers who make this traditional product. It has been produced for almost 500 years, originally with pork from the Cumberland pig. However, the breed became extinct around 1960, forcing producers to turn to other local stock. Until the 1950s every farm in the area had a few pigs which were butchered in the fall to provide meat for the winter. The best cuts were used for the sausages; the meat was salted, finely minced and spices were added. Recently the Cumberland Sausage has become so popular that many companies have started producing it industrially, to the detriment of quality and taste. Those making it by hand are working to protect the traditional recipe.

PRODUCTION AREA
Cumberland, England

COMMUNITY COORDINATOR
Peter Gott
tel. +44 1539567609
enquiries@sillfield.co.uk

Dumfries and Galloway food producers

Savour the Flavours, a local producers' association, has been operating in Dumfries and Galloway, a mainly agricultural area, since 2003. With the help of Scottish Enterprise, the Scottish economic development agency, in just three years its 500 members have built up their sales system and developed a trade mark for their meats, jams, cheeses, fish and alcoholic drinks All members are encouraged to work collaboratively and supply each other with ingredients. Recently the community has produced a brochure, supplying a "gastronomic itinerary" to visitors, which takes them round some of the association's farms, and every year there are awards for the best restaurant in the region and for shopkeepers promoting local foodstuffs.

PRODUCTION AREA
Dumfries and Galloway, Scotland

COMMUNITY COORDINATOR
Graeme Hume
tel. +34 1557870203
graeme@flavourofgalloway.co.uk

Farmers' market producers

The community is formed of producers in the National Farmers' Retail & Markets Association (FARMA), which has 15,000 members throughout the UK. Some work with the Soil Association nationally, some are involved with associations promoting local gastronomic traditions, all run small farms, rarely employing others. The FARMA members growing fruit use non-intensive methods, and bring consumers the choice of over 25 local varieties of strawberry and five types of raspberry; the fruit is sold fresh or made into jams and tarts. Those rearing cattle and pigs mostly raise indigenous breeds and use natural methods, mainly producing bacon and other cured meats.

PRODUCTION AREA
Throughout the country

COMMUNITY COORDINATOR
Gareth Jones
tel. +44 8454588420
gareth@farma.org.uk

Fishermen and restaurateurs

With plenty of low-cost fish on the market it is a difficult time for fishing in the United Kingdom. Yet small-scale fishing methods have less environmental impact, give higher quality fish and help fishing communities survive. Mindful of this, a group of UK restaurateurs are working with fishermen who respect the principles of sustainable fishing and who offer fish of excellent flavor, in return guaranteeing them a fair income. It's not easy for either side, because the restaurateurs need to be able to adapt their menus to what the fishermen have caught and the fishermen must always use sustainable fishing methods if they are to be part of the network.

PRODUCTION AREA
Throughout the country

COMMUNITY COORDINATOR
Malcolm MacGarvin
tel. +44 1807590396
macgarvin@modus-vivendi.co.uk

Guernsey Cow breeders

The community comprises the owners of three farms in Somerset who formed themselves into a cooperative, called Brown Cow Organics, bringing together 180 hectares of land, all farmed organically. They rear 100 Guernsey cows, a breed native to the island of Guernsey in the English Channel. It was once widespread in the United Kingdom but is now becoming rare. The herd gives excellent milk, its quality improved further by the completely natural, organic feed the cows receive: they graze on pasture in the summer and are fed with home-grown cereals in winter. Brown Cow Organic produce (meat, milk, yogurt, fruit and vegetables) is sold directly and at local farmers' markets.

PRODUCTION AREA
Somerset, England

COMMUNITY COORDINATOR
Judith Frean
tel. +44 1749890298
organics@browncoworganics.co.uk

Hand-made Marmalade and Jam producers

The community is formed of a fruit preserver in London and a group of fruit growers from Kent. The range produced includes jams, marmalades, chutneys and quince paste. Fruit preserves were originally imported into England from Portugal but home-based production started in the 17th century and they became a lynch-pin of the British breakfast. Where possible the community acquires its fruit from organic growers but it also tries to use local sources, to minimize the distances the fruit has to travel. The producers recently planted 330 new trees which will start to give fruit in 2009.

PRODUCTION AREA
London and Kent, England

COMMUNITY COORDINATOR
Sky Cracknell
tel. +44 2086920806
sky@englandpreserves.co.uk

Herdwick Lamb breeders

The community is a cooperative of 27 breeders from the Lake District, in Cumbria in northwest England, who rear lamb from the Herdwick breed, selling it directly. Although the origins of the breed are uncertain it is believed that it was introduced into the region by the Vikings. It is, however, known that the Cistercian monks of Furness Abbey were raising it in the Middle Ages. The Herdwick is a hardy breed, the sheep are solid with strong bones and short trotters; they roam freely on mountain slopes in both summer and winter, grazing on small plants, leaves and dried grass. The coat is mainly coarse-haired, forming an excellent rain barrier. The lambs are black when first born but as they grow the color lightens through brown, for the young lambs, to a pale grey for the mature animals.

PRODUCTION AREA
Lake district, Cumbria, England

COMMUNITY COORDINATOR
Andrew Sharp
tel. +44 1229588244
farmersharp@yahoo.co.uk

Highlands and Western Isles food producers

This north Scottish community comprises the Highlands and Islands Food Forum, which groups small-scale farmers, fishermen and dairymen, food science experts, lecturers and representatives of the local government. All the output is certified organic. The community crofters (who rent small plots) raise native sheep breeds, such as the Shetland or the Hebrides, which are resistant to the region's severe climate and which can graze on the islands' marshy coastlands. Some members rear Highland cattle, most notably the Black Kyloe, using natural feeding methods. The fishermen in the association produce organic smoked salmon, smoked over oak chips.

PRODUCTION AREA
Highlands and Na h-Eileanan Siar, Scotland

COMMUNITY COORDINATOR
Pam Rodway
tel. +44 1309676566
pam.rodway@virgin.net

Isle of Skye and Lochalsh food producers and distributors

The food community of Skye and Lochalsh is formed of a group of producers and traders in a joint production chain. Distribution is local, covering Skye, the best known and largest island in the Inner Hebrides, and Lochalsh, on the adjacent mainland. Community members concentrate particularly on mutton hams, venison bacon and wild boar sausages. All the animals, which are from local breeds, are reared naturally and the produce is sold at farmers' markets. The community also produces and sells fish, herbs, organic salad greens, jams, cheeses, ice creams, yogurt, sea food, beer and whisky. One of its most characteristic products is Scottish tablet, a traditional, hand-made fudge.

PRODUCTION AREA
Skye and Lochalsh, Highlands, Scotland

COMMUNITY COORDINATOR
Dede MacGillivray
tel. +44 1471833225-437
dedemacgillivray@hotmail.com

Jersey dairy farmers

The Jersey Dairy cooperative is formed of 33 dairy farmers on the island of Jersey who supply milk to its communal dairy. They mostly raise Jersey cows, one of the three breeds originating on the island, which lies in the English Channel. Jerseys, along with the Devon and the Guernsey, have often been exported from the island *en masse* but herds are not allowed to return, which has helped maintain the breed's pedigree. Abundant green pasture assures particularly rich milk leading to Jersey's great tradition for butter production. This is made by skimming off the cream from the milkings, leaving it to sour and then churning it until it thickens. Jersey butter is decorated with the island's traditional wedge- and diamond-shaped motifs. The cooperative's dairy also produces organic milk, cream, crème fraîche and cheeses.

PRODUCTION AREA
Isle of Jersey

COMMUNITY COORDINATOR
Christopher Journeaux
tel. +44 1534818502
christopher.journeaux@jerseydairy.je

Manx Loaghtan Sheep breeders

This community on the Isle of Man raises the Manx Loaghtan sheep, an indigenous breed which has four horns, as do all the breeds classified as primitive (the Hebrides, the Icelandic and the Norwegian). Up until the 18th century the Manx Loaghtan was the only sheep breed on the island but then more higher-yielding breeds were introduced from the mainland of Great Britain and the Manx Loaghtan underwent a rapid decline. Examples of the breed were exhibited at an agricultural fair in 1913. By then it had become almost extinct but a few Isle of Man breeders were determined to preserve it. Now there are just a few hundred head on the island, as well as a few herds scattered throughout the rest of the United Kingdom. The community's breeders let the animals roam free and their feed is natural. The butchering, and the sale of the meat and the wool, is handled by the Manx Loaghtan cooperative, of which the community members form part.

PRODUCTION AREA
Isle of Man

COMMUNITY COORDINATOR
George Steriopulos
tel. +44 7624492850
sales@manxloaghtan.com

Northumberland and Scottish Borders pig breeders

The community is formed of pig breeders from the Borders (which straddles Northumberland and southern Scotland) belonging to the British Pig Association. This groups those rearing native breeds, most of which have fewer than 500 sows throughout the United Kingdom and are therefore at risk of extinction. Its aim is to ensure the survival of these breeds. The Tamworth is the main breed raised by the community. This is believed to be a direct descendant of the Old English Forest, an ancient wild indigenous breed. The Tamworth was one of the few breeds not to have been crossed with Chinese stock, a widespread expedient taken to increase yields. It was long renowned for its bacon but in the 19th century it was superseded by more productive breeds. The community is trying to re-establish the Tamworth, and other breeds, for bacon and sausages.

PRODUCTION AREA
Northumberland, England; Scottish Borders, Scotland

COMMUNITY COORDINATOR
Graham Head
tel. +44 1289388543
grahampeterhead@yahoo.com

Oxfordshire cattle breeders

The Oxfordshire Food Group is a no-profit organization founded in 2000 with the aim of promoting the production and consumption of local foodstuffs. It comprises 66 members, who sell their produce at local farmers' markets. Of these, 13 raise local cattle breeds: the Hereford (which is a direct descendent of the Old Horned Hereford), the Devon (which was first identified in 1086) and the Sussex. The community members, most of whom use organic techniques, graze the cattle on clover pasture during the summer and feed them on barley, wheat, oats, broad beans and rye (all locally grown) in the winter. The cattle are butchered locally, thereby avoiding increased stress on the animals and ensuring easier traceability. Butchers in the area sell not just the fresh cuts of meat but also sausages, patties and salt beef.

PRODUCTION AREA
Oxfordshire, England

COMMUNITY COORDINATOR
Geoffrey Whittle
tel. +44 1491682568
ranger.organics@virgin.net

Real Ale brewers and drinkers

The Campaign for Real Ale (CAMRA) was founded in the UK by a group of beer lovers but then spread to other countries and now has 80,000 members across Europe, spanning brewers, pub owners and consumers. It works to support the production of real ale and spread awareness of its qualities, based on its objectives: to promote quality and the right to choose, to support the pub as the focal point of community life and to disseminate the value of traditional beers, ciders and perries as part of British culture. Real ale means a beer produced with natural ingredients and which, unlike normal ale, is cask-conditioned, remaining on its yeasts in the cask or bottle in which it matures and being served directly from that container. This means that fermentation continues and real ale remains "alive".

PRODUCTION AREA
Throughout the country

COMMUNITY COORDINATOR
Robert Stukins
tel. +44 7788641294
beerseeker@aol.com

Sussex fishermen

Most people in southeast England are unaware that within this densely urban area there is a small fishing community, whose history goes back hundreds of years. It is known for sure that the port of Hastings, in East Sussex, was famous for its fishing before 1066, when William of Normandy invaded England. Some of today's fishermen concentrate on catching herrings, mackerel and soles, using certified sustainable fishing methods. Most fishing is done at night, the catch being landed whole and sold to dealers and restaurants in the area.

PRODUCTION AREA
Sussex, England

COMMUNITY COORDINATOR
Paul Joy
tel. +44 1424722322
info@hastingsfish.co.uk

Traditional Scottish food producers

Scottish Food Guide is a network uniting 400 small-scale producers, distributors and restaurateurs in Scotland, all listed on the association's website. Of particular importance is the rearing of Ayrshire cattle, which have a characteristic red-white dappled coat. They are especially well adapted to Ayrshire's land formation and climate and, although primarily a meat breed, their milk gives excellent butter and local cheeses. Most notable among these are Dunlop, a cheese which was produced on more than 300 farms before the second world war, although now by only a few dairymen; and Dunsyre Blue, made from unpasteurized milk. Of no less importance are the bakery products, the jams, the fish specialties and the growing of fruit and vegetables.

PRODUCTION AREA
Scotland

COMMUNITY COORDINATOR
Wendy Barrie
tel. +44 1312203630
wendy@scottishfoodguide.com

Twickenham beekeepers

The Twickenham and Thames Valley Bee-keepers' Association was founded in 1919 and in 1987 was recognized as a registered charity. It is based near Twickenham, on the southwest corner of London. Members meet every week from March through to September, usually on Fridays, to learn new techniques and exchange ideas. The honey is sold at the local market. Its Bushy Park apiary comprises eight to 12 hives set within a clump of trees. They receive morning sunlight but are shaded for the rest of the day. The bees fly up to two miles away to collect pollen, nectar and water. The park, with its chestnut, hawthorn, linden and oak trees, supplies an excellent range of nutrients. The bees which feed on ripe plums produce a characteristic red-colored honey.

PRODUCTION AREA
Twickenham, Greater London, England

COMMUNITY COORDINATOR
Mike Gill
tel. +44 2089418250
mike.gill@bees.co.uk

Wales farmers

Dairy farmers from west Wales and other farmers in the region rearing Welsh Black cattle and Welsh sheep form the community, whose produce is sold at the regular Pembrokeshire farmers' markets. The lands of Wales are highly suited to livestock farming and, as a result, to cheese production. The Welsh Black is one of the most widespread cattle breeds in the country, and was once also of renown in the Midlands and on London markets. It is raised for milk as well as meat, the milk being used to make Caerphilly, a young, pressed, blue cheese named after the town (and county) in Wales where it was first produced. Caerphilly almost disappeared during the second world war, when British cheese production turned towards longer-aged cheeses, but recently a large number of farms have taken up its production again.

PRODUCTION AREA
Wales

COMMUNITY COORDINATOR
Margaret Rees
tel. +44 1558669116
margaret@culinaryprojects.com

Rosson Wild Fruits and Infusions

In the north of Belorus, not far from the borders with Russia and Latvia, is Rosson, in the district of Vitsebsk. Here, on the Nischa River, is the village of Kliastizy, a cluster of wooden houses with white doors and windows dotted about the hillside. More than 70% of the area is forested, with occasional wetlands and clearings exposed to the sun, an ideal environment for aromatic herbs and wild fruits: blackcurrant, wild strawberry, black and red blueberry, dog-rose, raspberry, willow herb (*Epilobium angustifolium*), St.-John's-wort, wild mint, thyme, spiraea olmaria (*Filipendula ulmaria*) and bisongrass (*Hierochloe odorata*), a local aromatic plant. Traditionally, these plants and berries are collected from spring to early autumn and are laid outside to dry for a day, but not in direct sunlight, on a piece of rough cloth on the floor. Then they are brought inside, and dried either over a large wood-stove or on wooden benches in a typical Russian bath-house. Kept in thick cloth or paper bags, the branches, berries, flowers and leaves are used to produce tisanes, which can be drunk cold or hot. Each recipe combines different ingredients and quantities, according to the aroma, flavor, color and medicinal effects desired. Usually, the tisanes are drunk with honey or a caramel-colored jam obtained by boiling yellow dandelion petals in a sugar syrup. In the nineties, when many of the *kolchoz* (collective farms) were disbanded, the population had to face unemployment and many were driven to alcoholism. Five of the women in this village got together with Alla Kharan, who had been assistant-director of the local *kolchoz* for 22 years, to assess how better use could be made of local resources, especially tourism, by opening an information center run by volunteers. The Presidium was set up through these women, in an endeavor to transform the tradition of making tisanes into an economic activity that would provide a livelihood. Lidziya Kukharava, expert on wild herbs and tisanes of the Central Botanical Garden at the Bielorussia National Academy of Sciences, is helping them to select the most interesting recipes and the local convivium, Slow Food Minsk, is helping them to wrap and market the tisanes.

PRODUCTION AREA
Rosson, province of Vitsebsk

PRESIDIUM COORDINATOR
Igor Danilov
tel. +375 296321131 - 172811336
danilov@gastronom.by

Pozegaca Plum Slatko

Slivovica is a world renowned plum distillate from the Balkans. In certain regions of the former Yugoslavia they still use the same variety of fruit, though less frequently than before, to make a preserve in syrup called slatko, meaning 'sweet'. In the upper valley of the Drina River, 120 kilometers southeast of Sarajevo near Gorazde, the women prepare the slatko with a particular variety of plum called pozegaca (*Prunus insititia*), which are gathered in the middle of September. They scald them in boiling water, peel them and then remove the pits with a skewer or a knitting needle. They firm them up by soaking them in water and lime for a half hour and then boil them in sugar water flavored with lemon slices, at times adding cloves and walnuts. Gorazde used to be a land of vineyards and orchards. Abandoned in the 1950s, they were replaced by war and chemical industries, swept away after 1989 by the dissolution of Yugoslavia. Today an attempt is being made to recover a farming economy that can once gain become a source of income for the population. The *slatko* from pozegaca plums, whose color varies from honey yellow to dark pink, has a creamy consistency and delicate flavor that is somewhat reminiscent of Turkish rose petal preserves. It is served with fresh cheeses and in Gorazde it is eaten with kaymak (a creamy cheese) or with goat's milk feta. And it is often served in little bronze bowls, containing a cooked plum each, accompanied by Turkish coffee. At present five women produce the Presidium *slatko*, but the group may grow. It all depends on how well it is commercialized. As a start, the group worked with elderly women to define the traditional recipe. Their *slatko* is prepared over a wood fire in the village of di Filipovici (Ustikolina-Gorazde), using plums grown on the banks of the River Drina. In November 2005 the group set up the Emina Association. For now the female producers sell the slatko locally (Gorazde e Sarajevo), but thanks to the Agropodrinje cooperative they plan to export it.

PRODUCTION AREA
Upper Drina valley, Ustikolina-Gorazde

PRESIDIUM COORDINATOR
Nefisa Medosevic
tel. +387 61206467
freni@bih.net.ba

PRESIDIUM SUPPORTED BY
Tuscany Regional Authority, Italy

Sack Cheese (Sir iz Mijeha)

The cheese is put in a light brown sack of sheepskin, turned inside out, and weighs 30-70 kilos depending on the size of the animals. It is the container itself, the sack, which makes this product so unique. Sack cheese is made in certain villages of Nevesinje, a harsh and mountainous region in southeastern Bosnia and Herzegovina and the grazing land for the local pramenka sheep (used for milk, meat and wool). It is made with top quality raw milk from sheep or cows, from two local breeds, the busa and the gatacka (now on the decline however) or from a combination of the two. Immediately after the milking the cheese is filtered through cheesecloth, rennet is added, and then after about an hour and a half the curd is broken apart into lumps the size of a walnut. The mass of curds are then placed on a cloth and pressed for about 12 hours. After the curd is broken up a second time, the cheese is salted and put into the sheepskin with the aid of a stick, being careful there are no air bubbles. The sack is then closed up and placed in a cool place to age for two to three months. To prepare the sack they need to butcher the sheep without damaging the skin, then shave it and wash it with boiling water and whey. When dry, they tie the legs and neck, fill the sheep with air and hang it to dry in a place where meat is usually smoked. It is then washed a second time and left to dry in the open air. The ripe cheese, white or slightly yellowish, is served as an appetizer, with boiled potatoes or with ham and *ustipci* (small fried focaccias). The Presidium was set up in collaboration with the Province of Arezzo and Ucodep, an Italian NGO that works in Bosnia and Herzegovina to promote certain local products. Its aim is to protect the indigenous breeds involved and to help the fifteen or so producers to work in accordance with the law and to sell, at least at a local level, the cheese made with cow's milk (in winter), sheep's milk (in summer) and a mixture of milk. It will also draw up a regulatory framework for production.

PRODUCTION AREA
Nevesinje region

PRESIDIUM COORDINATOR
Slavica Samardzic
tel. +387 65750427
slavica92000@yahoo.com

Giant Istrian Ox

With its imposing bulk (weighing up to a ton), white-gray coat, harp-shaped horns and majestic gait, the giant Istrian ox is a member of the Podolica family. Like the Chianina and Maremma breeds, this ox traces its ancestry back to *Bos taurus macrocerus*, a breed that gave rise the breed of the steppes and called Podolica because it was particularly prevalent in Podolia, an area that is today part of Ukraine. In Roman times the Boscarin worked in the fields, in the Venetian Republic it transported timber. Today, fewer and fewer animals are castrated, a step that develops their musculature to the full; the market for work animals has dried up, and a market for the animal's meat still does not exist. Consequently breeders prefer to sell young steers, crating them as soon as possible. From 50,000 heads at the end of World War II, the population has dwindled nearly to extinction. In 1986, when director Mirko Prijatelj's film *Boskarin* came out, the breed was reduced to a mere 30 animals in the Istrian hinterlans. Today, the population numbers around 200. Consistent restocking and remunerative prices for the breeders are necessary to save this breed and raise the profile of its meat, which is toothsome, well-marbled and tasty. The Presidium was established, with the help of the Tuscany Regional Authority, to support of a project in Istria to give eco-nomic aid to farmers helping to increase the numbers of the Giant Istrian Ox. When the cattle are no longer in danger of going extinct, efforts will then be directed to promoting their gastronomic value. In the meantime, courses will be organized to educate breeders, butchers, restaurateurs and chefs not only about the beef's culinary possibilities, but also about butchering and presenting and promoting the various cuts. In 2006, several representatives of the Presidium – two breeders, an agronomist and a butcher – visited the Italian Piedmontese Ox Presidium to compare methods of breeding and butchering.

PRODUCTION AREA
Istria

PRESIDIUM COORDINATOR
Graciano Prekalj
tel. +385 52619610
azrri@pu.t-com.hr

PRESIDIUM SUPPORTED BY
Tuscany Regional Authority (Italy)

Tsamarella

This product – goat meat is dried in the sun and covered with salt and oregano – is a real rarity whose secret lies in the utter simplicity of its preparation:. Unfortunately, few traces are left of the specialty in its native Cypress, perhaps only in the memories of the island's inhabitants. In a protected area high in the mountains, the indigenous tradition of goat herding yields both excellent cheeses and delicious meat. Tsamarella's dark, burgundy-hued cubes are not particularly inviting in appearance. However, its bold spiciness and pleasant gamey flavor are remarkable, and particularly good with zivania, the Cypriot grappa. The producers of the Presidium prepare tsamarella only from the thigh of the animal because it is the leanest and most highly valued cut and best provides the earthy, rustic flavor and smoothness they are looking for. The leg is butterflied and cut into strips, immersed in salt and oregano and left to dry in the sun for 7-10 weeks. The recipe is a lighter version of age-old *apokti*, a preparation that is said to have used the meat of goats that have died of old age. The Presidium, the first in Cyprus, aims to promote tsamarella in local markets and to bring it to more international attention as well. The most challenging aspect of the project, however, is saving a native goat breed, the *machaeras*, which is nearly extinct, despite it being particularly suited to grazing the dry and spiny scrub of the Cypriot hills with its long limbs and short coat. To this end, the production protocol includes a stipulation that a quota for this breed must be met. The few such animals still left live mainly in the western Troödos mountains.

PRODUCTION AREA
Pitsilia region

PRESIDIUM COORDINATOR
Photis Papademas
tel. +357 22 877220
photis@kss.com.cy

Barèges-Gavarnie Sheep

With its majestic peaks and wide valleys, the high Gave de Pau is a realm of mountain pastures. It is here that the rustic Baréges sheep have developed. With their thick wool and fine bone structure, they can stand the rigid Pyrenees climate and find food on even the most difficult of lands. This breed, which has recently been awarded AOC (certified origin denomination) recognition, traditionally yields meat products from two animals. One is the Doublon, a castrated ram of more than 18 months and over 23 kilos in weight, which must have spent at least two summers in the pastures (hence its name). Two years on the high slopes are also required for the Brebis de boucherie, a ewe of 2-6 years in age weighing at least 22 kilos. Both animals are far removed from the culinary customs of today, which demand only very young suckling lambs with lean meat and no odor or even flavor, since this supposedly guarantees a product that is tender, healthy and sufficiently 'rarefied' to satisfy 'sophisticated' palates. The meat from the Barèges-Gavarnie sheep, bright red in color, is tender, succulent, and melts in the mouth. The marbling fat is aromatic and velvety and leaves none of the strong after-taste of fleece, often typical of mutton. It is obvious that it will take more than an AOC recognition to remove preconceptions about the use of adult sheep, even if this is deeply rooted in the country's culinary traditions and the meat is excellent. This is what the Presidium has to do: namely, make people understand and appreciate the meat from the Barèges sheep and explain the value (also in economic terms, since a big difference exists between keeping an animal for two years instead of a few months) of an old meat produced following the high pasture cycles of our ancestors (in the summer higher than 2,000 meters and in the winter between 600 and 1000). It will also be necessary to establish with the producers the gustative profile for a breed that grows entirely outside in an area whose special geoclimate and perfect pastureland make it worthy of protection and promotion.

PRODUCTION AREA
17 municipalities of the Hautes-Pyrénées, between Barèges and Gavarnie

PRESIDIUM COORDINATORS
Raphaël Paya
tel. +33 562955647
terroir.gagnant@wanadoo.fr
Marie-Lise Broueilh
tel. +33 562923216
moutonbg@free.fr

PRESIDIUM SUPPORTED BY
Midi-Pyrénées Region

Bigorre Black Pig

That of the Gascony is the oldest pig population known in France. A pig of Iberian stock, it is completely black and originates from the foothills of Nébouzanne, on the edge of the High Pyrenees, High Garonna and Gers. It is a rustic, strong animal, with black skin and bristles and narrow ears set horizontally. Gentle and prolific, it is bred wild because it adapts to any climate and to grazing. With respect to the so-called improved breeds, it grows slowly with a daily increase in weight of just 450 grams (against 800 grams the other breeds) and with 43% of lean carcass (against an average of 56%), but the composition of its fat is exceptional in quality. It was the pig's poor adaptation to intensive breeding that almost led the Bigorre black pig to extinction, with a record minimum of just 34 sows in 1981. However, it was this nucleus that give life to the recovery project for the breed which culminated in 1992 in the Hautes-Pyrénées, with the setting up of a production chain, from breeding to the pork butchers, for the production and promotion of top quality cured meats. Thanks to this initiative in 2004 there were 600 sows spread around 50 pig farms. The Noir de Bigorre ham is sold with a product conformity certificate (CCP) which imposes very strict breeding and processing rules. This guarantees that all products from this breed – fresh and cured meat – present the best of its superb sensorial features, exalted by the fact that the animals grow and feed outside, with a density that never exceeds 25 head per hectare. Today the inter-professional association, Consortium du Noir de Bigorre, processes the meat of approximately 5,000 animals, but to free themselves from public support they need to increase production. The aim of the Presidium is to spread the culture of top quality ham in France, and thus introduce the Noir de Bigorre among top quality gastronomy products.

PRODUCTION AREA
Midi-Pyrénées, districts of Haute-Garonne and Hautes-Pyrénées

PRESIDIUM COORDINATOR
Armand Touzanne
tel. +33 562348735
a.touzanne@hautes-pyrenees.chambagri.fr

PRESIDIUM SUPPORTED BY
Midi-Pyrénées Region

Haute Provence Einkorn

For thousands of years, the history of einkorn (*Triticum monococcum*) has been closely linked to that of the Mediterranean. Until Roman times, this cereal was widely eaten, but later it was almost totally replaced by wheat, tender and durum, which ousted the various minor cereals, due to its higher yield and the fact it needed no processing. As einkorn has a hull, it must always be decorticated (with a similar technique to that used for rice). For a dozen or so years now, einkorn has enjoyed renewed interest, thanks to its rustic sturdy plant that adapts to rather dry climates and poor soil, to its nutritional and organoleptic qualities (it is rich in protein and magnesium). Haute Provence Einkorn (in French *petit épeautre*) from is a local plant, which can be traced back to 9000 B.C., and which is presumed to have arrived from the western coast of what is now Turkey. Today there are around 20 producers, with fields spread around 235 municipalities at an altitude of over 400 meters high, who have joined together in a syndicate and have obtained PGI recognition for their cereal and flour. They have established a very rigid protocol, strictly in conformity with the precepts of organic agriculture, promoting a product backed up by local restaurants and participation in markets and fairs. Einkorn has perfectly adapted to the difficult environment and its fields are alternated with fields of lavender and chickpeas, often with the crop rotation. The Presidium will seek to make this poor but versatile cereal (left to ferment, it can even be used to make good beer) popular outside France. It will also be necessary to establish the organoleptic profile and sensorial features that make *petit épeautre* so highly prized and distinctive, creating opportunities for producers to meet their counterparts in other parts of the world.

PRODUCTION AREA
Mevouillon, Haute-Provence

PRESIDIUM COORDINATOR
Vincent Clary
tel. +33 475285186
petit.epautre@wanadoo.fr

Pardailhan Black Turnips

The Pardailhan plain, about 40 kilometers from the Mediterranean coast, rises gently from 400 to 800 meters. For more than 200 years, the entire surrounding region has been dominated by vines and olive groves, while the colder and damper climate of the plain does not permit the cultivation of these products: around Pardailhan we find grazing cattle, meadows, flocks of sheep, forests and boar. The turnips produced in this small village have been famous since days gone by. In fact at the end of the 19th century they were preserved and sold at very high prices during international exhibitions. However, after the last war farming in Pardailhan slumped and all local produce was affected; only a few producers managed to continue selling the turnips to the nearby markets (Béziers, Saint-Pons, Narbonne...). The Noir long de Caluire variety, which takes its name from its original region, north of Pardailhan, has been acclimatized to this village for centuries, developing a unique flavor thanks to the special soil and microclimate. Here the turnips are broadcast sown at the beginning of August, when they can still enjoy the last summer rains, and grow and ripen before winter. In autumn, the rains give way to the fog: folklore says that the turnips 'drink through their leaves'. The manual harvest lasts from the beginning of November to the end of January. When eaten, the Pardailhan turnips, which have a black skin but white pulp, are very sweet, tender and delicate, with a flavor that recalls hazelnuts or pine nuts; they can be eaten cooked, cold in *vinai-grette*, hot and caramelized, or sautéed in goose fat with a pinch of sugar. The Pardailhan turnip producers association has formed a Presidium to spread knowledge about the excellence of this product, because by increasing production they could strengthen local agriculture, where there is abundant farmland (more than 4,000 hectares for just 165 inhabitants). One of the aims of the 14 producers is to restore some of the ancient preserves using the black turnips that Pardailhan was famous for (while nowadays they are sold fresh and the market thus lasts just three months a year). Furthermore, the producers intend to cooperate to follow the local market better, taking turns in participating in local fetes and promoting the activities of the Presidium during the 'Black Turnip Festival' held every year in Pardailhan.

PRODUCTION AREA
Pardailhan, Hérault, Languedoc-Roussillon

PRESIDIUM COORDINATOR
Elian Robert
tel. +33 467976544
e.m.robert@cario.fr

PRESIDIUM SUPPORTED BY
Parc Naturel Régional du Haut-Languedoc

Pélardon Sec

Pélardon is one of the 42 French (controlled origin denomination) AOC cheeses and, among these, one of the 12 goat's cheeses. The recognized production area extends from Cévennes to Montagne Noire, through to Hautes Corbières de l'Aude, following the southern profile of the Central Massif. There the landscape is characterized by Mediterranean scrub, which, together with a special, somewhat harsh climate and geomorphology creates this unique product. The milk used to make Pélardon is the sum of all these features: the herds are traditionally of just a few head, and they eat grass, broom, oak leaves, heather, chestnuts and other aromatic plants, which give the cheese a strong aroma of hazelnuts, flowers and honey. Pélardon is eaten while it is still quite fresh, after just 11 days, the minimum refining period, which allows the special aromas and right moisture level develop. This is why it is classified as a soft cheese. It is cylindrical in shape with rounded edges, about 2.2-2.7 centimeters high and 6-7 centimeters in diameter. It is made exclusively from raw whole goat's milk and uncooked lactic curd. Alas, the ripened version of this famous cheese — Pélardon Sec or Affiné, which ripens for at least one month — is disappearing. The gustative profile changes completely in just 30 days, becoming firm, complex and strong thanks also to the initial high moisture level, which accelerates the cheese's development. The fine rind is covered with mold that varies in color varying white to blue and the initially greasy, creamy cheese becomes compact and crumbly, while the aroma of goat grows stronger and is accompanied by a light and pleasant bitter aftertaste. The Presidium brings together a small group of producers who have decided to promote the traditional ripe version of Pélardon, harder to make and appreciate, as it is now considered as old, obsolete, with producers themselves regarding it as a stock remnant and selling it at the same price as the fresh cheese.

PRODUCTION AREA
Lozère, Gard and Hérault, Languedoc-Roussillon

PRESIDIUM COORDINATORS
Mélanie Fauconnier
tel. +33 499613045
melanie@slowfood.fr
Cécile Podeur
tel. +33 467 062357

Rennes Coucou Chicken

Until the Second World War, coucou chickens were highly appreciated and popular around Rennes and the whole of Brittany. Their slow decline began after 1950 due to industrialization and competition with 'modern' more productive breeds (Wyandotte, Sussex, Plymouth), to the extent that in the 80s the coucou was virtually extinct. In 1988 the Rennes Ecomuseum began showing interest in this ancient Breton breed, and managed to contact Monsieur Rouesné, an old farmer who gave them a few of his specimens, to safeguard the features of the bird. The following year the Ecomuseum got in touch with breeders and enthusiasts with the aim of gradually recovering and relaunching the breed. Today coucou chickens are an important part of Breton identity, especially in the Rennes region. They are elegant to watch of small-medium size, with wide shoulders, strong legs and wide jutting breast. The plumage is mainly grayish-blue and the feathers are run through by even black and white stripes. A rustic, slow growing breed, its meat is muscular firm and tender, with fine soft cream skin, that adheres well to the muscles. To conserve the organolpetic qualities and exalt the unmistakable aroma of hazelnuts, it is best slow cooked in the oven or a cocotte. The producers association of coucou chickens in Rennes, which is now the Presidium, has established very strict disciplines: the birds (no more than 500 per farm) are bred free range for at least 150 days, with a minimum of 10 square meters per head. Their food is 100% vegetable, excluding all genetically modified varieties. 18 breeders produce overall 25,000 chickens per year, a third go to wholesalers and restaurants and the rest are sold directly from the farms or on the market. The Presidium aims at helping the producers to maintain the high quality of their chickens, spreading knowledge of the excellence of the coucou and extending their markets.

PRODUCTION AREA
Ile-et-Villaine, Morbihan and Nord Loire-Atlantique, Bretagne and Pays-de-Loire

PRESIDIUM COORDINATOR
Paul Renault
tel. +33 299000590
bernadette.loisel@ille-et-vilaine.chambagri.fr

Roussillon Rancio Sec

A Banyuls in Roussillon, a small French region of Catalan culture, the eastern Pyrenees drop directly into the Mediterranean. Vines are cultivated directly on the coast (Cru di Collioure and Banyuls), and inland (Maury, Rivesaltes, Côtes-du-Roussillon). This wine ferments in an oxidizing environment partly exposed to the air, in barrels that are never topped up. To develop well in these conditions, it must have a high alcohol content. Rancio Sec – generally made from grenache (white or gray) or maccabeu, the same vines used to make the sweet wines of Banyuls, Maury, Rivesaltes – is centuries old and reflects the traditional wine making traditions of Roussillon. This was the wine of Banyuls before natural sweet wines were introduced, produced by adding sugar, hence alcohol (to block the natural fermentation), the success of which has drastically changed local taste. Rancio is far removed from any modern idea of wine: consumers, bar the Catalans, are simply not used to it. Connoisseurs drink it as an aperitif, served with tapas or salted anchovies, though Rancio could quite easily replace cognac or Armagnac with a good cigar at the end of a meal. The Rancio Sec Producers' Association was recently formed: it has about a dozen members and production is extremely limited (Rancio Sec is virtually impossible to find on the market). The Presidium was formed to raise the profile of the wine and ensure that better-informed consumers are aware of its special taste, especially in those countries where oxidized-type wines are more common and appreciated. This means that Rancio will be included in a series of guided samplings and Taste Workshops designed to study the right accompaniments to highlight its complex and fascinating organoleptic features, which on the palate express the notes of toast, vanilla, liquorice, hazelnuts typical of lengthy fermentation in the open air in oak barrels.

PRODUCTION AREA
Pyrénées Orientales, Languedoc-Roussillon

PRESIDIUM COORDINATORS
Brigitte Verdaguer
tel. +33 468290347
Rancy2@wanadoo.fr

PRESIDIUM SUPPORTED BY
Vinosafe

Saint-Flour Planèze Golden Lentil

In Alvernia, a region particularly renowned for cheesemaking, the growing demand for local cheeses in the late 20th century resulted in increased cultivation of animal fodder, to the detriment of grain and legume production. Lentils and peas have been cultivated for centuries on the lowest areas of Saint-Flour Planèze, a basalt plateau hemmed in by the Monts du Cantal and Margeride. Here, at the beginning of the last century, 1,500 hectares produced 1,200 tons of lentils, consumed locally and exported elsewhere. Production reached its peak in 1949 with 2,000 hectares devoted to this crop; since then, production declined steadily until it nearly disappeared. The trend was reversed in 1997, when a crisis in the milk market led several breeders to take up cultivation of these lentils – which was otherwise just a memory among the elderly. This was followed by extensive work to select varieties for cultivation and experimentation in the fields by farmers as well as the involvement of important chefs to put the lentils back on tables. Bright yellowish green, sometimes streaked with beige, Planèze lentils have very thin skins and thus cook quickly and absorb sauces very well. They have a sweet flavor and smooth texture that is never floury. Locally, the lentils are eaten both hot (with pork or cooked cured meats) and cold (with vinaigrette), while flour ground from the lentils is used to make traditional sweets. The producers association has 26 members who cultivate a total of 40 hectares (double that of two years ago), upholding high standards of quality, stabilizing retail prices and promoting commercialization. The Presidium aims to slowly expand the market beyond the immediate area – within which the product is well known – without compromising the product's quality. In 2006 three representatives of the Presidium took part in the Slow Food Foundation's exchange program, travelling to Sicily to meet the producers of the Ustica Lentil Presidium and to share their experiences.

PRODUCTION AREA
Cantal, Auvergne

PRESIDIUM COORDINATOR
Serge Ramadier
tel. +33 471605009
asso.lentilles@laposte.net

Mavrotragano Wine

The vine-growing area of Santorini is one of the few in the world where the vines grow on their roots, and the volcanic soil gives them natural defense against vine pest. However, the vineyards have fallen from 350 hectares in the 50s to just 140 today. Until seven or eight years ago, a few Mavrotragano plants, a rare red grape variety, could be found in small vineyards (no more than one hectare each, about 1% of the total on the island) and production never exceeded 1,500 kilos. The limited cultivation is because the grapes are very small, the bunches medium-sized and the yield 40% less than Mandilarià (another red variety in the Cyclades). The grapes are hand-harvested and the wine is left to ferment for nine days, when it is put into oak barrels and left for at least a year. Mavrotragano ripens at different times, it must be harvested often and small lots put to ferment. Santorini farmers have continued to cultivate it in small amounts to produce a *passito* wine for special occasions. Mavrotragano has recently attracted the attention of journalists and wine and food experts. It is a typical wine from the south, with a deep purplish color, full bodied, fruity, aromatic with a distinct tannin flavor, ideal for lengthy aging. The Presidium was formed to back up the work of two producers, Paris Sigalas and Haridimos Hadjidakis, who convinced the small producers in Santorini to plant Mavrotragano, recovering a few vines, selecting and reproducing the plants which cannot be found in nurseries. Later, Santo Wine, the largest cooperative on the island, began cultivating Mavrotragano as well. The Presidium has experimented various methods of fermentation to establish a protocol to guarantee a top quality product, and they worked to spread knowledge of the wine outside the island, with the contribution of Piedmontese vine growers in Italy, who call themselves Insieme, who went personally to visit the production area.

PRODUCTION AREA
Eastern part of the island of Santorini

PRESIDIUM COORDINATOR
George Hatziyiannakis
tel. +30 2286022249
selenegr@otenet.gr

Niotiko Cheese

The island of Ios, in the Cyclades, is an hour by ferry from Santorini and as soon as you leave the town center, it is just lonely mountains, Mediterranean scrub, stone walls, empty winding roads: this is tough land inhabited by shepherds breeding their goats, using their milk to make a rustic and fascinating cheese: Niotiko. The name means simply 'from Ios'. It is made with raw goat's milk, mixed with a part of sheep's milk and a small amount of curd, sometimes made locally using the goat's stomach. It is very simple to make: the curd is broken using a wooden branch, creating small rice-sized grains; the mass is left to deposit and is then collected with a skimmer and put into the moulds, without even pressing. After salting, the cheese is left in stone cellars to ripen. The remaining serum is boiled with a drop of milk to produce an excellent, soft ricotta: Mizitra. Niotiko is goat's cheese redolent aromatic herbs and salty winds. It is round with a golden yellow rind with yellowish white cheese with a fine and even grain. On the palate it is fatty, rich, doughy and, when it has ripened for at least two or three months, it is pleasantly spicy. A simple cheese, both in production method and sensorial features, which keeps extremely well. The Presidium was formed to protect stock raising on the island, uniting the shepherds in an association, to establish the best ripening method and guarantee a market for this ancient natural product. Niotiko is made respecting a few fundamental rules: only raw milk is used, no added enzymes to speed up coagulation, animals raised free range on the meadows and their diet integrated with only natural products. There are about 20 shepherds and five dairy farmers who intend working together to continue this long lasting tradition on the island.

PRODUCTION AREA
Island of Ios

PRESIDIUM COORDINATORS
George Hatziyiannakis
tel. +30 2286022249
selenegr@otenet.gr

TECHNICAL PARTNER
Avec-pvs
(Veterinary cooperation association
with developing countries)

Mangalica Sausage

Mangalica pigs have a small head and long, curly, mostly white or blond bristles (sometimes black, rarely red). The breed was introduced to Hungary at the end of 18th century and became immediately popular because it yielded plenty of fat. Yet these pigs were later replaced by modern cross-breeds, since they are incompatible with industrial breeding farms and hate to be enclosed. In the *puszta*, the great Hungarian plain, several producers in Bács-Kiskun county, 100 or so kilometers south of Budapest and home to one of the country's most important national parks, still rear Mangalica pigs in semi-free range conditions, integrating pasture with potatoes, pumpkin and topinambur (Jerusalem artichoke); they are slaughtered on reaching a weight of 150-200 kilos. Mangalica pork is oven roasted, stewed or cooking in broth and accompanied by sauerkraut, potatoes and stuffed capsicum peppers. In keeping with traditional techniques, breeders also produce smoked hams and sausages. The Presidium protects the puszta breed and the sausage - stuffed into pig intestines - that may even be one meter long. Preparation envisages fine ground lard and meat mixed with salt, pepper and paprika – the local products ensures a bright red color – and other spices, depending on the recipe of each producer. Handmade, the sausages are smoked cold, burning beech or oak wood, and cured for several months (the best require 60-90 days of curing). They are eaten sliced with fermented vegetables (cucumber and capsicum peppers stuffed with cauliflower). The Presidium was set up in 2003 and involves around a dozen producers who subsequently founded the Kiskunsagi Hagyomanyorzo Egyesulet Association, that in turn obtained organic certification; the meat and even the paprika are all 'home-grown'. In just a few years of activity, the Presidium has defined breeding and processing regulations, promoted this sausage throughout Europe, increased production and helped the association expand its membership.

PRODUCTION AREA
Bács-Kiskun county

PRESIDIUM COORDINATORS
Gabor Lövei
tel. +45 58113436
gabor.lovei@agrsci.dk
Olga Rendek
rendekbio@vodafone.hu

PRESIDIUM SUPPORTED BY
Slow Food Scandicci Convivium
(Florence, Tuscany, Italy), Sheepdrove Trust

Irish Raw Milk Cheese

Texts describing the green pastures and cheeses once produced in Ireland date to the 8th century, but the descriptions and names are very vague. We do know that the Irish cheesemakers produced a great variety of cheeses, including *tanag* and *grus*, pressed skim-milk cheeses, *faiscre grotha*, a fresh cheese, also pressed, and *tath* a tart cottage cheese. The variety of cheeses is also clear from the references that ancient texts make to the use of coagulants. Animal rennet from cows and sheep alone was not only used, but also moss and a particular type of violet (mothan). In the 1970s, an association of cheese makers reintroduced small-scale cheese production in the rural areas of Ireland, and in a short time there were as many as 30 cheese factories. Word of mouth and the need to earn a living with farm work encouraged the new generation of Irish cheesemakers to make use of techniques borrowed from around the world. Using the same raw ingredients that were already available to the ancient producers on the island, and making the cheese from raw milk, they began to produce a series of new cheeses that are not only a reflection of the territory, but also their personality and experiences. Irish cheeses have now achieved world recognition, but only a handful of the "new traditionalists" still use raw milk. To favor the survival of this outstanding product, the Presidium aims to celebrate the quality and promote the rebirth of the traditional island dairies. It currently includes eight dairies from the county of Cork and the Midlands, which are working to valorize the quality and diverse production methods. The objective of the project is to increase awareness of the quality of these cheeses among consumers, sellers and experts in the field of food health regulations.

PRODUCTION AREA
County of Cork and Midlands

PRESIDIUM COORDINATORS
Kevin Sheridan
tel. +353 469430373
kevin@sheridanscheesemongers.com
Colin Sage
c.sage@ucc.ie
Jeffa Gill
durruscheese@eircom.net

Acquaviva Red Onion

Each year the Acquaviva delle Fonti tourist office organizes a festival for the local onion. It takes place the first Sunday in October, attracting gourmands and the simply curious from neighboring regions as well. The particularly sweet, fresh taste of this onion contributes to the goodness of the classic focaccia rustica, filled with onions and a strong ricotta that has been acidified and aged for about three months. Local dishes made with the red onion also include baked lamb and the focaccia with olives, onions, anchovies and capers. But these red onions, whose iridescent carmine to mauve color gradually becomes white in the center, are also excellent when baked in the traditional terracotta pan called a tiella. Their cultivation is an important part of the local farming culture, which is tied to the abundance of subterranean waters and to the nature of the soil, which is deep, moderately compact, well-drained, aerated, potassium rich and rather limy. All of these qualities make it ideal for growing this characteristic flat onion, which is two or three centimeters thick, up to a handbreadth wide and weighs about one half kilo. Only grown in the territory of Acquaviva, the amount of land dedicated to this onion has decreased in recent years and the average yield per hectare – 200 quintals – is much lower than the national average (about 300). This is partly due to the intrinsic characteristics of the variety and partly to the type of cultivation required, mainly done by hand. Because the use of chemicals is kept to a minimum, an extra dose of work is needed in the field. The rows must be frequently hoed and weeded by hand and unfortunately this affects the price of the final product. The Presidium is working to see that the Acquaviva red onion becomes known and appreciated once again, on national markets as well, and can finally fetch a good price.

PRODUCTION AREA
Acquaviva delle Fonti, province of Bari, Puglia

PRESIDIUM COORDINATORS
Giuseppe Incampo
tel. +39 0803142866 - 3395484295
incamposlow@libero.it
Vito Abrusci
tel. +39 080762469 - 3391936517
abrusciserv@libero.it

PRESIDIUM SUPPORTED BY
Puglia Regional Authority, department of Agriculture and Forestry

Albenga Violet Asparagus

This unique variety of asparagus is characterized by its very thick and intense violet colored spears that become gradually lighter toward the base. Having 40 chromosomes instead of 20 like other asparagus, the violet cannot crossbreed with other varieties (the offspring would be sterile) and so cannot be genetically altered. The alluvial soils of the Albenga plain are perfect for its cultivation thanks to the deep layer of sand and limestone and the micro-climate in the area. Nevertheless, in the 1930s this variety was grown on more than 300 hectares, but in the year 2000 on fewer than ten. The Ligurian farmers, in fact, turned their attention to crops that were more profitable and with shorter production cycles I order to have at least two harvests per year. The violet asparagus is harvested from mid-March to early June, and because it is so late to mature it finds a market where other national and foreign varieties are already present. In an effort to speed up the harvest, the farmers have always devised a series of strategies. At one time, for example, they warmed the terrain with cotton waste (discards from the cotton mills) soaked with water. Today there are more modern methods, such as placing hot water tubing in the soil. Soft, buttery and non-fibrous, the violet asparagus goes very well with delicate foods like boiled, steamed or baked fish, white meats or refined sauces. Thick sauces, overcooking, refrigeration or freezing should be avoided. The Presidium has brought together six small producers from the Albenga plain with the aim of publicizing and promoting the original violet asparagus and reviving its cultivation. For a year now the members of a Committee of violet asparagus producers from the plain of Albenga have coupled completely manual cultivation with a veritable protocol for the protection and sustainable development of the area that would otherwise be at the mercy of indiscriminate building.

PRODUCTION AREA
Albenga, Ceriale and Ortovero (Albenga plain), province of Savona, Liguria

PRESIDIUM COORDINATOR
Lorenzo Montano
tel. +39 0182931059
lorenzo.montano@libero.it

PRESIDIUM SUPPORTED BY
Liguria Regional Authority

Alpago Lamb

This is a native breed of sheep of medium-small size with a thick, fine and wavy fleece from the knee and withers to the breast, with dark markings on the head and the lower parts of the legs. It originated in the Alpago high plateau and spread to nearby places, since it is well-suited to the Alpine environment and free range rearing - as well as being kept in stalls on farms. It has no horns and rather small ears: It was once best-known for its meat, milk and wool, while today it is almost exclusively reared for its firm yet tender and savory meat. The Alpago area has always been dedicated to free range pasture and is only a few kilometers from Belluno, between Cortina d'Ampezzo and Venice. The best lambs are slaughtered at 55-65 days from birth, when they weigh about 15-25 kilos. Regulations provide guidelines for rearing these lambs to produce high quality meat: free range with a diet based on pasture forage or semi-free range with integration of local hay and cereal by-products. This lamb melts in the mouth and ensures the right balance between fat and lean. Excellent when lightly grilled, stewed, with herbs and spit-roast, it is also an ideal accompaniment for certain traditional local dishes, such as patora (soup of maize and legumes) and bagozia, a kind of mixed purée once prepared with potatoes and beans and sometimes flavored with lard or pancetta. Like most native breeds, numbers fell drastically last century: today, the area boasts little more than 2000 head, a slight recovery compared to the early 1990s, when the European Union included the breed among local stock at risk of extinction. The Presidium has registered a trademark – Agnello d'Alpago – and ensures complete traceability of the product: the label affixed to meat products indicates the brand, name and address of the breeder and the codes of breeders and slaughterers.

PRODUCTION AREA
Communes of the Alpago plateau, province of Belluno, Veneto

PRESIDIUM COORDINATORS
Fabio Pogacini
tel. +39 0437937149
pogacini.fabio@tiscalinet.it
Alessandro Fullin
tel. +39 3356313705
alessandro.salce@tiscali.it

PRESIDIUM SUPPORTED BY
Veneto Regional Authority, Veneto Agricoltura, Puos d'Alpago Mountain Community

Amalfi Sfusato Lemon

This unique, relatively large lemon is pale yellow, with a tapered form, and is characterized by its juicy, moderately acidic pulp, few seeds and intense perfume, due to the richness of the essential oils and terpenes. According to a study conducted by the Department of Chemical and Food Engineering of the University of Salerno, the Sfusato has in some cases double the number of aromatic components of the lemons commonly found on the market. Its origins go back to Roman times: well-preserved frescoes depicting this lemon were found on the walls of the Casa del Frutteto in Pompei, destroyed in 79 AD by the eruption of Vesuvius. Deriving from the common Femminiello cultivar, this type of lemon is among the richest in vitamin C, and is excellent eaten fresh, served plain or dressed in a salad, as an accompaniment to fish and meat dishes, as a main ingredient in sweets and ice-cream and in the celebrated limoncello, an infusion of lemon peels and pure alcohol. Cultivated on typical terraces, the lemon trees are an integral element of the landscape, key to the rural architecture, local agriculture and also a useful method of protecting the zone's hydro-geological assets. The fruits are harvested throughout the year, but the most prized are those which ripen from March to July. Amalfi lemon growing is currently in a state of crisis due to the high production costs in relation to low sales prices, driven down by competition from large Sicilian plantations, and the difficulty of finding trained workers. The Presidium, which works side-by-side with the Consortium for the Protection of Amalfi Coast Lemons, intends to help consumers discover the quality which distinguishes citrus from Amalfi. Another fundamental aim is to raise the percentage of Amalfi lemons which are processed, currently only a paltry 5% or so of the total.

PRODUCTION AREA
Amalfi and another 11 communes in the province of Salerno, Campania

PRESIDIUM COORDINATORS
Giancarlo Capacchione
tel. +39 089753535
g.capacchione@libero.it
Marco Aceto
tel. +39 089853876 – 3471437979
cata@starnet.it
igpamalfi@tiscali.it

PRESIDIUM SUPPORTED BY
Salerno Provincial Authority

Aurina Valley Graukäse

Graukäse, or grey cheese, belongs to the family of acid coagulated cheese, made without rennet. It is so low-fat that the oil on the dry residue does not exceed 2%. In Alto Adige, it is particularly common in Aurina Valley and in the valleys of Selva di Molini and Rio Bianco. In recent decades, the production of Graukäse has been confined almost exclusively to the home, which is why the Presidium has decided to revive this important artisan tradition. Once skimmed, the milk is left in the container for two days, where the acid coagulation takes place. The mass is then slowly heated to 55°C. The curd is placed in a cotton cloth, hung up to drain and after about one half hour broken up with the hands. Then it is dry salted, possibly with a pinch of pepper. The mass of curds is then put into round or square molds (the forms vary from 500 grams to 7 kilos) and pressed by hand. The aging takes place in a temperate environment, at about 25°C with natural humidity, where the cheese ages for two or three weeks on boards of pinewood. The forms are not cleaned, but are turned over regularly. There is also a particular method of cold aging, in which the ripening at 25°C is interrupted after ten days or so and the forms

are moved to a colder place, where they remain for 12 weeks at most. During the aging process the Graukäse develops grey-green mold that gives it a strong flavor and a powerful, penetrating smell. The cheese, which does not have a crust, is marbled with a white center that can become yellow and oily and develop a strong odor according to the aging. It has a predominantly bitter taste, which becomes stronger depending on how much whey remains when the cheese is left to drain. It can be seasoned with oil, vinegar and onion or eaten with the typical Breatl bread made of rye, cumin and anise, butter and sour cream. It is also used in the traditional Pressknödel, roasted cheese dumplings.

PRODUCTION AREA

Tures and Aurina valleys from Gais to Casere, including the Selva dei Mulini, Lappago, Rio Bianco and Riva di Tures side valleys, province of Bolzano, Alto Adige

PRESIDIUM COORDINATORS

Martin Pircher
tel. +39 0474678495
despar.pircher@bestofdolomites.it
Angelo Carrillo
tel. +39 3398189965
angelo.carrillo@tin.it

PRESIDIUM SUPPORTED BY

Bolzano Chamber of Commerce, Industry, Crafts and Agriculture, Bolzano Autonomous Provincial Authority, Leader Plus

Badalucco, Conio and Pigna Beans

Having arrived from Spain in the 17th century, the beans found an ideal habitat in the Nervia, Oneglia and Argentina Valleys. Natural selection produced three cultivars in the small communes of Badalucco, Pigna, and in Conio, a hamlet of Borgomaro. The best terrains are those higher up, where the calcareous spring waters are filled with mineral salts. Sown in the month of May, the beans are harvested in September and then left to dry. The three types differ mainly in their shape and size. The Pigna bean is kidney-shaped and a bit larger and the other two (particularly the Conio) oval-shaped and smaller. In Badalucco the beans are called rundin, but there is also another less highly prized but similar variety, the mungette, which has a longer shape like the cannellino bean. Despite the very high gastronomic value (they are excellent both fresh and when dried), production is very scarce. Their preparation is rather lengthy because they must be soaked in water overnight. The best way to enjoy them is also the simplest: boiled in water, garlic, sage and bay leaf and then dressed with olive oil, salt and pepper. The beans are done when they are soft, but still firm and intact. They are an ingredient in many of the local dishes, but the ones that are emblematic of tradition are without doubt goat and beans and the frisceui (bean fritters), made with a mixture of mashed cooked beans and fresh chives that are fried in a batter of water, flour and salt. The main problem the Presidium wants to resolve is the poor distribution of the beans and a lack of interest on the part of the catering industry. For this reason a consortium of producers was set up to protect the white Badalucco, Conio and Pigna beans. The consortium gives all the members (on the basis of an annual statement of production) cotton sacks bearing the registered trademark and seal of guarantee, which helps them sell the product in a recognizable way and defend it from the numerous imitations on the market.

PRODUCTION AREA
Communes of Badalucco, Montalto Ligure, Castel Vittorio and Pigna, and the hamlet of Conio in the commune of Borgomaro, province of Imperia, Liguria

PRESIDIUM COORDINATOR
Fausto Noaro
tel. +39 3356511026
ventimiglia.im@coldiretti.it

PRESIDIUM SUPPORTED BY
Liguria Regional Authority

Bagnolese Pecorino

The Bagnolese is a breed of sheep native to Campania, which takes its name from Bagnoli Irpino, a town in the province of Avellino that is one of the most important breeding centers. From Irpinia, it has spread all over the Campania region, as far as the provinces of Caserta and Salerno. Today there are about 1,000 animals on the Laceno plateau, so they should not be at risk of extinction, at least in the immediate future. It is certainly a breed that deserves to be promoted, because of the high quality of the cheese – pecorino and fresh but above all salted ricotta – that is produced with its milk. It is fairly similar to the Barbaresca breed of sheep, which has distant North African origins and is now very common in Sicily. Quite large in size – adult males can weigh about 100 kilograms and females 60 – it has a white fleece with dark markings on the back and speckles on the head. It is rustic and adapts well to inaccessible pastures, with a good output of milk and meat. The lambs are used extensively in the local cuisine, being fed exclusively with their mother's milk, so that the meat is very tender and delicately flavored. In Irpinia they are reared primarily in a natural or semi-natural state, pasturing on grass with additional feed only in the Winter months. Nearly all the farmers have a few hundred animals and use the milk to produce an excellent pecorino, with a hard, compact rind that is yellow tending to dark brown, a hard fatty paste with a straw yellow color, which brings out its best organoleptic qualities when it has aged for at least two months. The Presidium proposes grouping the farmers of Irpinia together and encouraging them to produce cheese with pure Bagnolese milk. Fresh Bagnolese is a rustic, simple cheese with strong organoleptic characteristics, and it is always served in Irpinia, at the start or the end of a meal in the manner of the South, or cooked in various recipes. When it is aged it tends to become decidedly sharp and is used mainly for grating.

PRODUCTION AREA

Bagnoli Irpino, Chiusano San Domenico, Montella, Nusco and Volturara Irpin, province of Avellino, Campania

PRESIDIUM COORDINATOR

Luca Branca
tel. +39 0825765528 - 3480407059
luca.branca@virgilio.it

Bagolino Bagòss

Bagolino Bagòss is made with milk from the Alpine Brown Cow according to a very old artisan technique that calls for the addition of a teaspoon of saffron when the cheese curd is broken. Large copper pans are used and the cheese is heated over a wood fire. In summer the cheese is made in the pastures high up in the mountains, which is where the best forms are obtained. The aging process takes a long time: according to the production protocol it must age for at least 12 months, although it can continue for as much as 24-36. After one year, the cheese starts to become very hard and tends to flake, has a strong scent of saffron and a hint of green pastures, and tastes somewhat like almonds with a slightly piquant finish that increases with time. At this point the crust is rubbed with raw linseed oil, which gives it its characteristic ochre brown color. The rather large cheese forms (16-22 kilos) are made with raw, partially skimmed milk in Bagolino (Caffaro Valley), a small town in the upper Brescia region famous for its Carnival. While the cheese takes its name from the town, the locals affectionately call it the poor man's Grana. If well-aged, it does in fact lend itself well to grating, but is really an eating cheese that goes very well with strong red wines like Sfurzat della Valtellina and Amarone, or with a Spumante Metodo Classico. The Presidium producers, about 50 or so, have formed the Valle di Bagolino Cooperative. The Presidium promotes this great cheese and seeksto protect it from the many imitations on the market. And since 2004, a brand name on the forms makes it easy to recognize the cooperative's Bagolino *Bagòss*, which is the genuine article.

PRODUCTION AREA
Bagolino, province of Brescia, Lombardy

PRESIDIUM COORDINATORS
Massimo Scarlatti
tel. +39 0302306146 - 3287448206
mscarlatti@inwind.it
Marco Scalvini
tel. +39 0365904011
segreteria@comune.bagolino.bs.it

PRESIDIUM SUPPORTED BY
Commune of Bagolino, Valle di Bagolino Cooperative, Valle Sabbia Mountain Community, Brescia Provincial Authority

Banale Ciuiga

This simple dish from the Trentino peasant tradition has always been made with pork and cooked turnips at San Lorenzo in Banale, in the Giudicarie Esteriori (a valley wedged between Lake Garda and the Brenta Dolomites). At one time only lesser cuts of pork were used, but 150 years later it is now made with the choicer parts (shoulder, coppa, pancetta, throat) and a lower percentage of turnips (35-40%). The ciuiga has a curious history. In 1890, struck by the extreme poverty in the zone, priest Don Guetti decided to set up Friendly Society food cooperatives so that people who had the mon-ey available could invest it to the benefit of the less well-off. The Famiglia Cooperativa Brenta was founded right at that time and continues to produce ciuiga to this day. As this meat product is tied to the turnip season, production starts in autumn and continues until the spring. It begins with the cooking of the turnips, which are then squeezed and left to dry for a couple of days. The meat is added, the mixture is seasoned with salt, black pepper and chopped garlic and everything is minced in the meat grinder. The mixture is then stuffed into a pig's intestine and smoked for eight days. After three or four days of aging the ciuiga can be boiled in water for about 20 minutes and be eaten with boiled or mashed potatoes, shredded cabbage, or polenta and sauerkraut. It can also be eaten raw, cut in slices like salami, but in this case needs to age for about ten days. The Presidium aims to increase production of the traditionally prepared ciuiga, and wants to encourage restaurant owners and consumers to take an interest in this cured meat. The Banale ciuiga is an important part of the gastronomy in this area also known for its Bleggio walnuts, Lomaso potatoes and fine dairy products.

PRODUCTION AREA
San Lorenzo in Banale, province of Trento, Trentino

PRESIDIUM COORDINATOR
Alessandra Odorizzi
tel. +39 0465702626
alessandra.odorizzi@comano.to

PRESIDIUM SUPPORTED BY
Trento Autonomous Provincial Authority, Trentino SpA

Basilicata Podolico Caciocavallo

This symbol of the southern dairy tradition is made using the 'pasta filata' technique developed over the centuries in southern Italy to ensure the preservability and healthiness of cow's milk cheeses. The curd, obtained from the heated and coagulated milk, is cooked twice to make it elastic and stop it from breaking. Mozzarella, Scamorza, Provolone and Cacio-cavallo cheeses are all made using this method. *Caciocavallo podolico*, a particularly valued cheese, is made with milk from a specific breed of cow having the same name and still present in the southern Apennines. Once the most important breed in Italy, its numbers have now been reduced to about 25,000 heads. There are two main reasons for this: it produces little milk, albeit of outstanding quality, and must be raised in a wild or semi-wild state, making it a poor choice for intensive exploitation. Yet it must absolutely be safeguarded, since it is an integral part of the local area and because of the excellent cheese made from its milk. The Presidium was started by Anfosc, an association of cheese producers who raise the animals in pastures. The project that is underway intends to reactivate the entire production chain, increasing breeding of the Podolica in Basilicata for its meat and milk, and providing the breeders-producers with a cheese factory. Above all, it intends to equip a cave for aging the Caciocavallo, a cheese well-suited to long aging. The larger forms, from four to eight kilos, can remain perfectly intact even after four or five years of aging. In that case the taste is extraordinarily complex, with a range of aromas that can only be achieved with the excellent milk of the wild Podolico cattle. The taste is so pronounced that many attenuate it by serving the cheese with chestnut or strawberry flower honey.

PRODUCTION AREA
Abriola, Anzi, Calvello and Laurenzana of Camastra valley, province of Potenza; Accettura and part of the Gallipoli Cognato Park, province of Matera, Basilicata

PRESIDIUM COORDINATORS
Roberto Rubino
tel. +39 097672915
roberto.rubino@isz.it
Nicola Pessolani
tel. +39 0971923021
pessolani@libero.it

PRESIDIUM SUPPORTED BY
Anfosc (National Association of Open Air Cheeses)

Bazzone Prosciutto

Over and above etymological uncertainty – from the Lombard *bàsia* (jar, bowl) or Tuscan *bàgiora* (large wooden plate) – in Garfagnana 'bazza' means 'protruding chin'. Bazzone is also the name of a cured ham, typical of the upper and middle Serchio valley with a particularly elongated shape - the distance between the bone and the lower part is 12-18 centimeters. It is also very heavy - even 16-18 kilos at the end of long curing. This is because the thighs of pigs (the so-called gray pigs, when still available) slaughtered when they weigh 180-200 kilos, after about 15 months of mostly free-range rearing. The optimal diet is based on the floury remnants of spelt processing, a typical cereal in the Garfagnana area, windfall apples and pears, chestnuts, acorns and scotta, the processing waste from the small cheesemaking farms in the area. The thigh, after being trimmed to round off the profile, is kept under salt for two or three months, during which time it is 'massaged' several times. The excess salt is then eliminated and the thighs are washed and dried before going on with curing, that for hams with the Presidium 'mark' lasts for at least two years. Bazzone ham must be cut with a knife, not only for in view of its size but also to exalt its distinctive and delicately aromatic flavor. The Presidium includes three producers, who have taken up the challenge of re-creating an entire production and value chain in order to ensure both the origin of the pigs used and their diet. These methods are governed by regulations that define the traditional production approach – naturally without using additives and conservation substances – as well as the duration of curing in natural stores and cellars that must be no less than 24 months.

PRODUCTION AREA
Communes in the middle Serchio valley and Garfagnana, province of Lucca, Tuscany

PRESIDIUM COORDINATORS
Giordano Andreucci
tel. +39 3358258803
slowfoodgarfagnana@libero.it
Rolando Bellandi
tel. +39 058377008 – 3486520490
info@anticanorcineria.it

PRESIDIUM SUPPORTED BY
Middle Serchio Valley Mountain Community, Garfagnana Mountain Community

Biancoperla Corn

Held in higher regard than the yellow, more rustic variety typical of mountain areas, white polenta was common until the post-war period in the plains and hillsides, particularly in the Polesine area, around Treviso and Venice. It is made using biancoperla (pearly maize), a native variety grown in these areas for centuries. The cobs are long and streamlined; the grains are large, bright, glassy and pearl white. This variety was already mentioned at the end of the 1600s by Giacomo Agostinetti, an agronomist from Cimadolmo, in his *Cento e dieci ricordi che formano il buon fattor di villa* (One hundred and one hints for good villa managers). Since it kept for a long time, biancoperla maize was very popular in the late 1800s. Then, in the 1950s, it began to be replaced by floury hybrid varieties ensuring higher yields. Only a few growers, such as the Bellio company in Silea, still produce this crop and hold seed banks. Today, a group of agriculturists has set up an association with head offices c/o the Conte di Cavour State Professional Institute for Agriculture and the Environment at Castelfranco Veneto and has resumed production. This was also made possible thanks to the recovery and selection work launched by the Strampelli Institute of Genetics and Agrarian Experimentation in Lonigo. It offers many uses in cuisine: over and above the two classic local dishes (polenta and *speo*, polenta and *osei*), another excellent match is with "poor" river or lagoon fish dishes. The objective of the Presidium is to carry forward the work begun by the Strampelli Institute and identify the best eco-types among the ten varieties so far classified. At this stage, growers will be able to focus on the more productive varieties or those ensuring better quality for making flour. However, old-fashioned stone milling must also be promoted to exalt the optimal quality and sensorial features of the product.

PRODUCTION AREA
Provinces of Treviso, Padua and Venice, Veneto

PRESIDIUM COORDINATOR
Renato Ballan
tel. +39 0423490615
castelfranco@ipsaa.it

PRESIDIUM SUPPORTED BY
Veneto Regional Authority, Veneto Agricoltura

Bitto of the Bitto Valleys

Historically, Bitto cheese comes from the valleys of Gerola and Albaredo, where the torrent of the same name originates. The Celtic clans who settled there changed the local cheese making techniques so that cheeses would keep for a long time. The cheese making is supervised by the oldest caricature, who use traditional methods and play a key role in preserving Alpine biodiversity. A fat, semi-cooked, cylindrical cheese, it is made primarily in mountain dairies, at 1400-2000 meters, with whole milk from cows that graze in mountain pastures. Rotation pasturage is practiced. In the summer the animals are taken up to higher altitudes, with intermediate stops at itinerant mountain hut dairies known as *calècc*, which make it possible to process the fresh milk before the natural color is lost. Dry salted, Bitto is exceptionally well-suited to aging, which is never less than 70 days and can go on for as much as six months to three years – in some cases even ten. The cheese makers choose only the forms that are best suited for aging. The special aroma of the Bitto is because 10-20% of the milk is from Orobica goats that have been milked by hand. An excellent table cheese, it is also a basic ingredient of pizzoccheri, the symbol of Valtellina cuisine. The Presidium was set up to protect the mountain pastures in the historic area of Albaredo and Gerola valleys. Once Alpine meadows have been abandoned, they deteriorate quickly and in just a few years it is practically impossible to recover them. Associazione Produttori Valli del Bitto, which is bringing together the Presidium producers, is endeavoring to protect the cheese and the producers. Only

cheese forms deemed to be of exceptional quality and suited to a particular aging are branded with the logo bearing the image of the *calécc* and the name of the historic Alpine meadow where they were made according to the traditional methods established by the protocol.

PRODUCTION AREA
Albaredo and Gerola valleys and nearby Alpine meadows, commune of Sondrio, Lombardy

PRESIDIUM COORDINATORS
Maurizio Vaninetti
tel. +39 0342614800
info@osteriadelcrotto.it
Paolo Ciapparelli
tel. +39 0342635665
p.ciapparelli@libero.it

PRESIDIUM SUPPORTED BY
Coop Switzerland, Associazione Produttori Valli del Bitto Trading Spa, Commune of Gerola Alta

Black Cherry Wine

This cherry wine is called visciolato, visner or more commonly visciole. In the Marche there is an age-old tradition of making flavored wines that began in the Middle Ages with the lords of the region's castles and has been handed down to us today by farmer wisdom. The best area is in the towns of Candiano and Pergola, near Pesaro, and around the Castles of Jesi near Ancona. And the recipes for its preparation differ considerably from zone to zone. The traditional cherry wine is still made with the visciola, a very old variety of wild cherry (Prunus cerasus) having a dark red color and tangy taste, well-suited for marmalades and the famous Candiano amarene. The historic Pesaro recipe calls for picking the cherries when they are ripe in the first week of July and macerating them (partly whole and partly crushed) in the wine, which is almost always Montepulciano or local Vernaccia. The addition of sugar starts the fermentation that slowly creates the final velvety, fragrant product. In the area around Jesi, the cherries are left to dry in the sun after the harvest and then macerated with sugar until a dense syrup is obtained, which is added to boiling must during the grape harvest season. The wine has an intense yet delicate flavor, with a pleasant bitter aftertaste, and an aroma of ripe cherries. It goes well with rustic Marche desserts like nicino, ciambellone and ciambelle di mosto, and also holds its own with chocolate. The Presidium wants to preserve and promote this very old production by defining a protocol that calls for the conservation and replanting of visciola cherry orchards in the zone of origin, as well as rules for processing them. This means using local visciola cherries and wines historically tied to the area; a tie that helps to educate the taste to rediscover the age-old wealth of traditional Italian aromatized wines and liqueurs.

PRODUCTION AREA
The foothills of Mount Catria, province of Pesaro e Urbino, and the hills around the Jesi Castles, province of Ancona, Marche

PRESIDIUM COORDINATORS
Alfredo Palazzetti
tel. +39 3284558999
slowfood@abanet.it
Gianfranco Mancini
tel. +39 3388169718
direzione@italcook.it

PRESIDIUM SUPPORTED BY
Coop Svizzera, Pesaro e Urbino Provincial Authority, Commune of Pergola

Brigasca Sheep Toma

The Brigasca is a rustic, muscular sheep, most probably from the same stock as the Frabasona breed. Although somewhat less robust, they have a similar rounded profile and turned back horns (spiral-shaped in the males). The name derives from La Brigue, a French village in Val Roya that is famous for having once been the most important sheep-farming center in the area between Liguria, Piedmont and Provence. Throughout the area the sheep was the primary source of income. Then when the political and administrative borders were established in 1947 it became difficult to move the livestock, causing a decline in the numbers of herds. Today there are 1800 heads in Liguria and 800 in Val Roya. The Brigasca is raised for seven or eight months in mountain pastures and four or five months in bandia, the coastal zone where the herds can graze outdoors even in winter. Three cheeses are made from its milk: Sora, Toma and Brus. The Sora is made with raw sheep's milk from two milkings. Broken up with the classic wooden tool known as the spino, the curd is gathered up inside a rough cloth (raireura) and formed into a sort of bundle on which a stone is placed. After about 12 hours the mass is taken out of the cloth and cut into symmetrical parts. After ripening for two weeks, the cheeses are then rinsed in running water, dried and left to age in a cool place for at least two months. The Toma is made like the Sora except for the possible addition of goat's milk, the use of fascere (molds) to create the forms and a shorter aging period. The Presidium, with the support of the Liguria Regional Authority, is seeking to promote the raw milk tomas made in the few mountain pastures remaining on the watershed that marks the border with France and to support the crucial role that the shepherds play in safeguarding the natural environment. It is also working with some technicians to create a facility for making the cheese in the mountain pastures, making it possible for producers to process the milk immediately after the milking without having to refrigerate and transport it to the bottom of the valley.

PRODUCTION AREA
Mountain pastures in the Imperia valleys near the French border, Liguria

PRESIDIUM COORDINATOR
Maurizio Bazzano
tel. +39 019599767 - 3331035799
mauriziobazzano.apasv@quipo.it

PRESIDIUM SUPPORTED BY
Liguria Regional Authority

Bronte Pistachio

Its brilliant green color and pungently resinous aroma make this pistachio different from any other Mediterranean variety; it grows exclusively in Bronte, close to Catania, on lava soils rich in mineral salts. The trees, which produce a crop in alternate years, are not fertilized, treated or irrigated. In resting years, the farmers prune the dry branches and any buds that have sprouted, allowing the plants to conserve all their energy for the following year. The rough ground prevents the use of harvesters and the nuts are picked by hand. In late August, the town empties into the loci (pistachio orchards) where women, old men and children, teetering on lava boulders, with a cloth sack tied around their necks, grasp the branches in one hand and remove the nuts one by one with the other. A day's work will produce about twenty kilos; the nuts are then removed from the soft outer hull and laid out to dry. There isn't a shop, bar or pastry shop in Bronte that does not sell sweets made from pistachios: nut brittle, fillette (a sort of Savoy biscuit), torrone and torroncino, pastries and cakes... These are recently introduced sweets in which the pistachio has replaced the almond, whereas in traditional Sicilian confectionery, pistachios are sometimes found in torrone, ice cream, cassata, although generally the almond still takes pride of place. Around the world – in Germany, France, Switzerland and Belgium – the Bronte pistachio has become a key ingredient for the preparation of typical sweet and savory recipes. However, it cannot compete with the less strongly flavored but cheaper produce from Iran, Turkey and America. In fact, the main confectionery industries and the major Italian cured meat manufacturers – who previously purchased their pistachios from Sicily – now buy elsewhere. The aim of the Presidium is to ensure that consumers rediscover this exceptionally high-quality product, also by promoting the best Sicilian pasticceria, which is ideally placed to enhance its qualities.

PRODUCTION AREA
Bronte, province of Catania, Sicily

PRESIDIUM COORDINATOR
Pippo Privitera
tel. +39 3358455507
pippopri@tin.it

PRESIDIUM SUPPORTED BY
Sicily Regional Authority, department of Agriculture and Forestry

Caciofiore of the Roman Countryside

This raw milk sheep's cheese is the result of the proteolytic action of enzymes of wild thistles (*Cynara scolimus*), a cheesemaking technique that was already in use in Roman times. The flowers must be gathered when they are an intense violet blue color and then left to dry for four or five days in the dark. The dried petals are then put in water and the next day the maceration is filtered with a cloth. The rennet thus obtained is added to the sheep's milk, which is kept at a constant temperature of 38°C and coagulates in 60-80 minutes. The curd is broken into large cubes by using a long smooth blade, and after 20 minutes broken a second time into irregular pieces with a perforated ladle. The curds are then placed in square wicker containers so the whey can drain off. This creates the classic *mattonella* (brick shape), which is dry salted the next day and put in a room for aging, where it remains for 35-40 days at a temperature of 7-10°C and 90-95% humidity. It is turned over once a day during this period to prevent excessive mold from forming on the surface. When the aging is completed, the yellowish crust surrounds a soft cheese with slight air holes and, with particular aging, a very creamy center. It has the fragrance of wet straw and cooked field vegetables, and tends to melt in the mouth, releasing traces of vegetables and a

pleasant and equilibrated hint of fat. While it originated in Lazio, Caciofiore was also produced in the Abruzzo and Marche regions until a few years ago. The Presidium intends to support the recovery project. The Presidium producers in the mainly raise Sardinian and *Comisana* sheep, with a few crossbreeds, Massesi and Sopravvissane, which they leave free to graze in the farmlands around Rome. At the time of transhumance in the past, this was an area where the sheep would winter over before returning for the summer to the mountains of Abruzzo or the Mount Terminillo district.

PRODUCTION AREA
Farmlands in the province of Rome, Lazio

PRESIDIUM COORDINATORS
Stefano Asaro
tel. +39 067213195
stefano.asaro@alice.it
William Loria
tel. +39 0669792437
w.loria@romamercati.com

PRESIDIUM SUPPORTED BY
Rome Chamber of Commerce, Industry, Crafts and Agriculture, Azienda Romana per i Mercati

Campotosto Mortadella

They are prepared with choice cuts of lean, finely ground pork and seasoned with salt, pepper and a secret blend of herbs and spices, without any preservatives or additives. A stick of lard about ten centimeters long is inserted in the middle of the mixture, which is then tied with a double bridle knot. When ready, the mortadellas are hung on a pole and smoked for two weeks near a fireplace stoked with oak or beech wood. Then they are moved to rooms that provide the perfect temperature and humidity for drying the product because of the north wind and the elevation – we are at 1300 meters. After about three months they are aged just right and when sliced are compact and have a dark red color that contrasts with the sweet and crunchy white lardoon. They are made in Gran Sasso and Monti della Laga Park at Campotosto and usually sold in pairs (known locally as mule balls). Oval-shaped, tied two by two with a hand-knotted string, the Campotosto mortadellas are unique and inimitable and not to be confused with the industrial products hanging in butcher's shops and delicatessens for tourists scattered around Central Italy. The differences, which are obvious to the eye and the palate of experts, are substantial. The usual industrial mortadellas are made with presewn casings, frozen lardons, rubber ligature and lower quality meats. They also contain preservatives and additives not to be found in the original product. The Presidium was set up to highlight this difference and safeguard artisan methods. At Campotosto only two producers still make the mortadella the way the local families once did when they got together to prepare mortadellas that would be ready for Easter.

PRODUCTION AREA
Campotosto, province of L'Aquila, Abruzzo

PRESIDIUM COORDINATOR
Silvia De Paulis
tel. +39 086260521
silviadepaulis@gransassolagapark.it

PRESIDIUM SUPPORTED BY
Gran Sasso and Monti
della Laga National Park

Cannara Onion

Umbrian cuisine is one of the most interesting and distinctive in Italy. Plain and straightforward, its based on the fruits of the land, ingredients such as olive oil, pork, black truffles, pulses and vegetables, such as Trevi black celery, Colfiorito red potatoes and, naturally, enough the Cannara onion. Poor man's fare par excellence, these onions are indissolubly linked to the small town of Cannara, situated on land reclaimed from swamps (the name derives from canne, meaning reeds or canes). The sandy, damp soil and the climate here combine to provide perfect conditions for the cultivation of the vegetable. Golden and borrettane onions are also grown here but only the Cannara is so sweet and easy to digest as to be edible raw. Round with a bright red skin and coppery white flesh it is the pride and joy of the inhabitants of Cannara. It is cultivated entirely by hand. It is sowed in February and the soil is then hoed regularly and watered every seven or eight days. At the end of July, the onions are picked and arranged in fields to dry. Seven or eight onions are bound to form a plait (treccia), 25 or 30 plaits to make a bow (mazzocco), which are then taken to local markets and fairs (Cannara in the first fortnight in September, subsequently Spoleto, Foligno and Assisi). Thanks to the Presidium, the last onion growers left have joined together and increased production. Cannara onions are excellent eaten raw in salads with olive oil and salt and are a fine accompaniment to meat and game. Because of their extraordinary sweetness, they are particularly good with liver, lamb offal and foie gras.

PRODUCTION AREA
Cannara, province of Perugia, Umbria

PRESIDIUM COORDINATOR
Sonia Chellini
tel. 075 8296430
skelli@libero.it

PRESIDIUM SUPPORTED BY
Trasimeno-Medio Tevere Mountain Community

Caprauna Turnip

Turnips are herbaceous diuretic plants, rich in vitamins, of which the roots and tips of the scapes, commonly known as turnip tops, are eaten. In the high Tanaro Valley, between Piedmont and Liguria, where the province of Cuneo borders on those of Imperia and Savona, at 900 meters above seal level, is Caprauna. It is a small village in which the old terracing retained by walls of dry stone stand out, which over the past centuries made it possible to grow grain, barley, rye and oats at a high altitude. On the same lands sown previously with grain, at one time farmers cultivated turnips, because the presence of residues of stubble in the soil gave them a unique aroma and taste. Sowing occurred at the end of summer and the harvest continued through the winter. The specific features of this variety, combined with the high altitude and closeness to the sea, have made the turnips of Caprauna large, sweet, and delicate, of an unusual white color bordering on yellow. In cooking they are used to prepare flans to serve with *bagna caoda*, gratinated in the oven, used as a side dish and as condiment for a special kind of fresh pasta, *s-ciancui*, together with walnuts and mushrooms. Today the residents of Caprauna number no more than 130 and have an average age of 60; the dry walls are in ruins and the turnips are grown by a few pensioners only. The Presidium was set up by the public admin-istrations involved to target the promotion of a product of undisputed organoleptic qualities, but should develop into a land and environmental recovery scheme. This would also reintegrate the cultivation of turnips on the existing terraces, restore the damaged terraces and lead to a series of initiatives to encourage people wishing to revive this kind of cultivation. An important objective is the foundation of an association to represent the few growers left.

PRODUCTION AREA
Caprauna and Alto, province of Cuneo, Piedmont

PRESIDIUM COORDINATORS
Rinaldo Arnaldi
tel. +39 3488730153
curve@libero.it
Marco Costalla
tel. +39 3486701878
marco.costalla@libero.it

PRESIDIUM SUPPORTED BY
High Tanaro Valley Mountain Community

Carmagnola Grey Rabbit

The first projects to protect this breed were undertaken by the Department of Zootechnical Science at Turin University and the Professional Institute for Agriculture and the Environment in Verzuolo (Cuneo). This breed, which was common until the end of the 50s, is now the only Piedmontese rabbit of which any trace remains. The creation of a Municipal Center for the spread and promotion of the gray rabbit in Carmagnola, in the province of Turin, was followed by the organization of the Slow Food Presidium. This small farmyard animal used to be bred on all the Piedmont farms, but now is extremely rare; it has a soft, thick gray fur (lighter on the stomach, the limbs and the end of its tail), with a light triangular mark on its neck. It is medium sized, with a long body and muscular loins, and descends from a cross with chinchillas. Its delicate health and very fine skin make it difficult to breed in cages, and the ideal is a fenced field with a covered shelter in the case of bad weather, protected from draughts, damp and the overcrowding typical of intensive breeding farms. Its diet, which all the breeders with the Presidia follow strictly, is only natural grass and fodder. The animals are butchered when they weigh at least three and a half kilos, sometimes reaching four kilos for the females and five and a half for the males. The Carmagnola gray rabbit is known for its excellent yield: it has a very fine bone structure and the muscular mass is superior to that of other breeds. The meat is fine, tender, tasty, extremely white and not at all tough. Once upon a time rabbit with peppers made using the Carmagnola gray could be found on the menus in all the osterias, like the rabbit all'Arneis nel Roero, an ancient dish and direct heir of hare *civet* (meat marinated in blood and wine). More modern recipes suggest it sweet and sour, with chocolate, in egg sauce. Like those from cockerels, rabbit giblets give flavor to the sauces for *tajarin* and ravioli.

PRODUCTION AREA
Carmagnola, province of Turin, Piedmont

PRESIDIUM COORDINATOR
Renato Dominici
tel. +39 0119712673 – 3351370749

Carmagnola Ox-Horn Pepper

In Piedmontese cooking, pepper is the main ingredient of many traditional, simple, rustic dishes. It is eaten raw, dipped in oil, oven roasted or flash-fried, and is one of the essential vegetables for the *bagna caoda*. According to the season, you can taste it pickled, in oil, sweet-and-sour or in the old Piedmontese traditional way, *sota rapa*, soused in marc. The city of Carmagonla is one of the Italian capitals of pepper, or rather, of four different kinds of pepper: the Trottola, heart-shaped, the Quadrato, almost a cube, with four tips, the Tomaticot, a hybrid rounded at the center like a tomato (*tomatico* or *pomatico* in Piedmontese dialect), and the Corno di bue, or Ox-horn, long and cone-shaped. The latter comes in wonderful colors – intense yellow and green or vivacious red – and can exceed 20 centimeters in length with three or four lobes (modeled on the primordial *spagnolin*, the oblong pepper from the Americas). It has a sweet taste, a firm and fleshy pulp that improves with preservation, and a skin that is easy to remove after cooking. It is cultivated in flat, limey, sandy soils. It is sown between the last ten days of December and the beginning of April; at the beginning of February transplanting is performed in tunnels, and in May the peppers are cultivated in the open field. For mainly organic fertilization, cow manure is used. Scaled manual harvesting with shoulder sacks begins at the end of July. The Corno di bue pepper did not risk extinction, but it was debased by the habit of relegating it – often mixed with anonymous imported varieties- to the canning industry.

The Presidium was set up to create a new market for this vegetable with excellent organoleptic features: an appetizing table vegetable or a noble ingredient of traditional and creative recipes.

PRODUCTION AREA
Provinces of Turin and Cuneo, Piedmont

PRESIDIUM COORDINATORS
Renato Dominici
tel. +39 0119712673 - 3351370749
Domenico Tuninetti
tel. +39 0119721349 - 3470125334

PRESIDIUM SUPPORTED BY
Turin Provincial Authority

Carmignano Dried Fig

Color range from gray to beige and even hazel, while the sweet taste is set off by a hint of aniseed. The fig variety best for this type of preparation, and the most commonly used, is the dottato, with its characteristic white fruit. Other varieties are still to be found in Carmignano (verdino, St. Peter's fig, black brogiotto, corbo, perticone, pécciolo and rossellino) but this one covers 90% of the local fig production. These fruit trees have always dotted the countryside, growing in the marginal points of farms, by the roadside, close to dry walls, in the stoniest parts of fields and at the head of rows of vines. All the houses in Carmignano (not by chance nicknamed Carmignan da' fichi) had at least one fig tree, beside the door or in the vegetable garden. After a period of decline following the second world war, in recent years sales have resumed of figs prepared in accordance with the traditional technique. The fruit (siconi), after being picked, is cut longitudinally with a sharp knife to form the typical 'figures of eight'. Then they are left to dry in the sun on cane mats and doused with sulfur smoke to make the skins lighter in color. After four or five days of drying, they are left in a cool, dry place for 35-40 days, during which a coating of sugar (gruma) forms on the surface. At the end of drying, the dry figs are opened, the sugar is removed and a little aniseed is placed between each pair and the next. Traditionally, Carmignano dry figs are enjoyed as a dessert at the end of a meal, but today they are sometimes even served as an antipasto, accompanied by Prato mortadella and liver pâté. The Presidium was set up to help the few remaining producers through incentives to plant new figs and encourage the return of young people to an activity handed down from generation to generation for time immemorial.

PRODUCTION AREA
Carmignano and Poggio a Caiano, province of Prato, Tuscany

PRESIDIUM COORDINATOR
Alessandro Venturi
tel. +39 05744431105
info@slowfood.prato.it

PRESIDIUM SUPPORTED BY
Prato Province Authority, Commune of Carmignano

Carpino Broad Beans

Small, with a dimple on the underside, the Carpino broad bean starts out green and over time becomes a sandy white color. It is grown in calcareous, clay soils on plots of land of about one half hectare, in rotation with wheat, sugar beets, tomatoes and lupines. No fertilization or herbicides are used: the bean itself enriches the soil with nitrogen and the weeds are pulled by hand. The seeds are sown in October and November. When the plants begin to yellow in June, they are cut down, gathered in manocchi (sheaves) and left in the fields to dry. In the meantime a special circular area called the arij is prepared by wetting the ground and covering it with pressed straw to create a hard and compact layer to work on. In July, when the manocchi are good and dry, they are arranged on top of the arij. Then when the sun is high the pesa (crushing) phase begins: a farmer stands in the center of the arij while one or more horses go round in circles crushing the sheaves. The beans are then removed from the straw with traditional wooden forks and any remaining particles are eliminated by lifting the beans up with wooden shovels and tossing them in the air, taking advantage of the afternoon breeze. Since the plots of land used for cultivating Carpino broad beans are usually very small, only modest quantities are produced. The most common way to prepare them is by cooking them in terracotta pots over a fire in the fireplace. The tender, flavorsome broad beans are eaten as a side dish, anointed with extra virgin olive oil, or as a first course cooked with wild herbs, with squash or with pork. The Presidium producers also grow lupines and olives, from which they obtain extra virgin olive oil and eating olives.

PRODUCTION AREA
Carpino, province of Foggia, Puglia

PRESIDIUM COORDINATOR
Michele Palmieri
tel. +39 0884997474 - 3473159307
mickpalm@tiscali.it

PRESIDIUM SUPPORTED BY
Gargano National Park

Casentino Prosciutto

The upper Arno basin was once home to woodsmen and shepherds. Rustic dark-skinned pigs, probably the Anghiari Cappuccia, one of the three local breeds (the others were Casentinese and Casentino Red), were reared here in free or semi-free range pastures to produce highly prized cured hams. The traditional method envisaged that the thighs, after cooling for at least 24 hours, were trimmed and rubbed with a mixture of salt, garlic and spices, such as pepper, chili pepper, nutmeg and juniper. After a variable period of five-seven days, the residual salt was eliminated and the hams were 'massaged' again. Then came a second salting stage, that lasted for about two weeks. The excess salt was eliminated again and the hams were left to cure for 40-50 days; if they were to be slightly smoked, in keeping with tradition, they were exposed to a the smoke of wood fire with oak, beech and, to a lesser extent, juniper. After curing – for no less than 18 months – the ham was ready. These hams have a rounded shape that tends to flatten and weight 9-12 kilos. When sliced, the ham has a fine bright red color, with an appropriate percentage of very compact, white fat. The bouquet is intense and distinct and the tast delicate, at times with a closing hint of smokiness. The Presidiumn has saved this ancient tradition, beginning from experiments with raw materials. It is verifying the use of hybrids with Cinta Senese or Mora Romagnola (two ancient native breeds, respectively from Tuscany and nearby Romagna), Large White and Landrace. These animals, in accordance with the strict rules and regulations defined, are reared in the open with a diet essentially from free-range pasture (in the undergrowth of oak and chestnut woods), supplemented by natural vegetable products. The pigs are slaughtered only when they have reached a minimum weight of 120-160 kilos. The regulations that the producers and breeders belonging to the Presidium are finalizing envisage longer curing times to achieve optimal taste and sensorial results.

PRODUCTION AREA
Communes in the Casentino area, province of Arezzo, Tuscany

PRESIDIUM COORDINATORS
Vincenzo Tommasi
tel. +39 3397098418
schegge@inwind.it
Emanuela Nappini
tel. +39 0575507249
emanuelanappini@casentino.toscana.it

PRESIDIUM SUPPORTED BY
Arezzo Provincial Authority, Casentino Mountain Community, Arezzo Chamber of Commerce, Industry, Crafts and Agriculture

Casizolu

A spun cheese, old and prized, typical of Montiferru. It has at least two features: in one region where mainly sheep are bred, it is made with cow's milk (Sardo modicana or Brown sarda); the women prepare it, kneading the curd in the boiling water to shape it in the form of a pear. Having added the rennet (of lamb or kid) it is necessary to wait for the right moment to knead it, which can be in the evening, at night or at sunrise. The operation takes time, patience and hard work. The white water of the whey is kept; *s'abbagasu* is a tasty broth for aromatic soups with cheese. When it is well presented – the skin must be smooth, bright and wrinkle-free – the shape is wound on a canvas or a bran basket; after two or three days it is hung from the ceiling and to finish it is put in the cellar. The pasta of the Casizolu, with a yellow color with light surface holes, tends to flake with maturation. To the nose, when the shape is well-seasoned, it combines a touch of green grass tones and buttermilk with scents of wood and leaf. The same notes return with a good length and an almond finish on the palate. Other dairy products of the Montiferru are the Trizza (a plait made with the same pasta of the Casizolu and decorated with flowers, leaves and fruit, which should be eaten fresh) and the Fresa (an oval creamy cheese which is prepared only in autumn, preferably with the rich milk of pregnant cows). The women, in addition to making the cheese, also make the bread and process the pig. Today, many of them still make linen and cotton fabrics, woolen carpets and blankets with the loom. The Casizolu has all the right features to become a great product, first of all the exceptional raw material: the milk of the Sardo modicana (or the Brown sarda), rustic cattle bred all year in the natural state. The Presidium producers of the are united in an association and have a production protocol that guarantees the entire industry.

PRODUCTION AREA
Montiferru, province of Oristano, Sardinia

PRESIDIUM COORDINATORS
Corrado Casula
tel. +39 3401423951
corrado042004@libero.it
Gianpaolo Piu
tel. +39 0783551115 - 3385697976

PRESIDIUM SUPPORTED BY
Gal Montiferru Barigadu Sinis

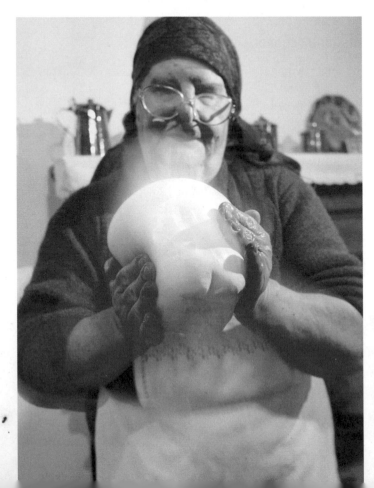

Casola Marocca

Chestnut flour, a little wheat flour, boiled and mashed potatoes, first-pressed olive oil, yeast dissolved in milk, a piece of 'pasta madre' and very hot water. These are the ingredients of the poor bread once baked by all the women in Càsola, a town in the Lunigiana area where most families, as in every other rural area of Tuscany, were sharecroppers. The dense woods in the Magra valley once boasted a rather special resource: chestnuts that, higher up where cereals could not be grown, also supplied flour for baking bread. Harvested in the fall, the chestnuts (carpanese, punticosa and rastellina varieties) were heated in stone jars known as metati or gradili over a fire of chestnut wood. The dried chestnuts were then slowly milled into flour in the numerous water mills in the valley. Every family had a wood oven and, usually on Sunday when people didn't work in the fields, baked bread for the entire week. The name 'marocca' seems to come from the dialect word marocat, which means 'not very malleable': this bread, in the past, was really hard! The recipe for marocca was rediscovered and production was re-started by a group enthusiasts living in the area with a passion for tradition. The loaves – round and measuring about 20 cm in diameter – are sprinkled with maize flour, left to rise for just over half an hour and then baked in a wood oven for about 45 minutes. The bread is dark brown with an intense bouquet of chestnuts and pleasantly sweet - and keeps well for days. Sliced bread flavored with extra virgin olive oil or spread with honey are an ideal accompaniment for fresh goat cheese, Tuscan cured meats and Colonnata lard. Consumption of marocca made all year round, since chestnut flour keeps very well, is today limited to a small number of families: only one bakery in Casola makes it regularly.

PRODUCTION AREA
Casola in Lunigiana, province of Massa Carrara, Tuscany

PRESIDIUM COORDINATOR
Daniele Rossi
tel. +39 058590131
matteodaniele@libero.it

PRESIDIUM SUPPORTED BY
Massa Carrara Provincial Authority -
Lunigiana Mountain Community, Massa Carrara
Chamber of Commerce, Industry, Crafts
and Agriculture Regional Park of the Apuan Alps,
Commune of Casola in Lunigiana

Castel del Monte Canestrato

This hard cheese is produced on the southern slope of Gran Sasso, in the Province of L'Aquila. The cheesemaking method is as old as the sheep farming in these pastures, whose rich forage encourages shepherds to bring their herds up for the summer from the Puglia plateau, Agro Romano, Maremma or the Terra di Lavoro near Caserta. On the plateau of the Gran Sasso and Monti della Laga Park, in the commune of Castel del Monte, Campo Imperatore has a long tradition of quality cheese making. At an altitude of 1800 meters, this summer pasture *par excellence* is populated by thousands of sheep from late spring to early autumn. The local shepherds still make this pecorino with raw sheep's milk so it keeps the extraordinary variety of flavors and aromas that characterize it. The milk, mainly from *Sopravvissane* or *Gentili di Puglia* sheep, is filtered and heated to about 35°C with the addition of natural lamb rennet. The curd is broken up into fine pieces, cooked for a quarter of an hour at 40-45°C (not by everyone), transferred to wicker molds and pressed to eliminate the whey. Once salted the forms are arranged on wooden tables in the cool and airy shepherds' huts, where they remain for two months to one year, regularly rubbed with oil to keep from drying out too much. Weighing from 500 grams to two and a half kilos, aged *canestrato* has a distinct tangy flavor and is excellent when sliced or grated. The transhumance tradition is gradually on the wane and fewer and fewer shepherds climb up to the Gran Sasso pastures, in part because of the lack of suitable cheesemaking facilities. The Presidium wants to draw attention to this situation and, with the help of Gran Sasso and Monti della Laga National Park, find ways to perpetuate traditional cheesemaking and turn it into an opportunity for employment and development.

PRODUCTION AREA
Barisciano, Calascio, Carapelle Calvisio, Castel del Monte, Castelvecchio Calvisio, Ofena, San Pio delle Camere, Santo Stefano di Sessanio and Villa Santa Lucia, province of L'Aquila; Filetto, Paganica, Camarda and Assergi hamlets of L'Aquila, Abruzzo

PRESIDIUM COORDINATORS
Silvia De Paulis
tel. +39 086260521
silviadepaulis@gransassolagapark. it
Giulio Petronio
tel. +39 3335814030
bioformaggi.gransasso@gmail.com

PRESIDIUM SUPPORTED BY
Gran Sasso and Monti della Laga National Park

Castellammare Violet Artichoke

Also known as the Schito artichoke, after a hamlet within the commune of Castellammare di Stabia, this is a subtype of the Roman artichoke, and is differentiated by its early development and the violet shading on the green leaves. It is particularly tender and pale because the flowers are protected from the sun's rays by little terracotta covers (known as *pignatte* or *pignattelle*) produced by local artisans. Farmers place these over the first clusters at the top of the plant, known as *mamme* or *mammolelle*. Every year the Castellammare artichoke is propagated by choosing the best new *carducci*, the shoots which appear around the mother plants, and transplanting them with a small portion of the rhizome. A traditional Campanian dish for Easter Monday is grilled artichokes, cleaned and dressed with extra-virgin olive oil, salt, pepper, spring garlic and parsley, then eaten with salame and soppressata, the typical cured meats of the Lattari mountains. Another typical preparation is *'mbuttunato*, artichokes stuffed with cured meats, cheese, egg, salt, pepper, grated Parmigiano-Reggiano and parsley, mixed with stale bread that's been soaked and then squeezed out as well as the finely chopped interior of the artichoke. The stuffed artichokes are then cooked for half an hour with some water, oil and salt and served with crostini soaked in the cooking liquid. Historically the plain that runs from the slopes of Vesuvius to Castellammare and to Sant'Antonio Abate was one of the centers of horticulture in the center and south of Italy. Unfortunately there has recently been a reduction in the amount of land dedicated to traditional agriculture, due particularly in the last 30 years to an uncontrolled building boom and an increase in floriculture. Through the promotion of a product which is emblematic of the cuisine of Campania and particularly Naples, the Presidium hopes to help return this land to traditional vegetable cultivation.

PRODUCTION AREA
Castellammare di Stabia, Gragnano, Pompei, Sant'Antonio Abate and Santa Maria la Carità, province of Naples, Campania

PRESIDIUM COORDINATOR
Sabato Abagnale
tel. +39 0813903300 - 3471135440
ab.sabato@tiscali.it

PRESIDIUM SUPPORTED BY
Province of Naples

Castelvetrano Black Bread

The round loaf of Castelvetrano Black Bread, called vastedda in Sicilian dialect, has a hard, coffee-colored crust, sprinkled with sesame seeds, and a soft, wheat-yellow interior. Famous throughout Sicily, Castelvetrano bread has risked extinction over the years because it needs to be made with stone-ground Sicilian grains and cooked in wood-burning ovens. The basic ingredients give the bread its color. The dough is made by mixing two flours, the Sicilian durum wheat and an ancient variety of local wheat called tumminìa, both whole grains that are milled by using natural stones. And it is thanks to the very rare tumminìa that Castelvetrano bread becomes black and exceptionally sweet and tasty, with an intense, unique toasted aroma. The long-rising dough also includes water, salt and natural yeast (lu criscenti, mother). Every baker has an old and airy warehouse to dry out the trimmings from olive trees, whose branches are used to stoke the stone ovens. The walls of the oven become red hot from the fire and can reach temperatures of 300°C. When the flame dies down, the oven is carefully cleaned with a curina, a long-handled broom made of miniature palm. Then the bread is put inside to slowly bake, away from direct flame, as the oven temperature gradually diminishes. When the oven is cool, the bread is done. The Presidium has united bakers who still make Castelvetrano black bread, and is now working with the Ballatore Consortium to reconstruct the entire production chain by increasing the cultivation of tumminìa and trying to revive the numerous local stone mills. Traditionally, the Castelvetrano black bread is cut in half while still warm and seasoned with extra virgin olive oil, salt, oregano, sliced tomato, local cheeses (primo sale or vastedda), anchovies or sardines and basil. When fresh it smells of malt or toasted almonds, which blend with the slightly aromatic scent of the olive wood with which it is cooked.

PRODUCTION AREA
Castelvetrano, province of Trapani, Sicily

PRESIDIUM COORDINATORS
Franco Saccà
tel. +39 0923559490
francosac@libero.it
Tommaso Rizzo
tel. +39 092481088

PRESIDIUM SUPPORTED BY
Sicily Regional Authority, department of Agriculture and Forestry, Gian Pietro Ballatore Consortium for research into specific sectors of the cereal production chain

Certaldo Onion

The Certaldo onion boasts an outstanding testimonial, Giovanni Boccaccio, with his short story dedicated to Frate Cipolla in the 6th book of the Decameron, and is inclusion in the town crest, with a motto: these two circumstances alone should suffice to underline the significance of this modest but tasty vegetable for this town in Valdelsa where, like all the mediaeval towns in the region, the bond between the town and the surrounding countryside has always been very strong. 'Famous all over Tuscany' even in the time of the author of the Decameron, onions are still cultivated, but to a lesser extent than in the past, in the loose soil around the ancient town, and sold loose on the nearby markets. There are two varieties, sown in different times of the year: the statina, which is round, light violet, juicy, sweet and tasty, and is eaten fresh in the summer, and the vernina, which is slightly flat at the ends, an intense red with a pungent flavor, and is found from late August all through the winter. Certaldo onions have their place all through the meal. They are excellent in soup: after sweating them in hot oil, mash them and add a little vegetable sock and a few potatoes to produce a dense cream, which is served with a little pepper, oil and crostini of Tuscan bread. Certaldo onions are an important ingredient of la francesina, or boiled meat re-heated the day after. A shin of veal, boiled and then cooled, is cut into small pieces which are fried with onion and tomato, then stock is added to keep it moist. The Presidium, which was started with the support of the Certaldo 2000 Consortium, aims to give a new boost to this crop, by recovering some abandoned fields and creating a cooperative to package and market the vegetable.

PRODUCTION AREA
Certaldo, province of Florence, Tuscany

PRESIDIUM COORDINATORS
Elisa Buti
tel. +39 3403788239
elbuti@libero.it
Eugenio Piazza
tel. +39 0571652130
info@certaldo2000.com

PRESIDIUM SUPPORTED BY
Commune of Certaldo

Cervia Artisan Sea Salt

Commerce was thriving in Cervia as early as Roman times. In 1968, the salt pans were so numerous that the sea waters endangered the city and the town was literally moved two kilometers away. In 1959 government monopolies assumed ownership of the salt fields, decided to make one large salt pan from the 144 in existence, and to collect the salt once a year with machines. Production ceased in 1998 as the result of a governmental decision, but the city of Cervia decided not to abandon the saltworks. This led to the formation of the Parco della Salina company, which later became part of the Delta del Po Regional Park Emilia Romagna. The method traditionally used at Cervia is multiple collection, particularly suited to the soil and weather conditions around the Adriatic. After completing the various evaporation phases, each salter divides his own salt pan into five small sectors. Everyday, as soon as a layer of one or two centimeters has formed, he manually collects the salt contained in one sector and in five days has removed it all. This method is only practiced at one salt pan today, the Camillone saltworks. It ensures the typical 'sweet' taste of the local salt because it prevents the formation of the bitterer salts that need more time to crystallize and higher concentrations, something difficult to achieve considering the average temperatures in this area. The artisan salt of Cervia is ideal for salting cheeses and cured meats, which is why the pork butchers from the Po plain used to get their provisions only at Cervia. The Presidium is made up of a small group of salters still practicing the traditional method of salt collection at the little salt pan of Camillone. Considering the success of the project and the great demand for this salt, it will open another salt pan soon that will be collected in the traditional way without the use of machines.

PRODUCTION AREA
Cervia, province of Ravenna, Emilia Romagna

PRESIDIUM COORDINATORS
Mauro Zanarini
tel. +39 0544530744 - 335375212
slowfoodravenna@libero.it
Oscar Turroni
tel. +39 3389507741 - 0544977592
info@salinadicervia.it

PRESIDIUM SUPPORTED BY
Society of Cervia Saltworks Park,
Po Delta Regional Park

Cetara Anchovy Traditional Extract

This flavorful sauce can be used for dressing fresh or boiled vegetables like chard, borage, escarole, broccoli and potatoes and also for livening up pasta and fish dishes. Product of an age-old sailors' tradition, it is similar to the Roman garum and obtained from the aging of salted anchovies during a long and labor-intensive process. The anchovies used are caught with a cianciolo (a kind of surrounding net) in the Gulf of Salerno from the end of March to the beginning of July, this being the period in which the fish have a low fat content. Once scapezzate (decapitated and gutted by hand) and laid head-to-tail in alternating layers with salt in a terzigno, an oak container, they are then covered with the tompagno, a wooden disk on which are laid stones from the sea. As the anchovies mature, a liquid forms on the surface, which little by little is gathered and conserved naturally, exposing it to the sun. After four or five months, generally between the end of October and the beginning of November, the concentrated liquid is poured back into the terzigno. After it has worked its way down through the various layers (hence the name colatura, or percolating), absorbing all the best flavors and aromas, it's collected from a hole at the base of the container with an instrument called a vriale, and transferred to another container. The final result is a translucent extract, with an amber color so deep it's almost mahogany, and a distinctive and full-bodied flavor. A traditional custom calls for every family to use some for dressing spaghetti and linguine during Christmas Eve dinner, a much-loved ritual which helps remind the people of Cetara of their seafaring history. The Presidium intends to ensure a future for this traditional product and create a protocol to define the characteristics of the classic production method.

PRODUCTION AREA
Cetara, province of Salerno, Campania

PRESIDIUM COORDINATORS
Secondo Squizzato
tel. +39 089261466 - 3335609785
squizzgio@tiscali.it
Giancarlo Capacchione
tel. + 39 089753535
g.capacchione@libero.it

PRESIDIUM SUPPORTED BY
Mountain Community of the Amalfi Peninsula

Ciaculli Late Winter Mandarin

The name of this fruit comes from the farming township of the same name in the Palermo area, and from their later ripening period compared to other varieties. It originated in the 1940s through a mutation of the Avana seedless fruit, and is a fairly small mandarin – juicy and sweet, with a pulp that has virtually no pips and with a very thin peel – light yellow or pale orange in color. It ripens from January to April. It was once to be found in a wide area around Palermo, in the "Conca d'Oro", but over the last fifty years the land given over to agriculture has been reduced by almost 80%, seriously affecting the hydrogeological conditions. Fortunately, the area including the townships of Ciaculli and Croceverde Giardina have remained intact; here, almost only mandarins are grown, in an agricultural park that has been created with financing from the European Union. Strict limits have been established on building activity and agriculture has been given a boost, with the promotion of local products by the Il Tardivo di Ciaculli consortium, a group of small organic growers. The late Ciaculli is a very resistant mandarin that needs no particular treatment and is delicious when eaten fresh, because of its high sugar content and pronounced flavor. The consortium packs them into wooden crates and smaller cardboard boxes marked with a common logo. Sicilian confectioners and ice-cream makers transform them into granitas, sorbets, jellies, fruit juices and liqueurs and, with the addition of lemon juice, into jams. The consortium has a membership of 180 small producers who own a total of around 280 hectares – all of them basically organic. The land is divided into small plots: given the low income they produce, the potential earnings from the sale of the lands are greater than the agricultural income deriving from the sales of the fruits. The Presidium's main priorities are to give visibility to the consortium of small mandarin producers, to publicize this variety with its undisputedly high quality and, especially, to safeguard what is left of the splendid gardens in the Palermo area.

PRODUCTION AREA
Palermo, Sicily

PRESIDIUM COORDINATORS
Nino Aiello
tel. +39 091 6628450
ninoaiello@tin.it
Giovanni D'Agati
tel. +39 0916301769 - 3392614123 info@tardivodiciaculli.it

PRESIDIUM SUPPORTED BY
Palermo Provincial Authority

Cilento Goat Cacioricotta

Cacioricotta is produced in the Cilento area of Campania, but also in Puglia and Basilicata using the same method. What distinguishes this Campanian Cacioricotta is the milk, which comes from native goats. The cheesemaking process involves two curdling methods, using rennet, as in other cheeses like cacio, and also heat, like ricotta. Once formed, the cheese can be eaten fresh or aged. When fresh it is delicious on its own, with honey or in a mixed salad. Once aged it becomes hard, compact, flaky and slightly piquant, perfect for grating and the ideal topping for the classic local dish of fusilli with mutton ragù. Like all the cheeses produced with milk from Cilento goats it has a distinctively complex aroma from the essential oils in the Mediterranean scrub plants on which the animals graze. The Bella Zootechnical Institute has demonstrated the extraordinary quality of the goats' milk, rich in unsaturated fatty acids, low in cholesterol and high in antioxidants. These characteristics underline the importance of the Cilento goat, raised principally for its meat but also an important milk source, even though yield is fairly low. The value lies in the goats' diet, based on pasturing and the trimmings from fig and olive trees and crown vetch, and the fact that the goats spend at least eight months out of the year in a semi-wild state. The goats' grazing actually helps keep the undergrowth tidy and fertilized, with beneficial effects for the development of the forest trees. Promotion of Cilento goat Ca-

cioricotta means offering a valid economic alternative to selling the flocks, often the only option remaining for local farmers. Among the objectives of the Presidium is the improvement of aging techniques for the Cacioricotta, so as to add value to a semi-aged product which can be enjoyed straight, helping the cheese find new markets outside its immediate production area.

PRODUCTION AREA
Cilento, province of Salerno, Campania

PRESIDIUM COORDINATOR
Raffaele Soriero
tel. +39 0975395215 - 3384897116
soriero@katamail.com

PRESIDIUM SUPPORTED BY
Cilento and Vallo di Diano National Park

Cinque Terre Sciacchetrà

'That bold Sciacchetrà that they press in the five leafy lands,' to quote D'Annunzio, is an amber-colored wine whose etymon seems to come from the Hebrew word shekar, the name of an alcoholic beverage. Put on the market after at least two years of aging, the wine can continue to evolve for as many as ten, twenty or even thirty years. It has a full, persistent and lovely amber color, with traces of dried fruit, apricot preserves, yellow peach and vanilla, chestnut honey and spices. Warm and full-bodied, velvety and soft, it is sweet to the taste but never cloying. This old and aristocratic passito (raisin wine) is made with albarola, vermentino and bosco grapes that are left to wither out of the sun. After the withering, the grapes are hand-picked from the bunches one by one. Then they are carefully selected to obtain (after the winemaking and aging) little more than 25 liters of Sciacchetrà from a hundred kilograms of grapes. It is a tiny quantity of wine made from sparing and difficult to grow vines that are planted on just a little over 4,000 hectares of harsh and mountainous coast, which winds its way along the Ligurian Riviera between Sestri Levante and La Spezia, sloping down to the sea on terracing known as cian. But the little dry stone walls the farmers built over the centuries are mostly abandoned by now and in ruins. So keeping alive the tradition of viticulture in this zone means preserving the landscape and ensuring a future for those who dedicate their lives to working the land. To do this, however, one needs to produce an excellent Sciacchetrà that has a remunerative price. Eight winemakers in the Cinque Terre have given themselves a rigorous protocol for producing top quality Sciacchetrà and formed the Associazione Piccoli Vignaioli delle Cinque Terre onlus, an essential tool for developing and maintaining quality viticulture. The aim of the Presidium is to clean up the uncultivated terraces, rebuild the dry stone walls, replant the vines and assist young people who want to cultivate the Cinque Terre vineyards in the future.

PRODUCTION AREA
Cinque Terre, province of La Spezia, Liguria

PRESIDIUM COORDINATORS
Barbara Schiffini
tel. +39 0187701098
schiffini1963@libero.it
Walter De Batté
tel. +39 0187920127

PRESIDIUM SUPPORTED BY
Cinque Terre National Park

Classic Bologna Mortadella

Despite having old and aristocratic origins dating to the Middle Ages, including a recipe by Cristoforo di Messisbugo from 1557, most mortadella is commercially produced today. Production has obviously changed a lot since then, and mortadella has gradually become a cured meat for mass consumption, almost synonymous with fast food. The Presidium's classic Bologna mortadella does not really look any different from the version normally sold in shops, but when sliced its distinctiveness becomes readily apparent. For one thing, the color tends towards light brown rather than the reddish or rosy pink we are used to and no additives or artificial aromas are used to enhance the natural fragrance, which is more delicate and complex than other mortadellas. It has a very distinctive consistency, with a sweetish flavor and a more savory aftertaste. This mortadella is at its best when served in very thin hand-cut slices, served with a glass of Spumante Metodo Classico or Champagne. The aim of the Presidium is to lend character and added value to an eminently artisan product. It has also identified the last remaining artisan still actively producing mortadella in Bologna, thus preserving the tie that the meat has with its old city of origin. The

Presidium mortadella is only made with meat from large-size Italian pigs. Practically no preservatives are used other than the tiny amounts of nitrites and nitrates that are permitted (two grams mixed with salt for every 100 kilos of meat to be exact). The mortadella is seasoned with salt, whole black peppercorns, ground white pepper, mace, coriander and crushed garlic and then cooked in stone ovens at an internal temperature of 75-77°C. Only a natural bladder casing is allowed.

PRODUCTION AREA
Bologna, Emilia Romagna

PRESIDIUM COORDINATOR
Alberto Fabbri
tel. +39 0516830187
centoggi@virgilio.it

PRESIDIUM SUPPORTED BY
Emilia Romagna Regional Authority

Classic Chianina Ox

This is one of the oldest and most important breeds of cattle in Italy. Wild, rustic, brown or black and rather coarse at the start of the last century, it has changed radically in the last 50 years, becoming an adult, powerful bovine – the largest in the world – with a white coat and a light, elegant head. Originally bred in Valdichiana (hence the name), it was used primarily as a beast of burden. After the World War II, with the spread of mechanized agriculture, it was almost entirely abandoned and risked extinction. Only the passion of a few farmers saved this important genetic, economic and cultural heritage. Rustic and suited to grazing, the Chianina has gradually shifted from the cowsheds of the plains to the mountains, and while it was once kept indoors it now roams free or semi-free: the cows are out at pasture from early May to mid November, and only closed in their sheds in the winter, when they are fed with hay harvested in the summer. Today Chianina meat is famous all over the world, which is why it is important to distinguish between the real thing and imitations, and to protect it. Capable of achieving very high weights (males up to 900-1000 kilograms), this breed has enormous potential for growth: bullocks are slaughtered at 16-17 months, with an average weight of 700 kilograms and they yield up to 65% when butchered. A protocol decides the rules to breed the Presidium Chianina, guaranteeing the high quality and absolute safety of the meat. Unfortunately a whole animal, in fact a whole breed – Chianina – has come to be identified with a single cut and a single dish: the *bistecca alla fiorentina*, or T-bone steak. As if only edible part of these splendid white bullocks were the rear end, the loin, which is what produces the T-bone steak (chops are cut from the front end).

PRODUCTION AREA
Provinces of Siena and Arezzo, Tuscany

PRESIDIUM COORDINATORS
Roberto Neri
tel. +39 3473820977
Stefania Veltroni
tel. +39 057520929
apaar@technet.it

PRESIDIUM SUPPORTED BY
Arezzo and Siena Provincial Authorities, Arezzo Chamber of Commerce, Industry, Crafts and Agriculture, Val Tiberina Mountain Community

Classic Genoese Focaccia

This poor man's food par excellence started out as morning refreshment and gradually became a popular breakfast, afternoon snack and appetizer. Its very old origins go back as early as the 16th century, when it was customary to eat the fugassa during benedictions in church, at weddings and even at funerals; a custom that was struck down when a bishop threatened to ban it. The ingredients are simple and few: flour, water extra virgin olive oil, coarse salt and occasionally a sprinkling of white wine from the valleys inland from Genoa. The result is a soft but never gummy focaccia, with a crispy crust and an intense aroma of oil and bread. The dough is the color of ivory, with small air bubbles and just the right amount of oil. Unfortunately the focaccia offered up by the hundreds of Genoese bakeries today is more and more often made with lard or, worse, with marc oil and prepared in a thousand different ways (with shrimp, rocket, gorgonzola, salmon and so on). None of which have anything to do with the traditional food. Traditionally the dough is left to rise for at least eight hours, but this has been considerably reduced with the more 'modern' product. The result is a focaccia that only keeps for a few hours and is not only less fragrant and flavorful, but also more difficult to digest. The classic Genoese focaccia, on the other hand, is less than two centimeters high and has an unforgettable aroma of yeast, warm bread and boiling oil. When you bite into it for the first time it should be crunchy and then soft and crumbly in texture, and glistening with oil on top. It is excellent by itself, but can also be enjoyed with figs, as in the past, or with the historical pork and beef Sant'Olcese, smoked sausage, traditionally made in upper Val Polcevera. The Presidium has brought together a group of Genoese bakers, who have drawn up a regulatory framework they all undertake to follow so the consumer can be sure of eating the classic Genoese fugassa.

PRODUCTION AREA
City and province of Genoa, Liguria

PRESIDIUM COORDINATOR
Livio Caprile
tel. +39 0105533046 - 3382391490
l.caprile@dolcap.it

PRESIDIUM SUPPORTED BY
Genoa Provincial Authority

Classic Robiola di Roccaverano

Roccaverano cheeses are 10-14 centimeters in diameter, 4-5 centimeters high and weigh about 400 grams. The cheese is fresh, soft and dense, and as it ages its very thin ivory-colored crust darkens to straw-yellow or brown, with reddish streaks. When eaten fresh the Robiola is delicious and has the aroma of yogurt, green grass and hazelnut. With aging it develops a slight aroma of goat and wild plants, while the taste becomes piquant and musky. The cheese is also excellent when preserved in oil. Produced in the harsh, untilled hills of the Asti Langa, it is the only historic Italian goat's cheese and the only one to have obtained the denomination of protected origin (POD), which was when it was given its official name. Fortunately, some breeders- cheese makers still make Robiola as tradition calls for. The Presidium protects a group of small artisans who produce the cheese the way people did 200 years ago and valorize the Roccaverano robiola by producing the 'classic' version made only with raw goat's milk, even though the present protocol allows them to use up to 85% cow's milk. The traditional cheese making technique varies little from producer to producer. Yet the differences between one Robiola and the next are considerable because the flowers, grasses and bacterial flora of the pastures and stables affect the quality of the cheese to the point that it is possible to define a veritable map of crus, just as it is with wine. Unfortunately, Roccaverano goats have declined drastically in numbers and have been substituted by other more productive breeds. Only 200 heads remained in 1990, but with the revival of Classic Roccaverano there are now important initiatives to safeguard and enhance this cheese.

PRODUCTION AREA

Bubbio, Cessole, Loazzolo, Monastero Bormida, Mombaldone, Olmo Gentile, Roccaverano, San Giorgio Scarampi, Serole and Vesime, province of Asti; Cartosio, Castelletto d'Erro, Denice, Malvlcino, Merana, Montechiaro d'Acqui, Pareto, Ponti, Ponzone and Spigno, province of Alessandria, Piedmont

PRESIDIUM COORDINATOR

Gian Domenico Negro
tel. +39 0144850000-3357219774
gd.negro@libero.it

PRESIDIUM SUPPORTED BY

Suol d'Aleramo (Erro, Orba and Bormida valleys) Mountain Community, Langa Astigiana Mountain Community,
Arbiora (Bubbio, Asti, Piemonte, Italy)

Coazze Cevrin

Some call it toma, and others, more appropriately, robiola, but in local dialect it is Cevrin. From spring to autumn in the Sangone Valley this cheese is made from goat's milk, which is not processed pure but mixed with varying amounts of cow's milk. After slow curdling, which is reached by adding liquid veal coagulant, halfway between lactic and rennet, the curd is broken, and then left to rest before being transferred into the cheese molds and shaped into forms of around 20 cm wide. Finally it is dry-salted on both sides and left to ripen for about three months in the mountain pastures inside natural caves, although the forms must be turned and cleaned every day. At the end of the process a cheese is obtained tasting of hazelnuts and butter, with certain spicy notes and intense long-lasting aromas ranging from dried wood to freshly cut grass, to animal fur. The cheese is yellow towards the outside and white inside, slightly granular, with a rough, damp, amber colored rind. The round forms weigh between 0.8 and 1.5 kilos, are about 10 cm high with face diameters between 15 and 18 centimeters. Cevrin could not be produced without the Alpine chamois, a goat similar to a steinbock, agile and slim, medium-small in size, with a reddish coat and wonderful backwards pointing horns. It is very like its wilder 'cousin', sharing its frugal attitude; it is enterprising and at its best in extreme conditions. This small ruminant lives in high often bleak pastures, and gives the milk for this cheese whose profile the Presidium wishes to raise, creating a new sales network to promote breeding of the goats to increase their milk production.

PRODUCTION AREA
Coazze and Giaveno, province of Turin, Piedmont

PRESIDIUM COORDINATORS
Franco Turaglio
tel. +39 0121 394556 - 3294151775
info@lanicchia.net
Maria Lussiana
tel. +39 011 9363903 - 3388015225
maria.lussiana@virgilio.it

PRESIDIUM SUPPORTED BY
Turin Provincial Authority

Cocomerina Pear

Judging from paintings by the Medicean artist Bartolomeo Bimbi, between the 17th and 18th centuries there were 115 different kinds of pears, only 17 of which have survived to this day. The cocomerina that has come down to us is a very old variety, carefully selected by farmers in the past according to the environment and use. The result is a very small, sweet and fragrant pear, weighing from 20-60 grams, that has an oval shape and dark green skin. The color of the pulp varies from a bright pink to a deep watermelon (cocomera) red, especially when harvested late, and this is where the name comes from (also called briaca or cocomera). It has a vague aroma of muscat and sorb apple and is very susceptible to scab. As it does not keep well it should be eaten when harvested, otherwise it loses its unique flavor and aroma, which is why it is particularly suited for jams and preserving in syrup. In the past it was grown mainly for home consumption, but starting in the 1950s it began to disappear like other older varieties of fruit because intensive cultivation of specialized varieties had become more widespread in Italy. Today a few trees can still be found scattered about the countryside of the Cesana Apennines in the Upper Savio valley, particularly in Le Ville di Montecoronaro, where the Presidium was started. There are two periods for the harvest: the early variety ripens at the end of August, while the late growers are picked at the end of October. In September a Cocomerina Festival is held. To promote and augment cultivation of this pear variety, the Pro-Ville di Montecoronaro growers' association was set up, which has taken a census of all the old trees and planted 200 new ones. Each year it harvests the cocomerina pears, sells them and processes them into jams and preserves using only natural ingredients. The Presidium also intends to create a space for teaching and experimentation.

PRODUCTION AREA
Ville di Montecoronaro and other areas in the communes of Verghereto and Bagno di Romagna, province of Forlì-Cesena, Emilia Romagna

PRESIDIUM COORDINATORS
Gianpiero Giordani
tel. +39 0547361728-3487682402
gianpierogiordani@libero.it
Manuela Biserni
tel. +39 3382971945
gia.ros@libero.it

PRESIDIUM SUPPORTED BY
Appennino Cesenate Mountain Community

Coggiola Paletta

The traditional paletta may be eaten both raw or cooked: piping hot, together with a plate of polenta or boiler potatoes, or raw, with sweet apple mustard from the Biella region. The name takes after the shape of the pig's shoulder bone, cut running lengthwise into two symmetrical pieces, then pickled for 15-30 days, and regularly turned and massaged. When the salt has been fully absorbed, the meat is seasoned with a mixture of local herbs and black pepper. Following this, it is put into a natural gut, usually the bladder, repeatedly poked in order to release the pickle. The bladder must adhere to the palette completely, protecting them from external agents and preserving their flavor. It should be tied with unbleached string. The cured meats are finally left to hang in a non air-conditioned room, at a temperature of 10 to 16°C. After 20 days they are ready, however, in order to be enjoyed raw the maturino process should continue at least four months, durino which the gut is kept damp and soft in order to prevent the meat from becoming too dry. The current production technique is the same as years back; it is carried out manually by artisans. Up until a few decades ago, the masaular – the man who butchered pigs door to door in the Val Tessera – made the paletta himself. He would prepare sausage, bacon, salami and ham: those made from thigh meat were destined for prelates and notables, those made from shoulder meat – such as the paletta – were for poorer people. After the Second World War, in Coggiola and the neighboring communes at least a dozen butchers were still active in the production of the valley's specialties.

Nowadays, two producers in the old part of town still make small prosciutti according to tradition, which means they employ a special mixture of local spices and age the meat in non air-conditioned rooms.

PRODUCTION AREA
Coggiola, province of Biella, Piedmont

PRESIDIUM COORDINATOR
Gianluca Foglia Barbisin
tel. +39 01578512
coggiola.sindaco@tin.it

PRESIDIUM SUPPORTED BY
Commune of Coggiola

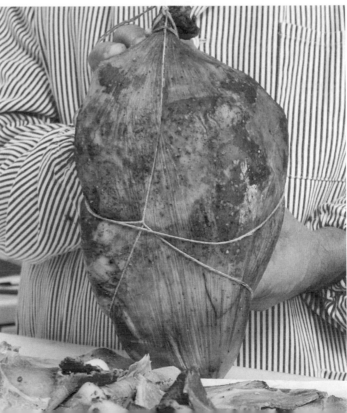

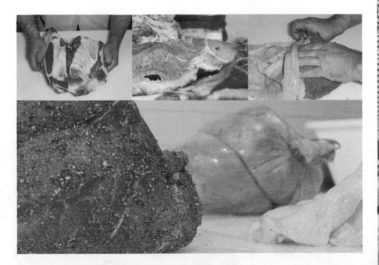

Colonnata Lard

In October 2004, Colonnata Lard obtained European recognition as a product with Protected Geographical Indication, granted on the basis of the production regulations developed by the promoter association of the Supervision. This also laid the legal basis for valorizing - in the sea of imitations - the only legitimate heir of the cured meat that was for centuries the daily food of Apuan quarrymen. Colonnata, near Carrara at an altitude of 550 meters, has been the tiny capital of marble since Roman times. And here, for centuries, pork lard was seasoned in marble jars aromatized with local herbs and spices. Not all marble, however, is suitable: only the right, dry and glassy marble serves the purpose. Among the many types to be found in the Colonnata quarry area, lard producers identified the marble from the Canaloni quarry. Processing is seasonal (from September to May) and the raw material, pig lard, is today mostly bought from selected breeders in central and northern Italy. A large cut is taken; the rind and the fatty lard is scraped away and then cut into thick pieces with regular sides. The pieces are then 'massaged' with sea salt. The pieces of lard are then arranged in a marble jar, alternating layers with a mixture of salt, black pepper, rosemary, fresh garlic and other flavorings, depending on family tradition: cinnamon, nutmeg, cloves, star anise, sage, bay leaf, oregano or thyme. When the jar is full it is closed and left so season at natural temperature for at least six months, although curing may even take as long as two years. Pure white, soft and perfumed, Colonnata Lard has a delicate and fresh taste that is extraordinarily sweet despite the large quantity of salt used (25 kg for 100 kg of lard). Every year, on 24 August, Colonnata holds a Lard Festival organized by a special association. The Presidium brings together the producers of the Colonnata Lard Tutelage Association.

PRODUCTION AREA
Colonnata, province of Massa-Carrara, Tuscany

PRESIDIUM COORDINATOR
Renata Ricci
tel. +39 0585758029
larderia.renataricci@tin.it

PRESIDIUM SUPPORTED BY
Massa-Carrara Provincial Authority –
Commune of Carrara, Massa Carrara Chamber of Commerce, Industry, Crafts and Agriculture, Colonnata Lard Protection Association

Comacchio Lagoons
Traditional Pickled Eel

Situated between the Po, the Reno and the Adriatic, the Comacchio area is part of Po Delta Park. The area is very important ecologically, but what really makes it special is the perfect integration of human activity and nature. In fact the entire process of fishing and marinating the eels is performed right here. As the eel fishing season is concentrated between November and January, marinating the eel is a way of preserving it for as long as possible. Indeed, marinated eel used to be the traditional dish at Easter. Eels born in the the Sargasso Sea, reach adulthood in freshwater zones such as the lagoons of Comacchio in the Po delta. Then when they are sexually mature they begin migrating to the sea to reproduce. When the eels arrive at the mouth of the lagoons and inland canals they are trapped in specially built cages (*lavorieri*) that block their migration. At one time the captured eels were transported to the many fish processing plants in the area, where they were sorted, cut, threaded on iron *schiodoni* and cooked before an open fire. Then they were put in pickling brine in metal vessels and, very occasionally in wood *zangolini*. This local tradition has been lost to us now, but thanks to the Po Delta Park, the Emilia Romagna Regional Authority and the commune of Comacchio, the Presidium has revived this local marinated dish in some of the restored rooms of the Manifattura dei Marinati, where the eels are cooked in front of the 12 original fireplaces in the *sala dei fuochi*. As in the past, there are three factors that determine the success of the final product: the wild eel itself, recognizable by the silver belly, the cooking and the composition of the brine which, according to the traditional recipe, should be made with 70 grams of Cervia sea salt (Slow Food Presidium), one glass of water per liter of white wine vinegar and a bay leaf. Pickled in this way, the eel conserves its flavor and aroma for several months.

PRODUCTION AREA
Comacchio lagoons, Po Delta Park, provinces of Ferrara and Ravenna, Emilia Romagna

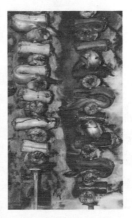

PRESIDIUM COORDINATORS
Alberto Fabbri
tel. +39 0516830187
centoggi@virgilio.it
Gianni Cavallini
tel. +39 053381159
giannicavallini@parcodeltapo.it

PRESIDIUM SUPPORTED BY
Emilia Romagna Regional Authority,
Po Delta Regional Park

Conca Casale Signora

The signora is a traditional pork sausage made in Conca Casale, a small mountain village above Venafro in Molise, where a small group of women keep up the age-old tradition by guarding the secret of its preparation. Not a poor man's sausage and rarely eaten by the people who make it, it was customarily presented to the doctor or the notary public, say, as a thankyou gift for a favor received. The fact that only one signora could be made from a single pig gave it added luster. Traditionally lean cuts of pork such as the fillet and the shoulder were used, with the addition of lard from the belly and back to provide the fat. Nowadays parts of the leg and the sirloin are also used. First the meats are chopped with the tip of a knife, one part finely minced and one part coarsely chopped to improve the blend. Then the mixture is seasoned with black pepper, coriander, ground hot red pepper and wild fennel. The mixture is left to marinate for a few hours before being made into sausage. In the meantime, the pork intestine casing, the so-called is carefully washed with raw corn meal, orange juice, lemon, vinegar and wine. The sausage is stuffed by hand with the aid of a sort of funnel and at this stage the artisan's skill is fundamental: for proper aging, the mixture must be distributed uniformly and all the folds in the intestine well-filled. The sausage is tied with a string, smoked for a few days and then aged for at least six months. Until a short time ago, the sausage was only homemade, but thanks to the Presidium and the municipal administration of Conca Casale, one producer decided to start making this ancient sausage again. As it is made in limited quantities, it is possible to maintain a strictly local production chain. The pigs that are used are organically raised in a semi-wild state, without the use of feed or additives. The flavor and texture of the signora are similar to coarse-grained salami with strong notes of wild fennel and citrus fruit.

PRODUCTION AREA
Conca Casale, province of Isernia, Molise

PRESIDIUM COORDINATOR
Francesco Martino
tel. +39 0865900377-3381048796
francesco.martino@tin.it

PRESIDIUM SUPPORTED BY
Commune of Conca Casale

Conciato Romano

Like Formaggio di fossa, a cheese aged underground, il matures in anaerobic conditions, undergoing a second fermentation. However this process does not take place in the ground, enabling the cheese to maintain its integral characteristics and giving it more balance and aroma. Milk from cows, sheep or goats is used, and the curds are formed with goat rennet. The small forms are then pressed by hand, salted, dried and cured. This final phase involves the cheeses being washed with the cooking liquid from *pettole* (a homemade pasta), then covered with a mixture of oil, vinegar, thyme and finely chopped chili pepper. The cheeses are then traditionally matured in a terracotta amphora, which these days is substituted by a glass container, so the development of the natural molds can be controlled. To ensure an even curing the jars are turned upside down periodically throughout the aging period, which can range from six months to two years. When ready the cheese has a hard texture, an uneven yellow color and an irregular rind which varies from yellow ochre to dark brown. To the nose it offers aromas of alcohol and ripe fruit, and in the mouth there's a very pronounced spiciness, typical of the so-called 'resuscitated cheeses', such as those which emerge from underground in Romagna or the Marche. The process of conservation and aging, in which it is cured, have led to the assumption that it is the oldest Italian cheese, going back to the pastoral civilization of the Samnites. The cheese can pair well with sweet preserves, like lemon marmalade, fig jam, chestnut honey or quince paste. However, the strong flavor clashes with ripe fruit. The Presidium has helped producers to return to traditional cheesemaking and the aging and curing in amphorae, creating a production protocol and helping promote this unique cheese.

PRODUCTION AREA
Castel di Sasso and surrounding area, province of Caserta, Campania

PRESIDIUM COORDINATORS
Vito Puglia
tel. +39 3298321284
vito.puglia@fastwebnet.it
Fabio Lombardi
tel. +39 0823878277
f.lombardi19@virgilio.it

PRESIDIUM SUPPORTED BY
Campania Regional Authority

Corno alle Scale Char

This char, a relative of the Fario trout and Alpine char, was imported from America at the end of the 19th century. It is very distinctive because of its bright colors: the fins edged in white; the brown back with yellow or olive green stripes; the sides dotted with yellow or red spots fringed with blue. In the mating season the colors become even brighter. The fish is raised in a 1930s plant in the town of Lizzano in Belvedere, in the province of Bologna. The town is part of the little Corno alle Scale Regional Park, in the Tuscan-Emilian Appenines. The chars reproduce in the month of December. Initially the fry are raised inside the plant, where there is spring water, and are moved into outdoor tanks when they are at least five centimeters long. No antibiotics or other chemicals are added to the water and the fish are nourished with a special food based on deep sea fish (not farmed), a composition created in collaboration with the University of Turin. GMOs and protein from land animals are prohibited. Sold fresh where they are raised, the Corno alle Scale Chars have compact white meat, whose fine and delicate flavor is enhanced by such classic recipes as *carpaccio* or foil baking. In any case, some caterers are successfully trying out new preparations, such as char paté. The Presidium involving the Il Salmerino (char) fish farm has drafted a protocol for raising the chars, which is characterized by the total sustainability of this kind of aquaculture; and in addition to the chars, it also raises Fario trout. It has a registered trademark - Il Salmerino – thanks to which it is possible to recognize the Presidium product and is making preparations to sell processed char products as well. For the moment one can only purchase fresh chars directly from the company in Lizzano in Belvedere.

PRODUCTION AREA
Lizzano in Belvedere, province of Bologna, Emilia Romagna

PRESIDIUM COORDINATORS
Roberto Ferranti
tel. +39 051522516
Giuliana Ori
tel. +39 053451291–3483036696
giulianaori@tiscalinet.it

PRESIDIUM SUPPORTED BY
Emilia Romagna Regional Authority, Corno alle Scale Regional Park

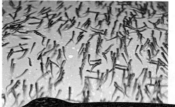
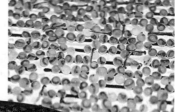

Cosenza Dottato Fig

Because of the ventilated climate, neither dry nor too rainy, Crati Valley near Cosenza is the perfect habitat for the dotato variety of figs. The trees flower twice a year. From mid-May to mid-August the fioroni are harvested and usually eaten fresh, while in August and September the forniti ripen, ideal for drying on cannizze (cane racks tied with mulberry branches). The yellowish medium-size figs stand out for their very tiny almost imperceptible seeds. The cannizze are put out in the sun during the day, raised up from the ground to keep out of the dampness, and then brought indoors at night. Turned over repeatedly for a week, when dry enough so that no pulp oozes out when pressed, they are ready to be baked, seasoned and stuffed. Three kilos of fresh figs yield one kilo of dried, which are then prepared in a great variety of ways: strung together in the shape of little crosses, circles or plaits; skewered; mixed with fig honey and shaped into characteristic balls; stuffed with orange rind and candied citron, with walnuts and almonds; spiced with cinnamon; coated with chocolate. They are also added to pitta 'chiusa, the traditional wedding sweet that is supposed to be prepared by the groom's family. In the 1950s, the province of Cosenza produced 650,000 quintals of fresh figs, today it produces barely 10,000. Before the Presidium was started, the individual farmers were giving up their fig cultivations (even though of superior quality) on account of foreign competition, from Turkey and Greece in particular. The Presidium has managed to reverse the trend and has brought together companies that still process Cosenza dottato figs in the traditional way. A consortium has been set up to protect the fig which is now working to guarantee the complete traceability of ther production system. The next step will be to organize a common collection center.

PRODUCTION AREA
Province of Cosenza, particularly Crati valley, Calabria

PRESIDIUM COORDINATORS
Raffaele Riga
tel. +39 0984462187
rafriga@hotmail.com
Angelo Rosa
tel. +39 0984949106
aziendarosa@tiscali.it

PRESIDIUM SUPPORTED BY
Gal Valle del Crati

Delia Cuddrireddra

In Delia, a farming town south west of Caltanissetta, all the local families are involved in the preparation of this bracelet-shaped sweet for Carnival. The term cuddrireddra derives from the Greek kollura (a ring-shaped biscuit), and means crown in local dialect, though it is virtually unpronounceable for anyone who is not Sicilian. In Sicily, and throughout the south of Italy, there are many kinds of fried donuts, but only in Delia does this complicated shape exist. Legend has it that the crown shape came about to pay homage to the ladies of the castle who lived in Delia during the Sicilian Vespers (1282-1302), in the medieval fortress which overlooks the town. It is made of durum wheat flour, yeast, lard, sugar, eggs, red wine, cinnamon and orange zest. The dough is kneaded on a wooden board called a scanaturi, until it reaches the right consistency. The most complicated part, which requires manual dexterity and experience, but which all the women of Delia know how to do, starts at this stage. Little strips of dough are wound round a stick, which is then removed. This spiral is then pressed against a comb – two wooden rods linked with a series of smoothed bamboo sticks – which was once part of a weaving loom – to make the characteristic grooves. Some of these combs are over 150 years old, and they are stored very carefully because there are no longer craftsmen able to make them. Once 'combed' the spirals are joined at the ends, forming the classic crown shape, and fried in extra virgin olive oil. The original cuddrireddra must be crunchy when cooked, sweet but not sickly, with a marked flavor of cinnamon and orange zest, and in the background a hint of red wine, which is one ingredient of the dough. They can now be found all year round, and make an ideal after-dinner treat served with passito siciliano.

PRODUCTION AREA
Delia, province of Caltanissetta, Sicily

PRESIDIUM COORDINATORS
Pasquale Tornatore
tel. +39 0934553777 – 348 3206302
pasquale.tornatore@thaos.it
Lelio Lunetta
tel. +39 0922820130
leliolunetta@virgilio.it

PRESIDIUM SUPPORTED BY
Commune di Delia, Chamber of Commerce, Industry, Crafts and Agriculture of Caltanissetta

Dried Calizzano and Murialdo Chestnuts

The very old technique of drying chestnuts in tecci was once common throughout the Ligurian Apennines and Piedmontese valleys. The tecci are small stone constructions consisting of a single room and a shingled roof made of wooden boards. Inside, two or three meters from the ground, the graia (a wooden latticework ceiling) allows the heat and smoke to reach the chestnuts. In the chestnut woods in Upper Val Bormida active tecci can be found hidden in the midst of the secular trees. After the harvest, the chestnuts, which mainly belong to the gabbina (or gabbiana) cultivar, are layered on the latticework ceilings, while the low and constant fire below is fueled by chestnut husks or by chaff. The smoking process goes on for a couple of months, and to ensure that it is uniform, the chestnuts must be turned so the bottom layers are brought to the top and vice versa. After this operation, they are smoked for another 5-10 days and then beaten to eliminate the peel. They can be eaten as is or as an ingredient in biscuits, preserves, creams and ice cream. At Christmas, the best fruit is used to make the traditional viette: the dried chestnuts are boiled for five hours in a pan with a weight on top so they always stay under the water. Particularly sweet, the flavor is reminiscent of candied fruit. The Presidium is seeking to promote the old methods of gathering and preserving the chestnuts through the Il Teccio cooperative, a group of gatherers and processors. And a strict production protocol defines the area for gathering the chestnuts as well as the methods for smoking, producing and processing them. Thanks to a questionnaire that the local chestnut gatherers filled out, it was possible to determine the true cost of producing the chestnuts and establish a higher selling price for them better than the going market price. As a result, the owners of the woods were encouraged to gather the chestnuts and keep the area clean, thus making it possible to recover tourist paths.

PRODUCTION AREA
Calizzano, Murialdo, Osiglia, Massimino and Bardineto, province of Savona, Liguria

PRESIDIUM COORDINATOR
Federico Santamaria
tel. +39 0197906065 - 3357708025
f.santamaria@tiscalinet.it

PRESIDIUM SUPPORTED BY
Liguria Regional Authority, Savona Provincial Authority

Fabriano Salami

The processing is done like it was in the past and still calls for the use of the leg – the choicest cut of pork. The lard from the back is cut into little cubes, salted and mixed with care. The leaner parts, the shoulder and leg, are cut up and finely ground and then blended by hand with the fat. Finally, the mixture is seasoned with salt and pepper and sometimes a touch of garlic. The ingredients are simple and few and make this salami an essential element of gastronomic history and part of Fabriano's identity. The casing is the lower pig's intestine (ideal for long aging), which is washed well and rinsed in either wine or vinegar before being stuffed with the meat mixture and then tied at the ends with string. The salami develops its characteristic flavor and aroma through an aging process lasting from 50-60 days, which starts with a few days exposed to a slow fire. The meat rarely takes on smoky taste, however, since the heat only serves to eliminate the humidity. When ready, the Fabriano salamis weigh 300-400 grams, are 6 centimeters in diameter and 30-35 centimeters long. They are rather hard and rough on the outside and covered with a soft dark brown mold. The compact, dark red meat emanates an intense aroma when sliced and the cubes of white lard are very apparent. The sweet, persistent vanilla taste, somewhat peppery, goes very well with Rosso Pi-ceno or sweet sparkling wines like Moscato and Verduzzo. The Presidium, which was formed to make this great product known, has taken on the problem of the raw ingredient. The best salamis have in fact always been made from locally raised heavy pigs (150-180 chili), which are difficult to find these days. For this reason a consortium of breeders and processors has recently been set up, armed with a protocol that regulates the feeding and raising of the pigs as well as the processing and aging of the salamis.

PRODUCTION AREA
Cerreto d'Esi, Genga, Sassoferrato and Fabriano,
province of Ancona, Esanatoglia, province of Macerata, Marche

PRESIDIUM COORDINATOR
Domenico Battistoni
tel. +39 07322016 – 073221066
inox@componendo.com

Farindola Pecorino

What makes this pecorino so unique is the use of pig rennet, a traditional preparation that has been handed down to the women in families ever since Roman times. The pig rennet and production technique give the cheese a very particular aroma and flavor as well as moistness even when aged. It is produced by heating the milk at 35°C and then breaking up the curds into tiny grains. Once removed from the cauldron, the mass is placed in rush baskets to drain, which creates the classic streaks in the crust. The cheese is dry-salted after 48 hours and the forms are left to age in old wooden kneading troughs, where they ripen for 40 days to one year, periodically oiled with a mixture of extra virgin olive oil and vinegar. Depending on the aging process, the color of the crust can vary from light yellow to saffron to dark brown. The straw-yellow cheese is granular and slightly moist, with an aroma of mushrooms, refined mould and dry wood. The mellowness is created by just the right balance of sheep's milk and spice. The milk comes from sheep that descend from the native Pagliarola Appenninica breed raised in the wild and the cheese is made in limited quantities, almost exclusively for home use, in an area along the eastern slope of the Gran Sasso massif. The Presidium was set up with the intention of protecting and reviving production of this singular cheese, while at the same time giving added value to the area of production. The main objectives are to promote this pecorino beyond the area where it is usually made and to consolidate its production. The producers have undertaken procedures to apply for a PDO (protected denomination of origin).

PRODUCTION AREA
Carpineto della Nora, Casanova, Civitella, Farindola, Montebello di Bertona, Penne and Villa Celiera, province of Pescara; Arsita, Bisenti and Castelli, province of Teramo, Abruzzo

PRESIDIUM COORDINATORS
Ugo Ciavattella
tel. +39 337912386
u.ciavattella@pecorinodifarindola.it
Silvia De Paulis
tel. +39 086260521
silviadepaulis@gransassolagapark.it

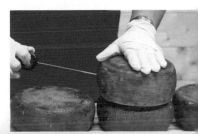

PRESIDIUM SUPPORTED BY
Gran Sasso and Monti
della Laga National Park

Favignana Bottarga

The time-honored tuna catch takes place in Favignana between May and June every year, but its role as a tourist attraction increasingly outweighs the socio-economic aspect of this type of fishing. Fewer and fewer tuna are caught, due to competition from large shipping companies which use big boats linked to aircraft with radar equipment. The enormous tuna processing plants which were in operation until the fifties have now been abandoned. All that is left of the island's wonderful preserving tradition is a small artisan company which produces botargo but has problems sourcing its raw materials in situ: the small number of tuna caught in Favignana – less than 100 a year – compared to the tens of thousands in the 19th century – are in fact sold and processed on the mainland. There are a number of varieties of fresh tuna, and blue fin is undoubtedly the most prized. Tuna preserved in oil varies in terms of the type of cooking, the oil used, the cut, the processing and so on. The most prized cuts are the belly (ventresca) and tarantello, rare and very costly. Then there is tuna botargo, usually darker and more sea-flavored than mullet botargo. Favignana botargo is outstanding in quality: with light notes of sea and salted anchovy, the saltiness is softened by the texture and length of the raw material. Tuna can be eaten fresh, but is ideal for preserving in oil. The dried, salted belly and guts can be roasted, the offal preserved in salt. Salt and pepper is added to the entrails to make a kind of sausage called ficazze, while dried botargo can be sliced and eaten, or grated, above all as a topping for pasta dishes. The Presidium wants to help those still left on the island, keeping the preserving tradition going, and encouraging other producers. The aim is to be able to process locally-caught tuna on the island.

PRODUCTION AREA
Island of Favignana, province of Trapani, Sicily

PRESIDIUM COORDINATOR
Franco Saccà
tel. +39 0923559490
francosac@libero.it

PRESIDIUM SUPPORTED BY
Sicily Regional Authority, department of Agriculture and Forestry

Ferrandina Baked Olive

Each year in December the majatica olive season gets underway and proceeds for two months. Grown in Vulture, in the lowlands of the Agri valley and on the hills around Matera, the olives are quite large. The stone is small in relation to the pulp, which makes the olive excellent for producing oil and for the traditional baking. The baked olives are particularly good when eaten alone, seasoned with extra virgin olive oil, pieces of fresh garlic and lemon and orange zest, but they also go very well with local salamis and aged pecorinos or when used in more complicated dishes such as white squash soup or stewed codfish. We know that these olives have been processed at Ferrandina since the 18th century. Today they are still prepared in the traditional way, which involves initial scalding for a few minutes in water at 90°C, then salting for a brief period of time. Then the partially dehydrated olives are placed on racks and 'baked' in special driers, where temperatures reach about 50°C. From 1910 they were no longer baked in wood fires but placed in hot air driers instead: these originally came from Germany and were later built in Naples according to the German model. The change in the processing technique has not compromised the original quality of the product. This method continues to bring out the natural goodness of the olive and, at the same time, its characteristic sweetness. It is likely that not all of the baked olives on the market are majatica as tradition would have it. So the Presidium intends to revive one of the most typical products of Basilicata, processed according to a recipe handed down for generations. The producers taking part in the project undertake to follow a strict protocol to ensure, first and foremost, that only the majatica olive is used.

PRODUCTION AREA
Accettura, Aliano, Cirigliano, Ferrandina, Gorgoglione, Salandra, San Mauro Forte and Stigliano, province of Matera, Basilicata

PRESIDIUM COORDINATOR
Angela Ciliberti
tel. +39 0835675270
info@lemacine.com

PRESIDIUM SUPPORTED BY
Gal Le Macine

Fiore Sardo
Shepherds' Cheese

Fiore sardo was the cheese most produced on the island until industrial dairy production took over from the shepherds and the most produced cheese in Sardinia became Pecorino romano. The name *fiore* – flower – is said to derive from the historic use of the thistle as rennet, or according to another version, from the fact that the pear or chestnut wood molds used in production had a flower carved on the bottom. It is a noble, ancient cheese with a strong personality, which may at times have an old-fashioned bitterness about it, especially when very mature. The traditional production method dates back to the dawn of civilization. Full-fat raw milk from Sardinian sheep is taken when just milked and placed in copper pots to coagulate at an average temperature of 32-35°C, using lamb rennet. After 20-30 minutes, depending on the season, the curd is broken into small pieces, about the size of a grain of rice, and left to settle on the bottom. Then without any type of cooking, this is patiently gathered from the bottom of the pot and placed in the characteristic cone-shaped molds known as *pischeddas*. The shepherds press the molds and shake them to remove as much whey as possible. When they are nice and firm, they are taken out and left to rest, then passed in brine. Then they are placed on reed mats, *sa cannizza*, by the fire and smoked for around two weeks. They are aged for a number of months in fresh, dry rooms. The Presidium was set up to safeguard the shepherds' production concerns in a number of small towns in the Barbagia area. Here artisan dairy production is still carried out by around 30 livestock farmers, mainly breeders of Sardinian sheep, who produce a few dozen quintals of raw full-fat milk pecorino cheese with home-made rennet, without the use of powdered cultures. The cheeses are given a natural smear coating, achieved by greasing the moulds with olive oil.

PRODUCTION AREA
A number of villages in the Barbagia area, province of Nuoro, Sardinia

PRESIDIUM COORDINATORS
Gianfranco Sotgiu
tel. +39 078436621
gfsotgiu@tiscali.it
Francesco Rubanu
tel. +39 0784529043
fioresardo-d.o.p.@tiscali.it

PRESIDIUM SUPPORTED BY
Gal Barbagia and Mandrolisai

Formadi Frant

In Carnia, the habit of never wasting anything that could be useful is a response to the extreme poverty and isolation of its valleys, which remain one of the most pristine natural environments in the Alpine chain. Without doubt, Formadi frant cheese is one of the symbols of this custom of salvaging mountain cheeses that were flawed or could not be aged because they were swollen or had cracked crusts. Nothing could be wasted in a farming civilization where everything was the fruit of sacrifice, let alone the cheeses made with milk from cows that grazed in the pastures; milk that imparted the aroma of the hundreds of wild grasses present in the forage. All of the imperfect cheese forms were gathered together, the fresh ones crumbled into small pieces and the more aged cheeses grated. Everything was blended with milk, top cream and salt and pepper until a homogenous mixture was obtained, which was then placed in the forms used to make Latteria cheese. The result was a particular product that varied from artisan to artisan and combined the mellowness and roundness of the cream with the fragrance and stronger flavors of the more or less aged mountain cheeses. Historically made only for home consumption, Formadi frant is still prepared in the same way today and is one of the most genuine and qualitatively excellent expressions of the farmer's art of reusing food, common to many Italian alpine areas. The Presidium was set up to protect this local tradition and motivate producers to continue it by linking it to mountain production in the Carnia area and the exclusive use of raw milk cheeses. This raises the profile of the artisan product and protects it from the attempts to imitate it with low quality cheeses often made with pasteurized milk not locally produced.

PRODUCTION AREA
Carnia, province of Udine, Friuli Venezia Giulia

PRESIDIUM COORDINATOR
Laura Rebagliati
tel. +39 3493526994
lreba@libero.it

Garbagna Bella Cherry

Bella di Garbagna, sweet and crunchy, is the classic cherry used in spirits, because it remains compact and tasty. It is ideal for *boeri* (chocolates filled with cherry and liqueur) or for making jams and liqueurs, while mixed with cinnamon or cloves, it is an unusual sauce to serve with meat. It has a brilliant deep red color, and a medium-long stalk; the trees are tall and vigorous, meaning the cherries have to be picked by had. Traditionally large amounts of different varieties of cherries were cultivated in Garbagna: Pistoia, Grisone and Bella. Once upon a time the entire valley was covered with cherry trees and in May, people used to enjoy walks under the trees in blossom. At the beginning of June the families got organized for the harvest: the youngest climbed up the trees, while the older held the rung ladders. Immediately on the ground the best cherries were selected and placed in low trays, which held five kilos of fruit at most. However, in the 80s the production of Bella cherries fell drastically from the thousands of quintals that were harvested every year down to just 40 quintals in the best seasons. This is due to the better resistance of other varieties to the damp climate, which split the Bella meaning they could not be used in confectionery, as whole, perfect cherries were needed. At the moment confectionery and chocolate industries mainly use the Vignola cherries, which is a more productive variety coming from the Emilia region. In Volpedo, a town close to Val Grue, there are the largest sellers and packers of fruit and all the local harvest goes to their wholesale warehouses irrespective of the type: no special value is granted to the Bella. However, the artisan confectioners of the past used to prefer them, and the Presidium unites the growers of Garbagna cherries and certain transformers who use them with excellent results.

PRODUCTION AREA
Garbagna and valley Grue, province of Alessandria, Piedmont

PRESIDIUM COORDINATORS
Nicola Piccinini
tel. +39 368917996 - 3389992833
nicola.piccinini@libero.it
Massimo Pisacco
tel. +39 3384392377
massimopisacco@tiscali.it

PRESIDIUM SUPPORTED BY
Curone, Grue and Ossona valleys
Mountain Community Commune of Garbagna

Garfagnana Biroldo

Biroldo, buristo, mallegato: three names from different parts of Tuscany for different recipes for sanguinaccio, a sort of black pudding made of offal and blood, with various seasonings, which is eaten cooked. The first term, which corresponds to the Ligurian dialect term berodo, could derive from the Latin bi(s)rotulus, meaning a roll of sausage. In the Serchio valley, biroldo is traditionally prepared by women from the head of the pig, with the addition of the heart and tongue, which are leaner and make the finished product softer. It is boiled for three hours, carefully boned and a small quantity of blood is added, with salt, pepper and other spices (the type and doses vary according to the tastes and habits of each family): nutmeg, cloves, cinnamon, anis, wild fennel, and sometimes a little garlic, but not the pine nuts which are used in the biroldo made in Lucca. The mixture is stuffed into the stomach of the pig and boiled for another three hours; then it has to cool at room temperature under a weight so that some of the fat runs out. Once there were endless varieties and every family was proud of the secret ingredient that made theirs unique. The sausage is eaten within 15 days, cut into slices half an inch thick. It is soft on the tongue and has a perfectly balanced flavor: the blood and the spices do not hide the taste of the lean meat of the pig's head, but give this rustic sausage a delicate, persistent aroma. It is best eaten with the typical bread of Garfagnana, made of chestnuts or potatoes. The Presidium has brought together the few remaining producers and intends to help them to promote biroldo outside the prevalently local market and consumption.

PRODUCTION AREA
Communes in the Garfagnana district and the Serchio valley, province of Lucca, Tuscany

PRESIDIUM COORDINATORS
Andrea Bertucci
tel. +39 058362192
andreabertucci1@virgilio.it
Luigi Angelini
tel. +39 0583666101

PRESIDIUM SUPPORTED BY
Garfagnana Gal, Garfagnana Mountain Community,
Media Valle del Serchio Mountain Community

Garfagnana Potato Bread

The tradition of making potato bread is very old and was widespread throughout continental Europe, especially in the years when the cereal harvest was meager. In Italy, the tradition is still alive today, particularly in the mountainous region of Garfagnana, surrounded by the Apuan Alps and the northern Apennines where the Serchio River flows. Known locally as garfagnino, it is made in the homes and can also be found in certain bakeries. The locally grown potatoes make the bread much softer and more flavorful than common Tuscan bread. Those cultivated at about 1,200 meters of altitude in the highest fields of Metello and Dalli (two hamlets of Sillano) are excellent. The dough consists of wheat flour, a little bran of durum wheat and tritello (cruschello), boiled and mashed potatoes (15%), coarse grains of sea salt, and mother yeast (plus a pinch of brewer's yeast to reduce the acidity). The dough is cut up and shaped into oval loaves weighing one or two kilos. Sprinkled with corn flour, they bake for about half an hour in an oven stoked with cerro hawthorn wood. Thanks to the natural humidity of the tubers, the Garfagnana potato bread keeps well for a few days. Curiously, it does not have a strong aroma or taste of potato. The large loaves, cut in slices, are an excellent accompaniment to the cured pork meats of the Garfagnana region (biroldo, mondio-

la, lard, pancetta), almost all very savory according to Tuscan tradition. The Presidium was formed because this bread has strong ties to local farm products like potatoes and wheat, and it is still possible to reconstruct a production chain in Garfagnana that joins the farms, stone mills and wood-fired ovens.

PRODUCTION AREA
Garfagnana, province of Lucca, Tuscany

PRESIDIUM COORDINATOR
Giordano Andreucci
tel. +39 3358258803
slowfoodgarfagnana@libero.it

PRESIDIUM SUPPORTED BY
Garfagnana Mountain Community

Gargano Citrus Fruits

With the exception of Gargano, there are no citrus fruits along the Adriatic coast. The citrus orchards, with their biodiversity of fruit – melangolo dolce, arancia bionda, limoncella, duretta and feminello – were already a characteristic feature of the Gargano coast in the 19th century, when the market and exporting were quite active. And even today they represent the cultural identity of many of the towns in the region. Rodi is still the town of lemons; Vico and Ischitella are still known for their oranges. In 1870, the uneven and difficult terrain here was cultivated with as many as 804 hectares of fruit orchards, producing about 150,000 quintals of citrus fruit annually. Until the depression in the early to mid-20th century that is. That was when the local farming economy collapsed people because began leaving the countryside or the land was and used for other purposes. The orchards, known as giardini in these parts, are located near the house and protected from the wind by cane, holm-oak or laurel fences and from the sea by dry stone walls. Irrigation is made possible by little canals carrying spring waters. Fragrant and juicy, the citrus fruits ripen all year: at Christmas, the seedless durette orange with the firm and crunchy pulp; from April to May, the bionda oranges, which remain sweet on the tree until September; in June, the limoncello lemons. The red melangolo

dolce (the best for duck with oranges) is a sweet-sour, medium sized orange with a very thin peel, crunchy pulp and little juice. The femminello is the oldest Italian lemon and in Gargano three types are cultivated: thin skin, seedless, and oval. The Gargano citrus fruits are used for making excellent marmalades, candied fruit and limoncello liqueurs. The Presidium has promoted a consortium to promote and protect the Gargano citrus fruits, which are now sold throughout Italy, fresh and in an interesting range of processed by-products.

PRODUCTION AREA
Vico del Gargano, Ischitella, Rodi Garganico, province of Foggia, Puglia

PRESIDIUM COORDINATOR
Alfredo Ricucci
tel. +39 0884966229
azagr.ricucci@tiscalinet.it

PRESIDIUM SUPPORTED BY
Gargano National Park

Gargano Goat

The Gargano Goat (*razza nustrala* in local dialect) is a very old indigenous breed native to the promontory of the same name, an area where livestock breeding has always played a fundamental role in the economy. Despite the rusticity and adaptability of this breed which is perfectly suited to the soil and climatic conditions of the Gargano area, there has been a dramatic reduction in its numbers. Raised in the wild for its meat, as well as its milk, it can be recognized on sight: long, smooth, jet-black hair, tuft of hair on the head and long beard under the chin, the horn slightly flattened at the side, twisted and diverging at points in an arc shape. Traditionally the milk from the Gargano Goat has been used to produce particular types of cheese: Canestrato, which according to the aging can be eaten fresh or grated, and Cacioricotta. The forms of Canestrato are not usually very large because the goats produce a limited quantity of milk. It has a brown crust and a straw-colored crumbly paste that has a strong aroma of grasses and dried fruit and a flavor that becomes more aromatic and piquant with age. Cacioricotta, on the other hand, was always produced in small quantities and used all of the milk proteins, including those of the ricotta. This cheese was historically tied to the more remote regions where the goat was called – not by chance – the poor man's cow. In these areas of transhumant shepherding food had to be preserved for the winter months. And the Gargano Goat was used to produce both cheese and *muscisca*, from the Arabic word *mosammed*, meaning hard thing; lean goat meat that had been deboned, cut into pieces and then salted and seasoned with wild fennel and hot red pepper before being left to dry in the open air.

PRODUZIONE AREA
Gargano promontory, province of Foggia, Puglia

PRESIDIUM COORDINATOR
Giuseppe Bramante
tel. +39 0882456288
giuseppebramante@tiscali.it

Gargano Podolica Cow

It appears to be a direct descendant of Bos primigenius, the wild bison from Asia, which probably arrived in Italy in two waves: the first following the Indo-European migration from central-west Asia and the second with the Barbarian invasions of the late Roman Empire. We do know that as early as the 5th century AD it was widespread throughout the Italian peninsula, from Istria to the tip of Calabria. It was particularly successful in Puglia (hence the name for Puglia beef), and especially in Gargano. This hardy, adaptable and disease-resistant breed has always been an important resource as a work animal. The Podolica is raised in the wild and not only provides very aromatic milk, but also healthy, flavorful meat rich in mineral salts. But this beef is not easy for the modern consumer because it does not conform to the usual esthetic canons: the fat is yellow (the animals graze on grasses filled with carotene, a substance not found in feeds and silage), the meat more fibrous, the flavor more distinctive and strong. All of these factors have caused the breed to be limited to only certain regions in the south (Puglia, Campania, Basilicata, Calabria), where it is usually a crossbreed, while in the past it was very common throughout all of central and southern Italy. The meat from the podolica cow must hang for a little longer after butchering, a procedure that a beef market of mainly young animals no longer makes necessary. Only an expert butcher can judge how much time the meat needs to age and how to suggest to consumers the cuts best suited to various preparations, especially those requiring long cooking. The Biogargano Association, of which the Orchidea Agro-animal Husbandry Consortium is a member, was founded in February 2001 to promote the meat from this breed.

PRODUCTION AREA
Gargano promontory, province of Foggia, Puglia

PRESIDIUM COORDINATOR
Giuseppe Bramante
tel. +39 0882456288
giuseppebramante@tiscali.it

PRESIDIUM SUPPORTED BY
Gargano National Park

Gargano Podolico Caciocavallo

It is probably one of the most representative cheeses of the old Capitanata, now the province of Foggia. Its goodness depends on the use of cow's milk from the podolica breed, which are distinguished by their long dignified horns, grey coat, great adaptability, rusticity and resistance to diseases. The milk from this cow is quite rare and only produced at certain times of the year however, so it is easy to understand how this breed that was once very common in Italy is confined to just a few areas of the South by now, where pastures are sparse and water is scarce. For this reason Podolico Caciocavallo is only produced for home consumption or a local market. This soft cream colored cheese has a sweet taste and a delicate aroma. It is made by heating the milk to 37°C and after one half hour breaking up the curd into grains the size of rice and then placing it in a tub containing whey to ripen. After this phase it is drained on an inclined wooden table for a variable period of time. Then it is cut into slices, put into boiling water and molded until it is shaped like a rounded flask with a head. At this point it is plunged into cold water and then put in brine. The cheese is aged in natural caves or in cellars with a certain degree of humidity for a few months to three years (sometimes as many as 8-10). During this time the Caciocavallo takes on a straw-yellow to ochre color and gradually stronger and tangier taste. This table cheese ages very well, and indeed it is only with time that it assumes those hints of freshly mown grass, bitter flowers, vanilla and spices that make it so distinctive. The Presidium wants to boost the production of podolica milk and cheese by reopening the traditional aging rooms and particularly the natural caves, which ensure better flavor and aroma.

PRODUCTION AREA
Gargano promontory, province of Foggia, Puglia

PRESIDIUM COORDINATOR
Giuseppe Bramante
tel. +39 0882456288
giuseppebramante@tiscali.it

PRESIDIUM SUPPORTED BY
Gargano National Park

Gavi Testa in Cassetta

A very old and elaborate recipe, *testa in cassetta* is a traditional cured meat that was 'studied' by farmers to preserve and make appetizing those parts of the pig left over after making prosciutto, coppe and salami. Prepared with both pork and beef, Gavi testa in cassetta is lean and delicate. Made only in the winter, it takes its name from the box (cassetta) in cui si poneva. It is an excellent appetizer when very thinly sliced and served cold; a main course when cut in thicker slices, heated and served with baked onions. The Gavi butchers all have their own recipe and the delicate flavor comes from the seasonings and the use of choice and less noble cuts of beef. In addition to the pig's head they make use of tongue, shin, and beef heart, considered essential for brightening up the color of the slice. The various cuts are cooked for a long time in salted water and then boned and coarsely chopped with a knife. The head, or *maschietta*, is boiled along with the other cuts, but minced instead with a crescent-shaped chopping knife until it becomes a semi-liquid mixture to which a little cooking broth is added. The other meat is then added to this 'purée' along with a blend of salt, pepper, cinnamon, coriander, cloves, nutmeg, hot pepper, pine nuts and a drop of rum. While the mixture is still hot it must be carefully stuffed into a cow's intestine, also called *mascone*. Once prepared, the testa is placed in a very cold room for one day. Some leave it outside for one night with a weight on top to give it the characteristic flat shape and make it more compact. At this point the *testa in cassetta* is ready to be eaten. The Presidium starts from a single producer who still makes it the way his grandparents did, without using even a gram of nitrates or nitrates.

PRODUCTION AREA
Gavi, province of Alessandria, Piedmont

PRESIDIUM COORDINATOR
Giovanni Norese
tel. +39 014379332 - 3355734472
gnorese@idp.it

Gioi Soppressata

Written documents show that this soppressata was produced as early as the 11th century. It is the only 'larded' cured meat made in Campania, though the technique is common in Abruzzo. It takes its name from the town of Gioi, a few miles from the Tyrrhenian coast, about 600 meters above sea level, but it is also produced in other towns in the neighborhood. It is similar shape to a small *paesana*, reddish brown in color and very aromatic, but the mineral and smoky overtones must not drown spicy musky aromas. It has a persistent, rich taste, with a final nuance of chestnut. Production is concentrated in the Winter. It is prepared with the fillet, leg and shoulder of pigs reared in a natural and semi-natural state, and fed naturally with acorns, chestnuts and leftovers from the kitchen. The sinews and cartilage are removed and the meat is chopped with a knife, seasoned with salt, pepper and, in some cases, chili and wild fennel, kneading it well by hand to amalgamate the ingredients. It is left to rest for about ten hours and then stuffed into gut, added a fillet of lardo at the center to keep the mixture moist. And this point it is sometimes smoked over a wood fire, and then left to age in a room with little ventilation. Gioi soppressata has the shape of a cottage loaf divided into two, and the reddish color of the skin and the meat is made even more intense by the contrast with the marbled white of the lardo inside. It can be preserved in olive oil or shortening so that it stays fresh all summer, and is excellent as a starter or a snack. Unfortunately it is produced almost entirely in the home. This is why the Presidium has been created, to safeguard what could become an important resource for the territory.

PRODUCTION AREA
Cardile, Gioi, Gorga, Orria, Piano Vetrale, Salento and Stio province of Salerno, Campania

PRESIDIUM COORDINATOR
Vito Puglia
tel. +39 3298321284
vito.puglia@fastwebnet.it

PRESIDIUM SUPPORTED BY
Cilento e Vallo di Diano National Park

Girgentana Goat

Typical of Girgenti, ancient Agrigento, this medium-size goat has a long, thick white fleece that is speckled with brown on the head and sometimes the neck. Locally it is known as *'nturcina*, meaning twisted, because of the spiral or corkscrewed horn, which in the males can be as long as 70 centimeters. It is also distinctive because of the shock of hair that covers the forehead (except in the billy goat) and the little beard. Native to Asia, it was introduced in Italy by some of the Greek colonies around 700 BC (or according to another theory by the Arabs in 800 AD). The breed gradually disappeared, however, even though it produced top quality milk, which was sold house to house in the 1930s and '40s by shepherds who milked the goats at the door. Often raised in the natural state, it grazed freely in the pastures by day and was sheltered in the stable at night, feeding on forage integrated with broad beans, barley, oatmeal and carob. The low profitability of the goat farms and strong competition from pasteurized, heat-treated milk are some of the factors responsible for the decline of the breed. With milk from the Girgentana the Presidium has started producing goat's cheeses (with calf, kid and wild artichoke rennet), Caciotta cheeses, fresh or briefly aged in ashes, and fresh and baked ricotta. It has also revived the production of *tuma ammucchiata*, 'hidden toma', so-called on account of the old custom of aging the cheese in crevices in gypsum or stone walls, safe from any possible thieves. The Presidium is working to identify and establish a top quality Girgentana cheese to be used in the finest restaurants, restore dignity and economic viability to the breeders and increase the goat herds.

PRODUCTION AREA
Provinces of Agrigento, Caltanissetta, Catania, Enna, Messina and Palermo, Sicily

PRESIDIUM COORDINATORS
Pippo Privitera
tel. +39 3358455507
pippopri@tin.it
Ignazio Vassallo
tel. +39 0922771681
i.vassallo@tin.it

PRESIDIUM SUPPORTED BY
Sicily Regional Authority department of Agriculture and Forestry, CoRFiLac

Goose in Onto

This is one of the symbolic Veneto dishes - a conserve prepared in the past in country homes using goose breasts and quarters that, after resting in salt for some days, were placed in the *onto* or *pignatto*, a terracotta or glass cooking vessel, alternating pieces of meat with melted goose fat and bay leaves. The jar was closed with a final layer of fat and then perfectly sealed. The meat therefore kept throughout Winter – and even for a couple of years – and was then enjoyed during the spring festivals, at Easter and on St. Mark's day: *risi* e *bisi* (rice and peas) with *oca in onto*. The geese were the gray or gray-white spotted species, once reared on every farm in the plains, only to be replaced by the white geese of Romagna. The local geese were used to make cured meats, hams, liver pâté and this conserve, that could be eaten much later. This was a winter production activity, not unlike the French confit, generally performed by the women-folk, when the first geese – the so-called 'pigs of the poor' – were slaughtered and eaten, usually for the festival of San Martino. The meat was usually slightly roasted before being placed under the fat. Today, *oca in onto* is almost impossible to find commercially and generally only made for family consumption. When needed, the amount of goose meat needed is taken, cooked in a casserole and served. It can be used as a condiment for pasta, as a main course or to flavor pasta and beans. It is excellent with horseradish sauce and a good glass of Veneto Cabernet Franc, with potatoes, *peperonata* (mixed capsicum peppers) and polenta. Today, *oca in onto* is mostly made from the meat of Romagna white geese. The traditional Veneto geese, in short, have more or less disappeared but there are some small breeders who are attempting to recover native breeds. The youngest producer belonging to the Presidium has more than 1,000 geese reared semi-free range on her farm holiday center.

PRODUCTION AREA
Provinces of Treviso, Padua and Vicenza, Veneto

PRESIDIUM COORDINATORS
Gino Bortoletto
tel. +39 3381313009
info@slowfoodtv.com
Manuela Tessari
tel. +39 0438933021
info@mondragon.it

PRESIDIUM SUPPORTED BY
Veneto Regional Authority - Veneto Agricoltura

Goyim Cuisine of the Tufa Towns

Pitigliano and Sorano are splendid little towns in the hinterland of the Maremma area built on tufa cliffs. Relative isolation and distance from power centers in the 16th century meant they became a refuge for Jews escaping the ghettos where they had been ordered to reside in Rome, Florence, Siena and Ancona. The Jewish community going back so many centuries has also left important marks on local gastronomy. Today, except for rare exceptions, there are no longer any kosher products: the Presidium decided to take its name from goyim (gentile, not Hebrew) cuisine precisely to emphasize this combination of Maremma and Israelite traditions. Attention focuses on two 'sweet' symbols of the Hebrew culinary culture: sfratto and bollo. Sfratto is a filled biscuit cut into slices: a fine short pastry shaped like a cigar (20-30 cm long by 3 cm in diameter), it has a rich filling of chopped walnuts, honey, orange peel, aniseed and nutmeg. Bollo is a risen sweetbread, round or eight-sided, soft and aromatized with aniseed. These two sweets are perhaps the most important products in the Hebrew tradition in Pitigliano and Sorano and symbolize the meeting between Hebrew and Maremma cooking. The presidiuim aims to expand its activities to include all such 'cross-breed' cuisines, which boast many dishes in the Maremma area: tortelli with sheep ricotta cheese sprinkled with sugar and cinnamon, pasta with chick peas, stuffed artichokes and lamb a' buglione or with an egg sauce. The Presidium has met producers to define the rules for making these two sweets: the raw materials must be local; bollo must be naturally risen.

In collaboration with producers and restaurateurs, initiatives are promoted to raise the profile of the local gastronomy and the extraordinary environmental significance of the 'tufa cities'.

PRODUCTION AREA
Pitigliano and Sorano, province of Grosseto, Tuscany

PRESIDIUM COORDINATORS
Giovanna Pizzinelli
tel. +39 3294284180
gio.pizzinelli@libero.it

PRESIDIUM SUPPORTED BY
Colline del Fiora Mountain Community, Grosseto Provincial Authority, Communes of Pitigliano and Sorano

Grappa Morlacco Cheese and Burlina Cow

The cattle grazed on the Grappa high plateau produce extraordinary milk, in turn valorized as 'morlacco' - also known in historic terms as 'murlak', 'murlaco' or 'burlacco'. A low-fat, uncooked cheese, it was once made from fully-skimmed milk – the cream was used to make butter then sold in the plains – and was the basic food of the mountain farmers from Morlakia, who settled in the area during the times of the Republic of Venice, eaten at lunch and dinner with polenta, boiled potatoes or home-made bread. The limited quantity of milk came from Burlina cattle, a native breed in the Veneto: small-built, with a black and white coat, they were well-suited to the poor pastures of the Grappa area. Today, very few remain – about 300 and almost all in the province of Treviso – but Morlacco cheese is still produced in Summer on the mountain cason (dairy farms), some of which date back to the 1600s. The skimmed milk of the evening is heated to 38-42°C together with the full-milk of the morning, liquid calf rennet is also added. The curds are then crumbled and transferred, after resting, to wickerwork baskets to drain the serum. The cheese forms are then salted several times a day 12 days, turning them over at every salting, and are sold 15 days after production (the cheese can also be matured for longer periods). Mild but not soft, clean to the cut yet moist, with a salty flavor that softens with aging to reveal hints of pasture and hazel - raw milk Morlacco from summer mountain pastures must be promoted and distinguished from the blander products of the dairies in plains made from pasteurized milk. The Presidium involving the mountain farmers and their summer produce on the pastures of Monte Grappa aims to safeguard not only such summer cheese of extraordinary quality but also the rearing of Burlina cattle, and has worked in recent years to produce forms of Morlacco matured for up to three months in specific facilities with exceptional results.

PRODUCTION AREA
Monte Grappa massif, provinces of Treviso, Belluno and Vicenza, Veneto

PRESIDIUM COORDINATORS
Gino Bortoletto
tel. +39 3381313009
info@slowfoodtv.com
Bruno Bernardi
tel. +39 0422422040
direzione@aprolav.it

PRESIDIUM SUPPORTED BY
Veneto Regional Authority, Veneto Agricoltura

Gressoney Toma

In the past, it was a valid substitute for meat; today, it is especially enjoyed as an end-of-meal cheese. Fine aromas of musk and mushroom, hints of pepper and vanilla stimulate the taste buds when this "toma" has been matured for at least three months, even if the ideal period is much longer - even up to 18 months. This product is the result of the typical processing techniques used for semi-fat cheese: the fresh milk of the evening is left to rest for 24 hours and then skimmed of the cream rising to the surface; it is then mixed with the morning milk, itself slightly skimmed after resting for 12 hours. It is then heated to 35°C; liquid calf rennet is added and left to coagulate. The curds are then finely broken up, removed and placed in wooden forms and salted (generally dry). As for other Alpine "toma" cheese made from uncooked milk, it is modeled in round forms but slightly smaller and higher: height varies between 5 and 12 centimeters, diameter between 20 and 30 centimeters and weight between 3 and 5 kilos. The body is slightly dimpled with a straw yellow color; the smooth, slightly greasy rind may have a reddish or gray-brown color depending on the curing. It is good fresh but becomes excellent after a year and, in any case, the processing technique is typical of mature cheese. The final production stage takes places in cellars at a temperature of 9°C and high humidity. For logistics reasons and convenience, today it is generally sold fresh. The Presidium was set up precisely to convince producers to extend aging and perhaps even to renovate abandoned, ancient cellars. Many producers, thanks to the help of local authorities, set up a consortium and defined production regulations. Maturing facilities will be soon be finalized thanks to renovation of several ancient cellars to be found in some of the towns in the area covered by the Presidium.

PRODUCTION AREA
Gressoney-Saint-Jean and Gressoney-La Trinité, Val d'Aosta

PRESIDIUM COORDINATOR
Valter Squinobal
tel. +39 0125355192 - 3297504447
comunegressoneystjean@tin.it

PRESIDIUM SUPPORTED BY
Aosta Valley Regional Authority, Communes
of Gressoney-Saint-Jean and Gressoney-La-Trinité

Grumolo delle Abbadesse Rice

In the 1500s, the nuns of the Benedictine Abbey of San Pietro in Vicenza undertook a series of structural works in the Grumolo delle Abbadesse area in order to grow rice. The small area midway between Vicenza and Padua saw land reclamation work, drying of pools and swamps, clearance of vegetation and the building of canals to carry water - many of which are still in use. The most important of these areas is Roggia Meneghina, from the River Tesina near Bolzano Vicentino as far as the center of the town. It was once the main route for large and small boats, hauled by horses along the embankments, carrying rice to the convent stores awaiting sale. Thanks rice growing, Grumolo witnessed decisive impact in economic and environmental terms, with both the water-channels and the splendid noble villas built in the surroundings by Venetian aristocrats, following donations by the Bishop of Vicenza of uncultivated land. And it was the only area in Vicenza to keep up rice-growing, overcoming all the recessions affecting this crop. The features of the local land and water ensure excellent quality vialone nano, a rice with tiny grains. Ideal for risotto, since it swells significantly and perfectly absorbs condiments, vialone is an essential ingredient in traditional dishes such as *risi e bisi* (rice and peas) or risotto with chicken livers. Today, land used to grow rice covers about 130 hectares - less than half the area in the 1600s. Yet the worst recession can in the last ten years: output has dropped since local vialone nano has a low yield and farmers began looking towards other crops. There are now only seven producers and three of these have very small husking facilities. The Presidium aims to safeguard and encourage the recovery of rice-growing in Grumolo by promoting a rice of excellent quality.

PRODUCTION AREA
Grumolo delle Abbadesse, province of Vicenza, Veneto

PRESIDIUM COORDINATORS
Gino Bortoletto
tel. +39 3381313009
info@slowfoodtv.com
Paolo Pavan
tel. +39 0444583792
riseria@libero.it

PRESIDIUM SUPPORTED BY
Veneto Regional Authority, Veneto Agricoltura

Heritage Canale Peach Varieties

In 1885 Ettore Ferrio, a farmer in the Roero, planted a few of the new American varieties of peach trees (Amsden and Brigg's Red May) at Vezza d'Alba, in Bricco San Martino. He wanted to find a crop to replace the vineyards decimated by marìn, peronospora and fillossera, diseases that had brought Italian and European wine producers to their knees. While the orchards appeared to be successful and the peaches gradually replaced the vines, a decline began in the 1930s, when peaches from Britain, Spain and other regions in Italy started to become popular. The local varieties, having a white pulp when there was a demand for yellow peaches and most of which ripened in July, causing a slump in prices were no longer suited to the market. The remaining orchards were converted to more productive varieties and the old types gradually disappeared. In terms of quality, some of the best peaches with white flesh are the botto (named for the first grower, Achille Botto) and the san pietro, which ripen in July. The yellow fleshed peaches include the giallo del porretto (with the distinctive yellow skin and pronounced center), which ripens between the end of July and mid-August and is excellent for preserving in syrup, and the krummel October, a late variety harvested at the end of September or early October. Five companies united in the Presidium have conserved several hundred trees of the botto, san pietro, giallo del porretto and krummel October peaches, which despite their intense aromatic fragrance and extraordinarily rich taste are penalized on today's market because of characteristics like a greenish skin, small size and irregular shape. The old peach varieties of the Roero fetch a good price with connoisseurs, but are little known outside the local market, and the Presidium wants to popularize them and see that they are cultivated once again.

PRODUCTION AREA
Corneliano d'Alba, Monteu Roero, Vezza d'Alba, province of Cuneo, Piedmont

PRESIDIUM COORDINATORS
Giorgio Reita
tel. +39 3477443729
giorgio.reita@unito.it
Giuseppe Destefanis
tel. +39 3406537917
dest@libero.it

Heritage Piedmontese Apple Varieties

Apples have been cultivated in Piedmont since time immemorial. As long ago as the Middle Ages, the monks were growing varieties that had survived the Barbarian invasions. Then in the 18th century, farmers from France crossed the Alps in search of work, bringing new grafts and growing techniques along with them. Almost all of the old varieties of apples keep very well and become more flavorful and aromatic with time. Among the Presidium varieties, the only exception is the Carla. This small, irregular, straw-yellow apple streaked with pink should be eaten fresh. The round, slightly flattened and rough Grigio Torriana is yellow with rust-colored spots. The Bura is related to the Grigio but more similar to the Renetta, both of which are excellent for baking. The Ronsé, an excellent eating apple, has a distinctive wine-red color, a shiny skin and is tangy, aromatic, and juicy. The somewhat flat, dark red Gamba Fina, with the white pulp, is delicate and sweet. The firm, red and compact Magnana has a tangy sweetness. The Dominici is large, somewhat oval-shaped, with a slightly rough skin and a crunchy cream-colored pulp. The Calvilla is the most aristocratic apple of all. Of the 50 types existing at the end of the 19th century only six have survived, the best of which are the white – soft and juicy, with a sweet and slightly tangy taste having a hint of raspberry – and the tangy sweet, crunchy and very flavorful winter red. In the early 20th century Piedmont still had thousands of varieties, but the expansion of industrial agriculture brought about a ruthless selection. Market preference is for foreign varieties that are larger, more attractive and more in keeping with modern tastes. But all is not lost. In marginal areas at the foot of the mountains in the Piedmont valleys, many of the old varieties have survived. Some of them can look forward to having a future – and not only as 'collector's items'– but because they are good, aromatic, rustic and hardy. The Presidium is endeavoring to get eight of these varieties back on the market.

PRODUCTION AREA

Bibiana, Pinerolo, Cavour, Bricherasio and Osasco, province of Turin, Verzuolo, Piasco and Caraglio, province of Cuneo, Piedmont

PRESIDIUM COORDINATORS

Franco Turaglio
tel. +39 0121394556 - 3294151775
info@lanicchia.net
Dario Martina
tel. +39 0121541010 012155620
malva@agribiocentro.org

PRESIDIUM SUPPORTED BY

Turin Provincial Authority

High Mountain Agordo Cheese

This semi-cooked cheese is typical of the Agordino area and is known locally as casél (nostrano-local) or formai (cheese). The area boasts cheese-making traditions going back many years: Canale d'Agordo, in short, saw Don Antonio Della Lucia in 1872 found of the first Italian co-operative dairy – a form of production he hoped would help the poorer shepherds. The dairy farmers-breeders go up to the mountain farms at various altitudes – Malga Ombreta at 1,904 meters, Malga Ciapela at 1,550 meters, both in the Rocca Pietore town council area – early in summer with Alpine Brown and Red Spotted cattle, to return to the valleys only in September. They always take with them a pair of donkeys and goats – that eat the poorest top growth of grass to reveal the superb pastures and their extraordinary variety of aromatic plants. Agordino is prepared by heating the partially skimmed evening milk mixed with the morning milk, adding rennet, to 33-36°C in tinned copper boilers. The curds are broken up twice: once roughly and then finely, after which the mass deposited on the base is removed, poured into metal dies and pressed. It is then processed with salt and water before beginning the maturing stage, that varies between two and eight months. On sale in the mountain farms, the cheese purchased at the end of Summer becomes increasingly harder as time goes by: the last 'forms' – stravecchi – are excellent as a condiment for polenta. Today,

the main priority is to safeguard production in these mountain pastures: the summer product is largely sold when the cheese is still rather fresh and has not had time to develop the best of its potential. The objective of the Presidium is to help producers mature their forms as long as possible and thus earn a higher and more remunerative price.

PRODUCTION AREA

Agordino, province of Belluno, Veneto

PRESIDIUM COORDINATORS

Fabio Pogacini
tel. +39 0437937149
pogacini.fabio@tiscalinet.it
Alessandro De Col
tel. +39 043762390
forestale.cma@agordino.bl.it

PRESIDIUM SUPPORTED BY

Veneto Regional Authority - Veneto Agricoltura, Agordina Mountain Community

High Mountain Honeys

The Alpine pastures are an essential resource for apiculture, and a number of excellent honeys are produced at altitudes above 1,200 meters. Rhododendron honey is white and intensely fragrant, delicate and not too sweet. Moreover, it is difficult to obtain because the flowers bloom for such a short time. Then there is the millefiori honey that can come from rhododendron, campanula, sainfoin, clover, raspberry, wild thyme and other varieties of mountain flora; a honey that varies from zone to zone and year to year. And finally the almost black honey (melata) made from the 'honeydew' resin of fir-tree, which tastes like caramel and has a slightly smoky aroma. It is made (though not every year) by bees that eat the resinous liquid from aphids that have fed on the sap from the white fir tree. Today the mountains are deserted and the pastures neglected. They now have fewer prized floral varieties, which have been choked out by wild bushes. On the other hand, the fact that the fields have been abandoned does have its positive side. The few roads are not heavily traveled by cars, so pollution is not a problem and the environment is uncontaminated. This means that there is a limited, if somewhat erratic, production of excellent honey that is very typical of the territory. The Presidium intends to promote the high mountain honeys and especially pure, virgin honey that has not been treated in any way. These honeys are excellent served with cheeses. The melata, which is not as sweet as nectar honeys, has an intense balsamic flavor, with hints of malt, and holds up well to medium-aged cheeses. Rhododendron honey and the millefiori, both very delicate and with a slight aroma reminiscent of marmalade made from small fruit, are better accompaniments to well-aged pecorinos and marbled cheeses that are not too strong. The Presidium unites about 60 beekeepers from Piedmont and Lombardy, who still take the apiaries to the high mountains. Making the honey is difficult and in a good season (only every four or five years) only a few hundred kilograms of honey is produced.

PRODUCTION AREA
Alpine chainabove 1,200 meters asl

PRESIDIUM COORDINATORS
Massimo Carpinteri
tel. +39 335205763
alberodellavitaapicoltur@tin.it
Armando Lazzati
tel. +39 038343858
info@apilombardia.it

PRESIDIUM SUPPORTED BY
Aspromiele, Unaapi (National Union of Italian Beekeepers), Apilombardia

Interdonato Lemon

This fruit came about by the grafting of a citron and a lemon of the ariddaru variety onto a bitter orange tree. It was invented by Giovanni Interdonato who, at the end of his career in Garibaldi'sd militia, decided to devote himself to his citrus groves in the Nisi valley, in Messina province. He obtained a highly scented, medium sized fruit, with a golden yellow peel, without bitter aftertastes and with a very fine zest, from which it gets its description as 'fine fruit'. The valley and the Ionian coast of Messina soon became well known for the lemon groves on the dry stone terraces with their delicate fruit, low in acid and rich in vitamins, that ripen between September and October. In the first of these months, it has no rivals, but then the market is invaded by Argentine, Spanish and Moroccan lemons which offer higher profit margins. The farms that grow them rarely have more than one hectare of surface area devoted to them and, since these are hilly areas, they don't always find life easy. In addition, the armacie or armacere that is, the low stonewalls that contain the soil of the terraces (the so-called gardens) on which the Interdonato lemon trees are cultivated need careful maintenance. In the 80s, this factor caused a commercial crisis that more than halved the crops. The Interdonato lemon is highly appreciated all over Europe and also much liked by the English in tea. Segments dusted in sugar and left to steep in the fridge for several hours, or flavored with oil, vinegar and salt, are excellent. Once upon a time, almost everyone managed to see their children through school thanks to income from the cota, that is, the lemon harvest, but today, this is no longer possible and in the coastal villages it is now only the old people who cultivate the 'fine fruit'. If this trend towards abandoning crop growing is not reversed in the next few years, the whole coast will be seriously affected by hydro-geological damage and desertification.

PRODUCTION AREA
Ionian coast from Messina to Letojanni, province of Messina, Sicily

PRESIDIUM COORDINATORS
Giorgio Foti
tel. +39 090810216
soat2@regione.sicilia.it
Attilio Interdonato
tel. +39 3807337406
attilio.interdonato@virgilio.it

PRESIDIUM SUPPORTED BY
Regional Office for Agriculture and Forestry 9th Regional department, Operational Unit no. 67 Peloritani District, Messina, Communes of Roccalumera, Alì, Nizza di Sicilia, Pagliara and Fiumedinisi

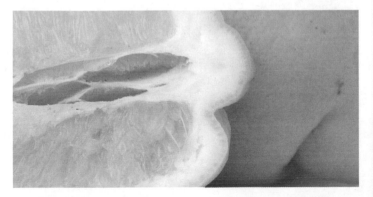

Ischia Cave Rabbit

There used to be two particular breeds raised in caves, the liparina (or liparota) and a' paregn, small and rustic, but these have now vanished due to years of crossbreeding with other populations. But even now the Presidium rabbits still live in caves dug out of the earth, up to 3 or 4 meters deep, from which branch out tunnels burrowed by the rabbits themselves. This activity and digging of warrens in an environment similar to their native habitat gives the rabbits' meat a firmer texture and better flavor than that from caged animals. The strong connection that the rabbits raised in this way have with local culture and customs, their role in communal society and their age-old symbolic value are evident from the fact that the rabbits are eaten particularly during holidays and for the traditional conigliata. This event used to be organized to inaugurate new domed houses and celebrate the collective effort of their construction, in particular the final phase when the roof was strengthened. This rabbit's innards are also eaten (the liver is particularly prized), but the ideal recipe for showing off the quality of the meat is coniglio all'ischitana. Pieces of the meat are browned together with a whole head of garlic in a traditional copper pan called a sartana. They are then transferred to a terracotta pot called a tiano, which evenly distributes the fire's heat and keeps the meat moist. White wine and tomatoes are added, as well as basil and parsley at the end of the cooking. Today there are seven active caves and each year they produce about 420 rabbits. The Presidium was born of the desire of a small group of farmers, Green Ground, to start from basics and rebuild a local production chain of traditionally raised rabbits. The starting point is the restoration of the old caves, many abandoned, which are spread around the island, of which there are estimated to be around a thousand. Studies are also being carried out on the best kind of diet for rabbits raised in this way.

PRODUCTION AREA
Island of Ischia, province of Naples, Campania

PRESIDIUM COORDINATORS
Riccardo and Silvia D'Ambra
tel. +39 081 902944
info@trattoriaalfocolare.it

PRESIDIUM SUPPORTED BY
Province of Naples

Lake Trasimeno Bean

This is a tiny bean with a oval shape and variable color: brown, black, salmon or white – the most common – and is also known as 'risina'. It has a soft, buttery and very flavorsome taste. It has always been grown in the area around Lake Trasimene. After being dried, this bean is excellent boiled and served with extra virgin olive oil (such as the superb oil from Polvese Island and the experimental olive groves in the middle of the lake). If eaten fresh (cornetto), it is best cooked with tomatoes and garlic. It was fairly common until the 1950s and then began to decline almost to the point of disappearing. Growing involves long, hard and still manual work, from sowing to harvesting and threshing. When they begin to ripen, the beans must be picked every day for a couple of weeks (since they ripen at different times). The plants are taken to the farmyard to be dried and are then threshed with forks and club; lastly, sieves are used to separate the seeds that are then placed in sacks. As people began to move away from the lakeside area, crops such as maize, sunflower and capsicum peppers consolidated their commercial value, while this bean was progressively forgotten. It is a truly very tiny reality: the agricultural companies are family owned and there are never more than three employees; overall production is seven or eight quintals of beans. The Presidium is working to promote the product so that it can be sold outside the local market (sales today are mostly direct) and thereby stimulate a small increase in production. The Slow Food Trasimeno Bean Presidium, in collaboration with the Monti del Trasimeno Mountain Community, local councils, producers, trade associations, the Agrarian Faculty of Perugia University and other authorities, has developed production regulations. In the meantime, a consortium of producers and a trademark have been established.

PRODUCTION AREA
Nine communes of the province of Perugia, Umbria

PRESIDIUM COORDINATOR
Sonia Chellini
tel. +39 0758296430
skelli@libero.it

PRESIDIUM SUPPORTED BY
Trasimeno Medio Tevere Mountain Community

Langa Sheep Tuma

At one time, farmers in the Upper Langa always raised a herd of a few dozen sheep on their farmsteads. With the milk from the sheep (and some goat's milk perhaps) they made the cheese that is typical of this part of Cuneo Province. Known in local Piedmontese dialect as toma 'd fe' or robiola, the cheese was put into wicker baskets and then sold at the markets in Murazzano, Alba, Bossolasco, Dogliani and Ceva. The milk traditionally used to make this cheese comes from the Langhe sheep, a breed having a rounded snout, long and slender limbs, white fleece and no horns. Once very common (more than 45,000 heads in 1950), today no more than 2,500 can be found on about sixty sheep farms in Piedmont and Liguria. The milk is heated to about 37°C and liquid calf's rennet is added. When the milk coagulates, the curd is broken and arranged in molds. The forms are turned over several times and then salted and placed in airy rooms where they are turned daily. The forms of soft, straw-white cheese, with a few eyes and no crust, are cylindrical in shape and weigh between 200-300 grams. The Tuma is ready for eating after ten days, but acquires a more complex taste and aroma after one month. It should not be confused with Murazzano cheese, which has the same origins but can contain up to 40% cow's milk. Toma prepared with milk from the Langa Sheep can also be bottled in olive oil (tome 'n burnìa in dialect), making it possible to eat the cheese all winter long. Forms that have aged at least one month and are then grated or crumbled and put in terracotta pots with a little grappa become bruss. The grappa causes the cheese to ferment again, making it creamy and piquant.

PRODUCTION AREA
Communes in the Upper Langa, province of Cuneo, Piedmont

PRESIDIUM COORDINATOR
Piercarlo Adami
tel. +39 3355757697
segreteriaonaf@libero.it

PRESIDIUM SUPPORTED BY
Mongia valleys, Cevetta and Langa Cebana Mountain Community

Late Harvest Leonforte Peach

Referred to as late because they are harvested in September, October and November, these peaches have always been grown in Leonforte, north-east of Enna. In June, when they are still green, they are wrapped, one by one, in parchment bags to protect them from the wind, hail and parasites. This means they can be left on the trees until they are perfectly ripe for picking. 'Bagging' the peaches takes a certain amount of practice and a lot of patience; the workers are paid a piecework rate: the fastest can bag up over 2,000 peaches. This is a unique technique for growing peaches and, although rather costly in economic terms, it does guarantee exceptional organoleptic quality. Even the harvest is labor-intensive and rather tricky: the fruit must be picked very carefully by slightly twisting the stalk, which must never be pulled off. Peach farmers in the area can offer a healthy and genuine product, which is completely free from pesticides, at a time of year when only imported peaches are normally available. While the rest of Italy has grown American varieties since the early 20th century and each year brings its new 'must-have' peaches, which are large and beautifully colored but lack any taste or scent, these late varieties of peach have survived in Leonforte, the outcome of natural crosses between old local cultivators. They are not particularly attractive – an intense yellow in color with slightly reddish streaks – but their scent is delicious. Their firm yellow pulp is sweet and uniquely flavored, reminiscent of candied fruit. They are delicious eaten fresh or in syrup; they can also be used to make wonderful juice, jam, sorbets and ice creams. These healthy, delicious peaches are barely known outside Sicily, but they could become an important asset for the revival of a town which, four or 500 years ago, was one of the island's most dynamic centers: this is why the Presidium was set up.

PRODUCTION AREA
Assoro, Calascibetta, Enna, Leonforte and Nissoria, province of Enna, Sicily

PRESIDIUM COORDINATOR
Salvatore Manna
tel. +39 0935904655 - 328 4206055 soat48@regione.sicilia.it

PRESIDIUM SUPPORTED BY
Sicily Regional Authority, department of Agriculture and Forestry

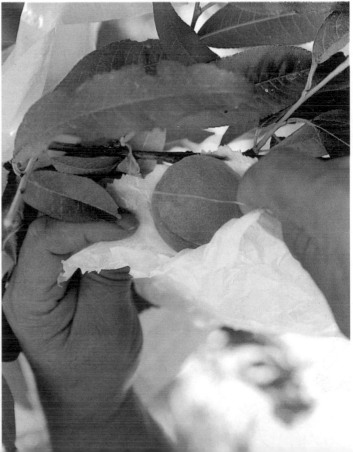

Leonforte Broad Bean

These broad beans were once highly popular and were grown in rotation with wheat; they enriched the soil with nitrogen and were a cornerstone in local gastronomic specialties. Cultivation today is still done entirely by hand, and is unfortunately very hard work and not sufficiently remunerative, so that fields of broad beans become fewer and fewer each year. The land is ploughed between November and December and the seeds are sown *a postarella* (in groups) and covered with soil. As soon as the shoots appear, the land is hoed to remove weeds and the earth is built up all around them. When the plants start to wilt they are cut and dried in small bundles, then beaten on a tarpaulin (once upon a time, they were trampled on using animals). To separate the *furba* (the remains of leaves and stems) from the seeds, they are tossed in the air with a pitchfork. The smaller beans are given to the animals and the larger ones are sold. They are delicious, they do not need a long soaking like other pulses, and they are easy to cook. As soon as they are harvested at the end of March, the green beans are steeped in salt with scallions and eaten with sheep's cheese (*favaiana e cipuddetti*) or they are cooked in *frittedda* that is, fried gently in extra virgin olive oil with bacon and onions. When they are dried, they are used in *pasta ccu' i favi a du' munni* and in *frascatula* (polenta with wild fennel and toasted broad bean and chick pea flours). Then there are *favi 'ngriddi, favi pizzicati, maccu*, and *favi vugghiuti* – broad beans boiled with herbs, flavorings and spices or stewed and flavored with wild herbs, depending on the recipe. And there are also *favi caliati* – dried broad beans roasted until they become reddish – to munch on every so often, like potato chips. The Presidium came into being to promote this area, a green oasis in the heart of the arid Enna countryside, through its key produce: broad beans and late peaches. A production protocol is currently being drawn up, and the aim for the near future is to establish a producers' consortium.

PRODUCTION AREA
Assoro, Calascibetta, Enna, Leonforte and Nissoria, province of Enna, Sicily

PRESIDIUM COORDINATOR
Salvatore Manna
tel. +39 0935904655
soat48@regione.sicilia.it

PRESIDIUM SUPPORTED BY
Sicily Regional Authority, department of Agriculture and Forestry

Lodi Pannerone

Once known as White Gorgonzola, though unrelated to the famous blue, it owes its name to the term panéra (cream in Lodi dialect) because it is made with whole milk. Before World War I this cheese was quite common throughout lower Lombardy (the communes near Lodi, particularly Casalpusterlengo, were the main producers), but today is rather difficult to find. Soft and rich, the cylindrical forms weigh from 12-13 kilos and are made with raw milk without any additives or salt, which is why the taste and aroma are never quite the same. When heated to 28-32° C, the milk coagulates very quickly. The curd is broken up into fine pieces and placed in ramin (basins) to start eliminating the whey. The curd is then removed with patte (cheesecloth), crumbled with the hands and placed in the molds for four or five days to finish draining. Once extracted, the forms are wrapped in special paper that is tightened with strips of wood and are left in stufatura (in a warm environment) to dry for one more day. They continue ripening at room temperature for 24-48 hours and then in the refrigerator (4-6°C) for 7-8 days. The final product has a thin, straw-yellow crust, cream colored center filled with eyes, and a sweet taste with just a hint of bitterness, the result of bacterial action due to the absence of salt. The cheese goes very well with uncommon accompaniments like fruit pickles, preserves, grapes, honey, wine distillates, etc. The Presidium started out with the only Pannerone producer remaining in the Lodi area, and has tried to involve other small businesses by promoting the product and defining a production protocol. Broadening the productive base and preserving the traditional methods is in fact the only way to ensure a future for this fine example of cheesemaking art.

PRODUCTION AREA
Lodi and surrounding towns, province of Lodi, Lombardy

PRESIDIUM COORDINATOR
Stefano Rancati
tel. +39 0371442461
stefano.rancati@provincia.lodi.it

PRESIDIUM SUPPORTED BY
Lodi Provincial Authority, Lodi Chamber of Commerce, Industry, Crafts and Agriculture

Lonzino di Fico

This traditional Marche sweet is made in a few of the communes in the province of Ancona: Serra de' Conti, Montecarotto, Maiolati Spontini, Cupramontana, Staffolo, Castelplanio and Rosora. Firm and compact, with the appearance of a large golden brown sausage, it is traditionally sliced fairly thickly and served with a firm, medium ripe cheese or with sapa, a slow-cooked grape must. There used to be a great quantity of figs cultivated in the Marche countryside, and since they all ripened at once, at the end of summer just before the grape harvest, fig cakes were a way to conserve the fruit for as long as possible. Picked at the end of September, the dottati or brogiotti variety of figs were dried in the sun and then mixed with almonds, pieces of walnuts, star anise seeds and at times a little sapa or mistrà (anise seed liqueur). The mixture was then wrapped in fig leaves and tied together with strings of wool or twine. Prepared like this, the fig cakes kept until spring and were an excellent snack for the children and a pleasant way to top off holiday meals. Today they are also vacuum-packed to keep them fresh year round. The cakes maintain the aroma of ripe fruit, with an enveloping note of anise, and have a mellow and well-balanced taste. Unfortunately, the fig cake is becoming a rarity today and can only be found in certain specialty fruit shops. Being a traditional peasant dish, it risks disappearing like the very world that created it. To prevent it from becoming a gastronomic relic, the Presidium has united the last remaining artisan producers in an effort to promote the fig cakes in local restaurants and elsewhere. It is a way to encourage the cultivation of figs, especially those varieties the market rejects because they are less plentiful or too delicate, but which nevertheless constitute a great patrimony of biodiversity.

PRODUCTION AREA
Castelli di Jesi and Media Vallesina, province of Ancona, Marche

PRESIDIUM COORDINATOR
Gianfranco Mancini
tel. +39 3388169718
direzione@italcook.it

PRESIDIUM SUPPORTED BY
Assivip (Maiolati Spontini, Ancona, Marche, Italy)

Macagn

This round cheese, weighing between 1.7 and 2.3 kilos, 18-25 centimeters wide and 5.8 cm tall, has a thick, springy texture. Its white, straw-like color turn more and more golden as it matures. It presents a few holes too. The crust is thin and smooth of a color which varies from straw to gray, with yellow and even orangey hues. Produced with cold whole milk from mountain pastures, it is a typical mountain cheese, smaller than the Piedmontese toma. It is important to point out that it is produced with each milking, therefore, twice a day: this method comes from the need to use the milk at its natural temperature. For this reason, and also being a summer cheese, it has an unusual scent, releasing pasture and pleasant flowery smells. It is advised not to leave this cheese to mature too long. Ideally between three and five months. The name takes after the Monte Rosa Alp, north of Biella. Nowadays it is produced around Biella and in the Valsesia region, in the Vercelli Province, especially in the Cervo, Sessera and Sesia valleys. An effort is to be made in order to further increase the average quality of the product, exploiting the differences In production techniques or in the pastures, while eliminating excessive unevenness and production diversities. In order to maintain the tradition of the Macagn and to acknowledge the work of those who continue to produce it in spite of the difficulties, the Biella Valleys and Valsesia Association for the conservation and exploitation of the Macagn cheese, groups producers, affineurs, but also local authorities and supporters together. The association follows strict rules to ensure that the production chain is completely transparent.

PRODUCTION AREA
Central and Eastern Pre-Alpine mountain area around Biella, province of Biella; Valsesia mountain area, province of Vercelli, Piedmont

PRESIDIUM COORDINATOR
Giacomo Bergamo
tel. +39 015737773 – 3357227572
agr.cmvmosso@ptb.provincia.biella.it

PRESIDIUM SUPPORTED BY
Biella Provincial Authority, Prealpi Biellesi, Valle Mosso, Valle Sessera, Valle Cervo, La Bürsch and Valsesia Mountain Communities, Biella Valley and Valsesia Association for the conservation and exploitation of the Macagn

Madonie Manna

The cultivation of the floweringash (*Fraxinuso ornus*), or manna, was the main activity of families in the Madonie area up to the 1950s, when thousands of tons of it were exported or processed by manna sugar factories in Italy. Today, the heritage of ash groves in northwest Sicily has been reduced to around 250 hectares, located in the Madonie Park between the boroughs of Pollina and Castelbuono, and only a part of this is still productive. The manna, a natural sweetener with a low glucose and fructose content, is collected between July and the first ten days of September, and is obtained from cuts made in the bark of the tree trunks by the *'ntaccaluòri* (harvesters) with a *mannaruòlu*. A pale blue, resinous substance comes out of the cuts, and this, when exposed to the sun, condenses to form whitish, light, spongy stalactites. The manna that remains in the clefts is scraped with a rasula and the runny part is made to flow into a large prickly pear leaf. The harvest is generally carried out once a week, but more frequently if storms are forecast since the rain does not allow it to solidify. The manna scraped from the bark has to be purified, while the manna that runs down to make stalactites is very pure and it is this that the Presidium wants to support. Manna is used as a sweetener in confectionery, and also in a transformed state by the cosmetic and pharmaceutical industries because of its depurative, diuretic and laxative properties. Today, there are around 150 manna harvesters grouped into a public consortium, and almost all of them are elderly. Manna is the main source of income for only two of them. The cultivation of the manna ash must be preserved for the further reason that it has an important value for the environment – it is a factor in preventing the deterioration of the Madonie area – and for its historical worth: the ash-groves could, in fact, be seen as a sort of open-air museum. The Presidium has brought together several manna ash growers who have decided on self-regulation with the aim of improving harvesting techniques, increasing the high quality manna harvest, and guaranteeing a natural product to counter the many imitations.

PRODUCTION AREA
Castelbuono and Pollina, province of Palermo, Sicily

PRESIDIUM COORDINATORS
Franco Saccà
tel. +39 0923559490
francosac@libero.it
Giulio Gelardi
tel. +39 0921425206 – 3298851889 - 3471370516
mannagelardi@libero.it

PRESIDIUM SUPPORTED BY
Sicily Regional Authority, department
of Agriculture and Forestry

Madonie Provola

This is a classic cow's milk cheese of the 'pasta filata' or spun curd variety, still made using the original techniques by the cheesemakers of the Madonie, a group of mountains facing the sea and one of Italy's richest terrains in terms of its biodiversity. Its shape is reminiscent of the classic round straw-covered bottle – this Provola is a little stouter than the one from the Nebrodi mountains. It has a smooth, thin rind which is pale-yellow in color, and a soft, compact texture that is delicately sweet in flavor. Many of the cheesemakers still make it using the original techniques. The whole raw cow's milk is heated to a temperature of 37–38°C and then left to coagulate in a wooden tina using sheep rennet paste. Once they have reached the desired density, the curds are broken into nut-size pieces and left to stand for a variable length of time, before being washed with water or hot whey. The mass is then placed on a wooden table to dry and cut into thin slices which again have to be washed in water at a temperature of 85°C. At this point the curds are stretched by pulling them by hand and with the help of a paddle in order to make them more elastic. The small cheeses are then molded into rounded pear-shaped forms with a very short neck. They are tied together in pairs and hung over a pole to mature for at least 10-15 days in a cool and well-ventilated room. A mild smoked version is also made. Provola is excellent with the local bread made using durum wheat flour, baked using *lu criscenti* (sourdough) in a wood-fired oven; when it is fresh it has an invitingly fresh milky scent. The Presidium brings together the best local producers and works to improve and guarantee the traceability and outstanding quality of this product. Together with the projects dedicated to Madonie Manna and the Polizzi Badda Bean, its aim is to add value to the exceptional ingredients and food from the Madonie Regional Park.

PRODUCTION AREA
Madonie Massif, province of Palermo, Sicily

PRESIDIUM COORDINATORS
Franco Saccà
tel. +39 0923559490
francosac@libero.it
Michele Macaluso and Achille Virga
tel. +39 0921680350
soat52@regione.sicilia.it

PRESIDIUM SUPPORTED BY
Sicily Regional Authority, department of Agriculture and Forestry

Magghia Masculina

Anchovies are the main candidate for catching in the close-knit, one-centimeter square mesh of the approximately 300-metre-long trawler nets (or *menaidi*) that are lowered in April, just before dawn, from the little boats of the same name in the gulf of Catania, along the coast leading from Ognuna (a few kilometers south of Aci Trezza) to Brucoli, near Augusta. In this stretch of sea, part of which comes into the Cyclops Islands Nature Reserve, techniques still survive that have remained unchanged for centuries, such as fishing with trawler nets and preserving anchovies by salting. The fish remain imprisoned in the mesh of the nets – thus they get their name *da magghia* (from "maglia", meaning "mesh") - and the blood drains out naturally, making them more tasty and sought-after, with meat that is firmer, white and sweet. The *masculini* are the same as those caught in Liguria and by the trawlers of the Cilento coast. Those that do not make their way to the Piazza Pardo market (*'a Piscaria*) in Catania are preserved in salt by the fishermen's wives using a technique that is the same all over the Mediterranean. In order to make use of the heads and the small pieces of anchovy that remain caught up in the nets, these women prepare an absolutely unique preserve - one which originated by accident because of the fact that, initially, the fishermen ate these leftovers in their boats, since they were impossible to sell. So their wives poured what remained into *cugnitti* (small terracotta pitchers) or glass jars and covered it with olive oil. The result was – and still is – a delicious ingredient to be used as necessary for making sauces. There are around thirty families who gain their livelihoods from this ancient craft – a tiny group divided between the little ports of San Giovanni li Cuti, Ognuna and Aci Trezza, and a few *civitotu* (as the inhabitants of the Civita district of Catania are called) in the port of Catania. At the present time, salted *masculina 'a magghia* are not on sale, but they can still be sampled in a few Catania restaurants or in the larders of fishermen's families. The newly set up Presidium is trying to reorganize production and marketing of these anchovies.

PRODUCTION AREA
Gulf of Catania, Sicily

PRESIDIUM COORDINATORS
Pippo Privitera
tel. +39 3358455507
pippopri@tin.it
Gaetano Urzì
tel. +39 3339713831
cooperativadelgolfo@tin.it

PRESIDIUM SUPPORTED BY
Sicily Regional Authority, department of Agriculture and Forestry

Maiorchino Cheese

This is a great sheep's cheese, in the sense both of physical size and of quality: it weighs around 12-18 kilos and its organoleptic properties – butter and herbs, with apple and vanilla tones – intensify during the maturing process, which can go on for up to 24 months. It is cylindrical in form, with an amber-yellow rind that becomes brown when very mature, and is a compact, white cheese, tending to a straw-yellow color. Traditional folklore links its origin with the festival of the Maiorchina, a very ancient game that still survives in the Messina area at Basicò and Novara di Sicilia: this consists of a competition at Carnival time to make a mature, whole cheese roll down the slope of the main street in the village and arrive at the finishing line with the least number of pushes. The cheese is produced from April to mid-June with milk from animals raised on pasturelands rich in the wild forage plants of the Peloritani Mountains. When the sheep and goats have been milked, the milk is poured off (70 and 30%) into the *quarara* (a tin-plated copper boiler), and heated to 36°C: it is then left to rest with lamb or kid's rennet paste. When the curd has broken up into minute grains, the cheese is placed in moulds and the air bubbles that gradually form in the cheese are pricked with a *minacino* – an iron needle – and the surface of the cheese is then pressed gently with the hands. This slow, patient operation can last two hours and is repeated, if necessary, after a second cooking. The cheeses are laid on wooden shelves in cool, damp underground rooms built in stone, and they are dry-salted for 20-30 days. Finally, they are left to mature for up to 24 months. The Maiorchino is an unusual cheese that is in serious danger of becoming extinct. The production technique is, in fact, very complex, requiring time, experience and great care, and the maturation period is long and costly. Thanks to the Presidium, production of the cheese has started up again, in limited quantities for now but with great potential for development.

PRODUCTION AREA
Seven communes in the province of Messina, Sicily

PRESIDIUM COORDINATOR
Pippo Privitera
tel. +39 3358455507
pippopri@tin.it

PRESIDIUM SUPPORTED BY
Sicily Regional Authority, department
of Agriculture and Forestry

Malga Monte Veronese

Lessinia is the mountain area overlooking Verona; it is rich in pastures and boasts cheesemaking traditions going back many years, with production of dairy cheese made from milk already skimmed to make butter. One such semi-cooked cheese is made with partially skimmed mountain farm milk from several milkings (*de pi monte*) is 'monte Veronese di malga'. It is cylindrical, slightly convex with almost flat faces, weighing 6-9 kilos; it must be matured for at least 90 days, if used as a table cheese, or six months-two years for grating. It has a thin, straw yellow rind, an off-white color with occasional holes; taste becomes delicately spicy as the cheese is aged. In past centuries, the Lessini Mountains boasted more than one hundred summer farms, some of which built centuries ago by the Cimbri who, as cattle farmers, were expert cheesemakers. Today, there are no more than thirty, of which only two still have cheesemaking facilities producing cheese exclusively using milk from the surrounding pastures. The rest of the milk from the cattle grazing in the mountain pastures is taken to cheese producers lower down in the valleys and mixed with the milk from cattle in stalls. The Presidium was set up to safeguard production in these mountain farms and pastures, several of which still reflect the characteristic architecture of the Cimbri. The risk is not only the loss of a great cheese but also changes to the mountain eco-system. The first step was to ask cheese-makers to keep separate the milk from mountain farms and the milk from cattle reared in stalls. The producer consortium then developed a trademark with an 'M' (for *malga*, or mountain pasture) applied to the cheese forms made using mountain milk. Currently, four producers mark their cheese in conformity with Presidium regulations.

PRODUCTION AREA
Monti Lessini and Monte Baldo, province of Verona, Veneto

PRESIDIUM COORDINATORS
Marco Brogiotti
tel. +39 3356371073
slowfoodverona@libero.it
Paola Giagulli
tel. +39 0456199054
paola.giagulli@monteveronese.it

PRESIDIUM SUPPORTED BY
Veneto Regional Authority, Veneto Agricoltura

Mallegato

Fresh pig blood, diced lard, salt, nutmeg, cinnamon, pine nuts and sultanas: this is the classic recipe for Pisan mallegato, especially made around San Miniato. There is also the Volterra 'variant' - lard, spices and blood (not fresh, in this case, but boiled for a couple of hours) are also mixed with breadcrumbs softened in water and then squeezed. In both cases, the outer gut lining is tied very 'loosely', only slightly compressing the mixture, so that it withstands cooking by immersion in already hot water. Once a robust lunch for workers and craftsmen, particular the alabaster workers in Volterra, this 'loose *sanguinaccio*' (blood sausage) is very dark – almost black – and has a flavor that may seem rather unsuitable for today's palates: aromatic from the spices and sweet from the blood. Made from October to end-February, it is best eaten cold, cut into slices even two cm thick, or tossed in flour and pan-fried, accompanied by legumes or certain slightly bitteri herb-vegetables that offset the sweet taste of the blood and sultanas. Cut into thinner slices, it is excellent with scrambled egg on top. The classic 'pairing' with potatoes is now joined by a less conventional but equally successful match with Certaldo onions (another Slow Food Presidium) baked in ashes. The Presidium, first of all, had to identify a suitable technique for processing the blood. Thanks to the Public Abbatoir Consortium in San Miniato and the collaboration of veterinary surgeon Luca Pasqualetti, it finalized a system for direct jugular pick-up from pigs using a suction knife. The producers subsequently agreed and signed regulations covering this delicate procedure. The Presidium now intends to launch efforts to promote this, a very interesting gastronomic specialty that deserves to be known and appreciated even outside the local area.

PRODUCTION AREA
Province of Pisa, particularly around San Miniato and Volterra, Tuscany

PRESIDIUM COORDINATORS
Carlo Gazzarrini
tel. +39 057134497
red@leonet.it
Sergio Falaschi
tel. +39 057143190
info@sergiofalaschi.it

PRESIDIUM SUPPORTED BY
Pisa Provincial Authority, Commune of San Miniato, Upper Val Cecina Mountain Community

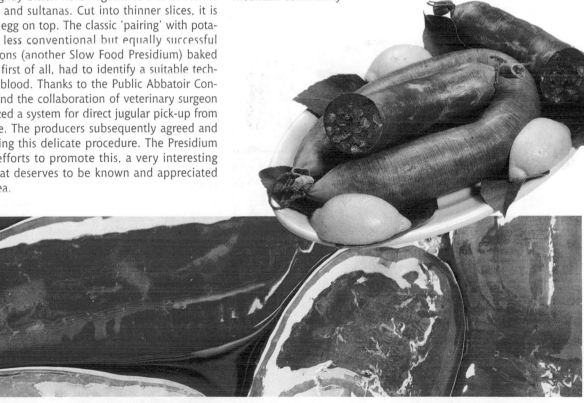

Mantuan Peasant Casalìn Salami

Casalìn, a traditional salami from the province of Mantua, is only made from the tender parts of the pig: the shoulder, loins, filets, and trimmed leg. Since the mixture must be soft and compact, without any hard parts, the muscles and nerves are not used. The meats are coarsely ground and then seasoned with salt, pepper and fresh garlic. The pork butchers from upper Mantua use all the parts, including ham and culatello, something considered a waste by those from the lower Mantuan region. The former also marinate the cloves of garlic in white wine and salt and then season the mixture with the infusion, which is why the sausage is less garlicky; the latter pound the garlic and then mix it into the meat. Everything is blended together, stuffed into a casing from the lower part of the pig's intestine (which is thicker and allows the mixture to withstand changes in temperature), and then tied by hand with string. There are also many other less important variations. The size of the pieces can change, the salami can vary in terms of length, diameter or grain, the peppercorns can be whole, broken or mixed, and the meat can be seasoned with grappa or Lambrusco, or with cloves or cinnamon. At the end of the aging period, which lasts from two to three months (5-6 if it weighs more than two kilos), the casalìn is a strawberry red color, soft and firm, and with a course grain and spots of white or pink fat. It owes its flavor to the damp air of the Po Valley and the harmless white and dove-gray mold that forms on the salami, which the *norcini* (meat curers) gently blow off from the surface. The Presidium plans to protect this very old product, made with pork from the pigs raised by the *norcini* themselves and the traditional methods for processing and aging it. It also wants to equip the processing plants and publicize this salami that has such a singular taste and aroma.

PRODUCTION AREA
Some communes in the province of Mantua, Lombardy

PRESIDIUM COORDINATORS
Gilberto Venturini
tel. +39 037647327
info@operaghiotta.com
Marco Boschetti
tel. +39 0376324889
info@agriturismomantova.it

PRESIDIUM SUPPORTED BY
Commune of Mantua, Banca Agricola Mantovana Gruppo Monte dei Paschi di Siena, ConfCooperative, Gazzetta di Mantova, Confederazione Italiana Agricoltori, Mantua Chamber of Commerce, Industry, Crafts and Agriculture, Consorzio Agrituristico Mantovano

Marceddì Arselle

The black clam (*Tapes decussatus*) is called *arsella* in Liguria and Sardinia. In the lagoons of Arborea, especially in those of Marceddì and Corru s'Ittiri – coastal pools between strips of sand which divide the sea from the mainland – these bivalvular mollusks live in numerous shoals, feeding on the plankton captured by aspiring through one of the two openings (siphons) which exit from the half-open valves. The *arselle* are 'sown' when they are small and grown freely, without providing food of any kind. They are distinguished from the Philippine clams, which have invaded the aquiculture systems and Italian markets, because they have separated siphons and valves with a particular stripe; the *cocciue pintade* are black and white, the *cocciue niedde* are totally black, and are considered the best. Mollusks of a different kind – *Cerastoderma edule* – less prized, have valves that are lighter, round and rough, or grey or black and slightly long. Until a few years ago there was a variety of larger-sized mollusks with an even better taste, the *Scrobicularia plana* (*cocciua lada*), but today it is almost disappeared. From May to August, the fishermen immerse themselves in the water up to their hips, equipped with only a special knife and a mirror, and extract the shells of the mollusks one by one from the seabeds. A highly selective fishing, which lasts a maximum of two to three hours and does not damage the seabed as no rakes or shovels are used as in other lagoons in Italy. The principal necessity of the fishermen is to defend the arselle from the numerous imitations on the market: the law also allows the Philippine clams cultivated in Italy to be called genuine. The fishermen of the Presidium are organizing themselves to package the Marceddì *arselle* with a label indicating the place and time of collection and, in perspective, they have set themselves the objective of opening a premises for retail and catering, to be managed independently.

PRODUCTION AREA
Lagoons of Marceddì and Corru s'Ittiri, commune of Terralba, province of Oristano, Sardinia

PRESIDIUM COORDINATORS
Corrado Casula
tel. +39 3401423951
corrado042004@libero.it
Mariano Aramu
tel. +39 078381634 - 3284031497
conspescamarceddi@tiscali.it

PRESIDIUM SUPPORTED BY
Sil Oristano, Oristano Provincial Authority

Maremmana Ox

Sturdy, with a whitish coat having shades of gray and long, lyre-shaped horns: the Maremmana cow is a descendent of *Bos taurus macroceros*, originating from the Asian steppes and later spread all over Europe. This breed was then crossed with cattle brought to Italy during the barbarian invasions, creating hybrids that over the centuries adapted perfectly to the swampy, malaria-ridden environment of the Maremma area. This breed especially came to the fore in the period between the two wars; then, the last land reclamation work and agricultural mechanization caused the breed to decline almost to the point of extinction. The recipe that best exalts the quality of its meat is a stew prepared with the leanest portions, chopped herbs and Maremma red wine. A simple yet savory dish using full-flavor meat thanks to free-range rearing. The Maremmana ox, in short, does not like to be kept in stalls: it is frugal and withstands the poor or little food available around the stagnant pools and open pastures. Between October and March, the cattle live in the open scrub and at the end of winter they are moved to fenced pastures to make the most of spring-time forage. At the end of May, the one-year-old calves are branded, while the adult cows and heifers are sorted into groups of 25-30 head for breeding. Early in fall, the bulls are taken from the herd and the other animals return to the scrub. All these stages are supervised by the *butteri*, the local 'cowboys' who are such an essential part of the Maremma landscape and culture. The Presidium aims to promote this excellent breed: Maremmana cattle, in short, could well become part of the menus in the best restaurants - those that currently serve Scottish Angus or American buffalo, overlooking the fact that Italy itself boasts native cattle reared in free range pastures that have nothing to envy of such more famous breeds. Today, the breed boasts about 20,000 head, distributed in three regions: Marches, Lazio and Tuscany. In Maremma itself, there are also two breeding farms owned by the Ministry for Agricultural Policy and the Colline Metallifere Mountain Community.

PRODUCTION AREA
Maremma, province of Grosseto, Tuscany

PRESIDIUM COORDINATOR
Roberto Tonini
tel. +39 0564329036 - 3397153654
roberto.tonini44@tiscali.it

PRESIDIUM SUPPORTED BY
Grosseto Provincial Authority

Mariola

Mariola is one of the most traditional cured meats from the Piacenzo area (a hilly zone affected by the mild and not overly damp air from Liguria, perfect for the aging), but is also made in limited quantities in the lower Parma area. It was, and is, prepared by using the first part of the large intestine (cecum) for the casing, which is why only one Mariola can be made from each pig. Raw Mariola was often the cured meatfor the Christmas holidays because of its size, characteristic flavor and very long aging process (even more than one year). The meats are taken from the loin, the shoulder and at one time also from the leg because prosciutto was not made around Piacenza. Even guanciale was used to give added fat to the mixture. Mariola can be eaten either raw or cooked. Long ago the local lords only wanted the cooked version, the most difficult to age. The poor, on the other hand, could not afford the luxury of a product that was so difficult to keep. The Mariola of the poor was the one that needed to be cooked (rather easy to find today), while the aged version, in just the right size, is rather rare. Those who produce It say it should look like a squat salamone, while others claim it should be shaped like a ball. In any case, the mixture is fine, garlicky and flavored with a little white wine (usually the local Fortana). What distinguishes the cooked mariola is the addition of spices like cinnamon, cloves, and mace (in the raw version only pepper is used) and the presence of fattier parts in the mixture like tongue, lard or rind, which give it the right degree of tenderness. The Presidium wants to valorize the raw mariola, the one that needs very long aging. When it is well-aged, the cut has the classic tear, which is a sign of goodness for very aged pork meats. The aroma is musky and complex, with a hint of spices and a pleasant note of mushrooms. The flavor is full, savory and a bit astringent, with a lingering aftertaste.

PRODUCTION AREA
Hills around Piacenza and the Parma plain, provinces of Piacenza and Parma, Emilia Romagna

PRESIDIUM COORDINATOR
Luisella Verderi
tel. +39 0523306056 – 3483844513
luisella@sinergia-pc.com

PRESIDIUM SUPPORTED BY
Emilia Romagna Regional Authority

Martina Franca Capocollo

Martina Franca is famous for its tradition of cured pork, the most celebrated of which is the capocollo, the name used in southern Italy to indicate the part of the pig between the neck and the ribs. It is made exclusively from locally-bred animals that have been fed with natural ingredients from the region. After the capocollo has macerated in salt for 15-20 days, it is washed with a solution of cooked wine and spices from the Mediterranean scrub, stuffed in a pig's intestine, wiped off with cloths and placed on wooden planks to dry for about ten days. When perfectly dry, it is then smoked in the traditional way by setting fire to twigs of thyme, myrtle, laurel and oak bark, which must burn without a flame. Another method is to burn the essences and bark of the small *fragno* oak in special fireplaces, which gives the meat a more subtle aroma but makes it easier to control the result. After this time the meat is aged for up to 90 days in damp, well-ventilated rooms. The final product is a wine-red color, with subtle traces of minerals and a strong aroma of spices. The light smoking, the long maceration in brine and the curing with cooked wine lend the meat a rich taste and aroma and are essential for keeping it wholesome and intact. Capocollo is fragrant and tender, with a winy taste that the quality of the meat stands up to very well. The aim of the Slow Food Presidium is to convince farmers to raise more pigs using natural methods and to make people throughout Italy aware of this cured meat. The Presidium is working to bring together meat processors and breeders in an association, and to this end has drawn up a protocol that makes provisions for raising pigs in the wild and semi-wild state as well as for processing and curing the capocollo.

PRODUCTION AREA
Martina Franca, province of Taranto; Cisternino, province of Brindisi; Locorotondo, province of Bari, Puglia

PRESIDIUM COORDINATORS
Michele Bruno
tel. +39 0831411430
Angelo Costantini
tel. +39 3337403370
costantiniangelo@libero.it

PRESIDIUM SUPPORTED BY
Commune of Martina Franca,
Terrae Maris Consortium of Tour
and Food and Wine Operators

Marzolina

The name of this cylindrical cheese derives from its history because at one time it was only made in March (marzo, in Italian), the month of the goat's first lactation. Originally production was concentrated on the slopes of the Aurunci Mountains, especially at Esperia, but it then extended to the Abruzzi border and the Comino valley in particular. Even today the milk (from two milkings) is coagulated with goat rennet and then broken up, salted (dry or in brine) and hand pressed before being put in special molds to drain. Although you can eat the cheese fresh, it is usually left to ripen a few days on wooden racks and then bottled up in glass jars for a few months. Traditionally there are two ways of doing this: some leave the forms of cheese as they are in the jars, while others cover them with olive oil. The Marzolina ages more slowly in oil and remains softer and mellower, and after eight months takes on an ivory white color. In any case, the forms have no crust, but rather a hard and dry skin. The cheese is compact and flaky in texture, with a few little holes, and aged without oil becomes rather hard. It has a goat-like fragrance and sweet, rich and oily taste, whose flavor intensifies with ageing, becoming stronger but not overly pungent. The Marzolina cheese making tradition had all but disappeared, but fortunately was kept up in the town of Esperia. A far-sighted female producer had the good sense to pass the recipe down to a young Campoli Appennino producer, who started up production again by raising goats once more. The monticellana, an indigenous breed of goat, is making a gradual comeback in the Aurunci Mountains now. It is hoped that other Presidium producers will become actively involved in regulating production in the future so the goats can graze in the wild for as much of the year as possible.

PRODUCTION AREA
Campoli Appennino, on the Lazio side of Abruzzo National Park, province of Frosinone, Lazio

PRESIDIUM COORDINATOR
Matteo Rugghia
tel. +39 0776830181 - 3395724767
ruma48@libero.it

PRESIDIUM SUPPORTED BY
Frosinone Chamber of Commerce, Industry, Crafts and Agriculture,
Commune of Campoli Appennino,
Gal Lazio slope of Abruzzo National Park

Matera Mountain Pezzente

The history of this sausage begins in the forests around Matera and the central Basento area, in the heart of Basilicata, most of which are now part of the Gallipoli-Cognato e delle Piccoli Dolomiti Lucane Park. Not so very long ago these forests were home to the Black Lucania pig, an indigenous breed now nearly extinct, which used to roam freely in the undergrowth, feeding on wild tubers, acorns, chestnuts and mushrooms. The farmers made pezzente out of the lesser cuts so as to conserve the meat for as long as possible and exploit every part of the pig. The Italian Touring Club guidebook of 1931 even mentioned it as one of the delicacies from Matera that was not to be missed. The finer cuts were used for pancetta, guanciale and soppressata. The throat, the nerves, the tougher muscles, the stomach, and the fat trimmings left over from other preparations were all cut into strips, minced and then seasoned with a mixture of ground sweet and hot Senise peppers, wild fennel, minced fresh garlic and sea salt. The pezzente is still prepared by hand today, and the most difficult step is still the *arricciatura*, or the blending of the meats and seasonings, because the mixture needs to be vigorously pressed with the fists until it becomes homogenous. Then a pinch is pan-fried and tasted to make sure the seasonings are just right. Once considered a meat substitute, pezzente aged 15 days is still used to prepare 'red sauce' for pasta, or is cooked as a tasty main course with vegetables, while the one aged for at least 20 days is sliced and eaten raw with good homemade bread. Only one producer sill makes it according to the traditional recipe, using meats from pigs raised in the wild in the Matera woods. In the future it is hoped that other pork butchers will join the Presidium and start making traditional *pezzente* again.

PRODUCTION AREA

Accettura, Aliano, Calciano, Garaguso, Gorgoglione, Oliveto Lucano, Stigliano and Tricarico, province of Matera, Basilicata

PRESIDIUM COORDINATOR

Angela Ciliberti
tel. +39 0835675270
info@lemacine.com

PRESIDIUM SUPPORTED BY

Gal Le Macine

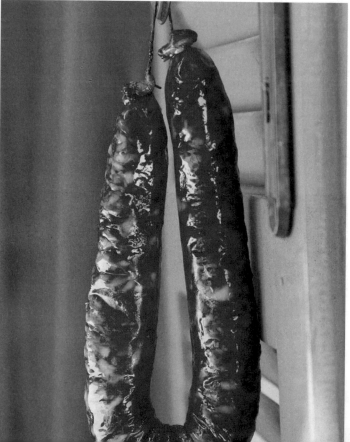

Menaica Anchovies

These delicate anchovies, with their pale pink flesh, are fished off the coast of Cilento using an ancient technique which has survived only around Marina di Pisciotta and Pollica. Between April and July, when the sea is calm, the fishermen go out at dusk in groups of no more than seven or eight boats fitted with nets. Both the boats and nets are called *menaica* or *menaide*. The nets are driftnets, not fixed to the sea floor, around 200 by 10 meters, held up by about 20 floats, and made by the fishermen. The diameter of the mesh changes during the season, following the growth of the anchovies themselves. Once trapped the fish start bleeding and in order to free them the fishermen have to remove their heads. Then they are gutted and brought to the shore in wooden crates, without ice or any other refrigeration. After being washed in brine they are then laid in terracotta jars, with alternating layers of salt, and left to mature for at least three months in the cool warehouses where boats were once stored. It's important that they don't dry out too much. The anchovies are eaten fresh or salted, raw or cooked. Some dishes are simple, like raw anchovy salad, dressed with oil, lemon, garlic and parsley, or anchovy cooked in a sauce with oil, cherry tomatoes, garlic and chili pepper, while others are more complex, such as *inchiappate* (stuffed with goat's cheese, egg, garlic and parsley then floured, fried and cooked in a tomato sauce), *ammollicate* (split and seasoned with breadcrumbs, garlic, oil and parsley) and *cauraro* (with potatoes, fava beans and wild fennel). All the fishermen salt the anchovies but only two of them have regulation workshops. The hope is that others will be able to have similar facilities so that a family custom can become a profitable source of income. The Presidium was created to help this group of fishermen make a living as well as to save an important tradition, a micro-economy and an important gastronomic product. The number of visitors who want to learn more about this ancient fishing technique is increasing, and in March and April, when the sea is calm and full of fish, the fishermen having been organizing fishing excursions for tourists.

PRODUCTION AREA
Pisciotta and Pollica, province of Salerno, Campania

PRESIDIUM COORDINATOR
Vito Puglia
tel. +39 3298321284
vito.puglia@fastwebnet.it

PRESIDIUM SUPPORTED BY
Cilento and Vallo di Diano
National Park

Minuta Olive

This rare and very ancient Sicilian cultivar is raised in the high hills of Nebrodi, at about 800 meters above sea level, where olive trees more than 100 years old, and still productive, can be found amidst hazelnut and chestnut trees. The minuta is known for its excellent nutritional value and is more resistant to adverse weather conditions than the santagatese and the ogliarola messinese, with which it is part of the Valdemone PDO, or the verdello. Though the yield is small and the cost of growing and harvesting the olives is expensive since the trees grow on uneven terrain, many olive growers use the minuta to produce multi-variety olive oils. The medium-small fruit ripen fairly early and are harvested from mid-October to mid-December, according to the degree of maturation and the altitude. The olives are hand harvested. First nets are arranged under the trees to catch the olives as they fall and to prevent them from touching the ground and then the olives are brought down by beating the foliage with a pole. Cold pressing the olives produces very delicate, fruity oil distinguished by very low acidity and just the right balance between bitter and tangy. It differs from other Sicilian oils, which usually have a stronger and spicier taste, and is ideal for fish dishes. The minuta olives are also good as table olives and are traditionally conserved a tinello, in a brine of water and sea salt flavored with the flora of the Nebrodi (wild fennel, garlic, bay laurel and rosemary), or a suppresso, layered with salt and aromatic herbs and then pressed in wood or ceramic containers. The Presidium brings together some of the minuta growers who produce a single variety oil according to a rigorous production protocol.

PRODUCTION AREA
17 communes in the province of Messina, Sicily

PRESIDIUM COORDINATOR
Vincenzo Pruiti
tel. +39 0941438179 - 3284206027 soat7@regione.sicilia.it

PRESIDIUM SUPPORTED BY
Commune of Sinagra

Modicana Cow

This breed of cattle, which spread from the county of Modica throughout Sicily and was exported to Sardinia to become the Modicana Sardinian breed, is of unknown origin: some say that it came from the Mediterranean, while others maintain that it was imported from continental Europe, in the wake of the Normans and Angevins. What is certain is that it is a very old breed, hardy and frugal, and unmistakable with its russet coat, in shades ranging from winey to black, above all in bulls. Its decline is linked to the introduction of mechanical equipment and its low yields in terms of milk (3,000 liters a year) and beef (below 55%); in addition, many farms have stopped processing milk directly into cheese. This means that while there were still 25,000 Modicana cattle in the 1960s, there are now only 2,000 left. Yet Modicana cattle used to be regarded as one of the best breeds for milk, beef and work: in fact, in the past they were valued for their ability to work on account of their exception-

ally strong legs and hooves. Moreover, being hardy, the cattle can withstand the hot summers and will survive on pasture alone, only requiring supplements when the grass is scarce. It roams freely all year round and the cows are only brought for milking. Their milk is not very plentiful but is excellent quality, the ideal raw material for one of Sicily's finest cheeses, Ragusano. The fact that the cattle are left completely wild guarantees the excellent quality – and healthiness – of the meat, although this asset is still relatively undervalued. Meat from animals who live in the wild is more difficult to butcher: if it is not left to hang for the length of time, it can be tougher than other kinds of beef. Therefore, the cattle are fed indoors for the last 40 days and professional butchering is required. The Presidium is working to improve the systems of production, finishing and hanging by involving a local butcher and trying to educate the consumer to notice the quality and flavor of the beef from this breed.

PRODUCTION AREA
Provinces of Ragusa, Enna and Palermo, Sicily

PRESIDIUM COORDINATOR
Giuseppe Licitra
tel. +39 0932660414
licitrag@tin.it
licitrag@corfilac.it

PRESIDIUM SUPPORTED BY
Sicily Regional Authority department of Agriculture
and Forestry, CoRFiLac

Moena Puzzone

This cheese is made in the Dolomites, in a few of the mountain dairies in Paneveggio-Pale di San Martino Park. The forms are branded on the surface with an M, which indicates that the milk was obtained in summer from mountain dairies, and that the cows grazed in mountain pastures and fed on grasses or other quality feed: no silage, no industrial by-products and no GMOs. Having a washed crust – something unique in Fassa Valley – it had always been known as nostrano (in Ladin spretz tzaorì), or 'local' cheese. Since the 1970s, however, it has gone by the name of puzzone (stinky), because of the intense and pungent aroma resulting from the long aging. Twice a day milk is transported to the Predazzo cheese factory from the mountain dairies. Heated to 34°C in copper cauldrons, it is mixed with artisan milk starter and made to coagulate with veal rennet. The curd is then broken and steamed at 47° C. When the mass settles to the bottom it is brought to the surface and gathered up in a cloth. Cut into pieces and arranged in wooden molds, it is delicately hand-pressed and left to drain. Then the forms are weighted down and pressed again, put into brine for four days, and then taken out to be aged. Each week the forms are washed with a damp cloth and turned one by one, a process that goes on for 60 days to six or seven months. It is not known where the tradition of washing the cheese in Fassa Valley comes from (the only other Italian cheeses with washed crust are Fontina and Taleggio). While there is no historical documentation, witnesses insist it has been like this ever since the time of their grandparents and great-grandparents. Washing the crust creates an oily layer on the cheese and favors bacterial fermentation, which gives the cheese its distinctive brick-red color. As the name implies, the Buzzone has a distinctively aromatic personality: smelly for some, a complex and penetrating bouquet for gourmets. When the cheese is cut there is an immediate aroma of fermentation and cellar, which gradually develops into hints of pasture, Alpine grass, ripe fruit and toasted hazelnut.

PRODUCTION AREA
Predazzo and Moena, province of Trento, Trentino

PRESIDIUM COORDINATOR
Giampaolo Gaiarin
tel. +39 3356674256
gaiarin.giampaolo@trentingrana.it

PRESIDIUM SUPPORTED BY
Trento Autonomous Provincial Authority, Trentingrana Concast

Moleche

These are the males of the green or common crab, a member of the most common species in the Mediterranean (Carcinus aestuarii), during the molting period, when they shed their shell and, soft and tender, can be eaten whole. They are green-grayish on the back but lighter on the belly and prefer the lagoon or shallower water near the ports, where there are plentiful supplies of decomposing organic substances. The Venetians call them moleche or moeche and have turned their harvest into a true art. Caught using nets in fixed positions in the shallows of the lagoon, the moleche are carefully graded to separate good crabs boni (ready for molting in one or two weeks) from the spiantani crabs, that need more time for the molt, and the matti thron back into the water since they will not molt during the harvest season. Placed separately in the vieri (large boxes) immersed in the water, the boni and the spiantani are checked at regular intervals and sold at just the right moment. The moleche are cleaned (eliminating the fragments of algae at-tached to their claws, washed, dried and cooked fried, tossed in flour or as an omelet. Alternatively, they are placed still alive in a terrine with beaten egg and, after a couple of hours, when they have fully absorbed the dressing, tossed in flour and fried on boiling oil. There are still around 50 fishermen dedicated to this type of catch and, after the recession in the 1980s, the sector seems to be enjoying a recovery. In any case, there is the risk that, over the next few years, this highly-prized specialty may disappear, not the least given the competition from breeding and rearing vongole veraci (clams). Yet the most serious threat is pollution, that harms the shallows where this crab lives, reducing the number and dimensions of the spiantani and boni ready for molting. Moreover, most fisherman in this trade are now rather old and, if a new generation does not come to the fore, there is the risk that their heritage of knowledge and experience will be lost - fundamental aspects in such as demanding activity.

PRODUCTION AREA
Venetian lagoon: Chioggia, Venice, islands of Burano, Mazzorbo and Giudecca, province of Venice, Veneto

PRESIDIUM COORDINATOR
Gigi Boscolo
tel. +39 3406142016
luigi.boscolo@provincia.venezia.it

PRESIDIUM SUPPORTED BY
Veneto Regional Authority, Veneto Agricoltura

Moliterno Casieddu

The name of the town of Moliterno possibly derives from the Latin term *mulctrum*, from *mulgere* (in Italian *mungere*), meaning to milk. With the addition of the suffix *ernum* (place) it becomes *mulcternum*, 'the place to do the milking'. In the summer months, the shepherds of Moliterno, in the Agri Valley, stop making pecorino cheese as the sheep no longer give milk, and start producing the goat's milk Casieddu, a traditional variant of Cacioricotta with herbs. First the goat's milk from two milkings is filtered through fern leaves and heated to 90°C in the *caccavo* (a tin-plated copper cauldron). During this phase *Calamintha nepeta savi* is added, a highly aromatic herb of the mint family, known locally as *nepeta*. When the milk has cooled to 38°C, a goat rennet paste is added, and as soon as the curd has reached the right consistency, it is broken up with a wooden stick called the *scuopolo* until the lumps are the size of grains of rice. After a few minutes, the curd is removed from the cauldron, pressed and shaped into rounds. At this point, if the cheese is to be eaten fresh, the forms are wrapped in fern leaves tied at the ends with broom stalks. Otherwise, the dry-salted aging can go on for 60 days or so. Casieddu cheese is smooth and compact, with a few air holes, and can vary from a chalk white to straw color depending on how long it is aged. It has a slight aroma of milk mixed with the delicate scent of *nepeta*, and the flavor has the same hints of mint in nice contrast to the sweetness of the goat's milk. A small group of local producers started the Moliterno Casieddu Presidium to ensure a future for this little-known product (Moliterno Pecorino is already quite famous) by establishing a rigid protocol and promoting the cheese on the national market.

PRODUCTION AREA
Moliterno, province of Potenza, Basilicata

PRESIDIUM COORDINATOR
Angela Latorraca
tel. +39 0975668511
comunemoliterno@rete.basilicata.it

PRESIDIUM SUPPORTED BY
Commune of Moliterno

Mondovì Corn Meal Biscuits

Corn meal biscuits are yellow, crunchy, they melt in the mouth and are neither greasy nor too sweet. The texture of the millstone-ground maize flour is grainy and in the mouth, just before swallowing, a toasted sensation hits the tastebuds. At times lemon rind, vanilla extract or honey are added, though none of these flavors interfere with the overall taste. Once upon a time they used to be prepared in the family, straight after baking the bread, mixing wheat and corn meal, adding butter, eggs, sugar and kneading the dough in various shapes and sizes. The recipe is the same today and the biscuits are round, oblong or crescent-shaped. Traditionally they were special occasion cookies, served at the end of a meal with a glass of red wine, such a the Barolo even, in which to dip them. In many less traditional restaurants they are nowadays served as a pudding together with warm zabaione, which our ancestors used to eat in between meals – in some cases with other dry cookies and fruit in syrup – on account of its high calorie count. Found in all cafés and bakeries in the region, these yellow, crunchy, fragrant and neither-thick-nor-thin biscuits are part of Piedmontese gastronomic culture, especially in and around Cuneo. The Presidium groups a few producers in the Mondovì area together in an association, and has created a unique brand and package for its very own biscuits. The production protocol only permits traditional procedures and high-quality ingredients: sugar, Alpine butter, fresh eggs, white flour and millstone-ground ottofile corn flour. No margarine, flavoring or preservatives are allowed. Most importantly, an entire high-quality production sector has been restored, and some farmers have started growing the old ottofile corn again.

PRODUCTION AREA
The communes of the Monregalese region, province of Cuneo, Piedmont

PRESIDIUM COORDINATORS
Gianni Ferrero
tel. +39 017447296 - 3356814854
info@leviedelmonregalese.com
Barbara Grigolon
tel. +39 017443564

PRESIDIUM SUPPORTED BY
Beppino Occelli (Farigliano, Cuneo, Piedmont, Italy),
Association for the conservation and promotion
of the Corn Meal Biscuits

Monreale White Plums

The plum, along with citrus fruit, mulberries, medlars and figs, is one of the traditional cultivations of the Conca d'Oro. Until 60 years ago, the area was one enormous fruit orchard, but the construction boom around Palermo invaded the inland areas and many fruit trees were eliminated; the 'paper-wrapped' plums that once filled the market stalls of Ballarò and Vuccirìa disappeared. The late plum, the *ariddu di core*, would keep until Christmas when wrapped in paper. Housewives used to package the fruit in long rolls of tissue paper closed and tied with string. Hung in a cool place, the fruit became dehydrated and shriveled, conserving its flavor and aroma. Monreale white plums are small and very sweet, with a light yellow skin. There are two varieties: the *sanacore*, which thanks to its aroma and taste is pleasing to the palate as well as the heart, and the *ariddu di core* (heart-shaped seed), so-called because of its distinctive seed. The *sanacore* is picked from early July to mid-August, while the very sweet *ariddu di core* is a late variety that ripens from mid-August to early September. Both of them are very delicate and must be handled as little as possible to avoid damaging the *pruina*, the white coating that covers them; and the peduncle must not be removed. The white plums have been revived thanks to the research on indigenous Sicilian germoplasm carried out by the Department of Tree Cultivations at the University of Palermo. But the passion of some of the older fruit growers has been responsible for preserving the trees of the older varieties. Most of the *ariddu di core* trees are conserved in a single orchard surrounded by buildings and cement in the commune of Monreale. The Presidium unites four growers who sell the plums directly or entrust them to the wholesalers of the Palermo and Trapani fruit and vegetable markets. The objective of the Presidium is to create a common trademark and a larger alternative market, but above all to revive the tradition of wrapping the *arridu di core* in paper.

PRODUCTION AREA
Monreale, province of Palermo, Sicily

PRESIDIUM COORDINATOR
Marilù Monte
tel. +39 3289714674 - 0916168151
mmonte@unipa.it

PRESIDIUM SUPPORTED BY
Palermo Provincial Authority, department of Agriculture and Forestry

Montébore

Montébore is a small village tucked away in the Val Curone, on the border between the Grue and Borbera valleys. An intact and little-inhabited corner of the Tortona area. The place is famous as it is linked to the production of two ancient types of cow's milk and ewe cheeses. They were first mentioned in 1153: a wealthy man from Tortona sent 50 cheeses to a high prelate as a gift to plead his brother's promotion to the priesthood. At the end of the 15th century it was the only cheese on the menu when Isabella of Aragon, daughter of Alfonso, married Gian Galeazzo Sforza, son of the Duke of Milan. Up to the middle of the 20th century, 1,200 kilos were produced a year. However, in 1982 the last producer ceased trade. The cheese has a typical wedding-cake shape inspired by the old village tower in Montébore, where it is made. 75% cow's milk is used in the preparation. It used to be local, but nowadays hardly any cows are left in the Tortona area. The remaining 25% is ewe's milk. No wonder a slightly animal, spicy flavor seeps out. The cheese is initially tastes milky and buttery, the chestnut and herb flavors only tickling the tastebuds as the mouthful is swallowed. The curd is cracked open with a wooden spoon and then placed into the moulds, turned upside down an salted. Extracted from the molds, three shapes of different sizes, from biggest to smallest, are put one on top of the other to mature for a length of time varying between one week and two months. In the beginning the crust is smooth and damp, then it becomes drier and wrinklier, the color also changing from white to yellow. The texture is smooth or with a few holes, and colored in white hues. The Montébore may be eaten fresh, semi-matured or used for grating. It literally "resuscitated" thanks to the Presidium, which contacted Carolina Bracco, the last connoisseur of the traditional Montébore production method in 1999. Two further producers followed her every move, gradually learning the ancient technique.

PRODUCTION AREA
Montébore in the commune of Dernice and surrounding communes between the Curone and Borbera valleys, province of Alessandria, Piedmont

PRESIDIUM COORDINATOR
Roberto Grattone
tel. +39 014394131
vallenostra@tiscali.it

PRESIDIUM SUPPORTED BY
Curone, Grue and Ossona valleys, and Borbera and Spinti valleys Mountain Communities

Monte Poro Pecorino

There are a number of reasons for the excellent quality of this sheep's cheese, made in the Province of Vibo Valentia. For one thing, the animals are raised in the wild, grazing on aromatic grasses in the Poro pasturelands. The cheese is made with sheep's milk, with the possible addition of goat's milk, and the goat rennet is produced at the factory itself. The curd is not heated after it is broken, which means that it needs to be pressed more vigorously and for a longer period of time to eliminate the whey residues. The small breeders make this pecorino in very limited quantities and sell it locally. The forms can weigh from 1.2 to 2.5 kilos and are about 12 centimeters high and 18 in diameter. It is dry-salted by rubbing the surfaces with sea salt, and before it is left to age in a cool place, at an even temperature, the crust is oiled with a mixture of olive oil and ground red peppers, giving it a reddish color on the outside. It is preferably eaten after five or six months' aging. When cut, it is firm and white with occasional 'eye's. It has a mellow consistency and a highly aromatic taste with obvious hints of mint, wild flowers, brushwood, in some cases dry hay and often animals. There is always a certain tangy flavor, which can be more or less pronounced, and a pleasant hazelnut finish. The Presidium is working to give the producers standardized facilities for processing and aging. With the help of CoGal Monte Poro, some of the producers are working with a technician to finally obtain adequate cheesemaking facilities and be able to market their product beyond the local level. They are also looking into the possibility of creating an association themselves.

PRODUCTION AREA
Rombiolo, Joppolo, Zaccanopoli, Nicotera, province of Vibo Valentia, Calabria

PRESIDIUM COORDINATOR
Raffaele Denami
tel. +39 0963332116
r.denami@libero.it

PRESIDIUM SUPPORTED BY
CoGal Monte Poro,
Salumificio Pugliese (Vibo Valentia,
Calabria, Italy)

Monterosso Anchovies

Fishing was once the main activity at Monterosso, and until 30 years ago there was a large cooperative of fishermen called the Monterossina. Even though there are only six fishermen left here now, the salted anchovies from this little village in the Cinque Terre are still famous and the method for preparing them the same. These tender, medium-size anchovies with the well-balanced flavor arrive in the Levant after a long journey that starts in the waters of the Atlantic. For the fishermen of the Cinque Terre, the magical day of the anchovies is June 29, but good fishing lasts until mid-July. Every evening the traditional rowboats, *gozzi*, set off for the night fishing towing the lamps. Attracted by the sight of the plankton, which is phosphorescent when illuminated, the anchovies become trapped in the nets. The salting used to be the responsibility of the womenfolk, who would clean the anchovies on the beach as soon as the boats docked and then layer them under salt inside terracotta containers. Since the fish are extremely delicate, the salting is a rather complex operation and the aging process needs to be done with great care. The Monterosso anchovies are the prime ingredient in many simple but wonderful dishes. They are excellent when they are split open, sautéed in a bit of oil, garlic and parsley and served very hot. If they are conserved in salt, they only need to have the salt removed and then be marinated for a few days in extra virgin olive oil with garlic and oregano. Anchovy fishing can still be a good job opportunity for young people, as well as an important economic resource. That is why the Presidium was founded. Currently there is a small cooperative of six fishermen from Monterosso and the salting is still done by women. A new salting facility, recently established at Monterosso in collaboration with the town and with the support of the Cinque Terre National Park, will be used for processing the fish and will also provide demonstrations on the traditional method of salting anchovies.

PRODUCTION AREA
Cinque Terre, province of La Spezia, Liguria

PRESIDIUM COORDINATORS
Barbara Schiffini
tel. +39 0187701098
schiffini1963@libero.it
Giuseppe Martelli
tel. +39 0187817053 - 3355396148

PRESIDIUM SUPPORTED BY
Cinque Terre National Park

Monte San Biagio Sausage

The origins of pork butchery in Monte San Biagio date back to the 6th century when the barbarian invasions arrived at Monticello, the present-day Monte San Biagio. The Lombard food traditions and the presence of a vast cork woods favored the establishment of a pork processing tradition. The sausage handed down to us today is still made without any additives by the pork butchers of Monte San Biagio and a few of the surrounding communities. The meat and fat are chopped by knife into good-size cubes. The lean part comes from all of the parts of the pig except the trotters, the innards and the head; the fat from the cheeks, lard and belly. Everything is mixed together in the traditional wooden containers called manielle (or in steel containers), with the addition of hot red pepper, sweet red pepper, toasted and ground coriander grown in the local gardens (petarda), sea salt and a little Moscato di Terracina. After the mixture has rested for at least 12 hours, it is stuffed into natural casings and lightly smoked with burning lentisk or myrtle wood. After the sausage has aged in natural grottoes for at least 18 days, it is ready to be eaten. It can be consumed fresh or preserved in lard or locally produced extra virgin olive oil. Savory and spicy, with a strong aroma of coriander and a slightly smoky aftertaste, the Monte San Biagio sausage is the focus of a Presidium project involving a five pork butchers. One of the objectives is to create a complete production chain that includes pig breeders that practice natural feeding, with the use of GMO-free cereals and proteins from the local area, acorns and tree roots. Another aim is to increase the pig farms in the large wooded expanses of the Ausoni and Aurunci mountains, today partly abandoned, by reestablishing valuable indigenous breeds like the Casertana.

PRODUCTION AREA
Mounts Ausoni and Aurunci, province of Latina, Lazio

PRESIDIUM COORDINATORS
Dionisio Castello
tel. +39 0773723974
d.castello@libero.it
Vittorio Iacovacci
tel. +39 3474729483
alek.mattei@tiscali.it

PRESIDIUM SUPPORTED BY
Commune of Monte San Biagio

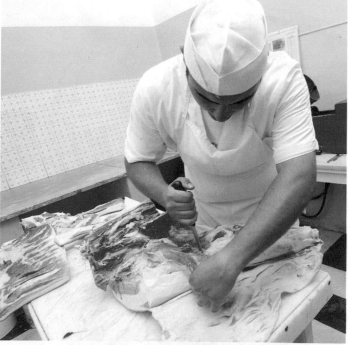

Monti Sibillini Pecorino

The history of the Sibillines is first of all the story of an important shepherding civilization and the transhumance. The National Park and the pecorino produced there both take their name from Mount Sibilla (2,173 m.). There are actually two Pecorinos: a fresh one made with pasteurized milk and produced year round by the industrial cheese factories, and the one supported by the Presidium, which is prepared with raw milk, semi-cooked and naturally aged. The latter method has remained the same for centuries: the rennet is still made by drying lamb or goat stomachs filled with milk, and according to a very ancient and now practically non-existent practice, some still flavor the curd with a little bunch of serpillo thyme. Traditionally the fresh milk is heated to 37-38°C in a copper cauldron and the natural rennet is added. The curd is broken after 20-30 minutes, reheated to 45-48°C and then the mass is arranged in the molds. The cheese is pressed and dry salted for a couple of days and then washed, dried and left to ripen in a cool and slightly damp place, where the forms are turned every two or three days to favor the formation of the crust. The cheese can be eaten after 30 days, but is best when aged for a few months. This produces forms with a golden, ochre or hazelnut colored crust and a bright yellow, compact and slightly oily cheese that has a grainy and flaky consistency, a strong, pungent aroma (often with notes of mushroom and truffle), and a pronounced and very persistent sharp taste. The Presidium has united some of the local producers, the ones with cheese making facilities that respect the health and sanitary regulations. It has worked out a detailed production protocol, whose main points regard the processing of raw milk and the aging in natural environments, without the use of air treatment systems. It is also endeavoring to set up an association and create a common seal of quality to distinguish the Monti Sibillini Pecorino of the Presidium.

PRODUCTION AREA
Sibillini mountains, provinces of Ascoli Piceno and Macerata, Marche; province of Perugia, Umbria.

PRESIDIUM COORDINATORS
Giocondo Anzidei
tel. +39 3395739475
anzideigiocondo@libero.it
Valerio Chiarini
tel. +39 3282868750
vchiarini@libero.it

PRESIDIUM SUPPORTED BY
Marche Regional Authority

Monti Sibillini Pink Apple

These small pink apples have an irregular, slightly flat shape and a very short stem. The sweet and slightly acidic pulp is intensely aromatic, while the color is greenish with tinges of color ranging from pink to red-violet. These apples have been cultivated in Marche since time immemorial, from the foothills to the Apennine valleys and the slopes of the Sibillini Mountains (especially at altitudes of 450-900 meters in certain communes of the province of Ascoli Piceno).The Presidium has identified eight ecotypes belonging to three different groups distinct in terms of basic color, overlying color and consistency of the fruit: green, with pink or yellowish-orange streaks and a firm and crunchy pulp; soft and yellow, with bright red markings from the sun; firm and green, with wine-red streaks. They were once much sought after because they kept so well. Harvested at the beginning of October, they were still excellent at the end of April; they actually improved with age because the firm, compact pulp softened with time. The cultivations were all but abandoned, however, because these apples had little success in a market where large, uniform and brightly colored apples are preferred. Albeit plain in appearance, these rustic pink apples are wholesome and healthy. It has only been in the past few years that the Monti Sibillini Mountain Community has reintroduced the ecotypes conserved by Assam (Marche Agribusiness Services Agency) and made it possible to resume production. An association of about 30 producers has been set up, a strict protocol providing for eco-compatible production has been drafted, and new production facilities are in the making. In addition to the fresh fruit, some members of the Presidium have also started making juices and jams from the pink apple.

PRODUCTION AREA
Sibillini mountains, in province of Ascoli Piceno, Marche

PRESIDIUM COORDINATORS
Graziella Traini
tel. +39 0736828276
Nelson Gentili
tel. +39 0736844379-3383913352
cmsibillini@libero.it

PRESIDIUM SUPPORTED BY
Marche Regional Authority,
Monti Sibillini Mountain Community

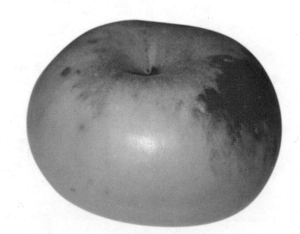

Mora Romagnola Pig

Strong, sturdy and good for fattening, the Mora Romagnola is a local breed that like many other old species is perfect for raising outdoors. It has distinctive dark brown skin tending to black, hence the name 'mora' (brunette), unusual almond-shaped eyes and particularly long tusks, especially in the males. These characteristics make the animal more similar to wild boars than to other breeds of pig. The Mora Romagnola grows much more slowly than the omnipresent Large White and its meat has more fat content than other breeds, which is why it was completely abandoned with the spread of commercial breeding and is now at risk of extinction. The nearly 22,000 heads that existed in 1949 were reduced to just 12 in 1997, miraculously preserved by Mario Lazzari, an old breeder from Faenza. Yet the animal's tasty, tender but compact meat is perfect for making excellent cured meats, as experimentations with *culatello* and *spalla cruda* have shown. The Presidium wants to save the Mora Romagnola from extinction. Thanks to the help of the WWF and the Department of Animal Husbandry Sciences at the University of Turin, a program was devised to recover the breed and appraise the quality of the meats from both pure and mixed breeds. Tests have been devised to assess the growth and the butchering yields of the breed, as well as studies on the various types of food and breeding methods. Copaf (Consortium for the Promotion of Appennino Faentino Products) is an association of breeders that have certified animals listed on the genealogical register of breeds at the Provincial Association of Breeders of Forlì and Cesena. Copaf is also collaborating with a few of the pork processing plants in the area. The aim is to produce quality cured pork products from the Mora Romagnola and to have a means of identifying its origins and safety assurances throughout the production chain.

PRODUCTION AREA
Provinces of Ravenna, Forlì-Cesena and Rimini, Emilia Romagna

PRESIDIUM COORDINATORS
Lamberto Albonetti
tel. +39 3473497668
slowfoodforli@aliceposta.it
Stefano Scalini
tel. +39 3357240538
scalini@libero.it

PRESIDIUM SUPPORTED BY
Emilia Romagna Regional Authority

Morozzo Capon

Around Christmastime in Morozzo, the townspeople Traditionally showed their appreciation to their doctors and notables by giving them a capon as a present. In fact, the meat is soft, tender and delicate and excellent used in simple preparations – boiled and soaked in salt or, at most, accompanied by the green *bagnet* (sauce), and also refined dishes like lasagne or stuffed. Genitals, topknot and lappet are all removed together and fried with chopped onion, rosemary and tomatoes, or used to make a giblet sauce, which is served on the most classic of Piedmont pasta the *tajarin*. When they are mature, capons have a long black tail with metallic hues, glossy brick red feathers, edged with blue or green without a topknot or lappet. During fetes and shows, they are calmly displayed in twos in the cages or baskets, behavior, which two cockerels would never accept. Only the women, with their small skilful hands are allowed to prepare them. The pullets are born in spring, and initially are fed with vegetable fodder and are left to run free straight away. The young cocks first and the capons after, have at least five square meters of open space to run around in and they are only closed in during the night. In august they are castrated, but they cannot be butchered until they are 220 days old, so they continue living for a further four or five months and are ready at Christmas. In a few years the Presidium has given new drive to their breeding: from 300 capons in 1999 there were 4,000 in 2005. An association was started with 31 breeders, and now has more than 60 breeders and the local butchers among its members, and is very well organized with boxes and ice, shipping capons throughout Italy. And, of course, the fete that is held every year on the third Monday of December has taken on new life; the capons are there in their thousands and are on show for selling, and the buyers have come back too: butchers, restaurateurs and private customers from all over Italy.

PRODUCTION AREA
Morozzo and twelve other communes in the province of Cuneo, Piedmont

PRESIDIUM COORDINATORS
Annamaria Molinero
tel. +39 0171772001
prenotazioni@capponedimorozzo.it

PRESIDIUM SUPPORTED BY
Commune of Morozzo, Opera Pia Peyrone, Association for the protection and promotion of Morozzo Capons and traditional bird rearing

Mountain Castelmagno

Valle Grana in the province of Cuneo boasts a pastures rich in forage and numerous indigenous varieties of herbs and flowers. The heart of the valley is Castelmagno ('Chastelmanh' in Provencal) but the entire area only has a population of about 150 inhabitants. The economy of the village is based on the artisan production of the cheese of the same name which, as early as the 13th century, local shepherds used to pay as rent for their pastures to the Marquis of Saluzzo. Today the Castelmagno you see in the shops is often produced in dairies, but there are still shepherds who make the cheese according to the old techniques. Those of the hamlet of Chiappi, for example, pasture their animals at an altitude of over 1,600 meters and have combined to set up a Presidium. The heady fragrance of the foraging herbs and meadow flora, composed of Gramineae of the *Poa* and *Festuca* genera exalt the aroma and flavor of this cheese which, in view of its supreme equality, received DOC recognition in 1982 and PDO in 1997. Each herb contributes in a different way not only to the aroma but also to the nutritional value of Castelmagno, and this is why the University of Turin is carrying out a survey of meadows to identify the finest crus. Made with the cow's milk from two consecutive milkings, the Presidium Castelmagno is produced following traditional techniques. First, the curd is broken up into nut-sized lumps and resulting mass left to drain for 24 hours in a knotted hanging canvas *(risola)*. After being chopped into cubes, it is gathered together again and left to acidify for three or four days with the whey before being minced, re-kneaded, salted and and pressed. The Presidium producers age the cheese in a natural environment to allow molds to spread and the characteristic blue veins and intense, piquant aroma to develop.

PRODUCTION AREA
Castelmagno, province of Cuneo, Piedmont

PRESIDIUM COORDINATOR
Giorgio Amedeo
tel +39 338 626 1222
terredicastelmagno@hotmail.com

Mozzarella in Myrtle

In the Basso Cilento, the zone included in the Cilento and Vallo di Diano National Park, most cheesemaking is dedicated to the production of Caciocavallo made mainly during the summer, in the highest pastures, using milk from Podolico cows or crossbreeds. However some of the milk is used by the cheesemakers to produce a cheese to be eaten fresh, Mozzarella stracciata. In the days before refrigeration or sterile packaging it became the custom to wrap it in leaves of myrtle, abundant in the mountains, so as to keep it fresh during transport down to the valley. A shrub with smooth, non-porous leaves and branches, the myrtle, *mortella*, provided a natural wrapping and also transferred its flavors and aromas to the cheese. Over time the *muzzarella co' a mortedda* or *indo a murtedda* became a recognized type among the many string cheeses of the south. The cheese is made using the classic mozzarella method, but the maturing of the curds takes place in the absence of almost any whey. The result is a white cheese with a dry and compact texture, elongated, flat and irregularly shaped, like a *stracciata*. When compared to regular mozzarella, the acidity is somewhat more pronounced. There is a market perfume of green herbs and sometimes also cedar and lemon, coming not just from the myrtle but also the pastures. At the highest altitudes the cows graze on the undergrowth of beech and chestnut forests, and at lower altitudes the fragrant Mediterranean scrub. Mozzarella in myrtle is an excellent cheese to eat straight, particularly as an antipasto, drizzled with a little extra virgin olive oil and perhaps with a pinch of oregano, and served with olives and tomatoes in oil. Given its strong aroma it would be unthinkable to use it on a pizza or in a calzone; instead it is best appreciated on its own. The Presidium was created to support the work of the few artisan producers who use raw milk from the area. A production protocol will control the entire production chain, from the raising of the cows to the cheese production itself.

PRODUCTION AREA
Cannalonga, Celle di Bulgheria, Futani, Laurito, Novi Velia, Montano Antilia and Rofrano in the province of Salerno, Campania

PRESIDIUM COORDINATOR
Vito Puglia
tel. +39 3298321284
vito.puglia@fastwebnet.it

PRESIDIUM SUPPORTED BY
Cilento and Vallo di Diano
National Park

Nassa Shrimp

Shrimps are decapod crustaceans of the suborder Macrura, having 10 thoracic limbs off a long abdomen which ends in a fanned fin, known in Italian as gamberi. The smallest are known as gamberetti, like the parapandolo (*Plesionika narval*). It's an elegant, pink little shrimp, with a long beak, and it is found in the underwater caves of the western Mediterranean. This preference for dark, hidden grottoes with strong currents makes them hard to catch with regular nets. As a result some fishermen from the villages of Marina del Cantone, Torca and Sant'Agata sui Due Golfi still use a traditional trap called a nassa, a basket of rushes or reeds and myrtle, closed at one end and with a funnel-shaped entrance: the fish enter, attracted by the bait inside, but cannot escape. The nassa traps are all still handwoven by the fishermen in the winter months. The pink shrimp from the Sorrentine Peninsula have a delicate, compact flesh, and are eaten raw, without even a squeeze of lemon. If one really wants to cook them, it's enough to sauté them briefly in a pan with a pinch of salt and ground pepper. The skill necessary for the construction of the nassa traps and the low productivity of this fishing system discourage younger fishermen from continuing the tradition; in the Sorrentine Peninsula there are only three remaining crews who earn the majority of their income from the pink shrimp. In an attempt to reverse this decline the Punta Campanella Marine Reserve, which protects the waters around the tip of the Peninsula, has decided to encourage this ancient technique with the inclusion of the nassa among the authorized fishing equipment that can be used in the protected area. The Presidium will help give this small community some visibility and recognize the fundamental role of the sentries of the sea: the presence of an active nucleus of coastal fishermen actually helps restrict illegal fishing practices as well as guaranteeing the continuity of a centuries-old tradition.

PRODUCTION AREA
Southern coast of the Sorrentine Peninsula, province of Naples, Campania

PRESIDIUM COORDINATOR
Mariagrazia Gargiulo
tel. +39 3334384134
ulixes@pescaturismo.org

PRESIDIUM SUPPORTED BY
Punta Campanella Marine Reserve

Neapolitan Papaccella

From the beginning of July to the first cold weather, the stands of Naples's markets abound with colorful peppers. However, few visitors to these markets are able to recognize the authentic Neapolitan papaccella at first glance. This pepper is on the small side (reaching at most 10 centimeters) and a little flat and ribbed, varying in color from a bold green to sunny yellow and garnet. Its flesh is sweet, meaty and very flavorful. The pepper's aroma is particularly intense, with herbaceous notes. Seeds are sown from the second half of March to the first 10 days of July, and the peppers are harvested – by hand – from the second half of July to the beginning of November. The gardens where this variety was once widely cultivated were situated in the Brusciano area, where many of the inhabitants have the last name Papaccio. Cultivation once took place around farms that produced vinegar used for making preserves. This vinegar was made solely from Piccirillo, a red wine that comes from grapes planted in rows supported by trees. The wine is tart and low in alcohol and should be drunk immediately after vintage. The peppers and other garden produce were preserved in the vinegar in wood barrels big enough to contain 150 kilos of whole peppers (never sliced). The Campania Regional Authority has recovered the genetic material of the Neapolitan pepper and are reproducing the original strain in an experimental plot and the resulting progeny will be planted at the residences of the Presidium's 11 producers. A strict production protocol has been drafted that guarantees high quality and sustainable production that respects the environment. The peppers can be eaten raw, roasted, sautéed, or stuffed with tuna or salted anchovies, breadcrumbs, raisins, pine nuts, *piennolo* cherry tomatoes and capers and baked in the oven. The peppers preserved in red wine vinegar are used in salads eaten during Neapolitan Christmas celebrations.

PRODUCTION AREA
Agro Acerrano, province of Naples, Campania

PRESIDIUM COORDINATORS
Vito Trotta
tel. +39 0818044295 - 3406001837
workinprogress@alice.it
Luigi Conelli
tel. +39 0818231528 - 339 2866189
luigiconelli@libero.it

PRESIDIUM SUPPORTED BY
Campania Regional Authority, department of Agriculture and Productive Activities

Nebrodi Black Pig

This very old native Sicilian breed is hardy and resistant to disease and bad weather; however, over the years, its numbers have plummeted because of a lack of market demand. These black swine – which are small in size with a dark coat, and closely resemble wild boar both in appearance and habits – live in the woods of the Nebrodi Mountains (50 thousand hectares of beech and oak, now mainly protected by a nature park), in the areas of Messina and Catania. They are reared semi-wild and wild in large areas where they can graze, feeding on acorns and berries. Only when a sow is about to farrow or in the last month before slaughter are the pigs given extra food in the form of beans and cereals. The farmers – most of whom are also producers – have small holdings and their produce is mainly reserved for family use or used in local barter; only rarely is the pork sold on the market. Over the past few years, the population of this hardy, rustic breed has dropped sharply and now numbers a few thousand. The extinction of this breed of pig would be a tragic loss for the genetic pool, for the local economy and for gastronomy: the black swine produce exceptionally high quality meat which can be used both fresh and to produce sausages and various cured meats. Salame di Sant'Angelo in Brolo, Nebrodi prosciutto and sausage, salami, capocollo and pancetta were once produced using black pork and their quality was guaranteed by their freedom of movement and natural diet. Many butchers specializing in cured meats are now forced to use hybrid breeds from industrial farmers, resulting in products that are less intensely aromatic and cannot be matured for long periods. The Presidium has identified seven farmers and brought them together, providing the necessary processing facilities to promote the rich and varied range of cured meats from this area.

PRODUCTION AREA
Nebrodi mountains, provinces of Messina, Etna and Catania, Sicily

PRESIDIUM COORDINATORS
Pippo Privitera
tel. +39 3358455507
pippopri@tin.it
Vincenzo Pruiti
tel. +39 0941438179 - 3284206027
soat7@regione.sicilia.it

PRESIDIUM SUPPORTED BY
Sicily Regional Authority, department of Agriculture and Forestry

Nebrodi Provola

A spun-curd cheese produced by hand from cow's milk using kid or lamb rennet; the curds are kneaded for a long time, like bread, and then spun by pouring hot water onto the mass. The cheesemakers are expert at shaping the forms with remarkable speed, handing down the cheesemaking techniques from father to son. They can even produce traditional figures for children: doves, baskets, little horses... The size varies depending on where it is made, ranging from one kilo in the north-western Nebrodi mountains – the area around Mistretta, Castel di Lucio, Caronia – to one and a half or nearly two kilos in the central Nebrodi mountains (the area around Floresta, Ucrìa, Castell'Umberto), and as much as five kilos in Basicò and Montalbano Elicona, in the eastern part of the Nebrodi mountains. This distinctively shaped cheese – an oblong, pear-shape with a round head that can be tied in pairs for hanging – is straw-colored when fresh, darkening to amber as it matures. The texture is soft and compact and it literally melts in the mouth with a sweet, delicate flavor. It is ripened in a building with thick walls for at least 10-30 days, if it is to be used fresh, or otherwise for three or four months. As it matures, the cheese acquires a strong, more piquant flavor. This cheese is excellent served at table and also for cooking, in particular as a key ingredient in a number of local dishes. The Presidium aims to add value to this ancient cheese and the wild, wooded area where it is made. Endemic pastures, a mainly native dairy herd and traditional cheesemaking techniques form a natural cultural microecosystem that encompasses the whole territory: man, animals, plants and soil. The Presidium aims to contribute towards the definition and possible improvement of the different types of Provola in order to encourage a longer ripening period and to introduce Provola dei Nebrodi to consumers throughout Italy, in particular restaurants and buyers.

PRODUCTION AREA
The whole area of the Nebrodi mountains, and the provinces of Messina, Enna and Catania, Sicily

PRESIDIUM COORDINATORS
Pippo Privitera
tel. +39 3358455507
pippopri@tin.it
Vincenzo Pruiti
tel. +39 0941438179 - 3284206027 soat7@regione.sicilia.it

PRESIDIUM SUPPORTED BY
Sicily Regional Authority, department
of Agriculture and Forestry,
University of Catania

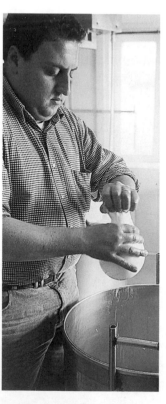

Nizza Monferrato
Hunchback Cardoon

The hunchback cardoon of Nizza Monferrato is the only one that can be eaten raw: the secret is the cultivation method. It is sewn in May in the sandy soils around Nizza Monferrato, Incisa Scapaccino and Castelnuovo Belbo. The cardoon growers in the Belbo Valley continue their age-old traditions, and the cardoons are not irrigated, fertilized or treated in any way. In September, when they are tall and strong, the cardoons are bent over and covered with soil. This way the ribs lose all traces of chlorophyll and become very white and tender and, in their attempt to free themselves and find the light, they curve round, giving them their characteristic shape. After a month, in October, they are ready to be unearthed, harvested and the outer leaves and ruined ribs are removed. The resulting hearts are amazingly sweet, extremely crisp and ideal for eating raw. They are a fundamental ingredient in a famous Piedmont dish: *bagna caoda*, a sauce made of garlic, extra virgin olive oil and anchovies, which simmers in a terracotta pan at the center of the table, while the guests dip vegetables into it. This is a real social ritual, and in Nizza Monferrato there exist the *Bagna Caoda* and the Hunchback Cardoon confraternities. However, there are numerous ways to cook the cardoon: stuffed, fried, in soups, flans, tarts, served with sauces or fondue. A few years ago there were very few cardoon growers and they were poorly paid, and the hunchback cardoons from Nizza Monferrato, while still an excellent product, were extremely hard to find. Outside help was therefore desperately needed. The Presidium drew up a discipline ordering that only the spade variety, the best and most traditional, could be used, and all the operations (cultivation, weeding, tying, burying and harvesting) are carried out manually, with no chemical fertilizers, herbicides or pesticides.

PRODUCTION AREA
Nizza Monferrato and eight communes in the province of Asti, Piedmont

PRESIDIUM COORDINATORS
Tullio Mussa
tel. +39 0141793350
botvinizza@libero.it
Claudio Vaccaneo
tel. +39 0141793044 – 3470776526
claudio.vaccaneo@libero.it

PRESIDIUM SUPPORTED BY
Asti Provincial Authority, Commune of Nizza Monferrato

Noli Anchovies (Cicciarelli)

Called cicciarelli in Italian, these anchovies have always been known as *lussi* or *lussotti* in Noli dialect. This little fish, more or less as long as a finger, is tapered, silvery and without any scales. The cicciarelli live in very large schools, which hide very quickly under the sand and only swim up towards the surface when the water is clear and the sun is high. At Noli there are still about 20 cicciarelli fishermen left, and they are between 30 and 70 years old. The heirs of a grand tradition, they belong to a cooperative that was founded in the early 1900s. They have always fished along the coast, with the *sciabica* net (sweep net) and always in groups: at least five or six fishermen on two different boats. When they catch sight of a black spot in the sea when looking through the *spegiu* (porthole), one of the boats 'stays on the fish, while the other surrounds it with the net, forming a sort of horseshoe shape. The fresh fish is sold on the beech in the morning. Unfortunately there are very few customers, mainly the elderly and at times old fishermen. Just a few kilometers away and nobody even knows what cicciarelli are. Even though they are excellent when fried or marinated, local restaurants tend to frown on them; maybe because they are little known or because the catch is not constant and is not practiced during the tourist season (when sweep nets are prohibited). To think that marinated anchovies could be an excellent traditional appetizer. The Presidium is seeking to promote this excellent fish and preserve the very ancient technique of fishing with the *sciabica* net. But it also wants to promote a wider campaign in defense of all the small fish in the Mediterranean, an important cultural, tourist and economic resource. To this end, with the help of OLPA (Ligurian Observatory for Fishing and Environment), an experimental project was realized that serves to demonstrate the selectivity of fishing with the *sciabica* net and therefore the full sustainability of the same. The objective is to obtain permission to fish from May to November, the best months for the cicciarello.

PRODUCTION AREA

Finale Ligure, Noli and Spotorno, province of Savona, Liguria

PRESIDIUM COORDINATORS

Attilio Olivieri
tel. +39 3409007618
attilio.olivieri@tin.it
Giuseppe Lepore
tel. +39 019850605
giuseppelepore@tin.it

PRESIDIUM SUPPORTED BY

Liguria Regional Authority

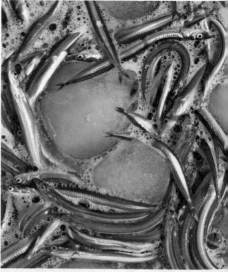

Non Valley Mortandela

Mortandela is a typical cured meat of Non Valley that is prepared with various cuts of pork, including the lungs, heart and throat. It has a slightly flattened spherical shape, a brown color and a very strong smoky aroma. To get the meat for the mortandela, local families used to buy a piglet at the All Saints' Fair and raise it for twelve months on potatoes, bran, vegetable scraps and hay. But today it is increasingly difficult to find heavy pigs that have been raised on natural foods, so fine for making this preparation. The meats trimmed of fat, gristle and nerves are minced and seasoned with salt and spices and then shaped into firm, but not overly stiff meatballs weighing about 200 grams each. The mortandele are then left to dry for 12 hours on wooden planks that have been sprinkled with buckwheat flour. Next they are smoked at a temperature of about 25°C, and to ensure that they dry and smoke evenly are turned over carefully one by one after six or seven hours. They are aged for at least one week, but are really best when eaten after one month. The aroma should be delicate and not overpowered by the taste of the meats or the spices. The pork butcher needs to trim the meats carefully so there is no sign of gristle or hard parts when eaten. A popular and rustic food, it can be enjoyed raw or cooked and served with polenta, potatoes or steamed field greens such as dandelion leaves. Because the meat is difficult to process and the local economy is based almost entirely on apple growing, traditional mortandela production has had its share of problems. Thanks to the involvement of young butchers and caterers, the Presidium has managed to revive production. The aim is to encourage the pork butchers involved to get their supply of pork from breeders willing to follow a natural production protocol that ensures top quality meat.

PRODUCTION AREA
Non Valley, province of Trento, Trentino

PRESIDIUM COORDINATOR
Massimo Corrà
tel. +39 0463536129
macelleriacorra@tin.it

PRESIDIUM SUPPORTED BY
Trento Autonomous Provincial Authority,
Trentino SpA

Noto Almond

Marzipan, *martorana, dolcetti da riposto, conchiglie, mustazzuoli,* amaretti, the Noto *faccioni,* torrone, cassata, etc.... Many Sicilian specialties in cakes and biscuits are almond-based. It was the Arabs who first processed these fruits, chopping them up with egg-white and honey, and the confectionery-making tradition started with them, later collecting elements from all sorts of places (from the Normans, the Spanish, The French, nobles, convents, pilgrims, etc.) and becoming a basic element of the island food. The most famous almond groves in Sicily are to be found in the Siracusa area, between Noto and Avola, where three varieties are cultivated: the Romana, the Pizzuta d'Avola and the Fascionello. The first of these gives the best fruit from the organoleptic standpoint (its flavor is intense and aromatic, and its color pinky-white) but it is the least appreciated by the market, because of its stumpy, irregular shape. The third variety lies midway between the first two, similar to the Pizzuta in the shape of its fruit and vigorous like the Romana. These ancient cultigens have thick, woody shells that hold in the fats and keep the flavor and the aroma of the almonds intact for a long time; however, they give a very low yield. The farmers work at the end of September to prune the trees, in December they graft on the wild plants, they plough the land three or four times a year and fertilize it with cow manure once a year. In July and August they beat the branches with long sticks and collect the almonds in tarpaulins spread over the ground; then they hull them, leave them to dry on the threshing-floor and pack them. All the subsequent phases (shelling, toasting and processing) are no longer dealt with by the farm workers, who only sell the raw material. The small sum of money they earn does not even pay for the work of harvesting, not to mention compensating for the uncertainty of cultivating almond trees, which are subject to the threat of frost. With the birth of the Presidium, a set of regulations has been drawn up and the almond farmers have joined forces in a consortium. The aim is to have the almonds hulled, dried, shelled, peeled and sold directly by the producers.

PRODUCTION AREA
Noto and another three communes in the province of Siracusa, Sicily

PRESIDIUM COORDINATOR
Carmelo Maiorca
tel. +39 3476557018
cmaiorca@sistemia.it

PRESIDIUM SUPPORTED BY
Sicily Regional Authority, department of Agriculture and Forestry

Nùbia Red Garlic

This takes its name from its bright red inner 'tunic' and because it has always been cultivated in Nùbia, a village near Paceco. The production area includes the town of Paceco, part of the area around Trapani, Erice and the northern part of Marsala and Salemi, around 3,000 hectares in total. Currently only 250 hectares are farmed, generally in dry conditions in dark, clay soil. This intense-flavored garlic has an outstanding quality: the Faculty of Agriculture in Palermo compared it with the main national varieties and detected an allicine content well above average. It is grown in rotation with melons, fava beans and durum wheat to ensure the terrain is not over-worked. Sowing takes place in November and December, sometimes also January, and the harvest (in May, if harvested fresh, or in June, if left to dry partially in the fields) is still carried out using traditional methods. It has to be picked in the evening – on very hot days it is necessary to wait for night fall – or very early in the morning, as the leaves, being damper, allow the bulbs to be plaited together by hand. In the past very large bunches were gathered – plaits containing 100 heads of garlic each, but now on the market there are smaller plaits, containing from 10 to 50 bulbs, each with 12 cloves. There are different names for these plaits depending on the diameter of the bulbs: *cucchia rossa* (50 millimeters), *corrente* (40), *cucchiscedda* (30) and *mazzunedda* (20-25). The plaits are then hung on the balcony, or in cellars or warehouses. Nùbia garlic is a key ingredient of many traditional Trapani dishes, including pasta *cull'àgghia* (with *pesto alla trapanese*) and fish couscous. The Presidium has brought together growers, all very small operations, under common production regulations and a brand which guarantees the provenance and quality of the garlic.

PRODUCTION AREA
Nùbia, a village by Paceco, Trapani, Erice and part of the area round Marsala and Salemi, province of Trapani, Sicily

PRESIDIUM COORDINATOR
Filippo Salerno
tel. +39 0923873844 - 3476673002 filipposalerno@trapaniweb.it

PRESIDIUM SUPPORTED BY
Sicily Regional Authority, department of Agriculture and Forestry, Banca Senatore Grammatico

Onano Lentil

Large, round and light brown, with shades of green, dark grey and ash marbling, this lentil is cultivated at Onano, a town in the upper Tuscia district in the province of Viterbo, and was even mentioned in one of the documents of the medieval city-republic back in 1561. It is also known that the papal court expressed its appreciation for this lentil in the 17th century and the last century as well. Then in the 1970s the oldest variety, the large, colorful one that is most highly prized, all but disappeared. A number of factors were responsible. The indiscriminate use of nitrogenous chemical fertilizers damaged the soil it grew in, more productive and more profitable varieties of lentils became available and some of the fields were simply abandoned. Highly flavorful, the 'lentil of the Popes' grows very well in the light, sandy, volcanic soil of Onano, which is ideal for legumes. It has a very thin, almost nonexistent skin, and a fine and creamy texture having the aroma of hay and chamomile. At the beginning of the last century it achieved recognition well beyond the local market as can be seen from the awards it received at the international expositions of Rome, Buenos Aires, London and Paris.

Very sweet, tender and delicate, the Onano lentil is excellent in soups with rice or the square egg pasta known as *quadrucci*. The legume also makes a very good and simple side dish prepared with a little tomato and a mixture of lightly sautéed minced *guanciale*, garlic, carrot and celery, or when it is stewed with wild game, particularly partridge. Today the Onano lentil is grown in family gardens, where an organic producer has carried out research on the seeds in an effort to bring the oldest variety back on the market. The aim of the Presidium is to increase the cultivation of this large lentil as potentially well-suited terrain is available but currently being used for other crops.

PRODUCTION AREA
Onano, province of Viterbo, Lazio

PRESIDIUM COORDINATOR
Marco Camilli
tel. +39 076378018 - 3284187301
marcocamilli@hotmail.com

PRESIDIUM SUPPORTED BY
Apabiol (Associazione produttori agricoli biologici del Lazio)

Orbetello Bottarga

The *cefalo volpina* (*Mugil cephalus*) is a gray mullet that thrives in the salty ponds of Sardinia, but also in the lagoons along the Tyrrhenian coast. In Orbetello the presence of this fish is combined with a preservation technique that was already recorded in the Middle Ages, and was perfected under Spanish dominion of the Garrison State. If smoked eel and fried fish marinated *in escabeche* (vinegar and herbs) probably derive from recipes that were originally Spanish, the name (*battarikh*) and the salting techniques the fish roe used for the botargo are of Arab origin. Botargo is prepared by delicately extracting the sacks of eggs from the female mullet (or the tuna, but with much less success), leaving them under salt for several hours, pressing them and drying them. The Sardinians age the botargo for up to six months, while the fishermen of Orbetello consider it ready after 15 days. The salted eggs become a solid but not dry block, amber in color, which is excellent as an antipasto, sliced very thin and drizzled with extravirgin olive oil, or as a sauce for spaghetti: a small amount of grated botargo is an excellent dressing for spaghetti with garlic and oil. Until not many years ago, the mullet from the lagoons were sent to Sardinia to remove the eggs and all that remained in Orbetello was some family production. Then 66 fishermen formed a cooperative to recover this ancient activity. Now they have a workshop which produces not only botargo but also smoked fillet of mullet and eel, and they run a shop and fish market, rear young bass and bream to restock the waters, and in the evenings they open a small restaurant that looks onto the lagoon, where they serve the day's catch prepared using local recipes. The Presidium wants to help them, working to promote their products and to maintain the lagoon habitat alive and healthy. The experimentation underway for the artificial restocking of mullet is part of this project.

PRODUCTION AREA
Lagoon of Orbetello, province of Grosseto, Tuscany

PRESIDIUM COORDINATOR
Massimo Bernacchini
tel. +39 0564860288
info@orbetellopesca.it

PRESIDIUM SUPPORTED BY
Grosseto Provincial Authority

Osilo Pecorino

Smaller than the classic pecorino sardo (narrower and taller), this cheese is produced in the area around the town of Osilo and in a number of surrounding towns (Ploaghe, Nulvi, Codrongianos and Tergu). It has a thin, straw yellow rind, like the cheese itself, which is soft, oily and greasy. It has a characteristic odor of sheep, with notes of wool, dry wood and in some cases, aromatic herbs, while on the palate it is very distinctive: buttery, melting, with notes of roasted hazelnuts. The key stages of production are the long pressing (sometimes with the help of rudimentary mechanical presses), after the curds have been broken into minute grains, and aging for five or six months, during which time the cheeses are turned regularly and washed with water and brine, and the surface is smeared with a mixture of oil and vinegar. Osilo Pecorino is unique, like the extraordinary, unique *ricotta mustia* made from the whey. This ricotta, shaped like a squashed bread roll, is amber in color with a slightly smoky flavor (the name indicates the final stage of the smoking process), and can be eaten fresh or aged at length. Unfortunately production is fragmented and much lower than full capacity: most of the shepherds sell their milk to the big dairies, as they do not have the facilities and equipment necessary to process, age and sell the cheese. The Presidium unites six Osilo producers and is working to set up an association. Strict production regulations have been drawn up, based on a key principle: Presidium pecorino can only be produced by local breeders and shepherds in the original production area, centered around the town of Osilo. Presidium regulations do not permit the production of cheese using milk from various farms, or worse, from farm-reared sheep.

PRODUCTION AREA
Osilo and four other towns in the province of Sassari, Sardinia

PRESIDIUM COORDINATORS
Fabrizia Fiori
tel. +39 3282514279
slowfood.sassari@hotmail.com
Gavinuccio Turra
tel. +39 07942695 - 360 498282
gavinuccioturra@virgilio.it

PRESIDIUM SUPPORTED BY
Municipality of Osilo, Gal Coros

Ozieri Copuleta

The sweet is traditionally tied to the important recurring and religious feast days of Ozieri (patron saints' days, weddings, baptisms) and one time it was commonplace in all families. As with many Sardinian sweets, sumptuous and difficult to prepare, the copuleta is at risk of extinction because the original recipes, handed down from mother to daughter, are difficult to adapt to the times and needs of standardization of modern bakeries. The preparation requires a considerable amount of patience and much manual work. It is begun with a flour mix, lard, water and salt, which is kneaded until a homogeneous consistency is reached. It is then rolled out like a thin sheet, from which a number of discs are cut with which metal profiles are lined with low rims, of oval or round shape, which are then filled with a compote based on sponge, grated lemon rind, finely chopped toasted almonds, with a dash of liquor. Cooked in the oven for 15 minutes at 200°C, the copuletas are then sealed with a topping of icing and left to cool for a few hours, presenting themselves as compact but delicate and soft at the same time. One cake shop and two confectionary companies of Ozieri, united in a Presidium, make them to order. Their copuletas are distinguished from other similar ones, which can be found in the different areas of the island, because of their almond filling, which substitute the sapa – in Sardinian *saba* – more commonly used. They must be eaten fresh and are, therefore, difficult to find outside of the town, known also for *spianata* (or fine bread) and *sospiri*, almond based pastries, now all over the national market. Ozieri is in the center of Northern Sardinia, an agricultural area where large quantities of almonds and lemons were grown. The aim of the Presidium is to rebuild a local industry and produce copuletas with raw materials from Sardinia: almonds, lemons, flour, from indigenous grains grown on the island.

PRODUCTION AREA
Ozieri, province of Sassari, Sardinia

PRESIDIUM COORDINATOR
Fabrizia Fiori
tel. +39 3282514279
slowfood.sassari@hotmail.com

PRESIDIUM SUPPORTED BY
Commune of Ozieri

Paceco Cartucciaro Melon

At the beginning of the 17th century, melon cultivations were very common in the farm communities near Trapani. In a text from 1609, *Storia di un borgo feudale del seicento*, we read that 'these people specialized in growing melons'; in another, written by a local historian in the mid-1800s, that 'in addition to extensive cereal crops, Paceco had broad tracts of olive groves, vineyards and vast melon fields'. After the late harvest (from mid-September on), people used to put the melons on their porches or hang them from the balconies. They did not touch them again until Christmas, when they cut them open during the holidays to find them still sweet and juicy. The cultivation of the yellow melon was at its height in the 1970s and '80s. Then there was a dramatic reduction in the crops because of competition from new yellow-skinned varieties and hybrids, esthetically very similar. They are all yellow, but the cartucciaro is a little more oblong than the common helios, more irregular and less perfect in shape, with a slightly curved point. The new varieties have proven successful because they are more productive and resistant to various pathogens. In recent years, the Faculty of Agrarian Sciences at the University of Palermo has started making a selection of the original seed of the Paceco cartucciaro ecotype, and with the help of some of the farmers has set up experimental fields. The work is still in progress. Each they try to isolate the best plants to obtain seeds that are resistant and capable of producing melons with the most consistent characteristics possible. The cartucciario is sown in stages from April to September and the harvest starts in early June. Its most distinctive characteristic is that it keeps so well. The Presidium, which brings together three farmers, wants to revive the tradition of conserving the melons, which today are kept in cool dry rooms. It also wants to postpone the sale until the winter holiday season to push up the market price and make the product more profitable for the producers.

PRODUCTION AREA
Paceco and part of the commune of Trapani,
province of Trapani, Sicily

PRESIDIUM COORDINATOR
Filippo Salerno
tel. +39 0923873844-3476673002
filipposalerno@trapaniweb.it

PRESIDIUM SUPPORTED BY
Sicily Regional Authority, department
of Agriculture and Forestry

Paduan Hen

Probably introduced to Italy in the 1300s by a nobleman from Padua, a doctor and astronomer, returning from a trip to Poland, these hens has a crest of long, slim feathers that open into a corolla and fall over the eyes. Black, white, gold, chamois or silvery, the hen has red, meaty nostrils meeting over the beak, a long beard, evident whiskers reaching to below the eyes and a rather hesitant gait - since it has to glimpse between its feathers to see where it is going. It can weigh up to two kilos; it has a thin skin and brownish meat, similar to that of pheasants and guinea fowl. In the 1960s, it was progressively replaced by more productive breeds. Production regulations now envisage a minimum area of four meters per bird, since it is a free-range animal, and a natural diet (grain, especially maize). Every bird within the Presidium has a ring with the breeder number and leaves the slaughterhouse accompanied by a label, a leaflet and, for restaurateurs, six edible wafers arranged on a serving dish next to each portion. The classic recipe is *a la canevera*: the hen is cooked with various flavorings in a pig bladder or wrapped in foil placed in a casserole full of water, using the *canevera* (a small bamboo cane) as a 'chimney': it is important that no flavor is lost to the cooking water and that all ingredients contribute to the final taste of the meat. It is served with a green sauce or *pearà* (peppery bread sauce). The are still a few small-scale breeders in Europe, while Italy boasts the San Benedetto da Norcia Professional Institute for Agriculture and the Environment in Padua. An association – Pro Avibus Nostris – has been set up to safeguard this breed, involving five companies: at the outset, the hens were only a kind of hobby, but then the Presidium was set up and, little by little, the Paduan hen found a small market, was included in the menus of restaurants and sold through poultry and specialist food shops in the city.

PRODUCTION AREA
Province of Padua, Veneto

PRESIDIUM COORDINATORS
Gianni Breda
tel. +39 049619814
giannibreda@tin.it
Gabriele Baldan
tel. +39 049720651
sbalengo@libero.it

PRESIDIUM SUPPORTED BY
Veneto Regional Authority, Veneto Agricoltura, Padua Chamber of Commerce, Industry, Crafts and Agriculture

Pestàt

In central Friuli, in the area around Fagagna, one of the loveliest and greenest in the region, the local economy is based almost entirely on farming and pig breeding, even though the land has gradually been given over to artisan settlements and small industry. A few smaller productions, historically associated with the important pork butchery tradition (San Daniele is very nearby), have resisted the changes underway. One of these is pestàt, which was typically made at home when families butchered a pig and is still produced in the traditional way by a very few butchers today. This simple method of using pork lard is a way to preserve the fragrance and flavor of garden vegetables and herbs in the autumn. The pigs, which originally belonged to an indigenous breed, are raised in the semi-wild state and fed naturally or come from local small-scale breeders. The excellent lard that comes from them is ground up and added to a mixture of carrots, celery, small pieces of onion, chopped sage, rosemary, thyme, marjoram, garlic and parsley. Salt and pepper provide the finishing touch and then the mixture is stuffed into a natural casing and left to age in cool damp cellars. The lard and the salt and pepper prevent the vegetables from fermenting and the gradual dehydration helps to preserve the mixture. The drying and aging processes ensure the proper amalgam and concentration of aromas and flavors, which reach their peak after about one year. Pestàt, which can also be consumed a few weeks after being made, is not eaten like a sausage but sautéed so the fat melts and the vegetables do not burn. It is an excellent base for many of the local dishes, especially for flavoring minestrones, *broàde e muset*, (a local dish of cotechino with turnips steeped in marc), stewed meats and skillet potatoes.

PRODUCTION AREA
Fagagna, province of Udine, Friuli Venezia Giulia

PRESIDIUM COORDINATOR
Laura Rebagliati
tel. +39 3493526994
lreba@libero.it

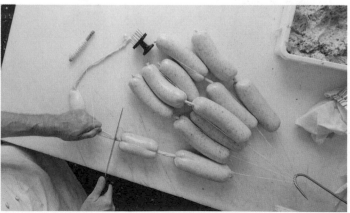

Piedmontese Blonde Hen and Saluzzo White Hen

The Piedmontese blonde hen (also known as Cuneo blonde, Villanova blonde, Crivelle red or 'nostralina') and Saluzzo white hen (also known as Cavour white) are types of chickens traditionally bred in Piedmont. Once upon a time these animals were destined for family consumption: typical dishes of the Cuneo area, such as boiled hen, served in its own stock, in jaspic or in salad, and pollo alla cacciatora, which tastes better and becomes more tender thanks to the sauce, the same which is then served on polenta. Today Charlie Zuchuat, of the Trattoria Società di Villanovetta di Verzuolo suggests gallina all'occitana, a recipe containing olives, tomatoes, dried peppers, anchovies and a drop of red wine from the hills surrounding Saluzzo. The blonde hen, bred almost everywhere in Piedmont, has golden suede-like feathers, a tall, black tail with a metallic hue, a yellow beak with four or six teeth, a full-grown upright crest. The Saluzzo white hen, similar to the blonde but bright white (including the tail) is rarer and is only bred in the ancient Marquisate of Saluzzo and a few municipalities to the north, such as Cavour, Villafranca and Garzigliana. Long ago in this area, many farms bred up to 200-300 hens, producing up to 10-15 dozens of eggs each day. Then in the 60s, intensive industrial and agricultural breeding, especially around Saluzzo, caused a steady decline in the production of these traditional breeds, which need the outdoors. Work on restoring the Presidium started with the help of the Verzuolo Professional Institute of Agriculture and the Environment. Farmers follow strict rules, so chickens each have five square meters outdoors in which to peck. In 2002 the installation of an incubator devoted to the chickens brought back the popularity of both breeds. The next project is the creation of a small abattoir. The process will then be complete.

PRODUCTION AREA
Provinces of Cuneo, Torino and Asti, Piedmont

PRESIDIUM COORDINATOR
Gianfranco Marengo
tel. +39 3389317319
gfmarengo@virgilio.it

PRESIDIUM SUPPORTED BY
Cuneo Provincial Authority, Verzuolo Professional Institute of Agriculture and the Environment, Commune of Saluzzo

Piedmontese Ox

The Piedmontese Ox is unique because of the very low levels of cholesterol and just the right fat content of its lean and flavorful meat. The raw beef, chopped with a knife and seasoned with extra virgin olive oil, salt and very little pepper is one of the most traditional dishes in Piedmontese cooking. It belongs to the classic regional cuisine that also makes use of this local beef for the *gran bollito misto*, mixed boiled meats to dip in salt and various *bagnèt* or sauces (green sauce, red sauce, *cognà*, *saossa d'avije*, horseradish sauce). The calf, the castrated bull, the ox and the cow (*la giora*) are all used in cooking. The Piedmontese White Ox has very ancient origins, but it was in 1886, at Guarene d'Alba (Province of Cuneo), that a bull with enormous buttocks and very muscular thighs was born by natural mutation. This specimen was the progenitor of the so-called *vitelli della coscia* (thigh calves) and would give rise to a new breed of white ox that was good as a work animal but also provided excellent meat. At one time, especially in the mountains, it was also used for milk. Piedmont became a major breeding area for this ox and was home to 680,000 heads at the beginning of the 20th century. In 1973, the Piedmontese Ox was the third most important Italian breed and the finest indigenous strain, and there were still over 600,000 heads in Piedmont in 1985. In the middle of the 1990s, however, production dropped by half, which is why Slow Food decided to set up a Presidium. Thanks to the work of veterinarian Sergio Capaldo, the La Granda association of small local breeders was formed. They follow a very strict protocol, using only natural feed such as maize, barley, bran, broad beans and hay (mostly grown by them) and no silage or vitamin supplements. In the La Granda butchers' shops every cut of beef is labeled with the date of butchering as well as the name, surname and address of the breeder. In the near future the labeling will also include the feed used and the organoleptic qualities of the meat.

PRODUCTION AREA
Communes in the provinces of Cuneo, Asti and Torino, Piedmont

PRESIDIUM COORDINATORS
Sergio Capaldo
tel. +39 3356770566
sergio.capaldo@libero.it - info@lagranda.it
Guglielmo Tomatis
tel. +39 017267265 - 017267422

PRESIDIUM SUPPORTED BY
Commune of Fossano, Fondazione Cassa di Risparmio di Fossano

Piennolo Small Tomato

These small cherry tomatoes, which are also known as *spongilli* or *piénnoli*, weigh about 20-25 grams and have always been grown on the slopes of Vesuvius, in the dark, sandy soil built up over the centuries by layers of lava flow, making it particularly fertile. The name refers to the ancient way of preserving them, which consists in tying them in bunches with strings of hemp and hanging them from the walls or ceiling in rooms with a suitable temperature and humidity, until the winter or the following spring. As time passes, they shrink but their taste and perfume increase. They differ from Pachino cherry tomatoes because they have two lateral furrows, which start from the stalk and produce a square shape, and a point or *pizzo* at the end. The skin is thick and resistant, the flesh firm and compact, dried by the sun that shines on the arid land around the volcano. They are sown in March and April and ripen in July and August, but by the age-old preservation process, they are harvested in bunches early in the summer and stored by hanging in rooms with a suitable temperature and humidity, until the winter or the following spring. Although every family has its bed of cherry tomatoes to use in the winter – the convenience of having an excellent *pummarola* on hand for many months – few grow additional quantities for the market, because it is hard work and not well paid. The best soil is hard to reach and to cultivate because it is higher up. These tomatoes are traditional fare for a quick mid-morning snack – seasoned with oil, salt, and basil and squashed on bread – or for quick sauces: vermicelli with clams, fish all'acqua pazza, meat alla pizzaiola. The Presidium is promoting this excellent vegetable: the main goal is to make the potential of the product known to more interested, curious consumers. *Piennolo* cherry tomatoes will also be offered to the best restaurants.

PRODUCTION AREA
Towns on the slopes of Vesuvius, province of Naples, Campania

PRESIDIUM COORDINATOR
Giovanni Marino
tel. +39 0813621048
agricola@casabarone.it

PRESIDIUM SUPPORTED BY
Naples Provincial Authority

Pietraroja Prosciutto

A few houses perched on the top of Monte Mutria, more or less 700 inhabitants and the fresh air of the hills: this is Pietraroja. The cellars of the old houses in this small town in the Sannio district are used to age extraordinary hams. For centuries the *salumieri* of the area have climbed up to the top of the hill with their trimmed hams, ready to be treated by hand and hung from the ceilings where, after at least 12 months but no more than 20, they will become excellent prosciutto at just the right stage of dryness: moist but not soft, delicately salted and with a lasting flavor. Pietraroja hams are not a recent discovery by some gourmet looking for new delicacies: as early as 1776, a historical document reveals that the Duca di Laurenzana di Piedimonte used to order this prosciutto for his table. The text mentions the *prigiotta*, the name of the tool used to press the prosciutto before curing. When they are ready, the hams weigh 9-13 kilograms and do not contain preservatives: they merely rest in a small quantity of rock salt for about 20 days – depending on the size of the ham – before being hung to breathe between the centuries-old stone walls. Output is limited, only 700 pieces a year, approximately one per inhabitant. In the past, the meat was provided by Casertana breed pigs – the famous *pelatelli neri* of Caserta – which were bred free in the countryside, an extraordinary raw ingredient that is now being recovered. The Presidium intends to recreate an entirely local production chain, even for the meat which is currently provided by common breeds of pig such as Landrace or Large White. For now, it is important to be able to say that in Pietraroja three small butchers are producing prosciutto from locally reared pigs, which are then cured with care. One interesting fact: Pietraroja prosciutto should not be sliced but diced, starting with a slice about half a centimeter thick and cutting small rectangles about five centimeters long.

PRODUCTION AREA
Pietraroja, province of Benevento, Campania

PRESIDIUM COORDINATOR
Gaetano Pascale
tel. +39 0824817840
gapasc@tin.it

PRESIDIUM SPONSORED BY
Benevento Chamber of Commerce, Industry, Crafts and Agriculture, Gal Titerno, Commune of Pietraroja

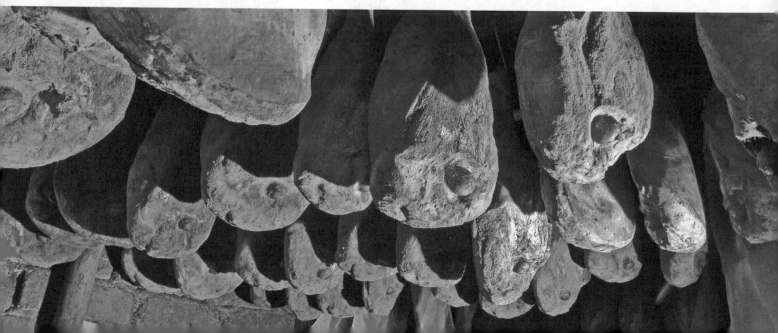

Pistoia Mountain Pecorino

Lead-gray fleece, shiny black skin, dark, spiral horns and bright, protruding eyes: the Massese is the most important Tuscan sheep breed. There are, especially in the north of the region, about 80.000 head, grazed in summer and, in winter, reared with hay, maize, bran and oats. The females give birth three times every two years and therefore provide milk in every season. Shepherds and dairymen in the mountains around Pistoia have used this milk, unpasteurized and blended with natural rennet, to make cheese that has remained the same for centuries. The milk is sometimes even taken by hand on the farms and used by dairymen-breeders to produce three types of cheese: fresh (best enjoyed after 1-3 weeks), *abbucciato* (matured for at least 35 days so that a rind is formed) and *pecorino da asserbo* (matured for two-three months up to one year). All three are round; the first two weigh 1-1.8 kilos, the third even up to 3 kilos. The rind is smooth, while its color changes with maturing from straw yellow to gray brown; the cheese is ivory white. Fresh pecorino (also named baccellone) has a milky aroma and herby flavor; it is the classic Cacio cheese enjoyed with pears, or broad beans in spring. The abbucciato and mature pecorino are ideal to close a meal and are also used grated. Abbucciato has a more intense aroma than the fresh cheese, with hints of game. It is best enjoyed with Tuscan bread, polenta, boiled potatoes, pears and *necci* (pancakes made with chestnut flour cooked in red-hot baking trays). Shepherds in the Pistoia mountains also produce two types of cheese for immediate consumption: Raviggiolo and ricotta. The Presidium embraces around 20 producers and aims to promote their cheese production, safeguard the pastures and ensure fair incomes for families deciding to remain in or return to the mountains.

PRODUCTION AREA
Borgo a Bussiano, Cutigliano, Lamporecchio, Montale, Pescia, Pistoia, Piteglio, Quarrata, Sambuca Pistoiese and San Marcello Pistoiese, province of Pistoia, Tuscany

PRESIDIUM COORDINATORS
Luciano Bertini
tel. +39 057333882
bertini46@yahoo.it
Renzo Malvezzi
tel. +39 0571584115 - 335331718
rmalvezzi@interfree.it

PRESIDIUM SUPPORTED BY
Pistoia Provincial Authority, Pistoia Apa, Pistoia Appennine Mountain Community

Pitina

The making of pitina and its variants – peta and petuccia – arose from the need to conserve meat in the autumn and winter months in poor regions like the valleys north of Pordenone. The venison from chamois deer or roe deer killed during the hunt, but also injured or ailing sheep or goats, were the main ingredient for the preparation of these specialties. The pitina (typical of Val Tramontina), the petuccia (traditional in Val Cellina) and the peta (a local specialty of Andreis) differ in terms of the aromatic herbs that are added to the mixture and the size. The round and slightly flattened Peta is larger and can weigh as much as a kilo. The meat, which is finely chopped in a hollowed out wooden log (*pestadora*) is seasoned with salt, garlic and coarsely ground black pepper. In Val Tramontina wild rosemary is also added, and in Val Cellina wild fennel and juniper berries. The meat is then shaped into small balls, dipped in corn flour, and left to smoke on the shelf of the *fogher*. Today one part lard or pork capocollo is added to the meat of roe deer, goat or mutton to counteract the slightly gamey taste. Various aromatic woods are used in the smoking process, especially beech wood. After it has aged for at least 15 days, the pitina can be eaten raw or cooked in a variety of traditional ways. It can be scalded in vinegar and served with polenta, browned in butter and onion and added to potato soup, or prepared *al cao*, i.e. cooked in fresh cow's milk. Before the Presidium was formed pitina ran the risk of disappearing. It was not known outside of the piedmont zone of Friuli and producers were rapidly on the decline. The Presidium is made up of producers who still make the homemade version and who adhere to a common protocol that prohibits using meat from refrigerated game, or any additives or artificial aromas.

PRODUCTION AREA
Val Tramontina and Val Cellina, province of Pordenone,
Friuli Venezia Giulia

PRESIDIUM COORDINATORS
Massimo Zecchin
tel. +39 3356353176
massimozecchin@katamail.com
Filippo Bier
tel. +39 042786189
info@pitina.com

PRESIDIUM SUPPORTED BY
Banca di Credito Cooperativo di San Giorgio
e Meduno, Montagna Leader

Poirino Tench

Typical in Roero cooking, the Presidium tenches are tender and flavorful, without that slightly muddy taste one usually finds in fish from lakes of inferior quality. Though some people prefer them fried, they are really at their best when prepared in *carpione* (a Piedmontese marinade of vinegar, white wine and aromatic herbs) and eaten cold during the hot days of summer. In any case, they are always served with a Roero Arneis. Many local restaurants regularly feature them on the menu today, but beginning in the 13th century they were raised exclusively for home consumption in the area straddling the provinces of Turin, Cuneo and Asti. Almost all the farming families had a small pond, equipped with a watering trough for the animals or a water tank for irrigation (*peschera* or *tampa* in Piedmontese), where they raised their own tenches. As the name implies, this relative of the carp family is hump-shaped and golden in color. In the past, tench fishing was practiced when the wheat was reaped. Today the fishing season is still concentrated in the summer, but can last from April to October. Only specimens having at least one year of age are fished and production is actually very limited, especially when compared with other species like trout, 50,000 tons of which are caught each year, or catfish (1800 tons). Of the more than 300 lakes on the Poirino plateau, there are only a hundred or so that can be fished today. Since the 1970s, in fact, farming has been abandoned in the area, and tench fishing was an integral part of the activity. Despite the commercial value of this indigenous fish, the tradition of tench fishing is on the decline. The Presidium producers are striving to rectify this problem by creating fish farms where quality tenches can be raised.

PRODUCTION AREA
Communes of the Poirino plateau, provinces of Turin, Cuneo and Asti, Piedmont

PRESIDIUM COORDINATOR
Leonardo Azzi
tel. +39 0119450114 - 3383539775
segreteria@comune.poirino.to.it

PRESIDIUM SUPPORTED BY
Turin Provincial Authority, Commune of Poirino

Polizzi Badda Bean

These medium-to-small sized beans, round in shape (from which the name *badda*, meaning 'little ball', derives), have been grown throughout the ages at Polizzi Generosa, but are practically unknown outside the Madonie area. They are two-tone in color, with shades varying according to ecotype: ivory with pink and orange spots (*badda bianca*) or ivory with dark purple, almost black spots (*badda niura*). Both of these ecotypes are well acclimatized in the gardens in the area, both in the Polizzi uplands, where they are sown during the first week of June – tradition requires them to be sown on the feast day of Saint Anthony of Padua – and at lower heights, where sowing is held back until the second half of July when the heat starts to lessen. As the shoots grow, they climb around four stakes arranged in the shape of a small hut , *'u pagliaru*. Harvesting the green pods begins after about two months and this can go on, depending on the height, until November, while the harvest of beans for drying is carried out in October and November before the pods open and drop their seeds. These tasty, creamy beans, with their herby and almost salty flavor, and with chestnut and almond overtones, are excellent fresh with homemade tagliatelle and tomato, and also dried, since they do not break up during cooking. They are a main feature of a lot of local recipes, including *cunigghiu*, which combines beans with *ventresca*, *baccalà* and vegetables, and badda bean soup with wild fennel and pork rind. The Presidium would like to further awareness of this bean and develop cultivation. A scientific study carrued out by the Italian Agriculture Ministry's Center of Agrifood Research (CRA) is seeking to identify the original seed morphologically, while the University of Palero is conducting studies to improve growing techniques.

PRODUCTION AREA
Polizzi Generosa, province of Palermo, Sicily

PRESIDIUM COORDINATORS
Nino Aiello
tel. +39 0916628450
ninoaiello@tin.it
Achille Virga
tel. +39 0921680350
soat52@regione.sicilia.it

PRESIDIUM SUPPORTED BY
Sicily Regional Authority, department of Agriculture and Forestry

Pompìa

The pompìa is a fruit which has grown naturally for over two centuries in the maquis and citrus groves of the coastal area of Baronia, between Budoni and Orosei, and which has survived thanks to being the main ingredient of a number of traditional Siniscola sweets. The tree, robust and hardy, looks like an orange tree with very thorny branches, and bears yellow fruits larger than grapefruits, with a thick, grainy rind. These are picked from mid November to January. The origins of the species are unknown: it is similar to the lime, but has a number of characteristics which do not correspond to that species. It is probably a natural hybrid which developed after cross-breeding among local varieties. It was first recorded in 1780 and is mentioned in a study of plant and animal biodiversity in Sardinia written by Andrea Manca dell'Arca. Its scientific name, *Citrus monstruosa*, is particularly apt: the fruits are lumpy with often very irregular, strange shapes. There are not many farmers who grow it as a commercial crop, most of them do so for family use. The juice is acidic and the fruit cannot be eaten fresh or juiced. The rind is used to make liqueur and the pith in a number of sweets. The process is very time-consuming: it takes about six hours, from the removal of the zest, attempting to keep the pith intact while the pulp is eliminated. What is left is a kind of hollow ball, which is soaked in blossom honey and then simmered for around three hours. This gives us *sa pompìa intrea*, which can then be filled with chopped almonds (*sa pompìa prena*). Slices of pompìa *intrea* and almonds, blossom honey and hundreds and thousands are used to make a cake called *s'aranzata*. The Presidium represents fruit growers, pastry chefs and Siniscola restaurants which offer sweets and liqueurs made with pompìa, with the aim of raising the profile of this citrus fruit outside the local market, and identifying new ways of processing and using it.

PRODUCTION AREA
Siniscola and the coastal area of Baronia, province of Nuoro, Sardinia

PRESIDIUM COORDINATORS
Gianpiero Lapia
tel. +39 0784810687
gplapia@tiscali.it
Francesca Pau
tel. +39 0784878762 - 3491243528
panecarasatupau@tiscali.it

PRESIDIUM SUPPORTED BY
Commune of Siniscola

Portonovo Wild Mussel

The wild mussel, or mosciolo (*Mytilus galloprovincialis*), a naturally reproducing species that lives attached to submerged rocks, was fished off the Cònero coast as long ago as the early 1900s. Even then the fishermen loved eating the mussels as soon as they were caught, cooked on a stone slab over the fire, without any seasonings, or steamed in a pan with garlic, parsley, olive oil and pepper (*alla marinara*). Mussel fishing was a rather limited activity until the post- Second World War period. With the use of row boats (*batane*), it was mainly done by the port workers and the farmers from Sirolo and a few hamlets of Ancona as a way to supplement their income. In the beginning they used a tool similar to a pitchfork to dislodge the mussels; at a later date the moscioliniera, a long pole equipped with curved iron teeth for scraping the rocks. Fishing increased considerably in the 1950s and was practiced by scuba divers as well. However, by the end of the '70s, because of the hardships associated with this kind of fishing and competition from farm-raised mussels, the quantity of moscioli taken from these waters dropped dramatically, as did the number of divers willing to take on such work. And today there are laws restricting wild mussel fishing to very limited stretches of the coast. It is important to maintain a healthy balance between the quantities fished and the ability of the mussels to reproduce, and production needs to be regulated to keep track of the mussels throughout the distribution chain and guarantee the origins. The Portonovo Pesca Cooperative, an association of fishermen, all members of the Presidium, still practices the traditional method of fishing and is a real tool for protecting this stretch of coast. Thanks to the work of the Presidium, there is a project in the pipeline to provide the fishermen with a workshop better suited to their needs, equipped with rooms for processing and selling the fresh mussels.

PRODUCTION AREA
Marche coast from Pietralacroce to Sirolo-Numana, province of Ancona, Marche

PRESIDIUM COORDINATORS
Franco Frezzotti
tel. +39 0712812404 -3477561090
franco.frezzotti@aliceposta.it
Sandro Rocchetti
tel. +39 071801166

PRESIDIUM SUPPORTED BY
Ancona Provincial Authority,
Commune of Ancona

Prato Mortadella

In and around Prato, traditions for this particular kind of cooked cured meat go back to the early 1900s and were dictated by the need to use second-grade cuts of pork and the leftovers from making prestige delicatessen meats such as finocchiona. The characteristic of this kind of mortadella (made until the last war) was its spicy flavor, achieved by marinating the meat in a blend of powdered flavorings and alchermes, a sweet liqueur, the recipe for which is attributed to the Florentine friars of Santa Maria Novella and made by the maceration of aromatic herbs and exotic spices in alcohol. Today, it is no longer necessary to process the meat with strong flavorings: meat is carefully chosen – the lean parts come from the shoulder and ham trimmings, fatty parts from the cheeks and lardons – and modern consumers no longer enjoy over-strong flavors. Today's Prato mortadella is a sophisticated cooked cured pork with a particular pinkish color that tends to become pale given the addition of the liqueur to the pulp, with an evocative, exotic aroma of spices. This mortadella comes in various shapes and sizes, mostly similar to salami or classic mortadella (depending on the producer), almost always weighing around 1 kg (yet other types vary in weight between 300-400 g and 2.5 kg). It is excellent fresh cooked or served at room temperature (if heated, it loses most of its taste characteristics). It is perfect with Prato bread (*bozza*) and Carmignano figs (*dottati*). The Presidium has brought together the still-active producers and convinced them to adopt a production regulations that harmonize (but not standardize) processing styles. These regulations envisages the use of national pigs, preferably from organic breeders, very limited use of preservatives, the type of processing (garlic, macis, pepper, coriander, cinnamon, cloves, alchermes) and packing in natural intestine.

PRODUCTION AREA
Prato and Agliana, province of Pistoia, Tuscany

PRESIDIUM COORDINATOR
Alessandro Venturi
tel. +39 0574 431105
info@slowfood.prato.it

PRESIDIUM SUPPORTED BY
Prato Provincial Authority

Provolone del Monaco

The name is misleading; this cheese is not really a Provolone, but rather a Caciocavallo, without the knob on top. Provolone del Monaco, literally 'Monk's Provolone': there's no point in asking who the monk might have been, although there has been some suggestion that the name refers to the cloak worn by the dairymen of yesterday, similar to a monk's habit. What we do know is that it has been produced for many years on the Lattari mountains, on the Sorrentine Peninsula, with the milk from Fresian or Bruno Alpina cows (even the almost extinct Agerolese is being reintroduced). The animals are reared almost entirely indoors, but much of their feed is still acquired by picking grass, leafy branches and spontaneous vegetation. Like all spun cheese, it is long and complicated to prepare. The raw milk is coagulated with goat rennet. Then the curds are broken up and scalded with very hot whey or water. The curds are left to rest in a cloth, sliced and wet with water at a temperature of 90-95°C. Certain stages of the stringing process needs two people who pull and twist the cheese as if it were a rope. When it is solid, it is made into the shape of a pear or a cylinder. And finally the cheese is soaked in brine, then dried and aging can being; it will last for four to six months, but even as much as a year and a half. When it is fresh, Provolone del Monaco is sweet and smooth; when it is aged, it gives off a scent of green grass, hazelnuts, and noble molds. The Presidium is working to create a consortium between the cheesemakers who undertake to use only the milk from local farmers; this is one way to promote their products and to support the reintroduction of the Agerolese breed. Up until a few years ago, there were just 75 pure-bred animals left, and it has taken a huge effort to draw up a breed register and start the process of strengthening it. We can only hope that this breed, which is currently found almost entirely in Agerola, will gradually spread all over the Lattari mountains, as in the past.

PRODUCTION AREA
Lattari mountains, province of Naples, Campania

PRESIDIUM COORDINATOR
Carmela Rita Abagnale
tel. +39 0818710157 - 3471135440
carmelarita.abagnale@email.it

PRESIDIUM SPONSORED BY
Monti Lattari Mountain Community

Purceddu d'Alcamo Melon

Melons are some of the oldest and most important products of Trapani agriculture. Sown between March and April, harvesting starts in the month of June. They are distinctive because they keep so well, still excellent up to Christmas and beyond (at one time they were kept as long as February), and even better with time. After the harvest, they are traditionally arranged on the terraces of the houses or hung on the balconies, which explains why they are known as winter melons, a name that indicates a family of old varieties now at risk of extinction. One of these is the *Alcamo purceddu*. Having a rough green skin and oval shape, it is a hardy variety that keeps a long time and grows in dry soil. The juicy white pulp becomes better and sweeter with time thanks to the progressive concentration of the sugar content. It is an excellent table fruit and an ingredient in ice cream and the traditional Sicilian *granita*. The melons grown in the Alcamo countryside and surrounding communities have always been purchased by big wholesalers from Campania to be sold at the markets in Naples, where they are highly prized and often sold as Campania melons. Sicilian growers derive little revenue from them, however, and the crop is becoming less and less profitable. For this reason a small group of farmers have joined together in a Presidium to try and sell the melons on their own. They have set up an association and found a place where they can leave the melons to ripen. A well-established method was to layer the melons on the floor of a cool and airy room and turn them periodically to prevent them from rotting. The Presidium growers have improved this technique by wrapping the melons in netting and hanging them one by one on wooden structures like sausages. This not only means they do not have to be turned, but also that it is easier to sort them according to size.

PRODUCTION AREA
Alcamo, province of Trapani and the communes of Camporeale, Roccamena and San Giuseppe Iato, province of Palermo, Sicily

PRESIDIUM COORDINATORS
Francesco Abate
tel. +39 3299870097
francescoabate@hotmail.com
Nunzio Bastone
tel. +39 320042493
info@cafisu.it

PRESIDIUM SUPPORTED BY
Sicily Regional Authority, department of Agriculture and Forestry, Commune of Alcamo

Radìc di Mont

The scientific name is *Cicerbita alpina*, but on the peaks of the Carnia Alps it is known as radìc di mont or radìc dal glaz. This very tender wild chicory, with the unusual violet color, is gathered at high altitudes (over 1000 meters) by local shepherds and many enthusiasts when the snow has receded. The height of season is in the first weeks of May. The foraging lasts 15-20 days and each step is controlled: each forager can take no more than one kilo of the chicory home on a given day. So as not to destroy the root, which is soft and offers no resistance, the *radìc* is gathered by gently pressing it just below soil level with the thumbnail or a small knife. And it is important not to put the herb in a plastic bag, otherwise it deteriorates. Radic is also gathered in other small alpine zones, but here in Carnia there is a long-standing tradition of conserving it in oil so it can be eaten for about one year. All the traces of dirt are carefully removed from the shoots, which are briefly scalded in a mixture of water, white wine, salt, a pinch of sugar and sometimes cinnamon or cloves. Once drained, they are left to cool for an entire day on dry cloths that are changed when they become too damp. Finally, they are bottled in small glass jars under a mixture of extra virgin olive oil, garlic and hot peppers. The Presidium brings together foragers and small food processing companies, who have endorsed a common production protocol and intend to keep up the tradition. But they are also striving to save from extinction a wild vegetable whose gathering techniques demand expertise and experience, as well as a healthy respect for the territory. Some of them are working on a project with the Friuli Venezia Giulia Regional Authority to assess the possibility of cultivating the radìc through seed reproduction.

PRODUCTION AREA
Carnia Alps 1,000 meters asl, province of Udine, Friuli Venezia Giulia

PRESIDIUM COORDINATOR
Manuela Croatto
tel. +39 0433467124
cirmont@cirmont.it

PRESIDIUM SUPPORTED BY
Cirmont (International Mountain Research Center)

Ragusano Cheese

Ragusano cheese is made from November to May, when the Iblei meadows offer an extraordinary variety of herbs. The milk comes from the Modicana cows, which have been in Sicily for centuries, but unfortunately risk extinction. Farmhouse Ragusano is cube-shaped, weighs 12-16 kilos and nears the marks of the cords used to tie it so it can be hung from the ceiling to age. It is prepared by heating up the milk from two milkings and adding lamb or goat rennet paste. When the *ruotula* (a stick) stands up straight when it is put into the mass, the curd is broken into grains the size of corn kernels. Left to rest on a wooden table, the curd is then scalded in hot water or boiling whey. It ripens for another 20-24 hours and then it is sliced and put into a wooden or copper *staccio* and blanched in very hot water (85°C). At this point is worked by hand or with a stick and shaped into a sphere when it begins to go stringy. The cube shape is obtained by putting the cheese on the *mastredda*, a wooden table where the cheesemaker shapes the cheese with heavy pieces of wood. To get the corners just right and to round the sides, the cheesemaker has to turn the form every 10, 30 and 60 minutes for 6-8 hours. Aged Ragusano (best at 8-24 months) has a smooth, thin and hard golden crust, while the straw-yellow interior is softish. The considerable complexity of flavors and aromas improves with time (fresh mushrooms, toasted bread, orange, freshly mowed grass and Iblei mountain flowers such as calendula, *anthemis*, *malva silvestre*, geranium, jasmine). The Presidium was formed to raise the profile of this heritage, not only gastronomic but also environmental and historical.

PRODUCTION AREA
All the communes in the province of Ragusa and a few in the province of Siracusa, Sicily

PRESIDIUM COORDINATORS
Giuseppe Licitra
tel. +39 0932660414
licitrag@tin.it
licitrag@corfilac.it
Ivana Piccitto
tel. +39 0932660414

PRESIDIUM SUPPORTED BY
Sicily Regional Authority department of Agriculture and Forestry, CoRFiLac

Ragusano Donkey

In days gone by donkeys were an important part of country life: in the south of Italy you would often see donkeys carrying loads, being used to turn mills or drag plows. In Sicily in particular there were local breeds such as Siciliana or Pantesca (the Pantelleria donkey, now declared extinct by the WWF), which were cross-bred over time, either with the Martina Franca donkey or, in some cases, wityh the Catalan donkey. The Ragusana breed is one of the newest: only in 1953 did the Institute of Equine Development in Catania manage to settle on a number of characteristics. A dark bay coat with 'grass snake or deer' shape belly, a gray muzzle with short hair, black mane and tail, not a heavy head, and almost straight profile, broad flat forehead, big eyes ringed with white, straight, medium length ears, a wide back and robust limbs. Like most local breeds of donkey, the Ragusana is also currently at risk of extinction: there are very few left, and only 89 females. The donkey, much longer-lived than the horse, can reach the age of 45, and not many are aware of its value. Its milk has very similar characteristics to human breast milk, and in the past country people used to replace breast milk with donkey milk. Nowadays, however, it is difficult to find lactating donkeys. The Presidium came about because one mother was looking for a way to deal with her child's multiple food allergies. Soya milk proved to be no good while donkey milk was a success. This is what led to the idea of making this product accessible, and the launch of Asilat, a company which produces and sells organic milk from donkeys of the Ragusana breed, Siciliana and cross-breeds of the old Pantesca breed. Donkey milk has a medium content of casein and albumin, similar to that of breast milk, and has a pleasant flavor thanks to its high lactose content, which also aids the absorption of calcium in the intestine.

PRODUCTION AREA
The whole of Sicily

PRESIDIUM COORDINATOR
Daniela Franchina
tel. +39 3339290042
danielafranchina@yahoo.it

PRESIDIUM SUPPORTED BY
Sicily Regional Authority, department of Agriculture and Forestry, CoRFiLac

Red Reggiana Cow

It is likely that the Red Reggiana cow came to Italy with the Lombards from Pannonia, present-day Hungary, about one thousand years ago. This would appear to be the case given its similarity to some of the breeds with similar red mantles still present in the Ukraine and central Russia. Since then these cow have been bred by local farmers, who have used them both as work animals and for their milk and meat. It is precisely the milk that is so highly prized, so much so that in distant times it stood godfather to the birth of Grana cheese. In the second half of the last century the breed gradually declined in number to the point that in the early 1980s fewer than a thousand head were left and it came close to extinction. During this period of time the indigenous breed was replaced by the *frisona*, the well-known black and white dappled cow capable of producing very large quantities of milk. The quality of the milk from Red Reggiana cows is far superior however; rich in protein, calcium and phosphorous and better suited to cheese making. It coagulates more quickly, the curd is firmer and more elastic, the whey is clearer and the cream rises to the surface better. It also yields more cheese: an additional kilo for every hundred kilos of milk that is processed. Parmigiano made with this milk must age for at least 24 months, but ideally for 26-28 months (12 months is sufficient for cheese made with milk from other breeds). Thanks to the dedication of a few breeders who believe in the importance of tradition and in the quality of this indigenous breed, it is slowly being revived. Today more than 2000 heads (1,200 of which are milk cows) are raised, mainly in the Province of Reggio Emilia. Slightly more than 4,000 forms of Parmigiano-Reggiano cheese from the Red Reggiana cow are produced annually. They are easy to recognize them because they are branded with the Parmigiano Reggiano delle vacche rosse dop seal. The Presidium is made up of 22 breeders and eight cheese factories.

PRODUCTION AREA
Province of Reggio Emilia, Emilia Romagna

PRESIDIUM COORDINATORS
Mirco Marconi
tel. +39 0522944203 - 3405530549
info@slowfoodreggio.it
Luciano Catellani
tel. +39 0522294655
granadoro@libero.it

PRESIDIUM SUPPORTED BY
Emilia Romagna Regional Authority, Province of Reggio Emilia

Regina di Londa Peach

Although the origin is unknown and specialized exploitation is relatively recent, this is without doubt an ancient variety. The plant was identified in the 1950s on an estate at Rufina, in Valdisieve, by forestry expert Alfredo Leoni, who realized its agronomic and commercial value – there was strong demand for late peaches at the time – and began cultivating it at Londa, a town crossed by the road, on the western slope of Monte Falterona, from Mugello to Casentino. Large, round and slightly squashed at the sides, the fruit has a white-light green skin, with many large bright red spots and markings on the parts most exposed to the sun; the pulp – firm, sweet and highly scented – is creamy white with bright red veins near the stone. This peach ripens in mid-September, so that it is also known as *regina d'autunno e tardiva di Londa* (Londa, late queen of fall peach). Since it grows well in areas that are not very humid at night, it is particularly suited to the Tuscan Apennines - dry and airy, totally uncontaminated and ideal for organic agriculture and integrated production. Although it ensures a high yield and is naturally resistant to attack by fungi, difficulties associated with growing have seen many people abandon this variety in recent years: it only takes a cooler summer to put the late harvest at risk. Moreover, regina is excellent immediately after picking but only retains its taste characteristics for a week after harvest. Today, barely one thousand quintals/year are grown and picked and sales are limited to local markets in Scarperia, Vicchio and Dicomano. The Presidium supports and valorizes the work of the last growers still active in the zone of origin. In an effort to save the Londa regina peach, an association of small fruit growers has been set up that applies strict regulations. In order to retain the taste and perfumes of regina peaches even over later months, producers belonging to the Presidium have started processing them to make conserves and syruped fruit.

PRODUCTION AREA
Londa and other towns in the valley of the Moscia torrent and its tributaries, province of Florence, Tuscany

PRESIDIUM COORDINATORS
Luigi Pittalis
tel. +39 3482259101
luigi.pittalis@libero.it
Tullia Benfenati
tel. +39 0558396635 - 0558396627
paf@cm-montagnafiorentina.fi.it

PRESIDIUM SUPPORTED BY
Florentine Mountain Community, Gal Start

Resia Garlic

Val Resia is a little corner of Friuli wedged between Austria and Slovenia. The ancestors of the local inhabitants probably came from the steppes of the Eastern Europe, settling here around the year 1000. The locals still speak a dialect of Slavic origin incomprehensible to people just a few kilometers away. This closed and protected valley, far from sources of pollution, boasts a culture that is truly unique. The isolation has also made it possible to conserve an interesting vegetable biodiversity. A study made by the Faculty of Agrarian Sciences of the University of Udine identified 30 different ecotypes of bean and a specific variety of top quality garlic known as *strock* in local dialect. Highly aromatic, and covered with a reddish skin, this garlic has small bulbs containing between six and eight cloves each. The crops in the valley are natural, cow manure is used for fertilizing and the use of pesticides is rare. After the harvest, which takes place between the end of July and early August, they used to plait long strings of garlic and hang them outside the houses to be used as needed, while today four or five bulbs are placed together in bunches. The *strock*, which keeps for as long as a year, is sweet and thus particularly suited for curing pork. To valorize this product, a project has been started up involving the town of Resia and the Prealpi Giulie Park, whose territory includes much of Val Resia. The Presidium hopes to counter the emigration of valley dwellers seeking work in the paper or electronic industries by reviving the cultivation of this product and giving vitality to a protected area that wants to be more than jus a natural museum. At present as many as 15 growers have undersigned a production protocol and given themselves a trademark to distinguish genuine Resia garlic from the Eastern Europe product sold as *resiano*.

PRODUCTION AREA
Resia valley, province of Udine, Friuli Venezia Giulia

PRESIDIUM COORDINATORS
Cristina Buttolo and Stefano Santi
tel. +39 043353001
direzione@parcoprealpigiulie.org
Manuela Croatto
tel. +39 0433467124
cirmont@cirmont.it

PRESIDIUM SUPPORTED BY
Cirmont (International Mountain
Research Center),
Prealpi Giulie Park,
Commune of Resia

Ribera Strawberry

These little Ribera strawberries, sweet, scented and bright red in color, are cultivated at the foot of lemon, orange and peach trees, which offer them shade from the intense heat. This is a local variety deriving from the replanting of seedlings that originated in mountain undergrowth, and that have found a perfect habitat in the Verdura valley with its particular type of soil and mild climate. They are very delicate and it only needs the Sirocco to blow for many of the flowers to wither and the whole season's harvest put in jeopardy. Their association with taller plants gives them greater protection against the torrid heat, but cultivation is still difficult and demanding. The harvesting period is short: the strawberries start to ripen in the first ten days of April and finish in June. They quickly go past their best, and should be consumed as soon as they are picked from the plant, or within two days at most. Rich in vitamins and minerals, they are excellent eaten just as they are or prepared in numerous ways – jams, syrups, ice-creams and jellies – while the dried leaves and roots are used on their own or with other medicinal plants to make natural herbal preparations and infusions to purify the body, promote diuresis and reduce pains in the joints. The original production area of these little strawberries has widened in recent times to include the neighboring boroughs of Sciacca, Caltabellotta and Menfi. Competition from other varieties of strawberries that have been revived has, unfortunately, drastically reduced the strawberry gardens in this area around Agrigento, and also the number of growers, who are discouraged by the low profitability of the product. Over the past few years, much work has been done to solve the problem of virus disease and today the plants reproduced in the experimental field under the auspices of Sicily Regional Authority technicians are stronger and more productive. Cultivation follows the principles of integrated plant management. The Slow Food Presidium would like to promote awareness of this delicate, highly scented strawberry as a fruit to be eaten on its own and in ice-creams and jams.

PRODUCTION AREA
Caltabellotta, Menfi, Ribera and Sciacca, province of Agrigento, Sicily

PRESIDIUM COORDINATORS
Antonino Bentivegna
tel. +39 092523071
ninobentivegna@hostariadelvicolo.com
Giuseppe Pasciuta
tel. +39 092586953
soat76@regione.sicilia.it

PRESIDIUM SUPPORTED BY
Sicily Regional Authority, department of Agriculture and Forestry, Commune of Sciacca, Commune of Ribera

Romagnola Cow

The Romagnola cow has a light grey, almost white coat (especially the females), with shades of grey on various parts of its body. The animal is remarkably muscular, with robust limbs and well developed black horns, shaped like a lyre in the females and crescent-shaped in the males. It is believed that the ancestors of this cow came to Italy with the Longobards or the Goths around the 4th century. Up until the 1950s, beef cattle farms flourished in the area of Emilia Romagna from Veneto to the north to Marche to the south. Then the general slump in the cattle-breeding industry caused a drastic reduction in their numbers, especially because of the propensity for intensive breeding and fruit cultivations. Today the breed is still raised in the pastures of the Romagnolo Apennines, particularly in the provinces of Forlì-Cesena, Bologna, Ravenna and Pesaro-Urbino (a total of about 15,000 head throughout Italy). This breed of beef cattle adapts extraordinarily well to difficult terrain. It is an excellent grazing animal that has little tolerance for being kept in a stable, and is the most climate-resistant of all the white breeds. The milk is only used for nursing the calves because the Romagnola is a breed that has been selected over time for its meat. It is butchered between 11 and 18 months of age, when it weighs 6-700 kilos. Traditional breeding methods provide for at least four months of free grazing and the use of exclusively natural feed, which is what makes the quality of the meat so superior. The rib steaks, in particular, can easily stand up to comparison with the more celebrated Chianina. The Presidium has drawn up a breeding protocol and has united 32 breeders from the historical zone of the five Romagna valleys of Savio, Rabbi, Montone, Bidente and Tramazzo. They are developing a project whose aim is to keep track of the origins of the beef throughout the production chain and the use of quality feed such as local forage, hays, cereals and no silage or soy.

PRODUCTION AREA
Province of Forlì-Cesena, Emilia Romagna

PRESIDIUM COORDINATORS
Gabriele Locatelli
tel. +39 0543970562 - 3805024260
g.locatelli@comunita-montana-acquacheta.fc.it
Piero Tassinari
tel. +39 0543956818

PRESIDIUM SUPPORTED BY
Emilia Romagna Regional Authority,
Acquacheta Mountain Community

Rose Syrup

It is not known why the processing of rose petals for making syrups, sweets and jams developed in Genoa in particular. Nevertheless, a book by Gian Domenico Peri, *Il negoziante* (1683), mentions 'the sweet jams and conserves made in Genoa as the finest that are prepared in any part of the world'. Roses, along with fig trees and a clump of erba luisa, used to be a constant presence on balconies or in gardens of Genoese homes. The rose syrup was a homemade preparation that was offered to guests in tiny crystal goblets. The roses most suited are the very fragrant musk roses, with silvery pink double fringed flowers having shades of violet and dark pink. These heirloom varieties, selected between the late 18th and early 19th centuries, are gathered from mid-May to early June when the corolla is wide open. The recipe for this infusion is really rather simple. The petals are put into boiling water with a little lemon and left to steep off heat for about 24 hours. The liquid is filtered, the petal residue is pressed and sugar is added. Then everything is brought to the boil for about ten minutes and poured into small bottles. Except for a few excellent artisans, including the outstanding historic Romanengo pastry shop in Genoa, the average production of rose syrup is almost always second-rate and made with artificial colors, preservatives, artificial aromas and glucose. The Presidium brings together people who still make the syrup according to the traditional Genoese recipe, using exclusively natural ingredients and rose petals cultivated biologically in their own garden. A group of cultivators and producers have formed the association called Le Rose della Valle Scrivia, based at the headquarters of the Antola Regional Nature Park at Busalla, in the Genoese hinterland.

PRODUCTION AREA
City and province of Genoa, Liguria

PRESIDIUM COORDINATOR
Livio Caprile
tel. +39 0105533046 - 3382391490
l.caprile@dolcap.it

PRESIDIUM SUPPORTED BY
Liguria Regional Authority, - Genoa Provincial Authority, Upper Scrivia Valley Mountain Community, Antola Regional Nature Park

Rotonda Red Eggplant

With their meaty pulp, intense and fruity aroma and piquant flavor with slightly bitter aftertaste, these small, round, red-orange vegetables streaked with green seem more like a persimmon or a tomato than an eggplant. It is no coincidence then that they are locally called *merlingiana a pummadora*. The Rotonda red eggplant (*Solanum aethiopicum*) arrived in Europe at the end of the 19th century, probably from Africa. It may have been imported by soldiers returning from the colonial wars, and in any case is not related to the common eggplant (*Solanum melongena*). Despite its excellent organoleptic qualities, it is known and produced only in the gardens of Rotonda in Pollino National Park, the largest nature reserve in Italy. The plants are bedded in the month of May and the harvest goes from August until the first frost. The methods of preserving them are also characteristic. The little eggplants are *nzertate*, tied together in bunches like peppers and cherry tomatoes, and then left to dry under rooftops. They are eaten preserved in oil or vinegar, and rarely just after being harvested. The tender leaves are quite different from those of the common eggplant and are highly prized for their spicy, unusual flavor. The pulp does not darken even after it has been cut for several hours, and it has an intensely fruity aroma reminiscent of prickly pears. The 'African' eggplant is only one of the many vegetables that have made Rotonda a unique little capital of traditional horticulture. The Presidium was set up so that this vegetable would be appreciated even outside the local market and so farmers would be able to sell their excellent preserves at a better price.

PRODUCTION AREA
Mercure valley, province of Potenza, Basilicata

PRESIDIUM COORDINATOR
Domenico Cerbino
tel. +39 3200241678
cerbino@alsia.it

PRESIDIUM SUPPORTED BY
Pollino National Park

Roveja

The roveja, also known as rubiglio or corbello, is a small legume similar to the pea with a color that varies from dark green to brown. In past centuries it was cultivated all along the Umbrian-Marche Apennine ridge, especially in the Sibillini Mountains. Resistant to cold temperatures and needing little water, it is cultivated in spring and summer. It also grows wild along escarpments and in fields, which is why some researchers claim it is a progenitor of the common pea. According to others it is a species (*Pisum arvense*) unto itself, different from the pea (*Pisum sativum*). Nevertheless, everyone agrees it is nutritious. The *roveja* is an excellent source of protein and when dried is very low in fat and high in carbohydrates, phosphorous and potassium. In Val Nerina it is sown in March (at an altitude of 600-1,200 m.) and harvested in late July and early August. It is reaped like lentils: when half the leaves have yellowed and the seeds are waxy, the stalks are scythed and left to dry in the field. Then they are taken to the threshing floor, where they are threshed and the grains sieved to remove any impurities. It can be cooked as is or stone-ground to make a flour for preparing excellent farecchiata (or pesata), a polenta seasoned with anchovies, garlic and extra virgin olive oil. It grows at high altitudes like lentils, so it is very laborious to harvest. The stalks are more than one meter high and it almost impossible to use mechanical threshers on the steep and rocky terrain. This has discouraged the cultivation of the *roveja* and other old varieties of legumes to the point that this small but tasty pea is relatively unknown today. The Presidium involves two farmers in Civita di Cascia, in Val Nerina, and is endeavoring to popularize this legume and engage other growers who currently grow *roveja* only for their personal use.

PRODUCTION AREA
Nerina valley, province of Perugia, Umbria

PRESIDIUM COORDINATOR
Gianluca Polidori
tel. +39 0743274134
gpolidori@castellodiporeta.it

PRESIDIUM SUPPORTED BY
Gal Valle Umbra e Sibillini

Salama da Sugo

The salama (or salamina) is one of the gastronomic specialties of Ferrara. It is made with prime cuts of minced pork, with a little bit liver and tongue, salt, pepper, at times cinnamon and cloves, and finally a red wine (at least 10%) made from the local vines of the Bosco Eliceo denomination or from vines native to the neighboring provinces. After the meat has been stuffed into the bladder casing it is tied tightly with a string so that eight segments are formed. Then the crucial aging phase begins, which can last 6, 12 or 24 months. To obtain the authentic flavor it is equally crucial to use the meat from farm-raised pigs. When the salama has aged it is closed in a linen bag (today they use special bags suitable for high temperature cooking) and boiled, hanging from a stick so it does not touch the sides of the pan. The flavor is strong, almost tart, so it is always served with mashed potatoes or, better still, mashed squash to soften its savory taste. In terms of flavor and aroma, it is one of the most complex of all cured meats. The slightly musty taste from the long aging process together with the flavor of the red wine and powerful spices is reminiscent of oriental flavors. It is an old-fashioned flavor suitable for strong palates, but at the same time refined and highly regarded even by Lorenzo de' Medici. There are still farmers in the Ferrara countryside who make the salama in the traditional way, processing the pork from pigs raised on the farm. One only needs to taste it to understand the difference in quality between this homemade salama and industrial versions. Unfortunately, very little of it is made and almost always for local consumption. The Presidium involves two companies that raise pigs using absolutely natural methods and which make artisan salama da sugo according to the traditional recipe.

PRODUCTION AREA
Province of Ferrara, except for the Adriatic coast, Emilia Romagna

PRESIDIUM COORDINATOR
Alberto Fabbri
tel. +39 0516830187
centoggi@virgilio.it

PRESIDIUM SUPPORTED BY
Emilia Romagna
Regional Authority

Salina Caper

Capers are a traditional crop on the islands around Sicily: all of them boast production of this perennial shrub, which is reckoned to be of tropical origin. Its use as food and for medicinal purposes is mentioned in the Bible, and the writings of Hippocrates, Aristotle and Pliny the Elder. But since the start of eighties there has been a dramatic fall in production. The labor-intensive harvest takes place at the hottest time of year – from the end of May to the end of July, every 8-10 days, and is usually performed by the women, whose smaller fingers are better at gathering the buds quickly. Because the caper is not the fruit of the plant (which is a small kind of gherkin called *cucuncio*), but the bud of the flower. The bushes with their unmistakable round leaves belonging to the *tondina* or *nocellara* variety, or the thorny *spinosa* variety, are present in most of the Sicilian islands, but in now Salina, thanks to the Presidium, they have become a new resource for the economy. The most widespread variety is the *tondina*, which is preferable to the *spinosa* because it produces firmer, heavier capers. It should be noted that this crop grows almost entirely without the use of anti-parasite treatments or chemical fertilizers. The pickers start around five in the morning, to avoid the midday sun, and the capers are laid out to dry on sackcloth in the shade, to make sure they do not flower. After a few hours the small capers are separated from the larger buds, about to flower. Then it is time for the salting process, where the capers are placed in barrels, *cugnitti*, alternated with layers of sea salt. In the following days they are transferred from one *tinedda* to another, to ensure that the combined action of salt and heat does not make them ferment, ruining them. After about a month they are ready to be eaten. The capers of Salina stand out for their firm texture, aroma and even surface. Compact buds will last over time, and can be kept in salt for up to two or three years.

PRODUCTION AREA
Island of Salina, provincia di Messina, Sicily

PRESIDIUM COORDINATORS
Rosario Gugliotta
tel. +39 3358391030
rguglio@tin.it
Massimo Loschiavo
tel. +39 0909843053 - 0909843014
jloschiavo@virgilio.it

PRESIDIUM SUPPORTED BY
Sicily Regional Authority, department of Agriculture and Forestry

Sambucano Lamb

The Sambucano breed first appeared on the Provencal hills of Val Stura, in the province of Cuneo, in the 18th century, and it adapted straightaway to the high meadows. In the 80s there were so few Sambucano sheep around that the FAO declared it a breed at risk. That was when the L'Escaroun Association was formed (1988), the farming cooperative Lou Barmaset (1991) and the ram selection center in Pietraporzio, and the brand 'Guaranteed Sambucano Lamb' was finally recognized. In the summer the Sambucano lives on the high slopes without any shelter, moving freely on the steep slopes and rocky faces, thanks to its inborn agility, then the rest of the year is spent in the stalls fed with hay. It is a medium-large size sheep with a wide, muscular neck, slender, solid and not very long limbs. It has a light head without wool or horns, slightly ram shaped and a narrow, woolly tail which grows down to its heels. The Sambucano is precious for its wool, a yellowish white color but, above all, for its meat. The lambs are butchered between 45 and 60 days old – weighing between 18 and 25 kilos, and they have a very fine skeleton and well-developed muscular mass, that is compact and without any greasy filaments. Their meat is tasty, not fatty and rich in protein, and this excellent flavor is given also by their natural diet. It is cooked in various ways: from roasting through to making liver pâté. Production peak is around Christmas, but there is also the tradition in the valley to eat the lamb from the end of October, when the butchers sell the large lambs (*tardun*) that were born at the end of spring and fed with their mother's milk and the pasture grass. On the last Sunday in October, in Vinadio, the Saints' Feast is the ideal event to exhibit the best examples of Sambucano sheep. The Presidium is proceeding with promoting and giving value to this breed.

PRODUCTION AREA
Pietraporzio, Sambuco, Vinadio, Aisone, high Valle Stura, Demonte, Moiola, Roccasparvera, in medium and low Valle Stura, province of Cuneo, Piedmont

PRESIDIUM COORDINATOR
Antonio Brignone
tel. +39 0171 955555
brignone@vallestura.cn.it

PRESIDIUM SUPPORTED BY
L'Escaroun Association to promote the sambucana sheep

San Gavino Monreale Saffron

Saffron is an aromatic spice with powerful coloring properties which originated in Asia Minor. The plant it comes from, *Crocus sativus*, has long, narrow deep green leaves, beautiful bell-shaped flowers with striped purple petals, and usually three red/orange stamens. One of the most prized varieties is the so-called 'Sardinian red' due to its scarlet stamens. It is cultivated in the town of San Gavino Monreale near Cagliari. This area has always been known for the cultivation of saffron, so much so that it is still Italy's leading production area. In the past both the cultivation and processing was carried out by women, whose hands are smaller and more delicate. They brought in some extra money by selling their produce to other women - the *zafferanaias* – who sold it in markets throughout Sardinia. The bulbs are planted between May and September and the plants flower from the end of October to the end of November. The flowers are picked at first light, when they are still closed or just starting to open, and layered in baskets. The petals are then opened using both hands, and the stamens removed. These are then very slightly moistened with organic Sardinian extra virgin olive oil and left to dry in the sun or by the fire: the heat must be very gentle to ensure that the process takes place slowly. Each hectare planted produces nine or ten kilos of dried saffron stamens, which stand out for their intense aroma and powerful flavor. Saffron is used in many Sardinian dishes: *fregula*, *malloreddus*, sausage ragù, soups, beef or mutton stock, and sweets including *pardulas* (pastries filled with ricotta or cheese and baked in the oven) and Carnival fritters. The Presidium numbers several growers from San Gavino, who must respect stringent production regulations, whereby the saffron can only be sold in filaments.

PRODUCTION AREA
San Gavino Monreale, province of Cagliari, Sardinia

PRESIDIUM COORDINATORS
Fabio Atzeni
tel. +39 3483393320
fabio.atzeni@tiscali.it
Antonio Casti
tel. +39 0709338034
rosipiras@libero.it

PRESIDIUM SUPPORTED BY
Commune of San Gavino Monreale

San Marzano Tomato

Until about twenty years ago the agro sarnese-nocerino, a very fertile vegetable-growing region near Naples, was cultivated almost exclusively with the San Marzano tomato. This very delicate variety retains its flavor even when conserved for a long time, but is difficult to grow and tend. Cultivations were scaled down as the result of a serious viral infection that destroyed the crops and then the reconversion to flower growing, which polluted the soil. Since then the canning industries manufacturing canned tomatoes began to acquire hybrids from other places that were more resistant to mechanical processing. As a result, the San Marzano risked extinction. The original ecotype is more flavorful, but also more delicate, and has a thinner skin than the many hybrids that have been produced and which can withstand canning better. The San Marzano tomatoes are harvested several times (seven, eight or even more) between July and September. As soon as they are picked, they have to be rinsed and arranged in jars and allowed to cook for 13 minutes without additives or preservatives. This process ensures they will keep in jars for at least one year, like puréed tomatoes and sun-dried tomatoes preserved in oil. The San Marzano is one of the ingredients of the Neapolitan pizza, *la margherita*. It is also used to prepare the *ragù*, or meat sauce, something considered a ritual in Naples. The Presidium united 11 growers who decided to bed out the original ecotype once again, identified by a mark, Smec20, which was retrieved in past years by technicians from the Cirio Research Center. The agronomists conducted research in the local gardens and selected the best plants, which in terms of distinctive characteristics were closest to the true San Marzano. Today the Cirio Center, called Eureco, has become public property, and thanks to a research project financed by the Campania Regional Authority conserves the Campania vegetable germoplasm. The same technicians are supervising the Presidium growers with the aim of valorizing both the canned and fresh tomato.

PRODUCTION AREA
Agro sarnese-nocerino, province of Naples, Campania

PRESIDIUM COORDINATORS
Patrizia Spigno
tel. +39 0818446048
patrizia.spigno@eurecompany.com
Vito Trotta
tel. +39 0818044295 - 3406001837
workinprogress@alice.it

PRESIDIUM SUPPORTED BY
Naples Provincial Authority

Sant'Erasmo Purple Artichoke

Tender, meaty, spiny and elongated, with dark violet outer leaves: this artichoke grows well in the clayey, well-drained land rich in mineral salts of Sant'Erasmo, an island in the Venice lagoon with many canals that since the 1500s can only be defined as a unique, huge market garden. In the past, *scoasse* (sweepings) or crab shells were used as fertilizers and to correct the acidity of the land. Still today the young plants are protected by preparing little piles of earth around the part facing the sea ("motte"). The season begins in April with the harvest of the superbly tender *castraùre* – the first, small tipped shoots that are nipped to encourage stronger growth of the other shoots and available for no more than 15 days – and continues through to late June. The harvested artichokes are then taken by boat to the Rialto and Tronchetto markets. These *articiochi* – as artichokes are known in the Venetian dialect – were introduced to Venice by the Hebrew community; they are excellent raw with a little extra virgin olive oil, pan fried or *garbo* (simmered slowly with garlic and onion over a low flame in a covered pan, adding a drop of vinegar or lemon one they are cooked). Accompanied by *schie* (lagoon shrimps), baby anchovies and sardines or boiled and flavored with a simple condiment of olive oil, pepper, garlic and parsley, they are an excellent *cicheto* (snack) ideal with *un'ombra de vin* (glass of wine) and interesting *ciacole* (chats). Today, they are grown by very few people - mostly older generation; connections with Venice are rare and transport costs are high, while competition by produce from Puglia and Tuscany (palmed off as Sant'Erasmo artichokes) is very strong. This is why a Presidium was set up to bring together the market-gardeners of the lagoon island: the objective is to distinguish and valorize the true artichokes grown on the islands around Venice and ensure better incomes for producers.

PRODUCTION AREA
Island of Sant'Erasmo and the islands of Vignole, Mazzorbo, Lio Piccolo, province of Venice, Veneto

PRESIDIUM COORDINATORS
Silvano Sguoto
tel. +39 3484705664
Carlo Finotello
tel. +39 0415282497-3470594687
carlo76@tele2.it
info@carciofosanterasmo.it

PRESIDIUM SUPPORTED BY
Veneto Regional Authority, Veneto Agricoltura

Santo Stefano di Sessanio Lentil

A very unusual biotype of lentil grows on the slopes of Gran Sasso, at over 1,000 meters above sea level in the National Park. The lentil is very small, round and dark violet-brown in color. The climate (long harsh winters, short and cool springs) and the calcareous mountain soils are just right for growing legumes, especially lentils, which were even mentioned in monastic texts as early as 998. The seeds are sown at the end of March and for four or five months the plant does not need much care. The harvesting in late July and early August, on the other hand, is long and laborious. The lentils mature gradually and at different times according to the altitude of the field. Sometimes fifteen days will elapse between the scything, almost always done by hand, and the threshing. Harvesting machines are hardly ever used because the fields are hard to get to, but mainly because the legumes grow very close to the ground. Most of the growers are elderly and grow the lentils almost exclusively for home use. Because of their very small size and extreme permeability, the Santo Stefano di Sessanio lentils do not need to be soaked before they are cooked. Exceptionally flavorful, the best way to appreciate them is in a very simple soup. They are covered with water in a pan, along with some peeled garlic, a few bay leaves, salt, and extra virgin olive oil, and then brought to a simmer with the lid on. After twenty minutes or so, the lentils are done. The soup can be completed with slices of toasted bread on top and a drizzle of local extra virgin olive oil. Like the Arssa Park project a few years ago, the Presidium wants to form a growers' association that can get a labeling and harvest control system in place to protect genuine Santo Stefano di Sessanio lentils from imitation varieties. But the primary aim is to increase cultivations in an effort to develop the area and give local young people a chance to find employment in this extraordinary terrioir.

PRODUCTION AREA
Barisciano, Calascio, Castel del Monte, Castelvecchio Calvisio and Santo Stefano di Sessanio, province of L'Aquila, Abruzzo

PRESIDIUM COORDINATORS
Silvia De Paulis
tel. +39 086260521
silviadepaulis@gransassolagapark.it
Donato Domenico Silveri
tel. +39 086433332
silveridonato@tin.it

PRESIDIUM SUPPORTED BY
Gran Sasso and Monti della Laga National Park

Saracena Moscato

Saracena Moscato is made with a number of different grapes: guarnaccia, malvasia, odoacra and moscatello, a local variety that is different from the moscato of Alessandria or Hamburg. The proportions of the various grapes can vary. Generally there are more guarnaccia and malvasi, with the addition of a small quantity of odoacra, a very aromatic grape. Harvested at the peak of ripeness, for 15-20 days the moscatello grapes hang from racks in the shade to wither and concentrate the sugars and aromas. The dehydrated grapes are then hand picked and gently pressed. After the grape harvest, instead, the guarnaccia, malvasia and odoacra are pressed and the must is boiled until reduced by a third, which increases the sugar and alcohol content. The two musts are then mixed together and begin a natural fermentation process in wooden barrels. The first siphoning is carried out after a couple of weeks, and then two more follow until the wine is bottled in about six or seven months. The result is an amber colored, intensely fragrant wine that has a hint of dried figs, exotic fruit, almonds and honey, along with resinous and aromatic qualities. It is very palatable, and has a refined, fairly persistent taste that is well-balanced with a pleasant bitter note. Saracena Moscato is not suited to long aging and is at its best in the first two years. The Presidium has selected six producers who work with the help of Mario Ronco, an enologist from Piedmont already collaborating with a group of Pollino wineries. The aims are to define a production protocol that will enhance the quality of Saracena Moscato and involve other wineries as well. The work of the commune of Saracena, the Pollino Park and other organizations in the region has also given rise to the Amici del Moscato di Saracena association, which is taking care of the paperwork to apply for a new Moscato di Saracena DOC label.

PRODUCTION AREA
Saracena, province of Cosenza, Calabria

PRESIDIUM COORDINATORS
Vittoria Maradei
tel. +39 098134162 – 098134865
Domenico Metaponte
tel. +39 3484093679

PRESIDIUM SUPPORTED BY
Commune of Saracena, Pollino Mountain Community, Pollino National Park

Saras del Fen

In Piedmont and Val d'Aosta the term *saras* (or *seirass*) – from Latin *seracium* – means ricotta, the milk product made from the whey left over from making cheese. *Fen*, on the other hand, is the hay that is put around the forms while they are being taken down to the valleys from the mountain pastures, which used to protect the cheese from insects and hold it together. These grasses and the milk added during the processing give the *saras* a unique aroma and taste. The initial grassy, milky bouquet gradually changes to a scent of mold as the cheese ripens, and the flavor is rich and persistent. The ricotta can be eaten fresh or aged, and as it ripens it takes on a creamy consistency and piquant aftertaste. The cheese is made by heating the whey to 70° C, adding milk or salts and bringing it nearly to the boil. The solids that have formed are then put in a linen sack and allowed to drain for 24-36 hours, salted and put on an inclined plane to dry for two days or so. For the next few months, no more than four, the ricotta will age in its hay covering. The *Saras del Fen* produced in the Waldensian Valleys, at more than 1,000 meters of altitude, is still made in the traditional way. 15 producers are still active in the shepherd's huts and each conserves his own cheese making style: some add milk, some press the cheese, some salt the cheese mixture and some dry salt the forms. There is even one producer who adds an infusion of herbs, spices and roots to the boiling whey. The Presidium protects the *Saras* and works to enhance the agrifood heritage of Val Pellice. And the work of restaurant owner Walter Eynard was fundamental from the very beginning. For twenty years he has been using this unusual ricotta to prepare *balotte*, stuff ravioli, season soups and enrich the cheese dishesoffered to the guests at his celebrated restaurant Flipot, in Torre Pellice.

PRODUCTION AREA

Over 1000 meters asl in the Val Pellice Mountain Community, the Chisone and Germanasca Mountain Community, and the Pinerolese Pedemontano Mountain Community, province of Turin, Piedmont

PRESIDIUM COORDINATORS

Franco Turaglio
tel. +39 0121394556 - 3294151775
info@lanicchia.net
Spartaco Fassi
tel. +39 01219524235
sfassi@valpellice.to.it

PRESIDIUM SUPPORTED BY

Turin Provincial Authority - Valle Pellice Mountain Community

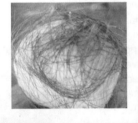

Sardinian Modicana Cow

This is one of Italy's most rural breeds, created at the end of the 19th century from a cross between local Podolica breeds and Modicana bulls imported from the Ragusa area. The cattle, with their characteristic long coppery red coats and black horns, live in the open on the pasture land of Montiferru all year round, including in winter and at night. Wild and hardy, they are a good working animal, adapt to any conditions and provide excellent milk, used by local women to make Casizolu, a characteristic local pear-shaped 'pasta filata' cheese. The tasty red meat features in a number of local recipes: *petza in brou* (meat boiled with thyme, oregano, mint, and wild fennel), *petza arrustida* spit-roasted by the fire, *ghisadu* (stew), *bombas* (meatballs) fried or in broth. It was much appreciated abroad too, until the beginning of the twentieth century when the breed became less popular, and this was exacerbated by the increasing mechanization of the production process and the importation of foreign breeds in the fifties and sixties. The population fell to around 3,000 and the market became exclusively local. Most of the farmers are getting on in years and it looked as if it would be difficult to relaunch commercial operations centered on the promotion of the breed. Thanks to the Presidium, which represents over thirty local breeders, agreements have been established with the breeders' consortium, set up in Seneghe four years ago, and butchers locally and in the province of Oristano, which brought financial returns for the farmers' work. The meat of the 'red ox' is present in various towns on the island. Production regulations stipulate that the calves must be fed by their mothers until they are weaned, then pasture-fed. In the finishing period before slaughter they are kept inside, and their fodder must exclude silage, meat and bone meal and GM blends.

PRODUCTION AREA
Montiferru, province of Oristano, Sardinia

PRESIDIUM COORDINATORS
Corrado Casula
tel. +39 3401423951
corrado042004@libero.it
Salvatore Porcedda
tel. +39 078354450 - 3386120280
e.montiferru@tiscali.it

PRESIDIUM SUPPORTED BY
Gal Montiferru Barigadu Sinis

Savona Chinotto

The chinotto, a small, round, bright green citrus fruit that turns yellow with time, is cultivated only in the Riviera between Varazze and Finale Ligure. Native to China, the plant was brought here in the 16th century. These sour oranges of Savona, famous for their quality and aroma, used to be preserved in maraschino and served in many French and Italian cafés. Since they are too bitter when fresh, they can only be eaten when preserved in syrup or candied. After the citrus fruit has soaked in brine for about three weeks (sea water was used in the past), they are peeled by hand to remove the thin rind that contains the bitterest essences and aromas. Placed in brine again, they are ready to be cured with successive boiling in ever sweeter syrups. Then they are candied or placed in liqueur (usually maraschino). The Silvestre-Allemand company (active in southeastern France ever since 1780) moved to Savona in 1877 and between that time and the 1920s, the local candied fruit industry was highly successful. Then short-sided economic policies and a series of winter frosts began causing problems for the industry, and today this product has practically been abandoned. There are a number of reasons for this: the processing is long and laborious (only one confectioner still performs it); little local citrus fruit is available (very few plants are grown in the Savona area now and the conservation of the species has been entrusted to botanical gardens and nurseries); the final selling price is inadequate. The objective of the Presidium is to revive cultivation and start the candying process up again. As a result, an association of growers and processors has been set up. A rigorous protocol has been drawn up that provides for systems of biological cultivation, the selection of plants from three reliable nurseries and the use of top quality ingredients for the various processed products.

PRODUCTION AREA
Riviera coast from Varazze to Finale Ligure,
province of Savona, Liguria

PRESIDIUM COORDINATOR
Danilo Pollero
tel. +39 3356230829
danilopollero1@tin.it

PRESIDIUM SUPPORTED BY
Liguria Regional Authority, Commune of Savona,
Oscar Tintori, Pescia
(Pistoia, Tuscany, Italy)

Serra de' Conti Cicerchia

In the second half of the 20th century, only a few farmers at Serra de' Conti were still cultivating the tiny, flavorful variety of cicerchia once so common in the Marche. Very small and irregularly shaped with a color ranging from grey to a light spotted brown, this pulse has a thin skin and a more bitter taste than other varieties of cicerchia. The traditional sowing season was spring, when the cicerchia seeds (like those of chickpeas and beans) were planted between the rows of corn to make good use of the space between one furrow and the other. In August the little plants ready for harvesting were placed in little bunches, taken into the barnyard and hung in the sun to dry. After a few days they were threshed to create a supply for the winter. After a long period of almost total abandon, a few years ago the cicerchia of Serra de' Conti was salvaged by a group of young farmers from the village association La bona usanza, now a full-fledged Ark of Taste project. Cicerchia began to be cultivated and sold again; packaged as a dry product with bay leaves and peppercorns, which ensure its natural conservation, or in glass jars. This has all been possible because a few farmers in Serra de' Conti have continued to grow this tiny and tasty variety of pulse in their home gardens, saving it from definitive extinction. Every year during the last week of November, a *Cicerchia* Festival is celebrated inside the medieval walls of Serra de' Conti. Ex-cellent in soups, puréed, or served as a side dish with the classic zampone (stuffed pig's trotter), it is also made into a flour for pastas like maltagliati and pappardelle. The Presidium is carrying forward the important work of salvaging, selecting the germ plasm, promoting and selling the cicerchia. New machinery has also been purchased and a production protocol has been drawn up.

PRODUCTION AREA
Serra de' Conti, province of Ancona, Marche

PRESIDIUM COORDINATOR
Gianfranco Mancini
tel. +39 3388169718
direzione@italcook.it

PRESIDIUM SUPPORTED BY
Marche Regional Authority

Sette Comuni Plateau
Malga Stravecchio

Stravecchio mountain cheese is an extremely rare product even if this may sound odd for an Asiago cheese. But this is no ordinary Asiago cheese: it is not the pressed cheese from dairies in the plains and their very high-quantity output, nor from breeders, very few of which come from the higher up areas. Stravecchio is made in the mountains, with milk from cattle grazed on summer pastures, and boasts extraordinary complex tastes, flavors and aromas. It has a smooth, regular dark yellow rind that tends to become brownish; the cheese itself is light in color, grainy, friable and has a few holes. Forms are 30-36 cm in diameter, 9-12 cm high and weigh 7-9 kilos. Although Fresian and Alpine Brown cows are also reared in the area, the milk used to make this cheese comes from Rendena cattle, with a dark chestnut coat tending to black. This is a rustic breed brought to these mountains from Trentino in the 1700s and is particularly suited to grazing even in poor pastures. Three breeders belonging to the Presidium have herds exclusively comprising Rendena cattle, traditionally brought down in September from the high plateau without using trucks: the descent from summer pastures is a festive occasion for everyone involved in the cattle drive. Stravecchio is usually free of the typical defects of low-fat or semi-fat cheese: too dry, too salty or tasting of caramel. Made using partially skimmed milk, this cheese is matured for a long time (the rules of Presidium involving 14 mountain producers indicate at least 19 months); its aroma recalls fresh-cut grass, musk and ripe fruit; the initial sweet taste becomes more pungent, with hints of toasted hazel nuts and bread. The Presidium aims to convince dairy farmers to set aside more forms of Stravecchio cheese for lengthy maturing and, especially, to make them increasingly aware of their fundamental role in preserving these mountains and safeguarding very ancient cultures and traditions.

PRODUCTION AREA
Asiago, Conco, Enego, Foza, Gallio, Lusiana, Roana and Rotzo, province of Vicenza, Veneto; Grigno in the province of Trento, Trentino

PRESIDIUM COORDINATOR
Dino Panozzo
tel. +39 042463848
panozzodino@virgilio.it

PRESIDIUM SUPPORTED BY
Veneto Regional Authority,
Veneto Agricoltura, Vicenza Qualità,
Gal Altopiano dei Sette Comuni

Sorana Bean

Sorana, near Pescia, is 10 kilometers north of the main town and has given its name to a pearl white dwarf bean (also known as *piattellino*) traditionally grown along the Pescia river in Valdinievole. It belongs to the haricot bean family, an original Tuscan variety held to be the best for drying, yet it is slightly curved and has a very thin skin. The legumes are harvested by hand in September, left in the sun for three or four days and then preserved throughout winter in special containers, adding grains of pepper, valerian roots or bay leaves. The recipe that best expresses their tastiness envisages cooking over a low flame in glass containers with a wide mouth (known as *gozzi*), with garlic, sage and spring water. Once cooked, they are flavored with Tuscan extra virgin olive oil and fresh-ground white pepper. The excellent quality of Sorana beans is the result of several climatic characteristics - optimal altitude (200-750 meters), plenty of water with little calcium scale, good air humidity, optimal exposure to sunlight and well-drained, loose and sandy soil. The best area extends for about four kilometers, especially on the left bank of the Pescia river, between the bridges at Castelvecchio and Sorana itself. The area was reclaimed under the De' Medici in the 16th and 17th centuries and split up among those who helped in the task: this is why still today there are many owners growing beans in small plots of land. With the creation of the Presidium, production has increased but annual quantities are nevertheless rather limited; and it can truly be said that the inhabitants of Pescia now know every single meter of the best land: the quantities of beans sold outside the Sorana area are utterly unjustified. For this reason, the producers belonging to the Presidium signed regulations that define the production area, govern agronomic activities and identify final bags of beans.

PRODUCTION AREA
Pescia valley in the commune of Pescia, province of Pistoia, Tuscany

PRESIDIUM COORDINATOR
Renzo Malvezzi
tel. +39 0571584115 - 335331718
rmalvezzi@interfree.it

PRESIDIUM SUPPORTED BY
Commune of Pescia, Pistoia Provincial Authority, Pistoia Apennine Mountain Community

Spalla Cruda

The Parma area is the historical epicenter of pork. No other region in the world boasts such a variety of processed pork products and so many ways of packaging them. In other regions, the *spalla* (shoulder) is ground and used to make salami and *cotechino* pork sausage, but here it becomes a great cured meat. Preparing a *spalla cruda* (raw pork shoulder) and curing it for up to 16-20 months is an example of the fine art of pork butchery. The front leg of the pig, including the muscles, is removed from the carcass. After trimming it and removing the rind, the meat is vigorously rubbed with coarse sea salt and pepper. Then the *spalla* is placed upside down in a basin, on supports that prevent the meat from coming into contact with the liquid that is released. The salting-cleaning operation is repeated for 6-8 days, depending on the weather. No additives or refrigeration are involved in this artisan method, which is why it is only done in the coldest months. At the end of the salting phase, when the excess salt has been removed, the *spalla* is put into the pig's bladder. The absence of any preservatives and the presence of the bone (increasingly rare in some cases) make the curing process anything but easy. The Presidium involves a few producers who still make this delicious cured pork. The whole *spalla* has a shape reminiscent of an oblong and slightly flattened *culatello* (ham). It must weigh at least 3.7 kilos. When cut, the slice of meat has a bright almost ruby red color, with visible nerves and fatty parts should be a bright and shiny white, perhaps only a little pink. It has an intense aroma with a slight suggestion of ammonia, typical of meats cured in the bladder, which wears off with time. The taste is sweet and fragrant, with hints of chestnut and a barely perceptible note of pepper.

PRODUCTION AREA

Busseto, Colomo, Polesine Parmense, Roccabianca, San Secondo Parmense, Sissa, Soragna and Zibello of lower Parma area, province of Parma, Emilia Romagna

PRESIDIUM COORDINATOR

Alberto Fabbri
tel. +39 0516830187
centoggi@virgilio.it

PRESIDIUM SUPPORTED BY

Emilia Romagna Regional Authority

 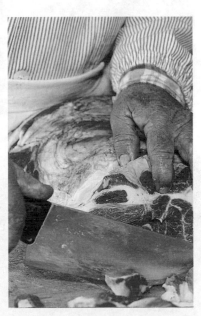 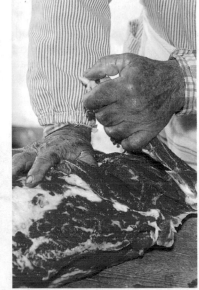 

Tenera Ascoli Olive

Tenera Ascoli olives have always been the gastronomic symbol of the rich and fertile Ascoli Piceno territory. Originally used only for home consumption, this variety of olive has reached a broad market only in the past 20 years. It was precisely the families in the province of Ascoli Piceno who saved one of the best eating olives in the Mediterranean (as well as the recipes for conserving and preparing it), making the tenera the emblematic dish in the area. These large oval olives are distinctive because of their thin skin and very tender flesh, the pale green color and the particularly sweet taste. The olives are grown on little more than 100 hectares of calcareous soils in the province of Ascoli Piceno; a very restricted area insufficient to meet market demands. The most common way to conserve them is in brine, but the most famous tenera olive is the one that is stuffed and fried. It is a highly refined preparation, probably of bourgeois origins, and there are as many recipes for it as there are families in Ascoli. Nevertheless, the ingredients must always include the tenera olive, beef and pork, and Parmigiano-Reggiano. Cooked this way it can be served with an aperitif, a ritual performed by practically all the cafés in the area (historic and otherwise). It can also be eaten as a main course, perhaps with other fried foods like artichokes, zucchini and lamb chops (a typical Ascoli recipe), and even as a side dish for grilled or baked meats. The Presidium producers follow a protocol that dictates a well-defined area for cultivating the olives and hard-and-fast rules for producing, harvesting and processing them. The most important objectives are to increase the olive cultivations by recovering abandoned terrains and to guard the authentic tenera Ascoli olive against imitations.

PRODUCTION AREA
Province of Ascoli Piceno, Marche

PRESIDIUM COORDINATORS
Emidio Bachetti
tel. +39 0736492369
emidio_bachetti@libero.it
Luigi Massa
tel. +39 0736880005
vinea@libero.it

PRESIDIUM SUPPORTED BY
Vinea (Offida, Ascoli Piceno, Marche, Italy)

Toritto Almond

The cultivation of almonds in the province of Bari is part of the local history and culture that shaped the landscape and inspired songs about the laborious hours spent trying to free the nuts from the hull. At Toritto a number of varieties have even been given the names of some of its illustrious inhabitants, testifying to the important role the tree and its fruit have played on the food and economy in many areas of southern Italy. The almond tree also grows well in dry and shallow soils. It is robust and rustic and no chemical fertilizers or special treatments are needed to keep the plant healthy. The nuts are oily and loaded with vitamins and protein. Even the leaves and hulls are of value: the former are an excellent feed that is particularly enjoyed by sheep, while the latter can be used to produce charcoal and ashes used as fertilizers. In Puglia the almond is appreciated in its natural state, after being lightly toasted, but most commonly it is used in confectionaries. Caramelized it makes an excellent almond brittle, and when mixed with other ingredients it livens up marzipan. At Toritto it is traditional to make almond milk served with a few grains of rice. The varieties that have developed in the area of this small village include the *antonio de vito*, the *genco* and the *filippo cea*, whose mother plant still survives in the village of Matite di Toritto. This latter variety, which is the most common, is very pasty, with lots of oil and polyunsaturated fats, low acidity and an intense but well-balanced taste. A number of young producers are investing in the *filippo cea* once again, recognizing that the flavor is superior to the more productive Californian varieties. A consortium to protect and promote the Toritto almond is currently being set up. The Presidium intends to support the entire cultural and economic activity with the aim of seeing to it that this traditional crop survives.

PRODUCTION AREA
Toritto and neighboring areas, province of Bari, Puglia

PRESIDIUM COORDINATORS
Pasquale Porcelli
tel. +39 0803389985 - 3356544642
pasqualeporcelli@libero.it
Emilia D'Urso
tel. +39 3494374955
amygdalea@alice.it

PRESIDIUM SUPPORTED BY
Puglia Regional Authority, department of Agriculture and Forestry

Tortona Strawberry

Sweet, aromatic and very perfumed, Tortona strawberries are like raspberries in shape and size, and they must be picked in the morning and eaten the same day because they are very perishable. They can be found for around ten days from the middle to the end of June, depending on the year, and traditionally are eaten whole sprinkled with sugar and a good Barbera wine. Their story began a century ago, when an excellent and precious variety was selected from the wild ones growing on the surrounding hills. It is a new strawberry, not much larger than a raspberry, with an intense perfume and sweet delicate flavor. They are sold in characteristic woven wood baskets, are mostly sold in the cultivation area and were one of the most important farm products for the local economy in the 30s. There were so many buyers that the local market was insufficient and the local council decided to build a new indoor market, the Gabbione. In the picking season, the factory workers leave their jobs to dedicate their time to the strawberries and many families, thanks to the excellent revenue, manage to supplement their budgets for the whole year. Immediately after the war, more economic, but less valuable varieties like the Volpedo, were more convenient to produce. Thus the serious crisis began, and reduced the harvest to just a few kilos in family orchards. Today production has recovered, thanks to a group of producers who, members of the Association to raise the profile of and protect Tortona strawberries, have started cultivating the variety in the areas near to the city and have created a brand and special packaging to distinguish the genuine Tortona strawberries on the market. If production is no longer at risk, they must still solve the problems however of promoting and distributing the strawberries outside local and regional areas.

PRODUCTION AREA
Tortona, province of Alessandria, Piedmont

PRESIDIUM COORDINATORS
Nicola Piccinini
tel. +39 368917996 – 338 9992833
nicola.piccinini@libero.it
Patrizia Lodi
tel. +39 0131817254 - 338 6471958
patrizia@carcassola.it

PRESIDIUM SUPPORTED BY
Commune of Tortona

Tortona Valley Salami

This raw salami is very good after three months of aging, excellent after one year. Val Curone, Val Grue and Valle, the three valleys giving their name to this product, are situated at the border of Piedmont, Lombardy, Emilia Romagna and Liguria. They are lands where pork breeding is an integral part of the farming culture. The typical salami of this zone is made with both the fat and lean parts of the animal. The lean meats are the shoulder (about 60% of the mixture), leg, loin, filet, coppa, lean parts of the pork belly and ham trimmings. The fatty part (20-30% of the total) consists of the throat and or pork belly. After the meat has been coarsely chopped, it is seasoned with salt, finely ground black pepper and a filtered infusion of garlic and local red wine. The mixture is then stuffed in the natural casing and the salamis are left to dry for a couple of weeks. The low hills in the region, with their cool and breezy microclimate and fairly even temperatures both day and night, are perfect for the aging process. According to the size of the salami, this phase can last for 3-18 months, during which time the salamis are moved from the cool cellars to rooms at higher altitudes to control the formation of mold better. The Presidium unites a small group of pork butchers from the Tortona valleys and aims to valorize the product by focusing on something that is rarely found in modern-day delicatessens: the availability of rooms for naturally aging the salamis. Now it is possible to use cellars and old aging rooms that are being restored by the Mountain Community, which is also overseeing the regulatory adjustments that are needed. The production protocol of the Presidium bans the use of preservatives, powdered milk or any other additives (except for modest amounts of nitrites and nitrates). The salamis must also be made with natural casings and aged for at least 90 days.

PRODUCTION AREA
Tortona valleys, province of Alessandria, Piedmont

PRESIDIUM COORDINATORS
Massimo Berutti
tel. +39 0131786198 - 3386174622
massimoberutti@libero.it
Alessandro Salimei
tel. +39 0131786198
cabannina@libero.it

PRESIDIUM SUPPORTED BY
Curone, Grue and Ossona valleys Mountain Community

Tosco-Romagnolo Apennine Raviggiolo

The first mention of this rather rare cheese dates to the Renaissance. It was 1515 when the Magistrate of Bibbiena gave Pope Leone X a gift of some Raveggiolo cheeses presented in a basket covered with fern leaves. Centuries later, in 1891, in his book *La scienza in cucina e l'arte di mangiar bene*, Pellegrino Artusi lists 'cacio raviggiolo' as one of the ingredients for the Romagna pasta known as *cappelletti*. The cheese is buttery and white, with a delicate, almost sweet flavor. The forms are 20-25 centimeters in diameter and 2-4 centimeters high. It should not be confused with the Tuscan cheese of the same name. The Presidium Raviggiolo is produced in some of the valleys of the Romagnolo Apennines (Montone, Rabbi, Bidente and Savio, partially within the Foreste Casentinesi, Monte Falterona and the Campigna National Park). The cheese is made with raw cow's milk and rennet, without breaking the curd but only draining the mass and salting it on top. It does not keep for more than four days so can only be found in the colder months, from October to March. Its extraordinary freshness and sweet flavor, with hints of milk and hazelnut, make it an excellent cheese to eat between meals, perhaps at breakfast or as an afternoon snack. Given its characteristics, it should be served with light wines, ideally a slightly sparkling white, fragrant but not aromatic. The Presidium was set up to safeguard the production of the raw milk Raviggiolo and to distinguish it from the Tuscan cheese of the same name. On the Casentino side of the Apennines, as in all of Tuscany, the Raviggiolo is made with sheep's milk, and usually on request. When the Presidium was first started there were only two producers and they were making Raviggiolo essentially for themselves. Today the number has doubled and some of the producers also raise Romagnolo cows. They have also designed a specific logo to highlight the Presidium Raviggiolo and created workshops to meet the rising demand.

PRODUCTION AREA
14 towns in the province of Forlì-Cesena, Emilia Romagna

PRESIDIUM COORDINATOR
Lamberto Albonetti
tel. +39 3473497668
slowfoodforli@aliceposta.it

PRESIDIUM SUPPORTED BY
Foreste Casentinesi, Monte Falterona and Campigna National Park

Traditional Altamura Bread

The loaf of Altamura bread, called *sckuanete* ('overlaid' in local dialect), looks like a wide-brimmed hat. It generally weighs one kilo, but there are also smaller half kilo loaves and some that weigh as much as five. It has a hard crust and keeps very well, and is still good, firm and perfectly fine to eat 15 days after it is baked. When fresh it has a pasty consistency that melts in the mouth, an aroma of toast or sometimes coffee, and an aftertaste with hints of vanilla. The baking method is traditional and the ingredients all natural: twice-ground durum wheat semolina flour, sour yeast, water and sea salt. Everything is amalgamated into an even dough and left to rise under a cotton cloth. Then the dough is kneaded, divided and shaped into the size of loaf desired. It rises again for another hour and then a circular incision is made all around the loaf before being put into the oven using the traditional very long-handled wooden paddle. It bakes for an hour and a half at 200-300°C, using only wood-burning ovens fueled with oak wood. The stone ovens used at Altamura and dotting the urban landscape with their tall chimneys are the same ones that were used in the 19th century, and can hold more than 300 kilos of bread. The Presidium of traditional Altamura bread starts with the raw ingredient: durum wheat grown and processed in five communes of the northwestern Murgia area. The second element is the oven, which must be fired exclusively with oak wood. To ensure quality and sincerity throughout the production chain, a rigid production protocol has been worked out and a census has been made on the durum wheat producers and grain mills in the zone.

PRODUCTION AREA
Altamura, province of Bari, Puglia

PRESIDIUM COORDINATOR
Giuseppe Incampo
tel. +39 3395484295 - 0803142866
incamposlow@libero.it

PRESIDIUM SUPPORTED BY
Altus Murus Cultural Association, Altamura, Bari, Puglia, Italy

Trapani Artisan Sea Salt

Traditionally harvested sea salt is produced by letting seawater evaporate in the salt pans, large basins built along the western coast of Sicily, between Trapani and Marsala, in an evocative scenario of water, windmills and white pyramids. The whole zone lies inside two beautiful protected areas: Trapani and Paceco Salt-Oriented Nature Reserve and the Salt pans of Stagnone, in the municipality of Marsala. The key elements required to produce this salt are seawater, sun, wind and the salter's hands; the salt is harvested by the salters and left to dry in piles covered by clay tiles. Production is concentrated in the summer months, particularly in July and August. There are usually three harvests, depending on weather conditions (a last harvest can take place in September). This traditional salt, protected by the Presidium, differs from industrial salt precisely because of the harvesting method used, but above all because of the processing techniques. Traditional salt is hand-harvested by the salters. Instead, industrial salt is harvested mechanically and, while it is being processed it may be refined and other mineral salts may be added. Because there are few traditional salt producers and they are not well organized, their salt cannot compete with industrial products and the so-called rock salt (from salt mines) because of its high production and sales costs. Compared to other cooking salts, sea salt contains more potassium, magnesium and iodine and less sodium chloride. This makes it saltier and, as a result, less needs to be used. Sea salt is used to salt botargo from Favignana, prosciutto and cheese, to make brine for tuna roe and other parts of the tuna, with better results in terms of preservation and aroma. The Presidium was set up to spread the culture of sea salt and to ensure that food manufacturers make increasing use of top-quality ingredients like this salt.

PRODUCTION AREA
Trapani, Paceco and Marsala, province of Trapani, Sicily

PRESIDIUM COORDINATOR
Filippo Salerno
tel. +39 0923873844 - 3476673002
filipposalerno@trapaniweb.it

PRESIDIUM SUPPORTED BY
Sicily Regional Authority, department of Agriculture and Forestry

Trentino Lucanica

The lucanica, the Trentino salami *par excellence*, is made of coarsely ground lean pork, lard, salt, pepper and garlic. So far, nothing unusual. The meat is stuffed into a natural casing, which can be even four meters in length, and then tied at regular intervals to form sausages that are 10-15 centimeters long and 3-5 centimeters in diameter. Hung to dry in a cool place, they are ready to eat after 45 days to 4 months. But there is more than one kind of lucanica. It can, for example, be smoked or not. The further one goes north towards Alto Adige, the more the *lucanica* salamis reflect the South Tyrol traditions, which call for smoking the meat over embers and the addition of a few juniper berries. In southern Trentino, on the other hand, they are rarely smoked. In the past, each of the Trentino valleys had its own variation. In some zones beef, lamb and goat were added to the pork (a way to use the meat from animals no longer suited for farm work) or wild game was used. The aging process differed as well. In some valleys they were aged longer and could be made more flavorful with a blend of cloves and cinnamon. Fresh lucanica is the classic ingredient in many typical dishes: canederli, the *tonco de pontesl* (a meat stew with *lucanica* thickened with toasted wheat flour), crauts cooked with the salami, the *smacafam* (a sort of quiche made by chopping the lucanica with smoked pancetta and cubed lard and adding milk, white flour and buckwheat flour). The meat mixture can be grilled and served with polenta or is used as a sandwich filling during country fairs and food festivals. When aged it is usually eaten alone. The Presidium has united a few producers who adhere to a strict protocol: the use of Trentino pork raised according to rules that ensure the healthiness of the meats, and only the addition of lard, salt, pepper and garlic.

PRODUCTION AREA
Province of Trento, Trentino

PRESIDIUM COORDINATOR
Massimo Cis
tel. +39 0464591023
cismassimo@cr-surfing.net

PRESIDIUM SUPPORTED BY
Trento Autonomous
Provincial Authority,
Trentino Spa

Tuscan Sea Palamita

A relative of tuna and mackerel, palamita (*sarda sarda*) is a streamlined, pelagic predator with a large mouth with sharp teeth even on its palate, small circular eyes and a body ip to 80 centimeters long covered with scales that on the back are dark blue to sky blue-green, with silvery sides and oblique blackish stripes. It is caught from late-Spring to early-Summer and again at the end of September, when it weighs up to five-six kilos. The fishing area extends along the entire coast of the Tuscan Archipelago, with several favorable points such as Capo d'Enfola, near Portoferraio, on the northern coast of Elba, where until a few decades ago there was still a *tonnara* dedicated to processing this fish. Large, open nets were once used for fishing (known as *palamitare*) that were even left in the sea for long periods. Today, on the other hand, large fishing boats are essentially used, alongside invasive methods harmful for the species that, for this reason, it now at risk of extinction. The meat of 'palamita fish' has a strong flavor with a delicate hint of acidity and can be cooked in various ways: grilled with fine herbs, oil and salt, or steamed with tomatoes, parsley, garlic, capers, olives and chili pepper (known as ginger in Tuscany). Yet the best way to savor palamita is preserved in olive oil: the larger fish are boiled after cutting them into fillets and kept under olive oil with bay leaves, pepper and the ever-present ginger. The result is very delicate fillets similar to tuna. The Presidium aims to encourage resumption of processing techniques and create a market value chain: at the time being, there are certain fishermen who would like to restore the use of ancient nets and restaurateurs interested in serving palamita in olive oil.

PRODUCTION AREA
Coast of the Tuscan Archipelago, provinces of Grosseto and Livorno, Tuscany

PRESIDIUM COORDINATOR
Stefano Ferrari
tel. +39 0586630822
stefano.ferrari34@tiscali.it

PRESIDIUM SUPPORTED BY
Grosseto Provincial Authority, Livorno Provincial Authority, Communes of San Vincenzo and Piombino, Tyrrhenian Promotour Consortium

Ur-paarl

A very old variant of the *vinschger paarl*, it is one of the typical 'long-lasting' breads of Alto Adige, edible even weeks after it is made. The complete name is *ur-paarl nach klosterart*, which roughly translated means 'original double-rye convent bread', and in fact it originated with the Benedictine monks of the Monte Maria convent in the town of Malles. A group of bakers in upper Val Venosta have revived the old recipe, making these breads with rye flour, spelt flour and mother yeast, and then seasoning everything with variable doses of fennel seeds, wild cumin and *trigonella cerulea* gathered in the valley pastures. Completing the production chain are the local farmers who have reintroduced the cultivation of rye, a cereal that until the 1950s was very common in the zone thanks to the dry climate. Since it is very resistant to cold and arid climates, the middle and upper Val Venosta have always been considered the breadbasket of the Tyrol and the rye grown here, even at very high altitudes, was sold all over Europe. The *ur-paarl*, which is 10-30 centimeters in diameter and 2-3 centimeters high, looks like a squashed figure eight, made by putting together two round and flattened pieces of dough. It has a soft, dark brown crust, a tender burnished center and an overwhelming flavor and aroma of fennel seeds. There is also a sweet version called *früchtebrot*, made by adding apricots, pears and wild berries to the dough. Dry *ur-paarl* is used in *Lottensuppe* (or paupers' soup), which is made with stock, pieces of meat or speck and pieces of the dry bread. The aim of the Presidium is to promote the *ur-paarl* made by the Val Venosta bakers. It also has a project in the works to reintroduce *schüttelbrot* the traditional flatbread of the Valle Isarco, and cultivate organically a variety of rye that used to be grown in the past.

PRODUCTION AREA
Upper Val Venosta, province of Bolzano, Alto Adige

PRESIDIUM COORDINATOR
Karin Huber
tel. +39 3357036533
karinhuber@dnet.it
Richard Schwrienbacher
tel. +39 3357495352
richard.schwrienbacher@ulterbrot.it

PRESIDIUM SUPPORTED BY
Bolzano Autonomous Provincial Authority, department of Economics and Finance, Bolzano Chamber of Commerce, Industry, Crafts and Agriculture

Ustica Lentil

Ustica lentils are the smallest in Italy – just a few millimeters in diameter – and perhaps the oldest in the world, since they have been cultivated for around 9000 years. They are dark brown in color and grow well on Ustica's particularly fertile lava terrain, without the need for fertilizers or herbicides (troublesome weeds are removed manually with a hoe). The lentils are sown in January and harvested in the first half of June. The shoots are left to dry in the field, then uprooted and grouped into bundles, and then placed on tarpaulins and beaten. Before the Presidium came into being, the bundles were pressed down by large stones dragged over them with the use of donkeys and then tossed in the air with a pitchfork, so that the wind a constant presence on the island could separate the lentils from the chaff. With the introduction of the fixed-position thresher the operation has become slightly less picturesque, but much easier, more functional and convenient: it takes just a couple of hours of work, whereas before it took one family two whole days. Several areas of land that had been abandoned have now been brought back into use, and the lentils, which were before destined only for local consumption, have begun to be marketed and known also outside the island. Ustica lentils are soft and tasty, easy to cook with no need for soaking, and they cook in just three quarters of an hour. They are used in two classic Ustica recipes: the *zuppa*, with a broth-like consistency, enriched with local vegetables and flavored with basil or wild fennel, extra virgin olive oil and a pinch of chili pepper, and *pasta e lenticchie*, made with spaghetti broken into pieces. Although there are only five producers making up a committee, Ustica lentils have started to go beyond the confines of their island, albeit rather timidly, and they have increased in quantity. This is a small step forward that has some appreciable effects from the environmental point of view as well: a lot of land that was previously abandoned has been recovered and given over to the cultivation of lentils.

PRODUCTION AREA
Island of Ustica, province of Palermo, Sicily

PRESIDIUM COORDINATORS
Giancarlo Lo Sicco
tel. +39 091362986
gilosicco@tin.it
Margherita Longo
tel. +39 0918449543
tramontana78@hotmail.com

PRESIDIUM SUPPORTED BY
Sicily Regional Authority, department of Agriculture and Forestry

Valchiavenna Goat Violino

This typical raw ham from the Valchiavenna, made with the leg and the shoulder of goat, is shaped like a violin (*violino*), with the hoof acting as the neck and the muscular mass as the body. The preparation and salting boast very old origins in Valchiavenna, but by now only a handful of artisans prepare these cured goat meats in the traditional way. The violino is unique because of its firm but moist meat, the burgundy color, the spicy flavor, and the aromas ranging from wild goat to smoked oak, juniper berry and at times beech wood, bay laurel or rosemary. The few artisans still making it in the traditional way each have their own jealously guarded recipe. The animals are raised in a semi-wild state in the Province of Sondrio, fed naturally (wild herbs and plants from mountain pastures, integrated with yellow bran flour) and carefully butchered. The sizes of the pieces vary according to which part is used: from one and a half kilos for the front shoulder to three and a half kilos for the rear leg. Naturally aged for three to twelve months in airy cellars without any artificial air-conditioning, the meat becomes more flavorful and aromatic with time. Produced in limited quantities, it is often made at home to be eaten at Christmas and New Year. Slicing the violino during the holidays is practically a ritual: it is passed from hand to hand and each guest holds it like a musical instrument, resting it on the shoulder and using the knife as a bow. According to tradition, it should not leave the table until it is finished. It is excellent served with rye bread and local wines such as Valtellina Superiore or a Sassella. The Presidium is a small group of breeders and producers who guard the secrets of preparing this specialty and are ready to protect it from the competition of market imitations.

PRODUCTION AREA
Chiavenna and Campodolcino, province of Sondrio, Lombardy

PRESIDIUM COORDINATORS
Teresa Tognetti
tel. +39 034332817 - 3356265071
teresa.tognetti@virgilio.it
Aldo Del Curto
tel. +39 034332312

PRESIDIUM SUPPORTED BY
Sondrio Provincial Authority,
Commune of Chiavenna

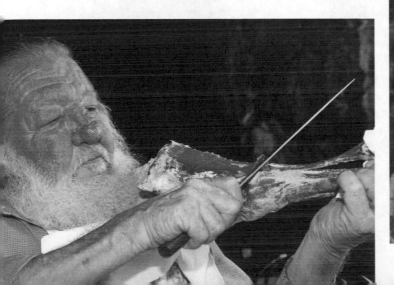

Valdarno Hen

Between Arezzo and Florence, where the Arno divides Chianti and Prato-magno, small-scale poultry breeding has been handed down since the times of share-cropping farmers: chicken and eggs, since they were excluded from the contractual rule of dividing half the produce with the owner and could therefore be sold directly on the market, were an important resource for families and managed by the womenfolk. The first indications of a hen with white plumage typical of the upper Valdarno date back tot he early 1900s, but it was participation in 1953 at the Cremona Poultry Exhibition that finally saw official recognition of the breed, that over the next decade achieved its maximum development, with 20-30 000 head sold every week. The decline of share-cropping and the expansion of intensive poultry breeding seemed to mark the end of this rustics breed, that was unsuitable for such methods. It was saved by the rural tradition of rearing a few hens in the farmyard for family consumption. The cocks are tall, streamlined with large thighs and a small breast; they weigh up to 2-2.5 kilos. They have white feathers that, over time, turn slightly wheat-ish in color, a crested tail with short, curved feathers, an upright blood red crest, very pronounced wattles, large cream eyes with red veins and yellow beak, claws and skin. The hens are smaller (1.5-2 kilos) and have a floppy crest. Valdarno chickens grow slowly and are never slaughtered before four months of age. The meat is excellent and the eggs are also superbly tasty, having and ivory white sheel and a deep yellow yolk. The Presidium was founded not the least with the collaboration of the Custodian Agriculturists Association and aims to safeguard Valdarno hens. All breeders apply regulations that envisage, among other things, natural diet – free range and feed, partly based on *quarantino*, a local variety of maize – and at least 10 square meters of land per bird.

PRODUCTION AREA

Communes in the upper Valdarno area, provinces of Arezzo and Florence, Tuscany

PRESIDIUM COORDINATORS

Camillo Duque
tel. +39 0559139238
vfduque@tin.it
Francesca Romana Farina
tel. +39 055967398
francescar.f@virgilio.it

PRESIDIUM SUPPORTED BY

Arezzo and Florence Provincial Authoritie, Commune of Montevarchi, Pratomagno Mountain Community, Arezzo Chamber of Commerce, Industry, Crafts and Agriculture

Valdarno Tarese

The term 'pancetta' indicates both a cut of meat (beef, pork, sheep) and the cured meat (bacon) prepared from fatty pork belly. In the second instance, unlike the rolled variety, the most common "pancetta" is flat, since it is prepared from a large, trimmed, salted and cured cut.. A typical produce of Valdarno, tarese is a flat pancetta of unusual dimensions – even 50 by 80 centimeters – since it is traditionally prepared from sows weighing more than two quintals. It is made using the entire rump of the animal, from the back to the belly, and thus includes the prized chine (*carré*). The cut is boned and excess fat is eliminated; it is then rubbed with pepper, red garlic, juniper and other spices – some even use orange peel – and, lastly, covered with rough salt. After 10-12 days, tarese is washed, dried and once again 'massaged' with garlic and spices; it is then cured for a variable period of 60-90 days. This pancetta has a characteristic, intense and persistent flavor yet, at the same time, is finer and more delicate than other cured meats made in similar ways. The fat of the chine ensures softness and mellowness; the bouquet is aromatic, thanks not the least to the spiced coating. The outer part has a thick and shiny skin that protects the softer parts; the inside is covered with pepper and natural flavorings, while the ribs are very evident and well-shaped. Traditionally, only sows weighing 200 kilos and more were slaughtered. For this reason, the valorization work of the Presidium began by re-creating a local value chain focusing on quality and tradition as the priority objectives of breeders and processors. One of the first steps was to reinstate the population of pigs historically reared in the area, that are best suited to making tarese. A by no means secondary objective was to define and regulate the processing techniques handed down by local families and butchers.

PRODUCTION AREA
Communes of the Valdarno: Bucine, Montevarchi, San Giovanni Valdarno and Terranuova Bracciolini, province of Arezzo, Tuscany

PRESIDIUM COORDINATORS
Camillo Duque
tel. +39 0559139238
vfduque@tin.it
Andrea Fantechi
tel. +39 0559102005

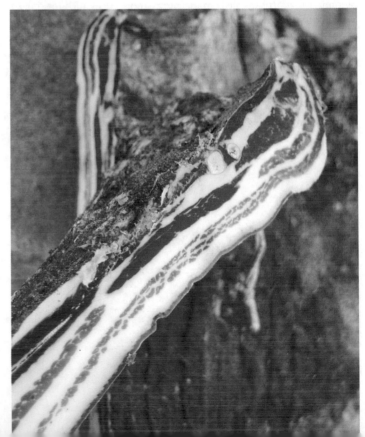

PRESIDIUM SUPPORTED BY
Arezzo Provincial Authority - Arezzo Chamber of Commerce – Commune of Montevarchi

Val d'Ossola Mortadella

The Val d'Ossola mortadella is different from the usual cooked, large, pink sausage, commonly known as Bologna. In reality, the traditional cured meat from the Ossola valleys is a salami sausage made with raw pork. The name dates back to earlier than the 17th century: mortadella comes from the word *mortaio*, 'mortar', indicating the meat's being mashed to a pulp. The local pork butcher keeps up this old custom and often uses the term instead of the more common word, salami. The mortadella is produced in the Val d'Ossola, an area between Piedmont, Lombardy and Switzerland. It is one of the valleys which has treasured the pork butchering tradition the longest, and it once was famous for its pork ham and goat ham, its salami, dry-salted beef and mortadella. Also famous were the pigs bred in a wild state, which in summer were taken to Alpine pastures wearing a ring on their snouts, in order not to spoil the pastures while grubbing. The production of the Presidium's cured meat is still very limited; it is carried out by only a few artisans. It is made of raw pork, (to which maximum 5% liver is added, though in the Val Vigezzo another variety contains 10% liver) and in some cases a sort of spiced, warm, mulled wine. The ingredients are all squeezed inside the pig's gut, and then left to season for about two months. Due to the ingredients used in the preparation, the mortadella of the Val d'Ossola has a sharp taste. Aged, it may be sliced and eaten, preferably with the local brown Coimo bread. Fresh, it may be boiled and served with potatoes or baked in the oven and then served with polenta *a fragai* (dry).

PRODUCTION AREA
Masera and the Val d'Ossola, province of Verbania, Piedmont

PRESIDIUM COORDINATOR
Massimo Sartoretti
tel. +39 0324 35035 - 3482202612
mara.sarto@libero.it

PRESIDIUM SUPPORTED BY
Coop, Verbania Chamber of Commerce, Industry, Crafts and Agriculture, Valle Ossola Mountain Community

Valle Bagnario di Strevi Moscato Passito

This sweet raisin wine is perhaps less famous than its *passito* cousins, Loazzolo, Caluso and Pantelleria, but it has a strong characterization and commercial potential which has yet to express itself completely, despite the fact that wine, Moscato especially, is part and parcel of the history and destiny of the town of Strevi, so. Up until about ten years ago the land of the Bagnarlo Valley was famous because the local vineyards, the most prestigious vines in the Strevi area, made the owners extremely rich. When everybody was still making wine during grape harvest, a very strong smell of moscato spread all through the valley. The quality of the grapes picked in these old, steep vineyards, where the typical scent of the vines meets a great balance in taste, rich but not sickening, is very high. These characteristics make the wine a good accompaniment for strong cheeses: excellent with matured goat's cheese Robiola, superb with natural Gorgonzola, Raschera and Bitto stravecchio. In order to obtain the Moscato Passito della Valle Bagnario di Strevi, the best part of the harvest is picked (in crates), that is to say the most intact bunches and *spargoli*, which are put to wither on racks. In November, part of the skin is removed of the pips and waste and put to ferment with the previously pressed grapes. This is an ancient method which allows the *passiti* from this area to keep intact and strong for decades. Despite this, the Moscato Passito di Valle Bagnario was about to disappear: too much work, poor wages for the amount of effort required, plus the remaining vine-growers were too elderly. Luckily, thanks to the work of a group of enthusiasts, the Presidium was born. An association now assembles all producers, who abide by strict rules, and tastings and experiments have kicked off in order to try and understand the most efficient techniques to produce such a great wine.

PRODUCTION AREA
Strevi, province of Alessandria, Piedmont

PRESIDIUM COORDINATORS
Enzo Codogno
tel. +39 0141888228 – 338 4364306
ecodogno@libero.it
Giampaolo Ivaldi
tel. +39 0144363459

Valli Valdesi Mustardela

The mustardela is a blood sausage which was originally part of the Provençal tradition, though this has never been documented. Producers state that they saw an identical product in France and Spain, near the Pyrenees. Today the mustardela is produced in the Val Pellice, Val Chisone and Val Germanasca areas, but not in the southern part of the valley, where another type of blood sausage is made with blood, milk and spices (*budìn*), similar to the one in neighboring France (*boudin*) and the one in the Val d'Aosta, particularly because it can also be prepared with turnips. The sausage produced in the Waldensian valleys is aubergine purple in color,

spicy, bittersweet, soft and doughy. It is 20-30 centimeters long, 6-7 cm wide and it is eaten boiled, with potatoes or polenta. It is a poor meat, like all other blood sausages, the idea being essentially that none of the parts of the pig were to be wasted. In fact, the head, throat, tongue and skin are boiled, removed of any bones and then ground. After that, scraps of pork fat, onions and leeks in fat are added, after which blood. Some like to add a little red wine with cinnamon for extra flavor. A pinch of salt, pepper and spices (nutmeg, cinnamon and cloves) before the entire mixture is put into an ox's gut called *torta*. It is tied and boiled for 20 minutes at 90°C (the water must not boil otherwise the sausage will split open). Producers are few and far between but they boast a long tradition and each of them owns their small abattoir: this is an extraordinary fact, unequalled anywhere else in Italy. The Presidium exploits this product, striving to make it known to a wider range of clients, not just locals. Producers abide by a strict set of production rules and have created a brand for the one and only mustardela of the Waldensian valleys.

PRODUCTION AREAS
Pellice, Chisone and Germanasca valleys, province of Turin, Piedmont

PRESIDIUM COORDINATORS
Franco Turaglio
tel. +39 0121394556 - 3294151775
info@lanicchia.net
Bruno Gonin
tel. +39 012191406 - 3355315885
chiotdlaiga@libero.it

PRESIDIUM SUPPORTED BY
Turin Provincial Authority

Valtellina Buckwheat

Also known as *furmentùn*, *fraina* or black flour, buckwheat (*grano saraceno*) is an ancient cereal that, over the course of time, was replaced by maize except in Valtellina. The name *saraceno* is said to come from the brown color of the kernels or the fact that it was brought to Italy by the Saracens. Rustic, resistant to the cold climate and rarely affected by parasites, it used to be a staple of the peasant diet. It also made it possible to use fallow farmlands after the crops of rye, potatoes or barley were harvested in the winter. Mentioned for the first time in Valtellina in 1616, this crop was at its peak in the first half of the 19th century. But since it was difficult and expensive to grow, the crops gradually declined, and in 1970 production had dropped to 3700 quintals. The buckwheat is broadcasted (sown by tossing handfuls of kernels on plowed land) and harvested in mid-September. The stalks are cut with a sickle, tied in bunches and placed in *caséle* (rows of small cone-shaped huts). Once they are dry, they are beaten with the *fièl*, a tool made of two sticks tied together at one end. The flour, which can also be used by people on a gluten-free diet, is a hazelnut grey color and has a slightly tart flavor. Buckwheat flour was not highly regarded in the past, while today the black polenta made from this *grano saraceno* flour alone, or mixed with maize, is one of the specialties of Valtellina cooking. Other dishes include polenta taragna, *sciatt* (saraceno and wheat flour fritters filled with cheese), pizzoccheri and the less common *kiscioeul*, a black flour focaccia filled with aged Casera, typical of the area around Tirano. Only a few small cultivations remain and most of the product processed in Italy is imported from abroad. The Presidium is resolved to reintroduce the local and organic *grano saraceno* variety, and is trying to recover the stone terraces in the valley so these lands will not be abandoned.

PRODUCTION AREA

Valtellina, province of Sondrio, Lombardy

PRESIDIUM COORDINATOR

Piero Roccatagliata
tel. +39 0342780152
furmentun@libero.it

PRESIDIUM SUPPORTED BY

Sondrio Provincial Authority, Valtellina di Tirano Mountain Community, Commune of Teglio

Vastedda del Belìce

Traditionally made in the summer by the cheesemakers of the Belìce valley who melted them at high temperatures in order to recover imperfectly shaped sheep's cheeses, the name of this cheese is linked to the dialect word for spoilt, faulty – *vasta* – or to the flattened, oval shape resembling the home-made loaves with the same name. It is the only spun-curd sheep's milk cheese and it is eaten very fresh: in fact, it's ready to eat after just one hour and it doesn't keep for more than three days. The milk, which still smells of meadow flowers, comes from a native breed, the Belìce sheep, a medium-sized animal with a thin, elongated and light head, strong legs and a white fleece. The processing method varies depending on where it is made and the individual cheesemaker. The raw milk from one or two milkings is usually coagulated at 35-36°C using lamb or kid rennet made on the farm; the curds are broken with a wooden pole, the *rotula*, and after a short pause the paste is then gathered into a linen cloth and placed on a table. It is cut into pieces after an hour, placed in a wooden container and covered with hot whey (55-60°C) to encourage fermentation. Once it has reached the right level of acidity, the mass is sliced into a wooden bowl; very hot water (90°C) is then added and the curds are worked with a wooden paddle, the *vaciliatuma*. In the final phase, when the curds have reached the right consistency, the mass is divided into portions which are molded by hand into balls and, once placed on pottery dishes, they become vastedda cheeses. The cheese is excellent served with extra virgin olive oil, tomato and oregano, but it is also used as an ingredient in some local dishes, including *cunzato* bread. The Presidium was set up by a couple of producers and has since expanded to include other cheesemakers from Belìce. Much still needs to be done, above all in terms of standardizing the systems of production, cheesemaking and storage, and providing efficient refrigerated transport.

PRODUCTION AREA
Belìce valley, province of Trapani, Agrigento and Palermo, Sicily

PRESIDIUM COORDINATOR
Franco Saccà
tel. +39 0923559490
francosac@libero.it

PRESIDIUM SUPPORTED BY
Sicily Regional Authority, department of Agriculture and Forestry

Vastese Ventricina

Because the casing for the *ventricina* is a pig's bladder, the sausage is round and weighs from one to two kilos. The filling consists of pieces of the choicest cuts of pork (leg, loin and shoulder), all carefully prepared and seasoned with salt, ground 'goat's horn' sweet peppers, sometimes wild fennel, and pepper. After the casing has been stuffed, it is tied with string and hung up to dry in a room where there is a fire going in the fireplace. The sausage then ages for three months in a cool and airy room, after which time the surface is cleaned of mold and covered with lard to protect it from insects and sudden changes in temperature. The ventricina is the most typical sausage in the mountainous area southwest of Vasto, between the Sinello, Treste and Trigno valleys in the southern part of the province of Chieti. The main ingredient used to be the pork from black or red pigs, but now the more common large white or Landrace breeds are acquired and home-raised until the butchering season in midwinter. The ventricina is ready to eat after seven or eight months. In its native area it is often coarsely chopped and put into meat sauce for pasta, but more commonly it is sliced and eaten raw. It has a reddish-orange color, interspersed with blobs of fat, and a fragrant aroma from the spices and long aging. At times there is a hint of citrus because of the habit of washing the bladder casing in water scented with oranges or lemons. But the overall flavor is hot and spicy, which in any case never overwhelms the flavor of the meat and seasonings. The Presidium is endeavoring to valorize this sausage by increasing production rather than raising prices (already quite profitable at the local level). It also intends to promote the breeding of heavy pigs in the production area according to a rigorous protocol.

PRODUCTION AREA
Middle and High Vasto area, province of Chieti, Abruzzo

PRESIDIUM COORDINATORS
Raffaele Cavallo
tel. +39 0872714195 - 337915112
raffaele.cavallo@libero.it
Luigi Di Lello
tel. +39 0873914173 - 3393086378
info@ventricina.com

PRESIDIUM SUPPORTED BY
Società Consortile Vastese Inn,
Accademia della Ventricina, Chieti

Vessalico Garlic

Vessalico is a small village in upper Valle Arroscia, in the hinterland of Alberga. In this area, especially in the less populated hamlets higher up, a very old variety of garlic continues to be cultivated thanks to the will of a few farmers who grow it in tiny plots of mountainous land, handing down from one generation to the next the particular methods for growing and packaging it in the traditional plaited strings. The heads of garlic, in fact, which are not cut from the plant or taken from the bunch, are dried, selected on the basis of size and then plaited in groups of two, forming a long interlaced reticulum. This delicate operation can only be performed in the morning and the evening, when the heads are damp and the leaves do not break off. Not cutting the plants keeps the garlic healthy and fragrant even 8-10 months after the harvest. The cultivation method is biological, using a system of solarization that makes it possible to sterilize the terrain with the heat of the sun. The perfect chance to buy it is at the 18th century garlic festival, which takes place on the Canavai meadow at Vessalico on July 2 each year

(when the date falls on a Sunday it is moved up to Saturday). Vessalico garlic is characterized by its delicate aroma, intense and slightly spicy taste and the fact that it keeps well for a very long time. The traditional dish, which brings out the best of its aroma and taste, is the *ajé*, a mayonnaise made with extra virgin olive oil and garlic crushed in a mortar (one of the many successors to the medieval *agliata*). It is best when eaten on crostini of baked bread or when served with boiled potatoes. The Presidium has made it possible for eight small producers to come together as the La Resta Cooperative, which produces authentic Vessalico garlic with a seal of quality and using certified biological methods. The Cooperative has also started a small-scale production of garlic by-products made according to the traditional Ligurian recipes.

PRODUCTION AREA
Valle Arroscia, province of Imperia, Liguria

PRESIDIUM COORDINATOR
Roberto Marini
tel. +39 0183382054 - 3386710534
roberto48@libero.it

PRESIDIUM SUPPORTED BY
Liguria Regional Authority, Upper Valle Arroscia
Mountain Community,Imperia Provincial Authority

Vezzena

This aged, semi-fat cheese is produced at the Lavarone cheese cooperative with milk rich in aromatic essences from the mountain pastures. The raw milk obtained from the cows in the evening is partially skimmed and the next day is added to the morning milk. It is all heated together with artisan milk starter and beef rennet is added when the temperature reaches 33-35°. The milk coagulates in 20-25 minutes or so and then the curd is broken up into grains the size of corn kernels and cooked at 45-48° C. When the curds have settled to the bottom, the mass is cut into blocks and arranged in wooden molds or *fascere* and pressed. In the evening the weights are removed and the forms are placed in a warm, damp room called the *frescura*. After the salting, either dry or in brine, the forms are placed on wooden planks for the aging process: once a month the cheeses are wiped clean and rubbed with linseed oil. The eyes disappear after 12-18 months and the yellow cheese tends to flake, releasing a flavor of grasses and spices. Even after it has aged a long time it remains buttery, with aromas that depend on the time of year the cows graze. With the June milk, for example, there is a slight hint of garlic. There is always a scent of chives, which experts say distinguishes the *vezzena* from the asiago di allevo. The Presidium Vezzena is the one made in summer with milk from the mountains and can be identified by the M for *malga* (mountain dairy) impressed on the forms. If the cheese is young, it goes well with a Trentino Lagrein or a Marzemino wine; if well-aged and somewhat piquant, a Trentino Vino Santo. Today the cheese is in the hands of Rodolfo Bertacchini, the cheesemaker who supervises production at the Lavarone cheese cooperative. There are eleven members of the cooperative, but Bertacchini makes the Vezzena with milk from two mountain dairies and mainly in summer. The breeders follow a rigorous protocol stating that the animals must be raised in pastures and that the feed only can be integrated with quality ingredients: no silage, no industrial by-products and no GMOs.

PRODUCTION AREA
All the communes of the Lavarone, Vezzena and Folgaria plateau, province of Trento, Trentino

PRESIDIUM COORDINATOR
Giampaolo Gaiarin
tel. +39 3356674256
gaiarin.giampaolo@trentingrana.it

PRESIDIUM SUPPORTED BY
Trento Autonomous Provincial Authority, Trentingrana Concast

Vino Santo Trentino

This singular passito (raisin) wine is made from the native nosiola vine, which is cultivated on about 110 hectares and represents 1.5% of grape production in the region. The nosiola has been a part of the history of Trentino ever since the Council of Trent, but today is in difficulty because of the tendency to plant international varieties like pinot and chardonnay, which are more market competitive. The zone of choice for the nosiola is in the Valle dei Laghi, where it grows on just ten hectares in small, old and isolated vineyards. The spargoli (bunches having few grapes) are harvested late and left to dry on the arele racks placed under the roof, where they can benefit form the Ora del Garda, the wind much loved by sailing enthusiasts that blows from the nearby lake. The withering goes on for more than five or six months, until Holy Week (hence the name). No other wine is made from grapes naturally withered for such a long time. Botrytis cinerea, a noble rot, develops inside the grapes. It intensifies the dehydration and, together with the effects of time and wind, causes the bunches of grapes to lose 80% or more of their volume. This means that just 15-18 liters of Vino Santo must is obtained from 100 kilos of fresh nosiola grapes. After the pressing, the wine is put into small oak casks, where the natural fermentation process begins. Because of the very high sugar content, this proceeds very slowly and goes on for at least six to eight years. And once bottled, the wine can even be kept for more than fifty years. Fruity and rich, but never cloying, and with just the right amount of acidity, it is traditionally served with local sweets like the fregoloti cake or renetta apple strudel. It is also excellent with blue cheeses and with paté of foie gras. This ancient tradition is kept alive by the sheer tenacity of a few producers. The Vino Santo Trentino doc association of six winegrowers was set up in April 2002.

PRODUZIONE AREA
Communes of Calavino, Cavedine, Lasino, Padergnone and Vezzano in the Valle dei Laghi, province of Trento, Trentino

PRESIDIUM COORDINATOR
Carlo Bleggi
tel. +39 3406282882
cableggi@tin.it

PRESIDIUM SUPPORTED BY
Trento Autonomous Provincial Authority, Trentino SpA

White Modena Cow

Less than 100 years ago about 52,000 heads of White Modena Cow were registered with animal husbandry consortia in the provinces of Modena, Ferrara, Reggio Emilia and Mantova, and numbers were growing. In the 1950s - the golden age for this breed - there were more than 140,000, but ten years later its numbers started to decline in step with the relentless expansion of Fresian cattle. The success of Parmigiano Reggiano cheese convinced breeders to substitute the two native breeds (the White Modena and the Red Reggiana) with breeds from Holland that were known for their productivity and with perfect udders for mechanical milking. White Modena cows, also called Val Padana (Po Valley) because of their close ties to that territory, only number a few hundred today, on about 20 small cattle-breeding farms. It is an animal with threefold 'talents': in addition to producing milk and meat, in the past it was also used for helping with work in the fields. The Presidium was formed by a few historical breeders who, with the help of the Modena Provincial Authority have started up a project to recover this indigenous breed. They have also achieved an important initial result: a mountain Parmigiano prepared only with the milk of the White Modena is produced at the Rosola di Zocca cheese factory, in the Apennines near Modena. One of the five cauldrons at the factory, well-separated from the others, is used exclusively for the production of two forms daily. Given the high levels of k-caseins in its milk, the White Modena is particularly well-suited to cheesemaking and thus for making quality Parmigiano Reggiano. Moreover, because the breed has preserved its genetic patrimony it matures fairly quickly, yields a good amount when butchered and has adapted perfectly to the environment. Its meat is tasty and well-marbled, making it perfect for quick cooking. In the future, when there are enough heads of cattle, it will be possible to develop an interesting project to promote the meat from this breed.

PRODUCTION AREA
Province of Modena, Emilia Romagna

PRESIDIUM COORDINATORS
Antonio Cherchi
tel. +39 059216969
antonio.cherchi@studio-professionisti.it
Graziano Poggioli
tel. +39 059209713
poggioli.g@provincia.modena.it

PRESIDIUM SUPPORTED BY
Modena Provincial Authority

White Pertosa Artichoke

Pertosa is a little village south of Salerno, within the Cilento and Vallo di Diano National Park, noted for its unusual caves, extraordinary natural chambers which formed following the creation of karst formations, over 35 million years ago. Here and in the neighboring towns of Auletta, Caggiano and Salvitelle one can find a few farmers who are growing a rare variety of artichoke in little allotments of just a few hundred square meters. The Pertosa white artichoke is distinguished by its very pale green color, almost white, with large, round, spineless flowers and a characteristic opening at the top. This is the lower valley of the Tanagro, a river which runs through the whole cultivation area, between 300 and 700 meters above sea level. The artichokes are grown almost exclusively for family consumption, without the use of any chemical treatments or fertilizers. The few producers have joined together in a consortium, with the help of scientific consultants from the Experimental Horticultural Institute in Pontecagnano. The white Pertosa artichoke has a number of unusual characteristics, namely its resistance to low temperatures and the extraordinary delicacy of the internal leaves. Much appreciated in the kitchen for its flavor, which is both intense and subtle, and the sweetness of the internal leaves, this artichoke is excellent eaten raw, dipped in the PDO Colline Salernitane extra-virgin olive oil from the same area. These two local products make a natural pairing, and it's common to see fields of artichokes alternating with groves of olive trees. The main goal is to find a market for this vegetable, aiming particularly at local restaurants. Given that this artichoke is also delicious preserved in oil, in Pertosa there's already a project underway which will create a modern processing facility to produce baby artichokes in PDO Colline Salernitane extra virgin olive oil.

PRODUCTION AREA
Auletta, Caggiano, Pertosa and Salvitelle, in the lower Tanagro Valley, province of Salerno, Campania

PRESIDIUM COORDINATOR
Andrea La Porta
tel. +39 3287123666
latendac@tiscali.it

PRESIDIUM SUPPORTED BY
Communes of Pertosa, Auletta, Caggiano and Salvitelle,
Vallo di Diano Mountain Community,
Valle del Tanagro Mountain Community

Zeri Lamb

Zeri is a municipal district of fewer than 1,400 inhabitants - although it had more than three times that number in the 19th century – comprising about 15 villages in the mountains of the Lunigiana area, west of Pontremoli, on the borders of Liguria and Emilia Romagna. Although it is not more than 20-30 kilometers from the bottom of the Magra valley, this district, which has three rivers, the Verde, Gordana and Teglia, is still somewhat isolated. However, this fact has encouraged the development of an *Ovis* ecotype which was recorded for the first time in 1845 by the agronomist Antonelli for the excellent output of young animals for slaughter, which took the name of the district. The rustic Zeri sheep has a white fleece and is medium-large in size, with a rather straight head. It spends most of the year in the wild and in the Winter is fed with hay from the local pastures. The milk is very rich in proteins, and is used to feed the lambs which are slaughtered when they are 60-65 days old and weigh 25-30 kilograms. The meat is tender, perfumed and sweet, extremely fragrant and with no hint of game. It is usually cooked in a copper pan with chopped lardo, garlic, herbs and tasty mountain potatoes, inside a *testo*, a pot of refractory material which is then heated on the coals. There are now about 3,000 Zeri sheep and the lamb is considered one of the gastronomic jewels of Italy. The Presidium has convinced the local farmers to concentrate on this activity, increasing the number of animals and linking up with local restaurants, traders and butchers, The consortium to promote and protect lamb from Zeri was created in 2001, with strict regulations. The chapter on food, for example, establishes that the sheep should be reared free with a supplement of local hay and meal products in certain periods of the year. The lambs must be fed with their mothers' milk until they are slaughtered, and they must go to pasture with their mothers.

PRODUCTION AREA
Bagnone, Filattiera, Mulazzo, Pontremoli and Zeri (at an altitude of over 800 meters), province of Massa-Carrara, Tuscany

PRESIDIUM COORDINATOR
Cinzia Angiolini
tel. +39 0187449178 - 3396397599
tercana@libero.it

PRESIDIUM SPONSORED BY
Massa Carrara Provincial Authority, Lunigiana Mountain Community, Commune of Zeri Town Council, Massa Carrara Chamber of Commerce, Industry, Crafts and Agriculture

Zibello Culatello

Despite its very ancient origins, culatello was barely mentioned in literature until the end of the 19th century. D'Annunzio made reference to it in 1891, and it was included among gastronomic specialties in Alfredo Panzini's dictionary published in 1905. It is long and laborious to prepare and made with the choicest part of the pig, the center of the leg. As such, it is considered one of the finest cured meats of the Italian pork butchering tradition. The area of production is limited to the area of the eight historic culatella towns of Zibello, Busseto, Polesine, Soragna, Roccabianca, Sissa, San Secondo and Colorno. Most of the culatello on the market today is commercially produced all year round, aged for only a year or so, and made with mediocre ingredients and synthetic casings. The Presidium is a group of about a dozen small artisan producers who still make the culatella by hand – and only in winter – and who age it in naturally ventilated rooms, without refrigeration. Adhering to a very strict and clearly defined protocol, they are committed to marketing only culatella that has been aged for at least 18 months (ideally 24). Some of the Presidium producers also raise their own pigs, often indigenous breeds, so they have a firsthand supply of the quality ingredient. The seasoned product has the typical pear shape, with a thin layer of fat on the surface, and is wound up in an openwork netting of string. When sliced, it is uniformly red with some white marbling. The slightly musky aroma, which it picks up from the damp floors during the aging process, is sometimes covered up by the taste of alcohol from the wine bath it is put in before being sliced. The aromatic and very complex flavor is almost honey-sweet at first and then with a slightly spicy aftertaste.

PRODUCTION AREA
Eight communes in the province of Parma, Emilia Romagna

PRESIDIUM COORDINATORS
Alberto Fabbri
tel. +39 0516830187
centoggi@virgilio.it
Massimo Spigaroli
tel. +39 052496136
info@cavallinobianco.it

PRESIDIUM SUPPORTED BY
Emilia Romagna Regional Authority

Zolfino Bean

Still very common in Tuscan cuisine (Florentines are renowned as bean-eaters), this legume from America spread rapidly all over the lands ruled by the Medici. It seems that Charles V introduced beans to Tuscany, immediately after the discovery of the New World, on donating them to Pope Clement VII, born Giulio De Medici. Alongside the more common *cannellini* and *toscanelli*, relatively rare varieties are also grown in the region, such as *coco nano* and, especially, *zolfino* - also known as *burrino* or *cento* (because it was planted on the 100th day of the year): small, globular, yellow with a lighter eye mark and a thin skin. The area where it grows best lies between the Arno valley near Arezzo and the Apennine crest of Pratomagno, at a variable altitude (250-600 meters); it is impossible to grow it in the plains because its roots are shallow and do not tolerate the least standing water. It is usually sown in April, often on the terraces beneath the olive trees: in this way, the water flows away between the stones of the dry walls. Since it suffers from significant climatic excursions – hot spells in summer, frosts in spring – and its distinctly lower yield than the more common varieties, zolfino beans have almost completely disappeared from markets. Production was recently re-launched thanks to the Zolfino Bean Association in Pratomagno and the Association of Custodian Agriculturists. Zolfino beans withstand long cooking (even more than four hours): dense and creamy, they melt in the mouth like butter. The are excellent boiled, flavored with a dash of extra virgin olive oil (best if strong, intense and fruity), served as a side dish for Florentine steaks or on toasted Tuscan bread. Families in the past - and still today - soaked them overnight in flasks or dishes in a wood oven. The Presidium aims to promote production, commerce and consumption of this old native variety.

PRODUCTION AREA
West side of the Pratomagno, communes of Castelfranco di Sopra, Castiglion Fibocchi, Laterina, Loro Ciuffenna, Pian di Scò and Terranuova Bracciolini, province of Arezzo; commune of Reggello, province of Florence, Tuscany

PRESIDIUM COORDINATORS
Viviano Venturi
tel. +39 0559172277
radici.radici@tin.it
Luigi Giovannozzi
tel. +39 0559705039
info@ilfagiolozolfino.it

PRESIDIUM SUPPORTED BY
Arezzo and Florence Provincial Authorities, Pratomagno Mountain Community, Arezzo Chamber of Commerce, Industry, Crafts and Agriculture

Aged Artisan Gouda

The cheese takes its name from Gouda, a city northeast of Rotterdam, where they produced thousands of tons of it at the end of the 17th century. Today we are mainly familiar with the mediocre industrial versions, but fortunately there are still a few small producers left who preserve the traditional method of production. Their survival, however, is compromised by the constant expansion of urbanized areas, rising production costs and competition from industry. The Presidium cheese, Boeren-goudse oplegkaas, is made with raw milk and only in the summer, when the cows can pasture on turf in the large 'Green Heart' of central Holland. Boeren means farmer and *opleg* is the equivalent of aged (in fact the forms are aged from two to four years). The processing is unusual in that the curd is washed: after the cut, the mass of curd is heated and then rinsed with warm water. This technique gives the cheese a well-balanced sweetness, containing the acidity and bitter taste in the forms that are aged longer. In addition, to start the coagulation they use starters made on site with milk from the previous day. The cheeses, weighing 20 kilos or more, are arranged in the traditional wooden forms lined with linen. The Presidium producers are trying out new techniques to eliminate the plastic coating that is applied to the crust today to give the it the classic shiny golden color, and are working to lengthen the minimum aging period (at present 24 months). For centuries Dutch artisan cheesemakers have been at the mercy of middlemen who resell their cheeses without indicating the origin. Slow Food is endeavoring to propose an alternative

to this system of commercialization by helping producers promote their own Boeren-goudse oplegkaas directly with the consumers.

PRODUCTION AREA
Green Heart, between the cities of Amsterdam, Rotterdam and Utrecht

PRESIDIUM COORDINATOR
Marjolein Kooistra
tel. +31 104678762
goudseboerenkaas@hotmail.com

Chaam Hen

The Chaamse hoen is a spotted hen with silver-white plumage scattered with black spots, named for a place in the Brabant, near Breda, where it was once raised. The first official description dates to 1911, but even in the 19th century the meats of the chickens and especially the Chaam capons were in great demand. Its decline started in the 1920s because of competition from more productive breeds like the North hollands blau. In 2001, a group of friends bought what were probably the last specimens remaining from an elderly chicken breeder of Rotterdam and began to raise them in the Chaam countryside. And in just a few years they achieved extraordinary results. A foundation for protecting the breed was set up, with the support of the Chaamsse Hoender club, and the number of hens rose to nearly 300. In addition to creating very strict guidelines, they designed a system for marking the animals to keep track of the origins of the meat. It has not been possible for now, however, to legalize the practice of castrating the male birds on the farm. For health reasons, this can only be done today at special health facilities, at a price that cannot be afforded. Through the Friends of the Chaam Hen Foundation, the Presidium is doing its best to revive the traditional method, which also gives better asroma and flavor. It also intends to help breeders and restaurant owners register the brand of the breed, to promote it and protect it. The chickens and hens belonging to the Foundation members live outside all year round (each animal has eight square meters of field available) and feed on local grass and cereals. Market availability is seasonal, and the meat can only be bought at butchers' shops or tasted at area restaurants from July to January.

PRODUCTION AREA
Chaam, Noord-Brabant

PRESIDIUM COORDINATOR
Victor van den Broek
tel. +31 611353643 - 161431866
vvdbroek@tiscali.nl

Oosterschelde Lobster

Because of the need to protect the land from periodically disastrous floods, man's intervention has played an important role in the history of the Oosterschelde lobster, as it has with much of the Dutch landscape and agrifood resources. The construction of dykes along the coast of Zeeland in the last two centuries (the last one, mobile, inaugurated in 1986) has barred the course of the Scheldt River, creating a perfect habitat for oysters and lobsters (*Homarus gammarus*)., to joined the mussels that were already present. The isolation of the Oosterschelde has caused the crustaceans to gradually become differentiated from their North Sea cousins and form a distinct sub species. Unlike Canadian or American lobsters, which are dark green, the ones from Zeeland are a cobalt blue color and have reddish orange stripes on their claws, and the meat is whiter and has a finer, softer consistency. They live hidden among the natural rocks and the foundations of the numerous dykes along the edge of the bay (up to 50 meters in depth), and take at least six years to reach maturity. The short fishing season lasts from April 1 to July 15, and artisan methods are used. The crustaceans are not caught in lobster pots or traps, but with a cylindrical net called a fulken. The lobster fishermen throw back the ones that are too small as well as the females with eggs. The male lobsters, at least 24 centimeters long, are kept in containers filled with sea water and sold alive. The Oosterschelde Lobster Presidium, a group of fishermen and volunteers, works to promote these sustainable fishing techniques among the local communities. Each year it celebrates the opening of the fishing season with a big festival in the city of Zierikzee and it has already involved restaurant owners in the area, who have pledged to use only locally caught fish.

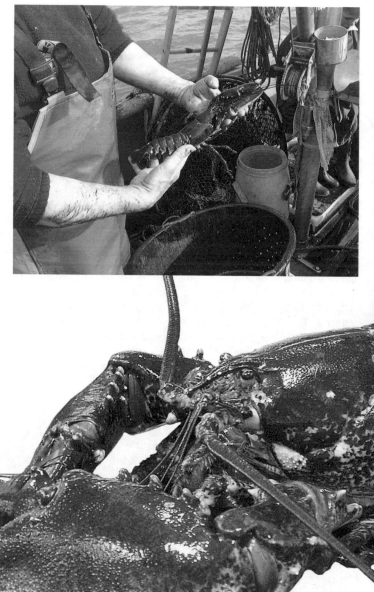

PRODUCTION AREA
Oosterschelde, Zeeland

PRESIDIUM COORDINATOR
Balth Roessingh
tel. +31 111644030 - 653353843
info@jcom.nl – schute@haansbeijsens.nl

PRESIDIUM SUPPORTED BY
Zeeland Provincial Authority

Texel Sheep Cheese

Texel is the name of the westernmost and largest area (157 sq. km.) of the Fresian Islands, but also of a breed of sheep that spread throughout the world from the coasts of the North Sea. Short and stocky, with broad shoulders and a muscular neck, it grows quickly and has a good yield when butchered. In the 19th century, it ended up replacing the indigenous sheep used for milk, raised for the production of the cheese that characterized the island for centuries. After World War II, the artisan version of the cheese of the same name disappeared. It made its reappearance only 40 years later thanks to the enterprising cheese maker Piet Bakker, who wanted to revive the traditional method of making the cheese. He tried to get quality milk again by experimenting with cross-breeds and selecting the most productive animals. *Texelse schapenkaas* weighs at least four kilos and is a dark yellow color with a persistent flavor of the sea, animal fleece and pastures. The cheesemaking process is unusual for the Netherlands. The mixture is semi-cooked and the curd is not washed. Reminiscent of a goat cheese from southern Italy or Greece, it is rustic, fragrant and, if well-aged, it tends to be hard and compact with very distinctive organoleptic qualities. Until the summer of 2003, Piet Bakker was the only producer actively making artisan raw milk *texelse schapenkaas*.

When the Presidium was established, a second cheese maker took up the challenge and began to produce raw milk. Currently they are trying to improve its quality. One of the cheesemakers is experimenting with the use of sheep rather than beef rennet. The aim is to make this cheese even more unique and the lamb rennet could well help to enhance the final taste. The Presidium also intends to publicize this product throughout Holland (for now it is only sold locally to the tourists) and support the work of recovering the Texel breed.

PRODUCTION AREA
Texel, northern Holland

PRESIDIUM COORDINATOR
Hielke van der Meulen
tel. +31 317427500
hielke.vandermeulen@hetnet.nl

Artisan Sognefjord Geitost

The villages scattered along the Sognefjord, the longest fiord in Norway, boast a very old tradition of making raw milk goat's cheese. *Geitost*, an unusual solid brown sweet caramel cheese has been produced there for over five hundred years using a technique that was common in Norway and Sweden, but practically unknown in the rest of Europe. At one time it was made throughout the zone, but now production is concentrated in Undredal, a village that until 1982 could only be reached from the sea. Made from whey, *geitost* is a by-product of processing the white goat cheese. The fresh whey is boiled, cream from cow's milk is added and everything is heated to 40°C for 8-10 hours. The lactose crystallizes during the cooking and gives the curd a brown color. Left to cool, it is then worked by hand and placed in rectangular wooden forms. After one day, the brown cheese is ready to be cut into very thin slices and eaten with warm bread. The cheesemakers of Undredal have always made the *geitost* with the raw milk from their goats, raised in pastures fro most of the year, but in 1991 the health authorities made it mandatory to pasteurize the milk. There was strong resistance to the new regulation at the Undredal Stølsysteri dairy cooperative, whose organizer Pascale Baudonnel founded the Norsk Gardsost an association of 140 Norwegian cheesemakers in 1997, Undredal Stølsysteri recently obtained the first authorization granted in Norway to produce raw milk goat's cheese. The Presidium is determined to involve consumers in the cheesemakers' battle to defend raw milk cheeses and to promote the products from the delicate ecosystem of the Sogne fiord. Currently the members of the Undredal Stølsysteri cooperative include six dairies and the two owners of the village shop where the product is sold.

PRODUCTION AREA
Sogne fiord

PRESIDIUM COORDINATOR
Ove Fosså
tel. +47 51665097
ovefossa@online.no

PRESIDIUM SUPPORTED BY
Fmla Sogn og Fjordane, Visit Mflån,
Aurland Kommune

Sørøya Island Stockfish

The island of Sørøya, at the edge of the Arctic Ocean in northern Norway, is in the heart of one of the zones having the most fish in the world. It has always been known for its cod fishing and the processing of the fish into tørrfisk (stockfish). The producers on the island are also trying out the same conservation technique with halibut, black cod, wolf fish and haddock. It is common practice at Sørøya to use small boats that go no more than 50 kilometers from the coast and deliver the fish very fresh, at most two hours after capture. The codfish for making stockfish is mainly caught with the *juksa* (hook), which prevents damaging the fish during capture and yields a more valuable finished product than one captured with nets. The fish is gutted, the head is removed and then it rinsed in sea water directly on the fishing boats. Once delivered to the processing plant, each cod is coupled with another one of the same size. The two fish are tied together at the tail with string and hung on the characteristic wooden racks called hjell. The stockfish are left there to dry in the open air during the winter, when temperatures are harsh and the air cold and dry. The drying process can last from two to three months according to the wind, the weather conditions and the size of the fish. While the stockfish are hanging, it is essential that there is enough room between them so the air can circulate freely. The Sørøya Island Stockfish Presidium has as its objective the promotion of this historic island product, fished with sustainable techniques and made from cod of the Barents Sea, one of the only two areas in the world (along with Iceland) where the cod supply is still buoyant. Slow Food will also try to expand the market for Sørøya stockfish beyond the confines of the region.

PRODUCTION AREA
Sørøya, county of Finnmark

PRESIDIUM COORDINATOR
Bjørg Hansen Alvestad
tel. +47 95765475
alvestad@hotmail.com

PRESIDIUM SUPPORTED BY
Hasvik i Utvikling

Sunnmøre Cured and Smoked Herrings

Herrings have been a mainstay of the Norwegian diet for more than a millennium and were once a very important part of the economy of northern European peoples. As early as the 13th century, a series of laws regulated herring fishing and the ways to conserve the fish in brine, in wooden barrels. In the 19th century, the coast was scattered with nearly 1,000 plants for processing the three traditional types of herring: the silver herring (smoked for no more than 12 hours), the golden herring (smoked for up to three days) and the hard cured herring (smoked from 10 to 12 days). From 1946 to 1968, the golden years of herring fishing, there were 35 processing plants in the region of Sunnmøre, 8 of which were at Naeroy, a fishing village on a coastal fiord near Ålesund. Competition from industrial production and ever rarer schools of herring eventually forced them all to close down. The only one left now is the family-run Njardar plant, located right at Naeroy. Founded at the beginning of the 20th century, it is the only Norwegian company that still practices the traditional methods of salting and smoking herring. During January and February, Njardar picks up the North Sea *storsild* (herrings) at the port of Naeroy. The herrings, which were fished by small boats no more than two hours earlier, are then taken to the plant and put in fir-wood barrels under salt for about 24 hours, after which time the brine is added. The pickling process can last up to 60 days. Then the herrings are rinsed in salt water, threaded on a sort of skewer, and smoked to get the three traditional variations. The final product is packaged in wooden boxes and sold in the company shop. The smoked and salted herrings are mainly eaten in salads (with honey and beets), as an accompaniment to boiled potatoes, or in omelets. The Presidium intends to increase consumer awareness of this product, revive techniques that risk being lost and keep alive this kind of small-scale sustainable fishing.

PRODUCTION AREA
County of Møre og Romsdal, region of Sunnmøre

PRESIDIUM COORDINATOR
Katrin Torvholm
tel. +47 70087850
katrin@alphafish.no

Villsau Sheep

The Villsau (wild) sheep descends from the Gammel Norsk Sau, one of the oldest breeds of sheep in northern Europe. Small and sturdy, the animals are well-suited to life in the open air along the western coast of Norway. They have a thick coat that can vary in color from white to grey to black, a spiral horn and a very short tail. The sheep feed on grass, algae and bushes growing wild in the moors, where they graze freely year round. This entirely natural diet gives the meat (very tender because the fat is well-distributed among the muscle fibers) a particular flavor. The lambs are used to prepare traditional dishes like pinnekjøtt (smoked ribs) and fenalår (smoked leg). The wool is used for weaving waterproof blankets and the hide for making rugs, and both are of good quality. Over the centuries, the Villsau risked extinction more than once, and in the 19th century the breed was gradually replaced by animals imported from abroad that were larger and better suited to industrial breeding. And the 1950s, only a few hundred head remained. Norsk Villsaulag, an association of Villsau sheep breeders, was founded to save the breed from extinction. Today it has about 400 members, who work along the coastlines of Nordland, Rogaland, Hordaland and Sør Trøndelag counties, and there are now 30,000 heads of Villsau. However, the economy associ ated with this breed remains poor and the survival of the animal depends on the passion of those who take care of them. In collaboration with the Heathland Centre of Lygra, a research center managed by the University of Bergen and working in close contact with local breeders, the Presidium will promote the breed and help the breeders make consumers and local institutions aware of their product. A rather serious problem has been the gradual disappearance of the local slaughterhouses in the last 20 years, which means the breeders have to travel hundreds of kilometers to have the animals butchered.

PRODUCTION AREA
Counties of Nordland, Rogaland, Hordaland and Sør Trøndelag

PRESIDIUM COORDINATOR
Hilde Buer
tel. +47 57744054 - 48126752
hilbuer@online.no

Oscypek

The milk is from the ancient sheep of the Polish mountain, which descend from a Carpathian breed, the Zackel. Taken to the pastures of the Tatra mountains by Wallachian nomad shepherds, they settled in here, encouraging the birth of the *batza*, who in May gather the sheep from the farmers and take them to higher ground to stay there until October. The fire burns day and night in their *basutzka* (wooden huts) for cheesemaking and smoking a cheese with a particular shape. To produce Oscypek, the morning milk, mixed with that of the day before, is heated in a copper cauldron. It is left to coagulate at 36°C, the curd is broken and, after half an hour, it is placed in a wooden vat, adding hot water and kneading it vigorously: it is pulled by hand, wrung well and pulled apart. The mass is then pressed in a wooden bowl, massaged, put back into hot water, and pressed again until an elastic firm ball is obtained. Threaded along the central axis of a bar and having removed the water, the shape is obtained, onto which some geometric symbols are impressed with a wooden stamp, the distinctive brand of each batza. After pickling for 24 hours, the Oscypek is laid out on wood shelves under the ceiling of the hut, where it hardens, assuming a yellow bronze color. It is served in thin slices or cooked on the grill with wine, beer and vodka. The Presidium wants to help the batza to overcome the regulatory obstacles (today it is very onerous to produce cheese with raw milk in Poland), spread the knowledge of Oscypek among the best Polish restaurants, and draw up production regulations. In spring 2004, thanks to a project of the Tuscan Provincial Authority, a group of representatives of the Presidium visited some Italian enterprises (Zeri Lamb and Pistoia Mountain Pecorino Presidia in Tuscany, Alpago Lamb Presidium in Veneto) and the visit was exchanged a year later by some Tuscan technicians. In 2005, Oscypek was the protagonist of an important event to present local Polish products in Krakow.

PRODUCTION AREA
Tatra Mountains, Malopolskie

PRESIDIUM COORDINATOR
Jacek Szklarek
tel. + 48 509093034
jacek.szklarek@slowfood.pl

PRESIDIUM SUPPORTED BY
Guido Berlucchi, (Corte Franca, Brescia, Lombardy, Italy)

Polish Mead

Together with vodka, mead was the traditional drink of festivals and prepared in all Polish families. Today the producers can be counted on one hand and only one of them, Maciej Jaros, a short distance from Warsaw, keeps the authentic artisan recipe, thanks to his mother Boleslawa, repository of the right dosages to use. In his small company, with 30 hives, he produces a dark aromatic honey, from which he has been making an excellent mead since 1991, the year in which the private activities became legal again in Poland. He also makes the terracotta bottles which contain it. There are different kinds of mead, depending on the ratio of honey to water: from one quarter honey and three quarters water, up to two thirds honey and one part water (the latter, the most prized, is called pultorak). The greater the quantity of honey, the longer the maturation times: from a minimum of four years to 10, 20 years and more. The preparation involves initial cooking of the honey in water with local herbs or with raspberry, apple or grape juice – fermentation in large steel casks and ageing. The honey drink produced by Maciej has nothing at all to do with the industrial products available on the Polish market, which are banal and prepared with young, artificial aromas. Essential, in fact, are the quality of the raw material and time. what discourages potential producers is mainly the requirement to wait at least four years before the first bottles can be sold. The Presidium was set up to protect and promote the authentic honey drink and ensure that the just remuneration can be obtained on the market. Only in this way can other producers overcome the fear of the initial investment (of time, above all) and recreate this old Polish product. In the first years of activity a production protocol was drawn up and the mead was promoted in Europe and the United States. In 2005 it was also the protagonist in an important event to present local products in Krakow.

PRODUCTION AREA
Lodz

PRESIDIUM COORDINATOR
Jacek Szklarek
tel. + 48 509093034
jacek.szklarek@slowfood.pl

PRESIDIUM SUPPORTED BY
La Petraia Holiday Farm in Radda in Chianti (Siena, Tuscany, Italy)

Mirandesa Sausage

The Mirandesa sausage was born from the need to use and preserve less popular cuts of beef or those coming from old animals and the great quantity of fat of local pigs. The cattle breed is the Mirandesa, one of the most prized, bred since medieval times, mostly on pastures, with the addition of hay, corn, oats and broad beans. Identifiable by a tuft of hair on its forehead, darker brown fur at the extremities and robust horns, it is a cow that originates from Miranda do Douro, while the Bisaro pig, which has black patches and large sagging ears, comes from Vinhais. Both municipalities are located in the district of Bragança, in the extreme Northeast of the country. To prepare the Mirandesa sausage, the meats 80% of the total according to custom are cut by knife and mixed with the coarsely sliced lard. It is macerated in wine and water, with salt, pepper (sweet and spicy), garlic and bay leaf for two or three days in a fresh dry place. Having removed the bay leaf, 400 grams of filling is put into the fine bowels of the calf, tying the ends with twine, and it is smoked for a few days on oak wood fuel. When it is perfectly dry, the sausage is ready to be eaten: raw, barbecued or stewed. The three artisans of the Presidium work under a Portuguese law which authorizes the regional kitchens to sell the product, but with the right kind of appreciation, this salami could go far beyond local consumption. This is the objective of Slow Food and the Association of breeders of Mirandesa cattle, aware of the fact that without a market for the less prized parts, risks penalizing the work of hundreds of people who keep the breed alive. They form an authentic community and meet each year to celebrate a feast in its honor with banquets, bull fights, auctions of the most beautiful specimens. A feast, which on this high plateau 'at the end of the world', as they say, takes on a totally unique charm.

PRODUCTION AREA
Miranda do Douro and Vinhais, district of Bragança

PRESIDIUM COORDINATOR
Fernando Sousa
tel. +351 273438120 - 273438121
frsousa@mail.telepac.pt

Serpa Cheese

The old town of Serpa, perched on the top of a hill and surrounded by its medieval walls, can be seen from miles away. The predominant color is white, the streets are made of stone cobbles and the walls of the older houses are made of mud and plaster. All around the town are low hills with cork-oak forests, olive-trees hundreds of years old, and sheep, cows, and pigs grazing. This landscape, which has a precise identity and name – montado – the equivalent of the Spanish dehesa, is famous for its black pigs. Here we are in the south of Alentejo, on the border with Estremadura, the traditional production area of the queijo serpa, a cheese made with raw ewe's milk and a coagulant made from cardoons collected in late spring. The petals are dried in the shade, put into a blender (once they were ground with a mortar and pestle) and are then soaked in water for a day. The liquid is filtered and used from October onwards. Initially, ewe's milk is used, mainly from the Lacauna sheep, a French breed which has replaced the Merino, because it produces more milk. Reared half-wild, they are milked twice a day. The milk is heated to 30°C-33°C and is passed through a cloth full of sea salt. The rennet is added and, after 40-90 minutes, the curd is broken up into tiny lumps about the size of a grain of rice, drained and put into the molds. The final weight of the cheese varies from 200 g to 2.5 kg, the height from 3 cm to 8 cm, and the diameter from 10 cm to 30 cm. The edges of the cheeses are delicately wrapped in thin gauzes, which are replaced and washed several times, to 'hold' the cheese and prevent cracks forming in the rind. The *queijo serpa* is protected by a PDO label, but the Presidium was formed to preserve the more traditional variety, which used to be matured in attics on beds of reeds and was consumed mature, a much more interesting type (hard and semi-hard) because of its organoleptic complexity and character. The protocol will have to define a much more restricted area than that of the PDO cheese, fix a minimum period of maturation and define a uniform size, given that, today, the name 'Serpa' is applied to a number of cheeses with entirely different characteristics.

PRODUCTION AREA
Southern Alentejo

PRESIDIUM COORDINATOR
João Nunes
tel. +351 213978369
joao.nunes@proap.pt

Brânzá de Burduf

The most prized and one of the oldest Rumanian cheeses, tied to the tradition of transhumance. The shepherds gather the animals from different owners to take them to pasture and, at the end of the summer, keep a part of what they have produced: with sheep's milk and variable additions of fresh goat's cheese they produce *telemea* – a fresh sweet cheese, which is pickled – and the *kas*, from which, with a second process, the long-life Brânzá de burduf is obtained. The *kas* is obtained coagulating the raw milk with veal or lamb rennet. The curd is then broken into fine grains, which are laid out for half an hour. The mass is collected with a cloth and the whey is removed, wringing the sack and submitting it to pressure, usually under a wood plank on which large stones are placed. After 24 hours work can begin to produce the Brânzá de burduf, placing the well-dried forms to ferment in an open wooden vat. After 24-36 hours they are extracted and finely minced with the addition of sea salt; they are then kneaded vigorously and laid out on a sheet of pine bark, which gives them pronounced resin notes. It takes between 40 days to a few months for the cheese to mature and develop a certain degree of spiciness. Many Brânzá producers also use cow's milk, in variable percentages with respect to the sheep's milk; the result is a cheese with a slightly less piquant taste. The Presidium, set up in collaboration with the Provincial Authority of Brasov, protects the Brânzá in its traditional area area, in the Bucegi mountains in southern Carpathians, where the abundance of pines has encouraged the use of the bark as container. The aim is set up an association of producers and draw up production regulations to define the diet of the animals and processing and aging times, thus guaranteeing the quality of the final product. Further attempts are being made to promote the Brânzá in Rumania and abroad.

PRODUCTION AREA
Province of Brasov

PRESIDIUM COORDINATOR
Mihai Pascu
tel. +40 268419056
mihaipascu2004@yahoo.com

PRESIDIUM SUPPORTED BY
Cav. G.B. Bertani (Grezzana, Verona, Veneto, Italy)

Saxon Village Preserves

The houses are low with hexagonal facades, painted blue, light-blue, purple, or green and arranged in two parallel rows along a wide dirt street. Opposite each, an old pear tree, behind a long cobblestone farmyard and, at the end, the chicken coop. This is the typical structure of the Siebenbürgen, the seven villages of Transylvania, today a kind of lost paradise, inhabited by Rumanians, Saxons, Hungarians and Roms. Mobile phones don't work here and there are no cars: only horse-drawn carriages, children, old people, dogs, cats, geese and silence. In the evening, the cows return in small groups to the barns from the pastures. The milk, sold to the large companies, is the only economic resource. The few cheeses produced are mostly fresh and consumed by the families, as are salami, jams, compotes and dulciazia, a kind of very sweet fruit in syrup. The fruit of the orchard and wild berries of the surrounding woods are used: the rhubarb, wild fruit (rose-hip, yellow plums, sour cherries, wild strawberries and blueberries), apple and cinnamon jams are typical (the apples are acidulous, grey green color and ripen between end of September and start of October). They are eaten at breakfast with bread, and are used to fill sweets and cakes. The recipes are simple: fruit, sugar, in some cases a small addition of natural pectin (made with unripe apples) and cooking over low heat for a short time, to retain the taste and aroma of the fresh fruit. The Presidium was set up thanks to the collaboration between Slow Food and Adept, a foundation which has been active in Rumania for a number of years and has run a hygiene course for a number of women so they can start producing; it has also recently opened an information point in one of the villages (tel. +40 748 0213 47). The jams, preserved in glass jars and sold in baskets handmade by a local family, will be presented to the public at the Salone del Gusto 2006. A pruning course and a workshop will also be organized this winter.

PRODUCTION AREA
Saxon villages of Transylvania

PRESIDIUM COORDINATORS
Cristie Gherghiceanu
tel. +40 748 2000 88
gher_cristi@zappmobile.ro
Jim Turnbull
tel. +44 1844 352385
JWTurnbull@bmc-ltd.com

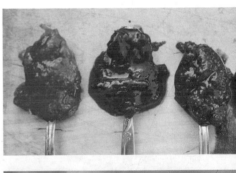

Euskal Txerria Pig

Until the early 20th century, there were no farms in the Basque region that did not rear pigs, which were sent to fairs all over Spain, mainly as lechones, as soon as they were weaned, only two or three months old. One or two animals were kept for family consumption, fed with scraps from the kitchen and garden, or what could be found in the woods. There were three native breeds in the Basque region: Batzanesa, Chato Vitoriano – both extinct – and Euskal Txerria, which was saved by the efforts of a French Basque farmer, Pierre Oteitza. By 1997 there were quite a few sows, but still none in the Basque lands of Spain. The Basque government sponsored the efforts made to recover this breed (in Euskera, urda-pilleta means a herd of pigs) by farmer Pello Urdapilleta and Mariano Gomez, a vet and biologist who specialized in local breeds. Euskal Txerria pigs have short legs, large hanging ears, and black marks on their heads and rear ends. The Presidium pigs live free, eating acorns, chestnuts, hazelnuts and grass, plus corn, fava beans and bran when they are being fattened up. When they reach 120 kilograms, they are ready to be slaughtered and their tasty meat produces chorizo (seasoned seven months, 70% lean and 30% fat, sweet paprika, salt and garlic), lomo (five months), salchichón (eaten fresh) and ham. Pello is experimenting with techniques and curing times that are more suitable for the region's difficult climate. His latest venture, with his wife, Matte Izaguirre Pello, has been to convert a small historical building into a restaurant, El Kontezeju Jatextea, where the Basque pig is the star of the menu. The Presidium plans to encourage other local breeders and artisans to follow the example of Pello who received the international Culatello d'Oro award on July 25, 2005, from the Culatello Consortium of Zibello. Early in the year, the Presidium was involved in an exchange between Italian and French butchers, where representatives of the best European meat products obtained from native breeds could meet and exchange ideas.

PRODUCTION AREA
Bidegoian, Basque Country

PRESIDIUM COORDINATOR
German Arrién
tel. +34 943322110
garrien@euskalnet.net

Ganxet Bean

The ganxet is a bean easily recognizable for the hook-shaped, squashed shape of its seeds, which remains unaltered even when cooked. As is the case of most traditional varieties, it is hard to establish the origin of the ganxet, though recent genetic studies suggest a relationship with the Mexican strain from which it probably derived, being brought to Catalonia at the start of the 19th century during migration to and from the New Continent. The productive cycle of this white-flowered creeper lasts 120 days. The seeds are sown at the start of July usually after a cereal cycle, and the beans are harvested in November. The ganxet's peculiar organoleptic qualities (very fine skin, buttery texture and delicate flavor) make it a particularly eclectic ingredient, suitable for a whole variety of recipes. It has always been noted for its unique taste and since it is a relatively unproductive but popular variety, it fetches high prices on the market. Unfortunately, this has led to a proliferation of hybrids and imitation ganxet beans, which have swamped market stalls and shops without check, confusing consumers no longer capable of recognizing the original variety but also attracting new ones. As a result of blends and sometimes deliberate crosses with other more productive varieties, genetically speaking the bean has drifted away from its original genotype. The Presidium has been set up to help those producers who joined together in a cooperative to reselect and cultivate the genuine ganxet with the support of technicians and researchers at the Agricultural College in Barcelona. By promoting the bean during events and guided tasting sessions, first at local level and with the help of restaurateurs, it will be possible to create discerning consumers prepared to pay the right price and aware farmers, motivated to grow a great bean without fear of imitations.

PRODUCTION AREA
Vallés, Selva, Maresme and Gironés, Catalonia

PRESIDIUM COORDINATOR
Valenti Mongay Castro
tel. +34 938110419
slowfoodgarraf@yahoo.es

Jiloca Saffron

Saffron is one of the most expensive and least known spices in the world, whose name refers to the stigmas of the flowers of the *Crocus sativus*, a member of the iris family that originates in the eastern part of the Mediterranean, and was introduced into Spain by the Arabs more than one thousand years ago. Here it has become an indispensable ingredient of numerous traditional dishes, but for centuries was used only by the upper classes, who even adopted it to perfume their clothes. Cultivation techniques have not changed much since then; in mid October the fields become an intense violent, streaked with the red of the precious stigmas: these are known as the *días de manto* and tell the farmers that the harvest – which takes place very day, by hand – can begin. The three stigmas are delicately separated from the flower when this is still fresh, taking care not to ruin or dirty them, or mix them with any other part. This meticulous work involved the entire family, who work incessantly so that the flowers picked in the fields at dawn do not wilt. The price may seem exaggerated, but it takes 100,000 flowers to make one kilogram of saffron. The Jiloca area, which is cut through by the river of the same name, has ideal geoclimatic conditions for the spice to grow (long, cold Winters and short, hot Summers, and an altitude of 700 to 900 meters). In the past, all the local farmers set some of their land aide for saffron, now they talk about it with a mixture or melancholy and bitterness, because they were not able to make more of it. Seven framers have now decided to try again, and they have formed an association under the Presidium, with the support of the Museum del Azafrán (run by the Casa de la Cultura of Monreal del Campo). The aim of this project is to promote this small output which risking extinction, and to transmit correct information about saffron to the consumer, with guided tasting sessions that compare foods seasoned with different types of the spice, including artificial types and those with added flavoring: this is certainly the most effective way of demonstrating the pleasure and sensations that the spice can produce.

PRODUCTION AREA
Jiloca, province of Teruel

PRESIDIUM COORDINATORS
Chusa Portalatín
tel. +34 976301408
chusap@terra.es
José Antonio Esteban Sánchez
tel. +34 978622070
A5881DU@hotmail.com

Sitges Malvasia

Only a few hectares remain of Sitges Malvasia, which is one of the 84 varieties recognized around the world. Legend has it that it was the Almogávares (mercenaries fighting against the Saracens, who has been around since the 12th century), who first introduced it into Garraf, on their way to fight for the Emperor of Byzantium. The vine's survival is due to the clear vision of the Catalan diplomat Manuel Llopis de Casades. The last heir to this family, one of the oldest in Sitges (mid-16th century), he left the ownership and management of all his property in Sitges to the Hospital de San Juan Bautista de Sitges, a charitable religious institute, with a clause: they should continue to make Malvasia in the vineyards on the estate. And so it survived, but there are only two and a half hectares now, surrounded by recent houses and buildings. Thanks to the limey soil, the sea breeze and the protection of the mountains, the small surviving allotments enjoy a unique microclimate, which is unsuitable for the commonest diseases of the vine. This variety has deeply indented leaves, long, flexible shoots and small, elongated grapes which tend to over-ripen. Two wines are produced, a sweet and a dry Malvasia. The former smells of honey and nuts, it is rich and has a high alcohol content; the latter has toasted overtones and a lasting after-taste, like a sherry. Annual output is limited and cannot meet demand which comes from Sitges, Vilanova, Barcelona and even Madrid, but the locals have priority. The Presidium has not been created just to promote the product, but rather to publicize this interesting reality, to protect the two and a half hectares in question from building speculation and to support any producers who wish to plant this vine in the surrounding area.

PRODUCTION AREA
Sitges, Catalonia

PRESIDIUM COORDINATOR
Valenti Mongay Castro
tel. +34 938110419
slowfoodgarraf@yahoo.es

PRESIDIUM SUPPORTED BY
Slow Food Emilia Romagna (Italy)

Tolosa Black Bean

The *Alubia negra* is a pearl-like, oval, glossy black bean with a white spot in the center, which was already famous in Tolosa in the early 20th century. It has always been grown in the Oria valley and, on Saturday mornings, it is sold in the covered market attended by local farmers. On November 23 and 24 every year, again in Tolosa, festivities are held to celebrate the new harvest. The bean was revived about ten years ago by a group of farmers who are now members of the Slow Food Presidium. They selected the two best varieties, a larger one (handia) and a smaller one (txikia). The beans are grown of very small plots, two hectares at most, at an altitude of between 140 and 600-700 meters. The pulses are sown between April and May and the plants sprout in July. The bean plants are tied to a mesh or to a support made from three stakes (inserted at a slant and tied at the top to form a sort of wigwam), or more traditionally they are grown alongside maize when the seeds are sown together. Weeds are removed by hand and only the only fertilizer is cow manure. The harvest is also done by hand, in stages. The plants are left to dry on frames before the beans are hulled by hand or using the association's machines. They are then separated by size and packed. These pulses do not need to be soaked (or at most just for half an hour if they are very dry) and, when they are cooked in water, with salt and a drizzle of extra virgin olive oil, they produce a wonderfully thick sauce but the beans remain whole, forming a deliciously smooth, tasty soup. The Presidium was formed to help the producers to spread the trade name of the real Tolosa bean (the entire Spanish market is flooded by fake beans), and to educate consumers and restaurateurs to tell the real beans from the fakes, also outside the Basque country, where the reputation of the *Alubia negra* is undoubtedly expanding.

PRODUCTION AREA
Oria valley, Basque Country

PRESIDIUM COORDINATOR
German Arrién
tel. +34 943322110
garrien@euskalnet.net

Reindeer Suovas

Reindeer meat was the traditional food of the Sámi, a European ethnic group that lived in the Sápmi region, a strip of land that crosses the northern zones of Sweden, Norway, Finland and Russia, even before the borders between these countries were established. Winter lasts for more than six months here and the temperature can fall below -30°C. Most of the tribe's traditional food is designed to be preserved and eaten when the Sámi are on the move. Since many of them are reindeer herders (a profession reserved for this ethnic group by law) their movements are associated with the raising of these semi-wild animals, which spend the winter grazing in the forests and then are taken to higher altitudes in spring and summer. One of their most typical preparations is *suovas*, a lean reindeer fillet that is simply salted and smoked over an open fire for 12 hours in the characteristic cabins with the peaked roof. At once flavorful, aromatic and delicate, it can be eat-

en thinly sliced or grilled. If aged, it is excellent when eaten plain with wild pickled mushrooms and lingonberries. When the herders are traveling they eat it with unleavened bread heated on stones around the fire. The Presidium wants to safeguard the production of aged *suovas* made exclusively from the inner and tender part of the leg (*innanlår*) of reindeer that graze naturally only in the pastures of the Sápmi. It will eventually involve all of the producers in the Sápmi region and is working hard to make people aware of this very old food product. It also discourages the practice of substituting reindeer meat with meats from other domestic animals that of used might prove unsuited, or even damaging, to the delicate ecosystem of the Sámi's land.

PRODUCTION AREA
County of Jämtland

PRESIDIUM COORDINATOR
Ola Buckard
tel. +46 703284455
ola.buckard@chello.se

PRESIDIUM SUPPORTED BY
Sámiid Riikasearvi, Association for the Protection of Sámi Culture

Locarno Valley Cicitt

This goat's meat sausage is traditionally produced in the valleys around the Swiss part of Lake Maggiore, near Locarno. It is made by mixing the less prestigious pieces of meat with the fat, the scalded stomach and the heart, seasoning it with salt, chopped garlic, pepper, cinnamon, cloves, and red and white wine. It looks like a pork sausage several meters long, dark red in color and with a strong aroma. The sausage is left to rest for several days before being eaten, preferably grilled. The history of the *cicitt* is linked to that of the goats in the Locarno valleys, which were once considered the 'poor person's cow'. Every family in Vallemaggia and Val Verzasca owned a few, and the 'mazza minore' took place in November, when the goats were slaughtered to make sausage. It seems that cicitt was first made in Cavergno, a small town high in the Vallemaggia. This is where two of the few remaining producers sill live, and here, on December 8, the Feast of the Immacolata is still also the Festa del Cicitt. The Presidium was created to protect this goat's sausage prepared by the traditional recipe. Sausages with this name are sold all year round in several parts of Canton Ticino, but they do not look, or more important still, taste like the pure goat originals. Corners are cut when preparing them, to accommodate modern tastes, and the flavor is softened by the addition of pork fat. The Presidium aims to give consumers a chance to choose between the real cicitt made entirely of goat that is typical of the Locarno valleys, and other similar products that are produced with less traditional methods.

PRODUCTION AREA
Locarno valleys, Canton Ticino

PRESIDIUM COORDINATOR
Meret Bissegger
tel. +41 918701300
meret@ticino.com

Muggio Valley Zincarlin

The traditional production of zincarlin is based in the mountainous region on the border between Italy and Canton Ticino. It is a raw-milk cheese, made with cow's milk and a small quantity of goat's milk. The curds are left to drain for 24 hours in a special cloth, without breaking them, but making a cut in the shape of a cross of the surface after 12 hours so that the whey is eliminated faster. The curds are kneaded and seasoned with black pepper and salt, and then shaped by hand into a form like an upturned cup, each cheese weighing about half a kilogram. Zincarlin is best aged for two or three months, so that the organoleptic qualities can evolve. In this time, it become greasy and the rind, which can be treated with white wine, becomes reddish-gray, with complex, penetrating aromas. The cheeses are stored in special *ole* (terracotta urns), where they maintain the right degree of moisture and softness. On the Italian side of the border, Zincarlino, or Cingherlino, is produced in the area around Besozzo and mount Generoso, in the province of Varese, where it is eaten fresh, seasoned with oil and pepper. Various types of industrial Zincarlin can be found all over Switzerland, even in supermarkets and food stores. The Slow Food Presidium was created to recover the original Zincarlin, made with raw milk and ripened for at least a month and a half. It is a complex process, which requires constant research by the cheese-makers involved, who aim to recreate the original techniques precisely, and identify the exact percentage of the ingredients (cow's and goat's milk, pepper, salt), elements that are essential to obtain a stable product. A first draft of the regulations was prepared in 2004 and a location where the cheese could ripen was chosen in Salarino, a district of Mendrisio. A company was then set up to collect, refine and market the zincarlin produced by the Presidium.

PRODUCTION AREA
Muggio valley, Canton Ticino

PRESIDIUM COORDINATOR
Luca Cavadini
tel. +41 916841816
slowfoodti@bluewin.ch

Artisan Somerset Cheddar

Thinking that a cheese risks extinction when two million tons of it are produced each year seems a contradiction in terms. But the fact is that almost none of the would-be cheddar found around the world has anything to do with the real thing, which takes its name from the town of Cheddar (Somerset) in the Mendips, the highest hills in Great Britain. The town of Cheddar was already famous for its dairy products possibly as early as the Middle Ages, and certainly at the end of the 16th century. The cow's milk cheeses were very large and just right for long ageing. An essential step during the processing was to heap up twisted strips of curd in ever larger mounds. With the exception of French cantal, this practice of cheddaring is exclusive to British cheeses and gives them a crumbly texture that industrial versions cannot match. In addition to the use of raw milk, artisan cheddar from Somerset is particular because lactic bacteria are added and the forms of cheese are wrapped in muslin that has been greased with lard. The Presidium cheddar weighs between 25 and 30 kilos, is aged for 11 to 24 months, and has abundant brownish-grey mold on the crust. The cheese is bright straw-yellow in color with complex aromas and hints of dry grass and hay, and a slightly smoky fragrance. Soft to the touch and buttery, it tastes of candied milk, with notes of hazelnut and bitter herbs. The three Presidium producers of make no more than 10 or 20 forms a day because each cheddar requires three days of work. The milk, which comes from the farms of the cheesemakers themselves, is not treated, and is processed within one day of milking, and local yeasts are used. The Presidium was formed to educate consumers to appreciate a different kind of cheddar, one that is handcrafted and produced with local fresh milk. It has thus worked to promote taste education by participating at local and international events to make people aware of traditional cheesemaking techniques and to favor sustainable farming.

PRODUCTION AREA
County of Somerset, England

PRESIDIUM COORDINATOR
Randolph Hodgson
tel. +44 2076453550
randolph@nealsyarddairy.co.uk

Cornish Pilchards

The scientific name for the pilchard is *Sardina pilchardus sardina* or *Clupea pilchardus*. The species is fished off the coast of Cornwall, in southwestern England, and then salted. Like all Clupeids, these fish with tapered bodies covered with shining scales make incredible vertical and horizontal migrations. When they reach the eastern Atlantic from the Mediterranean, the sardines are nice and plump and measure as much as 35 centimeters in length. Between June and March they are caught by small trawlers using traditional nets and then immediately sent to workshops for salting in large tanks, a process that goes on for weeks. The whole pilchards are then put into rectangular wooden boxes and gently pressed so the excess liquid drains off. Finally, they are arranged in the traditional wooden barrels, where they can age for up to one year. They have a strong and concentrated flavor, which is given a slightly bitter taste from the fermentation of the entrails. At the beginning of the 20th century, there were a number of factories in Cornwall for salting the pilchards, which were mainly exported to northern Italy. Then the market gradually went into a depression, and in 1960 only one company continued to package and sell pilchards. And it is the same one that continues this tradition today, using methods and equipment that are at least a century old. The Presidium was set up to valorize one of the historic foods of the British Isles. The members are the last remaining company and four fishermen. In addition to protecting a very old product (dating to the 16th century, but practically unknown today), the project aims to safeguard a kind of fishing that is attentive to the environment. The Presidium is working to recover the old pilchard market (in southern Europe), but also make the product known locally and find new sales channels in Great Britain.

PRODUCTION AREA
Coast of the county of Cornwall, England

PRESIDIUM COORDINATOR
Nick Howell
tel. +44 1736332112
nick@pilchardworks.co.uk

Fal River Oyster

The Fal estuary, in Cornwall, has one of the few remaining stocks of native oysters in the United Kingdom, and the only one of wild oysters. Belonging to the *Ostrea edulis* species, the mollusks live on the river bed or on the layer of shells deposited there. A law dating to 1868 makes it illegal to gather them with mechanical means or from crafts other than sail boats or row boats. The little fleet of oyster fishing boats from the port of Truro, the most important town in Cornwall, is the last one in the world to be made up entirely of sail boats and row boats, and the only one in Europe that is used for commercial purposes. Moreover, the oyster gatherers, united in the Port of Truro Oyster Fishermen's Protection Association, have drawn up regulations to protect this local resource. They use dredges, small hand- maneuvered nets, only capture mollusks with a shell larger than five centimeters in diameter, and have a very short fishing season. At the end of the hunt, they return to port and sell the oysters to the wholesalers (there are five along the Fal River), who take the oysters to one of two plants to be cleaned and then sell them to restaurant owners and shops in the county. Despite sustainability measures and the abundant supply, the Fal River oyster risks extinction because it is threatened by an infesting organism and the shoals are being damaged by the moorings of the yachts. Furthermore, the price of the mollusks has remained the same for more than 20 years, and the poor pay discourages young people from taking up the craft. The objective of the Presidium is to ensure that the fishermen and wholesalers get the best possible price for their oysters. It will endeavor to exploit the product better at the local level by creating a recognizable logo and promoting the particular characteristics of the oysters. To this end, for the past nine years the fishermen's association has organized the Falmouth Oyster Festival, which takes place in October, to coincide with the opening of the fishing season.

PRODUCTION AREA
Fal River estuary, county of Cornwall, England

PRESIDIUM COORDINATOR
Clare Leverton
tel. +44 1872270333
clare@swpesca.co.uk

Gloucester Cheese

Gloucester, capital of the county of the same name in the rural heart of Great Britain, was famous for its market of cheeses, butter and meat as long ago as the 16th century. Two centuries later, the double version of the local cheese was being exported as far as the North American colonies. A land of fruit orchards and pastures, the area of the Cotswolds hills, crossed by the Severn and Berkeley Rivers, still bears the signs of a very old tradition of dairy farming. There is often a place for ageing cheese in the old farmsteads and at many local festivals they practice cheese rolling, trying to block forms weighing four or five kilos made to roll down the steep slopes. The original Gloucester is a cheese made with the whole milk of the Old Gloucester Cow. This gradually evolved into two versions, single and double. Double Gloucester is still made with full fat milk (and so is higher in fat), while the single cheese, which is shaped in smaller forms, is made with partially skimmed milk (after the cream is used for butter) or in seasons when there is less pasturage. Double Gloucester, which is known for keeping well, used to be sold at the national level, while the single version was eaten locally by poorer people. The history of this cheese is closely tied to the vicissitudes of the Old Gloucester breed of cattle. Despite producing extraordinary milk for making cheese, the breed ran the risk of extinction. In terms of quantity, it simply could not compete with the specialized breeds that had become so successful in the 20th century. The Presidium intends to reestablish the old tie between the cow and the cheese, double and single, by working closely with the Gloucester Cattle Society. Indicating the origin of the milk and the name of the breed on the label could become an additional incentive for cattle breeding. The project hopes to encourage producers to use the milk of these cows and preserve the traditional method of making Gloucester cheese from raw milk. The Presidium will strive to promote the cheese, in particular at local shops.

PRODUCTION AREA
County of Gloucester, England

PRESIDIUM COORDINATOR
Marion Conisbee-Smith
tel. +44 1452770915
wdaniels@toucansurf.com

Old Gloucester Beef

The Gloucester (a name to which the affectionate adjective old was recently added) is a breed of cattle that originated in the county of the same name and was once found throughout southern England. As long ago as the 13th century, the cow was used for its meat, its milk and as a work animal at the farms in Gloucestershire. Its decline started at the beginning of the 18th century with the rise in popularity of specialized breeds of beef and dairy cattle. There was renewed interest in the breed around 1896, when the last two remaining herds were divided and sold to various breeders. In 1919 the Gloucester Cattle Society was founded and the first register counted 130 heads of cattle, which rose to 300 by 1925. But two years later, following an epidemic of hoof-and-mouth disease, the situation worsened again. Only 142 animals survived in 1930 and the Gloucester Cattle Society closed down. In 1972, when only one herd of 33 head of cattle remained, a group of farmers decided to set up the association again to save the breed from extinction. And in the next thirty years it manages to do just that. The old Gloucester cows are particularly robust and resistant animals. The meat improves with age, reaching its peak when the animals are two years old. It is the perfect ingredient for traditional dishes based on long, slow cooking. Extraordinarily flavorful, it is excellent when accompanied by traditional Tewkesbury mustard. The Presidium, which was set up in collaboration with the Gloucester Cattle Society, includes 99 producers who breed certified old Gloucester cows and provide for the final phase of their raising (at least six months) in Gloucestershire, though the animals can also be raised in other counties. The project aims to develop the local market and to involve chefs in the zone. Since the breed is still at risk of extinction, the Gloucester Cattle Society is encouraging producers throughout England to raise a few head of these cattle, though the final objective is to revive the old Gloucester in its native territory, where it has adapted best.

PRODUCTION AREA
County of Gloucester, England

PRESIDIUM COORDINATOR
Marion Conisbee-Smith
tel. +44 1452770915
wdaniels@toucansurf.com

Three Counties Perry

Perry is a pear cider, a drink made from the fermented juice of a very old variety of pear of the *Pirus* genus. It is a small fruit, having an astringent and rather bitter taste and practically inedible when raw. Produced for centuries in southern England, its name used to refer to the wild pear trees and the drink, which farmers made in small quantities mainly for personal use. The old orchards, with their tall and twisted trees, are an important feature of the British landscape. But in the past 50 years many of the dozen varieties of perry pears have seriously declined in numbers and may even vanish for good. Almost all English perry is made in the three counties of Herefordshire, Worcestershire and Gloucestershire. The drink is made in the same way as the more familiar apple cider. The fruit is harvested, crushed and then pressed to release the juice. Then the fermentation process begins, which can last a couple of days. Unlike apple cider, however, most perrys are also fermented a second time in the bottle. The classic accompaniment to the local Gloucester, Cheshire and Lancashire cheeses, true pear cider contains no additives and can be dry, semi-sweet or sweet, still or sparkling. The flavor varies a great deal, but even the driest version has a particular and unmistakable pear aroma. At present, the few remaining producers of perry are in serious difficulty because the market is continuing to decline even at the local level. The Presidium is working to promote authentic high-quality perry made with traditional bitter pears instead of common table or cooking pears. It is also trying to introduce stricter rules and regulations to guarantee the authenticity and typicality of the product, thus preserving the diversity of the various artisan perries. Finally, the Presidium producers are drawing up a complete list of the pear varieties traditionally used for perry.

PRODUCTION AREA
Counties of Herefordshire, Worcestershire and Gloucestershire, England

PRESIDIUM COORDINATOR
John Fleming
tel. +44 1584875548
info@slowfoodludlow.org.uk

Oceania

Australian Desert Lime producers

The community of Australian Desert Lime Producers consists of farming families and employees, specialist manufacturers, distributors, delicatessens, restaurateurs and chefs working in the Maranoa district in Queensland. The early plantation trees were propagated from cuttings taken from a handful of best fruiting native trees in the local area. The local native lime tree is being conserved and cultivated for its distinctively flavored fruit that is made into preserves, cordials, pastes, purées and ices. There has been a long history of desert limes being used by farmers in the outback to make refreshing drinks, jams and sauces.

PRODUCTION AREA
Maranoa district, Queensland

COMMUNITY COORDINATOR
Jock Douglas
jock@australiandesertlimes.com.au

Australian Rare Breed Meat producers and processors

The community is predominantly made up of producers across Australia who breed and conserve endangered farm livestock. There are approximately 450 producer members throughout Australia. The community is working to keep food diversity alive, by encouraging consumers to understand the diversity available and encouraging farmers to breed these diverse farm livestock. The community is made up of producers, processors and chefs who advocate the unique qualities of cooking with and eating rare breed meats. The meat products are accredited as rare breed meat and must be raised free-range in a traditional manner, for the animals to forage in the natural environment. It must also be a breed that is accredited by the Rare Breeds Trust of Australia as being endangered or at risk according to the UN/FAO criteria.

PRODUCTION AREA
The entire country

COMMUNITY COORDINATOR
Fiona Chambers
organic@fernleighfarms.com

Biodynamic Goat Cheese producers

The community of Biodynamic Goat Cheese Growers started farming in the early 1980s. After a couple of failed efforts at farm operations, they started making goat's milk cheese, partly for its nutritional benefits and partly for the ease of women handling goats. The community includes a minimum of four people throughout the year. The initial farming methods were chemical-free, wherever possible, and eventually evolved to organic and then bio-dynamic, and this is now the only fully Demeter-certified goat dairy in Australia. Kervella Cheese has always strived to produce healthy and nutritional produce and will continue to do so under Demeter Bio Dynamic Principles, said to be the future of farming. Since its early days of selling to health food shops around Perth, the farm has increased production of goat's cheese to meet rising demand and has won awards for the nutritional and taste quality of its produce.

PRODUCTION AREA
Gidgegannup, Avon Valley, Western Australia

COMMUNITY COORDINATOR
Gabrielle Kervella
kervella@activ8.net.au

Buninyong farmers' market producers

The food community of the Farmers' Market in Buninyong – a city in the state of Victoria - consists of local growers and chefs. It also includes consumers that are able to access local seasonal produce on a regular basis thanks to the presence of the farmers' market. The community includes 20 producers, 10 staff dealing with the organizational aspects of the market and the local residence who source their food directly from the growers. The operation is rather new, given that the farmers' market has been running since 2003. The produce includes sheep's and goat's cheese, olive oil and preserves, organic bread and garden vegetables, grown locally and in a sustainable manner.

PRODUCTION AREA
Buninyong, Victoria

COMMUNITY COORDINATOR
Dianne Ray
diray@ncable.net.au

Daintree Edible Rainforest Plant growers

The community is made up of producers, researchers, educators, tourism operators and cooks who take part in food conservation by collecting, documenting, growing, exchanging, promoting and creating new recipes of rainforest foods, many of which are rare or endangered in order to conserve the species and cooperate with people in other rainforest areas to enrich their diets and provide a more sustainable and ecologically acceptable form of agriculture. More than 500 species of tropical rainforest plants are conserved for the interest of biodiversity, food security, medicinal purposes and risk of extinction. These are grown within a botanical garden, which covers 12 hectares of the Daintree Rainforest in the region of the wet tropics of Far North Queensland.

PRODUCTION AREA
Daintree, Queensland

COMMUNITY COORDINATOR
Alan Carle
info@botanicalark.com

Daintree Organic Fruit growers

The community of Daintree Organic Fruit Growers is based on farming that works with a local supply chain that includes fruit growers, local farmers markets, small shops and a local winery in the wet tropics of far north Queensland, Australia. It grows tropical fruits such as Lychee, Rambutan, Mangosteen, Durian and Caimito. These fruits were first introduced to Australia by the Asian miners in the latter part of the 19th century. Although many of the original plants were lost, the community has continued to and improved the traditional way growing these fruits, by way of organic certification. The community also collects and conserves rare tropical plants with the emphasis on plants that are useful to human cultures. This includes conserving over 400 cultivars and species of rare tropical fruits.

PRODUCTION AREA
Daintree, Queensland

COMMUNITY COORDINATOR
Andre Leu
leu@austarnet.com.au

Gulf of Carpentaria fishermen

The community is a group of fishermen that have established and maintain a viable and sustainable fishery for 150 fishermen and processors. The native fish species, Barramundi and King Salmon, are caught in nets in rivers and foreshores. Both fish species are known as a favorite source of food for the indigenous Australians of the region, as well as in restaurants throughout Australia. The Barramundi inhabits a wide variety of habitats in rivers, creeks and mangrove estuaries in clear to turbid water. It shows a distinct preference for submerged logs, rock ledges and other structures in the water. Barramundi are a catadromous species: ie, it grows to maturity in the upper reaches of freshwater rivers and streams, and adults move downstream, especially during flooding, to estuaries and coastal waters for spawning. Barramundi are protoandrous hermaphrodites: ie, they start life as males, reaching maturity at around three to four years of age and later change gender and become females, usually at around age five. Due to the popularity of the fish species, the late maturing age of the female, strict fishing management is required to ensure that the species is sustainable.

PRODUCTION AREA
Gulf of Carpentaria, Queensland

COMMUNITY COORDINATOR
Gary Ward
gcward@bigpond.com

Nannup Sheep Cheese producers

The sheep cheese producers have been farming the same property since 1996 with the intention of milking sheep and value adding by making cheese. The farm has an area of 160 acres and is surrounded by forest; the closest neighbor is about 6 kilometres away. The community has been breeding a milking flock of ewes and has also planted an orchard which consists of citrus, stonefruit and avocados. The orchard has approximately 60 varieties of heritage apples and is maintained on a chemical-free basis. The milking flock is the result of a cross between the East Friesland breed (originating from the Dutch-German border) and a number of other breeds to create an animal that is hardier than the pure East Friesland. The soft cheeses that are produced are made by hand using traditional recipes: they are turned daily in a curing room with temperature and humidity control. All the cheeses are sold at the farm shop and at local farmers' markets and restaurants.

PRODUCTION AREA
Nannup, Western Australia

COMMUNITY COORDINATOR
Jane Wilde
cambray@westnet.com.au

Random Valley organic producers

The Random Valley Organic Producers farm beef, snails and grapes for wine, selling to local markets. The community consists of 10 people who assist with the planting, growing and production processes and selling to markets. The producers have had 10 years' experience learning how to develop a certified organic sustainable farming system involving grapes, beef and snails. All produce is grown under strict organic requirements for sustainability. They believe that human intervention in complex, uncertain and ambiguous natural ecosystems can only be revealed in terms of their consequences. Monitoring and observing the consequences of human intervention in natural ecosystems are two of the most important components of working and interacting with the land.

PRODUCTION AREA
Karridale, Western Australia

COMMUNITY COORDINATOR
Suzanne Little
organics@randomvalley.com

Swan and Chittering Valleys food producers

People have been producing a diverse variety of foods and wines, such as table grapes, citrus fruits, olives, fruit and vegetable crops in the Swan and Chittering Valleys since first settlement in 1829. Now these producers, from a variety of ethnic backgrounds such as English, Italian, Scottish and Slav, own and work the land. The community is made up of over 2,000 people. Grapes are a major produce for the valleys. Other produce includes fruit and vegetables, such as asparagus, stone fruit, citrus, tomatoes, cauliflower and table grapes. These crops are produced using traditional and mechanized methods. Farmers' markets are held regularly to sell the produce to the locals. Also a Spring Festival is held to celebrate the strong rural heritage of the valley community.

PRODUCTION AREA
Swan and Chittering Valleys, Western Australia

COMMUNITY COORDINATOR
Patricia Tew
info@foodsymphony.com.au

Wheatbelt biodynamic Grain and Cereal producers

The Wheatbelt Biodynamic Grain and Cereal Producers are based in the Southwest Wheatbelt, in the region of south-western Australia that is well known not only for grain growing but also for livestock breeding. The community is made up of 19 people who grow a wide range of organically certified cereals such as wheat, rye, barley, oats and triticale. These grains are sold in wholegrain form or as stone-ground flour. Merino sheep are also raised in accordance with biodynamic methods for the production of meat.

PRODUCTION AREA
Wheatbelt, Western Australia

COMMUNITY COORDINATOR
Terri Lloyd
edenvalley@wn.com.au

Williams River biodynamic farmers

The community of biodynamic farmers from Williams River grows and process a wide range of meats, nuts, fruits, olives for oil and preserves. The community is made up of five members, all involved with producing biodynamic produce. The wider community of Demeter-certified biodynamic farmers includes around 50 families in Western Australia and Australia. The community work to produce a high quality of biodynamic produce such as cereal grains, meats, fruits, wine, olives and berries. The animals raised for lamb and beef are fed on biodynamic grasses and only outdoors, under natural conditions. The animals are bred to be worm-resistant. The cattle are fed pasture hay grown as an autumn feed supplement and no grains are used. The animals are processed at a certified abattoir and butcher's shop and sold privately on the farm or at organic food shops or via the internet.

PRODUCTION AREA
Williams River, Western Australia

COMMUNITY COORDINATOR
William Newton-Wordsworth
william@williamsriverproduce.com.au

Willunga Almond growers

The Willunga Almond Growers are a small group of 10 farmers who have replanted heritage varieties that were first planted in the region over a century ago from European varieties. This production is significant not only due to the variety being heritage, but also because the Willunga Basin has seen a boom in grape growing. This has led to a decline in the number of farmers growing almonds in the region. The growers sell their produce directly at farmers' markets, restaurants, bakeries and health food shops. The almonds grown are brownskin hardshell as opposed to papershell. Thanks to the intensity of their flavor, they are much sought after by chefs and bakers around Australia.

PRODUCTION AREA
Willunga, South Australia

COMMUNITY COORDINATOR
Judith McBain
imcbain@ozemail.com.au

Maori Cereal and Vegetable growers

The 800 members of this community mostly belong to the indigenous Maori race. The main activity is organic cultivation, using traditional methods, of corn, potatoes, sweet potatoes (kumara: some varieties derive from the sweet potatoes brought in by the first settlers from Polynesia one thousand years ago), and zucchini. The traditional method of farming, known as maramatak involve observing the phases of the moon, the stars, the activity of birds and the flowering period of the plants. The farmers formed the Te Waka Kai Ora-Maori Organic Growers and Farmers association after the rise of diseases like obesity and diabetes among young Maoris, due to the consumption of unhealthy Western foods. The association certifies the products obtained using maramatak methods and sells them mainly on the internal market.

PRODUCTION AREA
The entire country

COMMUNITY COORDINATOR
Tipene Iwi Puihi
tel. +64 9404837
tipenep@xtra.co.nz

Maori Potato growers

This community numbers over 100 farmers, mostly belonging to the Maori race – who preserve and cultivate ancient potato varieties. Potatoes were imported into New Zealand by English colonizers at the end of the 18th century, and became a major part of the local diet. They have recently been the subject of a promotional campaign, and are now once more in demand on the market. There are around twenty varieties, and though the farming methods are the same as those used for newer varieties, the ancient Maori varieties are almost all late-harvesting. There are three native associations which grow these varieties organically, though the products are not certified. Many of the farmers cultivate shared land and sell their potatoes at the farmers' markets.

PRODUCTION AREA
Wellington region

COMMUNITY COORDINATOR
Harris Graham
tel. +64 45270482 - 211731535
graham.harris@openpolytechnic.ac.nz

Traditional food producers

Lying about 500 kilometers east of the Philippines, the archipelago of Palau is one of the youngest and least populated countries in the world. Near the capital, Koror, a community of 54 women affiliated to the Women's Resource Center are committed to preserving Palau's gastronomic traditions, based on the use of taro (a tuber rich in starch), tapioca, coconut milk and wild fruit. One of the archipelago's typical dishes is demok, prepared from taro leaves, coconut milk and land crabs. The ladies in the community intend to make their work a money-maker by selling traditional dishes to restaurants, school canteens and families celebrating special occasions.

PRODUCTION AREA
State of Koror

COMMUNITY COORDINATOR
Maria Goretti Masayos
tel. +680 4883929 - 4881126
giss@palaunet.com

The Network

The food communities were selected and their participation at Terra Madre made possible thanks to the collaboration of many associations, foundations, research agencies and so on.
We hereby wish to thank everybody involved – and we apologize if we have forgotten any names – indicating contact information, where possible, to enable them to be increasingly a part of the Terra Madre network.

NON-GOVERNMENT ORGANIZATIONS (NGOs)

Acav Trento Ong
Trento (Italy)
tel. +39 0461935893
acav@eclipse-net.it
www.acavtn.it

Acra
Milan (Italy)
tel. +39 0227000291 - 826
fax +39 022552270
acra@acra.it
www.acra.it

Afrique Verte Mali
Bamako (Mali)
tel. +223 2219760
afriqueverte@afribonemali.net
www.afriqueverte.org

Ccm
Comitato Collaborazione Medica
Turin (Italy)
tel. +39 0116602793
ccm@ccm-italia.org
www.ccm-italia.org

Cefa
Bologna (Italy)
tel. +39 051520285
fax +39 051520712
info@cefaonlus.it
www.cefa.bo.it

Cesvi
Bergamo (Italy)
tel. +39 0352058058
fax +39 035260958
cesvi@cesvi.org
www.cesvi.org

Cisp
Rome (Italy)
fax +39 063216163
cisp@cisp-ngo.org
www.cisp-ngo.org

Cisv
Turin (Italy)
tel. +39 0118993823
fax +39 0118994700
segreteria@cisvto.org
www.cisvto.org

Community Design Center of Minnesota
Minnesota (USA)
tel. +1 6512287073
rmurphy@comdesignctrmn.org
www.comdesignctrmn.org

Coopi
Milan (Italy)
tel. +39 023085057
coopi@coopi.org
www.coopi.org

Cospe
Florence (Italy)
tel. +39 055473556
cospe@cospe.it
www.cospe.it

Daa
Accra (Ghana)
tel. +233 21315894
daa@africaonline.com.gh

Ecofare
Kuching (Sarawak, Malaysia)
tel. e fax +60 82454811
tfanfare@tm.nrt.my
www.ecofare.com

Gtz
Quito (Ecuador)
tel. +593 22437399
fax +593 22439907
gtz-ecuador@gtz.de
www.gtz.org

Icei
Milan (Italy)
tel. +39 0225785763
fax +39 022552270
info@icei.it

Ipecon
Initiative for People Centered Conservation
Ulaanbaatar (Mongolia)
tel. +976 11329477
fax +976 11329259
ipecon@nzni.org.mn
www.nzni.org.mn

Lvia
Associazione Internazionale Volontari Laici
Cuneo (Italy)
tel. +39 0171696975
lvia@lvia.it
www.lvia.it

Mauritanie 2000
Nouakchott (Mauritania)
tel. +222 5256128 - 5746850
(Nouadhibou office)
fax +222 5254631
ongmauritanie2000@mauritel.mr

Mlal
Verona (Italy)
tel. +39 0458102105
fax +39 0458103181
info@mlal.org
 www.mlal.org

Oxfam
Guatemala
www.oxfam.org

Rabat Malik Ong
Uzbekistan

Re.Te
Grugliasco (Turin, Italy)
tel. + 39 0117707388 - 398
africa@reteong.org
www.reteong.org

Syfia International
Dakar-Liberté (Senegal)
tel. +221 8256908
fax +221 8245338
syfia@telecomplus.sn

Terra Nuova Kenya
Nairobi (Kenya)
tel. +254 204445511 - 12
tn.nairobi@tnea.or.ke
www.terranuova.org

Ucoped
Arezzo (Italy)
tel. +39 0575401780
fax +39 0575401772
info@ucodep.org
www.ucodep.org

Unhcr (AoR Gorazde)
Gorazde (Bosnia and Herzegovina)
tel. +387 38224120
bsngo@unhcr.org
www.unhcr.org

Wesm
Limbe (Malawi)
tel. +265 1643502
fax +265 1643765
wesm-hq@africa-online.net

Woodsta
Arusha (Tanzania)
tel. +255 057501165
rkihulya@yahoo.com

World Hunger Year
New York (USA)
tel. +1 2126298850
info@worldhungeryear.org
http://www.worldhungeryear.org

FOUNDATIONS

Adept Foundation
Brasov (Romania)
tel. +40 722983 771
fax +40 217464404
cristi@adeptfoundation.org

Akf - Aga Khan Foundation
Tagikistan Kirghizistan
The Aga Khan Development Network
Geneva (Switzerland)
tel. +41 229097200
fax +41 229097292
information@aiglemont.org

Avina Foundation
Hurden (Switzerland)
tel. +41 554151111
fax +41 554151150
foundation@avina.net
www.avina.net

Biotani Pan Foundation
Jakarta (Indonesia)
tel. +62 218296545
fax +62 218296545
biotani@rad.net.id
www.biotani.org

Clanrence E. Heller Charitable Foundation
California (USA)
tel. +1 4159899839
fax +1 4159891909
info@cehcf.org
http://cehcf.org

German Marshall Fund of the United States
Washington DC (USA)
tel. +1 2027453950 - fax 2022651662
info@gmfus.org
www.gmfus.org

Jhai Foundation
Vientiane (Laos)
tel. +856 205521037
vorasone@jhai.org
www.jhai.org/

Keystone Foundation
Kotagiri (India)
tel. +91 4266275297
mathew@keystone-foundation.org
keystone-foundation.net/web/

Navdanya Foundation
New Delhi (India)
tel. +91 1126535422 - 26968077
fax +91 1126856795 - 26562093
vshiva@vsnl.com
www.navdanya.org

Roots of Change Fund
California (USA)
tel. +1 4153910545 - fax 4159827989
http://www.rocfund.org

Siyath Foundation
Colombo (Sri Lanka)
tel. +94 112691433 - 112667176
fax +94 11269143
Siyath@zeynet.com
www.helpsiyath.org

Trace Foundation
New York (USA)
tel. + 1 2123677380
fax + 1 2123677383
info@trace.org
www.trace.org

FAIRTRADE

Alter Trade
Indonesia
altertradeindonesia@yahoo.com

Alter Trade
Negros (Philippines)
tel. +63 344410051 - 55
fax +63 344410051
atquery@info.com.ph
www.altertradegroup.com

Ctm Altromercato
Verona (Italy)
tel. +39 0458008081
fax +39 0458008020
info@altromercato.it
www.altromercato.it

Libero Mondo
Bra (Cuneo, Italy)
tel. +39 0172499169
fax + 39 0172499074
liberomondo@liberomondo.org
www.liberomondo.org

Mahaguti
Lalitpur (Nepal)
tel. +977 15533197 - 5532981
fax +977 15521493
mguthi@mos.com.np
www.mahaguthi.org

Pftc Panay Fair Trade Center
Philippines
pnyfair@skyinet.net

Scambi Sostenibili
Palermo (Italy)
tel. +39 04387841515
s.monachino@scambisostenibili.it
www.scambisostenibili.it

PRODUCERS' ASSOCIATIONS,
CONSORTIA, SYNDICATES,
DEVELOPMENT PROJECTS,
NONPROFIT ORGANIZATIONS

Aapi
Associazione Apicoltori Professionisti Italiani
Casteggio (Pavia, Italy)
tel. +39 0383 805452
lucaboniz@tiscali.it
www.mieliditalia.it/aapi.htm

Abrdp
Arsi and Bale Rural Development Project
Ethio-Italian Development Cooperation
Asella (Etiopia)

Accion Campesina
Mirando (Venezuela)
tel. + 58 2123214795 - 3643872
consultas@accioncampesina.org.ve
www.accioncampesina.org.ve

Agri Bio Piemonte
Associazione onlus dei produttori
e consumatori biologici e biodinamici
Cissone, Cuneo (Italy)
tel. +39 0173748211
fax +39 0173748728
www.agribionotizie.it
info@agribionotizie.it

Agtalon
Agro-Technical and Livelihood
Opportunities in the North
Philippines
agtalon_inc@yahoo.com

Aiab
Rome (Italy)
tel. +39 0645437485 - 6 - 7
fax +39 0645437469
aiab@aiab.it - www.aiab.it

Alce Nero
Isola del Piano (Pesaro and Urbino, Italy)
tel. +39 0721720221
fax +39 0721720209
alcenero@alcenerocooperativa.it
www.alcenerocooperativa.it

All National Associaton of Genetic Safety
Russia
tel. +7 0953088933
http://biosafety.ru/
eremurus@mtu-net.ru

Alternative Agriculture Network
Amphur Kuan KaLong
Satun (Thailand)
annet@ksc.th.com

Anpe Peru
Lima (Peru)
tel. +51 012419786
fax +51 012419784
anpep@ideas,org.pe

Apilombardia
Voghera (Pavia, Italy)
tel. +39 038343858
apilombardia@tiscali.it
www.mieliditalia.it

Are Vallebormida
Associazione Energie Rinnovabili Vallebormida
Cairo Montenotte (Savona, Italy)
tel. +39 019500523
are.vallebormida@libero.it

Associazione delle Casare e dei Casari di Azienda Agricola
Moretta (Cuneo, Italy)
tel. e fax +39 017293564
info@casarecasari.it
www.casarecasari.it

Aspromiele
Associazione Produttori Miele del Piemonte
Turin - Alessandria (Italy)
tel. +39 0131250368
aspromiele@aspromiele.191.it
www.mieliditalia.it/aspromiele

Assiette de Pays
tel. +33 0467978800
http://www.sunfrance.com/pays

Association Congolaise pour la Défense des Droits du Consommateur (Acddc)
Brazzaville (Republic of Congo)
tel. +242 5561882
Acddc_congo@yahoo.fr

Association Ibn Al Baytar
Rabat (Morocco)
tel. +212 37711692
zcharrouf@menara.ma
www.argane.de/main/associationibnalbaytar.htm

Associazione Patriarchi della Natura in Italia
Forlì (Italy)
tel. +39 3487334726
patriarchinatura@libero.it
www.patriarchinatura.it

Associazione Ram
San Rocco di Camogli (Genoa, Italy)
tel. +39 0185799087
fax +39 0185799214
info@associazioneram.it
www.associazioneram.it

Associazione Tin Hinan
tel. +226 50358275
tinhinanbf@yahoo.fr

Associazione Veterinaria di Cooperazione con i Paesi in via di sviluppo (Avec)
Donnas, Aosta (Italy)
tel. +39 0161433492
avec_pvs@hotmail.com
www.avec-pvs.org

Bees for Development
Troy Monmouth (UK)
tel. +44 01600713648
info@beesfordevelopment.org
www.beesfordevelopment.org

Bistrot de Pays
Forcalquier (France)
tel. +33 492752396
contact@bistrotdepays.com
www.bistrotdepays.com

Bikalpa Unnayan Karmashuchi (Buk)
Basisal (Bangladesh)
tel. +91 88043153854
bikalpa@bdcom.com

Center for Sustainable Development & Environment (Cenesta)
Teheran (Iran)
tel. +98 2166972973 - fax 2166400811
international fax +12533228599
cenesta@cenesta.org
http://www.cenesta.org

Civiltà Contadina
Pietracuta di San Leo (Pesaro and Urbino, Italy)
tel. e fax +39 0541924036
biodiversità@biodiversità.info
www.biodiversita.info

Confagricoltura Donna
Alessandria (Italy)
tel. +39 013143151
r.sparacino@confagricolturalessandria.it
www.confagricoltura.it

Connettivo terra/Terra
Rome (Italy)
tel. e fax +39 0621807855
forte@ecn.org
www.forteprenestino.net

Consorzio Apicoltori e Agricoltori Biologici Italiani (Conapi)
Monterenzio (Bologna, Italy)
tel. +39 051920283
info@mediterrabio.com
www.mediterrabio.com

Consorzio Etimos
Padova (Italy)
tel. +39 0498755116 - 654191
fax +39 0498755714
etimos@etimos.it
www.etimos.it

Consorzio Caffè Speciali Certificati (Csc)
Livorno (Italy)
cscoffee@tin.it
www.caffespeciali.com

Crossroad Resource Center
Minnesota (USA)
tel. +1 6128698664
kmeter@crcworks.org
www.crcworks.org

Cuisineries Gourmandes
Cordes-sur-Ciel (France)
tel. +33 563560658
contact@cuisineries-gourmandes.com

Culinary Alliance of Santa Cruz
California (USA)
tel. +1 8316888460
www.culinarysantacruz.com

Demeter USA
Oregon (USA)
tel. +1 5419297148 - fax 5419294387
demeter@peak.org
www.demeter-usa.org

Eco-Club Tapan
Yerevan (Armenia)
tel. + 374 1733322 - fax 1733322
tapan@acc.am

Egyptian-Italian Environmental Cooperation Program
Cairo (Egypt)

Fenagie-Pêche
Fédération Nationale des Groupements
d'Intérêt Economique de Pêcheurs
Quai de Pêche de Hann (Senegal)
tel. +221 8321100 - fax 8321101
fenagiepeche@sentoo.sn

Fongs/Acion Paysanne
Fédération des Ong Senegalaises
Senegal
fongs@sentoo.sn
www.fongs.sn

Gayo Mountain Cooperative
Indonesia
bachtiarusman98@yahoo.com

Granello di Senape
Bra (Cuneo, Italy)
tel. +39 017244599
segreteria@granellodisenape.org
www.granellodisenape.org

Ifoam
Bonn (Germany)
tel. +49 2289265010 - fax 2289265099
headoffice@ifoam.org
www.ifoam.org

Inades
Abidjan (Côte d'Ivoire)
tel. +225 22400216
ifsiege@inadesfo.ci
www.inadesfo.org

Ipo Associazione
Ponte Felicino (Perugia, Italy)
info@ipoassociazione.org
www.ipoassocizione.org

Isec
International Society for Ecology & Culture
Devon (UK)
tel. +44 01803868650
fax +44 01803868651
info@isec.org.uk
www.isec.org.uk/index.html

Istituto Agronomico d'Oltremare (Iao)
Florence (Italy)
tel. +39 0555061 1
iao@iao.florence.it

Italia Nostra
Consiglio Piemonte Valle d'Aosta
(Turin, Italy)
piemonte-valledaosta@italianostra.org
www.italianostra.org

Jvc
Japan International Volunteer Center
Tokyo (Japan)
tel. +81 338342388
fax +81 338350519
jvc@jca.apc.org
www.jca.apc.org/jvc

Locavores
Local Foods Wheel San Francisco Bay Area
California (USA)
www.locavores.com

Marin Organic
California (USA)
tel. +1 4156639667
fax +1 4156639687
info@marinorganic.org
www.marinorganic.org

Necofa Network for Eco Farming in Africa
satesfai@wiz.uni-kassel.de
www.necofa.org

Ofcd
Organic Food Development Center of China
Nanjing (China)
tel. +86 2585425370 - 8547 3103
fax +86 2585420606 - 8541 9083
info@ofdc.org.cn
www.ofdc.org.cn/english/about/about.asp

Pamalakaya
Philippine Federation of Fisherfolk Organizations
Philippine
pampil@skyinet.net

Podie
People's Organisation for Development
Import & Export
Negombo (Sri Lanka)
tel. + 94 3133773 - 75 - 24278
fax + 94 3133774
podie@sltnet.lk
www.catgen.com/podie/EN/index.html

Pof
Pakistan Organic Farm
Lahore (Pakistan)
tel. +92 426302778
fax +92 426361530
info@pakof.com
www.pakof.com

San Diego Roots Sustainable Food Project
California (USA)
tel. +1 6197226281
roots@sandiegoroots.org
www.sandiegoroots.org

San Francisco Food System
California (USA)
tel. +1 4152523937
fax +1 4152523818
info@sffoodsystems.org
www.sffoodsystems.org

Seeds of Change
(Distributor of certified organic seeds)
New Mexico (USA)
tel. +1 8887624240
www.seedsofchange.com

Soil Association
Bristol (UK)
tel. +44 01173145000
fax +44 01173145001
info@soilassociation.org
www.soilassociation.org

Sustain
Illinois (USA)
tel. +1 3129518999
fax +1 3129515696
lynn@sustainusa.org
www.sustainusa.org

Unaapi
Unione nazionale associazioni apicoltori italiani
Novi Ligure, Alessandria (Italy)
tel. +39 0143323778
fax +39 0143314235
unaapi@mieliditalia.it
www.mieliditalia.it

Union of Kazakhstan Farmers
Kazakhstan

Urban Village Farmers' Market Association
California (USA)
tel. +1 5107457100
fax +1 5107457180
urbanvillage@earthlink.net
www.urbanvillageonline.com

Wamip
World Alliance of Mobile Indigenous Peoples
Tehran (Iran)
tel. +98 2122964114 - 4115 - 4116
fax +98 212295 - 4217
aghaghia@cenesta.org
wamip@cenesta.org
www.iucn.org/themes/ceesp/wamip/wamip.htm

Wrc
Women Resources Center
Koror (Palau)
tel. +680 4883929
fax +680 4884502
giss@palaunet.com
www.palaugov.net

WWF Italia
Rome (Italy)
tel. +39 06844971
www.wwf.it

RESEARCH CENTERS, INSTITUTES, SCHOOLS, UNIVERSITIES

Ccs Aosta
Centro di Colture Sperimentali
Aosta (Italy)
tel. e fax +39 0112257473
ccs@envipark.com

Cedac
Centre d'Etudes et de Développement
Agricole Cambodgien
Phnom Penh (Cambodia)
tel. +23 880916
fax +23 885146
cedac@online.com.hk

**Center of Coordination of Research
and Development - Leisa Magazine**
Amersfoort (Netherlands)
tel. +31 0334673870
fax +31 0334632410
ileia@ileia.nl
http://www.leisa.info

Cerai
Centro de Estudios Rurales
y de Agricultura Internacional
tel. +34 963521878
fax +34 963522501
administracion@cerai.es

Cervim
Centro Ricerche Studi Salvaguardia
Coordinamento e Valorizzazione per la
Viticoltura Montana
Quart, Aosta (Italy)
tel. +39 0165775792
fax +39 0165771925
info@cervim.it
www.cervim.it

Cetdem
Centre for Environment, Technology &
Development Malaysia
Petaling Jaya (Malaysia)
tel. +603 78757767
fax +603 78754039
of@cetdem.org.my
www.cetdem.org.my

Crfa
Centro Ricerche Floristiche
Appennino Barisciano
L'Aquila (Italy)
tel. e fax +39 0862899025
crfa@gransassolagapark.it
www.gransassolagapark.it

**Department of Economic Development
and Productive Activities of the Rome
Provincial Authority**
Rome (Italy)
tel. +39 0667665553 - fax 0667665609
ass.attivitaproduttive@provincia.roma.it
www.provincia.roma.it

**Dwpartment of Soil Sciente and Plant
Nutrition - University of Florence**
Florence (Italy)
tel. +39 0553288211
dssnp1@agr.unifi.it
www.unifi.it/dssnp

Dover Adult Learning Center
New Hampshire (USA)
tel. +1 6037421030
dalc@dalc-online.org
www.dalc-online.org

Ecomuseo delle Acque del Gemonese
Ospedaletto di Gemona (Udine, Italy)
tel. +39 0432972316
ecomuseoacquegemonese@virgilio.it
www.mulinococconi.it

**Ecomuseo Regionale dei Terrazzamenti
e della Vite**
Cortemilia (Cuneo, Italy)
tel. +39 017381027
fax +39 017381154
ecomuseo@comunecortemilia.it
www.ecomusei.net

**Experimental Institute for Plant Nutrition
CRA
Council for Research
and Experimentation in Agriculture**
Turin (Italy)
tel. e fax +39 0117399714
isnp.to@entecra.it
www.isnp.it

Experimental Institute for Sheep Breeding
Rende (Cosenza, Italy)
tel. e fax +39 0984401858
istsperolivic@antares.it
www.isnp.it/cra/ISOliv.htm

Gfu
Global Facilitation Unit for Underutilized Species
Maccarese
Rome (Italy)
tel. +39 066118292
fax +39 0661979661
underutilized-species@cgiar.org
www.underutilized-species.org

Gruppo Abele
Turin (Italy)
tel. +39 0113841011 - 3841066
fax +39 01 3841031
segreteria@gruppoabele.org
www.gruppoabele.org

Icarda
International Center for Agricultural
Research in Dry Areas
Aleppo (Syria)
tel. +963 212213433 - 2213477 -2225112
fax +963 212213490 - 2225105
icarda@cgiar.org
www.icarda.cgiar.org

Icea Piemonte
Institute for Ethical
and Environmental Certification
Trofarello (Turin, Italy)
tel. +39 0116496450
fax +39 0116492542
www.icea.info
sot.piemonte@icea.info

Institute of Clinical Physiology
Cnr (National Research Council)
Pisa (Italy)
tel. +39 0503152328
www.ifc.cnr.it

Iucn
Russia
www.iucn.org

Osservatorio Ligure Pesca e Ambiente
Genoa (Italy)
tel. +39 010584368
www.olpa.info

Rec Caucasus
Regional Environmental Center
Tbilisi (Georgia)
tel. e fax +99532253649 - 253648
info@rec-caucasus.org
www.rec-caucasus.org

The Farm Institute
Food, Agricolture, Resource Management
Massachusetts (USA)
tel. +1 5086277007
fax +1 6277719
www.farminstitute.org
matthew@farminstitute.org

The Institute of American Indian Arts
New Mexico (USA)
tel. +1 5054242300
www.iaiancad.org

Vavilov Institute of General Genetics
Mosca (Russia)
asadova@mail.ru

Virgin Island Sustainable Farm Institute
Virgin Island (USA)
tel. +1 6789992143
info@ visfi.org
www.visfi.org

OTHER COLLABORATORS

Acquerello di Piero Rondolino
Livorno Ferraris (Vercelli, Italy)

Arsia – Tuscany Regional Authority
Italy

Associazione Abraham
Nichelino (Turin, Italy)

Auser Piemonte
Italy

Azrri
Agenzia per lo Sviluppo Rurale dell'Istria
Croatia

Berlinale Talent Campus
Germany

Massimo Bernacchini
Coordinator Bottarga di Orbetello
Presidium and Slow Food governor

Niccolò Biddau
photographer

Gianluca Cané
photographer

Manuel Carvalho
firm director

Centro Sperimentale di Cinematografia
Scuola Nazionale di Cinema
Piedmont Office, Animation Department
Chieri (Turin, Italy)

Cineteca di Bologna
Bologna (Italy)

Cisom
Corpo Italiano di Soccorso
dell'Ordine di Malta
Turin (Italy)

Commune of Lignana
(Vercelli, Italy)

Consorzio Pho-to.it
Turin (Italy)

Cooperazione Libico-Italiana
Tripoli (Libya)

Teresa Corção
Restaurateur and gastronome

Department of Animal Pathology
Faculty of Veterinary Sciences
University of Turin
Turin (Italy)

Department of Youth Policies City of Turin
Turin (Italy)

Raffaele De Lutio
Italian ambassador in Addis Abeba
(Ethiopia)

Jaya Deva
musician

Fabrica-Redazione Colors Magazine
Catena di Villorba (Treviso, Italy)

Bruno Fieno
musicologist

Owen Franken
photographer

Annette Frei Berthoud
journalist

Annamaria Gallone
documentarist

Guido Gobino Cioccolato e Giandujotti
Turin (Italy)

**Faculty of Agriculture
University of Turin**
Turin (Italy)

**Job Placement
Faculty of Letters and Philosophy
University of Turin**
Turin (Italy)

Ice
Amman (Jordan)

Laboratorio di Resistenza Dolciaria
Federico Molinari
Alba (Cuneo, Italy)

Liceo Vittoria di Torino
Turin (Italy)

Max Felchlin Ag
Schwyz (Switzerland)

**Meaningful People, Places and Food
Consulting and Design**
Wisconsin (USA)

Menodiciotto Il Gelato
Turin (Italy)

National Mercantour Nature Park
France

Orange Comunicazione
Turin (Italy)

**Parco Naturale Nazionale del Gran Sasso
e Monti della Laga**
Italia

Alberto Peroli
photographer

Protezione Civile
Turin (Italy)

Provincial Authority of Arezzo
Arezzo (Italy)

Regional Queyras Nature Park
France

Risi & Co-Gli Aironi di Michele Perinotti
Lignana (Vercelli, Italy)

**Sector of Rural Development
Provincial Authority of Grosseto**
Grosseto (Italy)

**Service of Agrifood System Development
Emilia Romagna Regional Authority**
Italy

Slow Food Imereti
Georgia

Slow Food Accra
Ghana

Slow Food Budapest, Central Region
Hungary

Slow Food Kenya
Kenya

Slow Food Kiev
Ucraina

Slow Food Beirut
Lebanon

Slow Food Minsk
Belorus

Staff Atrium
Turin

Topix
Torino Piemonte Internet Exchange
Turin (Italy)

Torino Film Commission
Turin (Italy)

Ufficio Volontariato Giovanile di Torino
Turin (Italy)

Yfy Biotech Co.
Taiwan

The 700 volunteers of Terra Madre

Country index

AFRICA 25

Algeria
Béni-Isguen Oasis Date Producers 26

Benin
Atacora Mountain Flower Honey Producers 26
Atacora Mountain Rice Producers 27
Cotonou Healthy Food Producers and Distributors 27
Fruit and Vegetable Producers...27
Honvié Angolan Pea Growers 27
Kalalé Peul Wagassi Cheesemakers 28
Matéri Mountain Rice Producers..28
Sakété Yovogari Producers 28

Burkina Faso
Bambara Pea Producers of Bobo-Dioulasso 29
Banfora Region fruit and cereal producers
and processors 29
Baobab Leaf and Shea Tree Larvae Gatherers 29
Black-eyed Pea (Niébé) Growers 30
Dried Mango Producers of Ouagadougou 30
Entomophagus Women of the Bobo-Dioulasso Region 30
Fonio and Palm Wine Producers of Orodara 30
Forest Food Promoters 31
Jujube Bread Producers 31
Okra Growers of Tanlili 31
Organic Sesame Producers of Gulmu...31
Organic Sesame Producers of Kongoussi 32
Ouagadougou Cheesemakers 32
Ouagadougou Peul Breeders..32
Pearl Millet Growers of Tanlili 32
Peul Zebu Cattle Breeders...33
Shea Butter Producers..33
Soumbala Producers...33
Zaban and Palm Juice Producers 34
Zamené Producers 34

Burundi
Banana Beer Producers of Cibitoke 34
Coffee Producers of the province of Ngozi 34
Farmers and breeders of Shombo, Mutumba and Nyabikere 35

Cameroon
Bambara Pea Producers of Djogona 35
Cassava Producers of Nyanon 35
Desert Date Leaf Gatherers 36
Growers and Processors of Black-Eyed Beans 36
Guiziga Bald-Neck Chicken Breeders 36
Guiziga Millet Growers 37
Honey Producers of Danay 37
Niébé (Black-Eyed Peas) Producers of Moutourwa.........................37
Ovangoul Okok Producers 37
Paradise Grain Producers 38
Rice and Sorghum Producers of Bizili 38

Cape Verde
Goat Cheese Producers of Santo Antão 38
Wine Producers of Chã das Caldeiras 38

Central African Republic
Cassava Growers...39

Chad
Kanembou Gatherers of Lake Chad Blue Algae 39
Kanembou Kouri Cattle Breeders 39
Lake Chad Maize Producers 40
Lake Chad Millet Producers 40

Comoros
Moroni Producers..41

Congo, Democratic Republic of
Dried Fish Producers of Kingabwa..41
Tanganyika Fishermen...41

Côte d'Ivoire
Cassava and Yam producers of Anyama..........42
Cocoa producers in Tiassalé 42
Coffee and Cocoa growers in Daloa 42
Fruit Juice producers of Abidjan 42

Djibouti
Animal breeders and milk and dairy producers
of Djibouti 43

Egypt
Bakers and Confectioners of Alexandria 43
Growers of Wadi El Rayan 43
Olive Producers of Sinai 44
Organic Vegetable and Aromatic Herb Producers
of Fayoum 44
Siwa Dates **90**

Eritrea
Vegetable Producers of Midrisien 44

Ethiopia
Coffee and Forest Honey Producers
of Dollo Mena 45
Coffee Producers of the Golocha Forest 45
Euphorbia Honey Producers of Tigrai 45
Hard Wheat Producers in Ejerre 45
Honey Producers of the Wonchi Volcano..........46
Incense and Myrrh Gatherers in the Filtu Area..........46
Kollo Producers of Dinsho..........47
Teff Producers of Debre Zeit 47

Gabon
Banana Growers of Mbenga 47
Cane Sugar Growers and Processors of Doumandzou 47
Cassava Growers and Processors of Makokouy 48
Coconut Processors of Bissok 48
Karkade Growers 48
Oil Palm Producers and Processors of Lambaréné 48
Taro Producers of Obout-Essangui 49
Traditional Spice producers in N'kart and Ngomessi 49
Wild Mango Gatherers of the Doum District 49

Gambia
Producers and Processors of Banjul 50
Producers and Processors of Brikama 50
Producers from the Methodist Mission of Kerewan 50

Ghana
Animal Breeders of Amuyaokope 51
Cassava Processors of Obom 51
Fish Smokers of Kokrobite..........51
Fishermen and Animal Breeders of Nyuiyui..........51
Maize Producers from Donkokrom 52
Pineapple Growers from Obodan 52
Pineapple Growers from the Central Region 52
Plantain Banana Growers of Amanease 52
Salt Producers and Processors of Nyanyano..........53
Vegetable Growers of Okushiebiade 53

Guinea
Beekeepers of Sampirin 53
Chilli Pepper Growers of Niégueré 53
Citrus Fruit Growers of the Pita Prefecture 54
Defenders of the Néré and Souombara producers of Fouta Djalon..54
Fishermen of Boulbinet..........54
Fonio Growers and Processors of Fouta Djalon 54
Ginger Growers and Processors 55
N'dama Cow Milk and Cheesemakers 55
Sintin-Sitirin Producers 55
Soumbara Producers of Lélouma 55
Taro Growers of Fello Diounguel 56

Kenya
Baobab Jam Producers of Kibwezi..........56
Camel Breeders of the Salato Tribe 56
Cereals Growers of Kathonzweni 57
Cow and Camel Breeders 57
Farmers of the Arid Areas of Kitui 57
Fish Farmers of Kisumu..........57
Herb and Fruit Gatherers of the Rift Valley forest..........58
Indigenous Chicken Breeders of Kilifi 58
Indigenous Chicken Breeders of Machakos 58
Macadamia Nut Producers and Processors..........58
Nettle Growers of the Rift Valley..........59

North Turkana Shepherds 59
Orange Sweet Potato Producers 59
Organic Farmers of Marsabit..59
Organic Infusion Producers of the Meru Region...........60
Organic Medicinal Food and Herb Producers 60
Organic Producers of the Suburban Areas of Gachie 60
Potato and Pea Growers of Nakuru 60
Pumpkin Growers of the Arid Areas of Homa Bay and Kilify 61
Seed Promoters and Savers in Molo and Makueni 61
Sesame Producers of Mount Elgon 61
Sustainable Food Producers of Kangemi 61
Taro Producers 62
Traditional Animal By-product Producers of the Rift Valley 62
Traditional Beekeepers of Pokot 62
Vegetable Growers of Embu 62
Waterlily Gatherers of the Baringo District....................63
Wild Mushroom Gatherers of Western Kenya................63

Lesotho
Vegetable Producers of Maseru 63

Libya
Local Date Variety Producers..64
Tuareg Breeders and Growers of Ghat 64

Madagascar
Andasibe Red Rice 91
Mananara Vanilla..92
Pink Rice Producers 64
Red Rice Producers of Antanafisaka 64
Strawberry Producers of Antsimondrano 65

Malawi
Fruit Juice, Jam and Purée Producers............................65
Honey and Fruit Juice Producers of Mwanza 65

Mali
Cereal and Legume growers and processors...................66
Cereal producers and merchants of Bamako and Ségou 66
Dogon Onion Growers 66
Goat Cheese and Dried Meat Producers of Gargando......67
Leaf Growers and Processors of Baguinéda 67

Mango and Vegetable Producers...................................67
Missira Market 68

Mauritania
Camel Breeders and Milk Producers of Nouakchott 68
Imraguen Women's Bottarga 93

Morocco
Argan Oil..94
Cheese and Honey Producers of the Mid-Atlas Mountains.............69
Dried Fruit Producers of Taounate 69
Goat Breeders of Souss-Massa-Draa 69
Mussel Fishermen from the Tiznit Province 69

Namibia
Farmers and Animal Breeders in the Khomas Region 70

Niger
Cheese and Curdled Milk Producers of Toukounous........70
Kouri Cattle Breeders of Sayam....................................70
Milk Producers of Kirkissoye 71
Takommar Cheese Producers of Timia 71
Tuareg Producers of Milk, Meat and Cereals 71

Nigeria
Beekeepers of Ijebu-Ode 72

Rwanda
Sorghum Drink Producers of Nyakinama........................72

Senegal
Artisan Fishermen of Saint-Louis 73
Artisan Fishermen of Ziguinchor 73
Cereal, Legume and Vegetable Growers of Keur Massar 73
Fish processors and sellers 73
Fonio Producers of Kedougou 74
Fruit Growers of the Diouloulou District 74
Groundnut Paste and Oil Producers of the Diourbel Region 74
Karkade Growers and Processors of the Dakar Region 75
Milk and Butter Producers of Koumpentoum...................75
Millet and Maize Growers and Processors of the Thiès Region 75
Niébé Producers in the Louga Region 76

Peul Animal Breeders and Milk Producers
in the Louga Region 76
Preserved Fish Producers and Sellers of Fatick 77
Producers and Processors of Diakhao 77
Rice Processors of Podor 77
Shea growers of Kedougou 78
Vegetable anf Fruit Producers and Processors of Thiès 78

Seychelles
Producers from the Island of Mahé 78

Somalia
Banana Producers of Lower Shabelle and Lower Jubba 79

South Africa
Beekeepers of the Pacaltsdorp District 79
Organic Producers of Klein Karoo 79
Rooibos Producers of Suid Bokkeveld 80
Rooibos Producers of Wupperthal 80

Sudan
Cereal and Fruit Producers of Wad Medani 80

Swaziland
Traditional Food producers, processors and cooks of Shewula 81
Vegetable and Legume Producers of Kambhoke 81

Tanzania
Bamboo Wine Producers of Njombe 81
Barabaig shepherds 82
Cassava and Coffee Producers of the Ileje District 82
Cereal and Legume Growers of the Kiteto District 82
Cheese and Milk Producers of Njombe 83
Fruit and Vegetable Producers of Morogoro...................83
Growers and Stock Breeders of Ngurudoto and Kikatiti 83
Hibiscus Growers and Processors of the Pwani Region 84
Masai Farmers of the Arusha Region 84
Milk and Nilk By-Product Producers of the Hai District 84

Togo
Cassava Growers and Processors of Attitogon...................85
Yam Growers of Kpéssi 85

Tunisia
Producers of Djerba Island 85

Uganda
Banana Growers of the Kampala District 86
Coffee Producers of Kibinge 86
Fishermen and Stock Breeders of Kasokwe 86
Honey Producers of Soroti 86
Local Chicken Breeders of Mukono 87
Organe Flesh Sweet Potato Growers of Luwero 87
Vegetable and Fruit growers and processors in the Masaka District..87
Wild Fruit Jam Producers 87

Zambia
Honey Producers of Kabompo 88

Zimbabwe
Gatherers of Mopane Worms 88
Ilala and Marula Wine Producers 88
Makoni Tea Producers...89
Natural Oil Producers in the Chivi District 89

AMERICAS **95**

Argentina
Andean Corn 216
Andean Potato growers...96
Caiman farmers 96
Cake-makers of Trelew 96
Carob Flour producers 96
Charqui producers 97
Cheese-makers of Estación Yeruá...............................97
Cheese-makers of Maciá 97
Edible wild plant gatherers 97
Farmers, growers and preserve producers of San Javier 98
Fruit and vegetable producers of El Hoyo 98
Fruit producers and farm tourism operators 98
Goat farmers of the Valle di Uco 98
Guaraní ka'aguy poty producers of Kuñá Pirú 99
Home-brewed Beer producers 99
Honey producers 99
Jam producers of Juella 99

Kiwicha and quinoa growers of the Quebrada de Humahuaca......100
Manioc growers and processors of Misiones 100
Muña liqueur producers 100
Mushroom growers 100
Oca growers of Coctaca 101
Oca growers of Iruya 101
Organic honey producers 101
Organic wine producers of Maipú..101
Organic wine producers of Mendoza..102
Pheasant farmers 102
Producers of cane-sugar honey and cane-sugar 102
Producers of chocolate and other cocoa derivatives...................102
Producers of dulce de leche 103
Producers of extra-virgin olive oil 103
Producers of fruit-flavored honey 103
Producers of goat's milk and cheese 103
Producers of honey and related products 104
Producers of honey, royal jelly and propolis 104
Producers of jam and spicy sweet and sour preserves 104
Producers of jam made from forest fruits 104
Producers of olives and extra-virgin olive oil 105
Producers of sheep's cheese and lamb 105
Producers of sweet products and liquerurs 105
Producers of traditional local wines..105
Producers of vegetables and regional specialities.......................106
Producers of wines, fruit and vegetables 106
Quebrada de Humahuaca Andean Potatoes **217**
Shellfish farmers...106
Smoked food producers of Rosario 106
Traditional food producers of Oberá 107
Vegetable growers of Corrientes 107
Vegetable growers of the Pereyra Iraola Provincial Park 107
Yacón **218**
Yerba mate growers 107

Belize
Cocoa producers...108

Bolivia
Coffee producers of Yungas...108
Goat farmers of Tarija...108
Pando Nut..**219**

Potato growers of Araca 109
Potosí Llama **220**
Wheat producers and processors of Totora 109
Women bakers of San Javier 109

Brazil
Abaetetuba Açaí and Cupuaçu by-product producers 110
Babaçu by-products producers 110
Barù Nut **221**
Beiju and Bolachinas de Goma producers 110
Brazil Nut and Copaìba Oil producers 110
Brazil Nut producers 111
Cacimbas Pequi producers 111
Cametá fruit by-products producers 111
Cananéia Oyster gatherers 111
Canapù bean **222**
Cantagalo Fava do Vale producers 112
Centro Popular de Saúde Yanten aromatic herbs producers 112
Cerrado fruit gatherers 113
Chapecó small-scale farmers 113
Cupuaçu producers and processors 113
Cupuaçu producers and processors 113
Farinha d'Água producers 114
Feira de Santana fruit producers and processors 114
Florianópolis Manioc Flour producers 114
Honey and Ouricuri producers 114
Itápolis Orange Juice producers 115
Iúna coffee producers 115
Jatobá Flour producers 115
Juçara Palm Heart **223**
Krahô Sweet Potato Flour producers 116
Lages Pine Nut producers 116
Lagoa Seca Caju Passa producers 116
Lima Duarte Honey producers 117
Macaúba Oil producers..117
Mata Atlântica resource promoters 117
Melipona bee's honey producers 117
Monte Claros fruit producers and processors 118
Montenegro Mandarin Juice producers 118
Nós Existimos...125
Pareci Novo fruit farmers and processors..................................118
Pintadas Honey producers 119

Pirarucu fishermen 119
Pirenópolis fruit preserve producers 119
Poço Fundo coffee producers 120
Praia Grande Valley banana producers 120
Rapadura de Melado producers 120
Red Chili Pepper producers....................................120
Rio Real tropical fruit and juice producers...............121
Santa Lizia do Itanhi fishermen.............................121
Santa Luzia Jam producers 121
Santa Rosa de Lima organic producers 122
Santana Velha Bacurí gatherers 121
Sateré Mawé Canudo Bee's Honey **224**
Sateré Mawé Native Waraná **225**
Serra do Salitre cheesemakers 122
Serra Gaucha Grape producers 122
Small-scale Cashew Nut producers 122
Spices producers...123
Sugar Cane growers 123
Teófilo Otoni young farmers 123
Turvo Pine Nut gatherers 123
Umbù **226**
Vale do Piancó Red Rice producers 124
Valente Manioc Flour producers 124
Vitoria De Santo Antão producers 124
Xingu Park fruit producers 124
Yerba Mate growers and processors 125

Canada
Acton Biodynamic Food producers 125
Alberta bakers 125
Alberta beekeepers and mead producers................126
Alberta Bison breeders 126
Alberta breeders...126
Alberta Cattle breeders 127
Alberta Lamb breeders 127
Alberta organic breeders..127
British Columbia farmers' markets producers...........127
British Columbia food producers.............................128
Cape Breton farmers' market producers 128
Dufferin Grove farmers' market producers..............128
Eastern Seaboard farmers' markets producers.........128
Grand Manan Island Lobster fishers 129

Gulf Islands farmers' markets producers 129
Gull Valley Vegetable growers 129
Hagersville Wild Plant gatherers 129
Ice Cider producers 130
Lake Superior fishermen 130
Newfoundland organic producers 130
Niagara Wine producers 130
Nova Scotia and Ontario Maple Syrup producers 131
Nova Scotia Wild Blueberry gatherers 131
Ontario farmers' market producers 131
Ontario producers and consumers..........................132
Ontario small-scale brewers 132
Ontario small-scale farmers...................................132
Ontario Wild Plant gatherers.................................132
Perth County dairy farmers 133
Red Fife Wheat **227**
Saint-Camille farmers' markets producers 133
Seed conservers 133
South Alberta food producers and restaurateurs 133
Southwest Vancouver fishermen and gatherers 134
Toronto organic producers 134
Vancouver Wild Plant gatherers.............................134
Yukon bakers 134
Yukon farmers' market producers 135
Yukon food tradition promulgators 135

Chile
Biological wine producers......................................135
Blue Egg Hen..**228**
Calbuco Brack-Bordered Oyster **229**
Garlic growers in Chilote..135
Mapuche Black Quinoa growers in Southern Chile......136
Merquén **230**
Mushroom pickers 136
País grape producers 136
Pichilemu Seaweed pickers 136
Pine nut producers 137
Potato growers in Chiloé..137
Producers of Chilean Hazelnuts.............................137
Producers of palustrine blueberries 137
Purén White Strawberry **231**
Robinson Crusoe Island Seafood............................**232**
Seed preservers 138

Colombia
Arhuaca farmers 138
Blueberry pickers Arhuaca farmers 138
Coarse Cane Sugar producers of La Vega 139
Cocoa producers and pig and sheep breeders 139
Fruit and vegetable producers and processors 139
Fruit producers and processors 139
Producers of aromatic herbs 140
Vegetable farmers of Cundinamarca 140
Vegetable farmers of Sabana de Bogotá 140
Zeri Foundation, coffee-producing center 140

Costa Rica
Organic producers of Talamanca 141
Raw milk cheesemakers of Turrialba 141
Sugar cane growers of Jaris de Mora 141
Sugar cane producers of San Ramón 141
Asociación de Cooperativas sin Fronteras 142

Cuba
Agricultural machinery producers 142
Farmers and stock breeders of Santa Barbara-Campo Florido 142
Producers of conserved foods 143
Tropical fruit farmers 143
Urban farmers 143
Proyecto Comunitario de Conservación de Alimentos 143

Dominican Republic
Coffee producers from the upper basin of the Yuna river 144
Jamao Coffee producers 144
Sierra Cafetalera Coffee **233**

Ecuador
Andean vegetable and cereal farmers 144
Cacao nacional **234**
Cereal farmers of Chimborazo 144
Cocoa producers of Nord Esmeraldas 145
Coffee producers of the South 145
Indigenous farmers of Cotacachi 145
Producers of aromatic herbs 145
Producers of honey and derived products 146
Producers of Salinas 146

Quinoa farmers of Chimborazo 146
Quinoa farmers of San Nicolas de Ichubamba 146

El Salvador
Producers of dehydrated fruit 147
Producers of cashew nuts 147
Producers of coarse cane sugar 147
Producers of honey 147

Guatemala
Growers and processors of medicinal plants 148
Huehuetenango Highland Coffee **235**
Ixcán Cardamon **236**
Pacaya and pepper growers 148
Southwest Honey Producers 148

Haiti
Northern cocoa producers 149

Honduras
Farmers, fishers and artisans of La Ceiba 149

Jamaica
Growers of organic products 150
Rastafarian producers of Ital Food 150

Mexico
Agave and Mescal producers of Chilapa de Álvarez 150
Agave Honey and Jam producers 150
Aires de Campo 159
Avocado growers 151
Bionexos 159
Bioplaneta 159
Chaya growers 151
Chili Pepper cultivators 151
Chinantla Vanilla **237**
Coffee and chocolate producers of San Rafael Toltepec 151
Coffee producers of Huatusco 152
Desiccated locust producers 152
Ecological food producers of Xonacatlán 152
Farmers and fishermen of Escuinapa 152
Flor de Jamaica producers 153

Fundación para la Productividad en el Campo 160
Fundación Renacimiento...160
Herbs, spices and passion fruit growers.....................................153
Honey producers 153
Maíz azul producers 153
Mescal producers of Teúl de González Ortega 154
Mescal producers of Tlacolula...154
Milk producers of Chiapas 155
Mushroom growers of Zitácuaro 155
Natural animal-based coloring producers 155
Organic cocoa and chocolate producers 156
Organic coffee producers 156
Organic food producers of Tlayacapan.......................................156
Organic fruit promoters 156
Peanut growers and processors 157
Pez Blanco fishermen 157
Prickly Pear cultivators and processors......................................157
Prickly Pear growers of Tlaxco...157
Red Lobster fishermen 158
Rice and zucchini cultivators 158
Salt producers 158
Sheep's cheese makers 158
Tehuacán Amaranth **238**
Traditional mescal producers of Durango....................................159

Nicaragua
Banana growers of Altagracia 160
Coffee growers of Estelí 160
Producers of cocoa and chocolate..161
Producers of honey 161

Panama
Cocoa producers of Bocas del Toro 161

Paraguay
Producers of cane sugar 162
Producers of herbs and infusions 162

Peru
Andean Kañihua **239**
Andean Sweet Potatoes **240**
Bean farmers of Chiclayo 162

Camu-camu growers of Ucayali..162
Chuin Flour and Starch producers of Yanallpa 163
Corn growers 163
Growers of medicinal plants 163
Mashua producers of Tuti 163
Organic vegetable farmers 164
Producers of citrus fruits 164
Producers of organic cocoa 164
Producers of special organic coffee 165
San Marcos Andean fruit **241**
Traditional Chuño Blanco **242**
Yaku tayta fishers and fish processors 165

United States of America
Alaskan Wild Salmon Fishermen 166
American Raw Milk Cheeses..**246**
Anishinaabeg Manoomin **243**
Arizona Seedsavers and Growers...166
Aroostook County Wheat Growers..166
Artisan Cheesemakers from the Uplands
of Southwestern Wisconsin 167
Asheville Producers...167
Austin Farmers 167
Berkshire and Taconic Region Biodynamic Farmers 168
Big Sandy Grain and Field Crop Producers.................................168
Bolinas Farmers 168
Boulder Farmers 169
Brentwood Organic Fruit Growers 169
Bristol Bay Wild Salmon Fishermen..169
Brooklyn Seedsavers and Gardeners 170
Brooklyn Urban Farmers 170
Burlington Farmers 170
California Ethnic Minority Farmers 170
Californian Artisan Bread Bakers 171
Camarillo Organic Farmers 171
Capay Valley Farmers and Ranchers 171
Cape Cod Hook Fishermen 172
Cape May Oyster **244**
Cascades Farmers' Market Producers 172
Catskills Region Agriculture Promoters.......................................172
Central Appalachian Farmers' Market Organic Farmers 173
Central Coast Heritage Poultry Producers 173

Central Indiana Organic Farmers 173
Central New Jersey Ice Cream Makers
and Vegetable Growers..173
Central Valley Peach and Raisin Growers 174
Chattanooga Breeders..174
Chattanooga Cooperative Farmers...174
Chattanooga Organic Bread Bakers 174
Chicago Green City Farmers' Market Producers 175
Chicago Producers 175
Community Supported Agriculture 209
Cornwall Hollow Breeders 175
Corona Ranchers 175
Creswell Farmers 176
Cromwell Vegetable Growers 176
Cuyahoga County Farmers 176
Dalton Small Grain and Row Crop Growers 176
Davenport Organic Berry Growers 177
Dungeness and Calallam County Organic Farmers 177
East Meredith Pig and Turkey Farmers...178
Eastern Colorado Plains Lamb Breeders..178
Esparto Vine Growers and Wine Makers 178
Farmers' Markets 190
Florida Panhandle Farmers 178
Food Justice 212
Fourth Corner Farmers' Market Producers 179
Georgia Family Farmers 179
Gulf of Mexico Seafood Harvesters 179
Gulf South Blueberry Growers 179
Hancock Educators..180
Healdsburg Farmers' Market Producers 180
Herscher Poultry Farmers 180
Homestead Tropical Fruit Growers 180
Honey Producers 181
Hudson Valley Agricultural Educators 181
Illinois Artisan Cheesemakers 181
Indiana Uplands Farmers 181
International Food Producers in National Parks 182
Iowa City Farmers..182
Jacksonville Farmers 182
Kalona Organic Sprout Growers...182
Lebanon Heirloom Apple Growers and Cider Producers..............183
Little Rock Agricultural Educators 183

Los Angeles Educators 183
Louisiana Farmers, Shrimpers, and Restaurateurs........................183
Madera Growers, Bakers, and Wine Grape Growers 184
Madison Educators...184
Maine Chocolatiers...184
Maine Organic Potato Farmers 184
Maine Organic Producers 185
Marin and Sonoma County Olive Oil Producers...........................185
Marin County Grassfed Livestock Ranchers 185
Marin County Producers 185
Marin County Vegetable Growers 186
Marin County Wine Grape Growers...186
Marshall Organic Dairy Farmers 186
Martha's Vineyard Aquaculturists 187
Maui Pineapple Growers..187
Mayan Corn Growers 187
Miami Student Farmers 187
Michigan Cider Makers..188
Michigan Specialty Grain Growers and Processors 188
Mississippi Cooperative Farmers 188
Morrilton Livestock Breeders..189
Napa Valley Farmers and Producers 189
Native North American Indigenous Delegation 212
Native Plants and Medicinal Herbs Gatherers 189
Navajo-Churro Sheep...**245**
New Britain Organic Farmers 189
New Florence Lamb Breeders 190
New Hampshire Farmers 190
New Mexican Benedictine Brewers 190
New Mexican Greenthread Growers and Gatherers 191
New Orleans Urban Gardeners 191
New Prague Organic Cattle and Dairy Farmers 192
New York City Greenmarket Farmers 192
New York City Organic Producers 192
North Carolina Piedmont Triad Food Producers 192
North San Juan Fruit Growers 193
Northern California Aromatic, Culinary
and Healing Herbs Growers 193
Norwich Dairy Farmers...193
O'ahu Food Producers 193
Ojai Valley Pixie Growers 194
Oregon and California Biodynamic Growers 194

Pescadero Goat Dairy Farmers.....................................194
Petaluma Geese and Pekin Duck Breeders 194
Philadelphia Growers 195
Pittsboro Educators...195
Pittsburgh Educators...195
Point Reyes Seashore Oyster Harvesters 195
Potter Valley Ranchers...196
Purcellville Livestock Breeders and Farmers 196
Redland Tropical Fruit Growers 196
Renewing American Food Traditions 212
Rhode Island Dairy Farmers 196
Russian River Wine Grape Growers 197
Sabinal Farmers and Ranchers...................................197
Saint Louis Brewers 197
Saint Paul Farmer's Market Lamb
and Sheep Breeders 197
San Diego Organic Farmers 198
San Diego Organic Tangelo Growers 198
San Francisco Brewers...198
San Francisco Educators 198
San Francisco National Parks Producers 199
San Francisco Organic Fruit Growers 199
Santa Cruz River Producers 199
Santa Fe Educators 199
Santa Fe Farmers' Market Producers 200
Santa Rosa Livestock Breeders and Vegetable Growers..........200
Sausalito Cooks and Fishermen..................................200
Shepherdstown Fruit Growers 200
Shushan Pig Breeders 201
Socorro Organic Poultry Producers 201
Sonoma County Brewers..201
Sonoma County Gravenstein Apple.............................**247**
Sonoma County Poultry Breeders 202
South Atlantic Farmers' Market Producers 202
South Florida Organic Farmers 202
South Londonderry Organic Vegetable
and Herb Growers 203
Southern High Plains Grassfed Livestock Breeders 202
Standing Rock Reservation Bison Ranchers 203
Tallahassee Region Farmers and Heirloom Seed Savers 203
Tea Purveyors...204
Tomato Seed Savers and Growers 204

Triangle Farmers' Market Producers............................204
Upper Columbia Poultry Breeders...............................204
Upper Connecticut River Valley Meat Producers 205
Vacaville Breeders...205
Vermont Bread Bakers 205
Vermont Farmers and Consumers...............................205
Vermont Maple Syrup Producers.................................206
Vermont Organic Producers..206
Vermont Wild Food Gatherers....................................206
Vernon Artisan Bakers and Cheesemakers 206
Virgin Islands Farmers...207
Waiahole Taro Growers..207
Waipi'o Valley Piko Poi Producers 207
Waltham Organic Farmers..208
Washington Chinook Fishermen 208
Waxhaw Organic Farmers..208
West Chester Herb Gatherers and Honey Producers......................209
West Concord Breeders...209
Westchester County Farmers, Chefs, and Educators 208
Wheatland Farmers 209
Willamette Valley lamb Breeders.................................210
Willamette Valley Wine Grape Growers 210
Wind River Indian Reservation Farmers and Ranchers 210
Windsor Fruit Growers...211
Winters Organic Walnut and Vegetable Growers 211
Wrightstown Organic Farmers 211
Yukon River Salmon Fishermen 211

Uruguay
Fishermen and processors of the Laguna de Rocha 213
Ñandú farmers..213
Producers of Colonia Valdense 213
Producers of goat's cheese 214
Vegetable and legume growers...................................214
Wine producers of San Juan 214

Venezuela
Artisanal producers of Cocuy 215
Casabe Galleta producers 215
Chocolate producers of San José de Barlovento..........................215
Preserve producers of Monte Carmelo 215
Barlovento Cacao..**248**

ASIA 249

Afghanistan
Jalalabad Olive Oil producers 250
Pistachio producers of Badghis 250
Raisin producers of Herat 250

Armenia
Ararat Valley fruit growers 251
Ararat Valley seed and vegetable producers 251
Breeders and fruit growers of Aragatsotn 251
Honey producers of central Armenia..................251
Lake Sevan fishermen 252
Local wheat producers 252
Motal **303**
Southern Armenia winegrowers 252

Azerbaijan
Indigenous sheep breeders 253
Ismailli beekeepers...253
Mazoni (fermented milk) producers 253
Sis village fruit growers.....................................253

Bangladesh
Barisal producers 254
Magura producers 254

Bhutan
Paro Red Rice producers 254

Cambodia
Takeo organic rice producers............................255

China
Organic beekeepers of the northeast.................255
Tibetan Plateau Yak Cheese **304**

Georgia
Abkhazia Tea producers 256
Aromatic Herb growers.....................................256
Cheese producers of the Tush ethnic group 256
Imereti beekeepers...256

Imereti wine growers 257
Kakheti wine growers 257
Kartli fruit growers 257
Khoni honey producers....................................257
Racha Ham producers 258
Samtskhe-Javakheti Wheat producers 258
Tbilisi organic producers..................................258
Wild Fruit and Herb gatherers..........................258

India
Amaranth growers of Agastyamuni 259
Bamboo producers of Sikkim 259
Banda Wheat growers 259
Barley growers of Ladakh 260
Bundelkhand producers of seeds for oil 260
Chitrakoot breeders 260
Coconut and Spice producers 260
Cumin and Fennel seed growers of Rajasthan Beawar 261
Dehra Dun Basmati Rice..................................**305**
Himachal Pradesh growers of local Walnut varieties 261
Karnataka Coffee growers 261
Karnataka Spice producers 261
Kashmir Saffron producers, ...262
Kotagiri Honey producers................................262
Legume growers of Uttar Pradesh 262
Mango growers of the pre-Himalayan areas 262
Medicinal herb and vegetable growers 263
Millet and Buckwheat growers of Kotdwara 263
Mumbai ready-to-eat food distributors 263
Orissa Mustard Oil Pickles **306**
Orissa rice and vegetable producers 263
Rajma growers of Uttaranchal...........................264
Sugar cane growers and processors 264
Turmeric producers of Erode 264
Varanasi producers of dairy products and sweets..........265
Wild Fruit gatherers of Chitrakoot 265

Indonesia
Aceh Coffee producers 265
Martabak producers of Java 265
Rice and Sweet Potato growers of Bali 266
Shrimp raisers of Java Island...........................266
Tempeh producers of Yogyakarta 266

728

Iran
Garmsar Cereal growers 267
Khorasan Spice producers...267
Nomadic shepherds of Fars...267

Israel
Goat's Milk Cheese producers of Mount Eitan 268
Olive Oil producers of Galilee 268
Traditional producers of Ela Valley 268

Japan
Aguni Island Sea Salt producers 269
Aigamo method Rice producers 269
Amarume Leek producers 269
Ancient Rice variety growers 270
Chikuma Apricot growers 270
Daikon growers of Akka 270
Daikon growers of Miura 271
Dried Persimmon producers 271
Hatahata fishermen and sauce producers 271
Hokkaido Maize growers 272
Japanese organic tea producers...272
Kobutakana producers of Unzen 272
Organic growers and breeders of Ayacho 272
Organic growers of Saitama 273
Organic growers of Uzumasa...273
Sakè Rice producers 273
Salted Anchovy producers of the Gulf
of Tachibana 274
Smoked Goby producers of the Gulf of Nagatsura 274
Tankaku cattle breeders 274
Unzen seed savers 275
Yuko growers 275

Jordan
Spice producers of Deir Alla 276

Kazakhstan
Kazakh nomadic breeders..276
Northern Kazakhstan producers 276
Uralsk producers 277

Kirghizia
Chon-Alaj yak breeders 277
Gulcho beekeepers 278
Issyk-Kul fishermen..278
Kirghis indigenous sheep breeders 278
Producers of Fermented Kumys...279
Talas Bean producers 279
Usgen Rice producers 280
Wild fruit and herb gatherers 280

Korea
Producers and processors of food for school cafeterias 280
Producers and processors of local cabbages
and radishes...281
Sea Salt producers 281

Laos
Bolaven Coffee producers...281
Paksong Tea producers 281
Vientiane organic growers 282

Lebanon
Beekeepers of Jdeideh 282
Chanklich Cheese producers 282
Chlifa growers 283
Darfiyeh **307**
Farmers' market of Beirut 283
Female producers of Mouneh 283
Female producers of Serdeleh...283
Fruit growers of Kab Elias 284
Herb gatherers of Adonis Valley 284
Kechel el Fouqara Cheese...**308**
Mouneh producers 284
Mount Kesrouan producers...285
Organic food producers 285
Organic food producers and distributors 285
Organic food producers of Beirut 285
Pine Nut producers of Rachaya el Wadi 286
Pine Nut producers of Rmeileh 286
Small-scale fishermen of Batroun 286
Traditional Bread producers 286

Malaysia
Bario Rice 309
Kampung fruit producers 287
Rimbàs Black Pepper 310
Selangor vegetable growers 287

Mongolia
Nomadic shepherds 287

Nepal
Chitwan producers 288
Gorkha district producers 288
Lalitpur Dafne Paper producers...............288
Madhuvan producers 288

Pakistan
Kinnow producers 289
Punjab Rice growers 289

Palestine
Bayta Olive Oil producers 289
Jenin Almond growers 289
Jericho Date producers 290
Jericho traditional food producers...........290
Tubas shepherds and Cheese producers...290
Land Research Center 290

Philippines
Balangon Banana and Sugar producers
of Negros Island......................................291
Oton Banana Chips and Sugar producers...291
Pangasinan producers 291
Rice and Cashew producers of Palawan....291
Small-scale fishermen 292

Sri Lanka
Coconut producers of the South 292
Negombo Spice producers 292
Pelmadulla Tea producers 293

Syria
Tadef dairy producers 293

Taiwan
Yuen Foong Yu Biotech organic producers 294

Tajikistan
Badakhshan fruit growers 294
Ishkashim Black Pea producers 294
Khorog Mulberry growers 295
Langar Wheat growers 295
Murgab breeders and dairy producers 296
Rasht Valley fruit growers 296

Thailand
Hin Lad Nai farmers................................297
Muk Island fishermen..............................297
Nan fruit growers 297
Ranong-Chumporn tropical fruit growers....297
Srisaket organic rice producers 298
Suphanburi White and Red Jasmine Rice...298
Yasothon organic rice producers 298

Turkmenistan
Wheat producers 299

Uzbekistan
Chimgan nomadic breeders 299
Khalva producers of Yangikishlok 299
Khashtak producers of Brichmulla 300
Khumsan Cheese producers 300
Producers of Karluk Melon Sweets 301
Sesame oil producers 301
Sheep breeders and dairy producers 301
Western Tian Shan wine growers..............301

Viet Nam
Chicken breeders of Hoa Binh..................302
Green Tea producers of Di Nau and Son Thuy ...302
Organic Rice producers of Hai Phong 302

EUROPE **311**

Albania
Dukati Black Goat breeders......................312
Elbasan Olive Oil producers 312

Iljare and Sukes grape-growers 312
Lepushe Food producers...........................312
Novosele Olive Oil producers 313
Përmet Food producers 313
Zadrima beekeepers 313

Austria
Bread bakers of Sarleinsbach 314
Cheese makers of the Salzburg region 314
Farmers of Lungau 314
Seed preservation and distribution specialists 314
Vineyard garlic cultivators........................315

Belgium
Producers of traditional Liegi Syrup 315
Promoters of typical products 315
Small-scale brewers of Flanders 316

Belorus
Central Belorus beekeepers.......................316
Kobrin Food producers............................317
Minsk Food producers 317
Producers of local varieties
of fruit and vegetables 317
Producers of traditional foodstuffs 317
Rosson Wild Fruits and Infusions **454**

Bosnia and Herzegovina
Bihac beekeepers 318
Growers of the Poljak Bean from Trebinje 318
Laksevine Fruit growers...........................319
Livno Cheese producers 319
Pozegaca Plum Slatko.............................**455**
Raspberry growers and processors 319
Sack Cheese (Sir iz Mijeha).......................**456**
Travnik Cheese producers 319

Bulgaria
Elena Ham producers 320
Haskovo cheese-makers 320
Karakachan nomadic breeders 320
Rhodope Mountains Bean producers..............320

Rhodope Mountains Tahan
(sesame cream) producers 321
Rose Jam producers 321
Smilyan dairy farmers 321
Troyan beekeepers 322
Troyan Rakya producers 322
Yogurt producers 322

Croatia
Crowns of Diocletian producers...................323
Giant Istrian Ox **457**
Isle of Unije food producers 323
Ljubitovica Garlic producers 324
Momjan Muscat producers 324
Producers of Extra-Virgin Olive Oil
from the Bianchera Istriana olive 324
Slavonia Kulin producers 325
Small-scale fishermen from Istria 325
Wild Berry fruit processors 325

Cyprus
Tsamarella **458**

Czech Republic
Boretice grape-growers and winemakers 326
Breeders and crop farmers 326
Chrámce fruit producers 326
Jablonec nad Nisou bread makers.................327
Kutná Hora wine producers 327
Prague organic producers 327

Denmark
Cider makers of Fejø.............................328
Food producers of Bornholm 328
Food producers of Greenland 328
Food producers of the island of Fyn 329
Fruit growers of Lilleø...........................329
Organic produce distributors of Barrit 329

Estonia
Dried and Smoked Flounder Producers 330

Finland
Bakers and food cultivators of Ekenäs and Nagu 330
Bakers of Parainen 331
Beekeepers of Pirkanmaa 331
Fishermen of the Åland archipelago 331
Food producers and distributors of Åland 332
Sausage and Salami producers of Turku.............................332
Snail farmers of Lumijoki 332

France
Bareges-Gavarnie Sheep **459**
Basque Pig breeders and processors 333
Béarn Cattle breeders 333
Bigorre Black Pig **460**
Bleu de Queyras producers 334
Breeders of Hardy Cattle from the Catalan Pyrénées 334
Breton Pie Noir Cattle breeders 334
Brittany seaweed gatherers and processors 335
Châteauneuf-du-Pape producers 335
Chemin Faisant 341
Espelette Chili Pepper producers 335
Forain Pink Garlic producers from the Tarn 336
Growers of grapes using animal traction 336
Haute Provence Einkorn **461**
Haut-Languedoc food producers, breeders and restaurateurs........336
Jurançon White Wine producers 337
Loire basin fishermen 337
Maine Anjou Cattle breeders 337
Mercantour Massif Cheese producers 338
Mercantour Olive growers..338
Pardailhan Black Turnip **462**
Pays Basque food producers 338
Pays de Thau Oyster breeders 338
Pélardon Sec **463**
Producers of the Sweet Basque Chili Pepper 339
Provençal Goat breeders and producers of Banon Cheese 339
Provence vegetable producers and consumers 339
Pyrenean Goat breeders 340
Rennes Coucou Chicken **464**
Roussillon Rancio Sec **465**
Saint-Flour Planèze Golden Lentil **466**
Seed producers..340

Tanche Olive Oil producers 340
Transhumance shepherds from Les Trois Vallées Béarnaises 341
Trébons Sweet Onion producers 341

Germany
Ahle Wurscht producers of Northern Assia 342
Animal breeders and dairy farmers of Langenburg 342
Bakers of Nordrhein-Westfalen 342
Beekeepers of Baden-Württemberg 343
Beekeepers of Nordrhein-Westfalen 343
Breeders of the Colored Pigs of Bentheim 343
Cattle farmers of Limpurg...344
Franconia Goat breeders 344
Goat breeders and cheese makers of Irmelshausen 344
Milbenkäse producers..344
Peat bog Sheep breeders of Diepholz 345
Potato growers of Svevia 345
Promoters of the regional produce of Oberes Werntal 345
Snail farmers of the Swabian Alb 346
Spelt farmers of Franconia 346

Greece
Aspra Spitia food producers and processors........................346
Ios Caper producers 346
Kavala Asparagus growers..347
Kos grape growers 347
Kythera beekeepers 347
Ladotyri Cheese producers 347
Lakonia Siglino producers 348
Local variety & breed conservers 348
Messolongi Gray Mullet Roe producers 348
Monopigado food producers and processors 349
Samos Olive and Grape growers 349
Tinos Pasta producers 349
Zakynthos dairymen 349
Mavrotragano Wine **467**
Mediterranean Association for Soil Health.........................350
Niotiko Cheese..**468**
Oiko Bio..350

Hungary
Baranya cheeses and traditional food producers 350
Breeders of indigenous Poultry breeds 350

Breeders of the indigenous Gray Cattle breed 351
Mangalica sausage **469**
Organic cereal producers 351
Organic producers in the Jászság region 351
Organic vegetable producers...351
Penyige Plum Compote producers...352
Szeged Paprika producers 352
Tokaj-Hegyalja winegrowers 352
Traditional food producers 352

Iceland
Breeders of Icelandic Goats and Sheeps 353

Ireland
Animal breeders and dairy farmers of North Kerry 353
Bellingham Blue cheese makers 353
Cheese makers of West Cork..354
Dairy farmers of Wicklow and Kilkenny......................................354
Food producers and educators of County Clare 354
Food producers of County Tipperary...355
Irish Raw Milk Cheese **470**
Organic farmers and growers of the West of Ireland 355
Organic farmers of Rossinver 355
Organic food producers of County Leitrim...................................356
Organic food producers of the Northwest 356
Seed savers 356
Sustainable food producers and consumers of Dublin 356
Sustainable food promoters of County Clare 357
Sustainable food promoters of Cloughjordan...............................357

Italy
Acquaviva Red Onion...**471**
Albenga Violet Asparagus..**472**
Alpago Lamb...**473**
Amalfi Sfusato Lemon **474**
Andarinos producers of Usini 357
Ansonica wine producers of the Isola del Giglio.........................357
Aole and carp fishers of Lake Garda 358
Artichoke growers of Chiusure 358
Artichoke growers of Perinaldo 358
Artisan brewers 358
Artisan Cupeta producers of Montepaone 359

Asparagus growers of Cilavegna 359
Aurina Valley Graukäse...**475**
Badalucco, Conio and Pigna Beans **476**
Bagnolese Pecorino **477**
Bagolino Bagòss...**478**
Bakers of Lentini...359
Banale Ciuiga...**479**
Basilicata Podolico Caciocavallo **480**
Bazzone Prosciutto **481**
Bean and vegetable growers of Pignone 360
Bean growers of Lucchesia 360
Bean growers of Paganica 360
Beekeepers of eastern Sicily 360
Beekeepers of Gran Sasso and Monti della Laga 361
Biancoperla Corn **482**
Biodynamic wine producers of eastern Sicily 361
Biscuit producers of Venafro 361
Bitto of the Bitto Valleys...**483**
Black Cherry Wine **484**
Botìro producers of Primiero 362
Bread bakers of Genzano 362
Breeders and cheese-makers of the Valnerina 362
Breeders and producers of Montefeltro..362
Breeders of black Calabrian Pigs 363
Breeders of calvana cattle 363
Breeders of cornella bianca sheep...363
Breeders of grigio alpina cattle 363
Breeders of pezzata rossa of Oropa 364
Breeders of varzese cow 364
Brigasca Sheep Toma **485**
Bronte Pistachio...**486**
Caciofiore of the Roman Countryside **487**
Campotosto Mortadella..**488**
Cannara Onion **489**
Caprauna Turnip **490**
Carmagnola Grey Rabbit **491**
Carmagnola Ox-Horn Pepper **492**
Carmignano Dried Fig **493**
Carpino Broad Beans **494**
Casentino Prosciutto..**495**
Casizolu...**496**
Casola Marocca **497**

Castel del Monte Canestrato................................498
Castellammare Violet Artichoke 499
Castelvetrano Black Bread 500
Certaldo Onion 501
Cervia Artisan Sea Salt 502
Cetara Anchovy Traditional Extract 503
Cheese and olive producers of the land between the two lakes 364
Cheese and salami makers of the Mugello................365
Cheese producers of the Alto Salento 365
Cheese producers of the Carso Triestino 365
Cheese producers of the Mugello and the Val di Sieve................365
Cheese producers of the Valle Elvo and the Serra 366
Chefs of Volterra detention center......................366
Chestnut flour producers of Pratomagno................366
Chestnut flour producers of the Garfagnana 367
Chestnut producers of Combai 367
Chestnut producers of the Valcamonica................367
Ciaculli Late Winter Mandarin 504
Cilento Goat Cacioricotta..................................505
Cinque Terre Sciacchetrà...................................506
Cinta senese pig breeders 367
Classic Bologna Mortadella................................507
Classic Chianina Ox 508
Classic Genoese Focaccia 509
Classic Robiola di Roccaverano..........................510
Coazze Cevrin 511
Cocomerina Pear 512
Coggiola Paletta 513
Colonnata Lard 514
Comacchio Valley Lagoons Traditional Pickled Eel 515
Conca Casale Signora 516
Conciato Romano 517
Corno alle Scale Char 518
Cosenza Dottato Fig 519
Custodian Farmers of ancient farming practices
of Vallo di Diano 368
Custodian Farmers of old varieties and local breeds
of Forlì-Cesena 368
Delia Cuddrireddra 520
Dried Calizzano and Murialdo Chestnuts................521
Fabriano Salami 522
Farindola Pecorino 523

Farmers and breeders of San Miniato 368
Farmers of Gran Sasso and Monti della Laga 368
Farro and mulberry growers of the Brescia plain 369
Farro growers of the Garfagnana........................369
Fatulì producers of the Val Saviore 369
Favignana Bottarga 524
Ferrandina Baked Olive 525
Fiore Sardo Shepherds' Cheese 526
Fishermen of Capo Teulada................................370
Fishermen of Lake Trasimeno 370
Fishermen of the Straits of Messina....................370
Fishermen of Tortolì 371
Florentine tripe producers................................371
Formadi Frant 527
Fruit producers of Mount Etna 371
Garbagna Bella Cherry 528
Garfagnana Biroldo 529
Garfagnana Potato Bread 530
Gargano Citrus Fruits 531
Gargano Goat..532
Gargano Podolica Cow 533
Gargano Podolico Caciocavallo 534
Gavi Testa in Cassetta......................................535
Gioi Soppressata 536
Girgentana Goat..537
Goose in Onto 538
Goym Cuisine of the Tufa Towns........................539
Grano solina growers of the Abruzzo mountains 372
Grappa Morlacco Cheese and Burlina Cow 540
Greek breeders and pork butchers of Calabria........372
Gressoney Toma..541
Growers of cappello del prete pumpkins 372
Growers of Controne beans................................372
Growers of durum wheat and bakers of Oristano........373
Growers of Lamon beans and agordino barley 373
Growers of marano maize..................................374
Growers of old maize varieties of Piemonte..........374
Growers of pericina pears 374
Growers of piccolo farro 375
Growers of red Cetica potatoes 375
Grumolo delle Abbadesse Rice 542
Heritage Canale Peach Varieties 543

Heritage Piedmontese Apple Varieties 544
High Mountain Agordo Cheese 545
High Mountain Honeys 546
Interdonato Lemon 547
Ischia Cave Rabbit 548
Lady chefs of popular festivals 375
Lake Trasimeno Bean 549
Langa Sheep Tuma 550
Late Harvest Leonforte Peach 551
Leonforte Broad Bean 552
Lodi Pannerone 553
Lonzino di Fico 554
Macagn 555
Madonie Manna 556
Madonie Provola 557
Magghia Masculina 558
Maiorchino Cheese 559
Maize flour producers of Storo 376
Maize growers of Vanoi-Primiero 376
Malga dairymen and shepherds of the Lagorai mountains...376
Malga Monte Veronese 560
Mallegato 561
Mantuan Peasant Casalin Salami 562
Marceddì Arselle 563
Maremmana Ox 564
Mariola 565
Martina Franca Capocollo 566
Marzolina 567
Matera Mountain Pezzente 568
Medicinal herb growers of the parks of Sicily 376
Menaica Anchovies 569
Minuta Olive 570
Modicana Cow 571
Moena Puzzone 572
Moleche 573
Moliterno Casieddu 574
Mondovì Corn Meal Biscuits 575
Monreale White Plums 576
Montébore 577
Monte Poro Pecorino 578
Monterosso Anchovies 579
Monte San Biagio Sausage 580

Monti Sibillini Pecorino 581
Monti Sibillini Pink Apple 582
Mora Romagnola Pig 583
Morozzo Capon 584
Moscato of Siracusa producers 377
Mostarda of Mantua producers 377
Mountain Castelmagno 585
Mozzarella in Myrtle 586
Mussel-farmers of La Spezia 377
Nassa Shrimp 587
Neapolitan Papaccella 588
Neapolitan vegetable growers 377
Nebrodi Black Pig 589
Nebrodi Provola 590
Nizza Monferrato Hunchback Cardoon 591
Noli Anchovies (Cicciarelli) 592
Nomadic shepherds of Piemonte 378
Non Valley Mortandela 593
Noto Almond 594
Nùbia Red Garlic 595
Olive farmers of the province of Pescara 378
Olive farmers of Umbria 378
Onano Lentil 596
Orbetello Bottarga 597
Organic fruit of Lessinia producers 379
Organic growers of the Abbazia di Monteveglio 379
Organic producers and fishermen of the Riserva di Torre Guaceto 379
Organic producers and transformers of Foresto 379
Organic producers of the Agro Romano 380
Osilo Pecorino 598
Ottofile maize growers of Antignano 380
Ozieri Copuleta 599
Paceco Cartucciaro Melon 600
Paduan Hen 601
Pasta producers of Gragnano 380
Pecorino producers of the Casentino 380
Pestàt 602
Piedmontese Blonde Hen and Saluzzo White Hen 603
Piedmontese Ox 604
Piennolo Small Tomato 605
Pietraroja Prosciutto 606
Pistoia Mountain Pecorino 607

Pitina..608
Poirino Tench...609
Polizzi Badda Bean..610
Pompìa...611
Portonovo Wild Mussel 612
Prato Mortadella 613
Producers and breeders of Migliarino San Rossore
Massaciuccoli 381
Producers of barena honey from the Venetian lagoon 381
Producers of Bose Monastery 381
Producers of Grecìa Salentina 381
Producers of piantone di Falerone olives 382
Producers of the Agro Nolano below Vesuvius................382
Producers of the Crete Senesi 382
Producers of the Val di Non 382
Producers of the Val Martello 383
Producers of Torchiato di Fregona wine 383
Producers on land confiscated from the Mafia...............383
Provolone del Monaco...614
Purceddu d'Alcamo Melon.....................................615
Radìc di Mont 616
Ragusano Cheese 617
Ragusano Donkey 618
Red garlic growers of Sulmona 383
Red Reggiana Cow 619
Red sausage producers of Castelpoto 384
Regina di Londa Peach..620
Resia Garlic 621
Ribera Strawberry 622
Rice-farmers, vegetable growers and transformers
of the Lomellina...384
Roero madernassa pear producers 384
Romagnola Cow 623
Rose Syrup..624
Rotonda Red Eggplant 625
Roveja 626
Roventino producers of Scandicci 385
Saffron growers of Cascia 385
Salama da Sugo 627
Salina Caper 628
Sambucano Lamb 629
San Gavino Monreale Saffron 630

San Marzano Tomato 631
San Patrignano producers 385
Sant'Erasmo Purple Artichoke................................632
Santo Stefano di Sessanio Lentil 633
Saracena Moscato 634
Saras del Fen 635
Sardinian Modicana Cow 636
Savona Chinotto 637
Sea snail fishermen of Francavilla al Mare 385
Serra de' Conti Cicerchia 638
Sette Comuni Plateau Malga Stravecchio 639
Sheep and goat breeders of the Valle d'Aosta 386
Shepherds and cheese-makers of the Alto Volterrano....386
Shepherds of the Abruzzo Appenines 386
Siddi pasta makers 386
Sorana Bean 640
Spalla Cruda 641
Strawberry growers of Maletto 387
Tenera Ascoli Olive 642
Terra/Terra market 387
Toritto Almond 643
Tortona Strawberry 644
Tortona Valley Salami 645
Tosco-Romagnolo Apennine Raviggiolo 646
Traditional Altamura Bread....................................647
Traditional Florentine Schiacciata producers 387
Traditional vegetable growers of Chioggia 387
Traditional vegetable growers of Mount Etna 388
Trapani Artisan Sea Salt 648
Trentino Lucanica..649
Turchesa potato growers of Gran Sasso and Monti della Laga 388
Tuscan Sea Palamita 650
Typical foods of Troina producers 388
Ur-Paarl 651
Ustica Lentil..652
Valchiavenna Goat Violino 653
Valdarno Hen 654
Valdarno Tarese 655
Val d'Ossola Mortadella 656
Valle Bagnario di Strevi Moscato Passito 657
Valli Valdesi Mustardela 658
Valtellina Buckwheat 659

Vastedda del Belìce 660
Vastese Ventricina 661
Vegetable growers of the Eremo dei Camaldolesi of Nola 388
Vegetable growers of the Giudecca detention center 389
Vessalico Garlic 662
Vezzena 663
Vine growers and producers of the Langa 389
Vine growers of the Pollino...............................389
Vino Santo Trentino 664
Walnut growers of Bleggio 389
White Modena Cow..665
White Pertosa Artichoke 666
Wild fruit gatherers of the Alto Tevere...................390
Wine producers of the Valle d'Aosta mountains...........390
Women's traditional food market 390
Young farmers of the Alto Savio 390
Zeri Lamb 667
Zibello Culatello...668
Zolfino Bean 669

Latvia
Janu sier producers..391
Rye bread producers 391

Lithuania
Black bread producers 392
Sheep farmers of Radviliskis 392

Macedonia
Vine growers of Tikvesh 393

Malta
Traditional food promoters of the island of Gozo.............393
Wine makers of La Valletta 393

Moldavia
Fruit and vegetable producers...........................394
Indigenous vine growers..................................394
Producers of Teleneflti 394

Montenegro
Ham producers of Tivat 395

Netherlands
Aged Artisan Gouda 670
Boeren-Leidse cheesemakers............................395
Chaam Hen 671
Dutch brewers 395
Edam and Remeker cheesemakers.....................396
Friesian Islands fishermen...............................396
Groningen Goat breeders and cheesemakers 396
Growers of traditional greenhouse
grape varieties 396
Oosterschelde Lobster 672
Sheep breeders from the Drenthe moorlands 397
Texel Sheep Cheese 673
Unpasteurized cheese producers and maturers 397
Unpasteurized cheesemakers............................397
Vechtdal food producers.................................397

Norway
Artesan Sognefjord Geitost 674
Bakers of spelt bread 398
Cider makers of Hardanger...............................398
Dried salt-cured cod producers of Kristiansund 398
Farmers and animal breeders of Lom 398
Mussel fishermen of the Hardanger Fiord 399
Producers of organic jams and fruit juices 399
Pultost producers of Hedmark and Oppland 399
Ringerik Potato growers 400
Sørøya Island Stockfish...................................675
Sunnmøre Cured and Smoked Herrings 676
Traditional Norwegian fishermen 400
Villsau Sheep 677

Poland
Apple growers of the Wisla Park 400
Apple-juice producers of Kalisz 400
Carp breeders of Zator 401
Growers and transformers of buck wheat 401
Organic producers of Mazovia 401
Oscypek 678
Polish Mead...679
Pradnicki bakers 401
Producers of Kielbasa lisiecka 402

Producers of wegierka plum jam.................................402
Producers of wizajny cheese 402
Swinia zlotnicka pigs breeders 402

Portugal
Batata doce producers of Aljezur 403
Broa de milho producers of Arcos de Valdevez 403
Mirandesa Sausage **680**
Oyster gatherers of Setúbal..403
Rock-salt producers of the Rio Maior 404
Sea salt producers of Castro Marim 404
Serpa Cheese **681**

Romania
Brânzá de Burduf..**682**
Breeders and cheese producers of Brusturoasa.............404
Cabbage growers and transformers
of Bucovina 404
Organic milk, cheese and bread producers 405
Producers of Vâlcea 405
Saxon Village Preserves **683**

Russia
Airan Producers 406
Bashkirian Honey Producers 406
Beekeepers and collectors in Zabajkalie......................406
Beekeepers in Krasnoznamensk...................................407
Beekeepers in the Urals 407
Biodynamic Producers 407
Bread Producers 408
Breeders of Kabardino-Balkaria....................................408
Butter Producers of Vologda 408
Cheese Producers of Kaliningrad 408
Cheese Producers of Ossetia 409
Cucumber Producers of Suzdal 409
Fishermen in the Gizhiga river.....................................409
Fishermen of Smolensk...409
Geese breeders..410
Goat breeders 410
Gray cow breeders of Altaj 411
Herb Gatherers of Kamchatka 411
Horse breeders..411

Kaliningrad Fishermen 412
Karachaeva sheep farming
in the Cherkessia region 412
Khalva Producers of Karachaevo-Cherkessia...............412
Organic Producers 413
Organic Producers of Kaliningrad 413
Preserves Producers of Kamchatka 413
Preserves Producers of Shoria 414
Producers of Goat's Milk Ricotta 414
Producers of Pine Nut Oil 415
Producers of Pskov 415
Producers of Reindeer Cheese....................................415
Producers of Siberian Pine Nuts 416
Reindeer farmers in the Kola Peninsula 416
Reindeer farmers in the Magadan region 416
Rye Producers of Vologda 417
Salmon Fishermen of Kamchatka 417
Salted Fern Producers 417
Talkan Producers of Tashtagol 418
Tuva sheep farmers..418
Watermelon Producers 419
Yak Cheese Producers of Tuva 419
Germoplasm bank of Saint Petersburg.........................419

Serbia
Backa bread producers 420
Indigenous livestock breeders of Srem 420
Kajmak cheese producers 420
Pozegaca Plum growers of Topola 421
Vojvodina organic producers......................................421

Slovakia
Bryndza producers 421
Organic cereal producers 421
Oscadnica sheep breeders..422

Slovenia
Droze bread producers 422
Goriska Brda wine producers 422
Organic producers of Stiria 423
Velika Planina cheese producers 423
Wild fruit and berry gatherers and processors 423

Spain

Álava pony meat farmers 424
Álava Txakolí producers 424
Alta Anoia cigronet growers 424
Ancient olive-tree farmers.......................424
Aragonese wheat growers and bakers 425
Artzai gazta cheese producers 425
Artzain Mundua 433
Asturias spelt producers 425
Caper growers of Ballobar 426
Casín cheese producers..........................426
Cheese producers of the Sierra de Espadán 426
Cocoa transformers..............................426
Dorondón Monegros 433
Euskal Oiloa chicken farmers....................427
Euskal Txerria Pig...............................**684**
Extensive system farmers, Sierra di Guara Cheese 427
Farmers of Asturian breeds 427
Farmers of Huesca poultry breeds 428
Fishermen of Mar de Lira 428
Galicia seafood gatherers 429
Gallecs farmers.................................429
Ganxet Bean **685**
Garraf vegetable producers 429
Jiloca Saffron **686**
Lágrima de Costa de Gipúzkoa pea farmers 430
Millo corvo growers and transformers...........430
Nomadic shepherds 431
Organic vegetable producers of Ademuz 431
Pink Álava bean producers 431
Producers of carranzana sheep's cheese 432
Sea salt producers of Añana 432
Sitges Malvasia **687**
Tolosa Black Bean **688**
Traditional preserve producers
of Muro de Alcoy...............................432
Vine and olive farmers of Urgell 433
Zalla purple onion growers......................433

Sweden

Biological producers 434
Craft producers of upplandskubb 434

Food producers and distributors
on the Stockholm archipelago...................434
Growers of early varieties of cereal crops 434
Halland county producers........................435
Jämtland goat's milk cheese makers 435
Koster Island producers 435
Lake Vänern fishermen...........................435
Linderöd pig breeders 436
Öland Island bean growers.......................436
Promoters of Gävleborg products 436
Promoters of sustainable agriculture
and stock farming...............................436
Promoters of Swedish food products.............437
Reindeer Suovas **689**
Small producers from the Kolmården region 437
Södermanland cereal growers and bakers 437
Sörmland producers 438
Västmanland producers 438
Västra Götaland cheese makers 438

Switzerland

Beer producers and consumers 439
Conservers of traditional apple and pear varieties 439
Locarno Valley Cicitt............................**690**
Maize farmers in the Rhine valley 439
Muggio Valley Zincarlin **691**
Organic producers in the Canton of Ticino 440
Producers in Val Lumnezia 440
Promoters of typical Sankt Gallen products 440
Raw milk Raclette cheese producers 441
Traditional distilled liquor promoters 441

Turkey

Ararat Apricot producers.........................441
Kars Cheese producers 442
Tulum Cheese producers of Tire 442

Ukraine

Buffalo breeders.................................442
Carpathian beekeepers 443
Crimean Wine producers 443
Rakhov Bryndza producers 443

United Kingdom
Aberdeenshire breeders and crop farmers 444
Anglesey Sea Salt producers 444
Artisan cornmillers 444
Artisan Somerset Cheddar **692**
Ayrshire food producers 444
Beer brewers and drinkers 445
Berkshire cereal farmers 445
Berkshire farmers 445
Cambridgeshire beekeepers 446
Cider Apple growers..446
Cornish Pilchard..**693**
Cornwall fishermen 446
Cornwall food producers 447
Cumberland Sausage producers 447
Dumfries and Galloway food producers 447
Fal River Oyster **694**
Farmers' market producers 448
Fishermen and restaurateurs 448
Gloucester Cheese **695**
Guernsey Cow breeders 448
Hand-made Marmalade and Jam producers 449
Herdwick Lamb breeders 449
Highlands and Western Isles food producers 450
Isle of Skye and Lochalsh food producers and distributors 450
Jersey dairy farmers 450
Manx Loaghtan Sheep breeders 451
Northumberland and Scottish Borders pig breeders.......................451
Old Gloucester Beef **696**
Oxfordshire cattle breeders 451
Real Ale brewers and drinkers..452
Sussex fishermen 452
Three Counties Perry **697**
Traditional Scottish food producers 452
Twickenham beekeepers 453
Wales farmers 453

OCEANIA **699**

Australia
Australian Desert Lime producers 700
Australian Rare Breed Meat producers and processos 700

Biodynamic Goat Cheese producers 700
Buninyong farmers' market producers...700
Daintree Edible Rainforest Plant growers 701
Daintree Organic Fruit growers 701
Gulf of Carpentaria fishermen..701
Nannup Sheep Cheese producers 702
Random Valley organic producers...702
Swan and Chittering Valleys food producers 702
Wheatbelt biodynamic Grain and Cereal producers 703
Williams River biodynamic farmers...703
Willunga Almond growers 703

New Zealand
Maori Cereal and Vegetable growers..704
Maori Potato growers 704

Palau
Traditional food producers 704

Alphabetical index

Abaetetuba Açaí and Cupuaçu by-product producers,
Brazil, Americas 110
Aberdeenshire breeders and crop farmers,
United Kingdom, Europe 444
Abkhazia Tea producers, Georgia, Asia..........256
Aceh Coffee producers, Indonesia, Asia 265
Acquaviva Red Onion, Italy, Europe **471**
Acton Biodynamic Food producers, Canada, Americas 125
Agave and Mescal producers of Chilapa de Álvarez,
Mexico, Americas 150
Agave Honey and Jam producers, Mexico, Americas 150
Aged Artisan Gouda, Netherlands, Europe **670**
Agricultural machinery producers, Cuba, Americas..........142
Aguni Island Sea Salt producers, Japan, Asia 269
Ahle Wurscht producers of Northern Assia, Germany, Europe 342
Aigamo method Rice producers, Japan, Asia 269
Airan Producers, Russia, Europe 406
Aires de Campo, Mexico, Americas 159
Alaskan Wild Salmon Fishermen,
United States of America, Americas..........166
Álava pony meat farmers, Spain, Europe 424
Álava Txakolí producers, Spain, Europe 424
Albenga Violet Asparagus, Italy, Europe **472**
Alberta bakers, Canada, Americas 125
Alberta beekeepers and mead producers, Canada, Americas 126
Alberta Bison breeders, Canada, Americas..........126
Alberta breeders, Canada, Americas 126
Alberta Cattle breeders, Canada, Americas 127
Alberta Lamb breeders, Canada, Americas..........127
Alberta organic breeders, Canada, Americas 127
Alpago Lamb, Italy, Europe **473**
Alta Anoia cigronet growers, Spain, Europe 424
Amalfi Sfusato Lemon, Italy, Europe **474**
Amaranth growers of Agastyamuni, India, Asia 259
Amarume Leek producers, Japan, Asia..........269
American Raw Milk Cheeses,
United States of America, Americas..........**246**
Ancient olive-tree farmers, Spain, Europe 424

Ancient Rice variety growers, Japan, Asia 270
Andarinos producers of Usini, Italy, Europe 357
Andasibe Red Rice, Madagascar, Africa **91**
Andean Corn, Argentina, Americas **216**
Andean Kañihua, Peru, Americas **239**
Andean Potato growers, Argentina, Americas..........96
Andean Sweet Potatoes, Peru, Americas **240**
Andean vegetable and cereal farmers, Ecuador, Americas..........144
Anglesey Sea Salt producers, United Kingdom, Europe..........444
Animal breeders and dairy farmers of Langenburg,
Germany, Europe 342
Animal breeders and dairy farmers of North Kerry,
Ireland, Europe 353
Animal breeders and milk and dairy producers
of Djibouti, Djibouti, Africa..........43
Animal Breeders of Amuyaokope, Ghana, Africa 51
Anishinaabeg Manoomin,
United States of America, Americas..........**243**
Ansonica wine producers of the Isola del Giglio,
Italy, Europe..........357
Aole and carp fishers of Lake Garda, Italy, Europe 358
Apple growers of the Wisla Park, Poland, Europe 400
Apple-juice producers of Kalisz, Poland, Europe..........400
Aragonese wheat growers and bakers, Spain, Europe 425
Ararat Apricot producers, Turkey, Europe..........441
Ararat Valley fruit growers, Armenia, Asia 251
Ararat Valley seed and vegetable producers, Armenia, Asia 251
Argan Oil, Morocco, Africa **94**
Arhuaca farmers, Colombia, Americas..........138
Arizona Seedsavers and Growers, United States
of America, Americas 166
Aromatic Herb growers, Georgia, Asia 256
Aroostook County Wheat Growers, United States
of America, Americas 166
Artesan Sognefjord Geitost, Norway, Europe **674**
Artichoke growers of Chiusure, Italy, Europe 358
Artichoke growers of Perinaldo, Italy, Europe..........358
Artisan brewers, Italy, Europe 358

Artisan Cheesemakers from the Uplands of Southwestern
Wisconsin, United States of America, Americas 167
Artisan cornmillers, United Kingdom, Europe................444
Artisan Cupeta producers of Montepaone, Italy, Europe.............359
Artisan Fishermen of Saint-Louis, Senegal, Africa 73
Artisan Fishermen of Ziguinchor, Senegal, Africa 73
Artisan Somerset Cheddar , United Kingdom, Europe **692**
Artisanal producers of Cocuy, Venezuela, Americas 215
Artzai gazta cheese producers, Spain, Europe................425
Artzain Mundua, Spain, Europe................433
Asheville Producers, United States of America, Americas 167
Asociación de Cooperativas sin Fronteras, Costa Rica, Americas 142
Asparagus growers of Cilavegna, Italy, Europe 359
Aspra Spitia food producers and processors, Greece, Europe 346
Asturias spelt producers, Spain, Europe 425
Atacora Mountain Flower Honey Producers, Benin, Africa 26
Atacora Mountain Rice Producers, Benin, Africa...............27
Aurina Valley Graukäse, Italy, Europe **475**
Austin Farmers, United States of America, Americas....................167
Australian Desert Lime producers, Australia, Oceania 700
Australian Rare Breed Meat producers and processos 700
Avocado growers, Mexico, Americas 151
Ayrshire food producers, United Kingdom, Europe....................444
Babaçu by-products producers, Brazil, Americas 110
Backa bread producers, Serbia, Europe 420
Badakhshan fruit growers, Tajikistan, Asia, 294
Badalucco, Conio and Pigna Beans, Italy, Europe................**476**
Bagnolese Pecorino, Italy, Europe **477**
Bagolino Bagòss, Italy, Europe **478**
Bakers and Confectioners of Alexandria, Egypt, Africa 43
Bakers and food cultivators of Ekenås and Nagu,
Finland, Europe 330
Bakers of Lentini, Italy, Europe 359
Bakers of Nordrhein-Westfalen, Germany, Europe 342
Bakers of Parainen, Finland, Europe 331
Bakers of spelt bread, Norway, Europe 398
Balangon Banana and Sugar producers of Negros Island,
Philippines, Asia, ...291
Bambara Pea Producers of Bobo-Dioulasso,
Burkina Faso, Africa 29
Bambara Pea Producers of Djogona, Cameroon, Africa...............35
Bamboo producers of Sikkim, India, Asia................259

Bamboo Wine Producers of Njombe, Tanzania, Africa 81
Banale Ciuiga, Italy, Europe **479**
Banana Beer Producers of Cibitoke, Burundi, Africa 34
Banana growers of Altagracia, Nicaragua, Americas 160
Banana Growers of Mbenga, Gabon, Africa 47
Banana Growers of the Kampala District, Uganda, Africa 86
Banana Producers of Lower Shabelle and Lower Jubba,
Somalia, Africa...........79
Banda Wheat growers, India, Asia...........259
Banfora Region fruit and cereal producers and processors,
Burkina Faso, Africa 29
Baobab Jam Producers of Kibwezi, Kenya, Africa 56
Baobab Leaf and Shea Tree Larvae Gatherers,
Burkina Faso, Africa...........29
Barabaig shepherds, Tanzania, Africa...........82
Baranya cheeses and traditional food producers,
Hungary, Europe 350
Bareges-Gavarnie Sheep , France, Europe **459**
Bario Rice, Malaysia, Asia...........**309**
Barisal producers, Bangladesh, Asia...........254
Barley growers of Ladakh, India, Asia 260
Barlovento Cacao, Venezuela, Americas **248**
Barù Nut, Brazil, Americas **221**
Bashkirian Honey Producers, Russia, Europe 406
Basilicata Podolico Caciocavallo, Italy, Europe **480**
Basque Pig breeders and processors, France, Europe 333
Batata doce producers of Aljezur, Portugal, Europe 403
Bayta Olive Oil producers, Palestine, Asia 289
Bazzone Prosciutto, Italy, Europe...........**481**
Bean and vegetable growers of Pignone, Italy, Europe 360
Bean farmers of Chiclayo, Peru, Americas 162
Bean growers of Lucchesia, Italy, Europe 360
Bean growers of Paganica, Italy, Europe...........360
Béarn Cattle breeders, France, Europe 333
Beekeepers and collectors in Zabajkalie, Russia, Europe 406
Beekeepers in Krasnoznamensk, Russia, Europe 407
Beekeepers in the Urals, Russia, Europe...........407
Beekeepers of Baden-Württemberg, Germany, Europe 343
Beekeepers of eastern Sicily, Italy, Europe 360
Beekeepers of Gran Sasso and Monti della Laga, Italy, Europe 361
Beekeepers of Ijebu-Ode, Nigeria, Africa...........72
Beekeepers of Jdeideh, Lebanon, Asia...........282

Beekeepers of Nordrhein-Westfalen, Germany, Europe 343
Beekeepers of Pirkanmaa, Finland, Europe 331
Beekeepers of Sampirin, Guinea, Africa 53
Beekeepers of the Pacaltsdorp District, South Africa, Africa 79
Beer brewers and drinkers, United Kingdom, Europe 445
Beer producers and consumers, Switzerland, Europe 439
Beiju and Bolachinas de Goma producers, Brazil, Americas 110
Bellingham Blue cheese makers, Ireland, Europe 353
Béni-Isguen Oasis Date Producers, Algeria, Africa.....................26
Berkshire and Taconic Region Biodynamic Farmers,
United States of America, Americas.............................168
Berkshire cereal farmers, United Kingdom, Europe......................445
Berkshire farmers, United Kingdom, Europe 445
Biancoperla Corn, Italy, Europe.........................**482**
Big Sandy Grain and Field Crop Producers,
United States of America, Americas 168
Bigorre Black Pig, France, Europe **460**
Bihac beekeepers, Bosnia and Herzegovina, Europe.....................318
Biodynamic Goat Cheese producers, Australia, Oceania 700
Biodynamic Producers, Russia, Europe.........................407
Biodynamic wine producers of eastern Sicily, Italy, Europe 361
Biological producers, Sweden, Europe................................434
Biological wine producers, Chile, Americas 135
Bionexos, Mexico, Americas 159
Bioplaneta, Mexico, Americas 159
Biscuit producers of Venafro, Italy, Europe.........................361
Bitto of the Bitto Valleys, Italy, Europe **483**
Black bread producers, Lithuania, Europe 392
Black Cherry Wine, Italy, Europe.........................**484**
Black-eyed Pea (Niébé) Growers, Burkina Faso, Africa 30
Bleu de Queyras producers, France, Europe 334
Blue Egg Hen, Chile, Americas **228**
Blueberry pickers Arhuaca farmers, Colombia, Americas 138
Boeren-Leidse cheesemakers, Netherlands, Europe 395
Bolaven Coffee producers, Laos, Asia 281
Bolinas Farmers, United States of America, Americas 168
Boretice grape-growers and winemakers,
Czech Republic, Europe 326
Botìro producers of Primiero, Italy, Europe 362
Boulder Farmers, United States of America, Americas.................169
Brânzá de Burduf, Romania, Europe **682**
Brazil Nut and Copaìba Oil producers, Brazil, Americas 110
Brazil Nut producers, Brazil, Americas 111
Bread bakers of Genzano , Italy, Europe........................362
Bread bakers of Sarleinsbach, Austria, Europe 314
Bread Producers, Russia, Europe 408
Breeders and cheese producers of Brusturoasa,
Romania, Europe 404
Breeders and cheese-makers of the Valnerina, Italy, Europe 362
Breeders and crop farmers, Czech Republic, Europe.....................326
Breeders and fruit growers of Aragatsotn, Armenia, Asia 251
Breeders and producers of Montefeltro, Italy, Europe...................362
Breeders of black Calabrian Pigs, Italy, Europe......................363
Breeders of calvana cattle 363
Breeders of cornella bianca sheep 363
Breeders of grigio alpina cattle 363
Breeders of Hardy Cattle from the Catalan Pyrénées,
France, Europe 334
Breeders of Icelandic Goats and Sheeps, Iceland, Europe 353
Breeders of indigenous Poultry breeds, Hungary, Europe 350
Breeders of Kabardino-Balkaria, Russia, Europe 408
Breeders of pezzata rossa of Oropa, Italy, Europe......................364
Breeders of the Colored Pigs of Bentheim, Germany, Europe 343
Breeders of the indigenous Gray Cattle breed,
Hungary, Europe 351
Breeders of varzese cow, Italy, Europe..........................364
Brentwood Organic Fruit Growers,
United States of America, Americas..............................169
Breton Pie Noir Cattle breeders, France, Europe........................334
Brigasca Sheep Toma, Italy, Europe **485**
Bristol Bay Wild Salmon Fishermen, United States of America,
Americas 169
British Columbia farmers' markets producers,
Canada, Americas..........................127
British Columbia food producers, Canada, Americas 128
Brittany seaweed gatherers and processors, France, Europe 335
Broa de milho producers of Arcos de Valdevez,
Portugal, Europe..........................403
Bronte Pistachio, Italy, Europe **486**
Brooklyn Seedsavers and Gardeners, United States of America,
Americas 170
Brooklyn Urban Farmers, United States of America, Americas........170
Bryndza producers, Slovakia, Europe.........................421
Buffalo breeders, Ukraine, Europe.........................442

Bundelkhand producers of seeds for oil, India, Asia 260
Buninyong farmers' market producers, Australia, Oceania 700
Burlington Farmers, United States of America, Americas................170
Butter Producers of Vologda, Russia, Europe 408
Cabbage growers and transformers of Bucovina,
Romania, Europe 404
Cacao nacional, Ecuador, Americas **234**
Cacimbas Pequi producers, Brazil, Americas................................111
Caciofiore of the Roman Countryside, Italy, Europe **487**
Caiman farmers, Argentina, Americas 96
Cake-makers of Trelew, Argentina, Americas 96
Calbuco Brack-Bordered Oyster, Chile, Americas **229**
California Ethnic Minority Farmers,
United States of America, Americas...170
Californian Artisan Bread Bakers,
United States of America, Americas...171
Camarillo Organic Farmers,
United States of America, Americas...171
Cambridgeshire beekeepers, United Kingdom, Europe 446
Camel Breeders and Milk Producers of Nouakchott,
Mauritania, Africa 68
Camel Breeders of the Salato Tribe, Kenya, Africa 56
Cametá fruit by-products producers, Brazil, Americas...................111
Campotosto Mortadella, Italy, Europe..**488**
Camu-camu growers of Ucayali, Peru, Americas...........................162
Cananéia Oyster gatherers, Brazil, Americas................................111
Canapù bean, Brazil, Americas **222**
Cane Sugar Growers and Processors of Doumandzou,
Gabon, Africa...47
Cannara Onion, Italy, Europe **489**
Cantagalo Fava do Vale producers, Brazil, Americas 112
Capay Valley Farmers and Ranchers,
United States of America, Americas...171
Cape Breton farmers' market producers, Canada, Americas 128
Cape Cod Hook Fishermen,
United States of America, Americas...172
Cape May Oyster, United States of America, Americas **244**
Caper growers of Ballobar, Spain, Europe 426
Caprauna Turnip, Italy, Europe **490**
Carmagnola Grey Rabbit, Italy, Europe..**491**
Carmagnola Ox-Horn Pepper, Italy, Europe **492**
Carmignano Dried Fig, Italy, Europe **493**

Carob Flour producers, Argentina, Americas 96
Carp breeders of Zator, Poland, Europe 401
Carpathian beekeepers, Ukraine, Europe 443
Carpino Broad Beans, Italy, Europe **494**
Casabe Galleta producers, Venezuela, Americas 215
Cascades Farmers' Market Producers,
United States of America, Americas...172
Casentino Prosciutto, Italy, Europe **495**
Casín cheese producers, Spain, Europe 426
Casizolu, Italy, Europe **496**
Casola Marocca, Italy, Europe...**497**
Cassava and Coffee Producers of the Ileje District,
Tanzania, Africa 82
Cassava and Yam producers of Anyama, Côte d'Ivoire, Africa 42
Cassava Growers and Processors of Attitogon, Togo, Africa 85
Cassava Growers and Processors of Makokou, Gabon, Africa............48
Cassava Growers, Central African Republic, Africa 39
Cassava Processors of Obom, Ghana, Africa 51
Cassava Producers of Nyanon, Cameroon, Africa 35
Castel del Monte Canestrato, Italy, Europe **498**
Castellammare Violet Artichoke, Italy, Europe **499**
Castelvetrano Black Bread, Italy, Europe **500**
Catskills Region Agriculture Promoters,
United States of America, Americas...172
Cattle farmers of Limpurg, Germany, Europe................................344
Central Appalachian Farmers' Market Organic Farmers,
United States of America, Americas...173
Central Belorus beekeepers, Belorus, Europe 316
Central Coast Heritage Poultry Producers,
United States of America, Americas...173
Central Indiana Organic Farmers,
United States of America, Americas...173
Central New Jersey Ice Cream Makers and Vegetable Growers,
United States of America, Americas...173
Central Valley Peach and Raisin Growers,
United States of America, Americas...174
Centro Popular de Saúde Yanten aromatic herbs producers,
Brazil, Americas 112
Cereal and Fruit Producers of Wad Medani, Sudan, Africa 80
Cereal and Legume growers and processors, Mali, Africa 66
Cereal and Legume Growers of the Kiteto District,
Tanzania, Africa 82

Cereal farmers of Chimborazo, Ecuador, Americas 144
Cereal producers and merchants of Bamako and Ségou,
Mali, Africa 66
Cereal, Legume and Vegetable Growers of Keur Massar,
Senegal, Africa 73
Cereals Growers of Kathonzweni, Kenya, Africa 57
Cerrado fruit gatherers, Brazil, Americas 113
Certaldo Onion, Italy, Europe **501**
Cervia Artisan Sea Salt, Italy, Europe **502**
Cetara Anchovy Traditional Extract, Italy, Europe **503**
Chaam Hen, Netherlands, Europe **671**
Chanklich Cheese producers, Lebanon, Asia 282
Chapecó small-scale farmers, Brazil, Americas 113
Charqui producers, Argentina, Americas 97
Châteauneuf-du-Pape producers, France, Europe 335
Chattanooga Breeders, United States of America, Americas 174
Chattanooga Cooperative Farmers,
United States of America, Americas 174
Chattanooga Organic Bread Bakers,
United States of America, Americas 174
Chaya growers, Mexico, Americas 151
Cheese and Curdled Milk Producers of Toukounous,
Niger, Africa 70
Cheese and Honey Producers of the Mid-Atlas Mountains,
Morocco, Africa 69
Cheese and Milk Producers of Njombe, Tanzania, Africa 83
Cheese and olive producers of the land between
the two lakes, Italy, Europe 364
Cheese and salami makers of the Mugello, Italy, Europe 365
Cheese makers of the Salzburg region, Austria, Europe 314
Cheese makers of West Cork, Ireland, Europe 354
Cheese Producers of Kaliningrad, Russia, Europe 408
Cheese Producers of Ossetia, Russia, Europe 409
Cheese producers of the Alto Salento, Italy, Europe 365
Cheese producers of the Carso Triestino, Italy, Europe 365
Cheese producers of the Mugello and the Val di Sieve,
Italy, Europe...365
Cheese producers of the Sierra de Espadán, Spain, Europe 426
Cheese producers of the Tush ethnic group, Georgia, Asia.............256
Cheese producers of the Valle Elvo and the Serra,
Italy, Europe...366
Cheese-makers of Estación Yeruá, Argentina, Americas..................97

Cheese-makers of Maciá, Argentina, Americas 97
Chefs of Volterra detention center, Italy, Europe...........................366
Chemin Faisant, France, Europe...341
Chestnut flour producers of Pratomagno, Italy, Europe..................366
Chestnut flour producers of the Garfagnana , Italy, Europe............367
Chestnut producers of Combai 367
Chestnut producers of the Valcamonica, Italy, Europe...................367
Chicago Green City Farmers' Market Producers,
United States of America, Americas..175
Chicago Producers, United States of America, Americas 175
Chicken breeders of Hoa Binh, Viet Nam, Asia, ...302
Chikuma Apricot growers, Japan, Asia 270
Chili Pepper cultivators, Mexico, Americas...................................151
Chilli Pepper Growers of Niégueré, Guinea, Africa 53
Chimgan nomadic breeders, Uzbekistan, Asia, ...299
Chinantla Vanilla, Mexico, Americas **237**
Chitrakoot breeders, India, Asia 260
Chitwan producers, Nepal, Asia 288
Chlifa growers, Lebanon, Asia 283
Chocolate producers of San José de Barlovento,
Venezuela, Americas...215
Chon-Alaj yak breeders, Kirghizia, Asia 277
Chrámce fruit producers, Czech Republic, Europe 326
Chuin Flour and Starch producers of Yanallpa,
Peru, Americas..163
Ciaculli Late Winter Mandarin, Italy, Europe **504**
Cider Apple growers, United Kingdom, Europe 446
Cider makers of Fejø, Denmark, Europe......................................328
Cider makers of Hardanger, Norway, Europe 398
Cilento Goat Cacioricotta, Italy, Europe **505**
Cinque Terre Sciacchetrà, Italy, Europe **506**
Cinta senese pig breeders, Italy, Europe.....................................367
Citrus Fruit Growers of the Pita Prefecture, Guinea, Africa..............54
Classic Bologna Mortadella, Italy, Europe **507**
Classic Chianina Ox, Italy, Europe **508**
Classic Genoese Focaccia, Italy, Europe **509**
Classic Robiola di Roccaverano, Italy, Europe **510**
Coarse Cane Sugar producers of La Vega,
Colombia, Americas 139
Coazze Cevrin, Italy, Europe **511**
Cocoa producers and pig and sheep breeders,
Colombia, Americas 139

Cocoa producers in Tiassalé, Côte d'Ivoire, Africa............................42
Cocoa producers of Bocas del Toro, Panama, Americas.................161
Cocoa producers of Nord Esmeraldas, Ecuador, Americas.............145
Cocoa producers, Belize, Americas 108
Cocoa transformers, Spain, Europe 426
Cocomerina Pear, Italy, Europe **512**
Coconut and Spice producers, India, Asia 260
Coconut Processors of Bissok, Gabon, Africa 48
Coconut producers of the South, Sri Lanka, Asia, ...292
Coffee and chocolate producers of San Rafael Toltepec,
Mexico, Americas 151
Coffee and Cocoa growers in Daloa, Côte d'Ivoire, Africa...............42
Coffee and Forest Honey Producers of Dollo Mena,
Ethiopia, Africa..45
Coffee growers of Estelí, Nicaragua, Americas 160
Coffee producers from the upper basin of the Yuna river,
Dominican Republic, Americas 144
Coffee producers of Huatusco, Mexico, Americas..........................152
Coffee Producers of Kibinge, Uganda, Africa 86
Coffee Producers of the Golocha Forest, Ethiopia, Africa................45
Coffee Producers of the province of Ngozi, Burundi, Africa 34
Coffee producers of the South, Ecuador, Americas 145
Coffee producers of Yungas, Bolivia, Americas 108
Coggiola Paletta, Italy, Europe **513**
Colonnata Lard, Italy, Europe **514**
Comacchio Valley Lagoons Traditional Pickled Eel,
Italy, Europe **515**
Community Supported Agriculture,
United States of America, Americas...209
Conca Casale Signora, Italy, Europe...**516**
Conciato Romano, Italy, Europe **517**
Conservers of traditional apple and pear varieties,
Switzerland, Europe 439
Corn growers, Peru, Americas 163
Cornish Pilchard, United Kingdom, Europe **693**
Corno alle Scale Char, Italy, Europe...**518**
Cornwall fishermen, United Kingdom, Europe 446
Cornwall food producers, United Kingdom, Europe 447
Cornwall Hollow Breeders,
United States of America, Americas...175
Corona Ranchers, United States of America, Americas 175
Cosenza Dottato Fig, Italy, Europe...**519**

Cotonou Healthy Food Producers and Distributors,
Benin, Africa 27
Cow and Camel Breeders, Kenya, Africa 57
Craft producers of upplandskubb, Sweden, Europe 434
Creswell Farmers, United States of America, Americas 176
Crimean Wine producers, Ukraine, Europe 443
Cromwell Vegetable Growers, United States
of America, Americas 176
Crowns of Diocletian producers, Croatia, Europe 323
Cucumber Producers of Suzdal, Russia, Europe 409
Cumberland Sausage producers, United Kingdom, Europe 447
Cumin and Fennel seed growers of Rajasthan Beawar,
India, Asia 261
Cupuaçu producers and processors, Brazil, Americas 113
Cupuaçu producers and processors, Brazil, Americas 113
Custodian Farmers of ancient farming practices
of Vallo di Diano, Italy, Europe 368
Custodian Farmers of old varieties and local breeds
of Forlì-Cesena, Italy, Europe 368
Cuyahoga County Farmers,
United States of America, Americas...176
Daikon growers of Akka, Japan, Asia 270
Daikon growers of Miura, Japan, Asia 271
Daintree Edible Rainforest Plant growers,
Australia, Oceania...701
Daintree Organic Fruit growers, Australia, Oceania 701
Dairy farmers of Wicklow and Kilkenny, Ireland, Europe 354
Dalton Small Grain and Row Crop Growers,
United States of America, Americas...176
Darfiyeh, Lebanon, Asia **307**
Davenport Organic Berry Growers,
United States of America, Americas...177
Defenders of the Néré and Souombara producers
of Fouta Djalon, Guinea, Africa 54
Dehra Dun Basmati Rice, India, Asia **305**
Delia Cuddrireddra, Italy, Europe **520**
Desert Date Leaf Gatherers, Cameroon, Africa 36
Desiccated locust producers, Mexico, Americas 152
Dogon Onion Growers, Mali, Africa...66
Dorondón Monegros, Spain, Europe 433
Dried and Smoked Flounder Producers, Estonia, Europe...............330
Dried Calizzano and Murialdo Chestnuts, Italy, Europe **521**

Dried Fish Producers of Kingabwa,
Democratic Republic of Congo, Africa 41
Dried Fruit Producers of Taounate, Morocco, Africa 69
Dried Mango Producers of Ouagadougou,
Burkina Faso, Africa 30
Dried Persimmon producers, Japan, Asia 271
Dried salt-cured cod producers of Kristiansund,
Norway, Europe 398
Droze bread producers, Slovenia, Europe...................................422
Dufferin Grove farmers' market producers,
Canada, Americas...128
Dukati Black Goat breeders, Albania, Europe 312
Dumfries and Galloway food producers,
United Kingdom, Europe 447
Dungeness and Calallam County Organic Farmers,
United States of America, Americas...............................177
Dutch brewers, Netherlands, Europe 395
East Meredith Pig and Turkey Farmers,
United States of America, Americas.................................178
Eastern Colorado Plains Lamb Breeders,
United States of America, Americas.................................178
Eastern Seaboard farmers' markets producers,
Canada, Americas...128
Ecological food producers of Xonacatlán, Mexico, Americas..........152
Edam and Remeker cheesemakers, Netherlands, Europe 396
Edible wild plant gatherers, Argentina, Americas 97
Elbasan Olive Oil producers, Albania, Europe 312
Elena Ham producers, Bulgaria, Europe.......................................320
Entomophagus Women of the Bobo-Dioulasso Region,
Burkina Faso, Africa 30
Esparto Vine Growers and Wine Makers,
United States of America, Americas.................................178
Espelette Chili Pepper producers, France, Europe 335
Euphorbia Honey Producers of Tigrai, Ethiopia, Africa 45
Euskal Oiloa chicken farmers, Spain, Europe 427
Euskal Txerria Pig, Spain, Europe **684**
Extensive system farmers, Sierra di Guara Cheese,
Spain, Europe..427
Fabriano Salami, Italy, Europe **522**
Fal River Oyster , United Kingdom, Europe **694**
Farindola Pecorino, Italy, Europe..**523**
Farinha d'Água producers, Brazil, Americas 114

Farmers and Animal Breeders in the Khomas Region,
Namibia, Africa 70
Farmers and animal breeders of Lom, Norway, Europe 398
Farmers and breeders of San Miniato, Italy, Europe 368
Farmers and breeders of Shombo, Mutumba and Nyabikere,
Burundi, Africa...35
Farmers and fishermen of Escuinapa, Mexico, Americas 152
Farmers and stock breeders of Santa Barbara-Campo Florido,
Cuba, Americas 142
Farmers' market of Beirut, Lebanon, Asia...................................283
Farmers of Asturian breeds, Spain, Europe.................................427
Farmers of Gran Sasso and Monti della Laga,
Italy, Europe..368
Farmers of Huesca poultry breeds, Spain, Europe 428
Farmers of Lungau, Austria, Europe..314
Farmers of the Arid Areas of Kitui, Kenya, Africa 57
Farmers, fishers and artisans of La Ceiba,
Honduras, Americas 149
Farmers, growers and preserve producers
of San Javier, Argentina, Americas.......................................98
Farmers' market producers, United Kingdom, Europe....................448
Farmers' Markets, United States of America, Americas 190
Farro and mulberry growers of the Brescia plain, Italy, Europe 369
Farro growers of the Garfagnana, Italy, Europe...........................369
Fatuli producers of the Val Saviore, Italy, Europe 369
Favignana Bottarga, Italy, Europe **524**
Feira de Santana fruit producers and processors,
Brazil, Americas 114
Female producers of Mouneh, Lebanon, Asia 283
Female producers of Serdelch, Lebanon, Asia 283
Ferrandina Baked Olive, Italy, Europe **525**
Fiore Sardo Shepherds' Cheese, Italy, Europe............................**526**
Fish Farmers of Kisumu, Kenya, Africa 57
Fish processors and sellers, Senegal, Africa.................................73
Fish Smokers of Kokrobite, Ghana, Africa....................................51
Fishermen and Animal Breeders of Nyuiyui, Ghana, Africa..............51
Fishermen and processors of the Laguna de Rocha,
Uruguay, Americas 213
Fishermen and restaurateurs, United Kingdom, Europe 448
Fishermen and Stock Breeders of Kasokwe, Uganda, Africa 86
Fishermen in the Gizhiga river, Russia, Europe 409
Fishermen of Boulbinet, Guinea, Africa......................................54

Fishermen of Capo Teulada, Italy, Europe 370
Fishermen of Lake Trasimeno, Italy, Europe 370
Fishermen of Mar de Lira, Spain, Europe......................428
Fishermen of Smolensk, Russia, Europe 409
Fishermen of the Åland archipelago, Finland, Europe................331
Fishermen of the Straits of Messina, Italy, Europe 370
Fishermen of Tortolì, Italy, Europe...............................371
Flor de Jamaica producers, Mexico, Americas 153
Florentine tripe producers, Italy, Europe 371
Florianópolis Manioc Flour producers, Brazil, Americas 114
Florida Panhandle Farmers,
United States of America, Americas.............................178
Fonio and Palm Wine Producers of Orodara,
Burkina Faso, Africa 30
Fonio Growers and Processors of Fouta Djalon, Guinea, Africa 54
Fonio Producers of Kedougou, Senegal, Africa 74
Food Justice, United States of America, Americas......................212
Food producers and distributors of Åland, Finland, Europe 332
Food producers and distributors on the Stockholm archipelago,
Sweden, Europe 434
Food producers and educators of County Clare,
Ireland, Europe 354
Food producers of Bornholm, Denmark, Europe 328
Food producers of County Tipperary, Ireland, Europe 355
Food producers of Greenland, Denmark, Europe 328
Food producers of the island of Fyn, Denmark, Europe 329
Forain Pink Garlic producers from the Tarn, France, Europe 336
Forest Food Promoters, Burkina Faso, Africa 31
Formadi Frant, Italy, Europe **527**
Fourth Corner Farmers' Market Producers,
United States of America, Americas.............................179
Franconia Goat breeders, Germany, Europe 344
Friesian Islands fishermen, Netherlands, Europe 396
Fruit and vegetable producers and processors,
Colombia, Americas 139
Fruit and vegetable producers of El Hoyo, Argentina, Americas 98
Fruit and Vegetable Producers of Morogoro, Tanzania, Africa 83
Fruit and Vegetable Producers, Benin, Africa 27
Fruit and vegetable producers, Moldavia, Europe 394
Fruit growers of Kab Elias, Lebanon, Asia...................284
Fruit growers of Lilleø, Denmark, Europe....................329
Fruit Growers of the Diouloulou District, Senegal, Africa.............74

Fruit Juice producers of Abidjan, Côte d'Ivoire, Africa 42
Fruit Juice, Jam and Purée Producers, Malawi, Africa 65
Fruit producers and farm tourism operators,
Argentina, Americas 98
Fruit producers and processors, Colombia, Americas 139
Fruit producers of Mount Etna, Italy, Europe 371
Fundación para la Productividad en el Campo,
Mexico, Americas...160
Fundación Renacimiento, Mexico, Americas 160
Galicia seafood gatherers, Spain, Europe 429
Gallecs farmers, Spain, Europe 429
Ganxet Bean, Spain, Europe **685**
Garbagna Bella Cherry, Italy, Europe **528**
Garfagnana Biroldo, Italy, Europe **529**
Garfagnana Potato Bread, Italy, Europe **530**
Gargano Citrus Fruits, Italy, Europe **531**
Gargano Goat, Italy, Europe **532**
Gargano Podolica Cow, Italy, Europe............................**533**
Gargano Podolico Caciocavallo, Italy, Europe................**534**
Garlic growers in Chilote, Chile, Americas 135
Garmsar Cereal growers, Iran, Asia 267
Garraf vegetable producers, Spain, Europe 429
Gatherers of Mopane Worms, Zimbabwe, Africa 88
Gavi Testa in Cassetta, Italy, Europe............................**535**
Geese breeders, Russia, Europe 410
Georgia Family Farmers, United States of America, Americas 179
Germoplasm bank of Saint Petersburg, Russia, Europe 419
Giant Istrian Ox, Croatia, Europe.................................**457**
Ginger Growers and Processors, Guinea, Africa.............55
Gioi Soppressata, Italy, Europe....................................**536**
Girgentana Goat, Italy, Europe **537**
Gloucester Cheese, United Kingdom, Europe.................**695**
Goat breeders and cheese makers of Irmelshausen,
Germany, Europe 344
Goat Breeders of Souss-Massa-Draa, Morocco, Africa 69
Goat breeders, Russia, Europe.....................................410
Goat Cheese and Dried Meat Producers of Gargando,
Mali, Africa 67
Goat Cheese Producers of Santo Antão, Cape Verde, Africa 38
Goat farmers of Tarija, Bolivia, Americas 108
Goat farmers of the Valle di Uco, Argentina, Americas 98
Goat's Milk Cheese producers of Mount Eitan, Israel, Asia 268

Goose in Onto, Italy, Europe 538
Goriska Brda wine producers, Slovenia, Europe 422
Gorkha district producers, Nepal, Asia........................288
Goym Cuisine of the Tufa Towns, Italy, Europe..............539
Grand Manan Island Lobster fishers, Canada, Americas 129
Grano solina growers of the Abruzzo mountains, Italy, Europe 372
Grappa Morlacco Cheese and Burlina Cow, Italy, Europe 540
Gray cow breeders of Altaj, Russia, Europe 411
Greek breeders and pork butchers of Calabria, Italy, Europe..........372
Green Tea producers of Di Nau and Son Thuy,
Viet Nam, Asia, ...302
Gressoney Toma, Italy, Europe 541
Groningen Goat breeders and cheesemakers,
Netherlands, Europe.........................396
Groundnut Paste and Oil Producers of the Diourbel Region,
Senegal, Africa 74
Growers and Processors of Black-Eyed Beans, Cameroon, Africa 36
Growers and processors of medicinal plants,
Guatemala, Americas 148
Growers and Stock Breeders of Ngurudoto and Kikatiti,
Tanzania, Africa 83
Growers and transformers of buck wheat, Poland, Europe 401
Growers of cappello del prete pumpkins, Italy, Europe...................372
Growers of Controne beans, Italy, Europe 372
Growers of durum wheat and bakers of Oristano,
Italy, Europe...........................373
Growers of early varieties of cereal crops, Sweden, Europe............434
Growers of grapes using animal traction, France, Europe 336
Growers of Lamon beans and agordino barley, Italy, Europe 373
Growers of marano maize, Italy, Europe 374
Growers of medicinal plants, Peru, Americas 163
Growers of old maize varieties of Piemonte, Italy, Europe 374
Growers of organic products, Jamaica, Americas 150
Growers of pericina pears, Italy, Europe.............................374
Growers of piccolo farro, Italy, Europe.......................375
Growers of red Cetica potatoes, Italy, Europe.......................375
Growers of the Poljak Bean from Trebinje,
Bosnia and Herzegovina, Europe..........................318
Growers of traditional greenhouse grape varieties,
Netherlands, Europe...........................396
Growers of Wadi El Rayan, Egypt, Africa 43
Grumolo delle Abbadesse Rice, Italy, Europe........................542

Guaraní ka'aguy poty producers of Kuñá Pirú,
Argentina, Americas 99
Guernsey Cow breeders, United Kingdom, Europe 448
Guiziga Bald-Neck Chicken Breeders, Cameroon, Africa 36
Guiziga Millet Growers, Cameroon, Africa 37
Gulcho beekeepers, Kirghizia, Asia 278
Gulf Islands farmers' markets producers, Canada, Americas 129
Gulf of Carpentaria fishermen,
Australia, Oceania.........................701
Gulf of Mexico Seafood Harvesters,
United States of America, Americas.....................179
Gulf South Blueberry Growers,
United States of America, Americas.....................179
Gull Valley Vegetable growers, Canada, Americas....................129
Hagersville Wild Plant gatherers, Canada, Americas 129
Halland county producers, Sweden, Europe.......................435
Ham producers of Tivat, Montenegro, Europe 395
Hancock Educators, United States of America, Americas..............180
Hand-made Marmalade and Jam producers,
United Kingdom, Europe 449
Hard Wheat Producers in Ejerre, Ethiopia, Africa 45
Haskovo cheese-makers, Bulgaria, Europe 320
Hatahata fishermen and sauce producers, Japan, Asia 271
Haute Provence Einkorn, France, Europe 461
Haut-Languedoc food producers, breeders and restaurateurs,
France, Europe 336
Healdsburg Farmers' Market Producers,
United States of America, Americas.........................180
Herb and Fruit Gatherers of the Rift Valley forest,
Kenya, Africa 58
Herb gatherers of Adonis Valley, Lebanon, Asia 284
Herb Gatherers of Kamchatka, Russia, Europe 411
Herbs, spices and passion fruit growers, Mexico, Americas............153
Herdwick Lamb breeders, United Kingdom, Europe 449
Heritage Canale Peach Varieties, Italy, Europe 543
Heritage Piedmontese Apple Varieties, Italy, Europe 544
Herscher Poultry Farmers,
United States of America, Americas.....................180
Hibiscus Growers and Processors of the Pwani Region,
Tanzania, Africa 84
High Mountain Agordo Cheese , Italy, Europe 545
High Mountain Honeys, Italy, Europe 546

Highlands and Western Isles food producers,
United Kingdom, Europe 450
Himachal Pradesh growers of local Walnut varieties,
India, Asia 261
Hin Lad Nai farmers, Thailand, Asia, 297
Hokkaido Maize growers, Japan, Asia 272
Home-brewed Beer producers, Argentina, Americas 99
Homestead Tropical Fruit Growers,
United States of America, Americas.....................180
Honey and Fruit Juice Producers of Mwanza, Malawi, Africa 65
Honey and Ouricuri producers, Brazil, Americas 114
Honey producers of central Armenia, Armenia, Asia 251
Honey Producers of Danay, Cameroon, Africa 37
Honey Producers of Kabompo, Zambia, Africa 88
Honey Producers of Soroti, Uganda, Africa 86
Honey Producers of the Wonchi Volcano, Ethiopia, Africa 46
Honey producers, Argentina, Americas 99
Honey producers, Mexico, Americas 153
Honey Producers, United States of America, Americas 181
Honvié Angolan Pea Growers, Benin, Africa.................27
Horse breeders, Russia, Europe 411
Hudson Valley Agricultural Educators,
United States of America, Americas.....................181
Huehuetenango Highland Coffee, Guatemala, Americas **235**
Ice Cider producers, Canada, Americas 130
Ilala and Marula Wine Producers, Zimbabwe, Africa 88
Iljare and Sukes grape-growers, Albania, Europe 312
Illinois Artisan Cheesemakers,
United States of America, Americas.....................181
Imereti beekeepers, Georgia, Asia 256
Imereti wine growers, Georgia, Asia 257
Imraguen Women's Bottarga, Mauritania, Africa **93**
Incense and Myrrh Gatherers in the Filtu Area,
Ethiopia, Africa...46
Indiana Uplands Farmers, United States of America, Americas 181
Indigenous Chicken Breeders of Kilifi, Kenya, Africa.................58
Indigenous Chicken Breeders of Machakos, Kenya, Africa.............58
Indigenous farmers of Cotacachi, Ecuador, Americas 145
Indigenous livestock breeders of Srem, Serbia, Europe 420
Indigenous sheep breeders, Azerbaijan, Asia 253
Indigenous vine growers, Moldavia, Europe.................394
Interdonato Lemon, Italy, Europe **547**

International Food Producers in National Parks,
United States of America, Americas.....................182
Ios Caper producers, Greece, Europe 346
Iowa City Farmers, United States of America, Americas 182
Irish Raw Milk Cheese , Ireland, Europe **470**
Ischia Cave Rabbit, Italy, Europe.................**548**
Ishkashim Black Pea producers, Tajikistan, Asia 294
Isle of Skye and Lochalsh food producers and distributors,
United Kingdom, Europe 450
Isle of Unije food producers, Croatia, Europe.................323
Ismailli beekeepers, Azerbaijan, Asia 253
Issyk-Kul fishermen, Kirghizia, Asia 278
Itápolis Orange Juice producers, Brazil, Americas 115
Iúna coffee producers, Brazil, Americas 115
Ixcán Cardamon, Guatemala, Americas **236**
Jablonec nad Nisou bread makers, Czech Republic, Europe 327
Jacksonville Farmers, United States of America, Americas.............182
Jalalabad Olive Oil producers, Afghanistan, Asia 250
Jam producers of Juella, Argentina, Americas 99
Jamao Coffee producers, Dominican Republic, Americas 144
Jämtland goat's milk cheese makers, Sweden, Europe 435
Janu sier producers, Latvia, Europe 391
Japanese organic tea producers, Japan, Asia 272
Jatobá Flour producers, Brazil, Americas 115
Jenin Almond growers, Palestine, Asia.................289
Jericho Date producers, Palestine, Asia 290
Jericho traditional food producers, Palestine, Asia 290
Jersey dairy farmers, United Kingdom, Europe.................450
Jiloca Saffron, Spain, Europe.................**686**
Juçara Palm Heart, Brazil, Americas **223**
Jujube Bread Producers, Burkina Faso, Africa.................31
Jurançon White Wine producers, France, Europe 337
Kajmak cheese producers, Serbia, Europe 420
Kakheti wine growers, Georgia, Asia 257
Kalalé Peul Wagassi Cheesemakers, Benin, Africa.................28
Kaliningrad Fishermen, Russia, Europe 412
Kalona Organic Sprout Growers,
United States of America, Americas.....................182
Kampung fruit producers, Malaysia, Asia.................287
Kanembou Gatherers of Lake Chad Blue Algae,
Chad, Africa...39
Kanembou Kouri Cattle Breeders, Chad, Africa 39

Karachaeva sheep farming in the Cherkessia region,
Russia, Europe 412
Karakachan nomadic breeders, Bulgaria, Europe 320
Karkade Growers and Processors of the Dakar Region,
Senegal, Africa 75
Karkade Growers, Gabon, Africa 48
Karnataka Coffee growers, India, Asia 261
Karnataka Spice producers, India, Asia 261
Kars Cheese producers, Turkey, Europe 442
Kartli fruit growers, Georgia, Asia 257
Kashmir Saffron producers, India, Asia 262
Kavala Asparagus growers, Greece, Europe 347
Kazakh nomadic breeders, Kazakhstan, Asia 276
Kechel el Fouqara Cheese, Lebanon, Asia **308**
Khalva Producers of Karachaevo-Cherkessia, Russia, Europe 412
Khalva producers of Yangikishlok, Uzbekistan, Asia, ...299
Khashtak producers of Brichmulla, Uzbekistan, Asia, ...300
Khoni honey producers, Georgia, Asia 257
Khorasan Spice producers Iran, Asia 267
Khorog Mulberry growers, Tajikistan, Asia, ...295
Khumsan Cheese producers, Uzbekistan, Asia, ...300
Kinnow producers, Pakistan, Asia 289
Kirghis indigenous sheep breeders, Kirghizia, Asia 278
Kiwicha and quinoa growers of the Quebrada de Humahuaca,
Argentina, Americas 100
Kobrin Food producers, Belorus, Europe 317
Kobutakana producers of Unzen, Japan, Asia 272
Kollo Producers of Dinsho, Ethiopia, Africa 47
Kos grape growers, Greece, Europe 347
Koster Island producers, Sweden, Europe 435
Kotagiri Honey producers, India, Asia 262
Kouri Cattle Breeders of Sayam, Niger, Africa 70
Krahô Sweet Potato Flour producers, Brazil, Americas 116
Kutná Hora wine producers, Czech Republic, Europe 327
Kythera beekeepers, Greece, Europe 347
Ladotyri Cheese producers, Greece, Europe 347
Lady chefs of popular festivals, Italy, Europe 375
Lages Pine Nut producers, Brazil, Americas 116
Lagoa Seca Caju Passa producers, Brazil, Americas 116
Lágrima de Costa de Gipúzkoa pea farmers, Spain, Europe 430
Lake Chad Maize Producers, Chad, Africa 40
Lake Chad Millet Producers, Chad, Africa 40

Lake Sevan fishermen, Armenia, Asia 252
Lake Superior fishermen, Canada, Americas 130
Lake Trasimeno Bean, Italy, Europe **549**
Lake Vänern fishermen, Sweden, Europe 435
Lakonia Siglino producers, Greece, Europe 348
Laksevine Fruit growers, Bosnia and Herzegovina, Europe 319
Lalitpur Dafne Paper producers, Nepal, Asia 288
Land Research Center, Palestine, Asia 290
Langa Sheep Tuma, Italy, Europe **550**
Langar Wheat growers, Tajikistan, Asia 295
Late Harvest Leonforte Peach, Italy, Europe **551**
Leaf Growers and Processors of Baguinéda, Mali, Africa 67
Lebanon Heirloom Apple Growers and Cider Producers,
United States of America, Americas 183
Legume growers of Uttar Pradesh, India, Asia 262
Leonforte Broad Bean, Italy, Europe **552**
Lepushe Food producers, Albania, Europe 312
Lima Duarte Honey producers, Brazil, Americas 117
Linderöd pig breeders, Sweden, Europe 436
Little Rock Agricultural Educators,
United States of America, Americas 183
Livno Cheese producers, Bosnia and Herzegovina, Europe 319
Ljubitovica Garlic producers, Croatia, Europe 324
Local Chicken Breeders of Mukono, Uganda, Africa 87
Local Date Variety Producers, Libya, Africa 64
Local variety & breed conservers, Greece, Europe 348
Local wheat producers, Armenia, Asia 252
Locarno Valley Cicitt, Switzerland, Europe **690**
Lodi Pannerone, Italy, Europe **553**
Loire basin fishermen, France, Europe 337
Lonzino di Fico, Italy, Europe **554**
Los Angeles Educators, United States of America, Americas 183
Louisiana Farmers, Shrimpers, and Restaurateurs,
United States of America, Americas 183
Macadamia Nut Producers and Processors, Kenya, Africa 58
Macagn, Italy, Europe **555**
Macaúba Oil producers, Brazil, Americas 117
Madera Growers, Bakers, and Wine Grape Growers,
United States of America, Americas 184
Madhuvan producers, Nepal, Asia 288
Madison Educators, United States of America, Americas 184
Madonie Manna, Italy, Europe **556**

Madonie Provola, Italy, Europe................................557
Magghia Masculina, Italy, Europe 558
Magura producers, Bangladesh, Asia.....................254
Maine Anjou Cattle breeders, France, Europe 337
Maine Chocolatiers, United States of America, Americas 184
Maine Organic Potato Farmers,
United States of America, Americas...........................184
Maine Organic Producers, United States of America, Americas 185
Maiorchino Cheese, Italy, Europe 559
Maíz azul producers, Mexico, Americas 153
Maize farmers in the Rhine valley, Switzerland, Europe 439
Maize flour producers of Storo, Italy, Europe 376
Maize growers of Vanoi-Primiero, Italy, Europe 376
Maize Producers from Donkokrom, Ghana, Africa 52
Makoni Tea Producers, Zimbabwe, Africa 89
Malga dairymen and shepherds of the Lagorai mountains,
Italy, Europe..376
Malga Monte Veronese, Italy, Europe 560
Mallegato, Italy, Europe 561
Mananara Vanilla, Madagascar, Africa.......................92
Mangalica sausage, Hungary, Europe 469
Mango and Vegetable Producers, Mali, Africa 67
Mango growers of the pre-Himalayan areas, India, Asia...........262
Manioc growers and processors of Misiones,
Argentina, Americas 100
Mantuan Peasant Casalin Salami, Italy, Europe 562
Manx Loaghtan Sheep breeders, United Kingdom, Europe............451
Maori Cereal and Vegetable growers, New Zealand, Oceania........704
Maori Potato growers, New Zealand, Oceania 704
Mapuche Black Quinoa growers in Southern Chile,
Chile, Americas 136
Marceddì Arselle, Italy, Europe 563
Maremmana Ox, Italy, Europe 564
Marin and Sonoma County Olive Oil Producers,
United States of America, Americas...........................185
Marin County Grassfed Livestock Ranchers,
United States of America, Americas...........................185
Marin County Producers, United States of America, Americas........185
Marin County Vegetable Growers,
United States of America, Americas...........................186
Marin County Wine Grape Growers, United States of America,
Americas 186

Mariola, Italy, Europe...565
Marshall Organic Dairy Farmers,
United States of America, Americas...........................186
Martabak producers of Java, Indonesia, Asia 265
Martha's Vineyard Aquaculturists,
United States of America, Americas...........................187
Martina Franca Capocollo, Italy, Europe 566
Marzolina, Italy, Europe 567
Masai Farmers of the Arusha Region, Tanzania, Africa 84
Mashua producers of Tuti, Peru, Americas 163
Mata Atlântica resource promoters, Brazil, Americas 117
Matera Mountain Pezzente, Italy, Europe 568
Matéri Mountain Rice Producers, Benin, Africa 28
Maui Pineapple Growers, United States of America, Americas 187
Mavrotragano Wine, Greece, Europe.........................467
Mayan Corn Growers, United States of America, Americas...........187
Mazoni (fermented milk) producers, Azerbaijan, Asia 253
Medicinal herb and vegetable growers, India, Asia 263
Medicinal herb growers of the parks of Sicily, Italy, Europe 376
Mediterranean Association for Soil Health, Greece, Europe 350
Melipona bee's honey producers, Brazil, Americas...........117
Menaica Anchovies, Italy, Europe 569
Mercantour Massif Cheese producers, France, Europe 338
Mercantour Olive growers, France, Europe..................338
Merquén, Chile, Americas 230
Mescal producers of Teúl de González Ortega,
Mexico, Americas...154
Mescal producers of Tlacolula, Mexico, Americas..........154
Messolongi Gray Mullet Roe producers, Greece, Europe 348
Miami Student Farmers, United States of America, Americas 187
Michigan Cider Makers, United States of America, Americas 188
Michigan Specialty Grain Growers and Processors,
United States of America, Americas...........................188
Milbenkäse producers, Germany, Europe 344
Milk and Butter Producers of Koumpentoum, Senegal, Africa..........75
Milk and Nilk By-Product Producers of the Hai District,
Tanzania, Africa 84
Milk producers of Chiapas, Mexico, Americas 155
Milk Producers of Kirkissoye, Niger, Africa..................71
Millet and Buckwheat growers of Kotdwara, India, Asia 263
Millet and Maize Growers and Processors of the Thiès Region,
Senegal, Africa 75

Millo corvo growers and transformers, Spain, Europe 430
Minsk Food producers, Belorus, Europe.......................................317
Minuta Olive, Italy, Europe...570
Mirandesa Sausage, Portugal, Europe 680
Missira Market, Mali, Africa 68
Mississippi Cooperative Farmers,
United States of America, Americas...188
Modicana Cow, Italy, Europe 571
Moena Puzzone, Italy, Europe...572
Moleche, Italy, Europe...573
Moliterno Casieddu, Italy, Europe...574
Momjan Muscat producers, Croatia, Europe 324
Mondovì Corn Meal Biscuits, Italy, Europe 575
Monopigado food producers and processors, Greece, Europe........349
Monreale White Plums, Italy, Europe...576
Monte Claros fruit producers and processors, Brazil, Americas 118
Monte Poro Pecorino, Italy, Europe...578
Monte San Biagio Sausage, Italy, Europe....................................580
Montébore, Italy, Europe 577
Montenegro Mandarin Juice producers, Brazil, Americas 118
Monterosso Anchovies, Italy, Europe...579
Monti Sibillini Pecorino, Italy, Europe 581
Monti Sibillini Pink Apple, Italy, Europe 582
Mora Romagnola Pig, Italy, Europe...583
Moroni Producers, Comoros, Africa 41
Morozzo Capon, Italy, Europe...584
Morrilton Livestock Breeders,
United States of America, Americas...189
Moscato of Siracusa producers, Italy, Europe 377
Mostarda of Mantua producers, Italy, Europe 377
Motal, Armenia, Asia 303
Mouneh producers, Lebanon, Asia 284
Mount Kesrouan producers, Lebanon, Asia 285
Mountain Castelmagno, Italy, Europe...585
Mozzarella in Myrtle, Italy, Europe 586
Muggio Valley Zincarlin, Switzerland, Europe 691
Muk Island fishermen, Thailand, Asia 297
Mumbai ready-to-eat food distributors, India, Asia 263
Muña liqueur producers, Argentina, Americas 100
Murgab breeders and dairy producers, Tajikistan, Asia, ...296
Mushroom growers of Zitácuaro, Mexico, Americas 155
Mushroom growers, Argentina, Americas....................................100

Mushroom pickers, Chile, Americas...136
Mussel Fishermen from the Tiznit Province, Morocco, Africa............69
Mussel fishermen of the Hardanger Fiord, Norway, Europe 399
Mussel-farmers of La Spezia, Italy, Europe.................................377
N'dama Cow Milk and Cheesemakers, Guinea, Africa 55
Nan fruit growers, Thailand, Asia,...297
Ñandú farmers, Uruguay, Americas..213
Nannup Sheep Cheese producers, Australia, Oceania 702
Napa Valley Farmers and Producers,
United States of America, Americas...189
Nassa Shrimp, Italy, Europe 587
Native North American Indigenous Delegation,
United States of America, Americas...212
Native Plants and Medicinal Herbs Gatherers,
United States of America, Americas...189
Natural animal-based coloring producers, Mexico, Americas 155
Natural Oil Producers in the Chivi District, Zimbabwe, Africa 89
Navajo-Churro Sheep, United States of America, Americas 245
Neapolitan Papaccella, Italy, Europe...588
Neapolitan vegetable growers, Italy, Europe 377
Nebrodi Black Pig, Italy, Europe..589
Nebrodi Provola, Italy, Europe...590
Negombo Spice producers, Sri Lanka, Asia,................................292
Nettle Growers of the Rift Valley, Kenya, Africa............................59
New Britain Organic Farmers,
United States of America, Americas...189
New Florence Lamb Breeders,
United States of America, Americas...190
New Hampshire Farmers, United States of America, Americas 190
New Mexican Benedictine Brewers,
United States of America, Americas...190
New Mexican Greenthread Growers and Gatherers,
United States of America, Americas...191
New Orleans Urban Gardeners,
United States of America, Americas...191
New Prague Organic Cattle and Dairy Farmers,
United States of America, Americas...192
New York City Greenmarket Farmers,
United States of America, Americas...192
New York City Organic Producers,
United States of America, Americas...192
Newfoundland organic producers, Canada, Americas...................130

Niagara Wine producers, Canada, Americas..................................130
Niébé (Black-Eyed Peas) Producers of Moutourwa,
Cameroon, Africa 37
Niebé Producers in the Louga Region, Senegal, Africa 76
Niotiko Cheese, Greece, Europe **468**
Nizza Monferrato Hunchback Cardoon, Italy, Europe.................**591**
Noli Anchovies (Cicciarelli), Italy, Europe **592**
Nomadic shepherds of Fars Iran, Asia 267
Nomadic shepherds of Piemonte, Italy, Europe 378
Nomadic shepherds, Mongolia, Asia 287
Nomadic shepherds, Spain, Europe.......................................431
Non Valley Mortandela, Italy, Europe **593**
North Carolina Piedmont Triad Food Producers,
United States of America, Americas 192
North San Juan Fruit Growers,
United States of America, Americas 193
North Turkana Shepherds, Kenya, Africa 59
Northern California Aromatic, Culinary and Healing
Herbs Growers, United States of America, Americas 193
Northern cocoa producers, Haiti, Americas 149
Northern Kazakhstan producers, Kazakhstan, Asia 276
Northumberland and Scottish Borders pig breeders,
United Kingdom, Europe 451
Norwich Dairy Farmers, United States of America, Americas 193
Nós Existimos, Brazil, Americas 125
Noto Almond, Italy, Europe **594**
Nova Scotia and Ontario Maple Syrup producers,
Canada, Americas...131
Nova Scotia Wild Blueberry gatherers, Canada, Americas.............131
Novosele Olive Oil producers, Albania, Europe 313
Nùbia Red Garlic, Italy, Europe.......................................**595**
O'ahu Food Producers, United States of America, Americas 193
Oca growers of Coctaca, Argentina, Americas.........................101
Oca growers of Iruya, Argentina, Americas 101
Oiko Bio, Greece, Europe 350
Oil Palm Producers and Processors of Lambaréné,
Gabon, Africa 48
Ojai Valley Pixie Growers, United States of America, Americas 194
Okra Growers of Tanlili, Burkina Faso, Africa 31
Öland Island bean growers, Sweden, Europe 436
Old Gloucester Beef, United Kingdom, Europe.......................**696**
Olive farmers of the province of Pescara, Italy, Europe 378

Olive farmers of Umbria, Italy, Europe.................................378
Olive Oil producers of Galilee, Israel, Asia 268
Olive Producers of Sinai, Egypt, Africa.................................44
Onano Lentil, Italy, Europe **596**
Ontario farmers' market producers, Canada, Americas 131
Ontario producers and consumers, Canada, Americas 132
Ontario small-scale brewers, Canada, Americas 132
Ontario small-scale farmers, Canada, Americas 132
Ontario Wild Plant gatherers, Canada, Americas 132
Oosterschelde Lobster , Netherlands, Europe........................**672**
Orange Sweet Potato Producers, Kenya, Africa 59
Orbetello Bottarga, Italy, Europe.....................................**597**
Oregon and California Biodynamic Growers,
United States of America, Americas......................................194
Organe Flesh Sweet Potato Growers of Luwero,
Uganda, Africa 87
Organic beekeepers of the northeast, China, Asia....................255
Organic cereal producers, Hungary, Europe 351
Organic cereal producers, Slovakia, Europe 421
Organic cocoa and chocolate producers, Mexico, Americas 156
Organic coffee producers, Mexico, Americas 156
Organic farmers and growers of the West of Ireland,
Ireland, Europe 355
Organic Farmers of Marsabit, Kenya, Africa 59
Organic farmers of Rossinver, Ireland, Europe 355
Organic food producers and distributors, Lebanon, Asia.............285
Organic food producers of Beirut, Lebanon, Asia 285
Organic food producers of County Leitrim, Ireland, Europe 356
Organic food producers of the Northwest, Ireland, Europe 356
Organic food producers of Tlayacapan, Mexico, Americas 156
Organic food producers, Lebanon, Asia 285
Organic fruit of Lessinia producers, Italy, Europe 379
Organic fruit promoters, Mexico, Americas 156
Organic growers and breeders of Ayacho, Japan, Asia 272
Organic growers of Saitama, Japan, Asia 273
Organic growers of the Abbazia di Monteveglio, Italy, Europe 379
Organic growers of Uzumasa, Japan, Asia 273
Organic honey producers, Argentina, Americas 101
Organic Infusion Producers of the Meru Region, Kenya, Africa 60
Organic Medicinal Food and Herb Producers, Kenya, Africa 60
Organic milk, cheese and bread producers, Romania, Europe.......405
Organic produce distributors of Barrit, Denmark, Europe 329

Organic producers and fishermen of the Riserva di Torre Guaceto, Italy, Europe 379
Organic producers and transformers of Foresto, Italy, Europe 379
Organic producers in the Canton of Ticino, Switzerland, Europe 440
Organic producers in the Jászság region, Hungary, Europe 351
Organic Producers of Kaliningrad, Russia, Europe 413
Organic Producers of Klein Karoo, South Africa, Africa 79
Organic producers of Mazovia, Poland, Europe 401
Organic producers of Stiria, Slovenia, Europe 423
Organic producers of Talamanca, Costa Rica, Americas 141
Organic producers of the Agro Romano, Italy, Europe 380
Organic Producers of the Suburban Areas of Gachie, Kenya, Africa 60
Organic Producers, Russia, Europe 413
Organic Rice producers of Hai Phong, Viet Nam, Asia, 302
Organic Sesame Producers of Gulmu, Burkina Faso, Africa 31
Organic Sesame Producers of Kongoussi, Burkina Faso, Africa 32
Organic Vegetable and Aromatic Herb Producers of Fayoum, Egypt, Africa 44
Organic vegetable farmers, Peru, Americas 164
Organic vegetable producers of Ademuz, Spain, Europe 431
Organic vegetable producers, Hungary, Europe 351
Organic wine producers of Maipú, Argentina, Americas 101
Organic wine producers of Mendoza, Argentina, Americas 102
Orissa Mustard Oil Pickles, India, Asia **306**
Orissa rice and vegetable producers, India, Asia 263
Oscadnica sheep breeders, Slovakia, Europe 422
Oscypek , Poland, Europe **678**
Osilo Pecorino, Italy, Europe **598**
Oton Banana Chips and Sugar producers, Philippines, Asia, ...291
Ottofile maize growers of Antignano, Italy, Europe 380
Ouagadougou Cheesemakers, Burkina Faso, Africa 32
Ouagadougou Peul Breeders, Burkina Faso, Africa 32
Ovangoul Okok Producers, Cameroon, Africa 37
Oxfordshire cattle breeders, United Kingdom, Europe 451
Oyster gatherers of Setúbal, Portugal, Europe 403
Ozieri Copuleta, Italy, Europe **599**
Pacaya and pepper growers, Guatemala, Americas 148
Paceco Cartucciaro Melon, Italy, Europe **600**
Paduan Hen, Italy, Europe **601**
País grape producers, Chile, Americas 136

Paksong Tea producers, Laos, Asia 281
Pando Nut, Bolivia, Americas **219**
Pangasinan producers, Philippines, Asia 291
Paradise Grain Producers, Cameroon, Africa 38
Pardailhan Black Turnip, France, Europe **462**
Pareci Novo fruit farmers and processors, Brazil, Americas 118
Paro Red Rice producers, Bhutan, Asia 254
Pasta producers of Gragnano, Italy, Europe 380
Pays Basque food producers, France, Europe 338
Pays de Thau Oyster breeders, France, Europe 338
Peanut growers and processors, Mexico, Americas 157
Pearl Millet Growers of Tanlili, Burkina Faso, Africa 32
Peat bog Sheep breeders of Diepholz, Germany, Europe 345
Pecorino producers of the Casentino, Italy, Europe 380
Pélardon Sec, France, Europe **463**
Pelmadulla Tea producers, Sri Lanka, Asia 293
Penyige Plum Compote producers, Hungary, Europe 352
Përmet Food producers, Albania, Europe 313
Perth County dairy farmers, Canada, Americas 133
Pescadero Goat Dairy Farmers, United States of America, Americas 194
Pestàt, Italy, Europe **602**
Petaluma Geese and Pekin Duck Breeders, United States of America, Americas 194
Peul Animal Breeders and Milk Producers in the Louga Region, Senegal, Africa 76
Peul Zebu Cattle Breeders, Burkina Faso, Africa 33
Pez Blanco fishermen, Mexico, Americas 157
Pheasant farmers, Argentina, Americas 102
Philadelphia Growers, United States of America, Americas 195
Pichilemu Seaweed pickers, Chile, Americas 136
Piedmontese Blonde Hen and Saluzzo White Hen, Italy, Europe **603**
Piedmontese Ox, Italy, Europe **604**
Piennolo Small Tomato, Italy, Europe **605**
Pietraroja Prosciutto, Italy, Europe **606**
Pine Nut producers of Rachaya el Wadi, Lebanon, Asia 286
Pine Nut producers of Rmeileh, Lebanon, Asia 286
Pine nut producers, Chile, Americas 137
Pineapple Growers from Obodan, Ghana, Africa 52
Pineapple Growers from the Central Region, Ghana, Africa 52
Pink Álava bean producers, Spain, Europe 431

Pink Rice Producers, Madagascar, Africa 64
Pintadas Honey producers, Brazil, Americas..................119
Pirarucu fishermen, Brazil, Americas 119
Pirenópolis fruit preserve producers, Brazil, Americas..................119
Pistachio producers of Badghis, Afghanistan, Asia 250
Pistoia Mountain Pecorino, Italy, Europe **607**
Pitina, Italy, Europe **608**
Pittsboro Educators, United States of America, Americas 195
Pittsburgh Educators, United States of America, Americas 195
Plantain Banana Growers of Amanease, Ghana, Africa 52
Poço Fundo coffee producers, Brazil, Americas 120
Point Reyes Seashore Oyster Harvesters,
United States of America, Americas..................195
Poirino Tench, Italy, Europe **609**
Polish Mead, Poland, Europe **679**
Polizzi Badda Bean, Italy, Europe **610**
Pompìa, Italy, Europe **611**
Portonovo Wild Mussel, Italy, Europe **612**
Potato and Pea Growers of Nakuru, Kenya, Africa 60
Potato growers in Chiloé, Chile, Americas 137
Potato growers of Araca, Bolivia, Americas 109
Potato growers of Svevia, Germany, Europe 345
Potosí Llama, Bolivia, Americas..................**220**
Potter Valley Ranchers, United States of America, Americas 196
Pozegaca Plum growers of Topola, Serbia, Europe 421
Pozegaca Plum Slatko, Bosnia and Herzegovina, Europe **455**
Pradnicki bakers, Poland, Europe 401
Prague organic producers, Czech Republic, Europe..................327
Praia Grande Valley banana producers, Brazil, Americas..................120
Prato Mortadella, Italy, Europe **613**
Preserve producers of Monte Carmelo, Venezuela, Americas 215
Preserved Fish Producers and Sellers of Fatick,
Senegal, Africa..................77
Preserves Producers of Kamchatka, Russia, Europe..................413
Preserves Producers of Shoria, Russia, Europe 414
Prickly Pear cultivators and processors, Mexico, Americas..................157
Prickly Pear growers of Tlaxco, Mexico, Americas..................157
Producers and breeders of Migliarino San Rossore
Massaciuccoli, Italy, Europe..................381
Producers and Processors of Banjul, Gambia, Africa 50
Producers and Processors of Brikama, Gambia, Africa..................50
Producers and Processors of Diakhao, Senegal, Africa..................77

Producers and processors of food for school cafeterias,
Korea, Asia..................280
Producers and processors of local cabbages and radishes,
Korea, Asia..................281
Producers from the Island of Mahé, Seychelles, Africa 78
Producers from the Methodist Mission of Kerewan,
Gambia, Africa 50
Producers in Val Lumnezia, Switzerland, Europe..................440
Producers of aromatic herbs, Colombia, Americas 140
Producers of aromatic herbs, Ecuador, Americas 145
Producers of barena honey from the Venetian lagoon,
Italy, Europe..................381
Producers of Bose Monastery, Italy, Europe 381
Producers of cane sugar, Paraguay, Americas 162
Producers of cane-sugar honey and cane-sugar,
Argentina, Americas..................102
Producers of carranzana sheep's cheese, Spain, Europe 432
Producers of cashew nuts, El Salvador, Americas 147
Producers of Chilean Hazelnuts, Chile, Americas 137
Producers of chocolate and other cocoa derivatives,
Argentina, Americas..................102
Producers of citrus fruits, Peru, Americas 164
Producers of coarse cane sugar, El Salvador, Americas 147
Producers of cocoa and chocolate, Nicaragua, Americas..................161
Producers of Colonia Valdense, Uruguay, Americas 213
Producers of conserved foods, Cuba, Americas 143
Producers of dehydrated fruit, El Salvador, Americas 147
Producers of Djerba Island, Tunisia, Africa 85
Producers of dulce de leche, Argentina, Americas 103
Producers of Extra-Virgin Olive Oil from
the Bianchera Istriana olive, Croatia, Europe 324
Producers of extra-virgin olive oil, Argentina, Americas 103
Producers of Fermented Kumys, Kirghizia, Asia 279
Producers of fruit-flavored honey, Argentina, Americas 103
Producers of goat's cheese, Uruguay, Americas 214
Producers of goat's milk and cheese, Argentina, Americas 103
Producers of Goat's Milk Ricotta, Russia, Europe 414
Producers of Grecìa Salentina, Italy, Europe 381
Producers of herbs and infusions, Paraguay, Americas 162
Producers of honey and derived products, Ecuador, Americas..................146
Producers of honey and related products, Argentina, Americas..................104
Producers of honey, El Salvador, Americas 147

Producers of honey, Nicaragua, Americas 161
Producers of honey, royal jelly and propolis,
Argentina, Americas 104
Producers of jam and spicy sweet and sour preserves,
Argentina, Americas 104
Producers of jam made from forest fruits, Argentina, Americas 104
Producers of Karluk Melon Sweets, Uzbekistan, Asia, ...301
Producers of Kielbasa lisiecka, Poland, Europe 402
Producers of local varieties of fruit and vegetables,
Belorus, Europe 317
Producers of olives and extra-virgin olive oil,
Argentina, Americas 105
Producers of organic cocoa, Peru, Americas 164
Producers of organic jams and fruit juices, Norway, Europe 399
Producers of palustrine blueberries, Chile, Americas 137
Producers of piantone di Falerone olives, Italy, Europe 382
Producers of Pine Nut Oil, Russia, Europe 415
Producers of Pskov, Russia, Europe 415
Producers of Reindeer Cheese, Russia, Europe 415
Producers of Salinas, Ecuador, Americas 146
Producers of sheep's cheese and lamb, Argentina, Americas..........105
Producers of Siberian Pine Nuts, Russia, Europe 416
Producers of special organic coffee, Peru, Americas 165
Producers of sweet products and liquerurs,
Argentina, Americas 105
Producers of Teleneflti, Moldavia, Europe 394
Producers of the Agro Nolano below Vesuvius, Italy, Europe 382
Producers of the Crete Senesi, Italy, Europe 382
Producers of the Sweet Basque Chili Pepper, France, Europe..........339
Producers of the Val di Non, Italy, Europe 382
Producers of the Val Martello, Italy, Europe 383
Producers of Torchiato di Fregona wine, Italy, Europe....................383
Producers of traditional foodstuffs, Belorus, Europe 317
Producers of traditional Liegi Syrup, Belgium, Europe 315
Producers of traditional local wines, Argentina, Americas............105
Producers of Vâlcea, Romania, Europe 405
Producers of vegetables and regional specialities,
Argentina, Americas 106
Producers of wegierka plum jam, Poland, Europe 402
Producers of wines, fruit and vegetables, Argentina, Americas 106
Producers of wizajny cheese, Poland, Europe 402
Producers on land confiscated from the Mafia, Italy, Europe 383

Promoters of Gävleborg products, Sweden, Europe 436
Promoters of sustainable agriculture and stock farming,
Sweden, Europe 436
Promoters of Swedish food products, Sweden, Europe 437
Promoters of the regional produce of Oberes Werntal,
Germany, Europe 345
Promoters of typical products, Belgium, Europe....................315
Promoters of typical Sankt Gallen products,
Switzerland, Europe 440
Provencal Goat breeders and producers of Banon Cheese,
France, Europe 339
Provence vegetable producers and consumers,
France, Europe 339
Provolone del Monaco, Italy, Europe 614
Proyecto Comunitario de Conservación de Alimentos,
Cuba, Americas 143
Pultost producers of Hedmark and Oppland,
Norway, Europe 399
Pumpkin Growers of the Arid Areas of Homa Bay
and Kilify, Kenya, Africa 61
Punjab Rice growers, Pakistan, Asia 289
Purceddu d'Alcamo Melon, Italy, Europe 615
Purcellville Livestock Breeders and Farmers,
United States of America, Americas 196
Purén White Strawberry, Chile, Americas 231
Pyrenean Goat breeders, France, Europe 340
Quebrada de Humahuaca Andean Potatoes,
Argentina, Americas 217
Quinoa farmers of Chimborazo, Ecuador, Americas 146
Quinoa farmers of San Nicolas de Ichubamba,
Ecuador, Americas 146
Racha Ham producers, Georgia, Asia 258
Radic di Mont, Italy, Europe 616
Ragusano Cheese, Italy, Europe 617
Ragusano Donkey, Italy, Europe 618
Raisin producers of Herat, Afghanistan, Asia 250
Rajma growers of Uttaranchal, India, Asia 264
Rakhov Bryndza producers, Ukraine, Europe 443
Random Valley organic producers, Australia, Oceania 702
Ranong-Chumporn tropical fruit growers, Thailand, Asia, ...297
Rapadura de Melado producers, Brazil, Americas 120
Rasht Valley fruit growers, Tajikistan, Asia, ...296

Raspberry growers and processors,
Bosnia and Herzegovina, Europe..319
Rastafarian producers of Ital Food, Jamaica, Americas 150
Raw milk cheesemakers of Turrialba, Costa Rica, Americas 141
Raw milk Raclette cheese producers, Switzerland, Europe 441
Real Ale brewers and drinkers, United Kingdom, Europe 452
Red Chili Pepper producers, Brazil, Americas 120
Red Fife Wheat, Canada, Americas **227**
Red garlic growers of Sulmona, Italy, Europe 383
Red Lobster fishermen, Mexico, Americas 158
Red Reggiana Cow, Italy, Europe...**619**
Red Rice Producers of Antanafisaka, Madagascar, Africa................64
Red sausage producers of Castelpoto, Italy, Europe 384
Redland Tropical Fruit Growers,
United States of America, Americas...196
Regina di Londa Peach, Italy, Europe **620**
Reindeer farmers in the Kola Peninsula, Russia, Europe 416
Reindeer farmers in the Magadan region, Russia, Europe 416
Reindeer Suovas, Sweden, Europe...**689**
Renewing American Food Traditions,
United States of America, Americas...212
Rennes Coucou Chicken, France, Europe **464**
Resia Garlic, Italy, Europe **621**
Rhode Island Dairy Farmers,
United States of America, Americas...196
Rhodope Mountains Bean producers, Bulgaria, Europe 320
Rhodope Mountains Tahan (sesame cream) producers,
Bulgaria, Europe...321
Ribera Strawberry, Italy, Europe **622**
Rice and Cashew producers of Palawan, Philippines, Asia, ...291
Rice and Sorghum Producers of Bizili, Cameroon, Africa................38
Rice and Sweet Potato growers of Bali, Indonesia, Asia 266
Rice and zucchini cultivators, Mexico, Americas...........................158
Rice Processors of Podor, Senegal, Africa 77
Rice-farmers, vegetable growers and transformers
of the Lomellina, Italy, Europe 384
Rimbàs Black Pepper, Malaysia, Asia..**310**
Ringerik Potato growers, Norway, Europe 400
Rio Real tropical fruit and juice producers, Brazil, Americas 121
Robinson Crusoe Island Seafood, Chile, Americas **232**
Rock-salt producers of the Rio Maior, Portugal, Europe 404
Roero madernassa pear producers, Italy, Europe 384

Romagnola Cow, Italy, Europe **623**
Rooibos Producers of Suid Bokkeveld, South Africa, Africa 80
Rooibos Producers of Wupperthal, South Africa, Africa 80
Rose Jam producers, Bulgaria, Europe 321
Rose Syrup, Italy, Europe **624**
Rosson Wild Fruits and Infusions , Belorus, Europe **454**
Rotonda Red Eggplant, Italy, Europe..**625**
Roussillon Rancio Sec, France, Europe..**465**
Roveja, Italy, Europe **626**
Roventino producers of Scandicci, Italy, Europe 385
Russian River Wine Grape Growers,
United States of America, Americas...197
Rye bread producers, Latvia, Europe 391
Rye Producers of Vologda, Russia, Europe 417
Sabinal Farmers and Ranchers,
United States of America, Americas...197
Sack Cheese (Sir iz Mijeha),
Bosnia and Herzegovina, Europe **456**
Saffron growers of Cascia, Italy, Europe 385
Saint Louis Brewers, United States of America, Americas 197
Saint Paul Farmer's Market Lamb and Sheep Breeders,
United States of America, Americas...197
Saint-Camille farmers' markets producers, Canada, Americas 133
Saint-Flour Planèze Golden Lentil, France, Europe **466**
Sakè Rice producers, Japan, Asia..273
Sakété Yovogari Producers, Benin, Africa......................................28
Salama da Sugo, Italy, Europe..**627**
Salina Caper, Italy, Europe **628**
Salmon Fishermen of Kamchatka, Russia, Europe 417
Salt Producers and Processors of Nyanyano, Ghana, Africa 53
Salt producers, Mexico, Americas..158
Salted Anchovy producers of the Gulf of Tachibana,
Japan, Asia..274
Salted Fern Producers, Russia, Europe 417
Sambucano Lamb, Italy, Europe **629**
Samos Olive and Grape growers, Greece, Europe 349
Samtskhe-Javakheti Wheat producers, Georgia, Asia....................258
San Diego Organic Farmers,
United States of America, Americas...198
San Diego Organic Tangelo Growers,
United States of America, Americas...198
San Francisco Brewers, United States of America, Americas 198

San Francisco Educators,
United States of America, Americas 198
San Francisco National Parks Producers,
United States of America, Americas 199
San Francisco Organic Fruit Growers,
United States of America, Americas 199
San Gavino Monreale Saffron, Italy, Europe **630**
San Marcos Andean fruit, Peru, Americas **241**
San Marzano Tomato, Italy, Europe **631**
San Patrignano producers, Italy, Europe 385
Sant'Erasmo Purple Artichoke, Italy, Europe **632**
Santa Cruz River Producers,
United States of America, Americas 199
Santa Fe Educators, United States of America, Americas 199
Santa Fe Farmers' Market Producers,
United States of America, Americas 200
Santa Lizia do Itanhi fishermen, Brazil, Americas 121
Santa Luzia Jam producers, Brazil, Americas 121
Santa Rosa de Lima organic producers, Brazil, Americas 122
Santa Rosa Livestock Breeders and Vegetable Growers,
United States of America, Americas 200
Santana Velha Bacuri gatherers, Brazil, Americas 121
Santo Stefano di Sessanio Lentil, Italy, Europe **633**
Saracena Moscato, Italy, Europe **634**
Saras del Fen, Italy, Europe **635**
Sardinian Modicana Cow, Italy, Europe **636**
Sateré Mawé Canudo Bee's Honey, Brazil, Americas **224**
Sateré Mawé Native Waraná, Brazil, Americas **225**
Sausage and Salami producers of Turku, Finland, Europe 332
Sausalito Cooks and Fishermen,
United States of America, Americas 200
Savona Chinotto, Italy, Europe **637**
Saxon Village Preserves, Romania, Europe **683**
Sea salt producers of Añana, Spain, Europe 432
Sea salt producers of Castro Marim, Portugal, Europe 404
Sea Salt producers, Korea, Asia 281
Sea snail fishermen of Francavilla al Mare, Italy, Europe 385
Seed conservers, Canada, Americas 133
Seed preservation and distribution specialists,
Austria, Europe 314
Seed preservers, Chile, Americas 138
Seed producers, France, Europe 340

Seed Promoters and Savers in Molo and Makueni,
Kenya, Africa 61
Seed savers, Ireland, Europe 356
Selangor vegetable growers, Malaysia, Asia 287
Serpa Cheese , Portugal, Europe **681**
Serra de' Conti Cicerchia, Italy, Europe **638**
Serra do Salitre cheesemakers, Brazil, Americas 122
Serra Gaucha Grape producers, Brazil, Americas 122
Sesame oil producers, Uzbekistan, Asia 301
Sesame Producers of Mount Elgon, Kenya, Africa..............61
Sette Comuni Plateau Malga Stravecchio, Italy, Europe **639**
Shea Butter Producers, Burkina Faso, Africa 33
Shea growers of Kedougou, Senegal, Africa 78
Sheep and goat breeders of the Valle d'Aosta, Italy, Europe 386
Sheep breeders and dairy producers, Uzbekistan, Asia, ...301
Sheep breeders from the Drenthe moorlands,
Netherlands, Europe...397
Sheep farmers of Radviliskis, Lithuania, Europe 392
Sheep's cheese makers, Mexico, Americas 158
Shellfish farmers, Argentina, Americas..............................106
Shepherds and cheese-makers of the Alto Volterrano,
Italy, Europe..386
Shepherds of the Abruzzo Appenines, Italy, Europe 386
Shepherdstown Fruit Growers,
United States of America, Americas 200
Shrimp raisers of Java Island, Indonesia, Asia 266
Shushan Pig Breeders, United States of America, Americas 201
Siddi pasta makers, Italy, Europe....................................386
Sierra Cafetalera Coffee, Dominican Republic, Americas **233**
Sintin-Sitirin Producers, Guinea, Africa..............................55
Sis village fruit growers, Azerbaijan, Asia 253
Sitges Malvasia, Spain, Europe **687**
Siwa Dates, Egypt, Africa **90**
Slavonia Kulin producers, Croatia, Europe 325
Small producers from the Kolmården region,
Sweden, Europe 437
Small-scale brewers of Flanders, Belgium, Europe 316
Small-scale Cashew Nut producers, Brazil, Americas............122
Small-scale fishermen from Istria, Croatia, Europe 325
Small-scale fishermen of Batroun, Lebanon, Asia 286
Small-scale fishermen, Philippines, Asia, ...292
Smilyan dairy farmers, Bulgaria, Europe 321

Smoked food producers of Rosario, Argentina, Americas 106
Smoked Goby producers of the Gulf of Nagatsura,
Japan, Asia..274
Snail farmers of Lumijoki, Finland, Europe...................................332
Snail farmers of the Swabian Alb, Germany, Europe.....................346
Socorro Organic Poultry Producers,
United States of America, Americas..201
Södermanland cereal growers and bakers, Sweden, Europe 437
Sonoma County Brewers,
United States of America, Americas..201
Sonoma County Gravenstein Apple,
United States of America, Americas..**247**
Sonoma County Poultry Breeders,
United States of America, Americas..202
Sorana Bean, Italy, Europe **640**
Sorghum Drink Producers of Nyakinama, Rwanda, Africa...............72
Sörmland producers, Sweden, Europe 438
Sørøya Island Stockfish, Norway, Europe....................................**675**
Soumbala Producers, Burkina Faso, Africa 33
Soumbara Producers of Lélouma, Guinea, Africa 55
South Alberta food producers and restaurateurs,
Canada, Americas..133
South Atlantic Farmers' Market Producers,
United States of America, Americas..202
South Florida Organic Farmers,
United States of America, Americas..202
South Londonderry Organic Vegetable and Herb Growers,
United States of America, Americas..203
Southern Armenia winegrowers, Armenia, Asia 252
Southern High Plains Grassfed Livestock Breeders,
United States of America, Americas..202
Southwest Honey Producers, Guatemala, Americas 148
Southwest Vancouver fishermen and gatherers,
Canada, Americas..134
Spalla Cruda, Italy, Europe **641**
Spelt farmers of Franconia, Germany, Europe..............................346
Spice producers of Deir Alla, Jordan, Asia 276
Spices producers, Brazil, Americas..123
Srisaket organic rice producers, Thailand, Asia, ...298
Standing Rock Reservation Bison Ranchers,
United States of America, Americas..203
Strawberry growers of Maletto, Italy, Europe 387

Strawberry Producers of Antsimondrano, Madagascar, Africa..........65
Sugar cane growers and processors, India, Asia 264
Sugar cane growers of Jaris de Mora, Costa Rica, Americas............141
Sugar Cane growers, Brazil, Americas 123
Sugar cane producers of San Ramón, Costa Rica, Americas............141
Sunnmøre Cured and Smoked Herrings, Norway, Europe..............**676**
Suphanburi White and Red Jasmine Rice, Thailand, Asia, ...298
Sussex fishermen, United Kingdom, Europe..................................452
Sustainable food producers and consumers of Dublin,
Ireland, Europe 356
Sustainable Food Producers of Kangemi, Kenya, Africa...................61
Sustainable food promoters of Cloughjordan, Ireland, Europe 357
Sustainable food promoters of County Clare, Ireland, Europe 357
Swan and Chittering Valleys food producers,
Australia, Oceania..702
Swinia zlotnicka pigs breeders, Poland, Europe............................402
Szeged Paprika producers, Hungary, Europe................................352
Tadef dairy producers, Syria, Asia..293
Takeo organic rice producers, Cambodia, Asia 255
Takommar Cheese Producers of Timia, Niger, Africa.......................71
Talas Bean producers, Kirghizia, Asia 279
Talkan Producers of Tashtagol, Russia, Europe 418
Tallahassee Region Farmers and Heirloom Seed Savers,
United States of America, Americas..203
Tanche Olive Oil producers, France, Europe 340
Tanganyika Fishermen, Democratic Republic of Congo, Africa 41
Tankaku cattle breeders, Japan, Asia...274
Taro Growers of Fello Diounguel, Guinea, Africa............................56
Taro Producers of Obout-Essangui, Gabon, Africa 49
Taro Producers, Kenya, Africa 62
Tbilisi organic producers, Georgia, Asia 258
Tea Purveyors, United States of America, Americas 204
Teff Producers of Debre Zeit, Ethiopia, Africa.................................47
Tehuacán Amaranth, Mexico, Americas......................................**238**
Tempeh producers of Yogyakarta, Indonesia, Asia 266
Tenera Ascoli Olive, Italy, Europe **642**
Teófilo Otoni young farmers, Brazil, Americas 123
Terra/Terra market, Italy, Europe 387
Texel Sheep Cheese , Netherlands, Europe..................................**673**
Three Counties Perry, United Kingdom, Europe **697**
Tibetan Plateau Yak Cheese, China, Asia **304**
Tinos Pasta producers, Greece, Europe..349

Tokaj-Hegyalja winegrowers, Hungary, Europe 352
Tolosa Black Bean , Spain, Europe................................**688**
Tomato Seed Savers and Growers,
United States of America, Americas.............................204
Toritto Almond, Italy, Europe **643**
Toronto organic producers, Canada, Americas 134
Tortona Strawberry, Italy, Europe **644**
Tortona Valley Salami, Italy, Europe **645**
Tosco-Romagnolo Apennine Raviggiolo, Italy, Europe **646**
Traditional Altamura Bread, Italy, Europe **647**
Traditional Animal By-product Producers of the Rift Valley,
Kenya, Africa 62
Traditional Beekeepers of Pokot, Kenya, Africa.............62
Traditional Bread producers, Lebanon, Asia 286
Traditional Chuño Blanco, Peru, Americas **242**
Traditional distilled liquor promoters, Switzerland, Europe...........441
Traditional Florentine Schiacciata producers, Italy, Europe 387
Traditional food producers of Oberá, Argentina, Americas 107
Traditional food producers, Hungary, Europe................352
Traditional food producers, Palau, Oceania 704
Traditional Food producers, processors and cooks
of Shewula, Swaziland, Africa 81
Traditional food promoters of the island of Gozo,
Malta, Europe 393
Traditional mescal producers of Durango, Mexico, Americas..........159
Traditional Norwegian fishermen, Norway, Europe 400
Traditional preserve producers of Muro de Alcoy,
Spain, Europe..432
Traditional producers of Ela Valley, Israel, Asia............268
Traditional Scottish food producers, United Kingdom, Europe........452
Traditional Spice producers in N'kart and Ngomessi,
Gabon, Africa...49
Traditional vegetable growers of Chioggia, Italy, Europe.............387
Traditional vegetable growers of Mount Etna, Italy, Europe 388
Transhumance shepherds from Les Trois Vallées Béarnaises,
France, Europe 341
Trapani Artisan Sea Salt, Italy, Europe **648**
Travnik Cheese producers, Bosnia and Herzegovina, Europe..........319
Trébons Sweet Onion producers, France, Europe 341
Trentino Lucanica, Italy, Europe **649**
Triangle Farmers' Market Producers, United States of America,
Americas 204

Tropical fruit farmers, Cuba, Americas 143
Troyan beekeepers, Bulgaria, Europe 322
Troyan Rakya producers, Bulgaria, Europe 322
Tsamarella, Cyprus, Europe...**458**
Tuareg Breeders and Growers of Ghat, Libya, Africa 64
Tuareg Producers of Milk, Meat and Cereals, Niger, Africa 71
Tubas shepherds and Cheese producers, Palestine, Asia 290
Tulum Cheese producers of Tire, Turkey, Europe............442
Turchesa potato growers of Gran Sasso and Monti della Laga,
Italy, Europe..388
Turmeric producers of Erode, India, Asia 264
Turvo Pine Nut gatherers, Brazil, Americas...................123
Tuscan Sea Palamita, Italy, Europe..............................**650**
Tuva sheep farmers, Russia, Europe 418
Twickenham beekeepers, United Kingdom, Europe 453
Typical foods of Troina producers, Italy, Europe 388
Umbù, Brazil, Americas **226**
Unpasteurized cheese producers and maturers,
Netherlands, Europe..397
Unpasteurized cheesemakers, Netherlands, Europe 397
Unzen seed savers, Japan, Asia...................................275
Upper Columbia Poultry Breeders,
United States of America, Americas..............................204
Upper Connecticut River Valley Meat Producers,
United States of America, Americas..............................205
Uralsk producers, Kazakhstan, Asia 277
Urban farmers, Cuba, Americas...................................143
Ur-Paarl, Italy, Europe **651**
Usgen Rice producers, Kirghizia, Asia...........................280
Ustica Lentil, Italy, Europe **652**
Vacaville Breeders, United States of America, Americas 205
Val d'Ossola Mortadella, Italy, Europe..........................**656**
Valchiavenna Goat Violino, Italy, Europe.......................**653**
Valdarno Hen, Italy, Europe **654**
Valdarno Tarese, Italy, Europe **655**
Vale do Piancó Red Rice producers, Brazil, Americas 124
Valente Manioc Flour producers, Brazil, Americas 124
Valle Bagnario di Strevi Moscato Passito, Italy, Europe **657**
Valli Valdesi Mustardela, Italy, Europe..........................**658**
Valtellina Buckwheat, Italy, Europe..............................**659**
Vancouver Wild Plant gatherers, Canada, Americas 134
Varanasi producers of dairy products and sweets, India, Asia 265

Vastedda del Belìce, Italy, Europe **660**
Vastese Ventricina, Italy, Europe **661**
Västmanland producers, Sweden, Europe 438
Västra Götaland cheese makers, Sweden, Europe 438
Vechtdal food producers, Netherlands, Europe 397
Vegetable and Fruit growers and processors in the Masaka District, Uganda, Africa 87
Vegetable and legume growers, Uruguay, Americas 214
Vegetable and Legume Producers of Kambhoke, Swaziland, Africa 81
Vegetable anf Fruit Producers and Processors of Thiès, Senegal, Africa 78
Vegetable farmers of Cundinamarca, Colombia, Americas 140
Vegetable farmers of Sabana de Bogotá, Colombia, Americas.......140
Vegetable growers of Corrientes, Argentina, Americas 107
Vegetable Growers of Embu, Kenya, Africa 62
Vegetable Growers of Okushiebiade, Ghana, Africa 53
Vegetable growers of the Eremo dei Camaldolesi of Nola, Italy, Europe..............................388
Vegetable growers of the Giudecca detention center, Italy, Europe 389
Vegetable growers of the Pereyra Iraola Provincial Park, Argentina, Americas 107
Vegetable Producers of Maseru, Lesotho, Africa 63
Vegetable Producers of Midrisien, Eritrea, Africa 44
Velika Planina cheese producers, Slovenia, Europe 423
Vermont Bread Bakers, United States of America, Americas 205
Vermont Farmers and Consumers, United States of America, Americas...........................205
Vermont Maple Syrup Producers, United States of America, Americas............................206
Vermont Organic Producers, United States of America, Americas............................206
Vermont Wild Food Gatherers, United States of America, Americas............................206
Vernon Artisan Bakers and Cheesemakers, United States of America, Americas............................206
Vessalico Garlic, Italy, Europe **662**
Vezzena, Italy, Europe **663**
Vientiane organic growers, Laos, Asia 282
Villsau Sheep, Norway, Europe **677**
Vine and olive farmers of Urgell, Spain, Europe 433

Vine growers and producers of the Langa, Italy, Europe 389
Vine growers of the Pollino, Italy, Europe 389
Vine growers of Tikvesh, Macedonia, Europe 393
Vineyard garlic cultivators, Austria, Europe 315
Vino Santo Trentino, Italy, Europe...........................**664**
Virgin Islands Farmers, United States of America, Americas 207
Vitoria De Santo Antão producers, Brazil, Americas 124
Vojvodina organic producers, Serbia, Europe 421
Waiahole Taro Growers, United States of America, Americas..........207
Waipi'o Valley Piko Poi Producers, United States of America, Americas.............................207
Wales farmers, United Kingdom, Europe 453
Walnut growers of Bleggio, Italy, Europe 389
Waltham Organic Farmers, United States of America, Americas.............................208
Washington Chinook Fishermen, United States of America, Americas.............................208
Waterlily Gatherers of the Baringo District, Kenya, Africa 63
Watermelon Producers, Russia, Europe 419
Waxhaw Organic Farmers, United States of America, Americas.............................208
West Chester Herb Gatherers and Honey Producers, United States of America, Americas.............................209
West Concord Breeders, United States of America, Americas 209
Westchester County Farmers, Chefs, and Educators, United States of America, Americas.............................208
Western Tian Shan wine growers, Uzbekistan, Asia, ...301
Wheat producers and processors of Totora, Bolivia, Americas........109
Wheat producers, Turkmenistan, Asia 299
Wheatbelt biodynamic Grain and Cereal producers, Australia, Oceania..............................703
Wheatland Farmers, United States of America, Americas 209
White Modena Cow, Italy, Europe.............................**665**
White Pertosa Artichoke, Italy, Europe.....................**666**
Wild Berry fruit processors, Croatia, Europe 325
Wild fruit and berry gatherers and processors, Slovenia, Europe 423
Wild Fruit and Herb gatherers, Georgia, Asia 258
Wild fruit and herb gatherers, Kirghizia, Asia 280
Wild Fruit gatherers of Chitrakoot, India, Asia 265
Wild fruit gatherers of the Alto Tevere, Italy, Europe.................390
Wild Fruit Jam Producers, Uganda, Africa 87

Wild Mango Gatherers of the Doum District, Gabon, Africa 49
Wild Mushroom Gatherers of Western Kenya, Kenya, Africa 63
Willamette Valley lamb Breeders,
United States of America, Americas 210
Willamette Valley Wine Grape Growers,
United States of America, Americas 210
Williams River biodynamic farmers, Australia, Oceania 703
Willunga Almond growers, Australia, Oceania 703
Wind River Indian Reservation Farmers and Ranchers,
United States of America, Americas 210
Windsor Fruit Growers, United States of America, Americas 211
Wine makers of La Valletta, Malta, Europe....................393
Wine Producers of Chã das Caldeiras, Cape Verde, Africa 38
Wine producers of San Juan, Uruguay, Americas 214
Wine producers of the Valle d'Aosta mountains,
Italy, Europe....................390
Winters Organic Walnut and Vegetable Growers,
United States of America, Americas 211
Women bakers of San Javier, Bolivia, Americas 109
Women's traditional food market, Italy, Europe 390
Wrightstown Organic Farmers,
United States of America, Americas 211
Xingu Park fruit producers, Brazil, Americas 124
Yacón, Argentina, Americas **218**
Yak Cheese Producers of Tuva, Russia, Europe 419
Yaku tayta fishers and fish processors, Peru, Americas 165
Yam Growers of Kpéssi, Togo, Africa 85
Yasothon organic rice producers, Thailand, Asia, ...298
Yerba mate growers and processors, Brazil, Americas 125
Yerba mate growers, Argentina, Americas 107
Yogurt producers, Bulgaria, Europe 322
Young farmers of the Alto Savio, Italy, Europe 390
Yuen Foong Yu Biotech organic producers, Taiwan, Asia, ...294
Yuko growers, Japan, Asia....................275
Yukon bakers, Canada, Americas 134
Yukon farmers' market producers, Canada, Americas 135
Yukon food tradition promulgators, Canada, Americas 135
Yukon River Salmon Fishermen,
United States of America, Americas 211
Zaban and Palm Juice Producers, Burkina Faso, Africa 34
Zadrima beekeepers, Albania, Europe 313
Zakynthos dairymen, Greece, Europe 349

Zalla purple onion growers, Spain, Europe 433
Zamené Producers, Burkina Faso, Africa 34
Zeri Foundation, coffee-producing center,
Colombia, Americas 140
Zeri Lamb, Italy, Europe ,....................**667**
Zibello Culatello, Italy, Europe **668**
Zolfino Bean, Italy, Europe **669**